Dictionary of Literary Biography

1 *The American Renaissance in New England*, edited by Joel Myerson (1978)

2 *American Novelists Since World War II*, edited by Jeffrey Helterman and Richard Layman (1978)

3 *Antebellum Writers in New York and the South*, edited by Joel Myerson (1979)

4 *American Writers in Paris, 1920-1939*, edited by Karen Lane Rood (1980)

5 *American Poets Since World War II*, 2 parts, edited by Donald J. Greiner (1980)

6 *American Novelists Since World War II, Second Series*, edited by James E. Kibler Jr. (1980)

7 *Twentieth-Century American Dramatists*, 2 parts, edited by John MacNicholas (1981)

8 *Twentieth-Century American Science-Fiction Writers*, 2 parts, edited by David Cowart and Thomas L. Wymer (1981)

9 *American Novelists, 1910-1945*, 3 parts, edited by James J. Martine (1981)

10 *Modern British Dramatists, 1900-1945*, 2 parts, edited by Stanley Weintraub (1982)

11 *American Humorists, 1800-1950*, 2 parts, edited by Stanley Trachtenberg (1982)

12 *American Realists and Naturalists*, edited by Donald Pizer and Earl N. Harbert (1982)

13 *British Dramatists Since World War II*, 2 parts, edited by Stanley Weintraub (1982)

14 *British Novelists Since 1960*, 2 parts, edited by Jay L. Halio (1983)

15 *British Novelists, 1930-1959*, 2 parts, edited by Bernard Oldsey (1983)

16 *The Beats: Literary Bohemians in Postwar America*, 2 parts, edited by Ann Charters (1983)

17 *Twentieth-Century American Historians*, edited by Clyde N. Wilson (1983)

18 *Victorian Novelists After 1885*, edited by Ira B. Nadel and William E. Fredeman (1983)

19 *British Poets, 1880-1914*, edited by Donald E. Stanford (1983)

20 *British Poets, 1914-1945*, edited by Donald E. Stanford (1983)

21 *Victorian Novelists Before 1885*, edited by Ira B. Nadel and William E. Fredeman (1983)

22 *American Writers for Children, 1900-1960*, edited by John Cech (1983)

23 *American Newspaper Journalists, 1873-1900*, edited by Perry J. Ashley (1983)

24 *American Colonial Writers, 1606-1734*, edited by Emory Elliott (1984)

25 *American Newspaper Journalists, 1901-1925*, edited by Perry J. Ashley (1984)

26 *American Screenwriters*, edited by Robert E. Morsberger, Stephen O. Lesser, and Randall Clark (1984)

27 *Poets of Great Britain and Ireland, 1945-1960*, edited by Vincent B. Sherry Jr. (1984)

28 *Twentieth-Century American-Jewish Fiction Writers*, edited by Daniel Walden (1984)

29 *American Newspaper Journalists, 1926-1950*, edited by Perry J. Ashley (1984)

30 *American Historians, 1607-1865*, edited by Clyde N. Wilson (1984)

31 *American Colonial Writers, 1735-1781*, edited by Emory Elliott (1984)

32 *Victorian Poets Before 1850*, edited by William E. Fredeman and Ira B. Nadel (1984)

33 *Afro-American Fiction Writers After 1955*, edited by Thadious M. Davis and Trudier Harris (1984)

34 *British Novelists, 1890-1929: Traditionalists*, edited by Thomas F. Staley (1985)

35 *Victorian Poets After 1850*, edited by William E. Fredeman and Ira B. Nadel (1985)

36 *British Novelists, 1890-1929: Modernists*, edited by Thomas F. Staley (1985)

37 *American Writers of the Early Republic*, edited by Emory Elliott (1985)

38 *Afro-American Writers After 1955: Dramatists and Prose Writers*, edited by Thadious M. Davis and Trudier Harris (1985)

39 *British Novelists, 1660-1800*, 2 parts, edited by Martin C. Battestin (1985)

40 *Poets of Great Britain and Ireland Since 1960*, 2 parts, edited by Vincent B. Sherry Jr. (1985)

41 *Afro-American Poets Since 1955*, edited by Trudier Harris and Thadious M. Davis (1985)

42 *American Writers for Children Before 1900*, edited by Glenn E. Estes (1985)

43 *American Newspaper Journalists, 1690-1872*, edited by Perry J. Ashley (1986)

44 *American Screenwriters, Second Series*, edited by Randall Clark, Robert E. Morsberger, and Stephen O. Lesser (1986)

45 *American Poets, 1880-1945, First Series*, edited by Peter Quartermain (1986)

46 *American Literary Publishing Houses, 1900-1980: Trade and Paperback*, edited by Peter Dzwonkoski (1986)

47 *American Historians, 1866-1912*, edited by Clyde N. Wilson (1986)

48 *American Poets, 1880-1945, Second Series*, edited by Peter Quartermain (1986)

49 *American Literary Publishing Houses, 1638-1899*, 2 parts, edited by Peter Dzwonkoski (1986)

50 *Afro-American Writers Before the Harlem Renaissance*, edited by Trudier Harris (1986)

51 *Afro-American Writers from the Harlem Renaissance to 1940*, edited by Trudier Harris (1987)

52 *American Writers for Children Since 1960: Fiction*, edited by Glenn E. Estes (1986)

53 *Canadian Writers Since 1960, First Series*, edited by W. H. New (1986)

54 *American Poets, 1880-1945, Third Series*, 2 parts, edited by Peter Quartermain (1987)

55 *Victorian Prose Writers Before 1867*, edited by William B. Thesing (1987)

56 *German Fiction Writers, 1914-1945*, edited by James Hardin (1987)

57 *Victorian Prose Writers After 1867*, edited by William B. Thesing (1987)

58 *Jacobean and Caroline Dramatists*, edited by Fredson Bowers (1987)

59 *American Literary Critics and Scholars, 1800-1850*, edited by John W. Rathbun and Monica M. Grecu (1987)

60 *Canadian Writers Since 1960, Second Series*, edited by W. H. New (1987)

61 *American Writers for Children Since 1960: Poets, Illustrators, and Nonfiction Authors*, edited by Glenn E. Estes (1987)

62 *Elizabethan Dramatists*, edited by Fredson Bowers (1987)

63 *Modern American Critics, 1920-1955*, edited by Gregory S. Jay (1988)

64 *American Literary Critics and Scholars, 1850-1880*, edited by John W. Rathbun and Monica M. Grecu (1988)

65 *French Novelists, 1900-1930*, edited by Catharine Savage Brosman (1988)

66 *German Fiction Writers, 1885-1913*, 2 parts, edited by James Hardin (1988)

67 *Modern American Critics Since 1955*, edited by Gregory S. Jay (1988)

68 *Canadian Writers, 1920-1959, First Series*, edited by W. H. New (1988)

69 *Contemporary German Fiction Writers, First Series*, edited by Wolfgang D. Elfe and James Hardin (1988)

70 British Mystery Writers, 1860-1919, edited by Bernard Benstock and Thomas F. Staley (1988)

71 American Literary Critics and Scholars, 1880-1900, edited by John W. Rathbun and Monica M. Grecu (1988)

72 French Novelists, 1930-1960, edited by Catharine Savage Brosman (1988)

73 American Magazine Journalists, 1741-1850, edited by Sam G. Riley (1988)

74 American Short-Story Writers Before 1880, edited by Bobby Ellen Kimbel, with the assistance of William E. Grant (1988)

75 Contemporary German Fiction Writers, Second Series, edited by Wolfgang D. Elfe and James Hardin (1988)

76 Afro-American Writers, 1940-1955, edited by Trudier Harris (1988)

77 British Mystery Writers, 1920-1939, edited by Bernard Benstock and Thomas F. Staley (1988)

78 American Short-Story Writers, 1880-1910, edited by Bobby Ellen Kimbel, with the assistance of William E. Grant (1988)

79 American Magazine Journalists, 1850-1900, edited by Sam G. Riley (1988)

80 Restoration and Eighteenth-Century Dramatists, First Series, edited by Paula R. Backscheider (1989)

81 Austrian Fiction Writers, 1875-1913, edited by James Hardin and Donald G. Daviau (1989)

82 Chicano Writers, First Series, edited by Francisco A. Lomelí and Carl R. Shirley (1989)

83 French Novelists Since 1960, edited by Catharine Savage Brosman (1989)

84 Restoration and Eighteenth-Century Dramatists, Second Series, edited by Paula R. Backscheider (1989)

85 Austrian Fiction Writers After 1914, edited by James Hardin and Donald G. Daviau (1989)

86 American Short-Story Writers, 1910-1945, First Series, edited by Bobby Ellen Kimbel (1989)

87 British Mystery and Thriller Writers Since 1940, First Series, edited by Bernard Benstock and Thomas F. Staley (1989)

88 Canadian Writers, 1920-1959, Second Series, edited by W. H. New (1989)

89 Restoration and Eighteenth-Century Dramatists, Third Series, edited by Paula R. Backscheider (1989)

90 German Writers in the Age of Goethe, 1789-1832, edited by James Hardin and Christoph E. Schweitzer (1989)

91 American Magazine Journalists, 1900-1960, First Series, edited by Sam G. Riley (1990)

92 Canadian Writers, 1890-1920, edited by W. H. New (1990)

93 British Romantic Poets, 1789-1832, First Series, edited by John R. Greenfield (1990)

94 German Writers in the Age of Goethe: Sturm und Drang to Classicism, edited by James Hardin and Christoph E. Schweitzer (1990)

95 Eighteenth-Century British Poets, First Series, edited by John Sitter (1990)

96 British Romantic Poets, 1789-1832, Second Series, edited by John R. Greenfield (1990)

97 German Writers from the Enlightenment to Sturm und Drang, 1720-1764, edited by James Hardin and Christoph E. Schweitzer (1990)

98 Modern British Essayists, First Series, edited by Robert Beum (1990)

99 Canadian Writers Before 1890, edited by W. H. New (1990)

100 Modern British Essayists, Second Series, edited by Robert Beum (1990)

101 British Prose Writers, 1660-1800, First Series, edited by Donald T. Siebert (1991)

102 American Short-Story Writers, 1910-1945, Second Series, edited by Bobby Ellen Kimbel (1991)

103 American Literary Biographers, First Series, edited by Steven Serafin (1991)

104 British Prose Writers, 1660-1800, Second Series, edited by Donald T. Siebert (1991)

105 American Poets Since World War II, Second Series, edited by R. S. Gwynn (1991)

106 British Literary Publishing Houses, 1820-1880, edited by Patricia J. Anderson and Jonathan Rose (1991)

107 British Romantic Prose Writers, 1789-1832, First Series, edited by John R. Greenfield (1991)

108 Twentieth-Century Spanish Poets, First Series, edited by Michael L. Perna (1991)

109 Eighteenth-Century British Poets, Second Series, edited by John Sitter (1991)

110 British Romantic Prose Writers, 1789-1832, Second Series, edited by John R. Greenfield (1991)

111 American Literary Biographers, Second Series, edited by Steven Serafin (1991)

112 British Literary Publishing Houses, 1881-1965, edited by Jonathan Rose and Patricia J. Anderson (1991)

113 Modern Latin-American Fiction Writers, First Series, edited by William Luis (1992)

114 Twentieth-Century Italian Poets, First Series, edited by Giovanna Wedel De Stasio, Glauco Cambon, and Antonio Illiano (1992)

115 Medieval Philosophers, edited by Jeremiah Hackett (1992)

116 British Romantic Novelists, 1789-1832, edited by Bradford K. Mudge (1992)

117 Twentieth-Century Caribbean and Black African Writers, First Series, edited by Bernth Lindfors and Reinhard Sander (1992)

118 Twentieth-Century German Dramatists, 1889-1918, edited by Wolfgang D. Elfe and James Hardin (1992)

119 Nineteenth-Century French Fiction Writers: Romanticism and Realism, 1800-1860, edited by Catharine Savage Brosman (1992)

120 American Poets Since World War II, Third Series, edited by R. S. Gwynn (1992)

121 Seventeenth-Century British Nondramatic Poets, First Series, edited by M. Thomas Hester (1992)

122 Chicano Writers, Second Series, edited by Francisco A. Lomelí and Carl R. Shirley (1992)

123 Nineteenth-Century French Fiction Writers: Naturalism and Beyond, 1860-1900, edited by Catharine Savage Brosman (1992)

124 Twentieth-Century German Dramatists, 1919-1992, edited by Wolfgang D. Elfe and James Hardin (1992)

125 Twentieth-Century Caribbean and Black African Writers, Second Series, edited by Bernth Lindfors and Reinhard Sander (1993)

126 Seventeenth-Century British Nondramatic Poets, Second Series, edited by M. Thomas Hester (1993)

127 American Newspaper Publishers, 1950-1990, edited by Perry J. Ashley (1993)

128 Twentieth-Century Italian Poets, Second Series, edited by Giovanna Wedel De Stasio, Glauco Cambon, and Antonio Illiano (1993)

129 Nineteenth-Century German Writers, 1841-1900, edited by James Hardin and Siegfried Mews (1993)

130 American Short-Story Writers Since World War II, edited by Patrick Meanor (1993)

131 Seventeenth-Century British Nondramatic Poets, Third Series, edited by M. Thomas Hester (1993)

132 Sixteenth-Century British Nondramatic Writers, First Series, edited by David A. Richardson (1993)

133 Nineteenth-Century German Writers to 1840, edited by James Hardin and Siegfried Mews (1993)

134 Twentieth-Century Spanish Poets, Second Series, edited by Jerry Phillips Winfield (1994)

135 British Short-Fiction Writers, 1880-1914: The Realist Tradition, edited by William B. Thesing (1994)

136 Sixteenth-Century British Nondramatic Writers, Second Series, edited by David A. Richardson (1994)

137 *American Magazine Journalists, 1900-1960, Second Series,* edited by Sam G. Riley (1994)

138 *German Writers and Works of the High Middle Ages: 1170-1280,* edited by James Hardin and Will Hasty (1994)

139 *British Short-Fiction Writers, 1945-1980,* edited by Dean Baldwin (1994)

140 *American Book-Collectors and Bibliographers, First Series,* edited by Joseph Rosenblum (1994)

141 *British Children's Writers, 1880-1914,* edited by Laura M. Zaidman (1994)

142 *Eighteenth-Century British Literary Biographers,* edited by Steven Serafin (1994)

143 *American Novelists Since World War II, Third Series,* edited by James R. Giles and Wanda H. Giles (1994)

144 *Nineteenth-Century British Literary Biographers,* edited by Steven Serafin (1994)

145 *Modern Latin-American Fiction Writers, Second Series,* edited by William Luis and Ann González (1994)

146 *Old and Middle English Literature,* edited by Jeffrey Helterman and Jerome Mitchell (1994)

147 *South Slavic Writers Before World War II,* edited by Vasa D. Mihailovich (1994)

148 *German Writers and Works of the Early Middle Ages: 800-1170,* edited by Will Hasty and James Hardin (1994)

149 *Late Nineteenth- and Early Twentieth-Century British Literary Biographers,* edited by Steven Serafin (1995)

150 *Early Modern Russian Writers, Late Seventeenth and Eighteenth Centuries,* edited by Marcus C. Levitt (1995)

151 *British Prose Writers of the Early Seventeenth Century,* edited by Clayton D. Lein (1995)

152 *American Novelists Since World War II, Fourth Series,* edited by James and Wanda Giles (1995)

153 *Late-Victorian and Edwardian British Novelists, First Series,* edited by George M. Johnson (1995)

154 *The British Literary Book Trade, 1700-1820,* edited by James K. Bracken and Joel Silver (1995)

155 *Twentieth-Century British Literary Biographers,* edited by Steven Serafin (1995)

156 *British Short-Fiction Writers, 1880-1914: The Romantic Tradition,* edited by William F. Naufftus (1995)

157 *Twentieth-Century Caribbean and Black African Writers, Third Series,* edited by Bernth Lindfors and Reinhard Sander (1995)

158 *British Reform Writers, 1789-1832,* edited by Gary Kelly and Edd Applegate (1995)

159 *British Short-Fiction Writers, 1800-1880,* edited by John R. Greenfield (1996)

160 *British Children's Writers, 1914-1960,* edited by Donald R. Hettinga and Gary D. Schmidt (1996)

161 *British Children's Writers Since 1960, First Series,* edited by Caroline Hunt (1996)

162 *British Short-Fiction Writers, 1915-1945,* edited by John H. Rogers (1996)

163 *British Children's Writers, 1800-1880,* edited by Meena Khorana (1996)

164 *German Baroque Writers, 1580-1660,* edited by James Hardin (1996)

165 *American Poets Since World War II, Fourth Series,* edited by Joseph Conte (1996)

166 *British Travel Writers, 1837-1875,* edited by Barbara Brothers and Julia Gergits (1996)

167 *Sixteenth-Century British Nondramatic Writers, Third Series,* edited by David A. Richardson (1996)

168 *German Baroque Writers, 1661-1730,* edited by James Hardin (1996)

169 *American Poets Since World War II, Fifth Series,* edited by Joseph Conte (1996)

170 *The British Literary Book Trade, 1475-1700,* edited by James K. Bracken and Joel Silver (1996)

171 *Twentieth-Century American Sportswriters,* edited by Richard Orodenker (1996)

172 *Sixteenth-Century British Nondramatic Writers, Fourth Series,* edited by David A. Richardson (1996)

173 *American Novelists Since World War II, Fifth Series,* edited by James R. Giles and Wanda H. Giles (1996)

174 *British Travel Writers, 1876-1909,* edited by Barbara Brothers and Julia Gergits (1997)

175 *Native American Writers of the United States,* edited by Kenneth M. Roemer (1997)

176 *Ancient Greek Authors,* edited by Ward W. Briggs (1997)

177 *Italian Novelists Since World War II, 1945-1965* edited by Augustus Pallotta (1997)

178 *British Fantasy and Science-Fiction Writers Before World War I,* edited by Darren Harris-Fain (1997)

179 *German Writers of the Renaissance and Reformation, 1280-1580,* edited by James Hardin and Max Reinhart (1997)

180 *Japanese Fiction Writers, 1868-1945,* edited by Van C. Gessel (1997)

181 *South Slavic Writers Since World War II,* edited by Vasa D. Mihailovich (1997)

182 *Japanese Fiction Writers Since World War II,* edited by Van C. Gessel (1997)

183 *American Travel Writers, 1776-1864,* edited by James J. Schramer and Donald Ross (1997)

184 *Nineteenth-Century British Book-Collectors and Bibliographers,* edited by William Baker and Kenneth Womack (1997)

185 *American Literary Journalists, 1945-1995, First Series,* edited by Arthur J. Kaul (1998)

186 *Nineteenth-Century American Western Writers,* edited by Robert L. Gale (1998)

187 *American Book Collectors and Bibliographers, Second Series,* edited by Joseph Rosenblum (1998)

188 *American Book and Magazine Illustrators to 1920,* edited by Steven E. Smith, Catherine A. Hastedt, and Donald H. Dyal (1998)

189 *American Travel Writers, 1850-1915,* edited by Donald Ross and James J. Schramer (1998)

190 *British Reform Writers, 1832-1914,* edited by Gary Kelly and Edd Applegate (1998)

191 *British Novelists Between the Wars,* edited by George M. Johnson (1998)

192 *French Dramatists, 1789-1914,* edited by Barbara T. Cooper (1998)

193 *American Poets Since World War II, Sixth Series,* edited by Joseph Conte (1998)

194 *British Novelists Since 1960, Second Series,* edited by Merritt Moseley (1998)

195 *British Travel Writers, 1910-1939,* edited by Barbara Brothers and Julia Gergits (1998)

196 *Italian Novelists Since World War II, 1965-1995,* edited by Augustus Pallotta (1999)

197 *Late Victorian and Edwardian British Novelists, Second Series,* edited by George M. Johnson (1999)

198 *Russian Literature in the Age of Pushkin and Gogol: Prose,* edited by Christine A. Rydel (1999)

199 *Victorian Women Poets,* edited by William B. Thesing (1999)

200 *American Women Prose Writers to 1820,* edited by Carla J. Mulford, with Angela Vietto and Amy E. Winans (1999)

Documentary Series

1 *Sherwood Anderson, Willa Cather, John Dos Passos, Theodore Dreiser, F. Scott Fitzgerald, Ernest Hemingway, Sinclair Lewis,* edited by Margaret A. Van Antwerp (1982)

2 *James Gould Cozzens, James T. Farrell, William Faulkner, John O'Hara, John Steinbeck, Thomas Wolfe, Richard Wright,* edited by Margaret A. Van Antwerp (1982)

3 *Saul Bellow, Jack Kerouac, Norman Mailer, Vladimir Nabokov, John Updike, Kurt Vonnegut,* edited by Mary Bruccoli (1983)

4 *Tennessee Williams,* edited by Margaret A. Van Antwerp and Sally Johns (1984)

5 *American Transcendentalists,* edited by Joel Myerson (1988)

6 *Hardboiled Mystery Writers: Raymond Chandler, Dashiell Hammett, Ross Macdonald,* edited by Matthew J. Bruccoli and Richard Layman (1989)

7 *Modern American Poets: James Dickey, Robert Frost, Marianne Moore,* edited by Karen L. Rood (1989)

8 *The Black Aesthetic Movement,* edited by Jeffrey Louis Decker (1991)

9 *American Writers of the Vietnam War: W. D. Ehrhart, Larry Heinemann, Tim O'Brien, Walter McDonald, John M. Del Vecchio,* edited by Ronald Baughman (1991)

10 *The Bloomsbury Group,* edited by Edward L. Bishop (1992)

11 *American Proletarian Culture: The Twenties and The Thirties,* edited by Jon Christian Suggs (1993)

12 *Southern Women Writers: Flannery O'Connor, Katherine Anne Porter, Eudora Welty,* edited by Mary Ann Wimsatt and Karen L. Rood (1994)

13 *The House of Scribner, 1846-1904,* edited by John Delaney (1996)

14 *Four Women Writers for Children, 1868-1918,* edited by Caroline C. Hunt (1996)

15 *American Expatriate Writers: Paris in the Twenties,* edited by Matthew J. Bruccoli and Robert W. Trogdon (1997)

16 *The House of Scribner, 1905-1930,* edited by John Delaney (1997)

17 *The House of Scribner, 1931-1984,* edited by John Delaney (1998)

18 *British Poets of The Great War: Sassoon, Graves, Owen,* edited by Patrick Quinn (1999)

Yearbooks

1980 edited by Karen L. Rood, Jean W. Ross, and Richard Ziegfeld (1981)

1981 edited by Karen L. Rood, Jean W. Ross, and Richard Ziegfeld (1982)

1982 edited by Richard Ziegfeld; associate editors: Jean W. Ross and Lynne C. Zeigler (1983)

1983 edited by Mary Bruccoli and Jean W. Ross; associate editor: Richard Ziegfeld (1984)

1984 edited by Jean W. Ross (1985)

1985 edited by Jean W. Ross (1986)

1986 edited by J. M. Brook (1987)

1987 edited by J. M. Brook (1988)

1988 edited by J. M. Brook (1989)

1989 edited by J. M. Brook (1990)

1990 edited by James W. Hipp (1991)

1991 edited by James W. Hipp (1992)

1992 edited by James W. Hipp (1993)

1993 edited by James W. Hipp, contributing editor George Garrett (1994)

1994 edited by James W. Hipp, contributing editor George Garrett (1995)

1995 edited by James W. Hipp, contributing editor George Garrett (1996)

1996 edited by Samuel W. Bruce and L. Kay Webster, contributing editor George Garrett (1997)

1997 edited by Matthew J. Bruccoli and George Garrett, with the assistance of L. Kay Webster (1998)

Concise Series

Concise Dictionary of American Literary Biography, 6 volumes (1988-1989): *The New Consciousness, 1941-1968; Colonization to the American Renaissance, 1640-1865; Realism, Naturalism, and Local Color, 1865-1917; The Twenties, 1917-1929; The Age of Maturity, 1929-1941; Broadening Views, 1968-1988.*

Concise Dictionary of British Literary Biography, 8 volumes (1991-1992): *Writers of the Middle Ages and Renaissance Before 1660; Writers of the Restoration and Eighteenth Century, 1660-1789; Writers of the Romantic Period, 1789-1832; Victorian Writers, 1832-1890; Late-Victorian and Edwardian Writers, 1890-1914; Modern Writers, 1914-1945; Writers After World War II, 1945-1960; Contemporary Writers, 1960 to Present.*

American Women Prose Writers to 1820

Dictionary of Literary Biography® • Volume Two Hundred

American Women Prose Writers to 1820

Edited by
Carla Mulford
Pennsylvania State University
with
Angela Vietto
Pennsylvania State University
and
Amy E. Winans
Susquehanna University

A Bruccoli Clark Layman Book
Gale Research
Detroit, Washington, D.C., London

Printed in the United States of America

The paper used in this publication meets the minimum requirements
of American National Standard for Information Sciences—Permanence
Paper for Printed Library Materials, ANSI Z39.48-1984. ∞ ™

Library of Congress Cataloging-in-Publication Data

American women prose writers to 1820 / edited by Carla J. Mulford, with Angela Vietto
and Amy E. Winans.
    p. cm.–(Dictionary of literary biography; v. 200)
"A Bruccoli Clark Layman book."
Includes bibliographical references and index.
ISBN 0-7876-1855-1 (alk. paper)
1. American prose literature–Women authors–Bio-bibliography–Dictionaries.
2. American prose literature–Colonial period, ca. 1600–1775–Bio-bibliography–
Dictionaries. 3. American prose literature–Revolution, 1775–1783–Bio-bibliography–
Dictionaries. 4. Women and literature–United States–Bio-bibliography–Dictionaries.
5. Women authors, American–Biography–Dictionaries. I. Mulford, Carla, 1955- .
II. Vietto, Angela. III. Winans, Amy E. IV. Series.
PS149.A54 1998
818'.1099287'03–dc21   98-42929
[B]   CIP

10 9 8 7 6 5 4 3 2 1

For the communities of women writers and their readers, past and present

Contents

Foreword: DLB 200 xiii

Plan of the Series xv

Introduction xvii

Abigail Adams (1744–1818) 3
 Edith B. Gelles, with Angela Vietto

Hannah Adams (1755–1832) 16
 Michael W. Vella

Susanna Anthony (1726–1791) 28
 Ellen Butler Donovan

Elizabeth Ashbridge (1713–1755) 34
 Cristine Levenduski

Abigail Abbot Bailey (1746–1815) 40
 Ann Taves

Martha Moore Ballard (1735–1812) 47
 Gail K. Smith

Ann Eliza Bleecker (1752–1783) 55
 Allison Giffen

Bathsheba Bowers (1671–1718) 62
 Sandra Harbert Petrulionis

Esther Edwards Burr (1732–1758) 67
 Sandra M. Gustafson

Jane Colden (1724–1766) 78
 Thomas Hallock

Hannah Mather Crocker (1752–1829) 85
 Constance J. Post

Elizabeth Drinker (1735–1807) 94
 Pattie Cowell

Hannah Duston (1657–1737) 107
 James A. Levernier

Sarah Pierpont Edwards (1710–1758) 113
 Donald R. Reese

Jenny Fenno (1765?–after 1803) 119
 David H. Payne

Hannah Webster Foster (1758–1840) 122
 W. M. Verhoeven

Winifred Marshall Gales (1761–1839) 132
 Jennifer Jordan Baker

Grace Growden Galloway
(1727–1782) 139
 Doreen Alvarez Saar

Sarah Prince Gill (1728–1771) 147
 Laurie Crumpacker

Anne MacVicar Grant (1755–1838) 154
 Edward J. Gallagher

Sarah Ewing Hall (1761–1830) 163
 Nicholas Rombes

Elizabeth Hanson (1684–1737) 168
 James A. Levernier

Anne Hart (1768–1834) 174
 John Saillant

Elizabeth Hart (1771–1833) 181
 John Saillant

Jane Fenn Hoskens (1693–1770?) 187
 Michele Lise Tarter

Anne Hulton (?– 1779?) 195
 Karen M. Poremski

Sophia Hume (1702–1774) 200
 Lee S. Burchfield

Susan Mansfield Huntington
(1791–1823) 206
 Erika M. Kreger

Susanna Johnson (1730–1810) 211
 Amy K. Ott

Mary Lewis Kinnan (1763–1848) 217
 Lisa M. Logan

Sarah Kemble Knight (1666–1727) 221
 Deborah Dietrich

Anne Home Livingston (1763–1841) 228
 Lorenza Gramegna

Deborah Norris Logan (1761–1839) 236
 Janice Durbin

Martha Daniell Logan (1704?–1779) 240
 George S. Scouten

Margaret Morris (1737–1816) 245
 Amanda Gilroy

Judith Sargent Murray (1751–1820)....................254
Sheila L. Skemp

Sarah Osborn (1714–1796)....................268
Philip Gould

Eliza Lucas Pinckney (1722–1793)....................278
Cynthia A. Kierner

Martha Laurens Ramsay (1759–1811)....................287
Joanna B. Gillespie

Martha Meredith Read....................294
Joseph Fichtelberg

Maria van Cortlandt van Rensselaer (1645–1689)....................299
Joyce D. Goodfriend

Mary Rowlandson (circa 1637–1711)....................304
Amy Schrager Lang

Susanna Rowson (1762–1824)....................313
Patricia L. Parker

Rebecca Rush (1779–?)....................326
Dana D. Nelson

Leonora Sansay (?–after 1823)....................330
Angela Vietto

Elizabeth Ann Seton (1774–1821)....................337
Frances Murphy Zauhar

Eunice Smith (1757–1823)....................345
Rosemary Fithian Guruswamy

Sarah Pogson Smith (1774–1870)....................351
Kirstin R. Wilcox

Tabitha Gilman Tenney (1762–1837)....................357
Joseph Fichtelberg

Caroline Matilda Warren Thayer (1785–1844)....................365
Mark L. Kamrath

Mary Palmer Tyler (1775–1866)....................373
Marilyn S. Blackwell

Sukey Vickery (1779–1821)....................380
Amy E. Winans

Mercy Otis Warren (1728–1814)....................385
Jeffrey H. Richards

Helena Wells (1758?–1824)....................399
Steven Hamelman

Eliza Yonge Wilkinson (1757–circa 1813)....................405
C. P. Seabrook Wilkinson

Anna Green Winslow (1759–1780)....................409
Ann E. Green

Margaret Tyndal Winthrop (circa 1591–1647)....................414
Rosemary Fithian Guruswamy

Sarah Wister (1761–1804)....................419
Etta M. Madden

Sally Sayward Barrell Keating Wood (1759–1855)....................429
Doreen Alvarez Saar

Appendix
Women's Work, Women's Sphere: Selected Comments from Women Writers....................439
Angela Vietto

Books for Further Reading....................465

Contributors....................469

Cumulative Index....................473

Foreword: DLB 200

This volume numbered 200 is actually the 252nd *Dictionary of Literary Biography* volume: 216 in the main series, including the early multi-volume titles; 18 in the *Documentary Series;* and 18 *Yearbooks.*

The Editorial Directors are frequently asked when the *DLB* will run out of material. Never. There are fields that have not yet been touched: e.g., the writers of the Orient, the Middle East, and India. Moreover, the volumes for contemporary writers require updating every generation as the writers already in *DLB* continue to write and new careers emerge. The 300th volume is now in the editorial pipeline.

The possibility of the *DLB* was introduced by Frederick Ruffner at a Ft. Lauderdale meeting on 22 November 1975. The initial planning session for the *DLB,* at the Yale Club library in 1977, was attended by Matthew J. Bruccoli, C. E. Frazer Clark Jr., William Emerson, James Etheridge, Richard Layman, Patrick O'Connor, Orville Prescott, Mr. Ruffner, Vernon Sternberg, and Alden Whitman. At this meeting Mr. Sternberg provided the rationale for the endeavor: each *DLB* volume covers writers belonging to a movement, chronological grouping, or another meaningful selection of writers. Accordingly, each volume is a literary history reference tool that can be utilized without recourse to other volumes.

The first *DLB* volume was published in December 1978, followed by volume two that year. Volume 100 was published in 1990. The first *DLB Yearbook* was published in 1981. The first *DLB Documentary* volume was published in 1982. The 252 volumes to date include 8,500 entries by 8,000 editors and contributors worldwide: more than 62,000,000 words.

Plan of the Series

The advisory board, the editors, and the publisher of the *Dictionary of Literary Biography* are joined in endorsing Mark Twain's declaration. The literature of a nation provides an inexhaustible resource of permanent worth. We intend to make literature and its creators better understood and more accessible to students and the reading public, while satisfying the standards of teachers and scholars.

To meet these requirements, *literary biography* has been construed in terms of the author's achievement. The most important thing about a writer is his writing. Accordingly, the entries in *DLB* are career biographies, tracing the development of the author's canon and the evolution of his reputation.

The purpose of *DLB* is not only to provide reliable information in a convenient format but also to place the figures in the larger perspective of literary history and to offer appraisals of their accomplishments by qualified scholars.

The publication plan for *DLB* resulted from two years of preparation. The project was proposed to Bruccoli Clark by Frederick C. Ruffner, president of the Gale Research Company, in November 1975. After specimen entries were prepared and typeset, an advisory board was formed to refine the entry format and develop the series rationale. In meetings held during 1976, the publisher, series editors, and advisory board approved the scheme for a comprehensive biographical dictionary of persons who contributed to North American literature. Editorial work on the first volume began in January 1977, and it was published in 1978. In order to make *DLB* more than a reference tool and to compile volumes that individually have claim to status as literary history, it was decided to organize volumes by

topic, period, or genre. Each of these freestanding volumes provides a biographical-bibliographical guide and overview for a particular area of literature. We are convinced that this organization—as opposed to a single alphabet method—constitutes a valuable innovation in the presentation of reference material. The volume plan necessarily requires many decisions for the placement and treatment of authors who might properly be included in two or three volumes. In some instances a major figure will be included in separate volumes, but with different entries emphasizing the aspect of his career appropriate to each volume. Ernest Hemingway, for example, is represented in *American Writers in Paris, 1920–1939* by an entry focusing on his expatriate apprenticeship; he is also in *American Novelists, 1910–1945* with an entry surveying his entire career, as well as in *American Short-Story Writers, 1910–1945, Second Series* with an entry concentrating on his short stories. Each volume includes a cumulative index of the subject authors and articles. Comprehensive indexes to the entire series are planned.

Since 1981 the series has been further augmented by the *DLB Yearbooks,* which update published entries and add new entries to keep the *DLB* current with contemporary activity. There have also been *DLB Documentary Series* volumes which provide biographical and critical source materials for figures whose work is judged to have particular interest for students. One of these companion volumes is entirely devoted to Tennessee Williams.

We define literature as the *intellectual commerce of a nation:* not merely as belles lettres but as that ample and complex process by which ideas are generated, shaped, and transmitted. *DLB* entries are not limited to "creative writers" but extend to other figures who in their time and in their way influenced the mind of a people. Thus the series encompasses historians, journalists, publishers, book collectors, and screenwriters. By this means readers of *DLB* may be aided to perceive literature not as cult scripture in the keeping of intellectual high priests but firmly positioned at the center of a nation's life.

DLB includes the major writers appropriate to each volume and those standing in the ranks behind them. Scholarly and critical counsel has been sought in deciding which minor figures to include and how full their entries should be. Wherever possible, useful references are made to figures who do not warrant separate entries.

Each *DLB* volume has an expert volume editor responsible for planning the volume, selecting the figures for inclusion, and assigning the entries. Volume editors are also responsible for preparing, where appropriate, appendices surveying the major periodicals and literary and intellectual movements for their volumes, as well as lists of further readings. Work on the series as a whole is coordinated at the Bruccoli Clark Layman editorial center in Columbia, South Carolina, where the editorial staff is responsible for accuracy and utility of the published volumes.

One feature that distinguishes *DLB* is the illustration policy—its concern with the iconography of literature. Just as an author is influenced by his sur-roundings, so is the reader's understanding of the author enhanced by a knowledge of his environ-ment. Therefore *DLB* volumes include not only drawings, paintings, and photographs of authors, of-ten depicting them at various stages in their careers, but also illustrations of their families and places where they lived. Title pages are regularly repro-duced in facsimile along with dust jackets for mod-ern authors. The dust jackets are a special feature of *DLB* because they often document better than any-thing else the way in which an author's work was perceived in its own time. Specimens of the writers' manuscripts and letters are included when feasible.

Samuel Johnson rightly decreed that "The chief glory of every people arises from its authors." The purpose of the *Dictionary of Literary Biography* is to compile literary history in the surest way avail-able to us—by accurate and comprehensive treat-ment of the lives and work of those who contributed to it.

The *DLB* Advisory Board

Introduction

It is sometimes argued that women writers of the early American past did not enter what has been called the American literary tradition because they were excluded from that tradition by men all along the historical way. Yet history, especially literary history, is more complicated than such assessments about women writers and the canon of early American literature seem to suggest. Even a cursory examination of the fifty-nine writers treated in this volume and their general level of output would seem to belie such assumptions about authorship by women. With the increased scrutiny given archives and the American cultural marketplace, one can no longer speak so readily about literary exclusionism that would seem, by implication, to have kept women from picking up their pens.

It is true, however, that women often believed their written works were being overlooked by men. Indeed, good evidence exists that many women felt as if their writings were not accepted by the men of their generation and not even by some of the women around them. Two of the most memorable lines about the authorship question, where women were concerned, occur in the poetic prologue to her book that Anne Bradstreet published in *The Tenth Muse Lately Sprung Up in America* (London, 1650), the first published book by a woman from English North America. Bradstreet wrote, "I am obnoxious to each carping tongue / Who says my hand a needle better fits than a pen." She continued by saying that "female wits" are not given the credit they deserve: "If what I do prove well, it won't advance, / They'll say it's stol'n, or else it was by chance." Bradstreet seems to have believed, if only for the creation of her poetic-authorial persona, that she would never receive appropriate credit for her merits as an author. In fact, records suggest that Bradstreet was highly praised as an author in her family, among her friends, and in the Puritan New England and London literary circles of people who knew about her poems. Bradstreet's expressions about feeling excluded from accolades as a writer *because* she was a woman might accurately have described her feelings, but such expressions about subservience were also part of the accepted way in which a woman could decorously offer her written works for public scrutiny.

In terms of the literary marketplace, the idea that a woman writer ought to be careful about seeking publicity through publication, which could quickly turn to notoriety, was a cultural commonplace that Bradstreet employed to her witty and timely advantage. By using the commonplace that women ought not put themselves *as authors* in the public eye, Bradstreet clearly marked for readers her sense of literary decorum and her upper-class social status. After all, Bradstreet was writing poetry, which was then considered the highest of genres, with epic poetry and poetic and dramatic tragedy considered the most serious of high literatures, so she needed to show an understanding of literature that reflected on poetry writing as a "high" literary endeavor. In addition, she came from a family whose social status placed them in the English aristocracy. Attitudes about presumed linkages among social status, genre, and literary inspiration surely affected this woman's sense of herself as "author" to her book.

The example of Bradstreet suggests that to take women's protestations about their exclusion from the literary world and from the "masculine" realm of the intellectual life as the whole picture, without examining closely the cultural system in which these women writers were circulating, is a partial way of going about the study of literary history. As the number and varieties of the women writers treated in this volume attest, women wrote a good deal, and their writings contributed in both aesthetic and cultural terms to the large canon of writings, especially prose writings, that emanated from the European colonies and then the new United States of America.

From the Renaissance through much of the eighteenth century, literature was considered to fall into categories or genres, which were often thought to have fixed and immutable properties. In Bradstreet's day, poetry was the genre most suitable for "high" literature and for scholarly or intellectual thoughts about one's place in the earthly world or the spirit world. Yet the writing of prose became more frequent, perhaps because of shifts in literary taste, in the numbers and social levels of those who were reading, and in the general distribution of wealth, so that more people could buy books and pamphlets. Many literary historians attribute the significant emergence and development of the prose genre less to shifts in particular literary tastes than to demographic changes indicated by changing religious attitudes (such as the influence of Protestantism above Catholicism) and by increased mobility of peoples of traditionally "lower" social status.

Changes in their living circumstances meant that women were engaged in adjusting to new kinds of labor, lifestyle, and belief systems. By the act of picking up their pens, it would seem, women were participating in the literary and cultural shifts of their day. Their writings, especially in prose, clearly had significant impact on the literary marketplace by the end of the eighteenth and the beginning of the nineteenth centuries. As literary and social historians such as Cathy N. Davidson (*Revolution and the Word,* 1986), Mary Beth Norton (*Founding Mothers and Fathers,* 1996), and Nina Baym (*American Women Writers and the Work of History,* 1995) have recently suggested, women's prose writings of the later eighteenth and earlier nineteenth centuries—often called the early national era or the era of the early (or new) republic—were the prime vehicles for social change. Such findings contradict the traditional story of the early national past, a story that told only of the political dealings of men. Women's prose writings—whether novels, histories, and essays, or religious, political, and educational tracts—were key markers of changing attitudes about writing, education, and politics within Anglo-American culture.

From the time of European contact in the Americas through 1820, prose writings for public audiences fell into fairly distinguishable modes of writing. For those in the Anglo-America inhabited by Anne Bradstreet, for instance, the key prose form was the sermon, the sole form dominated by men, the only acceptable members of official church clergy. In addition to sermons, prose genres at the time included writings on persons or qualities of persons. These writings were in the categories of *biography, autobiography,* and the literary *character,* a short and usually witty sketch of a distinguishable "type" of person, such as a "courtier," a "wise man," an "unhappy bachelor," or a "happy wife." Prose writings also included short pieces with clear didactic or instructional intent, such as *exempla,* stories that represented particular themes, usually drawn from sermons or biblical texts; *parables,* stories bringing home certain lessons by way of analogy with the circumstance discussed; and *fables,* short narratives indicating some abstract moral thesis or behavioral principle. Sometimes cultural instruction was also introduced in the form of *satire,* which generally used friendly or derisive laughter as a corrective to human follies. By the end of the eighteenth century, the most widely read prose writings fell into three modes: the essay (whether personal or formal, on a designated cultural topic), the short story, and the novel.

The women represented in this volume wrote in nearly all these accepted prose forms, thus contributing to the shifting literary tastes of their era. Yet they also created adaptations within the accepted familiar or domestic prose genres, adaptations that had significant impact on standards of literary acceptability. In the eighteenth century especially, women developed a whole cultural network around what might be called the converse of the pen. Most women who wrote adapted the formal prose genres of their day to meet needs and interests relevant to their views of the literary and aesthetic world. For women writers and readers, familiar essays on domestic or moral issues, letters to family members and friends (usually read aloud in mixed company), and journal, diary, or travel narratives took on great significance, and these modes clearly influenced what went into novels and fictions of the day. By the end of the eighteenth century, the ability to write a familiar letter well was a crucial marker of one's literary, cultural, and aesthetic abilities. The writing of didactic novels or sets of essays that inculcated domestic and national virtues became a mark of achievement for a writer, especially if that writer were a woman. Thus it is, for instance, that the essays of Judith Sargent Murray and Mercy Otis Warren, the fiction of many of the novelists represented here, including Murray, Susanna Rowson, Hannah Foster, and Tabitha Tenney, and the personal letters of writers such as Abigail Adams have come down to readers of the late twentieth century as signal cultural artifacts of an era that is said to have been dominated by men writers. Yet there were many, many more women writing than the few well-known female authors who have entered the canon of early American literature. Indeed, the sheer number of women who were writing attests not only to their resilience in the face of what they might have considered hostility to their literary output, but also to the ways in which women were, from the start, literary *makers* who developed important cultural influences on other women and on the men around them as well.

In their insistence that their personal lives were important and worthy of literary record, women writers helped to shift contemporary attitudes about what constituted "the literary" in written discourse. When European colonial ventures were taking place in the fifteenth century, it was understood that literature should represent the categorical and hierarchical human experience; that it was designed for those "high" in status; that it should be on social or religious issues and public in nature; and that it might be on political issues if it fell into certain categories. It was also understood that men more often than women should receive education in classical literature, history, and the arts. Yet with the influence of women in the literary arena by the end of the eighteenth century and the first quarter of the nineteenth century, notions of "the literary" were transformed to attitudes that accepted, indeed extolled, the virtues of private culture and domestic spaces. From literary "characters" about generalized qualities that were popular in the first half of the eighteenth century, for instance, fiction moved to specific narratives about proper behavior, education, and artistic expression for women. As critics such as Sharon M. Harris have suggested, principles of associativeness and interruptibility mark the writings of women (*American Women Writers to 1800,* 1996). By the end of the eighteenth century a discourse of interruption was commonplace in both men's and women's writings, whether they spoke of interruptions caused by servants or friends, by news "just received," or by errands that called them to other duties. As critics such as G. J. Barker-Benfield in *The Culture of Sensibility* (1992) and Nancy Armstrong and Leonard Tennenhouse in *Desire and Domestic Fiction* (1987) and *The Ideology of Conduct* (1987) have suggested, issues in women's lives—especially their domestic circumstances, their emotional responses, and their views about appropriate conduct in the world—drove the literary marketplace of Europe and America.

Women writers, whether they could recognize it or not, were thus having significant impact on the literary and cultural world in which they lived. The personal essay, the personal and formal letter, and the diary, the dominant forms of women's prose, clearly became central influences on the literary world they inhabited by the end of the eighteenth century—indeed, central parts of the literary world today. Far from having had no influence, in other words, and evidently despite what women writers might have thought was an absence of influence, women's interests and women's prose writings seem to have had a much greater influence than was once acknowledged. For the remainder of this introductory discussion of early American women prose writers, we will address two interrelated concerns by treating two key questions: what were the forms of writing that early American women writers of prose used most often, and what were the conditions of their lives that might have played into the sorts of prose they wrote?

In examining the forms that early American women's writing took, one must by necessity take account of the ways in which the European colonial project in the Americas forced adjustments in traditional written expression. Two points are worth noting. On the one hand, a breakdown in formal aspects of prose writing occurred for the obvious reason that there were no printing presses in the Americas for several decades after colonial contact occurred. The lack of printing capabilities, then, clearly affected the ways in which manuscripts would be prepared and presented to audiences, and even after presses were established in a few colonies, there were relatively strict expectations about what should reach print. The printing intricacies and extravagances of highly embellished typefaces were unavailable to generations of literate Americans. Nor were such extravagances sought after in the Puritan colonies, though they might have been accepted in other colonies, such as Virginia.

On the other hand, differences in colonial experiences forced changes on traditional generic categories. Where the aristocracy of Europe might have been preoccupied with reading discourses on the attributes of a good monarchy and the relationship between king and people, the colonial aristocracy was preoccupied with problems in setting up what John Winthrop called a "city upon a hill" or what William Penn called a "city of brotherly love," after the conception of the holy city of their God's heavenly kingdom. In considering the kinds of writing by women of this era, the reader must look at the ways in which their lived experiences as colonial women drove their writing interests, their literary concerns, and their methods of writing. As colonial women, they did not have to write imaginary narratives about journeys to other worlds, such as Samuel Johnson's *Rasselas* (1759), because they had onerous journeys of their own to relate. Their written expressions, in other words, came from actual experiences in the Americas. It is not surprising, then, that their prose writings took on different aesthetic and literary traits from those found in typical English and European prose forms.

With regard to the issue of writing and publication, it is useful to keep in mind that most writings by seventeenth- and eighteenth-century women did not reach print in their lifetimes. Until recently, scholars have tended to assume that if a work were not published during the writer's life, then it was not deemed "worthy" by the writer's contemporaries. Literary historians of the 1980s and 1990s have shown, however, that such hypotheses about printing, wide circulation, and acceptance belie the actual colonial circumstances of these writers and give only a partial picture of the literary marketplace during colonial times. Although some women's writing was private, many early women writers, like the men of their day, circulated their work in manuscript to significantly wide audiences, often of men and women. Also like the men around them, women writers established literary identities within networks of friends and family members, ministers, and acquaintances. Even diarists who were not part of a writing circle often wrote with specific audiences in mind. Esther Edwards Burr wrote for Sarah Prince, for example, just as Sarah Wister wrote for her friend Deborah Norris, and Anna Green Winslow wrote for her mother.

The circulation of manuscripts provided many women an avenue of "publicity," if not publication in print, even as it afforded them a sense of community among women and men. Works circulated in manuscript were in all genres of written discourse, although women often chose to circulate poetry, letters, journals, and memoirs. Writers of letters could assume that their letters would in all likelihood be read or heard by people other than the persons to whom the letters were addressed. Writers of diaries or memoirs could assume that family members might read their writings after the authors' deaths. Indeed, memoirs were often explicitly written for this purpose. Letters, memoirs, and journals might also be published by a woman's family to illustrate the moral life and model character of a woman relative. Published or not, such personal writing by women was considered a necessary and useful function of the woman's place within the family and her community. By modeling acceptable social virtues and attitudes in her person and her writing, a woman was fulfilling her duty as a mentor and monitor for those within her sphere.

In addition to diaries and letters, a form of life writing that was common among women has come to be known as spiritual autobiography. These narratives traced a subject's life specifically with reference to her spiritual growth, following the pattern of the Christian's search for the holy city that has been the goal of those within Christian communities from medieval times onward. Typically, these narratives trace the speaker's or writer's early indifference about spirituality and then move to descriptions of religious awakening and eventual conversion. This mode of self-expression was particularly important to women, who continually had to come to terms with their own mortality each time they faced the risks of childbirth. Some women wrote their own narratives, while others relied on their ministers to record their expressions. Indeed, some women's spiritual autobiographies were entirely composed by ministers in their communities. For many women, from Sarah Pierpont Edwards, a white Puritan woman living in seventeenth-century Massachusetts, to Elizabeth Hart, a free black woman living in early-nineteenth-century Antigua, spiritual narratives were an immensely important form of personal expression. By writing and speaking about their spiritual concerns, women were testing their own preparedness as Christians even as they were suggesting the means to spiritual salvation that other readers—especially their women readers living in colonial hardships—might follow.

Captivity narratives, which came about particularly as a result of colonial experiences, were often constructed, like spiritual autobiographies, to serve as spiritual and moral guides to personal salvation. Written by both men and women from the earliest era of contact between native peoples and Europeans, these accounts are about white men and women who were taken captive by Native Americans. They were immensely popular among colonists and their European observers. At first captivity narratives were brief, and they told only of the captive's observations and experiences while being held captive. By the middle of the seventeenth century, however, captivity stories—often mentioned in sermons and travel and trade accounts—became intermingled with accounts of spiritual regeneration. Early captivity narratives reflected the importance of the Puritan, Quaker, and Catholic religions of their writers. Most writers viewed their captivities in providential terms, believing that God used captivity to test their faith and, in some cases, to punish them for spiritual wrongdoing. Many captivity narratives thus served as spiritual autobiographies as well, so that "redemption," the usual conclusion of a captivity narrative, carried the double import of the captive's having been "redeemed" (that is, ransomed) and "Redeemed" (that is, elected or chosen for salvation in the hereafter). The model captive thus could become the model Christian within the same inspirationally constructed narrative journey.

The image of the woman captive was particularly significant in these early accounts because, culturally speaking, the purity of the religious commonwealth was understood, by analogy, to reside in the perceived purity of the woman's body. By the mid eighteenth century, the genre of the captivity narrative shifted somewhat, indicating a growing secularization of Anglo-American culture. In many instances the narratives functioned overtly as colonial propaganda that focused on the ways in which different peoples (such as Native Americans or competing European powers) were hindering further settlement. These narratives often appeared in almanacs or were published individually as relatively inexpensive pamphlets.

Although narratives based on actual incidents of captivity continued to be published into the nineteenth century, by the late eighteenth century fictionalized narratives of Indian captivity were forming the basis for poetry, drama, and prose. Early novels such as Ann Eliza Bleecker's *The History of Maria Kittle* (1793) demonstrate this important transition. Even prior to the appearance of recognizably fictional texts, distinguishing between fictional and historically verifiable "factual" accounts and establishing the authorship of narratives was quite difficult. Authorship was complicated by the fact that religious leaders, who often encouraged the publication of captivity narratives, sometimes served as editors and collaborators.

As the discussion of women's personal writing, spiritual autobiographies, and captivity narratives suggests, women were expected to provide models of and advice about good conduct. Given their relative isolation from other people—most people lived in relatively rural circumstances—women surely found consolation in reading about the lives and good conduct of other women in similar circumstances. By discussing conduct in their writings, women could conceive of themselves in ideal terms and center their roles within their local communities as necessary social monitors in an otherwise alien and worrisome environment. On the one hand, the writing of conduct materials would seem to fulfill a conserving tendency because women were instructing other women in preserving a submerged status within a patriarchally constructed social formation. On the other hand, conduct manuals often spoke explicitly to women about their central positions in civic development and improvement, thus illustrating the pivotal role women held in the ongoing social system.

A long tradition of European literature gave advice on conduct for both men and women. The literature directed toward women focused on instructing young women in the proper ways to behave in order to attract suitable husbands and then to be successful in running their households. Women's prose writing, then, focused on certain features of their lives as colonial women: what systems of gardening assisted family economy, what herbs produced the best cures for ailments, what levels of education were most appropriate for boys and girls, what was expected etiquette in different social circumstances, what amount of time could be suitably spent on reading, spinning, knitting, sewing, playing music, dancing, and singing. Of great concern were questions about how much of which activities

created high moral sentiments. These concerns, quite apart from specific issues in religious self-scrutiny (which was deemed necessary for one to be faithful), figured into women's conversations and writings in all genres but especially into their writings in prose.

Several popular European conduct manuals were read widely in the colonies and the new United States, although it seems clear that they had less utility for women in the Americas than for their European counterparts. For colonial women, the writing of conduct materials was an appropriately "feminine" employment; women would write about conduct to educate younger women and to help perpetuate women's domestic systems. Works such as those of Mary Palmer Tyler, who wrote the first American child-care manual, portrayed for readers the features of the ideal woman in the new republic. Conduct manuals also influenced much fiction written by or directed to women readers, as can clearly be seen in didactic works such as Hannah Webster Foster's epistolary novel, *The Coquette* (1797), and her book *The Boarding School* (1798), written as "lessons of a preceptress to her pupils."

Many women wrote novels during the early national era. Two of those women—Susanna Rowson and Hannah Webster Foster—wrote the two best-selling American novels before Harriet Beecher Stowe's *Uncle Tom's Cabin* (1852). Yet novel writing seems to have been a questionable activity for early women. Unlike poetry writing, the writing of novels was considered of dubious value for any writer, but particularly for women. Women novelists had to defend themselves against charges that they were neglecting their duties to their families by writing novels. Furthermore, many people—especially ministers, educators, and political figures—considered the novel a subversive genre, not only because it was *fiction* (as opposed to sermonic "fact") but because novels were presumed to influence the morals, intellect, and behaviors of readers, particularly young women readers. Part of the disavowal of novels had to do with the history of that form in Europe: chivalric romances tended to feature long-ago and far-away sites and experiences with knights-errant and women "in distress" whose chastity might be called into question. Foremost among the concerns in eighteenth-century Anglo-America, however, was the mere notion that people were reading fiction rather than spending their time getting to know factual phenomena. During an era when men preferred to think of women as moral guardians of the republic, novel writing and novel reading (especially when a woman might otherwise be "usefully" employed) were construed as potentially worrisome activities.

In response to widely voiced concerns about the impact of novel reading, novelists claimed that their novels were "tales of truth" or "true histories," and they opened their books with prefaces defending the moral usefulness of their particular tales. In the introduction to her novel, *Emily Hamilton* (1803), for example, Sukey Vickery explained that novels "which carry us too far from real life, and fill the imagination with a thousand enchanting images . . . impossible ever to realize . . . ought never to be read till the judgment is sufficiently mature to separate the truth from the fiction of the story." Vickery went on to defend novel reading overall, for those novels that "are founded on interesting scenes in real life, may be calculated to afford moral instruction to the youthful mind, in the most pleasing manner." Yet even after offering such a defense of her work, Vickery, like other men and women novelists, was not willing to have her name placed on the title page. In fact, most novels published prior to 1820 were published anonymously; the title page might state that the novel was written by "A Lady of Worchester" or, more simply, "By a Lady."

That the novel was a significant genre for women writers and readers is not surprising given the way in which novels drew on other genres typically used by women. Within many early novels are signs of religious tracts, travel and captivity narratives, advice books, diaries, and letters. Epistolary novels such as the best-sellers *Charlotte. A Tale of Truth* (1791, 1794) and *The Coquette* (1797) seem patterned not only upon their British predecessors—especially Richardson's *Pamela* (1740–1741), *Clarissa* (1747–1748), and *Sir Charles Grandison* (1753–1754)—but on women's letters and diaries. Novels tended to focus on similar issues: marriage, familial relationships, domestic economy, education and moral probity, and domestic topics of daily concern to women. More than writings in other genres, novels also seem to have been particularly accessible to women of diverse economic backgrounds because they were written in a manner that did not depend on specialized knowledge from an advanced education. Unlike many writers of poetry and essays, for example, novelists did not usually assume their readers' prior knowledge of classical writings, which would have been most familiar to well-educated men or to some elite-class women. Furthermore, the rise of subscription libraries (beginning around the 1760s) meant that novels were financially within the means of many women. By drawing on women's experiences and by employing materials familiar to them, novelists could assure themselves of a general, interested readership.

By contrast, drama was more accessible to the elite, who could afford to attend play productions, particularly during the postwar era. During the era of the American Revolution, dramatic performance was proscribed to colonial audiences as a cost- and potentially morals-saving effort. Indeed, during the Revolution, dramatic activity was described as a form of European-style luxury that more stable and moral colonials, if they were patriotic, should be happy to give up. Pamphlet plays from that era, such as those of Mercy Otis Warren, were designed to be read rather than performed, and they were thus widely circulated during the early 1770s. Perhaps because of the high-moral tone in discussions of drama and theater, many Anglo-Americans came to view the theater with suspicion. Yet during the years following the American Revolution, many members of the elite welcomed and encouraged dramatic activity. Some literary historians have suggested that the drama was an appropriate vehicle for promoting ruling-class interests over people who had just participated in an extended rebellion against political authority.

Writing in defense of dramatic performances, Judith Sargent Murray asked, "Doth not a virtuous theatre exemplify the lessons which [a] preacher labors to inculcate?" According to Murray, the author of two plays, the stage was "undoubtedly a very powerful engine in forming the opinions and manners of a people." Many men and women playwrights seem by their activity to have agreed with Murray's statements and shaped their work accordingly. By focusing their plays on historical, political, and patriotic issues, playwrights found a growing marketplace for their works. As Murray's comments suggest, plays could appropriately inculcate virtue in the citizenry, and they did so by exploring domestic issues and women's roles. Writing for the theater provided women an avenue whereby they could test the competing and conflicting positions taken by public leaders and educators about women's status within the community. Plays such as Susanna Rowson's *Slaves in Algiers; or, a Struggle for Freedom* (1794) used a current political situation—the enslavement of Americans in Algiers during the late eighteenth century—to explore the possible meanings of women's liberty in the postwar era. By focusing drama on historical or patriotic themes, women found ways to validate themselves and the dramatic fictions they were creating. The texts of many plays written and/or performed during this era do not survive, so the archive of dramas from the eighteenth and early nineteenth centuries is incomplete.

Another field in which women's authority was questioned was in the writing of history, long considered the province of men. From about 1750 on, however, the study and writing of history was considered an important educational goal for women as well as men. By writing historical treatises, women were entering a domain associated with the parliamentary and popular movements of the recent British past, movements that had resulted in the English Civil Wars and were thus anti-authoritarian at their core. In interesting ways, women were able to use to their advantage the expectation of their culture that they needed to become the key educators of the citizenry. The writing of history might have been considered anti-authoritarian and "masculine," but, because of their newly acquired roles as cultural monitors, women could appropriate the tradition of history writing to themselves. Following this line of reasoning, for instance, Mercy Otis Warren claimed that studying and writing history was a proper pursuit for women since it was so important to educating youth. Hannah Adams produced a history of New England designed—so the title said—specifically "for the use of young persons." Women's historical writing became even more common as the nineteenth century progressed and history became central to women's higher education. In other words, the historical writings of Warren, Murray, and Adams represent only the beginnings of a liberal, bourgeois trend that was to be of great importance for women writers who followed them.

Like the writing of history, the writing of essays offered middle-level and elite-status women a significant avenue for expressing their social and political concerns. Published in magazines, newspapers, and pamphlets, women's essays staked out positions on important issues of the day and displayed women writers' abilities to think and write with logic, reason, and probity, all qualities usually attributed to men's writing. The fact that women focused on issues such as marital relations, women's education, home cures, and infant and children's concerns demonstrates their commitment to improving their social circumstances even as incomes, literacy, and infant-survival rates began to rise during the early nineteenth century. From a range of political perspectives, essayists also considered topics such as relief for the poor and for children, temperance, and abolitionism. They also explored scientific concerns. Although even highly educated women seldom had scientific training, women such as Jane Colden and Martha Daniell Logan circulated their botanical writings in almanacs and letters.

Women relied on the circulation of their manuscripts as a means of "publishing" their works from the earliest colonial times. From about 1750 onward, however, women began to publish their writings in local and regional newspapers, and in books and pamphlets. The First Great Awakening in the English colonies (among those interested in Puritan theology, the time of religious ferment during the 1730s and early 1740s) afforded many women acceptable access to modes of public expression, and, in some cases, to publication of their pious writings. It should be noted that Quaker women had long been speaking publicly on varieties of issues, because the Society of Friends gave women key roles in family and community decision making. The American Revolution, perhaps even more than the First Great Awakening, offered women increased access to the public sphere, and women began on their own to seek publication of their writings. During the Second Great Awakening (a mass spiritual and revival movement of the 1790s that had special significance for rural dwellers, for the poor, and for nonelite peoples), greater numbers of women from the general population were prepared to assume more active speaking and writing roles than ever before. For pious women, writings on spiritual matters were the most accepted form of expression, and these writings became more and more popular toward the end of the eighteenth century. Sometimes a woman would seek publication of her own meditations, but in most cases a woman's writings were left for surviving family members to publish or not, as they saw fit. Memoirs of pious women entered the press with increasing frequency during the era of the new republic. After the death of Martha Ramsay, for example, her husband, David Ramsay, published *Memoirs of the Life of Martha Laurens Ramsay* (1811), a popular volume that includes Martha's private diary, along with a collection of her letters and a brief biography written by her husband. In other instances a bereaved widow would take on the task of completing her husband's memoirs. After her husband's death in Antigua, for instance, Anne Hart, a free black woman, completed his memoir.

In examining the general literary culture of women and the forms of their prose writings, it is also necessary to take into account key aspects of their experiences. By considering the conditions of the lives of women writers, we can see the extent to which their circumstances determined the nature of the writings they would create. One factor easy to overlook, given the great amount of written material that has survived, is that the culture of early America was primarily an oral one. More than 90 percent of the population lived on farms or in semi-rural areas. A population statistic like this one can reveal a good deal about the way in which information and attitudes were passed among people: transmission of cultural norms was primarily through oral networks if newspapers were scarce or unavailable within communities. Information was usually passed between people on a face-to-face basis. Literacy was less important in the predominantly rural, oral culture of colonial Anglo-America than it became during the mid to late eighteenth century. Accordingly, during the colonial era relatively few people received much—if any—formal training in letters and numbers. Access to education depended upon several variables in addition to gender, such as one's race, class, and religion, as well as one's locale. Typically, those who had the greatest access to education were white male children from elite (and in some cases middle-level) backgrounds, particularly those living in New England, in the Virginia colony, or in North Carolina. Although some wealthy children growing up on southern plantations had access to private tutors, most southern children had limited access to formal education.

Boys were given more extensive educations than girls, probably based on key cultural assumptions about women's appropriate positions in society and about their intellectual abilities. In 1643 John Winthrop explained to his Puritan community that one woman had become ill because of her intellectual endeavors. Anne Hopkins, Winthrop noted, had given "herself wholly to reading and writing, and had written many books." She might not have fallen ill, he insisted, "if she had attended her household affairs, and such things as belong to women, and not gone out of her way and calling to meddle in such things as are proper for men, whose minds are stronger." Winthrop's comment reveals the dominant cultural assumptions of his era: in the New England world, women were called on for household duties, not intellectual or scholarly ones.

Although both boys and girls were taught to read, often only boys were taught to write. The cultural assumption was that women would have no use for letters and instead needed to learn the domestic arts. As children, boys and girls were taught to read at home (usually by their mothers, sisters, or aunts, and sometimes by private tutors) or at small private schools, called dame schools, run by women. They typically learned reading from Bibles, catechisms, and hornbooks (so named because of the transparent sheet of horn that covered the pages). The religious content of their training prepared them well for the kind of reading they were expected to do throughout the rest of their lives. In-deed, religious texts remained the most popular material for primers and adult readers until the mid to late eighteenth century. Although most people had limited access to books, which were often quite expensive, many owned or had access to Bibles, psalm books, primers, catechisms, and various almanacs.

In terms of developing writing skills, young girls were often on their own, and it is likely that they taught themselves how to write by imitating the writing of the men in their families. When boys from well-to-do families were sent to learn writing from a writing master, girls were sent to study music and needlework instead. This separation reflected the fact that writing was considered a specialized skill, one that would prepare young men for jobs ranging from shipping clerks to ministers. Although some young women were tutored privately or sent abroad for further education and although by the mid eighteenth century some went to women's academies, they did not attend colonial colleges in any formal way. Yet women's literary circles did exist. The one hosted by Annis Boudinot Stockton for students at the College of Princeton (now Princeton University) became part of college life for young college men and young women from her social circle in the area.

For the most part, however, the largest portion of the population of women did not receive any formal training in letters. This situation produced an interesting circumstance for those who study women's written materials. Because the culture for women outside elite circles was largely oral, writings "by" women of color or women who were poor are not preserved in typical ways, where their authorship is known and where they themselves might have actually written their stories by themselves. Stories by and about members of nonelite status often appeared anonymously in newsprint, or they were dictated to members of the clergy who then retold their tales. Early settler women and Native American, African, and African-descended women received little if any formal training in reading and writing, so many accounts of these women's lives are not available, or, if they exist, they are dictated versions transcribed by someone who was literate. For that matter, early narratives of women's captivities were frequently included in sermons delivered by ministers.

The criminal narrative provides an intriguing instance of a dictated genre. Beginning in the late seventeenth century with execution sermons, criminal confessions and conversions reached print with greater and greater frequency, almost to the extent that criminal narratives became a separate kind of religious confession. The criminal, usually in concert with an editor who was sometimes a minister, composed a narrative of his or her life. Such accounts, in cases of women taken as criminals, are particularly important because they can offer information about women who had limited access to print culture, women about whom little would otherwise be known. *A Faithful Narrative of the Wicked Life and Remarkable Conversion of Patience Boston* (1738), for example, is the account of a Native American servant woman who from her earliest years rebelled against the conditions requiring her servitude. Evidently an alcoholic, she abused her husband and later avenged herself against her final master by drowning his grandson. While awaiting trial she spent much of her time reading the Bible, praying, and listening to sermons. The composition of her narrative, much of which was written in the first person, seems to have been a crucial part of her devotional activities prior to the moment of her hanging.

The rare instance of the conversion of Patience Boston provides a useful reminder: the lives of the women that can be recovered through their written words are typically those of women who had some degree of status within their communities. The instance also aptly indicates the extent to which these women's lived experiences were inextricably intertwined with their literary expressions. If we are to appreciate women's achievements as writers, we need to turn fully to the second question raised earlier in the introduction: What were the conditions of women's lives that affected the kind of writing they engaged in and how often they were able to write? Yet generalization across such a large expanse of time and geographical space is difficult. The women represented in this volume wrote over a span of two centuries. They lived in regions of North America from Maine to Florida and the Caribbean. Primarily from the Anglo-American colonies, they were of different religions, different social classes, and different ethnic backgrounds. In the remainder of our discussion, we will attempt to point out the key differences in women's experiences, even as we discuss the central issue they had in common—that they wrote prose and that their writings have been known to readers for centuries.

Regional differences occurred for women at the outset. In the English colonies of the Northeast, conceived as permanent settlements from the start, women tended to arrive as parts of established families. They also arrived in greater numbers than did women in the South, where the original English arrivals more frequently were either men of the elite class, who hoped to make fortunes from plantations and then return to England, or working men, who

came as indentured servants and hoped, after the expiry of their terms of indenture, to purchase their own land and become independent planters. In the South (known as England's staple colonies) during the earliest settlement era, the men who came over were less likely to bring families with them. Most women who did arrive in the South came as indentured servants. In the earliest Anglo-colonial period, then, there were more women in the English colonies to the North than in those to the South.

After the period of initial settlement, when it can be expected that women shared much of the daily labor with men, patterns of household work emerged that defined gender-specific domestic and agricultural activities. For most women throughout the colonies, daily life centered around household labor. As mentioned above, more than 90 percent of the settlers in Anglo-America lived on land they farmed—as plantation masters, as independent landholders, or as indentured or tenant farmers. The daily women's work in such households involved preparing and preserving food, making clothes (including spinning thread and weaving cloth), cleaning domestic spaces, and supervising children as well as servants or household slaves. Most farm women also engaged in heavy gardening chores that supplied food for the family; women's kitchen gardens, which they tended by themselves, sometimes provided them with money, if they could find a market for any surplus produce. The fields tended by men were generally reserved for cash crops. Wealthier women were more likely to be freed from heavy physical chores because they had access to the labor of servants or house slaves. Nonetheless, middle-level and wealthier women were involved with the household production of cloth and the stitching of garments, and they were responsible for supervising and coordinating the laborers of the household as well as the purchases made for it. Indeed, by the eighteenth century women married to southern planters were expected to manage relatively large household staffs, as plantations attempted to become self-sustaining communities. Middle- and upper-status women, depending on their husbands' positions, might also find themselves in charge of preparing for and entertaining important guests regularly. One of the key marks of a "goodly wife" was her ability to manage the domestic arrangements. This factor perhaps more than any other drove women's interests in writing didactic manuals about their gardens, households, domestic economy, and child rearing.

Regardless of class, the household was the key space in which women had authority and were expected to supervise. According to the theory of "separate spheres," the male head of a household alone represented the family in the public world (the sphere of action outside the home), and the public life of men was seen as clearly separate from the presumed domestic life of women. In actual experience, however, women's activities within the household strongly affected the public perception and the public reception given her family. A well-ordered homestead intimated to the world outside that a family was stable, productive, and reliable. Disorder within the family community could make a family a byword for failure in the world at large. As the example of Eliza Lucas Pinckney shows, Anglo-American women could and did take over the management of even such complex businesses as southern plantations. At different times in her life, Pinckney supervised the operation of her father's, husband's, and son's plantations. On a much broader scale, the Revolutionary War, which disrupted families and removed men from households, led many women to take on men's labor, from farming, smithing, and other physical activities to professional work such as accounting or printing. Public activity was common for women in colonies in regions other than the South as well. In New Netherland (New York), for example, it was common for women to hold nondomestic, public roles, even in administrating the manor holdings of their partners, as did Maria van Cortlandt van Rensselaer after the death of her husband. The theory of separate spheres for men and women in early America belies the lived historical experiences indicating that women's labors were central to a family's public role.

Although they certainly had public influence, women did not have legal status. Women's positions were defined by a colonial system based on English law. Single women could own property. Upon marriage, however, women conveyed all property, by a law of coverture, to their marital partners. In the language of the law, married women were *femmes coverts* (literally, "covered women"), because their legal rights were "covered" or absorbed by those of their husbands. The legal situation of coverture along with the social and domestic constraints that marriage brought to women were regularly discussed in women's writings, whether in those circulated among many readers or just a few. Today many readers know about Abigail Adams's letter to her husband, John, asking that he "Remember the Ladies" while drawing up the Constitution. Adams's plea is one commonly expressed by women of her era. The implied promise of equality offered in the act of the American Revolution did not reach full assent with the development of the U.S. Constitution and Bill of Rights, so that women's rights un-

der the law remained largely the same for decades after independence. The political situation, like women's domestic circumstances as a result of coverture, formed an oft-heard refrain in women's writing of the early national era.

Women wrote often and well about their marriages, their homes, and their families. Single women wrote about the blessedness of having a single life. In legal terms the situation of a single woman was always better than that of a married woman, because the single woman could control her own property. Also, in legal terms, the situation for women seeking divorces improved. Most of the former colonies broke from English tradition at the time the Constitution was written; they allowed absolute divorce, giving important new rights to married women whose husbands abused or deserted them. Changes in inheritance laws also gave daughters and widows greater rights to inherit property. Signs of women's concerns about how to manage themselves with probity if they possessed fortunes are indicated in the greater frequency with which their writings portrayed independent women. Julia Granby, a character in Hannah Webster Foster's *The Coquette* (1797), serves as an apt fictional model for young women who possessed independent fortunes: she is poised, decorous, self-possessed, and eminently moral and wise. Indeed, Foster gave Julia the concluding space of her novel, thus, by implication, indicating where the new nation might best seek its moral and social leadership.

Women's writings during the era of the new republic often featured marital and family concerns. This focus is not surprising given the demographic situation in the regions populated by Anglo-Americans (where population counts usually included white persons only). The average age of marriage for white women in this period was twenty-one or twenty-two. From early in their married lives until menopause, married women could expect to bear children on a regular basis, often spaced about two years apart. The average number of children a woman bore varied with her region, and it depended on her standard of living and the era in which she lived. Taking the average for most regions and most periods, women bore between eight and nine children. Childbirth was dangerous both for mother and child; the death of the mother in childbirth is estimated to have occurred for about one birth in every thirty. A conservative estimate, then, would be that the average woman had six childbirths. Infant mortality is estimated to have been as high as 25 percent. Statistics such as these explain the high incidence in women's writings, especially in their pious writings, of themes related to death, mortality, and the brevity of life. The potential losses of their own lives, along with the frequent loss of their infants and children, figured large in their lives and their written expressions contemplating life's vicissitudes.

Conduct books offered information on all the issues just mentioned—legal relations between the sexes, the independent lives of unmarried women, the management of husbands and children, and the facing of life's trials with patience, fortitude, and resignation. Advice changed over time, however, indicating women's shifting roles in the cultural marketplace. The traditional colonial model of the white family was hierarchical, with mother and children subordinated to the father as head of household and figural patriarch of the family community. After the Revolution a new conception of marriage as a more equal partnership emerged. Historians have argued that this conception of marriage was directly linked to republican ideology; that is, affectionate ties equally shared between husband and wife were seen as the model of voluntary union between citizens. An interesting change in advice books and articles about marriage occurred during the early national period. Whereas formerly men were advised to marry good housewives and dutiful women, books now advised both men and women to seek spouses who exemplified republican virtue, and they stressed women's roles in inspiring that virtue in suitors and maintaining it in husbands. The advice books also reflected similar changes in parent and child relations. In former years advice to parents emphasized a link between their roles as guardians of good discipline and the well-ordered system of their homesteads. During the Revolutionary era and later, however, parents seem to have loosened their controls over their children's lives, notably in giving young adults more freedom regarding marriage choices. Even as greater freedoms seemed to be allotted young adults, women's writings attest that higher expectations seem to have been placed on their becoming responsible mothers and guardians of youth.

In addition to their ties to husbands and children, women also formed important bonds with sisters and with other women relatives and friends. Much of women's fiction depends on a reader's understanding of the "sisterly community." During the period between childhood and marriage, most women found support from circles of women forming what they called their "sisterhood." The honest criticism and guidance that a relative could offer was also stressed as a duty of friendship. Young women were expected to seek guidance not only from women relatives but also from their circles of friends. Marriage could sometimes place a strain on such woman-to-woman relationships, a situation fictionalized in The Coquette. Evidence from correspondences such as those between Sarah Prince Gill and Esther Edwards Burr, however, indicates just how strong and long-lasting women's sisterly friendships could be, despite changes caused by time and by the marriage of one or more women. Fictional representations of women's relations frequently illustrated ideal and not-so-ideal views of friendship and parenting affiliations among women. To continue the example offered by Hannah Foster, Julia Granby acts toward Eliza Wharton with sincere kindness and sisterly affection, whereas Eliza's mother serves as a perfect example of a misguided, self-centered, and ineffective parent.

Women tended to find sisterly and communal fellowship when participating in religious communities, and many writers focus on their religious experiences. Religion was an important part of life throughout the colonies, with the major denomination varying regionally among European settlements. In New England a Puritan tradition established by the original settlers dominated throughout this era. Like the Anglican tradition in the southern colonies, the Puritan faith was patriarchal, and it reinforced the traditional European cultural norms that required women to be submissive and to refrain from public speech on public affairs. Some Puritan women made records of their religious experiences, but they did not normally serve in leadership roles within their congregations. When they attempted to do so, they were usually ousted from the community, as in the often-discussed instance of Anne Hutchinson, who was told to leave the Massachusetts Bay Colony.

In the Middle Atlantic English colonies the Society of Friends (known as Quakers to people outside their community) offered different roles for women. Quaker women wrote about their spiritual experiences, and they spoke publicly about them as well. The Quaker attitude about spirituality, which functioned around their conception of experiencing a divine inner light accessible to all, extended the possibility of religious inspiration and leadership to women as well as men. Like the former indentured servant Elizabeth Ashbridge, who wrote about her spiritual experiences as an Anglican woman who turned to the Society of Friends, Quaker women often spoke about attempting to resist the urge to speak but being forced to speak and write because of strong inner pressures from God that they speak their thoughts. Far from being exiled, Quaker women who took leadership roles often became highly respected within their communities. Indeed, both men's and women's writings attest that such earnest women were considered desirable as wives by wealthy Quaker men.

Women of other faiths also carved out public roles for themselves. Sarah Osborn, a Congregationalist, pursued writing, teaching, and evangelical work among local African and African-descended peoples in Newport, Rhode Island, and she persisted in this work in spite of criticism. Another woman, Jemima Wilkinson, who once called herself "the Universal Friend," founded her own sect. Wilkinson toured New England and Pennsylvania as a preacher, and she attracted an affluent, educated audience. Yet by attracting an upper-level congregation Wilkinson threatened the social order. Such independence as Wilkinson's often had dire consequences for women. During the course of her ministry, Wilkinson was charged with blasphemy, fraud, promiscuity, theft, and even murder, before she sought escape from her critics by founding a wilderness community of her faithful followers.

Religion was a key theme in women's written discourse, especially in the earliest colonial years. During the era of the new republic, discussions of education competed for space with discussions about creating a godly nation. From about 1785 onward, national leaders began to discuss—indeed, insist on—the importance of women's education. Because the success of the new republic was construed as depending on the existence of an informed populace, leaders emphasized the importance of general education. The instruction of women was particularly crucial to the future of the new republic, argued theorists of education such as Judith Sargent Murray and Benjamin Rush. Only educated women would be best prepared to help their children and husbands become virtuous and informed republican citizens. These ideas drew on common, later-eighteenth-century assumptions about men and women that were quite different from the ideas expressed by Winthrop a century earlier. For Winthrop, women's mental capacities were quite unlike men's, and women would become enfeebled by intellectual stimulation. By contrast, according to eighteenth-century educational theory, it was agreed that women's natures were different from men's—women were thought to have superior moral and religious sensibilities, for example. Yet women's capacities for abstract reasoning were considered to be nearly the same. Some historians have suggested that the shift in attitudes about women's capabilities can best be understood as a class-based reform movement that reflected the interests of an emerg-

ing elite in gathering power to its own culture-conserving agenda. Reading the situation more radically in terms of what it meant in the actual daily living circumstances for women, it is possible to find signs of greater responsibility being given white women for the nation's success or failure. It is also useful to remember that, despite changing ideas about education for women (ideas which were not necessarily put into practice), formal educational opportunities for children who were African or African-descended, Native American, or poor remained quite limited, and they were usually driven by missionary impulses rather than by assumptions about civic liberty, racial equality, and inherent ability.

Of course not all colonial women supported the American Revolution or were affected by it in similar ways. As their diaries and letters vividly illustrate, Loyalist women—women who wished to remain loyal subjects of the British crown—faced significant challenges during this era. They feared being tarred and feathered, and they worried about vandalism of their homes. They saw their entire way of life being taken from them by people whom they considered unjustifiably rebellious against the authority of England. They were often bereft of their husbands, fathers, and sons, who were arrested and imprisoned. Records of the Revolution indicate that the confusion and dislocation of the war had a different impact on the lives of women who were slaves or indentured servants. For serving women, whether enslaved or free, the Revolutionary War afforded an opportunity to run away or to attempt to negotiate freedom, based on wartime work with their masters (a term applied to both the owner of a slave and the owner of an indenture) or as camp followers. For some African-descended women who could not join the armies and whose family responsibilities often made running away impractical, the war represented different opportunities and challenges. In a case that helped to end slavery in Massachusetts, the enslaved Elizabeth Freeman successfully sued for her freedom in 1781, arguing that according to the state constitution, all were born free and equal. Yet freedom itself could present new challenges, particularly for elderly women. In her 1783 petition to the General Court of Massachusetts, a woman identified simply as "Belinda, an African" appealed for financial support after she was freed but left destitute when her master of fifty years fled Boston and abandoned her at the onset of the war.

At the conclusion of the Revolutionary War, the ideology of republican womanhood encouraged white women to assume a form of agency, though an indirect one, in the politics of the new nation. During the war married women were expected to take care of households and farms for months at a time in the absence of husbands. After the war, when husbands, fathers, and sons returned home, women's central roles in the ongoing operations returned to the more circumscribed domestic economy that had been expected of them prior to the war. A rhetoric of duty argued for the greater significance of the woman *in* the household rather than *running it*. If women assumed political roles outside the home, many warned, they would be neglecting their most important political duties: safeguarding the morals of their husbands and children inside their homes. It was a confusing time for women, as the conflicting written testimony about what constituted "right conduct" attests.

Early American women's writing is clearly marked by the conditions of their lived experiences. As those conditions changed over time, women's written endeavors shifted. In recent years, literary and social historians have come to view the study of women's materials as central to our ongoing discussion about life in early America. Far from having been excluded from the world they inhabited, women seem to have been central to its continued functioning. A volume such as this one attests to the resilience of the women of those former days even as it gives evidence of the important new scholarship on the lives and writings of the women thus described.

Because many of the paradigms used in the study of women's writing from 1820 to the present day are not applicable to the work of earlier women writers, scholars and general readers alike are attempting to develop historically and culturally reliable conceptual frameworks for the study of these writers. The reprinting of important works by seventeenth- and eighteenth-century women has facilitated their study and reassessment. In addition to studying the works of women such as Abigail Adams, who came from a socially prominent family and who was well-educated, it is now possible to study the works of indentured servants such as Elizabeth Ashbridge. Many important documents remain in manuscript form in archives, however, or they are currently out of print or available only in microform. In this regard, it is important to keep in mind that the study of early American women overwhelmingly favors the study of printed media and manuscript evidence, and it tends to overlook women associated with oral cultures, such as Native American women,

African and African-descended women, and poor women in general.

Choosing writers for inclusion in this volume was a challenging process. Although some much-studied writers (such as Abigail Adams, Judith Sargent Murray, and Hannah Webster Foster) were obvious choices, many writers who are only beginning to receive scholarly attention presented harder choices. In this volume we have included women who wrote primarily prose, who lived and published (or circulated) their works in North America and the Caribbean (with a focus on the area of the present-day United States), and who flourished before 1820. To assure general accessibility of these writers, we first selected those whose writings were published during their own lifetimes or are available in modern editions. When discriminating among writers who had published small numbers of works, we favored writers whose works have been reprinted. We also tended to select writers who have received significant attention from contemporary scholars, a decision that in some cases led us to include writers who had not been published during their lifetimes. Although some writers, particularly diarists and letter writers, might not have been formally published until long after their deaths, this fact by no means necessarily implies that their works were not read by or known to others, sometimes quite widely, because of circulation in original manuscript and manuscript copies.

After these initial considerations, we took into account several issues of representation. We tried to ensure adequate representation of the major prose genres of the early era. We also attempted to include more unusual genres to illustrate the wide range of fields in which women sometimes created written discourse. In addition, we attempted to include writers from underrepresented groups, such as those from the South, those who remained Loyalist, and those whose lives were less privileged.

Yet any selection process inevitably eliminates writers worthy of consideration. Our selection process reveals the problems those who study early American materials regularly face: much of the "American" literary past is primarily a study of the white Anglo-Americans' stories. We have tried within the necessary constraints of this volume to present the broadest possible range of significant works written by women during the colonial and early national periods. Volumes such as this one attest to the fact that, far from being excluded from the American cultural arena, women

have been participating in American literary-cultural processes, all along the way.
                                          —*Carla Mulford, with Angela Vietto and
                                                                Amy E. Winans*

Acknowledgments

This book was produced by Bruccoli Clark Layman, Inc. Karen L. Rood, senior editor for the *Dictionary of Literary Biography* series, was the in-house editor.

Administrative support was provided by Ann M. Cheschi, Tenesha S. Lee, and Shawna M. Tillman.

Bookkeeper is Neil Senol.

Copyediting supervisor is Phyllis A. Avant. The copyediting staff includes Brenda Carol Blanton, Christine Copeland, Thom Harman, Melissa D. Hinton, Jannette L. Giles, and Raegan E. Quinn. Freelance copyeditors are Rebecca Mayo and Jennie Williamson.

Editorial associate is Jeff Miller.

Layout and graphics staff includes Janet E. Hill, Mark J. McEwan, and Alison Smith.

Office manager is Kathy Lawler Merlette.

Photography editors are Margo Dowling and Paul Talbot. Photographic copy work was performed by Joseph M. Bruccoli.

Production manager is Marie L. Parker.

SGML supervisor is Cory McNair. The SGML staff includes Linda Drake, Frank Graham, Jennifer Harwell, and Alex Snead.

Systems manager is Marie L. Parker.

Database manager is Javed Nurani. Kim Kelly performed data entry.

Typesetting supervisor is Kathleen M. Flanagan. The typesetting staff includes Karla Corley Brown, Pamela D. Norton, and Patricia Flanagan Salisbury. Freelance typesetters include Deidre Murphy and Delores Plastow.

Walter W. Ross and Steven Gross did library research. They were assisted by the following librarians at the Thomas Cooper Library of the University of South Carolina: Linda Holderfield and the interlibrary-loan staff; reference-department head Virginia Weathers; reference librarians Marilee Birchfield, Stefanie Buck, Stefanie DuBose, Rebecca Feind, Karen Joseph, Donna Lehman, Charlene Loope, Anthony McKissick, Jean Rhyne, and Kwamine Simpson; circulation-department head Caroline Taylor; and acquisitions-searching supervisor David Haggard.

The editors of this volume would like to thank Judith Fetterly, who envisioned the DLB series on American Women Prose Writers and approached Matthew J. Bruccoli of Bruccoli Clark Layman with her idea. Her guidance through the early planning stages was essential.

We would like to thank our willing, interested, and painstaking contributors for making this volume possible. For suggestions of writers to include in the book we thank Joseph Fichtelberg, Steven Kagle, James A. Levernier, and John Saillant. We thank William Pencak for helping with some historical questions and Frank Shuffelton for answering our questions about Jane Colden. For their useful suggestions on illustrations we acknowledge the efforts of several contributors: Jennifer Jordan Baker, Lee S. Burchfield, Deborah Dietrich, Ellen Donovan, Edward Gallagher, Edith Gelles, Allison Giffen, Joanna Gillespie, Amanda Gilroy, Sandra M. Gustafson, Thomas Hallock, Mark Kamrath, Erika Kreger, Amy Schrager Lang, Lisa Logan, Etta Madden, Patricia Parker, Sandra Petrulionis, Karen Poremski, Nicholas D. Rombes, Doreen Alvarez Saar, Gail Smith, Michele Lise Tarter, Michael Vella, and Frances Murphy Zauhar.

Don Bialistosky, Head of the English Department at Pennsylvania State University, deserves a special note of thanks for giving the editors some departmental support while they developed the volume.

From start to finish, Karen L. Rood has been cheerful and resourceful. Would that all authors could have the good luck to work with such a fine editor as she. The editors wish to thank her and the staff at Bruccoli Clark Layman for their unflagging attention to the details we should have noticed earlier and surely would have noticed once the volume was in print.

Finally, the editors have some personal notes of thanks to extend. Carla Mulford thanks Louis Cellucci for his continued interest in her work and his attentiveness to her well-being. Angela Vietto thanks Alan Bilansky who, in addition to keeping the incoming and outgoing mail in order, helped with proofing and fact checking. Amy Winans thanks Windsor Morgan for his encouragement and his help with computer transmissions of texts.

Dictionary of Literary Biography® • Volume Two Hundred

American Women Prose
Writers to 1820

Dictionary of Literary Biography

Abigail Adams
(22 November 1744 – 28 October 1818)

Edith B. Gelles
Stanford University

with

Angela Vietto
Pennsylvania State University

BOOKS: *Letters of Mrs. Adams, The Wife of John Adams,* edited, with a memoir, by Charles Francis Adams (2 volumes, Boston: Little & Brown, 1840; revised edition, 1 volume, Boston: Wilkins, Carter, 1848);
Warren-Adams Letters, 2 volumes (Boston: Massachusetts Historical Society, 1917);
New Letters of Abigail Adams, 1788–1801, edited by Stewart Mitchell (Boston: Houghton Mifflin, 1947);
The Adams-Jefferson Letters: The Complete Correspondence between Thomas Jefferson and Abigail and John Adams, 2 volumes, edited by Lester Cappon (Chapel Hill: University of North Carolina Press, 1959);
Adams Family Correspondence, 1761–1782, The Adams Papers, Series II, 6 volumes to date, edited by L. H. Butterfield, Richard Alan Ryerson, and others (Cambridge, Mass.: Harvard University Press, 1963–1993).

Abigail Smith Adams is best known to the literary world for the letters she wrote during the half century crucial to U.S. nationhood. She is also historically important because she married John Adams (1735–1826), the second president of the United States (1797–1801); and she was the mother of John Quincy Adams (1767–1848), the sixth president (1825–1829). The letters she wrote from the early 1760s until the end of her life represent the most complete surviving record of a woman's expe-

riences during the Revolutionary and early national eras of American history.

Adams's letters reveal her efforts to fashion herself as a model woman according to the standards of the day: a capable and faithful wife, an effective household manager, a devoted mother and sister, and a discriminating reader and writer. They illuminate the public world of politics and the private world of domestic life that Adams and her family inhabited. As wife of one president and mother of another, she recorded her observations from a special perspective. She commented on the salient political issues of her time as well as voicing her concerns about social development, including religion, education, and child rearing. She noted details of everyday life, such as styles of dress and manners, and she wrote of philosophy, science, and poetry. She sometimes appears modern, as in her appeal to her husband during the Revolutionary War to "remember the ladies" by providing them greater legal protection under the new government. She functioned within a community of women—sisters, nieces, daughters, aunts, servants, and friends. Her correspondents included many of the great men of her time, including her friend Thomas Jefferson. The varied facets of her life give Adams's letters historical and literary importance, allowing the reader to learn about politics and society in early America.

Adams's letters have survived, thousands of them, because it was customary for people to preserve their correspondence. In addition, however,

3

Abigail Adams, 1766 (portrait by Benjamin Blyth;
Massachusetts Historical Society)

the Adamses, with their acute historical sensibilities, saved nearly everything they wrote. When first approached about publishing a selection of her letters in 1818, Abigail Adams responded, "No. No. . . . Heedless and inaccurate as I am, I have too much vanity to risk my reputation before the public." The first edition of her letters, heavily edited by her grandson Charles Francis Adams, appeared in 1840. The book was so popular that it was followed by three more editions during that decade.

In Adams's day letter writing was one of the most important literary genres for women. It was considered inappropriate for a woman to have a public role. Letter writing provided a respectable outlet for women's expression, because letters, while they were governed by literary conventions, were expected to be read privately. Adams's letters reveal literary talent and a distinctive and forceful voice. Her gifts were natural. Deriving her style from her sincerity, her cheerful temperament, her intelligence, and her keen powers of observation, she wrote with wit and expressed her emotions and opinions.

The eighteenth century is often considered the Golden Age of letter writing. The reliability of the mails was gradually improving, making regular correspondence easier. Moreover, English usage had become less formal, changing from the formulaic scholastic tradition of the Renaissance to a style more centrally concerned with human emotions and everyday experiences. The style that became the model for letter writers was adapted from conversation. Letters were considered a form of conversation in which the writer and reader carried on a written exchange with all the sociability of informal face-to-face discourse. The favored diction of letters was simple, economical, and direct, and the best letter writers, like the best speakers, took care to avoid pretentious language and long-windedness. Adams would have learned these epistolary conventions from any one of the many eighteenth-century letter-writing manuals designed to teach proper form and style to young women of her social class.

Abigail Smith was born on 22 November 1744 in her father's parsonage at Weymouth, Massachusetts. Her parents came from two respectable New England lineages. Her mother, Elizabeth Quincy Smith, descended from Quincys, Nortons, Shepards, and Winthrops—families who were, in the words of Charles Francis Adams, "the bedrock of the Bay Colony's Puritan theocracy." Her father, William Smith, came from a family of merchants and ship captains. Abigail Smith's youth—and, indeed, most of her adult life—was spent in the countryside around Boston. As was typical for young women, she was educated at home, where she read litera-

The house in Braintree, Massachusetts, where Abigail Adams lived for most of the first twenty years of her marriage

ture—popular, classical, and spiritual—and studied French. She had two sisters, Mary, who was two years older, and Elizabeth, who was six years younger. Her brother, William, seems to have been a disappointment to his family. He died in middle age of alcohol-related illnesses.

Abigail Smith met John Adams, a young lawyer, when she was sixteen and he was twenty-six. Her first surviving letters record their three-year courtship. In these letters Smith and Adams engaged in witty probing of one another's character. These letters are also flirtatious and amorous. "You was please'd to say that the receipt of a letter from your Diana always gave you pleasure," Smith wrote in September 1763, using her pen name Diana (an eighteenth-century convention) as a self-reference. "Whether this was designed for a complement (a commodity I acknowledg that you very seldom deal in) or as a real truth, you best know." Having challenged Adams on several fronts in one brief phrase, she continued: "Yet if I was to judge a certain persons Heart, by what upon the like occasion passes through a cabinet of my own, I should be apt to suspect it as a truth," persisting as though in conversation. "And why may I not? when I have often been tempted to believe; that they were both cast in the same mould, only with this difference, that yours was made, with a harder mettle, and

therefore is less liable to an impression. Whether they have both an eaquil quantity of Steel, I have not yet been able to discover, but do not imagine they are either of them deficient." The apt use of metaphor here is characteristic of her later writing.

Whether Abigail Smith's parents approved of Adams as a son-in-law is questionable. For his benediction at their marriage on 25 October 1764 Reverend Smith preached on the text, "For John came neither eating bread nor drinking wine, and Ye say, 'He hath a devil.'" In the memoir that accompanies his edition of Abigail Adams's letters, Charles Francis Adams claimed that a common prejudice against lawyers in that early era predisposed the Smiths to disapprove of John Adams's profession. Nevertheless, Abigail Smith chose to marry John Adams and moved with him to Braintree, where he inherited property from his father.

The first ten years of their marriage were Adams's childbearing years and were marked by the resistance to colonial rule in which John Adams became involved. Abigail Adams's letters from this period are sparse, likely because of her preoccupation with responsibilities as a young wife and mother. Within seven years five babies were born, four of whom would survive: Abigail (1765–1813); John Quincy (1767–1848), named for Abigail's maternal grandparent; Susanna (1768–1770); Charles (1770–1800); and Thomas (1772–1832). (Adams became pregnant once more, giving birth to a stillborn daughter in 1777.) Abigail Adams's extant letters from this period record the escalating events that led to the American Revolution. In these letters the contrast between public events and developments in the Adams family is striking. An early letter to a friend expressed her excitement with motherhood: "Your Diana become a Mamma—can you credit it?" she wrote in July 1765, still using her youthful pen name. A few years later, in May 1773, she exclaimed to her friend Mercy Otis Warren, "The tea that bainful weed is arrived," alluding to the tea that was subject to the British import tax that led to the Boston Tea Party the following December. "The flame is kindled and like Lightening it catches from Soul to Soul. Great will be the devastation if not timely quenched or allayed by some more Lenient Measures," she wrote to Warren.

For the next quarter of a century John Adams was involved in public service while Abigail Adams stayed at home most of the time. During that long period, excepting the years that she joined him in Europe or in the national capitals during his vice- presidential and presidential years, she communicated with her husband by letter. In summer 1774 John Adams was elected to serve as a delegate to the First Continental Congress, which met in Philadelphia. His return to Braintree in the late fall was short-lived, for within months the battle at Lexington occurred, and he departed once more to serve at distant places for the duration of the war. Thus began the torrent of letter writing by which the Adamses conducted much of their marriage. At first Abigail Adams wrote primarily as a means of communication about practical matters, such as the condition of the farm or the health of the family, but she gradually discovered that letter writing provided intellectual, emotional, and social benefits as well.

Her spontaneous recording of her experiences began in fall 1775, soon after John Adams departed for Philadelphia. A dysentery epidemic swept through the Boston area, and Abigail Adams's entire household—children, servants, farm laborers, and Adams herself—was afflicted. Despite her illness and with assistance from her mother, Adams served as nurse and physician to the sick. She wrote letters to her husband during the entire episode, describing the day-to-day course of the disease through their household and community. She also described how she sought scarce medicines, moved two of her healthy children out of the house to avoid infection, and endeavored to balance the needs of her various patients. Her letters about this epidemic make clear Adams's conception of her responsibilities as manager of an extended household and as its head in the absence of her husband.

Clearly Adams wrote not just to keep John Adams informed about conditions at home, but also as a means of coping with her feelings. Letter writing substituted for conversations with her husband. She wrote to invoke his presence, to "speak" through her pen the words she would have told him in person, and she found comfort in her writing. Her worries were well founded. The epidemic brought two fatalities to the Adams household: first one of her servants and then her mother. "Have pitty upon me, have pitty upon me o! thou my beloved for the hand of God presseth me soar," she pleaded in a letter to John Adams.

From this experience and others during the long and difficult years of the Revolution, Adams learned about letter writing as a means of coping with her emotions. In time she began to write with the intensity of one who enjoyed the process itself, having discovered that writing allowed her the satisfaction of re-creating her world in letters. In fact, she discovered that writing was a more effective medium than speech: "My pen is always freer than my tongue," she confessed to her husband in October 1775. "I have wrote many things to you that I suppose I never could have talk'd."

While Adams's letters are intelligent, sincere, and often poignant, they are also the products of a limited education. Typical of women in the late eighteenth century, her spelling and punctuation are faulty, reflecting limited schooling. Even her handwriting is untutored. In contrast to the polished literacy of her husband and most men of their social circle, her grasp of the grammatical foundations and of penmanship is rudimentary. (When her grandson Charles Francis Adams edited her letters for publication in the early nineteenth century, he corrected and standardized her English.) Like many women of her day, Abigail Adams learned to write out words according to the way they sounded to her ear. For example, she heard and wrote down "mar," for which her grandson substituted the more refined "mother." Though Adams might seem uneducated by modern standards, however, she was exceptionally well educated for a woman of the late eighteenth century. She grew up in a social class and a household where literacy was valued; yet compared to men of similar background, she was sparsely educated. The Bible and some English literature often represented the primary texts to which girls

The house in Auteuil, France, where Abigail and John Adams lived for ten months in 1784–1785

were exposed. While these books were good models, they paled in comparison with the intensity of the classical education that was available and often mandatory for young men. Throughout her lifetime Adams complained about the education afforded to women: "It is really mortifying Sir," she complained to her friend John Thaxter in January 1778, "when a woman possessd of a common share of understanding considers the difference of Education between the male and female Sex, even in those families where Education is attended too."

Pained by the shortcomings of her own education, Adams began early in her marriage to read the books in John Adams's vast library, and she became quite erudite. After his departure, especially, she read broadly in history, classics, politics, literature, medicine, and science. Her enterprise of making herself more learned is reflected in the content of her letters. Her spelling and punctuation, however, remained rudimentary, and her hand was never easily legible. In good part her poor handwriting was the result of the haste with which she wrote and the fact that she rarely recopied her letters to make them more legible. "My letters to you are first thoughts, without correction," she admitted to her sister Mary Cranch in May 1798.

Another way to appreciate Adams's letters is to consider them within the context of those written by her female correspondents. Such comparisons reveal much about the assumptions and self-constructions of the literate community within which Adams wrote. The letters of Adams's younger sister, Elizabeth Shaw Peabody, demonstrate a sense of herself and her readers as women of discriminating taste in literary and artistic matters. Peabody participated in popular modes of aesthetic discourse, and she often mentioned prominent literary figures, including William Shakespeare. On one occasion, she wrote, "Was anyone Blessed with the descriptive genious of a Thompson, had they the sublimity of a Milton, or the ease and perspicuity of the sweet Bard that Painted the Forests of Windsor and made men harmoniously quiver in his Lines, they could not give you an adequate Idea of the Glorious Scene, that this very moment ravishes my Sight and transports my Soul." It had snowed.

Adams's older sister, Mary Cranch, in contrast, was more serious than either of her sisters; she was neither as romantic as Elizabeth nor as witty as Abigail. Cranch's letters are those of an intelligent and literate woman making keen and wise observations about the world. Among the sisters she was a primary source of "gossip," that is, analysis of the behavior of individuals in their social group. "Parson Wibird visits me every other day," she informed Adams in winter 1787. "He still lives in that vile house. I told him the other day that nobody but he could live in it. . . . That house is so scandalous that in Boston the selectmen would tear it down." As scholars such as Patricia Meyer Spacks have suggested, such gossip has a cohesive force on society, expressing its rules and values. Cranch's writing demonstrates the utility of letter writing for this kind of social discourse.

Among Adams's correspondents none has achieved and deserved eminence more than Mercy Otis Warren, whom Adams first met in 1773 and with whom she exchanged letters for almost fifty years. Warren was a generation older than Adams, which accounts for a certain awkwardness in Adams's earliest correspondence with this venerated neighbor from Plymouth, Massachusetts. Unlike Adams, Warren had been well educated, sharing a tutor with her famous brother, James Otis Jr., a Harvard classmate and close friend of John Adams. Warren, moreover, was a published author, beginning with plays and poetry (published pseudonymously), and finally publishing her three-volume *History of the Rise, Progress and Termination of the American Revolution* (1806).

Adams's earliest letters to Warren indicate both her admiration for Warren's accomplishments and her sense of the value of exchanging letters with a woman whom she wished to emulate. "By requesting a correspondence you have kindly given me an opportunity to thank you for the happy Hours I enjoyed whilst at your House," Adams responded to Warren's invitation in July 1773. "Thus embolden'd," she continued, "I venture to stretch my pinions, and tho like the timorous Bird I fail in the attempt and tumble to the ground yet sure the Effort is laudable, nor will I suffer my pride, (which is greatly increased since my more intimate acquaintance with you) to debar me the pleasure, and improvement I promise myself from this correspondence tho I suffer by the comparison." Warren responded at length, and magnanimously: "I shall pass over in silence the Complementary introduction to your Letter, not because these Expressions of Esteem are frequently words of Course without any other design but to Convey an Idea of politeness as the Characteristic of the person the most Lavish therein." Warren's sincerity is apparent, but her letter—as this brief quotation may indicate—is marked by affected, elaborate, and obscure language. Typical of learned people of the time, Warren's sentences are wordy, overwrought, and ponderous. In comparison Adams's prose has a spontaneous and personalized expressiveness that makes her writing more accessible for many

readers. Indeed, in the twentieth century Adams is the better known and more frequently read of the two women.

Adams's unself-conscious literary legacy stands as an important historic record of social life, especially of women, in her era. Her temperament, her serious commitment to values, and her natural eloquence have survived the passage of time to give life and importance to her letters two centuries later. Yet one letter in particular has ensured Adams's relevance in the late twentieth century. On 31 March 1776 Adams wrote to her husband, who had traveled to Philadelphia the previous year as one of the Massachusetts delegates to the Continental Congress. She had recently learned that John Adams was serving on a committee to draft the Declaration of Independence, and understanding the significance of this appointment, she used the opportunity to approach him about an idea that had continued to take up her thoughts about American independence. Realizing that the past was being dismantled and the future was being shaped and stimulated by patriotic rhetoric about freedom and oppression, she proposed for his consideration an issue that seemed to her contradictory of the men's revolutionary impulses. In the middle of a paragraph about recent developments in Boston, she wrote, "I long to hear that you have declared an independancy." Affirming her revolutionary patriotism, she continued, "and by the way in the new Code of Laws which I suppose it will be necessary for you to make I desire you would Remember the Ladies and be more generous and favourable to them than your ancestors." Innocuously situated in midparagraph, those words have become the signal statement for which Abigail Adams is remembered. Especially during the twentieth century, the passage has resonated powerfully for those seeking greater rights for women.

Adams's thinking about the rhetoric of human freedom and equality had taken her in a direction that not many people of her time, men or women, had contemplated. Adams continued her 31 March letter with more-specific observations: "Do not put such unlimited power into the hands of the Husbands. Remember all Men would be tyrants if they could." She went on to criticize the founders for another paradox, this time about slavery: "I have sometimes been ready to think that the passion for Liberty cannot be Eaquelly Strong in the Breasts of those who have been accustomed to deprive their fellow Creatures of theirs." With this comment on the injustice of slavery, Adams touched on the sensitive issue that caused the greatest disagreement

Abigail and John Adams in the 1790s (portraits by Gilbert Stuart; National Portrait Gallery, Washington, D.C.; Gifts of Mrs. Robert Homans)

among the colonial representatives. Realizing perhaps that the radical nature of her outburst would appear ridiculous to the men in Philadelphia, she focused again on the issue of women's condition, this time teasing her husband. "If perticuliar care and attention is not paid to the Laidies," she wrote, "we are determined to foment a Rebelion, and will not hold ourselves bound by any Laws in which we have no voice, or Representation." Clearly, Adams did not mean to organize a revolt or break the law, but jokes provide a method for making a point, when a person knows that the cause is likely to be dismissed. Joking, furthermore, like teasing, is a device that is effective primarily among intimates. Adams often used this approach when introducing a sensitive issue to her husband. John Adams, understanding full well this private code, replied in a like vein.

Adams's admonition to her husband to "Remember the Ladies" has frequently been inflated to imply that she was a radical feminist for her time. She was not. Her argument continued with the request that men treat women humanely: "Regard us then as Beings placed by providence under your protection and in immitation of the Supreem Being make use of that power only for our happiness." She

did not ask for property rights, nor did she ever imagine that women might (or should) vote. What was notable for her time was that her few lines of complaint summarized and protested the subordinate social status of women and African Americans in revolutionary America. In this private communication to her husband, Abigail Adams appealed for consideration, recognition, and leniency from the men who were designing the future of the nation. She reminded them that they should specifically recognize the defenselessness of women before the law and restrict the power that men had to control women. She argued that they should break with the past. She observed that it would require laws to protect women, since men would continue to oppress women in the absence of legal restrictions on their unlimited power. She urged men to give up the title of "master"—invoking the imagery of slavery to which she had earlier alluded in this same letter—for that of "friend." In fact the Adamses referred to one another as "dearest friend," drawing on the contemporary notion of marriage as a material, emotional, and spiritual partnership. While scholars debate the extent to which such a conception of marriage could have been taken as a partnership of equals, drawing on this rhetoric would still have highlighted the presumably benevolent nature of companionate marriage.

Adams's statement is unusual among white Anglo-American women of her period. She ventured to use her influence as a wife of an important politician to affect policy. John Adams was in a position to introduce her ideas into the public debate in the same way that he could have raised the issue of slavery that she suggested. Yet the driving motive in John Adams's mission was to create unity among the diverse and quarrelsome colonies, and for him to support the dissolution of slavery or the rights of women to civil status would have ensured disunity. Consequently, after John and Abigail Adams joked briefly about the proposal, they seem to have dropped the subject.

A topic that Abigail Adams did continue to pursue, however, was women's education. She criticized a society that separated boys from their sisters at an early age, and in summer 1776 she waged a brief campaign regarding educational matters. "I most sincerely wish," she wrote to her husband, "that our new constitution may be distinguished for Learning and Virtue. If we mean to have Heroes, Statesmen and Philosophers, we should have learned women. The world perhaps would laugh at me, and accuse me of vanity," she continued, self-conscious at the audacity of her proposal. "If as much depends as is allowed upon the early Education of youth and the first principals which are instilld take the deepest root, great benifit must arise from litirary accomplishment in women." John Adams concurred in this case, as indicated by his response, "Your sentiments on the Importance of Education in Women, are exactly agreeable to my own." Even so, women's education was not to be a part of the constitutional program in the early republic, as the Adamses knew well.

When she challenged the legal subordination of women in her time, Abigail Adams was thinking progressively in a way that few women in her social group dared to contemplate. While she did not write again about changing women's civil status, she continued to advocate improvement in women's education for the remainder of her life. Her protests and her advocacy, however, appear only in letters to her private network of correspondents. She did not consider herself a public figure, nor did she aspire to public acclaim or a professional role, as did Mercy Otis Warren, among other early women writers. Adams's modern status as an author certainly would have surprised her. Indeed, it might have dismayed her.

For almost a decade, while her husband was away dealing with the problems of the nation, Abigail Adams supported herself, her children, and her household by taking over her husband's role as breadwinner. She managed their farm for four years before finally letting it out to tenants. She began a small business by selling locally items that John Adams sent from Europe. She negotiated for and purchased property (in his name, since married women could not hold land in their own names) so as to enlarge their estate. She speculated in currency and paid their taxes.

She undertook these activities with the understanding that they were her patriotic duties in wartime. "The unfealing world may consider it in what light they please," she wrote to John Adams in mid 1777. "I consider it as a sacrifice to my Country." Early in the Revolution, Adams had adopted a new pen name, calling herself "Portia," after the self-sacrificing wife of the Roman statesman Brutus. At the end of the hostilities in June 1782 she surveyed the scope of her sacrifices and declared: "Patriotism in the female Sex is the most disinterested of all virtues." She constructed a catalogue of the indignities that persisted, despite women's contributions to the war effort. "Excluded from honours and from offices, we cannot attach ourselves to the State or Government," she wrote dispiritedly. "Even in the freeest countrys our property is subject to the countroul and disposal of our partners, to whom the Laws have given a sovereign Authority."

Adams's lament—for she was complaining rather than petitioning for change—noted that women had no voice in making laws but were obliged nonetheless to submit to them. She was reminding John Adams of the irony of her case, given that lack of representation in Parliament had been a source of the colonial grievance with England. She continued: "Yet all History and every age exhibit Instances of patriotick virtue in the female Sex; which considering our situation equals the most Heroick of yours." She concluded with a stinging rebuke: "You can only die on the field of Battle, but we have the misfortune to survive those whom we Love most." Impassioned, angry, defiant, she wrote her last words on the subject: "I will take praise to myself," she announced; "I feel that it is my due, for having sacrificed so large a portion of my peace and happiness to promote the welfare of my country." Her sacrifices continued. In 1783, after the signing of the Treaty of Paris, John Adams remained in Europe, hoping that Congress would appoint him as the first American minister to Great Britain. Although his wife urged him to return, John Adams vacillated. Finally she decided to join him in Paris. In June of 1784 Abigail Adams, who had never before traveled beyond the environs of Boston, sailed for England with her daughter, Abigail, aboard the merchant ship *Active*.

The character of Adams's letters changed after her departure for Europe. In her youth she had begun to write letters as a social convention. Later she wrote as a means of maintaining contact with people, especially her husband. Once she had discovered the therapeutic benefits of the writing process, her letters had become a colorful patchwork of experiences, gossip, business, thoughts, observations, and feelings. They were mostly written spontaneously and with a distinct reader in mind. Beginning with her voyage to England in June 1784, however, her letters also become those of reporter or travel journalist. No longer did she assume that she addressed a discrete and private audience, for she was aware that her descriptions of her adventures and impressions of Europe would be circulated within her community of readers and friends and reach many people who would never have the same travel opportunities as she. (Of course, some letters were still particularly designed to conduct private business, such as the care of her sons or properties.)

Adams's travelogues began during the six-week voyage to England, when she composed a running commentary about shipboard conditions. For the first ten days she wrote between bouts of extreme seasickness, which afflicted her and all the unseasoned passengers aboard the four-masted vessel. Once recovered, however, she began to occupy her time by overseeing the cleaning of her cabin and the ship's galley. She also began to study the skills of navigation, to read the several books on politics and medical science that she had brought along, and to engage with other passengers in conversation and games. Probably not since childhood had she spent so leisurely a period of time, and she appreciated it. "I went last evening upon deck," she wrote to her sister Mary Cranch in July 1784, "to view that phenomenon of Nature, a blazing ocean. A light flame spreads over the ocean, in appearance, with thousands and thousands of sparkling gems, resembling our fire-flies in a dark night." She was filled, she added, with feelings of "the sublime." In this manner she began her travel reporting, recording the reactions of an American woman abroad in the 1780s.

From the time she and her daughter landed in England, Adams compared conditions in the Old World with those at home. While noting differences appreciatively, she most often concluded that things

—including people, food, customs, and church architecture—were better in America. Not only was this provincial attitude a defensive posture, but it was also a response to the language barrier in France and the cold reception of Americans in England in the wake of the war.

Her letters home provide vivid accounts of new experiences, some of them startling. When she described a holdup of her coach in Blackheath, a forest notorious for its roving bands of robbers, she sympathized with one of the bandits. She wrote that one, who "looked like a youth twenty only, attempted to lift his hat, and looked Despair." She also described the faded glory of their forty-room residence on the outskirts of Paris. On the first floor were the public rooms, including "the saloon . . . where we receive company." She called this room "very elegant, and about a third larger than General Warren's Hall," comparing it to the finest in Massachusetts. She loved attending the theater and was enchanted by the Marquis de Lafayette, a hero of the American Revolution. She met Jefferson, whom she called "one of the choice ones of the earth." She struggled to master French by assigning herself a play to read every day. Lacking fluency, she at times considered herself "in the midst of the world in solitude."

After ten months John Adams's appointment as American minister to Great Britain came through, and the Adamses moved to London. Abigail Adams left Paris somewhat regretfully, calling it a "dying leave" to see a place for the last time, but she was also relieved to enter an English-speaking world. Yet she and her husband entered that world as official representatives of former British colonies that had recently become states in a war that most English people did not understand. The stigma of the American Revolution made their three-year residence in London difficult for the Adamses. They were required to entertain on a scale that his minister's income could hardly support, and they had to make appearances at state functions and social activities that Abigail Adams (if not her husband) found boring. Her responsibilities were dauntingly strange, but the months in Paris had provided her with some opportunity to learn about the formalities of social life in the European diplomatic service.

Letter writing eased her nervousness before her first audience with the royal family. She wrote to her sister Mary Cranch in June 1785, describing the entire process from the dressing of her hair and the style of her outfit to the state of her mind. "I would gladly be excused the ceremony," she wrote. Afterward she recounted the processional through

Quincy June 30 1811

My dear neice

I promised to write you what I considered the state of your dear Mother, she has appeared since you left her to be mending slowly. has slept considerable at night her sleep has not been altogether quiet, a groaning which you no doubt observed attended it. she had [?] between the basket [?] times, but yesterday was obliged to quit it, her mouth and stomach being very sour, and her [?] tight, her nerves were much agitated, and a [?] cough very troublesome yesterday, which prevented her being down or sleeping, I think the cold change of weather obstructed her perspiration and brought on some fever. I thought her too low yesterday to be left without a watcher. Mrs Dexter was with her last night, and reported to me this morning that she rested the latter part of the night

Louisa was with her yesterday and is so again to day, I was with her in the afternoon of yesterday and shall see her again this afternoon —

Just returned from [your]
Seeing your Mother she is better to day, her mouth is very sour. the [spine?] is causing it, but her other complaints have subsided. She has slept some to day, your father is much better than he was last week — I hope my dear neice that both parents may be continued to their family and friends, and restored to health and usefulness again, I am most affec[tionate]ly
your Aunt A Adams

Letter from Abigail Adams to her niece Lucy Cranch Greenleaf (American Antiquarian Society)

the ornate chambers of St. James's Palace to the drawing room where her presentation (along with an audience of two hundred other people) took place. She liked the king, but "the Queen was evidentally embarrassed when I was presented to her. I had disagreeable feelings too." Clearly the Adamses' London years were difficult for them.

Official duties aside, Adams recorded her tours of England. English cultural life had features she admired and those she deplored. She watched celebrated actors perform in *Othello* and *Macbeth,* and she attended a performance of Handel's *Messiah* at Westminster. At her first ballet, she learned to appreciate the skill of the dancers. The cultural attractions were enlivening for her, but Abigail Adams's American moral principles—values she had learned during years of wartime deprivation—were troubled by some of her experiences. Reporting on a 1787 trip to Bath, she judged the famous resort as "not only for the infirm, but for the gay, the indolent, the curious, the gambler, the fortune-hunter and even the girl from the country who came *out of wonteness*." Her summary expressed the disdain that many in the new American republic felt for what they considered English luxury: "It is one constant scene of disippation and gambling," she concluded.

Adams was appalled at the conditions in which rural people, most of them poor, lived, and she commented that "whilst one part of the people, the noble and wealthy, fare sumptiously every day, poverty, hunger, and nakedness is the lot and portion of the needy peasantry." She observed the incongruity "in this land of freedom," this "boasted Island of Liberty" where "there is that inequality of property which renders the lower order abject and serviel, and the higher order insolent and tyrannical." Having seen firsthand what she had formerly read only as romance, she became more patriotic, reflecting on the advantages of people in America: "the ease with which property is obtained, the plenty which is so equally distributed, the personal liberty and security of life and property" reinforced her patriotic spirit of gratitude that she was an American.

In 1788 John Adams returned to the United States, becoming its first vice president. Abigail Adams's travel correspondence to her sisters and friends was posted from New York City until 1790, when the national capital moved to Philadelphia. Yet over the dozen years that John Adams served in national offices, she also spent much time at home in Quincy and wrote letters to him. The letters that Abigail Adams wrote during her husband's tenure as vice president and then president have a different quality from any of her earlier letters. They describe the exercise of power at the center of the new government as well as its social life. The vice president's residence in New York City, the capital during the first year of the Washington administration, was located on a lovely slope overlooking the Hudson River. The beauty of Richmond Hill (located in what is now Greenwich Village) made it an attractive locale. So did the opportunity to live with her daughter, Abigail, who had married William Stephens Smith in London and was now mother of two sons. Although Adams was unenthusiastic about leaving Quincy soon after their return from England, these attractions tempered the difficulties of performing her responsibilities as a public figure.

The following year, however, brought a less welcome change of residence. When the capital shifted to Philadelphia, the vice president's residence there was not at all to Adams's liking. Not only was the climate severe, but the only house that the Adamses could afford was located two miles from the city. Abigail Adams became ill and was housebound for most of that snowy winter. As soon as the weather and her health improved in the spring, she traveled home to Quincy, and for the remainder of John Adams's two terms as vice president (May 1791 through May 1797), she did not return to the national capital. Only after he became president did she rejoin him in the capital.

In fact, Adams did not even travel to Philadelphia in time to be present at her husband's inauguration in March 1797. Her lack of enthusiasm for the role she would play as First Lady was only one of the reasons she remained behind in Quincy for the first months of 1797. She had long performed most of the administrative and financial transactions for her family, and during that winter, when many building projects were under way at Peacefield (the name John Adams had given his new house), finances were tight. The Adamses even borrowed money to pay their taxes. In addition, many family and domestic arrangements had to be concluded before Abigail Adams could join her husband in Philadelphia. Soon after the inauguration, the new president summoned her in plea after impassioned plea. "I pray you to come on immediately," he wrote. "I never wanted your Advice & assistance more in my Life." It quickly became evident that John Adams had few trustworthy friends. "The Stillness and Silence astonishes me," he said. Abigail Adams concluded her business and hastened to

Philadelphia. For the next four years she served a taxing and exemplary role as her husband's companion, adviser, and friend.

Soon after taking office John Adams had discovered that unanticipated factions had developed around him. Even among his own allies, partisanship threatened his administration. He needed to talk about conditions and ideas with an intelligent and trustworthy person, and among his political entourage in those years, no one served him so well as his wife, who could listen sympathetically and respond with wisdom.

The position of First Lady was daunting. Following the Washingtons, whose popularity and style derived from the powerful persona and reputation of the president, the Adamses faced the prospect of creating their own mark on government. Abigail Adams knew that her husband lacked Washington's popularity and that his political position was more tenuous. Adams's letters during her husband's presidency describe delicate and potentially dangerous diplomatic and domestic situations that were known to her only because of intimate conversations between husband and wife. Many times Adams threatened to censor her own letters, noting the danger of sending sensitive information by post. As her husband's confidante, she did not create policies, nor did she influence the president against his own better judgments. John Adams was too opinionated and principled to need that kind of help from her. The presidency is a lonely office, and John Adams needed his wife's sympathy, intelligence, and loyalty.

During the presidential years Abigail Adams's letters to her sister Mary described a continual round of entertainments, dinners, receptions, and appearances at the theater and concerts, parades, and ceremonies. Adams outfitted her house with furnishings and plate, hired and supervised cooks and servants, and directed the purchase and preparation of immense quantities of food. "Today will be the 5th great dinner I have had," she reported to Mary soon after her arrival in spring 1797; "about 36 Gentlemen to day, as many more next week, and I shall have got through the whole of Congress, with their apendages." More elaborate entertainments were expected on "4 July . . . as we must then have not only all Congress, but all the Gentlemen of the city, the Governour and officers and companies, all of whom the late President used to treat with cake, punch and wine." Her years in Europe undoubtedly assisted her in preparing for these affairs of state, with the key difference that these affairs were her responsibility.

During these years the Adams family situation became more and more complex and troubled. John Quincy Adams married in London and was appointed to represent his country as minister to Berlin, with his youngest brother, Thomas, as his secretary. Daughter Abigail's marriage entered a critical phase when her unreliable husband disappeared for many months on a speculative venture. Charles Adams lost his battle with alcoholism and died a sad and lonely death in 1800. These woes provided a grim counterpoint to John and Abigail Adams's public life. Early in her husband's presidency Abigail Adams described her position as one of "splendid misery." More cynically, she wrote to John Quincy Adams that "None think the Great unhapy but the Great." She remained in the town of Quincy for months at a time during her husband's administration, in part because she found life as the president's wife trying. During the last year of John Adams's administration the circumstances of living in the uncompleted White House in the new capital city, named for the recently deceased first president, were most difficult. Putting the best light on her situation, Adams wrote her sister in November 1800, "This House is built for ages to come." For the present, however, the first family suffered the inconvenience of living in a building that was still under construction: "It is habitable by fires in every part, thirteen of which we are obliged to keep daily, or sleep in wet and damp places." Adams wrote of the dreariness of the surrounding area, "I have been to George Town. . . . It is the very dirtyest Hole I ever saw." When John Adams failed to be reelected for a second term, Abigail Adams was satisfied to return to private life and home. She left Washington in April 1801, just before her husband's departure and the inauguration of the new president, Thomas Jefferson. Once she returned to Quincy, Adams did not travel to distant places again in her lifetime.

Adams lived for nearly twenty more years at Peacefield. She administered a large household that fluctuated in size with the constant arrivals and departures of children, in-laws, grandchildren, members of her extended family, friends, political colleagues, and the curious. She read books and newspapers, maintained a keen interest in local and national politics, and wrote letters. In those letters she recorded happenings in the little circle of her family, in the broader sphere of local events, and in the great arena of the nation—for all those elements composed the running narrative that she considered her life. It was not always a bright narrative, as she detailed the deaths of her daughter, then her dear sisters, and a stream of her friends, including Mercy Otis Warren. She lived to see her son John Quincy

Adams, long the minister to St. Petersburg, Russia, return home and become the secretary of state. She counted among her blessings that John Adams survived. And she continued to worry about the survival of the nation.

As she grew old she most feared that she would lose her reason. She did not. She continued writing letters, but with a hand more tremulous and weak. Her handwriting became more wispy as she described her daily activities and her infirmities. Abigail Adams died after a bout with typhus on 28 October 1818, just a few weeks short of her seventy-fourth birthday.

Abigail Adams's letters have survived and have been studied at least in part because of her position in history, determined by her relations to politically significant men. Yet the letters have historical and literary value of their own. They reflect on the great political and social developments of the early American nation, as well as on the personal and domestic concerns of people of the age. Adams's letters provide an invaluable view of the concerns of eighteenth-century women and their participation in a literary sphere that existed independently of the world of print, but was nonetheless culturally significant. Abigail Adams's letters are, finally, the expression of a voice that continues to resonate today.

Biographies:

Janet Whitney, *Abigail Adams* (Boston: Little, Brown, 1947);

Charles Akers, *Abigail Adams: An American Woman* (Boston: Little, Brown, 1980);

Lynn Withey, *Dearest Friend: A Life of Abigail Adams* (New York: Free Press, 1981);

Phyllis Lee Levin, *Abigail Adams* (New York: St. Martin's Press, 1987);

Edith B. Gelles, *Portia: The World of Abigail Adams* (Bloomington: Indiana University Press, 1992);

Rosemary Keller, *Patriotism and the Female Sex: Abigail Adams and the American Revolution* (Brooklyn, N.Y.: Carlson, 1994);

Gelles, *First Thoughts: Life and Letters of Abigail Adams* (New York: Twayne, 1998).

References:

Charles Francis Adams, "Memoir of Mrs. Adams," in *Letters of Mrs. Adams, Wife of John Adams*, edited by Charles Francis Adams (Boston: Little & Brown, 1840);

Edith B. Gelles, "The Abigail Industry," *William and Mary Quarterly*, 45 (1988): 656–683;

Paul C. Nagel, *Descent from Glory: Four Generations of the John Adams Family* (New York: Oxford University Press, 1983);

Nagel, *The Adams Women: Abigail and Louisa Adams, Their Sisters and Daughters* (New York: Oxford University Press, 1987).

Papers:

The major collection of Abigail Adams's correspondence and manuscripts is at the Massachusetts Historical Society in Boston. All the Adams Papers are available from the Massachusetts Historical Society on 608 reels of microfilm. Reels 343 through 448 (Section IV) include Abigail Adams's correspondence. Other repositories of her letters are the American Antiquarian Society in Worcester, Massachusetts; the Boston Public Library; and the Library of Congress.

Hannah Adams
(2 October 1755 – 15 December 1832)

Michael W. Vella
Indiana University of Pennsylvania

BOOKS: *An Alphabetical Compendium of the Various Sects Which Have Appeared in the World from the Beginning of the Christian Era to the Present Day. With an Appendix, Containing a Brief Account of the Different Schemes of Religion Now Embraced among Mankind. The Whole Collected from the Best Authors, Ancient and Modern* (Boston: Printed by B. Edes & Sons, 1784); enlarged as *A View of Religions, in Two Parts. Part I Containing an Alphabetical Compendium of the Various Religious Denominations Which Have Appeared in the World from the Beginning of the Christian Era to the Present Day; Part II Containing a Brief Account of the Different Schemes of Religion Now Embraced Among Mankind; the Whole Collected from the Best Authors, Ancient and Modern* (Boston: Printed by J. W. Folsom, 1791; enlarged again, Boston: Printed by Manning & Loring, 1801; London: W. Button & Son, 1805); revised and enlarged as *A Dictionary of All Religions and Religious Denominations, Jewish, Heathen, Mahometan and Christian, Ancient and Modern* (London: Williams & Son / Button & Son, 1814; New York: James Eastburn / Boston: Cummings & Hilliard, 1817);

A Summary History of New-England, from the First Settlement at Plymouth, to the Acceptance of the Federal Constitution. Comprehending a General Sketch of the American War (Dedham, Mass.: Printed for the Author by H. Mann & J. H. Adams, 1799); abridged as *An Abridgement of the History of New England, for the Use of Young Persons* (Boston: Printed for the Author by A. Newell, sold by B. & J. Homans and John West, 1805; London: J. Burnett, Dunstable, printed by J. W. Morris, 1806);

The Truth and Excellence of the Christian Religion Exhibited In Two Parts. Part 1. Containing Sketches of the Lives of Eminent Laymen, Who Have Written in Defense of the Christian Religion. Part II. Containing Extracts from Their Writings (Boston: Printed by David Carlisle for John West, 1804);

Hannah Adams, circa 1827 (portrait by Chester Harding; Boston Athenaeum)

A History of the Jews from the Destruction of Jerusalem to the Nineteenth-Century (2 volumes, Boston: J. Eliot Jr., 1812; 1 volume, London: London Society House, 1818);

A Narrative of the Controversy between the Rev. Jedidiah Morse D.D., and the Author (Boston: Sold by Cummings & Hilliard, Bradford & Read, and Isaiah Thomas Jr., printed by John Eliot, 1814);

A Concise Account of the London Society for Promoting Christianity Amongst the Jews (Boston: Printed by John Eliot, 1816);

Letters on the Gospels (Cambridge, Mass.: Printed by Hilliard & Metcalf, 1824);

A Memoir of Miss Hannah Adams, Written by Herself
(Boston: Gray & Bowen, 1832).

The first professional woman of letters in the United States, Hannah Adams was the first woman to conduct research in the Boston Athenaeum, an early petitioner for national copyright, and a serious and scholarly writer of church history, comparative religions, and New England history. Most important, perhaps, was her role as an influential model for the next generation of female authors. Under a veneer of diffidence and self-effacement, Adams aggressively pursued her intellectual development, remained firm in her protofeminist convictions, and built a career writing on theology, comparative religions, and American history.

Like other women of her generation—including Judith Sargent Murray, Mercy Otis Warren, and Emma Willard—Adams was motivated by Enlightenment republicanism, whose principles posited the equality of women and men and whose rationalism tended to set forth the notion that "the mind knows no sex," that male and female faculties were equally grounded in universal reason. For these women, writing and language offered an opening to the public sphere and to general political discourses. While they often accepted the prevalent notions of woman's inherent physical weakness, they believed that only the want of education and opportunity prevented women from achieving equal footing with men in the arts and politics. Enlightenment values motivated Adams and other women of the Revolutionary War generation to pursue ways of contributing to the new republic, especially through patriotic writings that enhanced civic virtue. As a pre-Romantic writer unconditioned by Romantic notions of the writer as an individual, expressive creator, Adams considered the promotion of public virtue to be one of the writer's highest attainments, and she argued for rationality and lucidity in writing about religion and history, areas of discourse that she considered too given to partisanship.

Adams's contemporaries recognized her accomplishments. John Neal, for example, mentioned her in the series of essays on American authors that he wrote for *Blackwood's Edinburgh Magazine* (July 1824 – February 1826). About Adams, Neal wrote for the November 1824 issue, "Women, we look upon as a privileged class; but some of their amusements, it cannot be denied, are of a serious turn,—and some of their graver studies, rather amusing. This lady, for example, has written a large book—and a very useful book too, for the laity—which is called *A Dictionary of Religions*." William Emerson, Ralph Waldo Emerson's father, pointed out in *The Monthly Anthology* that until Adams wrote *A Summary History of New-England* (1799), the only cumulative histories of New England available to the nineteenth-century reader were those of Samuel Purchas (1625), Nathaniel Morton (1669), Thomas Prince (1735–1736), John Callender (1739), and John Winthrop (1790). Emerson also pointed out that by gathering and compiling many documents from New England history, Adams had made an important contribution to their conservation. Surveying Adams's works in his review of her *Letters on the Gospels* (1824) in *The North American Review (*April 1825), Jared Sparks wrote that Adams "has long been known to the public, as a successful writer on theological subjects, and as having rendered essential service to religion, by the productions of her pen." Other prominent figures, including her distant relative John Quincy Adams and William Smith Shaw, a principal founder of the Boston Athenaeum, also supported her literary endeavors.

Hannah Adams was born in Medfield, Massachusetts, on 2 October 1755 to Elizabeth Clark Adams and Thomas Adams Jr. Elizabeth Adams died when Hannah was ten. In the various drafts of her *Memoir* (1832) Adams emphasized that the early loss of her mother greatly affected her:

> The death of my mother was the first capital misfortune of my life. I lost that parent when about ten years old, an age which daughters have the greatest need of maternal direction and assistance.

At the same time she admitted her pain on the loss of her mother, she wrote that because of her, "I was educated in all the habits of debilitating softness."

Thomas Adams soon remarried, and he had four children by his second wife. After selling their family farm Thomas Adams channeled his passion for books into an indifferently successful bookselling business, acquiring the nickname "Book" Adams. Her father's bookishness provided Hannah Adams with intellectual and literary stimulation. Able to attend public schools only intermittently, she had free access to her father's library as well as his bookseller's inventory. In addition her father took in boarders as much to tutor Hannah as to supplement his income. In her *Memoir* Adams reported that she learned basic reading, writing, and arithmetic at school but nurtured her curiosity and passion for learning by reading extensively in her father's library and inventory. After reading about the Calvinist-Arminian discords in a tutor's copy of Thomas Broughton's *Historical Dictionary of All Religions from the Creation of the World to this Perfect Time* (1742), Adams became troubled by how such disagreements were contrary to her sense of funda-

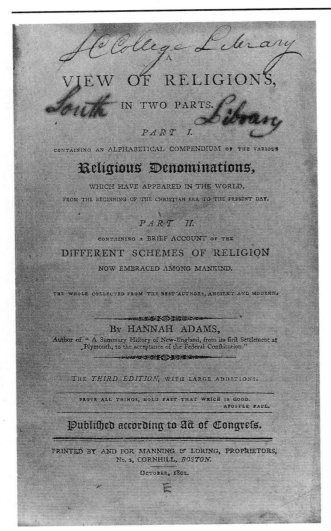

Title page for the first enlarged edition of Adams's attempt to present an objective description of all religions and theological doctrines (courtesy of Special Collections, Thomas Cooper Library, University of South Carolina)

mental Christian truth and was provoked to study theology, a discipline for which she felt ill equipped, having read mostly imaginative literature.

In 1778, while living in her family home in Medfield, she turned to the pen as a means of livelihood and began working on *An Alphabetical Compendium of the Various Sects* (1784). When her half-brother John Wickliffe Adams married in 1805, he moved into the household with his wife to care for his aged parents. The resulting overcrowding forcing Hannah Adams to find independent lodging. Throughout this period she struggled for financial independence. She considered launching a circulating library in Salem, Massachusetts, but circulating libraries profited most from lending novels, plays, and romances, which, she felt, had debilitating effects, especially on female readers,

and she gave up this project. She did work as a school mistress, often residing with the families of her students. Although it has been widely reported that she was reduced to supporting herself by weaving bobbin lace, in fact she confronted her circumstances and financial difficulties by writing and publishing more than by making lace. She remained committed to writing and intellectual inquiry throughout her life despite the many financial and gender obstacles she faced.

More than the next generation of New England women writers—such as Lydia Maria Child (1802–1880), Lydia Sigourney (1791–1865), and Catharine Maria Sedgwick (1789–1867), all of whom knew of Adams's precedent as a woman writer—Adams was a pioneer as a female independently gaining her livelihood by writing. Adams not only had to struggle against those internalized notions that led her to a lifelong struggle against self-deprecation and excessive timidity, she also battled the external forces of sexism prevalent in her era. While she was often deferential and self-effacing, she was also firm and resilient. In 1817 she attended a Swedenborgian service at a private Boston residence without an invitation, to conduct research by observing the sect in assembly. To explore Roman Catholicism she initiated a correspondence with the first American Catholic bishop, John Carroll (1735–1815). Later in her life she corresponded with Abbé Grégoire about Jewish history. Adams became a familiar figure to Boston booksellers, conducting her research in their inventories because she could not afford to purchase the books she needed. Not until 1827, with the support of William Smith Shaw, did the governors of the Boston Athenaeum allow Adams to use its collections; she was the first woman ever to do so. Her intellectual curiosity and her commitment to writing religious history prevailed over the gender constraints that would otherwise have kept her silent.

In *An Alphabetical Compendium of the Various Sects* Adams transcribed, compiled, and abridged theological documents that illustrate the distinctions among the diverse Christian denominations and other religions as well. Adams was a pioneer in the field of comparative religions in America, but her work was in part influenced by two European literary forms she had studied—philosophical dictionaries and religious compendia. Her book was influenced by philosophical dictionaries such as those composed by Pierre Bayle (1647–1706) and Voltaire (1694–1778) as well as by the religious compendia that began appearing as early as the seventeenth century. Adams's *Memoir* emphasizes the importance of her reading Broughton's *Historical Dictionary of All Religions* at a particularly formative moment in her development as a writer. Her ostensible goal in *An Alphabetical Compendium of the Various Sects* was to present an objective and cogent compendium of theology, religions, and beliefs, which gave precedence to no denomination over another. Yet the resultant work positions itself theologically by its effort to rationalize differences and suggest similarities across denominations, thereby enacting theological revisionism like the Unitarian and liberalized Christian theology that became widespread by the mid nineteenth century. In one respect her compilations situated her amid denominational and theological discords and represented her effort to enter into an arena dominated by male theologians, philosophers, and ministers.

Adams's preface discusses how she read romances and novels, and she accedes to prevalent notions of the potential deleterious effects that reading imaginative writing might have on the female sensibility. This statement was certainly meant as a concession to the convention of authorial self-effacement in prefaces, but it was also quite possibly a rhetorical maneuver intended to ease her into the male-dominated area of theological debate. More important, based on her own experience of reading broadly, Adams was committed to the necessity for female education and worked toward that end by compiling materials not readily available to the general readership, both male and female. By virtue of her compilation women interested in theology and religious history would not be as excluded from these "rational subjects" as she had been, nor would female readers be quite so limited to reading only the "lesser" forms of imaginative literature. Adams's summaries and paraphrases of diverse theologies amount to an intertextual response to male-dominated theology, an insertion of Adams's voice into an arena from which women for the most part had been excluded.

A good example is Adams's entry on Millenarians. In twelve pages it traces the millennial and eschatological "opinions of some celebrated modern authors" noting their disagreements, divergences, and similarities. Thomas Burnet and Cotton Mather are only two of the series of male theologians discussed, but Adams's compilation of their beliefs, without judgment or evaluation of their respective millennialisms, is representative of her compilation as a whole in its goal of developing a reasoned discourse on issues that often caused discord and opprobrium. Adams's entry on Antinomians, for example, accurately lists ten doctrinal points of their divergence from orthodox conceptions of the interplay of law and gospel. The entry presents chief tenets succinctly, citing scriptural authority without comment or evaluation. The first point reads, "That the law ought not to be proposed to the people as a rule of manners, nor used in the Church as a means of instruction; and that the gospel alone was to be inculcated and explained, both in the Churches and schools of learning." Though this point is the most controversial Antinomian tenet that had wracked the New England colonial enterprise, the entry states without comment: "Christians are not ruled by law, but by the spirit of regeneration; according as it is said, Ye are not under the law, but under grace." It is also noteworthy that the entry omits mention of Anne Hutchinson, one of the most controversial Antinomians.

Similar to Adams's entry on Antinomians is her entry on the Brethren and Sisters of the Free Spirit, who "plunged themselves, as it were, into analyses of the Divinity, acquired a most sublime liberty." One "who has ascended to God in this manner, and . . . became thus part of the Godhead" is "freed from the obligation of all laws, human and divine." Such groups were generally discussed as enthusiasts, heretics, and fanatics, but Adams treated them in dispassionate descriptions that leave the reader free to draw his or her own conclusions. Her treatment of more-orthodox denominations is similar, as her compendium rationally traces the tenets and theologies that historically often led to irrational conflicts and oppressions.

Adams's compendium did indeed advance the comparative study of religion over works such as Broughton's *Historical Dictionary of All Religions* in that she generally succeeded in avoiding classifications that privileged Christianity, and her coverage of non-Christian religions was considerably balanced and extensive. Broughton's book, for example, is arranged thematically, while Adams's is arranged as a dictionary, a format that permitted her more judicious selection and representation in the range of entries than thematic categories. Not only did she avoid deprecatory labels for non-Christian belief systems, but she also devoted more than thirty entries to heterodoxies that less tolerant writers might have termed heathen, pagan, or heretical.

The format for each entry consists of a brief history of the belief, a few lines sketching the historical founder or the origin of the theological position, a listing of its chief tenets that often cites claims to scriptural authority, a brief description of beliefs or practices, and citation of Adams's sources. Occasionally Adams inserted an anecdotal narration of an event—a claim to the miraculous or to

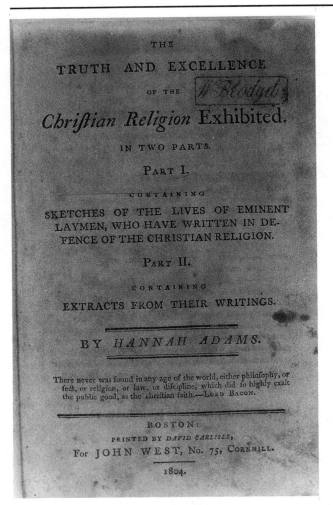

*Title page for Adams's brief biographies of some sixty men who
exemplified Christian piety*

Entries on the French Prophets and the Shakers
describe their ecstasies, but Adams did not use
words of approbation such as *enthusiasm, extremism,*
or *fanaticism.* Discussing the Quakers, Adams wrote,

> The appellation of Quakers was affixed on them early,
> by way of contempt. In their assemblies, it sometimes
> happened, that some were so struck with the remem-
> brance of their past follies, and forgetfulness of their
> condition; others so deeply affected with a sense of
> God's mercies to them, that they actually trembled and
> quaked.

About Mother Ann Lee, founder of the Shakers,
Adams wrote:

> Anna Leese, whom they style the Elect Lady, was the
> head of this party. They assert that she was the woman
> spoken of in the twelfth chapter of Revelation; and that
> she speaks seventy two tongues; and though these
> tongues are unintelligible to the living, she converses
> with the dead, who understand language. They add
> further, that she is the mother of all the elect; that she
> travails for the whole world; and that no blessing can
> descend to any person, but only by and through her....

American religious leaders such as Samuel Gorton
of the Gortonists and George Keith of the Keithians
also receive Adams's unbiased attention.

The book treats Islamic, Asian, and other
Eastern and Middle Eastern belief systems to the
fullest extent that the resources of her time
permitted. In short, her religious compendium is a
significant undertaking of scholarship and research
for its time, and its successive editions attest to its
popularity and influence.

Neither Adams nor her father, who assisted in
her publishing efforts, had made an adequate contract with the printer of the first edition of *An
Alphabetical Compendium of the Various Sects.* All four
hundred subscription copies were sold, but Adams
and her father received only fifty copies to sell or
distribute as they saw fit. In 1786, when she decided
to publish another edition of the book, she secured
copyright based on a Massachusetts law that had
been passed in 1783, and she subsequently published enlarged editions of her book in the United
States and Great Britain. Around 1790 she and
Fisher Ames petitioned Congress for a national
copyright law. When Adams published *The Truth
and Excellence of the Christian Religion Exhibited in Two
Parts* in 1804, it bore a copyright notice of the
District of Massachusetts, and copyright notices in
other editions of her books indicate Adams's
concern for protecting her authorial property.

The Truth and Excellence of the Christian Religion
comprises some sixty short biographical sketches of

revelation, for example—but she generally presented
such anecdotes as reported by others.

Adams studiously avoided negative judgments
even while treating the most enthusiastic and
fanatical sects. The tenets of unorthodox Christian
groups such as Gnostics and Manicheans, Fifth
Monarchy Men and Flagellants, Antinomians and
Gortonists, among others, are described with the
same controlled exposition as Congregationalists,
Calvinists, and Unitarians. Adams set such dispassionate treatment as her goal in the "Advertisement," which promises:

> To avoid giving the least preference of one denomina-
> tion above another: omitting those passages in the
> authors cited, where they pass their judgment on the
> sentiments, of which they give an account:
> consequently the making use of any such appelations,
> as Heretics, Schismatics, Enthusiasts, Fanatics, etc. is
> carefully avoided.

eminent men who expounded the revealed truths of Christianity. The subscription list for the book included John Quincy Adams and his mother, Abigail Adams. Nearly all the sketches in the book include short descriptions of their education, not surprising considering that education was an important issue for Adams. She was convinced that the prevalent notion of women's inferior intellectual capacity was the result of their being deprived of education. Some of the men portrayed in *The Truth and Excellence of the Christian Religion* have only limited connections with Christianity or theology. The description of Sir Philip Sidney, for example, emphasizes his heroic attributes more than his Christian traits, while that of Sir Thomas Browne stresses the literary qualities of *Religio Medici* (1642) more than his piety, and John Wilmot, Earl of Rochester, is included as an example of the prodigal converted. Other figures covered in the book include William Bradford, Sir Isaac Newton, and John Milton. The subjects of Adams's portraits exemplify Christian piety, but the cumulative effect of her brief biographies suggests that male prerogative yields the accomplishment and recognition denied women.

In 1799 Adams published *A Summary History of New-England, from the First Settlement at Plymouth, to the Acceptance of the Federal Constitution. Comprehending a General Sketch of the American War,* inserting her voice into an emergent American historiography as earlier she had entered into the discursive space of the theologians. *A Summary History of New-England* devotes many pages to the American Revolution, aligning the book with the movement to document the history of the new nation, an important undertaking given the brevity of time between the Revolution and the appearance of Adams's book in 1799 and the course, for example, of constitutional politics in those early years of the new republic. It is also important to recognize that history writing demands a high level of literacy, access to collections of documents and books, and political awareness—all of which were generally denied to women in Adams's time. Adams had attained a high level of literacy, but as with her compendia of religions, she faced obstacles in researching, such as difficulty in obtaining books and gaining access to collections. Like Mercy Otis Warren and Emma Willard, Adams was a product of the Revolution. Considering theirs a unique historical era, an important stage in human progress, they believed that the writing of American history contributed to that progress. As Nina Baym has noted, the Enlightenment belief that the mind has no sex, nor does language, enabled American women historians such as Adams to contribute to a developing national culture via the mediating discourses of history and religion. History at that time generally meant chronicling wars and diplomacy, explaining in part why Adams concentrated on the American Revolution. Clearly the egalitarian principles set forth in the Constitution as an explicit part of the national agenda spoke to Adams about her condition as well as that of other women in the early republic.

Continued financial difficulties and the success of *A Summary History of New-England* compelled Adams to consider abridging it. A shortened version would sell to a wider readership, and it might be adopted as a textbook in New England schools.

While she was at work on *An Abridgement of the History of New England, for the Use of Young People* (1805), Adams learned through the Cushing and Appleton bookstore in Salem, Massachusetts, that Jedidiah Morse and Elijah Parish intended to publish a new, cheap edition of *A Compendious History of New England, Designed for Schools and Private Families* (1804). A conflict developed between Adams and the two Congregational pastors over whether or not they had plagiarized from Adams's full-length history to prepare their book, and it was suggested by innuendo that Morse and Parish had maneuvered to preempt sales of Adams's abridged history with their own textbook.

The dispute over the competing texts is a product of the male-dominated field of American historiography in which Adams had placed her work, as well as increasing denominational differences between Unitarians and Congregationalists, differences in theology and ecclesiology that were never far removed from secular ideological and political conflicts between the Federalists and the Republicans. In this context Adams's Unitarian sympathies were evident to the Congregationalist Morse, and the ensuing conflict over their competing books was freighted with issues of denominational differences, gender politics, and secular ideologies.

Ideological differences do exist between Adams's book and that of Morse and Parish. Adams devoted 12 pages to the colonial Puritans, while Morse and Parish gave them about 120 pages. On the other hand, Adams's discussion of the American Revolution covers approximately 260 of 503 pages, while Morse and Parish devoted a mere 8 pages to it. In short, Adams's text is more concerned with national and Revolutionary history and her sense of the nation's future greatness; Morse and Parish's book tends to focus on prerevolutionary and

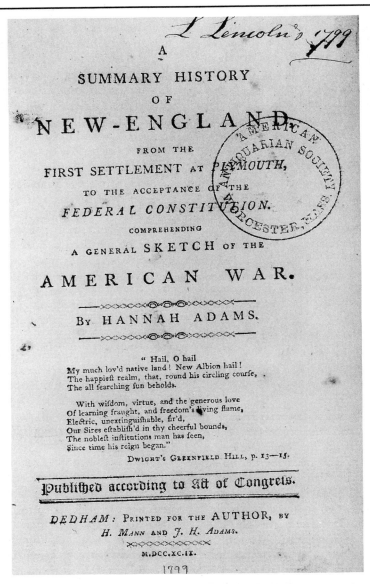

colonial history and is shaped by their devotion to their Puritan ancestors. Morse was one of many orthodox Congregationalist ministers who viewed postrevolutionary democratic enthusiasm with trepidation and regretted the loss of the politics of deference. In the debates over whether New England Puritanism was repressive and persecutorial or had within it the roots of American liberties and democratic principles, Morse, as a Congregationalist minister, viewed the Puritan past more sanguinely than did Adams. While patriarchy and the politics of deference are served in history books that give a larger role to orthodox, colonial ministers, gender

equality, and egalitarianism are served in historical records that focus greater attention on Revolutionary and Enlightenment principles. While the ideological differences apparent in the two textbooks were complicated by gender politics, so too was the litigation over authorial rights and plagiarism. Which textbook would be used in New England schools and whose vision of New England's past would be inculcated in its young people seemed at issue.

Since no statute covered Adams's complaints, adjudication was not possible. When Adams finally brought charges against Morse and Parish, she was allowed to choose referees, but these individuals could not decide the issue based on law, nor could they articulate Adams's copyright and intellectual property rights, both of which were ill defined. The prevalent gender biases also made common-law equity problematic. They wrote, "While the referees have express'd a conviction that there was not a violation in the case, of a right which could be judicially enforc'd, they conceive they have sufficiently manifested their opinion that the attention, respect & tenderness consider'd to be due Miss Adams, relative to her publications, should, in their just operation, have prevented the interference complain'd of, & ought now to restrain its continuance, unless reasonable offers of compromise should be made. . . ." Essentially the referees decided that Morse and Parish had a moral obligation to restrain from publishing their text and to reimburse Adams for her estimated losses. Morse resisted the referees, asking "Do these considerations give Miss Adams an exclusive privilege to write the History of New England?" In response to the referees' decision, Adams wrote,

> It is evident from this award, that the referees were desirous of sparing as much as possible the feelings and character of Drs. M and P. It decides, that they had not violated any such right of mine, as would entitle me to redress by the laws of the land. . . . It forbears also to any thing on the motives, which produced the interference of these gentlemen, or on the degree of their injustice in delaying so long to make me a reasonable redress. . . . It is satisfied with declaring, that I had suffered injury, without defining its magnitude. It admits, that there might be honest diversity of opinion with regard to the amount of my claims for compensation. It supposes . . . that the consciences of two clergymen would dictate to them the propriety of making such offers, as would be considered reasonable and ample.

Adams remained convinced throughout the dispute that the the issue of copyrights was complicated by gender. In a letter to William Smith Shaw, one of the referees, she wrote that the difficulties of being a writer "fall upon women with a double weight" and that women writers are "arraigned not merely as writers, but as women, their characters, their conduct, even their personal endowments become the objects of severe inquisition." The referees' decision was not legally binding; it carried only moral weight. Morse published his competing history, and no evidence exists to suggest he gave Adams any recompense.

Considering the allegations of plagiarism, it is important to note that the title page for the second edition of *An Abridgement of the History of New England*

(1807) bears the statement "Copyright Secured." Deprived of royalties on the sales of her first book and in conflict over the intellectual property and publication rights over her history textbook, Adams struggled to secure copyrights for her subsequent editions.

The conflict with Morse weighed heavily on Adams, and her health declined; her eyes progressively weakened; and her finances were depleted. To defray her debts, to help finance her litigation, and to subsidize her writing, Stephen Higginson, William S. Shaw, and Reverend Joseph Buckminster provided Adams with an annuity. According to Hannah F. Lee's preface to Adams's *Memoir,* the annuity "continued to her death, [and] was said to have been first suggested by ladies, but afterwards was put into the hands of Mr. Shaw, and other gentlemen mentioned in her memoirs. A few years previous to her death, a number of ladies at Salem sent her an annual sum as a testimony of their respect." Ten years after his conflict with Adams, Morse published *Appeal to the Public* (1814), reopening their dispute despite Parish's having warned him to keep silent. Adams described the conflict in *A Narrative of the Controversy between the Rev. Jedidiah Morse D.D., and the Author* (1814) and in *Memoir* (1832). Throughout the dispute Adams's supporters advised, encouraged, and respected her, responding to her commitment to authorship and expression.

From 1810 to 1812 Adams boarded in Dedham and worked on *A History of the Jews from the Destruction of Jerusalem to the Nineteenth-Century* (1812). Adams's interest in a just and fair treatment of the Jews arose from her involvement with Christian "benevolent" organizations seeking to convert them. In 1816 she founded The Female Society of Boston and the Vicinity for Promoting Christianity amongst the Jews and published *A Concise Account of the London Society for Promoting Christianity Amongst the Jews*. Adams admired the Jews' persistence in the face of persecution and recognized their long history of suffering at the hands of Christians. She wrote their history with the same effort at lucidity and evenhandedness she had brought to her earlier religious compendia, acknowledging Buckminster, who made his extensive library of theology and church history available to her, and materials on Jewish history sent by Abbé Henri Grégoire, known for his participation in the French Revolution and his influence on the first French constitutional assembly in assuring citizens' rights for Jews. In introducing her work, Adams wrote, "The compiler is sensible, that the subject is not calculated to engage the attention of those readers whose object is

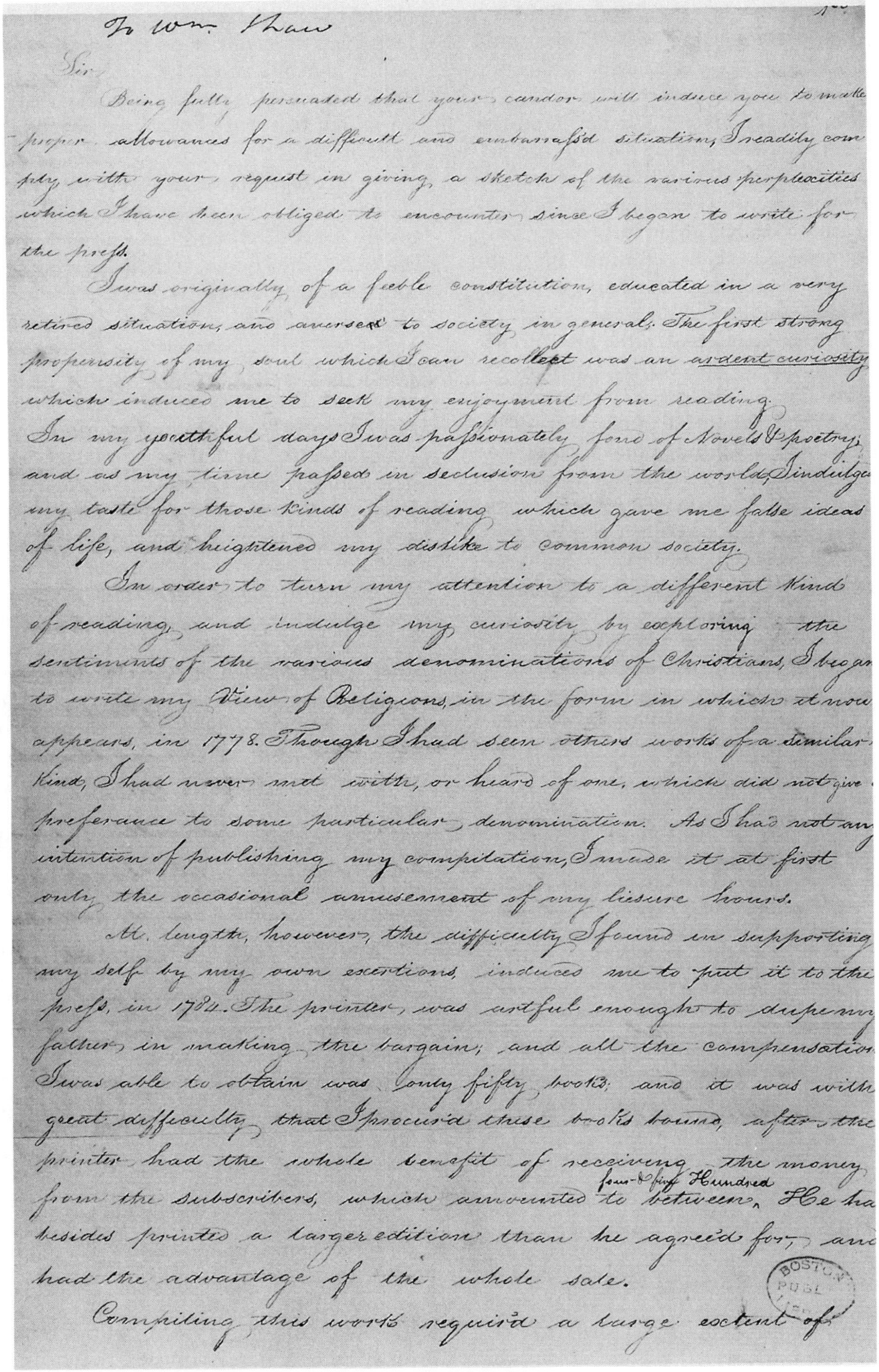

To Wm. Shaw

Sir

Being fully persuaded that your candor will induce you to make proper allowances for a difficult and embarrass'd situation, I readily comply with your request in giving a sketch of the various perplexities which I have been obliged to encounter since I began to write for the press.

I was originally of a feeble constitution, educated in a very retired situation, and averse to society in general. The first strong propensity of my soul which I can recollect was an ardent curiosity which induced me to seek my enjoyment from reading. In my youthful days I was passionately fond of Novels & poetry, and as my time passed in seclusion from the world, I indulged my taste for those kinds of reading which gave me false ideas of life, and heightened my dislike to common society.

In order to turn my attention to a different kind of reading, and indulge my curiosity by exploring the sentiments of the various denominations of Christians, I began to write my View of Religions, in the form in which it now appears, in 1778. Though I had seen others works of a similar kind, I had never met with, or heard of one, which did not give preference to some particular denomination. As I had not an intention of publishing my compilation, I made it at first only the occasional amusement of my leisure hours.

At length, however, the difficulty I found in supporting myself by my own exertions, induced me to put it to the press, in 1784. The printer was artful enough to dupe my father, in making the bargain; and all the compensation I was able to obtain was only fifty books; and it was with great difficulty that I procur'd these books bound, after the printer had the whole benefit of receiving the money from the subscribers, which amounted to between four & five Hundred. He had besides printed a larger edition than he agreed for, and had the advantage of the whole sale.

Compiling this work required a large extent of

First two pages of an eleven-page autobiographical statement that Adams sent to William Smith Shaw during her dispute with Jedidiah Morse (by permission of the Trustees of the Boston Public Library)

reading, and that of a kind for which my early education had render'd me ill prepar'd; And, as I am naturally timid, and constitutionally wanting in firmness and decision; examining so many various and contradictory systems had such an effect upon my feelings as to destroy my health by bringing on a train of the most painful nervous disorders which reduced me so low that my life was despaired of. After a long period of the most exquisite sufferings, I began to recover; and in 1786, had the precaution of securing the copy right to my View of Religions, agreeably to law which had been past in Massachusetts 1783. Not long after I received a letter from the printer; informing me, "that he had sold the greatest part of the first edition, was about to reprint it, and wish'd to know if I had any thing to add." I felt indignant at his insulting proposal, and return'd this laconic answer. "I have secured the copy right to my publication, and therefore take the liberty to forbid you to reprint it at your peril." He consider'd this as a vain threat, and said, as I am inform'd, that, "he should not pay any regard to what I had written, for admitting that I had secur'd the copy right, I was not able to reprint the book myself." I then engag'd a gentleman to call upon him, and inform him, that, "though I was destitute of the means of defending myself, I had friends who would protect me from such injurious treatment." This intelligence induced him finally to relinquish his design. The information that the first edition of my work was sold, gave me the idea of reprinting it for my own benefit. But my being entirely destitute of pecuniary resources, my retired situation, ignorance of the world, incapacity of conducting business myself, and the want of friends who were able and willing to assist me

merely amusement. Instead of a narration of new and entertaining events, they will find a tedious succession of oppressions and persecutions, and probably turn with disgust from the gloomy picture of human guilt and wretchedness," but she then argued for the inherent interest in the history of the Jewish people and their importance to the Jewish and Christian traditions of prophecy and ethics, and to the Gospel itself. In her *Memoir* Adams described her admiration for the profound determination and stamina of the Jewish people. *A History of the Jews* was published in England in 1818, and it was translated into German, appearing in Leipzig as *Die Geschicte der Juden* (1819).

In 1824 Adams turned to the edification of young women, publishing *Letters on the Gospels,* expositions that range throughout the history of Christianity, from primitive Christian sects such as the Essenes and the Gnostics to the Sermon on the Mount and the Beatitudes, drawing attention to the centuries-old tradition of Christian prophetical dissent. Believing that "the knowledge of the Sacred Scriptures, particularly the New Testament, is infinitely more important than any other kind of knowledge," Adams addressed her *Letters on the Gospels* to her "Dear Nieces," dividing the essays into "practical" letters designed to relate one's duties to God and to one's neighbors and "prophetic" letters discussing the character of the Messiah and the spiritual nature of his kingdom. She summarized her intent in one passage:

> Our Lord spoke with an authority which excited the astonishment of the people, because he delivered not the variable and contradictory opinions of men; but taught the doctrines which his heavenly Father commanded him to reveal. He also taught as "one having authority" because he enforced his doctrines by the highest sanction; that is, the sanction of a future state.

In short, Adams's text is calculated not only to advance the Christian edification of women but also to provide the maternal instruction that Adams felt she had been denied by her mother's early death. Inasmuch as virtue was crucial to the health of the republic, Adams's *Letters on the Gospels* fulfills the role of the republican mother, one in which the public and private spheres intermingle, yielding a discourse of edification and didacticism infused with gender politics, civic virtue, and Christian piety. *Letters on the Gospels* provided young women readings in theology and church history, domains that Adams considered best for offering young women rigorous and assertive thinking. *Letters on the Gospels* is not only a work of Christian piety; it is

also a serious and public effort at the edification of young women.

Adams wrote her *Memoir* (1832) at the request of friends shortly before her death on 15 December 1832 in Brookline, Massachusetts. In preparing for her litigation with Morse, both Higginson and Shaw had requested that Adams write a narrative of the events leading to the conflict as well as a sketch of her career. Various versions of this narrative exist in manuscript, and eventually these drafts became the raw materials that Adams used for her *Memoir*. The book briefly sketches the people and events in her life, the deaths of her mother and sister, her ailments, her litigation with Morse and Parish, and her endeavors to receive equitable remuneration for her authorship. In her characteristic understatement and humility, Adams presented the inequities she and other female writers faced in the new republic.

In a letter to Shaw, Adams described her experience as the first American professional woman writer:

> I have been necessitated to exert myself in doing business which is out of the female line. As I cannot but be sensible that my manners are remarkably awkward, this consciousness joined to the ignorance of the established rules of propriety has made me tremblingly apprehensive of exposing myself to ridicule. These feelings are, however, much less painful at present than they have formerly been. To reconcile myself to my fate? I consider, that what is *morally right,* and necessary to be done in the situation in which Providence has placed me cannot be in *itself improper;* and though my acting upon this principle may have exposed me to the ridicule of those whose ideas of propriety consist in conforming to the varying rules which custom and fashion has [sic] established, and not in following the undeviating law of *moral rectitude;* If I can have the approbation of my own heart, and the esteem of a few friends whose good opinion I most highly prize, I can rise superior to the ridicule or censure of the world in general.

Despite the problems she faced during her career as a writer, Adams refrained from castigating her adversaries, and despite her proclivity toward self-effacement, she communicated her independence, her resolve, and her perseverance. The *Memoir* reveals a woman who persevered against the obstacles of health, financial, and gender biases. The trajectory of her writing career moves from that of a discreet eighteenth-century woman who was a "voiceless" compiler to a reflective, self-aware nineteenth-century woman who wrote her memoir precisely as a woman writer. Throughout her career Adams remained committed to female authorship, high didacticism, and the professionalization of writing. She is buried in Mount Auburn Cemetery in Cambridge, Massachusetts. Her portrait, by Chester Harding, hangs in the Boston Athenaeum.

References:

Nina Baym, "Between Enlightenment and Victorian: Toward a Narrative of American Women Writers Writing History," *Critical Inquiry,* 18 (Autumn 1991): 22–41;

Nancy Cott, *The Bonds of Womanhood: "Woman's Sphere" in New England, 1780–1835* (New Haven: Yale University Press, 1977);

Gene Gleason, "A Mere Woman," *American Heritage,* 24 (December 1972): 80–84;

Elizabeth Porter Gould, "Hannah Adams: The Pioneer Woman in American Literature," *New England Magazine,* new series 10 (May 1894): 363–369;

Alma Lutz, "Hannah Adams: An American Bluestocking," *New England Galaxy,* 12 (Spring 1971): 29–33;

Olive Tilden, "Paper Presented to Medfield Women's Club at H. Adams Memorial Gathering May 15, 1896," *Dedham Historical Register,* 3 (July 1896): 64–87;

Thomas A. Tweed, "An American Pioneer in the Study of Religion: Hannah Adams (1755–1831) and her *Dictionary of All Religions,*" *Journal of the American Academy of Religion,* 60 (Fall 1992): 437–464;

Michael W. Vella, "Theology, Genre, and Gender: The Precarious Place of Hannah Adams in American Literary History," *Early American Literature,* 28 (1993): 21–41;

Conrad Wright, "The Controversial Career of Jedidiah Morse," *Harvard Library Bulletin,* 31 (Winter 1983): 64–87.

Papers:

The Hannah Adams Papers at the New England Historical and Genealogical Society in Boston comprise sixty items, including diaries and correspondence with Henri Grégoire, Stephen Higginson, Fisher Ames, Ezra Stiles, and others. Boston Public Library also has correspondence, including an eleven-page letter to William Smith Shaw that is one version of Adams's *Memoir;* the library also holds letters to several women—including Susanna Grant, Elizabeth Barstow, and Mrs. William Tuckerman—and a letter from Elijah Parish to Reverend D. McClure regarding Morse and Parish's controversy with Adams. The Hannah Adams Papers 1755–1817 at the Massachusetts Historical Society include correspondence, drafts for her *Memoir,* and materials relative to the Adams-Morse litigation. The Miscellaneous Collection at the same library includes items relating to Adams's writing career (receipts, contracts, and correspondence concerning her publishing activities); of particular interest are letters from John Adams (27 August 1800) and Jedidiah Morse (26 September 1804). The Alma Lutz Collection in the Arthur and Elizabeth Schlesinger Library on the History of Women in America, at Radcliffe College, Harvard University, has several letters. The Morse family papers in the Sterling Library at Yale University include copies of two letters from Adams to Morse and a copy of the original draft of the legal opinion of magistrates in the Adams-Morse litigation. Other materials are available in the Jedidiah Morse Papers at the New York Public Library and the William Smith Papers at the Boston Athenaeum.

Susanna Anthony

(25 October 1726 – 23 June 1791)

Ellen Butler Donovan
Middle Tennessee State University

BOOKS: *The Life and Character of Miss Susanna Anthony, who died in Newport, (R.I.) June 23, MDCCXCI in the sixty-fifth year of her age. Consisting chiefly in extracts from her writings, with some brief observations on them,* compiled by Samuel Hopkins (Worcester, Mass.: Printed by Leonard Worcester, 1796); republished as *Memoirs of Miss Susanna Anthony* (Clipstone, England): Printed by J. W. Morris, 1802);

Familiar Letters, written by Mrs. Sarah Osborn, and Miss Susanna Anthony, late of Newport, Rhode Island, edited by Hopkins (Newport: Printed at the Office of the Newport Mercury, 1807).

Though American women of the eighteenth century had few opportunities to publish their writings, many kept diaries or composed letters that their contemporaries viewed as valuable and instructive. Such was the case with Susanna Anthony, who—according to her editor, Samuel Hopkins—wrote a thousand pages of diary entries and maintained a copious correspondence. These writings record Anthony's spiritual life after her conversion during the major religious revival known as the Great Awakening. Her writings reveal an individual mind at work: Anthony's careful thought regarding doctrinal matters, her emotional and psychological distress at crucial periods of her life, and her accomplished prose convey a portrait of a woman who took advantage of her place in society to develop an independent and individual mind.

Little is known about Susanna Anthony's life except what Hopkins wrote in the introduction to *The Life and Character of Miss Susanna Anthony* (1796). Born in Newport, Rhode Island, on 25 October 1726, Susanna Anthony was the youngest daughter of Isaac and Mercy Anthony. Isaac Anthony was a goldsmith, and he and his wife raised Susanna in their Quaker faith. In 1741, in the midst of the revivalist preaching of the Great Awakening, Susanna Anthony experienced a spiritual conversion. She became an important member of the local Congregationalist congregation and was held in esteem by many, even at a young age. She never married and lived her entire life in her father's household, helping to support herself with needlework. She rarely traveled. She left Newport during the Revolutionary War and resided in the country, keeping a school and teaching the children of the families with whom she was staying. The published portions of her diary mention a trip to Boston in 1752 and a trip to Stonington, Rhode Island, in 1767. Though her life seems uneventful, however, her inner, spiritual and intellectual existence was rich indeed.

Susanna Anthony's writings first appeared in print because of Newport pastor Samuel Hopkins, a well-known revivalist minister who wrote and edited many religious works, helping to disseminate revivalist documents. The published version of Anthony's diary is Hopkins's compilation of various extracts. In his introduction Hopkins explained that he included "but a small part of her writings, the whole of which take up above a thousand pages" and that he "endeavored to select what is instructive and edifying." His selections include Anthony's description of her conversion, written when she was twenty-eight; diary entries made from 25 October 1743 to 25 June 1769; and passages from letters written to unidentified friends. A headnote explains that Anthony wrote in her diary almost daily until 1769 and that after that time, if she did keep a diary, she did not see fit to preserve it.

Despite his motivation to compile a devotional and inspirational book, Hopkins did not violate Anthony's account. A comparison of the only surviving holograph diary, which covers the period 1 November 1748 – 5 May 1751, with the extracts from it in the published version shows that Hopkins's selections are representative both in content and style. The manuscript diary, which Anthony headed "Continuing some more precious seasons of Communion and intercourse with God" does not include any entries that deal directly with Anthony's day-to-day material concerns, and no entries in it record more extreme spiritual states than the passages in the published version. Hopkins regularized punctuation and spelling and did not misrepresent or distort Anthony's prose style.

Anthony's independence and individuality is apparent early in her conversion narrative, which differs from the conventional pattern of most Great Awakening writings in this genre. In his *Faithful Narrative of the Surprising Work of God in the Conversion of Many Hundred Souls* (1737), Jonathan Edwards, one of the foremost leaders of the Great Awakening, identified the pattern he considered tantamount to true conversions. First, the individual would be moved by fear, anxiety, or distress at his or her sense of sinfulness in the sight of God. Next, the individual would recognize his or her complete dependence on God's mercy, made available in the death of Jesus Christ, and would experience inward peace, a sense of relief from distress coupled with a sense of joy at being accepted by God. The last stage is marked by the individual's abiding assurance of eternal salvation.

Anthony's narrative does not fall into these three distinct stages. Instead her narrative is influenced by Quaker beliefs and the conventions of Quaker conversion narratives. Quaker narratives are generally more detailed accounts of the spiritual experience than those of Puritans. Unlike Puritan conversion narratives, which emphasize the individual's unworthiness and God's mercy, Quaker narratives emphasize the individual's quest for the Inner Light and harmony with God. Quaker conversion narratives generally consist of six parts. First, the individual records early intimations of religious questioning, even as early as the age of five or six. Second, the individual attempts to ascertain from her current knowledge a basis for spiritual life. In many cases the individual is unaware of Quakers or their beliefs. Third, the individual records the initial contact with Quakers. Fourth, the individual struggles against God and the Quaker community. Fifth, the individual submits to the Inner Light, and sixth, the individual enters into the activities of the Society of Friends and defends its beliefs.

Like many Quakers, Anthony recognized early intimations of religious concerns in her experience as a child. The first part of her narrative describes her religious impulses as a child, including her awareness of her sinfulness, the religious training she received from her parents, especially her mother, and "a work of grace in my soul" that took place in her seventh or eighth year and that she considered the beginning of her conversion experience. She summarized her life from her eighth to her fourteenth year as vacillating between periods of temptation—"Childish vanities and plays"—and devotion to God, wonder at the grace of salvation,

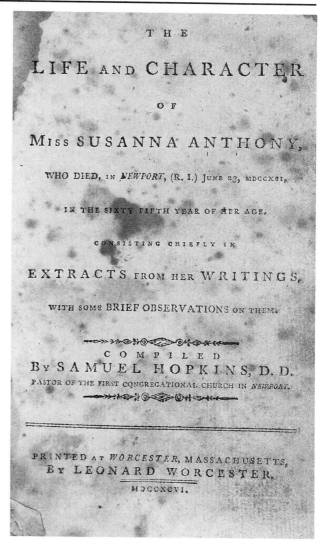

THE

LIFE AND CHARACTER

OF

MISS SUSANNA ANTHONY,

WHO DIED, IN *NEWPORT*, (R. I.) JUNE 23, MDCCXCI,

IN THE SIXTY FIFTH YEAR OF HER AGE.

CONSISTING CHIEFLY IN

EXTRACTS FROM HER WRITINGS,

WITH SOME BRIEF OBSERVATIONS ON THEM.

COMPILED
BY SAMUEL HOPKINS, D. D.
PASTOR OF THE FIRST CONGREGATIONAL CHURCH IN *NEWPORT*.

PRINTED AT *WORCESTER*, MASSACHUSETTS,
BY LEONARD WORCESTER.
MDCCXCVI.

Title page for Susanna Anthony's spiritual autobiography, excerpts from her diary and letters selected by her pastor (courtesy of the Lilly Library, Indiana University)

and delight in reading the Bible and in "all the exercises of religion," especially prayer. Anthony's inclusion of these childhood experiences was prompted by the Quaker belief that children could come to salvation through a gradual process of obeying the Inner Light.

In her thirteenth or fourteenth year, however, Anthony suffered a severe spiritual crisis. Her sister died suddenly, and Anthony was unable to restrain her soul from "foul, ungrateful wanderings." She lost confidence in her religious experience: "I was tempted to believe all the darkness and trouble I found was owing to my being so young, that I had not sufficient knowledge to engage in any thing of religion." In 1740, in the midst of this despair, she heard a sermon delivered by George Whitefield, a prominent Anglican revivalist preacher whose visit to America in 1739–1740 was a major event in the Great Awakening. The sermon encouraged Anthony to "give more diligence to make my calling and election sure," but her spiritual trauma did not diminish. On the contrary it caused depression and physical disorders. According to her account, she "cast off all regard for my body." She temporarily lost the use of one of her hands and developed an eating disorder: "I was tempted to mortify and cross my appetite. Every meal I was tempted to refrain from *that,* and so on. This the family soon began to perceive, that I withdrew at meal times, not knowing the occasion of it." Anthony also contemplated suicide.

Unable to sleep because of temptations to kill herself and fear of nightmares, Anthony picked up a book her sister had been reading, Samuel Corbin's *Advice to Sinners under Conviction to Prevent Their Miscarrying in Conversion* (1741). On the night of 19 October 1741, while reading a selection in this book, she became convinced that her temptations were from Satan, that God was powerful, wise, and good, and that God had granted her grace. On that night Anthony "engaged to be the Lord's and bound myself to him in a short written covenant."

Despite this written commitment, the salvation process was not yet complete. In the next portion of her narrative Anthony explained her investigation and analysis of doctrine, especially those of the Quakers. As a Quaker, Anthony did not observe such religious practices as baptism and the Lord's Supper. Sermons by local ministers and her reading of doctrinal books, however, convinced Anthony that baptism and the Lord's Supper were divinely ordained. Following this conclusion, another difficult period ensued. She decided to inform her parents of her decision to abandon her Quaker upbringing (which no other member of the family had done) and to apply for membership in the Congregational Church. Anthony recorded her mother's response: "She, with the utmost tenderness, assured me, that neither my father, nor she, would force my conscience. Only she intreated me not to be rash or hasty in what I did; but consider well of it." On 24 October 1741 Anthony was baptized and admitted to the Congregational Church.

The final portion of Anthony's conversion narrative summarizes her first twelve years of membership in the Congregational Church, showing how her belief and confidence in salvation gradually stabilized into a regulated faith. This section begins with an account of an ecstatic vision, which was followed by deep doubt. Anthony's main concern, however, was to show that, through trials such as

the deaths of her pastors or "bodily disorders," she remained confident in her faith.

Anthony combined the conventions of Puritan and Quaker conversion narratives, creating a text whose pattern resembles neither model. Like other Quaker writers, Anthony saw her experience as a long progression and described a longer period of her life than the typical Puritan narrative. Furthermore, the stages in Anthony's process are less discrete, more gradual and complicated than the pattern Edwards described. Anthony also distinguished her own experience from the assumptions people made about the conversion process. For example, she asserted that her moment of conversion came before the particular moment of relief in her spiritual struggle that her friends believed marked her conversion. While the emotional intensity associated with the Great Awakening is present in Anthony's narrative, particularly in the portion that describes her fourteenth year, that intensity is mitigated by Anthony's statements regarding her thinking about and reading of religious works. Though her language sometimes suggests her emotional turmoil, throughout the narrative she emphasized her rational thought processes. Anthony's narrative describes a private experience rather than the sort of public hysteria that was frequently associated with the Great Awakening. Part of the power of her narrative is in its privacy: Anthony resisted sharing her troubles with friends, family, or spiritual leaders. This quality further distinguishes her narrative from other autobiographical writings by women, which frequently emphasize identification, interdependence, and community.

Anthony's individualism characterizes much of *The Life and Character of Miss Susanna Anthony.* Though the diary records many instances of Anthony's interactions with other people—worshiping with others, attending to the sick, or conversing with friends—the details of these experiences are subordinated to the spiritual reflection they instigate. Similarly, difficulties and trials, including fears and illnesses, became opportunities for spiritual examination. Hopkins reported that Anthony was rather frail and from the age of twenty frequently suffered from a serious illness of unknown character. In the diary these bouts of illness are treated as spiritual trials—in part because they prevent her from public worship, especially from taking Communion—and also as moments of reflection on her readiness to meet her death and ascend to heaven. Frequently she regretted her recovery, as she wrote in this entry of May 1747: "When I was on the wing of desires, as it were, just on the entry of bliss; and joys unspeakable are opened to me, in the most ravishing prospects; my fluttering disorders tell me, it was but a dream I was in: I may yet live long." Thunderstorms also caused her anxiety (as they did Edwards) until she reached middle age. Her diary entries reveal that she recognized her fears as groundless, and the entries became opportunities to reassure herself of God's protection and to remind herself not to allow Satan to take advantage of her fear.

Despite her focus on her interior life, certain events and external circumstances make their way into the diary as a subtext. For example, Anthony recorded public days of fasting and prayer for God's blessings on the colonies. Anthony's entry for 26 June 1757 records her distress at the progress of the French and Indian War: "I lamented the general stupidity which had seized the whole nation; and that we appeared to be a people ripe for sudden and awful destruction; to be given up into the hands of our enemies that they should enter, not only into our borders, but into our bowels; that our nation and land should become a reproach among the heathen, and the scorn and triumph of our antichristian enemies."

While Anthony commented only infrequently on the larger political issues of the day, she also rarely discussed her personal relationships, even those of family members. In an entry dated September 1753, however, she wrote at length about the merits of her family, their affection, their "uncommon respect and lenity" in matters of religion, their "good repute" and good standing in the community. She also examined her own behavior to ensure that she was properly affectionate and respectful. The tolerance and affection that characterize the entry suggests that Anthony's move from Quaker beliefs to Congregationalism was not a cause of rancor in the household, nor did she feel obligated to attempt to convert her family members to her own religious convictions.

In another significant way Anthony's writing is distinct from the typical characteristics of diary literature. Unlike much diary literature, which is frequently discursive, loosely organized, and conversational, *The Life and Character of Miss Susanna Anthony* is remarkable for its range of style and repertoire of devices, polished writing intended for public exposure. Anthony's style ranges from conversational to formal and balanced. She used metaphors and other figures of speech to develop her ideas. In the same year that Anthony wrote her conversion narrative, she also wrote an entry in the tradition of *ars morendi*, a set piece common among religious writers of the sixteenth and seventeenth

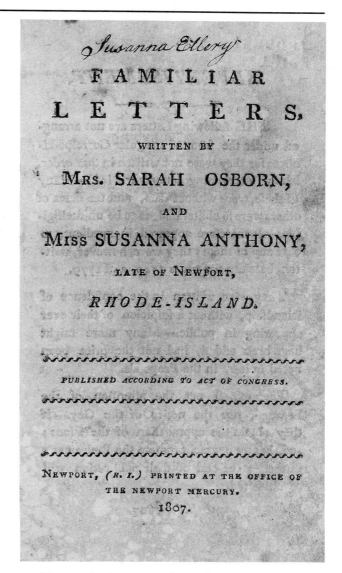

Title page for the correspondence of two women who had important roles in Newport, Rhode Island, religious circles during the middle of the eighteenth century (courtesy of the Lilly Library, Indiana University)

centuries that is written from the speaker's deathbed and provides an occasion for spiritual reflection. The entry is characterized by a formal style consisting of periodic and balanced clauses that crescendo and decrescendo in rhythm and power. It begins with relatively brief clauses of parallel elements that balance and build on each other: "If faith be the flight of the convinced distressed, self-despairing sinner, to Christ, for refuge and life; if it be a cordial choosing, receiving, embracing, and relying on him, as the only hope set before us in the gospel. . . ." As Anthony reviews her beliefs in God's graciousness and the efficacy of her faith, the clauses lengthen and become more grammatically complex: "if it be the effect of love, to look with indifference and contempt, on the most desirable objects of time and sense, and even wish to part with all, and with life itself, for the more perfect vision and fruition of him, whom she esteems the only amiable, the only desirable, object of love and admiration. . . ." Once Anthony's confidence is restored, the clauses shorten dramatically to reach her assertion, "I have an interest in Christ, and the promises of eternal life, through him." The individual clauses frequently consist of more than fifty words and the series of sixteen *if*-clauses concludes dramatically.

In other entries Anthony's formal prose style is also characterized by balanced elements, despite the intimacy and informality of the material. She almost always chose to include parallel grammatical elements:

> I have this day heard two excellent sermons on enduring temptation. My soul feels such a mixture of joy and grief as I cannot express. I feel an unspeakable joy in the liberty of public worship and yet I am melted in grief and sorrow, because deprived of secret retirement. I have had opportunity for this the last week: but what fixedness I have been allowed, has been in a common room; for I have not the privilege of a closet or a garret for retirement. This takes away almost all the relish of life.

The formality of the prose in this passage suggests that Anthony's models for writing came from the public genres of sermons and doctrinal works rather than more private forms such as meditations.

When the diary entries take the form of prayers, as they frequently do, the prose continues to show balanced elements, but on the whole it becomes more conversational and organized by extended metaphor. In an entry dated 18 December [1763?], Anthony developed her argument by comparing herself to a bankrupt merchant:

> O my great Redeemer, how many and great are my wants! Lord, I am ruined, if thou dost not appear to supply them. There are so many great and constant demands on me for every grace, arising from present circumstances, temptations, corruptions, duties, difficulties and relations, that I seem to have run all out, and, like a broken merchant, to have been making sham, sorry, mean and beggarly shifts, to keep up my credit. But I can shift no longer. A new supply I must have, or my credit is gone. And thine honor is concerned: I fall not alone.

Again Anthony's control of her prose style is evident. She took the time to develop her metaphor, embedding nouns and adjectives in subordinate clauses. At the end of the passage her short clauses

suggest her determination and create an imperative tone, and the final sentence is bold in its use of a veiled threat. Such clearly constructed prose indicates that Anthony's diary was not just an authentic record of her spiritual life but a literary record as well.

The surviving holograph diary reflects just such a conscientiousness on the part of the writer. Anthony must have re-read her entries during the composing process because she often revised with interlinear insertions of words or phrases, marking such insertions with carets. In some cases such revisions are merely the insertion of a previously forgotten word. In others the insertions provide balance to the structure and rhythm of the sentence.

Anthony's sophisticated and formal language as well as her use of multiple figures of speech suggest that she was better educated than many women of her time. She may have benefited from the Quakers' more liberal policy of educating girls, but her knowledge and ability surpass the formal education she would have received. As a member of a well-to-do household she may have had more free time to pursue learning. Her references to contemporary collections of sermons and devotional material suggest that she had access to books either through her connections in the Congregational Church or because she had personal wealth that allowed her to purchase them.

In 1807 Hopkins edited another volume of Anthony's writings, *Familiar Letters,* a selection of Anthony's correspondence between 1740 and 1779. The collection includes letters to Hopkins and others, but Anthony's primary correspondent was her lifelong friend Sarah Osborn. Both attended women's weekly prayer meetings in Newport. Such house meetings were common during the Great Awakening because this revival was in part a reaction to a laxity of doctrine among many congregations. Local church officials encouraged study groups, with the stipulation that if a woman led or taught a group, the membership should be composed only of women. Such groups were the only legitimate places at which women might lead discussions on religious matters. Later in her life Anthony also attended meetings led by Osborn, whose house meetings were controversial because they were attended by men and by slaves.

As in *The Life and Character of Miss Susanna Anthony,* the letters provide little information about Anthony's life. What information one might gain by reading the letters is limited by the lack of dates and a possibly nonchronological ordering of them. The reader finds brief references to the death of a sister (Letter LX), the death of a parent (Letter LXIII), the difficulties of having British troops garrisoned in Newport (Letter LX), and the deaths of Osborn's husband (Letter LI), her only child (Letter XXXIX), and a grandchild named for Anthony (Letter VI). Hopkins infrequently provided some context in editorial comments, such as the place the letter was written from or the occasion for the letter.

Hopkins's primary purpose in collecting and publishing the letters was to encourage devotion: "They [the letters] expect not the attention of the Learned, nor the notice of the Gay.—If they obtain the approbation of the Pious; and, in any degree, promote the Redeemer's interest; the end of their publication will be answered." The letters maintain a focus on Anthony's spiritual experiences rather than the material events or circumstances that prompt such experiences. For example, in Letter LX, Anthony devoted as much space to God's goodness as she did to three serious problems: the illness and death of her sister, Mrs. Osborn's illness, and the lack of wood for fuel during the cold weather (the result of the British occupation of Newport, according to an editorial footnote).

Letter LX also illustrates several important stylistic differences between the prose in *The Life and Character of Miss Susanna Anthony* and that of *Familiar Letters*. Individual letters are much more loosely organized, as is evident in this passage, which moves rapidly from the death of Anthony's sister to Mrs. Osborn's illness to the weather and the lack of wood:

> On the 7th November, I was called to part with my dear sister T——. Her pain and distress, increased fast upon her, after you left us. O, it was an affecting scene—to see the universal, extreme pain, in which she lay, without a murmuring word,—yea, with a cheerfulness, becoming the Christian character, to her last moments;—waiting for, and expecting, her dissolution! On Thursday, about ten o'clock, she expired! After I had attended on her through this finishing scene, and all was done for her that could be done, it appeared duty, to turn to my dear Mrs. O[sborn] who was *sick;* destitute; and in affliction; not knowing, but God would call me to attend her, through the like scene! But I found her better, though very weak.—At this time, and a little before, I had been brought to greater straits than ever.—More than two weeks, we were destitute of wood, only a little of which our dear Mrs. M. sent us; and the weather, was extremely cold.

Unlike the carefully shaped prose of Anthony's diary entries, the style of the letters is discursive and informal. The conversational voice and manner of the letters is apparent in the frequent use of exclamation points and dashes and the less-balanced sentence structure. Not every letter is written in this impromptu style. When she wrote to ministers to debate theological points Anthony employed the well-organized, formal style of the diary entries.

Susanna Anthony was not only an accomplished and admired spiritual adviser whose writings encouraged her friends and impressed the religious leaders of her community. She also engaged in the activities expected of an eighteenth-century woman. While nursing her sister, who was dying of pneumonia, Anthony became ill with the disease and died on 23 June 1791. Hopkins reported that while her final illness was "uncommonly distressing," Anthony was not troubled by spiritual concerns and died confident in her hope of heaven.

Anthony's writings convey her intellectual and spiritual independence, her insistence on the validity of her own experience over the patterns by which conversions and spiritual experiences were frequently judged. They reveal her extensive reading in devotional literature and her continual discussion of doctrinal and spiritual issues. Anthony's writings are careful expressions of an independent woman who acted on her thoroughly considered and fervently held beliefs.

References:
Carol Edkins, "Quest for Community: Spiritual Autobiographies of 18th-century Quaker and Puritan Women in America," in *Women's Autobiography. Essays in Criticism,* edited by Estelle C. Jelinek (Bloomington: Indiana University Press, 1980), pp. 39–42;
Steven E. Kagle, *American Diary Literature 1620–1799* (Boston: Twayne, 1979);
Ann Taves, "Self and God in the Early Published Memoirs of New England Women," in *American Women's Autobiography: Fea(s)ts of Memory,* edited by Margo Culley (Madison: University of Wisconsin Press, 1992), pp. 57–74.

Papers:
The only extant holograph portion of Anthony's diary, dated 1 November 1748 – 5 May 1751, is at the Connecticut Historical Society.

Elizabeth Ashbridge

(1713 – 16 May 1755)

Cristine Levenduski
Emory University

BOOK: *Some Account of the Fore-Part of the Life of Elizabeth Ashbridge* (Nantwich, England, 1774); republished as *Some Account of the Early Part of the Life of Elizabeth Ashbridge* (Liverpool, 1806; Philadelphia: Benjamin & Thomas Kite, 1807; Concord, N.H.: Published by Daniel Cooledge, printed by Geo. Hough, 1810); republished as *A Sketch of the Early Life of Elizabeth Ashbridge* (Brighton: Arthur Wallis, 1846); republished as *Some Account of the Forepart of the Life of Elizabeth Ashbridge* (Philadelphia: Printed for C.C.C. by Paul C. Stockhausen, 1886); republished as *Some Account of the Life of Elizabeth Ashbridge* (Philadelphia: Friend's Book Store, 1890?); republished as *Quaker Grey: Some Account of the Forepart of the Life of Elizabeth Ashbridge* (Guildford, England: Astolat Press, 1904); republished as *Remarkable Experiences in the Life of Elizabeth Ashbridge: A True Account* (N.p.: Edmund Hatcher, 1927).

Elizabeth Sampson Sullivan Ashbridge, a prominent eighteenth-century Quaker minister, traveled widely throughout the American colonies, England, and Ireland during the later years of her life, spreading the Quaker message. With her marriage to Aaron Ashbridge she became part of a large and powerful Quaker family in Pennsylvania, and her considerable skills as a preacher won her wide acclaim. Yet most of what is known about her life comes from a single surviving autobiography, a spiritual narrative telling of her conversion to Quakerism. In this document, republished many times throughout the nineteenth and early twentieth centuries, she spoke with a powerful voice about the early years of her life. As a woman, an indentured servant, and a Quaker, Ashbridge found herself continually in dialogue and often in conflict with the dominant colonial culture. While her position as a Quaker minister gave her sanction and occasion to write her story, the trials of her early years—not her later successes—dominate her self-characterization.

Her legacy to early American literature is her personal narrative of a life lived outside the realm of privilege enjoyed by many early authors. This text shows how Ashbridge's experiences and legacy reflected and even helped to shape the corporate history of Quakerism. Speaking to salient concerns in her time as well as in later American culture, Ashbridge's narrative is important because it challenges too-facile assumptions about colonial American life and offers insights about the place of pluralism in a democratic society.

Born in 1713 at Middlewich in Cheshire, England, Elizabeth was the only child of Thomas and Mary Sampson. Her father, a ship's surgeon, spent much of Elizabeth's early life at sea. Her mother, a devout member of the Anglican Church, bore the responsibility for Elizabeth's education, as well as for that of two other children from her first marriage. From her position as an adult autobiographer Ashbridge remembered her early years as characterized by a deep and somewhat precocious attention to religion and especially to ministers. She remembered wishing that she had been born a boy so that she might join the clergy.

Despite these early religious yearnings, Elizabeth's teen years were far from a model of piety. At fourteen, acting against her parents' wishes, she eloped with a poor stocking weaver. She was soon punished for her rebellion, she believed, when only three months after their marriage her young husband died, leaving her widowed and alone. Ashbridge later viewed this moment in her life as important because it marked the beginning of a life fraught with trials and persecutions and because it served as the occasion for the beginning of a journey that ultimately resulted in her position of power within the Quaker meeting.

Estranged from her father because of her "precipitate action," she spent her remaining teen years moving between the homes of two relatives in Ireland, one of whom was a Quaker. During this period of her life she not only had her first encounter with the Quakers, but she also began her search for her religious home. Unable to find this home with her relatives, she decided to immigrate to the American colonies. In her narrative this decision is represented as her final act of rebellion against her father. Throughout the experiences of her early life, Ashbridge reported in her autobiography, she had an almost obsessive need for paternal approval. If her father's sanction is interpreted as a voice of the broader patriarchal culture in which she lived, then Ashbridge's narrative becomes a complex critique of that dominant system. Throughout her narrative both her father and the system he represented mediate against her independence and her development of a sense of self-worth. Her decision to immigrate to the American colonies was the impetus for a journey toward that independence, but it was also a move away from what she remembered as the security of her father's home.

Descriptions of the ocean crossing from England to the American colonies are often central to conversion narratives such as Ashbridge's, but as with many of the conventions she seems to employ, Ashbridge's story deviates so dramatically from those told by her contemporaries that it sets her narrative apart from the genre. Instead of detailing rough seas and unseemly conditions on shipboard, she wrote of being kidnapped while she was preparing to emigrate by an unscrupulous woman who bought and sold indentured servants. Escaping, she returned, perhaps unwittingly, to the same ship on which she had been held captive and set sail for the colonies. During the voyage she overheard a mutiny being planned by a band of Irish servants, and by telling the captain she was successful in foiling their plans. Her efforts to save the ship notwithstanding, the captain took advantage of his authority over her while at sea and forced her to sign illegal indenture papers, committing her to four years of servitude.

When they landed in New York on 15 July 1732, the captain sold her contract to a cruel master. Elizabeth's indentureship was marked by a series of hardships, including a "difference" with her master, presumably of a sexual nature, that nearly resulted in a beating by the town whipper summoned to carry out the master's orders. The years of her servitude also had their brighter moments. Possessing considerable skill as a singer and dancer, she was befriended by some actors, and she considered a career on the New York stage. Although she apparently possessed the talent for this career, she abandoned the theater because of a fear that her father would disapprove of these activities. Her dreams unfulfilled, she used money earned from her needlework to pay off the last year of her contract, and she left her cruel master in 1735 to marry a Mr. Sulli-

van, a man for whom she says she felt no love but who was attracted to her because of her singing and dancing. These frequent references to her musical abilities during this part of her life are significant for the way they prefigure a scene in her narrative where her refusal to dance provides the most dramatic evidence of the lifelong abuses she described.

The height of her persecution came during her marriage to her second husband. Throughout the early years of this marriage Elizabeth continued her search for a religious center in her life and ultimately found this center while visiting relatives in Pennsylvania. When Sullivan arrived to meet her, he knew immediately by her speech and her actions that she had converted to Quakerism. So firm were her beliefs that she had already begun to use the characteristic Quaker "thee" and "thou," as she would later change her manner of dress to honor the Quaker testimony of plainness. Speech and actions became the means by which she set herself apart from those parts of the dominant culture that clashed with the Quaker teachings of equality and simplicity. Threatened by these "peculiar" habits as well as by her conversion, Sullivan attempted to "cure" her by removing her from the site of her newfound belief. At a tavern in Wilmington, Delaware, he realized the full power of Elizabeth's faith when, to hasten her return from Quaker habits, he tried to make her dance with him. As he pulled her from the tavern bench and dragged her across the floor, tears poured from her eyes. So poignant was this spectacle that the fiddler suddenly stopped playing so as not to prolong the new Quaker's misery.

This tavern scene, as well as other descriptions of the many forms of abuse Sullivan heaped on her for her Quaker faith, are particularly important in her narrative for the connection they make to the long history of Quaker persecutions throughout the seventeenth century in the colonies. Even though eighteenth-century Quakers were largely spared from the violence and horror of physical persecution, the stories of their martyred ancestors remained firmly planted in the cultural memory of later Friends. As Elizabeth Ashbridge sought to construct a character of herself from her retrospective view as an autobiographer, she understood and chose to represent herself as a victim of persecution not unlike that endured by the seventeenth-century martyred Quaker women whose faith she wanted to emulate.

Sullivan's physical, mental, and emotional abuse of his wife continued as Elizabeth began to preach at the Quaker meeting, the beginning of her path to renown. In order to move her away from a Quaker community, he led her on what, in her rec-

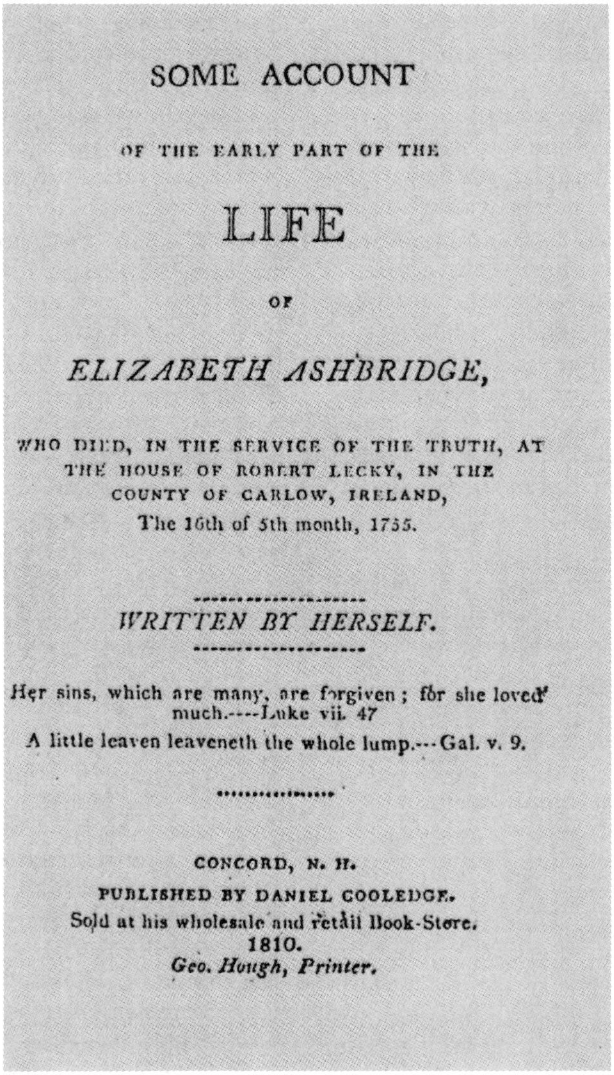

SOME ACCOUNT

OF THE EARLY PART OF THE

LIFE

OF

ELIZABETH ASHBRIDGE,

WHO DIED, IN THE SERVICE OF THE TRUTH, AT
THE HOUSE OF ROBERT LECKY, IN THE
COUNTY OF CARLOW, IRELAND,
The 16th of 5th month, 1755.

WRITTEN BY HERSELF.

Her sins, which are many, are forgiven; for she loved
much.----Luke vii. 47
A little leaven leaveneth the whole lump.---Gal. v. 9.

CONCORD, N. H.
PUBLISHED BY DANIEL COOLEDGE.
Sold at his wholesale and retail Book-Store.
1810.
Geo. Hough, Printer.

Title page for an early edition of the spiritual autobiography in which Elizabeth Ashbridge described the hardships of her early life and her conversion to Quakerism

ollections, seems to have been almost a forced march through the middle colonies. His efforts to prevent her from attending Quaker meetings ranged from denying her the use of their horse to attempts to restrain her physically at home. Yet eventually the Sullivans found at least some small measure of peace and stability within their marriage, both teaching school and keeping a comfortable home. Mr. Sullivan's opposition wavered, and occasionally he even attended the meeting with his wife—always making sure to leave before she rose to speak. Yet Sullivan's more civil behavior did not last. One night in 1740, in a drunken stupor, he left their New Jersey home, enlisted in the army, and was sent to Cuba. When called on to fight, however, he refused,

citing his belief in the Quaker testimony of pacifism. For his beliefs he was so severely beaten that he was sent to a hospital near London, where he died nine months later. Widowed again, Elizabeth continued to teach school and to sell her needlework, eventually paying off her husband's eighty-pound debt, a responsibility she was not required by law to assume.

On 4 November 1746, five years after Sullivan's death, Elizabeth married Aaron Ashbridge, a Quaker from Chester County, Pennsylvania. With this third marriage she moved into the kinship network of one of the most successful Quaker families in Pennsylvania. Unlike Elizabeth's story, the Ashbridge family saga is composed of continual financial and political successes. Immigrating to Pennsylvania in 1698, Aaron's father, George Ashbridge, immediately began purchasing several large tracts of land in Chester County. When Aaron was twenty-four, on the occasion of his first marriage, his father deeded a substantial piece of land to Aaron, who followed in his father's footsteps and built a sizeable estate of his own. Wealth gave the Ashbridge family leadership opportunities within the community, and several first- and second-generation family members assumed active roles both within the Quaker meeting and within the political life of the community. Aaron himself served as a justice of the peace, a position that brought with it privileges within and without the Quaker meeting. For Elizabeth, joining the Ashbridge family meant assuming a role of civic prominence, near the center of community activity, just as her own renown and expertise placed her at the heart of activity in the Goshen, Pennsylvania, meeting.

Little is known of her life with Aaron Ashbridge, in large part because her autobiographical narrative stops with the death of her second husband. It is known that she moved in prominent Quaker circles as her influence as a witness widened. Her name appears in contemporary documents among those of the best-known Quakers of her day. In his diary Pennsylvania assemblyman John Smith recorded his frequent dinners with leading Quakers, including Israel Pemberton, patriarch of another wealthy Quaker family; author Anthony Benezet; ministers M. Yarnal and Jane Hoskens; and Elizabeth and Aaron Ashbridge. Elizabeth Ashbridge's signature, along with those of such notable Quakers as Smith, Benezet, John Woolman, and Pemberton, also appears on a 1752 letter from the General Spring Meeting of Ministers and Elders of Philadelphia to their counterparts in London. Ashbridge's stature is further revealed in a letter written after her death from Aaron Ashbridge to Israel Pemberton, asking that the copy of his wife's narrative he enclosed with the letter be sent to John Woolman, who had asked permission to read it. Such prominence, however, also caused some friction. In 1751, for example, meeting records show that Hannah Eachus cast aspersions on Ashbridge's character. The Goshen meeting supported Ashbridge by disregarding the charges against her, issuing instead a complaint against Eachus for daring to bring such charges against an admired woman. Two months later the meeting disowned Eachus.

Less than seven years after acquiring her new status in the community, Elizabeth Ashbridge suddenly gave it all up. On 19 February 1753 Ash-

bridge asked the Goshen meeting for their support of her "concern to travel" to England and Ireland to testify to the Quaker truth. One month later, after appointing a committee to ascertain that her motivation was genuinely inspired by the voice within, the elders of the meeting signed a certificate that sanctioned her travel. Leaving behind the physical comforts and security of her new home as well as her husband, Ashbridge sailed to Great Britain on 11 May 1753. Although she did not write about her call to travel, many of her contemporaries did, and they often spoke of their "concern to travel" and preach abroad as an obsession that could not be ignored. They also detailed the agonizing process they went through to make their decisions, since traveling abroad usually meant leaving friends and family for at least a year, and two- or three-year trips were common.

Elizabeth Ashbridge's decision to leave her husband may have been extremely difficult because of the relatively short time she had enjoyed the security and privileges of her life with him. The lamentation Aaron Ashbridge wrote after her death supports this interpretation. He remained convinced that her call to travel in the "service of truth" was so strong that it was impossible to disobey the "Lord and Master" who called her to this service. Entries in the Goshen meeting records of the 1770s, however, some twenty years after her departure, raise the possibility that their marriage was a bit less idyllic than his lament suggests. After several prior complaints, Aaron Ashbridge, his prominence notwithstanding, was disowned by the meeting for public drunkenness. Had he been drinking heavily while still married to Elizabeth, she would certainly have been reminded of her miseries with Sullivan when he was drinking.

Whatever the reasons for her decision to travel, Ashbridge's successful ministry in the colonies made her a welcome guest throughout the transatlantic Quaker community, and owing to her work in England and Ireland, her reputation and influence among that community continued to grow. Her renown is attested to in spiritual narratives such as one by Sarah Stephenson, herself a Quaker minister. Stephenson wrote of her teenage memories of Ashbridge's visit to her uncle's home in England. Completely taken with Ashbridge and awed by her presence, the young Stephenson was affected so deeply by Ashbridge's casual but disparaging comment about the superfluity of her hair ribbon that she worked herself into a fevered sickness. She emerged from that sickness several days later with a commitment to the Quaker truth that led eventually to her own career as a Quaker speaker. Similar, if

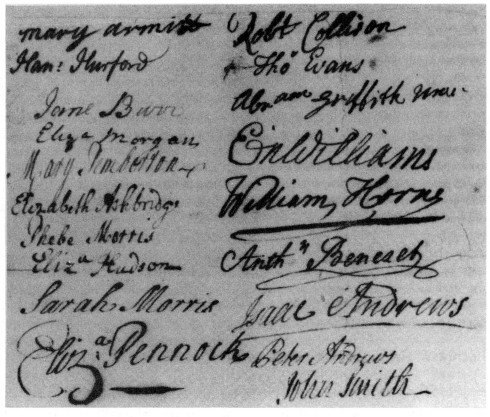

The only surviving example of Ashbridge's handwriting: her name (left, sixth from top) is at the end of a 1752 epistle signed by fifty-seven Quakers of Pennsylvania and New Jersey (Library of the Religious Society of Friends, Friends House, London)

less dramatic, accounts of the power of Ashbridge's presence and personality and of her message exist in testimonies written by Quaker meetings throughout England and Ireland on her death. These testimonies speak of her skill as a Quaker speaker and also of the power and reverence of her deportment in the execution of her duties. Finally, the publication of her spiritual narrative offers yet another measure of her achievement within the transatlantic Quaker community. Eighteenth-century women were seldom encouraged to write their autobiographies, and the fact that Ashbridge wrote hers suggests not only that she wanted to leave a personal memorial but also that members of her community considered her experiences worthy of record. All Quaker writings were brought before a committee appointed by the meeting, and only those deemed particularly edifying or powerful were approved for publication. Not only was her narrative published, but owing to its popularity, it was recopied and republished in many editions throughout the eighteenth and nineteenth centuries.

At the height of her power and prestige, Ashbridge fell ill while abroad. Accounts of her final months of traveling describe her as weak and in great pain, unable to move easily between towns. Yet despite these afflictions, all testimonies speak of the continued success of her ministry. She died in Ireland on 16 May 1755 at the home of Robert Lecky and was buried at the Friends' burial ground in Ballybromhill, County Carlow.

Elizabeth Ashbridge's story is much more than a Quaker conversion narrative. Ashbridge wrote not only as a Quaker but also as a woman, an indentured servant, and an immigrant who endured frequent experiences of displacement. She spoke from the margins of early American life and in so doing provided a perspective not found among the voices of the dominant culture. Writing within the tradition of Quaker spiritual narrative, Ashbridge used the story of her spiritual journey as an excuse to explain and explore the monumental changes she had experienced throughout her life. Knowing that opportunities for culturally sanctioned autobiographical acts were rare for eighteenth-century women, she constructed her story as a double-layered text that is at once a spiritual narrative as well as a stirring autobiographical tale of life lived against the grain.

Multiple cultural codes inform her narrative, and the image of herself that she constructed is layered. What unifies her text is her recounting of a seemingly unending series of abuses, trials, and adventures that made any sense of connectedness or belonging impossible for her. Despite continued attempts to find a sense of community, she found only a pattern of isolation and alienation. In its function as a conversion narrative, Ashbridge's text documents a spiritual search that took her from one religious denomination to another. Like her spiritual journey, her secular journey away from her family and her homeland was marked by breaks and ruptures of relationships. Throughout the autobiography she characterized herself as alienated, abused, and alone, and she placed herself continually on the edges of the society in which she lived. Even when she found her voice and was able to exert influence over those around her, she was empowered primarily among the Quakers, a people that even at their height knew they would never become the dominant colonial culture. The narrative strategy that links Ashbridge's spiritual journey with its analogous secular journey unifies the two layers of her text, the conversion narrative and the autobiography.

Her characterization of herself as a woman outside the cultural mainstream had resonances within the tradition of Quakerism. Historically, it linked her with the tradition of abuse and martyrdom endured by her seventeenth-century foremothers. Her narrative position as the outsider also meshed with the Quaker corporate identity of themselves as a "peculiar people," and it reinforced the Quaker practices that marked them as different from the dominant culture surrounding them. A feminist reading of her autobiographical narrative locates her as a strong, determined woman who was able to negotiate a position of relative power while still understanding herself as the marginalized "other." Through public speaking and, indeed,

through the act of writing her narrative, she was able to break the silence imposed on eighteenth-century women and to take an active part in shaping her life and in affecting those around her.

With women such as Elizabeth Ashbridge as their model, nineteenth-century Quaker women gained power and prominence through their oratorical skills and their willingness to assume positions of political leadership. These women became increasingly visible proponents of equality inside and outside the Quaker meeting. As Quakers became less preoccupied with defining themselves through difference, they participated in virtually all realms of life. Throughout the nineteenth century, in numbers disproportionate to their population, Quaker women assumed leadership roles in a variety of reform movements. They refused to accept the ideology of separate spheres for men and women, and they moved with ease into positions of public prominence, assuming activist positions that allowed them to exert power and to influence decisions about the shape of early American life.

References:

Wellington Ashbridge, *The Ashbridge Book* (Toronto: Copp, Clark, 1912);

Cristine Levenduski, *Peculiar Power: A Quaker Woman Preacher in Eighteenth-Century America* (Washington & London: Smithsonian Institution Press, 1996);

Levenduski, "'Remarkable Experiences in the Life of Elizabeth Ashbridge': Portraying the Public Woman in Spiritual Autobiography," *Women's Studies,* 19 (1991): 247–281;

Daniel B. Shea, "Elizabeth Ashbridge and the Voice Within," in *Journeys in New Worlds: Early American Women's Narratives,* edited by William L. Andrews (Madison: University of Wisconsin Press, 1990), pp. 119–146;

Shea, *Spiritual Autobiography in Early America* (Madison: University of Wisconsin Press, 1988).

Abigail Abbot Bailey

(2 February 1746 – 11 February 1815)

Ann Taves
Claremont School of Theology

BOOK: *Memoirs of Mrs. Abigail Bailey, who had been the wife of Major Asa Bailey, formerly of Landaff, (N.H.) written by herself,* edited by Ethan Smith (Boston: Published by Samuel T. Armstrong, 1815); republished as *Religion and Domestic Violence in Early New England: The Memoirs of Abigail Abbot Bailey,* edited by Ann Taves (Bloomington & Indianapolis: Indiana University Press, 1989).

Abigail Abbot Bailey was an eighteenth-century Congregationalist woman whose memoir describes her religious response to her husband's extended incestuous involvement with one of their teenage daughters. As one of a relatively small number of published memoirs by eighteenth-century American women, it illuminates the way in which women appropriated and lived out the teachings of New England Congregationalism in their everyday lives. Moreover, as the first autobiographical account of family violence published in the United States, Bailey's memoir provides an important source for understanding the problem of domestic violence, including father-daughter incest, in historical perspective.

The work published in 1815 as *Memoirs of Mrs. Abigail Bailey* was one of several documents written by Abigail Abbot Bailey and found among her possessions at the time of her death. While the others have not survived, her first editor, the Reverend Ethan Smith, included passages from her diary in the introduction and the appendix to the book. Bailey's memoir focuses on the four-year period from 1788, when her husband became incestuously involved with their daughter, until 1792, when Bailey forced her husband to agree to divide their property and leave town. Written after she obtained a divorce from her husband, *Memoirs of Mrs. Abigail Bailey* relies in part on diaries she kept throughout her life in the context of her regular private devotions.

Abigail Abbot was born in the newly settled town of Rumford (now Concord), New Hampshire, on 2 February 1746. She was the second eldest of the ten children born to James and Sarah Abbot, devout Congregationalists from long-established Massachusetts families. In November 1763, at the end of the French and Indian War, the Abbots, including seventeen-year-old Abigail, moved to the rich farmlands in the newly laid-out townships of Newbury (in what later became Vermont) and Haverhill, New Hampshire, on opposite sides of the Connecticut River, a three-day journey north of Concord. Abigail had been formally admitted to church membership in Concord on 4 September 1763, but soon after her arrival in Newbury she was converted at the age of eighteen under the preaching of a more evangelically oriented Congregationalist minister, the Reverend Peter Powers. Shortly thereafter, Abigail and her parents, both long-standing members of the church in Concord, joined with twelve others to found the Church of Christ in Newbury and Haverhill.

New England Congregationalism, and Puritanism in general, emphasized the conversion experience as a touchstone of the religious life. In early New England an account of one's conversion experience was institutionalized as the basis for full church membership. Although this requirement was relaxed over time, especially for the children of church members, it was reasserted during the "awakening" of the early eighteenth century by evangelically oriented New Light Congregationalists. Timothy Walker, Abigail's minister in Concord and a friend of Boston liberal Charles Chauncy, was the first minister in the region to speak out against the emotionalism of the Awakening in favor of a more reasoned approach to religion. The rational character of Abigail's decision to join the Concord church is suggested by Ethan Smith's comment that at eighteen, "being of a serious turn of mind, and of an unblemished moral character," she simply applied for membership. Both Ethan Smith and Peter Powers were more evangelically oriented than Walker and emphasized the importance of a conversion experience. Thus, it was only after moving to Newbury and hearing

Powers preach that Abigail was "convinced that she had no true religion at heart, and was thrown into great distress of mind."

New Light conversions were shaped by the Calvinist theological tradition to which the Puritans and their New Light descendants were heirs. They typically followed a three-stage pattern in which persons first awoke with fear and anxiety to a sense of their sinfulness in the eyes of God, then acknowledged their inability to save themselves and their consequent dependence on the mercy of God, and finally, with the bestowal of God's saving grace, experienced a sense of peace and joy. The excerpt from Abigail's conversion account quoted by Ethan Smith follows this pattern, beginning with "I saw myself to be a guilty and a very filthy creature," and ending "Now I saw that I had nothing to be, but to believe in Christ." Later in life, when she described herself as one who "had professed religion" and as "a great advocate for experimental and practical piety," she explicitly associated herself with the evangelical or New Light wing of New England Congregationalism typified by Jonathan Edwards.

While those who had experienced conversion were able to conform their lives to God's commandments both internally and externally, New Lights expected those who had not experienced conversion to conform their lives to God's commandments externally by attending church (in the hope of experiencing conversion) without receiving communion. When Abigail married Asa Bailey on 15 April 1767, she did so knowing that he was unconverted. There was, as she put it, "no evidence that he was a subject of true religion." Yet, she went on to say, "I did hope and expect, from my acquaintance with him, that he would wish for good regulations in his family, and would have its external order accord with the word of God."

After their marriage Abigail and Asa Bailey settled in the town of Haverhill. Asa's family had moved there from Salem, New Hampshire, where Asa had been born in 1745, the fifth of ten children. Asa's father was like Abigail Abbot's in many ways. Both were prosperous enough to buy the best available land along the Connecticut River; both were elected to the office of selectman and also filled other minor elected posts; and both had large families, each with ten children. The two families differed most obviously in their relationship to the church. While the Abbots were deeply involved in the life of the church both in Concord and in Newbury-Haverhill, neither Bailey's memoir nor local church records provide any evidence that Asa or any members of his immediate family ever joined

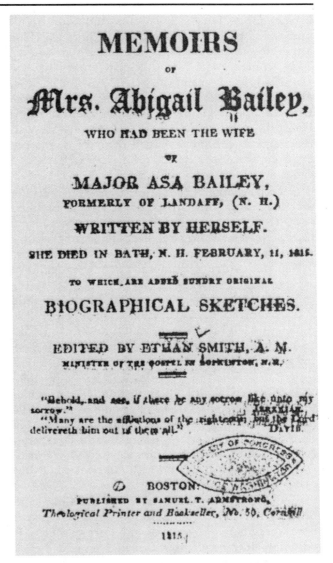

Title page for Abigail Bailey's memoir of her unhappy marriage to an abusive husband who committed incest with one of their daughters

the church. Perhaps because of their strong church ties, Abigail's parents and four of their eight adult children lived most, if not all, of their lives in the towns of Haverhill and Newbury. Members of the Bailey family, by contrast, all moved on to newer settlements within twenty years of Abigail and Asa's marriage.

Bailey's memoir reveals that her husband, a socially respected yet temperamental man, began physically abusing her within a month of their marriage, and three years later he had an affair with their hired woman. In 1772, after five years of marriage, Abigail and Asa moved to Bath, New Hampshire, a newly chartered town in the hills to the northeast of Haverhill. They were accompanied in this move by Asa's parents and four of his unmarried sisters and brothers. In July 1773 Asa attempted to rape another of their hired women. This woman took Asa to court, where he was acquitted by a grand jury in 1774 for lack of evidence. About 1780 Asa and Abigail moved from Bath to the neighboring town of Landaff, New Hampshire. In the course of their twenty-six-year marriage, the Baileys had a total of seventeen children, four born in Haverhill, five in Bath, and eight in Landaff.

In December 1788, after twenty-one years of marriage and the births of fourteen of their seventeen children, Asa began sexually abusing their sixteen-year-old daughter, Phebe. At that time Abigail was pregnant with their second set of twins. When the evidence of incest became undeniable, Abigail began pressuring her husband to divide their property and leave the area. Their last child was conceived in August 1790, just before Asa reluctantly left home for the first time only to return and leave repeatedly over the course of the following year.

Early in her marriage Abigail had kept silent about her marital difficulties. Not until her daughter Phebe turned eighteen and left home in April 1790 did Abigail speak to a minister about the incest and then only in vague terms. Some months later, after Asa left home for the first time, she told a few friends what had occurred, after which "the news . . . flew every way with great rapidity."

Compared to those in Great Britain and in other American colonies, New England divorce laws were liberal. In keeping with Puritan theology, colonial New Englanders viewed marriage as a covenant between husband and wife paralleling the relationships between God and the congregation and between a magistrate and a people. In all these relationships one partner was clearly subordinate to the other; nonetheless, both parties had certain rights and responsibilities. While it was the subordinate partner's duty to honor and subject oneself to the superior partner, this duty was conditional on the superior partner's fulfillment of the covenant. This understanding of marriage replaced the traditional concept of marriage as a sacramental union with a more contractual agreement. In New England, marriages were not viewed as indissoluble. They could be dissolved if either party failed to fulfill his or her responsibilities. Adultery, incestuous marriage (marriage to legally designated relatives), cruelty (wife beating), and desertion were all considered breaches of the marriage covenant and thus, especially in combination, grounds for divorce.

In theory Abigail Bailey could have petitioned for a divorce on grounds of cruelty and adultery long before the incest began. The way that the law was applied in practice, however, suggests that her chances of obtaining a divorce prior to the incest were slim. Even after the onset of the incest, she still faced practical difficulties. A divorce on the grounds of father-daughter incest, which was legally speaking a form of adultery on the part of her husband, was unlikely without her daughter's testimony. While Bailey pressured her daughter to testify during the months before she left home in 1790, Phebe Bailey was, according to her mother, "overwhelmed with shame and grief" and unwilling to do so. After Phebe left home, Abigail was apparently able to convince her to testify. Yet, when prosecution was possible, the prospect of a contested divorce in which both she and her daughter would be compelled to testify against Asa seemed so "inexpressibly painful" that she chose instead to pursue an informal property settlement with her husband. This decision opened the way for a protracted struggle in which Asa, who did not want a separation, was able to use his wife's desire for an informal settlement to his own advantage.

Conceived shortly before he returned home in December 1791, Asa's first plan was apparently to get Abigail to New York, where divorce laws were stricter, by convincing her to exchange their farm in Landaff for land owned by a Mr. Ludlow in New York state. After Abigail refused to go along with this plan, Asa then developed a more complex strategy. After blocking negotiations in Newbury, where Abigail had her family and friends to support her, Asa insisted that they go to his brother-in-law's farm in Bradford, Vermont, a few miles south of Newbury, to continue the negotiations. Although Abigail was afraid to leave her family and friends, she went. She agreed to trade their property in Landaff for Asa's brother-in-law's more salable farm in Bradford. After she and her children settled in Bradford in February 1792, Asa put off several local buyers for that farm and insisted that Abigail travel with him to New York State, where he claimed he could get a better price from a man he knew there. After crossing into New York that March, Asa revealed to Abigail that he had conspired with his relatives to get her away from her family and friends in the hope of bringing her "to terms, that would better suit himself."

Property records indicate that Asa had secretly sold the Bradford property back to his brother-in-law's son prior to leaving for New York to ensure that Abigail would have no legal right to it. Since Abigail was required to sign the deed, he

Last page of the second covenant of the Haverhill, New Hampshire, Church of Christ, which Bailey signed "Abigail Abbot" (second column, tenth signature) in the early 1790s (Haverhill Church Records, Town Clerk's Office, Haverhill, New Hampshire)

apparently forged her signature. On learning that she had been deceived, Abigail concluded that she should have listened to her relatives and church friends, who considered Asa "a cunning, crafty man," and not to her husband. In April, while she was ill from a smallpox inoculation, Asa left her alone in New York and started back to New Hampshire for the children. Defying her husband's expectations, she embarked alone on the 270-mile journey home. When she arrived in New Hampshire in June, with the aid of family and friends, she had her husband arrested and held in jail, threatening him with prosecution until he agreed to a property settlement. She divorced him on 4 May 1793.

Abigail's decision to rework her private diaries into the more public form of a memoir may have been made during the trip to New York. By the time Abigail and Asa left for New York, the community not only knew about the incest but also knew that Asa had left home several times only to be taken in again by his wife. When the Baileys' trip to New

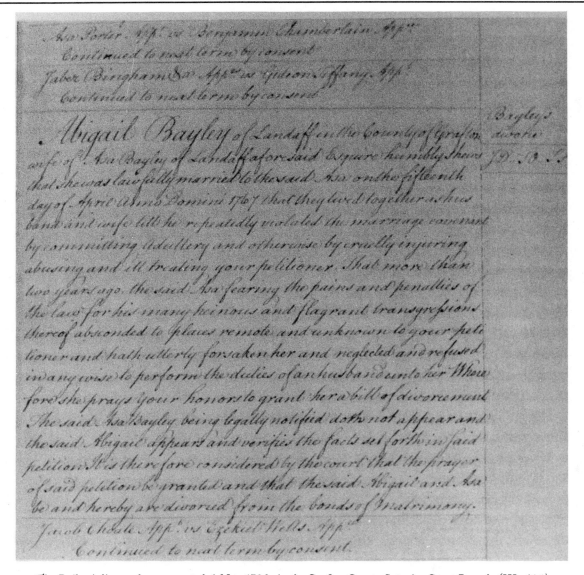

The Baileys' divorce decree, granted 4 May 1793, in the Grafton County Superior Court Records (III: 401)

York stretched on well beyond the planned two weeks, Abigail began to fear that her close friends would think she had abandoned her children. Moreover, during the trip Asa informed Abigail that some in the community thought she had been "too favorable to him, after it was believed he had committed such abominable crimes" and that she ought to leave town as well.

Many of the friends to whom Abigail referred were probably fellow members of the new congregation that had been founded in Haverhill in 1790. Abigail was deeply attached to the new congregation and longed to return to it. Given her church's strict enforcement of disciplinary standards and her fears that her friends, particularly her church friends, believed she had been unwise and perhaps even

deceitful, the memoir, as opposed to the diaries, may have been written after her return as a means of justifying her actions.

Thematically the narrative hinges on two mirrored developments: Abigail's increasing reliance on God (and others, especially her church-related circle of family and friends) and her emerging perception of her husband as her "enemy" and "captor." While Abigail's silence reflected her temperament, her belief that it was better to suffer in silence, her fear of her husband, and her desire to protect her husband and children from scandal, it may also have reflected her isolation from her church friends and family and the weakness of community institutions, especially the church, in northern New England in the period following the

Revolutionary War. From the time they left Haverhill, Abigail lived some distance (more than ten miles on horseback) from her extended family and from the church in Newbury (the only one in the area) but relatively close to many of her in-laws. Although she maintained her membership in the Newbury church throughout her marriage, the church was without a minister for much of the 1780s. Reverend Ethan Smith was not settled at the new church in Haverhill until 1790, two years after the incest began. The new congregation was a direct outgrowth of a revival of religion in the area that drew in clergy from other areas to preach and provided Abigail with her first opportunity to speak with a minister.

Abigail's tendency to keep silent about her husband was also reinforced by her dependence on him and her hope that he would reform. Much of the drama of the memoir centers on Abigail's gradual disillusionment and her increasingly negative perception of Asa. The process of separating the actual Asa from her idealized image of a husband was a slow one fraught with ambivalence. Initially she hoped that Asa might be converted; when that possibility began to seem unlikely, she hoped he might reform. After she ended their relationship, she hoped that he would honor his promise to divide the property and leave the state. Only when she realized that the trip to New York was a further attempt to avoid a property settlement did Abigail begin to see Asa as her "enemy" and herself as his "captive" rather than his wife.

The narrative as she constructed it is one in which she, like Job, is stripped by God of all that is of value to her in the world—her home, her children, and her husband—and then abandoned in New York, ill from a smallpox inoculation, while her husband returns to New Hampshire for her children. Maintaining her trust in God throughout this ordeal, she is assisted by strangers as she makes her way alone back to New Hampshire. Perhaps most significantly for someone who longed for friendship with her husband, she begins to refer to God as her Heavenly Friend during the return journey. By the end of the memoir, through God's mercy and the help of many in her community, she is delivered from her afflictions and reunited with her children, her extended family, and her church friends.

In her interpretation of her experience, Abigail relied not only on the Bible but also on the Indian captivity narratives popular in New England at the time. Abigail was familiar both with the narratives and with the actual threat of Indian raids, a threat to which she had been exposed while growing up on the New England frontier. In this mythic paradigm an individual, often a woman, stands as a passive captive awaiting God's deliverance. The task of the captive is to resist the temptations proffered by the captors and to maintain her faith and trust in God throughout the ordeal. Psalm 55, to which she frequently referred, provided her with a biblical basis for thinking about a husband who dealt treacherously with his wife and a friend who turned unexpectedly into an enemy. She set up this idea at the beginning of her memoir in a passage that summarizes the overarching framework of her narrative, stating that "God often suffers mankind sorely to afflict and oppress one another; and not only those who appear as open enemies;—but sometimes those who pretend to be our best friends, cruelly oppress." While in the captivity narratives open enemies become God's instruments for chastising his guilty people, in Bailey's memoir a hidden enemy becomes God's vehicle for chastising Abigail. In both instances chastisement means isolation and the violent disruption of family ties. In each case the question of salvation hinges on whether or not the captive can accept this disruption as a manifestation of God's grace and rely entirely on God for her deliverance.

The plot of the captivity narrative parallels that of the typical Puritan conversion narrative. In each case sinfulness or guilt is presupposed; punishment, whether damnation or chastisement, is understood as actual or imminent. Salvation or deliverance rests entirely in the hands of God, on whom the believer is absolutely dependent. Indeed, the devotional life of devout Congregationalists, such as Bailey, can be read as a series of recapitulations of the conversion experience, such that in the face of divine affliction the believer reenacted a pattern of self-abasement and absolute dependence only to be filled with the grace and power of God. This pattern of self-abasement and divine empowerment surfaced whenever Bailey felt the need for God's assistance, when, for example, she felt overwhelmed by emotions such as grief or despair, called upon to "reprove" or criticize another person, or helpless in the face of challenges such as traveling alone from New York to New Hampshire. Thus, while Bailey's memoir, like the captivity narratives, was intended both by the author and by her editor to testify to the necessity of total dependence on God, dependence on God was linked to divine empowerment.

Dependence on God was also linked to trusting God. As her disillusionment with her husband increased, Bailey's understanding of what it meant to trust God shifted as well. Through most of the narrative, she trusted that God would change

*Abigail Bailey's fourteenth child, the Reverend Phineas Bailey;
a Congregational minister whose memoir includes references to
his mother's sufferings*

her husband through conversion, reform, or a change of heart with respect to a property settlement. By the end of the journey back from New York to New Hampshire, she concluded "that trusting in God implies the due use of all proper means." This final shift in her understanding of what God wanted, an understanding that her "familiar connexions" had no doubt encouraged her to adopt, reflected a new willingness to rely on legal resources and the advice of her friends and extended family. In Bailey's case, dependence on God led to increased autonomy relative to her husband and increased dependence on others—strangers on the journey back from New York, her extended family and church friends, and, in the end, the legal profession and officers of the law. While captivity narratives carefully avoided any suggestion that the captives might have escaped their captors by virtue of their own strength or ingenuity, Bailey's memoir, like many of the captivity narratives, describes a woman who maintained her faith, acted independently of the man on whom she was legally dependent, and publicly legitimated her actions by writing about them.

At the request of friends and certain unnamed local "gentlemen," Reverend Ethan Smith edited Abigail Bailey's memoir for publication after she died. He arranged to have *Memoirs of Mrs. Abigail Bailey* published by Samuel T. Armstrong of Boston, a Congregationalist layman. It appeared alongside two other early published memoirs of Congregationalist women, the popular *Memoirs of Mrs. Harriet Newell* (1814), by a woman who died at nineteen en route to India with her missionary husband, and the virtually unknown *Writings of Miss Fanny Woodbury* (1815), by a woman who died at twenty-three having struggled most of her life with a hearing loss. With one print run of twenty-five-hundred copies, *Memoirs of Mrs. Abigail Bailey* was neither a best-seller nor a dismal failure. Among the earliest published memoirs of New England women, these volumes, all edited and published by Congregationalist clergy after the death of their authors, highlight the importance of such writings in the eyes of the clergy and the key role that religion played in the emergence of women's autobiography and in the definition of the exemplary female life.

References:

Ann Taves, Introduction to *Religion and Domestic Violence: The Memoirs of Abigail Abbot Bailey,* edited by Taves (Bloomington & Indianapolis: Indiana University Press, 1989);

Taves, "Self and God in the Early Published Memoirs of New England Women," in *American Women's Autobiography: Fea(s)ts of Memory,* edited by Margo Culley (Madison: University of Wisconsin Press, 1992), pp. 57–74.

Martha Moore Ballard
(1735 – May 1812)

Gail K. Smith
Marquette University

BOOK: Diary, published in part in *The History of Augusta: First Settlement and Early Days as a Town, Including the Diary of Mrs. Martha Moore Ballard (1785–1812),* by Charles Elventon Nash (N.p.: Printed by Charles Nash & Sons, 1904; published by Edith Hary, 1961); and in *A Midwife's Tale: The Life of Martha Ballard, Based on Her Diary, 1785–1812,* by Laurel Thatcher Ulrich (New York: Knopf, 1990); republished in its entirety as *The Diary of Martha Ballard, 1785–1812,* edited by Robert R. McCausland and Cynthia MacAlman (Camden, Maine: Picton Press, 1992).

Martha Moore Ballard, midwife and diarist, is known only through her diary, which she kept faithfully for more than twenty-seven years. Presented and interpreted by historian Laurel Thatcher Ulrich in *A Midwife's Tale: The Life of Martha Ballard, Based on Her Diary, 1785–1812* (1990) and published in full by a small press in 1992, the diary is of inestimable value as one of only a handful of surviving personal writings by American women of the late eighteenth century. Concentrating on her daily life, Ballard's diary offers a tantalizing glimpse into the network of her relationships and activities—whether at home or delivering a baby miles away—depicting the life of a dedicated healer and housewife in a newly settled Maine town during the years immediately following the American Revolution. The concerns of the diary—the relationship between women's and men's economies, the growing influence of male physicians, the legal consequences of debt, family quarrels, marriage and sexual mores, violent land disputes, murder and rape, and above all the professional life of a dedicated and energetic healer—provide details of hitherto almost unknown women's history, as well as the communal and social elements of early American history that contemporary men's diaries tend to ignore. Far from being "trivial and unimportant," as one critic complained, Ballard's daily entries, in their dailiness, are an invaluable resource for the study of early American culture.

Born in Oxford, Massachusetts, in 1735, Martha Moore was the daughter of Dorothy and Elijah Moore. The family was relatively well educated: one of the sons was a Harvard graduate who became a librarian and pastor, and an uncle was a Yale-educated physician. Martha Moore married Ephraim Ballard—a surveyor, mapmaker, and miller—in 1754. In 1769, after six of their children were born, a diphtheria epidemic that swept through Oxford took the lives of three of their four daughters in fewer than ten days. By 1775 several of their relatives had settled on Maine lands owned by the Kennebec Proprietors, a wealthy Tory company. In that year Ephraim leased Fort Halifax and its surrounding lands in Winslow, Maine, from the company. The property was soon confiscated by the Revolutionary army, however, after complaints about Ephraim's unfriendliness to the patriot cause. Ephraim moved down the Kennebec River from Winslow to the newly settled town of Hallowell (part of which later became Augusta), taking up the management of a landowner's acreage with its accompanying gristmill and sawmill. Martha and the five surviving children joined Ephraim there in October 1777; they remained in the Hallowell-Augusta area for the rest of their lives.

Martha Ballard's diary opens in Hallowell on 1 January 1785. By this time she was already skilled in many medical procedures, concocting medications and treating wounds and illnesses of all sorts in addition to delivering babies. She must have had some years of experience and observation in Oxford. Ballard noted in her diary that she first officiated at a birth in July 1778, less than a year after the move to Hallowell. Since a midwife typically learned her trade through years of participation in the customary "social childbirth," as one of the female friends and neighbors assisting at births, it is probable that Ballard assisted other midwives at many deliveries before the move to Hallowell. Her qualifications would have been greatly enhanced in the eyes of the public by her experience in giving birth to nine children. Moreover, her family seems to have had medical interests: one of her uncles and two of her brothers-in-law were physicians. In Ballard's case the time and the place may also have accelerated the usually gradual advancement from assistant to midwife; unlike Oxford, Hallowell was a young and growing town. Ballard was one of the few older female citizens, and she had experience.

Judging from the format of Ballard's diary, which mimics the style of an almanac—ruled margins, numbers for days of the week, and letters for Sundays—Ballard may have begun her diary in an almanac that no longer survives. It was not uncommon for eighteenth-century men to use the blank pages bound into printed almanacs to make sporadic notes on subjects such as the weather, their gardens, and social visits. Ballard's diary also shows characteristics of the other common form of everyday record keeping, the daybook, which typically contained daily accounts of expenses and income, with some short notes on family events or work performed. Whatever their length, every one of Ballard's entries records the weather, her whereabouts, and the people with whom she had contact that day. Every delivery is recorded, with an "XX" in the margin when it is paid for, and often the amount paid. Through most of the diary, marginal notes summarize the births, deaths, and major events in each entry. Her diary is thus part almanac, part personal journal, part town medical history, and part account book. Evidently Ballard wrote an entry every day, and she also used the diary for later reference to past events. While the entries often seem unpromisingly terse and factual, Ulrich explains the significance of the format: "Martha sometimes slipped the folded half-sheets from which she constructed her diary into her bag when she crossed the river or waded through snow to sit out a tedious labor, and when she felt overwhelmed or enlivened by the very 'trivia' the historians have dismissed, she said so, not in the soul-searching manner of a Puritan nor with the literary self-consciousness of a sentimentalist, but in a plain, matter-of-fact, and in the end unforgettable voice."

Ballard's diary reveals a great deal about the life patterns of a career midwife in postrevolutionary America. One might expect that just under one thousand deliveries in the course of a lifetime (814 in the years covered by the diary) would be enough work, but in twentieth-century terms Ballard was "simultaneously a midwife, nurse, physician, mortician, pharmacist, and attentive wife" as well as "keeper of vital records," as Ulrich attests. Dr. Daniel Cony, a member of the new all-male class of physicians, seems to have gotten town birth and death statistics from her records. Ballard was what Ulrich calls a "social healer." Unlike the new male physicians, who went through at least a formal apprenticeship of a specified length, joined professional associations, and assumed the title of "doctor," eighteenth-century midwives learned their trade in seemingly casual ways and went in and out of homes without fanfare, caring for the sick as women had always done, but with recognized skills above those of ordinary women. Their affiliations were personal rather than formal and professional, their reputations local rather than regional. The extent of their involvement in medicine also had a great deal to do with the amount of household labor they had to perform: when Ballard's childbearing years ended and her daughters began to take over the household weaving, her practice expanded considerably.

Though doctors are more visible in town and regional records, midwives were still presiding over the great majority of deliveries during Ballard's lifetime. Where Ballard averaged about forty deliveries a year, Dr. Cony, like most physicians, performed only eight or ten. As was typical, his medical practice was only part-time, and obstetrical cases were only a fraction of that work. He was a land proprietor and politician more than a doctor. Indeed, even when a doctor attended a birth, it was common for a midwife to be in charge. Their methods of treatment were not as different as one might think; midwives and physicians still relied primarily on the same time-honored remedies: "pukes" and "purges," medicines made from herbs, roots, hog's grease, blood, and alcohol. Unlike the physicians, however, midwives avoided dramatic methods such as bloodletting or the use of newer drugs such as laudanum or quinine. Ballard's diary shows her awareness of the town doctors' movements, as well as her occasional criticisms of their practice. Whereas physicians' records often fail to record the much greater work of midwives, Ballard's diary rights the proportion. Midwifery was Ballard's calling, not simply a professional interest. Her diary reveals her dedication to her practice and her pride in the physical stamina she brought to her work.

In three days of entries in April 1789, for instance, she outlined a harrowing series of calls in language reminiscent of Mary Rowlandson's:

[April 23] Clear & very Pleasant. I sett out to go to Mr Bullins. Stept out of the Canue & sunk in the mire. Came back & Changd my Cloaths. Maid another attempt & got safe there. Sett out for home. Calld at Capt Coxes & Mr Goodins. Was Calld in at Mrs Husseys. Tarried all night. A sever storm before morn.

[April 24] A sever Storm of rain. I was Calld at 1 hour pm from Mrs Husseys by Ebenzer Hewin. Crosst the river in their Boat. A great sea A going. We got safe over then sett out for Mr Hewins. I Crost a stream on the way on fleeting Loggs & got safe over. Wonder full is the Goodness of providence. I then proseeded on my journey. Went beyond Mr Hainses & a Larg tree blew up by the roots before me which Caused my hors to spring back & my life was spared. Great & marvillous are thy sparing mercies O God. I was assisted over the fallen tree by Mr Hains. Went on. Soon Came to a stream. The Bridg was gone. Mr Hewin took the rains waded thro & led the horse. Asisted by the same allmighty power I got safe thro & arivd unhurt. Mrs Hewins safe delivd at 10 h Evn of a Daughter.

[April 25] Rainy. I came from Mr Hewins to Mr Pollards. My hors mired & I fell off in the mud but blessed be God I received no hurt. Mr Hewins attended me to Mrs Husseys. We arivd at 11 hour morning. Mrs Norcross was in Travill. Her women were immediately Calld & Shee was Safe Delivrd at 5 hour 30 minutes Evening of a fine son. . . .

Yet this dramatic series of days is preceded and followed by more-mundane entries, the other side of Ballard's life: days spent knitting stockings, planting cabbages, sowing seed, and "warping" cloth. Ballard's midwifery accounts weave seamlessly into the household economy in which she operated as gardener, clothmaker, seamstress, cook, and supervisor. Much has been said in women's history about the ideology of "separate spheres" for men and women, with a focus on when and how those boundaries were crossed. Some historians have named the Revolution as a time when the female sphere began to gain political and public status, as wives and mothers were called to an appreciation of their roles in building future (male) citizens and leaders. Other analyses have looked not to "republican motherhood" but to women's leadership in the burgeoning voluntary reform movements of the nineteenth century as the source of women's increasing public activity. Ballard's diary does not contest the existence of separate spheres, but it does provide new evidence of the complexity of women's economic activity, which often took them beyond the household.

Judging by official town records or by the diaries of Ballard's male contemporaries in Hallowell, women's trade would seem almost nonexistent. Ballard's diary fills in the other side of the story. For instance, the women of Hallowell frequently bartered and traded household goods such as cloth, food, flax, yarn, and ashes among themselves. Ballard recorded many such exchanges and the visits during which they occurred. In addition, households exchanged daughters as often as

kettles, thread, or pumpkins. Between 1785 and 1800 Ballard had thirty-nine different young women in her household for varying periods to work at tasks such as spinning, weaving, harvesting, and laundering. The most skilled weavers were often employed for periods of days or weeks in others' households as trainers of young daughters. Ballard recorded her daughters' training in this way. This system of labor and exchange was almost entirely independent of male economic transactions. Ballard hardly ever recorded an exchange between men, recounting almost entirely the economic activity of women.

Ballard's records of contacts with the townspeople under varying circumstances provide a far more representative sampling of the town's actual makeup than the surviving diaries of males from Hallowell. Ballard's social and professional web included men and women, rich and poor. Her diary shows that, although social and economic distinctions typically divided a community, the "invisible" work of women helped hold it together. Ballard's medical skills, for instance, were extended to those who needed them, regardless of class and apparently of race as well. Where men's work in the town had titles and offices recorded in town records—including "selectman," "Packer of Fish," "Culler of Hoops & Staves," and "Sealer of Weights & Measures"—women's work, which was not mentioned in the records, was no less vital to community welfare. Ulrich suggests the beginnings of a collective consciousness among women in a few of Ballard's diary entries, especially those in which men are "diverting themselves" with military exercises and the women are keeping up the necessary household labor, even nursing the men who injure themselves by inept cannon firing at a muster. Diaries such as Ballard's reveal a full spectrum of the public and private, male and female life of a town.

Some historians have described the eighteenth century as a time of transition in family politics, during which the choice of a mate began to be influenced more by romantic love and less by economic considerations. Others have stressed the continued primacy of economic negotiation in marital contracts. Ballard's diary reveals the apparent free choice of spouses, as well as the prevalence of sex before marriage, but it suggests little if any romance in marital choices. At least from Ballard's perspective, economic factors seem primary, with weddings reported as simply one more event in the course of a day and the real focus being on when the couple began "housekeeping" together (often a month or more after the wedding), supplied with the

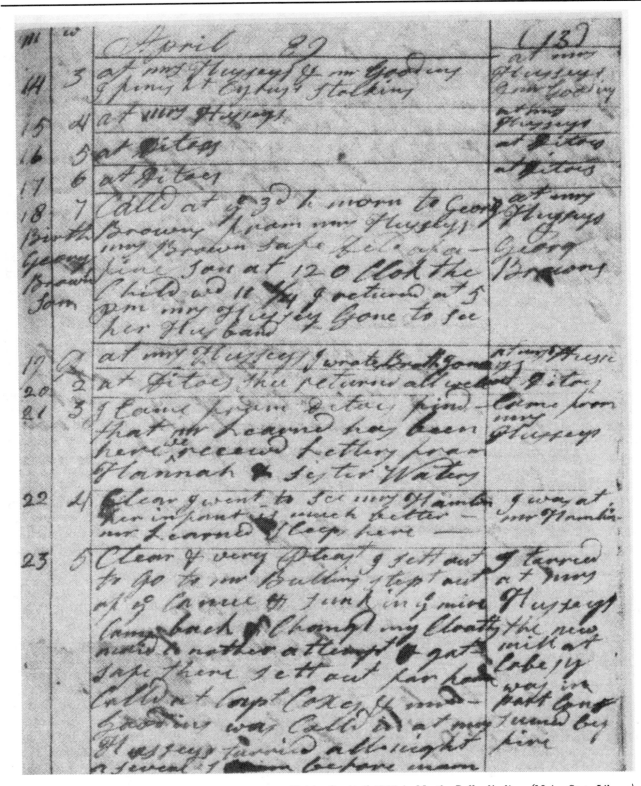

Entries for April 1789 in Martha Ballard's diary (Maine State Library)

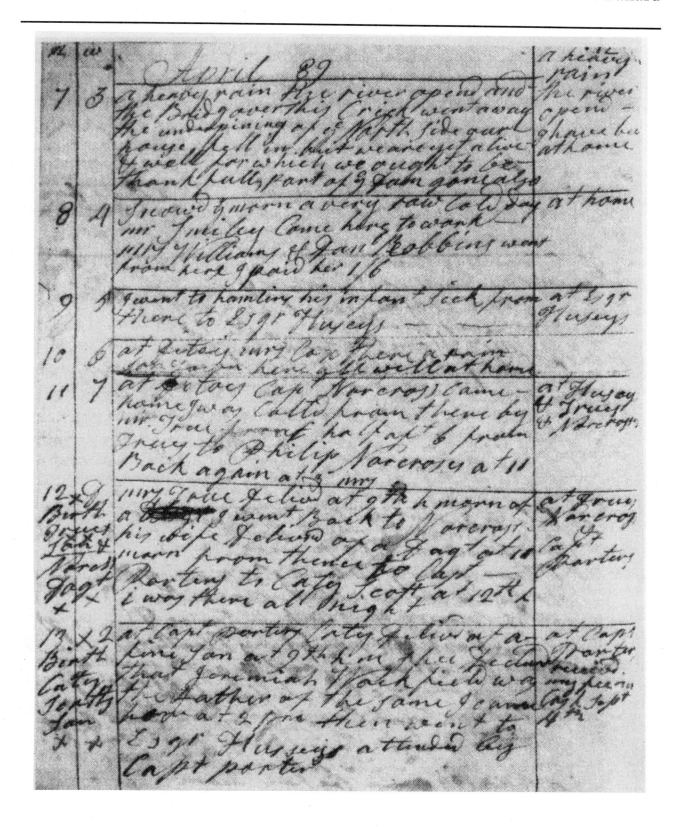

household goods that the women of the family manufactured. In Ballard's world, courtship—two people "keeping company"—seems to have been almost nonexistent, but mixed-gender social gatherings were common, with young men and women going off to taverns in groups, participating in husking bees, celebrating barn raisings or the completion of a quilt with a dinner and dance. For example, after several months of entries that occasionally mention a Ballard daughter socializing in groups with various male friends of the family, Ballard writes matter-of-factly that a Mr. Pitts asked for their daughter's hand in marriage. After a month of intensive work, including the preparation of a quilt for the couple, came the wedding, attended only by the family. The Ballards' daughter remained at home for a month before moving out to take up housekeeping with Mr. Pitts.

Sentimental novels of the time tended to present cases of pregnancy outside marriage as rare exceptions and viewed as dramatic catastrophes. Popular late-eighteenth-century novels such as Hannah Webster Foster's *The Coquette* (1797) or Susanna Rowson's *Charlotte: A Tale of Truth* (1791) feature seduced and abandoned women who either die in childbirth or live as miserable exiles. Ballard's diary, however, suggests a much calmer reaction to women in that circumstance. For instance, she recorded that Sally Pierce, an unmarried woman she attended in childbirth, named Ballard's son Jonathan as the father of the child. (It was the midwife's legal responsibility to ask for such testimony at the height of labor, since it was assumed that no mother would lie in that extremity.) In later diary entries Ballard worriedly recorded Jonathan's absence from home, until a few weeks later, when Jonathan, his new wife, and the baby came to visit. Ballard at first referred to the boy as "Sally's baby," but a few months later he became "Jack."

The evidence of Ballard's diary suggests that the sensational stories of wronged women were more a literary tradition than an historical pattern. The discomfort of forced marriages (Jonathan's absence may have been a protest) did not keep them from being the most common solution. Many new wives gave birth to their first babies a few months after the wedding. Nor did such cases usually go to court. By Ballard's time fathers of illegitimate children were rarely prosecuted, and even prosecutions of women for "fornication" dropped to almost nothing by the late eighteenth century in New England. Historians of sexual mores have focused on two main issues in early America: the evident double standard and the drop in prosecutions. Was the double standard, so roundly criticized in some novels of the day, fuel for a general societal debate over women's sexuality? Did the drop in court cases show the privatization of sexual mores, or perhaps a transition between Puritan and Victorian moral strictures? Using Ballard's diary, Ulrich argues that the decline in fornication cases may have resulted from the general effectiveness of informal, community-based methods of resolution such as those Ballard recorded. In Hallowell unmarried mothers were neither abandoned nor treated cruelly by the community. Instead they either married the father or (as in another case Ballard recorded) collected child support from him and later married another man without stigma.

The most dramatic story of sexual behavior in Martha Ballard's diary is a case that did go to court but remains inconclusive. In autumn 1789 Rebecca Foster, wife of the Reverend Isaac Foster, accused several prominent men in the town of raping her while her husband was out of town late that summer. The Fosters were already in trouble in the community: Reverend Foster had been dismissed from his pastorate because of doctrinal and personal conflicts with his parishioners. All that survives in the official records of the case are the indictment, the verdict, and an expense account. The Ballard diary, however, preserves Martha Ballard's testimony as well as her apparently after-the-fact addenda to entries from August 1789, when Mrs. Foster had made elliptical complaints: during the course of one week in August, men had thrown stones at her house and demanded that they be allowed in to "lodge with" her; Joseph North (a judge as well as a colonel) had, she said, definitely had intercourse with a woman other than his wife. Ballard recalled warning Rebecca Foster of the consequences of saying such things against a powerful man such as North. Eight and one-half months after the alleged attacks began, Rebecca Foster gave birth to a daughter. Though Ballard had urged Foster to keep silent, Ballard recorded in her diary that Foster swore rape complaints against three men, including North, and that Ballard was called to testify. As a friend of the Fosters, and a midwife, Ballard would have provided especially important testimony, since Foster first complained to her about the men's "abuses" only ten days after the first alleged attack—too early for a pregnancy to be confirmed, thus lending credence to her accusations. Ballard's diary entries suggest that she was impressed with Foster's calm and fearless court testimony and surprised by the eventual acquittal of the most prominent defendant, Joseph North, by the jury (which was, of course, all male). Compared to the scanty official trace of this case in court records,

Ballard's accounts give a fuller picture—though still an incomplete one—of an early American rape trial, giving a sense of the vulnerability of a woman whose husband had lost status, and the understandable reticence that may have prevented many women from taking rape cases to court in the eighteenth century.

As Martha Ballard aged and her daughters married and moved out of the household, the diary entries grew longer and more personal. Laments over housework became common since her chief labor supply was no longer easily available, and hired household help was difficult to keep. Accounts of days spent doing laundry—a task she described with a line from a popular song: "a womans work is never Done"—suggest her sense of oppression and abandonment. To add to her depression, her midwife practice began to fall off once she and her husband moved into a new house on Jonathan's land in 1799. At the top of a steep hill and farther from the center of Hallowell, they were far less accessible to neighbors in need. She wrote more and more often about difficulties with hired girls, gynecological illness, low spirits, a chilly period with her husband, and economic worries. There were other serious family troubles as well. Ephraim and his surveying party were attacked by angry squatters during surveying trips in 1795 and 1802. Martha's account of Ephraim's return from the 1802 trip on 28 August shows how much it disturbed him (he had a "fitt of shakeing" and in the night "dirtied the Bed") and troubled her (with a sleepless night and dutiful washing of the linen). Jonathan had embarrassing and violent outbursts of temper. In early 1804 Ephraim was imprisoned for debt. He had contracted with the town to collect the town's full tax bill (in addition to all his other work) and had eight hundred dollars still to collect when the yearly deadline came. It was well over a year before he was freed.

Most historians have studied imprisonment for debt as part of American economic and legal history. Martha Ballard's account of Ephraim's imprisonment, particularly in its effects on her and her role in the family, is a vividly human counterpoint, showing how a family's history and psychology was intertwined with its economic and legal fate. The 1804–1805 diary entries are full of fatigue, laments, and prayers for strength. With Ephraim unavailable, new problems loomed large. Lacking her husband as wood supplier, Martha chopped rotting logs with a hoe and burned old fence wood in the stove before overcoming her fierce independence and asking Jonathan to bring her wood. Some time into her husband's imprisonment, her status began to shift into that of a dependent widow: the hot-tempered Jonathan and his family

moved into the house with her, making her effectively a lodger in her own home, an uncomfortable situation detailed in the diary. Troubled by her daughter-in-law's temper and the noise and disrespect of Jonathan's family, Martha took to going to her old house during the day. Not until three months after Ephraim's release did Jonathan's family move out. The elder Ballards' dependent status was becoming more and more obvious.

During this period hard times in the community were taking their toll, and the Ballards did not escape the consequences of their neighbors' distress. When Captain Purrinton, a neighbor, went on a murderous rampage in his home on the night of 9 July 1806, attacking his wife and their eight children with an axe before slitting his own throat with a razor, the Ballards were among the first people on the scene. Martha's diary recounts how Jonathan went into the house in the early hours of 10 July, lighting his candle to see what had happened, and how she helped wash and lay out the bodies in the barn, as well as the "sollom specttacle" of the funeral, with the captain's coffin on the church porch topped by the axe and razor, and Martha's prayer to God to "Sanctify this affliction" to her and the community. Martha also recorded that the Ballards boarded the murderer's brother and the one surviving son for a short time following the funeral, and that Sally Ballard, Jonathan's wife, took in and nursed the Purrinton daughter who died of her injuries a few weeks later. Martha Ballard's account is spare but vivid, a picture of the network of neighborly services that operated at such a time. It says nothing of the ecclesiastical reflections that other accounts of the murders stress; Purrinton was said to be a believer in universal salvation, so that as he contemplated suicide he would have believed that ending the lives of his family as well was a kindness, saving them from the poverty that awaited them and bringing them with him to heaven. The particulars that Martha Ballard did give, however, record the town's reaffirmation of a more orthodox set of beliefs: Captain Purrinton's coffin was allowed only as far as the church porch during the funeral, and his body was carried in a cart at the end of the funeral procession and interred outside the walls of the churchyard. With its details and its conventional but heartfelt prayer, Ballard's diary entry is an attempt to bring order to a terrifying irruption of violence and chaos in the community.

Later, amid the sporadic violence of the "Malta Wars" of 1809—disputes between squatters and landowners during which the Ballards' nephew, Elijah Barton, was accused of murder—little of the outside world seemed to touch the diary. Instead Ballard concentrated on the work of hoeing, planting, and harvesting in the garden. Martha's careful planning and preservation of seeds and roots each year for the next year's planting meant that the care of the garden was almost a year-round activity, with cabbage and turnip roots stored in the cellar for replanting in early spring, bean and other seeds planted as soon as the ground could be worked, and multiple plantings extending the season into early winter for some crops. This area of endeavor was almost entirely her own: though Ephraim sometimes helped to hoe the ground in the spring, the rest of the work was Martha's, and she referred to the various plots as "my garden." When Elijah Barton was arraigned for the murder of a surveyor, Martha's diary entries conveyed her sympathy for his mother but concentrated on the ordering of her patch of the earth. While the surviving Hallowell diaries of Martha's contemporaries Daniel Cony and Henry Sewall mention gardening activities, only Ballard's diary gives the detailed daily account of the work that went into the intensive horticulture carried out by New England women. Martha's records of her eight kinds of beans and her many squash and cucumber plantings give a glimpse into a little-known world of women's work in early New England, as well as a hint of the therapeutic purposes of that work in a time of public and private disorder.

When the midwife Ann Mosier died in May 1809, seventy-four-year-old Martha Ballard began to be called more frequently to the bedsides of women in labor. She delivered almost as many babies in the last four months of her life in 1812 as in the first years covered in her diary. Yet her health continued to falter. After several years of intermittent illness, the last diary entries mention feebleness and "ague fitts," which were often incapacitating. In the final entry, dated 17 May 1812, Martha Ballard recorded that she was surrounded by friends and relatives, with the Reverend Benjamin Tappin conversing with her and making "a prayer adapted to my Case." Her funeral on 31 May was noted in Henry Sewall's diary. A one-sentence obituary appeared in the *American Advocate* on 9 June. Otherwise any official record of Ballard's life is almost nonexistent; censuses, tax records, merchant accounts, and the membership rolls at Augusta First Church mention only Ephraim Ballard's name.

The diary remained in Augusta, probably kept by the Ballards' daughter Dolly Lambard. Dolly's two daughters received it at her death, and they gave the diary to their grandniece Mary Hobart, a practicing physician, in 1884. Sometime before 1904 Charles Elventon Nash made an abridgment of the diary, reducing it by two-thirds and keeping references to public events such as the Purrinton murders and some representative examples of Ballard's work, but excising references to sexual matters (including the North trial) and family troubles and most of the passages about household labor. This abridgment was part of a projected two-volume history of Augusta, of which most of volume one was printed but not published in 1904. The uncut signatures were stored in the house of a Nash descendant until librarian Edith Hary, with the family's cooperation, had the signatures bound and published in 1961 as *The History of Augusta: First Settlements and Early Days as a Town, Including The Diary of Mrs. Martha Moore Ballard (1785–1812).* In 1930 Hobart donated the diary manuscript to the Maine State Library. In 1990 Ulrich introduced the diary to a wide spectrum of readers in *A Midwife's Tale,* highlighting its significance for students of early American culture and women's history. Two years later the whole diary was published by Picton Press as special publication number 10 of the Maine Genealogical Society. In the twenty-seven years of Martha Ballard's daily entries, the reader encounters the complexities of her life. Forced to reconsider stereotypical ideas about her era, the reader becomes acquainted with a courageous, dedicated, devout, hardworking, and exceptionally human woman of the early republic, a woman who turned to her diary to order her world.

Biography:
Laurel Thatcher Ulrich, *A Midwife's Tale: The Life of Martha Ballard, Based on Her Diary, 1785–1812* (New York: Knopf, 1990).

References:
Lynn Z. Bloom, "Auto/Bio/History: Modern Midwifery," in *Autobiography and Questions of Gender,* edited by Shirley Neuman (London: Cass, 1991), pp. 12–24;
James W. North, *The History of Augusta* (Augusta, Maine: Clamp & North, 1870; republished, Somersworth, N.H.: New England History Press, 1981).

Papers:
The manuscript for Ballard's diary is at the Maine State Library, Augusta.

Ann Eliza Bleecker

(October 1752 – 23 November 1783)

Allison Giffen
New Mexico State University

BOOKS: *The Posthumous Works of Ann Eliza Bleecker in Prose and Verse. To which is added, A Collection of Essays, Prose and Poetical, by Margaretta V. Faugeres,* edited by Margaretta V. Faugeres (New York: Printed by T. & J. Swords, 1793);
The History of Maria Kittle (Hartford: Printed by Elisha Babcock, 1797).

Ann Eliza Bleecker's letters, poems, and narratives depict her tumultuous experiences while living on the front lines of the American Revolution. Her letters in particular offer fascinating details and insights into the material lives of the ordinary men and women who participated in the War for Independence. They offer gossip about local premarital pregnancies, providing a satirical advertisement for much-needed husbands; they tell of a local "religious fanatic" who murdered his family and livestock; and they describe her feelings of betrayal by the acts of Benedict Arnold. Her work is also significant for its contributions to an emerging American literary tradition. Bleecker produced one of the first fictionalized Indian captivity narratives, an important and distinctly American genre. In *The History of Maria Kittle,* first published in *The Posthumous Works of Ann Eliza Bleecker* (1793), she transposed her own story of maternal loss onto the already popular form, contributing to a tradition of captivity stories by women that feature strong, active, female protagonists.

Bleecker's work is characterized by melancholy themes, and a large portion of it is dedicated to the specific expression of grief over the death of her young daughter, Abella. Consequently some scholars have seen Bleecker as an important precursor to the nineteenth-century poetess, exemplified by such writers as Lydia Sigourney whose antebellum poems are largely elegies and satirized by Mark Twain (Samuel Langhorne Clemens) in the figure of Emmeline Grangerford, who could write about anything "just so it was sadful," in *Adventures of Huckleberry Finn* (1884). Bleecker's mode of expression was influenced heavily by the eighteenth-century British cult of sensibility, and she wrote in the mannered, often hyperbolic, language of feeling. Indeed, her work reveals what happens when the British "Man of Feeling" is transformed into a mother in the American wilderness.

Born Ann Eliza Schuyler in New York City in October 1752 into a prosperous merchant family, she was the daughter of Brandt and Margareta Van Wyck Schuyler and acquired a local reputation as a precocious poetic talent. In 1769, at seventeen, she married John J. Bleecker, and the couple moved to Tomhanick, a town eighteen miles north of Albany, where John Bleecker had inherited land. Geographically isolated and far from the familiar urban context of her family and friends, Bleecker addressed all her work to friends to alleviate her loneliness. The central source of biographical information comes from her daughter, Margaretta V. Faugeres, who wrote "Memoirs of Ann Eliza Bleecker" as an introduction to her mother's *Posthumous Works.* Faugeres focused on her mother's loneliness and grief, suggesting that "being naturally of a pensive turn of mind, she *too* freely indulged" her sorrows.

The move to Tomhanick represents the first in a series of losses that, for Bleecker, characterized her life: she was the bereft artist, isolated, alienated, and grieving. In Bleecker's involvement in her grief the reader can sense that she was self-consciously fashioning a literary identity for herself, drawing heavily on sentimental virtues, particularly the tender emotions and compassion for suffering (that "tender contagion" as she called it in *The History of Maria Kittle*). Faugeres described her mother's melancholic temperament:

> She was frequently very lively, and would then give way to flights of her fertile fancy, and write songs, satires, and burlesque: but, as drawing a cord too tight will make it break, thus she would no sooner cease to be *merry,* than the heaviest *dejection* would succeed, and then all the pieces that were not as melancholy as herself, she destroyed.

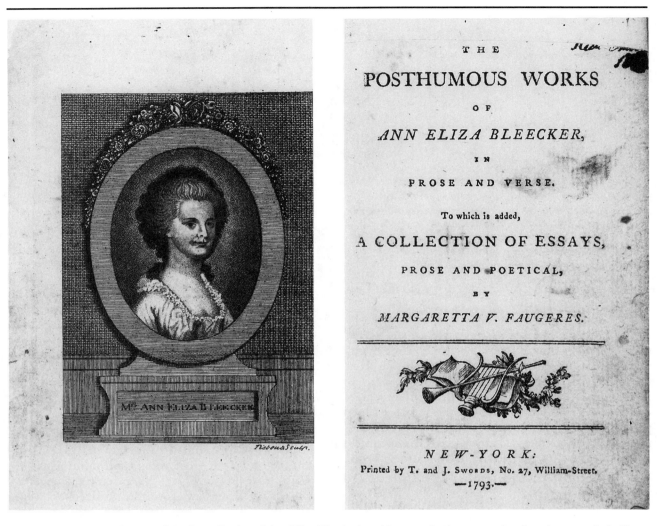

Frontispiece and title page of the first collection of Ann Eliza Bleecker's writings, works that express her "pensive turn of mind" (courtesy of the Special Collections Department, University of Virginia Library)

This passage explains in part why so much of Bleecker's work treats melancholy themes: she destroyed those works that did not conform to this dark pattern. This impulse to destroy her lighter works points to an awareness of audience and to an understanding of how that audience should receive her work. Bleecker was well read, and she enjoyed the literary tradition of the melancholic artist that was popular in the eighteenth century. Her poems and letters are filled with literary allusions, and she seems to have been fond of Thomas Gray, one of the British "graveyard poets" to whom she alluded frequently. Certainly, by destroying work that displayed too much levity, Bleecker revealed a strong interest in creating a career for herself as melancholic artist.

The central event that provoked Bleecker's intense and alienating melancholia occurred early in the American Revolution, in the summer of 1777.

Threatened by the approaching British troops of Gen. John Burgoyne, who led an expedition from Canada against the colonies, Bleecker was forced to flee her home on foot with her two daughters, six-year-old Margaretta and the infant Abella. This flight became the pivotal event of Bleecker's life. It colored everything she wrote afterward, and she never really recovered from its consequences. When the Bleeckers received word that Burgoyne's troops were near, John Bleecker went to Albany to find suitable housing for his family. While her husband was away, Bleecker learned that the troops were fast approaching. She was forced to flee with her daughters and joined her husband. The family fled south, and in the course of their flight Bleecker's infant, Abella, died of dysentery. They continued their journey and were joined in Red Hook by Bleecker's mother, who died soon thereafter. This death was followed by that of Bleecker's only sister, Caty Swits, who had joined them for their return trip to Tomhanick. Every generation in her supportive circle of women was devastated. Four years later, in 1781, John Bleecker was kidnapped by a band of wandering British soldiers. Though he was soon returned to his family, the trauma of the event led Bleecker to miscarry a pregnancy.

From that summer in 1777 until her death in 1783, Bleecker suffered from intense bouts of depression. In a letter to her brother, Samuel Schuyler, written just months before her death, she told the story of her flight from Burgoyne in 1777 and referred to the miscarriage, closely associating it with the loss of Abella. Maternal loss is always the central motif of Bleecker's story. Though Bleecker attributed her weakening health to the miscarriage, she concluded, "I have given you my little history that you may see that I die of a broken heart." In her memoir Faugeres also implied that her mother died from the trauma of loss, noting that "the idea of a far distant peace which should again restore her to her friends" sustained Bleecker through the distress of the Revolutionary War. When Bleecker finally revisited New York City after the war, she found her friends dead or gone and a good deal of the city destroyed. Faugeres wrote that "her sensibility was too keen for her peace," and she returned to Tomhanick, where "her health rapidly declined." Significantly, both mother and daughter relied on a popular eighteenth-century stereotype of the artist. Bleecker emerges as a kind of Young Werther, whose feelings are so refined and whose sensibility is so keen that the sorrows of this world cannot be endured.

Bleecker never published any of her writings in her lifetime, relying instead on a small audience of correspondents to whom she sent most of her work. After her mother's death Faugeres published a significant portion of the work in *The New-York Magazine* in 1790 and 1791 and then collected some of it in *The Posthumous Works of Ann Eliza Bleecker* (1793), which comprises twenty-three letters, thirty-six poems, *The History of Maria Kittle,* and an unfinished fragment, a short historical novel, "The Story of Henry and Anne," to which Faugeres added a conclusion. The reader can infer that most of these works date from the last six years of Bleecker's life, following the death of Abella. Though no other writings are now extant, it is apparent from Faugeres's memoir that she had writings dating as far back as 1769 when she selected the contents for the collection. Instead of publishing a representative sampling of her mother's work, Faugeres apparently

decided to focus primarily on writings dating from the last trauma-laden years of her mother's life.

Bleecker clearly felt isolated in Tomhanick, and much of her writing was driven by her desire for a supportive community of women. In her correspondence she sustained a fiction of communal presence, often referring to her letters as "conversations." Indeed, she seemed enamored of the letter form, and her work resists easy categorization because she often blurred the generic boundary between her letters and her other work. The titles of many of her poems are formulated as addresses to specific individuals, for example "To Mr. Bleecker" and "To Miss Ten Eyck"; yet Bleecker went a step beyond this fairly conventional strategy and often wrote a more personal address in the first line: "Peggy amidst domestic cares to rhyme / I find no pleasure and find no time"; "Dear Betsy now pleasure the woodland has left"; or "Come my Susan quit your chamber." Bleecker addressed many of these poems to the women with whom she corresponded, and the poems share with the letters an intimacy as well as a desire for her friends' presence. Bleecker framed *The History of Maria Kittle* as a letter to her half sister, Susan Ten Eyck, beginning the story with the salutation "Dear Susan" and interrupting her story intermittently to address Susan directly and comment on the action. In addition, she later included the narrative in a letter to her cousin, commenting on it and suggesting that, like Susan, her cousin might also benefit from the story. The context of the letters illuminates Bleecker's literary project in *The History of Maria Kittle,* in which she enscripted her desire for a supportive community of women who could accommodate her grief.

Bleecker's attachment to her women friends underscores the central role that women's friendships played in the emotional life of eighteenth- and nineteenth-century American women. As scholars such as Nancy Cott and Carroll Smith-Rosenberg have shown, these friendships were based on a model of familial relationships, specifically that of mother and daughter. Bleecker's work testifies to the power of these networks. In a letter to a friend with whom her correspondence had dwindled, Bleecker offered the model of their mothers' friendship:

> I sit down, dear Betsy, to congratulate you on a new occasion of happiness to your family, by the birth of another daughter. . . . you cannot look back to the period when your mother and mine interchanged the most delicate offices of friendship, and sat us an example of the brightest virtue, without a sentiment of gratitude and regret for their loss.

It is particularly revealing that Bleecker used this maternal model in a letter in which she congratulated her friend on the birth of a daughter. Emotional intimacy for Bleecker was bound up in a continuous, biological line, one that offered a powerful and stable model for a community of female friends. Bleecker's letters to her women friends are filled with passion and pain accountable, in part, by her traumatic losses of daughter, mother, and sister.

Bleecker's extant letters span the years 1779 to 1783, and her central correspondents were two of her cousins, Peggy and Maria Van Wyck and her half sister, Susan Ten Eyck, with whom she was especially close. These letters often include expressions of grief that are almost always accompanied by a bitter acceptance that her melancholy themes will not be well received:

> Your letters, Peggy's and Maria's I have received, often read, and wept over; but, conscious that my gloomy ideas would be unseasonable in the circle of pleasure, I omitted answering as much as possible. . . . Forgive my relapsing into melancholy: I will make one more exertion to be lively, and if I cannot succeed, will conclude my paper.

The "circle of pleasure" seems to be the circle that the exchange of letters inscribed around the friends. She wanted to participate in it; yet her anguish pulled her away. Bleecker noted in this letter that she was writing on the third anniversary of the death of Abella, and her words reflect an awareness that even the community of her closest female friends considered extensive and continued melancholy inappropriate. Filled with ambivalence, her letters reveal a writer torn between the desire to accommodate her readers and the desire to hold onto her alienating grief. The result was a correspondent who wrote about her own impulse to silence, naming and renaming it.

While Bleecker recognized that the expression of grief was not entirely welcome to her readers, she also believed it to be appropriate and consequently located failure, albeit indirectly, in her readers' inability to feel deeply and compassionately rather than in her inability to control her grief. Bleecker's primary correspondents, her cousins and Susan Ten Eyck, were younger and unmarried, and Bleecker's tone is that of a maternal counseling figure, one who would encourage or mock in order to lead the young ladies to greater maturity. In one of her gentler letters to a Van Wyck cousin, dated 1779, she wrote:

> I often suffer a constraint when I affect to be gay and trifle as formerly. But I am under no concern, my dear, of disgusting you by being serious, your judgment is

mature as my years, and puts us on a level: however I promise to be lively when I can. . . .

While Bleecker may occasionally have given her readers the benefit of the doubt, believing them to be mature enough to respond appropriately to her melancholic temper, more typically she resorted to sarcasm: "How shall I apologize my cousin, for writing in this strain to a fair lady who would chuse to hear of none but metaphoric deaths and innocent murders caused by her eyes?" At other times she became merely dismissive. In a letter in which she had enclosed one of her most significant poems, "Retreat from Burgoyne," she wrote: "I have enclosed some verses . . . composed at the time of our retreat from Burgoyne, the most melancholy period of my life; so if they are too serious for the volatility of a gay lady's ideas, hand them over to your good mamma. . . ." Bleecker used barbed wit as a distancing device to position herself as a figure of experience in relation to her unmarried correspondents.

Bleecker was interested 'in encouraging her women friends to indulge in "the luxury of grief," to participate in the kind of charged, yet refined, emotion typically associated with the cult of sensibility. She connected this response specifically with maturity and education and was at pains to distinguish herself and her women friends from the "sun-burnt daughters of labor," the local members of her rural community. She demonstrated this distinction most explicitly in her treatment of nature:

> we live perfectly retired, and see very little company at present, as the ladies in our vicinage are busy hoeing their corn and planting potatoes. As we are not quite so well calculated for this rare employment, we left the sun-burnt daughters of Labor yesterday and went on pilgrimage to the Half-Moon, to Visit Mrs. P***s.

Unlike her rural neighbors, Bleecker viewed nature as a place where one feels rather than works. Bleecker's letters are profoundly class inflected. They are literary performances meant to distinguish herself as urbane, educated, and of a higher class from the "rustic swains" and "silly chit-chat females" of Tomhanick. Her letters are filled with conventional poetic effusions about the beauties of her rural "prospect":

> we have erected a spacious arbor, closely shaded with annual vines, where we often drink tea and enjoy the prospect of a lovely collection of flowers on one hand, and a cool and shady orchard on the other; a luxuriant lot of herbage behind and directly opposite, a blushing vineyard in miniature. Here, often, when perusing Theocritus, Tasso, and Virgil, I drop those pastoral

enthusiasts, to reflect on the hours of friendship I have passed with my Susan. . . .

Typically such effusions evoke Bleecker's education, either indirectly through elevated poetic diction or directly, as in the passage above, where nature is a site of refinement and contemplation where one reads the classics.

Education marks one as upper-class, and this distinction had a specific benefit for Bleecker: access to a political identity. In one of the earliest extant letters, she offered an opinion about the local women and politics: "The most disagreeable of our hours are when we admit politics in our female circle: this never fails of opening a field of nonsensical controversy among our ladies." Of course, this female circle is not the "circle of pleasure" of Bleecker and her correspondents. It is composed of the local women, and Bleecker's "we" is highly qualified. In a letter to Peggy Van Wyck she humorously related a conversation with a local officer, informing her cousin that she "assur[ed] him you were a superior order of beings to our common chit-chat females. . . ." Though Bleecker's tone is slightly sarcastic as she (quite typically) teased her cousin about courtship, she did believe herself to be, to a certain extent, "of a superior order" and consequently permitted to participate in the political sphere.

Bleecker wrote patriotic poems commemorating the places and heroes of the Revolution and had a strong political identity as a patriot. She experienced little constraint when speaking in public and participating in the traditionally masculine political sphere. In an amusing letter to Susan, for example, she wrote of a conversation with the rebellious "Vermonters" in which she tried to show them the political error of their ways:

> I then began humbly to expostulate with these wise men of the east about the commencement of this civil war; and at length demanded how they could expect to support their jurisdiction, in the center of the states, who had not acceded to their claim? They replied, "The four eastern states were their own people, and would certainly assist them." I told them I could not see how they dared break through the confederacy while they were sensible all America's happiness depended upon the union.

Though Bleecker informed Susan that she "began humbly," her biting sarcasm in referring to the Vermonters as "these wise men from the east" obviously undercuts any sense of humility on her part. Bleecker delineated a political identity in terms of class. In this confrontation with the Vermonters,

Bleecker stood around a campfire with her husband and various officers, speaking for them as a representative American. She derived this authority from her education, from the fact that she read "Theocritus, Tasso, and Virgil."

Bleecker found ways to assert female agency and authority not only by defining herself against less educated, rural women but also by defining herself against a masculine racial other—Native Americans. Nowhere is this strategy more evident than in her fictionalized captivity story, *The History of Maria Kittle,* written sometime between 1777 and 1780. Captivity narratives were popular in the sensational literature of her day, and their appeal continued through the nineteenth century and well into the twentieth. *The History of Maria Kittle* first appeared in five installments in *The New-York Magazine* from September 1790 through January 1791, feeding a reading public hungry for tales of adventure and violence in the wilderness. Its popularity is suggested by the fact that after the novel appeared in *The Posthumous Works of Ann Eliza Bleecker,* it was separately published in 1797.

Typical captivity stories present sexually vulnerable women who are kidnapped by savage Native Americans and then ultimately rescued by white protectors. This popular plot objectifies women as sexual objects of exchange and seeks to justify Native American genocide. Bleecker's story participates in this racist model. She graphically depicted Native American violence, offering such gruesome details of carnage as the murder of a fetus from the body of a slain mother—a powerful indictment given Bleecker's sense of maternal loss. Couched between sentimental descriptions of domestic bliss and poetic apostrophes to nature, these bloody and specific descriptions are exceptionally jarring in Bleecker's tale. Toward the end of the narrative a minor character makes explicit the racist underpinnings of the story by calling for Native American genocide. Responding earnestly to a tale of violence and maternal loss, a Frenchwoman exclaims: "Would to Heaven! . . . that the brutal nations were extinct, for never, never can the united humanity of France and Britain compensate for the horrid cruelties of their savage allies." As in many other captivity plots, Native Americans stand outside the boundaries of humanity.

Yet Bleecker also strategically altered this model. In *The History of Maria Kittle* the central women characters are neither sexually vulnerable nor passive objects of exchange. Rather they are powerful, maternal figures who endure horrific violence (always at the hands of the "savage ally of France and England"). As in many captivity stories

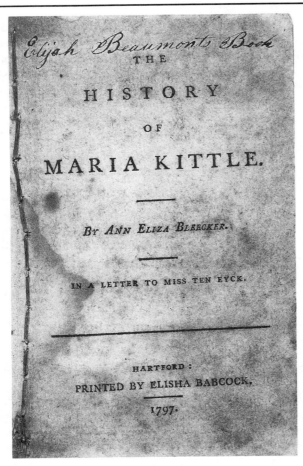

THE

HISTORY

OF

MARIA KITTLE.

BY ANN ELIZA BLEECKER.

IN A LETTER TO MISS TEN EYCK.

HARTFORD:
PRINTED BY ELISHA BABCOCK,
1797.

Title page for the first separate publication of the novel inspired by Bleecker's flight from the British during the American Revolution (courtesy of the Special Collections Department, University of Virginia Library)

by men, Bleecker's story is of threatened and lost innocence. It begins with an extensive description of the Kittles' idyllic family life. Sensitive and well educated, the mother, Maria Kittle, renders beautiful and harmonious all that she touches. She and her husband have two angelic children and are beloved by all. The Edenic quality of the Kittle estate can only suggest its imminent fall. Of course, this fall occurs as a result of Native Americans. Satanic figures of violence, they penetrate and destroy the innocence and purity of this domestic idyll. This racialized violence, presented as a kind of aggressive penetration of the domestic estate, threatens not the virginity of the women but the lives of their children. Indeed, in Bleecker's story women are never objects of exchange from dark men to light. Husbands play marginal roles, and there is never even a hint that the men will "redeem" their wives—they certainly cannot redeem their children. Rather the women redeem themselves through their collective action.

Once all the main plot points of the conventional Indian captivity narrative have occurred—Maria has suffered an Indian attack and watched her children murdered; she has been kidnapped and led from her home in New York on a strenuous journey to Montreal; and she has been returned to the white community in exchange for goods—a full third of the narrative concerns itself with the histories of loss as told by three American women, Maria, Mrs. Willis, and Mrs. Bratt. Their audience is a sympathetic circle of French and British women in Montreal. A kind of emotional redemption occurs through telling and receiving stories of loss. Maria's experiences in captivity carry less narrative weight than this final section, and the real focus of *The History of Maria Kittle* is this reconstructed female community distinguished by its mature acceptance and compassion for melancholy subjects. Given that Bleecker wrote this story in the form of a long letter to Susan Ten Eyck and later enclosed it in a letter to Peggy Van Wyck, her agenda is clear. Like much sentimental literature, this narrative performs what Janet Todd calls a "pedagogy of seeing." Bleecker was offering her less mature women friends a lesson in how to feel. She expected that the literary emotions she presented on the page would produce similar responses in her readers.

Within the circle of sympathy in Bleecker's novel, the women luxuriate in grief as the speakers find themselves liberated to recount their tales: "This ladies is the story of a broken hearted women; nor should I have intruded it in any other but the house of mourning." Clearly, no one present is intruding on her story, for in this home, "the eloquence of sorrow is irresistible." In fact the women derive great pleasure from indulging in these melancholy stories, as one of the Frenchwomen makes clear: "My heart is now sweetly tuned to melancholy. I love to indulge these divine sensibilities which your affecting histories are so capable of inspiring." After Maria relates her experiences, the reader is told that the women spent "some time . . . in tears and melancholy" and then request another story.

The greatest tragedy in these tales of woe is the loss of a child. The stories of Mrs. Bratt and Mrs. Willis share significant parallels with that of Bleecker, herself. Each woman has suffered a violent attack and has fled hostile forces with two children, and each has lost the younger of the two children. This similarity is intensified by intertextual echoes. For example, Mrs. Bratt's response to the death of her infant daughter closely resembles that of Bleecker in "Retreat from Burgoyne," her poem about the death of Abella. In both works mothers wail over their dead children, resisting the truth and seeking some kind of miraculous resurrection. Mrs. Bratt says, "I fell shrieking on the body of my child and rending away my hair, I endeavored to recall him to life with an unavailing lament." Reading these characters' stories in the context of Bleecker's poems and letters, Bleecker's intended audience, Susan Ten Eyck and the Van Wyck cousins, could not have failed to perceive the shadowy specter of Bleecker herself beside these women. These readers by extension must have identified themselves with the sympathetic women listeners. This didactic intent is perhaps most explicit in the narrator's occasional parenthetical remarks to "Susan": "But doubtless, my dear, your generous sensibility is alarmed at my silence about Mrs. Kittle. . . ." Bleecker literally injected Susan into the tale as a frame character, forcing the issue of her participation in the circle of sympathy.

Bleecker's fictional circle of sympathy transcends the confines of national identity. Mrs. Bratt, speaking of her prior bias against the French, says, "I now reject . . . all prejudices of education, from my infancy have I been taught that the French were a cruel, perfidious enemy, but I have found them quite the reverse." Since Bleecker set her story during the French and Indian War, this statement is a powerful one. The French in Bleecker's narrative are sympathetic women who "indulge these fine sensibilities." Though this circle of women may be able to overcome its nationalistic biases, it achieves this communal identity specifically by way of racism and classism. In order to cohere as a group, the women require a common enemy—Native Americans. In addition, Bleecker made a point of presenting all three mothers as well educated and, thus, of a specific class. Of Maria Kittle, she wrote: "as soon as the sun declined, she always retired with her books until the time of repose. . . ." Mrs. Bratt spent her widowhood educating her two sons, while Mrs. Willis is the daughter of a poor and ailing clergyman who, she says "amused himself by educating me." The "sun-burnt daughters of Labor" clearly are not welcome to participate in this communal identity.

The members of this circle are bound together by the narratives of the three grieving mothers as well as by the narrative of Bleecker herself. The women who tell their tales gain their "eloquence of sorrow" when they lose their children and are cast from their rural gardens. This fall from innocence leads to a new emotional maturity in which one accepts the essentially melancholic nature of existence. The narrative concludes not with Maria's returning home but with Mr. Kittle joining her in this specifically feminized site. Bleecker made clear that the eloquence of sorrow belongs to women. Earlier in the narrative, when Mr. Kittle learns of the death of his family, Bleecker described his expression of grief as inarticulate: "his disposition was entirely changed, his looks were fierce, his attitudes wild and extravagant, and his conversation, which was formerly sensible, commanding attention by a musical voice, now was incoherent. . . ." Maria, on the other hand, responds to her loss "with a stoical composure" and offers poetic exclamations describing the nuances of her grief. Her journey leads her to a new feminized site, a kind of postlapsarian community. Here the experience of loss permits women the ability to feel deeply, express grief eloquently, and respond to other such stories compassionately.

It is fairly certain that Bleecker's extant work dates from the last five or six years of her life, when she was struggling to survive on the front lines of the American Revolution and to deal with depression over the death of her daughter. Consequently her captivity narrative, letters, and poems are of a piece and share a consistent set of concerns. Bleecker had a strong sense of herself as a writer, and she drew on the literary influences of British sensibility and on her experiences as a woman living in a dangerous and newly settled part of America. The result is a distinctly American product that contributes significantly to a tradition of American women writers. She is an important precursor to such nineteenth-century writers as Catharine Maria Sedgwick and Lydia Maria Child, whose sentimental novels treat Native American themes. Bleecker's work has just begun to make its appearance in anthologies of American literature and has only started to receive scholarly attention. Thus far, most scholars have been interested in her treatment of race and gender. The increasing availability of Bleecker's work will certainly secure her a place among other significant early American women writers.

References:

Christopher Castiglia, *Bound and Determined: Captivity, Culture and White Womanhood from Mary Rowlandson to Patty Hearst* (Chicago: University of Chicago Press, 1996), pp. 125–136;

Julie Ellison, "Race and Sensibility in the Early Republic: Ann Eliza Bleecker and Sarah Wentworth Morton," *American Literature,* 65 (1993): 445–474;

Allison Giffen, "'Til Grief Melodious Grow': The Poems and Letters of Ann Eliza Bleecker," *Early American Literature,* 28 (1993): 222–241.

Bathsheba Bowers
(4 June 1671–1718)

Sandra Harbert Petrulionis
Pennsylvania State University, The Altoona College

BOOK: *An Alarm Sounded to Prepare the Inhabitants of the World to Meet the Lord in the Way of His Judgments* (New York: Printed by William Bradford, 1709).

Quaker writer and speaker Bathsheba Bowers wrote a spiritual autobiography, *An Alarm Sounded to Prepare the Inhabitants of the World to Meet the Lord in the Way of His Judgments* (1709), one of the first published religious testimonials by an Anglo-American woman. In a biographical sketch of Bowers written in 1879, William J. Potts referred to other works written by her, but none of these has come to light in scholarly research, and her reputation accordingly rests solely on her spiritual autobiography.

Although Bowers's work joined an established tradition of Quaker journals being written during her time by women in England, *An Alarm Sounded to Prepare the Inhabitants of the World to Meet the Lord in the Way of His Judgments* added an American dimension to this highly personal genre. It was not uncommon for English Quakers, men and women alike, to publish their journals, but in the early eighteenth century American women did not commonly publish their writings. Courageously defying contemporary norms, Bowers expected criticism for publishing her chronicle, and she confronted her readers with her rationale for doing so. Indeed this strong and individualistic woman almost defied the reader to disagree with her God-inspired feeling that she was led to share the story of her religious trials with the world.

Raised in Charlestown, Massachusetts, Bowers was one of twelve children born to Benanuel Bowers and Elizabeth Dunster Bowers, English Quakers who had settled in America. When the Puritan persecution of Quakers became intolerable in the late seventeenth century, her parents sent Bowers and three of her sisters to live in Philadelphia, a city known for its liberality and its large Quaker population. What little biographical information that exists about Bowers, in addition to what she revealed in her book, appeared in a diary kept by Bowers's niece Ann Bolton, who described the few

years in which she lived with the Bowers family. When Bathsheba Bowers was thirty-five years old, she moved from Pennsylvania to South Carolina, probably to spread the Quaker faith and to join the growing community of Friends there. Remaining single throughout her life, Bowers lived in South Carolina until her death in 1718, at the age of forty-six.

In Philadelphia, Bowers attended Quaker meetings, but she gradually isolated herself from the community, apparently preferring to spend time in her garden rather than with her neighbors. According to Potts, Bolton wrote that after Bowers "had finished her house and Garden, and they were as beautiful as her hands cou'd make them, or heart could wish, she retired herself in them free from Society as if she had lived in a Cave under Ground or on the top of a high mountain." The locals regarded her as an eccentric and referred to her garden as "Bathsheba's Bower" and "Bathsheba's folly." Praising Bowers's resolute faith in God when she was faced with an Indian attack after moving to South Carolina, Bolton nonetheless criticized what she regarded as her aunt's odd religious faith. In fact, Bolton wrote that Bowers's religious ideas were so strange that they hardly qualified as those of a Quaker. Quakers believed that an individual's physical drives and human needs too often supplanted the spiritual relation that he or she enjoyed with God. Although Bowers understood the necessity of overcoming what she viewed as her sins of ambition and pride, she was a strong-willed woman who did not easily transform herself into a Quaker. She agonized particularly over publicly speaking about her religious life, an obligation that most Quakers assumed to some degree.

Bowers received scholarly attention only in the late twentieth century. She is not discussed in most reference works about early Quaker writers or prominent Quaker women, but the inclusion of selections from her autobiography in the *Heath Anthology of American Literature* (1990) has led to a few critical inquiries.

Most likely published in New York by fellow Philadelphian and Quaker William Bradford (no relation to the Puritan William Bradford), who ran a prosperous printing business, *An Alarm Sounded to Prepare the Inhabitants of the World to Meet the Lord in the Way of His Judgments* is a twenty-three page narrative that relates Bowers's struggle to achieve and maintain a mystical union with God, a relationship Quakers believed was available to all who overcame human drives and passively awaited God's sign. Like other early Quaker-life writings, such as those of John Woolman and Elizabeth Ashbridge, Bowers's narrative documents her afflictions and anxieties about her faith as well as her lifelong battle to understand why God had subjected her to perpetual misery. Throughout the book Bowers doubted whether her moments of religious illumination would last, and the conclusion brought no resolution to these anxieties as she wrote, "O Lord God of Heaven, thou only knows how this Tormented me!" Only in a few rare moments did Bowers attain any semblance of inner peace. Instead, this written account of her life chronicles the depth of her spiritual questionings.

Whereas most colonial women's diaries provide a glimpse of what daily life was like for an early American woman, Bowers's work, like most Quaker journals, presents an intimate look at a woman's religious zeal. It records her spiritual strife and portrays her desperation to end her suffering. As Hugh Barbour and Arthur O. Roberts explain, "Quakerism demanded a protracted struggle," and thus early Quaker life stories record the torment these writers endured as they patiently awaited a sign from God. The spiritual autobiography documents a preoccupation with receiving God's grace, and it typically relates the author's spiritual transformation through a moment of illumination, an all too brief experience characterized by visions and apprehensions of the divine "light."

Quaker spiritual autobiographies nearly all follow the same stages of development: authors sometimes describe their childhoods, and then, with the onset of adolescence, they relate their search for a basis on which to build a religious life and their endeavors to follow a righteous path. Invariably these narratives depict troubled souls, as their authors suffer self-doubt and spiritual uncertainty. In *The Quaker Family in Colonial America: A Portrait of the Society of Friends* (1973) J. William Frost labels these stages of development "search and conflict, convincement, and conversion." Quaker women's spiritual narratives share this common refrain of inner struggle, moments of divine revelation, and attempts to forge a permanent relationship with God.

Yet whereas the author's bond with her community is central to many of these autobiographies, Bowers's story focuses on her personal travail.

Bowers's spiritual longing unfolds itself on every page of *An Alarm Sounded to Prepare the Inhabitants of the World to Meet the Lord in the Way of His Judgments,* and her language is that of a woman always emotionally on edge. She felt a "divine Sweetness" one moment, but that revelation was immediately followed by the statement that "the divine Ray with-drew." She heard voices telling her she "must come to further Sufferings" in order "to have the root or original of sin wrought out, to be made perfect." Her narrative thus documents its author's spiritual uncertainty as she doubted whether this precious moment of inner peace would return.

Bowers was alternately afraid, impatient, ecstatic, and anguished as she related her crises and anxieties. Her narrative does conform to the generic conventions of Quaker spiritual autobiography by offering a detailed recounting of her religious struggles, and like those by other Quaker women, it fails to provide the ending found in many of the autobiographies written by men, an ending indicating the author's spiritual resolution. Quaker men's autobiographical testimonies usually concluded with instructional messages for other Quakers, lessons in how to retain the divine spirit. Yet Elise Boulding explains that Quaker women rarely, if ever, "achieve peace of mind for once and all," and Carol Edkins writes that "in story after story, we hear the autobiographer reciting her struggles to find the inner light." Such conflict typifies *An Alarm Sounded to Prepare the Inhabitants of the World to Meet the Lord in the Way of His Judgments,* which ends as it began, with Bowers longing for spiritual certitude. In one grim moment Bowers wrote that she wished "that my Mothers Womb had been my Grave, and made me curse myself the day that I was born." She considered suicide but was afraid of God's retribution if she did not die.

Bowers's narrative begins by relating her spiritual journey according to a yearly progression, but unlike most Quaker journal keepers, she abandoned chronological sequence after she reached what she called "the first Covenant" with God in about 1694, when she was twenty-three. At this stage, after physical illness and emotional indecision, she surrendered herself to God and agreed to live according to his divine will. Prior to making this covenant, Bowers was, she wrote, an adolescent consumed in pride and mired in desire for material wealth and social position; in fact she deemed herself an "evil case" until the age of nineteen. Then, while seriously ill (a scene common in spiritual autobiogra-

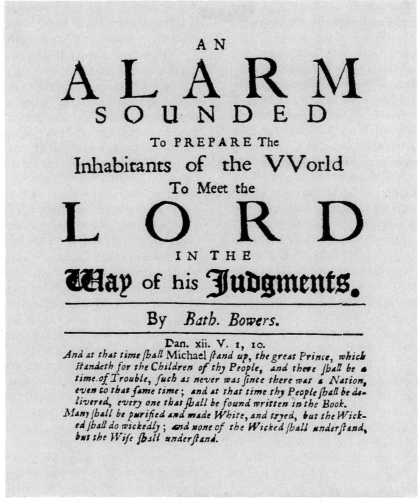

*Title page for Bathsheba Bowers's account of her "long and tedious Travail" in search
of salvation*

phies), she made a promise to God that, if he would
send her a sign that she would recover, she would
change her ways. At this same time her brother's
death from smallpox heightened her fear of incur-
ring God's wrath. This first covenant preceded the
onset of the severe emotional upheaval that Bowers
described throughout the remainder of her narrative. At this point she wrote, "Now I shall proceed in
recounting the Passages of my Travails or Pilgrimage after I received the Seal of Adoption or Heirship
to the Promises of God." This account of continually seeking after an elusive God refers only sporadically to specific months or years, instead depicting
the blind alleys and occasional glimmers of light she
encountered. An ordered account of her life seems
to have lost its purpose in light of an ongoing struggle to dedicate her life to God that ultimately caused
the years to blur in her memory. Life began to pass
not in years, but in stages of suffering.

Bowers battled what she called her sins of
pride and ambition, but, after her illness, she took
comfort in gardening, and she allowed this pastime
to replace her fixation with her physical appearance
and her love for society and material possessions.
When William Penn laid out the plans for Philadelphia, he emphasized gardens. Not only was the city
well situated for gardening, but the Quakers especially encouraged their members to be educated in
the husbandry of plants and herbs. Cultivating a
garden regularly fell to housewives as part of their
household supervision, but instead of managing a
garden for its various remedies and family food
sources, Bowers, as a single woman, tilled her soil as
a form of relaxation and artistic production and as a
way of giving free reign to her desire for ornamenta-
tion. Thus, she was able to shape her physical environment and satisfy at least one of her desires for
beauty.

Still, the young Bowers did not completely escape the temptation to what she considered sinful occupations. Although she had renounced secular concerns and appeared to have completely cast off her previous interests, Bowers continued throughout her life to be at war with herself and God, an abstract and distant deity who ignored her pleas for a sign that she did not seek him in vain.

An Alarm Sounded to Prepare the Inhabitants of the World to Meet the Lord in the Way of His Judgments discusses Bowers's hope that moving to the Quaker city of Philadelphia would strengthen her faith; yet Bowers wrote that attending Quaker meetings did not replace her need for the original sensation she had felt when she first accepted God into her life. Just as she was searching for her vocation as a Quaker, those who could have best guided her were embroiled in the serious theological controversy involving Quaker minister George Keith and others, a dispute that bitterly separated the Philadelphia Friends during the late seventeenth century and eventually divided Quakers in the entire region. A contributing reason for Bowers's dismay might also have been the city of Philadelphia itself, which was evolving from a frontier town to a thriving, cosmopolitan city that was also a center for trade. Bowers therefore lived in a diverse and exciting place that undoubtedly tempted her with the material possessions that she had renounced. For a young woman who rebuked herself for her pride and who tried to overcome her love for clothes and worldly goods, living in a such bustling city surely added to her trials.

Although she described her apprehension about public speaking—"the fear of Preaching fiercely invaded me—Bowers also feared that avoiding this duty meant certain doom. While she expressed reluctance to speak in meeting, she seemed to thrive on emotional public displays of religious piety. Scholars who study Quaker women, including Phyllis Mack, argue that many of them "preached to fulfill nonreligious needs" and that, through such public discourse, in which they often resembled Old Testament male prophets, they found an outlet for their "aggression and emotion." Since all Quakers were encouraged to speak at meeting when they were moved by the spirit, Bowers struggled to balance her desire and her fear of public address with her anxiety to know that her words were divinely inspired. The Quaker passivity in waiting for God's sign did not rest easy with the strong-willed Bowers, who may also have been troubled by her status as an unmarried woman. Although Quakers stressed gender equality, most of the women who had leadership roles in the Philadel-

phia Quaker meetings at this time were married and older.

Throughout her narrative Bowers revealed herself as an assertive woman, presenting a constructed authorial self to a public audience, a self who defended her work as originating from God. The book opens with Bowers's discussion and justification of her impulse to publish as she asserted her belief that God had called her to share publicly her spiritual saga: "Why it pleased the Almighty to bend his Bow and for me as a Mark for his Arrow, not only from my Youth, but even from my very Infancy up, I know not, but even so it has been." Bowers undoubtedly feared public rebuke. The Minutes of the Philadelphia Yearly Meeting of Friends in 1710, the year after Bowers's book was published, included this warning: "Whilst we are in Unity with the Body of Friends, we must be very careful that we Act, nor Do, any thing contrary to the Principle or Discipline of Truth, because there is no Person that is a member that is Exempted from the Censure of the Church." For many Quaker women, their own wills were regarded as enemies that had to be overcome. Bowers's emotional distress was palpable as she wrote, "Oh, that God would take away my Life from me! Oh, that I might have my Request, even to dye!" Yet she defended her public discourse, even while acknowledging her initial unwillingness to publish and her fight with the "potent Enemy (*Ambition*)." Bowers's ambition always worried her, and she confessed that for a long time she was "very unwilling . . . to appear in print at all; for it was, indeed, a secret terror to me to think of making a contemptible appearance in the world."

In the first paragraph of her book Bowers acknowledged the "smallness" of what she had written, excusing the content of her autobiography by stating that she had "diminished pretty much of what I had first intended to publish." She understood that with God's help she had overcome the sin of ambition by publishing a shorter work.

Bowers recorded only a few treasured moments of spiritual calmness, moments that were inevitably followed by periods of self-doubt and self-recrimination, lengthy tribulations that she characterized as "a profound Abyss of Torment." Bowers did not write calmly; her encounters with demons, whispers, and God's absence are narrated in tones of dread and all-consuming fear reminiscent of Puritan sermons. The fires of hell leaped before her eyes, and messengers from the underworld jeered at her faith as they worked to convince her that God dealt with her unfairly and had forgotten her. Unlike the Puritans, who believed that only an elect few were preordained to receive God's grace, the

Quakers believed that God would come to all who readied themselves and awaited his sign. When, after her first instance of heavenly connection, Bowers did not again feel the divine spirit, she feared that her anguish and uncertainty would be permanent, and she accused God of unjust treatment: "O Lord God! Remember, I beseech thee, what I have suffered at thy hand!"

Bowers's inability to achieve certitude and her fear that God would never return resulted in perpetual emotional torture. Tranquillity eluded her, and anger often replaced fear. Near the end of her spiritual autobiography, she wrote what could be regarded as the theme for the entire work: "I was no sooner arrived to the highest pitch of my paramount Desires, but I should be cast down to the lowest Hell." Seemingly every moment of divine understanding that she reached was offset by a corresponding moment of disconnection, which renewed her agony. The Quakers' insistence on a wholly personal relation with God appeared to be the source of Bowers's dilemma: she wondered how she could know that she had achieved this relation and what she could do when God seemed to disappear.

In describing her aunt's strong personality, Ann Bolton asserted that Bowers read the Bible so that she could argue with it. Bowers did not conform to the image of a Quaker as she hurled accusations at God. Although she tried to repress her forceful character and mold herself into the image of a proper Quaker, obedience to God did not come easily. Constantly railing at God, Bowers was not a meek, accepting servant. At times her expression of her desire to follow God's will seems to contradict her otherwise forceful tone, but Bowers reproved herself and quelled her curiosity, largely from the fear of hell. She never succeeded, however, in suppressing her independent spirit or her stubborn nature. "I submitted, tho' it was not without Tears," she wrote.

Yet Bowers struggled to leave her reader with some message of comfort, claiming that she had overcome her pride and that her moments of suffering grew more infrequent. She ended her book with this passage: "So, thus far having briefly hinted concerning some of the more material Passages in my long and tedious Travail in my spiritual Waifair; and if any part or parts, or the whole of it may be of Service to any, it answer, the end of her who can in truth Subscribe herself *'Their very humble Friend or Servant either.'*" Typically, Bowers wrote about her agonizing travail in an effort to support and increase the faith of others and to reassure them that some-

one else shared in the elusive human search to understand God's will. Her real passion, however, lay in her need for self-expression. The solace that she found in writing compensated, albeit meagerly, for divine reassurance.

References:
Hugh Barbour and J. William Frost, *The Quakers* (New York: Greenwood Press, 1988);

Barbour and Arthur O. Roberts, eds., *Early Quaker Writings 1650–1700* (Grand Rapids, Mich.: Erdmans, 1973);

Elise Boulding, "Mapping the Inner Journey of Quaker Women," in *The Influence of Quaker Women on American History,* edited by Carol and John Stoneburner (Lewiston, N.Y.: Edwin Mellen Press, 1986), pp. 81–150;

Howard Brinton, *Quaker Journals: Varieties of Religious Experience Among Friends* (Wallingford, Pa.: Pendle Hill, 1972);

Pattie Cowell, ed., *Women Poets in Pre-Revolutionary America 1650–1775: An Anthology* (Troy, N.Y.: Whitson, 1981), pp. 211–213;

Carol Edkins, "Quest for Community: Spiritual Autobiographies of Eighteenth-Century Quaker and Puritan Women in America," in *Women's Autobiography: Essays in Criticism,* edited by Estelle C. Jelinek (Bloomington: Indiana University Press, 1980), pp. 39–52;

J. William Frost, *A Perfect Freedom: Religious Liberty in Pennsylvania* (University Park: Pennsylvania State University Press, 1993);

Frost, *The Quaker Family in Colonial America: A Portrait of the Society of Friends* (New York: St. Martin's Press, 1973);

Phyllis Mack, "Gender and Spirituality in Early English Quakerism, 1650–1665," in *Witnesses for Change: Quaker Women over Three Centuries,* edited by Elisabeth Potts Brown and Susan Mosher Stuard (New Brunswick, N.J.: Rutgers University Press, 1989), pp. 31–68;

William J. Potts, "Bathsheba Bowers," *Pennsylvania Magazine of History and Biography,* 3 (1879): 110–112;

Daniel B. Shea Jr., *Spiritual Autobiography in Early America* (Princeton: Princeton University Press, 1968);

Jean R. Soderlund, "Women's Authority in Pennsylvania and New Jersey Quaker Meetings, 1680–1760," *William & Mary Quarterly,* 44 (1987): 722–749;

Suzanne M. Zweizig, "Bathsheba Bowers," *Legacy,* 11, no. 1 (1994): 65–73.

Esther Edwards Burr

(13 February 1732 – 7 April 1758)

Sandra M. Gustafson
University of Notre Dame

BOOK: *The Journal of Esther Edwards Burr 1754–1757,* edited by Carol F. Karlsen and Laurie Crumpacker (New Haven: Yale University Press, 1984).

Esther Edwards Burr was the author of a letter-journal that provides one of the earliest extensive accounts of a colonial American woman's daily life. Most women of her era wrote primarily for exchange with friends and circulation among acquaintances, and the letter-journal that Esther Burr exchanged with Sarah Prince was no exception. Writing on vellum with quill pens, Esther Burr recorded daily entries of varied lengths and then she bundled them into "paquets" of up to twenty pages whenever a suitable courier was available. These "paquets" also contained "privacies," secret enclosures recording candid opinions on mutual acquaintances that Sarah burned after reading them. In contrast to these evanescent texts, the letter-journal was designed to be preserved and shared among their circle of friends, a testament of Esther and Sarah's intertwined religious and intellectual lives.

While Sarah Prince's half of the correspondence has been lost, Esther Burr's letter-journal remained carefully preserved in manuscript until the twentieth century. Parts of the journal were first published by Jeremiah Rankin in 1902, in a volume that drew on Burr's manuscript but embellished it freely to create a document largely of Rankin's own invention. In 1930 Josephine Fisher published authentic excerpts and commentary in a scholarly journal. The complete work first appeared in Laurie Crumpacker's 1978 dissertation, and Crumpacker and Carol F. Karlsen edited the full journal for publication in 1984.

The semiprivate nature of Burr's work, its history of distorted and partial publication, and her relationship to three of the most prominent men in early America—Jonathan Edwards, Aaron Burr Sr., and Aaron Burr Jr.—all promoted the long eclipse of her literary significance. Since the publication of her

Esther Edwards Burr (Gallery of Fine Arts, Yale University, bequest of Aliner Burr Jennings)

complete letter-journal, Burr has emerged as an important contributor to the development of women's writing in America. Grappling with fundamental questions of female subjectivity and authority, marriage and friendship, spirituality and imagination, domestic labor and intellectual endeavor, Esther Burr articulated a set of interlinked concerns that dominated American women's writing for more than two centuries. In her prose style she participated in the adaptation of an evangelical aesthetic of spontaneity to American women's literature, and through her friendships with authors Sarah Prince and Annis Boudinot, she participated in a community of women writers committed to the formation of a public literary voice for women.

Aaron Burr Sr., who married Esther Edwards in 1752
(portrait by E. L. Mooney; Princeton University
Art Musuem)

Esther Edwards was born on 13 February 1732, the third of the eleven children born to Congregational minister and theologian Jonathan Edwards and his wife, Sarah Pierpont Edwards. Descended from prominent Puritan divines and exemplary pious women on both sides of her family, Esther Edwards was early immersed in a world of spiritual striving and turmoil. She was born in Northampton, Massachusetts, the Connecticut Valley town where her great-grandfather Solomon Stoddard had reigned as the "Congregational Pope" for many decades, and she was named for her great-grandmother Esther Stoddard, who was a woman of great spiritual authority in her own right. Before her death in 1736, Esther Stoddard led women's prayer groups and won a reputation for being even more forceful and learned than her distinguished husband. Jonathan Edwards assumed the pulpit of his influential grandfather upon Stoddard's death in 1729. Five years later Edwards sparked the famous Northampton revival of 1734–1735 that garnered him international attention. His fame spread after he published an important description of the revival in 1736 at the urging of Isaac Watts and other prominent evangelical leaders. *A Faithful Narrative of the Surprizing Work of God,* as it was titled in the revised edition of 1737, contributed to the emergence of the pietist strain in American Protestantism. That

strain culminated a few years later when English evangelist George Whitefield's 1740 preaching tour of the colonies sparked what historians have termed the Great Awakening. The Great Awakening altered colonial society in fundamental ways, transforming modes of worship, changing the relationship between ministers and congregations, introducing divisions into religious bodies, and altering the role of women in Protestant America.

In the published accounts of the Northampton revivals, Jonathan Edwards exemplified conversion through narratives of holy girls and women. These included Phebe Bartlett, who experienced conversion as a child, and young Abigail Hutchinson, whose saintly starvation mirrored the spiritual heroism of medieval women saints. The best known of Jonathan Edwards's holy women, however, was Sarah Pierpont Edwards, whose ecstatic conversion in 1742, when Esther Edwards was ten, provided her husband with an ideal type of the conversion experience. Sarah's mystical transports enabled her to negotiate her competing roles as a minister's wife devoted to the service of his needs and a person of spiritual authority in her own right. Her conversion ended her periods of illness and melancholy, during which she had withdrawn from her work and her community, and she emerged as a living type of female sanctity. Surrounded from childhood by women with spiritual authority, Esther Edwards received an early education in the contradictions and possibilities of female piety. Her letter-journal reflects her efforts to negotiate the conflicts arising from the Pauline beliefs that all souls are equal in Christ, but that women should remain subordinate within the earthly church.

Esther Edwards herself underwent conversion as a teenager, and in 1752 she followed the path of her great-grandmother and mother when she married a minister, the Presbyterian divine Aaron Burr. He was sixteen years her senior, self-assured and personally appealing. Celebrated for his erudition and compelling pulpit performances, he was known as an inspired teacher and a moderating force in church disputes. Born into a wealthy Connecticut family with extensive land holdings, Burr experienced conversion to evangelicalism shortly after his graduation from Yale College in 1735. After he was licensed to preach in 1736, Burr served in several pulpits before accepting a call to Newark, New Jersey. He continued to hold his Newark pulpit after he was chosen in 1748 to succeed Jonathan Dickinson as president of the newly founded evangelical College of New Jersey (which later became Princeton University). The evangelical clergy had founded the college out of concern over the fate of students such as David Brainerd, a protégé of Jonathan Edwards who was expelled from Yale College for criticizing the spiritual state of a tutor. Burr was a man of considerable social status and a mild, courteous, open demeanor. He invested the new college with stability and worked constantly to build it through his solicitation of contributions and other forms of support.

The theological controversies between New Light evangelicals and Old Light conservatives that led to the founding of the College of New Jersey had an immediate impact on the Edwards family in 1750, when Jonathan Edwards's Northampton congregation voted to remove him from his pulpit. He had demanded that anyone seeking to join the church offer a narrative of conversion, and the congregation refused to embrace his position. Economic difficulties and ostracism dominated the years following his expulsion. The family remained in Northampton, where he occupied the pulpit on a provisional basis. During this period the Edwards women made lace and painted fan mounts to supplement the much-reduced family income. The move two years later to the frontier town of Stockbridge, where Jonathan Edwards ministered to a community of Housatonic Indian Christians, added social isolation to the other changed circumstances of the Edwards's family life. When Aaron Burr made the long trip from New Jersey to Massachusetts to win Esther Edwards's hand in 1752, he had not seen her since she was fourteen. During the intervening years, Esther's piety, beauty, and charm had drawn much masculine attention. Despite her youth and their brief acquaintance, she soon accepted Aaron's proposal. Two weeks later she left for Newark, where they were married. That they married in Newark rather than in Stockbridge suggests that Esther's quick decision may have been reached out of unhappiness with the family's economic and social situation. The circumstances attending her marriage apparently proved the source of some friction within the family. In a letter of 20 August 1754, her sister Lucy Edwards warned of "how Little able she [Esther] was to bear to have any body say any thing as tho they did'nt like her way of marrying." Esther's sensitivity to criticism extended beyond her marriage, however. Lucy noted that "she never could bear pestering very well." Whenever Esther was subjected to disapproving scrutiny, she characteristically responded with a quick wit that sometimes became prickly. These features are particularly evident in her journal at moments when she confronted male assumptions about appropriate female behavior.

Despite its sudden and controversial beginning, the marriage of Aaron Burr and Esther Edwards Burr appears to have been loving and mutually respectful, based on shared intellectual interests and religious concerns. Yet Aaron was often away from home, traveling to raise money for the college, and Esther suffered in his absence. "Our house is very gloomy, as tis *always* when Mr Burr is gone," she wrote on 17 January 1755. Describing her affection for and dependence on her husband, she continued, "I am ready to immagine the *sun* does not give so much light as it did when my best self was at home, and *I* am in the glooms two, half *ded,* my *Head* gone. Behead a person and they will soon *die.*" Her traditional metaphors identify her husband as her head and link his authority with the sun of reason and divine truth. Esther relied on Aaron for companionship and guidance, but perhaps most for the encouragement he gave her as she developed her own sense of authority.

Esther's distance from her family enhanced her dependence on Aaron. Particularly in the early years of marriage as Esther adjusted to her new circumstances and responsibilities, she often felt isolated in her community and overwhelmed by her role as the wife of a minister and college president. Obligated to provide food and lodging for a steady stream of visitors, she could rarely find a moment for herself. Equally rare were the meaningful conversations with peers that she craved, surrounded as she was by young women cultivating gentility. She found their stylish pursuits superficial and their conversation insipid. On 12 January 1755 she wrote Sarah about her frustration with her local social circle and her hunger for substantive exchange: "for a whole week past I may say I have conversed with nobody but my other self, for Conversasion with any body elce I have about me, I dont call Conversasion. I dont know what to call it, but I believe *Chit-Chat* will do as well as any name, for indeed tis no easy matter to give a name to *Nothing.*" Esther had been given an education equal to that of most colonial men, and she longed for opportunities for shared intellectual life where she could engage as a full and equal participant.

With Aaron's encouragement Esther increasingly saw herself as engaged in matters of political and theological substance. She recorded her deep interest in the theological discussions that groups of ministers held at her home on 23 February 1757, describing such conversation as "a Heaven upon Erth!" The unusual nature of her relationship with her husband emerges in her 20 December 1755 comment upon her interest in political events such as the government conduct of the French and Indian

(29)   Newark   Nov͞br 24. 1754.   16   N͞o 10

Dear friend

Yesterday Just as I had Sent away
my No 9. Mr Foxcrafts Son came in with your dear Letter.
I am much refreshed with the good News you tell me
about Boston, O yt it may continue to go on & increase
mightily till Boston become a Mountain of holyness &
praise!   I rejoice with you my Dear yt you have found
the Lord to be with you of a truth, and yt you have experienced so much of his loving kindness to your Soul, &
have had his inlivening & quickning presence, I pray
God it may continue throu, out your life......

          I hope & pray yt dear Miss Sally may not
Miss this goulden Season, you my Dear friend have great reason to hope, & go on praying for her at Such a time
as this when the Spirit of God Seems to be Striving
among some.   I am unable to write any longer....

                    Monday A; M.

          This day is yt time apointed for our Sacrement-
ing, you have heard me Say what a time of confusion tis, I am almost Crazy, am not so well as
yesterday, but I dont wonder at yt..   You Say my
dear you believe you Shant answer Mrs Cummings
                                        Letter

Pages from Esther Burr's letter-journal, written for her friend Sarah Prince during the years 1751–1757 (Beinecke Rare Book and Manuscript Library, Yale University)

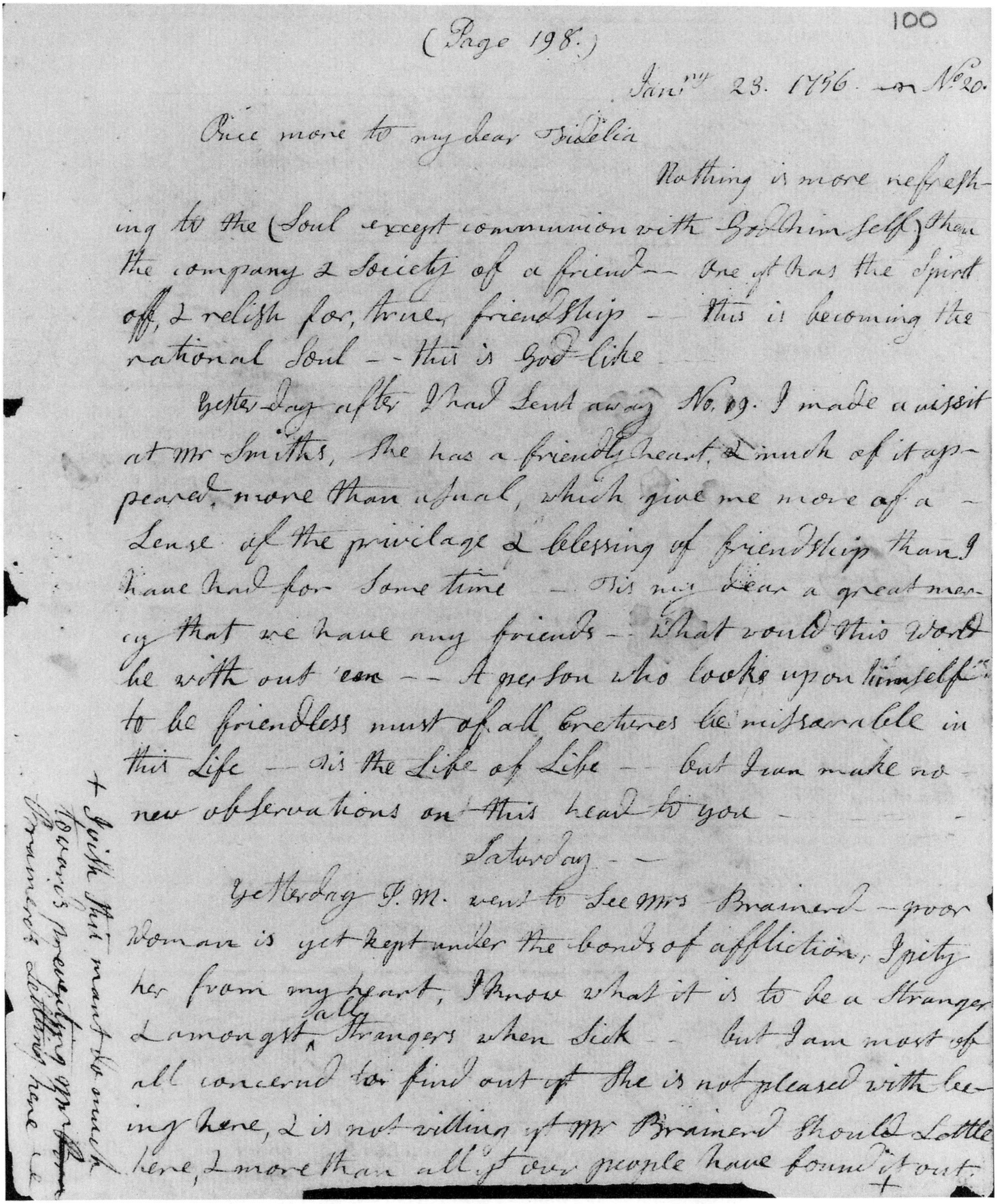

100

(Page 198.)

Jan'ry 23. 1756. — N.º 20.

Once more to my dear Fidelia

Nothing is more refresh-
ing to the (Soul except communion with God himself) then
the company & Society of a friend — One if has the Spirit
off, & relish for, true, friendship — this is becoming the
rational Soul — this is God-like —

Yester-day after I had sent away No. 19. I made a vissit
at Mr Smiths, She has a friendly heart, & much of it appeared more than usual, which give me more of a —
Sense of the privilage & blessing of friendship than I
have had for Some time — Tis my dear a great mercy that we have any friends — What would this World
be with out 'em — A person who looks upon himself
to be friendless must of all Cretures be miserable in
this Life — tis the Life of Life — but I can make no
new observations on this head to you —

Saturday —

Yesterday P. M. went to See Mrs Brainerd — poor
Woman is yet kept under the bonds of affliction, I pity
her from my heart, I know what it is to be a Stranger
& amongst Strangers when Sick — but I am most of
all concern'd to find out if She is not pleased with bee-
ing here, & is not willing if Mr Brainerd Should Settle
here, & more than all if our people have found it out —

+ Fidelia that meant to omitt
Burr's prevailing upon Brain-
Brainerd's settling here —

War: "The Men say (tho' not Mr Burr he is not one of that sort) that Women have no business to concern themselves about em." Fearful of French conquest and the imposition of Catholic worship that she believed would follow, she criticized the "great men" for their inadequate defense of the colonies, expressing her anxiety in the familiar language of the jeremiad. In passages such as these, Esther's journal reflects her growing sense of authority and Aaron's support for that authority.

A year and a half after Esther moved to Newark, her childhood friend Sarah Prince arrived from Boston for an extended visit. Prince was the daughter of Thomas Prince, the minister of the Old South Church in Boston, as well as a prolific writer and an early and constant supporter of Jonathan Edwards. Like her father, Sarah was an important force in the intellectual and social life of Boston. She formed a long-lived women's prayer group and later participated in an intellectual circle of republicans that included John Adams. Though her portion of the letter-journal has been lost, she also kept a daily journal that partially survives in manuscript. Moreover, she wrote poems and religious meditations, some of which were published posthumously as *Devotional Papers* (1773) under her married name, Sarah Prince Gill. Esther and Sarah had been friends for several years before this 1754 visit. They shared literary and intellectual interests and religious concerns. Their decision to keep journals for exchange with one another was designed to provide a medium for communicating those interests, for recording their spiritual progress as it registered in their daily lives, and for giving one another advice on matters spiritual and temporal. Aaron supported Esther's commitment to the journal form and to the exchange with Sarah, even writing for Esther at one point when she was ill. Esther observed that he admired the form enough to adopt it himself, keeping a letter-journal for her on one of his trips.

Around the end of Prince's visit, Esther Burr gave birth to her first child, her daughter Sarah, named for her closest friend and for her mother. Aaron Burr Jr. was born almost two years later, in February 1756. His birth was particularly difficult for Esther, for her husband was away and her mother was unable to attend her. She gave birth without the assistance of friends and relatives, finding solace in her proximity to God. The family moved to Princeton, New Jersey, with the relocated College of New Jersey in December of that year, after the Newark congregation finally released Aaron to devote himself full-time to his college duties. The move took place amid concerns over the French and Indian War, which absorbed Esther's attention because of her family's exposure to attack in frontier Stockbridge. Her trip back to Stockbridge with Aaron Jr. shortly after his birth, her first visit to the Edwards family home since her marriage, was cut short when the English defeat at Oswego intensified her fears of an Indian attack. Her father insisted that she subdue those fears and resign herself to God's will. Despite her efforts to calm herself, however, she could not alleviate the intensity of her anxiety. Her uneasiness became unbearable after her mother left home to help her sister Mary through childbirth. Close as she was to her father, seeking his advice on the spiritual matters that she described on 19 September 1756 as "my Christian warfare," her mother's departure transformed the house into a barren and gloomy place, one whose emptiness reenforced the near proximity of actual warfare. She left for home soon afterward.

A revival began at the college shortly after her return to Princeton, stirring up widespread anxiety among the students and townspeople that demanded Aaron's constant and intense labor with those seeking spiritual guidance. Esther celebrated the events of the revival in her letter-journal, finding in the spirit of the moment an intensified sense of commitment that she, like her mother before her, expressed in the language of the Magnificat: "My soul doth magnify the Lord for what he has done," she wrote to Sarah on 21 February 1757. In the midst of this "pouring out of the spirit" Esther befriended Annis Boudinot, a young woman who, like Sarah Prince, mingled spiritual devotion and literary ambition. Annis eased Esther's sense of isolation in Princeton. The intimacy of the women grew when Annis tended Esther's sister Lucy during a bout of smallpox and then contracted the disease herself. Together Esther and Annis briefly formed the core of a social group fostering literary creativity in the college community, which included college tutors John Ewing and Benjamin Young Prime as well as Richard Stockton. Annis eventually married Stockton, who became a patriot leader and signer of the Declaration of Independence. Through her youthful association with Esther Burr, Annis found her poetic ambitions validated. Esther recorded for Sarah a poem that Annis wrote about the events of the Princeton revival and another in celebration of Esther's friendship. She also shared Sarah's work with Annis, who later developed into a prolific and celebrated poet, publishing elegies on her husband's death and poems honoring George Washington.

The revival and other responsibilities hastened the pace of life in Princeton, and during the summer of 1757 Esther was often exhausted. The burst of creative energy that accompanied the beginning of the revival gave way to illness and distraction, and during these months she found less and less time to write in her journal. In September of that year her husband returned from one of his long trips feeling poorly, only to be called away immediately to deliver the funeral sermon for New Jersey governor Jonathan Belcher. Aaron returned home violently ill with malaria. Three weeks later he was dead. Esther's letter-journal ends abruptly with Aaron's departure to preach at the governor's funeral. When she took up her pen after his death, it was to seek solace from her family. She consulted her father for spiritual guidance in her grief. Eventually she received some consolation in an ecstatic moment reminiscent of her mother's conversion. She described that moment in a 2 November 1757 letter to her father: "my soul was carried out in such longing desires that I was forced to retire from the Famaly to conceal my joy." Soon afterward Jonathan Edwards agreed to take Aaron Burr's place as head of the College of New Jersey. He arrived in Princeton to assume his new duties in February 1758. Both he and Esther were inoculated for smallpox, and he died from the disease on 22 March. Esther died from a fever of unknown causes on 7 April.

Lamenting Esther Burr's death, Sarah Prince wrote in her private book of meditations on 21 April 1758 that "she was made for a Refin'd Friend." Friendship is a persistent theme in the letter-journal and one of the central paradigms shaping Esther Burr's insights. "Nothing is more refreshing to the soul (except communication with God himself)" she wrote on 23 January 1756, "then the company and society of a friend—One that has the spirit off, and relish for, true friendship—this is becoming [to] the rational soul—this is God-like." As Esther's remarks suggest, friendship meant far more to her than shared tastes and interests. The act of communicating spiritual, literary, and intellectual concerns elevated both women, she believed. Mutual trust permitted unhampered expression, including open criticism of the sort that Esther directed at Sarah's behavior toward her suitors. Esther suggested the social significance that she attached to female friendship in addition to its personal significance in her account of a dispute with college tutor John Ewing over women's capacity for friendship. Shortly after Annis Boudinot composed her poem soliciting Esther's affection, Ewing reflected on Boudinot's articulation of friendship as a female

ideal. In Esther's journal entry of 12 April 1757, she recorded his assertion that "*He did not think women knew what Friendship was. They were hardly capable of anything so cool and rational as friendship.*" Ewing implied that women's claims to friendship arose from their education, which he deemed improper. Esther identified Ewing's view with "Mr. Pop[e's] sordid scheam" of female irrationality and inferiority. In response, Esther insisted that the cultivation of friendship was a divine capacity that women fully share. She engaged in this battle in the war between the sexes with relish, noting with satisfaction that in the end "I talked him quite silent."

The "God-like" friendship between Esther and Sarah provided the legitimating social context for the production of the letter-journal and shaped both its content and its form in fundamental ways. As a dialogue, the letter-journal recast elements of the Puritan diary in a form that generated spiritual insight out of the interplay between the two women. The diary form was devoted to daily records of spiritual striving and the self-scrutiny that attended such striving. Esther's letter-journal incorporates the traditional diary themes of religious endeavor, a longing to be close to God through prayer, meditation, and devoted labor, and the repeated failure to sustain that ideal state. It also includes descriptions of daily life, such as the activities of her husband and children and accounts of her own reading, and advice to Sarah about the nature of marriage and the best way to respond to her various suitors. The interplay of daily life and spiritual realization is perhaps best captured in an exchange that Sarah initiated over the meaning of Solomon's good woman. Responding on 1 December 1754 to Sarah's query whether the good woman who "kept a candle a burning all Night" did not "set up to read," Esther first asked Aaron his opinion. When he responded with a jest, she began to record her own interpretation but was interrupted by guests. When she found time to return to the question eleven days later, she insisted that the good woman must sleep "unless she was made of some other sort of *Matter* than we be." In its context Esther's interpretation of the passage, with its telling play on words, registers her concrete sense of physical limitation. The previous day's entry reports William Tennent II's comment about her: "'Poor creature, she is to have no comfort in life I see! but always to be hurried to Death.'" While Esther insisted that "it has always been recond by me amongst my greatest pleasures to wait on my friends," her scriptural analysis attempts to mark some limit of an ethic of service to others. It also enacts an alternative

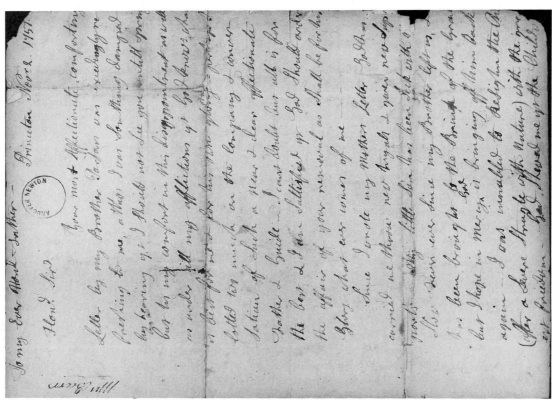

Esther Burr's 2 November 1757 letter to her father, Jonathan Edwards, describing an ecstatic moment of spiritual renewal (Franklin Trask Library, Andover Newton Theological School)

conception of friendship based on intellectual and creative exchange.

When Esther accepted Aaron's proposal of marriage, she chose the life of a minister's wife, which was in itself a religious calling. She knew this life well from her own upbringing. Her journal entries record her often heavy daily activities that included keeping house, training and supervising servants, entertaining guests, tending children, and visiting parishioners. They also offer reflections on her state of mind as she performed these duties. She aspired to sustain a sense of whole-hearted commitment, believing, as she wrote on 10 April 1757, that "my time is not my own but Gods." Yet her efforts to unite belief and action repeatedly failed to sustain that ideal level of elevation, and she routinely fell ill or slipped into melancholy after a period of intense devotion to the needs of others. These times of withdrawal were often the times when she turned to her journal. There she registered her dissatisfaction with the demands of her situation and with her imperfect acceptance of them. She longed for a visit with Sarah that would provide the communion often lacking from her activities as a hostess and minister's wife, and she responded with frustration to the repeated disruption of plans for such a visit. The journal was a substitute for Sarah's presence as well as a reminder of her absence, a doubleness that Burr captured on 12 April 1755, when she wished for a "*Long Letter* as long as from here to Bostn." On 8 February 1755 she imagined the fate of the text she was producing with a pressing intimacy: "What! These scrawls injoy the privilege of being handled in the most free and intimate manner and I deprived! *In short I have a good mind to seal up my self in the Letter and try if I cant Rival it.*" Burr linked the materiality of the letter with the limits of *"Matter,"* deploying the theological symbolism of presence and absence, matter and spirit, immanence and transcendence to redefine femininity.

The intensity with which Esther reflected on the means and processes of writing frames the act of writing itself as a holy discipline. She commented on the quality of her paper, complained of problems in getting good pens, criticized the clarity of her penmanship and the inadequacy of her prose style, described the physical ailments that made writing difficult, and reflected on the pressures on her time and attention that forced her to write while holding or nursing a child. Writing mimicked life. It required that the writer grapple with material and social constraints to produce the text that enacted even as it described her self-discipline. Moreover writing, like friendship, remained a controversial pursuit for a woman, even in an evangelical culture

that celebrated the exemplary value of holy women. When Cotton Mather urged pious women to write about their spiritual lives, he did so primarily as an alternative to having them speak publicly. When Jonathan Edwards sought to exemplify female saintliness in a written account, he chose girls and women whose life stories he could define. Of the three females whose conversion experiences he foregrounded, one was a small child too young to write; a second was dead; and the third was his wife, whose narrative he helped to edit and later recast in his own language. The ambivalence that surrounded women's writing permeates Esther's journal. On more than one occasion she wrote Sarah that she could not tell a female friend of the journal for fear that the friend would report their written exchanges to a husband likely to disapprove. Responding to these constraints, Esther and Sarah referred to themselves and their circle as the Sisterhood or the female freemasons. Together they cultivated a sense of privileged insight. In her letter-journal for 15 January 1756 Esther invested her words with an aura of secret knowledge, insisting that "these *Hes* shall know nothing about our affairs *untill they are grown as wise as you and I are.*"

The letter-journal provided Esther with a textual version of the sororal networks that took the form of prayer groups and social groups. From such groups eventually grew the woman suffrage movement and other reform movements of the nineteenth century. Esther recorded for Sarah's sympathetic eyes some of the beliefs in women's abilities that such groups fostered. She insisted that women should take an interest in public affairs, noting her disapproval of the way the war was conducted. She celebrated her ability to educate young Susannah Shippen in her entry of 14 January 1756, where she commented on the self-satisfaction evident in her own prose, writing "Did you ever see so many *Shes,* without one *He* before." The autonomy registered in such a passage characterized her spiritual life as well. Esther's work often left her drained and unable to attend church services. When she did attend church, however, she frequently observed her feelings of distraction and deadness. In contrast she celebrated the solitary communion that she sometimes enjoyed with God, for instance during her lonely ordeal giving birth to her son. Esther's sense of spiritual autonomy is particularly evident in her description of a Sabbath spent worshiping alone in the woods. On 29 August 1756 she wrote, "God does not want for means nor place," observing that while she had long sought the Lord at services, she finally found Him in a place and time outside the circumstances of her daily life.

Like these moments of spiritual insight, Esther's reflections on her reading fostered her confidence in her own judgment. Throughout the journal Esther commented on the literature that she read. The writings of Englishwomen such as the poet Mary Jones, the epistolary writer Elizabeth Singer Rowe, and the diarist Hannah Pearsall Housman provided models for her own endeavor. She read and critiqued the novels of Samuel Richardson, paying particular attention to his portrayals of women. She voiced her strong disapproval when she encountered his depiction of Pamela falling in love with her would-be seducer Mr. B. Esther also read for spiritual inspiration. While spending a wakeful night, she recalled the works of James Hervey and Edward Young on the gravelike silence of the night. Esther understood her own work as a contribution to a literary community. She employed literary pseudonyms in her journal, referring to Sarah as Fidelia and herself as Burrissa. Her insight into literary creation grew as she observed Aaron preparing a sermon for publication and responded enthusiastically to the works that Sarah periodically sent her. Esther's sense of her own artistry was often uncertain, however, and she commented in her entry of 16 April 1756 that "Tis impossible for one that has no better faculty of communicating then I have, to give you any Idea how full of those *peticular matters* I feel." The later journal entries manifest her literary development, growing more vivid and direct in their language and conception. Yet the many demands made on her time prohibited sustained endeavor.

Esther Burr had a context for the kind of to-the-moment, unrevised writing that she had time to produce. Aaron Burr cultivated an evangelical aesthetic of immediacy at those moments when he set aside a manuscript sermon to preach extempore. Richardson's heroines claimed to be writing under circumstances of household confinement similar to Esther's and with similar directness. Annis Boudinot wrote her poetic tribute to Esther on the spur of the moment, while standing ready to depart the Burr home. When Esther wrote to Sarah on 9 November 1754 that "I dont so much as look over what I send to you. You have my thoughts just as they then happen to be," she characterized her style in the dominant improvisational terms of her culture. The evangelical emphasis on spontaneity made forms such as the letter-journal into art of the most valued kind—an exemplary and redemptive register of God's workings in the soul. They could also be materializations of a "God-like" and transformative female friendship. The underlying human fragility of that quasi-divine friendship registered in the fragmentary and time-bound form of the letter-journal. Esther's journal breaks off with a chatty letter about her children and her neighbors that includes no hint of the impending series of tragedies that would end for her only with her death seven months later, on 7 April 1758. In its abruptness, the end of the journal captures the vulnerable materiality of both literary and human forms.

When Esther Edwards Burr died at the age of twenty-six, she left behind a work rich in historical and literary implications. Her letter-journal offers insight into the everyday activities of an economically and socially privileged colonial American woman. It also reveals the literary values and assumptions informing the writings of women such as herself, and the sense of a female community of readers and writers underlying those values and assumptions. Her work points toward the emerging world of women writers that flourished in the nineteenth century, when Harriet Beecher Stowe and Emily Dickinson produced their great works.

References:
Laurie Crumpacker, "Esther Burr's Journal 1754–1757: A Document of Evangelical Sisterhood," dissertation, Boston University Graduate School, 1978;
Josephine Fisher, "The Journal of Esther Burr," *New England Quarterly*, 3 (1930): 297–315;
Carla Mulford, Introduction to *Only for the Eye of a Friend: The Poems of Annis Boudinot Stockton*, edited by Mulford (Charlottesville: University Press of Virginia, 1995), pp. 11–17;
William J. Scheick, "Friendship and Idolatry in Esther Edwards Burr's Letters," *University of Mississippi Studies in English*, 11–12 (1993–1995): 138–150;
Ola Elizabeth Winslow, *Jonathan Edwards 1703–1758: A Biography* (New York: Macmillan, 1940).

Papers:
Esther Edwards Burr's letter-journal is in the Beinecke Library at Yale University. Other letters are available at the Franklin Trask Library of Andover Newton Theological School at Newton Centre, Massachusetts, and in the manuscript collections of the Princeton University Library.

Jane Colden

(27 March 1724 – 10 March 1766)

Thomas Hallock
Valdosta State University

BOOK: *Botanic Manuscript of Jane Colden, 1724–1766,* edited by H. W. Rickett (New York: Garden Club of Orange and Dutchess Counties, 1963).

OTHER: "Description of a new Plant," in *Essays and Observations, Physical and Literary,* volume 2 (Edinburgh: G. Hamilton & J. Balfour, 1756), pp. 1–7.

Jane Colden has been called the first woman to master the Linnaean system of botany. After learning taxonomy from her father, Cadwallader Colden, in the mid 1750s, she identified specimens native to the lower Hudson Valley and collected their names, with descriptions and drawings, in her *Botanic Manuscript,* published in part in 1963. Her manuscript catalogue, which did not circulate widely, nonetheless secured her reputation on both sides of the Atlantic among prominent colleagues who held up the daughter of Cadwallader Colden as an example to her sex. Such deserved recognition proved short-lived, however. Her marriage in 1759 brought the end of her study, and she died in 1766. The course of Jane Colden's career is an important indicator of the opportunities and limitations that women faced in neoclassical science. Botany did not become popular among English-women until the 1760s and among American women until the early nineteenth century, making Colden something of a pioneer in a field that tended not to acknowledge contributions from women.

The record of Jane Colden's early years is sparse, but she seems to have been reared in a progressive home that encouraged intellectual work. Both parents were children of Scottish clergymen and valued education for their children. Cadwallader Colden studied medicine at the University of Edinburgh and at London, immigrated to Philadelphia in 1710, and then returned to Scotland, where he married Alice Cristie. After crossing the Atlantic a third time, he began practice as a physician in Philadelphia and moved to New York in 1718 to accept the first in a series of public sinecures. The family settled ten years later at Coldengham, their estate near Newburgh, New York, where Jane Colden later took up botany. Colonial appointments provided Cadwallader Colden with a steady flow of income and abundant leisure throughout his life, allowing him to devote time to politics, study, and family. The influence of Alice Colden on her daughter is less clear. The family papers record that Alice was often in the garden, an interest that she passed on to her daughter.

The eight Colden children who reached adulthood seem to have enjoyed the elements of a solid education—regular visits to nearby New York City, a good library, and enlightened or well-connected visitors. As adults they acquired their parents' ability to circulate at any level of society. Jane married late for her generation and appears in the correspondence as a mainstay among her siblings. She was the one who reported on her sister's ailing health, recommended books, and remembered family recipes.

Jane Colden's most substantial piece of writing after her *Botanic Manuscript* is her "Cheese Book," a 1756 log in which she recorded over a seven-month period her improvements to the usual methods for making cheese. Published in its entirety in *The Letters and Papers of Cadwallader Colden* (1973), this singular document not only suggests an experimental turn of mind but also follows the same approach that its author brought to plant study, that is, to codify knowledge readily available around any home. Both projects brought scientific precision to the domestic sphere.

It was largely through her intellectually restless father that Jane Colden became known as a botanist. In a scientific age that divided its practitioners into two classes, collectors and philosophers, Cadwallader Colden aspired to the latter. He won early recognition for *The History of the Five Indian Nations Depending on the Province of New York* (1727) and turned his attention to natural history shortly thereafter. Colden, who had purchased one of the first copies of Carolus Linnaeus's *Genera plantarum* (1737) in the colonies, identified the plants around his estate and submitted a twenty-page catalogue, "Plantae Coldenghamiae," to

Jane Colden's parents, Alice and Cadwallader Colden (Metropolitan Museum of Art)

John Frederic Gronovius in Leiden. The work was applauded in Europe, and Colden became known as a source for descriptions and seeds from America.

Yet the provincial ties that brought Colden opportunities as a naturalist also limited him to the role of collector—one who could provide information but who should not dwell on systems. Chafing under this position on the lower tiers of natural history and probably bored with the relatively simple Linnaean method, Colden turned to physics, then considered a higher branch of learning. In *An Explication of the First Causes of Action in Matter* (1745) he undertook a problem that had escaped Isaac Newton: to explain gravitation. This bid for scientific immortality proved futile, however, meeting indifference on the Continent and confusion in America. Yet his scientific efforts opened the door for his daughter.

Socially progressive scientists had guardedly encouraged involvement by women in the enlightenment project of categorizing the natural world. Cadwallader Colden shared this view. In a 13 November 1742 letter to Peter Collinson he urged the British botanist to write in English: avoiding Latin would open the field to "Ladies," Colden argued, whose "idle hours" left ample opportunity for such pursuits. There have always been women who were knowledgeable about plants. (Joseph Banks, later president of the Royal Society, supposedly learned the rudiments of his study at

Eton, from women who "culled simples" for apothecaries.) The issue was one of recognition. Although largely invisible in the historical record, women participated at nearly every level of formal botany, save the reportage: they collected specimens, prepared herbaria, sketched, collaborated, and taught. Elite women, such as Jane Colden, could gain access to established institutions through kinship ties. Elisabeth Christina Linné wrote in the Swedish *Transactions* about "sparking" nasturtiums, a phenomenon discovered in her father's garden; the posthumous memoirs and correspondence of Sir James E. Smith, an important British botanist, were edited by his wife, Pleasance. These examples suggest consistent yet limited involvement by women. (Even Linnaeus discouraged his daughter from becoming too knowledgeable.) Those women fortunate enough to practice botany in the eighteenth century nonetheless were kept from the upper tiers of their community.

A 1 October 1755 letter from Cadwallader Colden to Gronovius, probably the most detailed account of Jane Colden's education, outlined her quick mastery of formal taxonomy and introduced her to the field. At least one critic has remarked on the demeaning tone of this notice, and Cadwallader Colden did take a surprisingly aloof air—considering that the subject was his daughter. He began with an apology for not responding to Gronovius sooner, probably a concession to his flagging interest in natural history, and catalogued the reasons for his waning correspondence with European savants: advancing age, failing eyesight, the Seven Years' War, and his gravity tract. Clearly anxious to shift the burden of seed exchanging to his daughter, Cadwallader presented the same case he had made to Collinson thirteen years earlier: curiosity and free time, plus the "variety of dress" in a garden, lend women to plant study. As proof, he introduced Jane, explaining how he had translated the Linnaean vocabulary into English for her and noting rather smugly that while initially discouraged by its Latin characters, she soon grasped the general method. This suspect remark about Jane's resistance to the language, however, fails to hide her relative ease with the overall system. The letter also boasts that she had prepared an extensive catalogue, made ink impressions of several leaves (now missing) and introduced at least two plants as new genuses (they were not). The letter ends with the suggestion that Gronovius direct future botanical correspondence to Jane Colden, who would have time for such fieldwork, and requests books that could compensate for her limited exposure to the important gardens in Europe.

The training described in this letter to Gronovius resulted most prominently in the *Botanic Manuscript*. Now in the British Museum (Natural History), this 341-page manuscript catalogue is the basis of Jane Colden's reputation. Most of the work remains unpublished. The 1963 abridgement includes fifty-seven selections from it. The more substantial entries in the catalogue run from seven to ten paragraphs, with the Latin and common names followed by remarks on the distinguishing features of each plant: cup (calyx), flower (corolla), chives (stamens), pestle (pistil), seed box or seed cover (capsule), leaves, roots, and random notes (such as location of the plants, curious traits, and medicinal value). Like her father, Jane Colden held few reservations about correcting authorities when the occasion permitted: her entry on *Polygala senega* (Seneca snakeroot) ends with a critique of Linnaeus. Largely because of its limited circulation, Colden's manuscript had little scientific impact. Twentieth-century commentators remark on her vivid prose. She had a keen eye and often peppered her descriptions with surprising comparisons to ordinary objects. These unexpected associations bring a fresh, spontaneous quality to her writing: the leaves of silk grass, also called butterfly weed (*Asclepias tuberosa*), are

"shaped like a Cat's E'ar," rising over the flower and bending over its middle. The relative lack of pretension in no small part accounts for the charm the work still holds for contemporary readers. An unguarded approach, moreover, served the purpose of the genre, which was to provide readers with the image of an unfamiliar object.

Provincial in the best senses of that word, the *Botanic Manuscript* also serves as a working handbook on the known uses of plants in colonial New York. The connection between medicine and botany was still quite strong in the mid eighteenth century, as the daughter and future wife of a physician would have known. Joseph Pitton de Tournefort's multivolume herbal (which Cadwallader Colden owned) indexes entries by ailment; the English-language *Elements of Botany* (from Linnaeus) was translated in 1755 by an apothecary. Writing from the margins of an international community, however, Jane Colden catalogued remedies from a humbler and considerably different perspective, one that was clearly colonial and probably gynocentric. Linnaeus acknowledged the medicinal uses of plants, but he grumbled about botanical names that fell outside a certain order (his own). In particular he cautioned against the inconsistent names that physicians assigned to their remedies. Hierarchical in regard to both its contributors and its formal structure, his system of genus, class, and species tended to erase any connection between plants and their local place. His distinctions were artificial and abstract, with little regional sense. The *Botanic Manuscript,* by contrast, includes plant origins and common names and uses, alongside the Latin taxonomy. Colden included tempting details about the provenance of her work: red mint (*Monarda didyma*) grows "wild in the Mohawks Country"; the "Country People" brew rattle (*Pedicularis tuberosa*) "for the Fever & Ague" and mountain mint (*Clinopodium*) for stomach pains; silk grass settles colic, a remedy "learned from the Indians." (Cadwallader Colden himself published case studies on pokeweed as an herbal remedy for breast tumors.) Although this point might easily be overstated, Tournefort and Linnaeus demonstrated considerably less inclination than Jane Colden to recognize their debts to everyday people. The *Botanic Manuscript* was one channel by which everyday lore became science.

Jane Colden published one short plant description in her lifetime, and that probably appeared without her prior knowledge. One of the most vocal of her supporters had been Alexander Garden, a Scottish transplant to South Carolina who corresponded often with the Coldens. Garden visited Coldengham in 1754 and took the liberty of forwarding her description of *Hypericum virginicum,* which she named "Gardenia" in his honor, to Robert Whytt in Edinburgh. (The plant now known by this name is *Gardenia jasminoides,* a native of South Africa.) A bilingual "Description of a new Plant" (Latin text by Garden and English by Colden) appeared in *Essays and Observations* two years later. This submission apparently caused some ill will. Garden cited "Miss Jenny Colden" as the rightful discoverer of the plant, but credit was not the issue: Jane Colden did not prepare her work for the public. She was the only female author in that series of the Edinburgh papers, and the transactions included no similar collaborations. Garden probably overstepped some boundaries by submitting this piece to the collection. His once chatty correspondence with the Coldens turned suddenly apologetic and then ceased altogether for a three-year period. Although the exact reasons are vague, a May 1756 note to Charles Alston hinted at the reasons for Jane's anger. In this letter Jane Colden specified quite clearly that any of her observations should be kept private until further study. Her indignation at Garden's actions provides a useful indicator to the etiquette of botanical exchanges, particularly with regard to gender. If women were to participate, the episode suggests, they were to remain behind the scenes. At least one woman naturalist recoiled at publishing her work, even under the aegis of a male sponsor.

Jane Colden received ample recognition through private correspondence. The importance of Coldengham as a stop for traveling naturalists, along with some relatively aggressive promotion by family and friends, ensured her rapid rise to renown as a scientist—with only a handful of her contemporaries having seen her *Botanic Manuscript.* The interest derived in part from the novelty of a woman practicing the Linnaean method. Writing before the Edinburgh submission, Garden could scarcely contain his enthusiasm for Cadwallader's "lovely daughter." Peter Collinson, a prominent liaison between the Continent and the colonies, claimed that she was the first woman to master the binomial system and recommended her as an example to the ladies of every country. John Ellis reported eagerly that her *Firbraurea,* or gold thread, constituted a new genus. Walter Rutherford paid similar tribute—adding for good

measure that she made "the best cheese I ever ate in America." This rush to honor Jane Colden provided the basis to some false claims that persist to this day. Drawing from this lively correspondence and her unwanted submission to the Edinburgh papers, commentators often credit her for naming the gardenia, though the plant she described is not the plant that now bears that name.

Enthusiasm for the *Botanic Manuscript* proved short-lived. Almost as quickly as she gained celebrity status in scientific circles, Jane Colden disappeared from view. She married Dr. William Farquhar on 12 March 1759. While the scant correspondence hints that the relationship was a happy one, she did not continue her plant studies. She died in 1766, the same year as her only child. Given the absence of details about her later family life, any explanation for her disappearance from the scientific record must remain speculative. A possible clue may lie in the example of Elisabeth Linné, a contemporary of Jane's who faced similar opportunities and limitations as the daughter of a prominent scientist. Two years after publishing her report on nasturtiums, Linné married and had a child. She soon separated from her husband, however, and raised the child in her father's home—without ever returning to her earlier botanical work. As one scholar maintains, Linnaeus encouraged plant study for a daughter but not for a mother. There is no evidence that Cadwallader Colden or William Farquhar shared this view of women's roles, but Colden clearly regarded botany as a hobby for a woman's "idle hours." The only other Colden child with an inclination for science, David Colden, followed his father into physics. He aspired to philosophy while his sister remained a collector. Tellingly, the word *curious* appears frequently alongside praise for the *Botanic Manuscript.*

Not until the twentieth century did scholars begin to recognize Jane Colden's place in the history of science. Largely overlooked for almost a century after her death, she now appears as a pathbreaker at the beginning of a tradition of nature writing that unfolded in the United States. By 1800 plant study had emerged as a popular pastime, leading to a boom of botanical literature by women. Slightly ahead of this trend, Jane Colden's career embodies the paradoxes that women naturalists faced in the eighteenth century. The *Botanic Manuscript* marks the intersection of science, culture, and gender in her time. Given its strain against the conventions of femininity and serious study, her work often yields insights that similar accounts by men do not

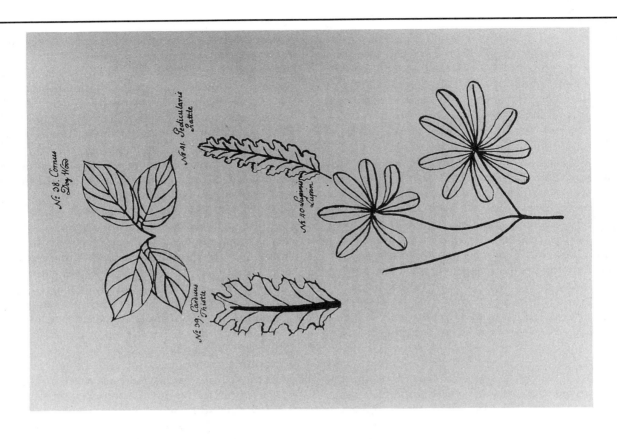

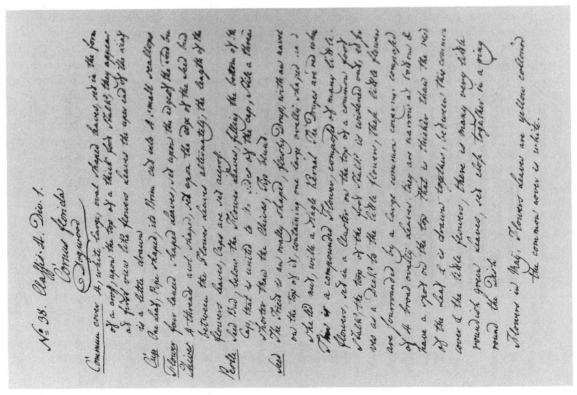

Descriptions and plates from Colden's Botanic Manuscript *(British Museum [Natural History])*

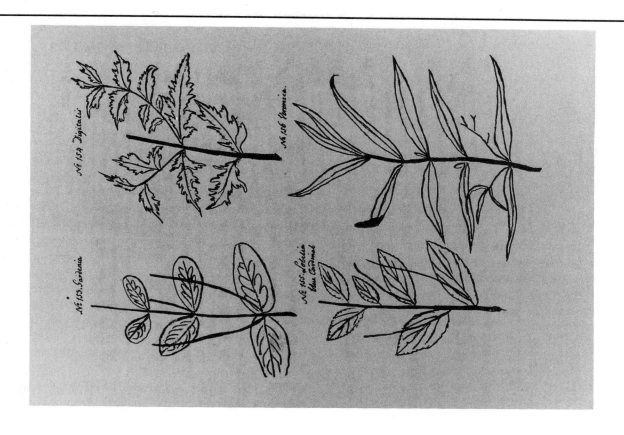

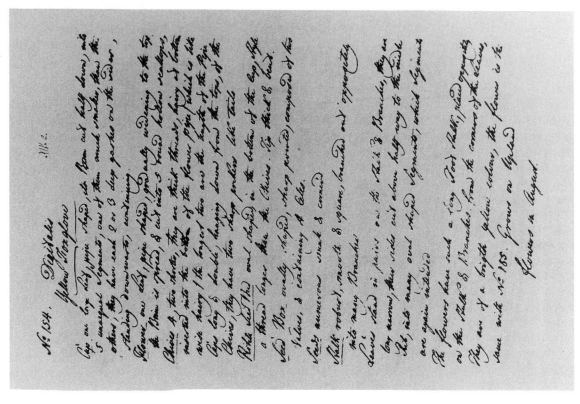

generally allow. The reception of her work suggests how a matrix of authority established overseas transformed ordinary observation into official knowledge. Jane Colden's unpretentious writing raises a significant question: did familiarity with nature qualify one as a naturalist or did natural history more successfully channel this familiarity into a larger web of correspondence, into a hierarchical system largely dominated by men? Given the later importance of nature writing in the United States and the tenuous hold of women at the forefront of that tradition, Jane Colden deserves to be recognized as a pioneer in her field.

Letters:
The Letters and Papers of Cadwallader Colden. New-York Historical Society Collections (New York: AMS, 1973).

References:
Marcia Myers Bonta, *Women in the Field: America's Pioneering Women Naturalists* (College Station: Texas A & M University Press, 1991), pp. 5–8;

Margaret Denny, "Naming the Gardenia," *Scientific Monthly,* 67 (1948): 17–22;

Brooke Hindle, "A Colonial Governor's Family: The Coldens of Coldengham," *New-York Historical Society Quarterly,* 65 (1961): 233–250;

Hindle, *The Pursuit of Science in Revolutionary America, 1735–1789* (Chapel Hill: University of North Carolina Press, 1956), pp. 42–43;

Ann B. Shteir, *Cultivating Women, Cultivating Science: Flora's Daughters and Botany in England* (Baltimore: Johns Hopkins University Press, 1996), pp. 50–57;

Raymond Phineas Stearns, *Science in the British Colonies of America* (Urbana: University of Illinois Press, 1970), pp. 565–567;

Joan Hoff Wilson, "Dancing Dogs of the Colonial Period: Women Scientists," *Early American Literature,* 7 (Winter 1973): 225–235.

Papers:
The unabridged *Botanic Manuscript* is in the British Museum (Natural History). Several of Jane Colden's letters (mostly on family matters) and her "Cheese Book" are at the New-York Historical Society. The Edinburgh University Library and the Linnean Society of London each hold one letter.

Hannah Mather Crocker

(27 June 1752 – 11 July 1829)

Constance J. Post
Iowa State University

BOOKS: *A Series of Letters on Free Masonry* (Boston: Printed by John Eliot, 1815);
The School of Reform, or Seaman's Safe Pilot to the Cape of Good Hope (Boston: Printed by John Eliot, 1816);
Observations on the Real Rights of Women, with Their Appropriate Duties, Agreeable to Scripture, Reason and Common Sense (Boston: Printed for the author, 1818).

The writings of Hannah Mather Crocker have received little attention. Although her *Observations on the Real Rights of Women* (1818) has been called the first "feministic" book in America, she has been omitted from most histories of American feminism. The neglect of Crocker's writings might be the result of her habit of relying on passages extracted from the writings of others; yet her texts that resemble commonplace books are valuable for what they reveal about reading practices of the period. Crocker's significance as a writer chiefly rests on her status as a "sublime amateur," a phrase applied to women writers of the period who wanted to avoid the criticism that professionalism was unfeminine. Crocker was no exception. By asking the reader of *Observations on the Real Rights of Women* to "gently draw the mantle of charity over all its imperfections," she adopted a pose of modesty that enabled her to deflect all criticism. Whether her request was a nod to convention or an apology for flawed writing, or both, Crocker's writings give ample evidence of a strong desire to express her ideas about contemporary issues.

As Susan Phinney Conrad notes in *Perish the Thought: Intellectual Women in Romantic America, 1830–1860* (1976), women with intellectual aspirations in this period usually had fathers who were professionals. Crocker was no exception. The daughter of Samuel and Hannah Hutchinson Mather, she belonged to what she called "the four-fold line of Mathers": Richard Mather was her great-great-grandfather; Increase Mather, her great-grandfather; Cotton Mather, her grandfather; and Samuel, Cot-

ton Mather's sole surviving son, her father. Born in Boston, Massachusetts, on 27 June 1752, Hannah Mather died in nearby Roxbury on 11 July 1829 and is buried in the Mather tomb at Copp's Hill, Boston. In 1779 she married Joseph Crocker, who graduated from Harvard College and served as a captain in the Revolutionary Army. Hannah Crocker waited until their ten children were grown before she took up the pen. Her timing was deliberate, as she believed that when children leave to form their own homes, "this is a fully ripe season to read, write, meditate and compose, if the body and mind are not enfeebled by infirmities." Her published works also appeared under the pseudonyms A Lady of Boston and A. P. Americana.

In her first publication, *A Series of Letters on Free Masonry* (1815), Crocker rose to the defense of the Society of Free Masons after the group was roundly criticized in 1810 for reportedly engaging in high revelry in its Boston lodges. Although she acknowledged "that it will be thought by many, a bold attempt for a female to even dare enter on the subject at all," she proceeded undaunted. The founder of a female Masonic society in the year before her marriage, Crocker gave her full support to Masonry in the correspondence between "Enquirer" and "Aurelia Prudencia Americana," for which she likely wrote both sides of the exchange. In his preface to the work the Reverend Thaddeus M. Harris acknowledged that he had urged Crocker to publish it.

Crocker conceded that the first letter, dated 7 September 1810, promotes the need for women to be educated instead of providing opinions about Freemasonry. According to Crocker, the society she established might have been the first to promote female education in Boston. At the time of its formation, "If women could even read and badly write their name it was thought enough for *them,* who by some were esteemed as only 'merely domestick animals.'" Crocker rested her authority on "the wise author of nature" who ordained women "as not only help-meets, associates and friends, not slaves to man." Her call for companionate marriage is accom-

85

panied by conventional warnings about wasting time "in frivolous calls" or "with some foolish novel" and ends on a theme to which Crocker returned in later works: the importance of cultivating virtue, which is best done by acquainting youth with the history of virtuous persons in their own country.

The next two letters respond directly to the request by Enquirer about her opinions concerning the Masons. Just as she would not stop going to church because of a member who "is irregular or immoral," Crocker saw no reason to withdraw from an association because of a member's conduct. Unwilling to judge another's heart and reluctant to censure behavior, she preferred instead to note that "every benevolent institution has a happy effect on society at large." Crocker believed that the good done for the poor by the Society of Masons to be of far greater consequence than any misconduct by a member, and she cited charity to the poor as one of the Masons' many benevolent activities that are consonant with their Christian duty. The exchange of correspondence is followed by three poems, the first two addressed to the female society of Masons and the last written in commemoration of Gen. George Washington.

A year after her letters on Masonry were published, Crocker's homily for sailors appeared as *The School of Reform, or Seaman's Safe Pilot to the Cape of Good Hope* (1816) by A Lady of Boston. In her exhortation to sailors to be guided by reason, Crocker began by quoting Benjamin Franklin on the debilitating effect of excessive drinking. Filled with nautical imagery used literally and figuratively, the essay inveighs against the habit of intemperance, which, warned Crocker, might start with the "morning cordial" and the "social glass" and end in degradation with dire consequences for the individual and for society. To prevent this end the sailor is enjoined to "Put on the new man; and by divine assistance you can work out your own salvation." On a larger scale the suggested remedy is to establish "schools of industry for males and females. Get youth an early habit of industry, for idleness will not only clothe a man with rags, but multiply many other vices." Despite her concern with the "too free use of ardent spirits," Crocker refrained from counseling total abstinence. Instead she admonished the sailor not to drink too hard nor too deep aboard the ship *Time*, whose owner is Christopher Columbus, thereby linking her twin concerns for private and public well-being.

That concern finds its fullest expression in *Observations on the Real Rights of Women, with Their Appropriate Duties, Agreeable to Scripture, Reason, and*

Common Sense (1818), one of the first books on women's rights written by an American to be published in America. (Judith Sargent Murray's *The Gleaner,* which appeared in 1798, is a compilation of pieces originally published in serial form.) By listing the author as H. Mather Crocker, the title page highlights her connection to the Mathers but obscures her female identity. Contemporary readers, however, were unlikely to miss the reference in the dedication to another Hannah, the British writer "Miss H. More."

Crocker's *Observations on the Real Rights of Women* comprises an introduction, eight chapters, and an appendix. The first two chapters concentrate on the religious roots of women's rights: the story of creation and the fall as it pertains to women's status in chapter 1 and women's restoration through the plan of redemption in chapter 2. After a review in chapter 3 of notable religious and secular women, chapter 4 maintains that contemporary women's writing is equal to that of any previous time and provides many examples. The next three chapters constitute the heart of Crocker's book by focusing on the last half of the title: *Agreeable to Scripture, Reason, and Common Sense.*

The argument chiefly rests on a series of correspondences whereby women's rights are linked in three ways: first, with their rights as Christians, based on scripture (chapter 5); second, with their rights as heirs of the Enlightenment, grounded in reason (chapter 6); and third, with their rights as citizens in a democracy depending, as it does, on common sense (chapter 7). The first four chapters, chapter 8, and the appendix reinforce the central idea of the book: the bond of mutuality as the primary means of assuring unity, whether it be that of husband and wife, members in an association, or citizens of a country.

The value of Crocker's *Observations on the Real Rights of Women* lies principally in its articulation of the ideals of freedom and equality for women that are linked to the American struggle against Great Britain during the Revolutionary War. Many of the assumptions underlying Crocker's text, however, were widely shared on both sides of the Atlantic by the time her book appeared in 1818. The belief that men possessed greater physical strength, for example, appears in most of the writings by advocates of women's rights, regardless of political affiliation. Nor did Crocker depart from the view that the mental powers of women are equal to those of men and that any apparent differences were attributable to education. On these and many other matters, those committed to the rights of women were in

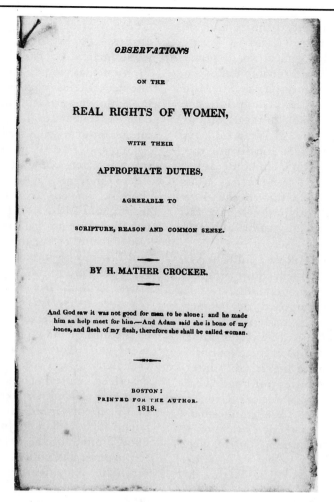

Title page for the book in which Hannah Mather Crocker argued that "a free, federal, republican government" would be strengthened by "the union and right understanding of the sexes" (courtesy of the Special Collections Department, University of Virginia Library)

agreement, especially on their ability to do more than cook and sew. As Crocker noted,

> There may be a few groveling minds who think women should not aspire to any further knowledge than to obtain enough of the cynical art to enable them to compound a good pudding, pie or cake, for her lord and master to discompound. Others, of a still weaker class, may say, it is enough for women scientifically to arrange the spinning-wheel and distaff, and exercise her extensive capacity in knitting and sewing, since the fall and restoration of women these employments have been the appropriate duties of the female sex.

Another sort of spinning occupied Crocker's attention: the swift rotation caused by political revolution in America, which not only transformed opinion about women's rights in the late eighteenth century but also changed the discussion about those rights in the United States.

Much of the debate after the Revolution centered on the need for both men and women to cultivate virtues essential for the survival of the republic, a requirement cast more as a duty than a right. The need to raise well-regulated individuals was deemed an important duty for women, but Crocker also extolled the indirect influence they could thereby exert on the course of public affairs as an important right. Allied with the need for well-ordered lives was the fear of luxury and dissipation, a fear frequently invoked by Crocker's forebears but one that took on a more pronounced political cast after the war. Crocker wrote approvingly of the period when women had time to pursue intellectual interests because "Luxury and the want of occupation had not introduced the fashion of sitting five or six hours at the glass to invent fashions." She similarly railed against wasting time in reading worthless novels and recommended instead the study of history. The emphasis on virtue was deeply rooted in the Puritan assumption that human nature is fallen but capable of regeneration; yet it also had roots in the ideas of Whig Liberty, especially those of Montesquieu. Succinctly put, this viewpoint meant, "No virtue, no Commonwealth." As Gordon Wood argues in *The Radicalism of the American of the Revolution* (1992), this emphasis on public moral character of the highest sort gave the American Revolution its "socially radical character."

By the time Crocker's book was published in 1818, two other events had influenced the progress of women's rights beyond the first tentative steps to challenge the boundaries imposed on women confined to making puddings and plying their needles: the scandal surrounding Mary Wollstonecraft and the French Revolution. In the eyes of the American public the two were inextricably intertwined. Noting that little attention had been devoted to women's rights in America, Crocker speculated that "Perhaps it has not been necessary in a land where the rights of women have never appeared a bone of much contention." Independent people, she argued, are likely to have ideas that "will be more liberal and expanded respecting the sexual rights." What did become a bone of considerable contention was William Godwin's *Memoirs of the Author of "A Vindication of the Rights of Woman"* (1798), which revealed that he and Wollstonecraft had lived together and had children without ever having married; an American edition of his book appeared in 1799, and another was published five years later. The effect on Wollstonecraft's reputation was disastrous, and those who defended her were open to charges of loose morals for private and public behavior. Crocker, however, praised Wollstonecraft's *A Vindication of the Rights of Woman* (1792) for its many "fine sentiments," even though she parted company "with her opinion respect the total independence of the female sex." She also faulted Wollstonecraft on the grounds that "her theory is unfit for practice." Coming as it did in 1818, the observation suggests that the passage of two decades had softened the criticism against Wollstonecraft and signaled a major shift in attitudes about women's rights. Radical and conservative forces seem no longer diametrically opposed.

For Crocker the treatment of women's rights through a series of correspondences began with the family circle and widened to include the entire nation. Noting that women in early America had always enjoyed the right to choose whom they would marry, Crocker did not explicitly repudiate the view that women were seen as inferior to men. She nevertheless challenged its assumptions by establishing a series of correspondences based on equality and mutuality, beginning, as most arguments about women's rights did at this time, with Adam and Eve. Echoing John Milton, Crocker informed her readers that the two "walk side by side, as mutual supports in all times of trial." They thereby served as models for other couples throughout history and received Crocker's praise because of the mutuality of their marriage. From the Old Testament she cited the marriage of Hannah and Elkanah as based on "one common interest." Her description of an ideal pair reflects what Lawrence Stone has identified in *The Family: Sex and Marriage in England, 1500–1800* (1977) as a movement toward "affective individualism" in marriage at the end of the eighteenth century. She lauded men who wrote about companionate marriage, especially Sir Thomas More, who in a letter described an ideal wife as serene, well educated, and a constant friend. Crocker likewise praised Jacques de Villamont for his insistence on women's capacity friendship and Samuel Johnson on the necessity of good humor for the happiness of the family. The importance she attached to marriage grounded in mutuality is evident by the frequency with which she returned to it in *Observations on the Real Rights of Women*.

Chapter 6 points out the advantage to both parties of a mutual marriage, especially in the matter of arguments. Although she maintained that many of these could be avoided if a woman reasonably conceded the point, Crocker did not advise that a man do the same in order to avoid matrimonial disharmony. She did, however, insist that a woman should "never assent merely to please a tyrant, for that betrays a servile mind; nor ever contradict merely to vex, for that shews an ill temper, and bad breeding." Ideally husband and wife are best friends, keeping no secrets "from each other but the secrets of another friend." Otherwise, secrets and strongboxes are to be shared by them together. Later, Crocker described the character of a good husband and a good wife, as well as a good father and a good mother, but not before she first declared that "it appears incontestably evident, that a happy marriage has in it all the pleasures of friendship, and all the enjoyments of sense and reason, and indeed all the sweets of life." As a final example, she ended the appendix with the story of Aurelius and Prudencia, a narrative "drawn from a

Having been repeatedly asked the question
What utility an Antiquarian Society can be of to
the world ingeneral; or what can possibly induce
any Lady in promoting such an institution.
with the most ardent desire of gratifying many
enquiring friends, I now take pen in hand.
wishing I may be ever ready, and able, to give
to give areason for the hope that sustains me.
Though I must acknowledge it is singular.
and perhaps I stand alone on female ground
as an advocate for masonry and awarm enthusiast
in the cause of antiquarian researches.
having been admited. I may say. when achild
to set at the feet of Gamaliel.
I was soon charmed with the tongue of the wise
and the learned, I then heard of ancient days
and ancient learning, and of the advantages.
that might be obtained by resorting to the original
languages. thus early in life I embibed the sentiment
that continues with me even in advanced age.
that if we would obtain knowledge, we must press on,

First page of the manuscript for Crocker's unpublished, undated essay on antiquarian research (American Antiquarian Society)

known couple in real life" who mutually supported each other in a marriage that lasted almost fifty years. This ideal couple is likely based on her parents. Their mutuality, which extended to other members of the family and to the community, represented what Crocker hoped might be achieved in the new republic.

The final chapter of *Observations on the Real Rights of Women* ends on a note of joyful anticipation of heaven, where the spiritual distinction of sexes does not exist, for all are equally redeemed. The advantage of forming "sacred love and friendship here," argued Crocker, is "that it shall be the foretaste of our future bliss." Recalling the biblical assertion that God is no respecter of persons or sexes, Crocker invited her readers to draw the conclusion that the same lack of distinction should be observed on earth. After all, she said—quoting Hannah More who in turn quoted a prelate—"women make up one half of the human race, equally redeemed by the blood of Christ." Crocker did not believe that women were relegated to the home as their sole area of influence, even though she accepted it as their dominant sphere. From the earliest days of American history, wrote Crocker, women availed themselves of the opportunity to be educated and were often consulted on matters of public concern. She pointed with obvious pride to Sarah Kemble Knight of Boston, whom she credited with wielding considerable influence in the early eighteenth century. Crocker also praised other women for "their writings and advice" during the American struggle for independence, a time when the bonds of domesticity were loosened, as Mary Beth Norton notes in *Liberty's Daughters: The Revolutionary Experience of American Women, 1750–1800* (1980).

An important way in which the redemptive or regenerative force of women was not confined to the individual household can be found in the many female associations, chiefly maternal or religious, the second in Crocker's series of correspondences. Insisting that "Women have an equal right, with the other sex, to form societies for promoting religious, charitable and benevolent purposes," Crocker went beyond advocacy when she formed a women's society of Masons. She also urged that an antiquarian society be established. Such mutuality, Crocker argued, would benefit the community and by extension the entire country.

The correspondences between mutual partners in a marriage and mutual members of an association are reinforced in *Observations on the Real Rights of Women* by the third in Crocker's series of correspondences, the mutuality of citizens. Here she parted company with Hannah More, Mary Wollstonecraft, and a host of other contemporaries, some of whom considered the role of women in raising good citizens but few of whom argued that a specific form of government was more congenial to women's rights. In chapter 7 Crocker argued that to maintain peace in "our American Israel," a phrase that resonates in the literature of early New England, "a free, federal, republican government . . . requires more sense and judgment to preserve it from disorder and disunion; therefore the union and right understanding of the sexes will have a tendency to strengthen, confirm and support such a government, and common sense must allow women the right of mutual judgment, and joining with the other sex in every prudent measure for their mutual defence and safety."

For women's contributions to the Revolutionary War effort, Crocker drew on the example in Mercy Otis Warren's *History of the Rise, Progress and Termination of the American Revolution* (1805), of Lady Ackland, cited for her fortitude in following her husband, a British major, from camp to camp before he was captured by American forces. To balance the picture, Crocker added Warren's examples of Martha Washington and a Mrs. Jackson, who joined her husband, Colonel Jackson, at the front with their six sons in tow. In so doing, they illustrate "the mutual virtue, energy, and fortitude" by which "the freedom and independence of the United States were attained and secured." Crocker was especially concerned that the egalitarian rhetoric of the Revolution might disappear and with it the right of a woman to participate directly in matters outside the home. That some women were already doing so in the postrevolutionary period was a source of obvious pride to Crocker, whose survey of the mutual accomplishments of the citizens of the new republic enlarges Thomas Jefferson's argument in his *Notes on the State of Virginia* (1785). Like Jefferson, Crocker claimed that "America, though as yet but young in the arts and sciences, will not long remain in the background." Unlike Jefferson, who concentrated on the accomplishments of men, Crocker stated that the country "can now claim the birth-right of many respectable female writers, both in prose and verse." Among those whom she praised are poet Sarah Wentworth Morton and historians Mercy Otis Warren and Hannah Adams. Although Crocker did not mention Jefferson, her argument contributes to the dialogue about American genius by offering evidence that women who lived during the Revolution were already extending its egalitarian ideals to a group not originally envisioned as a part of "We, the People."

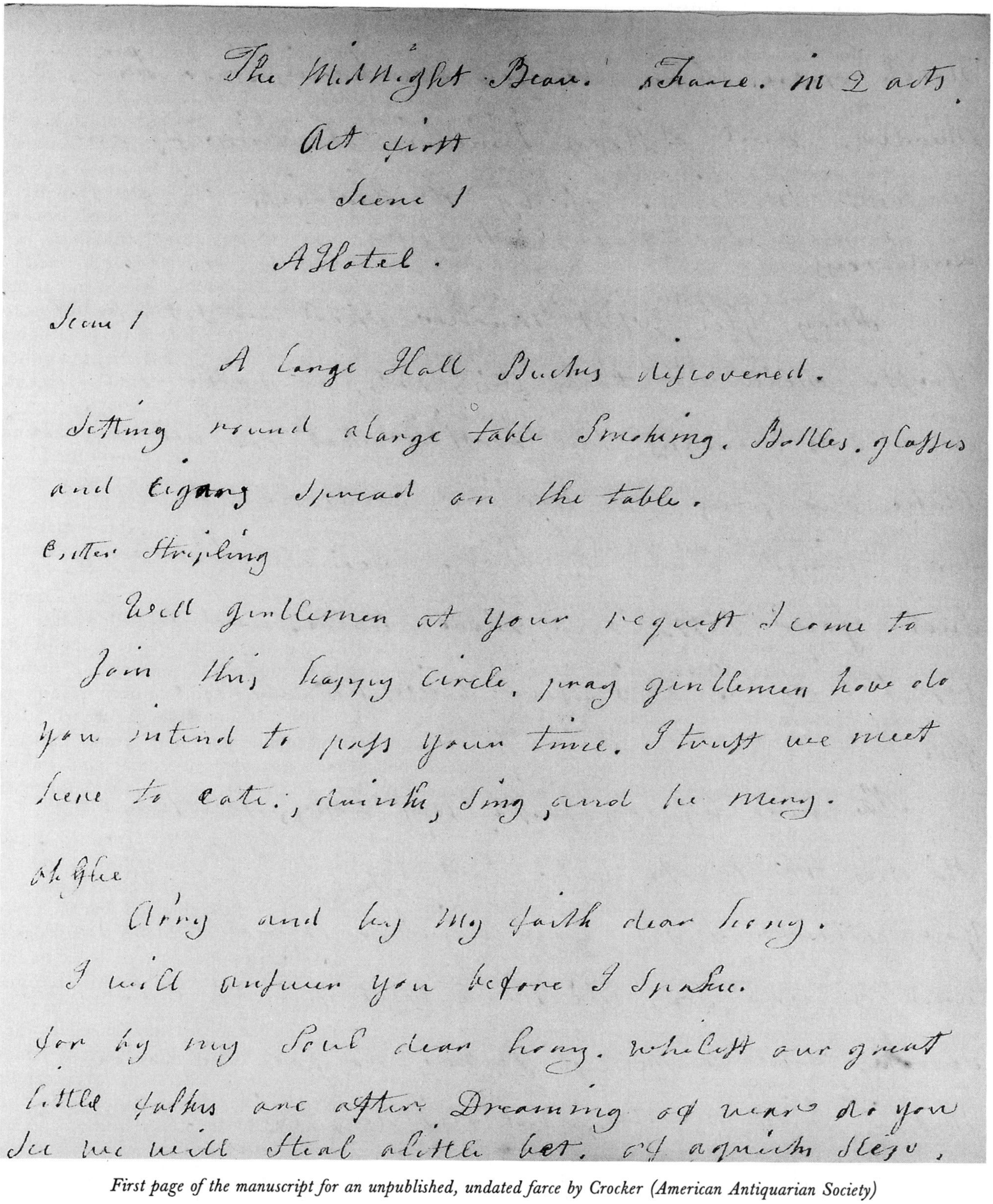

The Midnight Beau. a Farce. in 2 acts.

Act first

Scene 1

A Hotel.

Scene 1

A large Hall Bachus discovered.

Setting round a large table Smoking. Bottles, glasses and Cigars spread on the table.

Enter Stripling

Well gentlemen at Your request I come to Join this happy circle, pray gentlemen how do you intend to pass your time. I trust we meet here to eate, drinke, Sing, and be merry.

Oh Glee

A ring and bey My faith dear Hony.

I will answer you before I Spake.

For by my Soul dear hony, whilest our great little father are after Dreaming of war do you see we will steal alittle bet, of a quiet Sleep.

First page of the manuscript for an unpublished, undated farce by Crocker (American Antiquarian Society)

Concerned lest she be guilty of partiality in her *Observations on the Real Rights of Women,* Crocker ended with a roll call of illustrious men as a counterweight to the outstanding women listed in chapters 3 and 4. For example, the Old Testament figures such as Deborah, Ruth and Naomi, and Hannah in chapter 3 are offset in the appendix by Moses, Job, Solomon, and Isaiah; and ancient Romans Pliny and Cicero are used to balance Zenobia and Cornelia. Many of the men drawn from early modern history (including John Calvin, Martin Luther, Philipp Melanchthon, Francis Bacon, Voltaire, and David Hume) have no apparent counterparts in chapter 3; there are, however, exceptions. Crocker's praise of Marie de Gournay, Mary Shurman, Catherine Macaulay, and Mary Wollstonecraft as writers in chapter 3 is matched by her listing of John Dryden, Alexander Pope, Joseph Addison, and Samuel Johnson in the appendix, although perhaps unevenly. When she included selections from writers, those by men are much longer than those by women, not only in her listing of men in the appendix but especially in a separate section reserved there for "Miscellaneous Sentiments, moral and religious, From various authors." In chapter 4 Crocker maintained that contemporary women were equal in character and talent to those in earlier periods and mentioned approvingly Madame Germaine de Staël, Lucy Akin, Hannah More, Sarah Wentworth Morton, Hannah Adams, and Mercy Otis Warren. For the final three, the historians Jeremy Belknap and George Minot serve as counterparts in the appendix.

Crocker not only referred to illustrious men throughout the course of history but also gave high praise to many from her native land. "America has her worthies yet to claim," wrote Crocker, who mentioned more than thirty, including Christopher Columbus, Thomas Hooker, John Eliot, John Cotton, the Mathers, Benjamin Franklin, and George Washington. Were she to include "the catalogue of old Harvard, and the other Universities, it would swell our work to the frightful size of a huge folio." Grateful to writers who spared her the need to "wade through folio after folio" and wanting to keep her own from becoming too large, Crocker resumed her practice of culling passages from other sources for the rest of the appendix.

Crocker's unpublished writings include essays, sermons, a play, political commentary, poems, and a lengthy reminiscence. Several pieces are undated. In "The United Trinity or consistant Catholic Christian" Crocker cited many authorities in her attempt to reconcile Trinitarians to a belief in the unity of the Godhead and Unitarians to the recognition of the Trinity. Evident throughout its pages is Crocker's concern to balance opposing views. Signed "Candidus Maximus Originalis," the title page of the manuscript states that it was "Presented to the Am[erican]. Antiq[uaria]n. Soc[iety]. By Mrs. Hannah Crocker, the Authoress." A second essay, "Jephthah Vow explained," seeks to justify the rash action of Jephthah, who promised God that if Israel gained victory over the Ammonites he would sacrifice whomever he first saw coming from the door of his house on his return home. Crocker sympathized with the daughter, who was not offered as a literal sacrifice but was condemned to celibacy by serving in the temple. At the end of the essay Crocker noted that nunneries serve to commemorate the filial obedience of Jephthah's daughter. The essay is signed, "By Increase Mather Jun. Of the inner Temple (Mrs. Hannah Crocker, grand-daughter of Rev. Cotton Mather)."

Crocker also signed a political address and two sermons as "Increase Mather, Jun. of the Inner Temple" but without the parenthetical note about her paternal grandfather. In "An Humble Address to the reasons and Wisdom of the American Nation" she argued in favor of a strong navy for commercial interests, after devoting the first half of her essay to an exposition of the passage in I Kings about Solomon's fleet. Were the United States to have a strong navy, it "would be the glory of the American Constitution," Crocker believed. "Let me remind you, my Southern and Northern friends we are formed by nature as mutual helps." Fearful that the country might splinter into many groups, Crocker recalled its formation "under one federal hand, for the mutual support of the whole body politic," a theme to which she often returned in her writing.

Crocker signed both a "Fast Sermon," dated 20 August 1812, and a "Thanksgiving Sermon," dated 18 November 1813, as "Increase Mather of the inner Temple." She also indicated that the "Fast Sermon" was delivered on "Mr. Madisons fast day." This jeremiad attributes the War of 1812 to the sinfulness of the American people who were once "the happiest people on the Globe." Should they repent, Crocker believed, peace and other blessings would follow. The influence of President James Madison rather than the Mathers, however, can be seen in Crocker's remark that "if we differ in opinion we also differ in our looks, and we can no more make men think alike, then [*sic*] we can make them look alike." Crocker's "Thanksgiving Sermon" also blends religious and republican ideals. Noting that such a day had been celebrated from the time of the first settlement to the present day in

Massachusetts, Crocker used the occasion to recall that "no Nation ever enjoyed so wise an administration since the reign of Solomon." In reviewing the blessings of God on "our American Israel," which she extolled as the likely site of the last empire, Crocker offered thanks for many things, including antiquarian projects. The discoveries of antiquarians demonstrate that "all things in time shall become new."

The promotion of such activity informs Crocker's undated essay "Antiquarian researches, Exemplified pleasant and easy, By an original Antiquarian," which she signed with her own name instead of a pseudonym. Likening the preservation of literary and scientific antiquities to Solomon's care of records in the holy of holies, Crocker invested antiquarian research with a sacred errand by way of Masonic precepts and republican ideals. According to Crocker, such a society cannot bow to the will of a particular group but must have the good of the entire public in mind. Nor should the society place limits on those who conduct the research: just as Hannah, the mother of Samuel, preserved important patterns, so may a woman "be the means of saving a nation by prudently recording and preserving certain documents." Although Crocker pointed out that saving important papers may settle land disputes, her commitment to literary and scientific research reveals a bent that is intellectual rather than practical. Crocker herself contributed to antiquarian research in several ways. She gave the Mather family portraits and the Mather library, the bulk of which she inherited, to the American Antiquarian Society, which was founded by Isaiah Thomas in 1812. She also preserved family documents and created one of her own, a vast compendium titled "Reminiscences and Traditions of Boston." Dated 1829, the 478-page miscellany includes personal and regional history, expositions of Christian doctrine, political commentary, and poems. It also served as a commonplace book, which might account for its disjointedness.

Evidence of Crocker's far-ranging interests as a writer can be seen in the "Midnight Beau," an unpublished two-act farce in which several young men invite Joseph Stripling to join them for a night of revelry. The character Ludicrous suggests that they hunt cats, rats, or the chickens of an old woman as their sport for the evening, but Roland Nightramble urges instead that they hunt young women. Not finding any, they decide to storm the watch and then the quarters of Henry Philanthropus, where they meet Angelica. She warns Stripling to avoid the wrong crowd, lamenting the fate that befalls a woman "lost to virtue" because of the trust she places in a man. Thereupon Stripling vows to quit his night on the town and returns home, accompanied by Philanthropus. Stripling's mother, Prudencia, welcomes her prodigal son and expresses her confidence that children would not cause a parent such grief if they knew how sorely wounded are the feelings of a mother. Crocker's purpose in writing the play is revealed in the lines attributed to "Dr. Fran[klin]" that she appended to the bottom of the final page of the manuscript: "The Case was real, and gave rise to the fiction, in hope a song may Catch him whom a sermon flies."

This concern for the rising generation is a consistent theme throughout Crocker's writings, both published and unpublished. Aligning her with "the four-fold line of Mathers" whom she frequently invoked, the theme enabled her to remain within the traditions established by her forebears even as she took tentative steps in the direction of challenging the boundaries of those traditions. Although her ideas are rarely pathbreaking, Hannah Mather Crocker remains an important figure of the period.

References:

Sara M. Evans, *Born for Liberty: A History of Women in America* (New York: Free Press / London: Collier Macmillan, 1989);

Eleanor Flexner, *Century of Struggle: The Women's Rights Movement in the United States,* revised edition (Cambridge, Mass.: Harvard University Press, 1975);

Robert Riegel, *American Feminists* (Lawrence: University of Kansas Press, 1963).

Papers:

Unpublished manuscripts of works by Hannah Mather Crocker are held at the American Antiquarian Society and the New England Historic Genealogical Society.

Elizabeth Drinker

(27 February 1735 – 24 November 1807)

Pattie Cowell
Colorado State University

WORKS: *Extracts from the Journal of Elizabeth Drinker, from 1759 to 1807 A.D.*, edited by Henry Drinker Biddle (Philadelphia: Lippincott, 1889);

"Extracts from the Journal of Mrs. Henry Drinker, of Philadelphia, from September 25, 1777, to July 4, 1778," *Pennsylvania Magazine of History and Biography*, 13 (1889): 298–308;

"Verses by Elizabeth Drinker," *Pennsylvania Magazine of History and Biography*, 15 (1891): 246;

The Diary of Elizabeth Drinker, 3 volumes, edited by Elaine Forman Crane (Boston: Northeastern University Press, 1991); abridged by Crane as *The Diary of Elizabeth Drinker: The Life Cycle of an Eighteenth-Century Woman*, 1 volume (Boston: Northeastern University Press, 1994).

Although her works did not reach print during her lifetime, indeed were never intended to be published, Elizabeth Sandwith Drinker was among the most prolific of eighteenth-century North American women writers. Entry after entry in her diary notes cryptically that she found herself "in the reading and writing humour" or that she "spent this Afternoon up stairs writing." A woman of means, Drinker was able to cultivate her writing habit regularly from the 1750s until a week before her death in 1807. The resulting body of diaries, letters, and papers runs to thousands of pages. The 1991 complete edition of the diary gives the reader access to nearly 2,100 densely packed pages of Drinker's running commentary on family, friends, region, and nation.

At least since 1955, when Drinker's diary was placed on deposit at the Historical Society of Pennsylvania, scholars have recognized the importance of these documents. The diary is the most sustained narrative of an eighteenth-century woman's daily life in the North American colonies and the new republic. With only a few breaks, the thirty-three handwritten volumes comprise almost daily records of Drinker's family and community life and of her values as they were enacted in household work, relationships, and reading. Juxtaposing the mundane and the extraordinary, Drinker's diary depicts an everyday world that happened to include a revolutionary war, the birth of a nation, and the growth of a major metropolitan area. Her purposes in writing are more family focused than political, but family, region, and nation are bound together in the dailiness of anecdote: fire alarms, family births, soldiers marching, fishing, Quaker meeting, yellow fever, visiting friends, a daughter's elopement, Continental Congress, real-estate transactions, runaway slaves, and walking excursions in the countryside. Throughout, Drinker grounded her narrative line in the concrete events of everyday life.

Eighteenth-century Philadelphia provided Drinker with quite a spectacle. During her seventy-two years the population of Philadelphia grew from thirteen thousand to nearly seventy thousand, largely the result of successive waves of immigration. By 1800 the labor force of the city had been transformed from bound servants and slaves to free wage earners. Philadelphia became home to eight ethnic groups. Quaker control diminished as the Society of Friends became only one of fourteen sizable religious denominations. By 1800 Philadelphia had grown into the most diverse major metropolitan center in North America. It was a "walking" city, as Peter Thompson has described it, geographically compact enough that the young and rambling Elizabeth came to know it well.

Descended from Irish Quaker families, Elizabeth Sandwith was born to Sarah Jervis Sandwith (1708–1756) and William Sandwith (1700–1756) on 27 February 1735 in the same Philadelphia house "in second Street between Market and Chesnut" in which her "dear mother" had been born. Much of what is known of Elizabeth's youth is derived from diary entries she made in her last years and from the papers of the Jervis, Sandwith, and Drinker families. William Sandwith had emigrated from Dublin to Philadelphia in 1727. He was a successful ship captain and merchant, often away from home for long periods of time, a circumstance that might account for the scarcity of comment about him in the diary.

Silhouettes of Elizabeth and Henry Drinker (The Historical Society of Pennsylvania)

Young Elizabeth might not have spent a good deal of time in his company. She had an older sister, Mary (1732–1815), who never married, and a younger brother, William (1746–1747), who died in infancy.

Little is known of Elizabeth Sandwith's education, but she mentioned in passing that she had been "a schooler to Anthony Benezet," a well-known Quaker teacher and abolitionist who for a time ran a school for girls. She must have studied French at some point since her diary includes frequent examples of her rather meager accomplishments in this language. She often used her French to write about events or judgments that she sought to conceal, her schoolgirl French apparently working for her as a kind of code. In addition she mastered at least enough arithmetic to keep accounts, and like many women of her time, she learned needlework, practicing it with pleasure all her life. It seems appropriate that Elizabeth's diary opens in 1758 with a long list of items she had sewn, noting who each item was for and often indicating what varieties of stitches and materials she had used. A few months before her death she was still sewing: "needlework in silk or worsted was always pleasing to me.—I have done much of it in my time."

These slim details of Elizabeth's education cannot be the entire story. Her diary records multifaceted reading in literature, politics, memoir, history, biography, theology, parenting, natural history, and medicine. Those who scan the diary even hastily can have no doubt of the pleasure she found in reading. As her children grew older and she had more uninterrupted time, the record of her reading life grew correspondingly. In 1799 she began noting her year's reading in a separate list at year's end, though she also continued to comment on some items in her regular diary entries, much as she had from the early years.

Both Elizabeth's parents died in 1756, Sarah on 9 January of "a lingering illness" and William on 13 March suddenly "after 2 hours illness, of an Apoplexy." Perhaps in part a result of these deaths, Mary and Elizabeth developed a close bond. Their connection is graphically represented in the intertwining of the handwritten "MES" that Elizabeth used in the late 1750s when she wrote of the two of them. Though Mary Sandwith had an income of her own, she lived in her sister's household all her life, helping with household management and child-rearing.

Both Elizabeth and Mary were in their early twenties and financially independent when they were orphaned, but they were single and expected by their community to board in a family household. They lived for fourteen months with the family of Quaker philanthropist Thomas Say, where they followed their father's mercantile predilections by developing a small business in trading feathers with Edward Stephens of Dublin, Ireland. Early diary entries that allude to time given to "looking over accounts" presumably refer to this venture. Elizabeth and Mary then moved into the home of Ann Warner on Front Street and lived there for nearly four years. It was in the Warner household, on 8 October 1758, that Elizabeth began her diary. The diary indicates that these were happy years filled with friends. Though her bent for solitude developed early, in 1759 Elizabeth recorded her delight in frequent visiting with uncharacteristic immodesty: "Eight Women Friends dinn'd at AWs which made 14 of the best sort, our selves included." She did not explain what constituted "the best sort," but the running account of her social circle suggests that economic class was a lifelong part of her definition.

Drinker's personal characteristics can only be inferred from oblique references in her papers and from the scant commentary of others. She seldom gave herself away directly. The diary reveals that she weighed 130 pounds in 1776 and that her hair was dark. An undated silhouette suggests a woman of fine features. Her obituary recalled that the young Drinker was possessed of "uncommon personal beauty." She disliked travel in her later years, prized her solitude, and was addicted to snuff. She was not a gossip. The rest is inference.

Almost from the beginning readers encounter the emotional reticence that marks the entire diary. Elizabeth noted cryptically the repeated visits of widower Henry Drinker (1734–1809): "H Drinker drank Tea with us"; "HD spent the Evening"; "HD call'd after Evening Meeting"; "Henry Several times." Yet only readers who know the outcome of the story would discern the evolving courtship. Though Elizabeth made several notations on 13 January 1761, she neglected to mention that this date was the day of their marriage.

Elizabeth and Henry Drinker moved into a comfortable home on Water Street. Mary Sandwith moved with them. Ten years and four children later, they moved to larger quarters at 110 North Front Street on the corner of Drinker's Alley. Their new home was a three-story brick mansion next door to the Warner household in which Elizabeth and Mary had lived earlier. It was Elizabeth's primary residence for the rest of her life, though for many years the Drinkers also maintained a summer home on nineteen acres at Frankford on the main road to New York. In the 1790s they summered on a nearby farm they named Clearfield.

The Drinkers had nine children, five of whom lived past infancy: Sarah (Sally), 1761–1807, who married Jacob Downing; Ann (Nancy), 1764–1830, who married John Skyrin; William (Billy), 1767–1821, who suffered from tuberculosis for much of his life and never married; Henry (HSD), 1770–1824, who married Hannah Smith; and Mary (Molly), 1774–1856, who married Samuel Rhoads Jr. Elizabeth Drinker's days were consumed by child rearing for many years, as the diary records in both words and silences. The years of many pregnancies and small children have more gaps and shorter entries than later years. Nearly 80 percent of the extant text was written after 1789, by which time her youngest surviving child was fifteen. In later years, as a grandmother looking back on these strenuous years, Drinker commented that she had "often thought that women who live to get over the time of Child-bareing . . . experience more comfort and satisfaction than at any other period of their lives."

Available evidence suggests that the Drinker marriage was a happy one. Their letters to one another were consistently warm, full of solicitude, advice, and the everyday detail that mark comfort and caring. Elizabeth wrote often of Henry's absences from home for business and of missing him. She remarked on his heavy work burden and his generosity, particularly to the community of Friends: Henry "is perpetualy and almost ever employed; the Affairs of Society and the public, and private, out of his own family, or his own concerns, I believe takes up ten twelfths of his time, if benevolence and beneficence will take a man to Heaven . . . HD. stands as good, indeed a better, chance than any I know off."

Both Elizabeth and Henry Drinker were practicing Quakers throughout their lives, but Henry took a more public role in Society activity. Elizabeth recorded their frequent attendance at meeting in her early years, though she went less often as she aged and finally not at all. Still, she filled her diary with notations of meetings formed, meetinghouses built, the Society's organizational and philanthropic business, veiled allusions to schisms among groups of Friends, Quaker publications, marriages, and funerals. She noted with some distress that her children

Front and back of a sewing pocket embroidered by Elizabeth Drinker in 1757
(Rye Historical Society, Rye, New York)

seemed less serious about Quaker practice than she and her husband. Some fairly extended commentaries concern her daughter Mary's elopement with Samuel Rhoads Jr., a marriage that took Mary outside her parents' faith for a time and occasioned a family estrangement. The Drinkers were eventually reconciled with their daughter, but the seriousness they attached to the incident is a measure of their commitment to the Society of Friends.

Another measure of that commitment is revealed in their firm opposition to slavery. Elizabeth Drinker noted Quaker abolitionist efforts in her diary, and on at least two occasions the Drinkers acted to assist runaway slaves. Since Pennsylvania was a free state bordered by three slave states, many slaves made their way to freedom in or through

Philadelphia. As Gary Nash has noted, the African American population of Philadelphia increased twelvefold between 1770 and 1810. Drinker found many occasions to note the resulting cultural changes: African American Quaker meetings, weddings, burial processions, freemasons, preachers, and mass arrivals. She knew at least one of the leaders of the Pennsylvania Society for Promoting the Abolition of Slavery, and she recorded her sympathy with black individuals searching for lost family members.

Some of the strength of Drinker's convictions might have been reinforced by a recollection of her own culpability. When their parents died in 1756, Elizabeth and Mary Sandwith sold a slave girl Elizabeth referred to as "Black Jude" and "Black Judey." Drinker recalled the episode at length twice in her diary, once in 1799 and again in 1807 shortly before her death. Regretting their decision within a few weeks of the sale, Elizabeth and Mary had offered Jude's new owner a 60 percent return on her investment in an attempt to buy Jude back. The new owner declined their offer. Some years later Henry Drinker attempted to buy Jude from another owner, who also refused to sell, though he left Jude free at his death. Elizabeth Drinker reported the "uneasy hours" she spent over selling Jude, though she protested that she and Mary had "nothing to accuse ourselve of as a crime at that time." Still, it is always worth noting what a diarist records more than once. Drinker's "uneasy hours" over Jude's fate apparently persisted all her life.

Henry Drinker was already a successful merchant in the shipping firm of James and Drinker when Elizabeth married him. Though Elizabeth claimed that she was "not acquainted with the extent of my husbands great variety of engagements," the diary belies her protestations of womanly disengagement. She recorded many of his ventures in trade, real estate, and manufacturing. Thomas M. Doerflinger has found that Henry's trading business prospered so much that he was able to retire from it at age forty-two and derive a substantial portion of his income from an investment in iron manufacturing. Of course, the decision to curtail commercial trading was also influenced by the increased risk brought on by the Revolutionary War. Henry chose to collect outstanding debts from as many of his customers as he could before the currency severely depreciated. Then he invested in farms and rental properties. With construction at a standstill in wartime Philadelphia and food becoming increasingly scarce, Henry's financial strategy at least partly protected his wealth.

For a time, however, it did not protect his freedom. Though both Elizabeth and Henry were closet Tories, they lived the Quaker peace testimony and tried to stay aloof from Revolutionary conflicts and issues. For a time they succeeded. Yet in September 1777 Henry and sixteen other Friends were arrested and deported to Winchester, Virginia, for refusing to sign a loyalty oath to the rebel government. A series of moving letters between Elizabeth and Henry mark this period of their lives, though the probability of censorship kept their exchanges focused on mundane matters.

The wives and friends of these exiled Quakers were writing more than letters. In March 1778 Molly Pleasants drafted a petition to Congress for their release. In April, despite her aversion to travel, Elizabeth Drinker joined Pleasants, Susan Jones, and Phoebe Pemberton on a journey to deliver the petition to George Washington at his headquarters in Valley Forge. Washington gave them a pass to Lancaster, Pennsylvania, where they presented their petition to Timothy Matlack, the secretary of the Pennsylvania Supreme Executive Council.

The difficulties of the trip are detailed in Drinker's diary: gently persuading Quaker minister Nicholas Waln that the women's petition would be more effective than his, convincing Quaker merchant Isaac Morris that he need not act on their behalf before Congress, accepting and revising Molly Pleasants's petition, arranging for child care in their absence, seeking out reliable transportation, braving bad roads and late nights, fording rivers, facing delays, and dealing with unreliable public officials who "appeard kind, but . . . tis from teeth outwards." Their effort was successful. Within two weeks Henry and the other prisoners had joined the women in Lancaster for the journey home to Philadelphia.

Though her husband's imprisonment must have been the most trying Revolutionary event for Elizabeth Drinker, it surely was not her only stress. Whether Philadelphia was under British or American control, looting and violence were pressing dangers. During the British occupation of 1777–1778, the army sought to quarter its officers in private residences, a circumstance Drinker resisted for months, pleading issues of propriety since her husband was away from home in exile. Finally she had no choice but to accept Major J. Cramond, his three servants, and assorted horses, cows, sheep, and turkeys. Cramond established himself in Drinker's front parlor for several months, a burden made even more strenuous by the demands of her several small children and the scarcity of servants. Drinker's household was reduced from five to one by September 1778. American control was no less threatening to Drinker. When the British occupation ended and the Revolutionary government reestablished control of the city, confiscation of property of those considered disloyal to the rebels became commonplace. The homes of acquaintances Grace Galloway and Rebecca Shoemaker were forfeited in 1778, when their husbands were accused of treason.

Throughout the war Drinker's account of military, judicial, and political Philadelphia remained remarkably evenhanded. Though her sympathies were clearly with the Tories, she recorded injustices and hardships aplenty on all sides: British house burnings and plundering of townspeople, Patriot persecutions and lynchings of prominent Quakers, the austerities of wartime inflation, and random acts and threats of violence. Given her sources—the view outside her window, newspaper accounts, and rumor—Drinker's account is inevitably partial. But the force of its directness and immediacy gives it a value unavailable to later accounts.

Some readers have charged Drinker with trivializing Revolutionary events and with ignoring the political turmoil that accompanied the war. The furor of the times seems eerily flattened by Drinker's matter-of-fact prose. News of neighbor Abraham Carlisle's death sentence is sandwiched between a notation about a wedding and a gathering of friends for tea. Rumors of independence take second billing to a sick child and a sleepless night. But such juxtapositions reflect the texture of events. The demands of everyday life do not give way to single-minded preoccupations except when survival is immediately at stake. Political debate did not preempt the needs of children and friends; rather it became one piece of a multifaceted life narrative.

Henry's commercial successes put Elizabeth in elite Philadelphia circles throughout her life. In Elizabeth's none-too-modest opinion, their visiting networks consisted of "the best sort." Despite some Quaker predisposition to plain style, their homes had the comforts available to eighteenth-century well-to-do families: several servants, furniture of walnut and mahogany; clothing of silk, velvet, and cashmere; jewelry; an orchard and garden; a chaise and a carriage; and even new innovations such as a bathtub and an outdoor shower. Yet, like other Quaker families, they opposed the display of art as a matter of conscience. Neither Elizabeth nor Henry ever sat for a portrait, and Elizabeth reported on 6 August 1796 that when "a Man called this Afternoon to know if HD. would subscribe for a portrait of David Rittenhouse [a professor of astronomy at the University of Pennsylvania and president of the American Philosophical Society], I told him that my husband . . . was one that did not deal in pictures."

These details of family, business, home, and community describe much about the material circumstances of Elizabeth Drinker's life, but they do not explain her fifty-year writing habit. In keeping with eighteenth-century attitudes about women's roles, Drinker thought of her diary and letters as occupations for her leisure time only. Yet readers can hardly avoid noticing that for most of her adult life she was careful to make sufficient leisure for writing. Mary Sandwith's choice to live with the Drinkers freed Elizabeth from some of the responsibilities of household management. Affluence meant many labor-intensive tasks were assigned to a staff of servants. Drinker's penchant for solitude, avoidance of travel, and reputation as an invalid all worked to furnish "leisure." A representative comment reveals much about how Drinker gave herself permission to write. On 7 July 1795, just three days after moving an entire household from Philadelphia to their summer home at Clearfield, she remarked that she "spent this Afternoon up stairs writing, as I have but little work here as yet." Though Drinker articulated a strong, gender-specific work ethic throughout her diary, she kept her "work" sufficiently at bay to write prolifically.

She also wrote carefully. Diaries and letters were not nearly the private affair they often are in the late twentieth century. Friends and family were well acquainted with Drinker's diary-writing routine. Though her work was not published during her lifetime, her writing was widely enough known to be mentioned in her obituary in *Poulson's American Daily Advertiser* (2 December 1807). Drinker knew her writing would be in circulation and that her diary might well be read aloud at social gatherings. She had entertained and informed herself with similar manuscript materials from others. Her diary includes frequent instances of friends' visits that feature the reading of journal-like letters from absent spouses and family members. Diaries and journals were routinely exchanged among friends. Drinker noted the evening Billy Compton dropped by and "read great part of Dr. Smith's Journal to us" and the gathering of women who heard Betsy Moode read aloud from "Sammy Sansoms Journal." She recalled giving an entire morning to reading the journal of close friend Hannah Callender.

As a woman in her sixties, Drinker wrote retrospectively of the many kinds of diaries she had read over the years: "I have seen Diarys of different complections, some were amuseing, other instructive, and others repleat with what might much better be totally let alone." Such reading must have shaped her writing ethic: record events, not judgments; cause no pain. While she knew her audience would be limited, it was real and immediate. It included the circle of family and friends who mattered most to her. It might have been this perception of audience that led Drinker to conceal her feelings, avoid moralizing, and pronounce few judgments except against Thomas Paine and François Rabelais, who seemed to her beyond redemption. Emotional outbursts such as her expression of grief at her daughter Sally's slow death from breast cancer in 1807 are rare. Drinker's diary does not lack eloquence, but it is the unintended eloquence of dailiness. The narrative moves by accretion, its impact an enactment of the *lacrimae rerum* human experience.

Drinker's writing ethic also shaped her choice of subject matter and cryptic notational style. She wrote of those she cared about and for, and she

1759
June 1st — Stay'd at home all Day. —

2 Went in ye Evening to A. Mitchell's, to see H. Hicks, whose Brother Josey dyed this Morning. —

3 First Day; Went to Meeting 3 times went after, afternoon Meeting to the Burial of Joseph Hicks. call'd after Evening Meeting at S: Sansom's. —

4 Stay'd at home all Day: Sar: Sansom &c. spent ye Afternoon at T:d Warner's a hard Thunder Gust in ye Evening, several Houses struck with ye Lightening; but no great damage done —

5 Went to Meeting in ye Morning. — Hannah Modde call'd in ye Afternoon, H D spent the Evening. — — — — —

6 spent ye afternoon at T. Say's. — came home with ye sick Head Ake, — a Thunder Gust in ye Night. —

7 call'd at T. Say's in ye Morning. — Took an Emmetic before Dinner. — rain with Thunder. — — —

Entries for 1–7 June 1759 and 30 March – 1 April 1760 in Drinker's diary (The Historical Society of Pennsylvania)

March y 30: 1760

First Day: went to meeting as usual,
had a silent meeting in y Morning —
in y afternoon, Mary Kirby appeard,
S Morris in Prayer, in y Evening, B—y
Jones and D Stanton — —— —

31.st

Stay'd within all Day: Hannah Moode,
and Sam.l Emlen jun.r call'd this Morning,
Polly went out with them, H Moode, came
back with sister, — Peggy Parr call'd
after Dinner, stay'd but a little while,
she came to Town this Morning in y Boat.

April y 1:

Went to meeting this Morn.g M Kirby, and
Mor.i Yarnal, appeard in testimony, Sam.e
Emlen, and Mary Kir.y in Prayer, — spent
this afternoon with sister at Isaac Parrishs,
d M, there, H Hicks came after Tea to I P's,
she had been to our House to bid us Adieu,
intending for home tomorrow, took a
walk towards Evening with Hannah,
call'd after we parted from her, at Coll:
Whites, whoes spouse, is ill of y Head
Ake, — Peggy Parr, and H Ward, was
at our House, while we were out. —

wrote what seemed useful. She had little time for sentimental homilies and pieties. She lived in a material world about which she showed considerable curiosity, and she sought to record the natural and cultural events, discoveries, and innovations that impacted her experience. On any given day the activities of a legislature would compete for notice with the apricot tree blooming in her garden or the elephant on display in the market. Perhaps a measure of Drinker's recognition of the importance of health to all human activity, her diary is long on explicit descriptions of disease and medical treatments. She observed contemporary medical practice; knew the most prominent physicians in Philadelphia; learned herbal remedies; made tinctures, salves, poultices, and ointments; attended childbirths; and recorded symptoms, treatments, medical controversies, and epidemics in such detail that some have labeled her a hypochondriac.

Drinker's diary also includes copious records of the visits and activities of friends, neighbors, and family. She observed; she made note; but she seldom commented on the behaviors she described. As she explained on 31 December 1799 in her habitual "year-in-review" meditation, she had no desire "to write or record any thing that might in a future day give pain to any one," and most especially to "The Children or the Childrens Children of the present day." Drinker was always conscious of the public nature of her discourse, both for her contemporaries and for their descendants. Unlike William Byrd a century earlier, she kept no secret diary. Her reticence was chronic and deliberate:

> Could I write, instead of Trifles;
> That which most employs my mind:
> All thats here would be ommitted,
> Nor should I mark, how blew the wind?

Apparently unimpressed by the tabloid style of some eighteenth-century newspapers or by the disclosures of other diarists, Drinker did turn to the wind and the weather—and much, much more. If Drinker was clear about the materials she would not write about, she also detailed what readers could expect.

> I stay much at home, and my business I mind,
> Take note of the weather, and how blows the wind,
> The changes of Seasons, The Sun, Moon and Stars,
> The Setting of Venus, and riseing of Mars.
> Birds, Beasts and Insects, and more I cold mention,
> That pleases my leisure, and draws my attention.
> But respecting my Neighbours, their egress, and Regress,
> Their Coaches and Horses, their dress and their Address,
> What matches are making, whos plain, or Whos gay,
> I leave to their parents, or Guardians to Say:
> For most of those things, are out of my *Way*.

> But to those, where my love and my duty doth bind
> More than most other Subjects, engages my Mind.

—and I am not ashamed to own it.

Drinker's main business was family, of course, but family as it interacted with natural and cultural surroundings. As a consequence, the diary provides a richly textured social history and narrative in the cadences of a consciously chosen Quaker plainstyle: "prose in plain terms is better than ambiguous verse."

At least once Drinker tried to curb her pen, give up her narrative in favor of making the diary simply "a memorandum book." She announced her intention to discontinue the diary on 1 January 1799, "but seeing a fine snow falling this morning and being used to make observations on the weather," she kept on writing. At year's end, some 135 printed pages later, she remembered her New Year's resolution and blamed "the habit of scribling some thing every night" for leading her on. She justified her lapse from the self-imposed discipline of the memorandum book by reminding herself that the diary "answers no other purpose than to help the memory." Apparently she wanted to remember a great deal—moonlight, Henry's business dealings, garden foliage, walking with friends, reading, political news, complex interactions with servants, a grandson's upset stomach, runaway slaves who found their way to her door, a midnight fire alarm, a world passing by out her window. The writing habit was too ingrained to be overcome by anything so slight as a New Year's resolution.

Attentive readers may trace a variety of genres through Drinker's narrative: multigenerational family chronicle, political account, urban record, social register, health report, book review, nature writing, and local color. She became a master of the anecdote. Perhaps most surprising in so self-declared a homebody, Drinker included detailed travel narratives. She probably never traveled more than 125 miles from Philadelphia in her life, but some of the most colorful episodes in her diary and letters occur during her infrequent excursions.

A heightened attention to detail might be inherent in travel accounts since one effect of a trip is to remove the writer from habitual routines and places that have become almost invisible by familiarity. Travel can create fresh eyes, a different kind of seeing. Even in Elizabeth's younger and most cryptic days, her excursions and daytrips, with groups of friends or with Henry, elicited her most extended commentary: the logistics of travel, the destinations, walking in meadows near Philadelphia, spending idle moments at a beach on Long Island or on the banks of the Susquehanna, visiting a Native American family's wigwam, watching fireflies, playing a trick on a landlady who refused to change dirty sheets, shopping, checking on the site of a recent fire, stopping at a bookseller's, and taking tea with friends.

In later years, after repeated encounters with drunken carriage drivers, an accident, and more bad roads than she could easily count, Drinker became reluctant to travel. Even the trip to Lancaster in an attempt to free Henry during the Revolutionary War was undertaken with obvious hesitation. Only so extreme a circumstance as son William's dangerous relapse with tuberculosis convinced her to travel to New York in 1791. Drinker recorded her weeks in New York during William's recuperation in often daily letters to Henry rather than in her diary. These frequent letters were intended to keep Henry posted on William's condition, but they also measure the extent of Drinker's homesickness. As much as she had to say about her travels over the years, she grew to be a woman who enjoyed staying put.

Staying home allowed Drinker more time to pursue her passion for reading. Her detailed reading (and rereading) lists add an important document to studies of the history of the book. She had the means to frequent booksellers' establishments and the Library Company of Philadelphia. Many of her friends were educated to be readers themselves and had the habit of loaning their books and papers. Though the diary does not suggest that Drinker saw herself as building a personal library, it does reveal a woman who sought to engage the best minds that books could offer.

Drinker's tastes ran to the contemporary, but her reading practice seems to have been guided by three maxims: read much, read often, and read widely. She enjoyed variety and seldom read books in the same genre consecutively. A history was followed by a play, a medical tract by a volume of poetry, a Gothic novel by theology or natural history. While that might be a function of how books came to hand, it might also suggest something of Drinker's self-conscious choice to read expansively.

Drinker's literary tastes blurred boundaries between elite and popular culture. If she indulged in Gothic novels—Maria Edgeworth's *Castle Rackrent* (1800), Charles Brockden Brown's *Arthur Mervyn* (1799, 1800) and *Edgar Huntly* (1799), Horace Walpole's *The Castle of Otranto* (1764)—she also read John Milton, Alexander Pope, and Samuel Taylor Coleridge. She listed among her readings and occasionally comments on Plutarch, Pliny, Dante, John Bunyan, Daniel Defoe, Francis Bacon, Voltaire, François de Salignac de La Monte-Fénelon, Lady Mary Wortley Montagu, Samuel Johnson, Elizabeth Rowe, Mary Pilkington, Philip Freneau, Elizabeth Chudleigh, Henry Fielding, Hannah Foster, Samuel Richardson, Ann Radcliffe, Benjamin Franklin, and many more. Drinker identified Oliver Goldsmith as "one of my favourite authors," found that the more times she read Bunyan's *Pilgrim's Progress* (1678) "the better I like it," and thought William Wordsworth's *Lyrical Ballads* (1798) "Pretty enough Tho rather simple." She panned Jean-Jacques Rousseau's *Confessions* (1781, 1788) but thought Maria Edgeworth's volumes for young people were "pretty Stories."

As these cryptic pronouncements might suggest, Drinker became a master at thumbnail reviews. She wrote off the autobiographical *Life, Adventures, and Opinions of Col. George Hanger* (1801) as "a despicable work . . . very proper to light a fire with" and called *A Short Story Interspersed with Poetry* (1800) "By a young Lady" "a dismal ditty." A great many titles were listed without comment, others offhandedly noted as "mid'ling." Still others were praised as "very sutable," "tolerably good," "Excellent," "shocking," "a useful work," or "a Book worth reading with attention."

Drinker seldom explained her ratings, except in the most negative instances. She was embarrassed to have checked out Rabelais's works from the Library Company because she "found them filled with such obscene dirty matter." Often she let her judgments of literary merit rest on the character of the author rather than the text. Rousseau might be "a flowery writer," but he was "a man of bad principles." Laurence Sterne's works might convey "some good sentiments," but much of his writing was "very unfit for the pen of a Reverand Divine." Mary Wollstonecraft is mentioned several times, and Drinker admitted that she thinks her "a prodigious fine writer—and should be charmed by some of her peices, if I had never heard her Character."

It might be significant that Drinker turned so often to other women writers. A quick count of authors read in a randomly chosen year, 1803, reveals that nearly 40 percent of the writers listed are female. Perhaps Drinker found tacit permission for her love of books and writing from them. She often picked up books with titles such as *Sketches of the History, Genius, Disposition, Accomplishments, Employments, Customs and Importance of the Fair Sex* (1796), which speak to women's talents and abilities. When she first read Wollstonecraft's *Vindication of the Rights of Woman* (1792) in 1796, she commented that "in very many of her sentiments, she . . . *speaks my mind*," though she went on to add that she was "not for quite so much independance."

March 7. hazey morn: sunshine after, wind S.W — James Embree dined here — this evening my husband was abroad, he is bravely, William was also out, they both brough word of a fire that was cry'd about 8 o'clock, it was at the corner of Laticia Court in market Street, at an apothacarys of y name of Harris, it appeared to be a great fire, but we know not what damage was sustain'd — Will.m was at J Downings, dear Sally is very poorly — Anthony Woodward, our Peters father is dead, his wife was here this morning to ask for a Shirt to lay him out in, she said he died of a cramp in his stomach, poor old Anthony! I believe he was a sufferer in some respects — Nancy Skyrin was here this forenoon, she appears middling — a clear star light night. —

8. First Day: cloudy all day, rain at times. — wind N. E — H.D. went to morn: and even: meetings. James Embree and his daughter Phebe dined here. she came to town under some expectation of being employ'd as a School mistress, but another had stepd in the place — prices: daughter came with y bottle for liquid ladunum for poor friend Swett, she had very little sleep last night, her face very painful to day — I have heard nothing from any of my children this day — J.K. held his last meeting on sixth day even: and went home yesterday — cloudy

9. rain this morn: and again hard rain in the afternoon, wind N. E — moon chang'd this morning. W.D. went to J.D.; where was T. Thomas Phebe Downing — Eliza and Mary, J. and S. and a near

Drinker gave much of her attention to belles lettres, but literature was not her only interest. She read history, especially histories of Pennsylvania and the surrounding region. She sampled conduct manuals, medical tracts, lectures on health issues, and children's books. She pursued various versions of Scripture, followed current Quaker publications, and turned often to natural history, especially studies of the animal kingdom. She read lengthy theological studies, sought out biographies of writers whose work she had admired, and followed various accounts of the French Revolution.

As a woman in her sixties and seventies, Drinker increasingly chose to reread books she had known from her earlier years. As she put down a volume of Elizabeth Rowe's letters, for example, she remarked that many of her re-encounters were new reading experiences. Though Rowe "shows a lively imagination" and writes a "Flowery" language, Drinker did not "feel just as I did upwards of 50 years ago, when I first read the above in company with my dear friend E. Moode." Still, Drinker seemed drawn to rereading, sometimes obtaining whole volumes of old periodicals: *The Edinburgh Magazine, The Philadelphia Repository and Weekly Register,* even *The Tatler* and *The Spectator.*

Like many readers in a time when books were hard to come by and expensive to own, Drinker often wrote "extracts"—verbatim transcripts—of passages that were particularly meaningful to her. Schoolchildren learned to write by copying passages and poems, and the habit often persisted beyond the years of formal schooling. Drinker was so taken with the first volume of Thomas Stackhouse's *New History of the Bible* (1733), for example, that she "filled about 7 sheets of Large post paper, with extracts from it." At this rate, she exclaimed, she might never get to the second volume. As commonplace as writing extracts was in the eighteenth century, the extent to which Drinker embraced the practice was a mark of the seriousness of her reading. She read for amusement and inspiration, but she also turned her reading into disciplined lifelong learning.

Such application to study was often filled with cultural conflict for Drinker. Her conservative ideas of women's roles contradicted her intellectual habits. Throughout her diary she apologized for reading so much, as if it were a sign of indolence. She explained on 22 May 1795, for example, that she has never been "remarkably Bookish," but since the comment comes after a thumbnail review of a two-volume biography and a volume of memoirs she had recently finished, her protest may not have convinced even herself. She seems to have felt especially guilty about the attention she gave to novels

and romances. On 7 January 1796 she made one of her frequent attempts to excuse herself: "It may appear strange to some that an infirm old woman should begin the year reading romances—'tis a practice I by no means highly approve, yet I trust I have not sined—As I read a little of most things." Occasionally Drinker bracketed her comments on reading with lists of tasks accomplished—knitting stockings, binding a petticoat, making gingerbread. She explained that she made her list to "shew, that I have not spent the day reading." Guilty or not, Drinker read voraciously. Though such reading practice may have been common among educated eighteenth-century Americans, few were given to documenting their habit in such detail.

Elizabeth Drinker would not have thought of herself as a "writer" in the late-twentieth-century professional and creative uses of that label. She was a member of an eighteenth-century community that thought of authorship, at least in part, as a social activity. Like many of her friends, Drinker wrote for her intimate circle as a way of maintaining family and community ties. Her narrative became a kind of collective memory for well-to-do Philadelphia Quakers, recording lives and times with the immediacy and detail only an insider could provide. It functions differently now, having entered print culture and reaching a larger and more diverse group of readers than it did nearly two hundred years ago. Present-day readers come to the text with different purposes, and they require editorial annotations that Drinker's intended audience did not need. Modern readers find themselves immersed in the dailiness of another world, caught up in family dramas and community affairs. Drinker's careful account provides literary access to a culture about which too little is known.

References:

S. Carol Berg, "Elizabeth S. Drinker, Quaker Wife and Mother: Observations from her Diary, 1758–1807," *Valley Forge Journal,* 4 (1989): 333–339;

Carol Berkin, *First Generations: Women in Colonial America* (New York: Hill & Wang, 1996);

Carl Bridenbaugh and Jessica Bridenbaugh, *Rebels and Gentlemen: Philadelphia in the Age of Franklin* (New York: Reynal & Hitchcock, 1942);

Elaine Forman Crane, "Gender Consciousness in Editing: The Diary of Elizabeth Drinker," *Text: Transactions of the Society for Textual Scholarship,* 4 (1988): 375–383;

Crane, "The World of Elizabeth Drinker," *Pennsylvania Magazine of History and Biography,* 107 (1983): 3–28;

Margo Culley, ed., *A Day at a Time: The Diary Literature of American Women from 1764 to the Present* (New York: Feminist Press, 1985);

Cathy N. Davidson, *Revolution and the Word: The Rise of the Novel in America* (New York: Oxford University Press, 1986);

Thomas M. Doerflinger, *A Vigorous Spirit of Enterprise: Merchants and Economic Development in Revolutionary Philadelphia* (Chapel Hill: University of North Carolina Press for the Institute of Early American History and Culture, 1986);

Cecil Drinker, *Not So Long Ago: A Chronicle of Medicine and Doctors in Colonial Philadelphia* (New York: Oxford University Press, 1937);

Henry Sandwith Drinker, *History of the Drinker Family* (Merion, Pa.?, 1961);

Elizabeth Evans, *Weathering the Storm: Women of the American Revolution* (New York: Scribners, 1975), pp. 152–184;

Catherine Goetz, "A Woman of the 'Best Sort': The Diary of Elizabeth Drinker," in *Life in Early Philadelphia: Documents from the Revolutionary and Early National Periods,* edited by Billy G. Smith (University Park: Pennsylvania State University Press, 1995), pp. 131–154;

Linda K. Kerber, *Women of the Republic: Intellect and Ideology in Revolutionary America* (Chapel Hill: University of North Carolina Press for the Institute of Early American History and Culture, 1980);

Mrs. Wilmer Krusen, "Elizabeth Drinker," in *Notable Women of Pennsylvania,* edited by Gertrude Bosler Biddle and Sarah Dickinson Lowrie (Philadelphia: University of Pennsylvania Press, 1942), pp. 58–59;

Gary Nash, "Forging Freedom: The Emancipation Experience in Northern Seaport Cities, 1775–1820," in *Slavery and Freedom in the Age of the American Revolution,* edited by Ira Berlin and Ronald Hoffman (Charlottesville: University Press of Virginia for the United States Capitol Historical Society, 1983), pp. 4–12;

Mary Beth Norton, *Liberty's Daughters: The Revolutionary Experience of American Women, 1750–1800* (Boston: Little, Brown, 1980);

Anne Firor Scott, "Self-Portraits: Three Women," in *Uprooted Americans: Essays to Honor Oscar Handlin,* edited by Richard L. Bushman and others (Boston: Little, Brown, 1979), pp. 43–76;

Carole Shammas, "The Female Social Structure of Philadelphia in 1775," *Pennsylvania Magazine of History and Biography,* 107 (1983): 69–84;

Jean R. Soderlund, "Women in Eighteenth-Century Pennsylvania: Toward a Model of Diversity," *Pennsylvania Magazine of History and Biography,* 115 (April 1991): 163–183;

Peter Thompson, "A Social History of Philadelphia's Taverns, 1683–1800," dissertation, University of Pennsylvania, 1989;

Frederick B. Tolles, *Meeting House and Counting House: The Quaker Merchants of Colonial Philadelphia, 1682–1763* (Chapel Hill: University of North Carolina Press for the Institute of Early American History and Culture, 1948).

Papers:
Drinker's diary, letters, and papers are at the Historical Society of Pennsylvania in Philadelphia. Letters exchanged between Elizabeth and Henry Drinker when he was a prisoner of war in 1777–1778 are in the Haverford College Library.

Hannah Duston
(23 December 1657 – 1737)

James A. Levernier
University of Arkansas at Little Rock

WORK: "A Narrative of a Notable Deliverance Lately Received by Some English Captives, From the Hands of Cruel Indians, and Some *Improvement* of that *Narrative,*" in *Humiliations Follow'd by Deliverances,* by Cotton Mather (Boston: Printed by B. Green & J. Allen for Samuel Phillips, 1697).

Of the many hundred individuals of European descent whose stories of captivity among the native peoples of North America were written and published during the seventeenth through the late nineteenth centuries, Hannah Emerson Duston (also spelled Dustin or Dustan) is undoubtedly the most notorious and the most controversial. First published in 1697 with Cotton Mather's fast-day sermon *Humiliations Follow'd by Deliverances* as an example of "a Notable Deliverance from Captivity" and later republished by Mather with minor alterations in his *Decennium Luctuosum* (1699) and his *Magnalia Christi Americana* (1702), the story of Hannah Duston's captivity among the Abenaki Indians of New England and her subsequent murder and scalping of ten of her Indian captors, including several children, has fascinated generations of readers. It has also provoked a variety of responses, ranging from her near canonization as an early American saint to her condemnation as a ruthless killer of the innocent.

In addition to the attention it has drawn to the personality and actions of Hannah Duston herself, Duston's narrative provides insight into the handling, editorializing, and publishing of narratives by colonial American women, whose written voices were often suppressed and almost always controlled by male editors, even when they told stories of communal import, such as narratives of captivity among Indians. Always eager to publish narratives of personal experiences that they felt illustrated the workings of divine providence, early American Puritans collected and distributed dozens of stories about Indian captivity. Many of them concerned women, whose ordeals were often seen as divine chastisement and a warning to the community and whose

returns to their families and friends were considered an act of divine providence on behalf of themselves and their church. Yet Puritan women, who were encouraged to read and write, were generally not encouraged to publish their writings.

In early New England the publication of lengthy prose narratives was considered the prerogative of men, not of women. Only in instances where there were obvious lessons of benefit to the community were women allowed to publish narratives about their lives and then only under the careful scrutiny and editorial control of men who were usually clerics. Such, for example, was the case with Mary Rowlandson, whose captivity in the 1670s among the Indians of New England prompted the 1682 publication of the most famous Puritan captivity narrative, *The Soveraignty & Goodness of God, together, with the Faithfulness of His Promises Displayed.* This tremendously popular book was published with an introductory statement attributed to Increase Mather, who endorsed the narrative and pointed out lessons to be learned from her experiences, and it was printed with the last sermon delivered by her husband, Joseph Rowlandson, before his death. Only by framing the narrative within the safe confines of male authority was Rowlandson's story considered conventional and safe enough for publication.

The eldest of the fifteen children of Michael Emerson and Hannah Webster Emerson, Hannah Duston was born in Haverhill, Massachusetts, on 23 December 1657. According to a testimonial that she submitted in 1724 for full admission into the church at Haverhill, Duston received "a Good Education by My Father." This testimonial offers little other biographical information. On 3 December 1677 Hannah Emerson married Thomas Duston. Originally from Kittery in Maine, he had been living in Haverhill since June 1665, when his widowed mother, Elizabeth Duston, married Matthias Button and moved to her new husband's home in Massachusetts. During the years following their marriage, Hannah and Thomas Duston became prosperous

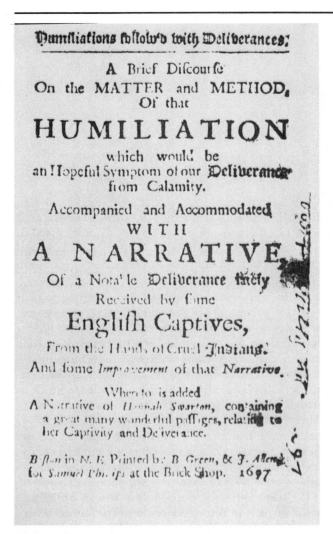

Title page for the book by Cotton Mather that includes Hannah Duston's account of her captivity and escape from Indians in spring 1697

members of the community. The family's landholdings were extensive, and Thomas Duston gained respect as a farmer, bricklayer, property owner, rising public official, and veteran Indian fighter. In 1676 during Metacom's War (also known as King Philip's War), he served as a soldier in the colonial militia.

At the time of her capture on 15 March 1697, Hannah Duston had given birth to twelve children, nine of whom were living. She was recuperating from the birth six days earlier of a daughter named Martha. Resting in an upstairs bedroom, Duston was captured along with her infant and a fifty-year-old nurse-midwife named Mary Corliss Neff, whose husband had died fighting Indians during King Philip's War. Duston's captors consisted of approximately twenty French and Indian soldiers. During the attack on Haverhill, nine houses were burned, twenty-seven inhabitants (including thirteen chil-

dren) were killed, and thirteen other colonists were taken away as captives. According to the historical record, Thomas Duston had left on horseback for a distant part of his farm when he saw the Indians heading toward his house. Gathering together his children, ranging in age from three to eighteen, Duston ordered them to flee. He is then thought to have tried to rescue his wife and baby but at her urging he left them so that he could protect their fleeing children. With his horse and rifle between himself, his children, and his assailants, Duston managed to lead the group to the safety of the garrison house of Onesiphorus Marsh, nearly a mile away. When he later returned to the farm, Duston found his infant dead, his house in flames, and his wife and her nurse gone. Duston's narrative states that the Indians had murdered the baby by knocking its head against a tree because the newborn could not be quieted. Whether or not the Indians actually killed the Duston infant is a matter of dispute. The killing of infants is a common motif in many captivity narratives and was also a common propaganda device used by Western writers to vilify their enemies. Possibly the Indians left the child in the snow near the Duston homestead because the crying of a baby was a danger to their collective safety. When the colonials found the dead infant, they may have embellished the means of its demise. It should also be noted, especially in the light of events that were to follow, that captured women were sometimes known to have accidentally smothered their own children in an attempt to quiet them.

Like Eunice Williams, Hannah Swarton, and many other New England captives of her day, Hannah Duston was apparently destined to march through the snow to Canada, where she would be sold into servitude. In the custody of an Indian family that included two men, three women, seven children, and an English boy known as Samuel Lennardson (probably Samuel Leonard's son), who in 1695 had been kidnapped from Worcester, Duston had been with the Indians for more than two weeks when, on 30 March, she made her escape. Told that when she arrived a few days later in an Indian town she would be stripped naked and tortured, Duston waited until her captors fell asleep, and then, with the assistance of Neff and Lennardson, she bludgeoned to death all but two Indians, who somehow managed an escape. In a deposition recorded in 1739 by another captive, "above penny cook the Deponent was forced to travel farther than the rest of the captives, and the next night but one there came to us one Squaw who said that Hannah Dustan and the aforesaid Mary Neff assisted in killing the Indians of her wigwam except herself and a boy, herself

The conversion narrative Duston submitted for admission to the Haverhill, Massachusetts, church in 1724 (Haverhill Historical Society, Haverhill, Massachusetts)

escaping very narrowly, shewing to myself & others seven wounds as she said with a Hatched on her head which wounds were given her when the rest were killed." Among those whom Duston had killed was a man named Bampico and another who had been in the employ of Mary Rowlandson of Lancaster before her capture by the Narragansetts in 1676. This man had later joined with the French and converted to Catholicism.

The scene of this massacre was a four-acre island north of Concord, New Hampshire, where the Contoocook meets the Merrimack River. After repairing a damaged canoe, Duston, Neff, and Lennardson had begun their journey home when Duston, remembering that the General Court of Massachusetts had offered a substantial bounty for Indian scalps and fearing that no one would believe her story without tangible evidence, returned to the island and scalped the bodies of her victims. After a reunion with her husband, Hannah Duston and the others went to Boston, only to discover that the bounty on scalps had expired the previous December. Petitioning the court for an extension of the bounty, Thomas Duston became the recipient of a 16 June resolution by the court "for allowing fifty pounds to Thomas Dustun in behalf of his wife Hannah, and to Mary Neff, and Samuel Lennardson, captives escaped from the Indians, for their service

in slaying their captors." In addition, the court allegedly gave Hannah Duston an engraved pewter tankard for her "services" to the community, and Gov. Francis Nicholson of Maryland is said to have sent her an expensive set of plate.

In October of the year following her captivity, Duston gave birth to her thirteenth child, a daughter named Lydia. In later life Hannah Duston again petitioned the court, this time for a pension that she eventually received. Duston died sometime in the early months of 1737, outliving her captivity by nearly forty years and her husband by four years. In her 1724 testimonial for admission to the church at Haverhill, Duston had this to say about her experiences among the Indians: "I am Thankful for my Captivity, twas the Comfortablest time that ever I had." After her captivity Mary Neff returned to Haverhill, where she lived with her son until her death on 22 October 1722. Samuel Lennardson was eventually reunited with his family, refusing throughout the rest of his life to speak about his experiences as a captive.

During the years since Duston's captivity, her reputation has undergone vast swings in public opinion. On her arrival home she was celebrated as a heroine. She even drew the attention of such notables as Samuel Sewall, whose diary for 12 May 1697 records that "Hannah Dustan came to see us." During the late eighteenth and early nineteenth centuries, however, writers such as Timothy Dwight, John Greenleaf Whittier, Henry David Thoreau, and Nathaniel Hawthorne, among others, began to question the morality of Duston's actions, and she came to be seen more as a villain than as an example of heroism and courage. In Hawthorne's words, "Would that the bloody old hag had been drowned in crossing Contocook river, or that she had sunk over head and ears in a swamp, and been there buried, till summoned forth to confront her victims at the Day of Judgment; or that she had gone astray and been starved to death in the forest, and nothing ever seen of her again, save her skeleton, with the ten scalps twisted round it for a girdle!"

Nonetheless, in yet another display of admiration, members of the American public rallied to her defense, and in 1861 Duston became the first American woman to have a statue erected in her honor. Still other such memorials followed. In 1874 a statue of Duston, with inscriptions reading "Heroum Gesta Fides–Justicia" (Faith Achíeved the Heroic–Justice) and "The War-whoop–Tomahawk–Fagot and Infanticides were at Haverhill, The Ashes of the Campfires at Night And Ten of the Tribe Are Here," was placed on the island where she massacred her captors. The dedication ceremony was attended by some five thousand spectators. Not to be outdone by its New Hampshire neighbors, Haverhill erected a similar statue in one of its town squares. This statue, like the one in New Hampshire, still stands, and around its base are four bronze panels valorizing the exploits of its subject.

In addition to the mythic implications of Duston's actions, her captivity is of primary interest to literary historians of American women writers because of the method of its transcription. Like the stories of many, if not all, Indian captivity narratives about women, the Duston narrative was processed through the filter of a male editor and member of the clergy, who took pains to guarantee that it be properly interpreted as a means of supporting the Puritan patriarchy. While it was once thought that Cotton Mather might have received the narrative from Duston's minister at Haverhill, the text is so replete with Mather's own moralizings that it seems almost certain that he transcribed the story from Duston, who, along with Neff and Lennardson, was in the audience when the sermon was delivered. Quotation marks at the beginning and end of the text indicate that the original text most likely belonged to Duston. The challenge to the reader, as Lorrayne Carroll has so carefully shown, is the disentangling of the two voices, Duston's and Mather's.

According to Carroll, Mather, perceiving the immediate threat to Puritan patriarchy that Duston's assault on her Indian captors represented, wished to make sure that God and the community, not Duston herself, were given full credit and central focus in the telling and interpreting of the narrative. He therefore took the narrative from Duston and, by retelling the story in the third person within quotation marks, forced her into the position of a passive listener of her own narrative, rather than an active participant in its recounting. He concluded the text with an afterword that exhorted Duston against taking pride in her release and thinking that as a woman she was somehow singled out for special favor by God because of her life prior to her captivity and her actions during it. "The *Use*" that Duston and the others should make of her captivity, Mather stated, "is, To *Humble* your selves before the Lord Exceedingly." "When you were Carried into *Captivity*," continued Mather, "We did not say, *That you were greater Sinners, than the rest that yet Escape it.* You are now Rescued from *Captivity,* and must not think, *That they are greater Sinners, who are Left behind in the most barbarous Hands imaginable*." "You are not now," enjoined Mather, "the Slaves of *Indians,* as you were a few dayes ago; but if you continue *Unhumbled,* In your Sins, you will be the Slaves of *Devils;* and, Let me tell you, A Slavery to *Devils,* to be in *Their* Hands, is worse than to be in the Hands of *Indians!*"

As Carroll and other commentators on the captivity-narrative tradition have pointed out, Duston was but one of many women captives whose voices were either suppressed, redirected, or edited so as to make their experiences—and not their skills as survivors and writers—the major interest of the text. While male captives such as John Williams were given free reign to write, interpret, and advance themselves through the telling of their narratives, women captives such as Mary Rowlandson and Hannah Duston were scrutinized so as to control the imaginative potential of their stories for equalizing the status of women and men within Puritan society. Thus, even though women often wrote captivity narratives about their own experiences, the New England clerical establishment maintained strict editorial control over how those stories could be published and told.

Laurel Thatcher Ulrich's recent discovery of dramatically significant biographical information about Hannah Duston and her family perhaps explains another reason why Mather went to such lengths to control the voice of the captive whose story he singled out for public attention. Only a few years before Mather told the story of Hannah Duston to the members of his Boston congregation, he had preached a sermon that included the narrative

*Statue of Duston on Contoocook Island, where she killed and scalped her captors. Erected in 1861, it is
the first monument honoring an American woman.*

of the activities of another member of Duston's family. On 22 September 1691 Elizabeth Emerson, the younger sister of Hannah Duston, was found guilty of having murdered the illegitimate twins she had secretly given birth to earlier that year. Then on 8 June 1693, after listening to Mather sermonize in church about her sinfulness, she was led to the gallows in Boston and executed. Mary Neff, who was captured along with Hannah Duston, had been among the Haverhill midwives who had discovered the murder of the Emerson infants. The father of the deceased children went undiscovered, but life in the Emerson household was apparently never peaceful. In 1676, for instance, Hannah Duston's father, Michael Emerson, was convicted in court for the "cruel and excessive beating" of his daughter Elizabeth. Such convictions and accusations were rare in the records of Puritan New England, but, according to another account, Michael Emerson was apparently known to the community for having a rather harsh disposition. His early neighbors in

Haverhill are said to have feared his temper and to have offered him a large tract of land if he would leave the town and "go back into the woods."

The possibility of additional abuse directed toward the daughters in the Emerson household, which might have established in them a susceptibility to fear, anger, and violence, will probably never be known. Certainly, however, a good deal could be inferred from Duston's 1724 conversion testimonial that she "had a Good Education by My Father, tho' I took but little Notice of it in the time of it" and that, although she long "had a great Desire to come to the Ordinance of the Lord's supper," she had not come forward for "fear" of giving "offence" and of her "own Unworthiness." No matter how the implications of the actions of the Emerson sisters are construed, both women were, in various ways at various times, as much victims as they were victimizers, especially in the way their life stories were interpreted and transmitted. It has even been suggested that Hannah Duston might have recognized a special bond with her sister, for after naming her first child Hannah (probably after her mother, Hannah Emerson), Hannah Duston named her second child Elizabeth. Although Duston went on to bear many more children, none were named after her father. Aware that scandal had previously shaken the Emerson-Duston families and equally aware of the irony that while one sister had been demonized and executed for the killing of children the other sister was singled out as a heroine for what could objectively be considered the same actions, Mather took control of the telling and transmission of the Duston captivity narrative, merging her story into his story, as was the case with the histories of many, if not all, of the early American captivity stories about women.

Of the many hundreds of Indian captivity narratives written and published from colonial times to the end of the nineteenth century, the story of Hannah Duston's captivity and escape is probably the most intriguing from the perspectives of scholarship and popular culture. Violent and dramatic, the Duston narrative provokes moral speculation about issues such as civilian involvement in war, Puritan concepts of providence, the role of women in early America, racism and genocide, and changing American attitudes toward heroism and gender. Nonetheless, perhaps because of its inherent controversies, the Duston narrative, like many other captivity narratives, traditionally has been assigned to the margins of the literary canon. Only as such narratives are given the scholarly attention they merit and are analyzed for their literary value as well as their historical and cultural significance are they beginning to take their rightful place in American literary history.

References:

Robert D. Arner, "The Story of Hannah Duston: Cotton Mather to Thoreau," *American Transcendental Quarterly,* no. 18 (1973): 19–23;

Albert T. Bartlett, "The Story of Hannah Duston and Mary Neff," *Daughters of the American Revolution Magazine* (1971): 806–809;

Lorrayne Carroll, "'My Outward Man': The Curious Case of Hannah Swarton," *Early American Literature,* 31 (1996): 45–73;

Kathryn Zabelle Derounian-Stodola and James Arthur Levernier, *The Indian Captivity Narrative, 1550–1900* (New York: Twayne, 1993);

Leslie Fiedler, *The Return of the Vanishing American* (New York: Stein & Day, 1968);

Tara Fitzpatrick, "The Figure of Captivity: The Cultural Work of the Puritan Captivity Narrative," *American Literary History,* 3 (1991): 1–26;

James Levernier and Hennig Cohen, eds., *The Indians and Their Captives* (Westport, Conn.: Greenwood Press, 1977);

Richard Slotkin, *Regeneration Through Violence* (Middletown, Conn.: Wesleyan University Press, 1973);

Laurel Thatcher Ulrich, *Good Wives: Image and Reality in the Lives of Women in Northern New England, 1650–1750* (New York: Knopf, 1982);

Alden T. Vaughan and Edward W. Clark, eds., *Puritans among the Indians: Accounts of Captivity and Redemption, 1676–1724* (Cambridge: Harvard University Press, 1981);

Kathryn Whitford, "Hannah Dustin: The Judgement of History," *Essex Institute Historical Collections,* 108 (1972): 304–325.

Papers:

The manuscript for Duston's conversion narrative, dated 1724, is in the collections of the Haverhill Historical Society, Haverhill, Massachusetts.

Sarah Pierpont Edwards

(9 January 1710 – October 1758)

Donald R. Reese
University of New Mexico

WORK: Conversion relation, in *The Life of President Edwards,* by Sereno E. Dwight, volume 1 of *The Works of President Edwards,* 10 volumes, edited by Dwight (New York: Converse, 1829–1830).

Sarah Pierpont Edwards was a religious mystic and the wife of Jonathan Edwards, one of the leading American evangelists of the mid eighteenth century. Of Sarah Edwards's entire literary output, which was not large, only a few letters and one spiritual narrative survive. To assume, however, that she had no great influence ignores the larger text that Sarah Edwards created. As Amanda Porterfield and other scholars have pointed out, Edwards's artistry took the form of her life itself, and that life has had a far-ranging influence on American letters, beginning with her acting as an example of true piety for her husband, not only as evidence in his text but as the source for many of his ideas about religious psychology. Indeed, the text of Sarah Edwards's life keeps showing up in American letters. Every minister who visited the Edwards household recorded her kindness, gentility, and inspiration. She was frequently cited by these ministers as a perfect, holy woman, and the famous evangelist George Whitefield prayed to God for a "daughter of Israel" just like her. Sarah Edwards reappeared in the nineteenth century in Harriet Beecher Stowe's novel *The Minister's Wooing* (1859), and many have noticed the similarities between Edwards's transports and those of little Eva in Stowe's *Uncle Tom's Cabin* (1852).

Sarah Edwards's life was recorded mostly through the pens of others, but it appears most dynamically and resonates most vibrantly through the short written narrative that she dictated to Jonathan Edwards and that was published in full in Sereno E. Dwight's biography of the theologian, evangelist, and minister. The text of Sarah Edwards's life was demonstrably her own, and it served both her immediate needs and the tradition within which she wrote her life story.

Edwards was born Sarah Pierpont in New Haven, Connecticut, on 9 January 1710. Her father, the Reverend James Pierpont (also spelled Pierrepont), was an American-born graduate of Harvard; her mother, Mary Hooker Pierpont, was a granddaughter of Thomas Hooker, who was one of the founders of the Plymouth Colony and was famous in England as a conversion preacher both before and after his immigration to the New World. Given this lineage, she was probably given as fine an education as a woman could receive in the colonies, and her family affiliation certainly lent prestige to her husband. (Not only was she related to Hooker, but she was also a distant cousin of Lady Mary Wortley Montagu.) By the time she was thirteen, Sarah Pierpont had met Jonathan Edwards and inspired perhaps his most-quoted piece of writing, an engagingly human adoration of the pious young girl who "hardly cares for any thing, except to meditate on [God, and who] expects after a while to be received up where he is, to be raised up out of the world and caught up into heaven." This close, loving relationship with God seems to have influenced, or at least corroborated, Jonathan Edwards's theological emphasis on beauty and love as the perceptions that could convince saints—in Calvinist theology, those predetermined to enjoy heaven in the afterlife—of the existence of God.

Sarah Pierpont married Jonathan Edwards on 28 July 1727, five months after he was ordained a minister in the Northampton, Massachusetts, congregation of his maternal grandfather, Solomon Stoddard. Less than two years later, on 11 February 1729, the formidable Stoddard died, and Jonathan Edwards took his place. As the minister's wife, Sarah Edwards was expected to be an example of holiness as well as seeing to the household economy, which she apparently did with strict efficiency. As a highly visible helpmate and model wife, she was strategically placed at the immediate left hand of the minister as he stood in the pulpit. Sarah Edwards understood this tradition of the minister's wife as paragon and had mastered the skills needed to take her place within this tradition.

It was at least partly to Sarah Edwards's credit when, in 1734, Jonathan Edwards sparked a remarkable religious fervor in his rural congregation. Young

Sarah Pierpont Edwards (portrait by Joseph Badger; from Frank W. Bayley, Five
Colonial Artists of New England, *1929)*

people whose behavior had been abominable became suddenly tractable and even eager for the minister's advice, and people all over town became concerned about whether they were saved or not. This
local revival died out two years later, when Sarah
Edwards's uncle, Josiah Hawley, committed suicide
at what he believed to be the urging of supernatural
voices. The revival had a lasting effect on the Edwardses. Jonathan Edwards's narrative of this event
(published in 1736)—featuring two female "case
studies" of exemplary piety (the conversion narratives of Phebe Bartlett, a four-year-old girl, and Abigail Hutchinson, a young woman who had recently
died)—inspired conversion preaching among ministers in England and the colonies and secured him
the literary fame that would allow him to begin publishing theological tracts. The revival was also re-

sponsible for bringing the Edwardses to the attention of George Whitefield.

Religious fervor arose again a few years later in
Northampton and the rest of New England. This
more widespread revival, often referred to as the
Great Awakening, was heightened by the arrival of
Whitefield, the most famous evangelist of the time.
With Whitefield's dynamic oratory, however, came
"excesses" that threatened the social order as citizens
suddenly found themselves possessed of the Lord. By
1740 the Great Awakening was under attack, and the
debate over emotional or "enthusiastic" religion raged
in Boston newspapers. During this time Jonathan Edwards, as a leading "New Light," was frequently absent from Northampton, preaching in other pulpits.
Other New Light ministers who were themselves traveling to preach in various pulpits often stayed in

Northampton and enjoyed Sarah Edwards's hospitality and pious company.

By 1742 Jonathan and Sarah Edwards's home was headquarters for this peculiar uprising. Revival preachers came there bringing news of sermons during which farmhands cried out and rolled on the ground, just as Jonathan Edwards rode off to speak in and carry the news to other towns. These activists for God must have carried on a running dialogue, sharing strategies and stories and speculations as to the final success of their work. Meanwhile James Davenport (among others) was carrying the revival to its extremes; more than once he burst into a minister's study, followed by members of the minister's congregation, and demanded to know if the man had been converted. "Lay exhorters," uneducated young enthusiasts, harassed ministers and disrupted services. In the midst of this turmoil—and as revivalists began to feel the stings of Bostonians' urbane response to the gyrations of the "hicks"—Jonathan Edwards was called on to defend the authenticity of the event.

By this time, however, religious fervor in Northampton had begun to cool again, and Edwards was having less success with his flock than he had once enjoyed. His well-known sermon *Sinners in the Hands of an Angry God* (1741) had far greater success in Enfield, Massachusetts, than it did in Northampton. Samuel Buell, one of his disciples, was able to rouse Edwards's congregation again to fervor, and Buell's success rankled Sarah Edwards's pride. When she "failed in some point of prudence, in some conversation I had with Mr. Williams of Hadley," her husband, never one to ignore character flaws in himself or any around him, had sharp words with her. He then left Northampton to preach elsewhere. While he was gone, Sarah Edwards went through an extraordinary seventeen-day religious experience that cleansed her of her jealousy of other preachers and left her "perfectly resigned to God, with respect to the instruments he should make use of to revive religion in this town."

This event was not her first mystical experience; she had been having periodic religious transports for quite some time, first as a child and then frequently beginning in 1734. When her husband returned at the end of her 1742 rapture, he recorded Sarah Edwards's story immediately. This text, altered substantially by Jonathan Edwards, was to become his greatest piece of evidence for the piety of the Great Awakening and the keystone to his argument that the revival could be managed. Sarah Edwards offered her husband a narrative that closely followed those he had used as evidence in his 1736 account. Rendering her husband's theory into experience just as that doctrine was coming under its heaviest fire from Boston, Sarah Edwards's account was a way to buttress her husband's

authority, as can be seen in her adopting the characteristics of the conversions he had described in his earlier narrative.

Sarah Edwards's account of her experience follows the outlines of the familiar conversion pattern, as well as those of Jonathan Edwards's earlier narratives: she had a brief sense of her sinfulness, then tried to subdue her pride through her own devices, and was finally visited by the Holy Spirit, who taught her to rely on God alone. Indeed, she acted out the ideal of submission to God's will to the point that her flesh became cold and the faithful in her household worried that she was going to be carried away to God. Moreover, her narrative focuses on her aesthetic experience, on the bodily sensations that resulted from her religious transport, in far more detail than those her husband had provided as earlier evidence. This deviation from the norm suggests that she was not only embodying Puritan conversion in its general outlines but also her husband's specific theology, with its emphasis on the apprehension of the beautiful and the body's response to it as a model for the way in which the saint can have an experience of the divine.

In his *Faithful Narrative Of The Surprizing Works of God,* written eight years earlier, Jonathan Edwards described Abigail Hutchinson as wanting to save the world through her own strivings. He also set forth four-year-old Phebe Bartlett's experiences in great detail, along with her family's reactions to her conversion. In both cases their relationships to Edwards are included. The narrative of her religious experience that Sarah Edwards dictated to Jonathan Edwards, or wrote herself, is also filled with particulars. For example, she pinpointed the times and durations of her transports of ecstasy: "I continued in a very sweet and lively sense of divine things, day and night, sleeping and waking, until Saturday, Jan. 23." Also, she related the personal jealousies and disputes that surrounded her experience.

Even more telling is the way in which Sarah Edwards's religious transport fulfills her husband's image of her specifically. When he was a tutor at Yale, Jonathan Edwards wrote that his future wife "expects . . . to be raised up out of the world and caught up into heaven." In 1742 Sarah Edwards managed, if only for a couple of weeks, to fulfill this image of her: "The presence of God was so near, and so real, that I seemed scarcely conscious of any thing else. . . . I seemed to be lifted above earth and hell." Indeed, Sarah Edwards seems to have acted out Jonathan Edwards's theology perfectly; in her text she described a visitation of the Holy Spirit that fits Jonathan Edwards's image in *A Treatise Concerning Religious Affections* (1746) of a fountain of love flowing from the saint to God in response to God's beauty: "my heart and soul

Jonathan and Sarah Edwards, circa 1740 (portraits attributed to Joseph Badger; Gallery of Fine Arts, Yale University)

all flowed out in love to Christ; so that there seemed to be a constant flowing and raffling of heavenly and divine love, from Christ's heart to mine." Sarah Edwards figured in the formulation of Jonathan Edwards's theology and acted it out once it had been written.

The various explanations that have been offered for Sarah Edwards's religious experience tend to focus on her social role. Laurie Crumpacker and Carol F. Karlsen see her experience as a response to her husband's criticism of her pride. Julie Ellison has argued that Sarah's second conversion was a withdrawal from the public life that had heaped so much pressure on her, a means by which she could find a new way to perform her role in the community. It has even been suggested that her experience was a response to marital tensions because 1742 marked the longest period since their marriage that she had gone without giving birth to a child. (The Edwardses eventually had eleven children in a marriage that lasted thirty-one years.) Yet Sarah Edwards also figured in her husband's intellectual life. Ola Winslow points out that the two apparently took walks during which they discussed theology at some length. Sarah Edwards's religious experience and the narrative she wrote about it were in some sense professional responses to a professional crisis. It seems likely, in other words, that her

experience was an intensely felt and intentional performance meant to ease domestic tension and prove the truth of doctrine.

This performance took on a far different form in print. Jonathan Edwards manipulated Sarah Edwards's narrative for a different set of needs than had been filled by the narratives of Hutchinson and Bartlett. The narrative in its first published form looks significantly different from the text as Sarah Edwards wrote it. In one sense the Edwardses seemed to be acting out a struggle over Sarah Edwards's disobedience. Her own narrative mentions Jonathan Edwards's displeasure as a motivating event for her experience. She seemed, in fact, to win a victory over her husband by resigning herself to his displeasure; she retreated, as Julie Ellison points out, in order to separate herself from his control, to find her own basis for agency that did not rely on his approval. That Jonathan Edwards describes in depth her sense of the justice of punishment for her sins as a corrupt human being as one of the causes of Sarah Edwards's religious experience—a sense of justice that she mentions only briefly and generally—suggests that he was gaining a measure of vengeance for her separation from him. If Jonathan Edwards used Sarah Edwards's experience to underscore his authority publicly, he also used his public authority as a way to deal with his personal struggle

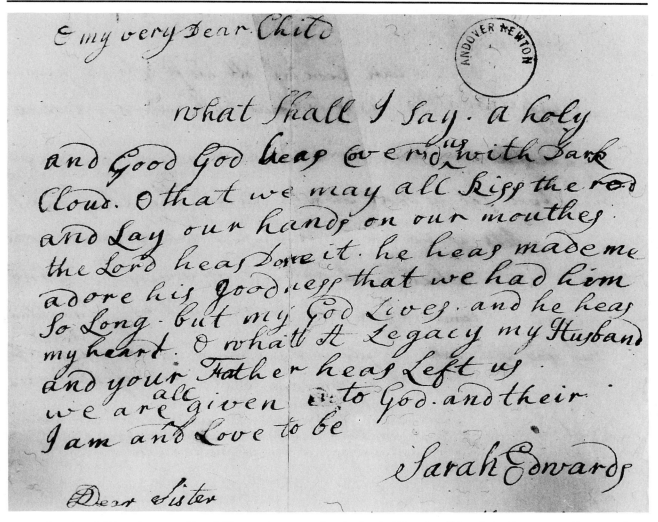

O my very Dear Child

what shall I say. a holy and Good God heas covered us with dark Cloud. O that we may all kiss the rod and Lay our hands on our mouthes the Lord heas done it. he heas made me adore his goodness that we had him so long. but my God Lives. and he heas my heart. O whatt A Legacy my Husband and your Father heas Left us. we are all given into to God. and their I am and Love to be

Sarah Edwards

Dear Sister

Letter from Sarah Edwards to one of her children, written soon after the death of Jonathan Edwards in March 1758 (Franklin Trask Library, Andover Newton Theological School)

with his wife. In Sarah Edwards's own account she upbraided herself for her pride when she felt jealous that other ministers were having greater success than her husband. At the same time she mentioned her too-great reliance on her husband's opinion of her. This narrative, however, did not appear in print until 1830. The first account of her experience was a sort of case study in Jonathan Edwards's *Some Thoughts Concerning the Present Revival of Religion in New-England* (1742). Removed from chronology, taken from agency, and displayed as a series of anonymous characteristics, she became "the person," and her story became a series of symptoms joined together with semicolons. The text of Sarah Edwards's life has been even more influential than the text that Jonathan Edwards made of it, as the list of her "appearances" in American literature indicates.

Eventually Jonathan Edwards was removed from the Northampton pulpit, and the Edwardses

were sent to Stockbridge, Massachusetts, where they more or less governed a remote outpost. They were responsible not only for a congregation but also for a missionary school and a garrison of troops. Once again Sarah Edwards's management skills became more important than her mystic visions. After seven years in the hinterlands of British America, Jonathan Edwards was offered the presidency of the College of New Jersey, later Princeton University, and accepted. He died of a smallpox inoculation only a few weeks after taking this post. In a brief, moving account of her grief, Sarah Edwards lamented that "a Good God hath covered us with a Dark Cloud." Seven months later, in early October 1758, she died of rheumatic fever contracted on a trip to visit her daughter, Esther Edwards Burr.

Amanda Porterfield has called Sarah Edwards an artist whose medium was her life; her experience was a creative working with the materials of the Puritan theology of salvation. Just as her husband was a minister from a family of ministers, Sarah Edwards was a holy woman in a line of holy women. She learned about religious practice from her mother and grandmother, whose names were watchwords for holiness in Massachusetts, and she became a better-known icon than either of them. She did so by embracing her role zealously, by acting out her identity with stunning success, becoming, it seems, the model for her husband's theories of conversion.

Fortunately the text Sarah Edwards wrote for her husband's use has survived, and a reading of that text brings all the richness of personal detail that Jonathan Edwards so assiduously erased from his version. The personal, the religious, and the political are all wrapped up together in her narrative; there is no purity in her motives but action out of near desperation. Sarah Edwards attained briefly the nearly impossible ideal of the Puritan saint to shore up her crumbling position in Northampton society. She created a dramatic self from a difficult and demanding creed. Since then, this self has served the needs of many New England religious and secular writers, beginning with her husband, but the text of her life remains her own.

Letter:

Letter to Esther Edwards Burr, in *The Journal of Esther Edwards Burr 1751–1757,* edited by Carol F.

Karlsen and Laurie Crumpacker (New Haven: Yale University Press, 1984).

References:

Esther Edwards Burr, *The Journal of Esther Edwards Burr 1751–1757,* edited by Carol F. Karlsen and Laurie Crumpacker (New Haven: Yale University Press, 1984);

Elisabeth D. Dodds, *Marriage to a Difficult Man: The "Uncommon Union" of Jonathan and Sarah Edwards* (Philadelphia: Westminster Press, 1971);

Julie Ellison, "The Sociology of 'Holy Indifference': Sarah Edwards' Narrative," *American Literature,* 56 (1984), pp. 479–495;

Perry Miller, *Jonathan Edwards* (New York: Sloan, 1949);

Amanda Porterfield, *Female Spirituality in America: From Sarah Edwards to Martha Graham* (Philadelphia: Temple University Press, 1980);

Patricia J. Tracy, *Jonathan Edwards, Pastor: Religion and Society in Eighteenth-Century Northampton* (New York: Hill & Wang, 1980);

Ola Elizabeth Winslow, *Jonathan Edwards: 1703–1758* (New York: Macmillan, 1940).

Papers:

Sarah Edwards's letters are at the Franklin Trask Library of Andover Newton Theological School in Newton Centre, Massachusetts.

Jenny Fenno
(1765? – after 1803)

David H. Payne
University of Georgia

BOOK: *Original Compositions, in Prose and Verse. On Subjects Moral and Religious* (Boston: Printed by Joseph Bumstead, 1791; revised edition, Wrentham, Mass.: Printed by Nathaniel Heaton Jr., 1803).

Jenny Fenno's poetry rarely surprises the reader. The steady couplets and expected imagery of her roughly seventy poems tempt one to think her not unusual or remarkable as a writer, and literary history has largely pigeonholed her into a "between points of interest" place in American literature. The steady features of her poetry, however, form a background for the fifteen often-surprising prose works that close her *Original Compositions, in Prose and Verse* (1791). Though most of her prose topics are rehearsed in her poetry, her essays escape many of the less interesting conventions to which much of her poetry adheres. While Fenno might be best known as another "dead children gladly lead us into heaven" poet, she brought the sentimental death and "Night Thoughts" approach to the imagination at an early point in American literature. The perhaps unconscious eroticism of her embrace of God points to a debt owed to Elizabeth Singer Rowe as much as to the Great Awakenings. Fenno's learned references (a toying mention of John Milton, a citation of Isaac Watts, imitations of Edward Young and perhaps James Hervey, and admirations of Rowe), her elegiac fluctuations between a stark grief that recalls Anne Bradstreet and the cloying response to death of the pre-Romantics, and her highly blurred picture of her own near death during illness—all make the reader vitally interested in learning biographical details about Fenno that are, so far, lacking.

Fenno was probably a member of the Boston Second Baptist Church, for which congregation she composed more than one elegy. Her level of education and obvious poetic control, as well as her social conservatism and subject matter, make her a likely representative of the growing post-Puritan middle class. Her writing implies that she remained single, though judging from her poetry, she might conceivably have been widowed by the sea (or perhaps some other person close to her suffered a maritime death). She might have been recalling a family scene when she lamented, "O what a scene of distress and wretchedness is exhibited to our view, when we behold the affectionate wife, the tender parent, the beloved child, and the kind sister deprived of their reason" ("On the Blessing of Reason"), but there is little concrete information on which to base a biography. One scholar, Jeanne Holland, has discovered a "Jennet Fenno" who was born in 1765, and Fenno's addition of two poems to the 1803 edition of *Original Compositions, in Prose and Verse* suggests that she lived into the nineteenth century.

Fenno's discussions of authority reflect much the same caution found in the writings of many of her contemporaries after the American Revolution, and she took her role as a religious writer seriously, asserting her responsibility to her new country as an ethical spokeswoman. Furthermore, her sturdy sense of self, even while acting in a role that demands great self-effacement, challenges any attempt to pass over her work. Critics remain divided on the degree of irony that might be found in Fenno's exclamation of humility in the preface to *Original Compositions, in Prose and Verse,* but her continued identification of herself with David the Psalmist throughout the book suggests that Fenno knew the value of her talent. Fenno explicitly compared herself to David, who was raised up from relative obscurity by a patron and substitute father figure; and, she pointed out, "Even David, the man after God's own heart, was accused of pride, because he attempted to do his duty." In like manner she prayed that "the feeble efforts of a young female, may tend to promote the glory of the adorable JEHOVAH!" Later in the preface, however, she added that while "this book may appear in the eyes of the learned world, like an insignificant pebble," she would be "happy . . . if it may be so slung as to smite one philistine." Though this statement appears modest, the reader should recall, as Fenno did, that "the little pebblestone was instrumental in destroying the enemy of this [David's] country." The temptation to read much into Fenno's use of David grows when the reader discovers that her longest poem, "David's Victory over Goliah," repeats

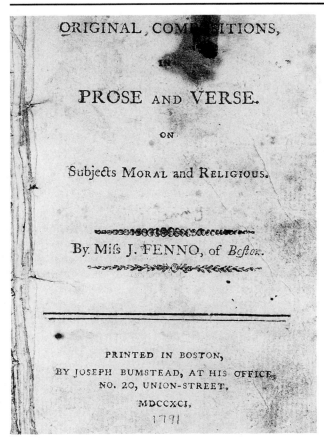

ORIGINAL COMPOSITIONS,

IN

PROSE AND VERSE.

ON

Subjects MORAL and RELIGIOUS.

By Miss J. FENNO, of *Boston.*

PRINTED IN BOSTON,
BY JOSEPH BUMSTEAD, AT HIS OFFICE,
NO. 20, UNION-STREET.
MDCCXCI.
1791

Title page for Jenny Fenno's only book, her sentimental musings on death and the consolations of religion (courtesy of the American Antiquarian Society)

the same story at great length and that the second edition of *Original Compositions, in Prose and Verse* includes further hints that Fenno identified with David the Psalmist in "An Acrostic addressed to the Author" and "The Answer." The acrostic "Ienny Fenno," supposedly addressed by a "Dear honor'd Sir" to Fenno, offers considerable temptation to earthly vanity that "The Answer" gracefully declines. The contrasting rapture with God follows in one of many passages whose near-erotic love of God rivals Rowe's, as "sovereign love . . . look'd upon me with compassion's eye." The answering poet notes that "Into my mouth he [God] put a song of praise," much as she later added in prose, "with the Psalmist we may say, all thy works shall praise thee" ("On the Greatness and Goodness of God").

Young's *Night Thoughts* (1742–1745) appears to have served as an apprentice's model in a writing such as "Evening Thoughts," and a reference to Hervey suggests that Fenno had read his *Meditations and Contemplations* (1746–1747), but it is Rowe whom Fenno most often praises directly, and one must assume that Fenno's descriptions of God owe something to Rowe. Not only is God thoroughly personalized in "Compas-

sion's eye," but throughout Fenno's poetry he takes on other characteristics of a divine lover. For example, both Fenno and Rowe use the term "Surprising love" in their descriptions of the divine. In the prose essay "God Alpha and Omega" Fenno commented, "Methinks I can adopt the language of dear Mrs. Rowe and say, I long to behold the supreme beauty, I pant for the original of all that is lovely." Plainly, physical love appears as the only image powerful enough to compare to the divine. As Fenno wrote in "God Alpha and Omega":

Thou art my boundless treasure, my infinite delight; my all, my satisfying portion. I can not be happy without thee, no more than I can see without light, or breathe without air. . . . I feel a desire which the most glorious creation could not satisfy, even if I could call it all my own, an emptiness which nothing but infinite love could fill.

In Fenno's prose the sea functions as a metaphor in much more original and suggestive ways than in her poetry, where the ocean appears largely as a stylistic commonplace, a home for the "finny tribe" and "scaly nations." In her prose the sea represents the afterworld. Fenno's preface points out that "I expected ere now to have launched out into the shoreless ocean; but just as I was expecting to change worlds, the scene changed, and I was sent back by unerring wisdom to finish this work I had begun to do." In fact her essay "The Ocean" addresses the ocean as familiarly as a Bostonian should: "What a grand prospect is here before us" in the sea, which would "certainly overflow" had not God "laid an embargo on the raging waves." God "holds the waters in the hollow of his hand" and "taketh up the isles as a very little thing," and, the essay exclaims,

how many millions are fed out of its inexhaustible shores! . . . There is something grand and exceeding beautiful in the ocean; but it is not only beautiful but beneficial to the world: there go the ships and do business in great waters, and foreign lands. America, this land of liberty, might forever remain undiscovered, if it were not for the advantages of navigation, by this, the glorious gospel came to our enlightened land; by this, the glad tidings of salvation were brought to this once howling wilderness.

The ocean reappears several times as the awesome hand of God, who "is a sea of love without a shore" ("Faith Surveying Eternity"). Fenno wrote, "O the height, the depth, the length, the breadth of the love of Christ. Here is an ocean in which I would ever swim" ("Christian Treasures"). Likewise, she asked, "Why do I abandon the full ocean in search of shallow streams" ("God Alpha and Omega").

Fenno's discussions of death range much more widely, especially in her prose, than might be indicated by the fact that some critics have associated her with the Graveyard school of poetry. In her preface Fenno's discussion of her own brush with death moves rather offhandedly, almost flippantly, as does her only other mention of this event, in her address to "the Rev. Mr. S.W. on his Recovery from Sickness": "Unto death's door you've been, as well as I." This poem challenges someone who appears to be a new minister to rise to his calling. Referring to religion, she added, "Oh may I practice this, while this you preach." Most of her other occasional poems on death console with the sentiments of "Reflections on the Grave," in which a wise man "Is led by choice to take a favorite walk, / Beneath death's gloomy, silent, cypress shade," where he gains the consolations now most often associated with the Victorians: by "the silent grave" he learns the "instructive lessons" that "friendly death is oft a sweet relief." Fenno's poetic consolation, then, consists primarily of a sort of muscular Christianity urging stoicism.

In Fenno's prose one finds far more realistic views of man and death, as in "Faith Surveying Eternity," which asserts: "Death's terror is the mountain faith removes." In her longest prose piece, "The Christians Treasure," Death is the final treasure and of far greater worth than riches, even higher than "reproach" and "infirmities." Death is the "king of terrors, and terror of kings," but to the faithful "thou appearest with an angel's face, and a deliverer's hand. . . . Welcome, thrice welcome thou kind messenger of heaven." While some of the themes in Fenno's prose might be influenced by Young or Hervey (note Hervey's "Meditations among the Tombs," "Upon Creation," "On the Night," and "A Winter-Piece"), some passages in Fenno's later essays—such as "On the Ocean," "Faith Surveying Eternity," and "Evening Thoughts"—let imagery do its work first before the writer interprets didactically, a restraint rarely found in Young or Hervey. "Evening Thoughts" in particular opens in quite undidactic terms, explicating the imagery after the word-picture is complete:

Now the evening approaches, drest in her sable robes, serene and solemn is the face of things. All around is silence. Now is the time for serious meditation. The glorious sun has now quitted our horizon, and left the world in shades. This may remind us of the evening of life, and the solemn night of death, which is approaching. Every day is succeeded by night, and all our lives will be followed by death.

In several comparable cases the imaginative object acts as the consciousness-mirroring world, in which Fenno further contemplated death.

Despite the momentous events of the last quarter of the eighteenth century in America—fires, plagues, and rebellions—only the Boston Fire of 1787 is mentioned in her work. Contemporary references do not provide any notable way of determining the sequence in which Fenno wrote her poems or essays. If there is an ordering principle to Fenno's prose essays in *Original Compositions, in Prose and Verse,* it arises from the sequence of gifts laid up for Christians in the discussion of "Christians Treasure," leading up to the ultimate gift of death. Her prose remains free of the occasion, and her poetry only slightly less so. Indians, for example, enter her work only as an example of "savage Indians, whose untutor'd mind / Sees God in clouds, and in the stormy wind" ("On Winter"). As often is the case in American letters, Indians become one with the "howling wilderness." It might be autobiographically meaningful that Fenno's "flagship" poem, "David's victory over Goliah" immediately precedes "To a Young Lady who was Reproached for Religion," directed toward a victim with whom Fenno clearly identified, and "On the President of the United States," which praises George Washington not so much for his actions as his character ("Greatness and good, both in him combine") and wishes him a role "Upon a nobler stage" of heaven, but Fenno was clearly impatient to return to her religious themes. "On the dreadful Conflagration in Boston, in 1787" combines both an expressive turn ("To see flames kindle, rage, and spread around") and an apocalyptic threat ("As if in fire we must have made our bed").

Fenno often praised reason in *Original Compositions, in Prose and Verse,* calling for a postrevolutionary return to balance and order in "The Answer" and in the poems "Filial Love and Obedience" and "On Reason." Her view of the order of this world is illustrated most clearly in the prose essay "The Christians Treasure," which reminds the reader, "You who are rich in this world are nobly distinguished, let not your mercies turn to weapons of rebellion; forbid it reason, forbid it gratitude." As at least one critic has noted, Fenno described a patriarchy that should include the maternal traits of mercy and kindness. While she placed human leaders well below God in a hierarchy of authority, the role allotted children and servants was clearly one of obedience. Given the time of its writing, the reader can easily believe that the American Revolution figures in this statement in "On Contentment": "The carnal mind is enmity with God, not being subject to his law, neither can be. No, the heart that is opposed to God, is not content that God should reign."

Hannah Webster Foster

(10 September 1758 – 17 April 1840)

W. M. Verhoeven
University of Groningen

See also the Foster entry in *DLB 37: American Writers of the Early Republic.*

BOOKS: *The Coquette; or, The History of Eliza Wharton; A Novel; Founded on Fact* (Boston: Printed by Samuel Etheridge for E. Larkin, 1797);
The Boarding School; or, Lessons of a Preceptress to her Pupils: Consisting of Information, Instruction, and Advice, Calculated to improve the Manners, and form the Character of Young Ladies. To which is added, A Collection of Letters, written by the Pupils, to their Instructor, their Friends, and each other (Boston: Printed by I. Thomas & E. T. Andrews, 1798).

Hannah Webster Foster is the author of one of the best and most successful sentimental novels of the early national period. Attributed only to "A Lady of Massachusetts," Foster's *The Coquette* (1797) was one of the two best-selling American novels of the eighteenth century. (The other is Susanna Rowson's 1794 novel, *Charlotte.*) Thirteen editions of *The Coquette* appeared in the thirty years that followed its first publication, with its greatest popularity occurring between 1824 and 1828, when it was reprinted no fewer than eight times. An epistolary novel of seduction in the style of Samuel Richardson's *Clarissa* (1747–1749), *The Coquette* portrays the tragic life and death of Elizabeth Wharton, a strong-willed and independent young woman who finds herself in a dilemma faced by many eighteenth-century sentimental heroines: how to be true to one's heart and at the same time remain a respected member of the established social order. In the late twentieth century Foster's novel enjoyed a remarkable revival, and *The Coquette* is now considered a key text in the canon of early American literature. No longer read exclusively for its sentimental and thrilling plot of seduction and betrayal, the novel is appreciated particularly for the intelligent and artistically convincing ways in which it reexamines familiar Enlightenment dichotomies, such as personal integrity versus social responsibility, personal versus universal free-

dom, and passion versus reason. Foster's second book, *The Boarding School* (1798), was much less popular than its predecessor. Dedicated to "the young ladies of America," the novel is essentially a series of lectures on female education and deportment. Disputing the accepted maxim that "reformed rakes make the best husbands," Foster's novel denounces seducers and pleads for more tolerance for their victims. Despite the tendency among critics to dispose of the novel as a mere moralistic tract, *The Boarding School* is in fact a critique of the submerged notions of public and private spaces that policed male-female relations at the end of the eighteenth century. The book thus confirms Foster's contemporary reputation as a major spokesperson in early American writing for greater female liberty.

Hannah Webster Foster was born on 10 September 1758 in Salisbury, Massachusetts, the daughter of Grant Webster, a wealthy Boston merchant, and Hannah Wainwright Webster. Although details of her childhood and adolescence are scarce, it is known that she was sent to a boarding school in 1762 following the death of her mother. In the early 1770s she was living in Boston, and in the 1780s she began publishing short political pieces in local newspapers. In 1785 Hannah Webster married the Reverend John Foster, a graduate of Dartmouth College, who later served as pastor of the First Church in Brighton, Massachusetts. Between 1786 and 1796 Hannah Webster Foster bore six children, the first of whom died shortly after birth. Despite her busy life as a mother of five and a minister's wife, Foster managed to find time to write her first novel, *The Coquette.*

Like most other novels from the period, *The Coquette* was said to be "Founded on Fact"; unlike most, however, the claim was accurate in the case of Foster's novel. The character Eliza Wharton is based on Elizabeth Whitman (1752–1788) of Hartford, Connecticut, a distant cousin of Foster's husband. The story of Elizabeth Wharton's elopement and her subsequent death of complications following the birth of her stillborn, illegitimate child at a

122

roadside tavern in Danvers (now Peabody), Massachusetts, was a cause célèbre that swept the nation in 1788. Both illegitimacy and maternal mortality were common enough during the late eighteenth century, but Whitman's decline and fall attracted widespread attention because she was by no means just another young and naive coquette who was seduced and abandoned by a licentious cad. On the contrary, Whitman, who was thirty-seven when she died, came from a long line of well-connected New England families and was the daughter of a highly respected minister. An intelligent and well-educated woman, she was, moreover, an accomplished poet and a popular and witty member of Hartford high society, who counted among her friends and acquaintances poets such as John Trumbull and Joel Barlow. At first an announcement in the 29 July 1788 *Salem Mercury* said that a "Mrs. Walker" had checked into the Bell Tavern and had died there after having given birth to a dead baby, but the news soon spread that "Mrs. Walker" was in reality Elizabeth Whitman, the vivacious New England wit. Ministers, maids, and moralists almost immediately filled newspapers and magazines with accounts that cast her tragic demise in terms of an awesome moral lecture and ultimate warning to all young ladies of America. Within months of Whitman's death, her sad history had been completely submerged into and replaced by a moral allegory of the dangers of licentiousness and coquetry. Furthermore, moralists quickly pinpointed the source of these evil passions. In the words of the *Massachusetts Centinel* (20 September 1788), Whitman owed her shameful fate to the reading of novels: "She was a great reader of romances, and having formed her notions of happiness from that corrupt source, became vain and coquetish." By the time Foster came to write her fictional tale "founded on fact," her prospective audience had already branded Whitman a "coquette" and had unequivocally identified reading too many romances as the fatal cause of her demise. As a creative artist, Foster knew that her words would be scrutinized and weighed carefully.

Writing within the narrow moral parameters dictated by the bourgeois sensibilities of the day, Foster at least superficially remained faithful to the circumstances of the original case. One of the most fascinating aspects of Foster's novel, however, is that while bourgeois morality and ideology certainly inform the surface discourse, there is some covert resistance as well.

Whitman's two suitors, the Reverend Joseph Howe (her parents' first choice, who died before the marriage could take place) and the Reverend Joseph Buckminster (who subsequently sought her hand)

are only slightly veiled in the novel as the Reverends Haly and Boyer, respectively. Foster reveals to the reader the fact that the death of the first suitor was not an entirely unwelcome event to the heroine (who in the opening letter quite boldly points up the disparity of their tempers and dispositions), and she portrays the second suitor, a respected clergyman, as rather too stolidly virtuous and even somewhat vain and pompous. Conversely, Eliza's seducer, Maj. Peter Sanford, whose real-life counterpart was generally assumed to be Jonathan Edwards's son Pierrepont (Aaron Burr, James Watson, and Joel Barlow have also been mentioned in this context), transcends the stereotypical debaucher of sentimental fiction and is actually quite a witty sparring partner to Eliza in their game of mutual seduction. Far from following the conventions of the traditional seduction novel, which would have presented Eliza's tragic end as the appropriate reward for having made a wrong choice of marriage candidate, Foster turned the choice itself into the real topic of her novel, suggesting that the challenge a talented and independent young woman such as Eliza faces is not so much the choice between virtue and sin, as the fact that, within the strict moral and ideological confines of the day, she has no real choice.

Eliza is by no means alone in her predicament: the choice of a suitable marriage partner being in essence a test of a woman's loyalty to the dominant bourgeois ideology. Many a young heroine in eighteenth-century novels found herself faced by the choice between society's candidate—in this case, Boyer—and the candidate of her heart—Sanford. This choice is much more intriguing in *The Coquette* than in other novels of the period not because Eliza's suitors are less predictable than their counterparts in the majority of sentimental novels, but because Eliza is a totally different sort of heroine. Describing herself as young, gay, and volatile, Eliza celebrates the fact that after the death of Haly she managed to extricate herself from the shackles that parental authority had imposed on her mind. From that point on she wants no one to interfere with the integrity of her self and proudly takes her fate into her own hands. It is not hard to see why so many contemporary readers warmed to Foster's liberated heroine.

To a large extent the popular success of *The Coquette* might be attributed to the dynamics of its epistolary mode. For example, it took only eight letters to set up the main plot, which pivots on Eliza and her two suitors, and also to develop a lively epistolary correspondence between Eliza and Lucy Freeman, between Boyer and Mr. Selby, and from

Sanford to Charles Deighton (this correspondence is not reciprocal). Although Lucy Freeman and Selby primarily function as the conventional confidants of epistolary fiction–being the more rational, wiser, and more conscientious counterpart of the person with whom they correspond–they are by no means mere colorless moralists. Lucy in particular turns out to be a character in her own right. She might not have the glamour and liveliness of the heroine, but she is far from insipid and not infrequently displays a witty sense of humor in her letters to Eliza.

Foster also uses the epistolary mode as a powerful means of characterization, creating personal levels of diction that vary from the formal, rational discourse of Boyer; to the colloquial, gossipy, and sometimes emotional discourse of Eliza; to the witty, ironic discourse of Sanford. Eliza's letters are especially successful, revealing her frequent changes of mood and temper. Whereas the correspondents in many other early American epistolary novels appear to be writing prepared statements drawn up for them by the author, the characters in *The Coquette* seem to write from their souls. In this way the reader gets the impression that instead of describing the tragic demise of the hero and heroine, Foster allowed them to enact and simultaneously document their own downfalls, giving the text a highly dramatic quality and resulting in a much more effective type of didacticism than one commonly encounters in sentimental fiction.

Another notable aspect of Foster's epistolary style is her multiple-point-of-view technique. On various occasions her main correspondents describe and comment on a single event from two or even three different angles. These partly overlapping accounts together form a double- or even triple-layered story. The power of this multiple-point-of-view technique is perhaps nowhere clearer than in Letters XL–XLII. This sequence relates a crucial episode in the heroine's tragic life, the exposure to the world of her clandestine intercourse with Sanford, after Boyer unwittingly discovers Eliza and Sanford having an intimate and illicit tête-à-tête in a secluded part of Richman's garden. The sequence of accounts that Boyer, Eliza, and Sanford give of the incident and their reactions to it reminds one of a multiple-camera-shot montage. These letters create a sense of dialogic opposition not only between each correspondent and his or her confidant but also between different textual accounts of the same event, greatly enhancing the dramatic as well as the discursive power of Foster's text.

If there is one element in *The Coquette* that alone fully warrants its recently enhanced status in American literature, it is the intriguing way in which Foster employed the various epistolary styles as part of an underlying critique of contemporary bourgeois morality. By setting up a dialogue between the dominant discourse of morality and an ironic counter-discourse, Foster effectively destabilized conventional models of morally responsible behavior. This dialogue is apparent in the following passages from two consecutive letters. In the first Eliza is writing to Lucy, expressing her humiliation over having been rejected by Boyer:

> Oh my friend, I am undone! I am slighted, rejected by the man who once sought my hand, by the man who still retains my heart! and what adds an unsupportable poignancy to the reflection, is self-condemnation! From this inward torture, where shall I flee? Where shall I seek that happiness which I have madly trifled away?

In response Lucy writes,

> Your truly romantic letter came safe to hand. Indeed, my dear, it would make a very pretty figure in a novel. A bleeding heart, slighted love, and all the et ceteras of romance, enter into the composition!

Similarly, a formal letter such as Letter XX, in which Eliza provides her mother with a report on the latest developments in the marriage market, is implicitly set off against the letter coming immediately before, an informal letter to Lucy dealing with the same issues but in a much more open-hearted manner. In the letter to her mother, whose motherly advice she says she is seeking, Eliza tells of Boyer's proposal of marriage but hints only vaguely at the existence of a competitor. From her letter to Lucy, however, it is clear that Eliza is deeply taken with the charms of Sanford and that she would much rather marry him than Boyer. As a result of this juxtaposition, the informal discourse of the gossipy letter to Lucy starts to interfere with the formal discourse of the letter to Mrs. Wharton, whereby the authority of the formal letter and the moral authority of the mother are implicitly undermined.

A similar tension exists in the clash between Eliza's two suitors. Eliza might for a while be under the impression that she can take her fate into her own hands, but it soon becomes clear that such a bid for self-determination was sadly illusionary in late-eighteenth-century America. In practical terms it is not Eliza choosing between two suitors, but two suitors dueling over who gets Eliza–a duel that, significantly, is not decided by an exchange of bullets but by an exchange of words and letters. Boyer's discourse is formal, rational, argumentative, full of good intent and moral rectitude, but utterly boring. Sanford's is glib, disrespectful of women and society, witty, yet entertaining. The most significant difference between the tactics of the two rivals, however, is that Boyer insists on communicating with Eliza in writing, whereas Sanford chooses the ephemeral medium of light-hearted conversation–witty small talk and flattery. Characteristically, Boyer sets great store by entertaining a formal epistolary correspondence with Eliza, to which she consents with evident distaste. Sanford, it needs to be emphasized, writes to Eliza only once–"a despairing letter," as he later confesses to Deighton, written only because he felt sure that Eliza was about to accept Boyer's offer of marriage.

The Coquette thus signals yet another kind of opposition, between the written language as employed in letters and the undocumented medium of speech. The novel treats epistolary discourse as a means of communication that, though ostensibly private, is sanctioned by society (hence Boyer's preference for it), presumably because it can be intercepted, opened, and read by others–which is indeed the rule rather than the exception in epistolary fiction. In contrast to writers such as Richardson, Pierre Choderlos de Laclos, and Charles Brockden Brown, Foster virtually ignored this somewhat Gothic aspect of the epistolary mode, which makes it all the more significant that the one letter that is intercepted in The Coquette happens to be Sanford's only written communication to Eliza (enclosed in Letter XLI). The most typical discourse of seduction is speech, undoubtedly because it is harder to monitor and control, especially when it occurs in intimate social spaces, such as the privacy of a secluded arbor, away from the inquisitive ears of guardians of virtue and morality such as Boyer and Mrs. Richman. Characteristically, Mrs. Richman asks Eliza to give an account of what Sanford said to her in the garden, fearing that the girl might be led astray by the "artful intrusions" of this "second Lovelace." Sanford, however, knows how to play the game successfully, and as a rule he makes use of the few opportunities sanctioned by the conventions of social intercourse to talk intimately to one's lover–as he does, for instance, while dancing with Eliza at the assembly or at Lucy's wedding ball.

The distinction that is made in the novel between the discourse of accepted social intercourse and the discourse of seduction corresponds to an equally sharp distinction made in ideological terms between the value system instituted in the established social framework and the moral wasteland that presumably lies outside this framework: a distinction between inside and outside, the known and the

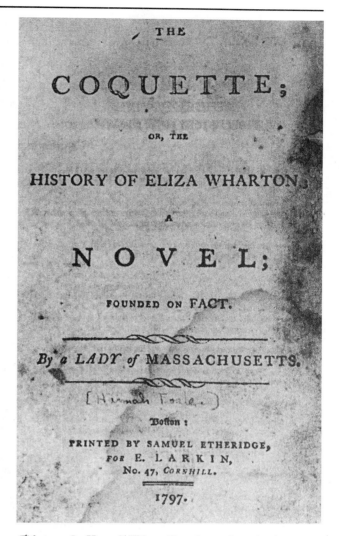

Title page for Hannah Webster Foster's popular tale of seduction and betrayal, one of only two eighteenth-century American novels that can be considered best-sellers

unknown, as well as between the conscious and the subconscious, the rational and the irrational. Within the ideology of the inside (essentially the ideology of the bourgeois state), the institution of marriage channels the social relations between the sexes. In the eyes of the representatives of the inside in Foster's novel, virtuous love as legitimized by marriage is the best guarantee of the solidarity and loyalty necessary to maintain the social fabric at all times: "Are we not all," Mrs. Wharton writes to her daughter, "links in the great chain of society, some more, some less important; but each upheld by others, throughout the confederated whole? In whatever situation we are placed, our greater or less degree of happiness must be derived from ourselves."

It is a central part of Foster's critical agenda in The Coquette to reveal how the concept of seduction functions as a ritual or social mechanism that helps a community build and uphold an ideological consensus. In the same way the concept of seduction helps to draw a fine line between the social, moral, and ideologically normative behavior that the social fabric condones and the kind of behavior that it denounces as disruptive. A person's good reputation is like a passport that society bestows on all those individuals who remain within the social framework—a passport that is immediately withdrawn from any person who is seduced into behavior that is not condoned by refined society, causing that person to become a nonbeing. Reputation, says Lucy, "is an inestimable jewel, the loss of which can never be repaired. While retained, it affords conscious peace to our own minds, and ensures the esteem and respect of all around us." Within this framework the seducer is the "assassin of honor" who is always prowling along the frontier between established society and its moral hinterland, ready to lure some unsuspecting fair maiden away from the flock with his insidious and subversive eloquence.

The resistance to this institutionalized view of seduction in Foster's novel is first apparent in the discrepancy that exists between the conventional rhetoric condemning the seducer as a degenerate rake and the way he is actually presented to the reader in all but the concluding stages of the novel: as the flamboyant ne'er-do-well from a picaresque novel. Similarly, Eliza is not at all the innocent, credulous young woman Lucy makes her out to be, but a self-conscious, intelligent woman in her mid thirties who knows exactly what she is doing when she seeks the company of Sanford. Eliza is far too complex a heroine for her not to see through the cheap rhetoric of Sanford's flattery, or to be blind to the voice of reason in Boyer's. The significance of Foster's novel in literary, historical, and cultural terms lies in the way it resists presenting Eliza's choice as one between virtue and sin; the way, that is, in which it lays out the familiar Lockean choice between Duty, or the pursuit of general happiness, and Desire, or the pursuit of personal happiness. Foster is not so much interested in depicting Sanford's rhetoric of seduction as such, as in showing the way it affects the heroine's freedom of mind and integrity of self. In subtle ways Foster allows the conventional rhetoric of the seducer to change from a discourse of sin and temptation into a discourse of desire. As a resistant heroine, Eliza is an active agent in the game, and on more than one occasion she announces to anyone who wants to hear it that she intends "to enjoy my freedom, in the participation of pleasures, suited to my age and sex" for a while, before she decides on a new commit-

ment. Clearly her open flirtation with Sanford is prominent among the pleasures in which she wants to indulge, and for a long while she is more than a match for him. Indeed, Eliza is such a formidable opponent that Sanford finds himself getting "so much attached to her" that he has come to the point where he would "sooner become a convert to sobriety than lose her." It is evident from their letters to their confidants that they are both having a great time, which Foster does not spoil with any intrusive moralistic digressions—until Eliza is caught in the garden with Sanford while she is supposed to be unwell and in her room.

Until that dramatic moment Eliza knows no better than to believe that she can actually determine the course of her life, that the choice between Duty (the moral obligation of every member of society to uphold its values) and Desire (the fulfillment of her individuality and of her womanhood) is a real one. Even after she has been unmasked by Boyer, she does not immediately realize what impact her mistake will have on her position in society: her naïveté is painfully underlined by her initial attempt to "go and try to retrieve my character." As a seasoned seducer Sanford knows only too well that when a woman has lost her reputation, it is only a matter of time before she will be ostracized by society and come falling into his lap: "Well, Charles," he writes to his friend, "the show is over, as we yankees say; and the girl is my own. That is, if I will have her." He is apparently so certain Eliza will never become a full member of society again and will be there for him to claim when it suits him that he can even leave her for a while to straighten out his financial problems by marrying the accommodating Nancy. Society, as well as Eliza's "sisterhood" of friends and protectors, responds exactly as predicted. With her reputation compromised, Eliza is doomed, even before she is seduced. Having seen her friend being handed into a chaise by Sanford, Julia Granby is convinced that

All is now lost; lost, indeed! She is gone! Yes, my dear friend, our beloved Eliza, is gone! Never more shall we behold this once amiable companion, this once innocent and happy girl. She has forsaken, and, as she says, bid an everlasting adieu to her home, her afflicted parent and her friends!

From this point onward Eliza is an isolated, drifting person who is so desperate as to write to Boyer, almost begging him to take her back even though it is obvious that she does not love him. Branded as a "fallen woman," Eliza is dead to society long before she breathes her last at the inn in Danvers.

It is not surprising that there is a marked change in Foster's treatment of Eliza and Sanford after he has married the innocuous Nancy. Eliza and Sanford's relationship becomes a threat not only to Eliza's virtue but also to the sanctity of marriage. While before Eliza was depicted as a victim of her volatile nature, she now becomes a downright sinner, consciously double-dealing her mother and female friends, and bent on consummating her relationship with her seducer. Sanford, who was before a charming rake (though a threat to every woman's virtue), suddenly becomes a callous cad, who at one point confesses unashamedly that his wife's unhappiness and her recent miscarriage give him neither pain nor pleasure. Still more significant is the dramatic change of tone in the letters written after the reader learns in Letter LXV that Eliza has lost her virtue. Where the previous letters are expressive of the mind and social position of each individual letter writer, the characters now all start to write conventional seduction rhetoric and post-mortem moralizing, a rhetorical about-face that culminates in Eliza's warning addressed to "the American fair" against the destructive consequences of associating with merciless profligates such as Sanford and against "risking their reputation by the practice of coquetry and its attendant follies," lest the sacred bond with parents, family, and society be severed forever.

The contrived didactic-moralistic ending of *The Coquette* to some extent belies the tale Foster told in the preceding letters. Whereas Foster first individualized Eliza's fate by showing that she was seduced at least as much by her own desire for Sanford as by his lust for her body, she finally turned her heroine into the conventional victim of the seducer's "base arts." For most of the novel the reader is given the impression that Sanford wanted to seduce Eliza because he desired her, but at the end it appears as if the drive to seduce Eliza is something completely outside him, as if seduction is an invisible evil force in the universe that uses Sanford as a mere, will-less tool. While it is clear that the collapse of a lively, dialogic epistolary discourse into a conventional moralistic-didactic sermon at the end of Foster's novel signals an overwhelming need for closure, it is less obvious to what extent the ending reflects Foster's purpose and ideological position.

The question of what makes a text, especially a popular-fiction text, ideologically subversive is hard to settle, and *The Coquette* is no exception. For most of the twentieth century critics have regarded Foster's novel, along with all other sentimental, didactic novels of the early republic, as aesthetically inferior echoes of Old World models, primarily designed to reinforce conventional pieties and established sexual politics and to generally propagate and consolidate the dominant bourgeois ideology. Characteristic of the twentieth-century reception of *The Coquette* roughly up to the 1970s is a remark by Joel Barlow's biographer James Woodress, who off-handedly dismissed the novel as follows: "Written in the tedious epistolary style of Samuel Richardson's piously immoral romances, this tale offered a generation of readers a titillating story of seduction and a Sunday-school tract on the wages of sin." In this now largely superseded reading of the novel, Foster's retelling of Elizabeth Whitman's tragic fate is seen as a cautionary moral tract, in which the heroine's death supposedly represents a just punishment for her transgressive behavior.

During the final decades of the twentieth century, however, several revisionist, cultural-materialist, and feminist critics have begun to challenge this approach to the sentimental novel in general, and to *The Coquette* in particular, arguing that the heavily encoded discourse of this type of fiction disguises a fundamental concern with contemporary cultural and sociosexual politics and that the sentimental tradition demonstrates covert resistance against the stifling domestic sphere to which most women in the young republic were confined. In the eyes of these critics the true significance of *The Coquette* exceeds the formulaic denunciation of the seducer and the mourning of the tragic heroine's demise at the end of the novel. While allowing that Foster might in the final analysis have been forced to sacrifice her heroine to the dominant ideology of the patriarchal society, they argue that she did so only after she forcefully dramatized how contemporary women had lost out on the promises of the American Revolution and the Enlightenment ideals on which the new nation was built: the promise of freedom, integrity of self, equality, and the right to personal happiness. It can be argued against this position that while there is indeed some resistance in the novel to the conventional (male) discourse of seduction and by extension to the disenfranchisement of women, nowhere in the novel did Foster indicate that she even for one moment sympathized with Eliza's invoking the Wollstonecraftian notion that "Marriage is the tomb of friendship." On the contrary, whereas a marriage such as that of Mr. and Mrs. Richman is presented as a model of social stability, equality, and enlightened relations, the social and moral "independence" of Eliza and Sanford is shown to have dire effects not only on their happiness but also on that of others—and not just in the moralistic sad ending but throughout the novel. Yet it would perhaps be unfair to try to reduce Eliza's fate to either that of an emancipatory heroine or a societal suicide, and it would probably do more justice to Foster's novel to regard Eliza as both a victim of circumstances and a rebel against them.

The Boarding School (1798), which appeared only a year after The Coquette, bears out the idea that creating a sociopolitical revolution of the kind Cathy N. Davidson and Carroll Smith-Rosenberg talk about in their analyses of The Coquette was far from Foster's mind. Published anonymously like its predecessor, The Boarding School introduces the reader to the widow of a respectable clergyman, Mrs. Williams, who—partly to preserve her little patrimony for the benefit of her two daughters and partly to provide edifying company for them—decides to open a modest boarding school. Her pupils having received the first rudiments of education before they come to her, Mrs. Williams's instructions are "more especially designed to polish the mental part, to call forth the dormant virtues, to unite and arrange the charms of person and mind, to inspire a due sense of decorum and propriety, and to instill such principles of piety, morality, benevolence, prudence and economy, as might be useful through life."

To interpret this statement as meaning that The Boarding School merely aspires to teach young women how to fulfill their prospective social roles as well-bred wives and mothers, however, would be an overly reductive reading of Foster's book. Like The Coquette, The Boarding School might not be the radically subversive text that some have claimed it to be, but it is not quite an ode to conventional bourgeois sexual politics either. In general, The Boarding School echoes many of the enlightened and emancipatory views on female education expounded in the deluge of treatises that flooded the market in America and Britain during the 1780s and 1790s, the best known of which is no doubt Mary Wollstonecraft's A Vindication of the Rights of Woman (1792). While she did not directly refer to Wollstonecraft's classic of radical feminism, Foster clearly shared some of its basic tenets, which can be summarized as follows: If young women are ignorant, it is because their parents have failed to educate them; if young women are narrow-minded—being, in the words of Mary Wollstonecraft, "brimful of sensibility, and teeming with capricious fancies"—then it is because their educators have withheld from them the lessons in rationality, practical knowledge, and understanding that they have given to young males; if young

women are weak, sentimental, coquettish, or slavishly dependent, it is because they have been conditioned to behave in such a manner by their fathers, brothers, and husbands; and if young women resort to lying, flattery, gossip, hypocrisy, and bribery, it is because they have been confined to social spaces in which to preserve necessary appearances is considered to be more valuable than to be honest and sincere. While it might be Mrs. Williams's stated aim to "domesticate" her pupils, for her this means

> to turn their thoughts to the beneficial and necessary
> qualifications of private life; often inculcating, that
>   "Nothing lovelier can be found in woman,
>   Than to study household good";
> and labouring to convince them of the utter insignifi-
> cance and uselessness of that part of the sex, who are
>   "Bred only and completed to the taste
>   Of lustful appetence; to sing, to dance
>   To dress, and troll the tongue, and roll the eye."

The Boarding School is thus firmly rooted in the conviction "that our improved countrywomen are superior to [the degrading pastime of the superficial and the giddy], and are able to convince the world that the American fair are enlightened, generous, and liberal. The false notions of sexual disparity, in point of understanding and capacity, are justly exploded; and each branch of society is uniting to raise the virtues and polish the manners of the whole."

Formally the book is a cross between an epistolary novel and a conduct book: virtually lacking plot, it is a series of thinly disguised lectures—duly illustrated with fitting allegories—on female conduct and virtue (ostensibly Mrs. Williams's farewell lectures to her pupils), followed by a series of letters gleaned from the correspondence between Mrs. Williams and some of her former pupils. The lectures are little more than a series of moral vignettes on conventional conduct-book topics ("Reading," "writing and arithmetic," "music and dancing," "miscellaneous directions for the government of the temper and manners," "dress," "politeness," "amusements," "filial and fraternal affections," "friendship," "love," "religion"), and the letters lack the narrative unity and the epistolary dynamics that Foster employed so successfully in The Coquette. Although commonly referred to as a novel, The Boarding School is in fact best seen as a "How to Survive in Genteel Society" guide designed for young middle-class women. Read as such, The Boarding School offers the twentieth-century reader fascinating, sociological insight into the daily life of the average American woman at the end of the eighteenth century.

While conduct books in general are concerned with promoting etiquette, decorum, and accepted morality, *The Boarding School* might be distinguished from many other conduct books because it underscores the importance of conformity, not so much in terms of self-denial as in terms of liberating young women from the gender stereotypes that have always made them appear foolish, vain, and superficial in the eyes of men and society. Thus, when Mrs. Williams warns her pupils against reading too many novels, she does so not because she fears that it might fatally poison their minds or threaten their mental stability, but because it might distract them from reading texts from which they might derive useful knowledge and practical instruction—because, that is, reading for mere amusement would confirm the notion that women are intellectually and rationally inferior to men. Similarly, when Mrs. Williams tells her pupils about the dangers of music and dancing, she is not so much afraid of young women falling into licentious ways as of their falling "prey to seduction"—that is, of encouraging men to believe that women who are not prudes and express themselves freely through singing and dancing must be flirts and therefore consenting objects of men's sexual desires. Likewise, contrary to what one might expect, Mrs. Williams does not tell her pupils that they should suppress their "various passions, affections, and propensities." Instead she admonishes them that they should become aware of such feelings, so that they can learn to control their emotions and desires and thereby become less susceptible to the deluding flattery of coxcombs and seducers and to all those who do not respect women for what they are but for what they want them to be.

Ultimately Foster was trying to teach young women how to cope with being the objects of the public gaze, which was predominantly male. She was, in other words, showing young women how others—notably, but not exclusively, men—see women. In this respect the brief moral interludes with which Mrs. Williams's lectures are interspersed act as mirrors in which her pupils can see themselves and their own behavior reflected. Thus the interlude about the lovers Leontine and Eudocia—in which Eudocia is at one point seen to descend from the carriage of Florio, a professed debaucher—is offered as an illustration of Mrs. Williams's warning that to be "culpable in appearance" is as fatal to a woman's reputation as to be culpable in fact. That Eudocia is innocent of any misconduct, and merely accepted Florio's offer to take her home because she was fatigued after a long walk, does not in any way diminish the seriousness of her transgression. As Leontine

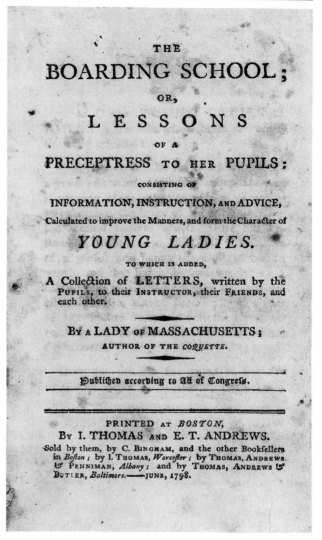

Title page for Foster's fictionalized version of a female conduct book, written in part to argue that properly educated American women "are enlightened, generous, and liberal" (courtesy of the Special Collections Department, University of Virginia Library)

explains, "though you have cleared yourself of guilt, in my apprehension, you will find it difficult to free your character from the blemish it has received in the opinion of the world."

As with *The Coquette*, the key question about *The Boarding School* is once more whether Foster was writing within the parameters of the male gaze, which she would then have accepted as a sociocultural given, or was she either implicitly or explicitly trying to subvert the gaze, possibly even to replace it by another, more equitable, perspective on gender and gender relations. Some critics have argued that *The Boarding School* constitutes a complex ideology of sisterhood, a separate sphere that presumably lies outside the male-dominated public sphere and that somehow exists independent of that sphere. Leaving aside the fact that it seems highly unlikely that late-eighteenth-century American culture would have allowed such a "separate sphere" to exist—even under the guise of a novelistic discourse—there are no indications in the book that setting up such a subversive sisterhood was part of Foster's plan in *The Boarding School*. For one thing the book never leaves any doubt as to the fate of any woman who endeavors to break away from the social rituals that define and police bourgeois America: she is invariably expelled from the genteel public sphere and ends in isolation and death. Nor are any of the female rebels set up as heroines of subversion; on the contrary, convinced that it is a woman's "duty and interest to enjoy life, as far as integrity and innocence allow," Foster posited that women should not "soar above, but accommodate ourselves *to* its ordinary state."

In the final analysis *The Boarding School* shows a fundamental concern for the stability and coherence of the social fabric, and the book accordingly seeks to consolidate the family as the cornerstone of society. In their capacity as daughters, sisters, and wives, *The Boarding School* argues, women have a key role in promoting the universal happiness of mankind, and the book attempts to prepare young women for this role. Foster might have been pleading for a revaluation of that role (hence for the democratization of filial, familial, and conjugal relations), but she was not arguing to change it. Though Foster was harsh toward male "pleasure-hunters" (commenting, for example, "That rakes make the best husbands, is a common, and I am sorry to say, a too generally received maxim"), she was even harsher toward female ones ("Still more unworthy are the insidious and deluding wiles of the coquette"). As Claire Pettengill has argued, female friendship is indeed an important aspect of the kind of social stability that Foster envisaged, and clearly Mrs. Williams's boarding school (aptly named Harmony-Grove) is offered to the reader as an emblem of such friendship. Yet Foster's book also makes it absolutely clear that "The highest state of friendship which this life admits, is in the conjugal relation." As Mrs. Williams's pupils flock out into the wide world, they are thoroughly persuaded that "Domestic happiness is the foundation of every other species" and that it is their right, as comanagers of the "little commonwealth" (the family), to expect their husbands to "bear an equal share of the burden."

While Foster's plain and pragmatic critique of conventional domestic gender relations has appealed to some modern, revisionist critics, it failed to impress her contemporary readers and reviewers.

Writing in *The American Review and Literary Journal* (1801), one critic reproached Foster for having failed to at least provide a good model for letter writing; arguing that the moral lessons proposed by Foster were by no means original, the reviewer felt that she should have called herself the editor, not the author, of the book. The reviewer concluded: "In these days, when so many books of questionable utility are published, it may be thought some commendation to say of the present volume, that if it is not calculated to do much good, it will do little harm, unless to the bookseller." *The Boarding School* was never reprinted.

Whether the lack of popular success of the book had anything to do with it or not, Foster did not write any other full-length books after *The Boarding School*. In the first decade of the nineteenth century she did, however, contribute anonymously to *The Monthly Anthology or Magazine of Polite Literature,* a Federalist journal that later became *The North American Review*. After her husband's death Foster went to Montreal to live with her two daughters, both of whom had embarked on literary careers of their own. Elizabeth Foster published two novels in 1824 and 1826 under her married name, Eliza Lanesford Cushing, and was co-editor of *The Literary Garland,* a monthly magazine in Montreal, while Harriet Foster published two books in 1824 and 1827 under her married name, Harriet Vaughan Cheney. Foster died in Montreal on 17 April 1840 at the age of eighty-one.

Even though critics are not unanimous on the ultimate sociocultural significance of Foster's work, few critics would contest the view that in *The Coquette* Foster created an original and subtly critical analysis of contemporary ideologies of seduction, marriage, loyalty, and authority. Much more than a mere novel of seduction, *The Coquette* thus addresses some of the fundamental gender and political issues of the 1790s in America, issues that are still relevant in the late twentieth century. In its revision of the tenets of conduct-book discourse, *The Boarding School* subtly shifts ideologies of gender, while *The Coquette* stands almost alone among early American sentimental novels as a work of exceptional dramatic quality and as one of the most imaginative critiques of the baneful effects of societal boundaries on women in the early republic.

References:

Charles Knowles Bolton, *The Elizabeth Whitman Mystery at the Old Bell Tavern in Danvers: A Study of Eliza Wharton, the Heroine of a Famous New England Romance* (Peabody, Mass.: Peabody Historical Society, 1912);

Herbert Ross Brown, Introduction to *The Coquette; or, The History of Eliza Wharton,* edited by Brown (New York: Columbia University Press, 1939);

Brown, *The Sentimental Novel in America, 1789–1860* (Durham, N.C.: Duke University Press, 1940), pp. 28–73;

Leonard Cassuto, "The Seduction of American Religious Discourse in Foster's *The Coquette,*" in *Reform and Counterreform: Dialectics of the Word in Western Christianity Since Luther,* edited by John C. Hawley (Berlin & New York: Mouton de Gruyter, 1994), pp. 103–118;

Caroline H. Dall, *The Romance of the Association; or, One Last Glimpse of Charlotte Temple and Eliza Wharton. A Curiosity of Literature and Life* (Cambridge, Mass.: Wilson, 1875);

Cathy N. Davidson, "Flirting with Destiny: Ambivalence and Form in the Early American Sentimental Novel," *Studies in American Fiction* (Spring 1982): 17–39;

Davidson, *Revolution and the Word: The Rise of the Novel in America* (New York & Oxford: Oxford University Press, 1986);

Gwendolyn-Audrey Foster, "The Dialogic Margins of Conduct Fiction: Hannah Webster Foster's *The Boarding School,*" *JASAT* (October 1994): 59–72;

Adam Goldgeier, "*The Coquette* Composed," *Constructions* (1990): 1–14;

Kristie Hamilton, "An Assault on the Will: Republican Virtue and the City in Hannah Webster Foster's *The Coquette,*" *Early American Literature,* 24 (1989): 135–151;

Sharon M. Harris, "Hannah Webster Foster's *The Coquette:* Critiquing Franklin's America," in *Redefining the Political Novel: American Women Writers, 1797–1901,* edited by Harris (Knoxville: University of Tennessee Press, 1995), pp. 1–22;

Jane E. Locke, "Historical Preface, Including a Memoir of the Author," in *The Coquette* (Boston: Etheridge, 1855);

Carla Mulford, Introduction to *The Coquette;* bound with William Hill Brown's *The Power of Sympathy* (New York: Penguin Books, 1996);

Claire C. Pettengill, "Hannah Webster Foster (1758–1840)," *Legacy: A Journal of American Women Writers,* 12, no. 2 (1995): 133–141;

Pettengill, "Sisterhood in a Separate Sphere: Female Friendship in Hannah Webster Foster's *The Coquette* and *The Boarding School,*" *Early American Literature,* 27 (1992): 185–203;

Henri Petter, *The Early American Novel* (Columbus: Ohio State University Press, 1971);

Frank Shuffleton, "Mrs. Foster's *Coquette* and the Decline of the Brotherly Watch," *Studies in Eighteenth-Century Culture,* 16 (1986): 211–224;

Robert L. Shurter, "Mrs. Hannah Webster Foster and the Early American Novel," *American Literature,* 4 (November 1932): 306–308;

Carroll Smith-Rosenberg, "Domesticating Virtue: Coquettes and Revolutionaries in Young America," in *Literature and the Body: Essays on Populations and Persons,* edited by Elaine Scarry (Baltimore & London: Johns Hopkins University Press, 1988), pp. 160–184;

John-Paul Tassoni, "'I Can Step Out of Myself a Little': Feminine Virtue and Female Friendship in Hannah Foster's *The Coquette,*" in *Communication and Women's Friendships: Parallels and Intersections in Literature and Life,* edited by Janet Doubler-Ward and JoAnna Stephens-Mink (Bowling Green, Ohio: Bowling Green State University Popular Press, 1993), pp. 97–111;

W. M. Verhoeven, "'Persuasive Rhetorick': Representation and Resistance in Early American Epistolary Fiction," in *Making America / Making American Literature: Franklin to Cooper,* edited by A. Robert Lee and Verhoeven (Amsterdam & Atlanta: Rodopi, 1996), pp. 123–164;

David Waldstreicher, "'Fallen under My Observation': Vision and Virtue in *The Coquette,*" *Early American Literature,* 27 (1992): 204–218;

Walter P. Wenska Jr., "*The Coquette* and the American Dream of Freedom," *Early American Literature,* 12 (1978): 243–255;

James Woodress, *A Yankee's Odyssey: The Life of Joel Barlow* (New York: Lippincott, 1958), pp. 60–64.

Winifred Marshall Gales

(10 July 1761 – 26 June 1839)

Jennifer Jordan Baker
University of Pennsylvania

BOOKS: *The History of Lady Emma Melcombe, and Her Family,* as A Female, 3 volumes (London: Printed for G. G. J. & J. Robinson, 1787);
Matilda Berkely, or, Family Anecdotes, as W. Brown (Raleigh, N.C.: Printed by J. Gales, Printer to the State, 1804).

OTHER: "Sunrise on the Potomac, 1821," "Musings in the Month of May," and "Lines of an Infant who Died at the Break of Day," in *Wood-Notes; or, Carolina Carols: A Collection of North Carolina Poetry,* 2 volumes, compiled by Tenella (Raleigh, N.C.: Warren L. Pomeroy, 1854), I: 111–116;
"O, what a goodly scene mine eyes embrace!" in *William Winston Seaton of the "National Intelligencer": A Biographical Sketch with Passing Notices of His Associates and Friends,* by Josephine Seaton (Boston: Osgood, 1871), pp. 130–131.

Winifred Marshall Gales was a novelist, memoirist, and poet who supported the British reform movement of the late eighteenth century and worked to bring civil libertarianism to her adoptive home of North Carolina. Exiled from England, she and her husband, printer Joseph Gales, spent their most productive years in the capital city of Raleigh, where they were staunch supporters of the American Unitarian movement and prominent members of Raleigh intellectual circles. Gales's best known work, *Matilda Berkely, or, Family Anecdotes* (1804), was the first locally published novel by a resident of the state of North Carolina.

Winifred Marshall was born on 10 July 1761 in Newark, England, the youngest daughter of John and Elizabeth Weston Marshall. Both her parents came from families that were respectable though not wealthy, and Winifred was distantly related to English aristocracy. At her father's insistence she received an education in both the classics and the political thought of the day. She later recalled in her memoir that her early readings included works by

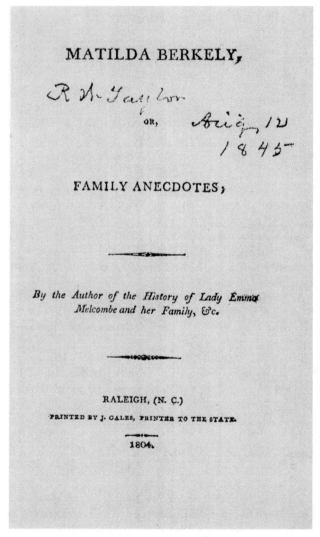

Title page for Winifred Marshall Gales's second novel, about a young woman who is ultimately rewarded for her virtue

Longinus, William Shakespeare, and Adam Smith, as well as various histories, topographical works, and periodicals. Other sources indicate that she was influenced by Homer, John Milton, William Cowper, Alexander Pope, and Joseph Addison. As a writer of stories and poems, she displayed literary talent at an early age. Some scholars have claimed that she published her first novel, a book titled *Lady Julia Seaton,* at the age of seventeen; however, no copy or record of this work exists today.

Winifred Marshall met her future husband, Joseph Gales, while he was a printer's apprentice in Newark-at-Trent. The two were married on 4 May 1784. Her husband, a tradesman and the son of a village schoolmaster, was a political liberal interested in the causes of parliamentary reform, labor reform, universal manhood suffrage, religious freedom, and the abolition of the slave trade. Although the Marshalls had been staunch Tories and political conservatives, Winifred embraced the causes of her new husband. The couple settled in Sheffield, where Gales's husband opened a bookshop. In 1787 he began publishing the Sheffield *Register,* a newspaper advocating political and religious reform. The first book printed by her husband's press was a folio Bible, for which she annotated the illustration plates. In 1785 Gales gave birth to their first child, a daughter who lived only a few hours. During the next five years she gave birth to four more children: Joseph, Winifred, Sarah, and Thomas. She took an active role in her children's educations, teaching them Latin and introducing them to literature.

Gales's first documented novel, *The History of Lady Emma Melcombe, and Her Family,* was published in 1787. She sold the copyright to a London publisher for twenty-five guineas, and that same year the book was published in Dublin as well. Set in England, this three-volume novel is the story of two orphaned children, Edward and Emma, and their search for their familial origins. The first volume primarily concerns the children's mother, Emma Melcombe. A woman born to high rank, she dies in obscurity after her marriage is discredited. Her children are declared illegitimate and unfairly denied their inheritances. This volume also includes a written narrative left by Emma Melcombe that chronicles her tragic past. It is to be given to her children when they reach twenty-one; thus, the "history" in the title of the book refers both to the novel and this narrative. In the second and third volumes the children uncover their origins, and by the end of the novel their titles and inheritances are restored. The final restoration, however, is a triumph only because the children's characters merit such distinction. The novel clearly conveys the message that lineage must be accompanied by virtuous behavior and that birth rank does not assure propriety.

This novel ultimately is concerned with vindicating virtuous behavior and demonstrating, for women especially, the dangers of unrestrained passion. Despite this didacticism, however, the novel does not entirely deny a woman's prerogative to follow her heart, especially in matters of matrimony. Various characters lament the prospect of arranged, loveless marriages, and the novel lauds women's decisions to choose their own husbands or to remain unmarried.

Modern scholars have often described *Emma Melcombe* as a typical sentimental novel, replete with melodramatic plot twists and emotionally volatile heroines. Gales was clearly well versed in the conventions of this genre. Volumes two and three are written in epistolary form, using the letters to present and contrast the private thoughts of several characters. Gales also prefaced her work with a conventional letter of gratitude addressed to her literary benefactor. Apologizing for her deficiencies as a writer, the letter presents the novel for the "candid judgement" of her readers. Gales wrote self-consciously as a woman. She published the novel under the pseudonym "A Female," obscuring her identity but not her gender. In the preface she discussed the merits of female writers: although she was quick to claim that male writers enjoyed superior literary abilities, she also celebrated the then- recent literary accomplishments of women such as Anna Barbauld, Anna Seward, and Hannah Cowley.

In 1794 Winifred Gales left England and never returned. The previous year her husband had been forced to flee England for Germany after local authorities became suspicious of his political activities. (He had sold the controversial writings of Thomas Paine, expressed sympathy for the French Revolution, and openly criticized the conservative government of William Pitt the Younger.) With her husband in exile Gales continued to run the newspaper and bookshop. While alone in Sheffield, she also became embroiled in the controversies surrounding her husband's participation in the parliamentary-reform movement. Gales eventually sold the business and followed her husband to Germany with their four children. They stayed briefly in the city of Altona, during which time she became acquainted with revolutionary emigrés from France and England and befriended American diplomat and poet Joel Barlow. During this time she also gave birth to her sixth child, a daughter named Altona in honor of the city.

When the Gales realized they could not safely return to England, they chose to immigrate to the United States. Philadelphia, then the national capital and a haven for revolutionaries such as Thomas Paine, was to be their new home. The immigration was distressful for Gales, who felt exiled from her mother country and torn from the relatives she had

Gales's 26 March 1815 letter to Edward Jones, commenting on the recently concluded treaty that ended the War of 1812 (Southern Historical Collection, The Library of the University of North Carolina at Chapel Hill)

left behind. She quickly adapted to life in America, however, and came to see her new homeland as a place where her political ideals might flourish. For the next three years she and her family lived in Philadelphia and maintained close contact with other European refugees. Her husband became a stenographer for the U.S. Congress and purchased the *Independent Gazetteer.*

Among these refugees was Joseph Priestley, the scientist and dissident who had first introduced Gales and her husband to Unitarianism in England. While in Philadelphia the couple renewed contact with Priestley and helped organize the Unitarian Society of that city. Gales was drawn to Unitarianism because she believed it fostered an intellectual and scientific understanding of the world. She maintained a pragmatic view of religion, believing that it should inspire virtuous action rather than blind adherence to doctrine. "Ample faith," she later wrote in a letter dated 11 June 1821, could not be a substitute for the "scanty practice" of Christian duties.

Owing in part to the yellow-fever epidemics ravaging the city, Gales and her husband resettled in Raleigh, North Carolina, in 1799. Here her husband established a new printing business and founded the *Raleigh Register,* a paper dedicated to promoting Jeffersonian Republicanism. He and his son-in-law, William Winston Seaton, later founded the thriving printing business of Gales & Seaton.

Winifred Gales quickly became a prominent member of Raleigh social and intellectual circles. She was especially good friends with Caroline Hentz, a North Carolina resident who enjoyed commercial and critical success as a playwright. By many accounts Gales was an exceptional conversationalist whose intellectual merits and progressive ideals earned her respect even within conservative Southern society. Following her immigration to the United States, Gales had four more children. Two daughters, Ann Elizabeth and Mary, were born during her stay in Philadelphia (Mary died in infancy traveling to Raleigh). After settling in North Carolina, Gales gave birth to Caroline Mathilda and Weston Raleigh.

Gales published her best-known work, a novel titled *Matilda Berkely, or, Family Anecdotes,* in 1804 under the pseudonym W. Brown. It was printed at her husband's press. Like *Emma Melcombe, Matilda Berkely* is a work of domestic fiction primarily concerned with demonstrating the merits of middle-class virtues. The main plot follows Matilda, a woman of "good connections" but orphaned since infancy, as she enters the alluring and often corrupt society of London. Her travel companion is Eliza Berville, also an orphan but of more obscure origins. Cosmopolitan society tests the two women as they must avoid the snares of lecherous and insolvent male suitors and suffer the haughtiness of high-ranking women.

Both women find happiness, though in far different ways. Matilda marries the virtuous and distinguished Charles Egerton (who must first forsake his fiancée, the vulgar Lady Blanche). Eliza is initially less fortunate, as she is kidnapped and hidden in a Russian monastery for years. Once released, having educated herself in the monastery, she resigns herself to a life of "blessed singleness." While most of Gales's writing exhibits little consciousness about the inferior social status of women, the fate of Eliza in this novel indicates that Gales did envision an alternative female life based on intellectual pursuits rather than marriage and children.

Unlike Gales's first work, *Matilda Berkely* does not preach to young female readers on the dangers of unrestrained passions. Rather the novel focuses on vindicating those unrecognized members of the middle class whose talents, learning, and refinement should, Gales suggests, rightly compensate for their lack of hereditary distinctions. The novel also goes to great lengths to poke fun at the excesses of high society, describing in comic detail the gaudy dress and incessant prattle of Lady Blanche.

It is important to note, however, that Gales's message is contradictory. As in her first novel, a virtuous character of unknown origins is revealed to be a person of notable lineage. In the final scene Eliza discovers she is Matilda's cousin and a woman of moderate distinction; thus, her virtuous behavior is, after all, validated by her familial line. While the novel satirizes the excesses of the aristocracy, it still harbors a nostalgia for hereditary social distinctions. Gales herself came from a family of "fallen aristocrats," and later, in her memoir, she wrote with mixed feelings about her British ancestors. She described her own "tender feelings" for their vestigial distinctions but simultaneously insisted that such distinctions were of little importance in a land such as America, where "honourable conduct" alone was to be the mark of nobility.

There is no evidence that *Matilda Berkely* received critical attention when it was published. Writing in *The Atlantic Monthly* in October 1860, one anonymous Southern historian stated that Gales's literary talent "won no approval" in her own day. A later critical review by Archibald Henderson, published in *North Carolina: The Old North State and the New* (1941), criticized the book for its "choppy" narrative style ("as if it had been jotted down in a notebook at intervals of leisure") and the "tears, faintings, and palpitating bosoms" associated with the cult of sensibility exemplified in the works of Samuel Richardson and Henry Fielding. Writing in the *North Carolina Historical Review* in 1850, Roger Powell Marshall noted the lack of American subject matter in *Matilda Berkely* and suggested that its distraught heroines would have appealed largely to teenage girls. As these reviews suggest, responses to Gales's work have tended to reflect a strong bias against the sentimental-novel tradition itself. Gales's novels have not received recent critical attention.

Matilda Berkely was Gales's last novel. In 1815 she turned to writing a memoir with the intention of providing her children with a genealogical record of their parents' families left behind in England. Gales wrote these reminiscences for the benefit of her family and expressed strong wishes that they never be made public. The second section of the memoir, which she took up in 1831, describes the political turmoil during the British parliamentary-reform movement of the 1790s and chronicles, with mixed emotions, the family's expatriation. Unlike the first section, which is a straightforward chronicle of family history, this second section covers with immediacy and vivid detail the events of the 1790s. It describes their passage from Germany to the United States, paying special attention to the inspiring yet terrifying experience of crossing the Atlantic. Invoking Longinus's notion of the sublime, Gales recalled the "vast wilderness of waves" that was the "most wonderful object in Creation." She also wrote of how a privateer captured the ship and how she was forced to use her celebrated conversational skills to negotiate its release.

During her time in Raleigh, Gales also turned to writing poetry in modes typical of her day: romantic nature odes, lamentations, and occasional poems. The handful of her poetry that remains was written in the 1820s as she was aging and looking back on her own life. All of the poems are pastoral, expressing awe for God's sublime manifestation in the natural world as well as a nostalgia for the simple life of her childhood in England. Some of this poetry was later collected in a regional literary anthology and in biographical works on the Gales family.

Always part of a political and literary community, Gales engaged in lively correspondence with several intellectuals, perhaps most notably Jared Sparks, a Unitarian minister and later the editor of *The North American Review*. From about 1820 until the end of her life, Gales and Sparks carried on a friendly, intellectual correspondence that included discussions of literature, American and European politics, and theology. In these letters Gales discussed her hopes for the Unitarian movement in the American South. She was especially concerned that the United States should forbid an established religion and maintain a Jeffersonian separation of Church and State. Although she considered orthodox religions to be superstitious and unenlightened, she always championed religious freedom. Her reasoning was in part practical; for she understood that Unitarianism would never take hold in the conservative southern state without there being tolerance of all religious beliefs. Above all, however, she supported religious freedom because she believed that an unfettered intellect was the basis of a progressive society: "a good man is not less estimable whatever sectarian creed he adopts," she wrote to Sparks on 18 July 1820. "Truth and virtue are immutable—and names are but finite distinctions."

Ultimately, Unitarianism failed to flourish in North Carolina. Unitarian churches began disappearing in the South, and orthodox movements, especially Methodism, spread quickly throughout the region. No longer comfortable in the increasingly conservative religious culture, Gales and her husband left North Carolina in 1833 and settled in Washington, D.C., where their oldest son, Joseph Gales Jr., edited *The National Intelligencer*. The youngest of Gales's children, Weston Raleigh Gales, assumed full charge of the *Raleigh Register* on his parents' departure. While in Washington, Gales's husband worked as the chief manager of the African Colonization Society.

In 1836 Gales resumed work on her memoir, but she did not live long enough to finish it. This brief final section chronicles her settlement in Philadelphia and Raleigh. She described the economic hardship her husband encountered when he was forced to start over in a new country and the emotional difficulties she faced as a perpetual wanderer in strange places. In her descriptions of Raleigh she decried the slave system, calling it a trade "in the blood and sinews of our fellow beings." She acknowledged, however, that she harbored "prejudices against colored servants, never having seen but 2 in England" and "would not suffer" black house servants to care for her when she was ill. She also admitted apologetically that the scarcity of wage labor in the South left the family no choice but to rely on slave labor for their printing business. It is clear that despite her commitment to social progress, she could not fully apply her libertarian views to the question of American slavery.

Toward the end of her memoir Gales related an amusing anecdote in which her doctor, while performing a painful procedure, distracted her by shouting "what's that in the street?" In this story Gales, full of the "World's Witch Curiosity," was easily enticed by the question and turned quickly to the window to see what was happening outside. She found the incident telling because she prided herself on her unflagging interest in civic life. The theme that surfaces repeatedly throughout Gales's memoir is her dedication to the civic causes to which her husband first introduced her in England. She wrote candidly of the personal sacrifices she made to accommodate his political activism, but clearly she believed that these causes were, save her children, the most important priorities in her life. Gales made no mention of her novels or other literary endeavors in her memoir.

On 26 June 1839 Gales died in Washington, D.C., after a painful illness. She was almost seventy-nine. Her husband appended his own recollections to the memoir she left behind. Writing the inscription for her tombstone, he eulogized her as a mother, as an emigré to the United States, and, above all, as a woman with a "strong and cultivated mind." Neither Gales's husband nor her oldest son, who wrote his mother's obituary, chose to remember her as a writer. The omission suggests that Winifred Gales and those who knew her considered her literary endeavors to be of secondary importance. It has been her role as a female intellectual and as the matriarch of a prominent publishing family that has determined her place in the cultural history of the American South.

References:

Margaret J. Boeringer, "Joseph Gales, North Carolina Printer," M.A. thesis, University of North Carolina, 1989;

Clement Eaton, "Winifred and Joseph Gales, Liberals of the Old South," *Journal of Southern History,* 10 (1944): 461–474;

"The National Intelligencer and Its Editors," *Atlantic Monthly,* 6 (October 1860): 470–481;

Josephine Seaton, *William Winston Seaton of the "National Intelligencer": A Biographical Sketch with Passing Notices of His Associates and Friends* (Boston: Osgood, 1871);

"Winifred Marshall Gales," in *Dictionary of North Carolina Biography,* 6 volumes, edited by William S. Powell (Chapel Hill: University of North Carolina Press, 1979–1996), II: 270;

"Winifred Marshall Gales," in *North Carolina Authors: A Selective Handbook,* prepared by a Joint Committee of the North Carolina English Teachers Association and the North Carolina Library Association (Chapel Hill: University of North Carolina Library, 1952), pp. 42–43.

Papers:

Papers of the Gales family are housed at the North Carolina State Archives in Raleigh and at the University of North Carolina, Chapel Hill. The combined "Reminiscences" of Joseph and Winifred Gales are in the Southern Historical Collection at the University of North Carolina, Chapel Hill. The original letters from Winifred Gales to Jared Sparks are at the Houghton Library, Harvard University, and a photostat of these letters can be found at the North Carolina State Archives in Raleigh.

Grace Growden Galloway

(1727 – 6 February 1782)

Doreen Alvarez Saar
Drexel University

WORKS: "Diary of Grace Growden Galloway," edited by Raymond C. Werner, *Pennsylvania Magazine of History and Biography*, 55 (1931): 35–94; 58 (1934): 152–189; republished, *Diary of Grace Growden Galloway*, Eyewitness Accounts of the American Revolution, Series III (New York: New York Times & Arno Press, 1971).

Once undervalued among literary scholars, diaries have been recognized in the late twentieth century as an important aspect of literature created by women. Among the most interesting diaries written during the American Revolution are those kept by a Loyalist, Grace Growden Galloway, while the world as she had known it was completely destroyed. The wife of a prominent Loyalist who was considered one of the greatest traitors to the American cause, Galloway wrote her diaries during the years 1778–1779, while she remained alone in Philadelphia (after her husband had fled) to fight for legal recognition of her right to her own property.

Produced by women whose literary output was often limited by circumstance, diaries have particular conventions that change with each literary period. Unlike modern diary writers, eighteenth-century diary keepers were not concerned with personal revelation. In the interpretation of a diary, biography provides essential context. Unfortunately, biographical information is not always available. Such is the case with Galloway. Most of her biography has been inferred from information about her male relatives, the most important of whom is her husband, Joseph Galloway. Like most women of her era, Grace Galloway lived her life in the shadow of men and derived her sense of self from her position as the wife of one of the most important men in Pennsylvania. Even when she felt scorned by society and abandoned by friends, she asserted her relationship to the male figures in her life as the sign of her own identity and as a means of validating her right to privilege:

I told them I was ye happiest woman in twown [*sic*] for I had been striped & Turn'd out of Doors yet I was still ye same & must be Joseph Galloways Wife & Lawrence Growdons daughter & that it was Not in their power to humble me for I shou'd be Grace Growden Galloway to ye last & as I had now suffer'd all that they can inflict Upon Me I shou'd now act as on a rock to look on ye wrack of others. (21 April 1779)

Grace Galloway's family history was not atypical of colonial American families. Her grandfather, Joseph Growden, a Cornish immigrant, settled in Pennsylvania and accumulated a large amount of property. His second son, Lawrence, sought his fortune as a merchant in England, where he married. Grace, Lawrence's second child, was born in England in 1727. After Lawrence Growden returned with his wife and two daughters to Pennsylvania in 1733, he served as a provincial councillor, a member of the Pennsylvania Assembly, and speaker of the assembly. In 1750 he was appointed second justice of the Pennsylvania Supreme Court, a position he held for fifteen years. At his father's death Lawrence Growden inherited land holdings valued at about £113,400, becoming one of the richest and most influential men in the colony.

According to Oliver Kuntzleman, her family's wealth and social standing made Grace attractive to many suitors in Pennsylvania. She, however, had a mind of her own. In 1747, while she was in England visiting her elder sister Elizabeth (Mrs. Thomas Nickelson), she fell in love with a Mr. Milner, son of the receiver of customs at Poole. In 1751 Grace's father heard about her attachment to Milner, deemed him unsuitable, and ordered Grace to return home. In 1753, fairly soon after her return to Pennsylvania, she married Joseph Galloway. Biographers have implied that the handsome, successful, and ambitious Galloway viewed the marriage as part of his ascent to the highest ranks of Philadelphia society. A Quaker, Galloway converted to Anglicanism in order to marry Grace Growden, and his conversion enhanced his political career.

139

Grace Growden Galloway (The Historical Society of Pennsylvania)

Like the Growdens, the Galloway family had risen to wealth and prominence in the New World in fewer than one hundred years. Joseph Galloway's great-grandfather, a Quaker, immigrated to Maryland in 1662. By the time Joseph Galloway was born in 1730, his family had land holdings and a mercantile business. Joseph Galloway studied with a lawyer and established a flourishing legal practice in Philadelphia, where he purchased a spacious mansion at Sixth and Market Streets.

Joseph and Grace Galloway prospered, but as Elizabeth Evans has indicated, both husband and wife were "strong-willed, and their marriage was a turbulent one." They had three sons and one daughter, Elizabeth, the only one of their children to live to an advanced age. It is evident from the diaries that Elizabeth (called Betsy or Betsay in the diaries) was the apple of her mother's eye.

A member of the American Philosophical Society and its vice president from 1769 to 1775, Joseph Galloway made his mark in intellectual and social circles, and he shaped history with his political activity. Galloway formed a political partnership with Benjamin Franklin that controlled Pennsylvania politics from the time of Galloway's election to the Pennsylvania Assembly in 1756 until the eve of the American Revolution. From 1766 to 1775 Galloway, who was known as the "Demosthenes of Pennsylvania," dominated politics as speaker of the assembly. His political success matched his financial achievements. Galloway was one of the richest men in the colonies. During the 1770s, when Grace Galloway inherited Trevose (444 acres), Belmont (574 acres), King's Place (297 acres), Richlieu (407 acres), a Delaware river tract (160 acres), and 30 percent of the Durham Iron Works, her wealth further enhanced their financial position.

Despite their worldly success, Grace Galloway's poetry includes indications that she was unhappy. In 1759 she wrote "[I] find Myself Neglected Loathed Dispised." Other poems describe male tyranny and a "wretched Wife / Whose Doom'd with him to spend her Life." In one poem she warned,

> never get Tyed to a Man
> for when once you are yoked
> Tis all a Mere Joke
> of seeing your freedom again[.]

The Galloways' luck changed when the colonies demanded independence. By 1775, living in retirement at Trevose, Joseph Galloway, who believed that remaining loyal to the British was the only sensible course for the colonies, passed the days in danger, threatened by patriotic mobs who wanted to "hang him at his own door." Late in 1776 Joseph Galloway left to join the British army in New Jersey while Grace Galloway remained at Trevose. In 1777 she complained of harassment to the Supreme Executive Council, which ordered the sheriffs and magistrates of Bucks County "to prevent so far as in your power, any insult being offered to Mrs. Galloway." Joseph returned to Philadelphia with the British army when it entered the city in August 1777.

The British occupation placed Joseph Galloway once again at the center of the political stage: he was made administrator of Philadelphia. For eight months during 1777–1778, Gen. William Howe occupied Philadelphia while the Revolutionary army spent the winter camped at Valley Forge. Feeling that Philadelphia offered her greater protection than Trevose, Grace Galloway joined her husband in 1778. While the British were promising bounties of land to Loyalists for enlisting, the Pennsylvania General Assembly acted against those it considered traitors to the patriot cause. In March 1778 it passed an act for "the attainder of divers Traitors." Joseph Galloway was on their list, and the assembly declared that his property, including the estates Grace Galloway had inherited, should be confiscated and sold. In May 1778, after hearing news of the French alliance with the Americans and their rejection of British offers for peace without independence, Sir Henry Clinton, who had replaced Howe in Philadelphia, evacuated British troops from the city. Three thousand Loyalists, including Galloway and his daughter, Betsy, accompanied the British army, going first to New York and later to England. Grace Galloway, however, stayed in Philadelphia, determined to salvage the estates that she had inherited from her father.

Her decision to remain was predicated on eighteenth-century British common law governing women's property rights. When a woman married, she maintained title to the realty that she owned. Her husband could use the rents and the profits from her land, but he had no permanent right to and could not permanently dispose of it without her consent, nor could it be taken to pay her husband's debts. After her husband's death a wife was entitled to claim the rents and profits from her land for her own use. If a wife predeceased her husband, title to her realty went to her children, who took possession of the land on their father's death. A primary thread in Grace Galloway's diaries is the record of her fight in the Pennsylvania courts to keep her realty. In her

view she made a proper maternal sacrifice when she remained in Philadelphia. While her husband was deemed a traitor and stood to forfeit his estates, Grace Galloway had not been declared a traitor, and she argued that she had a legal right to the estates she had inherited. Therefore, the family should be entitled to the rents from Grace Galloway's land, and her daughter should be able to inherit these substantial properties. Grace Galloway believed that the wealth that would accrue to Betsy from this property would have a substantial effect on her ability to marry suitably. As she wrote in a 23 September 1778 letter, "Should I leave this place they will not only take my income, but confiscate my estate, and then perhaps, my dearest child will become a beggar. Therefore, while I have the least shadow of saving something for her I will stay."

Some readers may question the wisdom of Grace Galloway's decision to remain among enemies in an embattled city. Yet she was not alone in this decision. Other Loyalist women remained for similar reasons. In his letters Joseph Galloway expressed concern about his separation from his wife, writing on 14 August 1778: "My dear, I cannot express the pain we suffer at our separation. I have as yet heard nothing certain from you. . . . Is your staying from us likely to be of any service. If not, make all the expedition to us possible." He also told her to consider an alternative: "Your own estate they can forfeit only during my life—get some friend to purchase that for you." Grace Galloway's diaries chronicle the events that befell her from 17 June 1778 until 30 September 1779. In summer 1778 Thomas McKean, chief justice of the Pennsylvania Supreme Court, ordered the seizure of certain Loyalist estates, including Grace Galloway's. While she was able to inhabit the Galloway mansion in Philadelphia for some time, on 20 August Charles Willson Peale, one of the agents for confiscated estates in Philadelphia, ejected her by force from that home, and she went to live with friends. Pursuing her legal battle, she watched the tide of the war turn against the British. Her diary records what happened when a sheltered, wealthy woman was forced to depend entirely on herself for the first time in her life. As Galloway frequently commented about her new situation, "I know not how to act."

Margo Culley has pointed out in her general study of the nature of the diary that the eighteenth-century secular diary "served a number of semi-public purposes and that the writers of many of these secular journals intended them to be read." Mary Sauter Comfort, the only critic to assess Galloway's literary achievement at length, bases her analysis of the Galloway diaries on Steven Kagle's

Friday 2d yͤ weather still very hot Mrs Cox
& Nancy Redman & Dr Chovet
& his wife drank tea with Me &
Daniel Mifflin they all went a way & Daniel
paid Me 40 pounds coming to me & I borrow'd
7 more of him Debby supped with Me & yͤ
Staid I am Determin'd to pay Craig as Daniel
says he will Make me pay had money should
times change Nothing Remarkable to day
Saturday 3 Debby took yͤ Mony to Craig but
there was some counterfeit bill & he return'd it
the weather extreamly hot that I cou'd not go
out & am very weak Drank tea & sat by Myself
all yͤ afternoon Debby supped with Me but
my spirits begins to sink as I can See no excep
else know not how to Act Sam Fisher put
in Jail this evening wish I was in England
Sunday 4th sat in My Room Hindred all day
it rain'd Drank tea by My self
Sally Janes came in & I asked her if she was
a whig in a Jesting way but I found she was atom
this only principle I was Much shocked at
being so Deceiv'd Mrs B Lawrence came in
& two Miss Rawles: they went soon but I prest
Mrs Lawrence & she stayd yͤ evening & supped
with Me I am not easy for fear I said something
that may not be proper & am vexed about Sally
Janes I wish I cou'd allways be on my Guard
Monday 5 Mrs Joe Morris & Mrs Craig & John
& Debby drank tea with Me Mrs Cadwallader call'd to
see me but did not stay: walked out in yͤ evening & at
my Return found Mrs Norris & Mrs Jones & Mrs Livingston
a deal of Talk but I fear I talk to Much wish

Galloway's diary entries for 2–5 April and 20–24 May 1779 (The Historical Society of Pennsylvania)

Thursday ye 20 Both Redman & Chovet came but Redman
treated me with such Contempt & disrespect that
I wish I had not sent for him he wou'd scarce hear what I had to
say & at last they prescribed a Natural Mixture but Redman said
I must send to ye Apothecarys for he had not Drugs & old Chovet is
so unfeeling & for making as much trouble so importantly & I
wish I had sent for Neither but they both told me Medecine wou'd
do me ye good as want of exercise was what I wanted I got so
frighted that I sent for Johnny Pembertons Chariot & rode
out with Neighbour Smith she is weak a woman but I cou'd get
No body else her whole discourse is of her own importance but
she was never in a Chariot I am convinced before in her life but
I let her go on for I think it Not worth while to talk to her she
is to weak & too conceited to be any way improved I was much the
worse after we came home & spent y^e afternoon in a most Nervous
some way Dr Chovet & Mr Goodman there. Mrs Pott is going
to New York she call'd on me for letters & I got Mr on looking
up belongs pocket book where I found two letters that ____ far be
a balm they were a Dagger to my mind as I find my child is not
happy. Hannah Jones was Married this day to Amos Foulk
I was invited to the wedding but cou'd not go but they sent me
some good things seem'd much better & Cheerful

Friday y^e 21 was bravely to day went to Smiths but
had not been there long before Molly Law came
came to see me I talked very freely to her of Johns & Mrs Bonds
behaviour in short I spoke of ye ill treatment with spirit & I found
she was rather pleased at my resentment their surprized thing
with me as a friend she stayed but a little while but I told Debby we
talked the things I have appointed her but I care not strong of
love my will hold out their hand to beleive me very the spirit
Saturday y^e 22 I was very low & Humphries with y^e Debby down
the coffee the My Goodloe went after ____ to Smiths
but Nothing entertaining there supped by myself & Debby in my
own Nurse very unwell serious cold what with it all dark
Sunday y^e 23 Nurse I much worse of y^e Lip early I was in
good spirits & much better than before
seen a great while walk in y^e Entry all y^e afternoon by myself
was a little unwell of a Cause at Night there took Laudice &
Nouring Neighbour Smith here a little while with Mrs
Francis & Nancy Powel Debby & I supped together ____ Chear
ful & better Mrs Debby went to Bristol a Mob is raised in
Monday y^e 24 y^e County they are taking Up Tories and are
were much alarmed I say We will assert our about to Smiths he was
very serious but I hid is much frighted we are quite alone

notion in his *American Diary Literature, 1620–1799* (1979) that the diary as a form is both "a work and a fictional person to whom the work is directed." Noting that Galloway's diaries have no specifically named audience, Comfort argues, there are three implied audiences, each associated with the different tensions in Galloway's life.

The first audience is the diary as witness to Galloway's private and secret concerns, allowing her to express her opinions while keeping them secret from those who would use them against her. The second audience is the diary as psychotherapist and friend as she fell from an exalted status to one that made her vulnerable to many slights and harms. In fact, she saw herself as a victim and the revolution as a sign of the decline of all human society. Functioning as a sympathetic ear, the diary enabled her to share her troubles and perceived slights when she knew that it was impolitic to express her anger openly: "I hope all will be right yet & I shall ride when these Harpies walk as they Use to do before they Plunder'd me & others" (1 December 1778). The third audience is future generations, for whom she used her diaries as a canvas on which to create a flattering self-portrait. For this audience she created a suspenseful narrative in which she is noble and courageous, presenting herself as a heroine to counterbalance her loss of status. The diary became her friend, and she made herself responsible to the diary, sometimes apologizing for having "neglected" to write. Comfort believes that the diary took on the characteristics of Galloway's absent companions and became the "ideal friend," welcoming "full explication of events and sometimes, interpretation of those events." More receptive than perceptive, "the diary not only tolerates but actually requires exposition."

Comfort adds that the character of Galloway's diaries is revealed by the diarist's changing physical interaction with them. At first Galloway wrote on ledger paper and used a ledger format. The opening entries, which comprise dates, public events, and visitors, are typical of eighteenth-century diaries. As Galloway's needs changed, she soon began to ignore the format of the book and wrote across the lines, adding information about herself and the weather. Her style changed from "accounting to exposition" as she turned to recording her distress, writing the first such entry on 27 June 1778: "Col Mattlack his behaviour Convinced me their is no dependance on him & he threw Me into a state of Dejection." The accounting mode does not entirely disappear, but it is supplemented with description and exposition, as in the entry for 10 July 1779, in which she wrote, "saw Neighbour Zanes there is something so honest & blunt in that plain woman that I prefer her company to most others."

Galloway's relationship with her husband is another provocative element in the diary. Although Galloway sometimes complained of her treatment by her husband, she never challenged the basis of their relationship. What she said about him varied according to her view of how political and personal events were progressing. In July 1778, when Joseph and Betsy Galloway were still in New York, she insisted that "was I assured that My husband and child was happy nothing cou'd make me very wretched." Yet at the same moment she admitted the awfulness of her own situation, "I am fled from as a Pestilence." Letters from Joseph Galloway buoyed her spirits; as the war continued, however, she heard less and less frequently from him. In her diary she attempted to value him fairly, saying for example that he "has his foibles but he was an Honest Man" (24 June 1779). Yet she found that he had mismanaged their lives and wanted sagacity: "Jg is two sanguin & these creatures Underminds him." Even in the midst of her despair she rejoiced in her newfound freedom from the bonds of marriage: "as to Myself I am happy & ye Liberty of doing as I please Makes even poverty more agreeable than any time I ever spent since I married" (25 November 1778). In the same entry she reflected that his "Unkind treatment makes me easey Nay happy not to be with him & if he is safe I want not to be kept so like a slave as he allways Made Me in preventing every wish of my heart." Her anger flared up whenever she reviewed his financial mismanagement, as, for example, his telling tenants that he would not ask rent from them (December 1778). Yet she still defended her husband publicly, as on 2 May 1779, when she wrote:

> Neighbour Smith came in & she said Many of the Army disliked Mr. G I was very warm & am provoked he did so Much for Nothing while people thinks he was so well paid but a vain Man will Neglect his family for a Name & he might have been as Much respected if he had been well paid but this woman is a fool.

After August 1779 Galloway's attitude toward her husband became more critical. Accusing him of "vanity & baseness," she wrote that she was "now truly set against him." She found him guilty of "Ungenerous conduct," hurting "me more than all the proventials . . . had done." To the outside world she had to declare their mutual support for one another and to hide his mismanagement. In a world where she had once been pampered and petted she found only coldness and baseness. As husband, friends, and advisers failed her, she became mistrustful. Galloway summed up her situation in her penultimate diary entry: "I seem'd like an Outcast & as I belong'd to Nobody Nobody cared for Me" (27 September 1779). Her diary had become her only confidante.

Because of her Loyalist affiliations, commentators read Galloway's personality differently. Mary Beth Norton sees her as a "desperately unhappy" wife while Linda Kerber calls her "formidable" and "resentful," arguing that Galloway did not understand how her private life had a particularly public dimension. Beverly Baxter finds that Galloway demonstrated a "mixture of spoiled juvenility and haughty courage," and Lina Leff decries Grace's lack of objectivity and her selfish focus on abandonment and betrayal. On the other hand, Comfort praises Galloway's "personal heroism and commitment." These different readings of Galloway's character probably spring from her often vehement comments, such as:

> I bleam'd them for conversing with ye French & violent Wiggs & said they desarvesd ye ill treatment they met with in short I am determin'd to carry on No More face Unless these people will treat me as My station in life requires: they may as well Whine and Make Mouths where as to me they Make More Noise about a few pounds than I do with all I have lost. . . . (19 April 1779)

In her diaries Galloway always blamed her collapse in social status on her husband. Certainly she was treated in a way that would have been unthinkable before the Revolution. For example, she was manhandled during her ejection from her house; she was unable to procure a carriage in which to take exercise; she had to think about money and how to procure food; and she walked alone and unprotected in the evenings. In one entry she wondered what her daughter "wou'd say to see her Mama walking 5 squares in the rain at Night like a common Woman & go to rooms in an Alley for her home" (13 November 1778). Her misfortunes cost her her health. As external events went against her, she suffered a series of internal maladies.

For many years historians believed that Pennsylvania was a Loyalist stronghold, but recent studies have demonstrated that it was not. Galloway's accounts of her treatment support this contention. Her diary entries reveal that even Loyalists were critical of the British. The Loyalist community blamed them for the failure of the war, believing them not to be sufficiently fervid: "the King's greates[t] enemies ar[e] his own Armies," Galloway wrote on 20 July 1779. Earlier she had charged, "the English Deserves Not the Name of Brittons" (30 June 1779). In her disparagement of the British, she shared the opinion of her husband: Joseph Galloway believed that if the British had behaved properly, Pennsylvania would indeed have been a Loyalist stronghold. Like many Pennsylvanians, he chafed at British indifference to Pennsylvania and complained of personal losses at their hands. In particular, he blamed Howe, whom his wife called "the Author of all our ruin."

The reader is also given glimpses of well-known and even heroic Americans from a Loyalist's vantage point. For example, in Galloway's eyes Charles Willson Peale was a villain for forcibly ejecting her from her home. Gen. Benedict Arnold appears as the indifferent American commandant of Philadelphia, who told Galloway that "he cou'd do Nothing in ye Case" (6 July 1778). Other prominent patriots were helpful; for example, George Bryan, vice president of the Supreme Executive Council of Pennsylvania, offered her advice on her legal case.

Other prominent Philadelphians are mentioned in Galloway's diaries. Her doctor was Abraham Chovet, one of the best-known anatomists and physicians of that period. Prominent Quakers such as Warner Mifflin and Benjamin Chew (who became chief justice of Pennsylvania) are pictured as self-serving. For some reason the appearance of the French ambassador in Pennsylvania on 12 July 1778 aroused strong personal feelings: "I look out & saw the Cannon & soldiers & I thought it was like the execution of my husband." She particularly noticed events unfavorable to the Revolutionary cause, such as the trial and execution of John Roberts and Abraham Carlisle for giving aid to the British. Both men had served in the British administration during the occupation of Philadelphia, but they had performed humanitarian offices and, as history has proved, were innocent of the charges brought against them.

In August 1779 Grace Galloway admitted for the first time, "I know all is lost." She never saw her husband or daughter again and died "blessed with a silent, peaceful exit" on 6 February 1782. According to Evans, "a large crowd gathered at the burial, although Anna Rawle [another Loyalist] believed that Grace had been 'cruelly deserted by her gay acquaintances.'" In her last will and testament, dated 20 December 1781, Galloway devised all her estates to her daughter.

Joseph and Betsy Galloway did not have an easy time in England. In 1782 Betsy wrote, "What a humiliating situation are the refugees reduced to from a state of independent affluence, to *rejoice* at the bounty of the public." Considered the leading Loyalist in exile, Joseph Galloway remained in England until his death. In the 1790s Betsy married William Roberts, a barrister. The couple agreed to a postnuptial contract giving Betsy and her heirs sole ownership of her estate after her father's death. The couple had one child, Ann Grace, and separated soon after her birth. At his death in 1803 Joseph Galloway left a will clearly stating that his wife's estates were to go to Betsy. The trustees immediately began legal proceedings on Betsy's behalf in Pennsylvania, and the common law prevailed. In 1804 Grace Galloway's heirs were judged to have legal right to her realty. The court decided that the attainder on Joseph Galloway's property rested no claim to Grace Galloway's real estate and that, given his death, the property should legally pass to her heirs. Grace Galloway would have been pleased to know that her sacrifice had not been in vain.

References:

Beverley Baxter, "Grace Growden Galloway: Survival of a Loyalist, 1778–79," *Frontiers,* 111 (1975): 52–57;

Wallace Brown, *The King's Friends: The Composition and Motives of the American Loyalist Claimants* (Providence, R.I.: Brown University Press, 1966);

Mary Sauter Comfort, "The Literary Styles of Four Women Diarists of the American Revolution," dissertation, Lehigh University, 1985;

Margo Culley, ed., *A Day at a Time: The Diary Literature of American Women from 1764 to the Present* (New York: Feminist Press at the City University of New York, 1985);

Elizabeth Evans, *Weathering The Storm: Women of the American Revolution* (New York: Scribners, 1975);

John E. Ferling, *The Loyalist Mind: Joseph Galloway and the American Revolution* (University Park: Pennsylvania State University Press, 1977);

Linda Kerber, *Women of the Republic* (Chapel Hill: University of North Carolina Press, 1980);

Oliver Kuntzleman, *Joseph Galloway, Loyalist* (Philadelphia: Temple University Press, 1941);

Linda Ringer Leff, "Seven Women Diarists of Eighteenth-Century Philadelphia," dissertation, Oklahoma State University, 1987;

Mary Beth Norton, *Liberty's Daughters* (Boston: Little, Brown, 1980);

Wilbur Henry Siebert, *The Loyalists of Pennsylvania,* Ohio State University Studies, no. 5 (Columbus: Ohio State University, 1920);

Raymond C. Werner, Introduction and notes to *Diary of Grace Growden Galloway,* Eyewitness Accounts of the American Revolution, Series III (New York: New York Times & Arno Press, 1971).

Papers:

Galloway's diaries are at the Pennsylvania Historical Society. Other miscellaneous papers are scattered in various collections, including the Cairns Collection in the Department of Special Collections at the University of Wisconsin-Madison Memorial Library; the Bucks County Historical Society; the Pennsylvania Historical Society; and the Library of Congress.

Sarah Prince Gill
(1728 – August 1771)

Laurie Crumpacker
Susquehanna University

WORKS: Devotional exercises, in *A Sermon Occasioned by the Death of Mrs. Sarah Gill, Late Consort to Mr. Moses Gill, Merchant,* by John Hunt (Boston: Printed by Edes & Hall, 1771); separately published as *Devotional Papers Written by the Late Mrs. Sarah Gill, of Boston, Together with Her Touching Letter as from the Dead* (Norwich, Conn.: Printed by Green & Spooner, 1773); republished in *Dying Exercises of Mrs. Deborah Prince and Devotional Exercises of Mrs. Sarah Gill, Daughters of the Late Thomas Prince, Minister of South Church Boston* (Edinburgh, 1785; Newbury-Port: Printed & sold by John Mycall, 1789).

Sarah Prince Gill, a model of eighteenth-century evangelical piety, was a diarist, a letter writer, and a leader in the female religious circles of Boston. As was often the case, even among influential women of her day, she published nothing during her lifetime. Manuscripts of her personal diary and meditations remain, however, revealing daily events and her spiritual life; and ten of her devotional exercises were published with the funeral sermon preached at her death in 1771. Her letter-journal, addressed to Esther Edwards Burr, is not extant, but Burr's responses have survived and present a picture of the lively letters that must have occasioned them. Gill was considered a leader and exemplar in religious circles, exerting powerful influence among family and friends, in her church, through her correspondence, and in regular prayer-group meetings with other women.

Sarah Prince was born in Boston, Massachusetts, in 1728, the daughter of the Reverend Thomas Prince of Boston (1687–1758) and Deborah Denny Prince, a recent immigrant from Suffolk, England. Sarah Prince was the first of four daughters and one son born into this Puritan family. Her father, a Harvard graduate and later a noted preacher and historian, was pastor of the Old South Meeting House, the first Congregational Church of Boston. His children grew up in an at-

Sarah Prince Gill, circa 1764 (portrait by John Singleton Copley; Museum of Art, Rhode Island School of Design, Providence, Jesse Metcalf Fund 07.118)

mosphere of intellectualism and piety. Using his extensive library Thomas Prince educated his daughters. Thus they would have been well-read in the classics and would probably have read the works of some of the leading liberal thinkers, such as John Locke. The Prince household was a center for religious intellectuals such as Jonathan Edwards and George Whitefield, leaders of the evangelical or "New Light" Protestant revivals of the mid eighteenth century, which historians have called the Great Awakening. Discussions of the political, religious, and intellectual issues of the times were regular occurrences; and Sarah, her mother, and her sis-

147

ters would have been observers and participants in these events.

Sarah Prince and Esther Edwards met as young girls when their families visited one another and their fathers exchanged pulpits. Esther Edwards was the daughter of New England theologian Jonathan Edwards of Northampton, Massachusetts, and his wife, Sarah Pierpont Edwards. The two girls met frequently as their fathers engaged in confrontations with orthodox Congregationalists (Old Lights) who did not support the revivals of the Great Awakening. Deeply interested in these controversies Sarah and Esther shared the belief of their fathers and other proponents of the Great Awakening that ministers should show evidence of having undergone personal conversion experiences before they were qualified to preach and convert others. This stipulation led Jonathan Edwards, Aaron Burr, and others to abandon their alma mater, Yale, after that school repudiated the evangelical clergyman David Brainerd. In the 1740s Burr and Edwards felt called to establish the College of New Jersey (later Princeton University) to train evangelical New Light ministers.

Writing after these events but still during the revivals of mid century, Esther and Sarah praised some ministers for their heartfelt piety and excoriated others for their failure to inspire their flocks. The two women greatly admired the evangelists George Whitefield, David and John Brainerd, and Gilbert and William Tennent, as well as the hymn composer and religious writer Isaac Watts, whom Sarah quoted frequently in her religious journal.

In 1752 Esther Edwards married Aaron Burr, the second president of the College of New Jersey, and moved to Newark, New Jersey, where the school was then located. She and Sarah agreed to maintain their friendship and the network they shared with other evangelical women by sending one another letter-journals. (Their network also included Elizabeth Royall of Medford and Annis Boudinot, who later married New Jersey governor Richard Stockton.) From 1752 until Esther Burr's death in 1758, Esther and Sarah corresponded almost daily and vowed to preserve one another's letters. They used their letter-journals as a way to share information and to guide one another's spiritual, intellectual, and emotional lives. Indeed their friendship was so close that Esther wrote to Sarah in October 1754, "I have not one Sister I can write so freely to as to you the Sister of my heart." As evangelical women they saw friendship as exemplary of Christian love and asserted their right and duty to establish their friendships in the name of Christian

brotherhood and sisterhood. They also linked friendship and intellectual attainments, with Sarah stating in her third devotional exercise that "friends are precious [and] . . . intellectual attainments far better."

There are many references to Sarah's wide and eclectic reading in her own and Esther's journals. For example, Esther's letters in March 1755 reveal that both women were influenced by Samuel Richardson's novels, *Pamela* (1740) and *Clarissa* (1747–1748). Sarah preferred *Clarissa,* arguing that *Pamela* (subtitled "Virtue Rewarded") was flawed because the author "rewarded" the virtuous serving maid Pamela by marrying her to the deceitful, profligate, upper-class "Devil," Mr. B. The fate of the "fallen woman" Clarissa, who suffered a lonely death, was in Sarah's view a logical outcome of yielding to seduction. Even though Esther found "many useful lessons" in *Pamela,* she deferred to her friend's viewpoints, telling her, "Your judgment my dear has a very great influence on mine." This interchange is typical of the epistolary interactions that make Esther Burr's journal an especially rich source of knowledge about Sarah Prince Gill as well as about eighteenth-century friendship networks among American women.

At all times Esther Burr and Sarah Prince deplored the criticisms of opponents of religious revivals. Although they wrote and prayed about religious topics, they apparently did not always participate openly with men in conversations about these controversial topics. Their boundaries are clearly delineated in an October 1754 letter in which Esther pictures the events of a typical evening in the Prince home: "You all set in the middleroom, Father has the talk, and Mr Burr has the laugh, Mr Prince gets room to stick a word in. . . . The rest of you set and see, and hear, and make observations to yourselves . . . and when you get upstairs you tell what you think and wish I was there too." While they sometimes fell silent in mixed conversations on serious religious topics, it is clear that Esther and Sarah often conversed with men on more "appropriate" topics such as friendship, and no topic was excluded from their constant conversations among themselves and with other women.

Letters from Esther in the 1750s, along with Sarah's journal of meditations and other devotional writings, make it possible to follow the evolution of her thinking and spiritual life. It is difficult to determine the chronology of her published devotional exercises, but they clearly demonstrate the evangelical fervor that characterized her entire life. Part of a long tradition of introspective religious writings, mostly by men, her writings, follow a similar formula. Few such writings by eighteenth-century women have survived, placing Sarah Prince Gill in a select group that also includes Sarah Osborn and Sarah Edwards.

For Sarah Prince Gill, who did not need material wealth, simple peace of mind and some assurance about the state of her soul must have been the rewards of her spiritual pilgrimage. Yet assurance of salvation often seemed distant. Her short devotional pieces express her religious doubts and questions and demonstrate the process by which she found comfort and reassurance. Exercise #1, "Christian Magnanimity," suggests that life is a "scene of threats" and that the sole option for a pilgrim is a humble dependence on God; only that "will quiet the mind under deserved calamities." Later exercises expand on the theme of human frailty and unworthiness, with Sarah designating herself in Exercise #3 a "worthless worm, a clod, . . . nay, a sinful nothing." These phrases appeared often in the preaching and prayers of evangelical clergy during this period, and originality was not essential to achieving the requisite humility and receptivity to God's grace.

For latter-day Puritans or Calvinists such as Gill, the conversion experience was central to religious life and had certain comfortingly predictable steps—all of which were repeated frequently and often agonizingly in their lives. She alluded to the steps of a conversion experience in her devotional works and detailed them in her private journal of meditations. The process began with agonizing self-doubts and accusations of personal unworthiness. Gill chose many metaphors for her sinful state including an October 1744 reference to herself as a "barren figtree," which "it would be just in God to cut . . . down as a cumberer of his ground." In July 1756 she called herself "a patient sufferer." In September 1756 she had a "hard heart and a stubborn will," and in January of the next year she found her "heart vain and carnal and unwatchful." Quite often in her meditative journal she used water metaphors, as in a passage written in January 1757, when she referred to herself as a dry "water brook, . . . thirsting after God." As she moved beyond this first stage into a second predictable phase, she humbled herself and recognized her own helplessness. At this stage, in February 1757, she described her feelings as "unconceivable confusion and anguish."

The difficult preparatory steps eventually led to a third stage in which the pilgrim was supposed to recognize that it is impossible to find satisfaction in earthly pleasures and then to place total reliance on the power of God. In her devotional exercises she gradually dispensed with "earthly pleasures" and thereby began to understand the "freedom grace brings." At that point she maintained, one's " soul shall be sweetly attempered to the business and blessedness of . . . God" (Exercise #10). In her private journal, after a lengthy period of trials in May 1757, she at last achieved "Peace of mind flowing from a desire to approve myself to God—from a subjection of soul to Him and a reliance on his Covenant. Faithfulness attended me . . . renewing my choice of Him for my only God. I felt a most happy serenity." Having completed the requisite steps of the cycle, like other religious pilgrims, she achieved a sense of peace.

In Gill's writing the process of moving from complete humiliation and despair to ecstatic joy is repeated over and over in predictable cycles. As in most spiritual autobiographies, particular triggers for despair and self-doubts were her own and others' illnesses, the deaths of friends and family members, overwork and exhaustion, facing difficult decisions, and preparations for the Sabbath—especially those involving the sacrament of the Lord's Supper. In all instances Gill as the pilgrim had to admit her unworthiness in order to recognize her compete helplessness and necessary reliance on the gift of God's grace. The suffering could be intense, but the rewards for this writer were immense, bringing serenity and renewed energy and accomplishments. Gill's writings are a window on the spiritual rhythms in the lives of pious women of her time, connecting spirituality to all the events of such a woman's life.

The deaths of loved ones and friends were particular trials throughout Gill's life. In 1743 her infant sister, Grace, died, and in July 1744 her sister Deborah died at the age of twenty. At that time Sarah wrote in her private diary of her own anguish that her sister was not certain of salvation: "It was enough to melt the hardest heart to see her . . . as she was in great darkness and distress of soul." Sarah was unable to stay in the room until her sister Mercy brought her word that "every cloud was scattered and God had . . . [shined] the light of his countenance on her." Although at first in her grief Sarah experienced tremendous anxiety and doubts, she finally sought comfort in her prayers and begged to "hear the call of God" in Deborah's death and "prepare for my own." In 1757 and 1758 Sarah was desolated by the deaths of Aaron and Esther Burr. As was her custom, she personalized her response to Aaron's death, writing in October 1757, "God in holy and righteous sovereignty has now touched me in a near and heart-rending stroke. The

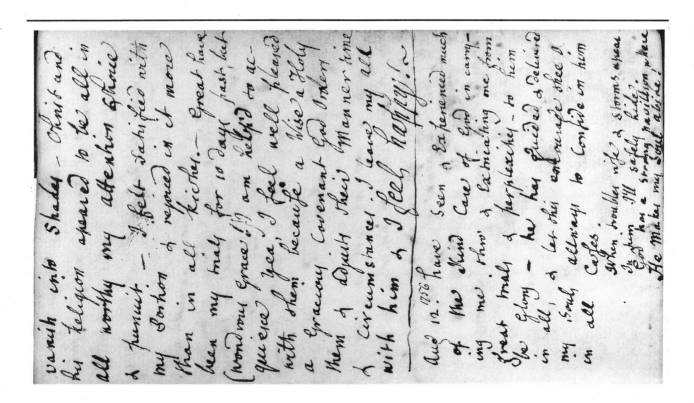

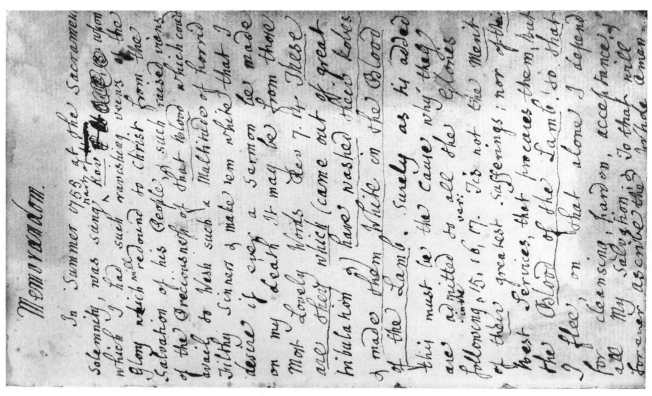

Pages from Sarah Prince Gill's journal of meditations (courtesy of the Trustees of the Boston Public Library)

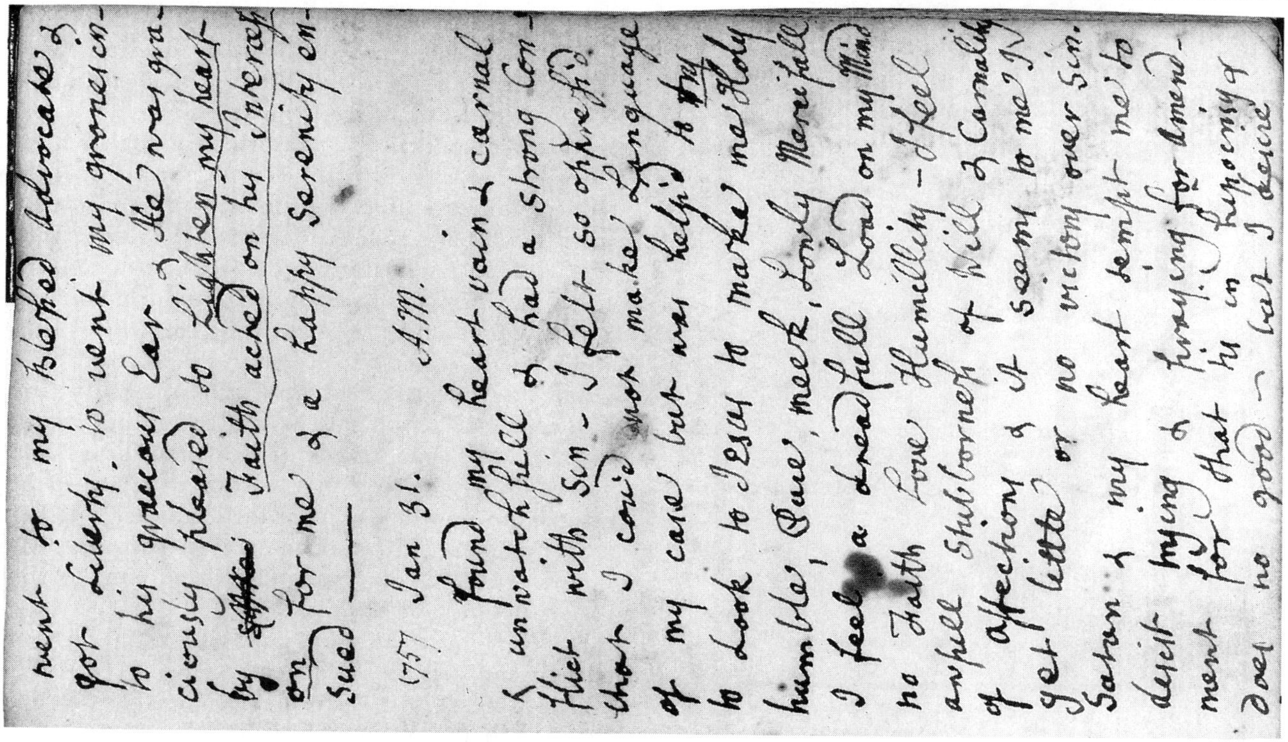

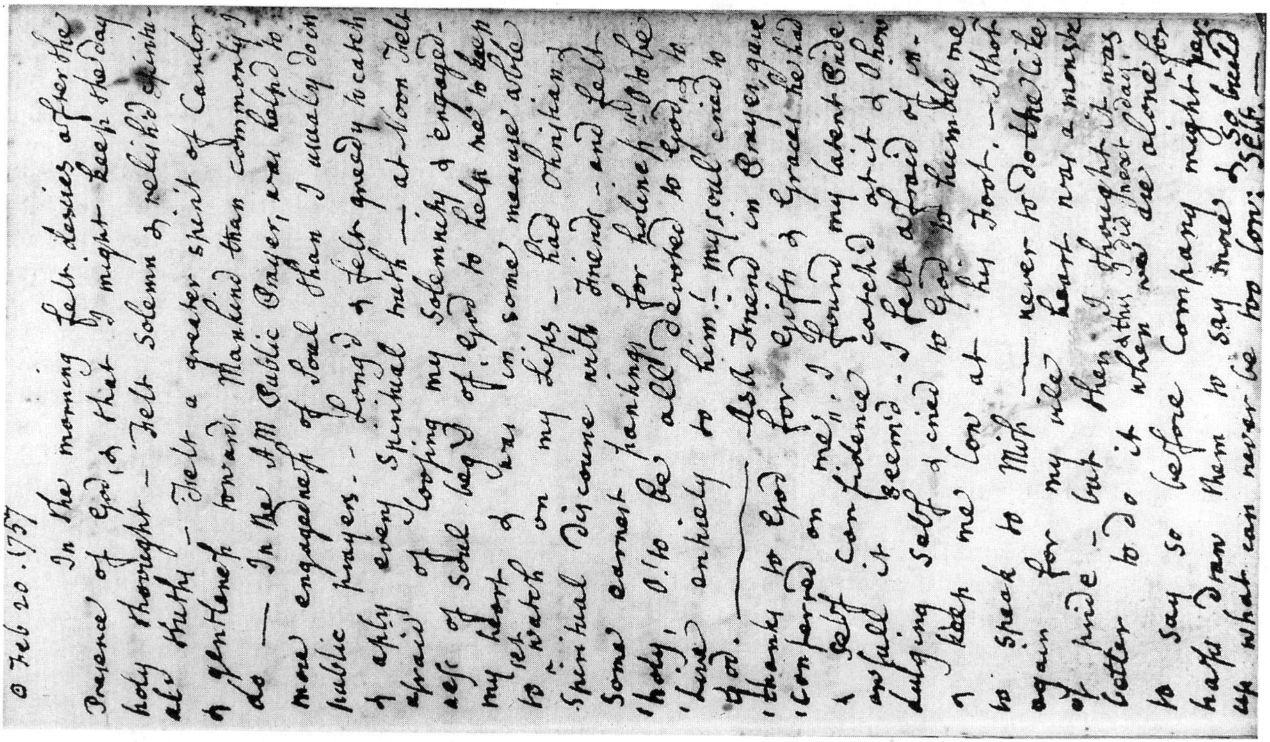

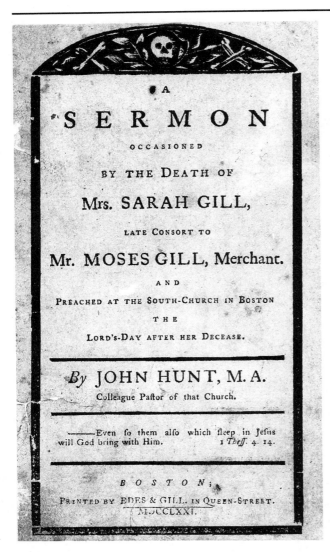

Title page for the book that includes Gill's devotional exercises, personal aids to meditation that reveal her evangelical fervor (courtesy of the Trustees of the Boston Public Library)

death of the most useful and valuable friend I ever had! (Except my Brother and Sisters and Mrs. Burr). . . ." Again she began to despair but caught herself with this admonition: "I dare not complain (even in thought) of God. I see He has done justly—I see the rod pointed at ME and I own I have deserved it. . . . But still selfish as my vile heart is I mourn more for the dear Relict [widow] than for myself . . . and O that I may get more ripened for glory by it."

Sarah found Esther Burr's death in March 1758 even more devastating, and this event occasioned some of her most moving prose. She wrote in her diary on 21 April 1758, "'GOD will have no rival in the heart which he sanctifies for himself.' God in Holy but awful severity has again struck at one of my principle springs of earthly comfort in taking from me the beloved of my heart, my dearest Friend Mrs. Burr. . . . Her natural powers were superior to most women . . . her accomplishments fine. . . . In friendly quality none exceeded her . . . how faithful? how sincere? . . . how tender, how careful, how disinterested—And *she was mine!*" This passage makes obvious the importance of female friendships to eighteenth-century evangelical women. Later in this outpouring of grief Sarah again sought resignation to the will of God and lessons for herself: "O painful separation," she wrote, "a desolate world, now barren. . . . My God hides his face . . . What shall I do, whither shall I turn?" She began finally to feel comforted and vowed to lay herself at the foot of God, to be resigned to his will. She faced the death of her father in September 1758 and again went through the familiar stages of agony followed finally by resignation to God's will.

Not long after the deaths of her father and close friends, she decided to marry widower Moses Gill (1734–1800), a Boston merchant. He was not the first man to court her. She had received a marriage proposal in 1756, leading to diary entries in September about her "great perplexity" because "the path of duty is not plain and I have been deliberating seriously and solemnly consulting with friends, but no help. . . ." Two of the friends she had consulted were Esther and Aaron Burr, and in her letters to Sarah at that time Esther spoke of her distress at her friend's "perplexed state." She instructed Sarah to trust in God and not "*to stand upon points too much.*" She added, in answer to Gill's apparent anxiety about her suitor's piety, that her own parents had taught her "some other things were more necessary to happyness in a married state." In a letter dated 23 October 1756 Esther concluded by advising Sarah that "if upon mature deliberation and serious consideration you find that you can't think of spending your days with that gentleman with complacency and delight, *say No.*" This interchange affirms the right of eighteenth-century women in Sarah's circle to choose their own mates, and it also underlines the tremendous importance placed on a decision to marry. Her refusal of the 1756 proposal attests to her full life at that time. Her friends Esther and Aaron Burr and her father were still alive, and her duties in her father's house still occupied most of her time.

On her marriage to Moses Gill in March 1757 Sarah Gill wrote in her diary of her delight that God had acted as a fatherly adviser to her and had "led me to think of changing my state." She was also grateful that her "consort" was a pious person who had made her once again the "head of a family." Finding a pious husband must have been important after the loss of so many of her spiritual advisers.

Sarah and Moses Gill did not have children of their own, but he had two adolescent sons. In the early days of her marriage Sarah Gill confided to her diary that she experienced a "mixed dispensation" with the considerable challenges of housekeeping, her own "lameness," and her obligation to guide both her new family and her "forward and ungovernable, ungodly" servants toward salvation. As she noted in an April 1759 diary entry, to find time for personal devotions she first procured a trustworthy and pious housekeeper and then established a schedule that allowed time each day for personal and family devotions. This schedule also provided for the completion of the housework by Saturday so the entire household could prepare properly for the Sabbath. With her new family, her new duties, and her carefully scheduled life, Gill appears to have had more time for religious reflection and writing and for social and political pursuits. It was at this time, for example, that she gathered together a group of praying women to offer counsel about choosing a new pastor for the Old South Meeting House.

In the decades leading up to the American Revolution, Gill developed a reputation as an intellectual. In her funeral sermon the Reverend John Hunt noted that "her natural inclination led her to books, and her many private papers discover a good acquaintance with them." Further evidence of her important intellectual and political contributions appears in a 1770 letter from John Adams to the British republican author Catherine Macaulay. In this letter Adams spoke of Sarah Gill as "a very learned lady in Boston." Macaulay herself mentioned writing to Gill and asking her about Adams. It is therefore likely that in 1770 Gill was instrumental in initiating the well-known correspondence between Adams and Macaulay—an exchange that influenced Adams's thinking about liberal politics and the necessity for colonial independence. Gill might well have been an active sympathizer with the republican ideology and activities leading up to the Revolution. Her obituary in the *Boston Evening Post* (12 August 1771) supports this contention, stating that "to her latest hour she fervently wished and prayed for the liberty of the world in general, and of her own Country in particular." After the American Revolution, Moses Gill became lieutenant governor of Massachusetts.

Although few of Gill's writings are published or available to scholars, those that are accessible contribute significantly to the understanding of the lives of eighteenth-century religious women. Gill's writings reveal that religion had both positive and negative effects on eighteenth-century women's lives. Even learned pious women such as Gill and her friends usually deferred publicly to ministers' views. They chastised themselves for not living up to standards of perfect piety. Yet some of these women saw their piety as a mandate to write of their experiences for the instruction of others. They also felt empowered to make choices for themselves, especially in choosing a marriage partner. Finally, in the name of Christian love and benevolence, these women claimed a mandate to develop friendships among themselves and to establish organizations to succor those in need and prayerfully influence certain public issues. They often interpreted the word of God for themselves and judged the piety of others, including ministers and political leaders. Gill's writings make it clear that her own and other women's self-esteem increased as they grew in piety.

Even the revolutionary events at the end of the eighteenth century could not be predicted when, after a long and painful illness, Gill died in August 1771. Her obituary in the *Boston Evening Post* praised her intellectual genius as "uncommonly strong and penetrating" and noted her "ever amiable" personality as well as her reputation as a "constant and warm friend." In the sermon preached for her funeral the Reverend John Hunt reassured the congregation that Sarah Gill died as she had lived: "With utmost calmness of mind . . . she made a happy exchange, we trust, of this life for heavenly glory." He was also accurate in his final appraisal that "Religion was both the business and pleasure of her life."

References:
Carol F. Karlsen and Laurie Crumpacker, eds., *The Journal of Esther Edwards Burr, 1754–1757* (New Haven: Yale University Press, 1984);
Monica Letzring, "Sarah Prince Gill and the John Adams-Catherine Macaulay Correspondence," *Proceedings of the Massachusetts Historical Society,* no. 88 (1976): 107–111;
John E. Van de Wetering, "Thomas Prince, Puritan Polemicist," dissertation, University of Washington, Seattle, 1980.

Papers:
The manuscript for Gill's journal of meditations (1743–1764) is in the Rare Book and Manuscript Collection at the Boston Public Library. A transcript edited by Rebecca Husman is in the Kellogg Library at Bard College.

Anne MacVicar Grant
(21 February 1755 – 7 November 1838)

Edward J. Gallagher
Lehigh University

BOOKS: *Poems on Various Subjects* (Edinburgh: Printed for the author by J. Moir and sold by Longman & Rees and J. Hatchard, London, 1803); revised as *The Highlanders, and Other Poems* (London: Printed by C. Whittingham for Longman, Hurst, Rees & Orme, 1808; Philadelphia: M. Carey, 1813);

Letters from the Mountains; Being the Real Correspondence of a Lady, between the Years 1773 and 1803 (3 volumes, London: Longman, Hurst, Rees & Orme, 1806); enlarged as *Letters from the Mountains; Being the Real Correspondence of a Lady, between the Years 1773 and 1807* (3 volumes, London: Longman, Hurst, Rees & Orme, 1807; third edition, 1807; 2 volumes, Boston: Printed by Greenough & Stebbins, 1809);

Memoirs of an American Lady; With Sketches of Manners and Scenes in America, as They Existed Previous to the Revolution, 2 volumes (London: Printed for Longman, Hurst, Rees & Orme, 1808; Boston: W. Wells, 1809; New York: S. Campbell, 1809);

Essays on the Superstitions of the Highlanders; To Which Are Added, Translations from the Gaelic; and Letters Connected with Those Formerly Published (2 volumes, London: Printed for Longman, Hurst, Rees, Orme & Brown, sold also by J. Hatchard, Mrs. Cock, and Manners & Miller, and by John Anderson, Edinburgh, 1811; 1 volume, New York: Eastburn, Kirk, 1813; Boston: Bradford & Read, 1813);

Eighteen Hundred and Thirteen: A Poem, in Two Parts (Edinburgh: Printed by James Ballantyne for Longman, Hurst, Rees, Orme & Brown, London, 1814);

Memoir and Correspondence of Mrs. Grant of Laggan, edited by J. P. Grant (London: Longman, Brown, Green & Longmans, 1844).

OTHER: Previously unpublished poems, in *Memoirs of an American Lady, With Sketches of*

Anne MacVicar Grant

Manners and Scenes in America as They Existed Previous to the Revolution . . . with Unpublished Letters and a Memoir of Mrs. Grant, edited by James Grant Wilson (New York: Dodd, Mead, 1901).

Mrs. Grant "of Laggan," to distinguish her from several other Mrs. Grants of her time, lived in several distinct worlds. She spent her childhood on the frontier of America, half her adult life on the northern frontier of Scotland, and the other half in Edinburgh, one of the great centers of Western culture. She was an isolated and imaginative girl, a dutiful minister's wife, a mother of twelve, and then a literary lioness. In America she received the stamp of a prerevolutionary multicultural society, the Albany Dutch, and of a traditional Dutch American woman, Margaretta Schuyler, both of which Grant vividly depicted in a little-known work of American history, *Memoirs of an American Lady* (1808). She then took her "American" values to the Highlands of Scotland, where she became the first effective apologist for the ancient pastoral society of that region at a time when it was coming under assault by intellectual and industrial revolutions. Without formal education and as a woman, a Tory, and a "Highlander," she wondered early in her publishing career what chance she could have for success in the male literary world, but a success she was.

Anne MacVicar Grant was born on 21 February 1755 in Glasgow. Her mother, Catherine MacKenzie MacVicar, was descended from the Stuarts of Invernahyle, one of whom was the model for the Baron of Bradwardine in Sir Walter Scott's Waverley novels. Her father, Duncan MacVicar, born in Craignish in Argyllshire, an officer in the British army, was sent to America in 1757 during the French and Indian War. His daughter's earliest memory was at two years old wandering alone to the edge of town, "going to America to seek papa." Mother and daughter followed Duncan MacVicar in 1758, settling in Claverock, a Dutch settlement near Albany, just prior to the battle of Ticonderoga. MacVicar retired from the army in 1765 to found an "estate" at Clarendon, in what is now Vermont, where lands were granted to soldiers. Homesick, in ill health, and discouraged by hostility against Tories, he precipitately moved the family back to Scotland in 1768, ending his young daughter's dreams of becoming an "heiress."

Grant lived in America, which she called "her foster-mother," from ages three to thirteen, the formative years, in circumstances that made her a self-described "anomaly." In her posthumously published memoir she recalled that she was often alone, that "no one fondled or caressed" her, that she did not possess "a single toy" until she was six, and that she and her mother were the first upper-class females to penetrate "the then trackless wilderness." By necessity she developed an "active imagination" and "uncommon powers of memory." She was not subject to the usual forces of cultural conditioning. What made her "very different" was her originality, her readiness to live and think outside established social structures.

Among the "primitive worthies" in the Dutch settlement of Claverack, Grant learned to admire "simplicity and truth" and to love the

Indians, but the most important thing that happened to her in America was meeting Margaretta Schuyler (1701–1782). Madame or "Aunt" Schuyler was "the most distinguished woman in the province of New York, perhaps on the American continent," a woman whose ancestors were the "aristocracy of the province," whose understanding gave her "great weight in society," whose liberality earned her the love of that society, and whose home, the Flatts, was the hub of the community. Grant regarded Aunt Schuyler as the "Minerva of my imagination," and the connection between Grant and Schuyler was the turningpoint in Grant's life. A friend of her father's had given the six-year old a copy of the works of John Milton, and the normally shy Anne became a "great favourite" of Aunt Schuyler when "the spirit moved" the child's uncommon memory to interrupt a conversation on dreams with a long quotation from *Paradise Lost* (1667). After this moment Grant lived with Schuyler for long periods, slept in the same room with her, and read with and to her. Acknowledging that she "owed whatever culture my mind received" to Schuyler, Grant eventually wrote a book about her. Schuyler even offered to keep Anne when her family returned to Scotland in 1768.

In Glasgow, Grant set about establishing her "usual source of felicity," faithful friends, and when her father returned to army life in 1773, moving the family to Fort Augustus in the Highlands, her distress triggered a lifetime of letter writing. (Walter Scott once described her as "the maintainer of an unmerciful correspondence.") In 1779 she married James Grant, a minister, and moved to his cottage at Laggan. They eventually had twelve children. She outlived all but one, a son who edited her letters. Grant began to write regularly after she returned to Scotland, and though friends urged her to write for publication, she gave away all her "occasional scraps" and devoted herself to a tender, affectionate, and delicate husband, who "made my society and attendance essential to him." Even when writing her memoir at age seventy, Grant saw this sacrifice as "gratifying."

Grant's move to Laggan foregrounds another activity she had been involved in since 1768–becoming Scottish. Essentially Grant spent her early years in a "foreign" culture, though even there a soldier gave her a copy of "Wallace" by Blind Harry, balladeer of Scottish liberty, from which she came to understand the Scots language and caught an "enthusiasm for Scotland." Near Glasgow, she spent three summers with the Pagan family frequenting peasant cottages, raiding "their

The Flatts in Claverack, New York, home of Margaretta Schuyler, with whom Grant lived for long periods of her childhood

smoky bookshelves," experiencing the best of "genuine Scottish character," and enriching her memory with "Scottish history and manners." Once settled in Laggan she took "pride and pleasure" in overcoming the Highlanders' dislike of strangers "by adopting the customs, studying the Gaelic language, and, above all, not wondering at any thing local and peculiar." Her empathy with the brutally stereotyped Highlanders is the basis of three books.

The death of her husband in 1801 left Grant at age forty-six with eight children and "not free from debt." She was forced to write to live. Faithful friends engaged the patronage of the duchess of Gordon and enlisted three thousand subscribers for Grant's *Poems on Various Subjects* (1803), republished in 1808 with slight changes as *The Highlanders, and Other Poems*. The first edition includes "The Highlanders," a five-part poem with notes that composes one-third of the book. It also includes twenty-nine other poems (one dated as early as 1774), two translations from the Gaelic with a preliminary letter on the importance of the

oral tradition, and two songs—including her popular song "The Blue Bell of Scotland." (In the second edition one poem was repositioned and four poems and the songs were dropped.)

Grant saw the Highlanders of northern Scotland—whose culture was as foreign to her as the Dutch or the Indians in America—as proud, noble, energetic, cohesive, ancient, insulated, fiercely independent people whose way of life was much maligned and was being destroyed by a far inferior "modern" culture from the south. Scotland was originally settled by Celts from Ireland, who successfully fought off England under Robert Bruce at the turn of the fourteenth century and remained independent until 1707. After the British monarchy passed to the house of Hanover in 1714, the Highlanders twice rebelled unsuccessfully—the Jacobite rebellions in 1715 and 1745—to restore the Stuart line. As a consequence of the Forty-five Rebellion, England instituted reforms designed to take power away from the Highland clan chiefs and to assimilate the region more fully into a united Britain. During the period from 1773, when Grant moved to Fort Augustus, to 1810, when she moved to Edinburgh, the Highland culture was disappearing through encroachment and emigration, seemingly without a ripple of concern in the outside world. Grant called attention to what was being lost.

Like James Macpherson, Grant asserted the value of Highland culture in the face of passionate prejudice. A reviewer for the *North British Review* (1844) said that before Grant it was impossible for the Saxon mind to imagine the Highlanders as anything but the "uncouth semi-clad savages . . . ravenously gorging on the food proper to horses, and mowing down with scythes gentlemen of the highest respectability" during the Forty-five Rebellion. Grant's poem "The Highlanders" sets up a pastoral community ruled by the wisdom of an old patriarch, bound together by the songs of a poet, adorned by a beautiful maiden, and aligned with the seasons. Characterized by care for and play with each other, Grant's characters offer examples of quiet, selfless heroism by noncombatants during the war of 1745. In the preface to her Gaelic translations Grant asks if it is possible for "generous and tender sentiments" to reside in people thought "so savage and barbarous." As an answer she offers the "exalted notions of probity and honour" she experienced among contemporary Native Americans and the "considerable influence" women had among the Celts. The conclusion of "The Highlanders" expresses the need to foster these simple, frugal "Nature's children" as a necessary antidote to a contemporary culture in which "honour, conscience, truth, are cheaply sold, / And none deny the omnipotence of gold."

In 1803 Grant "unwillingly" moved to Stirling, near Glasgow, where in 1805 she turned her letters into the resource necessary to assist her son, dishonorably discharged from the army, to achieve a commission in the East India Company. By the time the third edition of *Letters from the Mountains* (1806) appeared in 1807, the book comprised 134 letters written from 1773 through 1806. Needing money but reluctant to publish—realizing especially that male critics treated female writers "with unqualified scorn"—Grant met with solid financial success: in addition to her contractual profit, her publishers made her a liberal additional "gift," and the book attracted an eminent New England lady, who had it republished there and forwarded all the royalties to Grant. At last Grant was able to say that her family's "quiet sphere" was secure.

Letters from the Mountains is full of Highland scenes and people, for which it was duly praised and for which it remains interesting. It is also clearly a woman's book. As her introductions make evident, the letters were written by a woman without much time to write. The letters are "interrupted sketches" written in "the most remote obscurity" about the feelings of a woman who "in the secret shades of privacy" cultivates "the simple duties and kindly affections of domestick life" and is supported by friends whose sympathy is "the solace" of her afflictions. Predictably such letters received condescension, if not scorn, from male critics, who dismissed them as "chit-chat," "much of the merest tittle-tattle," with correspondents unknown beyond the family circle.

Letters from the Mountains begins with the "scarce seventeen" year old going "she knows not where, to do she knows not what, and live with she knows not whom." Regardless of many pleasing associations with the Highlands, that world is harsh. She lived so far from markets that, "unless the ravens were commissioned to feed us," they had to grow all their own food. The "diary of one July Monday" is curtly punctuated with "Spare your pity." From that other world she reached out to her friends, chiding them for not writing. Lonely and "seized with longings," she signed letters "unalterably yours." With her friends she shared confidences—wondering if she would marry, speculating on the value of marrying into a ready-made family to escape "mother Eve's penalty," assessing nearby husband material, pinpointing what she most wanted in a man, and admitting that she entered marriage without the vulnerability of "sanguine expectations." Later she recounted the death of her husband and the sicknesses and deaths of children, with the desolations and consolations that follow. She made an album for her friends' letters from a "great old goose of a book" and exulted that enduring female friendships redeem a fallen world.

The image of womanhood that Grant enshrined in her albums and inculcated in her children is traditional. Needlework, she said, habituates "peaceful and still-life pleasures; which form the chief enjoyments of every truly amiable woman." Purity, the basis for "the order and virtue of society," makes women "consequential beings": impudent and licentious women signal the downfall of nations. The only reason for women to study science is to "adorn conversation," for who would understand a woman who

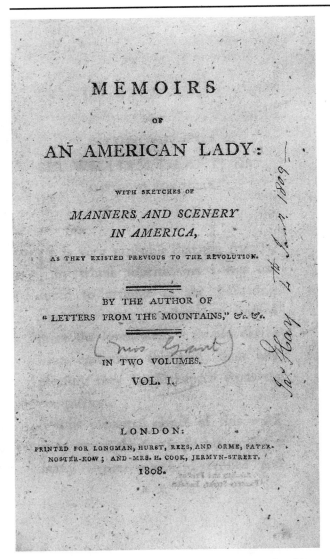

MEMOIRS
OF
AN AMERICAN LADY:
WITH SKETCHES OF
MANNERS AND SCENERY
IN AMERICA,
AS THEY EXISTED PREVIOUS TO THE REVOLUTION.

BY THE AUTHOR OF
"LETTERS FROM THE MOUNTAINS," &c. &c.

IN TWO VOLUMES.
VOL. I.

LONDON:
PRINTED FOR LONGMAN, HURST, REES, AND ORME, PATER-
NOSTER-ROW; AND MRS. H. COOK, JERMYN-STREET.
1808.

Title page for Grant's book about Margaretta Schuyler, "the most distinguished woman in the province of New York" (courtesy of the Lilly Library, Indiana University)

talked profoundly on philosophy, astronomy, or chemistry? "The insatiable love of change" is "the great and growing evil of the age," and her extended views on Mary Wollstonecraft at times verge on parody. Grant considered Wollstonecraft "dangerous" and warned, "this intellectual equality that the Misses make such a rout about, has no real existence." For Grant, women were more gentle, benevolent, and virtuous than men, and their minds were delicate. Wollstonecraft reminded Grant of a kitten who put her head in a teapot, broke the pot trying to get it out, and ran wildly about the house with her neck in a "moveable pillory," making peace impossible for everyone. If "Mary's" revolution succeeded, exclaimed Grant, one-third of the female members of the national council would be "lying-in,

recovering, or nursing," but, she noted ironically, these babies would not interfere with debate for "children that suck in philosophy with their milk" would not cry like "vulgar brats."

As early as 1773 Grant mentioned her desire to write a memoir of Margaretta Schuyler, but the proximate motivation was suggestions by friends and the proximate function was "blunting the stings" of the deaths of two daughters within five months in 1807. *Memoirs of an American Lady* (1808), reprinted within three months of its publication, combines main elements of the first two books in its depiction of a passing culture with a powerful traditional woman at its center. In Grant's view Dutch families such as the Schuylers, Rensselaers, and Cortlands were natural aristocrats who succeeded for a brief time before the American Revolution in establishing a pastoral paradise of "equality, simplicity, and moderation" around Albany. She depicted independent patroons who wisely ruled a culture in which public service was instinctual, Europeans lived in harmony with Indians who acknowledged white superiority, and in which slaves were few, well-treated, and happy in their servitude. In this edenic setting children communed in summer picnics and winter sledding. Their rites of passage involved perilous adventures, while Arcadian forests stirred dreams of social bliss and the thunderous thawing of the Hudson occasioned a "perfect saturnalia." The analogy between the Highlands and Albany, though unspoken, is palpable.

Aunt Schuyler supported her prominent husband, Col. Philip Schuyler (1696–1758), with a "spirit worthy of a Roman matron." Around the liberal table of the Flatts, for instance, Aunt Schuyler's "calm, temperate wisdom" and "easy versatile manners" taught her Dutch, English, and Indian guests not only toleration but esteem for all cultures and races. On the front porch of the Flatts the whole town gathered with pleasure when word was heard that "Aunt Schuyler is come out." Having no children of her own, Schuyler made her house an "academy," and over the years she "adopted" fifteen children, providing girls "a perpetual school for useful knowledge" instead of raising them "to dance, to dress, to roll the eye, or troul the tongue." She had an "indefatigable mind," created leisure hours for reading, invited upper-class guests to casual "lyceums" on questions of religion and morality, and sat in "tribunal" for new settlers who needed assistance or advice. Roused from depression after her husband's death during a raid by the French, Aunt

Schuyler continued the family role in public affairs. After male leaders neglected to follow her good advice and incurred negative results, she became a "public oracle" who was "resorted to and consulted by all."

Memoirs of an American Lady ends on the brink of the Revolution and offers some reflections on the American national experience. According to Grant the approaching war brought "demons of discord" such as lawyers, merchants, and "fierce republicans" into paradise. A new population arrived, "let loose, like Samson's foxes, to carry mischief and conflagration wherever they went." The peaceful asylum became "a refuge for the vagabonds and banditti of the continent." Aunt Schuyler could see the chaos and carnage of civil war and felt the dilemma of not being able to live with England or without her. And from her vantage point of forty years, Grant included a long, scathing, Tory indictment on the present state of affairs, which included statements such as: "The gangrene of the land has not healed"; "When the spirit of extermination walks forth over prostrate thrones and altars, ages cannot efface the traces of its progress"; "A total subversion of a long established government is like an earthquake"; "It is wonderful how little talent or intellectual preeminence of any kind has appeared in this new-born world"; and "Is there any person whose dubious or turbulent character has made him unwelcome or suspected in society, he goes to America." America killed the virtuous Alexander Hamilton (who was married to a Schuyler) and raised a "cold blooded philosopher," Benjamin Franklin, while ignoring the laudable pacifism of Quaker society in Pennsylvania. For Grant one faint hope for America remained, a new frontier, perhaps the last resort of the pastoralist, this time in Canada, a severe land peopled by royalists and "tribes" of emigrants—such as Highlanders—who wanted to continue their established cultures rather than creating new ones. Even the few remaining Mohawks, true to their alliance with England through the Schuylers, had also emigrated there.

In 1810 Grant moved to Edinburgh, where she "arrived" as a writer when Francis Jeffrey did a retrospective review of her writings in the prestigious *Edinburgh Review*. The occasion for his essay was the publication of *Essays on the Superstitions of the Highlanders* (1811). This work comprises nine related essays on superstitions, a tenth explicating a Highland song, and fifteen letters. In the book Grant confronted analytically a basic question hindering acceptance of Highland

culture—in effect, what good could be said of a people in the "enlightened" nineteenth century who believe in ghosts? A belief in ghosts, Grant argued, bespeaks vivid imagination, not low intellect, and it has the good effect of developing courage and strengthening personal attachments. Every soul longed for a glimpse of the unknown, she suggested, and an intelligent person should acknowledge "divine beneficence" at every stage of human existence. Furthermore, she said, Philip Dormer Stanhope, Lord Chesterfield, would have been "mortified" to discover that the rules of good breeding he had laid out in his popular, posthumously published letters to his nephew (1774) were already familiar to the lowest ranks of Highlanders. If there was superstition on one side of the "smothered animosity" between Highland and Lowland, she implied, there was bigotry. Ultimately, however, Grant knew that Highland culture was disappearing, and the best she could do was to preserve some art that would otherwise perish.

Grant thought *Essays on the Superstitions of the Highlanders* would "close my literary life," but she published one more book in her lifetime, *Eighteen Hundred and Thirteen: A Poem, in Two Parts* (1814), which celebrates the year in which the tide finally turned in the war against Napoleon Bonaparte. In this long poem she gloated over a people's revolution that, unlike the American uprising, would not succeed. The internecine feuds between Highland and Lowland and Scotland and England are replaced in this poem by an image of a prospering England, Scotland, and Ireland unified against "the demon power from Gallia." Untouched by revolution, Britain remained for Grant "the home of liberty," which was waiting for the Old Testament-like scourge of Europe to subside before serving as the divinely ordained "minister of fate" to restore peace. "High-gifted bards"—George Gordon, Lord Byron; Joanna Baillie; Maria Edgeworth; and Walter Scott—would "Inspire new zeal for freedom's holy cause" and make all countries look to Britain as a model society. Britain's only interest would be to sway minds and gladly share her ideas, while she restored boundaries, allowed countries to be themselves again, guarded against the future rise of a giant power, and established the "good of all" as the goal of political activity. *Eighteen Hundred and Thirteen* is stentorianly patriotic, and for once Grant was able to frame her conservative values in an approaching mainstream future rather than in a disappearing frontier past.

Though she continued to write letter after letter (there are 392 in her son's 1844 edition) and

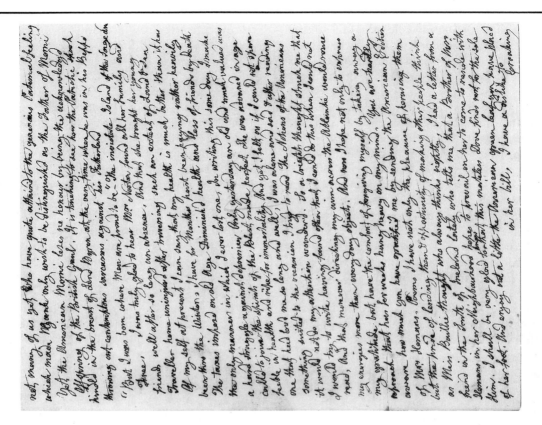

Letter from Grant to Andrews Norton, editor of The North American Review *(Anne MacVicar Grant Collection, 7369-A, Clifton Waller Barrett Library, Manuscripts Division, University of Virginia Library)*

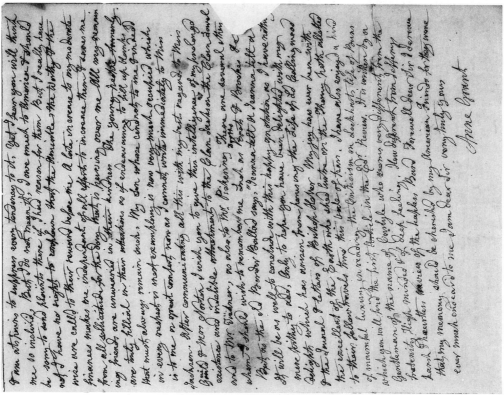

poetry (including "Lines Written on Her Eighty-Third Birthday"), Grant's celebrity in Edinburgh during the latter part of her long life was based on her wit and conversation and on the literary elite who gathered at her modest house. Her circle included Scott, Byron, Henry Mackenzie, William Wordsworth, Thomas De Quincey, Felicia Hemans, Robert Southey, Baillie, Washington Irving, George Ticknor, and Germaine Necker, Madame de Staël, among many others. Ticknor said her conversation was better than her books, while Scott tagged her a "blue-stocking gossip." Southey praised her description of the Hudson River thaw. Irving called her a "great Tory" who always gave Americans a cordial welcome while Henry Thomas, Lord Cockburn, remembered her "amusing horror" at Whig principles. Grant's *Memoirs of an American Lady* inspired James Kirke Paulding's *Dutchman's Fireside* (1831), and historians tapped her knowledge of Scottish history. No longer might critics carp that her correspondence was limited to unimportant females.

Grant became so well known and so widely revered that she received legacies from friends and a pension from the government. Scott wrote a memorial for her contributions to national pride and patriotism. After 1820, lameness from a series of falls limited her mobility, and at seventy-six she made the melancholy remark that "in my old age, when worldly pursuits and even praise are weighed and found wanting . . . I feel pained and alarmed when people come, not to see, but actually to look at me." Yet at her death in 1838 she left behind images of the good life in America, in Scotland, and in a future Europe that still serve as chastening mirrors for Progress.

Letters:
Memoir and Correspondence of Mrs. Grant of Laggan, edited by J. P. Grant (London: Longman, Brown, Green & Longmans, 1844);
"Letters Written by Mrs. Grant of Laggan concerning Highland Affairs and Persons Connected with the Stuart Cause in the Eighteenth Century," edited by J. R. N. MacPhail, *Publications of the Scottish Historical Society,* 26 (1896): 251–330;
Memoirs of an American Lady, With Sketches of Manners and Scenes in America as They Existed Previous to the Revolution . . . with Unpublished Letters and a Memoir of Mrs. Grant, edited by James Grant Wilson (New York: Dodd, Mead, 1901).

Biography:
George Paston, *Little Memoirs of the Eighteenth Century* (New York: Dutton, 1901).

Sarah Ewing Hall

(30 October 1761 – 8 April 1830)

Nicholas Rombes
University of Detroit Mercy

BOOKS: *Conversations on the Bible* (Philadelphia: Harrison Hall, 1818; London, 1821);
Selections from the Writings of Mrs. Hall, Author of Conversations on the Bible, with a Memoir of Her Life (Philadelphia: Harrison Hall, 1833).

Sarah Ewing Hall, whose writings on topics ranging from women's education to biblical criticism were widely read in her day, is perhaps best known for her *Conversations on the Bible* (1818), which was popular in America and England. Hall contributed to the influential *Port Folio,* a significant and successful early American literary periodical, which sold more than two thousand copies per issue. Founded by Joseph Dennie and later edited by Hall's son, John Ewing Hall, the journal provided an outlet for Sarah Hall, who contributed criticism, verse, and essays on a broad range of topics, many of them treating issues affecting women. Indeed her writings reveal her concerns about women's roles in the public life of the nation as well as her broader concerns about the development of an American literary nationalism.

Sarah Ewing Hall was born in Philadelphia in 1761, the daughter of the Reverend John Ewing and Hannah Sergeant Ewing. At the time of her birth, her father was the pastor of the First Presbyterian Church and a tutor at the College of Philadelphia. Later he served as provost of the University of Pennsylvania. Although she was not formally educated, Sarah Ewing gained an extensive knowledge of the ancient classics by listening as her brothers recited their Latin and Greek lessons to their father. In 1782 she married John Hall, the son of a wealthy Maryland planter, and for the next eight years the couple lived on a farm on the Susquehanna River in Cecil County, Maryland. Around 1790 the family moved to Philadelphia, where John Hall served as secretary of the land office and as U.S. marshal for the district of Pennsylvania.

Although her eleven children kept her busy, Sarah Hall remained an active reader, taking advantage of the cosmopolitanism of Philadelphia to educate herself. Nearly every night, after her family was asleep, she is said to have spent hours reading, writing, and studying. During this time she socialized with members of the Tuesday Club, a literary circle that included Joseph Dennie, who established *The Port Folio* in January 1801 and made the club members the nucleus of his writing staff. Other members of the club and contributors to *The Port Folio* included fiction writers, poets, and historians such as Charles Brockden Brown, John Blair Linn, Charles J. Ingersoll, and Philip Hamilton, son of Alexander Hamilton. Other women who wrote for *The Port Folio* included Harriet Fenno, Gertrude Meredith, and Elizabeth Graeme Ferguson. Despite the fact that she and her husband lived in Lamberton, New Jersey, in 1801–1805 and then resided in Maryland in 1805–1811, Hall was among the select group of *Port Folio* contributors for its entire existence, writing for the journal periodically under the pen names Constantia and Florepha until it ceased publication in 1827. In Philadelphia, to which the Halls returned in 1811, her home was often a center of activity among authors, editors, and friends. According to Samuel L. Knapp, Sarah Hall's

> disposition was cheerful and she looked on the bright side of every thing. At her hospitable mansion, the feverish scholar [Dennie] found more charms to cure his misanthropy than could be found elsewhere. . . . When the evil spirit came over him . . . he went, to use his own words, to the house of Mrs. Hall, to drive off all his blue devils. Her conversations abounded in classical recollections, in playful remarks, and in delicate satire, and, like the harp of David, gave new soul and life to the gloomy editor.

By 1811 the Halls had settled permanently in Philadelphia, where, because of her husband's ill health, Sarah Hall helped to support the family. (John Hall died in 1826.) In 1811, at age fifty, she began to learn Hebrew, preparing to write her 365-page *Conversations on the Bible.* This book, which went through three American editions and one British edition in

Hall's lifetime, takes the form of a dialogue between various family members and "Mother," who usually introduces each biblical book and then, in response to questions and comments, discusses its major themes, its likely authorship, and its historical and cultural context. Although much of Mother's analytical commentary is rooted in contemporary biblical scholarship—parenthetical references and footnotes point readers to other biblical scholars—it is also frequently informal and conversational, features for which the book was praised in Hall's day.

Indeed much of the appeal of the work comes from the seamless and easy textual transitions between biblical scholarship and fairly casual dialogue. In the "conversation" on the Book of Job, for instance, Mother tackles the difficult question of disputed authorship, a question that "divides commentators." Mother enters the scholarly debate with her own theory: "From the language of Elihu, he would seem to be the author of this whole narrative. In the introduction to his speech, he says—'When I had waited,' (for they spake not, but stood still, and answered no more,) 'I said, I will answer my part, I will also show mine opinion'; thus speaking in the first person, whereas the other speakers are always quoted in the third." In other sections, however, the commentary is much more informal and diffuse, as in the "conversation" on the Book of Ruth. Here, after listening to Mother's summary of the story, Fanny notes that it "bears so strong a resemblance to the Palemon and Lavinia of our favourite Thomson." This comment leads to a rather lengthy dialogue about the differences between the narrative qualities of the biblical version and poet James Thomson's version of Ruth.

On one level Conversations on the Bible is at pains to defend the Bible as authentically divine. Indeed it resists the larger secular drift of the Enlightenment. On another level, however, Hall's book on the Bible enacts the same kind of rationalist ideology that it attacks. That is, while Hall never wavers in her conviction that the Bible is the literal Word, she nonetheless provides ample space for rationalist-skeptical voices in her text, as she does in her discussion of Job: "Some writers, more fanciful than wise, have imagined the whole book to be an allegory, or fable, agreeably to the eastern mode of giving lessons." Later she notes that another "argument against the reality of the whole story is assumed, from its metaphorical style, in the debate between Job and his companions." Instead of shielding her listeners from the potentially subversive logic of skepticism, Mother provides it space in the text in order to argue against it rationally and critically.

Twentieth-century readers have sometimes characterized Hall as conservative or conventional; yet it is important to note that the dialogues in Conversations on the Bible are often between women. These conversations show women grappling with moral, intellectual, and political issues while traditionally authoritative male voices—usually in the form of biblical scholars—are confined to parenthetical asides or footnotes. By positioning herself in a larger, male sphere of scholarly biblical criticism and by routinely offering her own interpretations that are sometimes at odds with the official critics, Hall asserted her voice into a traditionally male world.

Some of the concerns about women's status, which are only hinted at in Conversations on the Bible, are made more explicit in the essays Hall published in The Port Folio during the 1810s and 1820s. Many of them address the tensions between a woman's domestic "duties" and her potential for finding a public voice in the republic. Like Benjamin Rush, Judith Sargent Murray, and others who wrote specifically about women's education in the young republic, Hall advocated expanding educational opportunities for women, but only by carefully situating such opportunities in the context of domestic usefulness. Although some twentieth-century critics have labeled Hall a "conservative," her essays on young women's education, while they do not call for an expanded public role for women, do in fact highlight women's limited options, addressing in detail women's domestic duties and lack of formal education. For example, in "Defence of American Women," published in The Port Folio in 1818 and collected in Selections from the Writings of Mrs. Hall (1833), Hall responds to criticism that American women are increasingly ignorant of "every species of domestic usefulness and economy" and are failing in their duties as republican mothers. According to Hall, the real problem is not that young women do not give due attention to domestic matters but that they cannot give due attention to their education: "too soon after they leave their schools, their books are abandoned in order that they may not be in 'ignorance of economy.' They must sew for their brothers! they must assist their mothers in the care of the house." Hall further suggests that instead of expanding their minds by continuing to study "the sciences" they began to learn at school, these young girls are too occupied by "things which, although they may be of the very first importance in domestic life, require no great time or ability to learn." Thus, an essay that at first appears to be a defense of women against the charge that they have abandoned "domestic economy"

CONVERSATIONS

ON

THE BIBLE.

BY A LADY.

PHILADELPHIA:
PUBLISHED BY HARRISON HALL,
N° 133, Chesnut-street.
J. Maxwell, printer.
1818.

*Title page for Sarah Ewing Hall's popular interpretation of
the Bible, in which a mother discusses the Scriptures with
her family*

turns out to be quite different: an essay explaining how women's domestic duties interfere with their educational development. If the essay is "conservative" in that it is throughout governed by the assumption that domestic duties are of paramount importance, it is less so in its indictment of an educational and social system that makes it difficult for women to benefit from extended educational training.

In another essay regarding women's options, "On Female Education" (*The Port Folio,* 1825; collected in *Selections from the Writings of Mrs. Hall*), Hall also couches her somewhat radical propositions in a familiar rhetoric of domesticity. Conceding that there "was a time when the female mind was consigned to a state of darkness," Hall asserts that this "unhappy state of things has passed away; men have discovered that women can learn and that they may learn, and they are now admitted to the benefits of mental cultivation." Clearly not as radical or specific as writers such as Judith Sargent Murray in her claims for women's higher status in public life, Hall is careful to point out that women should *not* receive the same education as men because women are not interested in active public life and that "domestic and social life is her proper sphere." Yet, she suggests, women could exhibit the same "mental powers" as men were they simply afforded the opportunity. This strategy allows Hall to speak in some detail about women's current conditions and limited options. For instance, Hall notes that most boys stay at school for several years beyond girls, whose formal education normally ends at "fourteen or fifteen" years of age. Then while boys are at school a girl "must learn to sew and keep house; for these mysteries, which in the time of our grandmothers, constituted the *summum bonum* of a woman's character, cannot be entirely neglected. They force themselves upon us, receive them with what mind we may. Now the young lady marries, and care rises upon care." At points throughout "On Female Education" Hall's detailed descriptions of women's domestic duties and her word choices (such as domestic duties "force themselves upon us") suggest a carefully rendered critique of the status quo, a critique that is characteristic of much of her prose writing.

"On the Extent of Female Influence, and the Importance of Exerting it in Favour of Christianity," collected in *Selections from the Writings of Mrs. Hall*, treats another of Hall's major concerns, the confluence of female domesticity and Christianity. Like "On Female Education," "On the Extent of Female Influence" speaks with a kind of doubleness that, while reminding women of their places and duties as wives and mothers, also advocates activity that would gradually move women further from the domestic sphere. Hall's message is conservative when she reminds her readers that we "are not of those who plead for equality in domestic government; obedience in a wife is a scriptural doctrine." Yet despite her stress on the importance of republican motherhood, she also advocates women's active roles in evangelizing through writing "tracts" for the "western country . . . where gospel ordinances are not yet established." Hall concludes her essay by calling for a kind of female activism: "Let not diffidence withhold the female pen. We know not what we can do until we assay our strength. Let everyone then remember, that no talent must be hidden, that can in any way subserve the cause of christianity." In this essay and other writings Hall conflates issues of domesticity and female activism in a rhetoric that advocates social change even while claiming that such change would not disrupt women's domestic obligations.

In addition to her more-public writings Hall's private correspondence during the 1820s is of interest. It sheds light on a network of female authors and frequently comments on the special difficulties they faced as writers, and it also comments on the broader concerns of literary nationalism in general. Of special interest are the letters that speak to the unique obstacles many women faced when presenting their work to the public. For instance, in an unpublished 23 September 1825 letter to Anne Harris, who had sent Hall a copy of her book *The Alphabet of Thought* (1825), Hall revealed how she had disguised Harris's gender when she secured someone to review the book for *The Port Folio*: "I have committed it to my friend Dr. Beasley, the provost of the University—who has himself written pretty largely on metaphysics. That you may not be prejudg'd, I have concealed the petticoat, leaving him to suppose—if he pleases—that a man *must* have written it." In a 28 August 1827 letter to Harris, Hall commented on novels written by women: "Our ladies are beginning to shew themselves to advan-

tage in the literary world. Miss Sedgewick, the author of 'Redwood' has added to her reputation by her 'Hope Leslie.' You have probably seen these novels, although I suppose, new books, travel slowly to Bellefonte." Indeed, much of Hall's correspondence reveals an interest not only in other female authors but on the general state of authorship in the young republic as well. Her letters help illuminate the intersections of authorship and gender in an era of growing literary nationalism. Writing to an unknown correspondent in Scotland in 1821, for instance, Hall noted that

> literature has no career in America. . . . We are a business-doing, money-making people. And as for us poor females, the blessed tree of liberty, has produced such an exuberant crop of bad servants, that we have no eye nor ear, for anything but work. We are the most devoted wives, and mothers, and housekeepers, but every moment given to a book, is stolen.

This concern about how women are to find time for intellectual pursuits and writing while attending to domestic duties is an overriding one in Hall's letters. In fact, it is addressed much more directly in her correspondence than in her public writings, which tend to be more indirect in their treatment of the tension between domestic and intellectual concerns. In her 23 September 1825 letter to Harris, for example, Hall wondered how "you even could obtain leisure of quiet, in the business and bustle of a family to think so profoundly. My own experience says, that not an hour without visitors—orders—questions, can be found amidst the multitudinous paraphernalia of house keeping." Here and elsewhere Hall's letters provide an inside view of the obstacles many women writers faced, regarding not only public acceptance of their work but also production of the texts themselves.

Hall's correspondence also reveals how much she aided her son John Ewing Hall as he edited *The Port Folio* from 1816 through 1827. Until recently most commentators have not realized the full extent of her involvement with *The Port Folio* and her efforts to keep the journal afloat during its slow demise from the late 1810s until 1827, a period during which subscribers failed to pay and contributors were difficult to find. As circulation of *The Port Folio* gradually declined during the 1820s, Sarah Hall, along with other members of her family, wrote much of the original material published in the magazine. She was also active in seeking out new contributors. Typical of her frequent attempts to find new writers is her query to Anne Harris in her 1 June 1826 letter: "Could any *literary* or *patriotic* names, be found in your part of the world to support the drooping plant [*The Port Folio*]?" Letters such as these reveal Hall's behind-the-scenes influence on *The Port Folio* as well as her nationalist interest in finding American voices.

Sarah Ewing Hall died in Philadelphia on 18 April 1830 and was buried at the Third Presbyterian Church. Her writings, partly obscured by the growing dominance of fiction and the novel, offer valuable insights into the changing roles of women in the early nineteenth century and into the cultural production of "literary nationalism" during that period. Her shifting voices between "private" and "public" and her interesting and varied stances on women's rights make her a valuable and fascinating figure with regard to the development of national, cultural, and literary identities. She raised eleven children, was primarily responsible for supporting her family during her husband's ill health after 1805, and still managed to write on a remarkable number of subjects in a voice that still speaks to readers nearly two hundred years later.

Letters:

Letters to Anne Harris, in *Harris, Dunlop, Valentine and Allied Families,* compiled by William M. Mervin (Philadelphia: Printed by Edward S. Pared, 1920), pp. 88–89.

References:

Nina Baym, *American Women Writers and the Work of History, 1790–1860* (New Brunswick, N.J.: Rutgers University Press, 1995);

Samuel L. Knapp, *Female Biography* (New York: Published by J. Carpenter / Baltimore: Phoenix, Wood & Company, 1834), pp. 268–269;

Gertrude Boiler Middle and Sarah Dickinson Lawrie, eds., *Notable Women of Pennsylvania* (Philadelphia: University of Pennsylvania Press, 1942), pp. 79–80;

Frank Luther Mott, *A History of American Magazines: 1741–1850,* 4 volumes (Cambridge, Mass.: Harvard University Press, 1938–1968), I: 223–246;

John T. Queenan, "'The Port Folio': A Study of the Significance of an Early American Magazine," dissertation, University of Pennsylvania, 1955;

Randolph C. Randall, "Authors of the *Port Folio* Revealed by the Hall Files," *American Literature,* 11 (1940): 379–412;

Thelma M. Smith, "Feminism in Philadelphia, 1790–1850," *Pennsylvania Magazine of History and Biography,* 68 (July 1944): 243–268.

Papers:

The Bellefonte Historical Society in Bellefonte, Pennsylvania; the Historical Society of Pennsylvania; and the Lilly Library at Indiana University have collections of Hall's letters.

Elizabeth Hanson
(1684 – 1737)

James A. Levernier
University of Arkansas at Little Rock

BOOK: *God's Mercy Surmounting Man's Cruelty, Exemplified in the Captivity and Redemption of Elizabeth Hanson* (Philadelphia: Sold by Samuel Keimer and by W. Heurtin in New York, 1728); expanded as *An Account of the Captivity of Elizabeth Hanson, Now or Late of Kachecky, in New-England* (London: Printed & sold by Samuel Clark, 1760).

Elizabeth Meader Hanson is known primarily for the popular eighteenth-century frontier narrative about her experiences in 1724 as a Euro-American captive of American Indians. First published in 1728 as *God's Mercy Surmounting Man's Cruelty, Exemplified in the Captivity and Redemption of Elizabeth Hanson* and later expanded and republished as *An Account of the Captivity of Elizabeth Hanson, Now or Late of Kachecky, in New-England* (1760), the narrative of Hanson's captivity among the Indians of North America merits analysis for a variety of reasons. Once relegated to the margins of the American literary canon, captivity narratives such as Hanson's reveal significant information about the literary culture of Euro-American women living on the New England frontier in the early eighteenth century and about the relationship between Native American peoples and the European newcomers during the formative years of the United States of America. In addition the Hanson narrative provides considerable insight into Quaker perceptions of Native Americans, and it is an excellent example of eighteenth-century Quaker women's writing.

Collectively called "Indian captivity narratives," stories such as Hanson's were immensely popular among European and Euro-American readers during colonial times. Such narratives were put to a variety of often conflicting and sometimes quite ignominious cultural uses, ranging from spiritual edification, to various forms of propaganda, to entertainment, and beyond. The earliest captivity narratives, written during the sixteenth and early seventeenth centuries, were essentially by-products of

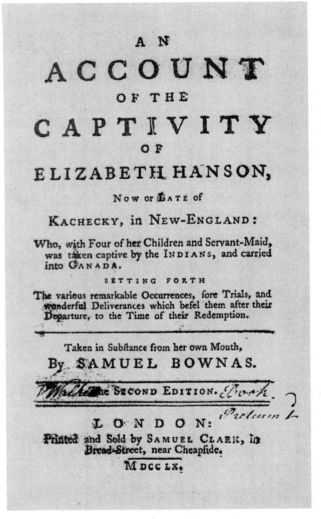

Title page for the expanded edition of Elizabeth Hanson's account of being held for ransom by Indians for more than a year in 1724–1725

European attempts to explore and colonize the New World. Often printed in the context of larger works about the experiences of Europeans in the New World, they provided Old World audiences with their first glimpses into the cultures of the native peoples of the Americas. Eager for such information, European audiences found in these narratives a vision of the New World that was simultaneously thrilling, dangerous, alluring, and exotic. The story of Capt. John Smith's captivity by the Powhatan Indians of Virginia in December 1607 and his subsequent rescue by Pocahontas is a famous example of this phase of the captivity-narrative tradition. First published in Smith's *Generall Historie of Virginia, New-England, and the Summer Isles* (1624), the story adds drama and ethnological data about Indian customs and culture to a larger text about Smith's explorations of North America. With the arrival of the Puritans in New England, captivity narratives increasingly became the locus of religious concerns. Interpreting Indian captivity within a typological framework, Puritans saw themselves as neo-Israelites and the Indians as neo-Canaanites, and they used captivity narratives to depict what they perceived as the divine afflictions and triumphs inherent in their conflicts with the Indians. In such works as Increase Mather's *An Essay for the Recording of Illustrious Providences* (1684), for example, captivity narratives function in this capacity. Similarly, narratives such as those of the Quaker woman Elizabeth Hanson and of Catholic priests in the *Jesuit Relations* provided religious interpretations of the experience of Indian captivity from the Quaker and Roman Catholic perspectives.

From the last decade of the seventeenth and through the early nineteenth centuries, captivity narratives were essentially propagandistic in their aims. During the period of warfare known as the French and Indian Wars, which began in 1689 and ended in 1763, when Great Britain and France finally settled their border disputes in North America, captivity narratives were written to vilify the French, who were described as using their Indian allies to kill and capture British settlers from Maine to the Carolinas. At the time of the American Revolution, captivity narratives were used to accuse the British of similar crimes against humanity. When Great Britain finally withdrew its troops from North America, writers and publishers of captivity stories focused their attention on the Indians, who were depicted as irredeemable, brutish, and barbaric in order to justify the extermination of them. During the nineteenth century, captivity narratives also formed the substance of novels by writers such as Catharine Maria Sedgwick, James Fenimore Cooper, and William Gilmore Simms. Indian captivity was also the subject of plays, folklore, Southwestern humor, dime novels, poetry, and even children's literature. In the twentieth century the subject continued to surface in movies, television dramas, and the ever-

popular "Westerns" so familiar to contemporary audiences.

Like many Europeans who published detailed records of their captivity experiences, Elizabeth Hanson offered few details about her life except those that related to her captivity. Other than the fact that she was born in 1684, nothing is known about her early life and background. At the time of her capture on 27 August 1724, she was living on a farm in Dover Township, New Hampshire. Her "dear Husband," John Hanson, was a Quaker. According to the narrative, he and the other men on the farm were "gone out of the Way," perhaps to tend to work on the far reaches of the property, when the homestead was attacked by French and Indian assailants. Being Quakers and pacifists, the Hansons were probably unarmed and did not intend to defend themselves when attacked. Two of the Hansons' six children were killed at the time of the attack or shortly thereafter. During the attack Elizabeth, a maid in her employ, and four other children—a six-year-old son, two daughters (one fourteen and the other sixteen), and a two-week-old infant—were taken into captivity.

Colonial records on the subject are obscure, so the exact identity of Hanson's captors is difficult to ascertain. During the French and Indian Wars, war parties of the sort described in the Hanson narrative generally consisted of French officers leading small groups of Indians from one or more of the tribal units living along the borders between New England and New France. Throughout these conflicts the French and the British eagerly recruited Indian tribes to assist in the war efforts and encouraged their Indian allies to take captives from among the enemy. Indians occasionally tortured and killed their captives, a fate Hanson feared for herself and her children, but most captives, particularly women and children, were intended for adoption into the tribe as a way to replenish numbers decimated by war and diseases stemming from contact with Europeans or for the ransom captives might bring from the French and the British. Increasingly dependent on Europeans for trade goods and weapons, the Native American populations of New England used the ransom to support and protect themselves in their commerce and in warfare with other tribal groups and the Europeans. The experiences of the Hanson family were by no means unique in colonial New England, where literally thousands of English captives were taken by French and Indians and brought to Canada for ransom.

The events described in the Hanson narrative reveal that Hanson and three of her children were almost certainly intended for ransom. After a captivity that lasted for one year and six days, Hanson, her maid, and three of her children were ransomed by the French and later "redeemed," to quote the terminology of eighteenth-century captivity narratives, by her husband, who found them at Port Royal, Canada. As in the case of many captives, including the well-known Eunice Williams of Deerfield, Massachusetts, the Hansons' later attempts to retrieve their daughter Sarah, who stayed among the Indians, proved unsuccessful. Like many other English captives taken to Canada during the eighteenth century, she chose to remain among the Indians and the French, eventually marrying a man of French descent and converting to Catholicism. Elizabeth Hanson survived her captivity by thirteen years. She died in 1737 at the age of fifty-three. John Hanson died shortly after his wife's redemption, during a trip in the attempt to recover his lost daughter. Elizabeth Hanson described his death in some detail at the conclusion of the narrative.

Exact authorship of the Hanson narrative is difficult to ascertain with absolute certainty. In this regard it resembles many other early captivity narratives, especially those by or about women captives. Told in the first person in the relatively plain, clear, straightforward style characteristic of Quaker journals during the early part of the eighteenth century, the narrative appears to be written or at least dictated by Hanson herself. Belonging to a religious denomination noted for its simplicity and directness in all matters from dress and diet to literary style, Quaker writers of the eighteenth century eschewed complicated sentence structures in favor of more-direct forms of expression. Because they believed that truth was its own best witness, Quaker writers believed that facts spoke for themselves, and they valued clear, direct first-person prose narratives as the most effective means for expressing the religious truths they hoped to reveal in their accounts of personal experience.

Nevertheless, by the middle decades of the eighteenth century, first-person prose by no means guaranteed the historicity of a given captivity narrative, even among Quakers. Appropriated for purposes of sensationalism, propaganda, titillation, and profit, first-person captivity narratives were often fabricated from fictions. Indeed, some narratives, such as Ann Eliza Bleecker's *The History of Maria Kittle* (1793), had little connection with historical reality and were in fact totally fictitious epistolary novels. In the case of the Hanson narrative, external and internal evidence strongly suggests that Hanson's is indeed the primary voice behind the narrative, but whether or not she wrote the narrative or told it to someone else who in turn transcribed or even "interpreted" or "improved" the story is unclear. According to a brief third-person introduction published in the 1728 edition, the narrative "was taken from her [Hanson's] own Mouth, by a Friend" and "differs very little from the Original Copy, but is even almost in her own Words (what small Alteration is made being partly owing to the Mistakes of the Transcriber)."

Who the "friend" mentioned in the introduction might be is a matter of speculation, but it was probably Samuel Bownas, an English preacher of Quaker background traveling in America at the time the narrative was written and whose autobiography was published in 1756. The somewhat revised, 1760 edition of the Hanson narrative stated that the original narrative was "Taken in Substance from her own Mouth, by Samuel Bownas." Especially when they were about the experiences of women, many of the historical captivity narratives required at least the imprimatur, if not the outright collaboration, of clerics, who frequently edited or shaped the captivities to ensure their public credibility and appropriate salutary impact. Fearful that narratives written by ordinary people might encourage the publication of texts not in keeping with the orthodox religious structures of the day, clerics and publishers throughout New England exercised strict control over much of the print medium. While women were encouraged by the establishment to learn to read and write, only in rare instances were they encouraged to publish what they wrote or even to write with a view toward publication. Because captivity narratives about women were considered a powerful public means of testifying to God's providential control over human affairs, they constituted a form of writing that women could undertake, but only under the scrutiny of male editors. Although captivity narratives such as Hanson's reveal considerable literary sophistication, rarely if ever did their authors publish anything else during their lifetimes. Despite the commercial popularity of their texts, it was the didactic religious concerns of the captivity experience, not the literary skills or potential of the authors, that such texts were intended to emphasize.

As Increase and Cotton Mather had done in their day for the captivities of Mary Rowlandson and Hannah Duston and as John Todd would later do for Frances Slocum and Royal B. Stratton for Olive Oatman, Bownas, or another male editor, seems to have taken upon himself the task of making "respectable" the telling of the Hanson narrative. Consequently, when approaching a captivity narrative such as Hanson's, the reader must sometimes make a deliberate effort to disentangle the speaker's voice from the editorial voice imposed on hers. The 1760 edition of the Hanson captivity includes, for instance, information, credited as Hanson's own words, that is not in the first edition. These additions are often violent, sensationalistic, and incendiary in political intent and decidedly not in keeping with the more gentle spirit of Quaker humanism evident in the earlier text. After a description of the practice of "scalping," the 1760 edition states: "And it has been currently reported, that the French, in their wars with the English, have given the Indians a pecuniary reward for every scalp they brought to them." Clearly, propagandistic and sensationalistic statements such as this one seem not to have been written by Hanson, who presented a relatively unbiased account of intercultural and international wartime rivalries. Probably such statements were not even by Bownas, for they were also not in keeping with his mission as a Quaker preacher. They would, however, be congruent with an anonymous British editor's attempts to contextualize the narrative within the framework of the anti-French sentiment prominent in England around 1760 and to capitalize on such sentiment for purposes of increasing notoriety and hence sales among the British reading public. Thus, the Hanson narrative might, as recent commentary has suggested, be a compilation of multiple voices and hands, with Hanson's voice submerged somewhere in the text.

Identifying the role an individual captivity narrative plays in the historical and literary evolution of the theme has usually proven an effectual means of assessing the significance of a given narrative, but the tradition is complex, with undercurrents and impulses that often overlap and intersect. Care must be taken when contextualizing these narratives, and the Hanson captivity narrative is a case in point. Historically associated with a transitional phase when the impulse toward anti-French and anti-Indian propaganda became the dominant impetus behind the captivity tradition as it moved from propaganda and sensationalism to fiction, *An Account of the Captivity of Elizabeth Hanson* actually has much more in common with the pietistical religious dimensions of the seventeenth- century Puritan captivity narratives than with the propaganda narratives of its day.

Indeed, remarkable similarities between the Hanson narrative and Mary Rowlandson's *The Soveraignty & Goodness of God* (1682), the popular Puritan text that identified and established the pattern for all American captivities to follow, suggest that either Hanson or her editor had read the Rowlandson narrative and used it as a structural and mythic model. Both narratives are similar in length, and both begin with a preamble written by a "friend" who explained that the narrative was published at the request of others so that the world might learn that "Remarkable and many have been the Providences of God, towards his People for their Deliverance in a Time of Trouble." Both narratives end with concluding statements reiterating the lessons to be gained from a reading of such texts. In addition both narratives include scriptural allusions and typological references that function as interpretive frameworks for the sequence of events they describe. At one point in the narrative, for example, an allusion to the captivity of the Israelites in Babylon helped to sustain Hanson in her trials. At the request of their Indian captors, Hanson's daughter Sarah was made to sing a song for her captors. "At the Side of one of these Runs or Rivers," states the narrative, "the *Indians* would have my eldest Daughter *Sarah* to sing them a Song: Then was brought into her Remembrance that Passage in the 137th Psalm, *By the Rivers of* Babylon *there we sat down, yea we wept when we remember'd Zion; we hanged our Harps on the Willows in the midst thereof; for there they that carryed us away captive required of us a Song, and they that wasted us, required of us Mirth.*" Rowlandson structured her narrative around a series of "Removes," and Hanson's is the only other captivity narrative to use the term "Remove" in the same context as Rowlandson.

Finally both writers thanked Providence for their deliverances; both dwelt extensively on the metaphors of hunger and food as ways of understanding their experiences; and both drew attention to the "civility" that the Indians showed them in matters of sexual decorum. About the behavior of Indian men toward her, Rowlandson wrote, "I have been in the midst of those roaring Lyons, and Salvage Bears, that feared neither God, nor Man, nor the Devil, by night and day, alone and in company, sleeping all sorts together, and yet not one of them ever offered me the least abuse of unchastity to me, in word or action," and Hanson wrote, "the *Indians* being very civil toward their captive Women, not offering any Incivility by any indecent Carriage, unless they be much overgone in Liquor, which is commendable in them so far."

Such similarities in texts might be just that—coincidental similarities common to the theme; yet they might equally indicate how the subject of Indian captivity so saturated and fascinated the imagination of the reading public of the late seventeenth and early eighteenth centuries that barriers of dogma and sect were easily broken through when the subject matter was Indian captivity. While religious concerns might have dominated the minds of the clergy and publishers who edited, printed, and distributed captivity narratives, readers were probably far more interested in the drama and adventure of the narratives than they were with morals and theology. Thus, from the start captivity narratives developed into a literary tradition that by virtue of its readership defined itself apart from the religious concerns of the male clergy who often supervised their publication. Reprints of Rowlandson's famous account of her captivity were common in the early eighteenth century and would have been easily accessible to a writer looking for commercially successful precedents on the subject. In a possible reference to individually published narratives such as Rowlandson's and books that included captivity accounts, such as Increase Mather's *An Essay for the Recording of Illustrious Providences* and Cotton Mather's *Magnalia Christi Americana* (1701), the introduction to the Hanson narrative acknowledges a familiarity with the captivity tradition among "our modern Histories." In the words of Hanson's narrative, "our modern Histories have plentifully abounded with Instances of God's Fatherly Care over his People, in their sharpest Trials, deepest Distresses, and sorest Exercises by which we may know *he is a God that Changeth not, but is the same Yesterday, to Day, and for ever.*"

Comments such as this one frequently appear in the introductory matter of captivity narratives published throughout the seventeenth, eighteenth, and nineteenth centuries. Writing in the nineteenth century about the captivity of Mary Jemison, James Seaver summarized the long-standing tradition of captivity stories in the popular literature and culture of his day, stating that "In those days, Indian barbarities were the constant topic of the domestic fireside, the parlor, the hall, and the forum." According to Seaver, "It is presumed that, at this time, there are but few native citizens that have passed the middle age who do not distinctly recollect the hearing of such frightful accounts of Indian barbarities, often repeated, in the nursery and in the family circle, until it almost caused their hair to stand erect, and deprived them of the power of motion." Clearly a distinct body of oral and manuscript literature accompanied the published record about Indian captivity, and all potential writers were probably familiar with this material.

Perhaps what most distinguishes the Hanson narrative from others of its kind, however, is not its piety or its anti-Indian and anti-French sentiment but its lack of sensationalism and its focus on the

human dimensions of Hanson's experiences. Much has been made of grouping the Indian captivity narratives into a single American genre, but much of the literary significance of these narratives resides more in their generic differences than their thematic similarities. Captivity narratives were actually written in a variety of forms, including spiritual autobiographies and sermons, folk narratives and ballads, journals and diaries, and novels and short stories. What binds the narratives together in a literary tradition is theme and subject matter. The generic manifestation of the theme of Indian captivity varied with the literary tastes and forms of the time of the writing and publication of individual narratives. In this regard Hanson's narrative shares far more with the humanitarian concerns of eighteenth-century Quaker journals such as those by Elizabeth Ashbridge and John Woolman than it does with the providential concerns of the early Puritan narratives or with the propagandistic concerns of others of its kind in the eighteenth century. Moreover, the method of its publication and distribution confirms that its early editors and publishers considered it a form of Quaker journal. Indeed, at the conclusion of her narrative, Hanson directly stated that her text, given the nature of her experiences, was as close as she could come to approximating the form of the Quaker journal: "Thus, as well, and as near as I can from my memory, (not being capable of keeping a Journal) I have given a short, but a true Account of some of the remarkable Trials and wonderful Deliverances, which I never purposed to expose."

Nowhere are the Quaker concerns of the Hanson narrative more evident than in her descriptions of her Indian and French captors. Unlike her Puritan predecessors and many of her contemporary counterparts, Hanson was loathe to vilify her enemies. Instead she credited them for acts of humanity toward her and her family, and she even individualized particular Indians and Canadians in cameo vignettes that illustrate and highlight their personalities and concerns. Whereas earlier Puritan narratives, such as Rowlandson's, interpret any acts of kindness shown captives during their ordeals as signs of God's predominant providence over even their "savage" captors, and whereas the propaganda captivity writers of the eighteenth century fulminated with rage and excess at lurid descriptions of Indian cruelty, Hanson was relatively unbiased and objective in analyzing the motivations and behaviors of the Indians and French, even though they were responsible for the murders of her children. On the contrary she attributed these acts less to cruelty than to "Fright" among the Indians about "the

Danger of a Discovery that might arise" from the cries of the young children.

Throughout her narrative Hanson drew attention to her captors' acts of kindness. During their flight toward Canada, for instance, Hanson stated that the "Captain" of the party, "tho' he had as great a Load as he could well carry, and was helped up with it, did for all that, carry my Babe for me in his Arms, which I took to be a Favour from him." About the difficulties she had in climbing "some very high Mountains" with her children in hand, Hanson wrote that "the *Indian* my Master, would mostly carry my Babe for me." "Nay," she stated, "he would sometimes take my very Blanket, so that I had nothing to do, but take my little Boy by the Hand for his Help, and assist him as well as I could." "When we came at very bad Places," she continued, her master "would lend me his Hand, or coming behind, would push me up before him: In all which, he shewed some Humanity and Civility more than I could have expected." Other Indians, she stated, carried "my Boy on their Shoulders," and whenever the occasion came for crossing through rivers, swamps, or thickets, in such "Places my Master would sometimes lead me by the Hand a great Way together, and give me what Help he was capable of under the Straits we went thro'." About Indian society in general, Hanson stated that "these People [were] very kind and helpful to one another, which," she noted, "is very commendable." Mary Rowlandson would never have made such statements. For her, Indians were "hell-hounds," "merciless Heathen," "ravenous Beasts," and "Barbarous Creatures." Thus, while Rowlandson's description of Indian culture reflected her Puritan background, Hanson's description of her captors revealed the more humanitarian, egalitarian views of the Quakers toward Indians.

Attitudes and remarks such as Hanson's, as well as the relatively straightforward unadorned manner in which they are recited, are in keeping with Quaker thinking and writing, and the narrative is by no means the anti-Indian propaganda document that it has often been called. Hanson was especially moved by the kindness shown her by Indian women. When for want of milk Hanson found herself unable to feed her baby, "One of the *Indian* Squaws perceiving my Uneasiness about my Child, began some Discourse with me" about how walnuts could be mixed with water to produce what

"look'd like Milk." Hanson credited the advice and concern of this woman with saving the life of her child. On another occasion, when Hanson's master became angry with her and threatened her life, she mentioned the sincere solicitation shown for her welfare by her master's mother-in-law: "the poor old Squaw was so very kind and tender, that she would not leave me all that Night, but laid her self down at my Feet, designing what she could to asswage her Son-in-law's Wrath." About her French captors, she similarly remarked that they were "very civil to me" and their remarks about her future "very sensible."

From the 1940s, when serious scholarship on the captivity narrative began to be written, to the mid 1990s much attention has been given to interpreting the captivity tradition as a whole. This work certainly needed to be done, but it was sometimes done at the expense of overlooking the significance of individual narratives such as Hanson's, which were either eclipsed by more-spectacular manifestations of the theme such as those by Rowlandson, John Williams, and Mary Jemison or contextualized into theoretical frameworks that diminished their importance. That situation is now being rectified, and narratives such as Hanson's have begun to receive the full critical attention they deserve.

References:

Kathryn Zabelle Derounian-Stodola and James Arthur Levernier, *The Indian Captivity Narrative, 1550–1900* (New York: Twayne/Macmillan, 1993);

Gary L. Ebersole, *Captured by Texts: Puritan to Post-Modern Images of Indian Captivity* (Charlottesville & London: University Press of Virginia, 1995);

Roy Harvey Pearce, "The Significances of the Captivity Narrative," *American Literature,* 19 (1947): 200–217;

R. W. G. Vail, *The Voice of the Old Frontier* (Philadelphia: University of Pennsylvania Press, 1949);

Alden T. Vaughn and Edward S. Clark, eds., *Puritans among the Indians: Accounts of Captivity and Redemption, 1676–1724* (Cambridge, Mass.: Harvard University Press, 1981);

Richard VanDerBeets, ed., *Held Captive by Indians: Selected Narratives, 1642–1836* (Knoxville: University of Tennessee Press, 1973).

Anne Hart
(1768 – 18 July 1834)

John Saillant
Western Michigan University

WORKS: "Memoir of John Gilbert," in *Memoir of J.G., Esq., Late Naval Storekeeper at Antigua, to Which Are Appended a Brief Sketch of His Relic, Mrs. A. Gilbert, by the Rev. W. Box, Wesleyan Missionary, and a Few Additional Remarks by a Christian Friend* (Liverpool: D. Marples, 1835);

"History of Methodism," in *The Hart Sisters: Early African Caribbean Writers, Evangelicals, and Radicals,* edited by Moira Ferguson (Lincoln & London: University of Nebraska Press, 1993).

One of the earliest black women to write in English, Anne Hart offered a view into eighteenth-century African American Christianity, a religious approach to the lives of enslaved women in a West Indian plantation society, and valuable information about African practices among New World slaves. Her writings about Antiguan Methodism and enslaved women were preserved by a British missionary and came to light only in the 1990s. They are particularly valuable because writings by African American women of the eighteenth century are extremely rare.

Anne Hart's literary ambitions were rooted in her family and bloomed in a slave society. Her father, Barry Conyers Hart, collected books by English authors and published his own poetry in an Antiguan newspaper. The author of a history of Antiguan Methodism and a loving memoir of her husband, John Gilbert, Anne Hart spent years instructing Antiguan slaves in reading and Christian doctrine and regularly read evangelical periodicals such as the *Arminian Magazine* and the *Methodist Magazine.* Her sister, Elizabeth Hart, was the author of another history of Antiguan Methodism and other works, also unpublished in her lifetime. The Hart sisters left accounts of their intimacy, most likely one that allowed each to encourage the other's literary enterprises.

Anne Hart was born in 1768 into a free-black family on the West Indian island of Antigua, then a British colony. Nearly all eighteenth-century Antiguan blacks were enslaved, and the free status of the Harts almost certainly resulted from white men's manumission of slave women who had borne their children. In the Anglo-American colonies the free or enslaved status of a child was nearly always that of the mother, and Hart's maternal grandmother, Frances Clearkley, had probably been freed by an Englishman with whom she had a child. Thus, Hart's mother, Anne Clearkley Hart, a free woman, transmitted her freedom to her daughters. Anne Hart's father, Barry Conyers Hart, was a free man (possibly a mulatto) and the owner of slaves who served him as agricultural laborers. Although Hart's ancestors probably included Africans and Europeans and although she was probably considered a "mulatto" during her childhood and early adulthood, by the time of her death she was considered "black" according to the terminology then in use.

Among Hart's family were some of the first Antiguans who subscribed to the Methodist movement within the Church of England. The usual way of becoming part of this evangelical movement was to join a Methodist Society, which was visited by missionary preachers and which sustained its own spiritual warmth through prayer meetings and "love feasts." Methodist missionary work was so intense in eighteenth-century Antigua that it was known as the "mother of West Indian Methodism." In her "History of Methodism," written in 1804 and first published in 1993 (but based on an essay Hart composed in the early 1790s), Hart recalled that her maternal grandmother cherished for years her first admission ticket to a Methodist meeting. Frances Clearkley became the spiritual guide of her granddaughters after her own daughter, their mother, died in 1785. Anne Hart was baptized in 1786 under the guidance of an itinerant Methodist who was seeking converts in Antigua.

Hart labored to spread Methodism among Antiguan blacks. Although ministers (generally white men) exhorted blacks to convert to Christianity, the regular prayer meetings, also called "love feasts," were held by women such as the Hart sisters, who are credited with keeping the faith alive. Although the formal doors to the church were controlled by white men, its day-to-day life was in the hands of black women. In the late eighteenth century, black Methodists outnumbered white Methodists in Antigua. The planter elite was mostly Anglican. (In the late twentieth century the majority of Christian Antiguans are Anglicans.) The separation of the Methodist Church from the Church of England in 1795 confirmed the differences in style and membership—not the least among them the large number of black Methodists—that were apparent in Antigua, as in other places in England and the Americas. Hart's family legacy of pious Methodists, her close contact with slaves, visits by itinerant Methodist preachers, and her devotion to literacy shaped her life after 1786.

Although she wrote no hostile words about her father, it is evident in her writing that she was critical of his slaveholding and his enjoyment of secular literature. Whatever her relationship with her father, however, it is clear that she carried on his literary sensibility at the same time she carried on her grandmother's faith. John Gilbert, whom she married in 1798, seems to have been quite different from her father—pious and committed to his wife's evangelical work among slaves. Yet he was also unable to maintain good enough relations with the secular authorities to keep himself employed.

Beginning in the 1790s the Hart sisters offered religious instruction and reading lessons to slaves, both children and adults. The population of eighteenth-century Antigua guaranteed the Hart sisters a large audience among which they might proselytize. Settled by the British in 1632, Antigua in the eighteenth century was a complex of sugar factories. The island continually received victims of the slave trade, transshipped slaves to areas where their labor was desired, and attracted those Britons and Anglo-Americans who would manage the plantations or serve in a British naval outpost. The Hart sisters hoped to convert to Christianity a large enslaved black population, which was ruled by mercenary whites and freed only in 1834, the year Anne Hart died. Students in the Hart sisters' classes sometimes numbered in the hundreds. In 1809 the sisters established a Sunday School for slave and free children alike, and in 1815 the sisters established the Female Refuge Society of Antigua, devoted to the instruction and moral improvement of slave women. In 1817 Anne Hart began supervising the girls' Sunday School in English Harbour, where she had moved with her husband as he searched for employment.

Much of the home instruction in Methodist principles and practices in Antigua had been carried out by black women who followed lessons learned from missionaries. Indeed, some of the hard labor of building places of worship was performed by black women. The Hart sisters continued these efforts in a more genteel way; yet they made a special effort to credit the slave women who had helped to construct places of worship, providing labor, preparing food for the workers, or donating petty cash. In her "History of Methodism" Hart discussed ways in which a church that relied on itinerant white male ministers cast its roots into a colonial society by drawing on the resources of enslaved women: "The most decent, and creditable of the black women did not think it a labour too servile to carry stones and marl, to help with their own hands to clear the Land of the rubbish that lay about it, & to bring ready-dressed victuals for the men employed in building the House of God."

The Methodists decried unofficial liaisons between black women and white men as acts of prostitution or fornication. The Hart sisters cast themselves as the rescuers of such women and scourges of the system of "Concubinage." Hart threw her energy into preaching abstinence to girls and women and believed that she had successfully undermined the process by which women prepared their daughters for such liaisons: "I see with heart-felt joy that prostitution is now esteemed abominable & disgraceful by the greater part of the Colour'd Women in St Johns."

In Antigua during Hart's time, as in most slave societies in the Americas, free and enslaved black men far outnumbered free and enslaved black women. Furthermore, white men in Antigua outnumbered white women. This relative shortage of women led to a situation in which they became commodities far more accessible to high-status men than to low-status men, more to white men and free blacks than to slaves. Hart's family and her own life exemplify this pattern. Her father, probably of mixed blood, married twice, and both she and her sister married white men. As literate and accomplished black women, the Hart sisters would have been much sought after in a society where women were relatively scarce. Still, commodification of women did not always lead to good treatment, such as the Hart sisters seem to have received. They saw much abuse in the lives of the enslaved women around them.

To The Reverend Richard *[...]*

37

Antigua English-Harbor 1st June 1804.

W T

My Dear Sir!

Having seen most of the accounts transmitted to our Brethren in Europe, respecting the rise, progress & present state of Methodism in the West-indies; and having, I think matter of fact, & the concurrent opinions of other impartial persons on my side, for differing with some in many, and with others in a few particulars; I feel some reluctance to giving you the information you require of me, lest the testimony of those that have gone before should render my time so employed, uselessly disposed of. I will however venture; hoping at least to profit my own Soul by calling to mind the wonders God has wrought in this benighted Land.

In the Year 1798 One of our Preachers who is now in Europe, requested me to inform him by letter, of all that I knew respecting the rise & progress of Methodism in Antigua: I endeavour'd at that time, to collect all the information I could get, and having part of a copy of that letter now in my possession, I will give you the substance of it as far as it goes.

The remotest period to which I can trace the Preaching of the Gospel, in these Islands, is in the year 1671: By William Edmundson a Quaker, who with five other friends visited Bermudas, Jamaica, Barbadoes, Antigua Barbuda Nevis & St Christophers. He made the attempt at Mountserrat also but was not suffered to land, Colonel Stapleton, the Governor, having heard that by means of their preaching seven hundred of the militia had turned Quakers & that Quakers would not fight. They were obliged to return immediately to Antigua from whence they came, and were again graciously received: To give you the paragraph from his own

First two pages of Anne Hart's "History of Methodism," in a letter dated 1 June 1804 (Missionary Society Archives, School of Oriental and African Studies, University of London)

Journal———— "After we had laboured sometime in Barbadoes, we were
"moved in our minds to visit the Leeward Islands; & Colonel Morris of
"Barbadoes, would go with us; so we took ship & in four days we landed
"in Antigua, where we had large & heavenly meetings & many were
"convinced & turned to the Lord. Sev'ral Justices of the Peace, & Officers, &
"Chief men came to the meetings, & confessed the truth which we declared
"in the power of God. When we left Antigua Colonel Windthorpe (who
"had been Governor, being convinced, he & his family received the truth; we
"had several large & heavenly meetings in his house) would go with us to
"Nevis, & having a vessel of his own Shipped us in it with himself, Colonel
"Morris, their waiting men, & Seamen; so we set sail from Antigua, & in
"the way we touch'd at a little Island called Barbuda where we made a little
"stay & preach'd the truth."

This Colonel Windthorpe, was I doubt not ancestor of the person
mentioned by Mr Nathaniel Gilbert in his letter to Mr Wesley called
"The Dawn of a Gospel Day". and published in the 3d Volume of the
Arminian Magazine. He calls her Miss Molly Windthorpe a first
Cousin of his Wifes. In the year 1683 after spending sometime in
America, W. Edmundson returned to Ireland, from whence he came.
To the best of my knowledge the Islands were destitute of a Gospel ministry
till the year 1756 when a Moravian Mission began. The clouds of sin
and error began to disperse among the Slaves by their instrumentality;
and while they preached the truth, they laboured with their hands
to forward the Work in which they were engaged. But yet, darkness"
covered the Land & gross darkness the hearts of the people". In the
Year 1760, The Lord rais'd up Messrs Nathaniel & Frances Gilbert.
The Slaves at this time were in a state of inconceivable darkness &
diabolical superstition. The torch of Moral & divine truth was carefully
                                                                    hid

The Hart sisters were among many Anglo-Americans drawn to Methodism around 1800. The rapid growth of Methodism in the late eighteenth century can be attributed to the willingness of Methodist ministers and missionaries to seek out hearers even among the unchurched and the enslaved as well as to the Methodist message of purity, simplicity, and the possibility of a direct emotional encounter of the believer with God. Moreover, in the 1780s the leading Methodists renounced the Calvinist doctrine of predestination, emphasizing more forcefully than earlier preachers that salvation is open to anyone, no matter what race or class. These facets of Methodism easily merged with resentment against the social elite throughout the English-speaking world of the late eighteenth century. One source of the appeal of Methodism was its capacity to allow ordinary people, even the lowliest in society, to articulate their resentment in a religious vocabulary. In Antigua—where the local elite were not aristocrats in the European sense but rather a rough mercenary class making a living in the Atlantic slave trade and relying on the forced work of unfree labor— Methodism gave Hart an instrument with which to attack the enforcers of the plantation system. In her writings she contrasted the purity, simplicity, and piety of the black Methodists with the corruption and vice of the plantation owners and overseers and the white women of their society. She considered the white plantation owners to be "Learned & polished Heathens of the present day," given to "Debauchery, Drunkenness, Duelling, & Sabbathbreaking," and she called their wives "vain Women of the World" who were preoccupied with "Tea-parties & feasts" laid on "the tables of the Wicked."

Hart was also critical of the liberals in the Anglican Church, labeling some Antiguan Anglicans as immoralists and latitudinarians and finding heartening evidence of evangelical Christianity in black women. Charging that a white minister who misled his hearers caused them to decline in spirituality and become "friends with the world & inwardly enemies to God & his people," she asserted that "a praying remnant held fast where unto they had attained." The leaders of those who maintained their "simplicity, purity & love of the cross" were "Mary Alley a Mulatto Woman & Sophia Campbel a black." As in her own family, the day-to-day responsibilities of nourishing the faith were taken up by black women. Still, Hart was not immune to a feeling of her own superiority over the enslaved. Although

she lauded Mary Alley's and Sophia Campbel's faith, she noted that "it cannot be said, that they abounded in knowledge, brightness of reason or soundness of speech." Generally, Hart accepted the argument about black intellect that had been made by Thomas Coke, the Methodist missionary who baptized her in 1786 and who, with Francis Asbury, had founded the American Methodist Episcopal Church in 1784. Coke argued not only that natural depravity had crushed the intellect of black men and women, as was the case with all humans, but also that blacks had a natural ferocity that could be diluted only through Christian faith. For Coke and his followers the solution to the degradations of slaves' lives was to give them enough instruction to allow them to comprehend the Christian message; then an infusion of grace could replace ferocity with mildness. Both racism and the hope that religion would make slaves docile are evident in this view. Indeed, in 1794 the Society for the Conversion and Religious Instruction and Education of the Negro Slaves in the British West Indies, an Anglican association with Methodist members, began to evangelize among Antiguan slaves in order to increase their compliance and thus their value as slaves.

Hart's mixed beliefs about black intelligence, even her tendency to associate enslaved blacks with animals, can be seen in her statement that when some Methodist missionaries proselytized among them, "the slaves . . . were in a state of inconceivable darkness and diabolical superstition. The torch of Moral and divine truth was carefully hid from them, lest by it they should discover that they were Men, and Brethren, and not Beasts, and Reptiles." Readers in the late twentieth century may see these words as ironic, but Hart lived in a time and place in which blacks' mental and moral faculties were scorned, and only Christian conversion, many believed, elevated blacks to humanity. She did not challenge those views and insisted that slaves without Christian religion differed in "few respects from the Beasts that perish."

Yet Hart was not unquestioningly accepting of the itinerant Methodist ministers whom she heard preach from her adolescence onward. Although she believed that some of them faithfully preached the Word of God, she presented others as betrayers and sinners who misled their hearers and fell into the sin, sensuality, and worldliness of the West Indian plantation life. She never explicitly mentioned which sins these itinerants were likely to commit, but several times she recounted tales of men who concealed sins that were later made public. Because she characterized these secret sins as those of a slave society and because her condemnation was often violently phrased, it seems likely that some, if not all, of the ministers whom she condemned as sinners and deceivers were involved in sexual liaisons with slaves.

Many early Methodists were opposed to slavery, but they were little inclined to challenge the secular and commercial powers in the Anglo-American Atlantic. Hart was abolitionist, but not in a modern sense of opposing slavery as a violation of individual liberty. Instead, she opposed slavery as corrupt because it encouraged informal sexual relations between white men and black women and undermined the stability of black families by dividing women's loyalties between their white patrons and their black home communities. She favored manumission because the former slave could be "saved from vice." In particular, freed girls and women were liberated from "degradation and impurity." For Hart, then, the point of emancipation was virtue, not liberty, but she was loath to countenance postponing virtue until liberation. She insisted that, just as enslaved women could be effective church workers, so they should communicate virtue to their daughters: "One happy effect of seeing the Gospel seed sown in the hearts of their Mothers" is that girls and young women learn the value of "chastity, tho' accompanied with labour & self-denial." Seeing sexual "vice" as a flash point in Antigua, Hart interpreted the evangelical idea of "total renunciation of self, and entire dependence on the atonement of our blessed Saviour" to imply that enslaved women should renounce "Concubinage," whether with white men or black.

Among the most interesting features of Hart's history of Methodism are her accounts of Antiguan slaves' African practices, which she recorded only to condemn them as heathen and satanic. Despite Hart's bias against African practices, readers of her history can gain valuable information about Africanisms in Antigua around 1800. Because of their position between African societies and Euro-American societies, many literate black men and women of the eighteenth century and early nineteenth century, including Hart, left information and insights that cannot be gleaned from other sources. Hart described funeral processions in which the mourners carried the dead while "beating upon an instrument they call a Shake Shake. (This is a large round hollow Calabash fixed upon the end of a stick, with a few pebbles in it.)" She recorded the mourners' "heathenish account of the Life & Death of the deceased; invoking a perpetuation of their friendship from the world of Spirits with their Surviving friends and relations, & praying them to deal destruction among their enemies." She noted slaves' intense preoccupation with witchcraft and with the "Obeah men & women" who met the slaves' needs for charms and protection against spells. She described a Christmas festival in which enslaved men and women left cooked meat and yams and poured rum on the ground at the graves of deceased friends and relatives. She explained the spells that slaves used to manipulate their masters, the techniques they used to make horses race faster and to identify evildoers, and the magical use of "grave-dirt." She also condemned whites who relied on blacks for magic spells, and she lamented that white ministers were so little aware of the extent of "diabolical work" among the slaves of Antigua that "they pass too lightly over the sin of witchcraft."

Hart's last years were difficult. John Gilbert proved inept at providing for his wife, partly because his intense religiosity put him at odds with men of commerce and the military and partly because the couple's voluntary work contributed nothing to their sustenance. They were proud that they owned little but gave much to the poor and enslaved around them. Both Hart and her husband became ill in the 1830s. Gilbert contracted a lingering malaise that led to his death on 16 July 1833. Hart was diagnosed with "erysipelas" (also known as "St. Anthony's fire"), an inflammation of the skin indicating an infection, which she believed she had contracted while handling fish. She and her husband may have had pellagra, a disease resulting from a deficiency of niacin in the diet and characterized by all the symptoms exhibited by Hart and Gilbert—fatigue, digestive disturbances, disorientation, and darkened skin that was painful to the touch. The disease was common in slave societies, and instances of pellagra even among the free black Antiguans suggest that the diet of slaves was so poor as to be life threatening. Anne Hart died on 18 July 1834.

Between the composition of the second version of her history of Methodism in 1804 and her husband's death, Hart wrote nothing that has survived. Her memoir of her husband is a continuation, in her own words, of an autobiographical essay that John Gilbert had partly completed before his death. Hart's memoir recounted their hard times, their devotion to their benevolent work in Antigua, and their faith that

God would watch over them providentially. In remembrances included in *Memoir of J.G.* (1835) one eulogist commemorated Hart as "a leader, a shepherdess, a pattern, a pillar of the first magnitude [and] a burning and shining light—a city set upon a hill, which could not be hid—a righteous woman." Another eulogist recalled her as "almost the founder" of "those religious and moral principles which distinguish the Antigua negroes." Hart's writings are a valuable resource for scholars of West Indian slavery and African American culture around 1800. She revealed some of the inner dynamics of the life of black women in the late eighteenth century—rebelling against her father's ways, affiliating herself with her grandmother's faith, voicing her concern for enslaved women and children, and choosing a husband who respected her values. She recorded important details of African practices in Antigua, described how Methodism cast its roots into slave society, and expressed a pre-liberal view of abolitionism based on slaves' potential for virtue.

Reference:

Moira Ferguson, Introduction to *The Hart Sisters: Early African Caribbean Writers, Evangelicals, and Radicals,* edited by Ferguson (Lincoln & London: University of Nebraska Press, 1993), pp. 1–54.

Papers:

Anne Hart's "History of Methodism" is in a letter dated 1 June 1804, English Harbor, Antigua, at the Missionary Society Archives, School of Oriental and African Studies, University of London.

Elizabeth Hart
(1771 - 1833)

John Saillant
Western Michigan University

WORKS: Correspondence, hymns, and poetry, in *A Voice from the West Indies: Being a Review of the Character and Results of Missionary Efforts in the British and Other Colonies in the Caribbean Sea, with Some Remarks on the Usages, Prejudices, etc., of the Inhabitants,* by John Horsford (London: Alexander Heylin, 1856);

"History of Methodism," in *The Hart Sisters: Early African Caribbean Writers, Evangelicals, and Radicals,* edited by Moira Ferguson (Lincoln & London: University of Nebraska Press, 1993).

Elizabeth Hart, who was among the earliest black women to write in English, showed that popular understanding of theological issues in a time of debate between Calvinists and Arminians conditioned opinions about slavery and that moderate opposition to slavery, far removed from nineteenth-century abolitionism and twentieth-century intolerance for slavery, seemed a viable option for a black woman around 1800. Theodicy, the examination of the role of evil in a world created by a benevolent deity, influenced her thoughts on slavery, which she opposed less as an infringement on individual liberty than as a trap in which slaves were led into vice. Her major writings are "History of Methodism," written in 1804 at the request of a British minister, Richard Pattison, and a 1794 letter that was published in an 1856 collection of missionary documents relating to the West Indies. This collection also includes several hymns and poems by Hart.

Hart was born into a free, mixed-race family in Antigua. In her childhood and young adulthood she would probably have been considered a "mulatto" in the Anglophone New World, but by the time she died most people of mixed African and European descent in the Anglophone Americas were called "black." She and her older sister, Anne Hart, were reared in a family in which several generations of women were noted for their piety. Her maternal grandmother, Frances Clearkley, an early affiliate of the Methodists in Antigua, provided spiritual guidance to her granddaughters after their mother, Anne Clearkley Hart, died in 1785.

Their father, Barry Conyers Hart, seems to have been a worldly individual who owned slaves and published his poetry in an Antiguan newspaper. His daughters apparently merged his literary interests and ambitions with their mother's and grandmother's piety.

A major part of Elizabeth Hart's "History of Methodism" treats the way in which black women were drawn into the church by white evangelical itinerant preachers and describes the intellectual and emotional process of compunction, despair, and revivification that constituted religious conversion in Methodist societies during the late eighteenth century. Hart's conversion experience, which took place sometime between 1786 and 1804, followed years of religious tutelage and prayers. In her case, as with many blacks in the Anglo-American world during the late eighteenth century and the nineteenth century, conversion engendered a determination to help improve the lot of black men, women, and children.

The Hart sisters were baptized in 1786, when the noted Methodist evangelist Thomas Coke made a revival tour of Antigua—a typical Methodist itinerancy of the late eighteenth century in which blacks as well as whites were exhorted to strive for conversion. The Hart sisters devoted themselves for decades to philanthropic work among Antiguan slaves, particularly women and children. Elizabeth Hart married Charles Thwaites in 1805. (She and her sister both had white husbands who aided them in their benevolent endeavors.) In 1809 the Hart sisters established a Sunday School for slave and free children, and in 1813 Elizabeth Hart and her husband began offering Sunday School classes to slaves and erected a schoolhouse. In 1815 the Hart sisters founded the Female Refuge Society of Antigua.

According to Elizabeth Hart's "History of Methodism": "My beloved sister Anne Gilbert, joined the Methodists at the same time that I did. . . . Blessed be God, we are at this Day of one heart and

31

The Reverend Richard Pattisson   St. Johns, May 5th 1804

My Dear Sir,

        I am induced by two considerations to a compliance with your request, one is, that I would be obedient, and the other, that in so doing in this case, I afford myself a fresh opportunity of making mention of that goodness and mercy which have followed me, the most unworthy, all my days. Knowing the Interest you take in the concerns of Immortal Souls, I would give you a more circumstantial detail of my spiritual course, and for your satisfaction, add some account of others with whom I am acquainted, but time will not at present admit, I hope to write you again on the subject. I am as you know, a native of Antigua. My deceased Grandmother, who was converted to God by the ministry of the Rev.d Francis Gilbert, & who died in the Faith, with my dear Mother (gone to Glory) were united to the Methodists & trained up the younger branches of the Family (myself among them) in the Fear of God & the observance of religious duties. I was also blest with an affectionate Father who ever watched with the tenderest solicitude over the morals of his Children, as did others of our near Relations, who by their kind attention prevented our feeling the want of Mothers care after her Death. Having soon imbibed a great regard to the duty of Prayer, and beliving in its efficacy, I never omitted the performance of it

First two pages of Elizabeth Hart's "History of Methodism," in a letter dated 5 May 1804 (Missionary Society Archives, School of Oriental and African Studies, University of London)

it without feeling some compunction, and upon all occasions of danger or difficulty, I would either retire to prayer, or at the moment, lift up my heart to Heaven for assistance or direction; notwithstanding this, I was from my earliest days, subject to many painful temptations concerning the being of a God and of a future state, and would often be led into such labyrinths of inward reasonings on some parts of Scripture and things that I could not comprehend as have made me wretched.

After my Mother's death, I principally attended the Preaching of the United Brethren in St. Johns; the retirement of their situation, together with the simplicity of their manners and Preaching, greatly pleased me, and their Preachers used to dwell in such a pathetical manner on the sufferings and death of the Saviour, as never failed to affect my heart. I thought they were happy, and in the midst of my Childish follies, often wish'd that I was of their communion.   About this time, one night several severe Earthquakes were felt all over the Island. I was exceedingly terrified, and spent most of the night on my knees, imploring mercy and resolving that if the Earth did not open and swallow me up, but I was spared, that I would be very religious. Towards morning the shocks ceased, but not my tormenting fears; all the day following I was sad and could not take pleasure in any thing. On being told, in the Evening that Mrs. Mary Gilbert (now in England) was to have a public prayer meeting at her house, I made haste to go, hoping there to find ease to my troubled mind, but I became worse, as I thought

soul." Although the circumstances of their lives reveal no important difference between the sisters, Elizabeth's writings suggest a habit of introspection and theological reflection lacking in Anne's. Elizabeth Hart described her thoughtful nature when she wrote that she was often "led into such labyrinths of inward reasonings on some parts of scripture and things I could not comprehend" that she was rendered "wretched." Her racial identity and her faith were both subjects of her introspection. Reservations about interacting with slaves and opinions about debates on religious doctrine appear in her writings but not in her sister's. For instance, Elizabeth Hart revealed that she was initially reluctant to attend prayer meetings with slaves and so stood aloof at first from the Methodist Societies. Yet, once she joined the Methodists, she came to serve as a leader in prayer and religious instruction to "a Class of young women who were Slaves." Feeling herself to be more virtuous and more refined than the enslaved women, she found herself at first unable to speak to her students of her own religious experience—her initial compunctions, her faith, her desire to be sanctified, and her grief over the persistence of temptation. Her freedom and perhaps her mulatto status also made her reticent to open her inner being to slaves; yet she felt that as a black woman she had a special calling to instruct enslaved girls and women. Then she realized that she was teaching a formal, outward religion because of her inability to reveal her inner self to the slaves. To teach such a religion was, she believed, a useless exercise—indeed it was a violation of Methodist piety—and she learned how to open her heart to the slaves. Her account of the way in which her spiritual awakening was linked to her efficacious instruction of slave girls and women is a remarkable text in African American religious history. No matter how much she believed in spiritual communion among black women, however, she never lost her sense of social superiority to the slaves. For example, reflecting on the differences between the life of a free black woman and that of a slave in her "History of Methodism," she noted that while enslaved girls and women were tempted by "Unchastity," she herself was beset by the temptations of "Company, conversation and Books which did not tend to the Glory of God, together with Music's charms." While she had become able to criticize herself for her perhaps un-Christian distance from slave women, she showed no self-criticism in her comments about the difference in social status that she implied when she delineated the different temptations of slave life and free life. Whatever her religious anguish, she seems to have felt secure in the cultivation she believed enslaved women lacked.

Hart's comments on religious doctrine reveal that the theological discussions and disputations pursued at the highest levels in Protestantism had repercussions in a West Indian slave society far from the seminaries, colleges, and cosmopolitan centers of discourse. African American Christianity is often understood as primarily emotional, but Hart's writing (like that of many other writers) demonstrates that doctrine was also important for some black believers. Missionaries and missionary publications probably carried news of cosmopolitan theological disputes to the West Indies. The Hart sisters became active in the church just at the time when doctrinal disputes about predestination versus free will in effecting one's salvation were preoccupying Methodists. The founders of Methodism, John Wesley and Charles Wesley, renounced the Calvinist doctrine of predestination in favor of the Arminian belief in free will. (Two other Methodists who were well known as patrons of literate blacks, George Whitefield and Selina Hastings, Countess of Huntingdon, remained Calvinist. The Huntingdonians, including some black congregations, seceded from the Church of England over the issue of free will.) The difference between Calvinism and Arminianism was important to thinking about slavery, especially for those in the antislavery camp. Believing in an omniscient, omnipotent deity who predetermined all, Calvinists held that God had ordained slavery for some good purpose, even if those trading and holding slaves were sinning in those deeds. Indeed, for Calvinists it was a sign of divine majesty that God overruled human sin by bringing good out of evil, just as the Resurrection followed from the Crucifixion. Believing that God left people free to choose good or evil and to choose salvation or not, Arminians of the antislavery persuasion held that trading and owning slaves was a sin, but as freely chosen human misdeeds, these activities lacked any larger significance implanted by God. For those convinced by the Calvinist argument, the sufferings of black people under slavery were part of a divine plan and so held a meaning that transcended individuals' miseries and travails. For those convinced by the Arminian argument, the transcendent meaning of slavery was nonexistent, and the fact that slavery was the result of human misdeeds meant that individuals themselves could eradicate slavery from the world. Either form of Christianity could inform opponents of slavery, but each form led to different understandings of slavery and different hopes for a postslavery society.

Like most Methodists, the Hart sisters considered themselves Arminians, but they were aware to some degree of the eighteenth-century Calvinist tenets of an omnipotent, overruling deity, a divinely ordained plan for the universe, and the divine use of sin and sinners in that plan. Elizabeth Hart dismissed "Fatalists," who posed as "good Christians"–an obvious allusion to Calvinists. Anne Hart was familiar with some of the key concepts of late-eighteenth-century Calvinism–an "over-ruling" God, a "relish" for holy things, a "directing" and "providential" deity. Because the Harts heard many missionary preachers beginning in the 1780s, including some Irish Protestants who were almost certainly Calvinists, they might have had some lingering sympathy for Calvinism despite their professed Arminianism. Most likely this mix of beliefs existed among many Methodists in the transitional decades of the 1770s, 1780s, and 1790s. While they, as well as other Christians, might have believed that they were free to effect their own salvation and that sinners were acting utterly on their own, not as instruments in a divine plan, the remnants of predestination and a God who uses sin in a divine plan still held tenaciously to many hearts and minds.

Indeed, Elizabeth Hart's writings suggest that she was torn between predestinarian and free-will religion. Her 1794 letter to an acquaintance with Calvinist sensibilities is among the most important documents of early African American Christianity. Although her correspondent's letter did not survive, it is apparent from her response that he had broached the possibility that slavery was part of a divine design and a punishment for the sins of black people. She assented to his predestinarian view of the cause of slavery,

> But you . . . ask: Is it not, at least, permitted by the all-wise Governor of the universe, and will He not do all things well? Might there not be some clue to it quite unknown to us, such as the sins of the Africans, as it was the case of the Israelites before their bondage in Babylon? I readily allow there being in a state of servitude is permitted by the Almighty and I do not question but He may intend bondage for this race of men; but I account the abominations that follow to be purely the will and work of corrupt, fallen man, and displeasing to God. He doeth all things well.

Calvinists, of course, had argued that the evildoers were still sinning even if God was using them as instruments to bring what is truly good out of what is truly evil. Unable or unwilling to argue forcefully against the Calvinist view, Hart wrote,

> I do not give full assent to your proposition at the conclusion of your queries, that the perpetrators of guilt, whether fair, black, or brown, are doing God's work. He has, and does still make use of the wicked (being most fit) as His sword to punish wickedness; but if these are in this case doing God's work they have mixed so much of their own with it, as at length to be bringing the same sort of punishment upon themselves.

Insofar as Hart believed these words, she shared something essential with the Calvinist "Fatalists"–as did many African American Christians of her day.

Hart's comments on slavery also show a tension between an older notion that enslavement was an unfortunate, though justifiable, state and a newer understanding that it was an immoral system designed to strip away from laborers the value of their work and production. She wrote that the immorality of slavery lay in its promotion of vice, not in its forced extraction of labor from the unfree. Of the immorality of slavery she wrote, "That which pains me the most is, that every contrivance is made, by the generality of those who have rule over them, to baffle their efforts for decency and virtue." By contrast she wrote of slave labor, "Truly labour and want are not the evils of slavery (horrid system!) though they, as well as the Oppressor's yoke, cause many still to groan." Neither "servitude" nor "penury" nor "much labour" seemed to her greatly objectionable. Rather she objected to the viciousness of slavery: its violence, its evident enervation of Christianity, its subjection of slave women to lecherous masters and overseers, and its disruption of family life. (Not only were slaves sometimes sold away from their families, but also masters who owned several plantations, sometimes in both the American mainland and the West Indies, moved laborers from one to another often without regard for the family unit.)

The philanthropic work of the Hart sisters and their husbands was intended as a means of instilling virtue in the enslaved. Still, Hart saw flashes of a new form of thought when she noted that slaves received little of the value of their labor. "Free men may enjoy the fruit of their labours," she wrote, "but slaves are allowed a very small portion of their earnings." Although she was horrified by the morals of the oppressed–those "half-clothed and half-fed" by their masters "are consequently thieves"– she still perceived that slavery stripped the unfree of the value they produced. The path she recommended, however, was not the reclamation of that value but the cultivation of piety and virtue. Freedom from slavery came at last for black Antiguans in 1834.

Charles Thwaites recorded many details of Elizabeth Hart's benevolent activities in an 1829 letter. She was devoted to the religious instruction of enslaved children, and she warned all slaves against such seeming evils as dancing. He also reported that she had been called before the bar of the House of Assembly because her benevolent work aroused the fear that she was an abolitionist. She had once before been interrogated and had refused to answer questions that seemed to be leading to a charge of antislavery activities as well as to endangering the slaves among whom she had proselytized. This time, threatened with jail and knowing that it was not illegal to offer charity to slaves, she unflinchingly answered all questions put to her by the House of Assembly, and she walked away free from the interrogation.

Elizabeth Hart's writings, though few, are of enduring significance for those who seek to understand African American history and culture of the late eighteenth century and early nineteenth century. She was a member of a generation of black Christians who thought in a characteristically eighteenth-century manner about slavery and freedom and who thus shared little with nineteenth-century abolitionists. Barely interested in individual liberty and unable to imagine that the social landscape around her could be quickly transformed into a land of freedom, she saw slavery as a corrupter of virtue and considered some degree of unfreedom in society to be unavoidable. Her writings demonstrate that black thought in the era of the first abolitionists was psychodynamically complex since even her moderate antislavery views entailed a rebellion against her slaveholding father. They also illustrate a similar complexity in the black literature of this era, since in her writing and her reading in missionary publications she departed from her father's secular tastes. Moreover, her writings lend credence to the notion that the Christianization of African Americans did not have to await a free-will version of Protestantism (as most interested scholars have argued) but that predestinarian religion attracted at least some of her generation of slaves and free blacks. Probably she was representative of African Americans who found in predestinarian religion, whether derived from Protestantism or from one or more African religions, both an explanation for the suffering of blacks under slavery and a hopeful way of thinking about a divinely ordained future.

Reference:

Moira Ferguson, Introduction to *The Hart Sisters: Early African Caribbean Writers, Evangelicals, and Radicals,* edited by Ferguson (Lincoln & London: University of Nebraska Press, 1993), pp. 1–54.

Papers:

Elizabeth Hart's "History of Methodism" is in a letter dated 5 May 1804, St. Johns, Antigua, in the Missionary Society Archives, School of Oriental and African Studies, University of London. Charles Thwaites's 5 May 1829 letter describing his wife's activities is in the Methodist Missionary Society Archives, School of Oriental and African Studies, University of London, West Indian File.

Jane Fenn Hoskens

(1693 – 1770?)

Michele Lise Tarter
Eastern Illinois University

BOOK: *The Life and Sufferings of that Faithful Servant of Christ, Jane Hoskens, a Public Preacher among the People Called Quakers* (Philadelphia: Printed & sold by William Evitt, 1771).

Jane Fenn Hoskens was an exemplary minister and writer of eighteenth-century America. In many ways her life story bears testimony to the possibilities for women who joined the transatlantic Society of Friends (Quakers) at that time. At age nineteen, feeling a calling to go to Pennsylvania, she left behind all her family and relations in England and immigrated to America. She rose from the state of indenture to being one of the most well-respected and well-traveled Quaker ministers and writers of the century, carrying her prophetic message throughout the colonies, Barbados, and Great Britain.

Although her autobiography, *The Life and Sufferings of that Faithful Servant of Christ, Jane Hoskens, a Public Preacher among the People Called Quakers* (1771), is her only published record, many letters and journals of other Friends, in manuscript and in various publications, attest to Hoskens's influence throughout the religious society and early American society at large. In particular, she joined the network of Quaker women ministers and writers who were diligently traveling long distances to visit women's meetings, preaching, corresponding with these women to sustain their sisterhood, and even initiating a large body of autobiographical writing among women Friends. In her own narrative Hoskens constructs the identity of a marginalized woman who finds her self and her voice as she evolves in relationship with her spiritual family. In turn her autobiography, considered a classic and widely circulated in the Quaker transatlantic community, served as a prototypical model of edification, hope, and power to many Friends on their own journeys as spiritual seekers, speakers, readers, and writers.

Carefully considering her Quaker audience, Hoskens chose to begin her autobiography with the moment she was divinely called to the Friends' religious society. Born in London, England, in 1693, Jane Fenn was raised and strictly educated by Angli-

can parents. At the age of sixteen she became extremely ill and feared she might die, which led her to negotiate with God and offer her devoted service in exchange for the preservation of her life. In recounting this transforming experience in her memoir, Hoskens actually quotes the distinct, divine voice she heard in response to her request: "if I restore thee, *go to Pennsylvania.*" The phrase "go to Pennsylvania" served as a trope for going to the Quaker community of Pennsylvania; yet she was not aware of this meaning in her initial encounter with God. Rather, looking through the lens of a sixteen-year-old girl, Hoskens reported that she quickly agreed to follow this charge, soon recovered, and then altogether ignored her promise.

As a Quaker minister writing her autobiography for future generations, Hoskens then noted what resulted from her attempts "to stifle the witness of God, which had been raised in me." Often when she was alone, she was haunted by her promise and could find virtually no peace of mind. In her memoir she transcribed parts of her dialogue with God, inviting the reader to undergo her gradual process of discernment and awakening: "What shall I do in a strange country, separated from the enjoyments of all my relations and friends?" she asked of God, bringing to light the concern and fear that many eighteenth-century women and men might feel in leaving their friends and families to follow the unconventional Quaker path. The response she received reassured her as well as her readers: "Go, there shalt thou meet with such of my people as will be to thee in the place of near connexions; and if thou wilt be faithful, I will be with thee." In effect this divine message names the Quakers of Pennsylvania as God's people, and it presented Hoskens with an absolute test of faith, calling her to leave behind her earthly family and follow this spiritual one.

When Hoskens told her relatives of this calling to go to Pennsylvania, her father was adamantly opposed to such a journey, knowing full well what it connoted. As she recollects in her autobiography, "I remember the remark my father made on these arguments, was, 'the girl has a mind to turn *Quaker.*'" Her father's position in the autobiography shrewdly reflects the extreme prejudice that he and others felt toward the Society of Friends. Anti-Quaker sentiment was widespread in England and had been so for nearly a century, dating back to the founding of this religious group in 1648. Anglicans and Protestants were vehemently opposed to the Quakers' nonconformist socioreligious practices, including their nonhierarchical form of worship, their unusual speech and body codes incorporating "plain" language and dress, and their inclusion of women in the ministry.

Hoskens insisted that she had no acquaintance with Friends nor any of their religious principles at the time of her religious calling. When her father forbade her to go to Pennsylvania and ordered her never to bring up the idea in conversation again, Hoskens, as a dutiful daughter, initially resolved that her father's "will was as a law to me" and once again conveniently dismissed the divine leading. Her mother, equally dismayed by the thought of her going, carefully detailed the dangers she might face in traveling as a single woman to a strange country.

In her autobiography Hoskens ultimately cast her father in direct opposition to God the Father, illustrating the importance of surrendering completely to the will of the Lord. Tormented by her unfulfilled promise, she reported that she could no longer sleep or feel any contentment. Ultimately, she re-inscribed paternity and authority to God alone, resolving to go to Pennsylvania despite all familial or social consequences and hoping that God would direct her "like a little child" in a new world. Herein began Hoskens's act of self-definition as an obedient daughter to God, homeless but faithful in her spiritual path; she was a single woman leaving behind family, friends, and earthly security to pursue her courageous errand across the seas.

Hoskens departed for America in 1712 with the help of a Welshman, Robert Davis, who was moving to Philadelphia with his wife and two daughters. He offered to pay for her passage, without any signature for this loan, agreeing that she would reimburse him once she was living and working in America. Within three months of settling in Philadelphia, however, Davis reneged on his word and insisted that Hoskens sign an indenture, binding herself as a servant to a complete stranger for four years. Utterly deceived by his breach of word and trust, Hoskens refused, and Davis turned to the law and enforced her confinement.

The experience of transatlantic immigration and forced indenture was a common and extremely humiliating experience for young immigrant women in eighteenth-century America. In addition indentured servants were generally perceived as escaped criminals or penniless and helpless vagabonds, and they were often exploited. Yet Hoskens rewrote such a traumatic experience in positive and hopeful terms: trusting in the will and work of God, she recounted how she underwent extreme humiliation but was ultimately rewarded by it, for she was led to the Society of Friends.

Learning of a position as a schoolmistress for four Quaker families in Plymouth County, Hoskens applied for the job and asked the Friends to pay her debt of £12 currency to Davis. She then willingly indentured herself to the Quakers for three years, moving to their community and teaching the children to read and write. While living in Plymouth, moreover, she learned about the Friends' religious principles and attended their meetings, although at first she admittedly went as a "spy" to see what they did in their worship services.

The Quakers had settled Philadelphia and its environs as early as 1681, when William Penn established their colony to be a "Holy Experiment." In the religious meetings Friends worshiped as spiritual equals, regardless of one's gender, race, age, or social position. Rid of any hierarchical structure and without any paid ministers, the meetings fostered the living ministry, or "that of God," in every human being. Out of their gathered silence, Friends would wait to feel "moved" by God to speak and were often viscerally affected by the pouring of spirit unto flesh. These moments of divine stirring were upheld by Friends as the most sacred union with God. They became God's living instruments, the children in the "new birth."

As a "child" of God in her new world and as an observant "spy" attending the Quaker meetings, Hoskens positioned herself in her autobiography as a marginalized figure seeking a spiritual home. As she relayed the process of acquainting herself with the Friends, she paid careful attention to the changes she underwent as she became increasingly affected by the Quakers' religious practices, ever striving to identify with this group: she adopted the Quaker manner of plain dress, eschewing all forms of superfluity in fashion and thus honoring the simplicity of Christ's path on earth; she walked three to four miles to attend meetings regularly; and she became extremely meditative and introspective. Many Friends noticed the change in her countenance. Indeed, she wrote, "In that time I became a wonder to many" while also assuring her readers that such behavior was accepted tenderly by Friends around her.

Hoskens revealed the uncertainty and fears she had of becoming a Quaker as she recollected the visit of traveling Friends Thomas Wilson and James Dickinson in 1714. These men were part of a widespread movement among Friends to foster relations among meetings and to keep alive the spirit of Quakerism on a transatlantic scale. As traveling ministers, they would visit Quaker meetings and families living anywhere from large cities to remote villages on the frontier. They would preach and inspire worshipers; carry with them news of other meetings they had visited; check on the business of regional monthly, quarterly, and yearly meetings; uphold the traditions of keeping minutes and writing epistles; and distribute Quaker literature, often circulating spiritual autobiographies to the Friends in attendance.

As Hoskens described the gathering around Wilson and Dickinson in her narrative, she focused on Friend Wilson's message regarding female ministry and service, particularly highlighting the biblical passage of the "captive maid" and her complete surrender to God's service. Identifying strongly with this image, Hoskens overheard Wilson telling Friends that she was like the captive maid in whom the Lord was at work, fitting her for religious service, but she noted that she left the room to avoid his further notice. Her inclusion of this experience in her autobiography is fascinating, for she depicted herself as someone fleeing recognition as a minister. Still positioning herself as a marginalized figure set apart from the Quaker community, Hoskens nonetheless revealed that Friends were beginning to recognize the prophet in her. This exchange, she recorded, was one of the many "hints" that helped reassure her during times of spiritual distress and doubts about her public voice and prophetic persona.

When Hoskens felt called by God to speak in a meeting for the first time, she was utterly filled with terror. Describing this moment, she noted that many observed her body trembling, a true sign of her receiving divine motion to speak, and yet she refused to comply, for she had denounced women speaking in public. In resisting the act of preaching Hoskens reflected the dramatic cultural transformation necessary for a woman becoming a Quaker in the eighteenth century. For the next seven months, she wrote sadly, Hoskens suffered a state of desolation and even stopped going to meetings, feeling embarrassed and ashamed that she might distract other attenders by her mere presence. Here, she illustrated the pain of resisting divine motion as well as her self-enforced isolation.

Hoskens then revealed the power of her spiritual epiphany when she finally acquiesced and spoke for the first time in a Quaker meeting. At once, in her state of submission and concomitant speech, she revealed the surrender necessary for speaking as a

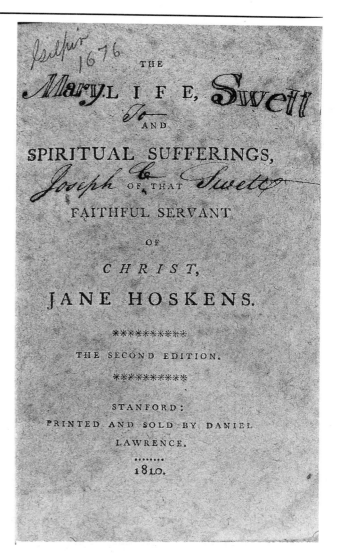

Title page for the 1810 edition of Jane Fenn Hoskens's spiritual autobiography, which describes her rise from indentured service to prominence in the Society of Friends (courtesy of the Historical Society of Pennsylvania)

prophet: "Lord, I will submit, be thou with me, take away the fear of man, thou shalt have my whole heart," she prayed. Within moments, she wrote, she stood and spoke only a few words "like a child." Friends all around her felt the joy and release of her powerful prophecy. She thus inscribed herself as a child of God, breaking forth into language, and her autobiography is the extension of such a prophetic threshold as she captured the spirit of that breakthrough in her narrative and proclaimed her entry into public prophecy. For this brief moment Hoskens felt completely centered in this religious community at Plymouth, although she knew that this was not her permanent home.

After Hoskens's three years of indenture were completed, she elected to stay an additional three months and serve the Friends there, repaying them for their kindness and support. Indeed, as a true Quaker, she recorded that she felt blessed to live her life as a servant to others.

In 1716, when Hoskens was no longer legally bound to anyone, she chose to move to the Welsh Quaker community of Haverford, Pennsylvania. She attended meetings in that area, worked on a month-to-month basis for Friends, and otherwise retired from social engagements, truly devoted to cultivating her spiritual awakening. Again she returned to the position of marginalization as she entered this new Quaker community, waiting patiently for divine leading and invitation.

During this time she witnessed Friend Elizabeth Levis visiting and speaking to the Haverford meeting. Levis's ministry deeply touched Hoskens and inspired her own voice. Many diaries, journals, and letters of women Friends noted that the spoken ministry of Quaker women directly affected and moved other women to speak and witness. Hoskens's autobiography attests to the rising community of women Friends who inspired each other and created a socioreligious space for themselves and their voices in early America. Hoskens's own ministry work and writing was catalyzed by Levis's preaching, and the two became close friends and traveling companions in their collaborative religious work.

Also during her residence in Haverford, Hoskens became acquainted with Grace and David Lloyd, affluent Quakers from Chester who were visiting her meeting. When they entered the worship room one First Day (Sunday), Hoskens was instantly struck with the divine message that she was to go and settle with the Lloyds; yet she doubted such a leading because of their level of distinction, still casting herself as "a poor destitute orphan . . . in a strange land." Her inner voice, however, reassured her that the Lloyds would, in fact, seek to meet her, which they did immediately following the service. To other Friends the Lloyds revealed that they had been moved during the service to take Hoskens under their care and to prepare her for the Lord's service.

Hoskens's description of her initial interaction with the Lloyds poignantly illustrates the Friends' principles concerning social position: in the meeting structure there were no hierarchical or divisive lines, for it was believed that everyone was equally open to receiving divine testimony. When the Lloyds recognized the preacher in Hoskens, they embraced the opportunity to uphold her prophetic voice and help in whatever way they could. Her autobiography is a lasting testament to this Quaker principle in action.

Hoskens moved to Chester, and closer to her spiritual home, when she accepted employment as a maid for Friend Benjamin Head in 1718. Attending a First Day meeting in Chester several months later, Hoskens witnessed a large gathering of Quakers congregating around traveling Friend John Danson from Great Britain. Her account of meeting Danson is perhaps one of the most striking features of her autobiography, for it reveals the depths of uncertainty and insecurity that she felt about her religious identity at that time. With elaborate detail she recounted the many ways in which she tried to evade a conversation with this Friend, until he sought her out and pursued her attentively.

Danson, she wrote, announced that he wanted to speak to her after the meeting, declaring that he had a message to deliver to her from God. She overheard this statement, trembled, and went away until the Lloyds called for her. When the Lloyds insisted that she come to their home to join their guest Danson, she immediately declined but was persuaded to come along. Finally, at the Lloyd home Hoskens carefully noted the great company of Friends in the parlor, but, as she wrote in her autobiography, she had no intention of sitting with them: "not thinking myself worthy, I would not thrust myself among them, intending to go among the servants." She joined the company only when she was invited to do so by Danson and was then seated directly next to him.

In her narrative Hoskens described how he took her hand, looked closely at her, and, after a period of silence, encouraged her in her prophetic work and divine service. She noticeably withheld any further content of their conversation, telling the reader that she did not have "freedom" to relate it. This silence is one of only a few instances in her text where she preserved her privacy as a Quaker woman, minister, and autobiographer. She concluded her description of this scene by remarking that Friends around her and Danson acknowledged and were moved by such a powerful interaction and that she herself was deeply touched by his vision and his voice.

Danson, as a messenger, told the Lloyds to make Hoskens their "adopted child" and to give her the freedom to go wherever she felt divinely led. The Lloyds immediately accepted such a charge, which was in accord with the leading they had experienced at the Haverford meeting. By the end of the evening Grace Lloyd had taken Hoskens aside and offered their home and care to her, and Hoskens gratefully accepted. This evening marked a turning point in Hoskens's journey, for she had found her spiritual family, security, and a Quaker identity and voice through these intimate and supportive relations.

Concluding her seven-month stay with the Head family, Hoskens moved to the Lloyd household and was given the position of "upper servant," or housekeeper, of their large estate, thereby being granted much trust and responsibility in their home. Although she lived there in the station of a servant, Hoskens always ate meals with the Lloyds, and when Quakers came to visit the household, she took part in conversations and enjoyed their company. Indeed, as Hoskens describes this time in her life, she characterizes the Lloyds as if they were her spiritual parents, and she did nothing without their permission and acceptance.

While in residence at the Lloyds, Hoskens was granted the freedom to attend to her spiritual leadings and ministry work. She spoke often in meetings at this time, noting that she felt many eyes on her. She recorded that she was like "a city set on a hill," and it was her responsibility to shine in her conversation. As a prototype of Quaker ministers, Hoskens devoted the majority of her time and care to setting an example for others.

As a result her autobiography begins to document the meetings she visited as a minister. In 1721, along with Friend Elizabeth Levis, Hoskens began journeying to meetings near her home. She remained Levis's companion, or "helpmeet," for the following four years. In the Society of Friends, ministers generally traveled in pairs, adhering to a long-standing Quaker tradition that had its origins in Christ's apostles traveling two by two. Among women, the pair usually consisted of an elderly matron with a younger, single woman; yet Hoskens and Levis were both young and equally diligent in their work. Their experiences as ministers illustrate the unusual possibilities offered to women of this religious society.

Notably among Friends, women were generally not pressured to marry, for Quakers believed that women could serve many other roles besides wife and mother. In fact, in the eighteenth century there was a rising number of women Friends who chose to remain single and devote their lives to service. They ministered, traveled, wrote, took part in the women's meetings, and actively contributed to social issues and concerns. For those women who became traveling ministers, close ties grew from their intimate network of support. These women journeyed across seas, through forests during wartime, and often to extremely remote areas of the colonies and rural areas of Great Britain in order to visit—and sometimes even found—women's meetings, thus ever widening and consolidating their transatlantic sisterhood.

Hoskens began her official ministry in 1722, receiving her first certificate from Friends to travel with Levis to meetings in Maryland, Virginia, and North Carolina. By the eighteenth century Quakers had begun to regulate the number and quality of traveling ministers through the act of issuing certificates. Before a member received approval to minister publicly, she had to undergo a series of business meetings with members of the monthly and quarterly meetings as well as through the Select Committee of Ministers and Elders, all of whom considered if the said Friend demonstrated sound preaching and "conversation" in daily life; if her health and family situation were acceptable for such a journey; if a traveling companion was available; and, finally, if her calling was sound and true.

After returning from their first trip, Hoskens and Levis obtained a certificate and sailed in 1725 to Barbados, where they visited and spoke to large gatherings of people on the island. On their way back home they traveled on horseback through Rhode Island, Nantucket, New England, New York, the Jerseys, Maryland, and Virginia, journeying wherever they felt a divine leading to go. As a result of this trip, which lasted more than a year, their relationship grew strong and intimate. Hoskens paid tribute to Levis in her narrative: "I hope the love which subsisted between us when young, will remain to each other forever; mine is now as strong to her as then." While many Quaker ministers' autobiographies focus on the writers' attendance at meetings and their travel as preachers, Hoskens's focuses more on the importance of female companionship that fostered her spiritual development and ministry.

In 1726 Hoskens met Abigail Bowles, a traveling Friend from Ireland, and joined her on a visit to Delaware, Maryland, Virginia, and then the Jerseys, covering roughly seventeen hundred miles together on horseback. Then she felt moved to journey overseas for the first time, continuing service with her Irish helpmeet. Receiving a certificate from her meeting, she departed with Bowles and other Friends in 1727 to travel extensively throughout England and Ireland. On board the ship *Dorothy* she and the others held meetings for worship during their five-week voyage. When they arrived in England, Bowles continued on her trip home to Ireland, but Hoskens remained in London and held meetings nearly every day.

Never once referring to this pilgrimage as a return to her homeland or mentioning her biological family, who resided there, Hoskens recorded her perseverance in her ministry work in London, trusting in divine motions to direct her path as a traveling minister. After a month spent in the city, she then began to travel throughout the countryside, speaking, worshiping, ministering to Friends about their spiritual conditions, and awakening many of those who witnessed her preaching.

In 1728 Hoskens sailed to Dublin and continued her successful ministry work in Ireland. As she recounted visiting many Quaker families living in the city, she also mentioned her daring task of holding meetings in many areas where there were no Friends at all. Her autobiography acknowledges people of other religious denominations who observed her prophesying and treated her kindly, many proving receptive to hearing about Quaker principles. She shared that she was particularly affected by this religious mission, and she even used a metaphor of sustenance and renewal to describe its success: "The doctrine of Truth descended as the small rain upon the tender grass, whereby many were refreshed, and a living greenness appeared," she wrote, thus fusing the literal greenness of the Irish countryside with the figurative growth and fertile richness of her spiritual travels and connections.

After five months she departed from Dublin and returned to Lancashire, resuming her visits to many meetings throughout the British countryside until she felt clear to return to America. She arrived home in 1730, concluding her first transatlantic voyage, which had lasted nearly two years and eight months. During that time she had met hundreds of Friends and undoubtedly affected their lives by way of her visitations, prophecy, spiritual counseling, and even by the Quaker literature she left with them for future reading and inspiration. Indeed, traveling Friends distributed the writings of men and women in their religious society, believing in the power of written testimony as strongly as they did in the living Word.

When Hoskens returned to the Lloyds' home in Chester, she no longer lived there as a hired servant but rather as a friend. Shortly after her return in 1731, David Lloyd died, leaving £25 to Hoskens in his will. She mourned his death, noting that she had lost a father and a friend, and she stayed with Grace Lloyd for many more years at the widow's request. Hoskens remained at home with Grace for much of the year following David's decease and then resumed traveling in 1732 (incorrectly printed as 1742 in her memoir), receiving a certificate for her second trip to Barbados and New England with companion Rebecca Minshall. Afterward Hoskens returned to Pennsylvania and continued visiting meetings in Philadelphia and its environs. Then she decided to marry Friend Joseph Hoskens in 1738. She mentioned her marriage in only one brief sentence of her memoir, focusing much more intently on the widow Lloyd, for whom she continued to care until her maternal friend died. Indeed, it seems apparent that Hoskens placed much more importance on her fe-

male friendships, at least in terms of her spiritual identity and autobiographical record.

By 1740 Hoskens had begun to travel extensively again, visiting Long Island meetings that year, Philadelphia meetings in 1741, and the yearly meeting of Maryland in 1742. Two years later, with companion Margaret Churchman, Hoskens received a certificate and traveled south for a second time, visiting Friends in Maryland, Virginia, and Carolina. Deeply moved by this trip, she noted that the people received their ministry with great openness and even followed them from meeting to meeting, granting them much respect and kindness. Unlike many Quaker women ministers, whose autobiographies detail the abuses they received for public preaching and nonconformist appearance and behavior, Hoskens never once presented any conflict she might have encountered in her ministry. Hers is a narrative of public approval and success, once she became a public Friend and no longer a marginalized persona. In 1748 Hoskens, then fifty-five years old, was approached by twenty-six-year-old Elizabeth Hudson, who was feeling called to travel to England and Ireland with her. The monthly meeting of Philadelphia conferred with Hudson's parents and concluded that the companionship was suitable, trusting in the wisdom and guidance of Hoskens as a spiritual mother of their religious society. The pair set sail on their transatlantic journey that same year.

The intimacy shared by these spiritual companions is evident in the letters they exchanged during their pilgrimage. While in England, Hoskens became ill and was not able to travel on horseback a great deal, so Hudson often had to leave her with Quakers in London and travel to various counties without her maternal companion. Sending Hudson affectionate and supportive letters, Hoskens often began with the address of "Dear Child," and the intimate tone and language of these epistles reveal the women's attachment as "helpmeets" in their ministry as well as their difficulty in being separated. As she wrote to Hudson on First Day, August 1749, "The want of thy company makes everything insipid."

Many Friends' meetings in England, Scotland, and Ireland reported through meeting minutes and epistles that these women favored them with their exemplary conversation and refreshing testimony. Yet in her narrative Hoskens referred sparingly to this trip, commenting that it was one of the most painful experiences in her life and never even mentioning companion Elizabeth Hudson by name, the only time that she omitted such an important detail in her narrative.

Only recently have Hudson's narrative and letters been retrieved from Quaker archives and published in a collection of Quaker women ministers' diaries, *Wilt Thou Go On My Errand?: Three Eighteenth Century Journals of Quaker Women Ministers* (1994). In her account Hudson wrote tenderly of her companion, but she did allude to a tense parting. She also added that Hoskens had to end their trip suddenly, much to Hudson's dismay, when she received a letter from her husband stating that he was not well and requesting that she return home as soon as possible. The women arrived back in America in 1751, having been on their "errand" for more than three years and three months.

In 1756 Hoskens received a certificate and traveled with Philadelphia minister Susannah Brown to visit Quakers in New England, first delivering ministry in many meetings throughout New York and Rhode Island. Many Friends from New York, in fact, accompanied them to Rhode Island and then attended its yearly meeting, where Hoskens was in the company of such well-respected ministers as John Woolman. They then sailed on a sloop to Nantucket to attend its yearly meeting. While disembarking Hoskens reported vaguely that she "received a hurt" but was still able to attend the daily gatherings and remained on the island for two weeks. Yet she and her companion were detained for eight weeks in Boston because of Hoskens's "lameness," at which time many Friends and non-Friends alike helped the women. In her autobiography Hoskens seems to have been determined to underplay any physical struggles or hardships of her journey and to focus on the kindnesses and the divine favor she received during her travels.

When she and Brown were finally able to go to meetings in the area, Hoskens documented the large numbers of people in attendance, responding enthusiastically to the women's public appearances and ministry. Many of these men and women followed the ministers through New England, joining large crowds at each of the worship gatherings. Her autobiography celebrates Hoskens's reception as a minister in eighteenth-century America despite the prevalent anti-Quaker sentiment in the colonies. As a well-respected public preacher in the company of her female companion, recording these experiences for future generations, she inscribes the influence she had on thousands of women and men in her daily prophetic work.

While visiting Long Island, New York, during this trip, Hoskens experienced a sudden memory loss, even to the point that she could not remember her name. She was taken to Flushing for respite and gradually recovered there. Friends then accompanied her and Brown on every step of their journey back to Pennsylvania, as they held meetings in cities

and towns along the way. At the age of sixty-three Hoskens had made her fourth and last visit to New England, and she concluded her account of this trip by praising her companion.

Hoskens expounded on the importance of companions near the end of her narrative, honoring them when they are "firmly united" in their ministry and thus bearing a living witness to the meaning of Christian fellowship. This bond, she wrote, is critical to the work of ministers because it testifies to the comfort and strength they provide for each other and grants authority to their ultimate message. While Hoskens wrote of these attributes, immediately following her praise of companion Brown, she remarked to her readers how disappointing it was when this unity did not occur and prayed that God would help those who have strayed from "the right path." Some critics believe that this comment is a reference to her relationship with Elizabeth Hudson, but Hoskens never spoke disrespectfully of another Friend by name.

In 1760 Grace Lloyd died, leaving Hoskens to reflect on her significant relationship with the Lloyds and its effect on her life as a minister, speaker, writer, and Friend. Little is known about Hoskens's life after this year, other than that she continued to attend yearly meetings in Philadelphia despite her growing infirmity and that she died sometime around 1770.

Hoskens's narrative was published posthumously by the Society of Friends in 1771 and republished in 1837 in the first volume of the *Friends' Library,* a nineteenth-century compendium of classic journals written by Quakers over the centuries. The tradition of writing and publishing spiritual autobiographies has long been considered an integral part of ministry work among Friends, who have historically perceived the prophetic and recorded texts of these men and women to be divine testament for all to read, learn, and integrate into their faith. As Hoskens noted in the first line of her autobiography, she felt a "concern" to leave her story for future readers. These autobiographies were read religiously by Quakers, appreciated for their edification as well as their inspiration, and often shared with children as solid, timeless examples of spiritual development and expression. For twentieth-century readers this body of autobiographical literature also bears testimony to eighteenth-century American life and culture, as Hoskens's narrative, for example, recounts the language and customs of Pennsylvania Friends and her experiences in traveling as a woman preacher throughout the colonies and overseas.

Hoskens's narrative also portrays a striking alternative model of eighteenth-century womanhood: she courageously left behind her family to travel overseas, thus freeing herself to obey a divine calling; she surrendered to the experience of prophesying despite her disapproval of women speaking publicly; she traveled with several female companions over a period of thirty-five years, preaching to thousands of Friends and non-Friends alike in the colonies and overseas; and she recorded her life story for future readers, testifying to the public reception of women's ministry and work.

Hoskens's story also celebrates nontraditional roles available to women through membership in the Society of Friends. Never a mother, she recorded her life's devotion to the Quakers, God's Children of Light; as a wife, she mentioned her marriage at the age of forty-five in only one sentence of her otherwise quite detailed life story. Indeed, Hoskens served as a role model to many women during her work as a traveling Friend, and her autobiography and letters are a lasting testament to her influence.

Historically the number of published journals by men Friends far exceeds that of journals written by women in this religious society. In large part this discrepancy can be traced to a censoring committee established in 1672, the Second Day Morning Meeting, which determined every text to be endorsed and published by the Society of Friends. Evidence exists that reveals the silencing of Quaker women's narratives by this committee, as men Friends' life stories were favored for publication and Quaker representation. Scholarship, in turn, has generally conflated male and universal experience, ignoring the critical consideration of gender in analyzing early Quaker ministers' experiences and writings. Many women's diaries and letters are still lodged in archives throughout Pennsylvania and in England, and these buried texts challenge many of the assumptions made about Quaker prophesying and women's expression at that time. These manuscripts, for example, reveal the intimate network of women ministers and their influence on transatlantic women's meetings. Ministers such as Hoskens visited many meetings and told the women in attendance to keep a vigilant record of their spiritual experiences, thus initiating a large body of early American women's autobiographical writing. Traveling Friends sustained this community by their arduous journeys and visiting patterns, their prophecy, and ultimately through their autobiographical record. Moved to speak publicly, to travel, and to write, Jane Fenn Hoskens committed her life to religious service and touched many lives with her voice, her agency, and her text.

Hoskens's influence is evidenced in many memoirs of Friends who met, worshiped, or even traveled with her. The best-known of these journals include those of Friends Thomas Chalkley, Samuel Bownas,

Daniel Stanton, and John Woolman. These published accounts, as well as private diaries and manuscript letters by women Friends, are located in the Quaker Collection at the Haverford College Library and in the Friends Historical Library at Swarthmore College.

References:
Margaret Hope Bacon, *Mothers of Feminism: The Story of Quaker Women in America* (San Francisco: Harper & Row, 1986);

Bacon, ed., *Wilt Thou Go On My Errand? Three Eighteenth Century Journals of Quaker Women Ministers* (Wallingford, Pa.: Pendle Hill, 1994);

Howard Brinton, *Quaker Journals: Varieties of Religious Experience Among Friends* (Wallingford, Pa.: Pendle Hill, 1972);

Mary Maples Dunn, "Women of Light," in *Women of America: A History,* edited by Carol Ruth Berkin and Mary Beth Norton (Boston: Houghton Mifflin, 1979), pp. 115–136;

Carol Edkins, "Quest for Community: Spiritual Autobiographies of Eighteenth-Century Quaker and Puritan Women in America," in *Women's Autobiography: Essays in Criticism,* edited by Estelle Jelinek (Bloomington: Indiana University Press, 1980), pp. 39–52;

Willard C. Heiss, ed., *Quaker Biographical Sketches of Ministers and Elders, and Other Concerned Members of the Yearly Meeting of Philadelphia, 1682–1800* (Indianapolis: Privately printed, 1972);

Cristine Levenduski, *Peculiar Power: A Quaker Woman Preacher in Eighteenth-Century America* (Washington, D.C.: Smithsonian Institution Press, 1996);

Phyllis Mack, *Visionary Women: Gender and Prophecy in Seventeenth-Century England* (Berkeley: University of California Press, 1992);

Daniel B. Shea, *Spiritual Autobiography in Early America* (Princeton: Princeton University Press, 1968);

Caroll Smith-Rosenberg, "The Female World of Love and Ritual," *Signs,* 1 (1975): 1–29;

Nancy Tomes, "The Quaker Connection: Visiting Patterns among Women in the Philadelphia Society of Friends, 1750–1800," in *Friends and Neighbors,* edited by Michael Zuckerman (Philadelphia: Temple University Press, 1982), pp. 174–195;

Christine Trevett, *Women and Quakerism in the Seventeenth Century* (York, U.K.: Ebor Press, 1991);

Luella Wright, *The Literary Life of Early Friends: 1650–1725* (New York: Columbia University Press, 1932).

Papers:
Haverford College has some Hoskens papers.

Anne Hulton
(? – 1779?)

Karen M. Poremski
Emory University

BOOK: *Letters of a Loyalist Lady: Being the Letters of Anne Hulton, Sister of Henry Hulton, Commissioner of Customs at Boston, 1767–1776,* edited by H.M. (Humphrey Milford?) and C.M.T. (Cambridge, Mass.: Harvard University Press, 1927).

PERIODICAL PUBLICATION: "An Eighteenth-century Lady and her Impressions," edited by E. Rhys Jones, *Gentleman's Magazine,* 297 (August 1904): 195–202.

Most of what is known about Anne Hulton comes from the letters she wrote to her friend Mrs. Adam Lightbody between 1763 and 1776. Of Hulton's published letters the most frequently studied have been those written during 1767–1776, collected in *Letters of a Loyalist Lady* (1927). Scholars first noticed Hulton through her brother, Henry Hulton, who was a commissioner of customs (a tax officer) in Boston during the nine years preceding the Revolutionary War. Hulton's letters were examined more recently, during the bicentennial and the second wave of the American feminist movement, in studies of women's experiences of the Revolutionary War. The letters offer a firsthand, personal view of political relations in the prewar period as well as Loyalist views of the Revolution. They also chronicle the everyday life of an upper-class eighteenth-century woman in colonial America, and they portray a friendship between two women who worry about one another's health, share news of friends and relations, and maintain their correspondence even in wartime.

Hulton's work offers the modern reader insight into various facets of life in the colonies: social relations, gossip, and fashions; agricultural practices, observations on native plants and animals, and domestic economy; diseases and cures; and the family ties and responsibilities of single women in the eighteenth century. Hulton did not characterize herself as a writer. To Lightbody, she commented, "Nothing but necessary business, or to keep up a

communication with some valuable friends, who will indulge me in the pleasure of hearing from them, woud ever prompt me to use my pen." Yet her letters are full of exciting stories, moving personal reflections, witty remarks on society and individuals, and informative descriptions of places and customs foreign to most English women of her time.

Anne Hulton's birth date is unknown. E. Alfred Jones has noted that her father was John Hulton of Chester and that she never married. She did, however, become an important member of her brother's growing family, which consisted of Henry, his wife, Elizabeth, and the four sons whose births were noted in Hulton's letters.

Shortly before December 1763 Henry Hulton returned to London after having served George III in Germany by helping to settle the accounts of the Seven Years' War—a job that placed him in danger of assassination. On his return to London, Anne Hulton lived in Westminster with him, and he worked at a much safer job in the London Customs House, where he took part in the regulation of trade between Great Britain and its colonies (America) and plantations (the West Indies).

In winter 1763–1764 Hulton accompanied her brother to Bath, where many of the people she met were "West Indian" agents of the British government who knew her brother. She witnessed and took part in the various recreations and dissipations the resort town offered—going to balls, gambling, meeting new people, buying new fashions—but she assured Lightbody of her constancy of character: "You might imagine by all this that I am commenced for the fine Lady, but I think I need not tell you it is a character I am not suited for, neither by nature or inclination."

Hulton returned to London in late January 1764 amid the chaotic festivities associated with the marriage of Princess Augusta (a sister of George III) and Charles William Ferdinand, Duke of Brunswick. Hulton's descriptions of London as a seemingly foreign place express the extent of the confusion there. Mobs attacked upper-class people trying

Castle William, the fort in Boston Harbor where Anne Hulton and other Loyalists spent several months in 1768, fearing violence from the Sons of Liberty (engraving from J. F. W. Des Barres, The Atlantic Neptune, *1780)*

to make their way to the royal court, to the opera, and to plays. Several people suffered broken limbs or had jewelry stolen; one man had even lost a false leg. Although she does not seem to have directly experienced this violence, the details Hulton provided indicate a possible connection between her social circles and the royal court.

A three-year gap in Hulton's letters deprives the reader of an account of Henry Hulton's wedding to Elizabeth, which took place in 1766.

In September 1767 Hulton announced two exciting events: Henry's appointment to a post in the colonies and the birth of his first child. Henry and his wife wished Anne to accompany them to their new home, and he had promised to take good care of her there. She also laid out her intentions to do something productive in the colonies. Repudiating once again the part of the "fine Lady," she planned to establish herself as either a merchant or planter, writing: "some usefull employment as Traffick or cultivat^g a small Plantation in the Country will be most agreeable to my genius & inclinat^n & best for health. . . ." In a comment hinting that she might have had previous experience in trade, she assured her friend that she would venture alone on her business in the New World, as she was wary of partnerships—she had "seen enough of that."

Although she was proud of her brother's important position, Hulton expressed some concern about his new appointment. She anticipated trouble for him in the colonies, noting the "Turbulent Folks" there. Henry Hulton left England ahead of

his family, arriving in Boston in November 1767. Anne Hulton left for the colonies early in 1768, traveling with Elizabeth and baby Thomas.

On her arrival in Massachusetts five weeks later, Hulton got a clearer view of the political vicissitudes of life there, which presumably deflated her ideas of becoming a tradeswoman. The first letters she wrote from the colonies were posted from Castle William, a fort in Boston Harbor to which the family had retreated (along with other families of government agents) because of the threat of violence to them. Hulton presented a mixed view of her circumstances, intermingling both lighthearted and darkly foreboding first impressions of her new home. While she presented her assignment as "Mistress of the Ceremony of the Tea table" with good-natured wit, socialized often with other families at the castle, and referred to their life there as "romantic," she also reported the chaos of the rebellion. Mobs in the colonies were different than those in England. It took more to disperse them than a few torches, and no one would stand up to the rebels. On her arrival Hulton had met a Mrs. Burch, who reported that the Sons of Liberty had surrounded her house, howled hideously like "the Indians," and threatened violence. In her letters Hulton sometimes referred to the Sons of Liberty by the name she devised for them after she had heard of their doings: the "Sons of Violence." Hulton was shocked not only that the colonists categorically denied the right of Parliament to tax them but also that they were being incited to violence even from the pulpits. In a short and dramatic postscript to one of her letters, Hulton reported that Gov. Francis Bernard told the company "two more such years as the past & the Brit[ish] Empire is at an End."

After a peaceful six months the family moved into lodgings in Boston in 1769 while Henry searched for a house. Although less turbulent, the atmosphere was still delicate: The family's safety depended on the presence of the army and navy, and they made a practice of not talking politics with their friends and neighbors. The Hultons socialized a good deal during this period, attending concerts and a dancing assembly of about sixty couples.

By May 1770 the Hulton family had finally made their home in Brookline, in a house that Henry and Elizabeth found agreeable. (The Boston Massacre of March 1770 is unmentioned in the letters.) The family had many visitors—up to twenty people in the house at once—and Henry and Elizabeth took a trip to Rhode Island while Anne looked after her two nephews. Their peace was short-lived. In the middle of the night on 19 June, a mob of men disguised as "Negroes" attacked the Hulton house, smashing the first-floor windows with boards and rocks and threatening to set the house on fire. Hulton said she awoke to the noise downstairs and shrieking upstairs with a feeling "I can't describe, & shall never forget." Once again the family lodged in Castle William, where Hulton called them "prisoners." She complained bitterly to her friend that they had little hope of justice, as the few witnesses were being threatened and probably would refuse to testify. Hulton asked Lightbody not to repeat the events she reported, possibly because she preferred people in England to hear about the incident through her brother's official report. After living at the castle for five months, the family moved back to their home in Brookline with augmented security—soldiers encamped nearby, a dog, and a bell at the top of the house. Hulton also mentioned the solicitude of their neighbors: "every one seems desirous to make our Situation agreeable to us, & to banish the prejudices we may have receivd against it."

Although Hulton apparently dropped the idea of becoming a merchant in the economically and politically volatile atmosphere of Massachusetts, she participated in running her brother's small farm, which he cultivated to improve his health rather than for a profit. She not only studied the crops and gardening practices of the farms nearby but also planted vegetables new to the area, learned about pest control, and used the innovation of the greenhouse to extend the growing period of Massachusetts, which has long winters. Henry hired a farmer,

who probably did most of the physical labor, while Anne acted as manager of the small farm, earning the whimsical title "Director General of the Vegatible Tribe."

In addition to providing detailed information about her assignment, Hulton described other concerns of domestic economy, including the varieties and characteristics of game and wild fowl colonists regularly ate and the prices of meats such as beef, mutton, pork, and fish. She observed that the cost of living in the colonies was not as low as she had expected and also provided observations on Massachusetts weather. It tended to vary between extremes of heat and cold, she said, and the variations themselves were extreme, with freezing cold following on the heels of melting heat.

Between March 1771 and November 1773 the political climate became calm enough for Hulton to write mostly about other things, though in several letters she equated politics with the weather in its tendency to shift rapidly between extremes. In March 1771 family members and their domestic needs—as well as her own—occupied her concern. She worried about a young male relative (possibly a cousin) named I. Hincks, whose overabundance of wit, lack of prudence, and tendency to make fun of others had made him enemies on the Board of Commissioners. Hulton asked Lightbody not to repeat her worries to Hincks's "poor mother" for fear it would add to her "afflictions."

During this time Hulton made a request that indicates the strength of her friendship with Lightbody. She asked Lightbody to acquire eight pairs of shoes for her and a set of Staffordshire ware for the family, to ship them to Boston from London and Liverpool, and to collect reimbursement from Hulton's cousin, Suky Hincks. The detailed nature of the request itself as well as the payment arrangements hint at the trust the two women felt in one another. (It was a well-founded trust; the goods arrived in May 1773.) Hulton later asked Lightbody's assistance in the complicated details of the settlement of a lawsuit. Hulton's description of the matter is somewhat opaque, but it once again exhibits her reliance on Lightbody as a personal friend and a trusted representative in business matters.

In a longer letter (occasioned by her use of large sheets of paper) Hulton reported on church politics and social politics. She noted the large number of meetinghouses in their neighborhood and that one new meetinghouse had hosted evangelist George Whitefield, whom she heard give "a kind of consecration Sermon." On the social scene she reported a recent scandal among the neighbors.

Conclusion of a 17 January 1776 letter to Mrs. Adam Lightbody, in which Hulton, who had recently returned to England, expressed her concerns about Loyalist friends who were still in Boston (from Letters of a Loyalist Lady, 1927)

Elizabeth had made specific efforts to avoid meeting with a particular woman in her visits, as the woman and her husband carried on extramarital affairs; he "entertaind his Ladies in one Part of a great House, & She her Gentlemen at the other."

During the period of relative calm between 1771 and 1773, Henry and Elizabeth took two long trips (to North Carolina and Canada), and Anne took one relatively short trip of 260 miles (to an unspecified destination). Hulton remarked that the distances traveled in the colonies were typically greater than in England and that they offered a "variety of Noble Prospects," but that the cost was "much fatigue bad roads & hard fare." Henry and Elizabeth's 1772 trip to Canada became a topic of conversation among their neighbors. The journey was thought to be virtually impossible at the time, given the unreliability of colonial roads. Anne stayed home to take care of her nephews during Henry and Elizabeth's journeys; perhaps they felt free to travel because Anne—not just a servant—was available to take care of the boys.

Hulton expressed concern about servants in several of her letters. In an August 1772 letter she claimed that one of the two major problems presented by living in the colonies was finding good servants. In a remark that highlights the differences of class relations in England and Massachusetts, Hulton said the difficulty with servants was that no one in the colonies wanted to call another person "Master."

Hulton also expressed concern about children's education in the colonies, claiming that it was the second major problem faced by people living there. She argued that youths were too often indulged and therefore learned only vice. She told Lightbody that her nephews would probably eventually go to England for schooling. In the meantime she gave Tom his lessons.

In her letter of 25 November 1773 Hulton reported increased hostilities over tea ships scheduled to land in Boston Harbor. She said the level of violence was "beyond anything of the kind since we came here." Just two months later Hulton reported that the situation in Boston was "too shocking for me to describe." Although the Hulton family took refuge in Castle William for only a short time, the tea consignees were trapped there by an agreement on the part of surrounding towns not to protect them. Hulton described the cruel treatment of a particular man, a Loyalist who was tarred, feathered, and beaten while being carried around the city in a cart for five hours. She told Lightbody not only of the details of the horrible event but also of the man's bravery: "when under Torture they demanded of him to curse his Masters The K[ing,] Gov[ernor,] &c which they coud not make him do, but he still cried, Curse all Traitors. . . . The Doctors say that it is impossible this poor creature can live. . . ."

In July 1774 Hulton's letters carried more bad news from the colonies. The port of Boston was closed. The family had moved into the city from Brookline, but it was a gloomy setting in which they lived. Most families had left; the port was blocked; and warships sat in the harbor. The families who remained quarreled with each other. Even getting a return letter from Lightbody would be difficult, as it would have to be routed through New York or Philadelphia. Hulton reported that the rhetoric of rebellion was being used by ministers and pamphlet writers to incite the passions of the ignorant country people. She even quoted arguments put forth by a "Dr. Frankland" (presumably Benjamin Franklin) that inflamed the spirit of the rebellion. Yet she also found fault with the Tories because their feelings of loyalty issued from their own economic interests rather than their principles. Despite all this turmoil, in 1774 Hulton still expressed some hope that she would yet see peace in the colony.

An end to this hope came a few months later. Hulton sent Lightbody an account of the Battles of Lexington and Concord in April 1775, telling her to feel free to publicize certain passages that she had marked. Hulton provided a graphic account of the characteristic fighting techniques of the rebels–shooting from behind things and then running away–as well as their cruelties–scalping and cutting the ears and noses off wounded British soldiers. She heaped praise on Sir Hugh Percy, who brought reinforcements to the British troops marching between Lexington and Concord. Her description of him engaged in a flash of rhetoric that, rather than focusing on his specific deeds, emphasized his strength of character, noting that he possessed "all those qualities that form the great Soldier–Vigilent Active, temperate, humane, great Command of temper, fortitude in enduring hardships & fatigue, & Intrepidity in dangers."

After the battle Boston was surrounded by twenty thousand rebel soldiers occupying the heights above the city. Hulton indicated that the people in the town, including her family, were protected by British troops. The fact that she kept up her correspondence at this time attests to her friendship with Lightbody but also hints at a recognition of her own value as a witness and recorder of historic events.

Hulton left the colonies on a ship with about fifty passengers in late 1775. Her next letter, written from Chester in January 1776, expressed her worries about those whom she had left behind. Henry, his family, and many of her friends were still in Boston and still in great danger. She decided not to go on a pleasure trip to London, as she could not enjoy herself while others were in such peril. Other bad news from the colonies contributed to her depression: an outbreak of smallpox necessitated inoculation for the boys, and the Loyalists trapped in Boston were low on supplies. Hulton appended a second, slightly more cheerful letter to this one for fear of being too gloomy. In the second letter she reported that the boys were better and that some provisions had been received by the Loyalists. Fuel, however, was at a crisis point, and the cruelties of war continued.

Although she was no longer in Boston, Hulton still served as an important news link between the colonies and her friends in England. She wrote of the report she had received about a man being buried alive merely for voicing his support of the British troops. An instance of particular cruelty toward a Loyalist woman also shocked her. During the woman's lying-in, rebel guards had stripped her and her children and made them into a kind of sideshow for other rebel soldiers.

Hulton was much relieved in April 1776 with the news of her brother and family arriving safe and healthy in Halifax, and she reported their being back in England several months later. She expressed poignantly her anxiety while waiting to hear about them: "How long & painful the suspence I have been in, agitated between hope, & fear. It has indeed been a time of severe trial to me."

Hulton seems to have moved into new lodgings on her own shortly thereafter. Although her next letter was dated only "November 10" (without specifying a year), it seems to have been written shortly after her ordeal. She expressed wonder at the contrast between what she had been through and the safety and peace she enjoyed. She noted that she no longer worried about cannons or awoke with anxious thoughts; she could walk outside, and, instead of seeing deserted streets, she saw plentiful markets and happy faces.

Although the precise date of Anne Hulton's death is unknown, it is known that Henry announced her death to Lightbody in a letter dated 13 January 1779.

Hulton's writing offers readers an example of the art of letter writing, a portrait of an enduring friendship between two women, and an unusual perspective on an important moment in American history. Finally, and perhaps most important, her letters illuminate the ways in which women negotiated the personal effects of political events.

References:
Cheryl Cline, *Women's Diaries, Journals, and Letters: An Annotated Bibliography* (New York: Garland, 1989);
Norma Olin Ireland, *Index to Women of the World from Ancient to Modern Times: A Supplement* (Metuchen, N.J.: Scarecrow, 1988);
E. Alfred Jones, *The Loyalists of Massachusetts: Their Memorials, Petitions and Claims* (London: St. Catherine Press, 1930);
H. M., Introduction to *Letters of a Loyalist Lady* (Cambridge, Mass.: Harvard University Press, 1927);
Selma R. Williams, *Demeter's Daughters: The Women who Founded America, 1587–1787* (New York: Atheneum, 1976).

Sophia Hume

(1702 – 26 January 1774)

Lee S. Burchfield
Louisville Free Public Library

BOOKS: *An Exhortation to the Inhabitants of the Province of South-Carolina, to Bring their Deeds to the Light of Christ, in their Own Consciences* (Philadelphia: Printed by B. Franklin & D. Hall, 1748; Bristol, England: Printed by Samuel Farley, 1750);

An Epistle to the Inhabitants of South Carolina, Containing Sundry Observations Proper to be Considered by Every Professor of Christianity in General (London: Luke Hinde, 1754);

Extracts from Divers Ancient Testimonies of Friends and Others (London: Luke Hinde, 1760?; Wilmington, Del.: Printed by James Adams, 1766);

A Caution to Such as Observe Days and Times, to which is Added, an Address to Magistrates, Parents, Masters of Families, Etc. (London, 1760; Newport, R.I.: Printed & sold by Solomon Southwick, 1771);

A Short Appeal to Men and Women of Reason: Distinguished by Titles of Worldly Honour, or by Riches Exclusive of Titles: Who May be Walking According to the Course of this Evil World, Living in the Pleasures thereof, and Frequenting Theatres, Balls, &c. (Bristol, England: Printed by E. Farley, 1765);

Remarks on the Practice of Inoculation for the Smallpox, second edition (London: 1767).

Sophia Wigington Hume was a preacher and writer associated with the Religious Society of Friends, or Quakers. Her writings address common Quaker concerns and indicate an exemplary facility with leading scholarship in Quaker and wider Protestant intellectual traditions. Particularly noteworthy is her extensive expression of various defenses of women's involvement in public religious leadership. This activism was tempered by her private reservations about her own fitness for such a role and about the general appropriateness of it. In her most extensive works, *An Exhortation to the Inhabitants of the Province of South-Carolina, to Bring their Deeds to the Light of Christ, in their Own Consciences* (1748), and *An Epistle to the Inhabitants of South Carolina, Containing Sundry Observations Proper to be Considered by Every Professor of Christianity in General* (1754), she aimed to present a defense of Quaker principles, to call all Christians to a renewed commitment to their historic ethos, and to suggest to a wide audience the need for greater awareness of and adoption of evangelical zeal.

Born in Charleston, South Carolina, in 1702, Sophia Hume was the daughter of Henry Wigington, a leading figure in the colony as politician and property owner. Her mother, Susanna Bayly Wigington, was a Quaker and the daughter of the well-known Quaker controversialist Mary Fisher. Despite her extended family's prominence among the Friends in Charleston, Hume was nurtured and educated in the Anglican tradition of her father, which she adopted as her own with little careful reflection. By all accounts Hume's gracious early life typified the gentility of the Southern aristocracy. The habits and tastes she developed during this time served later as a source of guilt and a target of her tireless jeremiads.

By 1719 Susanna Wigington had returned to the Friends tradition and made efforts to influence her family likewise, but Sophia remained an Anglican. Brief and unspecific autobiographical references indicate that she was fond of the arts, fiction reading, dances, concerts, and fine clothes, all of which were criticized by Quakers. At least in part she favored Anglicanism for the liberty it granted in these respects. In 1721 she married Robert Hume (died 1737), an attorney and politician. She had two children, Susanna Wigington Hume (born 1722) and Alexander Wigington Hume (born 1729), and presumably lived a quiet and private life. (Little is known of her affairs during this period.) In her writings Hume made reference to two illnesses that affected her intellectual outlook. Following shortly after the death of her husband in 1737, these brought her to a point of spiritual crisis. By 1740 she had become convinced of a connection between her resplendent lifestyle and her illnesses. She believed that she was being punished for her wickedness and that her recovery could be effected only through repentance. She destroyed many of her possessions and vowed to live simply and humbly as a Quaker.

By that time Susanna Hume lived in England, and after Sophia's recovery from illness she moved to London to be nearer her daughter. In 1741 Sophia joined the Society of Friends and became active in the local meeting. A sensation of divine calling compelled her to deliver a prophetic message of reproof in South Carolina and, despite her children's disapproval, she traveled there during the latter part of 1747. On her arrival in Charleston, Hume was instrumental in reviving the regular meeting of Friends. Through her public speeches at the meetings, opposed by some, she delivered a fiery message calling for the colonial Quakers to return to the austerity and strict ethos that previously had been their norm. Believing her message to be of crucial import, she attempted to disseminate it more widely by writing *An Exhortation to the Inhabitants of the Province of South-Carolina*. The work consists of an extended and sometimes rambling presentation of her conservative opinions regarding proper Christian life and thought.

An Exhortation to the Inhabitants of the Province of South-Carolina is Hume's first printed plea for Quakers to take seriously their spiritual destiny and to contemplate the impact of their everyday actions on the state of their souls. She wanted to warn them that if they continued in their present course they were indeed endangering themselves. Her fear for their welfare is evident in the anguished tone and exhausting patience with which she carefully and tediously presented her arguments. Believing the case to be urgent, she even traveled to Philadelphia to locate a publisher. While there she continued to speak publicly to Quaker meetings.

Hume's first work touches on the themes that also appear in her later works. Her message is built on the foundation of the Quaker belief in an Inner Light that guides seekers toward truth and aids them in knowing what it means to be in perfect obedience to God. Hume's purpose in writing was to show her readers what it meant to be called a Christian and how their own behavior departed from the ideal. Before addressing these issues directly she included a defense of her prophetic role, using extensive citations from biblical materials, other writers, and her own experience to justify her radical behavior. At the center of this rationale is her belief that she acted out of a true divine calling.

Hume stated her desire to honor God and to promote the welfare of those she loved, deflecting any praise that she might receive. She also denied that she sought any personal gain from her efforts and, having mentioned greed, used its specter to accomplish her transition from apology to reproof. Here begins a series of extended discussions on common activities that Hume considered spiritually destructive and socially dangerous. First she attacked extravagance, whether in clothing, money, or personal vanity. Then she turned her attention to recreation. Her litany of evils, which is repeated with minor variation throughout her writings, includes card playing, attending plays and "music gardens," reading fiction, and behaving foppishly. In contrast to these activities Hume advocated pious worship that sought in all things to glorify God. She spoke specifically to pride as the source of many evils and devoted several pages to a discussion of habitual "detraction" or slanderous criticism of others. Christmas, along with the traditional means of celebrating that season, also received particular attention. Hume saw such behavior as ill suited to the occasion it celebrated.

An Exhortation to the Inhabitants of the Province of South-Carolina was published first by subscription and later in many other editions in England and America. After spending most of 1748 in Philadelphia, Hume returned to London, where she continued to speak and write. By 1763 the London Friends had granted her standing as a minister, not previously forthcoming despite her experiences in the colonies. Her second published work was occasioned by a devastating hurricane that caused much damage and suffering in Charleston. Hume learned about the event when she received a newspaper item dated 15 September 1752. A ten-foot storm surge had pounded Charleston as the eye of the storm passed nearby. All hope seemed lost when, seemingly without cause, the winds shifted and the flood waters inexplicably receded, dropping five feet in ten minutes. In this event Hume saw the design of a merciful God seeking to express displeasure and to call followers to careful self-examination and immediate repentance.

In her *An Epistle to the Inhabitants of South Carolina* published in London in 1754, she reproduced the newspaper account and informed readers that it was indeed the power of God that had turned back the storm. She advocated reverent acknowledgment of God's mercy and called survivors of the storm and flood to renew their commitment to their faith. Hume also pointed to other recent events, including the Indian War, droughts, and fires as signs that God intended to exact universal worship whether "in mercy or judgement."

Hume remained concerned with the same issues she had discussed in her first book, specifically attacking cursing, greed, and luxurious tastes. Identifying these vices as the provocation of the

Letter from Sophia Hume congratulating a fellow Quaker on her marriage (Library of Haverford College)

divine wrath expressed in the violent weather, Hume reissued a call to holiness and repentance. She urged her readers to purify themselves not only in their relationships with each other but especially regarding their relationship to God. God had been forsaken and, Hume believed, was directly and indisputably chastising the disobedient.

On this basis Hume built a critique of so-called natural religion, or deism, arguing that the reversal of the wind was "contrary to the common course of nature." What was at work in this modern marvel was not a deus ex machina but was the hand of Providence—"a visitation from the Lord." Along with her supposed refutation of deism Hume also defended several important doctrines that, as she suggested in her title, are broadly applicable not only to Quaker believers but also to all Christians.

Classic authors are cited, among them Daniel Whitby and Matthew Henry. In her explication of scripture, her commonsense logic, and her sometimes prolific quotation of other writings, she returned many times to foundational themes of orthodox evangelical belief: experimental or "heart" religion, personal morality, individual responsibility for sin, God's judgment against the unrighteous, and God's mercy toward the repentant. At the same time she advocated several important ideas that commonly distinguished Quakers and other "radical" groups: concern for the poor, opposition to denominational organization, and vigorous antimaterialism.

Given its lack of autobiographical insight, *An Epistle to the Inhabitants of South Carolina* is of less interest to scholars than Hume's first work. Nevertheless, its prose is among her most melodic and typifies her eloquent phrasing and repetitive reinforcement of her primary points. As an example of her rhetorical style, it is less encumbered, more mature, and—given her interpretation of the hurricane—perhaps more useful for understanding her intellectual framework. The first edition in 1752 was followed by a second in 1754, and the work was bound with other short works in subsequent editions.

In 1756 Hume published her most scholarly work. *Extracts from Divers Ancient Testimonies* is an anthology of materials by both Quaker and non-Quaker writers. The work suggests that Hume had extensive exposure to the leading thinkers of her era as well as significant knowledge of early Christian history. The texts are grouped according to five general topics: education, getting and spending riches, feasting at marriage ceremonies, paying tithes, and trade and merchandising. The excerpts are quoted without introduction or commentary,

separated only by short citations of sources. The sections begin with general passages summarizing particular ethical positions that grow more explicit and specific, often citing examples or testimonials to the dangers of wicked behavior. Hume occasionally included a paragraph or two of summary based on her own perspective or experience.

The basic premises are a reflection of Hume's strong commitment to Quaker principles. In educating the young she believed that there should be no teaching of classical, or "pagan," languages. Children should not be exposed to anti-Christian (that is, secular) literature. Some of her strongest protests are directed as well at the practice of teaching "superfluous needlework" and other fashionable skills that impede sobriety and induce vanity and excess.

On the gaining and expenditure of wealth, Hume first cited Fathers of the Church to establish a valid Christian tradition of asceticism. She then turned to modern authors and anecdotes to illustrate the inherent danger of Christians giving a place to fashion and luxury. While acknowledging the need to provide for family and to earn money to support the poor, Hume sternly warned against the "love of money" as the source of many evils. Similarly, she criticized lavish feasts and celebrations. Her primary concern was with wedding feasts, but here and in other works she opposed feasts for almost any occasion, suggesting instead that money be given to the needy.

A short section is also included on the paying of tithes. This form of taxation was opposed by Quakers, who were dissenters against the churches that benefited from the proceeds. Hume was concerned that some people paid tithes to avoid any possible penalties for nonpayment. She urged her readers to stand firm, citing two particularly influential stories of the emotional discontent engendered by duplicitous conformity. She concluded the work with a series of excerpts concerned with the Christian's choice of vocation and the necessity of mercantile trade. Any time one's choice of a trade was motivated by a lust for material benefit Hume saw it as a violation of the higher ethic to which Christians are called. The end result, she wrote, was greed and vanity, which would always assert themselves in evil actions.

Hume wrote only ten of the eighty-five pages in *Extracts from Divers Ancient Testimonies*. Her brief introduction is largely a call to repentance and an urgent plea to conform to the Quaker tradition of simplicity and humility. The great significance of this work is its suggestion that Hume was reading the Church Fathers, history, theology, and partici-

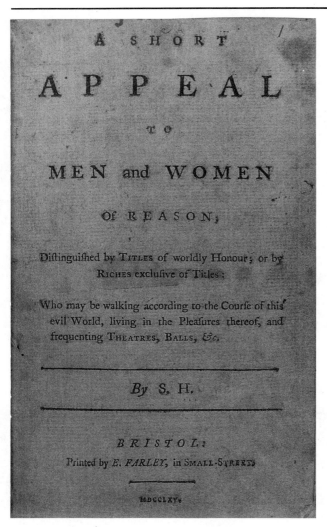

Title page for the pamphlet in which Hume called on the upper class to renounce luxury and live sober, pious lives

pating in public intellectual dialogue on these subjects, all at a much earlier date than women's public religious leadership is often acknowledged.

During 1757 Hume traveled to Holland with Catharine Phillips (1726–1794), a Quaker whose writings were addressed to a British audience and discussed social problems, religious issues, and missionary endeavors. Afterward Hume resumed her writing career in London. A brief work (thirty-eight pages in the 1771 edition), *A Caution to Such as Observe Days and Times* (1760), is more focused than Hume's earlier writings. It is an impassioned critique of public and private immorality, especially as practiced in connection with Christmas celebrations. The work consists of two distinct parts, one clearly written several years earlier. The first section includes Hume's rationale for warning against Christmas celebrations. The second is a somewhat more general "Address to Magistrates,

Parents, and Masters of Families," which echoes earlier themes of moral reform.

The main premise of *A Caution to Such as Observe Days and Times* is that Christians were using the commemoration of Jesus' birth to justify many forms of behavior that Hume found inconsistent with the Christian's life. This view is consistent with her stance on luxurious living, humility, and sobriety. The thirteen-page essay draws on her experiences, using them as an example of common seasonal activities and contrasting them with Hume's ideal of Christian morality, which she based on scriptural teaching, especially the lifestyle of Jesus reflected in the Gospels. She appealed to her readers to be attentive to the guiding light of truth in their hearts, which would result in the recognition of their shortcomings.

The second section asks the leaders of society to question their role in societal reform. Hume accuses them of being too tolerant toward immorality, citing cursing, "intemperate drinking," gaming, and harlotry as typically popular vices. The general lewdness of London society was the chief impetus for Hume's writing, and she expresses her dismay at the extent to which the city accepted corruption. She described the environment, citing statistics on the number of ale houses, and pointed out its effect on everyday behavior. She also defended her place in the desired reformation as she again made the case for women's public leadership.

Hume invoked the threat of divine judgment as an incentive for reform and made clear her belief that the wicked would be held accountable for their disobedience. In this idea lies the key to understanding the career of Sophia Hume. She believed that Christians had a duty not only to live moral lives but also to inform fellow believers when their lifestyles departed from the ideal. This common and resilient compulsion, simultaneously compassionate and judgmental, constitutes the heart of Hume's motivation. Her belief that failure to call others to repentance damaged her own innocence must account for her intensity and endurance. In her "Address to Magistrates, Parents, and Masters of Families" she informs those in leadership of their own similar responsibility, hoping thereby to enlist their aid.

A Caution to Such as Observe Days and Times was republished in many editions in Britain and America. Its nonsectarian call for reform was useful for diverse movements opposed to the character of public morality. It is not only one of Hume's last writings but also her most insightful, revealing more about her intellectual character and personal ambitions than any of her previous works. It is also a rich resource for suggestive descriptions of urban life in London.

Hume wrote two other short books. *A Short Appeal to Men and Women of Reason* (1765) called on the wealthy to acknowledge their responsibilities as custodians of the world's riches. It repeats earlier themes and arguments, calling on the upper class to forsake the trappings of aristocratic living, to spurn luxury beyond what is necessary, and to honor God with practical and sober lives. *Remarks on the Practice of Inoculation for the Smallpox* (1767) is a short critique of inoculation as an example of human trespass against divine prerogative. Both pamphlets are quite rare, and no copies of the first edition of the latter are known to exist.

Hume returned to Charleston in 1767, responding to the decline of the Charleston Friends meeting. In the midst of legal questions about ownership of the meeting's property she attempted to win funding for a new building from Quakers in London and Philadelphia. Aiming for a Quaker revival, she spoke to reportedly large crowds but failed to win many converts or sufficient capital for a new meetinghouse.

At this time Hume produced another work, which was published in Newport, Rhode Island: *The Justly Celebrated Mrs. Sophia Hume's Advice and Warning to Labourers* (1769). This two-column broadside may have appeared earlier in a 1750 London edition with a similar title. In it Hume described the dangerous lifestyle that her intended audience had adopted (visiting pubs, blasphemy, cursing, and other unspecified corruption), delivering a stern warning and trying to elicit a reformation in her readers' character. She appealed to reason, building a careful and logical argument that God created each person and requires conformity to a high standard. Failure, she bluntly warned, would result in judgment and damnation to hell. As a short example of Hume's biblically imitative style, the broadside is a valuable introduction to her rhetoric and her logic.

Frustrated by her failures as a reformer and fund-raiser, Hume returned to London late in 1768 and there spent her remaining years. She died at Gracechurch Street, London, on 26 January 1774 and was buried at Friends' Burial Ground, Bunhill Fields. Despite her significant literary output, her early role in women's public leadership, and her participation in important intellectual trends, she is ignored by historical and literary scholarship. Her harsh condemnation of social mores and her intellectual dexterity create a rich and unexplored resource for scholars.

References:

Margaret Hope Bacon, *Mothers of Feminism: The Story of Quaker Women in America* (San Francisco: Harper & Row, 1986);

Carol Stoneburner and John Stoneburner, eds., *The Influence of Quaker Women on American History* (Lewiston, N.Y.: Edwin Mellen, 1986);

Mabel L. Webber, "Records of the Quakers in Charles Town," *South Carolina Historical Magazine,* 28 (1927): 22–43, 94–107, 176–197.

Papers:

Manuscripts by and about Sophia Hume are scattered. The most useful collection is that of the Philadelphia Yearly Meeting in Philadelphia. The collections at the Historical Society of Pennsylvania and the Friends House, London, are also useful.

Susan Mansfield Huntington

(27 January 1791 – 4 December 1823)

Erika M. Kreger
University of California, Davis

BOOKS: *Short Address to Sick Persons Who Are Without Hope. And, Letter to a Friend Recovered From Sickness* (Andover, Mass.: Printed for New England Tract Society by Flagg & Gould, 1818);

Little Lucy, or The Careless Child Reformed (Cambridge, Mass.: Printed by Hilliard & Metcalf, 1820);

Memoirs of the Late Mrs. Susan Huntington, of Boston, Mass., consisting principally of extracts from her journal and letters; with the sermon occasioned by her death, edited by Benjamin B. Wisner (Boston: Crocker & Breasted, 1826; London: R. Baines, 1827).

Susan Mansfield Huntington

Susan Mansfield Huntington was a New England philanthropist, diarist, religious writer, and poet. She is best known for her letters and journals, posthumously collected and published as *Memoirs of the Late Mrs. Susan Huntington, of Boston, Mass.* (1826). Concerned primarily with questions of faith and duty, Huntington's writings exemplify the intense self-scrutiny that characterized Christian women's autobiography in the early national period. Such pious memoirs—typically Protestant women's personal diaries and correspondence collected by family members after the writer's death—were widely read by evangelicals in the new republic and Europe. The reception of Huntington's writing reflected the popularity of the genre. Her memoir sold out two editions of one thousand copies each in its first year of publication. By the time the third American edition came out in 1829, the book had already gone through five British editions.

A minister's wife active in organizing the first American benevolent societies, Huntington wrote at a time when women's religious role was becoming increasingly public. She saw herself not only as a mother responsible for helping her children find salvation but also as a citizen responsible for the moral guardianship of her community. Her writings constitute a spiritual record, documenting the struggle inherent in attempting to reconcile the complete self-denial demanded by Protestant belief and the implicit self-assertion involved in charitable work. Like other authors of pious memoirs, Huntington constantly doubted her faith, questioning the genuineness of her repentance. Her sense of inadequacy, however, derived partly from her belief in the enormous influence of her domestic role. In her discussions of motherhood and education she not only emphasized female moral duty but also argued for women's rational nature and equality before God. Although lacking the idiosyncratic self-expression and descriptions of events valued by twentieth-century readers, Huntington's letters and journals illustrate a worldview shared by many New England women of her day, as well as reflecting the early development of the religiously sanctioned female empowerment that changed American women's lives in the succeeding decades.

Susan Mansfield was born in Killingworth, Connecticut, on 27 January 1791. Her father, Achilles Mansfield (died 1814), was a minister, and her mother was a descendant of the famous "Indian Apostle," John Eliot (1604–1690) of Roxbury, Massachusetts. The youngest of three children, Susan attended common school and spent two seasons at a "classical school" in Killingworth, but she was mainly educated at home. Her reading most likely included the religious writings of her noted Puritan ancestors, such as John Eliot's *The Christian Commonwealth* (1659) and the published sermons of her maternal great-grandfather, the Reverend Jared Eliot (1685–1763), as well as her father's *Christianity the wisdom and power of God* (1791).

As might be expected from a child raised in a devout family, Susan showed a religious tendency early in life. She recalled that when she was only five years old she "was brought by the holy spirit to consider the duties and consequences of becoming a Christian," and at that time she chose "God for her portion." In 1807, at the age of seventeen, she made a public profession of faith and joined her father's church. This same year she began her first journal, which she destroyed before her death.

On 18 May 1809 Susan Mansfield married Joshua Huntington (1786–1819), junior pastor of the Old South Church in Boston. Also a descendant of a respected Puritan family, Joshua had recently graduated from Yale. Known for his correct and pious deportment while a student, he had overcome a stammer to become such an effective speaker that when he preached as a candidate, he was courted by several different parishes. Susan knew, as she wrote in a letter of 1 January 1810, that the married state "must be very happy, or very miserable" for women. She categorized her own marriage as a happy one, describing her husband as the "friend of my bosom." She credited the success of her marriage in part to her husband's piety. As she wrote to a friend on 20 December 1810, "Oh! the importance of religion in order to render the married state a blessing!"

Soon after her marriage, expressing sentiments she repeated throughout her life, Susan wrote in a 30 May 1809 letter that she feared her own inadequacies but trusted in God, who called her to the "arduous duties" of a minister's wife. Those duties continued to multiply in the following years. The first of her six children, a daughter also named Susan, was born in September 1810. The next year,

following the senior pastor's death, the young Reverend Huntington, ordained only three years earlier, was left solely responsible for his congregation. Church attendance grew steadily and rapidly during his tenure, and his wife was an active participant in founding the benevolent societies initiated during these years. She later advised a young preacher considering marriage, "it is of great importance that a minister have the right sort of wife. It is surprising how much his usefulness may be retarded or promoted by her influence."

Opinion varied, however, about how to define the right sort of wife. When her husband became the senior pastor, Susan Huntington knew she would be held under close surveillance. As she noted in a letter of 15 August 1811,

> the wife of a clergyman is more narrowly watched than almost anyone else. Her deviations from duty are very seldom overlooked; her opinions are minutely examined and often repeated. She is thought to take her notions from her husband; and, of course, he suffers if she is imprudent.

Huntington knew she was held up as a model, as she explained in a 24 February 1814 journal entry, "I am emphatically like a city set on a hill. I am required to exhibit the fruits of a full grown tree, when I am but a feeble plant." She recorded her frustration with this position in her journal on 5 January 1815:

> How difficult, how hopeless is the task of pleasing everybody! A fortnight since a lady said to me with a tone and manner which gave peculiar emphasis to the words, "How is it possible you can go out so much, visit your people so frequently, and be engaged in so many charitable societies, without neglecting your family?" This week . . . I am censured for doing so little in a public way, and confining myself so much to my family.

Always attempting to submit to God's will, Huntington throughout her life struggled to balance and rationalize the conflicting demands of her public and domestic duties.

In 1812, soon after the birth of her second child, Joseph Beckley, Huntington began another journal that survived to be included in her printed memoir. Her stated purposes for keeping these "written memorials of special mercies" are to praise God, reinforce her sense of duty, inspire trust in divine will, and remind herself of her own weakness. Such goals echo those of other Protestant women memoirists, whose editors emphasized the personal nature of their writing. The editor of Hun-

MEMOIRS

OF THE LATE

MRS. SUSAN HUNTINGTON,

OF

BOSTON, Mass.

CONSISTING PRINCIPALLY OF

EXTRACTS FROM HER JOURNAL AND LETTERS:

WITH THE

SERMON OCCASIONED BY HER DEATH.

By BENJAMIN B. WISNER,

PASTOR OF THE OLD SOUTH CHURCH IN BOSTON.

SECOND EDITION.

BOSTON:
PUBLISHED BY CROCKER & BREWSTER,
No. 47, Washington Street, late 50, Cornhill.

1826.

Title page for the second edition of Huntington's popular autobiography, which went through eight editions in the United States and Great Britain between 1826 and 1829

tington's memoir, Benjamin B. Wisner (1794–1835), included the expected comments in his introductory essay that she never intended her letters, "written for the eye of friendship only," and her journals, "written for the eye of her own spirit," to be published, but her privacy must be sacrificed so that others might learn from her example.

As Joanna Bowen Gillespie points out, despite such "ritual disclaimers," young girls inspired by female memorials adopted the literary and religious conventions of the genre in their own writing. The similarity in women's narratives was seen as a mark of the authenticity of their religious feeling. Huntington mentioned and quoted several well-known memoirs, including *The Power of Faith: exemplified in the life and writings of Mrs. Isabella Graham* (1816), about a famous New York widow who began a girls' school and organized many charitable societies, and the memoirs of Harriet Newel (1793–1812), which describe the Christian suffering of a young missionary wife who died at nineteen. Newel's and Graham's popular life stories were credited with inspiring interest in the missionary and benevolence movements. Huntington admired these pious role models. She wrote of Newel that "there was an elevation and spirituality in her character, seldom met with in the present day. No one can help but admire her excellence. Christians will be humbled by its contemplation, and stimulated to greater activity in the service of Christ." Wisner later quoted these words as an apt description of Huntington herself, describing both women as "invisible agents" whose "works are preserved to exercise unceasing influence."

Huntington believed Christian women could exert great influence in life as well as after death, and therefore, like the other memoirists mentioned in Gillespie's study, she did not find her position in the domestic sphere restrictive. Huntington wrote in a 22 January 1813 journal entry, "When I hear females, as I sometimes do, deprecating the contractedness of domestic life . . . I am led to think that my life, in the little sphere of my family, must be more varied than theirs, or they could not consider the duties of the domestic circle as unimportant." In Huntington's view God saw the person who "performs a self-denying duty" as "greater than the hero or the conqueror," so the complaining woman "virtually professes to value the praise of men more than the praise of God."

Certainly, Huntington's "little sphere" grew to encompass the larger family of her community as she became active in many societies and organizations in the years following 1813. The organization of women's charitable societies that had begun in Boston in 1800 continued in the succeeding decades, encouraged by ministers whose congregations and resources had been depleted by westward migration. Societies were founded in rapid succession: The New England Tract Society in 1814, the American Education Society in 1815, and the Boston Society for Religious and Moral Instruction of the Poor in 1816. Active in all these groups, Huntington by the end of her life was director of both the Boston Female Tract Society and the Boston Maternal Association, a subscriber to another three charitable organizations, as well as a life member of six other benevolent societies.

While Huntington's philanthropic activities multiplied, her family continued to grow as well.

Three daughters, Sarah Ann, Elizabeth Moore, and Mary, were born in 1813, 1815, and 1816, respectively. Her writings indicate that she continued to view her role as mother as her primary responsibility, never forgetting that, as she noted in her first journal entry on 21 May 1812, her most important duty was "at all times by my precepts and by my example, to inspire my children with just notions of right and wrong." Huntington's letters reflect the goals and activities of the maternal association she founded in the year of Mary's birth. This society celebrated the mother's role in helping children convert, encouraged women to support each other, and circulated religious and educational materials.

Educating the child, not just for this world but also for the next, was a primary mission of the maternal association. Like many of her contemporaries, Huntington believed in John Locke's notion that the child was a blank slate that might be written on by either the Holy Spirit or the emissaries of Satan. It was thus crucial, through example and instruction, to impress virtuous ideas on children's minds. Following in the tradition of educational writers she admired—such as the former president of Princeton University the Reverend John Witherspoon (1723–1794) and Elizabeth Hamilton (1758–1816), whose *Letters on Education* were first published in 1804—Huntington emphasized the importance of the mother's religious influence in child rearing. Huntington's advice received a wider audience in 1818, when three of her letters were published. The New England Tract Society printed two of Huntington's letters as a *Short Address to Sick Persons Who Are Without Hope. And, Letter to a Friend Recovered From Sickness* (1818). The first of these letters reminds a sick individual of the need for earnest repentance. After recovery, however, this person seems to have forgotten the lesson that "the soul that sinneth shall die." The second letter admonishes the recipient, "You know beyond the shadow of a doubt, that if you die unrenewed, you must be eternally separated from God; and yet you feel no concern about it!" It then offers a list of directions that will help the receiver find "peace and joy in believing." Huntington's advice here, and in later letters to her children, reflects the belief that chastisement is a way to show love. Believing that, as she had written on 22 November 1808, "we are naturally in a state of enmity to God, entirely depraved," she feared that if we "look with too charitable an eye upon the experiences of others" these loved ones might "at the judgement day . . . rise up and accuse us of having been the means of lulling them to sleep" when they should have been earnestly repenting.

Another of Huntington's letters appeared in the *Boston Recorder* in 1818 (and was later published in her memoir). Having read the memoir of the Reverend Richard Cecil (1748–1810), Huntington took issue with his claims that ministers should not mingle with women. In her letter she stated, "I am not pleased with his remarks upon my sex. . . . I object to his insinuations, not as a woman, but as a Christian, as a member of God's universal family." Throughout the discussion she presented her views emphatically: "My opinion has been, that, by cultivating habits of rational intercourse between the sexes, the real good of both parties would be promoted." She argued that women whose reason was not developed through education would be denied their family's respect and their children's obedience. Equal in the eyes of God, women should be treated accordingly: "There are those who think, that if women are treated as equals, they will aspire to dominion, or will not 'be in subjection, with reverence,' to their husbands. I am of the contrary opinion. . . . We are always the most generous, when left free. The enlightened obedience of a sensible woman is consistent, because it is the dictate of reason." Yet Huntington considered it "idle" and a "waste" to "dispute the point of equality with our brethren." Despite her forceful claims about women's nature and ability, she concluded her letter with the expected assurance that the woman who "steps out of her proper sphere" ceases to be "either amiable or respectable."

In 1820 Huntington published a book of moral instruction for children, aimed at making the next generation of young women "amiable and respectable." *Little Lucy, or The Careless Child Reformed* shows the influence of both Hannah More's widely distributed moral tracts and the popular children's stories written by Maria Edgeworth and her father. Although Huntington shared the evangelical disapproval of fairy tales and novels—she mentioned the dangers of Walter Scott's Waverley novels and chose not to read Edgeworth's adult fiction—she praised works such as More's in which "religious sentiments are inculcated under the form of a story." In the Edgeworth books—which began with *Harry and Lucy* in 1801 and continued through *Harry and Lucy Concluded* in 1825—boys and girls are rewarded for being honest, cheerful, and industrious. Huntington, who remarked in a 25 December 1816 letter that Edgeworth's stories "evince an uncommon knowledge of the human mind," might have modeled her own child protagonist after the girl in the Harry and Lucy series. Written in an era when parents' increased leisure time resulted in a growing demand for children's books, Huntington's was one of the first "Little Lucy" books, but dozens of similarly titled stories by other authors—such as *The History of Little Lucy and Her Dhaye* (1822), *Lucy or the little enquirer* (1824), and *Little Lucy or the pleasant day: an example for little girls* (1825)—were published over the next twenty years.

On 11 September 1819 Joshua Huntington, who had often been ill, died at the age of thirty-three. Susan Huntington's journal describes his death in detail, and many of her remaining letters focus on her attempt to interpret God's will in the face of affliction. Her last child, Joshua, was born three months after his father's death. Huntington published an elegy for her husband and a poem about her new baby in the *Boston Recorder* in 1820. (All her published verse is collected in her memoir.) In 1821 two-year-old Joshua succumbed to dysentery, and less than a month later six-year-old Elizabeth, who had been an invalid most of her short life, also died. This same year a new minister filled Joshua Huntington's post, which had been vacant for seventeen months, necessitating that his widow move her family to another house. Coping with her new circumstances in 1822, she wrote letters to her oldest son, who was away at Andover, and her oldest daughter, who was visiting friends. These late letters remain remarkably consistent with the beliefs expressed throughout her life.

After an illness Susan Mansfield Huntington died on 4 December 1823. Wisner preached her funeral sermon, which he based on Romans 8:28: "And we know that all work together for good to them that love God, to them who are called according to His purpose." James Montgomery later wrote a poem about Huntington based on the same passage. Wisner and other early-nineteenth-century readers valued Huntington's writings because they depicted "an exemplification of Christian character in the female sex, rising into grace, expanding into beauty, and flourishing in usefulness." The next generation emphasized her usefulness in particular. In 1883, for example, biographer Phebe Hanaford included Huntington in a chapter on "Philanthropic Women" along with Isabella Graham, Dorothea Dix, and Clara Barton. For readers in the late twentieth century, as Ann Taves argues, memoirs such as Huntington's provide insight into the daily existence of a minister's wife in the early nineteenth century and highlight the centrality of religion in the development of American women's self-definition.

Biography:

Huntington Family Association, *The Huntington Family in America: A Genealogical Memoir of the Known Descendents of Simon Huntington from 1633 to 1915* (Hartford, Conn.: Huntington Family Association, 1915), pp. 460–463.

References:

Joanna Bowen Gillespie, "'The Clear Leadings of Providence': Pious Memoirs and the Problems of Self-Realization for Women in the Early Nineteenth Century," *Journal of the Early Republic,* 5 (Summer 1985): 197–221;

Phebe A. Hanaford, *Daughters of America, or Women of the Century* (Augusta, Maine: True, 1883), pp. 132–133;

Joshua Huntington, *Memoirs of the Life of Mrs. Abigail Waters: who died in Boston November 22d, 1816, in the 96th year of her age: to which is prefixed the sermon preached on occasion of her death* (Boston: Samuel T. Armstrong, 1817);

Mary Hallam Huntington, *Memoirs of Mary Hallam Huntington of Bridgewater, Mass.* (Boston: Printed for Samuel T. Armstrong by Crocker & Breasted, 1820);

"Memoir of Joshua Huntington," *Panoplist,* 16 (December 1820): 529–535;

Leonard I. Sweet, *The Minister's Wife: Her Role in Nineteenth-Century American Evangelicalism* (Philadelphia: Temple University Press, 1983);

Ann Taves, "Self and God in the Early Published Memoirs of New England Women," in *American Women's Autobiography: Fea(s)ts of Memory,* edited by Margo Culley (Madison: University of Wisconsin Press, 1992), pp. 57–74;

Benjamin B. Wisner, *The History of the Old South Church in Boston: in four sermons, delivered May 9, & 16, 1830, being the first and second Sabbaths after the completion of a century from the first occupancy* (Boston: Crocker & Breasted, 1830).

Papers:

Some of Susan Huntington's letters are included in the papers of John Trumbull (1756-1843) at Yale University. Other Huntington family papers are at the Connecticut Historical Society.

Susanna Johnson

(20 February 1730 – 27 November 1810)

Amy K. Ott
University of Delaware

BOOK: *A Narrative of the Captivity of Mrs. Johnson. Containing an account of her sufferings during four years with the Indians and French* (Walpole, N.H.: Printed for D. Carlisle Jr., 1796; Glasgow: Printed by R. Chapman for Stewart & Meikle, 1797; "corrected and enlarged" edition, Windsor, Vt.: Printed by Alden Spooner, 1807; "corrected and considerably enlarged" edition, Windsor, Vt.: Printed by T. M. Pomroy, 1814).

Susanna Willard Johnson was a historian, writer, mother, and survivor who made a home on the New Hampshire frontier despite war, captivity, and poverty. Her Indian captivity narrative is one of the most thoroughly detailed, politically astute, and historically accurate of the genre. Writing her narrative in 1796, almost forty years after her captivity among the Abenaki and French in New France at a time when the new republic was just testing its federal powers, Johnson exposed the injustice of women's social and political disenfranchisement, speaking for the thousands of American women who could not speak for themselves.

Born in Groton, Massachusetts, on 20 February 1730, Susanna Willard was the daughter of Lt. Moses Willard and Susanna Hastings Willard. Lieutenant Willard was descended from Maj. Simon Willard, the original purchaser of Concord, Massachusetts, from the Indians. In 1742 Moses Willard moved his family to the sparsely settled wilderness where stockade Fort Number Four, New Hampshire, was erected in 1744. (The settlement was renamed Charlestown in 1757.) Susanna Willard was not with her parents on this move. At the age of eight she had been placed in the care of Lt. Col. Jonathan White of Leominster, Massachusetts, where she remained until her marriage to James Johnson in 1747, when she was seventeen and he was about ten years her senior.

An Irishman, James Johnson was ten years old when Susanna's great-uncle Josiah Willard pur-

chased him at a wharf in Boston. The circumstances of James Johnson's servitude are suspicious. Susanna Johnson later suggested that her husband had been a ship boy for his uncle, a sea captain, whose death had precipitated the crew of his ship to commandeer vessel and cargo and remove the boy witness by selling him as an indentured servant. He purchased his freedom at the age of twenty, a year before his indenture was complete, and made a success of himself, as is apparent by the large allotments of land he received in the division of Fort Number Four township. He also had a house at Fort Number Four and a large outbuilding designed for storing the goods he traded for fur with Indian trappers. Susanna Johnson moved to her husband's home at Number Four in 1749, reuniting with her father and mother and bringing her first son, Sylvanus, aged one and a half. She was also carrying her second child, Esther, who was born in December 1749 and died less than two months later.

In 1749 Fort Number Four was little more than an outpost along a well-traveled Indian trading route, and it suffered frequent French and Indian attacks, largely because of the mercurial nature of Anglo-French diplomacy. In addition, an ongoing border dispute between Massachusetts and New Hampshire often left this northernmost British outpost in New England bereft of a military presence. New Hampshire pled poverty as an excuse for leaving it defenseless. Massachusetts resented the necessity of manning the strategically placed fort. In fact, "Two or three days after my arrival," Susanna wrote in her narrative, "orders came from Massachusetts to withdraw the troops: government placed confidence in the proffered peace of Frenchmen, and withdrew even the appearance of hostility." As Johnson's foreshadowing indicates, the fort was attacked a short time later. On 26 June 1749 a group of Indians attacked the men of the fort, who were out harrowing their fields. Johnson's father and brother were among the missing after the attack and were feared dead. Although they eventually re-

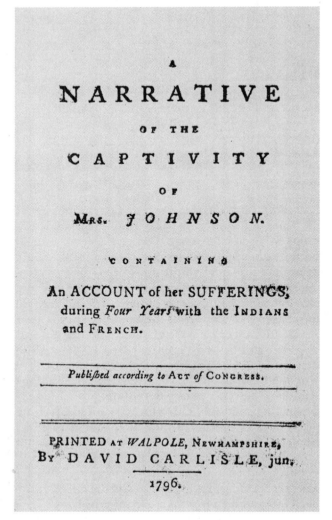

Title page for Susannah Johnson's account of her capture by Abenaki and her exposure "to the malice of exasperated Frenchmen" in Canada during her husband's extended efforts to raise the money for her ransom

turned unharmed to the fort, it is clear from Susanna Johnson's analysis of government frontier policy that the attack and the general insecurity of her family home left a lasting impression, one only deepened by her capture and captivity.

In the introduction to her narrative Johnson employed the tropes and language of earlier New England historians, among them John Winthrop and William Bradford, to draw an analogy between her frontier community and the first Puritan settlements: "The situation of our ancestors has often been described in language that did honor to the hearts that conceived it. The boisterous ocean, with unknown shores, hemmed them in on one side, and a forest, swarming with savages, yelling for their blood, threatened on the other. . . . I have in all my travels felt a degree of pride in recollecting, that I belonged to a country whose valor was distinguished and whose spirit had never been debased by servile submission." By expanding through implication the typology of Puritan historians to include her own experiences of frontier America, Susanna Johnson appropriated patriarchal authority. In the same way she continually linked her experiences in captivity with her experiences once freed, making a direct connection between what she had suffered and the rights and freedoms to which she was entitled in return for her suffering. Thus, she criticized British imperial frontier policy, as in the following example: "Had there been an organised government, to stretch forth its protecting arm, in any case of danger, the misery might have been in a degree alleviated. But the infancy of our country did not admit of this blessing."

Not all her experiences on the frontier were filled with fear and misery. The five years following the Johnsons' removal to Fort Number Four were relatively good ones for the Johnson family. Susanna and James had two more children, Susanna and Mary (Polly), born on 19 December 1750 and 8 November 1752, respectively. The family moved out of the fort and into a log house outside the stockade, and James Johnson's business boomed. In fact, the Johnsons, their servants, and their neighbors were celebrating his return from a successful trading trip with "watermelons and slip" on the night before their lives were to change dramatically.

In 1754 Massachusetts once again withdrew military support at the garrison, despite increasingly frequent Indian raids on the westernmost borders of New England. Early on the morning of 30 August 1754 neighbor Peter Labarree knocked at the Johnsons' door to awaken the men for work. When the door opened, a raiding party of eleven Abenaki Indians rushed in, capturing James and Susanna Johnson; their three children; her fourteen-year-old sister, Miriam Willard; Ebenezer Farnsworth, a boarding laborer; and Labarree. Thus began a harrowing, two-hundred-mile trek along the Connecticut River and across Lake Champlain to the Abenaki's home, the Jesuit mission village of St. François-du-Lac on the St. Lawrence River above Montreal. Unlike some captives in her situation, Susanna Johnson, who was in an advanced stage of pregnancy, was not killed for slowing the party down. On 31 August 1754 she gave birth on the trail to a daughter, whom she named Captive. In her narrative she remarked that her captor responded to the birth of Captive by gleefully proclaiming, "two monies for me, two monies for me." Though weakened from childbearing, scantily clad, and ill-shod, Johnson, with the help of her fellow captives, survived the journey.

Johnson's narrative indicates that her captivity among the Abenakis was relatively painless. She was not abused or treated as a slave but adopted as a family member. The Indian captivity portion of Susanna Johnson's narrative is remarkable for its details of Abenaki culture and lifestyle and her generally unbiased observations. On occasion she expressed appreciation for the unity and harmony of Abenaki culture and the way in which they welcomed her into their tribe and family. She forgave the Abenaki any cruelty by remarking that they have "no claim to the benefits of civilization." Because of the brief duration of her captivity among the Abenaki, however, this section is only a small part of her narrative.

Johnson's husband, sister, little Susanna, and Polly were sold to the French shortly after their arrival at St. François-du-Lac. Captive remained with her mother, and Sylvanus was sold to an Abenaki hunter and carried into the wilderness with a hunting party. In November 1754 Susanna and Captive were finally "ransomed" by the French and joined the rest of the family, all of whom had been bought by respectable, genteel French families. In the second to last chapter of her narrative Johnson remarked with typical frankness on "leaving a country where I had suffered the keenest distress, during two months and a half with the savages—been bowed down by every mortification and insult, which could arise from the misfortunes of my husband, in New England; and where I had spent two years in sickness and despair, in a prison too shocking to mention." The euphemistic "misfortunes" to which Johnson alludes occurred from late 1754 through mid 1755, when her husband was given a two-month parole from French captivity to return to New England and petition the government for ransom to release his family and other New Englanders. He appealed first to Gov. William Shirley of Massachusetts and received ten pounds from the House of Representatives of Massachusetts "to defray his expenses. He got no further assistance in Massachusetts." After successfully petitioning Benning Wentworth and the New Hampshire House of Representatives, James Johnson made arrangements to return to Montreal with the ransom. He was stopped, however, by counterorders from Shirley, who cited a change in the political atmosphere of colonial New France as his reason for delaying him. Shirley's delay caused James Johnson to violate his parole, and "his credit in Canada lost: his family exposed to the malice of exasperated Frenchmen, and all his good prospects at an end," he spent months attempting to return to his family.

When he finally succeeded in returning to Montreal, Luc de La Corne, who was to act as his agent in ransoming the family and other New England captives, proved treacherous. The Johnsons were left penniless and out of favor with the government of New France. James Johnson was jailed in July 1755, and on 22 July 1755 the family was put on a ship bound for Quebec. On their arrival in Quebec they were jailed in the criminal prison, where they suffered smallpox, starvation, and the ravages of a Quebec winter, having only one blanket each to keep out the cold and dirty straw to keep them off the floor. In January 1756 the final in a series of petitions they had been sending to Gov. Pierre François de Rigaud de Vaudrieul of Quebec was answered, and they were moved to the civil prison, where they had better facilities and a degree of freedom. In the autumn of 1756 Susanna Johnson received word that in June of the same year her father had been killed in an Abenaki attack on Fort Number Four. In December 1756, still in prison, she gave birth to a child who survived only a day. She and her family remained in prison until 20 July 1757, when Susanna Johnson, Captive, Polly, and Miriam Willard were placed on a cartel ship bound for Plymouth, England, where they arrived on 19 August 1757. After a series of minor delays they were placed on board a man-of-war bound for New York City. They debarked at Sandy Hook, New Jersey, on 10 December 1757, having been captives for more than three years.

James Johnson, who had gone by land through New France and been detained in prison in Massachusetts for having lost the ransom money he gave to La Corne, was reunited with Susanna, Polly, and Captive on 1 January 1758. "Happy new year," Johnson exclaimed in her narrative. Her happiness was marred, however, by the absences of her ten-year-old son, Sylvanus, and of little Susanna, who was still in the care of the Mesdames Jaisson and who was being raised as a Catholic Frenchwoman.

Johnson's portrayal of French captivity, which she suffered for more than two-and-a-half years, is longer and less objective than her portrayal of Indian captivity. Johnson made glowing exceptions for "some benevolent friends, whose generosity I shall ever recollect with warmest gratitude," among them Rine DuQuesne, an affluent Montreal merchant; Joseph Perthius, commissary of the royal prisons in Quebec and member of the Conseil Superieur; Mrs. Hubelie Bisson; and the Mesdames

Jaisson, whose care of her daughter Susanna she highly praised. Yet most French do not fare so well in Johnson's narrative. Indeed, she noted bitterly, "the French, who give lessons of politeness, to the rest of the world, can derive no advantage from the plea of ignorance." She went on to cite French Catholic superstition and its influence on "the common herd" as the "sources [to which] I attribute most of my sufferings."

Her happiness on her reunion with her husband was short-lived. In order to raise money to pay debts incurred during captivity, James Johnson accepted a lieutenancy in the colonial militia and was killed at the Battle of Ticonderoga on 8 July 1758, only days after receiving word that a child born to his wife in March had died. The battle was widely considered a military fiasco. After the competent and celebrated Lord George Augustus Howe had died in a skirmish on 6 July 1758, the strategically inept Gen. James Abercrombie, armed with false information, led a troop of reluctant regulars and untrained provincials against the impressively fortified Ticonderoga. James Johnson was one of several colonials who fell trying to breast an abatis formed from interlaced trees.

Of James Johnson's death, Susanna Johnson remarked, "The cup of sorrow was now replete with bitter drops." She brought all of her bitterness to bear on the one man whom she held representatively responsible for their captivity, subsequent imprisonment in Quebec, and her husband's death: Gov. William Shirley. Johnson targeted Shirley's role in the Louisbourg Expedition of 1745, a battle widely celebrated by contemporary historians and still considered a definitive moment in American military history. Susanna Johnson had a different view of the campaign. Calling the attack on Louisbourg a "Quixotic expedition . . . the success of which originated from the merest accident, rather than from military valor or generalship," she accused Shirley of having "visionary schemes" leading to "impolitic" or "wild" projects. She further noted that the expedition "drained the thinly inhabited state of New-Hampshire of most of its effective men." As a result "the frontiers sustained additional miseries, by having the small forces of the state deducted for purposes which could be of no immediate service to them. The savages committed frequent depredations on the defenceless inhabitants, and the ease with which they gained their prey, encouraged their boldness."

Johnson constructed her revisionist view of the popular military victory from the overlooked perspective of remote frontiers people, specifically women, who were left to "hold down the fort," sometimes literally, while their few men were fighting battles in distant places. As Johnson noted, Indian attacks continued despite the glories and honors gained by Shirley.

Johnson gained some consolation from the return of Sylvanus. In October 1758 she received word that he was "sick of a scald" in Northampton, Massachusetts. When she arrived to recover him, he had no recollection of her and spoke no English. He had entirely assimilated to Abenaki culture.

Susanna Johnson's encounters with the Abenaki were not over. In summer 1760 her brother-in-law, Joseph Willard; his wife; and their five children were captured two miles from Susanna Johnson's home and taken to Montreal. When they returned to New England four months later, they brought with them little Susanna. Of the meeting Johnson wrote movingly, "My daughter did not know me at her return, and spoke nothing but French; my son spoke Indian, so that my family was a mixture of nations." Johnson's comment reflects her sorrow at her children's estrangement from her and a spirit of perseverance that allowed her to make the best of her situation.

The elements of Johnson's physical captivity and her suffering as a direct result of captivity make up only half of her narrative. The rest—a long introduction, a lengthy concluding chapter, and a document appendix—represents Johnson's struggles with captivity of a different nature: legal and social powerlessness.

Referring specifically to her attempts to settle her husband's estate, Johnson noted: "When New-England was ruled by a few men who were the creatures of a king, the pleasures of dissipation were preferred to the more severe attention to business, and the small voice of a woman was seldom heard." Although James Johnson had been wealthy, his captivity, his consequent loss of trade, and his expenses in trying to rebuild a farm and business had left him in debt, and he had died intestate.

As administratrix of her husband's estate, Susanna Johnson struggled for years after James Johnson's death to get out from under the debts incurred during their years in captivity. Among others, she owed Col. Peter Schuyler and John H. Lydius, both of New York, for money they gave the Johnsons to ease the burden of their captivity. Johnson petitioned the New Hampshire House of Representatives for relief on 2 February 1760, citing the circumstances of their captivity and her husband's faithful service in "that unhappy attack under Gen. Abercromby" in her favor. She also notes, "That your Petitionr Considering that the Deceasd was a Person very Serviceable to his

Country in General & Died in Defence of it was encouragd by sundry Gentlemen of Note to Petition the General Court in the Province of the Massachusetts to Grant her some Relief under her Desolate & Oppressing Circumstances But they Refused because the Deceased was an Inhabitant of this Province." She had already petitioned Massachusetts for help on 12 January 1759 and been denied six days later. In March of the same year the Massachusetts House of Representatives allowed her the wages that had been owed James Johnson before his death, with the stipulation that said wages be considered in any action taken concerning the disposal of the estate. New Hampshire granted her the sum of £41. On 8 September 1761, more than three years after James Johnson's death at Ticonderoga, the New Hampshire Court of the Probate and Wills handed down a decision favoring James Johnson's creditors and ordering Susanna Johnson to sell what household goods and real estate necessary to pay the debts they had incurred. Ironically, she retained the log home in which she was captured. In all she had made twenty trips to Portsmouth, Boston, and Springfield, Massachusetts, to settle the estate.

In the midst of this legal nightmare Susanna Johnson had finally come into her share of Moses Willard's estate, left to her on his death in 1756 while she was in captivity. At the time of his death her mother had been evicted from the Province house to which Willard had been entitled as an original grantee. She had built a house outside the fort, and Johnson and children were sharing this house with her mother and running a store with her younger brother, Moses Willard Jr., in order to support the family.

Throughout the settling of James Johnson's estate, one name appears several times in the probate records concerning estate assessment: John Hastings Jr. In 1762 Susanna Johnson married Hastings, who was also an original inhabitant of Charlestown, New Hampshire. His father had been a grantee and the town doctor. Little is known of the junior Hastings, except that in several lawsuits he brought against others in the Inferior Court of Common Pleas, he is identified as a "yeoman." Town records indicate that in 1769 he owned an inn somewhere in Charlestown or its immediate vicinity. He and Susanna Johnson had a total of seven children, five of whom died in infancy. Two daughters survived to adulthood, but only one married: Theodosia wed Stephen Hassam (Johnson spelled it Hasham), a noted New England clockmaker and carpenter who played an important role in Susanna Johnson's life.

The third American edition of her narrative, prepared in 1810 and published posthumously in 1814 by the Universalist pastor Abner Kneeland, corrects and adds details of her later life to the second edition of 1807. Sometime between 1798 and 1801 John Hastings Jr., "with [Susanna's] consent and agreement," gave the Johnson home to Stephen Hassam. Hastings was living out of town, although for what purpose is unclear, and Susanna was living in the Hassam household. In the third edition of her narrative she noted that once Hassam owned her house, "my life and living were so immediately under his controul that my situation was rendered very unhappy. But a respect for the feelings of the surviving relatives will prevent my going into a detail of my sufferings, while under Mr. Hasham's roof; which, considering the different treatment I had a right to expect, under the care and protection of a son-in-law, I sometimes found almost as painful to be borne, as my savage captivity." By overtly connecting physical captivity with social convention, she was pointing out the injustices of the custom that required the elderly to turn over their estates to the eldest child in order to assure themselves care in their old age.

What cruelties Hassam enacted are unclear, but town history records that he was an inveterate "free-thinker" who regularly and spiritedly flaunted his views in public. Among his colorful acts were washing his yellow barouche on the sidewalk on a Sunday, in full view of faithful parishioners of the Methodist Church across the street, and carrying his dead daughter in her coffin on a wheelbarrow to the churchyard, burying her in the family vault without benefit of ceremony.

To Susanna Johnson, a faithful Universalist, Hassam must have been trying at best. Her narrative never refers to her daughter's presence in the household. She complained of her son-in-law's behavior, as though Theodosia did not exist (which legally she did not). The bitterest pill for Johnson was her powerlessness, that she had no choice but to live under almost unbearable conditions, despite the fact that she was in civilized and not "savage" company. Social convention prevented her from voicing her exact complaints about Hassam's treatment.

In 1803 Captive Johnson, now Elizabeth "Captive" Kimball, returned to New England with her husband and a daughter from where they had been living in Lower Canada. On hearing Susanna Johnson's story, they took her in. When they returned to Ontario, Johnson moved in with another daughter and son-in-law, Susanna and Samuel Wetherbee. In 1804 John Hastings Jr. died, and the following year Susanna Johnson returned to Charlestown with Wetherbee and "concluded a settlement with Mr. Hasham, in which I received the rents of certain pieces of land yearly, to continue during my natural life, which is sufficient to support me comfortably, and I can expend it where I please." There is some pleasure in Johnson's tone, though there is irony in her settling to receive money from an estate that was once hers. She lived with a niece and traveled, spending time with other relatives until she died on 27 November 1810. At the time of her death she had thirty-nine grandchildren and four great-grandchildren.

In her narrative the majority of Johnson's criticism is aimed at the "creatures of a king," the colonial governor who detained her husband and caused him imprisonment in Quebec and Boston and the royally appointed judges who took so long to settle her husband's estate. Yet she also criticized the Massachusetts House of Representatives, a locally elected group of men responsible for overseeing the affairs of colonial Americans. Much of Johnson's critical view of government was added to the second, 1807 American edition of her narrative. Just as she extended Puritan typology to justify and authorize her history of New England, Johnson was drawing an implicit connection between British colonial government and the new republican government still being shaped in 1807, implying that not much had changed for women from pre-revolutionary America, when "the small voice of a woman was seldom heard," to new republican America, where a woman still had to take on the identity of her husband upon marriage, had no voice in the government, and could be forced in her old age to live at the mercy of a cruel son-in-law who gained her estate by custom alone.

Yet Susanna Johnson did not write her narrative merely to complain of patriarchal government and its injustices to women. Carefully appropriating traditionally male forms and subverting their meaning, she rewrote history not only to highlight legal and social injustices but also to offer a solution to the imbalance of power between government and its female constituents. She cited the act of storytelling itself as empowering: "Twice has my country been ravaged by war, since my remembrance; I have detailed the share I bore in the first. . . . The savages are driven beyond the lakes, and our country has no enemies." Johnson celebrated the "thrifty farms" grown from "gloomy wilderness," the peaceful Sundays that no longer have to be spent "guarding a fort," and the "sickle and plough-share" replacing "tomahawk and scalping knife." She

ended her narrative by noting, "My numerous progeny often gather round me, to hear the sufferings once felt by their aunt or grandmother, and wonder at their magnitude." Here she painted a picture of a new America, employing biblical imagery to recount the changes she had witnessed as the nation grew from infancy to its more prosperous youth. In sharing her story of the birth of the American nation with her "progeny," Johnson passed on to them the authority vested in her experiences, embodying in her self and in her survival the seeds of new generations of Americans.

Susanna Johnson asserted that the growth of America from ravaged colonies to prosperous nation was in part a direct result of her participation in frontier history and her procreation of Americans to people the country. The path to further glory, she implied, came in raising more children, especially females, to be like her, self-authorizing and proliferative. Thus she offered a final commandment, which came from her mother and which she passed down to her female children: "Arise daughter, and go to thy daughter, for thy daughter's daughter has got a daughter."

Little evidence survives about the public and critical reception of Johnson's narrative. In the fourteen years between its first publication in America and Susanna Johnson's death, two American editions and at least four British editions were published. The Reverend Abner Kneeland expurgated some of Johnson's references to bureaucratic ineptitude from the third American edition. Throughout the nineteenth century Johnson's narrative was frequently anthologized, showing up in local-history collections and anthologies of captivity narratives. Though abridged and often expurgated, Johnson's factual, unsensational, and nonsentimental captivity narrative survived in one form or another into the twentieth century. In fact, in many nineteenth- and early-twentieth-century histories of New Hampshire, one can find Susanna Johnson's own unattributed words offered as a historically accurate account of frontier New England.

References:

Martha McDonalds Frizzell, *Second History of Charlestown, New Hampshire, the Old Fort Number Four* (Littleton, N.H.: Courier Printing, 1955);

Henry H. Saunderson, *History of Charlestown, New Hampshire, No. 4 Embracing the Part Borne by its Inhabitants in the Indian, French and Revolutionary Wars . . . Also Genealogies and Sketches of Families from its Settlement to 1876* (Claremont, N.H., 1876).

Mary Lewis Kinnan

(22 August 1763 – 12 March 1848)

Lisa M. Logan
University of Central Florida

BOOK: *A True Narrative of the Sufferings of Mary Kinnan, Who Was Taken Prisoner by the Shawanee Nation of Indians on the Thirteenth Day of May, 1791, and Remained with them till the Sixteenth of August, 1794* (Elizabethtown, N.J.: Printed by Shepard Kollock, 1795).

A captive of the Shawnee and Delaware from 1791 to 1794, Mary Lewis Kinnan escaped and told her story to New Jersey printer Shepard Kollock, who added embellishments and published the fifteen-page account as *A True Narrative of the Sufferings of Mary Kinnan* (1795). Widely read by a public hungry for sensational stories about Native American warfare on Western settlers, the pamphlet represents a curious mix of Kinnan's and Kollock's voices and the melding of providential narrative, sentimental fiction, and political propaganda that is characteristic of popular fiction and the captivity genre during the late eighteenth century.

Kinnan was the second child and eldest daughter of Zephaniah Lewis and Ann Doty Lewis of Basking Ridge, New Jersey. Little is known about Mary Lewis's early life. On 8 January 1778, at age fifteen, she married Joseph Kinnan, a sergeant in the New Jersey Regiments during the Revolutionary War. In 1787 the couple and their two children, Lewis and Joseph Jr., were part of a group that left New Jersey to settle in what is now Tygart's Valley, Randolph County, West Virginia.

The Kinnans lived in a two-room log house with their two sons and their daughter, Mary, born in western Virginia, as well as Jacob Lewis, Mary Kinnan's brother; Mary Ward, a widow, and her three children; and a young man named Canley or Ralston. In 1791 the British-backed Shawnee Indians, responding to increased white Westward expansion, began attacking settlements along the Ohio River and ranging into Pennsylvania, Kentucky, and Virginia. On 13 May 1791, a little after dark, two Shawnee surprised the Kinnan household, killing Joseph, young Mary, and Mary Ward's daugh-

ter; the rest of the household escaped from the house, but Mary Lewis Kinnan, whose flight was hampered by her attempts to rescue her daughter, was taken captive. She and her captors traveled northwest into Ohio, finally reaching the Shawnee towns in late July, when she was made a slave to her captor's wife and then sold to a Delaware woman. The following spring she managed to slip a letter addressed to her New Jersey relatives to a trader, who took her message to Detroit, where it was recopied and sent east in late July. In what might be termed a bizarre stroke of bad luck, the messenger carrying Kinnan's plea died of yellow fever in Philadelphia, and the letter, along with his personal effects, was buried until danger of infection passed. When the letter was exhumed, it was sent on its way and finally read before the Presbyterian congregation in Basking Ridge.

With funds from friends and neighbors, Jacob Lewis traveled for three months to Detroit, and five months later, in August 1794, he finally helped his sister escape. In late October the siblings returned to New Jersey, where Kinnan lived her last fifty-four years with relatives.

From the testimony of Susan Lewis Anderson, Kinnan's grand-niece, and from evidence from the narrative itself, Oscar M. Voorhees observes that Kollock "used his own gifted talents for much of the language, including, of course, the poetical quotations" in the narrative, but that he based the story "wholly on what Mrs. Kinnan herself told him." Such collaboration explains the use of literary allusions and sentiment in the work of a woman who was probably not well read.

After a brief three-sentence introduction that situates Kinnan's experience in sentimental and providential traditions, the narrative shifts to a first-person account that traces her capture, travels, ill treatment, and escape. About half of the fifteen pages concerns Kinnan's capture, forced march, and physical and emotional hardships among her captors. The remainder of the narrative describes her

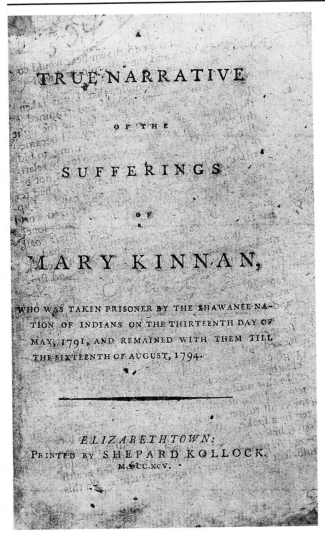

Title page for Mary Lewis Kinnan's captivity narrative, which taught her "to place my dependence on the beneficent dispenser of good and evil" (courtesy of The Newberry Library, Chicago)

escape plans in the context of the Western wars between the United States Army and the Native American nations of Ohio and Michigan (1790–1794) and her animosity toward the British for their interference in these wars and therefore in her escape. While it is impossible to distinguish Kollock's ideas from Kinnan's, the aim of the text is clear: captivity becomes a site for examining the importance of domesticity and white womanhood to the new, expanding republic.

A True Narrative of the Sufferings of Mary Kinnan evinces an ambivalence about domesticity that might be best understood in the context of Kinnan's experiences during and after her captivity. The narrative opens with an idyllic first-person description of domestic life in the western Virginia wilderness. Kinnan is "blest with the affections of the best of

husbands, and the love and esteem of the most dutiful of children." The words "affections," "love and esteem," and "dutiful" suggest the ideal republican marriage, an egalitarian union of virtuous citizens crucial to the survival of the new nation. This "exalted happiness," however, is countered in the following paragraph by the Shawnee attack and its scenes of domestic horror. Kinnan observed that her husband, "scalped and weltering in his blood, fixed on me his dying eye, which, though languid, still expressed an apprehension for my safety." Her youngest child was likewise "scalped and slaughtered." Thus stripped of her role of wife and mother, Kinnan entered captivity and the wilderness, an experience that challenged the assumptions of her former domestic life.

As Kinnan began her recollections of captivity, she emphasized her feminine weakness: "my bosom heaves impetuous; the cold sweat of fear stands on my brow; and the burning tear glistens in my eye." Kinnan's actions during and after captivity, however, suggest a strong, assertive resourcefulness uncharacteristic of the sentimental heroine the narrative sometimes portrays. For example, at the time of the attack Kinnan tried to rescue her child and broke away from her captors three times before making "signs of submission." Her flight, rescue attempt, and decision to acquiesce are not the acts of a passive woman. Further, the reader learns that her "soul acquires . . . vigor" and that she exerts "faculties, which till then were not possessed, or at least lay dormant." The wounded Kinnan, faint through loss of blood, rest, and refreshment, marches "over the most rugged rocks and mountains, wet and slippery with rain." She was "beaten severely," and when she arrived at the Shawnee towns, she was forced to run the gauntlet while "each person then struck me with great violence over the head and face, till I could not see." In addition to these and other regular abuses, her captors tormented her with the trimmed and cured scalps of her husband and child and later those of U.S. soldiers.

The text uses three narrative techniques to compensate for its subject's removal from the domestic sphere and assertion of unfeminine traits: it allies unwomanliness with Kinnan's captors, who are depicted as savage and uncivilized; it characterizes her unseemly thoughts and acts as providential; and it presents her plight in the larger context of British attacks on the new nation.

Daily life among her captors—as with the Shawnee attack itself—challenges the domestic values of Kinnan's former life. The narrative observes the "humiliating condition" of Native American women, who, "instead of polishing and improving the rough manners of the men, are equally ferocious, cruel, and obdurate." The "convulsive groans" of a tortured captive are described as "music to their souls." The behavior of Shawnee women shocked Kinnan, who–the reader is led to assume– possessed "that benevolent disposition and warm sensibility to the sufferings of others, which marks their [women's] characters in more civilized climes." These passages reflect the republican notion of womanhood and women's moral influence over their husbands and children, citizens of the new nation, asserting that civilized women are by nature of a "benevolent disposition and warm sensibility." Since Native American women were apparently unfeminine and equal to their husbands in "rough manners" and since such dispositions seemed to arise from the culture or "clime" in which they lived, the passage seems to ask whether women can continue to be feminine in the wilderness. Moreover, it asks if the captive Kinnan, who was asked to perform according to the dictates of these less "civilized" women, was womanly. As a slave, she endured the "degradation" of "the most menial and laborious offices." She chopped and carried wood, endured physical abuse, and was "fed in a very scanty manner." While her survival depended on her obedience to a "ferocious, cruel, and obdurate" standard of womanhood, the narrative emphasizes that her feet were frozen and that she caught and nearly died of fever. In this way the text illustrates Kinnan's resistance to Native American or "savage" models of femininity, women who "quaff with extatic pleasure the blood of the innocent prisoner, writhing with agony under the inhuman torments inflicted upon him."

While instances of feminine sensibility in the way Kinnan's story is narrated would seem to restore Kinnan's displaced domesticity, events in the text and Kinnan's later life counter such restoration. As Sharon M. Harris notes, the work lacks the restoration scene typical of the captivity genre. Instead the narrative breaks off after reporting, "We descended in a batteau to the Genessee river, and thence traveled to New Jersey, where I arrived amongst my friends on the eleventh day of October, 1794." The narrative then concludes with a paragraph about the usefulness of her story. The absence of a restoration scene is consistent with Kinnan's later life. After returning to New Jersey she lived among relatives and never remarried or returned to the grave sites of her husband and daughter. Essentially, Kinnan never was restored, and her life after captivity is a kind of testimony to the limited possibilities for women who chose or were forced by circumstance to remain unmarried

and as a result were marginalized from traditional domestic roles. Known as Aunt Polly, Kinnan depended on friends and relatives for the remainder of her life. At seventy-five–destitute, feeble, and living with her unmarried son, Joseph Jr., who had been tomahawked in the raid at Tygart's Valley but had survived–she was granted a pension from the U.S. government on the basis of her husband's service in the Revolutionary War.

The narrative also counters Kinnan's marginalization from domesticity through an insistence on the usefulness of her story, which is placed, like earlier Puritan narratives, in a providential framework. A third-person narrator introduces her text: "It will display the supporting arm of a Divine Providence: it will point to the best and surest support under danger and adversity: and 'it will teach the repiner at little evils to be juster to his God and to himself.'" Kinnan resisted suicide, endured depression, and escaped death through the "spirit of Christianity," "a fervent prayer to Heaven," and "the good providence of God." These assurances and the pious one-sentence conclusion anticipate a moral reminiscent of Mary Rowlandson's captivity narrative, *The Sovereignty & Goodness of God* (1682). Kinnan stated, "I have been led to place my dependence on the beneficent dispenser of good and evil, and to withdraw my affections from that world, where the ties by which mankind are in general so firmly bound are indissolubly broken." Kinnan urged her readers "who are pierced by the darts of misfortune" to "imitate my example" and "recline on the bosom of your Father and your God." This conclusion displaces Kinnan's survival, self-sufficiency, and strength to a patriarchal God and shifts her narrative status as subject to that of object. These displacements return her to a domestic paradigm and the role of modest, virtuous, and passive woman.

Finally, *A True Narrative of the Sufferings of Mary Kinnan* situates Kinnan's loss of domesticity in anti-British sentiment and the Western wars of 1790–1794. Writing in his *Held Captive by Indians* (1973), Richard VanDerBeets has pointed out that captivity narratives written during the late eighteenth century were vehicles for condemning British aggression against the new nation. Citing the Declaration of Independence, which asserted the British aim to "bring on the inhabitants of our frontiers the merciless Indian savages," VanDerBeets notes that captivity narratives of this period used sentiment and sensation to promote patriotism and sales. Kinnan's narrative places the responsibility for the suffering of its innocent subject on the British army, at whose orders "the Indian murderer plunges his knife into the bosom of innocence, of piety, and of virtue; and drags thousands into captivity, worse than death. The cries of widows, and the groans of orphans daily ascend, like a thick cloud, before the judgment-seat of heaven. . . ." This passage emphasizes the sundering of family life that renders wives widows and children orphans and ravages the domestic innocence, piety, and virtue at the center of the new republic. Kinnan and her shattered household become metaphors for the new nation and its agrarian and domestic vision that covers over U.S. aggression onto Native American lands.

Much of Kinnan's narrative directly concerns the ways that British efforts on the part of her captors lengthened her captivity and made it more difficult. Her progress toward escape is presented in the context of key events in the western wars, including Gen. Arthur St. Clair's defeat by the Miamis and Wyandots in November 1791; the failure of President George Washington's peace deputation in May 1793; Gen. Anthony Wayne's attempts to force the Western Indian confederacy to acknowledge U.S. sovereignty in November 1793; and Wayne's victory at the Battle of Fallen Timbers in August 1794. The narrative reports instances of British interference in U.S. interests, including supplying provisions to Native Americans and sending agents to advise them against negotiation. Kinnan's escape occurred at the time of Wayne's victory at Fort Miami, when the British withdrew their support; and her journey home continued to be complicated and delayed by the British, who occupied forts along the Great Lakes. In all these senses Kinnan's account casts her experience in a larger, patriotic narrative of a new and innocent nation under attack by savage and ill-motivated "foreigners." The loss of home and Kinnan's rough and unwarranted treatment figures forth the danger these "non-Americans" pose to the survival and growth of virtuous U.S. citizens.

Popular during her lifetime, Kinnan's narrative was republished in 1801 by William W. Morse of New Haven. The narrative then seems to have disappeared, however, until 1926, when a copy was discovered in the Newberry Library of Chicago and republished in the *Magazine of History-Biography* of the Randolph County, West Virginia, Historical Society. In the 1970s scholars began to reconsider the importance of the captivity narrative to U.S. literary history, and Kinnan's text has been republished and has received the attention of critics interested in popular fiction and women's writing. The text is usually viewed as an example of the captivity narrative as propaganda in the late eighteenth century, of the links between captivity plots and sentimental fiction, and of the importance of captivity narratives to U.S. women's literary history and expressions of female subjectivity.

References:

Christopher Castiglia, *Bound and Determined: Captivity, Culture-Crossing, and White Womanhood from Mary Rowlandson to Patty Hearst* (Chicago: University of Chicago Press, 1996);

Kathryn Zabelle Derounian-Stodola and James Arthur Levernier, *The Indian Captivity Narrative, 1550–1900* (New York: Twayne, 1993);

Sharon M. Harris, ed., *American Women Writers to 1800* (New York: Oxford University Press, 1996), pp. 227–228;

Jan Lewis, "The Republican Wife: Virtue and Seduction in the Early Republic," *William and Mary Quarterly,* 44 (1987): 689–719;

Boyd B. Stutler, *The Kinnan Massacre, Including the True Narrative of the Sufferings of Mary Kinnan* (Parsons, W.Va.: McClain Printing, 1969);

Richard VanDerBeets, ed., *Held Captive by Indians: Selected Narratives, 1642–1836* (Knoxville: University of Tennessee Press, 1973);

VanDerBeets, *The Indian Captivity Narrative: An American Genre* (Lanham, Md.: University Press of America, 1984);

Oscar M. Voorhees, "A New Jersey Woman's Captivity Among the Indians," *New Jersey Historical Society Proceedings,* 13 (April 1928): 152–165;

Voorhees, "The Pension Secured for 'Aunt Polly' Kinnan," *Somerset County Historical Quarterly,* 5 (April 1916): 106–108.

Sarah Kemble Knight

(19 April 1666 – 25 September 1727)

Deborah Dietrich
California State University, Fullerton

See also the Knight entry in *DLB 24: American Colonial Writers, 1606–1734.*

BOOK: *The Journals of Madam Knight, and Rev. Mr. Buckingham. From the Original Manuscripts Written in 1704 & 1710,* by Knight and Thomas Buckingham, edited by Theodore Dwight Jr. (New York: Wilder & Campbell, 1825).

Editions: "The Journal of Sarah Kemble Knight," edited by Sargent Bush Jr., in *Journeys in New Worlds: Early American Women's Narratives,* general editor William L. Andrews (Madison: University of Wisconsin Press, 1990);

"The Journal of Sarah Kemble Knight," in *Colonial American Travel Narratives,* edited by Wendy Martin (New York: Penguin, 1994).

Sarah Kemble Knight's published journal recounts the trip she made from her Moon Street home in Boston to New Haven and New York City and back between 2 October 1704 and 3 March 1705. Her five-month, two-hundred-mile journey, undertaken to settle her cousin Caleb Trowbridge's estate on behalf of his widow, enabled her to negotiate cultural restrictions on women's freedom and identity. At the time of Knight's journey the road, though increasingly well traveled, was still treacherous and might have tested the hardiest of horsemen. The thirty-eight-year-old Knight, however, viewed her situation with humor, and despite her occasional expressions of fear and helplessness, her bravery and sense of adventure contradict the stereotype of the passive and delicate woman who was forced to abandon her home and friends by a husband blind with wanderlust. Leaving her husband and daughter in Boston, she was neither passive nor fearful. She was physically, emotionally, and financially independent. The vitality and enthusiasm with which she met any experience make her

descriptions of each inn, each river crossing, and each town along the way distinct and memorable.

Written in 1704–1705, the manuscript was published by Theodore Dwight Jr. in 1825 in *The Journals of Madam Knight, and Rev. Mr. Buckingham. From the Original Manuscripts Written in 1704 & 1710.* Knight's journal was printed from the original manuscript, which was complete except for the bottom half of the first sheet, which was torn away, causing two breaks in the narrative. Soon after Dwight published his edition, the original manuscript was lost, raising doubts concerning the authenticity of the narrative. Some of the skepticism regarding the authorship might have been triggered by the misogynism of the male-dominated literary establishment of the 1820s and by reviewers' disbelief that a woman could write such a witty narrative. There have been several editions of Knight's journal since Dwight's, but his remains the authoritative text. Dwight wrote in his introduction that his edition "is a faithful copy from a diary in the author's own handwriting, compiled soon after her return home, as it appears, from notes recorded daily, while on the road." For Dwight the value of early American travel narratives in general and Knight's journal in particular lay in the information they provided about America, from which the reader could gauge and evaluate the material and moral progress of the nation since Knight's day.

Dwight was correct. Knight's travel account is remarkable for the vantage point it offers readers for observing continuity and change in colonial America. From William Bradford's *Of Plimmoth Plantation,* written in 1630–1650, to the *Itinerarium* written in 1744 by Alexander Hamilton of Annapolis, the modern reader can see intolerance giving way to moderate lenience, the emergence of the individual from the confines of the community, and a shift from the seventeenth-century emphasis on God's plan to an eighteenth-century emphasis on reason. The image of the land itself evolves from a vast and howling wilderness to a very wild and romantic place. The increasing sophistication and the prosperity of the cities deepen the contrast with the areas in the backwoods. Sarah Kemble Knight's narrative, standing almost midpoint between the Pilgrims' emigration in 1620 and the outbreak of the Revolutionary War in 1775, is a crucial document of these changing conditions in early America. No other account quite like her journal survives. Dwight's timing of the publication was a response to the general inclination of many American writers of his time to produce an American literature that was firmly grounded in an American landscape and culture. He recognized that her journal would be a contribution to a growing body of texts that were truly native.

Sarah Kemble was born in Boston, Massachusetts, on 19 April 1666. She was the first daughter of Thomas Kemble, a merchant and reportedly an agent of Oliver Cromwell in selling prisoners of war, and Elizabeth Terice Kemble of Charlestown, Massachusetts. A document dated 17 April 1688 and signed by Knight's father and her future husband, Richard Knight, stating Knight's intention to marry the "Spinster Daughter" of Thomas Kemble is in the Boston Public Library. Her marriage to Captain Knight, a shipmaster and London agent for an American company, occurred shortly after that date. Their only child, Elizabeth, was born on 8 May 1689. While her husband was abroad, Sarah Knight was the head of the household. She supplemented the family income by a variety of employments: she taught handwriting, ran a boardinghouse, worked as a court scrivener, kept a shop on Moon Street, and taught school, which, it has been reported, might have been attended by Benjamin Franklin and Samuel Mather. Knight became a widow in 1706. In 1712 she moved to Connecticut, where she kept a shop and an inn and engaged in Indian trading and farming. Public records indicate that she gave a silver cup to the church of Norwich, Connecticut, and in 1717 she was given permission to sit in a designated pew in the church meetinghouse in Norwich. Records show that although she paid a twenty-shilling fine for selling liquor to the Indians, she complained that a misguided servant was the one at fault. At her death she left a formidable estate of £1,800, further evidence of her skill as a shrewd businesswoman.

As a businesswoman Knight was confident of her middle-class status, and in her journal she took special care in noting the courtesy and hospitality she was shown by people of ranks higher than her own. For example, as a result of Gov. Fitz-John Winthrop's attentions, she stayed

a day longer in New London than she had initially intended. The next morning, when she crossed the ferry to Groton, she was careful to detail that she "had the Honor of the Company, of Madam Livingston (who is the Govenors Daughter) and Mary Christophers and divers others to the boat." It is interesting to note that eight years later and after Mary Livingston's death, widower John Livingston married Sarah Kemble Knight's daughter, leaving his two sisters appalled that their brother had stooped beneath their family's social status in his choice of a wife.

Knight's journey was a business trip, not a divine enterprise. As such it is representative of the shift in the New England character as well as the changing attitude toward New World travel. Knight sought to capture the distinctive flavor of the emerging cosmopolitan and backwoods regions in America. Knight's cultural narrowness at the beginning of the journal changes over the course of her narrative. At the start her descriptions of the frontier inns and taverns and the customs of the people she met along the way are filtered through her civilized Boston vantage point. She frequently complained about the accommodations she found along the road. For example, although the chocolate was prepared in a "little clean brass Kettle" at Mr. Havens's, when she went to bed she was unable to sleep because "of the Clamor of some of the Town tope-ers in next Room. . . ." On 4 October 1704 she set out for Kingston, but the road was poorly furnished with lodging for travelers, and, she wrote, "we were forced to ride 22 miles by the post's account, but neer thirty by mine, before wee could bait so much as our Horses, wch I exceedingly complained of." She arrived in Rye, New York, on 7 December and found lodging at an "ordinary" kept by a French family. The fricassee she was served being contrary to her "notion of Cookery," she went to bed supperless. Though exhausted, she could not sleep: the covers were too scanty, and the bed was noisy from the rustling of the corn husks in the mattress. These descriptions of frontier lodgings and taverns provide a rare glimpse of the cramped quarters and lack of privacy awaiting early- eighteenth-century travelers. The details also contribute to the portrait of Knight herself. As a civilized Bostonian her sense of propriety frequently was offended by her uncomfortable and often filthy surroundings.

Knight often commented on the customs of the people she met along the way. She was indignant when she learned that some blacks in Connecticut were allowed to eat with their masters. She disdainfully remarked on the rudeness of the backwoodsmen. If she did not like something, she referred to it as "Indian." When the food was not up to her standards, for example, she called it "Indian-fare." She called one poor backwoodsman an "Indian-like Animal." Usually, however, she looked tolerantly on customs that differed from her own: for example, the unusual wedding customs in Connecticut or the marriage and divorce practices of the Indians. While her portraits of backwoods men and women are unsympathetic, Knight's humor allows her to critique their morals and manners without appearing overly insensitive.

For Knight, New York City was the antithesis of backwoods America. It was "pleasant, well compacted," and situated on a "commodious river." She liked the buildings and noted that the "hearths were laid with the finest tile that I ever see." She described an auction and expressed her delight at her acquisition of one hundred reams of paper from Holland, purchased "very Reasonably" and at the opportunity to make the acquaintance of many women who "curteosly invited" Knight to their houses. Although she observed that the auctions made good money because the customers drank so liberally that they "pay for't as well, by paying for that which they Bidd up Briskly," Knight felt she was treated fairly.

In contrast to New York, Connecticut was for Knight a combination of backwoods wretchedness and New York civility. The man "wth his alfogeos full of Tobacco" is a symbol of the Connecticut position. He spat and scraped his shovel-like shoe. Finally, "hugging his pretty Body with his hands under his arms," he stood and stared "like a Catt lett out of a Baskett." Ill-bred and yet mannerly, he asked if the merchant had any ribbons for hatbands.

The journey changes the traveler. It challenges old beliefs by uncovering facts previously unknown. For earlier American travelers such as William Bradford, new experiences were valued to the extent that they supported old truths. As travel writing developed, the traveler increasingly incorporated new knowledge into new ways of thinking. Knight's travels took her beyond her controlling Bostonian point of view. During the first two-thirds of her trip almost everything she saw fell short in its comparison to Boston, but by the time she arrived in New Rochelle the case was changed. She described the town as a "very pretty place well compact, and good handsome houses, Clean, good and passable Rodes, and situated on a Navigable River, abundance of land well fined

and Cleerd all along as wee passed, which caused in me a Love to the place, wch I could have been content to live in it." This description marks a fundamental change in the narrator. Instead of viewing New Rochelle against her Bostonian yardstick, she altered her way of thinking to the extent that she was able to relocate a vision of home and herself. Her experiences on the road gave her fresh insight, weaning her away from her Boston measure.

As the early American travel narrative evolved, humor began to play a more significant role. Seventeenth-century immigrants were busy establishing themselves in a wilderness. Only after they felt comfortable in their new surroundings could they view their situation lightheartedly. With Knight's journal the reader sees the beginning of the American comic imagination and certainly one of the earliest examples of American humor by a woman. No longer overwhelmed by the New World landscape or under pressure to instruct, explain, self-examine, or justify, travel narrators such as Knight could use humor for the sole purpose of entertainment. Knight's spontaneous reactions to New England bumpkins (the ancestor of the archetypal Yankee), cantankerous innkeepers, and dull-witted country wenches are cleverly drawn. Lightly mocking the backward rustics and Indians, she satirized life in the wilderness. At times her descriptions of her adventures are reminiscent of Ebenezer Cook's *Sot-Weed Factor* (1708), a satirical narrative of Maryland. Like Cook, Knight used satire to record social contrast. Her humor not only provided a way for her to reach out to her readers, but it softened her satire. As a middle-class Bostonian observer, she might easily have approached the backwoods men and women with a critical eye. Instead Knight used humor to portray the range of behaviors she observed. Her comic portrayals anticipated the increasing emphasis on the delight that later travelers took in drawing character sketches of unsavory, lower-class types. As in Knight's journal, the humor in William Byrd II's *Secret History of the Line* (written in 1728) and Hamilton's *Itinerarium* is at its best when the authors described the characteristics and the dialects of the strange people they encountered during their travels. Byrd and Hamilton were also similar to Knight in their confidence of their place in society, and they recorded comments about those of lower status with an amused air.

Frequently the vernacular itself provided Knight's humor. One such example is her retelling

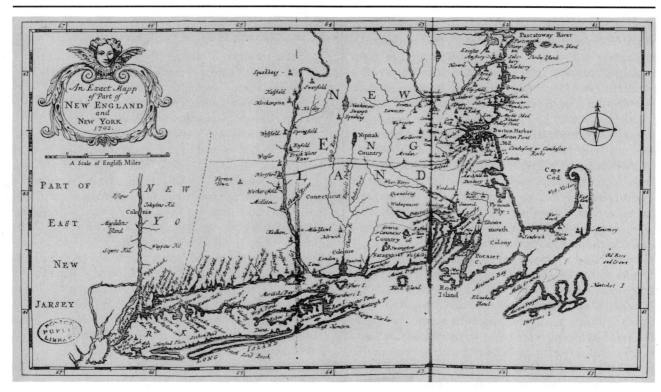

Map of Sarah Kemble Knight's 1704–1705 journey from Boston to New York City and back (from The Journal of Madame Knight, *1920)*

of a story she heard about a pair of justices: "You Indian why did You steal from this man? You sho'dn't do so—it's a Grandy wicked thing to steal. Hol't Hol't cryes Justice Junr. Brother, You speak negro to him. I'le ask him. You sirrah, why did You steal this man's Hoggshead?" Often she used comic colloquialisms and humorous metaphors. For example, at Billings's Inn a pretentious innkeeper's daughter ran upstairs, put on two or three rings, returned, and placed herself before Knight. According to Knight, the girl was "showing the way to Reding, that I might see her Ornaments, perhaps to gain the more respect. But her Granam's new Rung sow, had it appeared, would [have] affected me as much." At the second stage of the Post she was served a "sause of a deep Purple, wch I tho't was boil'd in her dye Kettle . . . but my stomach soon cloy'd, and what cabbage I swallowed serv'd me for a Cudd the whole day after." At Western Post she was unsuccessful in her attempt to find a guide because the tavern guests were "tyed by the Lipps to a pewter engine." Even Knight's self portrait is humorous. She frequently portrayed herself as less than competent as she made her way along hazardous roads and across swollen rivers. In describing her matronly figure she noted that the stairs to her sleeping chamber in Rye, New York,

had "such a narrow passage that I was almost stopt by the Bulk of my Body." On another occasion she described herself sitting up in bed and composing a poem relating her resentment of the "Town tope-ers" in the next room. Even when she imagined herself falling into one of the dangerous rivers, she was able to view herself with a humorous eye. She described herself as emerging from the waters "like a holy Sister Just come out of a Spiritual Bath in dripping garments."

The connection of Knight's journal with folk and mock-epic traditions places it close to popular colonial forms, especially Indian captivity narratives. For example, captivity narratives and Knight's journal share a similar structure: removal, testing, and reconciliation. A comparison with a contemporaneous Puritan writer, Mary Rowlandson, illustrates this connection. Rowlandson was abducted by the Narragansett Indians in 1675 and forced to travel more than 150 miles. She marked her descent into the wilderness in "removes," spatial and spiritual moments away from Puritan light into Satan's darkness. The nadir of her captivity was "twenty removes" away from civilization. Her physical removal typologically signifies her spiritual testing. Figuratively she fell from grace and was in a type of metaphysical hell. Her eventual ransom and ascent to the Puritan fold was a restoration of her old life but with newly opened eyes. Like Rowlandson, Knight left her familiar surroundings to journey into the woods. Her "removes" are marked by the various rustic stages in which she found lodging at night, and they are climaxed by her stop at Mr. Devills's "habitation of cruelty." As Puritan captives such as Mary Rowlandson quoted scripture and called on God their protector in moments of need during their wilderness ordeals, so Knight broke into verse, and mocking the Puritan travel-narrative tradition, she paid homage instead to "Fair Cynthia," the pagan goddess of the moon, and later identified with Hecate of the underworld. Rowlandson and Knight both crossed many treacherous rivers, but instead of reconciling herself to the ordeal and praising God for keeping her feet dry, Knight simply shared her sense of entrapment in the canoe. Her single most absorbing consideration was always to keep the raft afloat. As Mary Rowlandson finally met Metacomet, better known as King Philip and the mastermind behind the war to which his name was given, so Knight encountered a backwoods counterpart: "an Indian-like animal . . . who fumbles out his black junk, dips it in the ashes, and . . . fell to sucking like a calf, without speaking, for near a quarter of an hour."

Like Rowlandson, Knight illustrated the dual sensibilities of William Bradford. At times she is like the disengaged narrator in book one of Bradford's narrative. Her apostrophe to the pagan goddess Cynthia and her description of the "Glorious Luminary" are examples of her attempts to remove herself from the midst of the journey itself and back into a literary and disengaged position. Her literary disengagement allowed her to control the uncomfortable and forbidding environment. At other times, however, she was like the engaged and vulnerable protagonist of Bradford's book two. From the first sentence of Knight's journal the narrator plunges into the action of her trip: "About three o'clock afternoon, I begun my Journey from Boston to New-Haven; being about two Hundred Mile." Never removed from the action for long, Knight is at her best when she places herself in the thick of things and describes her situation with a vividness that earlier retrospective narratives usually lack. Her invigorating word choice accents the hurried movement and sense of the unexpected circumstances of early New England travel.

Even as members of tightly knit communities, seventeenth-century Puritan travelers understood that the journey to salvation was made alone with God as their guide. Knight's dependence on her secular wilderness chaperon anticipates the search by later writers for companions for themselves or their protagonists. William Byrd's Ned Bearskin, Rip Van Winkle's escort to the wilderness amphitheater, Natty Bumppo's Chingachgook, Goodman Brown's Black Man, and Ahab's Fedallah are all fellow travelers whose comradeship in more civilized circumstances would be unthinkable. These guides provide the wilderness expertise that enables the naive traveler to penetrate successfully beyond known boundaries. Unfamiliar with the landscape, Knight was completely dependent on the local guides or the "Posts," the mail carriers who traveled between the colonial settlements. As she made her descent into the wilderness with her first guide, John, she recalled the heroes in Emmanuel Forde's *The History of Parismus* (1598) and *The Famous History of Montelion, Knight of the Oracle* (earliest surviving edition, 1633), and, she added, "I didn't know but I had mett with a Prince disguis'd." She realized that all the good manners and culture of Boston would not help her in her current situation, and she was dependent on the backwoods' escort she had earlier ridiculed as a "shade on his Hors [who] resembled a Globe on a Gate post."

Knight's journal offers further evidence of her indebtedness to literary figures when it refers to "The Babes in the Wood," an English ballad in which two children are taken out to the woods to be murdered and instead are left by their uncle to die during the night. Her comment that the setting sun, that "Glorious Luminary, with his swift Coursers arrived at his Stage," is a reference to Helios's ride across the sky. The thickness of the trees in the distance filled her imagination "with the pleasent delusion of a Sumptuous citty . . . Grandeurs which I had not heard of, and which the stories of foreign countries had given me the Idea of. . . ." Her literary references and her explicit debt to "stories of foreign countries" remind the reader that she was an educated Bostonian and not to be confused with the rustic men and women she met in the backwoods settlements. Many later travel narratives share her genteel, educated disdain.

Knight is also indebted to the picaresque tradition in popular European fiction. The episodic plot of her journal is held together by the narrator's self-determined personality. Like the picaresque hero, Knight was an outsider whose marginality gave her an independence not usually permitted women. When she was on the road, she capably chose her guides and then bargained with them for a fair price. The oddity of finding a woman traveling alone at night was expressed by one young woman at Billings's Inn. At the sight of Knight on her doorstep, she exclaimed: "I never see a woman on the Rode so Dreadfull late, in all the days of my versall life." Although Knight mentioned the dangers of wilderness travel, she frequently undercut the description of her fears with humor, allowing the difficulties to appear as temporary obstacles and nothing that she would be unable to surmount. Like the picaro, she allowed herself to be an object of amusement. She was the genteel greenhorn who slept in lumpy beds, whose efforts to hire a guide were thwarted because the patrons' lips were stuck to "a pewter engine," who vomited after a meal at an inn and then was able to make a joke of it: "It was down and coming up agen which it did in so plentifull a manner that my host was soon paid double for his portion, and that in specia."

Another characteristic of the picaresque that Knight incorporated in her narrative is her emphasis on the realistic as opposed to the pastoral. Knight's frontier contained wretched poverty, lumpy beds, greedy bumpkins, inedible food, and noisy pub crawlers, and when she was in the wilderness, she emphasized not the natural, but the domestic, whenever possible. She focused on the inns and taverns; she noted how the moonlight altered the trees into "Buildings and churches"; and she ignored the typological significance of the land. Once in New York she became the tourist who delighted in describing the manners and habits of those members of higher ranks of society than her own. She liked the "stately and high" brick buildings "laid in checkers," which, "being glazed, look very agreeable." In contrast, the less-urban Connecticut was a mix of moral rigidity and sloppy manners. Its towns were often flawed. For instance, Stamford was "a well compacted town, but with a miserable meeting house," and in Norwalk the "church and tavern are next neighbors."

As with a typical picaresque hero, Knight's travels expanded her awareness of the social differences between herself and the people she encountered during her five-month journey. When she returned safely home, she was able to entertain her family and friends with her satirical observations, and with Theodore Dwight's publication of her narrative more than one hundred years later, she was able to leave a permanent record of the growing diversity of colonial American society.

Twentieth-century critics disagree on the generic categorization of Knight's journal. Robert O. Stephens has described Knight as an epic heroine, and Peter Thorpe was the first critic to examine the influence of the picaresque on Knight's narrative. Kathryn Zabelle Derounian-Stodola follows Thorpe's argument and concludes that Knight's work is truer to the form than later female picaresques that are restrained by the influences of the eighteenth century. Alan Margolies has provided a thorough examination of the history of the narrative. Recent criticism has centered on Knight's contribution to the American comic tradition, with Robert D. Arner suggesting that Knight's journal represents the direction that later American humorists have taken. Others who have examined her use of humor include Peter Thorpe, Jacqueline Hornstein, and Hollis L. Cate. The most recent fully annotated editions of Knight are the Penguin edition (1994) and Sargent Bush Jr.'s annotated edition in *Journeys in New Worlds* (1990). Observing that Knight's journal resembles a picaresque work by Tobias Smollett, John Seelye has included an excellent discussion of her narrative in his *Prophetic Waters: The River in Early American Life and Literature* (1977). In *The Adventurous Muse: The Poetics of American Fiction, 1789–1900* (1977) William Spengemann examines the tension between Knight's disengaged Bostonian voice and her engaged, experiencing voice. Arguably the best piece of scholarship to date on Knight's journal, Spengemann's discussion describes the influences of early journey narratives on Knight and her contribution to American travel literature.

Knight's journal is not only a charming narrative; it parallels the journey of America into a new age. Whereas many earlier American travel narratives were moral justifications or tales of spiritual triumph, Knight's journal is often lighthearted. She was able to laugh at human folly, enjoy the travel for its own sake, and allow herself to get caught up with the journey to the extent that she was noticeably changed by her experiences on the road. Like her traveling ancestors, she was constantly expecting the unexpected, but unlike them she took pleasure in it when it occurred. Her purpose in writing was in part to describe the transforming effect of the journey and the new person she became as a result of it. Her perceptions and responses are integral with the journey itself. Marking the beginning of the American comic imagination, Knight's journal portrays the country in transition between the old ways and the new and one woman's response to a changing and at times strange and foreboding landscape.

References:

Robert D. Arner, "Wit, Humor and Satire in Seventeenth-Century American Poetry," in *Puritan Poets and Poetics: Seventeenth-Century American Poetry in Theory and Practice,* edited by Peter White (University Park: Pennsylvania State University Press, 1985), pp. 283–284;

Hollis L. Cate, "The Figurative Language of Recall in Sarah Kemble Knight's *Journal,*" *CEA Critic,* 43 (1980): 32–35;

Kathryn Zabelle Derounian-Stodola, "The New England Wilderness Frontier and the Picaresque in Sarah Kemble Knight's Journal," in *Early American Literature and Culture: Essays Honoring Harrison T. Meserole* (Newark: University of Delaware Press, 1992), pp. 122–131;

Jacqueline Hornstein, "Comic Vision in the Literature of New England Women before 1800," *Regionalism and the Female Imagination,* 3 (1977): 11–19;

Alan Margolies, "The Editing and Publication of *The Journal of Madam Knight,*" *PBSA,* 58 (1964): 26–28;

John Seelye, *Prophetic Waters: The River in Early American Life and Literature* (New York: Oxford University Press, 1977);

William Spengemann, *The Adventurous Muse: The Poetics of American Fiction, 1789–1900* (New Haven: Yale University Press, 1977);

Robert O. Stephens, "The Odyssey of Sarah Kemble Knight." *CLA Journal,* 7 (1964): 247–255;

Peter Thorpe, "Sarah Kemble Knight and the Picaresque Tradition," *CLA Journal,* 10 (1966): 114–121;

Faye Vowell, "A Commentary on *The Journal of Sarah Kemble Knight,*" *Emporia State Research Studies,* 24 (1976): 44–62.

Anne Home Livingston

(24 February 1763 – 23 August 1841)

Lorenza Gramegna
Illinois State University

See also the Livingston entry in *DLB 37: American Writers of the Early Republic.*

BOOKS: *Sacred Records Abridged in Verse. Consisting of Some of The Parables and Miracles, The Life, Death, Resurrection and Ascension of the Blessed Saviour* (Philadelphia: Printed & published for the author by T. S. Manning, 1817);

Nancy Shippen, Her Journal Book; The International Romance of a Young Lady of Fashion of Colonial Philadelphia, with Letters to Her and About Her, edited by Ethel Armes (Philadelphia & London: Lippincott, 1935).

Anne Home Livingston, born Nancy Shippen, was the author of one of the most interesting and best-written diaries of early America. The two manuscript volumes of her journal, which cover a period of roughly ten years, served as Livingston's response to the tensions caused by her abusive husband, a situation beyond her endurance and control. Her journal entries display her exceptional ability to report events, convey images and atmosphere, and express deep emotions. In addition to its historical and literary value, this personal document is valuable for women's studies in its descriptions of how Livingston responded to and lived out a woman's assigned role in eighteenth-century American middle-class society.

Livingston's story is in both personal and literary terms a tragedy resulting from women's dependence on their parents' presumably wiser guidance on the choice of marriage partners. Brought up to be submissive to her father and later to her husband, Livingston, like most women of her age, was taught that marriage and motherhood were a woman's greatest form of self-realization. Although the American Revolution and the Romantic movement produced a new interest in the individual, many women in Livingston's time still lived in the shadows of their fathers or husbands, a situation that made it difficult for a woman to express her individuality. Livingston's journal, which

Anne Home Livingston (portrait attributed to Benjamin Trott; from Nancy Shippen, Her Journal Book, *1935)*

covers the historically important era between 1783 and 1791, shows how she found herself forced into a part she had not chosen and played the role her society created for and expected from her. Her narrative is the story of gradual disillusionment regarding her husband's improvement. Yet, in moments of self-revelation, the diary shows that a new consciousness was emerging in Livingston, one barely convinced of its worth, yet timidly searching for freedom from her assigned role.

Originally from England, the Shippens were one of the oldest and most powerful families in Philadelphia. Dr. William Shippen III, an ambitious man, earned his medical degree in England, where he had met Alice Lee, a member of a less affluent branch of the prestigious Lee family of Virginia. The two married and settled in Philadelphia, where the first of their two children, Anne Home Shippen (called Nancy), was born on 24 February 1763.

During the American Revolution the British occupied Philadelphia, and many Philadelphians left the town. Shippen House, formerly a meeting place for revolutionaries, was closed. Not all the Shippens supported the patriot cause, but Dr. William Shippen served as director of the American military hospitals. Nancy Shippen was safe from the dangers of war at Mistress Rogers' Boarding School for Young Ladies in Trenton, New Jersey. There she was educated according to the criteria of her times. She learned some French and read British authors such as John Milton, Samuel Richardson, and Oliver Goldsmith, as well as the popular British periodical *The Spectator*. Great emphasis was placed on learning to curtsy, move with grace, sew, embroider, play the harpsichord, sing, and dance.

When the Shippens returned to Philadelphia in 1778, they came in contact with the French diplomats who had arrived as a result of the American alliance with France. Many events were organized to welcome the French ambassadors. Probably at one such party Livingston met Louis Guillaume Otto, a young French attaché. Later she informally accepted his proposal of marriage. As William Shippen explained in a 27 January 1781 letter to his son, Thomas Shippen, he recognized that his daughter was in love with Otto and that she felt only esteem for the much older Col. Henry Beekman Livingston of New York, her father's preference for her future husband. William Shippen wanted his daughter to act in accordance with his conviction that economic security and social position were more important than love. Though Otto belonged to a distinguished French family, he was just at the beginning of a promising diplomatic career, and his wealth did not compare to that of Colonel Livingston. Thus, after Livingston proposed marriage to the seventeen-year-old Nancy, Dr. Shippen successfully arranged a separation between her and Otto, convincing his daughter to disregard her earlier promise to Otto and to enter into a financially and politically advantageous marriage to Livingston. As Dr. Shippen noted in his letter to his son, "A Bird in hand is worth 2 in a bush." Alice Shippen, who had at first been partial to her daughter's relationship with Otto, seems ultimately to have favored the marriage to Colonel Livingston, possibly out of a desire that her daughter should have a life of affluence. The wedding, organized in secrecy and haste, took place on 14 May 1781.

Only later did Livingston learn of her husband's jealous, violent, and libertine nature. Notorious for his arrogance, selfishness, and profligacy, he was the black sheep of his illustrious and wealthy New York family. Colonel Livingston's mother, Margaret Beekman Livingston, told her daughter-in-law that he was the father of illegitimate children. Much appreciated and loved by her mother-in-law, Anne Livingston played her new role with dignity, accepting the custom of her times by which "a wife who had an unfaithful husband must not expostulate, but feign ignorance of his misconduct" and try to win him back. After two years of marriage and after giving birth to a daughter, Peggy, Anne Livingston realized that she could no longer put up with her husband's increasing jealous abuse and groundless accusations of infidelity. After learning from her mother-in-law that her husband planned to have all his children, including Peggy, gathered in the same house, she found the courage to leave him. Early in 1783 she returned with her daughter Peggy to her family's home and, at the age of nineteen, started her diary.

Livingston approached her diary as if it were a confidant. In addition to recording her daily activities and social visits in it, she also expressed her wretchedness and her growing awareness of her female identity. This identity was at times in conflict with the subordinate place that, she had been taught, was proper for a woman and challenged the expectations that her parents and her culture had for her as a woman. Writing in her diary helped Livingston to clarify the disparity she felt between her changing self-conception and the public self she had constructed in accordance with social expectations. While she had been submissive and obedient, she was unhappy. She turned to her journal as to a friend who might help her discover the means to control the disturbing events of her life. At one point she even entered a plan for daily activities. Unfortunately, Livingston had neither close, wise women friends nor, despite a bond of obvious affection, any deep relationship with her mother.

When she first began keeping her journal, Livingston did not seem thoroughly aware of the tragic nature of her situation. The earliest entries are written in romantic and sentimental tones, most probably because Livingston expected a happy ending, perhaps provided by external interposition. It is, however, clear from the first entry that she was experiencing a fracture in her life, one that challenged romantic expectations and led her to question the current ideas on the status of woman and wife. Indeed, on reading Madame Françoise d'Aubigné de Maintenon's advice to

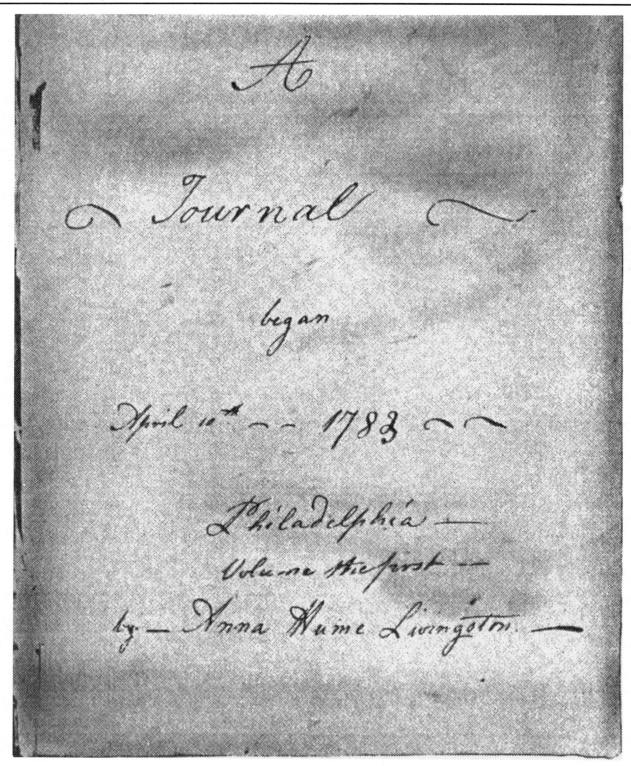

Title page and entries for 16–17 May 1782 in Livingston's diary (Library of Congress)

May 6.

    Papa told me this morn'g at break-
fast that I must send my darling Child to its
Grand mama Livingston, that she had desird Mr. Montgomery to request it of me, as
a particular favor — I told him I coud not
bear the Idea of it, that I had sooner part
with my life almost than my Child — he
told me it was for the future interest of
my baby, that its fortune depended on
the old Lady's pleasure in that particular — begd me to think of it, & to be reconciled to it — If I'm now my own heart
I never can — When will my misfortunes
End! If I placed my happiness in her! she is
my all — & I must part with her! cruel
cruel fate ——

May 7.   10 o'clock at night ——
I have been so an happy all day that I have not
stird out of my room except to dinner —

women, Livingston expressly disagreed with the idea that women are born to "suffer & to obey." She wrote in her diary on 15 May 1783 "that men are generally tyrannical I will own, but such as know how to be happy, willingly give up the harsh title of master for the more tender & endearing one of Friend. Equality is the soul of friendship: marriage to give delight, must join two minds, not devote a slave to the will of an imperious Lord." This passage endorses the new idea of companionate marriage, while recognizing that society continued to make unreasonable demands on women. Her journal is the direct and concrete consequence of a marriage not based on friendly equality. Some entries even raise the possibility that Livingston's husband abused her verbally and physically.

Although she had escaped a dreadful situation, Livingston's unusual status of separated wife was not an easy one. On 6 October 1784, visiting a soon-to-be-married acquaintance, she was not "pleased with the reception" she received, observing that the bride-to-be might have been among those who believed that Livingston was at fault in her conduct toward her husband. Early in the diary Livingston was not ready to reject the demands of a patriarchal society and to take control of her own future. While denying her husband's right to control, she was still not prepared to reject her father's authority. Dr. Shippen's judgment and his morals proved not to be trustworthy either. In January 1780 he had been arrested on the charge of having speculated with hospital stores and was only barely acquitted. Yet Livingston lived under his control. She kept repeating in her journal that she felt "calm and composed" and pleased herself "with the reflection of having conform'd to the will" of her parents "in the most important action" of her life. In May 1783, when her father told her that for the future well-being of her child she had to send the baby to live with her grandmother Livingston in Clermont, New York, she protested and cried, but in the end, in utter humility and self-abnegation, she acquiesced. The only comfort she was allowed was to accompany the baby on the journey.

The journey was not pleasant. As she wrote on 7 July 1783, Livingston experienced a further humiliation when, during a pause at an inn, the landlady, oblivious of Livingston's identity, spoke of Colonel Livingston as "a very bad" man who had recently almost killed one of his servants. Yet Livingston hoped that the child would be the means of her reconciliation with her husband, that he would be glad to see her, repent his mistreatment of her, be happy of her willingness to forgive him, and even become a new man. Yet a few days preceding her journey she had received letters in which he, among other malicious slanders, ac-cused her of being unfaithful. Her innocence, supported by all that she had been told in her youth, allowed her to continue believing that even a partner such as her husband might suddenly "soften" and "relent," as she wrote on 9 June 1783, before beginning her journey. Unable to realize that she was not living a fairy tale with a happy ending, she continued thinking according to traditional assumptions of her society, which held that a woman's total submission was the key to her happiness.

A slight change in her attitude can be detected in the entry for 10 September 1783, after her return from Clermont. As a mother she was painfully aware that she had lost her child. She had become conscious of the immediate repercussions of her predicament, although she was not yet aware of what caused it. The presence of her child might have spared Livingston some of her suffering; still she did not accept that her father's judgment was deficient and that complying with his will was like an admission that she was somewhat at fault regarding her husband's reproaches. According to her diary, she still viewed her father as a dear, indulgent man, and she never blamed him or her mother for her misery. Far from rebelling, she even forced herself not to complain. For example, in her entry for 10 September 1783 she concluded, "I will not repine. I have done my duty." As for her husband, the journey to New York fully convinced her that if she were to live with him "with all the discretion that ever fell to the lot of woman," her life would still be "made miserable by him" because of his jealousy. Although Livingston does not seem to have been aware of the injustice of the "discretion" that she, as a woman, was expected to have, she seems no longer to have been willing to show any such "discretion" toward her husband. Because he would not reform his ways, to give him up was her only reasonable course. Unfortunately, however, Livingston did not go further in this direction. Instead, she criticized such speculations as unprofitable: "But why these reflections, they will do me alass no good." Such language suggests that she might have been afraid of questioning the legitimacy of the "duties" society expected of a woman in her situation.

Livingston was next allowed to see her baby almost a year later, when she took a long, tiresome journey to New York. Her joy at the prospect was immense. On 14 April 1784 Livingston wrote in the last entry of the first volume, "Tomorrow & Tomorrow & one day more, & then I shall see my Lovely Child. The Thought alone makes me happier than I can express. My heart has been as light as a fly all day. & I have thought of nothing else hardly all day."

She spent only a few days in New York, however. After that, for a long time and despite her efforts, she had to be happy with having relatives or even strangers talk to her about her daughter. By 2 May 1784 Livingston was back in Philadelphia, where, much to her surprise, she found her house let to the Spanish ambassador. Probably because of financial difficulties and Alice Shippen's poor health, both women had to move to the country, where Livingston spent many tedious days until mid September 1784. As the months elapsed, Livingston's miserable state of mind did not improve. Finally she openly lamented her dull and lonely life in the country with her sick mother. She eventually returned to Philadelphia, but the change of scene was not of much help. Her diary entries reflect her utter misery. She had already started to become impatient with her father; yet she continued to behave obediently and to comply with his desire for her to live a retired life. Knowing no other role, she played the only part she knew, that of the perfect, dutiful daughter. Indeed, Livingston played her role so well that a good portion of the journal seems to be written for her parents. Lacking both the strength and the faculty to make decisions about her life, Livingston seems to have relied more on hoping than acting: "Sweet hope," she wrote on 30 October 1784, "now & then comes into my relief that a change for the better may take place in my hitherto variagated life."

On 24 February 1785, three years after she had last seen her husband, Livingston made one last attempt at reconciliation, at having "a prospect of living happily with him" and her "darling Child," but her hopes were shattered by a sharp letter from the colonel. On 5 March she wrote in her journal that even her father "sees it will never do for" her to go back to her "inflexible husband." As her disillusionment increased, Livingston started to skip entries in her diary. Her life, she wrote, was not worth recording.

In September 1785 Otto, with whom she had kept up a friendly correspondence, returned from France with a title and a higher position. The consideration of what she had lost, and what her life was doomed to be, led Livingston to resume her journal in order to express her utter wretchedness. The woman writing at this point is not the same person who started the journal. She acknowledged her father's responsibility for her situation and expressed the realization that she should not have obeyed him passively but rather should have taken a more active part in deciding her future. She found only minor satisfaction in the knowledge that her father had come to realize his mistake. As she wrote on 6 September 1785, "what is my unfortunate situation—A wretched slave—doom'd to be the wife of a Tyrant I hate but from whom, thank God, I am separated."

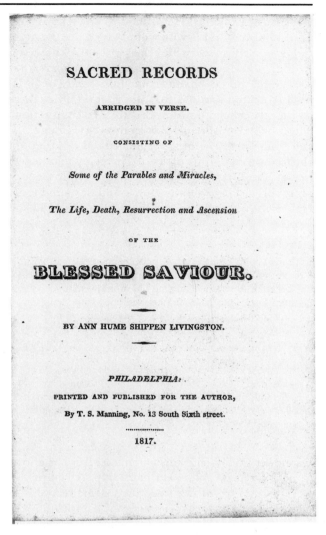

Title page for Livingston's verse account of "the most important history in the world" (courtesy of Special Collections, University of Virginia Library)

Livingston's only consolation was that she was separated from her husband. Her romantic belief in a happy ending gave way to cries of despair: "O! my God teach me resignation to thy divine will, & let me not suffer in vain!" Livingston's parents could offer little help; her insensitive father still did not really understand what his daughter was experiencing, and her mother, though probably more aware of her part in creating her daughter's misery, was suffering from chronic depression and seeking isolation. Alone, Livingston tried to suffocate her sufferings in "retirement" and "resignation to divine will."

Livingston next picked up her journal in October 1785. With Otto returned, she saw one last opportunity to have a chance of happiness. She tried to obtain a divorce, which would have left her free to marry Otto; yet, in addition to his other defects, her husband was also revengeful. He offered to consent to a divorce, but only if his wife would give up her daughter, a condition to which he probably knew she would never consent. Moreover, it appears that though her parents had become fully aware of Colonel Livingston's true nature, they let their daughter down at a crucial point in the divorce transactions and took her husband's side against her. Livingston gave up hope. Becoming reconciled to her situation, she found "an infinite pleasure" in trying to improve herself, and having determined "to employ every hour" of her day usefully, she found her mind to be "much more composed." On 15 October 1785 she wrote:

Thus I enjoy at present a negative happiness—disturb'd it is occasionally, by some few cross accident[s] & disagreeable reflections. Now and then I hear of my child—& some times form plans of having her with me, & as often I am disappointed. My husband (what misery, alass to me, that I have one) lives in his old way trying to deprive his wife & lawful heir of their property by throwing it away on miserable undeserving objects. I have a new source of woe, for the authoriz'd separation that I have so long been expecting to take place, is given over entirely. Thus am I situated differently from all the human race, for I am deprived of all hope of ever being more happy in this world—the next I leave to HEAVEN.

Prompted by a further disappointment in her efforts to be with Peggy, she next picked up her journal in December 1785. At this stage the journal records her turn toward religion as a source of consolation. On New Year's Eve 1785 she wrote in her diary that "happiness consists more in our minds being at ease, than in all the variety of accidental circumstances." It had become clear to her that her family and society had made her unable to change her situation, and she lacked the strength to rebel. She concluded that to be "compleatly" happy she had only to "persevere in the path of" her "duty, & always remember that a virtuous life insures happiness, & eternal felicity."

After January 1786 Livingston did not write regularly in her diary. Her last substantial entry, written on Christmas Day 1791, shows her utter misery:

I have consider'd my life so uninteresting hitherto as to prevent me from continuing my journal & so I shall fill up the remainder with transcriptions—It is certain that when the mind bleeds with some wound of recent misfortune nothing is of equal efficacy with religious comfort. It is of power to enlighten the darkest hour, & to assuage the severest woe, by the relief of divine favor, & the prospect of a blessed immortality. In such hopes the mind expatiates with joy, & when bereaved of its earthly friends, solaces with the thoughts of one friend, who will never forsake it.

Livingston wrote in her diary only as long as she thought she would eventually find happiness. After all her dreams and romantic illusions had been irremediably shattered, she no longer felt the need to keep a diary. In her last entry she sounds wholly detached from earthly life. Unable to change her plight, Livingston turned toward spirituality and tried to convert the pain she felt into religious acquiescence. The nature of her acceptance is apparent not only in the frequency with which she recorded going to church and in her meditations on religious matters but also in the religious transcriptions she included at this stage of her journal.

Although the diary is typically a form in which one can attempt to redefine the self and escape the definitions and expectations of the world, the final image created in Livingston's journal is that of a woman too accustomed to conforming to the expectations of her society to realize that she could rebel. She gained some self-knowledge, but she usually had difficulty making distinctions and choices according to a personal standard rather than the social code of her age. Caught amid conflicting demands, she was unable to gain power over her life and thus assumed the role of a victim.

At the beginning of her journal, Livingston so accepted society's standards that she was unable to understand the real nature of the people around her. She described her situation as if she were a romantic heroine in a work of fiction. She even identified the people close to her by pseudonyms that seem to have come from British sentimental novels and Restoration plays. "Lord Worthy," the name she used for her father, can be traced to eighteenth-century British novels and reflects the way she saw her father when she started keeping her journal. She identified her husband as "Lord B.," a name that echoes Mr. B., the villain in Samuel Richardson's novel *Pamela* (1740–1741). Livingston's Lord B. is indeed the villain of her story. She called Otto "Leander," who in the legend of Hero and Leander drowns in the Hellespont while trying to reach the woman he loves. The true romantic hero of Livingston's story, Otto, like his literary counterpart, was probably expected to make heroic efforts to be with Livingston.

Livingston called herself "Amanda," a name that comes from the Latin "Amandus," suitable to be loved. It was the name by which Otto addressed her in one of the letters he wrote her during their courtship. Her self-portrait has much in common with the depiction of the persecuted maiden in many works of romantic fiction. Her hope that Colonel Livingston could make the transition from villain to good husband is an expectation taken from such fiction, including *Pamela*, in which the reformed profligate makes a model husband. It is significant that Livingston was well acquainted with another of Richardson's novels, *Clarissa* (1747–1749), in which the heroine is not united with the rake who succeeds in raping her and dies virtuous but alone. She considered it "a charming book fraught with instruction," some of which she thought worth adopting. Initially Livingston probably considered her situation to be better than that of Clarissa Harlow because, unlike her, Livingston had obeyed her parents and married the man they chose for her. For example, in her entry for 19 May 1783 she recorded the story of a young woman "who was sacrificed to the avarice & ambition of her parents to a man she hated—& . . . death was the natural consequence of her misery"; yet she did not realize that the event she recorded almost exactly mirrored her own situation. She could not yet see that "the avarice" and "ambition" of her parents were the cause of her ultimate death in life.

Livingston did not write in her journal with any thought of publication, nor did she consciously aim to create art. Her audience seems at first to have been her parents rather than herself, a point that may explain why she was so complimentary toward them and their values. She was probably never concerned to any great extent with style; yet her writing displays an unconscious art. Livingston's style is straightforward. She often used plain language to express her feelings with a clarity and simplicity that must have been typical of her personality. The style of individual entries varies according to content and perspective. When drawing conclusions from her musings, Livingston's entries tend to be longer than those in which she wrote about her sufferings. The entries that express her emotional and psychological pain are marked by unsteady writing and short sentences. Some entries can be considered little narratives and show Livingston's natural skill. She had an ability to capture on paper her different reactions to events. When she tried to express strong emotions, her language became poetic, but as she grew more resigned to her situation, her entries became shorter and more prosaic, until finally they served only to record trivial events and to transcribe religious material.

Her acceptance of heavenly will is also apparent in the book that she had privately printed in 1817. Aside from the family, religion was the only major sphere in which women were allowed free movement. Religion was the shelter in which Livingston took ref-

uge, and during a period of seclusion caused by illness, when her only consolation was reading the Gospels, Livingston wrote *Sacred Records Abridged in Verse,* a collection of verses in which she sought to summarize the main events of Jesus' life. In the "Introductory Address" to the collection she explained her decision to express in verse parts of what she considered "the most important history in the world," as it might "be committed to memory with greater facility than prose" and be useful for young minds. Livingston's verse is competent but undistinguished; its content, derived from the New Testament, shows little creativity; and the collection is loosely strung together. *Sacred Records* was dedicated to the Reverend E. S. Ely, apparently a much esteemed friend and one of the few people who had any contact with mother and daughter during their years of seclusion.

Livingston died on 23 August 1841, having spent her last years as a religious recluse. She was assisted only by her daughter, Peggy, who had renounced all the comforts of the Livingstons' manors as soon as she had come of age. In early 1797 she joined her mother in her self-imposed isolation from the world.

Livingston's reputation as a writer rests primarily on her journal. Its pages give insight into the hopes and challenges she faced and reveal in detail the construction of female subjectivity. The tragedy caused by her difficulty in perceiving and accepting the nature of her predicament is eased by an attitude toward life that seems almost heroic.

References:
Margo Culley, ed., *A Day at a Time. The Diary Literature of American Women from 1764 to the Present* (New York: Feminist Press, 1985);
Lorenza Gramegna, "The Journal of Anne Home Livingston (Nancy Shippen): A New Approach," dissertation, Illinois State University, 1991;
Carolyn G. Heilburn, *Writing A Woman's Life* (New York: Ballantine, 1988);
Steven E. Kagle, *American Diary Literature* (Boston: Twayne, 1979);
Randolph Shipley Klein, *Portrait of an Early American Family: The Shippens of Philadelphia* (Philadelphia: University of Pennsylvania, 1975).

Papers:
Livingston's journal is with the papers of her brother, Thomas Shippen, at the Library of Congress.

Deborah Norris Logan

(19 October 1761 – 2 February 1839)

Janice Durbin
University of Missouri–Columbia

BOOKS: *The Norris House* (Philadelphia: Fair-Hill Press, 1867);

Memoir of Dr. George Logan of Stenton, edited by Frances A. Logan (Philadelphia: Historical Society of Pennsylvania, 1899);

"The 'Worthy' and the 'Irrelevant': Deborah Norris Logan's Diary," edited by Marleen S. Barr, dissertation, State University of New York at Buffalo, 1980.

OTHER: *Correspondence of William Penn and James Logan,* 2 volumes, transcribed and annotated by Deborah Norris Logan, edited by Edward Armstrong (Philadelphia: Historical Society of Pennsylvania, 1870, 1872).

Born into one of the leading Quaker families in colonial Philadelphia, Deborah Norris Logan was immediately involved in or surrounded by the events that led to the founding of the United States. Her family played host to many important figures in the American Revolution, including John Hancock, Henry Laurens, Francis Lightfoot Lee, George Washington, and Thomas Jefferson. As a result of the constant stream of visitors to her family home, Logan became well versed in the political events of the day. When she was fourteen years old, she heard the first public reading of the Declaration of Independence as she stood at the fence in her own yard. As a young girl Logan developed an appreciation of the importance of recording important events for future generations. Recognizing the significant opportunity afforded to her by the location of her childhood home, she paid tribute to it in a work published after her death as *The Norris House* (1867), a brief, illustrated description of the family residence. She is best remembered, however, for her diary and for her work in transcribing the letters of William Penn and James Logan, which document the founding of Pennsylvania.

Logan began her education at the Friends Girls' School of Anthony Benezet, who used the

Deborah Norris Logan

standard curriculum for young women, which included basic reading, arithmetic, music, and needlework, skills that society expected women to master. She did not devote herself fully to her studies, preferring to have fun. At some time after she left school (the records are unclear on the exact date), she developed a self-education program that she continued throughout her life. Through her extensive reading she developed her interest in literary pursuits.

In 1781 Deborah Norris married George Logan, a physician and farmer from a leading Philadelphia family. A devoted wife, she was blessed with a happy marriage and a husband who trusted her judgment and gave her full control of his affairs when he was away from home. Although married women could not legally control property at this time, during the Revolutionary era it was not uncommon for women to act as "deputy husbands," managing the family lands while their husbands were away. Whenever her husband left home on business, Deborah Logan managed the family's agricultural endeavors. As her diary suggests, her duties included not only overseeing preparation and preservation of food, cleaning, sewing, and gardening but also monitoring larger farm operations such as planting, harvesting, and storing crops as well as buying new equipment, land, and seeds.

Political events of the postrevolutionary era affected the personal lives of George and Deborah Logan. Deborah Logan was well known for her impeccable manners and her personal charm. Many visitors to Stenton, her husband's home, sought her company or turned to her for advice and information. Throughout the late eighteenth and early nineteenth centuries she corresponded with many leaders of the early republic, including Thomas Jefferson and Robert Walsh, editor of the *National Gazette*. She backed her husband's political activities. George Logan had become actively involved in politics after the American Revolution, and he increasingly supported Jefferson and James Madison's newly formed Democratic Republican Party, also known as the Jeffersonians. The Democratic Republicans believed that John Adams's Federalists threatened the integrity of the new nation by usurping federal power and threatening individual liberties. Her husband's political activities led her to fear for his personal safety and caused her to be ostracized by Federalist friends. Criticizing the Federalist Party, including President Adams or members of Congress, could have led to George Logan's being jailed or fined under the provisions of the Alien and Sedition Acts of 1798. Despite such risks, George Logan took a daring and forceful stand on his beliefs.

During the quasi war with France in 1798, George Logan sailed to France as a private citizen to conduct private negotiations with the French government on behalf of the United States. After meeting with highly placed members of the French government and receiving praise in Paris newspapers for his pacifism, he returned to the United States to share what he had learned with the government. The Federalists accused him of treasonous behavior, however, and Congress passed the Logan Act, which forbade private citizens from undertaking such missions in the future.

During her husband's absence Deborah Logan experienced "political excommunication" by friends who failed to understand her husband's mission, but Vice President Jefferson visited her at Stenton and encouraged her to continue her regular duties by going out in public rather than trying to hide from her husband's critics. Although she might earlier have been aware of the political danger faced by public figures, in 1798 Logan was forcefully reminded that impeccable manners could not protect her and her family from attacks by the political opposition.

As a Quaker, Logan was sustained by her faith during this and other difficult periods of her life. She believed in living a life of faith, simplicity, and beauty. Attending Quaker meetings regularly provided her with a support network that helped her cope with the challenges she faced. As her writings illustrate, however, her faith did not alter her belief that class status was an inherited position and that family background was even more important than wealth. Members of the elite, she believed, did not toil on a daily basis in the same way as people of other classes. She wrote about visiting friends, holding tea parties, and overseeing her servants, who performed the actual labor of the household. She described the tasks of managing the household and gardens, but not the physical work involved in caring for a large home. While Logan's attitudes about social position and wealth might seem inconsistent with Quaker doctrine, many wealthy Philadelphia Quakers had similar attitudes. This division between Quaker beliefs and practice separated city-dwelling Quaker merchants from rural Friends. Echoing some of the beliefs of their Puritan neighbors in New England, wealthy Quakers asserted that God had granted them wealth and social position because of their devotion and worth; thus, they believed they had a hereditary right to be treated as members of the elite. Logan's interest in preserving the family history and heritage also reflected her belief in the importance of her family's social status and her desire to maintain it.

Logan did not begin her literary career until 1814, when she began the laborious task of transcribing the correspondence between William Penn and her husband's grandfather James Logan, who had been Penn's agent. She stumbled on these letters, which became her most important contribution to American history, in the attic at Stenton. Recognizing the piles of old, worn, worm-eaten papers as the correspondence between two early Pennsylvania leaders, she began the process of copying, deciphering, and annotating thousands of pages of the old correspondence, which reveals how Penn and Logan assisted in colonial development and eventually in the creation of a new nation. At the time she began this process, there was little interest in colonial history, and Logan realized that if she did not undertake her task, the valuable information in these documents might be lost. Logan had no intention of publishing her efforts. Rather, seeking to ensure that her family's contribution to American history was recorded properly for posterity, she donated her transcription and the entire collection to the American Philosophical Society in Philadelphia. The Historical Society of Pennsylvania eventually published the letters in two volumes in 1870 and 1872.

Clearly believing that her role as a wife and mother was most important, Logan used her writing as a means of reinforcing the importance of mothers and wives to the survival of the new republic. Society expected women in the early republic to be good republican mothers, and reading and writing history was a task that enhanced women's responsibilities for educating their children. Furthermore, Logan's concept of "home" extended into the public arena, at least as far as her intellectual pursuits were concerned. Intellectually, at least, women of Logan's era were assumed to have parity with men while the physical differences between men and women dictated inequality in strength. Thus, while men had the physical task of building a new nation, women had the task of preserving for future generations the knowledge of the important men who shaped the young nation. Women's history writing became an important patriotic tool and a way in which women could participate in the public political world. Women were not politicians, but they documented and preserved the record of public actions. By transcribing the correspondence of Penn and Logan, Deborah Logan was attempting to ensure that the documents survive for future generations. She was not advocating political equality for women.

In January 1815 Logan began keeping a diary that she maintained regularly until her death in 1839. In preserving and annotating the Penn and Logan correspondence, Logan had concerned herself primarily with issues of national, political import. In contrast, the diary is a remarkable collection of observations about daily life as well as including transcriptions of letters she or her husband received from political leaders such as Jefferson. She wrote about interactions with neighbors and friends, included copies of her poems, and reflected on politics and life in general. As she noted in an introduction to the first volume of her diary, "I have been induced to begin this book as a means to *preserve* fresh in my memory passing events and because I have frequently reflected on the probability that a great mass of curious and interesting facts and information are lost to posterity from a want of record." This opening statement indicates that Logan intended her diary to become part of the public record rather than considering it a personal journal. The possibility that she intended the diary to be made public raises questions about what Logan might have omitted. Yet Logan's diary provides a wealth of detail on daily life and people in Philadelphia in the early republic, making it a useful tool for scholars. She wrote about topics as diverse as Napoleon's activities in Europe to butchering hogs and tending her gardens. For example, in her 27 April 1815 entry Logan wrote,

> It is beyond a doubt that Napoleon has reascended the throne of France. What will be the result? What a want of foresight to trust him in Elba! How will Talleyrand settle this business? Surely it will task his art severely to blind the eyes of his old master and satisfy him that he was effectually serving his cause and procuring for him "ships, colonies and commerce," as in fact is now the case while swearing fidelity to the Bourbons. The eagle has reposed in Elba for a short time. Meanwhile, armies are disbanded, France again receives her numerous veterans who were captured abroad, her ships and colonies are restored, the bands of her commerce removed and its hopes again looking up. And the eagle shaking its ruffled plumes from the "dark lands of slumber," will again glance "the lightening of his eye" upon his foes. And if not prevented by an overruling providence will again tear with his beak the hapless prey.

Logan was conscious of the difficulties faced by Europeans who were trying to restore order after Napoleon's first defeat, and she echoed the fears of many who worried that exiling Napoleon would not be enough to prevent him from attempting to regain power.

Although Logan did not publish any of her prose writings during her lifetime, she did publish some of her poetry anonymously in the *National Gazette* after 1815. She explained in her diary that she enjoyed poetry and believed that writing good poems was a difficult task. Her verse reflects on her life at Stenton and her various interests, as in this sonnet from 22 January 1815:

Pure, and not transient, are the joys I have
Beyond the boast of power, or Fortune's slave,
Or Pride's gay Robes with rainbow radiance coy.

This is my pleasure—that the active mind,
The present, past and future can survey.
In science, nature, and at Home can find
Employment ample as the summer's day:

And more, as Faith directs her nobler flight,
Dwells in immortal worlds of living light.

Logan's simple phrases presented the picture of a woman who was content with her life. She took pleasure in studying diverse subjects such as science and nature; yet the poem also reflects Logan's belief that caring for her home and family was her first priority.

Logan continued her efforts to record her family's important role in Pennsylvania history when she wrote a memoir of her husband after his death in 1821. She wrote at the beginning of her *Memoir of Dr. George Logan of Stenton* (1899) that she intended the book as a tribute to her husband's life and a truthful statement about his role in American history. In the memoir Logan recounted the major events of her husband's life, his education and study abroad, and his interest in politics. She described the circumstances that surrounded his trip to Paris and the accusations and threats they both endured. She made herself the subject in the chapters describing the years he was in France, revealing how she coped with the accusations hurled at her husband and the anxieties and fears she had for him. Although the rejection she suffered from former friends hurt Logan deeply, her faith and trust in her husband's integrity, as well as the support of other friends, helped her to overcome the pain she suffered during this period.

In her *Memoir of Dr. George Logan of Stenton* Logan also published transcriptions of correspondence between her husband and many prominent political leaders, including the marquis de Lafayette and other French leaders, James Madison, Thomas Pickering, John Dickinson, and James Monroe. Once again, Logan used prose writing as a means of recording her family's prominent position in the political history of the United States.

Women such as Logan saw history as progressive and realized that understanding history could help shape the development of a national identity and ideology. While her historical writings are chiefly concerned with public, political events, her more personal writings, such as her diary, reveal her concern with social issues. Thus Logan's work as a whole describes public events that helped to forge a new country and the often unacknowledged private happenings that allowed political change to succeed.

Her efforts at preserving her family's correspondence and her understanding of the importance of the period in which she lived allowed Logan to extend her role as caretaker of the family to guardian of family history and to secure her family's place in the history of early America. In so doing she demonstrated that women of the early republic were not always passive observers of the dynamic events of history. As Nina Baym has argued, Logan, as a good republican mother, found a way to serve her country through her writing. Using family as the structure around which she wrote, she created an historical narrative in which women actively participated in shaping the new country, whether as recorders of prominent political events and mundane details of daily life or as participants in the discussions and debates surrounding important political events. Studying Logan's life can help modern scholars to understand the evolution of the diverse and complex roles of men and women in the early republic.

References:
Marleen Barr, "Deborah Norris Logan, Feminist Criticism, and Identity Theory: Interpreting a Woman's Diary Without the Danger of Separatism," *Biography—An Interdisciplinary Quarterly,* 8 (1985): 12–24;

Nina Baym, "Between Enlightenment and Victorian: Toward a Narrative of American Women Writers Writing History," *Critical Inquiry,* 18 (1991): 22–41;

A. C. Myers, "Sally Wister's Journal," *Pennsylvania Magazine of History and Biography,* 9 (1885): 318–333, 463–478; 10 (1885): 51–60;

S. B. Wister and A. Irwin, *Worthy Women of Our First Century* (Philadelphia: Lippincott, 1877), pp. 279–328.

Papers:
The bulk of the Logan family papers are at the Historical Society of Pennsylvania.

Martha Daniell Logan

(29 December 1704? – 28 June 1779)

George S. Scouten
University of South Carolina

WORK: "Gardners Kalendar," in *The South-Carolina Almanack for the year of our Lord 1752* (Charleston, S.C.: John Tobler, 1751); republished as "DIRECTIONS *for managing a Kitchen-Garden every Month in the Year*," in *The South-Carolina Almanack for the year of our Lord 1756* (Charleston, S.C.: John Tobler, 1755), pp. 18–21; enlarged as "Gardener's Calendar," in *Palladium of Knowledge: or, the Carolina and Georgia Almanac for the year of our Lord 1796* (Charleston, S.C.: Printed by W. P. Young, 1795), pp. 44–48; enlarged again as "Gardener's Calendar," in *Palladium of Knowledge: or, the Carolina and Georgia Almanac for the year of our Lord 1798* (Charleston, S.C.: Printed by W. P. Young, 1797), pp. 39–44.

Best known for her immensely popular "Gardner's Kalendar," the first American treatise on gardening, Martha Daniell Logan earned a reputation not only as a woman of letters but also as a savvy businesswoman and a gifted horticulturist. Logan's writings are an essential source for information about women's culture in the colonial South. Her treatise on gardening, for example, not only describes the sort of work expected of women in the colonial South but also expresses many shared cultural values. Furthermore, Logan's treatise and letters must be viewed in the context of the immense interest in botany and scientific classification that arose on both sides of the Atlantic in the mid eighteenth century. Logan's writing and gardening allowed her access to some of the most influential horticulturists of her day, and her exchange of plants and letters with such well-known figures as John Bartram placed her at the forefront of a cultural exchange that was vital in contributing to European knowledge about American flora.

Martha Daniell was born in St. Thomas Parish, South Carolina, to Robert and Martha Wainwright Daniell. Several sources suggest that she was born in 1704, but discrepancies in her year of birth exist even in documents dating from her lifetime, as evidenced by a 1773 title dispute, the resolution of which rested in part on when she was born. As the daughter of Robert Daniell, Martha was a member of one of the most prestigious families in colonial South Carolina. Her father was highly respected as a prominent landowner and for his distinguished military service against the Spanish troops in Florida. In 1715 Robert Daniell became a landgrave—the highest title in the semifeudal South Carolina system of government—and during the following year he served as deputy governor and then as governor. The proprietary lords, who ruled South Carolina under a grant from the king, removed Daniell from the governorship in 1717 because of his procolonist stance in a political dispute. One year later, when Martha Daniell was about thirteen years old, Robert Daniell died.

Although little is known about Martha Daniell's childhood, her family's high social and political status must have given her access to the sort of education unavailable to most young women in the early eighteenth century. It is evident from her later accomplishments and her emphases as a teacher that she learned reading, writing, arithmetic, and needlework. In addition, as a young woman from an elite Charleston family, she would have learned dancing and possibly French. In May 1719, one year after her husband's death, Martha Daniell's mother married Col. George Logan, a respected citizen of Charleston and a good friend of the late Robert Daniell. Later that same year, on 30 July 1719, Martha married George Logan Jr., Colonel Logan's only son from a previous marriage; Martha was about fourteen; her husband was roughly ten years her senior. Like his father, George Logan Jr. was an active member of the Charleston community and served as a member of the Commons House of Assembly and as a justice of the peace. He died in 1764.

Martha Logan was a highly motivated woman. She not only maintained a large household, raising eight children (six of whom lived to adulthood), but she also participated in matters of business and law. Her husband was occasionally out of the colony, and beginning in 1739, she was given power of attorney over all his lands and slaves. She seems to have had a great deal of control over the family's estate and was frequently involved in the leasing and releasing of properties. At one point she even acted as legal counsel for one of her sons in the sale of a property he owned.

In addition to her participation in traditionally masculine arenas, Martha Logan is notable for her ability to transform her domestic roles into those of a businesswoman. As early as 1742 Logan ran advertisements in the *South Carolina Gazette* announcing her intentions to open a boarding school for the children of the wealthy families in Charleston. Her advertisement in the 6 March 1742 issue is interesting because it also offers for sale 500-acre and 120-acre tracts of land, two lots in Charleston, and one lot in "Beauford." The juxtaposition of the two advertisements suggests the entrepreneurial spirit with which Logan undertook her various projects. Both the sale of land and the school were designed as sources of income. Her school was not in continuous operation. In 1750 she placed an advertisement for a new school, and the 1 August 1754 issue of the *South Carolina Gazette* included the news that "Martha Logan (who lives in a pleasant airy Situation . . .) again proposes to keep a BOARDING SCHOOL."

While Logan may have received some recognition as a teacher, she acquired far greater acclaim as a horticulturist. Her friend and mentor Elizabeth Lamboll is credited with having the first impressive garden in the Charleston region, but Martha Logan's garden followed soon thereafter. To keep one of the most impressive gardens in the region was no small feat, especially since the transatlantic enthusiasm for botany ran particularly high in Charleston. In addition to amateur gardeners such as the Lambolls, the city boasted several professional botanists, including Dr. Alexander Garden, who influenced Linnaeus's classification of plants and was also the person for whom the gardenia was named. In eighteenth-century Charleston a large, well-maintained garden with a variety of trees, flowers, and shrubs was a mark of wealth and refinement, and Logan's garden provided her access to some of the most important botanists in North America. She became highly respected for her horticultural abilities and was consulted by these botanists more than once.

In addition to providing her with social distinction, Logan's garden became a source of financial security. Unlike that of Elizabeth Lamboll, Logan's garden served a highly utilitarian purpose. She grew plants designed to please the eye, but like most women of her day, she also grew them to help feed her family. She acquired a reputation as a skilled gardener and sold all sorts of plants, bulbs, and seeds. In the 12 November 1753 issue of the *South Carolina Gazette* she and her youngest son placed an advertisement announcing, "Just imported from London . . . a parcel of very good seeds, flower roots, and fruit stones of several kinds." Various other advertisements published over many years indicate that Logan's nursery business was quite successful. By 1768 she had moved from her location at Trott's Point to Meeting Street in Charleston as she continued to sell everything from "garden seeds and flower roots" to "flowering shrubs and box edging." Reference to her nursery also appears in the writings of contemporary diarists such as Ann Manigault, who in 1763 recorded going to "Mrs. Logan's to buy roots."

Logan's publishing career, which was closely linked to her nursery business, began in 1752 with the inaugural issue of John Tobler's *The South-Carolina Almanack*. An advertisement for the almanac noted that, among other features, the publication would contain a "GARDNERS KALENDAR, *done by a Lady of the Province* and esteemed a very good one." Logan's "Gardners Kalendar," a set of instructions for managing a kitchen garden, was frequently republished during Logan's lifetime in almanacs such as Tobler's *South-Carolina Almanack* and James Johnston's *South Carolina and Georgia Almanac,* but the work was never attributed to her in print during her lifetime. There are no known copies of the 1752 almanac; Tobler's almanac for 1756 states that the calendar is "Done by a Lady."

The first almanac in which Logan's treatise was attributed to her was the *Palladium of Knowledge* for 1796, published nearly seventeen years after her death. This version of the "Gardener's Calendar / from Mrs. Logan / known to succeed in Charleston and Vicinity for many years" is much more extensive than the earlier versions, featuring additional notes on growing strawberries, raising cauliflower and broccoli, and killing worms at the roots of peach trees. The *Palladium of Knowledge* continued to feature Logan's treatise through the first decade of the nineteenth century, when it was eventually displaced by that of Robert Squibb. In 1811 the *Palladium of Knowledge* still included an abbreviated version of Logan's calendar but referred readers to "Squibb's Gardener's Calendar" for additional information. The fact that "Squibb's Gardener's Calendar" was published by W. P. Young, who also

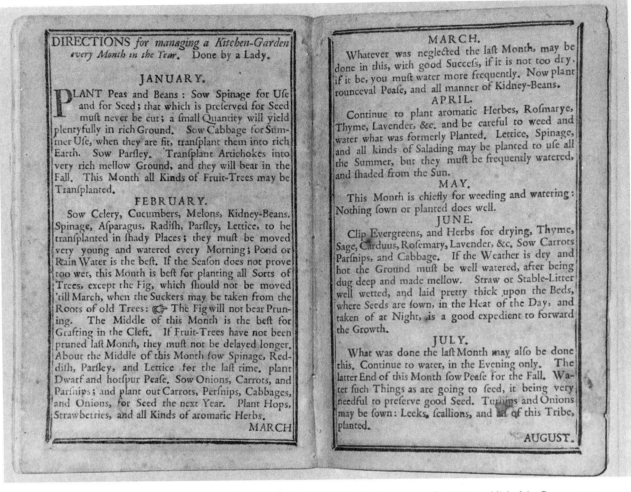

DIRECTIONS *for managing a Kitchen-Garden every Month in the Year.* Done by a Lady.

JANUARY.

PLANT Peas and Beans : Sow Spinage for Ufe and for Seed ; that which is preferved for Seed muft never be cut ; a fmall Quantity will yield plentyfully in rich Ground. Sow Cabbage for Summer Ufe, when they are fit, tranfplant them into rich Earth. Sow Parfley. Tranfplant Artichokes into very rich mellow Ground, and they will bear in the Fall. This Month all Kinds of Fruit-Trees may be Tranfplanted.

FEBRUARY.

Sow Celery, Cucumbers, Melons, Kidney-Beans. Spinage, Afparagus, Radifh, Parfley, Lettice, to be tranfplanted in fhady Places ; they muft be moved very young and watered every Morning ; Pond or Rain Water is the beft. If the Seafon does not prove too wet, this Month is beft for planting all Sorts of Trees, except the Fig, which fhould not be moved 'till March, when the Suckers may be taken from the Roots of old Trees : ☞ The Fig will not bear Pruning. The Middle of this Month is the beft for Grafting in the Cleft. If Fruit-Trees have not been pruned laft Month, they muft not be delayed longer. About the Middle of this Month fow Spinage, Reddifh, Parfley, and Lettice for the laft time. plant Dwarf and hotfpur Peafe. Sow Onions, Carrots, and Parfnips ; and plant out Carrots, Perfnips, Cabbages, and Onions, for Seed the next Year. Plant Hops, Strawberries, and all Kinds of aromatic Herbs.

MARCH

MARCH.

Whatever was neglected the laft Month, may be done in this, with good Succefs, if it is not too dry, if it be, you muft water more frequently. Now plant rounceval Peafe, and all manner of Kidney-Beans.

APRIL.

Continue to plant aromatic Herbes, Rofmarye, Thyme, Lavender, &c. and be careful to weed and water what was formerly Planted. Lettice, Spinage, and all kinds of Salading may be planted to ufe all the Summer, but they muft be frequently watered, and fhaded from the Sun.

MAY.

This Month is chiefly for weeding and watering : Nothing fown or planted does well.

JUNE.

Clip Evergreens, and Herbs for drying, Thyme, Sage, Carduus, Rofemary, Lavender, &c. Sow Carrots Parfnips, and Cabbage. If the Weather is dry and hot the Ground muft be well watered, after being dug deep and made mellow. Straw or Stable-Litter well wetted, and laid pretty thick upon the Beds, where Seeds are fown, in the Heat of the Day, and taken of at Night, is a good expedient to forward the Growth.

JULY.

What was done the laft Month may alfo be done this. Continue to water, in the Evening only. The latter End of this Month fow Peafe for the Fall. Water fuch Things as are going to feed, it being very needful to preferve good Seed. Turnips and Onions may be fown : Leeks, fcallions, and all of this Tribe, planted.

AUGUST.

Pages from Martha Daniell Logan's "Gardners Kalendar" in Tobler's Alamanac *for 1757, published in Germantown, Pennsylvania (South Carolina Historical Society)*

published the *Palladium of Knowledge,* suggests that the decision to phase out Logan's calendar speaks less about the popularity of her treatise than about Young's desire to sell Squibb's work.

Logan's "Gardners Kalendar" appeared in several different forms—the primary difference concerning the amount of additional gardening advice after the monthly planting schedule that was central to every version of the treatise. Many versions of the treatise, especially in its early appearances in the *Palladium of Knowledge,* include additional information on garden management and advice for growing difficult plants. For this reason certain versions of the treatise are more than double the length of others. The shortest versions of the work provide the reader with a monthly schedule for the creation and maintenance of a kitchen garden of vegetables and herbs. The directions in the calendar range from straightforward commands—

"Plant peas and Beans"—to more in-depth suggestions on how to maximize the growing potential of a garden during the hot, dry month of June in South Carolina.

The fact that Logan's instructions are for a kitchen garden suggests that her work may have been primarily directed at women. The maintenance of such a garden was a central responsibility of the colonial housewife, regardless of her social status. The kitchen garden—located behind the principle dwelling—was often a primary source of food for the household, and kitchen gardeners focused mainly on growing edible and medicinal plants. Lesser attention was given to exotic plants, such as citrus trees and ornamentals. Logan's calendar mentions some ornamentals—such as honeysuckle, jessamines, and flowering shrubs—but the overwhelming focus of her calendar is on growing foodstuffs. According to Logan's calendar, a good kitchen garden should contain more than thirty types of vegetables, various fruits and herbs, and even some grains, including hops and oats.

Because so much of a family's diet was dependent on the kitchen garden, Logan placed a particular emphasis on thrift and economy. For example, she suggested that spinach should be sown for "Use and Seed," and described separate processes for each purpose. Logan always sought to offer means of maximizing the crop yield of a garden while preparing for its continuation in future years. Her method is an excellent example of orderly, small-scale crop management; yet it is not so rigid that it does not leave room for flexibility. Logan's calendar demonstrates an understanding that the demands of one's other obligations occasionally disrupt the care of the garden and that the weather does not always cooperate. In her treatise she tried to help her readers to prioritize their tasks. The text provides ample room for "Whatever was neglected last Month" while emphasizing what "must not be delayed longer."

The calendar also indicates the emphasis Logan placed on a solid work ethic. In discussing the growth of Jerusalem artichokes, for example, her treatise warns that in the absence of sufficient manure, it is best to dig at least six inches to reach the "Untry'd Earth." While Logan clearly recognized that the task of digging further into the ground created additional toil, she claimed that it was well worth the extra work and would "amply reward the Labour." Logan used economic terms to suggest that an initial investment of labor is prerequisite to a high crop yield.

While the "Gardners Kalendar" focuses exclusively on the kitchen garden, Logan's own gardening went well beyond these limitations. In addition to garden writing, keeping a nursery, and maintaining her own garden, she actively studied many plants. For example, she apparently examined the effects of soil and climate on plants. In one such instance, she noted that a pool of urine around the base of a fruit tree is not only nourishing for the tree but also repulsive to many insects that might otherwise attack the plant.

Logan was also actively involved in the promotion of various plants. While her location in Charleston brought her in contact with some of the major figures in American botany, she did not confine her communication to those in South Carolina. She was involved in exchanging plants with people on both sides of the Atlantic. By far the most prominent horticulturist with whom she corresponded was John Bartram, the Philadelphia botanist who later became King's Botanizer Royal

for America. While Bartram visited Charleston on several occasions, he met Martha Logan only once. Nevertheless, Logan's friendship with Bartram spanned several years, and the letters that resulted from that connection display a slightly different side of the author of "Gardners Kalendar." While her publication placed an emphasis on practical plants, Logan's letters focus on the acquisition of new varieties of plants, often flowers and shrubs for ornamental purposes. Her focus on sharing plants and her knowledge about them made her letters a valuable part of an ongoing transcultural exchange. Logan and Bartram regularly sent one another seeds and plants, and because Bartram was also linked to the scientific elite of Europe, the exchange became a transatlantic one as well. Logan was able to introduce European species to her own garden while Bartram was able to pass along knowledge and samples of species from the American South.

Unfortunately, the conversation between Logan and Bartram is incomplete because Bartram's letters to Logan have never been found. It is possible that they were destroyed along with her Bible and her copy of the calendar when Gen. William Tecumseh Sherman burned the city of Columbia, South Carolina, in February 1865. Yet even though Bartram's letters to Logan are unavailable, the extant letters written by Logan reveal that both horticulturists encountered challenges in their gardening. For example, Logan indicated that she was not uniformly successful with her transplanted species. In a letter dated 14 September 1760, Logan lamented that "the mainy Shrubs & plants you have be Stowed on me have Succeded so badly that I am quite dishartned from trying Varity & Shall Confine my desires to what I know will doe," and on another occasion she admitted that mice had eaten up some of the bulbs she had set out to dry. Similarly, her letters also reveal that Bartram had failures as well, such as the "Striped Stockgilly Flowers" Logan encouraged him about in her 20 December 1760 letter. The mutual encouragement they offered one another is indicative of the spirit of knowledge sharing that marked this cultural exchange.

An examination of Logan's relationship with Bartram and her treatise on gardening suggests that Logan played an important role as an advocate of the region. In her exchange of seeds, bulbs, and insights with Bartram, Logan was effectively promoting species indigenous to the southern colonies to the entire western world. Her treatise on gardening also has distinctly regional elements. In an advertisement for Tobler's *South-Carolina Almanack* for 1752 the publisher claimed, "If this should meet with favourable Reception (which we hope it will as it is the first [almanac] calculated in and for this Province, and printed in it) a Continuance may be expected. . . ." While most almanacs are inherently regional to some degree or another, Tobler's comments reveal that Logan's calendar was part of an attempt to foster Southern writing and publication—one way in which Southern knowledge could be shared with the world.

The regional emphases in Logan's "Gardners Kalendar" and her correspondence with Bartram were transformed into a national emphasis during the Revolutionary War. Like her father in the earlier dispute with the proprietary lords, Martha Logan sided with the colonists against the British; she had children and grandchildren fighting in the war, and her son John was captured by royal troops and held as a prisoner of war. Logan loaned the U.S. government £3,500 to help finance the war, indicating her comfortable financial status at the end of her life. Following her death in 1779, her heirs continued to receive interest from the loan.

Martha Logan lived to be nearly seventy-five years old and led a full life by any standards. In addition to her full-time domestic responsibilities, she filled the roles of entrepreneur, teacher, horticulturist, scientist, and writer. Her writings about horticulture linked her not only to the average colonial housewife but also to some of the most highly esteemed botanists of her era. Well after her death, many people continued to revere Martha Logan as a woman of many talents. Indeed, her character seems to reach near-mythical proportions in one 1870 chronicle of Charleston families, which describes her in her later years as having been "wasted but majestic still, shrunken yet neither melancholy nor austere, never enveloping her house in gloom, nor banishing comfort from her board; but happy and cheerful to the last." The work also claims that Logan was "of a high order of intellect, great energy and a noble perseverance, crowned by sound practical piety, and busy in good works." Yet Logan's renown arose chiefly from her treatise on gardening, and because of that, the chronicle points out, "Her name will ever live as associated with horticulture."

Letters:

"Letters of Martha Logan to John Bartram, 1760–1763," edited by Mary Barbot Prior, *South Carolina Historical Magazine,* 59 (1958): 38–46;

"The Letters of Martha Daniell Logan," edited by Sharon M. Harris, in her *American Women Writers to 1800* (New York & Oxford: Oxford University Press, 1996), pp. 105–108.

References:

Buckner Hollingsworth, *Her Garden Was Her Delight* (New York: Macmillan, 1962), pp. 18–22;

Ann Leighton, *American Gardens in the Eighteenth Century: "For Use or for Delight"* (Boston: Houghton Mifflin, 1976), pp. 128–129, 211–215;

Elizabeth A. Poyas, *Days of Yore, or Shadows of the Past* (Charleston: W. G. Mazyck, 1870), pp. 16–34.

Papers:

Martha Logan's letters to John Bartram can be found at the Historical Society of Pennsylvania.

Margaret Morris

(21 November 1737 – 10 October 1816)

Amanda Gilroy
University of Groningen

WORKS: *Private Journal Kept During a Portion of the Revolutionary War for the Amusement of a Sister,* edited by John Jay Smith (Philadelphia: Privately printed, 1836);

"The Private Diary of Margaret Morris, Daughter of Dr. Richard Hill," in *Letters of Doctor Richard Hill and His Children: or, the History of a Family as Told by Themselves,* edited by Smith (Philadelphia: Privately printed, 1854), pp. 337–367.

Margaret Morris was a prolific writer. Between 1751 and 1774 she kept a private diary in which she recorded the inspirational messages of a devout Christian woman. She was also an assiduous correspondent and exchanged many letters with family members, especially her sister Milcah Martha (often called Patty) and her granddaughter Margaret Morris Collins. These letters deal with a range of topics including domesticity and suffering, faith and female conduct. Her most significant work is her Revolutionary War diary, written to keep her youngest sister, Milcah Martha, informed about events in Burlington, New Jersey. The journal begins on 6 December 1776, when Sir William Howe's British troops arrived in New Brunswick, New Jersey, about thirty-five miles north of her home, and ends at the time of the American victory over Howe in June 1778. It provides a vivid, and often amusing and satirical, commentary on the fate of noncombatants in Burlington, a town that was the object of contending armies. While other women, including Sarah Wister and Grace Growden Galloway, wrote Revolutionary War diaries, Morris's is especially precise about military detail, and it has been a resource for studies of the military history of the Revolution. The main focus of Morris's spiritual diary is the private loss and spiritual introspection caused by the death of several family members. In the war diary, however, she recorded the public disturbances of the war, and this work demonstrates a correspondence between public events and personal spiritual evolution.

Margaret Hill, circa 1752, about five years before her marriage to William Morris (portrait by A. Newsam; from Letters of Doctor Richard Hill and His Children, *1854)*

Margaret Hill Morris was born at South River, near Annapolis, Maryland, on 21 November 1737, one of the twelve children (two of whom died in infancy) of Quaker parents, Dr. Richard Hill and Deborah Moore Hill. Her father was the grandson of Richard Hill, a sea captain who immigrated to Maryland in 1673 and was granted a patent for 150 acres of land on the Eastern Shore. Her mother was the granddaughter of Thomas Lloyd, the friend of William Penn and the first governor of Pennsylvania. For eighteen years after his marriage in 1721, Richard Hill resided at South River, practicing as a physician and shipping merchant. (He also held several slaves.) In 1739 financial problems caused him to remove with his wife and two of his daughters to Funchal on the island of Madeira, where he established a successful wine business. Six other children—including Margaret, who was not yet two years old—were left in Philadelphia to be looked after by a fifteen-year-old sister, Hannah Hill Moore, the wife of Dr. Samuel Preston Moore. Margaret's two brothers, Richard Jr. and Henry, subsequently followed their parents to Funchal and became partners in their father's flourishing business; another sister, Deborah, also went to Madeira, and Milcah Martha was born on the island. Margaret's mother died in 1751, and her father returned to Philadelphia shortly thereafter. He died on 29 January 1762.

Little is known of Margaret's childhood, but her subsequent devotion to her sister Hannah suggests that she was a tender surrogate mother. The Hill children left in Philadelphia received an education at the best schools, and it is recorded that at least one of the girls was a pupil of Anthony Benezet, a Quaker abolitionist and egalitarian schoolteacher. The family's strong Quaker practice is evident throughout Margaret Morris's writings. Beginning in May 1757 Margaret was dangerously ill with what she calls "a nervous fever" for a year, an illness that apparently delayed her marriage to William Morris on 23 September 1758. Her husband was a dry-goods merchant and a direct descendant of the first Anthony Morris, who had come to Pennsylvania in the time of William Penn. The marriage seems to have been one of mutual affection. In a diary entry for January 1760 Morris described herself as "happy in the tender affections of a beloved husband." That happiness was cut short, however, by her husband's death in December 1765, leaving her with three surviving children, John, Deborah, and Richard Hill. Another daughter, Gulielma Maria, was born in August 1766; two other children had died in infancy. In June 1770 Margaret Morris removed her family to the home of her sister Sarah Dillwyn, wife of George Dillwyn, a Quaker catechist, on the Green Bank in Burlington, New Jersey. Their riverside home had previously been occupied by William Franklin, royal governor of New Jersey and the illegitimate son of Benjamin Franklin. She returned to Philadelphia some years later and was there during the yellow-fever epidemic of 1793. She subsequently moved back to Burlington, where she raised her orphaned granddaughter Margaret Morris Collins.

Morris's private diary, published in *Letters of Doctor Richard Hill and His Children* (1854), covers the early years she spent in Philadelphia, with only two entries written after her first removal to Burlington in 1770. She began this spiritual diary on her fourteenth birthday, 21 November 1751, opening it with a meditation on the frailty of the body and the sublimity of the soul. Morris made entries sporadically until 1774, and the diary forms a compendium of the heterogeneous materials of everyday life. It includes prosaic information about the arrival or departure of friends and relatives, especially the visits of family members living in Madeira. Like many women of her generation, Morris used her diary to record births, deaths, and marriages, notably her own marriage to William Morris. In her diary Morris emerges as a pious young matron grateful for the moral habits of her merchant husband. Events that endanger others but which did not harm her own family, such as a "very dreadful fire" in September 1760, are also recounted, as well as the intimate joys of her domestic life, notably her repeated survival of the dangers of childbirth and the delivery of healthy babies. Many entries deal with her concern for her children and, more broadly, with the moral economy of her whole household. Thus, an entry of 1761 recounts a fairy-tale-like dream in which she was lost in a strange place and was guided home, through briars and thorns and over a river, by an old woman who said she was a prophetess and who remained with Morris to care for her children. The dream was interpreted by a friend to mean that the Church would care for Morris's children. The gift of a Negro boy from her deceased father occasioned a meditation on slavery in April 1763. Morris found slavery "inconsistent" with Christian principles, but while the institution existed she endeavored to convert it to "an easy servitude" and to fulfill a parental role in relation to her servants. A memorandum inserted in her diary on 1 January 1768 records that she had neglected the practice of keeping household accounts while absorbed in sorrow during the two years following her husband's death. Her resumption of the practice of meticulous financial management was a practical response to the limitations of her widow's income, but it is also a sign that she was keeping good spiritual accounts.

It is personal tragedy that most often led to Morris's diary entries and a sense of the spiritual renewal that could come from keeping a faithful record of her life events. In September 1760 Morris wrote: "My darling first-born child thou hast been pleased to take from me." She later wrote of the deaths of "my dear little daughter" on 14 February 1765, of her parents, and of both her husband and sister-in-law in her entry for 11 December 1765. These tragic events are not, however, recounted in detail. Rather, she saw them as tests of her faith and

Green Bank, Burlington, New Jersey, where Morris wrote her Revolutionary War diary (engraving after a drawing by John Collins)

as occasions for spiritual introspection, so that the writing of the diary became a type of spiritual discipline. The brief records of these events are followed by prayers for humility or guidance, or by meditations on their spiritual significance. A "constant theme of gratitude" to God, her "adorable Creator," is characteristic of those occasions when Morris was spared from a general calamity, such as a sickness that afflicted the community, but it was in heroic submission to personal loss that Morris confirmed the strength of her faith. Again and again she registered her desire to "live loose" from those she loves, so that she might be able to relinquish them according to God's will. Yet the pathos of her petitions to God testifies to the strain of suppressing secular ties in favor of spiritual ones. Morris reached toward a "sweet resignation" of her maternal affections, precisely those feelings most valued by the culture in which she lived.

The difficult negotiations between secular and spiritual concerns also dominated Morris's war diary, written in Burlington between 6 December 1776 and 14 June 1778, and finally published in 1836 as *Private Journal Kept During a Portion of the Revolutionary War for the Amusement of a Sister*. She wrote about the effects of war on a thriving religious community, for Burlington was one of the earliest Quaker settlements in the colonies, and by 1776 some one hundred and thirteen men and women gathered at the Society of Friends hexagonal meetinghouse. The journal is in fact a compilation of diary "scraps," which Morris collected to send to her sister Milcah Martha in Montgomery Square, Penn-

sylvania, and it was not intended for publication. However, like many women, she expected her diary would be circulated among family and friends, and in a letter prefacing the diary she hopes for friendly readers who will "turn the critic out of doors" in order to attend to her heartfelt words.

Morris's war journal begins in one of the darkest periods of American history: Sir William Howe's troops arrived in New Brunswick, New Jersey, on 6 December 1776, and on the next day Gen. Charles Cornwallis's British division, including Hessian troops (German mercenaries), marched south, threatening Philadelphia. They arrived at Trenton on 8 December, as the last of George Washington's troops were retreating across the Delaware River into Pennsylvania. Panic reigned, and many of the inhabitants of Philadelphia fled the city. Although rumors and warnings were rife, Margaret Morris decided to trust in Providence and to stay put. In diary entries over the next year and a half, Morris details the movements and behavior of Hessian and rebel troops in Burlington and on the Delaware River, including the American bombardment of Burlington in early December, as well as reports of action further afield, such as Washington's surprise attack on the Hessians at Trenton at Christmas 1776. She also wrote of her concealment of a Tory refugee, Dr. Jonathan Odell, while her house was searched by armed men, and she provided a vivid picture of how rumors circulate in a time of crisis, their vagueness frequently compounding the feeling of danger.

December 6th 1776 – Being on a Visit to my frd. M S, at Haddonfeild. I was preparing to return to my Family, when a Person from Philada told us the people there, were in great Commotion, that the English fleet was in the River & hourly expected to sail up to the City; that the inhabitants were removing into the Country, & that several persons of consi= derable repute had been discoverd to have formd a design of setting fire to the City, & were summoned before the Congress & strictly injoind to drop the horrid purpose – When I heard the above report my heart almost died within me, & I cried surely the Lord will not punish the innocent with the guilty, & I wishd there might be found some interceeding Lotts & Abrahams amongst our People. – On my Journey home I was told the inhabitants of our little Town were going in haste into the Country, & that my nearest Neighbors were already removed – When I heard this, I felt my self quite Sick I was ready to faint – I thought of my S D (the beloved Companion of my widowd State) her Husband at the distance of some hundred miles from her – I thought of my own lone= ly situation, no Husband to cheer, with the voice of love, my Sinking spirits, my little flock too, without a Father to direct them how to Steer, – all these things crouded into my mind at once, & I felt like one forsaken – a flood of friendly tears came to my releif – & I felt an humble confidence, that he, who had been with me in six troubles woud not forsake me now – While I cherishd this hope my tranquility was restord, & I felt no Sensations but of humble Acquiescence to the Divine Will – & was favo= ord to find my Family in health, on my Arrival, & my Dear Companion not greatly discomposd, for which favor I desire to be made truly thankful – 7th a letter from my neas= ghbors Husband at the Camp, wishd her to be gone in haste

The first entry in Morris's Revolutionary War diary (Library of Haverford College)

and many persons coming into Town today, brought
intelligence that the British Army were advancing towards
us - 8th every day begins & ends with the same accounts,
& we hear today the Regulars are at Trenton - some of
our Neighbors gone, & others going, makes our little Bank
look lonesome; but our trust in Providence is still fixt.
& we dare not even talk of removing our Family.. 9th, this
Evening we were favord with the Company of our faithful
Frd & Br: N.W. this testimony of his love was truly acceptable to us. 10th today our Amiable frd E.C, & her Family
bid us adieu, my Br: also left us, but returnd in less than an
hour, telling us he coud not go away fast as the Hessians were
entering the Town - but no Troops coming in we urged him
to leave us next morning, wch he concluded to do, after preparing
us to expect the Hessians in a few hours - A number of Gallies
had been lying in the River, before the Town for 2 days past
11th after various reports from one hour to another of light horse, &
approaching, the people in town had certain intelligence that a
large body of Hessians were come to Borden town, & we might
expect to see them in a few hours -

About 10 o'clock in the morning of this day (the
eleventh) a party of about 60 men, marchd down the
Main Street, as they past along, they told our Docto:
& some other persons in the Town, that a large
number of Hessians were advancing, & would be in
the Town in less than an hour — This Party
were Rifle men, who it seems had crost the
River some where in the neighborhood of Borden
Town to reconnoitre, & meeting with a Superior
number of Hessians on the road, were then
returning, & took Burlington in their way back

As a member of the Society of Friends, Morris was opposed to war, and in a March 1777 letter she claimed that "the height of my politics" is the heartfelt wish that "the now contending parties shall shake hands, and all be friends once more." In this desire Morris was in accord with most Quakers of the period, who did not support a revolutionary break with Britain and who hoped for a reconciliation between the mother country and the colonies. Often their neutrality was interpreted as sympathy toward the Tories. Some of Morris's entries, however, reveal an underlying sympathy with the successes of her fellow countrymen. She sometimes referred to the victories or losses of "our people," meaning the American soldiers. At least one page of the diary manuscript was inadvertently or deliberately destroyed, possibly by members of Morris's family prior to the publication of the journal in 1836, in order to avoid any entanglement in the ongoing arguments about questions of loyalty during the Revolutionary War. What emerges most clearly in the diary is Morris's aversion to war, which she called "a horrid Art" with "a Woeful tendency . . . to harden the human heart against the tender feelings of humanity." She sympathized with the soldiers' mothers and with the straitened circumstances of her neighbors as a result of the "calamities of war."

In a letter to Milcah Martha, Morris explained that parts of the journal were "written in a serious, others in a waggish mood, and most of it after the family were abed, and I sat up to keep guard over my fences, &c., while the soldiers were next door, for fear they should pull them down to burn." This tension between the serious and the humorous characterizes the narrative style of the diary. Though she dealt sympathetically with the havoc the war wreaked on the land, Morris also made dangerous events amusing as part of a satiric strategy to expose irrational or inappropriate behavior. Thus, in contrast to the panic of her neighbor James Verree (called J.V. in the diary) that their homes would be pillaged by a marauding army and that Hessians will be billeted on them, Morris represented herself as a hostess caught unprepared for the entertainment of a large company. Her response to events tended to be pragmatic: she started to teach her children some German phrases in preparation for the Hessians she might be required to accommodate, and she located a possible interpreter in a neighbor's Dutch maidservant. In describing what happened when Tory hunters invaded her home in search of Odell, Morris displayed her storytelling skills, especially her ear for dialogue. The Tory hunters spoke "rudely" and searched incompetently for the refugee; "strange where he could be," Morris reflected wryly. While she claimed to have been "ruffled," she put on a "simple look" for the benefit of the searchers and pretended to think that they were Hessians.

The war diary, unlike Morris's earlier journal, is seldom religious in tone. Lacking the prayers and meditations that characterize Morris's spiritual diary, the war diary is nevertheless more than a document of public events: it is also the agent of personal evolution. Morris's focus on the temporal served spiritual ends, for she was concerned with how war could impair faith (as in the cases of her neighbors who fled in the face of rumors). Indeed the public ravages of the war were trials that tested her faith. She often marveled that she was not discomposed by the dangers to which she was exposed, but faith gave her confidence. Though the rebel soldiers could not understand what hindered them from firing on her home, she attributed her safety to the protection of "the Guardian of the Widow & the Orphan." Throughout the journal staying in one place is seen as a demonstration of faith, and she thanked God who "kept our feet from Wandering from the habitation his goodness has allotted to us"; thus, she was able to keep calm while people all around her were panicking.

Morris's charitable acts, especially her protection of and medical assistance to soldiers on both sides of the conflict, were rewarded beyond her expectations in ways that validated for her the values of community in a time of strife and indicated the hand of God in secular life. The Tory refugee whom she protected appears to have prevented the cannonading of her house by the British fleet. A rough-looking naval man, whose wife Morris successfully treated for "itch fever," repaid her kindness by taking some gifts to her family in Philadelphia. Each act of charity seemed to generate more good deeds, for the man returned with a letter and provisions for her, including salt, tea, coffee, and sugar. Morris thanked God for "such seasonable supplies" and proceeded to share the salt with the local poor: like Christ's feeding of the multitude, Morris asserted, their "little store" seemed "increased by distributing it." Such entries reveal the divine pattern beneath the surface of social chaos and show how spiritual and practical concerns were intimately bound together in her life.

Morris was a prolific correspondent, writing to members of her family throughout her life. As with her diaries, she used letter writing to cope with stress, and she saw correspondence as a necessary form of record keeping. She vividly described the ravages of the yellow-fever epidemic in Philadelphia

Memo Potatoes, Turnips, Carrots, Parsnips, Beets & Radishes shoud be planted, in the decrease of the moon —

12th month 1806 —
The produce of my Garden this year has fallen much below what it had been for several years past, which I attribute to the want of good attendance, having let it to the Shares &c.
The Potatoes, first Crop were very poor, & the last planted yeilded but little more than what was put into the ground — the Onions were fine tho the crop was very small —
The Cucumbers & Melons intended for Pickles were nearly destroyd by weeds & did not afford a single Mango to Pickle — the Peppers destroyd by weeds —
This Memo is meant to be referrd to, in case of my living to the return of another Season for Gardening —

Page from Morris's gardening notes (Library of Haverford College)

in 1793, when she stayed in the city to nurse family and friends against advice to leave for a place of safety. She wrote that this "post" was "assigned" to her by "Infinite Wisdom." Once again her spiritual faith survived severe trials, notably the death of her son Dr. John Morris, and again she wrote to surmount any "murmuring thought" against God and reach "the road to peace." Following the death of her son and his wife, she took over the care of her infant granddaughter and namesake, Margaret Morris. A letter to this granddaughter, written before her marriage to Isaac Collins in 1810, was published as a separate pamphlet by Morris's great-grand-daughter E. P. Smith in 1886 for its "wholesome

advice" on female conduct within marriage. (A few sentences on the indecency of public expressions of marital affection are omitted from this publication.) The letter sums up Morris's thoughts on a woman's duties: she enjoins wifely obedience and frugality, "blameless deportment," and a daily application to God's wisdom.

Throughout her writings Morris documented her medical skills, from treating feverous soldiers during the Revolution and yellow-fever patients in Philadelphia to curing the upset stomach of a small child who had eaten too many currants. In a 1794 letter to her sister Morris fretted that her "quack-ings" might be harmful but hoped that her good

Morris at seventy-six (engraving by Morris Smith)

intentions would protect her from censure. In accordance with traditional attitudes about the correlation between the mind and the spirit, Morris believed that healing the physical person would also help to heal the spiritual person and that strength of spirit could enhance strength of person. Many women's diaries include medicinal recipes, but Morris was remarkable in that she was publicly recognized as a skillful doctor and dispensed healing to others outside her family. The demand for her services in Burlington was so great that she visited her patients in a carriage that was regularly brought to her door for the purpose. At one point she had thirty smallpox patients under her care, and she is said to have bled a fainting woman using only a common razor because no lancet was available.

Morris often relied on remedies she had jotted down in notebooks. Her undated "Recipe Book" is a blend of the domestic and the scientific, with recipes for "Potted Beef" and instructions on how "To preserve cream to use at sea" alongside advice on skin care and how "To destroy Bed Bugs," as well as cures "For the bleeding Piles" and for rheumatism

and ringworm. A letter from about 1780 documents her plan to open a small pharmacy in order to capitalize on the townspeople's long-standing practice of applying to her for every "dose of physic." Unfortunately the townspeople seem to have preferred the old system of gratuitous dispensation, and the new venture was soon abandoned.

Morris's reference to the medicinal efficacy of breast milk in her private diary—as a young woman "languishing" under a nervous fever she was cured by breast milk—suggests the importance of the maternal as a healing force in life. When her sister Patty was unwell, she wrote of wanting to "nurse" her and "nourish thee with milk from my own breast." She sympathized with other mothers during the Revolutionary War, and throughout her life she defined herself in familial terms, signing her letters as "thy tenderly affection mother" (or sister). Her unwavering spiritual commitment is embodied in her lifelong commitment to maternal nurturing. In a diary entry for 5 September 1762 she described herself as "a hopeful mother": ultimately, she was a mother whose care for bodily and spiritual well-being extended beyond her immediate family to the wider community.

Margaret Morris lived out her declining years in Burlington, her lifelong devotion to her family amply repaid in the loving care of her grandchildren. She was carried in a sedan chair to the Friends meetinghouse, a few doors from her dwelling, and she was frequently visited by friends and neighbors. She was engaged in writing and domestic pursuits until the end of her life: a letter from Margaret Collins found her grandmother, her daughters, and "two or three damsels . . . busy at the quilting-frame." In 1811 Morris recorded making shirts for her grandson. A letter of May 1813 calmly recorded a slight paralytic stroke; Morris died on 10 October 1816.

Morris's voluminous correspondence, her private diary, and her war journal provide a picture of Quaker womanhood in the second half of the eighteenth century. Since its first publication in 1836, Morris's revolutionary journal has been republished several times: in 1854 (in the collection of her family's letters), in 1865, in 1919–1920 in the *Bulletin of Friends' Historical Society,* in 1949 and 1969, and in Elizabeth Evans's *Weathering the Storm* in 1975. This diary has a significant place in the history of Quaker women's writing. Morris's private diary, which was also published in the 1854 collection of her family's letters, received little scholarly attention. Feminist critics, however, might find much of interest in this diary and in Morris's letters, especially in her treatment of femininity and spirituality.

Letters:

Letters of Doctor Richard Hill and His Children: or, the History of a Family as Told by Themselves, edited by John Jay Smith (Philadelphia: Privately printed, 1854), pp. 368–463;

A Family Letter. Margaret Morris to her Grand-daughter, Margaret Morris, 1810 (Germantown: Privately printed, 1886).

References:

Mary Sauter Comfort, "The Literary Styles of Four Women Diarists of the American Revolution," dissertation, Lehigh University, 1985, pp. 23–59;

Elizabeth Evans, *Weathering the Storm: Women of the American Revolution* (New York: Scribners, 1975), pp. 73–109;

Steven E. Kagle, *American Diary Literature: 1620–1799* (Boston: Twayne, 1979), pp. 131–135.

Papers:

Margaret Morris's manuscripts, including her unpublished "Recipe Book," and her correspondence are housed in the Quaker Collection at the Library of Haverford College.

Judith Sargent Murray

(1 May 1751 – 6 July 1820)

Sheila L. Skemp
University of Mississippi

See also the Murray entry in *DLB 37: American Writers of the Early Republic.*

BOOKS: *Some deductions from the system promulgated in the page of divine revelation, ranged in the order and form of a catechism, intended as an assistant to the Christian parent or teacher . . .* (Norwich, Conn: Printed by John Trumbull, 1782);

The Gleaner: A Miscellaneous Production, 3 volumes (Boston: Printed by I. Thomas & E. T. Andrews, 1798).

Editions: *The Gleaner* (Schenectady: Union College Press, 1992);

Selected Writings of Judith Sargent Murray, edited by Sharon M. Harris (New York: Oxford University Press, 1995).

PLAY PRODUCTIONS: *The Medium; or Virtue Triumphant,* Boston, Federal Street Theater, 2 March 1795;

The Traveller Returned, Boston, Federal Street Theater, 9 March 1796;

The African, Boston, Federal Street Theater, 1808.

OTHER: John Murray, *Letters and Sketches of Sermons,* 3 volumes, edited by Judith Sargent Murray (Boston: Joshua Belcher, 1812–1813);

John Murray, *Life of John Murray,* edited, with a continuation, by Judith Sargent Murray (Boston: Munroe & Francis, 1816).

SELECTED PERIODICAL PUBLICATIONS:
"Desultory thoughts upon the Utility of encouraging a degree of self-complacency, especially in female bosoms," *Gentleman and Lady's Town and Country Magazine; or, Repository of Instruction and Entertainment,* 6 (October 1784): 251;

"On the Equality of the Sexes," *Massachusetts Magazine,* 2 (March and April 1790): 132ff.;

"On the Domestic Education of Children," *Massachusetts Magazine,* 2 (May 1790);

Judith Sargent Stevens, circa 1770, about eighteen years before she married John Murray (portrait by John Singleton Copley; private collection)

"The Gleaner," *Massachusetts Magazine,* 4 (February 1792) – 6 (August 1794);

"The Repository," *Massachusetts Magazine,* 4 (September 1792) – 6 (July 1794).

An American poet, essayist, and playwright, Judith Sargent Murray was surpassed in her day only by British feminist Mary Wollstonecraft in her willingness to examine and probe the limits that her society placed on women. Murray's views were traditional in many ways: she exhibited little interest in voting rights for women, disapproved of divorce, and looked at politics and society through the lens of an elite Federalism that valued order and hierarchy over equality. Yet her willingness to demand the fruits of independence and liberty for women; her insistence that in most instances masculinity and femininity were human constructs, not natural or God-given reality; and her assertion that the mind has no gender gave her work a feminist edge that set her apart from most of her American contemporaries.

Judith Sargent was born in Gloucester, Massachusetts, on 1 May 1751. The oldest of eight children, four of whom lived to adulthood, she grew up with a quiet sense of her family's superiority in a world where lineage and wealth mattered a great deal. Indeed, Murray's character and views were shaped as much by her inherited social position as they were by the changes in America wrought by the Revolution. Her father, Winthrop Sargent (1727-1793), was, like his father and grandfather before him, a prosperous ship's captain and merchant. Her mother, Judith Saunders Sargent (1731-1793), whose paternal ancestors had settled in Gloucester at the turn of the eighteenth century, also came from a successful seafaring family.

Until she was two years old, Judith Sargent was an only child. In 1753, however, with the birth of her brother Winthrop (1753-1820), her sense of entitlement was challenged for the first time. If she enjoyed the automatic respect accorded her family name, she discovered that as a female her opportunities were limited. Winthrop was given the best education that his parents' money could buy. He attended Boston Latin School, and in 1771 he graduated from Harvard. For her part Judith had a reading teacher, briefly attended a local writing school, and sat in on some of the lessons that Winthrop endured with the local Congregationalist minister, John Rogers. Her parents steadfastly ignored her pleas for further formal education, especially for an introduction to the classics.

Sargent used what skills she had attained to read voraciously and indiscriminately–novels and poetry, history and essays, and drama–especially the works of William Shakespeare–and religious works. By the time she began to write for publication, she had read and absorbed the work of European women writers such as Mary Astell, Madame Madeleine de Scudéry, and, most important, Whig historian Catherine Macaulay. Sargent's resentment at what she considered to be her inferior education made her especially receptive to the examples of women who had managed to transcend their circumstances and to enter the world of print.

In the short run no such possibility seemed likely for young Judith Sargent. She "scribbled" constantly, writing poetry and what she called a "little history," but she shared her work with only relatives and close friends. On 3 October 1769, a year after the birth of her youngest brother, FitzWilliam (1768-1822), she married John Stevens (1741-1787), a Gloucester sea captain and merchant whose social credentials were at least as impressive as her own. If the marriage was not unhappy, neither did it meet Judith's expectations, which had no doubt been elevated by the romantic novels she had devoured as a young girl. She admired John but did not love him. The family's finances were precarious. Most unfortunately from her perspective, the marriage was childless.

Judith Stevens's life changed dramatically on 3 November 1774, when the Universalist itinerant minister John Murray arrived in Gloucester at the invitation of her father and her uncle Epes Sargent. Murray had left England for America in 1770 and had begun preaching up and down the New England coast shortly thereafter. The Sargents, Stevenses, and some of their Gloucester friends were already familiar with the views of Murray's mentor, English minister James Relly, and they were delighted with the opportunity to meet one of Relly's disciples. While Murray's brand of Universalism embraced the traditional Calvinist notions of original sin and predestination, his theology was suffused with the optimism of the European Enlightenment. He stressed God's rationality, love, and benevolence rather than his role as judge. While Murray agreed that all humans deserved eternal damnation, he believed that because Christ had died for the sins of all, ultimately everyone would be saved. Sin would be punished on this earth, he said, not in the hereafter. Because the Universalists believed that humans were originally purely spiritual beings who were once united with Christ, they not only saw the human body as an inessential, artificial, and destabilizing construct, but they also thought that all people had a common blood and a common spirit. As persecuted dissenters who distrusted human authority in religious affairs, they were firm advocates of the separation of Church and State. While Judith Sargent Murray rarely discussed her theological views in public, the tenets of Universalism, particularly its emphasis on the spiritual essence of humanity and its support of religious liberty, were apparent in everything she wrote.

In 1776 Murray's supporters quit attending Gloucester's First Parish Church, and in February 1777 the church elders formally suspended fifteen of its recalcitrant members, including Judith, her parents, and her uncle Epes Sargent. The following January the remnant group formed an Independent Church of Christ, designating John Murray as their minister. Both Judith and John Stevens signed the Articles of Association that created the first Universalist Church in America.

Having rejected her old religion and rebelled against the Puritan establishment of Massachusetts, Judith Stevens began to question other human traditions and constructs as well. The religious views that cost her so dearly in social esteem ultimately gave her the courage to disagree with her detractors in other areas. By submitting to God's will as she understood it, she learned to reject the authority of mere mortals whose views of women did not conform with her own understanding of human nature. In particular, her notion that the body is merely a temporary home for the soul and that the eternal and genderless soul controls and defines the body meant that in intellectual and spiritual matters women were equal to—indeed no different from—men.

Most important, her religious views led to her first publication, *Some deductions from the system promulgated in the page of divine revelation, ranged in the order and form of a catechism, intended as an assistant to the Christian parent or teacher . . .*, published anonymously in 1782. Originally she intended to employ this catechism to help her teach two young orphans—distant relatives of her husband—who had been entrusted to her care. When her Universalist friends urged her to publish the work, she reluctantly complied. The introduction reveals her fears that as a woman she was going well beyond her sphere in discussing theological issues in a public forum. She defended her action as a mother, a woman, and a Christian. She wrote the catechism, she insisted, to fulfill her motherly duty to her two young charges. She proclaimed that in spiritual matters women and men were equal and that, as a Christian, she was obliged to use her God-given ability in the service of true religion. Thus, from the beginning Murray linked her religion with her views on gender. Once she had entered the public realm, she was reluctant to quit the arena. She had begun her literary career in the service of God; she continued that career in pursuit of earthly renown and eventually profit as well.

Even as she abandoned the faith of her fathers, her own countrymen were declaring their independence from England. Judith Sargent Murray later credited the American Revolution with forcing her to question the legal, political, and economic limitations that all American women endured in the eighteenth century. While her religious views gave her the courage to question women's place, the Revolution gave her the language with which to challenge the gender-based strictures that defined her world. In many ways the war did little to change women's lives and did much to reinforce traditional views of gender relations. As men marched off to war, leaving women and children behind, they reconfirmed the notion that helpless women needed men to protect them and that there were certain public spaces—particularly the battlefield—where most women could not go. Still, a war fought in the name of liberty, equality, and independence was a liberating experience for some women, and Thomas Jefferson's plea for the natural right of all people to "life, liberty, and the pursuit of happiness" struck a chord for many others, including Judith Stevens.

Most of Judith's relatives were patriots, although Epes Sargent remained loyal to England and was forced to flee Gloucester for his safety. John Murray served briefly as a chaplain in the Continental Army until bad health forced him to resign. Despite his active support for the American cause, the Gloucester Committee of Public Safety accused him of spying for the enemy and tried to banish him from Gloucester.

The treatment of John Murray and Epes Sargent reconfirmed Judith's conviction of the importance of toleration for unpopular opinions. It also contributed to her lukewarm support of the war effort. She viewed the war in the same way as many women of her era. As many of her poems indicate, to her the war meant the potential deaths of loved ones and the disruption of her normal, domestic routine. Moreover, as she watched the coarsening effect of the war on her brother Winthrop, an officer in the Continental Army, she became convinced that military service and traditional morality did not mix. She also became convinced that war supported the "masculine" values of civic republicanism, which were grounded in public virtue and heroic self-sacrifice on the battlefield. As she began to entertain thoughts of earning literary fame for herself, she realized that so long as the war dragged on, the private and mundane sacrifices of women would pass unnoticed. Only at the end of the war could the poet and historian reap the praises of their countrymen.

It is hardly surprising that Judith Stevens began writing an essay on the equality of the sexes in 1779. She did not publish it until more than a decade later, but in 1784, just a year after the United States celebrated its official independence from England, she published "Desultory thoughts upon the Utility of encouraging a degree of self-complacency, especially in female bosoms" in the October issue of *The Gentleman and Lady's Town and Country Magazine* under the pen name Constantia. The essay foreshadowed many of the themes of her later writings, as it emphasized women's innate rationality and the need for women to value themselves if they were to achieve their full potentials. Women who had no confidence in their own abilities, she insisted, were likely prey for wily seducers or unworthy husbands. The essay spoke as well to the one issue that dominated her writing from that time forward: the need for better educational opportunities for women. The editors of the magazine begged for more essays from Constantia, but the journal closed its doors after only a few issues, and Judith temporarily abandoned her hopes for literary fame.

Indeed, the years immediately following the Revolutionary War were not a good period for Judith and John Stevens. Although she wrote quite a few essays and poems in the 1770s, many of which she published decades later, Judith was preoccupied with more-mundane concerns in this period. A postwar economic slump hurt all the merchants in Gloucester. John, who was a reckless businessman, was devastated by the contraction in merchant activity. In 1786 his creditors demanded immediate payment of all his debts. Unable to comply, he fled his house—arguably the finest private edifice in Gloucester at the time—and sailed for the West Indian island of Saint Eustatius, where he hoped to recoup his losses. In the early spring of 1787 he fell ill, dying on 8 March before he could return home. Judith Stevens was left alone to face her husband's creditors.

While she eventually managed to resolve her financial affairs, the experience left an indelible mark. She remained obsessed by a need for financial security for the rest of her life. Her "Gleaner" essays are replete with sympathetic stories of worthy debtors who fall from positions of affluence through no fault of their own. Moreover, her financial problems made her realize how important it was for women to be prepared to take care of their own needs. As wives, eighteenth-century American women lived under the system of coverture, which meant that they did not exist as independent economic or legal entities. As single women, whether they were widows or had never married, they were "femmes soles," but in general they had few marketable abilities and even fewer economic opportunities to take care of their own needs. Women, insisted Judith Sargent Murray, had to be educated not simply to achieve self-esteem but to develop the skills to fend for themselves. Thus, unlike many of her contemporaries, her public pleas

for better education for women were grounded not only in her desire to make women better wives and mothers but also in her conviction that women should never be solely dependent on men for their material welfare.

Although she had often declared that she would never take a second husband, Judith Stevens married John Murray on 6 October 1788. While the marriage did little to ease Judith's financial worries, it was by all accounts a happy union, approaching the standard of the companionate marriage that had become the ideal if not the reality among elite Americans by the end of the eighteenth century. Their attraction was based on a judicious mixture of mutual esteem and respect, rationality and passion. In 1789 Judith was overjoyed to discover that she was pregnant, and devastated when her son, George, was stillborn on 5 August 1789. A little more than two years later, her daughter, Julia Maria, was born on 22 August 1791.

The 1790s were Judith Sargent Murray's most prolific period as a writer. In January 1790, using the pen name Constantia, she started publishing her poetry in the *Massachusetts Magazine,* beginning with the autobiographical "Lines, occasioned by the Death of an Infant." In March and April 1790 her two-part essay "On the Equality of the Sexes" appeared in the same periodical. The essay contended for the intellectual equality of women, as Murray maintained that women possessed the essential qualities of imagination, reason, memory, and judgment in the same degree that men did. If women used their abilities to frivolous or fanciful ends, she argued, they did so because they had no education to guide them and no reason to assume that their efforts would result in economic success or even the approbation of posterity. It was nurture, not nature, that condemned women to their vain and circumscribed lives. She agreed that most men were superior to women in physical powers, but she contended that bodily strength bore no relationship to strength or rationality of mind. The body, she said repeatedly, was simply a transient "earth born tenament." Murray was careful not to assert that women should be liberated from responsibility for their traditional duties. She merely thought most domestic activities required so little mental ability that women could easily exercise their minds while performing their ordinary household tasks. With a little effort they could even find time to write down their thoughts, snatching a few moments here and there or forgoing the frivolous round of visits and gossip that occupied all too much of most women's days.

the declaration of Jehovah is surely worthy of all acceptation, and the record which God hath given of himself, proclaims the universality of his love, and of his power, the restitution of all things, the wiping of every tear from every eye. The individuals

Those individuals who were, upon this occasion, assembled in the chamber of death, continued silent, they tacitly consented that the Heretic, if in her power, should soothe the agonized mind of their departing friend, nay their countenances were descriptive of approbation. A gleam of hope seemed also to light up the features of the dying, but this apparent gleam was only the notice of the moment, her apprehensions returned, and despair enwrapped her soul!!!

Yet few persons have deserved more than Amanda, her life was amiable, useful, and benevolent. How indispensable, how truly important, is an acquaintance with the great and consolatory truths of our most holy Religion.

Penetrated by the goodness of my God, and wrapt in the robe of Emmanuel's righteousness, I prostrate at the feet of the Most High.

     Cleora

    May 31st 1777   Saturday evening

A White day this — I have hailed Cleora the joyful Mother of a second pledge of connubial love. It is a sweet smiling Girl, her infant countenance prognosticates future loveliness, and the lines of her pretty face, already indicate a number of latent beauties. How enchanting is innocence, how sweetly interesting, how endearingly prepossessing. The scene at Cleora's was replete with high toned rapture! It was about four O'clock in the afternoon, that the God of our salvation gave us this new cause for gratitude, for immeasurable joy. With what transport did I hasten to gratulate the tender fair One, and to hail the New born Stranger. Alternately we pressed to our bosoms the lovely infant, while the gentle Matron appeared absorbed in extatic contemplation; and her every wish, in that delicious moment, seemed amply gratified. The partner of her life, in a delirium of joy, hardly knew to which to address himself, the tender female who had thus blessed him, or the little unconscious pledge of their mutual love. For Cleora, a virtuous blush suffused her pale countenance, as the Father of her children approached, her eyes proclaimed him the chosen of her heart, and every feature was expressive of the unutterable tenderness with which her fond bosom is replete. Happy, thrice happy Cleora, silken are the bands in which thou art holden — May the Almighty continue to thee, the blessings which he at present giveth thee so abundantly to enjoy. Their first hope, their eldest blossom was introduced, here was a new source of pleasing sensations

Pages from the manuscripts for two unpublished essays by Murray (Mississippi Department of Archives and History)

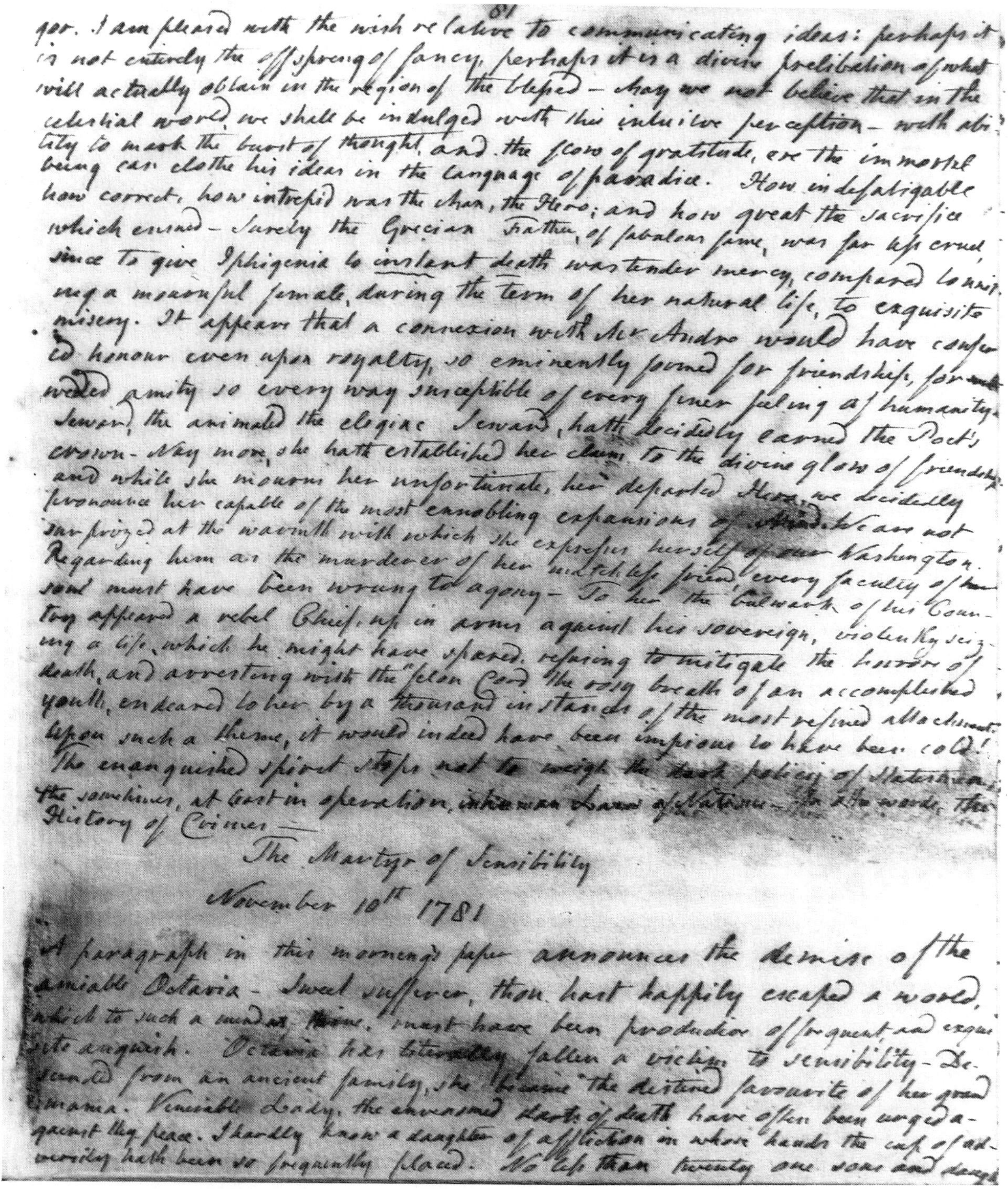

you. I am pleased with the wish relative to communicating ideas: perhaps it is not entirely the offspring of fancy, perhaps it is a divine prelibation of what will actually obtain in the region of the blessed — May we not believe that in the celestial world we shall be indulged with this intuitive perception — with ability to mark the burst of thought, and the flow of gratitude, ere the immortal being can clothe his ideas in the language of paradise. How indefatigable, how correct, how intrepid was the man, the Hero; and how great the sacrifice which ensued — Surely the Grecian Father, of fabulous fame, was far less cruel, since to give Iphigenia to _instant death_ was tender mercy, compared to inuring a mournful female, during the term of her natural life, to exquisite misery. It appears that a connexion with Mr André would have conferred honour even upon royalty, so eminently formed for friendship, for wedded amity so every way susceptible of every finer feeling of humanity, Seward, the animated the elegiac Seward, hath decidedly earned the Poet's crown — Nay more, she hath established her claim to the divine glow of friendship, and while she mourns her unfortunate, her departed Hero, we decidedly pronounce her capable of the most ennobling expansions of — We are not surprized at the warmth with which she expresses herself of our Washington. Regarding him as the murderer of her undelibed friend, every faculty of her soul must have been wrung to agony — To her the bulwark of his Country appeared a rebel Chief, up in arms against his sovereign, violently seizing a life, which he might have spared, refusing to mitigate the horror of death, and arresting with the "felon Cord" the only breath of an accomplished youth, endeared to her by a thousand instances of the most refined attachment. Upon such a theme, it would indeed have been impious to have been cold! The enanguished spirit stops not to weigh the dark policy of Statesmen, the sanctimes, at least in speculation, which was a chann of Statesmen — the Records the History of Crimes —

The Martyr of Sensibility

November 10th 1781

A paragraph in this morning's paper announces the demise of the amiable Octavia — Sweet sufferer, thou hast happily escaped a world, which to such a mind as thine, must have been productive of frequent and exquisite anguish. Octavia has literally fallen a victim to sensibility — Descended from an ancient family, she became the destined favourite of her grand mama. Venerable Lady, the envenomed shafts of death have often been urged against thy peace. I hardly know a daughter of affliction in whose hands the cup of adversity hath been so frequently placed. No less than twenty one sons and daugh

In May 1790 the *Massachusetts Magazine* published another essay, "On the Domestic Education of Children," which spoke to one of Judith Sargent Murray's most abiding concerns. In a treatise suffused with the spirit of Lockean environmentalism, Murray laid the groundwork for what historians now call "Republican Motherhood." Citizenship in the new nation was defined in terms of gender, race, and class, thus denying all women any direct political voice. Still, if they did not have power, women such as Murray tried to claim influence for themselves. Arguing that the fate of the nation depended on an educated citizenry and maintaining that mothers nurtured their children in their formative years and played a significant part in forming the character of budding American citizens, she insisted that the future of the republic was in the hands of its women and the survival of the republic demanded that women be accorded an education equal to that enjoyed by any man.

The essay sent a mixed message to the women who read it, however. It maintained in the strongest possible language that women were more suited to educate their children than men were, because women were naturally gentler and more empathetic than their male counterparts. It also implied that women were rational creatures who could guide and correct their young charges, leading them along an appropriate path to virtue. Still, Murray's determination to claim the quality of rationality for women led her to encourage mothers to repress all their emotions and passion. Moreover, while she clearly believed that young girls and boys could benefit from the same education, she conceded that at some point boys would leave home to complete their classical studies while girls would remain at home.

In 1792 Murray began submitting two series of essays to the *Massachusetts Magazine*. Her "Gleaner" essays appeared for the first time in February; the initial "Repository" essay was published in September. Both appeared every month for nearly two years. Murray had written many of the "Repository" pieces, which she once again submitted under the name Constantia, in the 1770s. Most were relatively short discussions of religious and moral issues, characterized by paeans to virtue, benevolence, and serenity or condemnations of slander and dueling. A handful were less conventional. Numbers three and six celebrated the pleasure of rational friendship between members of the same or the opposite sex, as they valued the mind and soul over the body. Number sixteen deplored the sexual double standard, insisting that a seduced woman deserved pity rather than condemnation and holding out the possibility that a fallen woman might

eventually become virtuous even if she could never recover her reputation. Number seventeen, written in 1775, entered the realm of politics, characterizing the American Revolution as a civil war and calling for toleration of Loyalists of good character who were not active supporters of the Crown. No one, she insisted, should be punished merely because he or she held unpopular beliefs.

The authoritative voice in which Murray presented all her "Repository" essays indicates that she was one of a handful of American women in her era who was not content merely to influence public affairs indirectly, as a sister, a wife, or a mother. Like historian Mercy Otis Warren and playwright and novelist Susannah Haswell Rowson, Murray wanted to enter the public sphere, to have a direct and immediate impact on her world. While writing for publication was surely less radical than an attempt to vote or hold public office, it was nevertheless an act of assertion that helped Murray blur the lines that divided the private from the public world and to renegotiate the boundaries that defined male and female. Physically she remained in her home. Yet by writing for publication she participated in the vigorous public dialogue that dominated American intellectual and political life in the postwar years, thus implicitly claiming some rights of citizenship for herself.

Of more lasting importance than the "Repository" essays was Murray's "Gleaner" series. Murray abandoned the pseudonym Constantia for these essays, adopting a male persona instead. As a man, the Gleaner was free to wander through public spaces, talking and listening to strangers, gathering news and opinion, and commenting on everything he heard with the confidence that his views would be taken seriously. As the Gleaner, Murray could write as a disinterested generalist and as a dispassionate observer. The Gleaner represented the enlightened ideal of someone who is politically neutral and speaks for the public good rather than for any particular private interest. In a sense her decision to take on a male persona reflects Murray's belief that the mind had no gender, that an intelligent woman could comment on any topic rationally and analytically. Yet the fact that she saw such a disguise as essential indicates that Murray continued to believe that society tended to discount arguments emanating from a woman's pen. Only men could speak for the public good. Only men were rational enough to rise above the petty interests of the day. As she explained when she revealed the identity of the Gleaner in 1798, Murray feared that if she wrote as Constantia, her readers would view her opinions with "contempt" or at best dismiss them with a *"significant shrug."* For this reason, she claimed, she had decided to assume a "borrowed character."

The Gleaner's most popular essays centered on the character of Margaretta, told from the perspective of yet another man, Mr. Vigillius, who with his wife, Mary, had adopted the orphaned title character. The serialized story, which discusses Margaretta's education, courtship, and marriage, encouraged young women to live virtuous lives and to eschew the seductive temptations of a dangerously immoral world. Murray's main audience was parents, not their daughters. She clearly hoped her essays would help mothers and fathers, especially mothers, to develop a rational educational program for their progeny.

Like many of her contemporaries, Murray was ambivalent about the effect that romantic fiction might have on impressionable young girls. She especially feared that novels would raise women's expectations of marriage to unrealistic heights. Still, she admitted that moral novels in which virtue was rewarded and villainy punished might—at least in small doses—do no harm. In fact, the story of Margaretta is a thinly disguised novel. As fiction, it broke no new ground. It is filled with stock characters and standard ploys. The account of Margaretta's near seduction, a fate she escapes only as a result of her rationality, her virtue, and her willingness to heed the advice of her loving parents appears conventional. The pages of this tale are filled with the misunderstandings and cases of mistaken identity that are typical of the genre.

If Margaretta's story appears stylistically hackneyed, its message was not. It challenged traditional notions of gender difference at their core. It empowered women, emphasizing the value of women's education as it assumed that women were potentially rational beings who could be trusted to control their passions and to make intelligent decisions about their futures. Women, in other words, were possessed of the qualities that were essential to citizenship in the new nation. Yet both Mr. Vigillius and Margaretta's husband, Edward Hamilton, exhibit the emotional and sentimental characteristics that were beginning to be associated with femininity.

It is Mary Vigillius who devises and superintends Margaretta's educational program. To be equipped for this task, her husband notes, Mary needs to be proficient in geography, history, writing, arithmetic, astronomy, music, and drawing. She must also be conversant in French but not, interestingly enough, in Latin or Greek. Margaretta reaps the benefits of her stepmother's exacting regimen,

while at the same time she remains thoroughly "feminine." She is proficient at all sorts of needlework, is an excellent cook, and is clearly prepared in every way to assume her duties as republican wife and mother.

A creature of her time, however, Murray managed to soften, if not to subvert, her message. While she created a heroine who was intelligent, rational, and raised to value herself, the fact that Margaretta's highest aspiration is a good marriage partially undercuts Murray's insistence that women needed to be educated for independence. Moreover, while Mary Vigillius devises and administers Margaretta's educational program, Murray authorized the validity of that program through the voice of a man. It is Mr. Vigillius's approval that gives the reader permission to view Mary's efforts as worthy of serious consideration. Still, Murray's use of her characters to blur gender distinctions and her insistence that domestic subjects were worthy of serious consideration turned the "Margaretta story" into a significant attack on traditional values.

Only twelve of the twenty-seven original "Gleaner" essays center on the story of Margaretta. The rest are wide-ranging in scope and do not confine themselves to conventional women's topics. In them Murray discussed politics and history, theology and the classics with a sense of confidence and assurance that derived in part from her borrowed male character. Indeed, her "Gleaner" essays include many borrowed characters. They are interspersed with letters to the author written by fictional men and women, lower-class seamen as well as elite merchants, who comment on the Gleaner's views or tell him how his advice has changed their lives. These letters, a common eighteenth-century literary device, serve several purposes. By taking on the personae of these characters Murray once again contended that the mind had no gender. Moreover, the letters were designed to prove that private writing had public consequences. Both a "Sea Commander" and "Rebecca Aimwell" wrote to the Gleaner to proclaim the salutary effect that his account of Margaretta's education had had on their own conduct, and a "Bellamour" promised to reform his spendthrift ways if Margaretta would marry him. Clearly, a writer's influence went well beyond the little closet in which she wrote. The line between private and public life, between domesticity and the world of politics and business, was blurred if not erased whenever a woman picked up a pen.

The letters also reflect Murray's social conservatism. While she thought differences between men and women were artificial, Murray wanted to main-

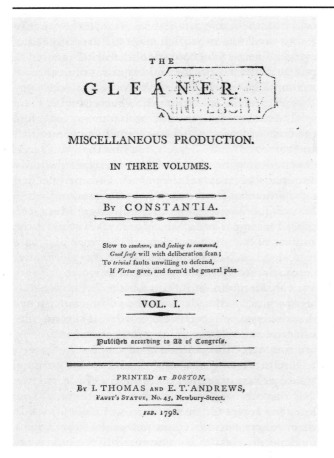

THE

GLEANER.

A

MISCELLANEOUS PRODUCTION.

IN THREE VOLUMES.

By CONSTANTIA.

Slow to *condemn*, and *seeking to commend*,
Good sense will with deliberation scan ;
To *trivial* faults unwilling to defend,
If *Virtue* gave, and form'd the general plan.

VOL. I.

Published according to Act of Congress.

PRINTED at *BOSTON*,
By I. THOMAS and E. T. ANDREWS,
Faust's Statue, No. 45, Newbury-Street.

FEB. 1798.

*Title page for the first of three volumes in which Murray collected
the "Gleaner" essays she wrote for the* Massachusetts
Magazine *(1792–1794), as well as previously
unpublished essays, poems, and plays (courtesy
of John Carter Brown Library at
Brown University)*

tain the class distinctions and the deferential relations that characterized the orderly world she valued so highly. All of Murray's elite characters write with one voice. It is virtually impossible to distinguish the letters Mary Vigillius writes to her daughter from the prose style of her husband. Both exhibit the qualities of intelligence and rationality that characterized acceptable public discourse in the new nation. Letters from a "Sea Commander" and "Rebecca Aimwell," however, are replete with grammatical errors, poor syntax, and laughable logic. For Murray it was clearly class, not gender, that divided worthy republican citizens from their unworthy inferiors. Indeed, it was essential for elite women such as Judith Sargent Murray to distance themselves from lower-class men and women. They saw themselves as more akin to rational, orderly men of their own class than to working women, who became an increasingly visible and troubling part of national urban culture in the years after the American Revo-

lution. By identifying with elite men, by valuing their intellectual over their bodily attributes, women such as Murray could deny any connection to the vulgar and sexual women beneath them. To claim their own rationality, purity, and spirituality, they asserted their identity as genteel, orderly, and respectable Americans who deserved the same fruits of citizenship and independence that they were willing to deny to others.

While Judith Sargent Murray had entered the world of print with considerable trepidation, by the mid 1790s she had become comfortable with her role as published poet and essayist and could even defend her desire for literary fame with relative ease. In 1793, after the death of her parents, the Murrays moved to Boston, where John had agreed to become minister of the first Universalist Church in that city. The family moved into a house at 5 Franklin Place, part of a new complex of buildings located in fashionable south Boston, the heart of elite Federalist society. The abode was modern, spacious, and clearly more than a struggling minister's family could afford. Moreover, Julia Maria was fast approaching the age when Murray would no longer be able to teach her. Murray longed to imitate Mary Vigillius's example and educate her daughter at home, but her lack of confidence in her own abilities made that impossible. She wanted to be able to give Julia Maria the best possible education.

Some time before the spring of 1795 Murray began to write with an eye to earning fortune as well as fame. She had always disdained women who wrote for profit, and she found it difficult to justify her change of heart. She did so in a manner that echoed her old defense of her catechism. She entered the marketplace, she said, as a loving mother who sacrificed her sense of propriety for the sake of her daughter's future. She did so not as a poet or an essayist but as a playwright.

Although Americans in general and denizens of the Massachusetts Bay Colony in particular had always been suspicious of the theater, Murray had harbored a fascination for drama for years. In 1790, when a few Gloucester men decided to produce a sanitized version of George Farquhar's *The Recruiting Officer* (1706), she accepted their invitation to write an epilogue for the play. For the next two years she wrote poetic prologues and epilogues for Gloucester thespians, six of which were published in the *Massachusetts Magazine*. Her twenty-first "Gleaner" essay (February 1794) is a spirited defense of the dramatic art.

That same year a group of theater lovers in Boston defied Puritan custom, taking advantage of the recent repeal of a law banning theater in Massachusetts by opening the Federal Street Theater under the management of Englishman Charles Powell. Though theater was more accepted than it had been in Boston before the Revolution, an aura of disrepute continued to hover over actors. The theater was, moreover, much more a male venue than the world of print. Men greatly outnumbered women in the audiences, and most playwrights were male. Because the theater was an undeniably public space, it took a certain amount of courage for a respectable woman to demand a place for herself as an actor or writer.

Nevertheless, Murray almost immediately began to contemplate writing a play of her own. She was confident in her ability to tell an interesting story. Many of her personal letters had a dramatic quality. Women playwrights on both sides of the Atlantic served as proof that drama need not be the exclusive purview of men. The Murrays were struggling to make ends meet, and a successful playwright might hope for handsome profits.

Murray's comedies, *The Medium* (later retitled *Virtue Triumphant*) and *The Traveller Returned,* were performed in 1795 and 1796, respectively, and both were collected in volume three of *The Gleaner* (1798). The first play by an American-born writer to be produced in Boston, *The Medium* was also the first play by an American woman known to have been produced professionally. Both plays appeared anonymously, but Murray's authorship was impossible to conceal. Neither production received critical or popular acclaim. Indeed, Robert Treat Paine's *Federal Orrery,* after first admitting that *The Traveller* exhibited some merit, later retracted its kind words, characterizing the script as dull, moralistic, and artificial. Neither production earned its author any profit, and Murray gained nothing substantial from her efforts but a private box at the Federal Street Theater. She always remained convinced that her plays deserved a better reception. The first had suffered from the ill effects of poor actors who botched their cues and forgot their lines. Moreover, she was sure that the hostility with which her work was greeted could be explained by the unpopularity of the Universalist religion. The real object of her detractors' disapproval, she always maintained, was John Murray.

Murray's plays are peopled with strong female characters, some of whom are happily single, virtually all of whom call into question the circumscribed sphere within which respectable women were confined in the late eighteenth century. Matronious Aimwell in *The Medium* and Louisa Montague in *The Traveller Returned* are not only ideal republican mothers whose advice to younger women guides their charges along rational paths. They also run their business affairs and their own households with intelligence and dexterity. Both plays also proclaim the value of a companionate marriage. Eliza Clairville in *The Medium* refuses to marry the man she loves because she fears that his wealth and her poverty will make their relationship an unequal one. Both plays demonstrate that young women are capable of choosing their own husbands without parental interference. Indeed, Harriot Montague in *The Traveller Returned* takes an active part in her own courtship, initiating a tryst with her admirer, Alberto Stanhope, and politely but firmly rejecting her mother's pleas that she wed Major Camden—a wise choice, as it turns out, for Camden is in fact her brother.

While Murray created heroines who are rational and educated, active and outgoing, her treatment of lower-class characters of either sex is, as in the "Gleaner" essays, patronizing at best. Her servants provide little more than comic relief. In *The Traveller Returned* Dorothy Vansittart, who runs a boardinghouse with her husband, serves as an example of the folly of anyone who tries to transcend the class position to which he or she "naturally" belongs.

Murray's brief career as a playwright brought her neither immediate fortune nor lasting fame. The same cannot be said of her most important production, *The Gleaner.* Shortly after she withdrew *The Traveller Returned* from production, Murray began to assemble some of her previously published essays into a collection of her "miscellaneous work." In the end her ambitious effort filled three volumes. The first comprises primarily her old "Gleaner" essays, but she added five new pieces, combined and rearranged some others, and made some minor alterations to many of the poems that introduce each selection. The other two volumes include previously unpublished essays as well as some new material—including a continuation of the story of Margaretta—that she wrote specifically for the book. Volume three also includes both her plays as well as a few letters that had appeared in the Boston press attacking and defending the plays. Taken in its entirety, *The Gleaner* provided an opportunity for Murray to present herself to her public as a poet, essayist, playwright, and novelist. Her four-part "Observations on female abilities" also demonstrated her talents as a historian.

The Gleaner covers a wide variety of subjects, from praise of virtue and philanthropy to a defense of the Federalist Party, from essays on economy to her plea for educational opportunities for women. Together, the essays reflect Murray's belief that an

238

To Matilda, upon receiving a number of letters from her
friendly and elegant pen – 1784 –

    If things inanimate could feel,
To these fair sheets I would appeal,
They should my gratitude express,
The warmest thanks to thee address,
For all the kindness thou hast shown,
Favors repeated, which have flown,
In melting numbers from thy hand,
And records of thy friendship stand.
    Matilda, well I know thy worth,
Thy honor, faithfulness, and truth,
And though the paper cannot feel,
It may my sentiments reveal
And can in glowing language tell,
The wishes which my bosom swell,
    The big emotions which controul
Each painful movement of the soul:
Happy the line which thus bestows,
The joys from Amity which flows,
    Yea, though unconscious – greatly bless'd,
Which is of such a pow'r possess'd:
    Besides, perhaps some vital spark,
Of life is hid, which serves to mark –
    Through matters variegated whole,
A universal moving soul,
If this in very deed is so,
    My feeling which most ardent flow,
To this white surface will convey,
    Their fervor, truth, and genial ray.

To a Gentleman who informing me of the arrival of a great Artist in our Coas-
t, immediately followed that intelligence with an account of his death – 1784
        Important news your letter brought to view,
    Most interesting and authentic too,

Manuscript for "To Matilda," a poem by Murray (Mississippi Department of Archives and History)

intelligent woman could comment on any topic: women's intellectual ability knew no bounds. Yet she continued to write as a man, although her adopted persona had long since lost its usefulness, and the title page designated the author of *The Gleaner* as Constantia.

The Gleaner is no doubt best known for "Observations on female abilities." Murray saw this essay as a supplement to her "On the Equality of the Sexes," as she sought to provide examples to substantiate her previous general statements concerning the intellectual abilities of women. She renewed her demand for women's education even as she proclaimed her pleasure that in her own lifetime "female academies [were] every where establishing." While she continued to argue that education would enhance a woman's ability to perform her domestic duties and to be a loving wife and a good mother, in "Observations on female abilities" she declared that there was virtually no task a woman could not perform. Women were strong, heroic, and brave; they were patriotic, energetic, and eloquent. They could be business people, soldiers, and statesmen. Most important, they were "equally susceptible of every literary acquirement." Her historical and contemporary examples of women who excelled on the battlefield and the printed page, in the counting house and the corridors of political power, was a virtuoso effort to refute the assumptions about the two sexes with which most Americans continued to view their political and social world.

While she blurred the distinctions between men and women in some ways, however, Murray upheld them in others. She argued that women were defined more by their humanity than by their sex; yet she welcomed a society that protected women from the corruption and degradation of the public sphere. While she believed that women could be statesmen, warriors, and farmers, she generally implied that only exceptional women in exceptional circumstances should actually attempt to do so. While she saw a single life as preferable to an unhappy marriage and hoped that women would be educated to support themselves so that they would never feel compelled to marry an inappropriate suitor simply to survive, she nevertheless saw marriage as the happiest end for the characters in her plays and essays. Though she wanted her daughter to study Latin, she did not see the classics as a stepping stone for a woman's career in medicine, the ministry, or the law. They merely prepared Julia Maria to converse intelligently with her husband and to help her sons with their lessons.

In the end Murray believed that if men and women were intellectual equals, they were neverthe-less different. "Nature," she wrote to her brother in November 1796, "although equal in her distributions is nevertheless various in her gifts." Her problem was to devise a way to defend both equality and difference. In "Gleaner" essay number twenty-seven Murray described a farm family that faced anarchy and chaos when it abolished "the series of subordination" that made any society function smoothly. Proclaiming their equality with men, the women of the household refused to do what custom designated as women's work. When they refused to prepare breakfast, the meal was a disaster. Work in the field was similarly ruined. With no one in charge, anarchy reigned, and at the end of the summer there were no crops for anyone to reap. For Murray a society without order, where people refused to fulfill their proper roles, was one where strength substituted for law, where brute force ruled, and where no one was safe. Because women as a group were physically weaker than men, women in particular enjoyed the blessings of an orderly society in which each contributed his or her designated part to the good of the whole and in which the contributions of each member were valued. Hierarchy, subordination, rank, and degree remained essential to Murray, despite her professed admiration for equality and independence.

Unlike many women authors, Murray assumed full responsibility for every detail of the difficult process of publishing *The Gleaner*. Adopting the prevailing practice of her day, she had to garner subscriptions for the book before the printers would set one line of type. Writing to relatives, friends, and strangers, she managed to obtain 759 subscribers, including such notables as George and Martha Washington, John Adams (to whom she dedicated the book), and Mercy Otis Warren. Murray was sufficiently confident of the value of her work to order one thousand copies of the book. She agonized over each entry, proofread the entire book, and mercilessly badgered those individuals who were reluctant to pay for their copies once the finished product was in their hands.

The Gleaner had admirers and detractors. President Adams was by no means the only subscriber to offer effusive praise of Murray's work. In 1806 the Reverend Robert Redding expressed an interest in publishing the volumes in England. Unfortunately, Redding died before the project got off the ground. Not everyone lauded Murray's effort. Still, it is clear that her most virulent critics were either Jeffersonian Republicans or individuals who disapproved of Murray's Universalism. Although she never sold all the copies of her book, and in later years she actually gave them away to new acquaintances, she nevertheless sold enough to purchase the mortgage on the house on Franklin Place and to send her daughter to the Federal Street Academy in Boston. The reception of her book may not have been as grand as she had hoped, but her effort was not a failure.

Murray's career as a writer virtually ended after the publication of *The Gleaner*. To a great extent she was too preoccupied with domestic affairs to devote much energy to her writing. In 1800 her brother's stepchildren—Anna, James, and David Williams—came to Boston to live under the Murrays' roof. After following a peripatetic military career in the Ohio Territory, Winthrop Sargent had moved to Natchez, Mississippi, in 1798. There he became the first territorial governor, a post he retained for two years until newly elected President Thomas Jefferson demanded the arch-Federalist's resignation. In Natchez, Winthrop Sargent married wealthy widow Mary Williams and assumed control of her plantation, which he named Gloster Place in honor of his boyhood home.

With the arrival of the Williams children, Judith Murray was responsible for the education of four children, three of whom were strangers. Then, in 1806, Winthrop's son William Sargent entered the Murray household. He was followed in quick succession by Adam Bingaman, the son of one of Winthrop's Natchez acquaintances, and Washington Sargent, Winthrop's youngest son. The boys caused no end of trouble. David and William were both suspended from Harvard. In 1816 Winthrop finally came to Boston to take charge of his two youngest children. He blamed Judith's progressive methods of education for their behavior and removed them from her home.

While Judith Murray spiritedly defended the philosophy of child rearing about which she had written for so many years, she was distraught and embarrassed by her failures. The problem as she framed it, was her sex. On 5 June 1815 she wrote to her brother explaining her views. American society taught boys of a certain age to disdain "petticoat government," she said. Moreover, once youths began to learn Latin and Greek, they understandably lost respect even for older women, to whom they began to feel superior. As Murray interpreted it, her experience was an object lesson in the value of according women an equal education with men.

Murray coped with Winthrop's children by herself. Her husband's health had always been frail, and in 1801 John Murray suffered a stroke, losing all ability to use his right hand. Eight years later, he had another, more debilitating seizure. On 3 September 1815, almost six years to the day after his second stroke, he died.

Even as she tended to her husband and tried to control her nephews, Murray had to deal with yet another personal problem. When Adam Bingaman had arrived in Boston in 1807, both mother and daughter were impressed by him. Adam was handsome and intelligent—he graduated at the top of his Harvard class—highly moral and apparently well fixed financially. He seemed like an ideal match. It was clear from the beginning that Adam was as fond of Julia Maria as she was of him. In 1811 the young people declared their intention to marry. Judith gave her consent, as did Adam's parents, although everyone urged them to wait until Adam's financial prospects were on solid footing.

Instead, right after Adam's graduation from Harvard in 1812, the two were secretly married before Adam returned to Natchez to visit his parents. In January, Julia Maria admitted to her mother that she was pregnant, and in April she gave birth to a daughter, Charlotte Bingaman. Even then the couple's affairs were not settled. Although Adam visited Boston occasionally, it was not until 1818, six years after her marriage, that Julia Maria left Massachusetts to join her husband.

Surprisingly, Judith Sargent Murray managed to find time for some writing after 1798. In 1804 she wrote a third play, *The African*. It took her four years of nonstop lobbying to persuade the manager of the Federal Street Theater to produce the play anonymously. Once again, she was the victim of poorly trained actors who forgot their lines, and she demanded the immediate return of all copies of her manuscript. She no doubt destroyed them, for no copy is extant.

After her husband's second stroke Murray assumed responsibility for finishing the autobiography he had begun and for preparing an edition of his correspondence for publication. Although her eyesight was failing and she was discouraged by her failure to achieve the fame that had always been her fondest desire, Murray submitted an occasional poem for publication to the *Boston Weekly Magazine* and its successor, the *Boston Magazine,* under the pen name Honora-Martesia.

After the failure of *The African* Murray lost all interest in writing, even for her own pleasure. She had been more hurt by criticism of *The Gleaner* than she cared to admit. A humiliating public quarrel with her cousin Lucius Manlius Sargent left an even greater mark on her psyche. In 1808 she vowed never again to "venture upon so fluctuating an ocean as public opinion." Her career as a writer was over.

Murray traveled to Mississippi with her daughter and granddaughter in 1818, living her last two years as a dependent in her son-in-law's home. She died on 6 July 1820. Julia Maria died two years later, a few months after giving birth to a son, Adam Lewis Bingaman Jr.

Judith Sargent Murray always harbored an unabashed hunger for fame. During her lifetime that hunger was only partially assuaged. Her poetry and her "Gleaner" essays found a following, but her plays were not well received. With the rise in interest in women's history during the 1970s, Murray's writings began to attract new attention. Her work reveals the limits as well as the possibilities that American women faced in the years after the American Revolution. Unlike her English counterpart, Mary Wollstonecraft, she could not contemplate a society that destroyed class lines along with gender distinctions. In some ways, particularly in terms of the importance she placed on women's roles as wife and mother, she laid the groundwork for the nineteenth-century cult of domesticity. Yet Murray's work challenged the religious and philosophical basis for gender distinctions that pervaded eighteenth-century discourse, as she dared to urge women to transcend the limits that conventional society had set for them and to claim the American promise of equality and independence for themselves.

Letters:

Judith Sargent Murray: Her First One Hundred Letters, transcribed by Marianne Dunlop (Gloucester: Sargent-Murray-Gilman-Hough House Associates, 1995).

Biographies:

Vena Bernadette Field, *Constantia: A Study of the Life and Works of Judith Sargent Murray, 1751–1820* (Orono: University Press of Maine, 1931);

Sharon M. Harris, "Judith Sargent Murray," *Legacy,* 2 (1994): 152–158;

Sheila L. Skemp, *Judith Sargent Murray* (Boston: Bedford Books, 1998).

References:

Madelon Cheek, "'An Inestimable Prize,' Educating Women in the New Republic: The Writings of Judith Sargent Murray," *Journal of Thought,* 20 (1985): 250–262;

Madelon Jacoba, "The Novella as Political Message: *The Margaretta Story,*" *Studies in the Humanities,* 18 (1991): 146–164;

Amelia Howe Kritzer, "Playing with Republican Motherhood: Self-Representation in Plays by Susanna Haswell Rowson and Judith Sargent Murray," *Early American Literature,* 31 (1996): 150–166;

Sheila L. Skemp, "The Judith Sargent Murray Papers," *Journal of Mississippi History,* 53 (1991): 241–250;

Kirsten Wilcox, "The Scribblings of a Plain Man and the Temerity of a Woman: Gender and Genre in Judith Sargent Murray's *The Gleaner,*" *Early American Literature,* 30 (1995): 121–144.

Papers:

The Judith Sargent Murray papers, which include eighteen letterbooks, comprising 2,500 letters written by Murray between 1765 and 1818, and one manuscript volume of unpublished essays and poetry, are located at the Mississippi Department of Archives and History in Jackson, Mississippi.

Sarah Osborn

(22 February 1714 – 2 August 1796)

Philip Gould
Brown University

BOOKS: *The Nature, Certainty and Evidence of true Christianity: in a letter from a gentlewoman in Rhode-Island to another, her dear friend, in a great darkness, doubt and concern of a religious nature* (Boston: Printed for & sold by S. Kneeland, 1755; London: Printed by T. Bayley, 1763);

Memoirs of the Life of Mrs. Sarah Osborn, who Died at Newport, Rhodeisland, on the Second Day of August, 1796, edited by Samuel Hopkins (Worcester, Mass.: Printed by Leonard Worcester, 1799);

Familiar Letters, Written by Mrs. Sarah Osborn, and Miss Susanna Anthony, late of Newport, Rhode-Island, edited by Hopkins (Newport: Printed at the Office of the Newport Mercury, 1807).

Educator, revivalist, spiritual leader, autobiographer, and decidedly "public" figure, Sarah Osborn gained eminence in Newport, Rhode Island, during the series of mid-eighteenth-century religious revivals known as the Great Awakening. Her life and writings demonstrate not only the importance of women to this movement but also the unconventional roles that women might fashion for themselves when they acted in the name of the Lord.

Born in London on 22 February 1714 to Benjamin and Susanna Guyse Haggar, Osborn briefly attended a boarding school near London, where she received largely religious instruction. At the age of eight she emigrated with her mother to join her father in Boston. After moving around southeastern New England for several years, the family settled permanently in Newport, Rhode Island, when Sarah was a teenager. The piety that Osborn emphasizes in her spiritual autobiography, *Memoirs of the Life of Mrs. Sarah Osborn* (1799), was apparently accompanied by a rebellious spirit. In Newport she immediately became attached to the staunchly Calvinist minister Nathaniel Clap, whose First Church was losing influence to the more moderate Second Church, whose pastor was Ezra Stiles, the future president of Yale College. Defying her parents, Sarah went to hear Clap preach, and she was there-

after affected by the spiritual rigor of Puritan piety. Clap became her spiritual mentor, and she joined the First Church in 1737.

Osborn's willfulness is apparent in the early sections of *Memoirs of the Life of Mrs. Sarah Osborn.* In the course of fulfilling the formula of Puritan spiritual autobiography and portraying the sinner in need of grace, Osborn also revealed an energetic woman. Time and again the autobiography shows Osborn's resistance to parental authority. For example, she ignored their warnings about the dangers of the river near their home, and when she took the canoe out at night, or walked on the ice during winter, she found herself endangered by natural forces beyond her control. True to the conventions of Puritan narrative, these scenes show how the stubborn sinner is preserved by the precarious ties of Providence and allegorize the saint's gradual understanding of the uncertainty of the mutable world and hence the sinner's need for grace. Yet Osborn's autobiography unfolds dual levels of narration. In addition to offering spiritual lessons, these scenes (and others like them) also reveal the irrepressible energy (the presence, in Puritan terms, of the unregenerate "self") that was later harnessed to serve God in Osborn's extraordinary career.

Osborn's adult life was fraught with hardships that paradoxically tested and strengthened her religious faith. In 1731 she defied parental authority by marrying a young sailor named Samuel Wheaton. He died at sea two years later. Widowed and the mother of a one-year-old child, Osborn turned to teaching school as one of the few vocations that were open to a colonial woman who needed to earn a living. Her career in education continued for most of the next forty years. Her first school failed in 1741, but she returned to teaching in 1744, and by the late 1750s she was boarding students in her home. In addition to suffering anxiety over constant financial woes, Osborn struggled spiritually.

During the evangelical revival that occurred in Newport in 1740 Osborn heard the preaching of the well-known itinerant ministers George Whitefield

Sarah Osborn's house in Newport, Rhode Island (The Newport Historical Society)

and Gilbert Tennent, and afterward she began to experience greater assurance about the state of her soul. She corresponded with Tennent during the 1740s and read influential works by Jonathan Edwards. Yet her spiritual autobiography in part one of her memoir, and her diary entries that portray her spiritual life during the 1740s through the 1760s, illustrate the important fact that Puritan "conversion" was not so much a single occurrence as an ongoing process.

In 1741 a group of about fifty women in the First Church asked Osborn to direct what became known after her death as the Religious Female Society. The society reflected the New Light Calvinist sense of social and spiritual solidarity, which derived from the theological belief in the separation of the elect (or "visible saints") from the population at large. The women met twice each week for spiritual meditation and edification, observed special days of fasting and prayer, and helped to raise money for alms and ministerial support. At its height the society had more than sixty members, but at the time of Osborn's death in 1796 there were only half this number. (In 1826 the name of the group was changed to the Osborn Society in her memory.)

Through the society the women of the First Church played an important role in colonial evangelical culture. The support of such women proved crucial during the 1766–1767 revival in Newport as well as to the selection of Jonathan Edwards's protegé Samuel Hopkins as the new minister of the First Church.

Soon after the formation of the female society, Sarah married Henry Osborn, a widower with three sons. The family's economic security proved to be short-lived. Henry Osborn's tailoring business and his health failed a few months after their marriage. This hardship compelled Osborn to return to teaching so that she could support the family. During this period her grief at the death of her twelve-year-old son was somewhat eased by the friendships she forged in the society.

One particularly intense relationship for Osborn was her friendship with Susanna Anthony. In her "dear Susa" Osborn found a kindred spirit who experienced intense spiritual longings. Osborn's first published writing, *The Nature, Certainty and Evidence of true Christianity* (1755), derived from a letter to Anthony, who was suffering at the time from religious doubt. The publication of this familiar letter not only demonstrates the degree to which Osborn

The First Church of Newport, which Osborn joined in 1737 (detail from "Newport R. I. in 1730," an 1864 lithograph by J. P. Newell)

Puritan severity, the text displays in theological and emotional terms the prominence of God's supporting love.

Many of the same rhetorical and thematic features are apparent in the correspondence that Osborn and Anthony exchanged between 1740 and 1779. *Familiar Letters, Written by Mrs. Sarah Osborn, and Miss Susanna Anthony* (1807) includes letters to other friends and ministers (such as Hopkins) in addition to those between the two women. The "Advertisement" to the book makes clear that its publication served the didactic and utilitarian ends of shoring up piety in a supposedly backsliding era. One is certainly impressed with the religious rigor to which Osborn and Anthony adhered in their epistolary exchange. Both consistently emphasized the necessity of the individual's submission to God. Even secular details, such as severe sickness, infant mortality, the tumult of the American Revolution (during which the British occupied Newport) are couched ultimately in religious metaphysics. Rhetorically saturated with the conventional language of Protestant spirituality—the "darts" of Satan, the port of redemption at the end of the storm of life, the pollution of selfhood, and those cups of affliction that saints are forced to drink—these letters testify to the extreme variations of the psychological dynamics of Puritan piety. Both Anthony and Osborn complained about the presence of Satan as the dullness of religious sensibility. Both oscillated between anxiety over spiritual deadness and the utter exaltation of spiritual assurance. In these letters such moments were often cast in the erotic language of God's ravishing of the soul.

Yet these letters do not merely follow the conventional discourses of Protestant spirituality. They are intimate personal exchanges between two women who needed one another. In their shared intimacy of ecstasy and pain, these letters move in and out of confessional and sermonic modes, varying from serene and personal to hortatory and oratorical. Much of their writing, in other words, mediates between private and public discourses, as though these women were testing public voices with one another, voices that were often difficult, if not impossible, for women to use in the public sphere of Newport society. Moreover, the power of feeling suggests a generic link to eighteenth-century sentimentalism.

The spiritual guidance that Osborn provided her friend indicates her exceptional qualities of initiative and benevolence. These characteristics were among several factors that eventually led to Osborn's leading role in the revival that swept Newport in 1766–1767. The re-emergence of the female

already was respected in religious circles but also provides evidence that colonial women's letter writing was considered a serious literary pursuit, a form that complicates the distinction between the "public" and "private" spheres. Following the convention of the era, the text was published anonymously, but in any case Osborn had no wish to draw attention to herself as an aspiring theologian. In this tract Osborn offered her own experience as an exemplary model for the dispensation of God's grace. Her realization of the inefficacy of the self and the absolute necessity of grace was crucial for her and, by implication, for Anthony. Osborn's consistent focus on the mediating influence of Christ was intended to quell Anthony's anxieties, which are personified in the figure of Satan, who voices doubt over the viability of religion. Yet she did not wish to reduce her friend's experience to her own, and she admitted that God deals differently with each individual. Osborn ingeniously struck the right rhetorical balance in admitting her chronic anxieties while maintaining a spiritually empowered persona for the sake of her immediate audience. Dispelling the stereotype of

society during the early 1760s, the fact that Osborn already had students boarding in her home, the moribund institutional leadership in the First Church, and the newfound piety of the free blacks and slaves of Newport—all brought people to her home for devotional exercises, biblical study, singing, general religious instruction, and, perhaps most important, social exchange. The daily traffic made her home a "public" place: on Sunday nights a group of young men arrived; on Monday evenings there came teenage girls; Tuesdays were reserved for boys; on Wednesdays the regular meetings of the female society were held; Thursdays and Saturdays were reserved for catechism lessons for children, and Fridays for the heads of families. By July 1766 more than 300 people met each week in the Osborn home, and by January 1767 that number had risen to 525.

Osborn's religious sincerity and her capacity for nurturing allowed her to fill a gap left by the enervated ministry of the First Church. Clap's successor, William Vinal, apparently suffered from alcoholism and was forced to resign in 1768. Vinal's failure to offer spiritual guidance during this period of spiritual awakening thrust Osborn into a position of prominence that she might not otherwise have attained. Indeed, she may well have been the only woman to lead an eighteenth-century revival.

Osborn's public role created frustration as well. Her transgression of societal norms that confined women to the "private" sphere was not lost on many people in Newport society. As her private correspondence attests, Osborn felt the pangs of social ostracism and patriarchal rebuke by several local ministers and church leaders. Her letters to her longtime correspondent Reverend Joseph Fish of Stonington, Connecticut (whose two daughters attended Osborn's school), address these issues directly. In one letter, written between 28 February and 7 March 1767 (republished in 1976 by Mary Beth Norton), Osborn complained that during the revival she sought advice and assistance from the religious leaders of Newport but received little help. In contrast to the letters to Anthony, this correspondence appears much more prosaic, worldly, and subdued. As Osborn was becoming overwhelmed with the sheer numbers of proselytes meeting in her home, Deacon Coggeshall of the First Church began to hold meetings in his home and to assist Osborn in instructing men at hers. She was especially sensitive about her position as a woman teaching men and tried not to take an openly authoritative stance toward them. Her husband or male friends may have actively led the men's religious discourse and devotions. Osborn's outward style of chastened humility appears to have ensured her relatively

long-term success as an unconventional woman. Yet her correspondence affirms that her anxiety about social proscription never precluded the gratification that she gained from her leading role in Newport revivalism.

Perhaps the major point of controversy surrounding Osborn's role in the revival involved her relations with the African American population of Newport, which placed her in the burgeoning antislavery movement that arose in late colonial and Revolutionary-era America. During the revival, African Americans, who composed roughly 10 percent of Newport's population, were the first group in Newport to flock to Osborn and the last to leave. (They were still meeting in her home as late as 1768.) As early as spring 1765, black slaves had begun to hold prayer meetings in the Osborn home on Sunday evenings, and by June of the following year an Ethiopian Society composed of free blacks was meeting there on Tuesday evenings. One of Osborn's letters to Fish suggests that the religious fervor of African Americans actually helped to energize—and perhaps even inaugurate—the Newport revival by attracting neighborhood youths to her home. The radical potential of African American enthusiasm, however, was not lost on Osborn, and she reassured Fish that spiritual edification was not meant to be disruptive socially. She specified the conditions on which she allowed slaves to attend meetings, insisting that they obey their masters and go straight home after Sunday sessions. She also assured everyone that she did not intend to foster pride in the blacks of Newport. Such comments must be understood in context of the hierarchical arrangement of dependence and submission that characterized eighteenth-century colonial society. Yet in spite of these restrictions Osborn obviously provided spiritual support and educational opportunities for Newport African Americans. As many historians have noted in other contexts, the spiritual forms of religious revivalism at least implied a kind of social egalitarianism.

The political ramifications of Osborn's public role and her humanitarian connections with the antislavery movement converge in her relationship with Samuel Hopkins, whose relative openmindedness toward women and African Americans made him an attractive candidate for pastor of the First Church after Winal's resignation. The inspiration of Osborn and the female society was crucial to Hopkins's appointment, the history of which is a complicated one fraught with political factions and vituperative propaganda. Even Ezra Stiles, the minister of the Newport Second Church, viewed Hopkins suspiciously. After the First Church voted to

grant a blessing upon this medicine, Let it accomplish the desird Effect: but this I ask with submission to thy will, and only in subordination to thy glory. o Lord Let me not with holy Bassel be too earnest with thee to remove this inveterate Head-ach. Lest I should Provoke thee to remove it and Let Loose some Lust upon me, o Lord Let thy will be done, continue what bodily disorders thou Pleasest yea afflict me in any way thou Pleasest rather than Let Loose one Lust o! I deprecate this I tremble at the thought of this Let sin be crucified Let that goes and die: let grace grow and flourish Let union be more compleat; and sencible communion with thee be more obtaind, Lord make me Holy, and all is well: infinite ly well. I ask with importunity, as no more I desire no more: but to be Like thee and to enjoy thee, that knowest is all my Joy and all my salvation. Let flesh and heart fail, Let it cry out or shrink from Pains as even the innocent Nature of Jesus did

Pages from the spiritual journals that Osborn kept from 1753 through 1784 (The Newport Historical Society)

(94)

I knew it with in some measure
prevent my Leaving family
with out the care there of
following me into my retirem[ent]
that God will order all thin[gs]
well for me, and so engage
my heart for himself when hen[ce?]
that nothing may be able to
divert my tho'ts from him
yesterday call'd to Part with another
of my Scholars by Death will
God sanctifie this blow to all
the school to me, and in spe=
cial to her Poor distrect mother
O Lord if it be thy will Pre
serve the vse of her reason
and Grant her a quiet sub
mission to thy will oh may
she more than Ever give up
her whole heart to thee and
choose thee for her all Lord
support her for Jesus sake

(margin, written vertically) of Jonathan clarks Daughter many No 19 1765

Advertisement for Osborn's school in the 19 December 1758 issue of the Newport Mercury

reject Hopkins's candidacy in March 1770, Osborn and her "sorority," as Stiles referred to the female society, politicked in favor of Hopkins and eventually prevailed. Working within the socially legitimate context of piety, Osborn and the society had considerable political leverage.

Osborn's support of Hopkins's candidacy indicates the shape of her remaining career. The antislavery movement and the American Revolutionary struggle were inextricably linked, as antislavery proponents pointed out the hypocrisy of a republic in which citizens owned slaves. Only a few years after his appointment as minister of the First Church, Hopkins published an antislavery tract, *A Dialogue, Concerning the Slavery of the Africans* (1776). Osborn's support for Hopkins is further evidence of her connection to the movement and, at the very least, her empathy for African American slaves. Some scholars believe that she forwarded Phillis Wheatley's first published poem, "On Messrs. Hussey and Coffin," to the *Newport Mercury,* which published it on 21 December 1767. It is also possible that she influenced the decision of that newspaper to publish its first antislavery article in 1767. The American Revolution provided the language and ethical context for people such as Osborn to oppose slavery, and her activity also reflects the element of social reform imbedded in New Light millennial thinking. Osborn's growing sensitivity to the plight of slaves evolved from her relative intimacy with them in her home. In theory, religious benevolence made no distinctions based on race.

Osborn's close relationship with Hopkins had literary ramifications as well. The vast majority of the manuscripts that Hopkins edited for *Memoirs of the Life of Mrs. Sarah Osborn* are no longer in existence. As Hopkins noted, Osborn left more than fifty volumes of personal and religious writing, each volume ranging from about one hundred to three hundred pages. Osborn wrote in most of the traditional Puritan forms—spiritual autobiography, journals, letters, and occasional writings such as the religious poem "The Employment and Society of Heaven" (which is included in *Memoirs of the Life of Mrs. Sarah Osborn*). The purpose of her writings was internal examination and moral edification of her friends, family, and descendants. In negotiating the private spaces within her own soul and the public social spaces recorded in her diaries and letters, Osborn cultivated a powerful identity as a colonial woman.

A major spiritual narrative by a colonial American woman, *Memoirs of the Life of Mrs. Sarah Osborn,* was published soon after Osborn's death in 1796. Edited by Hopkins with assistance from his colleague Levi Hart, the text consists largely of extracts from Osborn's diaries. Because Hopkins may have significantly edited certain sections and also provided considerable commentary, the text may be seen as an ongoing dialogue between editor and author/subject, between the New Light divine and the woman whose piety was intended as an example for backsliders in an increasingly secularized age.

Hopkins divided the book into four sections. Part one, "Containing an Account of the first thirty years of her life," briefly introduces Osborn and then lets her spiritual autobiography (written when she was about thirty years old) speak for itself. Part two, "Containing a general Account of Her Life," is mainly Hopkins's recitation of the major events of her life, including her formation of the female society and her role in the Newport revival of 1767. At

Oct 22 1794 this day it is my will
that when I depart my Gold necklace
and Locket with my silver table
spoon marked s°s with all my
House hold goods and clotheing
(excepet what reserves I have made
on the enclosed papers) shall be
sold every thing that will fetch
a peney and ~~thing~~ after my
just debts and funeral charges
are paid the money that is left.

shall be put out to intrest and one
~~half~~ the intrest be paid yearly to the
ministers of the first congregati
onal church in Newport, and the
other half to the poor of that
church. if I Leve any money
it must be put to the same
uses as the above is mentioned
Witness my hand   Sarah Osborn

Osborn's will (The Newport Historical Society)

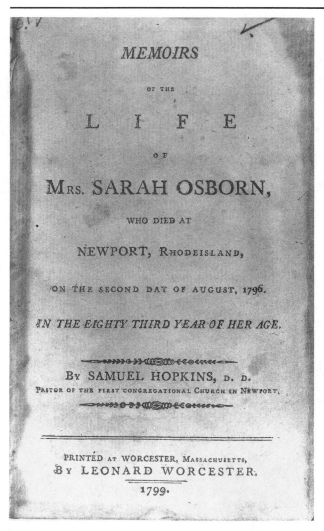

MEMOIRS

OF THE

LIFE

OF

MRS. SARAH OSBORN,

WHO DIED AT

NEWPORT, RHODEISLAND,

ON THE SECOND DAY OF AUGUST, 1796.

IN THE EIGHTY THIRD YEAR OF HER AGE.

BY SAMUEL HOPKINS, D. D.
PASTOR OF THE FIRST CONGREGATIONAL CHURCH IN NEWPORT.

PRINTED AT WORCESTER, MASSACHUSETTS,
BY LEONARD WORCESTER.
1799.

Title page for the spiritual autobiography that Osborn's pastor compiled from her more than fifty volumes of personal and religious writings (The Newport Historical Society)

ion, emphasizes the great discrepancy between this world and the next and presents a vision of a heaven that includes all groups of God's elect. (A similar motif occurs in the work of Phillis Wheatley.) As Hopkins noted, Osborn began writing poetry in her later years to enhance her spiritual life.

The style of Osborn's autobiographical writing is reminiscent of seventeenth-century Puritan discourse. In her spiritual autobiography as well as her diaries, Osborn recorded the classic cycles of faith and doubt, presumption and humility, and hope and despair that are found in Puritan spiritual narratives such as Thomas Shepard's and Michael Wigglesworth's journals. This evaluation, however, is not meant to oversimplify Osborn's writings. Most modern scholars of Puritan spiritual autobiography have abandoned older critical models of the genre that emphasize repression and self-doubt. Instead they stress that Puritan conversion was a complex—and ongoing—process fraught with extreme theological and psychological tensions. Like the good Puritan struggling to make meaning of the self, Osborn relied on scrupulous examination of the inner workings of her soul and the outward signs of providential intervention in her life. Her diaries reveal her attempt to bring divinity into close proximity. Moreover, her search for providential signs led her to include in her writing significant secular details of her daily life. It would be unwise to liken *Memoirs of the Life of Mrs. Sarah Osborn* to a work such as Samuel Sewall's diary, for Osborn's piety appears much more rigorous than Sewall's, and, in her oscillations between assurance and anxiety, she much more consistently emphasized the individual's need for grace. Yet *Memoirs of the Life of Mrs. Sarah Osborn* also portrays a woman who was much involved with public matters and whose home became a public (and political) place of sociability. Thus the book captures the Puritan paradox of spiritual power-through-powerlessness as well as one in which female identity is socially empowered through pious humility.

The end of Osborn's life was characterized by poor health and the disruptions of the Revolutionary War. According to Hopkins, Osborn's health problems might have been related to an overdose of mercury prescribed by a physician. During the Revolution, after Hopkins and other ministers fled occupied Newport, church buildings were converted to military and hospital centers, and Osborn's home became a place for religious meetings. Each week members gathered there in formal prayer. Twenty years later Osborn died in poor health and with an estate valued at less than fifty dollars. Her characteristic benevolence was consis-

times he employed her diary entries to confirm his assessments of her.

By far the longest section of the book, part three comprised detailed extracts from diary entries from 1744 to 1767. Hopkins also included selections from Osborn's commentaries on Genesis and the Gospels, informing readers that they were composed, not by a theologian, but by a woman engaged in devotional exercises. When she commented on Matthew 16 and 25, Osborn altered the biblical text to insert herself in its narrative and dramatic action. By making the Bible speak to her personally, she established intimacy between the Lord and herself. Part four, "The Conclusion of her Life," offers Hopkins's final remarks about Osborn's exemplary piety. The volume concludes with "The Employment and Society of Heaven," which, in Augustinian fash-

tent to the end. She ordered that after her meager property holdings were sold and her debts were paid, the remaining funds should be distributed equally between the poor of Newport and the minister of the First Church.

This final act exemplifies Sarah Osborn's piety and benevolence. Her indisputable importance in American religious and literary history derives as well from her position in women's history. Osborn's intense piety and stern religious self-scrutiny are akin to older Puritan practices that had waned by the time she was born. Yet the social uses to which Osborn put such piety prefigure the religious means that later generations of American women employed to cultivate public roles for themselves. Osborn, in other words, is an early example of an American woman who appropriated the acceptable ideology of female benevolence to break down the cultural boundaries that prevented women from participation in public affairs. In so doing, she subtly resisted patriarchal authority by relying on the higher authority of God. For Osborn this transgression of societal mores was conducted cautiously, and it apparently gave her both joy and pain.

References:

Joseph A. Conforti, *Samuel Hopkins and the New Divinity Movement: Calvinism, the Congregational Ministry, and Reform in New England Between the Great Awakenings* (Grand Rapids, Mich.: Christian University Press, 1981);

David Grimsted, "Anglo-American Racism and Phillis Wheatley's 'Sable Veil,' 'Length'ned Chain,' and 'Knitted Heart,'" in *Women in the Age of the American Revolution,* edited by Ronald Hoffman and Peter J. Albert (Charlottesville: University Press of Virginia, 1989);

Charles E. Hambrick-Stowe, "The Spiritual Pilgrimage of Sarah Osborn (1714–1796)," *Church History,* 61 (1992): 408–421;

Sheryl Anne Kujawa, "Religion, Education and Gender in Eighteenth Century Rhode Island: Sarah Haggar Wheaton Osborn, 1714–1796," dissertation, Columbia University, 1995;

Kujawa, "The Great Awakening of Sarah Osborn and the Female Society of the First Congregational Church in Newport," *Newport History,* 65 (1994): 133–153;

Barbara Lacey, "The Bonds of Friendship: Sarah Osborn of Newport and the Reverend Joseph Fish of North Stonington, 1743–1779," *Rhode Island History,* 45 (1986): 127–136;

Mary Beth Norton, *Liberty's Daughters: The Revolutionary Experience of American Women, 1750–1800* (Boston: Little, Brown, 1980);

Norton, "'My Resting Reaping Times': Sarah Osborn's Defense of Her 'Unfeminine' Activities, 1767," *Signs: Journal of Women in Culture and Society,* 2 (1976): 515–529.

Papers:

Many of Osborn's letters may be found in the Sarah Osborn Letters collection at the American Antiquarian Society in Worcester, Massachusetts. Some of the private journals that she kept between 1753 and 1772 are located at the Newport Historical Society.

Eliza Lucas Pinckney

(28 December 1722 – 26 May 1793)

Cynthia A. Kierner
University of North Carolina at Charlotte

BOOKS: *Journal and Letters of Eliza Lucas, Now First Printed* (Wormsloe, Ga.: Privately printed, 1850);
Recipe Book of Eliza Lucas Pinckney, 1756 (Charleston: Committee on Historic Activities of the South Carolina Society of the Colonial Dames of America, 1936);
The Letterbook of Eliza Lucas Pinckney, 1739–1762, edited by Elise Pinckney (Chapel Hill: University of North Carolina Press, 1972).

Chiefly remembered as the young plantation mistress who pioneered the cultivation of indigo in colonial South Carolina, Eliza Lucas Pinckney was also the author of a remarkable collection of letters that chronicled her experiences as a planter, wife, mother, and patriot in eighteenth-century America. Pinckney's early letters discuss her intellectual and social activities, as well as the important agricultural experiments she conducted at her father's plantations in South Carolina. Her later letters, which focus more on family and domestic concerns, also reveal her continuing interest in the world beyond her household. Letter writing gave elite women, many of whom lived in relative seclusion, a means of sharing ideas, emotions, and experiences with those outside their immediate families. Pinckney's lively and vividly descriptive letters give modern readers insights into the lives and concerns of such early American women.

Both in quantity and quality, Pinckney's surviving writings are unusually rich for an American woman of her era. Spanning the years 1739 through 1762, her letterbook provides a compelling portrait of its author and, along with other scattered letters and documents, constitutes a literary legacy unrivaled by any other Southern woman of the colonial era. That legacy reflects a privileged life in which ambition and intellect coexisted with more-conventional feminine ideals and values.

Elizabeth Lucas, better known as Eliza, was born in the West Indies in 1722. She was the oldest of four children of Lt. Col. George Lucas, a British army officer, and his wife, Ann, of whom little is known. As a girl, Eliza traveled to England, where she attended school for several years. After completing her education she returned to her family in Antigua, where her father held a military commission and later attained the office of lieutenant governor. In 1738 George Lucas, seeking a more healthful climate for his sickly wife, took her, Eliza, and Eliza's sister Polly to a plantation he owned on Wappoo Creek, near Charleston, South Carolina. When war with Spain forced him to return to his military post in Antigua the following year, he entrusted seventeen-year-old Eliza with the management of his property in South Carolina. Ann and Polly Lucas remained with Eliza until shortly after 27 May 1744, when she married forty-five year old widower Charles Pinckney of Charleston, a prominent member of the South Carolina bar and former speaker of the provincial assembly. The couple had four children, one of whom died in infancy.

Eliza Lucas wrote her earliest surviving letters in 1739, and when she assumed responsibility for her father's land in South Carolina. Her correspondence reveals that reading, writing, and plantation business were her main occupations as a young single woman, though she also found time for social visits and for the ornamental accomplishments that women of the colonial elite increasingly cultivated. Lucas's daily routine began at 5:00 A.M., when she got up and read for two hours before eating breakfast. Then she practiced her harpsichord for one hour and spent the next reviewing French, shorthand, or some other subject that she had studied during her school days in England. In the hours before dinner she tutored her sister and two slave girls. After dinner and another hour of playing music she did needlework until she could see no longer without the aid of candles. From dusk until bedtime she read, took care of plantation business, and attended to her business and personal correspondence. Although she enjoyed socializing, the diligent young planter went visiting only on alternate Fridays and left her estate no more than once a week.

In her rural isolation Eliza Lucas self-consciously labored to continue her education. Her reading was unusually varied and wide-ranging, reflecting her own tastes and the influence of two male mentors, her father and her future husband. On 2 May 1740 Lucas informed an English friend, "I have a little library well furnished (for my papa has left me most of his books)." She supplemented this supply of books by borrowing from her friend Charles Pinckney. Pinckney encouraged her to read John Locke's *Essay Concerning Human Understanding* (1690), an influential treatise on human psychology that Lucas found fascinating. She also borrowed Pinckney's edition of Virgil and thoroughly enjoyed studying the works of that ancient Roman. Lucas also read the works of Plutarch, John Milton, Miguel de Cervantes, Isaac Newton, and Robert Boyle, as well as Thomas Wood's two-volume *Institute of the Laws of England* (1720), in the five years before her marriage.

Lucas's tastes in reading accorded well with the spirit of Enlightenment rationalism, but they contrasted markedly with those of most of her female contemporaries. She enjoyed the classics and nonfiction far more than the sentimental novels that were increasingly popular, especially among women. Like many of her contemporaries, Lucas read Samuel Richardson's *Pamela* (1740–1741). Unlike most of them, however, she criticized the novel because its sentimental heroine was irrational and immature and because she disparaged Locke, whom Lucas admired greatly. Moreover, unlike most women readers, Lucas did not favor the sermons and devotional tracts that typically constituted the bulk of women's reading in eighteenth-century America. Although she attended the services of the Church of England regularly and considered herself religious, hers was a rational piety that blended belief in the deity with the Enlightenment's faith in the power of human reason.

Lucas readily reconciled her deep-seated rationalism with a Christian faith in the infinite wisdom and beneficence of God, in which she took comfort during times of crisis. In March 1742 she vigorously declared that "God is Truth it self and. . . . The Christian religion is what the wisest men in all ages have assented too." While Lucas conceded that certain Christian teachings, such as the resurrection of Christ, might be beyond the power of humans to comprehend fully, she, nonetheless, insisted that Christianity was a rational belief system. Indeed, Lucas maintained that people who ridiculed or rejected Christianity acted contrary to the dictates of reason. On the other hand, she condemned the outpouring of religious emotions precipitated by the revivals of the Great Awakening as a perversion of Christianity, maintaining that a rational reading of the scriptures was the surest path to true religion.

Lucas brought the same faith in the efficacy of reason to the business of plantation management, which dominated her life and letters in the years before her marriage. She supervised her father's overseers at Garden Hill plantation, a 1,500-acre estate that produced mainly pork and naval stores, and on some 3,000 acres of rice-producing land along the Waccamaw River. In addition, she personally oversaw the management of the 600-acre estate at Wappoo and its twenty resident slaves. At Wappoo, the young planter experimented with a variety of new and exotic crops both to indulge her own interest in horticulture and to enhance the profitability of the land. In 1740 she planted indigo, ginger, cotton, and alfalfa on a trial basis. Two years later she installed a fig orchard and a cedar grove on the estate. She also planted many oak trees, which she expected to increase in value over the coming years. In 1743 this self-consciously accomplished plantation mistress sent rice, corn, peas, pickled pork, grapes, and eggs preserved in salt to her father in Antigua. She had produced all these items on his South Carolina estates.

The successful cultivation of indigo was Eliza Lucas's chief triumph as an experimental farmer. Decades earlier, South Carolinians had planted indigo, but they had found the dyewood difficult to grow and soon abandoned it for rice, a much more lucrative agricultural staple. By 1740, however, war in the Caribbean disrupted South Carolina rice exports to the West Indies, and Col. George Lucas sent his daughter some indigo seeds, encouraging her to experiment with them on his Wappoo Creek plantation. Frost destroyed the first crop, planted in 1740, but the 1741 planting was somewhat more successful. On 14 October Eliza Lucas reported to her father the production of a quantity of indigo dye under the direction of herself and Nicholas Cromwell, an experienced dye maker from the West Indian island of Montserrat whom the colonel engaged to assist his daughter. According to Eliza, however, the dye was mediocre. She accused Cromwell of sabotage, suggesting that he purposely spoiled the dye because he worried that competition from Carolina indigo would ruin the West Indian planters.

Undeterred, Eliza Lucas continued to experiment with indigo. Though her crops failed in 1742 and 1743, her efforts came to fruition the following year. In 1744, with the assistance of another expert dye maker, Lucas produced seventeen pounds of indigo, six of which were sent to England, where bro-

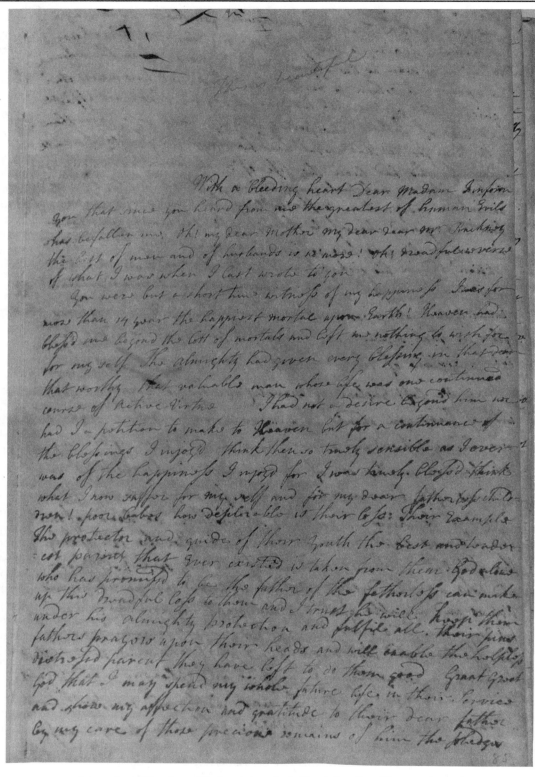

A page from Eliza Lucas Pinckney's letterbook (South Carolina Historical Society)

kers judged it comparable in quality to the excellent and much-coveted dyes produced in the French West Indies. Colonel Lucas included the Wappoo indigo crop in his daughter's dowry when she married Charles Pinckney in 1744. The Pinckneys saved most of that valuable crop for seed, much of which they gave away in small quantities to planters throughout the Low Country to promote the cultivation of indigo in coastal South Carolina.

Largely through the efforts of Eliza Lucas indigo became a viable agricultural staple in South Carolina, where production of the costly blue dye increased significantly during the last three decades of the colonial era. By 1747, only three years after Lucas attained her first successful crop at Wappoo, South Carolinians exported more than 135,000 pounds of indigo; they produced more than a million pounds a year by the 1770s. Second only to rice in value, indigo accounted for more than one-third of South Carolina's total exports on the eve of the American Revolution.

Eliza Lucas derived immense satisfaction from her work as a planter and experimental farmer. "I have the business of 3 plantations to transact, which requires much writing and more business and fatigue than you can imagine," she informed an English friend on 2 May 1740, "But least you should imagine it too burthensom to a girl at my early time in life . . . I assure you I think myself happy that I can be useful to so good a father. . . ." In addition to serving her beloved father, however, Lucas also developed a proprietary interest in the estates she oversaw and in the improvements she made on them. She believed her plan to dry and export figs, for example, would net her big profits. "I have reckoned my expence and the prophets to arise from these figgs," she wrote in April 1742, "but was I to tell you how great an Estate I am to make this way, and how 'tis to be laid out you would think me far gone in romance." Similarly, Lucas regarded the oak trees she planted as her own property though they stood on her father's land. When the trees grew and their wood became valuable, she intended to sell it and use her profits for philanthropic purposes. Even late in life, she remained proud of the achievements of her youth, contentedly reminiscing about her role in the introduction and promotion of indigo cultivation in South Carolina.

Entrepreneurial-minded and intellectually ambitious, Eliza Lucas enjoyed an unconventional life, but she saw her activities and interests as ultimately compatible with the prevailing gender ideals of her era, which deemed women subordinate to men and sharply circumscribed their public roles. Despite her pride in her success as a planter, Lucas saw herself first and foremost as a dutiful daughter who acted as her father's agent or deputy in South Carolina. Indeed, like most white women who performed nondomestic work, she did so not to gratify her own ambitions but to contribute to a family economy. Lucas sought no public recognition for her horticultural experiments, though they were of great public significance. In 1744, with his bride's blessing, Charles Pinckney took public credit for the successful cultivation of indigo at Wappoo and for the generous division of indigo seed among their Low Country neighbors.

Gently reassuring skeptics, Lucas also defended her studious habits as appropriate training for her future domestic life. In spring 1742 a neighbor warned her that too much reading and plantation work would make her tired and old looking and, consequently, render her unmarriageable. Lucas responded with neither indifference nor defiance but with the happy thought that "what ever contributes to health and pleasure of mind must also contribute to good looks" and hence improve her marriage prospects. Shortly before her nuptials, she thanked her father for the expenses he incurred for her education, which was unusually good for a girl of her time and place, declaring it would make her a more appealing companion for her future husband.

Eliza Lucas was fortunate in choosing a spouse who shared and encouraged her intellectual interests. Though Charles Pinckney's status as an English-educated planter, lawyer, and officeholder placed him in the first rank of the South Carolina elite, like growing numbers of women of her class, Eliza Lucas married more for affection than wealth. Four years earlier eighteen-year-old Eliza had rejected an elderly suitor of her father's choosing, respectfully asserting in her letter of 17 March 1740 that "the riches of Peru and Chili if he had them . . . could not purchase a sufficient Esteem for him to make him my husband." Steadfast in her conviction that wealth alone could not provide the foundation for an acceptable marriage, Lucas eventually married a man whose character and abilities she knew and esteemed, having become friendly with him shortly after her arrival in South Carolina. Charles Pinckney's first wife, Elizabeth Lamb Pinckney, had died in January 1744, after a long illness. In May of that year, Eliza Lucas married the widower she came to idealize as the best of husbands. Not long afterward, she blissfully described their marriage as a union of souls.

Eliza Lucas Pinckney appears to have written relatively few letters during the early years of her marriage, perhaps because her new domestic responsibilities kept her busy or because she was now

Charles Pinckney, who married Eliza Lucas in 1744 (portrait by Mary Roberts, painted between 1738 and 1753; private collection)

discussing with her husband the topics that characteristically dominated her letters. The young wife cultivated indigo at Belmont, Charles Pinckney's home plantation on the Cooper River, and she also experimented with silk production, a project that her husband encouraged. The couple divided their time between Belmont and the new townhouse that Charles built overlooking Charleston harbor. Eliza gave birth to four children within five years: Charles Cotesworth (born in 1746), George Lucas (born and died in 1747), Harriott (born in 1748), and Thomas (born in 1750).

Eliza Lucas Pinckney self-consciously strove to be an exemplary wife and mother. Some time early in her marriage, probably around 1750, she composed a private prayer in which she recorded her ideals and aspirations for domestic life. Listing what she believed to be her familial duties, Pinckney resolved "by [God's] Grace . . . to improve in every virtue" so that she might perform them commendably. Pledging to "make a good Wife to my D[ea]r Husband . . . [and] to make all my actions Correspond with that sincere Love and Duty I bear him," she resolved to preserve Charles's physical health, to promote his spiritual welfare, and "to do him all the good in my power; and next to my God to make it my [duty] to please him." The young mother also averred her desire to nurture her children physically and intellectually and, above all, to guide their religious and moral development. "I am resolved to make a good Mother to my Children, to pray for

them, to set good Examples, to give them good advice, to be careful both of their Souls and bodys, to watch over their tender minds, . . . and to instill piety, Virtue, and true religion into them," she wrote. Pinckney's childrearing strategy balanced praise with discipline. She promised both "to correct them for their Errors whatever uneasiness it may give my self and never omit to encourage every Virtue I see dawning in them."

In March 1753 the entire Pinckney family traveled to England, where Charles served briefly as the colonial agent for South Carolina. The main purpose of the trip, however, was to enroll Charles Cotesworth and Thomas in an English school, which the Pinckneys, like many elite South Carolinians, considered superior to any in provincial America. After a round of sightseeing and social life the Pinckneys' sons began their schooling while Harriott remained with her parents and presumably was tutored by her mother. Charles, Eliza, and Harriott settled into a house at Ripley, outside of London, where they lived for nearly five years. Then, in May 1758, leaving the boys behind in school, they returned to South Carolina.

Soon after their arrival in Charleston, Eliza Lucas Pinckney suffered what she later described as the greatest crisis of her life. Charles contracted malaria in June, and he died on 12 July. Eliza professed to accept Charles's death as God's will and urged her children to do likewise. Nevertheless, the grief of the thirty-five-year-old widow was so profound that she was unable to write to her sons with the sad news until some time in August. By then she had also turned her attention to business, for Charles had named her executor of his sizeable estate.

As a widowed mother, Pinckney returned to the occupation she had pursued before marrying, working now to preserve and enhance the prospects of her children, particularly her sons, who became coexecutors of their father's estate when they attained their majority. Charles Pinckney's estate included his home at Belmont, Pinckney Island, and five other plantations, in addition to property and two houses in the city of Charleston. With the help of several overseers Eliza Pinckney managed these properties, dividing her time primarily between Belmont and Charleston. She supervised crops and harvests, pored over plantation accounts, and dealt with merchants in Charleston and in London. She worked hard and took pride in her management of her family's business interests, as she had in the years before her marriage.

For Pinckney work was still a challenge, a source of self-esteem, and a family obligation, but it also became an activity that eased the pain of wid-

Letter from Eliza Pinckney to her husband, June or July 1744 (from Harriott Horry Ravenel, Eliza Pinckney, *1896)*

owhood, particularly in its early stages. "Had there not been a necessity for it," she observed on 14 March 1760, "I might have sunk to the grave by this time in that Lethargy of stupidity which had seized me after my mind had been violently agitated by the greatest shock it ever felt," the death of her beloved husband.

Because Charles Cotesworth and Thomas continued their studies in England for more than a decade after their father's death, Eliza Pinckney's chief companion was her daughter, Harriott, who resided with her mother until she married Daniel Horry in 1768. Educating young Harriott was one of Eliza's chief preoccupations. Harriott, like her mother, was fond of learning, and Eliza believed that her daughter had great intellectual potential. Using her own intellectual abilities to good effect, she tutored Harriott in academic subjects, as well as teaching her cooking, dairying, and other skills useful in housekeeping and plantation management. Harriott probably studied her mother's book of culinary and medicinal recipes, which she compiled in 1756, during her days as an English housewife. Harriott recopied twenty-six of her mother's recipes in a book

of her own, which she began two years after she married.

Although Eliza Pinckney's influence on her sons' development was necessarily less direct, her letters to them suggest that she readily stepped in to monitor their moral and intellectual development after the death of their father. Believing that her sons' happiness depended on their receiving an appropriate education, she decided that they should continue their studies at Oxford and the Inns of Court, despite her intense desire to reunite her family. From South Carolina, however, she advised the young men to persevere in their studies and to avoid the sordid temptations of London life. "For be assured, my dear child," she informed Charles Cotesworth on 7 February 1761, "I would not hesitate a moment were it in my choice whether I would have you a learned man with every accomplishment or a good man without any." An affectionate mother, Pinckney nevertheless held her sons to high standards of conduct and moral responsibility. On 15 April 1761 she reminded her eldest that "the welfair of a whole family depends in a great measure on the progress you make in moral Virtue, Religion and

Charleston in 1774 with the Pinckneys' mansion, begun in 1745, at center (detail from an engraving by Samuel Smith, after a painting by Thomas Leitch)

learning, and I dont doubt but the Almighty will give you grace and enable you to answer all our hopes, if you do your part."

Pinckney's letterbook indicates that the volume of her correspondence increased markedly after the death of her husband. Writing letters helped her to retain contact with her sons, her English friends, and the world beyond South Carolina. During the first year or so of her widowhood, Pinckney vented her grief in letters to a variety of English correspondents. While many later letters pertained to business or to her children's education and general welfare, others discussed English acquaintances and personages and fashionable life in London.

During this period, the letters Pinckney wrote and received gave her an opportunity to wax nostalgic for the happy time she passed in England with her family and afforded her access to information and ideas that may have enhanced her status among her Low Country neighbors. Pinckney's friends in South Carolina appear to have regarded her as exceptionally well informed on cosmopolitan topics. For instance, when Princess Charlotte Sophia of Mecklenburg married King George III in 1761 and was installed formally as queen shortly thereafter, Pinckney's South Carolina acquaintances assumed that she had news from London about the new

queen and her coronation. "You cant think how many people you have gratified by your obliging me with so particular a discription of the Queen," she declared to an English correspondent on 27 February 1762, explaining that South Carolinians "had no picture of her Majesty nor discription that could be depended upon till I received your favour." Maintaining her English contacts also allowed Pinckney to keep up with the latest London fashions. When an English friend sent twelve-year-old Harriott a fan and a suit of clothing, her happy mother reported that all their acquaintances admired the gifts, which were the first of their type to arrive in provincial South Carolina.

Before the imperial crisis that culminated in the American Revolution, Pinckney's letters occasionally mentioned political and military matters, but such concerns clearly were not among her chief preoccupations. As the daughter of one colonial official and the widow of another, Eliza Lucas Pinckney was naturally attuned to imperial affairs; consequently, her letters sometimes included passing references to British politicians or colonial officials or news about the French and Indian War (1754– 1763). Like most colonial women, however, Pinckney appears to have accepted the prevailing gender conventions of her culture, which regarded politics as the domain of men and relegated women and their opinions, at least in theory, to the margins of public life.

The changing tone and content of Pinckney's letters demonstrate the extent to which the imperial crisis and the subsequent War of Independence enhanced the political consciousness of some women in eighteenth-century America. By the late 1760s Pinckney's correspondence had dwindled, partly as a result of Charles Cotesworth's return to South Carolina in 1769 to assume responsibility for his father's estate. From then on, however, Eliza Pinckney's surviving letters focused on public affairs, which she followed avidly and unapologetically during those critical years. Not only did she discuss political and military matters, but she also took increasingly partisan stances on the public news she reported to correspondents both in England and in America.

While in 1767 Pinckney, like many politically conscious Americans, hoped for a peaceful repeal of offensive parliamentary statutes, by 1775 her letters had begun to reflect a fervent support for an increasingly militant patriot movement and contempt for those who opposed it. On 2 August 1775, as colonial troops prepared to defend "Divine Liberty" in the months after the battles at Lexington and Concord, Pinckney wrote that "Britain surely will be shortly taught by our successes, & continued unanimity in spite of all their base acts to disunite us that America determines to be free, & that it is beyond their force of arms to enslave so vast a Continent." Those who refused to join the struggle she reviled as a "few base Souls . . . who, leaving penury, & want in their own Country, have lived Luxuriously in our land, & . . . now spurn at their benefactors, & betray the place that has been their Asylum." To the "misrepresentations of such wretches" she attributed "much of our present calamity."

The Revolution profoundly affected Eliza Lucas Pinckney and her family. Both Charles Cotesworth and Thomas, who returned to South Carolina in 1774, served during the entire war as officers in the American army. Charles Cotesworth was taken prisoner after the British occupation of Charleston in May 1780, while Thomas's leg was shattered in battle at Camden, where he also became a prisoner. Like most other civilians, Eliza Pinckney struggled with inflation, high taxes, and scarcities during the war years, and, like other American patriots, she was driven from her home when the British confiscated the property of all South Carolinians who refused to swear allegiance to the king in September 1780.

Harriot Pinckney Horry, Eliza Pinckney's only daughter (miniature attributed to Walter Robertson; from Frances Leigh Williams, A Founding Family, *1978)*

Although she and her sons reclaimed their property after the war, the Revolution and its aftermath brought financial hardship to Eliza Pinckney and her family. "It may seem strange, that a single woman, accused of no crime, who had a fortune sufficient to live Genteely in our part of the world . . . should in so short a time, be so intirely deprived of it as not to be able to pay a debt under sixty pound Sterling," she explained to an impatient creditor on 14 May 1782, "but such is my singular [lot] after the many losses I had met with, for the last three or four desolate years, from fire, and plunder, both in Country and Town, as well as from the death, and destruction of slaves."

Eliza Pinckney took pride in the American Revolution and in her family's prominence in it. Shortly after the signing of the Treaty of Paris, which formally ended the war and recognized the United States as a sovereign nation, she extolled the exemplary patriotism of her sons for the benefit of her grandson Daniel Horry, whose own father had fled to England in 1780. Advising him that virtuous children were any mother's greatest treasure, she urged young Daniel to follow the same principles of honor and patriotism that inspired his heroic uncles. Perhaps the unflagging patriotism she saw in her own sons led the aging matriarch to look confidently to the future. Despite the devastation and suffering created by the war, Pinckney looked forward to a new era of liberty, peace, and prosperity for her own family and for America.

After the Revolution, Pinckney resided mainly at Hampton with her daughter, Harriott, who was widowed in 1786. The household at Hampton included not only Harriott's two children but often also those of her brothers, whose political business frequently took them away from South Carolina. In May 1791 President George Washington acknowledged the importance of the Pinckney brothers—and by extension, that of their entire family—when he toured the Southern states to solidify support for the new national government he headed. During his tour, Washington visited Hampton, where he enjoyed an elaborate breakfast with Eliza Lucas Pinckney and her family.

Less than a year after she received Washington as a guest at Hampton, Pinckney discovered that she had cancer. Her condition deteriorated, and in April 1793 she and Harriott went to Philadelphia to consult a physician who was known to specialize in the treatment of that disease. On 26 May 1793, Eliza Lucas Pinckney died at the age of seventy in Philadelphia, where she was buried in St. Peter's churchyard. By his own request, President Washington served as one of her pallbearers.

Pinckney's obituary, which appeared in the *Charleston City Gazette* on 17 July 1793, revealed the stature she enjoyed in her own right in addition to that which her contemporaries bestowed on her as a mother of patriots of the American Revolution. In an era when newspapers usually published only the most perfunctory notices of women's deaths, Pinckney's obituary celebrated the moral and intellectual qualities that made her at once exemplary and unusual among women. "Her understanding . . . had been so highly cultivated and improved by travel and extensive reading, and was so richly furnished, as well as with scientific, as practical knowledge, that her talent for conversation was unrivalled . . . ," the anonymous essayist intoned. "Her religion was rational, liberal, and pure. The source of it was seated in the judgment and the heart. . . ."

A valuable source of women's history, Eliza Pinckney's writings situate her unusual abilities and experiences in a cultural context she shared with many eighteenth-century Americans. Although she was undeniably exceptional in many respects, Pinckney's letters reveal her commitment to her children and her family, her taste for reading, her decorous piety, and her growing political awareness—all of which were characteristic of elite women of her generation. Pinckney recognized herself as an elite female, and she accepted the conventions that governed class and gender relations in the society in which she lived. Her letters re-create the cultural environment of her time and place, chronicling the domestic, business, and social relationships of their gifted and privileged author.

Biographies:

Harriott Horry Ravenel, *Eliza Pinckney* (New York: Scribners, 1896);

Frances Leigh Williams, *Plantation Patriot: A Biography of Eliza Lucas Pinckney* (New York: Harcourt, Brace & World, 1967);

Elise Pinckney, "Biographical Sketch," in *The Letterbook of Eliza Lucas Pinckney, 1739–1762,* edited by Elise Pinckney (Chapel Hill: University of North Carolina Press, 1972), pp. xv–xxvi.

References:

Frances Leigh Williams, *A Founding Family: The Pinckneys of South Carolina* (New York & London: Harcourt Brace Jovanovich, 1978);

Nancy Woloch, *Women and the American Experience* (New York: Knopf, 1984).

Papers:

There are collections of Pinckney's papers at Duke University, the Library of Congress, and the South Carolina Historical Society.

Martha Laurens Ramsay

(3 November 1759 – 10 June 1811)

Joanna B. Gillespie
University of Arizona, Tucson

BOOK: *Memoirs of the Life of Martha Laurens Ramsay,* edited by David Ramsay (Philadelphia: Printed by James Maxwell, 1811; London: Printed for Burton & Briggs, sold also by J. Hatchard, 1815).

The literary legacy of Martha Laurens Ramsay is found primarily in a slender leather-bound volume, *Memoirs of the Life of Martha Laurens Ramsay* (1811), compiled and edited after her death by her husband, Dr. David Ramsay. This single publication, republished and excerpted frequently during the nineteenth century, remains important for its passionate tone and for the quality of its spiritual and psychological self-analysis. Ramsay's sophisticated use of religious concepts in her attempts to understand her struggles reveals that she was less intent on autobiographical self-disclosure than on mental grapplings with theological issues. She aimed for spiritual rather than literary immortality. To learn about her life—her ambitions, her probable response to the Revolutionary War, and the emergence of a distinctive "American" identity, even her complex emotions about being a slaveholder married to an antislavery advocate—the reader must examine her writings in the context of the lives and writings of the men who shaped the course of her life. This information may be found in the papers of her father, Henry Laurens, and in Arthur H. Shaffer's biography of her husband.

Martha Laurens was born in Charleston, South Carolina, on 3 November 1759, the third living child of Eleanor Ball Laurens and Henry Laurens, an importer and civic leader with English and Huguenot bloodlines. Raised in a wealthy, Anglican home, she was nurtured in the religious liturgy of St. Philip's Church and educated by tutors with her elder brother, John (a sister between them died at age eight, when Martha was five). Martha was taught to "measure" the newly invented celestial and terrestrial globes her father sent from his Continental travels, along with mathematics and geogra-

Martha Laurens, circa 1767, about twenty years before her marriage to David Ramsay (portrait by John Wollaston; private collection)

phy. As a daughter, however, she also mastered the domestic skills of sewing, making puddings, playing harpsichord, and making "drawings from nature" (botany). Her mother died when Martha was eleven. She and her newborn infant sister were sent to live with their uncle and aunt James and Mary Laurens, who had no children of their own. Henry Laurens was often in Europe for the schooling of Martha's elder brother and her two younger brothers, Henry Jr. and Jemmy.

Because of her uncle's failing health, his household, including Henry Laurens's two daughters, relocated to England in 1775. Trapped there by the outbreak of hostilities, they moved to Nîmes, a more hospitable location in Protestant southern

France, until the war ended and peace negotiations were completed. (Henry Laurens was one of three negotiators for the United States.)

There are few extant writings by Martha Laurens from the period when her uncle's household was located in France; none is included in the published record. She spent her early twenties nursing sick relatives, tutoring her sister Polly, and instituting a school for children in the village of Vigan. She was an excellent caregiver and manager, the only healthy adult in the household, and its only speaker of French competent enough to negotiate with the surrounding Huguenot community. When Martha was eighteen, her youngest brother, Jemmy, who was only ten, died in a tragic accident at his English boarding school. Next came the trauma of war with their mother country, trapping Martha an ocean away from her father and her homeland's birth struggles—except through her vicarious identification with her brother John, an officer under George Washington's command in the Revolutionary Army. The larger context of her European displacement was her newly formed identification of herself as "American." Its ultimate bitter fruit came with brother John's death in late 1782 during one of the last sorties of the war. None of these traumas, however, was recorded in any of her writings that were included in the *Memoirs*.

Martha Laurens had always idolized her dashing brother John, a military hero and idealist. The impact of his death at age twenty-seven, intermixed with devotion to a father whose health had been broken by his imprisonment in the Tower of London, finally resolved the standoff that emerged between father and adult daughter during that same painful year.

With the tacit approval of James and Mary Laurens, Martha had allowed a local French merchant to court her. She was nearly twenty-three and may have felt trapped in an invalids' home, fearing she might never have the opportunity for a home of her own or the culturally legitimate role of married matron. Whatever her motive, she had not asked paternal permission for this courtship. Her independence unleashed a barrage of anguished letters from her father, alternately raging at her disregard of his authority and pleading that she not be deceived by a fortune hunter.

Unfortunately only Henry Laurens's side of this battle has survived. His attacks on female independence are a set piece of rationalization for paternal control. His daughter apparently remained obdurate for about ten months, waiting for divine or human leading to help her choose between life as a French matron, oceans away from father and native

country, and life as a spinster managing an honored patriarch's household. Ultimately her heart may have been softened by her father's palpable despair at losing his dearest daughter to life in a foreign land and by the dubious civil status of an American wife to a French Huguenot. When the news of John Laurens's death finally arrived in Europe and plunged the family into shock, she chose in her father's favor. Released from the Tower and needing her care, Henry Laurens had requested the services and company of this beloved daughter who had been the pillar of his brother's household from the age of sixteen, with books and correspondence the only source of her prodigious "self-improvement." In early 1783 she traveled alone from southern France to her father's side in Bath, England, to nurse him back to health and to become his hostess and secretary—the best he ever had, her father later told David Ramsay. Henry Laurens expressed his alarm and gratification at his daughter's independence in the new postrevolutionary vocabulary, calling her "a true American woman."

James and Mary Laurens died in France, and the remaining members of the Laurens family returned to Charleston in 1785. At that time Martha Laurens met David Ramsay, a recently widowed physician who was attending her ill father. On 28 January 1787 she became his third wife.

Among letters in the Caroliniana Library at the University of South Carolina, a gossipy note by one of their female contemporaries in Charleston deplores the new Mrs. Ramsay's enthusiasm for being "in the family way." Martha's unconcealed joy in a "matrimonial partnership" was unseemly, the neighbor wrote, because it forced an observer to "bring to mind the act of sweet Dr. Ramsay" that produced it. For his part David Ramsay was delighted to have a third wife who survived longer than a first wedding anniversary, since each of his previous two wives, also daughters of distinguished men, had not. His second wife, Frances Witherspoon Ramsay, had left behind an infant son, John Witherspoon Ramsay, for David and Martha to raise. The doctor's own reproductive ambitions were expressed in an exuberant note to Martha Ramsay about a backcountry Carolina couple who had seventeen children. Though he denied aiming that high, he and Martha had eleven children in their twenty-four year marriage. Four daughters and four sons were living when she died.

On her deathbed Martha Ramsay told her husband about a secret cache of her writings, including a diary. David Ramsay was an established figure on the national literary horizon, having published a history of the Revolution in South Carolina in 1785 and a complete history of the American Revolution in 1789. He had several motives for creating a published memorial to his wife. At that time biographies of distinguished women were primarily from Britain or New England. Presenting a national female exemplar for the new nation fit into Dr. Ramsay's pattern of relating history through brief biographies of "great characters." The need for didactic models for citizens of the new nation was ample justification: Martha Laurens Ramsay could be a prototype for the new American woman, her scholarly level of reasoning and writing proof of the advanced capabilities of educated American females.

David Ramsay's decision to fill out the memoir with writings other than the diary was also logical, editorially and quantitatively. He amended the limited prose he could extract from her diary, sixty-seven pages in a completed memoir of more than two hundred, with several long footnotes, one of which illustrated her model of self-education: a comprehensive abridgment (in outline form) of a British preacher's treatise on "heart religion." He supplemented the core of her memoirs—the diary excerpts labeled Appendix V—with five other appendices and a forty-seven-page biography of laudatory anecdotes, testimony to her self-education and household management, her family "school," and her beautiful death scene.

The memoir is arranged chronologically. After the biographical introduction, Appendix I features "war letters" written to young Martha Laurens from her father during 1771–1776, paternal adjurations to a beloved oldest daughter with forebodings about horrendous "civil war" with England. The worried father restated the societal prescriptions for female behavior in which his daughter had already been schooled, including the mandate that she must pray without ceasing for her country and her father. He also warned that she must prepare herself to earn her own living if the vast financial losses he dreaded came to pass, a somewhat surprising admonition for a daughter of the Charleston elite. This first appendix provides a clearer picture of Henry Laurens as a father than of young Martha as a daughter. Yet these six emotionally charged letters from the pen of the one-time president of the Continental Congress (1777–1778) and the highest ranking American diplomat to be captured by the British and imprisoned in the Tower of London (1779–1781) provided additional justification for memorializing Martha Laurens Ramsay in print.

Appendix II is the earliest surviving document by Ramsay. According to the introduction, she destroyed her childhood writings in 1775, lest they fall into the wrong hands while she was in England. The

Dr. David Ramsay, who edited his wife's writings for publication after her death (portrait attributed to Charles Willson Peale; Gibbes Museum of Art/Carolina Art Association, Charleston, South Carolina)

work in Appendix II is a "Self-dedication and Solemn Covenant with God," written when she was "fourteen years and seven weeks old." Created as an "adult" response to a family crisis, the document shows that she was mature enough to understand the impact of a 1772 scandal that hurt the respected Laurens name in Charleston. Confiding it to no one, she transformed the trauma of this crisis into a spiritual rite of passage.

The incident involved illicit sex as well as issues of patriotism and loyalty. Henry and James Laurens's niece Molsy, only a few years older than Martha, had been seduced by a British appointee who made her pregnant with an illegitimate child and then smuggled her onboard a ship sailing for England. Young Martha's awareness of her elders' dismay apparently led her to seek a principle for self-management, an internal moral armor. Using a model in a 1763 edition of British theologian Philip Doddridge's *The Rise and Progress of Religion in the Soul,* one of many popular devotionals her uncle's book-importing business made available, she wrote out a contract committing herself to be God's "co-worker." This action may well have been the catalyst for the two "voices" in her diary entries and personal letters. She adopted the elevated tone of published religious authorities for writing about ultimate goals and highest spiritual vows. In contrast, the written voice in letters to neighbors, family, and friends was conversational and less constrained, but always elegantly phrased.

Martha Laurens's "Covenant," carefully preserved through her young-adult years, is a prime example of eighteenth-century high-English Calvinist self-inquisition. It is filled with sweeping apostrophes to the all-powerful Creator and contrasting terms of self-reference such as "a wandering sheep, a prodigal daughter, a backsliding child." The word change from "prodigal son" to "prodigal daughter" is the only alteration she made from Doddridge's original. Outraged over her cousin's sordid adventure, as well as expressing her youthful quest for self-importance, Martha could well have relished Doddridge's emphatic vocabulary and occasional arcane verbs, as in "I *avouch* and declare myself . . . one of his covenant people." Copying out the phrase "May . . . I . . . be a fellow citizen with the saints" reinforced her awareness that citizenship for females would be found only in heaven, even for daughters of leading citizens.

Doddridge's model concluded with an aspiration deeply inscribed in the psyche of teenage Martha and reiterated in her deathbed commission: her diary should be "preserved as a common book among the family." She and other women whose memoirs she admired expressed the devout hope that if their writings were ever seen by others, they should become "the means of making serious impressions on their mind." Aspiration to be the cause of others' profound concerns about the meanings of life, death, and salvation was the reigning cultural goal for self-perfecting Christians, and young Martha vowed to become one. As her editor-husband recognized, any understanding of his wife's adult writings depended on young Martha's formative spiritual "Covenant" and its role in her psychological as well as spiritual evolution.

Appendix III dates from the earliest days Martha Laurens spent in England, a brief religious supplication, "For a Beloved Relative," written in 1776–1777 about the illness of her guardians. Appendix IV comprises some twenty meditations returned to David Ramsay after his wife's death by a British woman in whose safekeeping they had been left. These writings provide a fuller revelation of young Martha's character between the ages of sixteen and nineteen.

Each short essay or meditative fragment is typically focused on a single theme of self-chastisement for its spiritual implications. For example,

one deplores the female obsession with ribbons and finery, which interferes with a woman's concentrating on "the hillocks of immortality." Another laments frivolous conversation and "shocking levity," again because it undermines her desired self-image: "I hate all company, all amusements, all business that diverts my mind from spiritual things." Religious language cloaks these youthful struggles for poise and social confidence in a foreign context: "Let not the fear of singularity make me a babbler," she begged God. "If I can bear no innocent and useful part in conversation, keep me silent." These self-focused meditations reveal the anxieties of a young female who often felt like a social misfit, one who could not help being attracted to "things of the world" but at the same time one who was too pious (by which she undoubtedly meant "serious") to be much of a success at afternoon tea.

Several features of the excerpts from Martha Laurens Ramsay's diary that are published in Appendix V of the *Memoirs* are puzzling to present-day readers. Although the entries were written during her years of intensive childbearing and child rearing, they include few references to such domestic concerns. The diary writings are filled with spiritual anxieties, fears, and self-accusations, not thanksgivings and rejoicing. Even the birth of David Jr., the first male child after four daughters, in 1795 was not recorded. She also did not mention or explain her distinctive naming practice: giving each of the daughters both her father's names as a middle name (as in Eleanor Henry Laurens Ramsay) until his death in 1792. The diary primarily details Martha Ramsay's negotiations with fate, variously called Providence or God. For example, if he would let her dangerously ill infant daughter survive, she would pledge new depths of devotion; if somehow they could survive a period of financial difficulty, she would be more vigilant in prayer. There is little doubt that her editor-husband was selective in excerpting from her diary and family letters. Still, out of respect for her mental and spiritual capacities and her sophisticated social background, David Ramsay would not have presumed to add words to her accounts or to slant the selection of diary entries toward a focus on sin. He may well have omitted her thoughts on slavery or other morally fraught topics, both to protect her posthumous literary reputation and to prevent controversial opinions from inhibiting sales of the *Memoirs*. The most likely interpretation of the obsessive self-focus of her diary was Martha Ramsay's unrelenting conscience, her drive toward religious achievement—her "duty to God." She constantly tested herself against the spiritual standard she had set for herself in her "Covenant."

Turning diary introspection into life interrogations was one way she could discharge that awesome obligation.

Her self-indictment is apparent in the arresting phrase "my easily besetting sin," which appears at least five times in the *Memoirs*. She so belabored herself with this concept that her editor-husband declared his bafflement about her intention. The appearance of this phrase in her diary seems to be associated with occasions when she had dared to juxtapose her will against God's. Fervent prayers, unrewarded in the way she had hoped, were transformed into some sort of self-blame; the effort to make sense of disappointments resulted in ever more strenuous vows against that "easily besetting sin." She knew no other way to "advance in the spiritual life" than by resubmitting her will to the divine will.

A relatively concrete example of "easily besetting sin" appeared when she could no longer ignore her husband's financial mismanagement—something she only implied in praying for her "dear husband's judgement and steadiness of mind, in the duties of his profession." She was determined to avoid the critical, antimale tone for which she and many contemporaries criticized Mary Wollstonecraft in spite of their applause for her views on female education. If "easily besetting sin" was sometimes a euphemism for spiritual pride, any thought of competing mentally or spiritually with her husband's authority could be reason for self-censure. During 1795 the diary entries trace a downward spiral into despair, which she called "spiritual darkness," her label for midlife feelings of helplessness. This episode, akin to clinical depression with a spiritual component, was Martha's "dark night of the soul." It undermined her confidence in her powers of reason and competence. After a psychic collapse, she gradually restored her health through the use of her "reason"—reading, taking notes, and writing. The contradiction in her inner life—trying to write her powerful sense of self into religious submission in her diary, while at the same time educating her mind in the superior skills of Enlightenment rationality—forced her to a psychic surrender that she could explain to herself, finally, only in the mysteries of Christian conversion and a rebirth of faith.

One of the few anecdotes in Ramsay's diary demonstrates her ability to construct a cautionary moral from a concrete experience—the style of logic and "philosophical" interpretation or mindset that characterized much popular literature, including Sunday school library books, through the nineteenth century. In 1802, once again anxious about

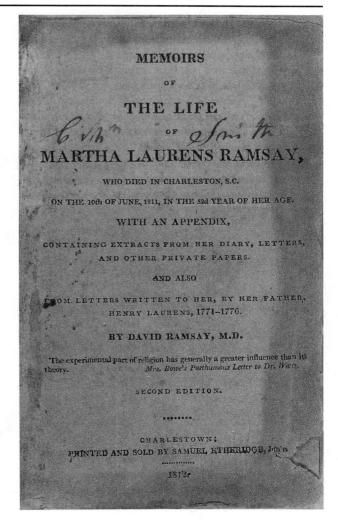

Title page for the second edition of Ramsay's writings, which form an account of her spiritual struggles and psychological self-analysis from age fourteen until two months before her death at age fifty-one (courtesy of the South Caroliniana Library, University of South Carolina)

debt and the household cash flow, she felt besieged by tensions arising from the gap between her expectations of their midlife circumstances and their realities. Even as she rocked in her chair seeking comfort from her Bible, her mind was tormented by the "sharp pinching" economies necessary in her house "full of dear children." Suddenly an answer to that prayer arrived: David Ramsay interrupted her anguished meditations with an "unexpected payment" from a long overdue bill. In her diary Martha Ramsay recorded that blessing, lecturing herself for a lack of faith in God's providential goodness, and she turned such "miraculous provision" into a prayer that their souls would be fed with spiritual food. The "bread of life" was far more valuable than actual food, she reminded herself—a fact easier to celebrate when real food was no longer unobtainable.

Death was the second most frequent subject of Martha Ramsay's diary reflections—as though putting her thoughts about death and dying into words was a religious ritual for her. Deaths of people among the civic leaders in the Ramsays' social circle, among their many relatives, among the slaves in her own household, or among members of the church congregation in which she and her husband were considered pillars all led her to write in her diary, honoring the departed life and examining it for spiritual meanings. No occurrence was without its religious significance, she believed.

By comparison with the intense ego-and-soul focus of the diary, the approximately thirty letters David Ramsay collected in Appendix VI are outward-focused and gregarious, almost playful in tone—except when she wrote spiritually elevated letters of condolence. She acclaimed her daughters' felicitous expressions of sorrow "a sacred duty" and "a tender feeling" when Miss Futerell, their British mother's helper, returned to England. She wreathed maternal instructions in blessings and scriptural citations. She compared novelist Samuel Richardson's early practice of letter writing for pay with her sons' disinterest in writing and jested that none of them would ever produce a novel like Richardson's *Pamela* (1740–1741). She borrowed and recommended books; she rhapsodized about the "fair face of nature" while cutting flowers for her nieces in the early morning garden; and she praised the "sweet elasticity" of her daughter Sabina's "virtuous mind." Against the unrelieved somberness of the diary, the letters often read like verbal bouquets.

This final appendix concludes with a collection of ten monitory letters to their son David Ramsay Jr. at Princeton. David Ramsay instantly recognized them as a sort of citizenship curriculum for sons of the elite in the new nation. Written in 1809–1810, they addressed classic parental and patriotic concerns that still exist in the late twentieth century: write home more often, study harder, be serious about preparation for earning your future livelihood. Martha Ramsay characterized her maternal advice as "an overflowing tide of affection." She warned against being spendthrift with his parents' hard-earned money and against being misled by foppish, indulged fellow Carolinians. Those letters were written during the "long, lingering illness" from which Martha Ramsay died. Her final letter, written in March 1811, was a heart-rending benediction.

The originals of Ramsay's diary and most of her letters are no longer extant, but a few letters in her hand, written during the Revolutionary War, may be found in collections of the correspondence of Benjamin Franklin and John Adams, early American diplomats to whom she wrote for help in obtaining her father's release from the Tower of London. These well-written, politely demanding letters from an unmarried female are further evidence of her independence and practicality. Ramsay's hand, like her father's and brother's, is bold, legible, and masculine in style—and in marked contrast with her husband's erratic physician's scrawl. It was obviously a product of her father's belief that penmanship indicated character, breeding, and social responsibility.

Ramsay's religious views were widely esteemed among early nineteenth-century Protestants. Her *Memoirs* were republished and excerpted in a variety of religious volumes, most notably Sarah Josepha Hale's *Women's Record: Sketches of Distinguished Women* (1855). The excerpts selected were usually expressions of soul-searching agony from her diary, evidence of the uneven cultural weight assigned to the less elevated discourse of letters. Formal (male) religious language and psalmodic intensity were the telling theological qualities that appealed to nineteenth-century editors.

Ramsay wrote in the two prose forms available to all literate women of her era: diary and letters. Epistolary communication was as natural as breathing for her, and letter writing was important in her father's agenda for his children. Yet diaries connoted a different level of introspection, and as such they were accorded greater cultural significance by both the diary keeper and the reading public. A diary was assumed to be a safe place in which to confide one's fears, hopes, and dreams, to write one's deepest self into being. The act of pouring oneself into a diary, ostensibly for the writer's eyes only, promised compelling insight into the writer's central autobiographical quest. For a compiled memoir such as Ramsay's, that framework provides the necessary coherence. Letters were expected to be less significant. In Ramsay's *Memoirs* both verbal forms in the same book provided two contrasting voices from the same writer.

Martha Ramsay may well have been reaching for some earthly immortality when she requested that the writings she had hidden be preserved. As with many of the learned Christian females whose memoirs she had admired, Ramsay's deathbed request gave the imprimatur for turning her writings "toward a more enlarged sphere of usefulness." Whether or not the dying middle-aged woman recalled her youthful determination to "do honor to that last finishing scene . . . with my expiring breath," the mournful watchers at her bedside believed her departure from this life fully exemplified the Christian memoirist's ideal.

The picture presented in Ramsay's *Memoirs* is the portrait of a woman who set out to exemplify the dutiful daughter and respectfully submissive wife—the patriarchal expectations of the female Christian in her era and class—as the highest cultivation of her powers of intellect and judgment. The writings preserved in the *Memoirs,* published to honor her virtue and piety in that accomplishment, also unwittingly reveal a disjunction between her willed adherence to prevailing social expectations and her inner spirit's struggle within and against those boundaries. Since all her writings are religious in imagery, language, and psychology, it has been easy to stereotype them as evangelical. For most readers the spiritual intensity and self-criticism of the diary overshadows the more accessible human being visible in her notes and letters.

Yet modern scholars are interested in Martha Ramsay because she employed the only psychologically analytic language available to her for self-development and self-management—making religion the template for her life writing. She was a rare eighteenth-century female: at home with the sophisticated vocabulary and concepts of theologians, historians, memoirists, and poets, she was also capable of writing personal letters that reveal glimpses of a warm human being struggling through and surviving politically and personally turbulent times. Her prose writings offer rich insights into the sensibility and soul of an elite Southern woman in early America.

References:

Joanna B. Gillespie, "David Ramsay Jr. and Martha Laurens Ramsay: Filiopietism as Citizenship," *Early American Literature,* 29 (1994);

Gillespie, "Many Gracious Providences: The Religious Cosmos of Martha Laurens Ramsay," *Colby Library Quarterly,* 25 (September 1989): 199–212;

Gillespie, "1795: Martha Laurens Ramsay's Dark Night of the Soul," *William and Mary Quarterly,* 47 (January 1991): 68–92;

Gillespie, "Martha Laurens Ramsay: A Case Study of Diary as Autobiography," in *A Women's Diaries Miscellany,* edited by Jane Dupree Begos (Weston, Conn.: Magic Circle Press, 1989);

Gillespie, "Martha Laurens Ramsay, Prototypical Citizen in the Constitutional Era," in *A Selection of Papers from Women and the Constitution: A Bicentennial Perspective,* edited by Joyce M. Pair (Atlanta: Communicorp, 1990);

Henry Laurens, *The Papers of Henry Laurens,* 15 volumes to date, edited by Philip M. Hamer, George C. Rogers Jr., David R. Chesnutt, and C. James Taylor (Columbia: Published for the South Carolina Historical Society by the University of South Carolina Press, 1968–1998);

George C. Rogers, "Martha Laurens Ramsay," in *Notable American Women, 1607–1950: A Biographical Dictionary* (Cambridge, Mass.: Harvard University Press, 1971), pp. 111–113;

Arthur H. Shaffer, *To Be an American: David Ramsay and the Making of the American Consciousness* (Columbia: University of South Carolina Press, 1991).

Martha Meredith Read

Joseph Fichtelberg
Hofstra University

BOOKS: *Monima, or The Beggar Girl* (New York: Printed by P. R. Johnson for I. N. Ralston, 1802);
Margaretta; or The Intricacies of the Heart (Philadelphia: Samuel F. Bradford, 1807; Charleston, S.C.: Edmund Morford, 1807).

SELECTED PERIODICAL PUBLICATIONS–UNCOLLECTED: "A Second Vindication of the Rights of Women," *Ladies' Monitor* (22 August and 5 September 1801).

Martha Meredith Read was one of several early national writers who drew on the rancorous political imagery of the Federalist era. Her fiction, replete with references to the French Terror, the slave rebellion in St. Domingo, and the yellow-fever outbreak of 1793, expresses a conservative resistance to republican passions—a reaction consistent with her own patrician background. At the same time, however, Read's fiction displays a marked feminism and an awareness that human suffering is caused by many of the same institutions that enforce social order. Her work may thus be seen as a call to address some of the inequalities that surfaced in the early republic without sacrificing the elite dominance on which Federalists and old-line republicans had insisted. The fact that her second novel was published just as Federalist dreams were disintegrating points to the critical and experimental nature of her fiction.

Little is known about Read's life and career. Neither her birth date nor her death date is known. A member of the Philadelphia elite, she was the daughter of Margaret Cadwalader Meredith and Samuel Meredith, a brigadier general during the Revolutionary War and the first U.S. treasury secretary. She married John Read Jr. on 25 June 1796 and had five children, one of whom, John Meredith Read III, served as chief justice of the Pennsylvania Supreme Court at the end of his career. Her literary productivity seems to have been confined to the first few years of her marriage. On 8 August 1801 Isaac Newton Ralston, a printer and publisher Read

probably knew in Philadelphia, where he ran the *Supporter* and *The Ladies Museum* in 1800, inaugurated his New York venture *The Ladies' Monitor* with the first chapter of *Monima, or The Beggar Girl* (1802). The novel was serialized until 26 September, after which Ralston sold the paper to P. Heard and announced that he would publish the complete work in a single volume. On the title page Read was identified only as "An American Lady," a pseudonym used in her other publications if she was identified at all. During the same period *The Ladies' Monitor* also began to publish "A Second Vindication of the Rights of Women" (22 August and 5 September 1801), Read's answer to Mary Wollstonecraft's *Vindication of the Rights of Woman* (1792). Only two installments of the essay have survived. Six weeks after the first chapter of *Monima* appeared, Ralston began serializing *Margaretta; or The Intricacies of the Heart* (12 September – 3 October 1801), which he abandoned along with the other projects on 10 October—all casualties of the high cost of early American publishing. Read apparently revised *Margaretta* over the next six years, seeing it published in Philadelphia and Charleston in 1807.

Monima is a melodrama with a social conscience. The title character, a beautiful sixteen-year-old French emigrée, lives on the fringes of Philadelphia society, repeatedly facing starvation as she tries to provide for her decrepit father, M. Fontanbleu. Behind her sufferings lie two persecutors—Ursala Sonnetton, jealous of the attention her benevolent husband has paid to the girl, and Sonnetton's lover, Pierre De Noix, who has conspired against the Fontanbleus on both sides of the Atlantic. Although Monima occasionally finds work as a seamstress, she is more often reduced to begging while her father gives in to grief-stricken melancholy. Facing the full range of sentimental catastrophes, Monima is kidnapped, imprisoned for theft, stricken with yellow fever, and assaulted by De Noix, whom she wounds with his own pistol. She is an unusual amalgam of passivity and daring, as industrious and active as she is submissive and oppressed. Read's heroine thus allows her to explore

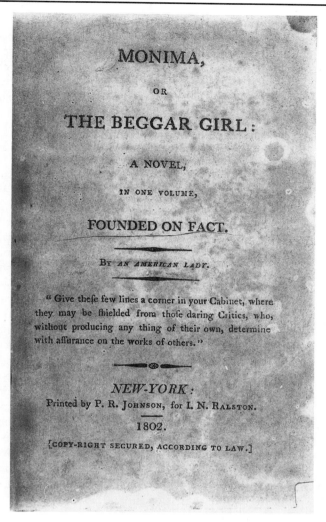

MONIMA,

OR

THE BEGGAR GIRL:

A NOVEL,

IN ONE VOLUME,

FOUNDED ON FACT.

BY AN AMERICAN LADY.

"Give thefe few lines a corner in your Cabinet, where
they may be fhielded from thofe daring Critics, who,
without producing any thing of their own, determine
with affurance on the works of others."

NEW-YORK:
Printed by P. R. JOHNSON, for L. N. RALSTON.
1802.
[COPY-RIGHT SECURED, ACCORDING TO LAW.]

Title page for Martha Meredith Read's melodramatic novel about a virtuous young woman
who is kidnapped, assaulted, wrongfully confined several times, and nearly starved to
death before she finds happiness with a benevolent husband (courtesy of the Special
Collections Department, University of Virginia Library)

social and structural tensions in the early republic in a context that accepts its dominant institutions.

One aspect of Read's challenge to patriarchy involves the weakening of family ties that is evident among the Fontanbleus. In France, Fontanbleu was the patriarch of a prosperous family, a merchant whose son, Ferdinant, received the finest education and who would have undoubtedly increased the family fortune. Both father and son are imprisoned on false charges, however, and Ferdinant later dies in a duel. His demise signals a retreat of patriarchal authority that touches almost every family in the novel, from De Noix's uncle, the Marquis de la Montte, who dies prematurely after learning of his nephew's plots, to the well-meaning but fatuous M. Sonnetton, ignorant of his wife's scheming and philandering as well as of her vicious persecution of Monima. Along with this collapse of authority comes revolutionary chaos and counterrevolutionary oppression, including a host of nightmare institutions to which the Fontanbleus are subject. In addition to the French prisons that break both father and son, Fontanbleu faces an American debtors' prison, while Monima, whose infancy was largely spent in a prison cell, is by turns confined to a Philadelphia workhouse and a lunatic asylum, arraigned at the mayor's court, and nearly starved to death in the Sonnettons' summer house, which takes on the airs of a Gothic edifice. Weakened fathers, the novel implies, invite such abuses, permitting the onslaught of passion best exemplified in St. Domingo, where the Fontanbleus, seeking refuge from the French Reign of Terror, are pursued and nearly murdered by rebellious slaves. Ironically, then, Monima's sufferings originate with her father, whom she is attempting to shield.

Those sufferings reflect challenges to the national family that were increasingly decried during the 1790s. In his Farewell Address, for example, George Washington cautioned against the "jealousies and heart-burnings" of international hatreds and sectional passions alienating "those who ought to be bound together by fraternal affection." Washington's warning came amid heightened domestic tensions that had already included a tax rebellion in Pennsylvania and heated factional disputes over France that would culminate in the Alien and Sedition Laws of 1798. This domestic contention demanded extraordinary responses; and just as Washington prescribed affection as the antidote to sectionalism, so Read saw in benevolence the answer to national ills. If the weakening of Federalist authority had unleashed destructive social passions, then the answer was to reassert control through a mild but firm benevolence. Like a reverse image of Charles Brockden Brown's Arthur Mervyn, who runs himself ragged dispensing virtuous aid, Monima provides the occasion for others to display compassion, allowing the reader to discriminate between socially destructive and socially supportive characters. Thus, by the end of the novel she has not one but two benevolent suitors, each willing to sacrifice his fortune to preserve Monima's surpassing virtue. Her marriage to Sonnetton, whose first wife has died of apoplexy and a bad conscience, signals that members of the social elite have it within their power to restore moral order. The abysses Monima has glimpsed are the result of bad management, not bad morals, and the social order remains fundamentally sound.

This pragmatic feminism is also evident in "A Second Vindication of the Rights of Women." Although Read, like Wollstonecraft, sought a radical solution to the "evil" of women's subjection, she was shrewd enough to realize that the remedy had to proceed from men. As in Monima, that remedy is both institutional and familial. Girls' schools must educate the mind, not the manners, persuading their charges that they have a duty higher than the "foolish display of their own vanity." Similarly, parents ought to be more socially conscious, realizing that they are primarily responsible for perpetuating or eradicating ills. Mothers ought to recognize that it is in their power to break the chain of error that dedicates daughters to a life of frivolity and irrelevance. Fathers should take time from business to impress their daughters with a knowledge of the wider world, which bright women have as great a role in maintaining as do men. Here Read evoked widely held beliefs of the Revolutionary and post-Revolutionary era, beliefs that brought a political dimension to the private sphere by stressing the virtuous capabilities of the republican mother and wife. Yet Read also added a distinctive note of her own by urging that women learn self-respect and that parents nurture that self-respect through judicious love. Imagine the evils of a marriage in which the wife has more genius and talent than her husband, but who must nevertheless display a servile deference, she urged. In a republican society, tolerance and ability should not be so coldly suppressed. It is imperative, then, to nurture in both boys and girls the authority of natural affection rather than the corroding demands of custom. A sentimental education under the firm but compassionate direction of fathers and mothers would ensure social felicity.

Read's novel Margaretta was a further attempt to explore these themes, this time in a manner that may have been stimulated by events preceding the War of 1812. As American merchants, whose ships were increasingly attacked or impounded by British and French forces, sought to portray themselves in memorials to Congress as sentimental victims ravaged or ruined by rapacious foes, the effects of sentimental claims became an object of national concern. At the same moment when American prosperity was in jeopardy, spokesmen evoked an older sentimental rhetoric, long the preserve of novelists such as Read, a discourse in which the exchange of money was subordinate to an exchange of feeling. Commerce, as one writer put it in the Boston Patriot (1809), had become "the sensorium of our national sensibility." In many ways the obverse or complement of Monima, Margaretta presents a heroine who circulates in that same international sphere, exposed to the scrutiny and occasional attacks of a host of treacherous observers. In a manner far more radical and self-conscious than was true of most contemporary works, the novel thus evokes the opportunities and perils of a woman addressing the public sphere through the affections. By appropriating the discourse of mercantile politics, Read forged a space for activist women.

The problem of female authorship may have been stimulated by Read's encounter with Judith Sargent Murray's Margaretta stories, first serialized in the Massachusetts Magazine in 1792–1794 and later collected in The Gleaner (1798). In these essays Murray often imagined the Gleaner as an anonymous, almost invisible observer scrutinizing her critics, to whom Murray responded by urging that it was the "intrinsic" merit of her writing, not the fluctuating currency of public opinion, that would ensure its value. Similarly, the seventeen-year-old heroine of

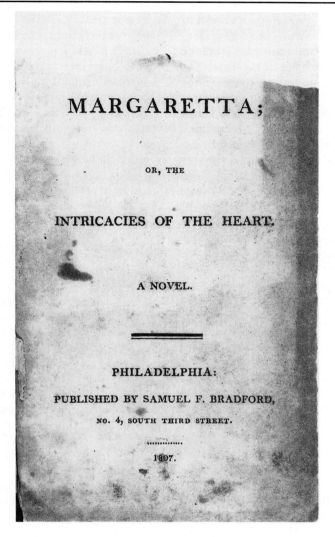

MARGARETTA;

OR, THE

INTRICACIES OF THE HEART.

A NOVEL.

PHILADELPHIA:

PUBLISHED BY SAMUEL F. BRADFORD,

NO. 4, SOUTH THIRD STREET.

1807.

*Title page for Read's second novel, about a young woman who narrowly escapes rape,
marriage to her father, and an incestuous relationship with her uncle before she is
re-united with the reformed rake who finally deserves her hand in marriage
(courtesy of the Special Collections Department, University of Virginia Library)*

Margaretta is a rural orphan whose intrinsic merits are demonstrated not only by her moral triumph over many perils, but also by her eventual reunion with her aristocratic English parents, who make her heiress to a vast fortune. Here Read elaborates on a subplot in *Monima* involving Julia Frenton, an illegitimate daughter of a marquis who inherits a large estate before dying. Both versions of what Michael McKeon calls "aristocratic romance" suggest the attractiveness to Read of a reinvigorated patrician order. Intrinsic value is ultimately rewarded by social esteem.

Margaretta Wilmot moves rootlessly through Maryland, St. Domingo, and English society. At each stage she is subjected to the penetrating scrutiny that Murray associates with the public sphere.

In her rural home, where she falls under the observation of well-heeled visitors, Margaretta soon senses that only her native virtue will protect her. When she finds herself falling in love with the rakish William De Burling, who eventually renounces his betrothal to the wealthy St. Domingo heiress Arabella Roulant in order to possess her, she flees rather than compromise De Burling's social status. Tricked into taking refuge on St. Domingo with Roulant's father, she must escape his advances on a slave plantation before retreating to the benevolent Edward Montanan. Like Roulant and De Burling, Montanan falls under her spell, honorably proposes to her, and is on the verge of marriage when accident reveals he is her father and he is reunited with his actual wife, Margaretta's long-lost mother. Yet even this reconstituted family does not put an end to Margaretta's jeopardy. As long as she remains single, she is vulnerable to the abduction and slander that were the lot of many sentimental heroines. Not coincidentally, however, abduction and slander were also themes surrounding contemporary merchants, who sought to portray their trials in sentimental terms. The confluence of those two domains points to the most serious public claim of Read's fiction.

Like the impulse behind *Monima,* that claim has both a regressive and a progressive aspect. Twice in "A Second Vindication of the Rights of Women," Read urged fathers to become more responsible by invoking the specter of incest. Errant fathers, she warned, had been known to seduce unsuspecting daughters. From an opposite perspective she warned husbands to respect their wives by arguing that were the husband to have a married daughter, he would not "brook" her ill treatment. This penetration of the father's influence in the daughter's affairs, akin to the penetrating scrutiny cast on authors in the public sphere, becomes a recurring motif in *Margaretta.* In each of the three settings, Maryland, St. Domingo, and England, Margaretta is approached or threatened by a familiar figure—first by De Burling, who desires disingenuously to be her affectionate brother; then by Roulant, whose silvery locks brand him as a fatherly intruder; and last by her actual father. Restored to her own family, she is briefly abducted by her uncle, who thinks her an impostor, and she is once again menaced by incest. Such encounters possibly suggest a fear of exposure to public scrutiny that created the tension in Murray's Margaretta stories, but they also suggest Read's pragmatic recognition that, despite her attempts in "A Second Vindication of the Rights of Women" to claim for women a zone of intrinsic, sentimental purity, there was no way to maintain that purity as an activist or author. To enter the public sphere was to submit to its capricious, often compromising demands.

Margaretta, unlike Monima, grows as a result of her experience, in a manner highly suggestive for women addressing the public sphere. Whereas Monima is eloquent only in her testaments to suffering, Margaretta is literate, articulate, and increasingly aggressive. Her eloquent "sentences" initiate De Burling's reform, and her blunt defense of her human rights saves her from rape on the Roulant plantation. That self-defense is a turning point for Margaretta, providing a new resolve that she takes with her to England. Vaguely unsettled by Montanan's fervor, she bluntly tells him she "hates" his

passion, and she calls another rakish suitor "criminal." Abducted by her uncle, she boldly claims a "law for women, which will, independent of her voice, plead for me"—thus laying claim to the same abstract principles of justice that had motivated republicans since the Revolutionary era. When Margaretta returns to republican America, fabulously wealthy and wed at last to the reformed but penniless De Burling, she is in a position to articulate a republican world as it should be:

> In the wife I would have an ardent disposition to acts of benevolence, in the husband, a passive compliance, or an approving smile of complacency, to urge her to the exercise of them. I would have the wife to have a vivid understanding, with a correct taste; and the husband, to have sense enough to know how to appreciate their value.

Virtue and intrinsic worth allow the wife to control the sphere of benevolence, thus ensuring social order. Yet that order is also linked to a keen intelligence and active spirit, before which the husband may evince no more than passive admiration. It was a bold but subdued claim, a recognition of women's proper sphere into which trailed vestiges of the writer's assertiveness. At the same time it was a renewed claim to patrician control amid a political scene that was rapidly sliding into war. Read shrewdly understood the temper of her time and responded with a fiction assuring anxious readers that the old order was still viable. Benevolence and compassion, she believed, would cleanse the world of its excesses, and wealth would secure virtue.

Although Read is not known to have published any more fiction, the two novels and her feminist tract establish her as an important early American writer. Within the constraints of her culture and class she sought to portray active and independent women capable of industry as well as feeling. Her fiction also resonates with contemporary concerns, helping to legitimize the novel at a time when it was denigrated. Her work is a serious attempt to carve out a place for women in the public sphere.

References:

Herbert Ross Brown, *The Sentimental Novel in America 1789–1860* (Durham, N.C.: Duke University Press, 1940);

Cathy N. Davidson, *Revolution and the Word: The Rise of the Novel in America* (New York: Oxford University Press, 1986);

Henri Petter, *The Early American Novel* (Columbus: Ohio State University Press, 1971), pp. 231–236.

Maria van Cortlandt van Rensselaer
(20 July 1645 – 24 January 1689)

Joyce D. Goodfriend
University of Denver

BOOK: *Correspondence of Maria van Rensselaer 1669–1689,* translated and edited by A. J. F. van Laer (Albany: University of the State of New York, 1935).

Maria van Cortlandt van Rensselaer is one of only a handful of seventeenth-century Dutch-American women whose lives can be documented from personal and family correspondence. The van Cortlandt and van Rensselaer names conjure up images of wealth and privilege, but in many respects Maria van Cortlandt van Rensselaer's personal history mirrors the course of all Dutch women's lives in early America.

As daughter, sister, wife, mother, widow, businesswoman, and church member, Maria experienced many of the same pleasures and trials as her female counterparts in New Netherland and early New York. Yet her connections to the elite van Cortlandt and van Rensselaer families, as well as her early widowhood, forced her to deal with business and legal matters that ordinarily were beyond the purview of seventeenth-century women. Maria van Rensselaer's letters, all dating from the period after her husband's death, enable the modern reader to gain entrance to the interior world of a Dutch colonial woman who had much in common with her contemporaries but who also faced an unusual set of problems.

Maria van Cortlandt was born in New Amsterdam on 20 July 1645, the second child of Oloff Stevensen van Cortlandt and his wife, Anna Loockermans van Cortlandt, natives of Holland who had been married in the Dutch Reformed Church of New Amsterdam in 1642. Oloff achieved prominence in New Netherland, first as an employee of the Dutch West India Company and then as a merchant and entrepreneur. One of the wealthiest men in New Amsterdam at the time the colony was taken over by the English in 1664, he was recognized by his peers as a community leader. Maria grew up with three brothers and three sisters in what appears to have been a close-knit family. The bonds forged during childhood proved durable, and Maria's siblings later offered much-needed support during her widowhood. Maria was taught to read and write and probably to cipher, since she was later able to keep accounts.

Religion was a dominant force in the van Cortlandt household. Both of Maria's parents were communicants of the Dutch Reformed Church, and there is little doubt that she regularly attended worship on the Sabbath and participated in Bible reading and family prayers. Her affinity for religion was demonstrated by the fact that she joined the church even before she had reached the requisite age of sixteen.

Maria's piety impressed her future husband, Jeremias van Rensselaer, director of the patroonship of Rensselaerswijck, a vast estate created in 1629 from land purchased from the Indians. On this estate near what later became Albany, New York, tenant farmers and craftsmen worked to enhance the profits of the van Rensselaers. When Jeremias wrote to his widowed mother in Amsterdam on 19 August 1662 describing his new bride, he extolled Maria's spiritual qualities, noting that he was grateful to have "a wife who has always led a good moral life and feared the Lord God."

Maria was not quite seventeen when she married Jeremias van Rensselaer on 12 July 1662. A critical alliance between two of the most prominent families of New Netherland, the marriage also united two individuals who seem to have been attracted to one another. In his 19 August 1662 letter Jeremias confessed to his mother that "I had been thinking of her already a year or two before, when now and then I did an errand at the Manhatans."

Though quite young, Maria successfully shouldered the burdens of housekeeping, and her skills in household management seem to have pleased her husband. Despite the thirteen-year age difference between them, Maria and Jeremias enjoyed a mutually satisfying relationship that rested on respect and love. On 11 May 1663 Jeremias expressed his gratitude that "the Lord God has

Maria van Rensselaer's husband, Jeremias, whose death in 1674 left her with the responsibility for supervising Rensselaerswijck, his vast estate near Albany, New York

granted me such a good spouse, with whom I can get along so well and live with peaceably."

In addition to customary housekeeping tasks, Maria, like many Dutch housewives in the Netherlands as well as New Netherland, was involved in business activities. While growing up she had worked in her father's brewery, and after her marriage her husband took up brewing for her sake, explaining in a letter of 15/25 April 1665 that Maria had formerly been in charge of "the disposal of the beer and helping to find customers for it." Maria also apparently looked forward to engaging in trade. On 10 June 1668 Jeremias wrote his father-in-law regarding Maria's dowry, asking "whether it would be convenient for you to let us have in Holland the promised money of my wife, your daughter? My wife would then start to trade with it a little and order some goods for it."

Dutch women in seventeenth-century New York could typically expect to become mothers within two years of entering the state of matrimony. Jeremias wrote his brother in Holland on 11 May 1663: "You may perhaps be longing to hear whether we have any baby yet. My answer is no, but that my wife is pregnant and that, please God, she will be in childbed in two or three months at the longest."

Their first child, Kiliaen van Rensselaer, was born in August 1663. Maria's reproductive history followed the pattern prevalent among colonial mothers, as she gave birth roughly every two to two and one-half years. Over the next eleven years Maria bore six more children, one of whom died shortly after birth, an exceptional survival rate in that era of high infant mortality.

Maria van Rensselaer was also more fortunate than many of her counterparts in colonial New York because she survived the rigors of childbirth seven times. Maternal mortality was high in seventeenth-century America, but Maria did not escape childbirth unscathed. During her first delivery, an injury occurred to one of her legs, which never healed correctly. For the remainder of her life she was crippled and frequently could not get around without crutches or a cane. Maria also suffered from a host of other ailments, including chicken pox and a persistent sore throat, and her health was always frail.

Being a mother was a joy to Maria, who cherished her children and derived great pleasure from them. Jeremias hinted at the intense emotional attachment between mother and child on 27 August 1663, when he referred to newborn Kiliaen as "a beloved child to his mother and a welcome son to his father." Kiliaen was going to school before his fourth birthday, and religious instruction was also of paramount importance to his parents. In their joint will, made in October 1674, just a few days before Jeremias's death, they directed that their children should be "trained in godliness."

Despite ill health, the loss of a baby, and the difficulties of living on a frontier, Maria had much to be grateful for in her married life with Jeremias, but her life swiftly changed on 12 October 1674, when Jeremias died suddenly. At the time, Maria was pregnant with her last child, a son who was born soon after his father's death and whom she named Jeremias in his honor.

Losing a husband at an early age was not exceptional in the seventeenth century, when epidemic disease was prevalent and the state of medical knowledge was primitive, but the young widow's failure to remarry was unusual. Maria had compelling reasons for not remarrying—the complex matter of her children's inheritance, the precarious state of her health, and the fact that she already had four sons and two daughters, all under the age of eleven. Moreover, her position at the top of the social ladder meant that the pool of eligible partners was small.

Maria van Rensselaer faced what seemed insurmountable problems—overcoming her grief at the loss of a beloved husband, seeing to the welfare of six young children, supervising Rensselaerswijck and attempting to safeguard its legal status in turbulent political times, and attempting to prevail in the interminable negotiations over the inheritance with her husband's brother in the Netherlands. Her difficulties were compounded by her illnesses and disability. The letters that the widowed Maria wrote provide detailed evidence of how she met her obligations while offering a rare glimpse of the affective life of a seventeenth-century Dutch colonial woman.

Only twenty-seven of Maria van Rensselaer's letters are extant, but it is probable that she wrote other letters that have not survived. These twenty-seven existing letters were all written in Dutch between 1675 and 1688. Twelve of them date from 1683, and no more than two were written in any other year. All but two short letters were directed to members of her own family or to her husband's kin in the Netherlands. The great majority of the letters were written to Richard van Rensselaer, her deceased husband's youngest brother and the person responsible for settling his estate, and to her brother Stephanus van Cortlandt. Her correspondents also included her father and her son Kiliaen. None of the extant letters was addressed to a woman, although the existence of several letters written to Maria by her sister, Catharina Darvall, implies that Maria also wrote to Catharina.

Maria's letters are not literary compositions; they are practical communications. Written in concrete language, they convey news about the activities of family members, Rensselaerswijck's tenant farmers, and members of the larger Albany community. They include Maria's observations on the condition of the local Dutch Reformed Church, the economy, and the colonial government. On occasion they reveal the young widow's attitudes toward current events. At the time of King Philip's (or Metacom's) War, Maria confided in a December 1675(?) letter that "we live here in great fear on account of the great war between the English and the Indians around the north and of New England."

In an important sense Maria's letters are business letters. They reported on finances, land sales, the demands of tenants, the condition of gristmills, and the prices of commodities. They are not, however, the modern sort of business correspondence in which transactions are described in a neutral tone. In seventeenth-century New York, economic affairs were grounded in personal relationships, and success or failure hinged on the ability of individuals or families to gain the favor of powerful persons. Maria was acutely aware of the way New York politics worked, and though she had entree to the circles of power, she found it difficult to counter the influence of Robert Livingston, who claimed the van Rensselaer lands by virtue of his marriage to the widow of another member of the van Rensselaer family. "We have no Friends at New York, so that Livingston will have his way, for he has the governor on his side and the governor himself told me that he would not benefit the van Rensselaers who are in Holland," she wrote on 12 November 1684. She was not always able to offer such a dispassionate assessment of her family's conflict with Livingston. Her hostile feelings toward him surfaced in a letter of January 1682(?) in which she admitted "I cannot bear to see him any longer in possession of the patroon's garden, where my husband, my child, and brother, deceased, lie buried, [and to know] that he is the master of it." Maria's letters are filled with other personal comments on the motivations of individuals and the courses of action they pursued.

Though the role of businesswoman was thrust on Maria by her husband's untimely death, it was not a role for which she was unprepared. Dutch women routinely engaged in trade, and their activities in the marketplace were sanctioned by law and custom. Maria had developed considerable business acumen through her involvement in the brewery and other van Cortlandt family enterprises. Yet in January(?) 1683 she reflected that "it often saddens my mind to have to deal with things with which heretofore I never had anything to do."

Maria's talents were pressed to the limit during her widowhood, as she endeavored to manage the daily affairs of Rensselaerswijck while making every effort to reach a settlement of her husband's estate with his family in Europe. Dutch inheritance law and customs were not prejudicial to women, and therefore Dutch widows in seventeenth-century America stood in a favored position with respect to the acquisition of family property. Yet the case of the van Rensselaer estate was complicated. It included property in America and the Netherlands. The legal status of the colony under English rule had yet to be defined, and the interests of the Livingston and Schuyler families, both of whom had claims to the estate, clashed with those of Jeremias's heirs. Moreover, Maria was unable to represent her own interests in public, since English law in the colony of New York curtailed a woman's right to act independently. She had to delegate responsibility for conducting her public business to her brother Stephanus, who, because he was married to a member of the Schuyler family, was faced with a conflict of interest regarding his sister's inheritance.

Over the years Maria's attitude toward her brother altered as she became increasingly suspicious of his motives. Initially content to follow his

CORRESPONDENCE

OF

MARIA van RENSSELAER
1669–1689

Translated and edited

by

A. J. F. van Laer
Archivist, Archives and History Division

ALBANY
THE UNIVERSITY OF THE STATE OF NEW YORK
1935

Title page for the book that includes all of Maria van Rensselaer's surviving letters, which are for the most part devoted to her successful efforts in a dispute over her sons' inheritance of their father's property

instructions, she later was willing to go against his advice, realizing that Stephanus's primary loyalty lay with his in-laws. By November (?) 1683 she had reached the conclusion that "one dares not trust one's own brother." The following year, on 12 November 1684, she confessed "I never thought my br[other Stev]en would have deserted us so."

Maria's letters are largely taken up with the details of the inheritance dispute. She pleaded with Richard van Rensselaer to treat his brother's children equitably and chided him for making financial decisions that she felt were not in the family's best interest. Repeatedly, she argued that she and her children should be guaranteed assets commensurate with their rank in society. Maria never minced words, stating bluntly to Richard on 15 August (?) 1683, "I can not live with my family on 200 schepels of wheat and then receive calls from the most prominent people every day. I pray brother to take that

into consideration sometime and to [help] a sorrowful widow."

Maria's children were never far from her mind as she struggled to protect their inheritance and to prepare them for adulthood. As a widowed mother, Maria was forced to enlist the help of family members in arranging schooling and apprenticeships for her children. Although she had the option of sending one of her sons to Holland to be educated by the van Rensselaer family, she followed her own family's advice and decided that it would be best for her sons to learn trades. Kiliaen was apprenticed to a silversmith in Boston, and Hendrick went to live with a New York merchant. Maria probably played a crucial role in arranging the marriage of her daughter Anna to her cousin Kiliaen van Rensselaer (the son of Johannes van Rensselaer), who became the first lord of the Manor of Rensselaerswijck in 1685.

As her children matured, Maria came to feel that she could rely on them. Kiliaen in particular proved a boon to his ailing mother, as he assumed responsibility for managing the estate. He "can get along very well with the farmers and also knows the patroon's cattle, yes, down to the calves," she wrote on 15 August (?) 1683. "This year I let him settle with the farmers about the tithes."

Despite sometimes meager resources, Maria consciously strove to maintain her family's position of social eminence and to cultivate a standard of living appropriate to her station. A concern for the reputation of her family and perhaps a measure of personal pride were responsible for this attitude. Indeed, she made a point of noting that she had entertained two English governors at Rensselaerswijck. Upholding her status also involved teaching her offspring to keep their distance from people presumed to be social inferiors. One of Maria's sons, most likely Hendrick, apparently violated this rule of conduct, prompting his mother to request assistance from her brother in reminding the boy of his social position. During her more than fourteen years of widowhood Maria did her utmost to ensure the wealth, position, and moral character of her sons and daughters.

Maria derived emotional succor from her children, but it was her parents who seem to have given her the strength to go on in the face of what she felt was the van Rensselaer family's betrayal of her children's rightful claim to their inheritance. Oloff van Cortlandt not only gave Maria financial support, but he also attempted to intercede for her in gaining a settlement of her husband's estate. He also offered her spiritual counsel. When her father and then her mother died in spring 1684, Maria was emotionally devastated, but the deep-seated religious faith that her devout parents had nurtured in her enabled her to persevere until her family's legal problems were finally resolved.

Throughout her widowhood, Maria found meaning in her suffering by turning to God. After her husband's death, she wrote in December 1675(?), "as it has pleased the Lord to afflict me with such a great sorrow, I must put my [trust] in God's will. May He make me patient and strengthen me in all adversity and in my infirmity, from which at present I suffer great pain, through Jesus Christ, who gives me strength and who through His mercy will further [sustain] me." After his 1680 visit to Maria van Rensselaer, whom he described as "polite, quite well informed, and of good life and disposition," the usually critical Labadist missionary Jasper Danckaerts was convinced that she had "experienced several proofs of the Lord" but "had borne herself well."

For Maria religion was communal as well as individual. She manifested a strong attachment to the Dutch Reformed Church and was exceedingly pleased when her son Kiliaen became a church member. In November 1675(?) she expressed dismay at "the sad dissensions which prevail here in God's church . . . so that one person is turned against the other."

The guiding principles of Maria's life were drawn from the Word of God as set down in the Bible. She treasured the scriptures, and on several occasions she quoted biblical passages in her letters as a way of emphasizing a point. As one who led a godly life, she expected the same from others. When they failed to live up to scriptural precepts, she excoriated them, being careful to leave the final judgment to God. In October (?) 1683 she averred that Mrs. Schuyler "thinks as little of God's word and law as written in Exodus, ch. 22, where God speaks of the widows and orphans, but where there is money, there is power. But God, who will take care of the widows and orphans, will not desert me and my six children." Maria hoped that people who had spoken evil words or committed immoral acts would repent and be forgiven by God.

Toward the end of her life Maria's frail health compelled her to lean on her eldest son, Kiliaen, more and more in running the estate. When she died on 24 January 1689, from what is believed to have been septic arthritis, Kiliaen was in charge of Rensselaerswijck, by then an English manor. Ultimately, Kiliaen and his siblings gained legal control over the van Rensselaer family's land, just as their mother had wished.

In her letters Maria van Rensselaer revealed herself as a woman who was at home in the seventeenth-century world of affairs. Well informed on matters of law, business, and politics, as well as an astute observer of the family rivalries that festered in early New York, she drew on every resource available to her as a woman to resolve her family's inheritance problems. As an advocate for her children, she expressed herself forcefully and directly to the powerful men with whom she dealt. She chose her words carefully; yet she did not conceal her emotions, and she never hesitated to condemn those whom she believed to be acting from venal motives. A woman of high moral purpose, she wrote with an intensity that could come only from deep conviction.

References:

Linda Briggs Biemer, *Women and Property in Colonial New York: The Transition from Dutch to English Law, 1643–1727* (Ann Arbor, Mich.: UMI Research Press, 1983), pp. 45–57;

Joyce D. Goodfriend, "Recovering the Religious History of Dutch Reformed Women in Colonial New York," *de Halve Maen,* 64 (Winter 1991): 53–59;

A. J. F. van Laer, Introduction to *Correspondence of Jeremias van Rensselaer 1651–1674* (Albany: University of the State of New York, 1932);

S. G. Nissenson, *The Patroon's Domain* (New York: Columbia University Press, 1937).

Papers:

Maria van Rensselaer's letters are among the Rensselaerswijck manuscripts at the New York State Library in Albany, New York.

Mary Rowlandson

(circa 1637 – 5 January 1711)

Amy Schrager Lang
Emory University

See also the Rowlandson entry in *DLB 24: American Colonial Writers, 1606–1734*.

BOOK: *The Soveraignty & Goodness of God, Together with the Faithfulness of His Promises Displayed; Being a Narrative of the Captivity and Restauration of Mrs. Mary Rowlandson, Commended by her to all that Desire to Know the Lord's Doings to, and Dealings with Her. Especially to her Dear Children and Relations.* (Cambridge, Mass.: Printed by Samuel Green, 1682); republished as *A True History of the Captivity & Restoration of Mrs. Mary Rowlandson, A Minister's Wife in New-England: Wherein is set forth, The Cruel and Inhumane Usage she underwent amongst the Heathens for Eleven Weeks time: And her Deliverance from them. Written by her own Hand, for her Private Use: and now made public at the earnest Desire of some Friends, for the Benefit of the Afflicted* (London: Sold by Joseph Poole, 1682).

At sunrise on 10 February 1676, a little more than a year after the confederated colonies of Massachusetts, Rhode Island, Plymouth, and Connecticut declared war against the Algonquian tribes allied under the leadership of the Wampanoag Metacom, or "King Philip," a band of Indians descended "with great numbers" on the English frontier settlement of Lancaster, Massachusetts. Among the twenty-four English settlers captured during the raid on Lancaster were "God's precious servant and hand-maid," Mary White Rowlandson, wife of the Lancaster minister, and their three children. Were it not for this raid and her captivity, modern readers would be unaware of Mary Rowlandson's existence, for her renown arises only from the account she wrote for her children of her three-month sojourn with the Narragansetts. Although Rowlandson was not the first white settler to be captured by Native Americans, her account originated what scholars usually consider the first Euro-American literary genre, the captivity narrative, which persisted well into the

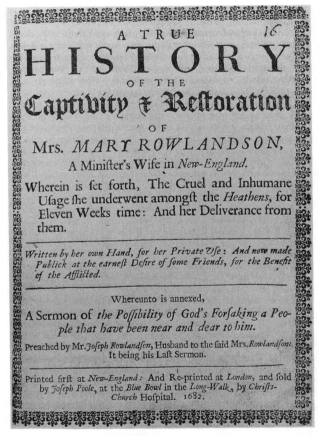

Title page for the first British edition of Mary Rowlandson's account of the three months she spent as a prisoner of the Narragansetts in 1676

nineteenth century and influenced the form of the novel in America. One of the earliest examples of women's autobiographical writing and in some respects a precursor to later slave narratives, Rowlandson's story has a special significance in the literary history of the United States.

Born to John and Joan White of Somerset, England, around 1637, Mary White, the sixth of their ten children, was raised from infancy in New England, living first in Salem, Massachusetts, and then

304

in the frontier town of Wenham, Massachusetts. The Whites were among the original settlers of Lancaster, arriving there in 1653, when the still unincorporated town numbered only nine families. At that time John White was the wealthiest landholder in the settlement. In 1656 Mary White married the English-born, Harvard-educated Joseph Rowlandson, Lancaster's first minister. She bore four children, the first of whom died in infancy. Mary Rowlandson's "near relation to a *Man of God*" set her apart from her neighbors and contributed in large measure to the attention accorded her narrative.

Because she was the wife of a well-known minister, Rowlandson's captivity was widely regarded as an especially forceful sign of God's dealings with his people. For the same reason, Rowlandson was of special value as a captive, a fact as fully recognized by her Indian captors as by the New England colonists. As a casualty of the Lancaster raid, however, Rowlandson was hardly distinctive in her familial relationship to the town's minister. At the time of the attack, Joseph Rowlandson and his brother-in-law, Henry Kerley, were en route to Boston to plead with the colonial government for Lancaster's protection. They returned to find their family decimated. Mary Rowlandson's sister Elizabeth Kerley and two of her children had been killed in the Rowlandson garrison, as had the husband and son of Mary's sister Hannah and a Rowlandson nephew. Of those captured, thirteen were members of the Rowlandson family.

Taken with Mary Rowlandson were her daughters—six-year-old Sarah, who was wounded in the raid and died a week later, and ten-year-old Mary—and her son, Joseph, then fourteen. Captives ordinarily became the possession of the particular Indian by whom they were taken, but as Rowlandson's narrative indicates, they were on occasion purchased or traded. As a consequence of this practice, Rowlandson was separated from her two older children immediately, she having been captured by a Narragansett, her son by a Nipmuck, and her daughter by a member of another, unidentified tribe.

For eleven weeks and five days Rowlandson lived and traveled with the Narragansetts. Her "master" and "mistress," as she designated them in her narrative, were a Narragansett sachem, Quanopen, and Weetamoo, the sachem consort of the Pocassets, who by 1675 had joined the Narragansetts in Nipmuck territory. On 3 May 1676, after "much prayer had been particularly made before the Lord on her behalf," Rowlandson was ransomed by the English in exchange for goods valued at £20. In late June, Joseph was released by the Nipmucks, and

Mary was brought to Providence by an unidentified Indian woman.

Lancaster had by then been destroyed, and the Rowlandsons spent the following year in Boston, supported by their friends. In spring 1677, they moved to Wethersfield, Connecticut, where Joseph Rowlandson was called to the ministry. He died the following year at age forty-seven. Until David L. Greene brought new information to light in 1985, historians had believed that Mary Rowlandson died shortly after her husband. This assumption lent itself to a melodramatic view of a languishing Rowlandson, unable to resume a normal life after her captivity. It has been established, however, that Rowlandson was not dead but only lost to view because nine months after her husband's death she married a Connecticut leader, Capt. Samuel Talcott. Mary White Rowlandson Talcott died on 5 January 1711, at the age of seventy-three.

This new knowledge of Rowlandson's life after her captivity not only sets the historical record straight but clarifies several literary and logistical problems that have absorbed readers of her narrative. The most important of these concerns the publication history of Rowlandson's narrative. Internal and external evidence suggests that it was written shortly after the Rowlandsons' arrival in Wethersfield in 1677 and before her husband's death in November 1678. Apparently intended for private circulation among friends and relatives, it was not published until 1682.

The assumption that both Rowlandson and her husband died in the late 1670s had left the means of publication of her narrative unexplained, but scholars now believe that Mary Rowlandson Talcott published her narrative well after her husband's death with the encouragement of the Reverend Increase Mather, minister of the Second Church in Boston and a prominent political leader in the Massachusetts Bay Colony. The style and the substance of the preface, signed "*Per Amicum*" and included in all the seventeenth-century editions of the narrative, suggest that Mather, the author of *A Brief History of the Warr with the Indians in New-England* (1676), was the friend responsible for introducing Rowlandson's work. Some scholars have argued further that the orthodoxy of Rowlandson's interpretation of her experience and the aptness of her biblical allusions point to Mather's extensive involvement in the production of the narrative. The extent of the Rowlandsons' association with Mather is unknown, but it was apparently sufficient to allow Joseph Rowlandson to appeal to Mather for assistance in negotiating the release of his wife. Beyond this evidence of direct contact between Increase

Mather and Joseph Rowlandson, it is known that in the early 1680s Mather began to gather the accounts of providential events in New England that would compose the substance of *An Essay for the Recording of Illustrious Providences* (1684). Rowlandson's narrative may well have been included among these accounts, and many scholars argue that Mather promoted its separate publication. Mather's long-standing connection with the Boston printer responsible for the first printing of Rowlandson's work further suggests his involvement in its publication, although other theories have been proposed. It seems clear in any event that the no longer extant 1682 Boston edition was the only one of the early editions to be set directly from Rowlandson's manuscript and that Rowlandson herself played no part in the publication of subsequent editions.

The captive Rowlandson's visibility as a minister's wife and the notoriety of the Lancaster raid ensured the immediate success of her account of her captivity. Four editions appeared during its first year in print; it was advertised and sold in England and New England. The first extant edition was printed in Cambridge, Massachusetts, in 1682 by Samuel Green with the assistance of James the Printer, a Christianized Indian who plays a minor part in Rowlandson's narrative, and bore the title *The Soveraignty & Goodness of God, Together with the Faithfulness of His Promises Displayed; Being a Narrative of the Captivity and Restauration of Mrs. Mary Rowlandson, Commended by her to all that Desire to Know the Lord's Doings to, and Dealings with Her. Especially to her Dear Children and Relations.* The printer of the 1682 London edition dropped the devotional title and republished the narrative under the title by which it is now best known, *A True History of the Captivity & Restoration of Mrs. Mary Rowlandson, A Minister's Wife in New-England: Wherein is set forth, The Cruel and Inhumane Usage she underwent amongst the Heathens for Eleven Weeks time: And her Deliverance from them. Written by her own Hand, for her Private Use: and now made public at the earnest Desire of some Friends, for the Benefit of the Afflicted.* This edition corrected minor omissions and errors in the Cambridge edition and is generally regarded as the most reliable version of the text. Like most existing seventeenth-century editions of Rowlandson's narrative, the London edition includes, in addition to Mather's preface, Joseph Rowlandson's last sermon, preached in Wethersfield, Connecticut, on 21 November 1678. By 1828 twenty-three editions of *A True History of the Captivity and Restoration of Mrs. Mary Rowlandson* had been published. By 1998 at least forty editions of the narrative had appeared.

After Rowlandson published her account the narrative of Indian captivity became a staple of American letters. The early examples of these narratives, including Rowlandson's, were vehicles for Puritan religious expression. They confirmed the election of God's people, the piety of the captive, and the rightness of the Indians' removal by the colonists. By the middle of the eighteenth century, however, the religious concerns of the captivity narrative had been overtaken by propagandistic ones. The highly sensational narratives written in this period were designed to demonize Native Americans and to generate support for the wars against them by recounting the suffering of white captives in lurid detail. By the 1790s, Indian captivity—particularly the captivity of white women—was being exploited by novelists such as Charles Brockden Brown and, later, James Fenimore Cooper. Popular demand for gruesome tales of life among the "heathens" remained great enough in the nineteenth century to encourage the production of fictionalized captivity narratives. Throughout the eighteenth and nineteenth centuries, authentic narratives, sensationalized revisions of earlier narratives, and wholly fictional accounts of Indian captivity competed for popular attention.

Early captivity narratives adhere for the most part to a formula that can be traced to *A True History of the Captivity and Restoration of Mrs. Mary Rowlandson*. Beginning with an account of an Indian raid and the taking of the captive, they relate the experience of the captive during a forced march or journey, which concludes with a period of detention in one location while the terms of sale or trade of the captive are negotiated. This period ends with either the release or the escape, often highly dramatic, of the white captive. The interpretation of events in these early narratives depends, as a rule, on two ideas central to seventeenth-century Puritan thought. A providential theory of history locates the experience of the captive within a larger design, according to which God governs not only saints but sinners as well, while a doctrine of afflictions assures the captive that her suffering is both just and efficacious.

In Rowlandson's narrative these ideas are invoked from the start in the anonymous preface. Beginning with a highly ambiguous account of the decision by the colonial council of war to withdraw its forces from Nipmuck territory, a decision that left Lancaster open to attack, the preface represents Rowlandson's affliction and redemption as a "strange and amazing dispensation" of the Lord toward his "Hand-maid." Her suffering is at once a sign of her worthiness and God's power. In addition to providing an historical and doctrinal framework within which to understand Rowlandson's narrative, the preface defends the author of the narrative against charges of unfeminine immodesty. Writing a private "*Memorandum* of God's dealing with her," Rowlandson, the preface insists, had no intention of bringing her narrative before the public. Only "her gratitude toward God" and the judgment of her "Friends" that it was "unmeet that such works of God should be hid from present and future Generations" persuaded her to allow the publication of her account. According to the preface, the value of Rowlandson's narrative to those later generations is twofold: not only does it provide a crucial firsthand account of the horrors of Indian captivity—for "none can imagine, what it is to be captivated, and enslaved to such Atheistical, proud, wild, cruel, barbarous, brutish . . . diabolical Creatures"—but it offers "an instance of the Faith and Patience of the Saints, under the most heart-sinking Tryals" and of the spiritual benefits of such affliction.

The preface interprets Rowlandson's experience in the terms of Puritan political and theological orthodoxy, with which Rowlandson herself struggles in the narrative. Like many colonial spiritual autobiographies, *A True History of the Captivity and Restoration of Mrs. Mary Rowlandson* begins with the rupture of ordinary life, with a violent end to the daily rounds of the Puritan wife and mother. The narrative opens with a brief but graphic account of the violent attack on the Rowlandson compound and the unsuccessful efforts of the thirty-seven people garrisoned there to defend themselves. This description is cast in conventional language as a battle between innocent Christians and "the bloody Heathen," "infidels," and "hell-hounds." The account of the raid concludes with the narrator's confession that, whereas once she had thought she would rather be killed than taken alive by the Indians, so "daunted" was she by their "glittering Weapons" that she "chose rather to go along with those . . . ravenous Bears, than that moment to end my daies."

"All was gone," Rowlandson told her readers, "my husband gone . . . my children gone, my relations and friends gone, our house and home . . . all was gone (except my life)." Stripped of affectionate relationships, social identity, and familiar surroundings, Rowlandson was forced to re-create herself. As a woman, a wife, a mother, she had to define her "life" in the absence of everything that once constituted life. As a faithful Puritan, she had to find meaning in her affliction, uncover the spiritual failings that prompted her punishment, and submit to God's will. The captive of an alien people on whom she dared not depend for even the barest necessities of life, she had to learn to provide for herself. In making a new life—or, more accurately, a new

Frontispiece for the 1770 edition of Rowlandson's captivity narrative, which went through twenty-three editions by 1828 (Houghton Library, Harvard University)

self—she moved simultaneously toward submission and self-sufficiency.

Rowlandson's narrative carefully records the physical and social details of her 150-mile trek through the woods of western Massachusetts and southern New Hampshire with the Narragansetts. Cut off from their stores of food in the eastern Bay Colony and pursued by colonial troops, the displaced tribes were continually on the move. From the outset Rowlandson's narrative leads the reader through a landscape at once literal and symbolic. The darkness of the "thicket" is indistinguishable from the darkness of the soul when God has averted his face; redemption is both release from captivity and assurance of salvation. Time is marked in space as "Removes" from European "civilization" and from the light of the gospel, and each remove is represented by a separate section within the narrative. These removes provide a formal structure for Rowlandson's account of daily life with her captors and offer as well a means by which to represent her symbolic journey.

The first three "removes" focus on Rowlandson's desperate efforts to care for her dying daughter. Carried further and further into the wilderness of the Indians' territory by her captors, she was also carried further and further into despair by her inability to aid her "poor wounded Babe." Sarah's death after nine days, her unsanctified burial in the woods, and Rowlandson's captors' unwillingness to allow her to see her distraught older daughter, who was held in the same Indian encampment, brought the author of the narrative to the brink of suicide. Unable to "sit still," "going up and down, mourning and lamenting," she prayed for a "token," a "sign" of mercy from God. Two such signs of God's goodness marked the end of this crisis: her son was brought to see her from an Indian camp six miles distant, and an unnamed Indian gave her a Bible, part of his plunder from an attack on Medfield. Initially, her "dark heart" finds neither mercy nor hope but only confirmation of her doom in the Bible. Yet with the Lord's help, as she understood it, she was led eventually to read Deuteronomy, in which she found "mercy promised again, if we would return to [God] by repentance; and though we were scattered from one end of the earth to the other, yet the Lord would gather us together, and turn all those curses upon our Enemies."

Rowlandson's discovery of God's promise to his captive people marks a turn in the narrative. From the fourth remove on, Rowlandson's narrative details the difficulties and the victories of daily life in captivity, describing river crossings by raft and canoe, the temporary dwellings of the Indians, their rituals, behavior, and dress, her own and the Narragansetts' efforts to find food and the preparation of that food, her meeting with King Philip, the kindnesses and cruelties meted out to her by the Indians with whom she interacted, the intelligence she received of the war, her rare meetings with her son, and finally the negotiations for her release. The order of events is chronological, and their meaning is invariably spiritual. Each incident of Rowlandson's life in captivity—from the fact that she did not get her feet wet in her first river crossing to her new distaste for tobacco—confirms the justice of God's past and present dealings with her, and each finds its type in the Bible.

These biblical types provided consolation to the captive, but they function as well to indicate the significance of her experience in sacred as well as secular history. As scholars have long noticed, the many biblical passages and allusions that punctuate Rowlandson's narrative are drawn almost exclusively from the Old Testament, and particularly from the cycle of biblical captivities. For the orthodox Rowlandson, as for her Puritan teachers, Israel of the Old Testament was the type of New England: like the ancient Israelites, the colonists were a people chosen by God, sent forth into a wilderness to found a model society, a theocratic "city upon the hill." In her captivity narrative Rowlandson stands as their representative, the image of *Judea capta*, Israel in bondage. In this sense the meaning of her experience is not personal but public, not individual but communal. Some students of the Puritans have proposed that Rowlandson's orthodox use of the Bible indicates the heavy-handed intervention of her minister husband or of Increase Mather in the production of the narrative. By the end Rowlandson's survival has come to signify not merely God's graciousness toward the individual sinner but the eventual victory of the faithful, of the New Israel, over its heathen enemies.

For all the orthodoxy of Rowlandson's exegesis, however, tension is evident in the two different voices of *A True History of the Captivity and Restoration of Mrs. Mary Rowlandson*. This tension has been characterized in a variety of ways, as between description and interpretation, between colloquial and "biblical" voices, or between narrative independence and conventionality. Scholars have suggested that the dissonance of the narrative renders the border world between the known and the unknown through which Rowlandson travels or the threshold of her subjectivity as she adjusts to an alien culture. Most commonly this narrative dissonance is ascribed to the psychological trauma of captivity or regarded as a feature of the "survivor syndrome" from which some scholars believe the liberated Rowlandson to have suffered. However this tension is described, the voice of the Christian crying out to her God from the wilderness is distinct from the voice of the survivor obsessively recording details of Indian diet, ritual, garb, and social organization, and the two voices are often in conflict.

The wilderness, as Rowlandson described it, reiterates this doubleness. On the one hand, it is an untracked, menacing place in which she is unable to travel one mile without getting lost, in which she is unable to find food or shelter without assistance. On the other hand, it is a spiritual and psychological "condition" carrying both personal and corporate significance. The spiritual darkness to which Mary Rowlandson is relegated by God and from which she can be redeemed only when she repudiates the "vanity of this world" and acknowledges her "whole dependence" on God is also a Babylon in which the American Israel is captive. Intimacy with the wilderness—even the intimacy of aesthetic appreciation—must be resisted. Traveling through the pristine woodland of New England, Rowlandson makes no mention of the landscape in which she finds herself. She sees no beauty in untamed nature, only terror.

Yet Rowlandson's apparent failure to learn the ways of the wilderness—her inability to find food or shelter or her way—attests not to feminine fragility but to spiritual strength. As *Judea capta,* her part in the cosmic drama called King Philip's War is, as she tells her reader again and again, to "wait upon the Lord." In this character Rowlandson acts as a spiritual interpreter and guide. The literal wilderness continually thwarts her efforts, but she is mistress of the symbolic one. She may have lost her way in the woods, but she plots her course unerringly through the wilderness of Christian exegesis, citing the Old Testament passage appropriate to each incident of her captivity and drawing the conventional lesson from it.

The process of spiritual fulfillment requires patience and passivity, but physical survival makes different demands. The prisoner of a people she regards as "heathen" and "barbarian," Rowlandson nonetheless has to make her place among them. The Christian self who continually urges her to "Be still," who believes that her salvation rests in a Job-like submission to affliction, is paired with a self that is faced with the problem of negotiating a foreign culture from a position of powerlessness. Perhaps inevitably, Rowlandson's progress toward passive acceptance of God's will goes hand in hand with a movement toward active accommodation to the Indian world, but the second radically disrupts the first, for her physical survival depends on seeing the Indians as something more than types of Satan.

The difficulties posed by this necessary accommodation to Indian life may be illustrated by Rowlandson's attitude toward food, a subject that necessarily receives a great deal of attention in her narrative. As Rowlandson explains, the Narragansetts were starving. Foraging for food in the woods, they were reduced to eating whatever they could find, from acorns and bark to bear, beaver, and "horses's guts." For Rowlandson, the eating of the Indians' "filthy trash" signifies capitulation to the "howling wilderness," but resistance proves impossible. The first week of her captivity she fasts; the second week weakness overcomes revulsion, but only barely. By the third week, however, she finds,

to her amazement, that food that once turned her stomach tastes "pleasant and savory." Like other adjustments required by her captivity, the ability to eat with relish food that once revolted her is highly ambiguous in its representation. Insofar as "civilization" and Christianity are paired, to savor the food of the wilderness calls into question her understanding of herself as "civilized." At the same time her tolerance of "savage" food enables her survival and had, therefore, to be accepted as a token of God's mercy.

Just as she learns to eat Indian food, so Rowlandson learns to distinguish between her various captors. The "wild beasts of the forest" gradually reveal themselves as distinct individuals—some, like Metacom, are generous; others are cruel. By the middle of the narrative, she can speak of Quanopen as "the best friend that I had of an Indian," whereas the "proud gossip" Weetamoo's vanity, ruthlessness, and imperiousness become more and more pronounced as the weeks go by. Although the Narragansetts figure more often as the agents of Satan in the cosmic drama of New England's affliction than as independent actors in Rowlandson's narrative, she scrupulously records their acts of kindness as well as those of apparently gratuitous violence. She acquits her captors of the customary charge of drunkenness and sexual abuse of female captives and describes the rituals of the Narragansetts with genuine interest, if considerable disdain. Rowlandson's highly individual portraits of the Narragansetts have led some scholars to argue for her sympathy with her Indian captors, a sympathy founded in the shared oppression of white women and Indians by the Puritan patriarchy. Others find an antitypological impulse in Rowlandson's humanizing of the forces of Satan, evidence of the failure of Puritan typology to accommodate the fullness of Rowlandson's experience.

The shift in Rowlandson's representation of the Narragansetts is paired with a change in her status. Faced with the need to find food and sometimes shelter, Rowlandson discovers her own resourcefulness. She not only learns to subsist in the wilderness, but she carves out a place for herself in the Indians' barter economy. Knitting and sewing in exchange for food and shelter, she describes herself as sufficiently secure to negotiate the terms of barter and, on one occasion, to attempt to refuse an offer of work on the Christian Sabbath. As her time with the Narragansetts lengthens Rowlandson becomes increasingly competent to supply her own needs and increasingly willing to assert herself without fear of violence.

A
NARRATIVE
OF THE
CAPTIVITY, SUFFERINGS AND REMOVES
OF
Mrs. *Mary Rowlandson*,

Who was taken Prisoner by the INDIANS with several others,
and treated in the most barbarous and cruel Manner by those
vile Savages : With many other remarkable Events during her
TRAVELS.

Written by her own Hand, for her private Use, and now made
public at the earnest Desire of some Friends, and for the Benefit of the afflicted.

BOSTON:
Printed and Sold at JOHN BOYLE's Printing-Office, next Door
to the *Three Doves* in Marlborough-Street

*Title page for the 1773 edition of Rowlandson's book, the model
for many of the Indian captivity narratives that were popular
into the early nineteenth century*

On the one hand, then, *A True History of the Captivity and Restoration of Mrs. Mary Rowlandson* offers the daily record of a meticulous and not altogether unsympathetic observer of Indian life during King Philip's War. It depicts a Mary Rowlandson who managed, despite her repugnance, to negotiate the wilderness condition into which she was thrust by her capture. Yet like the stories of other survivors, her story is fraught with unspoken ambivalence. The narrative indicates, though rarely explores, her worries about whether her accommodation to her wilderness condition is a form of political or spiritual complicity with the "heathens," about the morality of taking food from a captive child too young to chew it, about what it is that enables her son to grieve for his father when she cannot, and, most important, about why her life has been spared when so many others have been lost.

Nonetheless, the survivor Rowlandson who argued with Weetamoo, who manages to find enough to eat and a place to sleep in the "vast and howling wilderness," remains always secondary in the narrative to the pious woman who moves from desolation and affliction to faith and dependence on God. The first Rowlandson acts while the second, in the fashion the author of the preface so admired, simply records: "God's dealing with her." This pious Rowlandson understands, retrospectively if not immediately, the twofold lesson of her captivity: that suffering and adversity are God's way of chastising his disobedient children and that his "overruling" providence governs even the "most unruly" of heathens. At each juncture in her narrative Rowlandson finds the appropriate public meaning in private experience. She attempts to normalize the extraordinary experience of captivity by assimilating it to the familiar patterns of her own culture. Yet the tone of the narrative swings between hope and despair—hope of salvation, both physical and spiritual, and a guilty despair at her condition, both physical and spiritual.

While it has been proposed that Rowlandson moved beyond the familiar boundaries of female experience in her narrative, it is her remarkable capacity to bring her experience and emotions as a captive into perfect accord with the meanings offered by official Puritan culture that authorized her public speech in a social context in which women's voices were largely silenced. As the author of the preface suggests, she can "come . . . into the publick" to tell her story because she had learned through her affliction "how . . . to talk of God's acts and to speak of and publish His wonderful works." She can, without loss of modesty, "thrust" her story "into the press" because her story is, paradoxically, one of not telling, but a story of being "still" and awaiting the Lord.

"I can remember the time," Rowlandson muses at the close of her narrative, "when I used to sleep quietly without workings in my thoughts, whole nights together; but now it is otherwise with me." This allusion to insomnia is Rowlandson's only concrete indication of the lingering psychological effects of her captivity, but her narrative is shot through with expressions of grief, anxiety, and guilt, with a sense of her alienation from quotidian life. So pronounced are these feelings that one scholar has argued that *A True History of the Captivity and Restoration of Mrs. Mary Rowlandson* enacts a conflict between an exemplary tale of *Judea capta* with broad social meaning and an intensely personal account of mourning for a lost child and a lost self. According to this reading of the narrative, Rowlandson's desire to restore her sense of membership in the Puritan community and her understanding of the religious and political significance ascribed to her experience by that community push her to represent her captivity in ways that, however orthodox, could not adequately express the trauma of her experience or her grief at the loss of her daughter. The narrative, thus, becomes a defense of mourning even as it works to translate private grief into public providence. Hard as she tried to see her private distress, her weeping in the night, as a type of "the wonderful power of God" that has brought her safely out of the wilderness, her language reveals the painful ambiguity of her encounter with the Narragansetts and the private mourning that was its outcome. The pious Rowlandson, schooled in the meaning of affliction, understands that her encounter with the Indians is tragic only

from the vantage point of the present, of the survivor; seen rightly, as part of God's eternal design, her captivity is her salvation. She has, she insists, "learned to look beyond the present and smaller troubles, and to be quieted under them." Yet the narrative makes apparent the insufficiency of this explanatory model in the face of the extremity of Rowlandson's experience of loss.

Rowlandson wrote of only one brief moment in her life, one that has no recorded prelude or aftermath. There is no account of her life prior to the raid on Lancaster and only scant information about her life as she reconstructed it after her release from captivity. Her narrative is, in this sense, like other spiritual autobiographies, and in this sense too *A True History of the Captivity & Restoration of Mrs. Mary Rowlandson* is typical of the stories of colonial women's lives, stories that have come to modern readers most often as fragments—glimpses from letters, diaries, or jottings—or as records of moments of heightened experiences of such great social significance that the strictures against women's public speech are briefly lifted.

Rowlandson was saved physically and spiritually, and her words were saved as well. Her captors were less fortunate. On 6 August 1676 a party of Indians was captured near Taunton, Massachusetts. Shortly thereafter, the body of an Indian woman was found in the same vicinity. According to Increase Mather, the English "cut off her head, and it hapned to be Weetamoo." On 12 August, shortly after his wife and nine-year-old son were captured to be sold into slavery in the West Indies along with many other captive Indians, Metacom was killed while trying to escape the English on Mount Hope peninsula. The officer in charge ordered him decapitated and quartered. The quarters were hung on trees; the head sent to Plymouth, one hand to Boston, and the other to the Indian who shot him. On 24 August, Quanopen was executed in Newport, Rhode Island, along with two of his brothers.

As the author of the earliest known Indian captivity narrative, Mary Rowlandson figures importantly in the literary history of the United States as a definitive spokesperson for the experience of colonial captives and as the originator of a new and long-lived narrative genre. Long regarded as a straightforward vehicle for orthodox Puritan doctrine and mined for information about the conduct of the Indians toward their captives and the attitudes of the English colonists toward their Indian opponents, *A True History of the Captivity & Restoration of Mrs. Mary Rowlandson* has come more recently to be seen as articulating the difficulty of translating private experience into public ideology. As one of the few extant examples of seventeenth-century women's writing, Rowlandson's narrative has figured as a central text in reconstructing the lives of women in colonial New England.

References:

Mitchell R. Breitweiser, *American Puritanism and the Defense of Mourning: Religion, Grief, and Ethnology in Mary White Rowlandson's Captivity Narrative* (Madison: University of Wisconsin Press, 1990);

Michelle Burnham, "The Journey Between: Liminality and Dialogism in Mary White Rowlandson's Captivity Narrative," *Early American Literature,* 28 (1993): 60–75;

Margaret H. Davis, "Mary White Rowlandson's Self-Fashioning as Puritan Goodwife," *Early American Literature,* 27 (1992): 49–60;

Kathryn Zabelle Derounian, "The Publication, Promotion, and Distribution of Mary White Rowlandson's Captivity Narrative in the Seventeenth Century," *Early American Literature,* 23 (1988): 239–261;

Derounian, "Puritan Orthodoxy and the 'Survivor Syndrome' in Mary Rowlandson's Indian Captivity Narrative," *Early American Literature,* 22 (1987): 82–93;

Robert K. Diebold, "A Critical Edition of Mrs. Mary Rowlandson's Captivity Narrative," dissertation, Yale University, 1972;

Deborah J. Dietrich, "Mary Rowlandson's Great Declension," *Women's Studies,* 24 (1995): 427–439;

David Downing, "'Streams of Scripture Comfort': Mary Rowlandson's Typological Use of the Bible," *Early American Literature,* 15 (1980/1981): 252–259;

Tara Fitzpatrick, "The Figure of Captivity: The Cultural Work of the Puritan Captivity Narrative," *American Literary History,* 3 (1991): 1–26;

David L. Greene, "New Light on Mary Rowlandson," *Early American Literature,* 20 (1985): 24–38;

Annette Kolodny, *The Land Before Her: Fantasy and Experience of the American Frontiers, 1630–1860* (Chapel Hill: University of North Carolina Press, 1984);

Lisa Logan, "Mary Rowlandson's Captivity and the 'Place' of the Woman Subject," *Early American Literature,* 28 (1993): 255–277;

David L. Minter, "By Dens of Lions: Notes on Stylization in Early Puritan Captivity Narratives," *American Literature,* 45 (1973): 335–347;

Roy Harvey Pearce, "The Significance of the Captivity Narrative," *American Literature,* 19 (1947): 1–20;

Richard Vanderbeet, "The Indian Captivity Narrative as Ritual," *American Literature,* 43 (1972): 548–562.

Susanna Rowson

(February 1762 – 2 March 1824)

Patricia L. Parker
Salem State College

See also the Rowson entry in *DLB 37: American Writers of the Early Republic.*

BOOKS: *Victoria, A Novel. In Two Volumes. The Characters Taken from real Life, and Calculated to Improve the Morals of the Female Sex, By impressing them with a just Sense of The Merits of Filial Piety,* 2 volumes (London: Printed by J. P. Cooke for the Author & sold by J. Bew and T. Hookham, 1786);

A Trip to Parnassus; or, the Judgment of Apollo on Dramatic Authors and Performers. A Poem (London: Printed by & for John Abraham, 1788);

The Inquisitor; or Invisible Rambler (London: Printed for G. G. J. & J. Robinson, 1788; Philadelphia: Printed & sold by William Gibbons, 1793);

The Test of Honour. A Novel. By a Young Lady, 2 volumes (London: Printed by & for John Abraham, 1789);

Charlotte. A Tale of Truth, 2 volumes (London: Printed for William Lane, 1791; Philadelphia: Printed by D. Humphreys for Mathew Carey, 1794); republished as *Charlotte Temple: A Tale of Truth* (Philadelphia: Printed for Mathew Carey by Stephen C. Ustick, 1797);

Mentoria; or the Young Lady's Friend, 2 volumes (London: Printed for William Lane, 1791; Philadelphia: Printed for Robert Campbell by Stephen Harrison Smith, 1794);

Rebecca, or The Fille de Chambre (London: Printed for William Lane, 1792); republished as *The Fille de Chambre, A Novel* (Philadelphia: Printed for H. & P. Rice and J. Rice & Co., 1794); revised as *Rebecca, or The Fille de Chambre* (Boston: Published by R. P. & C. Williams, printed by J. Belcher, 1814);

Slaves in Algiers; or, a Struggle for Freedom: A Play Interspersed with Songs, in Three Acts (Philadelphia: Printed for the Author by Wrigley & Berriman, 1794);

Susanna Haswell Rowson (Susanna Haswell Rowson Collection, Clifton Waller Barrett Library, University of Virginia Library)

Trials of the Human Heart, A Novel, 4 volumes (Philadelphia: Printed for the Author by Wrigley & Berriman, 1795);

The Volunteers. A Musical Entertainment as performed at the New Theatre, by Rowson and Alexander Reinagle (Philadelphia: Printed for the Author, 1795);

Americans in England; or, Lessons for Daughters. A Comedy (Boston, 1796);

Reuben and Rachel; or, Tales of Old Times. A Novel (1 volume, Boston: Printed by Manning & Loring for David West, 1798; 2 volumes, London: Printed for William Lane, 1799);

Miscellaneous Poems (Boston: Printed for the Author by Gilbert & Dean, 1804);

An Abridgment of Universal Geography, Together with Sketches of History. Designed for the Use of Schools and Academies in the United States (Boston: Printed for John West, 1806);

A Spelling Dictionary, divided into Short Lessons, For the Easier committing to memory by Children and Young Persons; and Calculated to Assist Youth in Comprehending What They Read (Boston: Published by John West, 1807);

A Present for Young Ladies; Containing Poems, Dialogues, Addresses, &c. As Recited by the Pupils of Mrs. Rowson's Academy, at the Annual Exhibitions (Boston: Published by John West, printed by E. G. House, 1811);

Sarah, or The Exemplary Wife (Boston: Published by Charles Williams, printed by Watson & Bangs, 1813);

Youth's First Step in Geography. Being a Series of Exercises Making the Tour of the Habitable Globe. For the Use of Schools (Boston: Published by Wells & Lilly, 1818);

Biblical Dialogues Between a Father and His Family: Comprising Sacred History, From the Creation to the Death of Our Saviour Christ. The Lives of the Apostles, and the Promulgation of the Gospel; with a Sketch of the History of the Church Down to the Reformation. The Whole Carried on in Conjunction with Profane History, 2 volumes (Boston: Richardson & Lord, 1822);

Exercises in History, Chronology, and Biography, in Question and Answer. For the Use of Schools. Comprising Ancient History, Greece, Rome &c. Modern History, England, France, Spain, Portugal, &c. The Discovery of America, Rise, Progress and Final Independence of the United States (Boston: Published by Richardson & Lord, 1822);

Charlotte's Daughter: or, The Three Orphans. A Sequel to Charlotte Temple. To Which is prefixed A memoir of the Author (Boston: Richardson & Lord, 1828).

OTHER: "A Dirge," in *Sacred Dirges, Hymns, and Anthems, Commemorative of the Death of General George Washington, The Guardian of His Country, and The Friend of Man* (Boston: Printed by I. Thomas & E. T. Andrews, 1800);

"Hymn" in *Hymns and Odes Composed on the Death of General George Washington* (Portsmouth, N.H.: Printed at the United States Oracle Office by Charles Peirce, 1800);

"Ode. To the Memory of John Warren," in *An Oration Occasioned by the Death of John Warren,* by Josiah Bartlett (Boston: Printed for C. Stebbins, 1815).

Author of the first American best-seller and the first American writer to find an audience for fiction, Susanna Haswell Rowson also became widely known during her lifetime as an accomplished actress, playwright, songwriter, poet, and educator. Her best-selling novel, *Charlotte. A Tale of Truth* (1791), later retitled *Charlotte Temple,* has gone through more than 150 editions, including 9 editions in three languages other than English. Rowson has earned a permanent place in American history for her accomplishments in women's education and for her portrayals of female independence on stage and in print. Her drama *Slaves in Algiers* provoked a pamphlet controversy in Philadelphia in 1794 for its assertions of female equality. Her life and works epitomize the importance and interrelatedness of the arts in early America.

Susanna Haswell was born in February 1762 to Susanna Musgrave Haswell and William Haswell in Portsmouth, England. Her mother died soon after Susanna's birth. Her father came from a naval family, and when the Royal Navy sent him to the colony of Massachusetts in 1763, he left his small daughter with relatives. William Haswell settled in Nantasket (now Hull) and remarried. In 1766 he brought his daughter to join him in America. Rowson recalled the adventurous journey twenty-five years later in her novel *Rebecca, or The Fille de Chambre* (1792), describing how her ship arrived in Boston Harbor during a sleet and snow storm. This vivid childhood memory is the source of the shipwrecks or dangerous adventures at sea in six of Rowson's novels.

In Hull, Susanna Haswell benefited from her father's small library of books by David Hume, Edmund Spenser, John Dryden, and William Shakespeare, as well as from conversations with patriot James Otis, who, according to Samuel Knapp, called Susanna his "little pupil" and often invited her to his home. Her happy childhood was brought to an end by the onset of the American Revolution. Her father's affiliation with the Royal Navy and his house overlooking the entry to Boston Harbor invited the suspicion of local patriots, and in October 1775 the family was taken prisoner, moved further inland, and kept under house arrest for three years. Then, like so many other people suspected of siding with the British, they were taken to Nova Scotia, exchanged for American prisoners of war, and shipped to England.

At age sixteen Susanna Haswell found herself in London among hundreds of other refugees from America, their families deprived of property and livelihood by the war. At first the Haswells waited for an end to the hostilities, hoping to return to

America and resume their lives. Without income and deprived of their American land, they passed the time exploring London, its free parks and monuments. American refugees frequently attended the Drury Lane and Covent Garden theaters, where three-to-five-hour performances cost one or two shillings. Susanna Haswell delighted in the performances of Hannah Cowley, Elizabeth Inchbald, and Harriet Lee. As the end of the war extinguished hope of return to America and diminished prospects of financial redress from the British government, responsibility for family finances fell on the shoulders of young Susanna.

Susanna Haswell's first literary productions may have been song lyrics. Stage managers needed a constant fresh supply of songs for plays and for entr'acte entertainments. Singers in pleasure gardens such as Vauxhall needed new material every week. Rowson had a natural inclination for coining catchy phrases, and she wrote lyrics throughout her life although she could not have earned much money from such writing. Rowson's fictional protagonists are often young women who find themselves forced to seek employment to support themselves and their aging parents. These characters regard work as an ennobling necessity, and they enter the working world with pride and determination. As governesses, milliners, or instructors in schools for girls, they live virtuously and are rewarded with happy marriages. None of Rowson's heroines becomes an author or an actress. In 1786 Susanna Haswell became both.

Her first experience with publication was not pleasant. She took her first novel, *Victoria* (1786), to printer J. P. Cooke, who recommended that instead of writing original fiction she should copy stories from magazines and offer them to the public as new work. She was dismayed at his suggestion that she engage in such an immoral practice and at his request for "a story full of intrigue, wrote with levity, and tending to convey loose ideas," so she never again did business with him. She published her novel by subscription. The preface includes a list of 270 subscribers, including friends and acquaintances from Covent Garden Theatre as well as well-known people such as the American patriot Samuel Adams and the British Revolutionary War veteran Gen. John Burgoyne. Doubtless many of the better-known subscribers were recruited by Georgiana Cavendish, Duchess of Devonshire, a patron of the arts and a frequenter of the Covent Garden Theatre. Haswell may have met the duchess at the theater. Although it is frequently said that Haswell served as governess to the duchess's children, there is no evidence to substantiate this assertion.

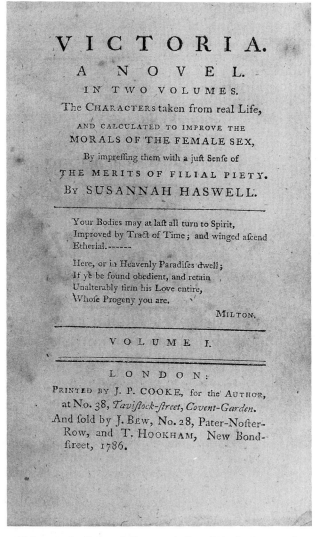

Title page for Rowson's first novel, for which she drew on her own difficulties with making her way in the world (courtesy of the Lilly Library, Indiana University)

As a first attempt at fiction, *Victoria* relied heavily on Haswell's own experiences with finding "a position" in a heartless world, experiencing a storm at sea, and enjoying contemporary theater. References to hotels, service, and tourist sights in Brussels suggest the author's firsthand acquaintance with travel, perhaps as a governess, and allusions to the "late war with America" reveal the author's sensitivity to the profound effect of the war on the lives of British citizens. The novel employs the standard plotlines of seduction, abandonment, and death. The daughter of a deceased naval officer, Victoria Baldwin resists an attempted seduction only to be taken in by a sham marriage. Soon pregnant and abandoned, she gives birth to a son, becomes insane, and dies. The theme of filial piety runs through the five subplots and several brief stories within stories.

Also in 1786, Susanna Haswell married the minor actor and singer William Rowson and began a new career as an actress. According to Philip H. Highfell Jr., she may have performed that summer with a company of London actors at Brighton, and it is likely that the Rowsons and his sister Elizabeth joined a group of "strolling players" who traveled in provincial towns for months at a time. Her intimate acquaintance with the personalities and issues of the London stage is apparent in *A Trip to Parnassus* (1788), Rowson's lighthearted poetic evaluation of thirty-four actors and writers at the Covent Garden Theatre. This thirty-page pamphlet established Rowson as a strict moralist among theatrical people, whose sometimes-scandalous private lives often became the subject of public gossip.

Marriage did not alleviate Rowson's need to earn her living. William Rowson was seldom given acting roles and never earned much money. If the couple did perform in provincial companies, their salary would have been low. To supplement their income Susanna Rowson wrote a second novel, *The Inquisitor* (1788), a loosely structured, picaresque series of heartrending domestic scenes unified by a male narrator. As Rowson pointed out in the preface, the narrator responds to the events he describes in the fashion of Laurence Sterne's *A Sentimental Journey Through France and Italy* (1768). Rowson's imitation of this sentimental tradition could carry her only so far; her desire to teach young women readers the dangers of such fiction required that she satirize the effects of excessive sentimentality and romantic, unrealistic plots. Thus with comic abruptness the Inquisitor's tale of Annie, born to affluence and educated on sentimental authors, shows the ill effects of reading such drivel. This early novel demonstrates Rowson's lifelong and often-repeated conviction that women should be guided by reason rather than emotion. *The Inquisitor* also introduces Rowson's concern for the woman as artist, describing booksellers who urge aspiring women writers to plagiarize and a public that often disapproves of their literary ambitions.

The Inquisitor met with little public acknowledgment. Reviews were brief, as they had been for *Victoria. The Critical Review* disparaged the device of the magic ring that allows the Inquisitor to become invisible, but the reviewer approved of the affecting pathos that spoke to the heart (June 1788). *The Monthly Review* found nothing exceptional in the novel and therefore approved of it for "young readers" and commended the author for her "feeling heart" (August 1788). These two influential literary magazines held different standards for women than for men. Assuming that women wrote only for women and children, reviewers accepted any woman's writing so long as it held a reader's interest and threatened no moral harm. Rowson's first book of poetry, *Poems on Various Subjects* (1788), mentioned in the first edition of *The Inquisitor,* received no reviews, and no copy of this book is extant.

The Rowsons' continuing financial difficulties can be inferred from Rowson's next novel, which she published anonymously probably because she was embarrassed by it. In need of money, she had rewritten material obtained from a publisher. The publisher and probable source of the material was John Abraham, who ran a circulating library. Such libraries rented books to those who could not afford the five-shilling purchase price of a book. *The Test of Honour* (1789) appealed to the lower-middle-class women who patronized these libraries. The young woman protagonist displays an independent spirit and a moral sense far superior to that of the wealthy aristocrat who refuses to let his son marry her. At the same time she is also blessed with an awareness of the ways of the world, as when she demands that an unscrupulous ship captain give her a receipt for her payment so he "cannot pretend to deny receiving the money." Aware of her audience's desire for entertainment, Rowson introduced innocent humor as well as suspense and drama. She enlarged the standard sentimental domestic plot to include a sea adventure and a captivity narrative. Posing as a first-time author, Rowson insisted in the preface that she had written this novel for her own entertainment and claimed no truth for her story, but she defended her heroine in a position consistent with the view articulated in *The Inquisitor,* that fiction is acceptable if didactic and not excessively sentimental. Defying the tradition of prefacing women's novels with obsequious comments about their lack of quality, she offered no apology.

The Test of Honour follows the adventures of orphan Mary Newton from childhood to her marriage perhaps fifteen years later. Her adventures include a trip to Jamaica in an attempt to recover a bequest from a rich uncle, being shipwrecked on a deserted island with the man she loves, the loss of an inheritance to a scheming cousin, a lawsuit to recover her fortune, and her final marriage to the man she has refrained from marrying until she can become his financial equal. One of the three subplots to the novel anticipates Rowson's later play *Slaves in Algiers* (1794). The main plot and the subplots amply demonstrate the rewards of virtue. Mary typifies other Rowson heroines in her independence, her knowledge of the ways of the world, and her adventurousness, but the action is couched in a style so sentimental as to suggest parody.

William Rowson's minor roles at the Covent Garden Theater could only barely support the couple, who–though childless themselves–had been supporting William's younger sister since the death of his parents. It is quite likely that Susanna Rowson earned money not only by writing novels but also by writing magazine stories and songs for the stage or open-air entertainments such as those at Vauxhall and Ranelagh. In 1791 she published two works whose didacticism suggests her growing desire to offer instruction to her audience. *Mentoria* (1791) is a collection of ten letters, three short stories, and an essay, compiled for women who do not read novels. The title character, Helena Askam, has served as governess, or female mentor, to the four Winworth daughters. Now that they have grown and moved to London, Helena writes them letters signed "Mentoria." Each letter usually begins with an account of what Mentoria has heard about the young ladies' behavior, continues with a short sermon on how they ought to behave, and ends with a brief narrative for illustration. The tone is friendly but firm, as proper conduct is essential for the girls' reputation and happiness. "You must early learn to submit," writes Mentoria to her charges, "without murmuring to the will of your father." This direct admonition expresses a theme that is less explicit in Rowson's other fiction.

The story "Lydia and Marian," which occurs between Letters VI and VII, fictionalizes some of the doctrines of the letters. The story recounts the fates of two generations of women seduced by young noblemen who promise to marry them but leave after sham or illegal marriages. The moral is that a woman should not aspire to a class above her own. Rowson's "Essay on Female Education," which follows the letters, repeats the attack on boarding schools that she had earlier made in *The Test of Honour*. This essay may have inspired *The Boarding School* (1798), by American writer Hannah Webster Foster, although the subject of schools for girls and women often provoked controversy in England and the United States. *Mentoria* ends with two stories that had earlier been published in magazines. With its combination of letters, stories, and essays, *Mentoria* resembles a female courtesy book such as Eliza Haywood's *Female Spectator* (1744–1746). Rowson's didacticism in this book is evidence of the practical bent she later put to use in her schools. Middle-class women needed to know how to manage a household: to budget, to make and mend clothes, and to cook. The morals of the stories in *Mentoria* relate in a variety of ways the false allure of social ambition as well as Rowson's favorite

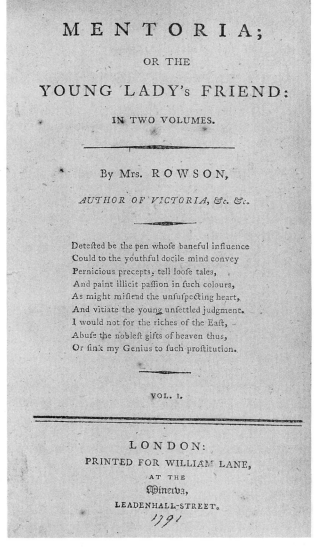

MENTORIA;

OR THE

YOUNG LADY's FRIEND:

IN TWO VOLUMES.

By Mrs. ROWSON,

AUTHOR OF VICTORIA, &c. &c.

Detested be the pen whose baneful influence
Could to the youthful docile mind convey
Pernicious precepts, tell loose tales,
And paint illicit passion in such colours,
As might mislead the unsuspecting heart,
And vitiate the young unsettled judgment.
I would not for the riches of the East,
Abuse the noblest gifts of heaven thus,
Or sink my Genius to such prostitution.

VOL. I.

LONDON:
PRINTED FOR WILLIAM LANE,
AT THE
Minerva,
LEADENHALL-STREET.
1791

Title page for Rowson's version of a female courtesy book, in which a fictional governess advises four young ladies (courtesy of the Lilly Library, Indiana University)

themes of filial piety and the importance of female friendships. Editions of *Mentoria* were published in Dublin (1791) and in Philadelphia (1794), and the book was listed in booksellers' catalogues in Albany, Boston, New York, Philadelphia, and Worcester from 1797 to 1891.

In 1791 Rowson published in London *Charlotte: A Tale of Truth,* the novel that later became the first American best-seller. The simple plot centers around Charlotte, a fifteen-year-old boarding-school student who is seduced and brought to America by a dashing young army officer, Lieutenant Montraville. Once in New York, Montraville reneges on his promise to marry Charlotte. He soon falls in love with the beautiful and wealthy Julia Franklin, but his guilt over Charlotte prevents his proposing marriage. Montraville's false friend Belcour treacherously convinces Montraville that Charlotte is unfaithful and persuades Charlotte that Montraville has left her for another woman. Pregnant and abandoned, Charlotte is turned out of her lodgings and struggles through a snowstorm to seek assistance from her former friend and French teacher, Miss LaRue. LaRue, however, has been installed comfortably in a luxurious house and refuses to jeopardize her social position by assisting Charlotte. Charlotte is taken in by poor servants, gives birth to a daughter, and loses her senses. Her father arrives from England just in time to forgive her before she dies, and he brings home to his heartbroken wife not their lost daughter but their orphaned grandchild, Lucy. The novel ends with Belcour's death in a duel, LaRue dying penniless and alone, and Montraville suffering for the rest of his life from "fits of melancholy."

Some readers have attributed Charlotte's downfall to her youth and inexperience and to the trust she places in Miss LaRue. Pampered by overly protective parents, Charlotte has no defenses against the selfish wiles of such a worldly and clever woman. LaRue is Rowson's most fully developed villain, proof that vice has no respect for gender. Montraville, the actual seducer, is more complex than LaRue, as Cathy N. Davidson has shown in her *Revolution and the Word* (1986). He pursues Charlotte with thoughtless impetuosity and seems not to consider the consequences of their elopement. He too is victimized by one he considers a friend, and his guilt and suffering contribute to the air of credibility in the novel. The narrator blames Charlotte herself: "No woman can be run away with contrary to her own inclination."

Charlotte is the shortest of Rowson's novels and is narrated in third person with occasional first-person commentary by the author. Rowson addressed her reader in the first person in her earlier novels, though the effect had been somewhat less personal. In *The Inquisitor,* for example, she forthrightly expressed her old-fashioned views of the novelist's moral purpose while at the same time insisting upon the reader's right to amusement. In *Charlotte* the maternal authorial line of discourse reinforces the narrative discourse of female companionship and advice giving and may account in part for the popularity of the novel.

These authorial asides create a level of discourse between the reader and author. In nine separate passages the author interrupts the narrative discourse in favor of a personal address to the reader. If, as Davidson says, women readers needed and

sought advice about how to make the most important decision of their lives, *Charlotte* offered an authoritative advice giver whose sole concern, it seemed, was the reader's welfare. This discourse is directed at both young unmarried readers and mothers of prospective brides. The authorial asides and the narrated story warn about the dangers of seduction and, more importantly, offer advice about the whole idea of family.

While similar novels often include one or more subplots about unrelated characters, in *Charlotte* the single subplot introduces the reader to Charlotte's parents. The account of their love marriage and their willingness to forego Mr. Temple's inheritance and live within their modest income informs the main narrative and helps to explain Mr. Temple's generosity at his daughter's deathbed. A loving man who years before waived wealth and position to establish a family based on love, he readily forgives Charlotte and adopts his grandchild. Conventional eighteenth-century literary treatments of the theme of the pathetic, seduced maiden often portrayed the maiden's father as chief victim and focused on his suffering and deprivation as much as or more than the suffering of the seduced. Mr. Temple refuses revenge and makes no complaint about the unjust deprivation of his daughter. He grieves but carries on.

The last novel Rowson published in England was *Rebecca, or The Fille de Chambre* (1792). This tale of Rebecca Littleton, daughter of a retired army lieutenant, is Rowson's most autobiographical work. The preface to the 1814 edition tells readers that the heroine's adventures have been those of the author. Rebecca's vain and cruel employer Lady Ossiter deprives Rebecca of her inheritance; Lord Ossiter attempts to seduce her and drives her from the house. Rebecca's sea voyage recalls Susanna Haswell's own early journey and her idyllic New England village life shattered by the onset of the American Revolution. The novel repeats Rowson's favorite themes of filial piety and the virtues of the middle class, which may be one reason why it, like *Charlotte,* became popular in America.

In 1792 Susanna Rowson, but apparently not William, performed at the Edinburgh Theatre Royal during the winter season. Then, frustrated by their inability to earn a living in England, the Rowsons suddenly decided to emigrate. When Thomas Wignell came to England to recruit performers for his new theater in Philadelphia, the Rowsons joined a full company of actors, including several other married couples, who sailed for America aboard the *George Barclay* in July 1793. Yellow fever prevented them from landing in Philadelphia, so they opened briefly in Annapolis. In February 1794 the troupe moved to Wignell and Alexander Reinagle's New Theatre in Philadelphia.

In Philadelphia, Susanna Rowson soon became recognized as an accomplished comedienne. She worked harder but more happily than in London, performing thirty-five roles in the first season of four and a half months, twenty-two additional roles during the next season (December to July), and at least seventeen others from December 1795 to July 1796. Rowson found American audiences more responsive than the British. Americans expressed their pleasure by applauding and cheering loudly, but they could be distracting and even dangerous when they hissed, whistled, or threw fruit and beer bottles. Though she never attracted the acclaim of great British actresses such as the beautiful and talented Sarah Siddons, Rowson seems to have been regarded as a competent actress. Never idle, she continued writing despite her demanding schedule.

Rowson's first American play, *Slaves in Algiers* (1794), capitalized on the current attacks on American ships by Barbary pirates. Her interest lay not in Algeria but in the idea of tyranny, and she appealed to her American audience by means of her patriotic American characters. As evidence of her developing interest in the position of women, she expanded considerably on the basic captivity narrative from *The Test of Honour*. She extended the idea of political liberty to include love of sexual liberty, and the play includes her most staunchly feminist statements. Political writer and satirist William Cobbett grew incensed by the feminism in her play and attacked Rowson personally and politically. John Swanwick, a congressman from Pennsylvania, defended her in a pamphlet exchange with Cobbett, while Rowson refrained from commenting on Cobbett until the preface to her next novel, *Trials of the Human Heart* (1795). Rowson's next dramatic effort, *The Volunteers* (1795), dealt with an event called the Whiskey Rebellion of southwestern Pennsylvania. Written in 1794, the script to that play has not survived, but the songs, with music by Alexander Reinagle and lyrics by Rowson, are still extant. The script for Rowson's third dramatic effort of that same year, *The Female Patriot; or, Nature's Rights,* also no longer survives. Rowson continued to compose lyrics to popular songs, often in collaboration with Reinagle or Raynor Taylor, as her theatrical association brought her into close contact with actors and musicians, many of whom were new British immigrants like herself. All circulated freely from city to city, catering to Americans' desire for entertainment. The musicians often gave lessons, held concerts, and

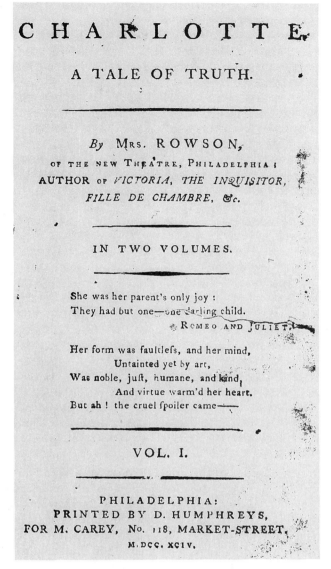

CHARLOTTE.

A TALE OF TRUTH.

By MRS. ROWSON,
OF THE NEW THEATRE, PHILADELPHIA;
AUTHOR OF *VICTORIA, THE INQUISITOR,
FILLE DE CHAMBRE, &c.*

IN TWO VOLUMES.

She was her parent's only joy :
They had but one—one darling child.
ROMEO AND JULIET.

Her form was faultlefs, and her mind,
Untainted yet by art,
Was noble, juft, humane, and kind,
And virtue warm'd her heart.
But ah ! the cruel fpoiler came—

VOL. I.

PHILADELPHIA:
PRINTED BY D. HUMPHREYS,
FOR M. CAREY, No. 118, MARKET-STREET.
M.DCC.XCIV.

Title page for the first American edition of the book that became the first best-selling novel in the United States (courtesy of the John Carter Brown Library at Brown University)

opened music stores or musical publishing houses while writing music for theaters. Such contacts proved useful when Rowson left the theater.

During her busy first year in America, Rowson also found time to arrange for American editions of three of her books. *Rebecca* was published in Philadelphia under its subtitle, *The Fille de Chambre.* Published the following year in Baltimore and in 1814 in Boston, the novel was listed in booksellers' catalogues for the next forty years. *Mentoria* was also published in 1794 in Philadelphia, but Rowson's real success was *Charlotte,* which Mathew Carey of Philadelphia published in 1794 and republished in 1797 as *Charlotte Temple,* the title of many subse-

Susanna Haswell Rowson

quent editions of the novel. Robert W. G. Vail has called this book "the most popular of all American novels" before *Uncle Tom's Cabin* (1852). How much income Rowson realized from the success of *Charlotte* is not known. In 1933 Vail documented 161 editions, including 59 in New York, 39 in Philadelphia, 12 in Hartford, and 9 in other countries.

In her preface Rowson attested to the authenticity of the story. Despite the widespread use of such disclaimers in eighteenth-century novels, Rowson's American public believed her, and by the early years of the nineteenth century, fans had concluded that Charlotte was in fact Charlotte Stanley, daughter of the eleventh earl of Derby (an assumption that historical fact makes improbable) and that Montraville was in real life a cousin of Rowson. Evidence does support the conclusion that Montraville was based on Lt. John Montresor, the son of Susanna Rowson's paternal aunt Mary, who married John Gabriel Montresor, an army engineer.

American readers liked Rowson's maternal authorial voice, and the fact that the novel was partially set in America with a British officer as the villain appealed to their sense of patriotism. Another factor contributing to the popularity of the novel is

the way Rowson's didacticism presents a worldview in accordance with the bourgeois ideology of the literate young women who constituted Rowson's American audience. *Charlotte* emphasizes middle-class virtues: the wisdom of marrying for love rather than money, provided one lives frugally; the need for parental guidance; and parents' duty to provide children with a proper preparation for life. American audiences responded more enthusiastically than British to these ideas, and the novel held American interest for more than a century.

Another appeal of the book was that its fictional representation of decision making offered not only instruction but also vicarious satisfaction for women readers who as daughters and wives were allowed little opportunity to make decisions and no legal power. Because Charlotte is portrayed as having had decision-making power at the crucial times, the narrator holds her accountable. At the same time Charlotte's parents have taken too little responsibility for instructing their daughter in the ways of the world.

As she continued her heavy performance schedule, Rowson also began a new novel, *Trials of the Human Heart* (1795). She chose to sell this work, as she had her first novel in England, by subscription, a publication method that had passed out of favor in the United States as it had done in England. The four-page list of subscribers included impressive names such as Martha Washington and members of leading Philadelphia families as well as managers and members of the New Theatre Company. The book is dedicated to socialite Anne Bingham, a patron of the New Theatre.

Trials of the Human Heart is written in epistolary form, which Rowson had not used since *Victoria*. Meriel Howard, the protagonist, relates some sixteen years of adventures in a series of letters to her friend Celia, a resident in the French convent that Meriel has just left. Like some earlier Rowson heroines, Meriel is thrust into the world to support herself. As a "sport of fortune" or a "child of adversity," Meriel endures sixteen years of suffering before finding her reward. She believes in endurance, saying, "We ought not to complain: every trial, however painful to be borne, is inflicted for some wise purpose." Meriel's multiple trials include marriage to a man she does not love, but in the end she succeeds in settling down with her true love, Frederic Rainsforth. The novel is notable for its autobiographical references, including a female character whose father is a retired naval lieutenant, a male character who leaves for naval duty from Portsmouth, and a heroine who seeks a writing career and undergoes a terrible storm at sea. The heroine attends a theater production of *Jane Shore*, a play in the New Theatre Company repertoire for 1795.

Trials of the Human Heart reiterates its author's favorite themes, compassion for the "fallen" woman and the democracy of virtue. A lower-middle-class woman who has suffered repeated trials from family and others, Meriel forgives even the woman who has slept with her husband, saying, "whatever had been her errors, she was now penitent and in distress. . . . I did not hesitate in resolving to become her friend." Meriel extends kindness to any woman in need, even if she has treated Meriel unjustly. The moral superiority of people at the bottom of the social scale to people of wealth and rank is an idea that occurs in many of Rowson's works.

In September 1796 the Rowsons joined their colleagues in a mass defection from the Philadelphia New Theatre, whose managers were having money troubles. The actors went to the Federal Street Theater in Boston. In addition to higher salaries they enjoyed a large theater, designed by Charles Bulfinch and managed by John Williamson, known to Rowson from her season in Edinburgh. Williamson cooperated with the Reverend Jeremy Belknap, pastor of the Federal Street Church, agreeing never to perform on nights when church services were held. Two of Rowson's half brothers were living in Boston, and she soon began collaborating with the British immigrant musicians of Boston to produce songs for theatrical productions. In April 1797 her drama *Americans in England; or Lessons for Daughters* was performed. Only the list of characters survives.

Despite all the efforts of the company, audiences dwindled, and Williamson's theater plunged immediately into the red. On 26 December 1796 their problems were compounded by the opening of a competing theater. By March 1797 the Rowsons had received their weekly salary of $40 only once. When Williamson left town that summer, overcome by debt, Rowson's hopes for her theatrical career disappeared with him. It was time to change direction. She gave up her stage career and turned to women's education, a field that had always held her interest and was then generating popular concern and debate. That fall she opened a private school, Mrs. Rowson's Young Ladies' Academy on Federal Street, the first of its kind in Boston.

Rowson's Young Ladies' Academy opened with one pupil, the adopted daughter of Mrs. Samuel Smith, and within a year the school had grown to accommodate more than one hundred students. Rowson combined her lively imagination with the charm and conversational skills she had developed during her years in the theater to persuade the best Massachusetts families of the need to educate their

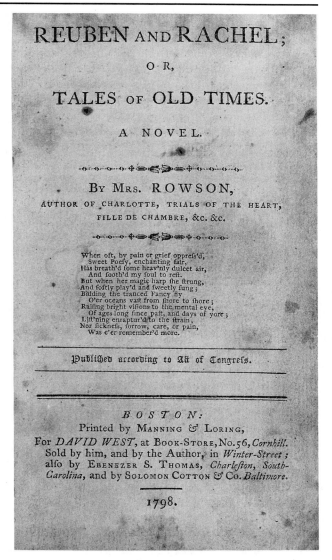

Title page for Rowson's fictionalized survey of more than two and one-half centuries of world history (courtesy of the Lilly Library, Indiana University)

daughters. The Young Ladies' Academy moved in 1800 to a scenic estate in Medford. In 1803 Rowson's friend and patron Gen. William Hull offered her his mansion in Newton for use as her school building. In 1807 her academy moved back to the city of Boston, and in 1809 the Rowsons bought and remodeled a large and beautiful house on Hollis Street, where the academy remained for the rest of Rowson's career. As an educator, Rowson was known for her strict discipline and for setting a rigorous course of study designed to motivate and hold students' interest.

Despite her responsibilities as headmistress, Rowson still enjoyed writing fiction. Her novels had always been forms of moral instruction, but *Reuben and Rachel; or, Tales of Old Times* (1798), published the year after she opened the academy, added instruction in history. This ambitious work, which spans more than two and one-half centuries in at least six countries, was designed "to awaken in the minds of . . . young readers a curiosity that might lead them to the attentive perusal of history in general, but more especially the history of their native country." The title characters are twins whose ancestry is traced from Christopher Columbus to the eighteenth century. The history remains fairly accurate as the action moves to America in the late seventeenth century, when the Dudley family settles in New England and participates in King Philip's War. When the twins are introduced, they experience many of the adventures of other Rowson characters, including a fair share of unhappiness and poverty, but after shipwrecks, a lost inheritance, and the slandering of Rachel's good name, the twins unite with their true loves and settle happily in Pennsylvania. The novel repeats Rowson's favorite themes of loyalty to parents, the virtue of the lower classes (which includes portrayal of morally upright, dignified Indians), and the advantages of a community of women. Rowson idealized places and things American, perhaps to present herself as a suitable educator for the daughters of the best Boston families. Her depiction of Indians is remarkably balanced, describing in detail both the colonists' plundering of Indian settlements and the Indians' brutal attacks in revenge. One passage, unusual for its time, defends Indians as human beings with both strengths and weaknesses, neither "noble savages" nor "infernal fiends." Despite their enforced helplessness, the white women in the novel display remarkable fortitude. The book was popular enough to merit a second edition, published in 1799, and Vail found *Reuben and Rachel* in booksellers' catalogues until 1819.

As the number of students and extent of the curriculum expanded, Rowson's administrative duties somewhat slowed her creative output. She cultivated the goodwill of community leaders and entertained them in her parlor, and she hired and supervised teachers, including music and dancing teachers from the theater. She put in practice the theories of women's education she had outlined in her novels, stressing women's rationality over emotion and teaching young women not simply superfluous accomplishments but skills they would need as wives and perhaps widows. In 1802 she held her first "exhibition" for which she wrote addresses that were delivered by her students.

Several sources have documented that Rowson's marriage was less than happy. For many years William Rowson earned no steady income. Indeed, despite his constant association with the theater, he clearly lacked acting talent, and evidence indicates that he drank heavily. The couple raised William's illegitimate son. In 1803–1804 Susanna Rowson published a novel that revealed some of her situation. *Sarah, or The Exemplary Wife* (1813) first appeared serially in the *Boston Weekly* under the title "Sincerity." Claiming in the preface that many scenes had been "drawn from real life," Rowson attempted to hide their autobiographical connection by adding that they occurred "in another hemisphere, and the characters no longer exist," but even Elias Nason, Rowson's defender and biographer, admitted that much of the plot paralleled her own experiences and that the quotation on the title page, "Do not marry a fool," related to her own sufferings.

The novel traces the marriage of Sarah and George Darnley. Sarah marries reluctantly, unwilling to allow relatives to continue to support her. George proves unfaithful, thoughtless, and hostile to his wife's values. Sarah suffers from excessive pride and keenly dislikes dependence on a man inferior to her. She tries her best, however, to serve him as a dutiful wife, even going off and supporting herself after George claims he prefers to live without her. On her own, she tries to earn a living as a lady's companion and governess, suffering trials similar to those of other, younger Rowson heroines. She adopts her husband's illegitimate son and later meets a man she might have loved and married. She dies early, her dignity intact, but without ever having attained happiness.

More overtly than in any of her other works, Rowson created an intelligent heroine who suffers not only from a bad marriage but also from social restraints that deny her any hope of setting or attaining goals. Her pride and integrity ensure that she fulfill her duties, but she maintains her inner independence. Sarah marvels that women can be so passive as to "assent implicitly to his [a husband's] opinions, however absurd, and . . . not exert their own mental power to think or decide for themselves. . . ." When Darnley strikes her, she realizes she is "dishonoured–insulted," and she knows hers is not simply the human condition; her problems exist because she is a woman. She resigns herself, saying, "the law will not redress my grievances, and if it would, could I appeal publicly?"

The epistolary form provides several points of view, enhancing the reader's understanding of Sarah's situation. The strong women characters take up the issue central to the novel: what makes an ideal woman? A good woman is kindhearted but scornful of the cult of sensibility that leads to swoons. She is proud because she is aware of her own sincerity and personal worth, but she knows when to show prudence and discretion, and she sticks with her husband, poor choice though he may have been. As Nason noted, this novel "opens where such productions generally terminate, with the wedding day." The book ends with the heroine's death, not her happiness, an ending so uncommon that Rowson felt obliged to justify it in the preface.

Much of Rowson's creative energy during her last twenty years went into poems for public occasions, occasional newspaper pieces, and textbooks, including two geography books. Geography had become an indispensable part of academic curricula in the new United States. Rowson's *An Abridgment of Universal Geography* (1806) describes regions and countries of the world in its first seventy-three sections. The large section on America includes descriptions of each state and its territories, including location, geographical description, and information about inhabitants, their occupations and customs, manufacturing and natural resources, and sometimes its discovery. Following the text is "Geographical Exercise," perhaps for memorizing, and finally "Historical Exercise," noting great events. In it Rowson decried slavery and displayed a clear preference for European culture and history, especially British over any other, but she praised the potential of America, especially New England. The book is particularly interesting for its probably widely held views of other cultures. Yet Rowson's distinctive views of the poor treatment of women in non-Christian and non-democratic countries probably placed her in a liberal minority. In her *Youth's First Step in Geography* (1818) her style became more factual, as she used a question-and-answer format, probably designed for memorization by younger students.

Like her geography texts, Rowson's *Spelling Dictionary* (1807) was written to serve her teaching needs and shows her remarkably ahead of her time. To help her students who could "read" but did not understand the meanings of words, she combined the qualities of spelling books, dictionaries, and grammar books to make students associate ideas and think so that they could continue their educations independently. She argued that "it is better to give the young pupil one rational idea, than fatigue them by obliging them to commit to memory a thousand mere words."

The success of Rowson's academy was demonstrated not only in the register of young ladies' names but also in its annual exhibitions. To an audience of parents and friends and anyone willing to pay the fifty-cent admission charge, students recited poems, dialogues, and essays written by Row-

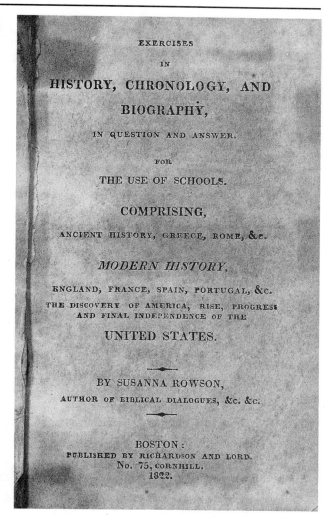

Title page for one of the textbooks Rowson published after she established her Young Ladies' Academy in Boston in 1796 (courtesy of the Lilly Library, Indiana University)

son herself. In 1811 Rowson collected these pieces as *A Present for Young Ladies*. The book reveals that the academy was an unconventional institution where women learned self-respect and the importance of education, both practical and artistic. Many selections call for women's educational and intellectual equality with men. How is a woman to manage studying "huge volumes" of history and five- or six-hundred-page poems? By "Order, regularity, and habitual industry," exactly as Rowson had educated herself while fulfilling her domestic, social, and career responsibilities. Audiences particularly enjoyed the "Sketches of Female Biography" and the dialogues performed by groups of students. At a time when women usually apologized for daring to speak in public, Rowson's students publicly recited encomiums against tyranny, especially against women.

During her years as educator Rowson preferred writing poetry and formal essays rather than novels. In 1804 she collected and published *Miscellaneous Poems*. She wrote unsigned essays for the *Boston Weekly Magazine,* including a series called "The Gossip," whose moralistic and rambling style resembled *The Inquisitor* and *Mentoria*. It seems unlikely, however, that she served as editor of the magazine, as early biographers claimed. In her last year she also contributed to the weekly *New England Galaxy,* usually essays on religious or moral topics and several religious songs.

As her health declined and she suffered the losses of people she loved, Rowson's creative output diminished. Her last works were produced intermittently between bouts of illness. *Exercises in History, Chronology, and Biography* (1822) is a series of questions and answers, tracing the history of the world from the time of Creation to the founding of the American Republic. Like her contemporaries, Rowson made no distinction between biblical and secular history. Her history includes art, literature, architecture, and invention as well as colorful personalities and politics. Consistent with Rowson's lifelong interest in women, she catalogued significant women of history, including Boadicea, warrior queen of early Britain, and Margaret of Anjou, wife of Henry VII and supporter of his government when he became incapacitated. Rowson was thus among the first American women historians to search out women's role models.

In 1822 Rowson published *Biblical Dialogues Between a Father and His Family*. Work on this eight-hundred-page, two-volume work exacted its toll as the author grew older and her health declined. The book retells all the main stories of the Old and New Testaments together with some "profane" ancient history and some history of the medieval church. To appeal to young readers Rowson created a family dialogue among an authoritative father who dominates and guides the family discussions; a mother who, though more gentle, patient, and less quick to express opinions than her husband, nonetheless creates a climate in which her daughters are encouraged to ask rational questions; and children whose authority over one another derives from age rather than gender. In the Bible stories themselves, however, the children find women characters relying on sources other than male authority for guidance. *Biblical Dialogues* stresses the aspects of Christianity mostly likely to encourage respect for women. Rowson included biographies of courageous and clever women from the Bible and from secular history. The book stresses Rowson's belief in a rational rather than emotional approach to re-

ligion, thus distinguishing Rowson from nineteenth-century women writers whose characters rely on male guidance.

Rowson's last years were unhappy. Her three half brothers had predeceased her, and in 1821 her good friend Catherine Graupner died. Her husband mortgaged their Hollis Street house, and she was unable to pay it off. Still, she managed to write one more novel, which was published posthumously as *Charlotte's Daughter: or, The Three Orphans* (1828; better known as *Lucy Temple* after the 1842 edition). It opens eighteen years after the end of *Charlotte Temple*. Set in Hampshire, England, the story revolves around three orphans, Charlotte's daughter Lucy Blakeney, Mary Lumly, and Aura Melville, all under the guardianship of the kindly Reverend Matthews. As the three young women come of age, their actions reflect their early upbringing and the educational efforts of their guardian. Mary Lumly demonstrates the misguided values learned from her mother when she elopes with a deceitful young man who marries her only to obtain her inheritance and then leaves her. Aura Melville, though penniless, marries a wealthy man attracted by her fine qualities. Lucy Blakeney plans to wed John Franklin but learns just in time that he is her half brother, the son of Montraville, the seducer of Charlotte Temple. While John goes off to India in remorse, Lucy reconciles herself to a single life and opens a school for girls.

Echoes of the earlier novel appear in the rapid pace and concise narration that made *Charlotte* easy to read, but the sequel uses more detailed and vivid descriptions. Though most of the characters remain one-dimensional, some surprise the reader with turns of personality. Dialectic language briefly provides humor not often found in Rowson's fiction. The villain of *Charlotte,* John Montraville, is known in this novel as "Lt. Franklin," having taken his wife's name many years ago. Again Rowson relied on her cousin John Montresor as the basis for Montraville-Franklin. On his return to England after years abroad in the army, he has received "royal thanks for his intrepidity," has established himself in an elegant house in Portland Place, and keeps a summer residence in Kent. Such details were all true of Rowson's cousin, who was still living in his Portland Place home when Rowson left England in 1793.

The book seems an expression of Rowson's old age, reflecting her increasing interest in religion and charitable causes and her nostalgia for times and places of her youth. After years of advocating women's independence and rights, Rowson suggested in this novel that women take their happiness in the happiness of others. Yet the title character chooses not to marry and selects a career that will bring her independent satisfaction. In a break with sentimental tradition the character of Mary Lumly suffers the usual seduction, bad marriage, and pregnancy, but she recovers from her madness and rejoins the Matthews family to live out a quiet and relatively happy life. The book teaches the same lessons about sexual behavior that Rowson offered in all her fiction, but it ends more realistically. The novel enjoyed considerable popularity and went through at least thirty-one editions. It received mixed reviews, but John Greenleaf Whittier liked the characters, the "moral beauty" of the book, and its language of nature.

Rowson has stirred favorable scholarly interest since the late 1970s, her rise in critical reputation paralleling the women's movement. Readers have particularly responded to Rowson's consistent advocacy of equal education and personal as well as political freedom for women. These ideas developed and intensified after Rowson moved to the United States in 1794 and suggest the influence of democracy. Her enlightened views of women are reflected in strong, adventurous, thoughtful heroines whose positive attributes surpassed the weaknesses of Rowson's plots. On stage Rowson helped to make the theater a respectable career choice for women, and her development from actress to novelist to educator made her a remarkable career woman in the new republic. After two hundred years *Charlotte* still has its fans, and many of Rowson's other works invite further study.

Bibliographies:
Robert W. G. Vail, *Susanna Haswell Rowson, The Author of Charlotte Temple. A Bibliographical Study* (Worcester, Mass.: American Antiquarian Society, 1933);

Edward J. Piacento, "Susanna Haswell Rowson: A Bibliography of First Editions of Primary Works and of Secondary Sources," *Bulletin of Bibliography,* 43 (1986): 13–16;

Devon White, "Contemporary Criticism of Five Early American Sentimental Novels, 1970–1994: An Annotated Bibliography," *Bulletin of Bibliography,* 52 (December 1995): 293–305.

Biographies:
Samuel Lorenzo Knapp, "A Memoir of the Author," preface to *Charlotte's Daughter: or, The Three Or-*phans (Boston: Richardson & Lord, 1828), pp. 3–20;

Elias Nason, *A Memoir of Mrs. Susanna Rowson, with Elegant and Illustrative Extracts from her Writings in Prose and Poetry* (Albany, N.Y.: Munsell, 1870);

Patricia L. Parker, *Susanna Rowson* (Boston: G. K. Hall, 1986).

References:
Eva Cherniavsky, "Charlotte Temple's Remains," in *Discovering Difference: Contemporary Essays in American Culture,* edited by Christoph K. Kohmann (Bloomington & Indianapolis: Indiana University Press, 1993), pp. 35–47;

Cathy N. Davidson, "The Life and Times of *Charlotte Temple:* The Biography of a Book," in *Reading in America: Literature and Social History,* edited by Davidson (Baltimore: Johns Hopkins University Press, 1989);

Davidson, *Revolution and the Word: The Rise of the Novel in America* (New York: Oxford University Press, 1986);

Blythe Forcey, "*Charlotte Temple* and the End of Epistolarity," *American Literature,* 63 (1991): 225–241;

Susan Greenfield, "*Charlotte Temple* and *Charlotte's Daughter:* The Reproduction of Woman's Word," *Women's Studies,* 18 (1990): 269–286;

Klaus P. Hansen, "The Sentimental Novel and Its Feminist Critique," *Early American Literature,* 26 (1991): 39–54;

Philip H. Highfill Jr., Kalman A. Burnim, and Edward A. Langhans, *A Biographical Dictionary of Actors, Actresses, Musicians, Dancers, Managers & Other Stage Personnel in London, 1660–1800,* 12 volumes (Carbondale & Edwardsville: Southern Illinois University Press, 1973–1987);

Eve Kornfeld, "Women in Post-Revolutionary American Culture: Susanna Haswell Rowson's American Career," *Journal of American Culture,* 22 (Winter 1983): 56–62;

Wendy Martin, "Profile: Susanna Rowson, Early American Novelist," *Women's Studies,* 2 (1974): 1–8;

Julia Stern, "Working Through the Frame: *Charlotte Temple* and the Poetics of Maternal Melancholia," *Arizona Quarterly,* 49 (Winter 1993): 1–21;

Dorothy L. Weil, *In Defense of Women: Susanna Rowson (1762–1824)* (University Park: Pennsylvania State University Press, 1976).

Rebecca Rush
(1 January 1779 – ?)

Dana D. Nelson
University of Kentucky

BOOK: *Kelroy: A Novel* (Philadelphia: Bradford & Inskeep / New York: Inskeep & Bradford, 1812).

Edition: *Kelroy: A Novel,* edited, with an introduction, by Dana D. Nelson (New York: Oxford University Press, 1992).

Little is known about the circumstances of Rebecca Rush's life, her authorship of *Kelroy* (1812), what she did after she published her novel, or even when she died. Thanks to the Rush family archives, which are devoted largely to the person and direct descendants of Dr. Benjamin Rush, Rebecca's uncle and a signer of the Declaration of Independence, something more is known about her parents. Her father, Jacob Rush (1747–1820), who became a noted Pennsylvania jurist, graduated from Princeton in 1765. On 17 November 1777 he married Mary Wrench, or Rench, two months after being admitted to the Pennsylvania Bar. He practiced as an attorney in Philadelphia, serving as Third Circuit Court judge in Reading, Pennsylvania (1791–1806), and then as presiding judge in the Court of Common Pleas in Philadelphia from 1806 until his death in 1820. Like his well-known brother, Jacob Rush published essays on a range of topics.

Before she married Jacob Rush, Mary Wrench had been locally known as a painter of miniature portraits and had supported her mother and younger brother by her earnings. She knew and had perhaps even studied with the painter Charles Willson Peale. Her friendship with the artist apparently continued after her marriage. In 1786, when Rebecca was seven years old, Mary Rush sat for a portrait painted by Peale. She gave up portraiture after her marriage, insisting, according to Peale biographer Charles Coleman Sellers, that she had begun painting only to help support her family.

The Jacob Rush family Bible lists Rebecca's birth on 1 January 1779. She was their first child and was followed by four more daughters: Sarah

(born 24 January 1781), Mary (born 24 January 1783), Harriet (born in 1784?, died in 1798), and Louisa (born in 1786?). While the family made its home in Reading, Rebecca spent time in Philadelphia living with her uncle Benjamin and his family, probably taking care of the children. Correspondence between her uncle and his wife, Julia, reveals that when Rebecca was fourteen, while the yellow-fever epidemic of 1793 was raging in Philadelphia, she was caring for young Benjamin at her uncle's country estate, Rose Hill. Correspondence between her father and her uncle attests that Rebecca also visited Benjamin Rush's family for a time in 1804, when she was twenty-five. Rebecca's mother died in 1806, and six years later Rebecca published *Kelroy,* when she was thirty-three. According to Samuel A. Allibone, "Miss Rush"–apparently still single–was paid $100 for her novel by the publishers Bradford and Inskeep. This payment record is the basis for establishing her authorship of *Kelroy,* which was published under the pseudonym "A Lady of Philadelphia."

Kelroy did not attract much critical notice when it was published, perhaps in part because it appeared right before the official onset of the War of 1812. Bradford and Inskeep's advertisements in local newspapers were quickly overshadowed by anxiously awaited news about the hostilities between the United States and Great Britain.

There is no information about Rebecca Rush's life after the publication of her novel. Scholars have not located marriage or death information in any Philadelphia or Reading church or historical registers. Perhaps she married elsewhere, but she might have remained single and done nothing of public note. When her father died in 1820, his will bequeathed to Rebecca his "Cambridge Bible."

Since the late nineteenth century *Kelroy* has repeatedly provoked the interest of literary critics and historians, some of whom have called Rush's novel one of the best works of fiction produced during the early years of the new republic. Rush's handling of character and subject in her novel is

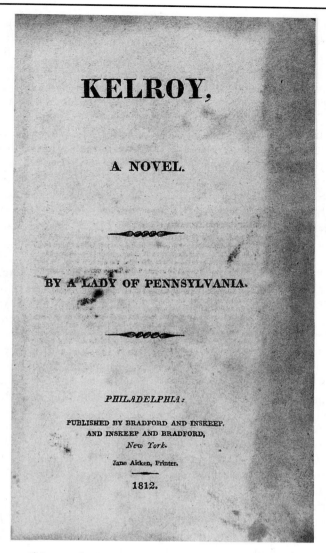

Title page for Rebecca Rush's only novel, in which the title character and the young woman he loves both die of grief after learning that they have been tricked into ending their engagement (courtesy of the Lilly Library, Indiana University)

frequently compared to that of Jane Austen, who published her first novel the year before the appearance of *Kelroy*.

Variously characterized as sentimental, didactic, and a novel of manners, *Kelroy* defies any easy categorization of its plot or characters. The novel interweaves a plot of jeopardized finances with one of thwarted love. The title character, Kelroy, is left in a socially compromised position when his father dies after overreaching his family's resources through speculation. In the midst of engineering plans to remake his fortune through colonial mercantile ventures, Kelroy falls in love with the young and beautiful Emily Hammond. Emily,

who has noticed Kelroy's fine sensibilities and attachment to poetry, soon returns his love. Emily has also lost her father, who, unbeknownst to Emily or Kelroy, has left his family in financial danger. Mrs. Hammond has carefully kept this information from her daughters, Emily and Lucy, as part of her scheme to marry them off to wealthy men, thereby ensuring not just her daughters' future but also her own. Alarmed by Kelroy's lack of wealth, Mrs. Hammond immediately begins scheming to prevent Emily from marrying the man she loves.

Mrs. Hammond, whose villainy constitutes the center and the energy of the novel, is a complex character who sustains reader interest. More than the other characters in *Kelroy,* Mrs. Hammond has an intricate personality and tangled motives. Described by the narrator as a "woman of fascinating manners, strong prejudices, and boundless ambition, which had extended itself to every circumstance of her life," Mrs. Hammond schemes not just to survive but also to gain notice in a world that refuses to accept public ambition in women. Increasingly, as many scholars have recently argued, women in the early years of the nation were called on to conform to the new ideal of republican motherhood, and later true womanhood—cultural models that prescribed for women to be self-effacing, self-sacrificing exemplars of moral purity. The narrator's attitude toward Mrs. Hammond seems to reflect these demands, sneering at her self-interest, castigating her pride, and excoriating her deceptions. Indeed, the narrator repeatedly encourages her readers to adopt a position of disgust toward this woman, and in so doing, to align themselves with the values of sensibility: romantic love, seeming self-effacement and self-denial, the virtuous embrace of poverty and hard work, and the appreciation of the sufferings of others.

Yet the narrator seems ambivalent about this agenda. The characters who exemplify the virtuous characteristics the novel seems to forward are not as interesting as Mrs. Hammond, nor are they particularly rewarded for their virtue. As alternatives to the craven financial concerns of Mrs. Hammond, the narrator offers the characters of Emily and Kelroy, who exhibit an emotional economy known through its Scottish-school advocates as "sensibility." Careful not to take sensibility to its caricatured excess, the narrator depicts Emily as having "none of those unpleasant variations which are usually attendant on strong sensibility." In true form Emily falls ill in the face of emotional betrayal and is always left speechless by rudeness. Yet she can also laugh vigorously at good jokes and is able to recover from most bad fortune, such as when she learns of Kelroy's betrayal of their engagement.

The narrator is at pains to emphasize the sensible nature of Emily's sensibility, but it could be argued that Emily dies as much of excess sensibility as in response to the shock she receives when she learns of Kelroy's faithfulness to their engagement after she has married the wealthy man her mother has chosen for her. Yet Mrs. Hammond's plot for deceiving Emily has been surprisingly easy to accomplish. Despite her passionate attachment to Kelroy, it has taken only two forged letters for her mother to detach Emily from him and, after a short courtship, to attach her to the

wealthy and kind Dunlevy. Just as problematic for this paragon of sensibility is Emily's utter inability to estimate correctly her mother's motives and feelings. In the end Emily seems not so sensibly sensible, after all.

As the male exemplar of fine feeling, Kelroy also has a marked proclivity to fall into mistaken judgment. Though he deduces Mrs. Hammond's intentions to separate him from Emily, he believes his counterfeit letter from Mrs. Hammond. After Kelroy learns of her base deceits and realizes how easily he fell into her trap, he, like Emily, almost immediately dies of grief.

The tragedy of the novel resides in the sad end of Kelroy's romance with Emily. Yet it is difficult to overlook the fact that the narrator is far more interested in detailing the "career" of Mrs. Hammond. What fascinates the narrator and provides the structure of the story are the details of how a woman of "boundless ambition" negotiates a suitable economic situation for herself when she must start with no resources in reserve and with severely restricted avenues for achieving her financial goals. Accustomed to living in wealth, Mrs. Hammond must do what she can to salvage a life for herself and her daughters. In her mid forties, she is too old to count on an economically advantageous second marriage for herself. Mrs. Hammond pays her husband's debts out of his estate and then carefully calculates her resources and options for a comfortable future.

Her first move is to retire to the country for the years it will take to prepare her daughters to enter the marriage market. There her most significant investment is to hire people to school Lucy and Emily in the social graces that will win them high standing in society. When she returns with her daughters to Philadelphia, the reader sees that Mrs. Hammond's estimation of the market has been exactly right, however base her maneuvers might seem to the narrator. High-society matchmaking does most certainly revolve around the question of money. At such events as Mrs. Hammond's Washington's birthday ball, potential suitors are interested in the Hammond girls either for their supposed wealth or for how the young women's drawing-room skills and elegant demeanor might complement the fine furnishings and estates the suitors already possess. Several characters ridicule women who lack the Hammond girls' supposed combination of wealth and good looks. Rush's story forces readers to realize that Mrs. Hammond's mercenary nature is a response to the cruel and competitive market on which their futures depend.

Mrs. Hammond's character flaw is the same as her husband's: overconfidence in her chances on the market. Eager to perpetuate the illusion of their wealth, she overspends and begins to rely heavily on credit. In debt to dressmakers and grocers, she becomes mired in a domestic version of the web of credit in which her husband and Kelroy's father were caught. Mrs. Hammond is rescued by chance: a forgotten lottery ticket pays off. Her gamble is a scaled-down version of the gamble Kelroy plans to restore his fortune: a trading venture in India. The narrator excoriates Mrs. Hammond's behavior at the same time as the novel highlights how successful she is at managing the game of capitalist speculation in the domestic arena.

Whatever attitude the narrator encourages the reader to take toward Mrs. Hammond, the careful reader realizes that the novel offers a striking portrait of the contradictions middle- and upper-class women faced in the rapidly changing economy of the early republic. The ideological and economic tensions of *Kelroy* offer a window into a period of cultural adjustment during which political and economic gains made by "middling" women during the Revolution were disappearing, as both the public sphere and market were claimed as exclusive domains for masculine achievement. *Kelroy* shows what it meant for women to struggle within the shifting gender constraints of the emerging socio-economic context of the early United States, as they became increasingly dependent on the economic gambles and fortunes of their husbands and fathers and were left with ever-narrowing economic recourse of their own.

References:

Herbert Ross Brown, *The Sentimental Novel in America, 1789–1860* (Durham, N.C.: Duke University Press, 1940);

Cathy N. Davidson, *Revolution and the Word: The Rise of the Novel in America* (New York: Oxford University Press, 1986);

Kathryn Zabelle Derounian-Stodola, "Lost in the Crowd: Rebecca Rush's *Kelroy* (1812)," *American Transcendentalist Quarterly*, 47–48 (Summer-Fall 1980): 117–126;

Lillie Deming Loshe, *The Early American Novel, 1789–1830* (New York: Columbia University Press, 1907);

Harrison T. Meserole, "Some Notes On Early American Fiction: Kelroy Was There," *Studies in American Fiction,* 5 (Spring 1977): 1–12;

Dana D. Nelson, Introduction to *Kelroy: A Novel* (New York: Oxford University Press, 1992);

Henri Petter, *The Early American Novel* (Columbus: Ohio State University Press, 1971).

Papers:

The Rush family papers are housed at the Historical Society of Pennsylvania and the Library Company of Philadelphia.

Leonora Sansay

(? – after 1823)

Angela Vietto
Pennsylvania State University

BOOKS: *Secret History; or, The Horrors of St. Domingo, in a Series of Letters, Written by a Lady at Cape Francois, to Colonel Burr, Late Vice-President of the United States, Principally during the Command of General Rochambeau* (Philadelphia: Bradford & Inskeep, 1808); revised and expanded as *Zelica, The Creole: A Novel,* 3 volumes (London: W. Fearman, 1820);
Laura (Philadelphia: Bradford & Inskeep, 1809).

The novels of Leonora Sansay are fascinating examples of early American fiction. She dealt with social issues such as revolution, slavery, and yellow-fever epidemics as well as a more typical theme of novels by women of her era—seduction. Her treatment of these subjects is unusual, as is her approach to the genre of sentimental fiction. Revealing political and social ideas that diverged somewhat from dominant beliefs, Sansay's novels can enrich the modern reader's understanding of the social outlook of early American fiction.

Little is known about the early life of Leonora Sansay; even her name is somewhat uncertain. Basing his conclusions on an inscription in a copy of her anonymously published first novel, Philadelphia book collector Philip S. Lapsansky has asserted that Sansay was likely the daughter of William Hassall, a Philadelphia innkeeper, but that attributions of the novel to "Mary Hassall" are probably based on the incorrect assumption that the first name of the book's narrator was the same as the author's. There is no evidence that Sansay's given name was Mary. Yet it is also somewhat questionable that Leonora was her given name. On more than one occasion Aaron Burr Jr. referred to her as "known as" or "spoken of under the name of Leonora," suggesting that "Leonora" may have been a nickname or adopted name.

These speculations regarding Sansay's birth and name are the biography available for the period of her life before her marriage to French-born merchant Louis Sansay and her romantic involvement with Burr, third vice president of the United States.

There is some uncertainty regarding the date of Leonora's marriage to Louis Sansay, who was operating his business from New York after selling his Santo Domingo coffee plantation to revolutionary leader Toussaint-Louverture in 1795. Some evidence suggests that the marriage may have occurred as early as 1797, and it is clear that the couple must have been married by 1800. The first suggestions of the involvement between Leonora Sansay and Burr appear in two letters Burr wrote to Boston physician William Eustis in 1797 and 1798. If the references to "L.S." in these letters are to Leonora, they place her in New York in fall 1797, in Boston the following winter or spring, and back in New York by summer. They also indicate the nature of the early relationship between Sansay and Burr.

Burr's 16 July 1798 letter to Eustis indicates that Sansay had developed a somewhat scandalous reputation, about which Eustis informed Burr: "You have excited my curiosity to an extreme—How could such an Animal be Months in my Vicinity & I not even hear of her?" The same letter also suggests that Burr set out rather consciously to seduce Sansay, as he recriminated Eustis for not keeping him informed of her departure from Boston and assured him, "I shall certainly talk of you—there is no speaking of Boston without it—but there are Various Ways of doing the thing—and it will so be done, you may be assured, as shall not criminate you or prejudice my interests."

Whatever the details and whatever Burr's original intentions, it is clear from their correspondence that Sansay began a romantic relationship with Burr sometime during this period. Their correspondence lasted nearly twenty years. While sporadic, their relationship seems to have been intense, both romantically and intellectually. Sansay referred to Burr as her "mentor" while he praised her high degree of "sense & information."

In 1802 events occurred that dramatically affected the direction of Sansay's life and were significant in shaping her career as a writer. Like many other French planters, Louis Sansay decided to return to Santo Domingo in that year. The arrest and deportation of Toussaint-Louverture gave them hope that French rule would be reestablished, and like other planters, Sansay hoped to recover his property. In March, Leonora visited Burr in Washington, D.C., ostensibly to obtain letters of introduction for their trip. Louis Sansay, however, was afraid Leonora intended to leave him and wrote several letters to Burr, asking him to ensure Leonora's return to New York and promising to settle $12,000 on her in case of his death. Leonora did return to New York, and the Sansays arrived in Santo Domingo together in late May or early June.

French merchants who returned to Santo Domingo in 1802, including Sansay, were quickly disappointed in their hopes. Efforts to regain control of the island were hampered by resumed war between France and Great Britain and continued black resistance. By 1803 the French had withdrawn, and in 1804 Haiti was established as an independent nation under black rule. Continued unrest between 1802 and 1804 drove away many of the French residents who had returned so hopefully in 1802. By 1803 the Sansays had gone to Santiago, Cuba, where Burr attempted to aid one or both of them financially. Sometime before 1806 Leonora Sansay, apparently without her husband, returned to Philadelphia. It is not clear whether Leonora took this opportunity to leave her husband (as does the character in her novel), or whether he lost his life in the unrest, or agreed to a separation.

As early as 1803, when she mentioned the idea to Burr in a letter, Sansay had conceived of basing a work of fiction on her experiences in Santo Domingo. The same letter introduces the character of Clara, whom Sansay implies is a representation of herself and who would figure prominently in the romantic plot of *Secret History* (1808). The letter also includes passages that appear almost verbatim in *Secret History,* as well as expressing some anxiety about her writing style: "Do tell me if I write frenchified english, I dread that, of all things; it has so much the air of affectation." Whether Sansay began revising her letters into a novel while she was still in the Caribbean is not clear. *Secret History* was not published until 1808.

During the intervening years, Sansay's involvement with Burr seems to have remained important to her. It is clear that Burr had not forgotten her during her absence. Before his duel with Alexander Hamilton in 1804, in instructions to his son-in-law regarding the disposition of his effects in case of his death, Burr wrote, "Madame Sansay, too well known under the name of Leonora, has claims on my recollection." At that time Sansay was still in Cuba. When she returned to the United States, she was evidently as committed to Burr as ever. According to Lapsansky, she traveled with other Burr supporters to New Orleans in 1806, using the name Madame d'Auvergne. There she awaited Burr's anticipated arrival, thus risking implication in the allegedly treasonous plot by Burr to take control of the western territories of the United States.

By August 1808 Sansay had returned to the East, along with other Burr supporters whose hopes had been disappointed. She settled again in Philadelphia, where Burr's supporter Erich Bollman wrote of her that she was "well and industrious" and had "nearly finished a little novel, which will be read with avidity." He may have been referring to *Secret History,* which was published that year, or to *Laura,* which came out the following year, attributed only to "A Lady of Philadelphia."

The title of *Secret History; or, The Horrors of St. Domingo* likely led Sansay's contemporaries to expect an account filled with atrocities committed by blacks against whites during the Haitian revolution. Such accounts were common in U.S. newspapers and magazines during the 1790s and early 1800s. Indeed, only a year earlier, Charles Brockden Brown's *American Register* had featured an "Account of the Massacre in St Domingo, in May, 1806," which focused on the perils of whites and the brutality of blacks, including a scene in which an entire white family is murdered by blacks in their home—the parents hanged, the baby "mashed" in the hands of the blacks, and the children strangled. *Secret History,* however, did not share this intense focus on black atrocities, as a contemporary noted in an 1808 review of the novel in *The Monthly Anthology and Boston Review:* "From the impression given by the title of this book, we were agreeably relieved by its perusal. The Horrours of St. Domingo are so dreadful, so recent, and so numerous that the bare recital would be an inhuman task."

As the reviewer implied, *Secret History* does not satisfy the most obvious expectation created by its title. Rather the novel presents a sentimental story about an unhappy marriage (presumably modeled on the Sansays' marriage) combined with accounts of a variety of events that might be considered "horrors," including interracial violence in which both blacks and whites are aggressors and incidents of cruelty and violence between men and women, across and within races. The tie between the two themes seems to be an implicit argument that unchecked power—whether in the social structure or within marriage—leads to outrageous abuse.

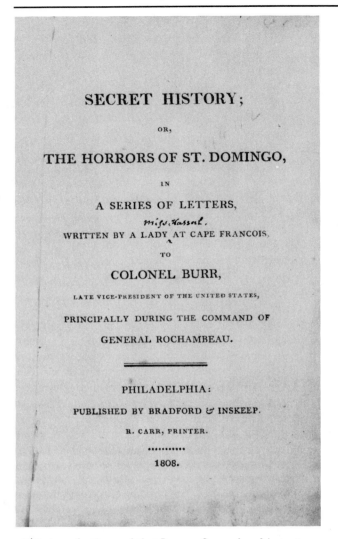

SECRET HISTORY;

OR,

THE HORRORS OF ST. DOMINGO,

IN

A SERIES OF LETTERS,

miss Hassal.

WRITTEN BY A LADY AT CAPE FRANCOIS,

TO

COLONEL BURR,

LATE VICE-PRESIDENT OF THE UNITED STATES,

PRINCIPALLY DURING THE COMMAND OF

GENERAL ROCHAMBEAU.

PHILADELPHIA:

PUBLISHED BY BRADFORD & INSKEEP.

R. CARR, PRINTER.

············

1808.

*Title page for the novel that Leonora Sansay based in part on
letters she wrote to her lover, Aaron Burr Jr., while she was
living in Santo Domingo with her husband, a French planter
(courtesy of the Library Company of Philadelphia)*

Secret History is an epistolary account of a trip
to Santo Domingo that coincides with the dates
during which the Sansays were there. Sansay must
have used incidents she witnessed and stories she
heard from people she met to depict the "horrors" of
which her title speaks. The work is also clearly fictionalized: Mary, the writer of the letters, is an unmarried woman who has traveled to Santo Domingo
with her sister Clara, who is married to a French
officer, St. Louis. Much of the plot revolves around
Clara and her difficulties with her obsessively jealous husband. The letters also recount the military
developments in the area and many anecdotes of
violent "horrors" that the narrator witnessed or was
told about.

Sansay's explicit commentary on the racial
conflict in Santo Domingo is sparing. The few com-

ments she does make reveal a conflict between a
nostalgic attraction to the luxurious white lifestyle
enabled by black slavery and an egalitarian attitude
that seems to champion liberty for the enslaved. On
one hand, the narrator wishes that the blacks were
"reduced to order" so that she could experience the
indolence of a slave-owning culture: "walk on car-
pets of rose leaves and frenchipone; be fanned to
sleep by silent slaves, or have my feet tickled into
extacy by the soft hand of a female attendant." On
the other hand, she recognizes the uprising as a
natural result of the slave system: "More than five
hundred thousand broke the yoke imposed on them
by a few thousand men of a different colour, and
claimed the rights of which they had been so cruelly
deprived." Whites who suffered at the hands of the
rebels were victims of a disaster that they helped to
bring about: "Unfortunate were those who witnessed the horrible catastrophe which accompanied
the first wild transports of freedom! Dearly have
they paid for the luxurious ease in which they rev-
elled at the expense of these oppressed creatures."

These strikingly joined contradictory impulses
may be read as symptomatic of conflicting attitudes
about slavery and race during the era in which
Sansay was writing. As Winthrop Jordan wrote in
The White Man's Burden (1974), Americans "delighted to talk about freedom but wished their slaves
would not. . . . assumed that their Negroes yearned
for liberty but were determined not to let them have
it." This tension between pragmatic economic
concerns and the ideals of the American Revolution,
which had at least implicitly questioned the validity
of slavery, was resolved temporarily in the early
nineteenth century by the rise of scientific theories
of racial difference that would be used to justify
race-based slavery. Rather than seeing slave revolt
as inevitable because of the natural desire of all men
for liberty, the new ethnology defined races as so
different that slavery seemed the inevitable condition of blacks.

While the explicit commentary on racial
conflict in *Secret History* is sparse, the novel abounds
with narratives of violence and cruelty, though not
concentrating exclusively on scenes of blacks killing
whites. Most of this sort of material is included in
two letters rather late in the novel, which describe
the massacre of whites that occurred after the
withdrawal of the French general Rochambeau.
These letters describe how white men were "assembled in a public square, where they were slaughtered by the negroes with the most unexampled
cruelty," how young girls were killed trying to
protect their fathers, and how the remaining whites
lived with "the sword suspended over their heads"

by "their savage masters." There is no question that this section depicts blacks as cruel and savage and whites as innocent victims. Yet these late passages follow many others that provide a more balanced picture of victims and aggressors.

The horrific events depicted in the earlier parts of the novel cover a wide range of acts of violence and cruelty between various kinds of people. Interracial violence is often involved, but not always. Cruelty, both physical and mental, occurs between men and women within various racial groups and between the French military and the Creole whites born in Santo Domingo. In addition the scenes that depict violence between the races feature both blacks and whites as malicious aggressors. The broad scope of the narratives effectively shifts the focus away from race.

Some incidents show the brutality of slave owners toward their human chattel. In one case a slaveholder's wife believes her husband is enamored of "the beautiful negro girl" she keeps "continually about her person." The mistress orders another slave to behead the girl and presents the head to her husband at dinner. "Shocked beyond expression," the husband leaves for France, "in order never again to behold such a monster." This incident, of course, occurs during French rule. During black rule the wife of a black chief is depicted as equally vicious in her jealousy. Her husband has a habit of ordering white women to meet him for romantic assignations. If a woman refuses, he has her killed, but if she complies, she is "as sure of being killed by his wife's orders. . . . Jealous as a tygress, she . . . never failed to punish" the subjects of her husband's attention. The "horror" in each of these two cases proceeds from extreme sexual jealousy combined with the indisputable power to order death, a power held in one case by the slave's mistress, in the other case by the wife of the black chief. Given the same power, Sansay suggests, black and white women are capable of behaving with precisely the same degree of barbarity.

Whites are also depicted as brutalizing each other, specifically in violence between the French military and the local Creole French. In a notable example the French commander Rochambeau, Napoleon's representative, victimizes a young Creole against whom he has some private grievance. He orders the Creole "to pay into the treasury, before three o'clock, twenty thousand dollars on pain of death." When the Creole refuses, Rochambeau has him imprisoned. When the Creole's brother brings the money, Rochambeau accepts it but has the prisoner executed anyway, while imprisoning the brother who had come to his rescue. Rochambeau's behavior is clearly reprehensible, and a few days after this incident he imprisons nine more merchants, again demanding large sums of money. Although he is talked into levying a property tax instead, the whites continue to fear for their lives: "everyone trembles lest he should be the next victim of a monster from whose power there is no retreat." This point about excessive power links the stories of this sort of violence to other stories dealing primarily with violence by men against women.

Sansay's picture of relations between the sexes in Santo Domingo is one in which men are granted great power to terrorize women. In one case a young white woman rejects a suitor because she is engaged to another man, but a few days before her wedding, on her way home from church, she is stabbed and killed by a man at the door of her own house. Everyone believes the killer is the girl's rejected lover, but nothing is done. This state of affairs, the reader is told, is typical in Santo Domingo: "Nothing is more common than such events. They excite little attention, and are seldom enquired into. How different is this from the peaceful security of the country in which I first drew breath."

In another case a father lets his daughter die through sheer neglect. Having taken a mistress, he not only lavishes all his money on the mistress but also cuts off support to his wife and daughter. Although wealthy, he refuses his daughter a dowry, and when she becomes ill with fever, he refuses even money for a doctor, and she dies. This account ends with a specific reference to the excessive power of the husband and dependency of the wife: "How terrible is the fate of a woman thus dependent on a man who has lost all sense of justice, reason, or humanity." The problem is not just the cruelty of the husband; it is the wife's subordination to him that seals her fate.

Finally a series of incidents between Clara and her husband make male brutality against women a central thread of the novel. St. Louis has fits of jealousy in which he throws his wife on the ground, drags her by the hair, and then locks her in a small dressing room. In reference to his penchant for locking Clara up, the narrator suggests that, as in the case of the woman murdered out of jealousy, the cruel behavior is socially sanctioned: "This does not accord with the liberty French ladies are supposed to enjoy. But I believe Clara is not the first wife that has been locked up at St. Domingo." In addition to locking her up, St. Louis abuses his wife emotionally, and Clara even hints at sexual violence: "Often, whilst pouring on my head abuse which would seem dictated by the most violent hatred, he

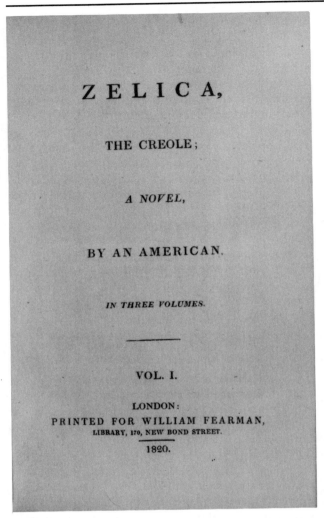

ZELICA,

THE CREOLE;

A NOVEL,

BY AN AMERICAN.

IN THREE VOLUMES.

VOL. I.

LONDON:
PRINTED FOR WILLIAM FEARMAN,
LIBRARY, 170, NEW BOND STREET.
1820.

Title page for the revised and expanded version of Sansay's novel about life in Santo Domingo (courtesy of the Library Company of Philadelphia)

has sought in my arms gratifications which should be solicited with affection, and granted to love alone." When Clara finally leaves her husband, it is because he has threatened to kill her or to disfigure her.

"Horrors" perpetrated by white men against white women thus play an important role in *Secret History*. One of the important functions of these incidents is to make it perfectly clear that not all the horrors of Santo Domingo have to do with race. Rather, what connects the various horrific incidents in *Secret History* is the excessive power that enables the violent and malicious actions. Although Sansay never explicitly draws a connection between interracial violence and violence against women, the final victory of the blacks provides a resolution to the story of Clara's unhappy marriage by making it possible for her to escape her tyrannical husband,

who is unable to find her and flees to France. The critique of Santo Domingo society in *Secret History* revolves around the abuse of excessive power. American democracy is implicitly praised: Americans are the only group who are consistently shown in a favorable light, and the abuse of women, it is suggested, would never be tolerated in the United States.

The review of *Secret History* in *The Monthly Anthology* was generally positive. It is not known what remuneration Sansay received for her first novel, but she evidently felt encouraged to continue her literary career, because she followed *Secret History* quickly with *Laura* (1809). On the surface *Laura* seems to be a more conventional novel than *Secret History*. Its setting is Philadelphia and its environs, not the exotic Caribbean, and its subject is the wooing, seduction, and premarital pregnancy of the title character. In its general outlines *Laura* shares a great deal with many novels of seduction published in the eighteenth and early nineteenth centuries. Yet *Laura* offers unconventional attitudes about seduction and sexual mores.

Laura is essentially an orphan. Her mother eloped from Ireland to Philadelphia to marry the man of her choice; then she was widowed and remarried out of necessity. As the novel opens, Laura's mother has died, and she is left with a stepfather who shows little interest in her. Laura meets Belfield, who will become her lover, while she is crying about her mother's death. This familiar situation initially sounds as though it can only lead to exploitation on Belfield's part: "The friendless state of Laura, rendered his approaches to her easy," but it quickly becomes apparent that sexual seduction is not Belfield's only interest in Laura: "he considered with astonishment the extent of her intellectual powers. Her understanding was excellent, her memory uncommon, and she possessed a degree of refinement very unusual."

Belfield sets to work improving Laura's education, furnishing her with books that "increase her intellectual stores" but also lead her to romantic misconceptions. Their relationship proceeds on a platonic basis until another man proposes marriage, and Laura's dying stepfather agrees to the match. To prevent her marriage Belfield engages lodgings at a farmhouse and persuades Laura to run off with him. They live together, and Belfield promises to marry her when he has finished his medical studies. When yellow fever comes to Philadelphia, Belfield becomes ill, and only Laura remains to nurse him.

After his recovery, Belfield is forced by the farmer's suspicions to move Laura's lodgings into what turns out to be a house of ill repute. When the madam approaches Laura to "entertain" a customer, Laura flees and sleeps on her mother's grave. Taking refuge with a friend whose husband has deserted her, Laura refuses for a time to be reconciled to Belfield, but she has conceived a child, and Belfield is constant in his desire to be reunited with her and to marry her. Belfield's steadfastness is different from that of most seducers in sentimental fiction. He is not really a villain. Moreover, he justifies his actions with an appeal to a Romantic notion of higher laws: "he now considered their marriage as already registered in heaven." Like a truly romantic hero, Belfield dies in a duel defending Laura's honor.

It is in the ending of the novel that *Laura* diverges most widely from the typical novel of seduction. Pregnant and left alone again by the death of her lover, Laura seems to be helpless, but the dying Belfield has asked a friend to protect her. This friend not only treats Laura as Belfield requested but also recognizes "her worth amid the shades of the deepest affliction." In typical seduction-novel language, the reader is informed that "happiness remained a stranger to her bosom," but this warning seems hollow when at the same time "her beauty continued unimpaired" and "her mind acquired new brilliancy." Like Clara running away from her husband in *Secret History*, Laura breaks conventional mores, living with a man and conceiving a child without benefit of wedlock, but she receives no concrete punishment for her crime. In fact society accommodates her unconventional behavior quite easily.

In its ending *Laura* challenges the didactic purpose of much fiction about seduction by refusing to punish the heroine with death or disgrace. Moreover, in its description of Laura and Belfield's romance, the novel challenges conventional attitudes toward romantic relationships. While Belfield is initially attracted to Laura by her appearance, his love seems to grow primarily because of her intellectual qualities. He not only recognizes her intellectual ability but also instructs her and encourages her to increase her knowledge. Based on this representation of the romance, it seems that Sansay was portraying some idealized version of her relationship with Burr. Sansay, who often wrote to Burr that she never felt as happy as in his presence, was, like Laura, never seriously punished for her violation of conventional mores. In Sansay's fiction and her life the transgressing woman survived and moved forward.

A January 1809 review of *Laura* in the Philadelphia magazine *The Port-Folio* was favorable. A later comment by Sansay suggests it may have received more praise elsewhere as well. In a 29 July 1812 letter to Burr she reflected that "my self-love, inordinate as it may be, was amply satisfied by the praises bestowed on that little work." Yet she earned only $100 for the novel. Other means of support were needed. In 1809 she and Erich Bollman began experiments in artificial-flower making. They found their efforts profitable and set up a larger-scale manufactory in a house west of Philadelphia.

Bollman took nearby lodgings, and the two seem to have become quite close. When Sansay wrote to Burr on 29 July 1812 (shortly after his return to the United States), she not only told him about her manufacturing activities but also informed him in detail about Bollman's health and his literary efforts. She also proposed relocating to be near Burr, or at least meeting during an August vacation. There is no indication that Burr accepted her offers.

Aside from a few more letters to Burr (the last written in 1817), Sansay's activities after this point are unknown. Her literary efforts seem to have continued. In 1820 a revised version of *Secret History* was published in London as *Zelica, The Creole*. Attributed only to "An American," this later version of the novel was considerably expanded, with a new focus on a mixed-race character. The racial dimension of the conflict is highlighted. Clara, who in *Secret History* was victimized by her French husband, in *Zelica* becomes a murder victim, killed by a black revolutionary. If Sansay did, in fact, revise the novel herself, she made a major stylistic change: the epistolary form of *Secret History* is abandoned in favor of third-person omniscient narration. These major changes create a notably different work. As Lapsansky has said, in *Zelica* the story has been "transformed from a nearly journalistic account into a brooding romantic thriller."

Despite the London publication of *Zelica*, there is no indication that Sansay had relocated to England; the publisher noted that the work was "transmitted from America," and, according to Lapsansky, advertised two forthcoming novels by the same author, one of which, *The Scarlet Handkerchief*, was published around 1823. No copies are known to survive. The second, *A Stranger in Mexico*, seems never to have been published, although it may have appeared under a different title. There is no way to be certain that Sansay wrote these books, but the possibility of her authorship of *The Scarlet Handkerchief* offers evidence that tentatively places Sansay's death sometime after 1823.

While Sansay's novels received generally favorable contemporary reviews, they were not best-sellers. In the late twentieth century they are not widely available to the general reader, although *Secret History* was translated into French in 1936 and republished in English in 1971. Neither *Laura* nor *Zelica* has been republished. Yet Sansay's novels deserve attention for the light they shed on the history of early American fiction.

As with so many women of her era, many of the details of Sansay's birth, education, family, and death are unknown. If she had not written novels, the record of her life experience would amount to no more than a few footnotes in the life of Burr. Yet she lived during a time of important political and social events, and her writings reflect a free-thinking attitude toward issues such as slavery and marriage. No Wollstonecraftian polemicist, Sansay left behind no overt arguments for women's rights. Yet her novels, in their reflection of her unconventional life, demonstrate that not all women in early America lived and died by the code of the republican wife and mother. Her writings reveal the workings of an independent mind and spirit.

Letters:

Matthew L. Davis, *The Private Journal of Aaron Burr, During His Residence of Four Years in Europe, with Selections from His Correspondence* (New York: Harper, 1838);

Charles Burdett, *Margaret Moncrieffe: The First Love of Aaron Burr, A Romance of the Revolution. With an appendix containing the letters of Colonel Burr to "Kate" and "Eliza" and from "Leonora"* (New York: Derby & Jackson, 1860).

References:

Mary-Jo Kline, ed., *Political Correspondence and Public Papers of Aaron Burr* (Princeton: Princeton University Press, 1983);

Philip S. Lapsansky, "Afro-Americana: Rediscovering Leonora Sansay," in *The Annual Report of the Library Company of Philadelphia for the Year 1992* (Philadelphia: Library Company of Philadelphia, 1993), pp. 29–46.

Papers:

Letters of Leonora Sansay are scattered among Aaron Burr's correspondence. The largest collection of Burr papers is at the New-York Historical Society. These and other Burr papers have been made available in the microfilm edition of the Papers of Aaron Burr. A transcription of a poem attributed to Sansay (identified as Madame d'Auvergne) is in the Benjamin Henry Latrobe papers at the Library Company of Philadelphia.

Elizabeth Ann Seton

(28 August 1774 – 4 January 1821)

Frances Murphy Zauhar
Saint Vincent College

BOOKS: *Memoir, Letters and Journal of Elizabeth Seton,*
2 volumes, edited by Right Reverend Robert
Seton (New York: O'Shea, 1869);

A Daily Thought from the Writings of Mother Seton,
edited by Reverend Joseph B. Code (Emmits-
burg, Md.: Daughters of Charity of St.
Vincent de Paul, 1929); republished as *Daily
Thoughts of Mother Seton* (Emmitsburg, Md.:
Mother Seton Guild, 1957);

Letters of Mother Seton to Julianna Scott, edited by Code
(Emmitsburg, Md.: Daughters of Charity of
St. Vincent de Paul, 1935);

Selected Writings, edited by Erin Kelly and Annabelle
Melville (New York: Paulist Press, 1987);

*Elizabeth Ann Seton: A Woman of Prayer: Meditations,
Reflections, Prayers and Poems Taken from Her
Writings,* edited by Sr. Marie Celeste, SC (New
York: Alba House, 1993).

Elizabeth Ann Seton

A religious figure and educator in the early
nineteenth century and the first native-born American saint, Elizabeth Ann Seton founded the Sisters
of Charity and established several schools that provided religious and secular education to wealthy
and poor children alike. Her private struggles and
her public work are recorded in detail in the many
letters and several journals she wrote throughout
her life. Sent to private schools as a young girl, she
was carefully tutored at home beyond the custom of
her contemporaries, and she was well versed in
French and English literature, contemporary philosophies, and the natural sciences, especially in
medicine. Her youthful thinking was influenced
somewhat by the writings of Voltaire and Jean-
Jacques Rousseau, but the greatest influence on her
thought was the enthusiastic yet intellectual Protestant Episcopal spirituality prevalent in her social
class during the late eighteenth century in America.
The love of personal Bible reading and the practice
of scrupulous self-examination that Seton learned as
a girl remained with her after she converted to Roman Catholicism in her early thirties, and they pro-

foundly influenced her religious practices as a Catholic, as well as the practices of the religious order
she founded and the students they taught. Seton's
intense temperament and spirituality are strongly
reflected in her writings. In her letters and journals
she revealed an evangelistic enthusiasm, a deep
faith in God, and a consistently activist sense of
civic duty, especially as it related to her responsibilities as an educator.

Seton never wrote a comprehensive account of
her life or work, and it is unclear whether she ever
intended her writings to be read beyond her immediate circle of family, friends, and religious sisters.
Throughout her adult life, however, and especially

337

after her religious conversion, she corresponded with several women, specifically intending to influence the direction of their lives. Three friends of her girlhood, Julia Sitgreaves Scott, Catherine Dupleix, and Eliza Craig Sadler, remained lifelong correspondents. Seton attached great importance to women's correspondence, and her letters are filled not only with the quotidian events of her family life as a society matron, the hardships of her husband's economic decline, the horrors of his final illness and death, and the day-to-day matters of running a lively household of students and young teachers, but also with detailed reflections on civic virtue and private spirituality. She wrote many significant letters to family members, including her father; her sisters-in-law Rebecca, Cecilia, and Harriet Seton; her daughter, Anna Maria; and her sons, William and Richard; to friends Amabilia, Philip, and Antonio Filicchi, as well as to the friends of her girlhood; to spiritual directors and advisors, in particular to Reverend Pierre Babad, Reverend Simon Bruté, and Bishop (later Archbishop) John Carroll. With Babad and Bruté she maintained particularly intense correspondences about the circumstances of her relationship to the Roman Catholic Church hierarchy, whose dictates concerning her fledgling community were often at odds with her own insights and preferences, and about her emotional state and spiritual condition as well. In addition to her wealth of letters, Seton also kept journals at various periods in her life, starting in her girlhood. In particular she kept them when she accompanied her husband to Italy, when she defied her family to enter the Catholic Church, and when she left New York to found the community of sisters and their school in Emmitsburg, Maryland.

Elizabeth Ann Bayley was born on 28 August 1774 in New York City, the second of three children born to Dr. Richard Bayley and Catherine Charlton Bayley. Elizabeth Bayley's father, an eminent physician, was the first professor of anatomy at King's College (later Columbia University) and health officer of the Port of New York. Her mother died when Elizabeth was three years old, and her father remarried. His second wife, Charlotte Barclay, bore him several children, including James Roosevelt Bayley, who, like his sister, converted to Catholicism. He entered the priesthood; was consecrated first bishop of Newark, New Jersey; and later became the archbishop of Baltimore. As a young girl, following the practice of her family, Elizabeth Bayley was baptized and confirmed in the Protestant Episcopal Church. Like all the Bayley children, she was sent to "Mama Pompelion's," a small private school near the Bayley home, where she learned to play the pi-

ano and speak French. After she had completed the curriculum offered there, her father directed her studies, using the resources of his own library. Under his guidance she read works in history and philosophy and continued her studies in French and music. She also spent at least an hour every day reading and studying the Bible. For her father's inspection she kept a journal on her studies and her experiences. In one such entry she compared what the result would have been on a particular evening, when she attended a party and was courted by an eventually unsuccessful suitor, if the time had by contrast been devoted to her studies: "The consequence would have been . . . I would have been pleased with myself; M___ would have been pleased with me; even they to whom the sacrifice was made would have liked me better; and, the heavenly consideration, my God would have blessed me."

On 25 January 1794, at the age of nineteen, Elizabeth Bayley married William Seton, a New York merchant in the prosperous Seton-Curson firm, which had valuable connections in Europe. Like her, William Seton was from an old New York family, also members of the Episcopal Church. After their marriage Seton seems to have begun seriously reading French philosophy. It is clear from letters she wrote to Julia Scott and Eliza Sadler that she read both Voltaire and Rousseau and that she enjoyed their writing, although in retrospect she considered their influence a dangerous one. She also continued her serious reading and study of the Bible, as evidenced by the many reflections on individual passages that she recorded in the journal-letter she kept with her sister-in-law Rebecca Seton. In letters to her father and her husband, she wrote on the subjects of medical treatments, public health, and business. In one letter to her father, she reported:

> I had the pleasure to hear a Mr. Delmas, a French physician, refer a number of strangers, both French and English, to a publication, called the *Monitor* [by Richard Bayley], as the best thing written on the subject of yellow fever, and as the only one that points out its true cause and origin. He said he did not know who was the author, but he must be the best friend of humanity, and should be considered by the Americans as their best adviser. I imagine my eyes were larger and blacker at that moment than usual.

As a privileged member of New York society, Seton fulfilled her philanthropic obligations as a founder and active member of the Widows' Society in New York, an organization that cared for widows and orphans. Also at this time she became the primary confidante of her father, who often visited briefly

Elizabeth and William Seton at about the time of their marriage in 1794 (Sisters of Charity of Mount Saint Vincent-on-Hudson)

with her when he made his rounds as health physician for the Port. The two exchanged letters almost daily, writing not only about medical matters, but also in reflection on Bayley's often peripatetic career, which had kept him apart from his first family when his daughters were little. In one note Seton revealed significant insight into her father's personality with a roundabout story: "Mr. Sitgreaves thinks that men of active genius should never be more than one month in the same place. Who does that apply to? . . . No bonds, no restraints, the air, the ocean the whole earth—and not even that, I believe, would satisfy the restless spirit of the object now present to my mind." His death in August 1801, apparently the result of exposure to ship fever, cost Seton the individual who was perhaps her closest intellectual companion at that time.

In 1800 William Seton's financial affairs suffered a permanent reversal, which also severely affected his already fragile health. By this time the couple had four children: Anna Maria, William, Richard, and Catherine Josephine. (The Setons' youngest child, Rebecca, was born in 1802.) In 1803 the Setons embarked on a long sea journey in the hopes

of improving William's health. They lodged their four younger children with relatives, and taking their eldest daughter, Anna, they left New York in October, bound for Livorno, Italy, to stay with the family of Antonio and Philip Filicchi in whose counting house William Seton had worked as a young man. They made the trip in five weeks. Because yellow fever still raged in New York, the ship was quarantined on its arrival in Livorno on 18 November, and the Setons were required to stay at the lazaretto, the official place of quarantine, for a month after reaching Italy. During this time William Seton lay seriously ill with a fever; Anna Maria developed whooping cough; and Elizabeth Seton was required to nurse them under the harshest of circumstances. Her journal from this period, kept as a record for Rebecca Seton, indicates that her duties were extremely taxing and that she often responded to the circumstances with weeping and distress. At the beginning of the quarantine section of her journal, she wrote:

How eagerly would you listen to the voice that should offer to tell you where your "dear sister" is now—your soul's sister. Yet, you could not rest in your bed if you saw her as she is, sitting in one course of an immense prison, locked and barred with as much ceremony as any monster of mischief might be, a single window double-grated with iron, through which, if I should want anything, I am to call a sentinel with a fierce cocked hat and a long rifle-gun—that is, that he may not receive the dreadful infection we are supposed to have brought from New York.

The journal also indicates, however, that after the first week, she rallied herself and provided tirelessly for her family, nursing them in their illnesses and reading to them from the Bible. While they slept, she often read the Bible to herself to allay her fears and wrote in her journal about her hopes for their future. On 20 November she began,

> The matin bells awakened my soul to its most painful regrets, and filled it with an agony of sorrow which could not at first find relief even in prayer. In the little room . . . I first came to my senses, and reflected that I was offending my only friend and resource in my misery, and voluntarily shutting out from my soul the only consolation it could receive. Pleading for mercy and strength brought peace. And with a cheerful countenance I asked William what we should do for breakfast.

The family was released from quarantine after a month and taken to the Filicchi residence at Pisa, where William Seton died twelve days later, on 27 December 1803, after suffering terribly. He was buried in the Protestant cemetery.

Seton's account of her family's journey and her husband's suffering and death bears remarkable similarity to the captivity narratives of early American Puritan women. She wrote painstakingly careful accounts of the events she experienced and remarkably accurate descriptions of the places and the people that surrounded her. Her willingness to face her emotions, to describe them and their effect, and to explain them rationally as well as spiritually testify not only to her skills as a writer but also to her sound intuitions about human psychology. Throughout her life Seton's writing reflected her understanding that human spirituality and human experience reacted practically to one another. Seton also indicated that she understood something of the relationship between spiritual and physical realities. She related to Rebecca Seton the following dream she had the night before her husband's death:

> I saw in my slumber a little angel with a pen in one hand, and a sheet of pure white paper in the other. He looked at me, holding out the paper, and wrote in large letters "JESUS." This, though a vision of sleep, was a great comfort. [William] was very much affected when I

told him and said a few hours before he died, "The angel wrote 'Jesus.' He has opened the door of eternal life for me, and will cover me with his mantle." I had a similar dream the same night. The heavens appeared a very bright blue. A little angel at some distance held open a division in the sky. A large black bird like an eagle flew toward me and flapped its wings round and made everything dark. The angel looked as if it held up the division waiting for something the bird came for. And so, alone from every friend on earth, walking in the valley of the shadow of death, we had sweet comfort in our dreams, while faith convinced me they were realities.

Seton's account to her sister-in-law is remarkable for its detail and its clarity, as well as for its eloquence and unsentimental realism. It is a compelling record of a horrible sojourn.

After her husband's death, Seton remained in Italy for about three months. The Filicchi family used this opportunity to acquaint her with some of the precepts of the Catholic faith, and her letters to her sister-in-law Rebecca indicate that she was moving closer to the Catholic tradition. When Seton and her daughter left for America on 8 April 1804, her husband's friend Antonio Filicchi accompanied them. By the time Elizabeth Seton arrived in New York in late May, she had decided to convert to Catholicism. About six weeks after her return, Rebecca Seton died after a long illness. Rebecca's death deprived Seton not only of her most beloved female relative, but also of the one individual in her family who might not have so vehemently opposed her about her developing religious convictions.

Over the next twelve months Seton was subject to her family's and the Filicchis' constant attentions to and questions about her religious beliefs. Both parties lobbied tirelessly, in person and by letter, for her to choose between the Episcopal and the Roman Catholic traditions. Seton experienced great distress and confusion over their strongly conflicting opinions on this matter, as her journals and letters from this period clearly demonstrate. In particular her letters to Amabilia Filicchi record the intense lobbying of her Seton relatives and the extreme pressure she felt. She eventually resolved these doubts, and on 25 March 1805 she made her first communion as a Roman Catholic. As a result she was alienated from her relatives, disinherited, and forced to rely on the Filicchis, who never failed to recognize what her decision had cost her and were unflagging in their moral and material support. They readily provided for the education of her sons and wrote letters of introduction for her to several influential American Catholics. Antonio Filicchi also arranged a subscription of annual

Seton in 1796 (engraving after a portrait by Favret de St. Mesmin)

support for her family from some of her American friends. After his return to Italy, however, and probably under pressure from her relatives, most of the subscribers withdrew. The Filicchis paid for a substantial portion of the educations of William and Richard Seton. For the rest of Elizabeth Seton's life, her letters to the Filicchis indicated her gratitude for their support. Likewise, her letters to Julia Scott and Eliza Sadler reveal that she became a regular subject of their charity throughout the remainder of her life.

After seeing that her sons were provided for, Seton sought to secure a place of safety and some comfort for herself and her daughters. At first she considered Antonio Filicchi's offer to have all three of them placed in a convent in Montreal, where Seton could open a school for girls while her daughters were trained in Catholicism, but the priests who were her principal advisers at this time persuaded her to wait until a similar situation was available in the United States. Their letters from this period show that they recognized Seton's leadership potential and were extremely reluctant to allow someone of her character and charisma to leave the fledgling American church for Canada. Her letters from this time indicate how difficult it was for Seton to abide by the wishes of these men and ignore the advice of the Filicchis and her own inclinations. Seton was seldom willing to denigrate her own ability to discern what she believed to be the hand of God in her life, but she recognized in a practical sense that Bishop Carroll provided a more immediate temporal protection from her family's virulent anti-Catholic attacks than the Filicchis could from their home in Italy. At this time the Catholic Church in the United States constituted a small and relatively powerless minority: of the approximately 2.2 million people living in the United States, about forty thousand were Catholic, mostly poor rural farmers descended from German and Irish immigrants and settled in Maryland and Pennsylvania. The Carrolls were one of the few truly affluent families who had remained Catholic and active in politics. Seton probably recognized Bishop Carroll as something of a kindred spirit because of their similar family backgrounds. Nevertheless, she seems to have found it difficult to follow his dictates when they did not correspond to her own inclinations. Her letters to him reveal her thinly veiled discomfort when their opinions clashed, and her obedience to his dictates is often qualified and conditional. Her letters to Julia Scott are usually more candid. While Seton was never openly critical of Carroll, she was often open about her misgivings.

For a while Seton taught a coeducational school run by a Mr. Harris in New York. In 1808, on the advice and with the financial support of her spiritual director, Father William Valentine DuBourg, she moved herself and her daughters to Baltimore, where her sons were enrolled at St. Mary's College and where she began a school for Catholic girls.

During this period Seton had considered making a formal declaration of her commitment to religious life, but it was not until December 1808 that this hope seemed likely to become real. The change in possibilities occurred when one of the priests with whom she worked sent to her a young woman, Cecilia O'Conway, who had determined to return to Europe to enter a convent until she heard that Seton also wanted to enter religious life in the United States. She became Seton's first companion and fellow teacher.

At about the same time as she began making plans to take vows committing herself to religious life, Seton revealed to her spiritual director her wish to redirect her efforts to educating poor children, and she began making written inquiries among the wealthy Catholic community in Baltimore toward this end. Under the financial sponsorship of Samuel Cooper, a wealthy Catholic living in Baltimore, Seton and her household retired to rural Emmitsburg, Maryland, and prepared to open another school. In 1809 several other women traveled to Emmitsburg to live in the religious community Seton had started and to join in her educational work. On 1 June of

that year the women made a formal dedication as a community. Shortly after this date, Seton's young sisters-in-law, Cecilia and Harriet Seton, visited her in Maryland. Cecilia, who had already converted to Catholicism, also hoped to join the religious community there. It was during this visit that the younger sister, Harriet, also converted to Catholicism, much to the dismay of the rest of the Seton family. Later that year, when an epidemic of fever swept the convent, Harriet fell ill and died on 22 December 1809. Cecilia, whose health had long been tenuous, died in April 1810. Seton's letters to Julia Scott record the final days of both young women and, like her earlier journal-letter to Rebecca Seton, they reveal Seton's anguish and suffering and her skill as a detailed observer and eloquent writer.

The Sisters of Charity, as the community was called, finally opened their school in May 1810. By June there were forty students enrolled. Seton was successful in recruiting young Catholic women to her community and in persuading both poor and affluent Catholics to send their children to her school. Her work at Emmitsburg earned her the title "foundress of the parochial school system in America," and she is credited with creating the model for the Catholic parochial schools that provided free education to thousands of Catholic children, especially in urban dioceses, during the nineteenth and early twentieth centuries. Often ill herself, Seton seldom taught at the school. She served as principal, supervising the spiritual development and temporal work of the other sisters. At first she was also heavily engaged in fund-raising activities, most of which were only partially successful. During the first two years of the school, the community of teachers and students living at Emmitsburg often endured penetrating cold and damp for days and nights on end in buildings that were ill equipped to withstand the harshness of the winter. They often went without heat and developed a regular program of physical activity more to ward off the cold than for any other physical benefits. Letters to Bishop Carroll and to Julia Scott spare little detail in the reports of what the community suffered. While Seton dreamed of operating a free school to provide for the full education of poor Catholic children, the school at Emmitsburg always had a preponderance of paid boarders, most of whom were the daughters of wealthy Catholics. (The paying boarders usually outnumbered the "pensioners" by about four-to-one.) Seton's reluctant decision to take paying students was the only way to enable the school to survive and flourish.

In addition to the material concerns of the school and her growing religious order, Seton also found herself in the middle of several controversies regarding the leadership of the community. As had been her practice before her conversion to Catholicism, Seton avidly read the Bible, and she corresponded regularly with her spiritual director about the state of her soul and the mission that she believed God intended for her. Pierre Babad directed her spiritual life when she first moved to Maryland, and the two continued to exchange letters after the religious community retired to Emmitsburg. Bishop Carroll considered Babad an officious meddler in the affairs of the fledgling community, and he formally placed the group at Emmitsburg under the authority of the Sulpician fathers who taught at nearby St. Mary's Seminary, hoping that this action would remove Seton from Babad's influence. Babad and Seton continued to correspond, however, and her devotion to this priest put her in conflict with her bishop for several years, nearly resulting in the demise of the Emmitsburg community. Her letters to Babad and Bishop Carroll are full of diplomatic but strongly worded complaints about the restrictions the bishop sought to place on her correspondence with Babad. Seton eventually acceded to the wishes of the clergy who were her official religious superiors, and the young priest whom they placed in charge of her spiritual direction, Simon Gabriel Bruté, proved to be a suitable complement to Seton's headstrong and emotional temperament.

Bruté became Seton's spiritual director at a crucial time in her life, shortly after the death of her oldest daughter. Anna Maria Seton was two months short of her seventeenth birthday when she died on 12 March 1812, after a long and painful struggle with tuberculosis. Elizabeth Seton was practically inconsolable, and in the months after Anna Maria's death, she was almost unable to run the day-to-day affairs of the school, much to the consternation of Bishop Carroll and her superiors at St. Mary's Seminary. Bruté helped her move beyond her grief and achieve the sense of resignation and faith that had comforted her after the deaths of her husband and sisters-in-law. While they met in person on a regular basis, the two also often corresponded by letter. He encouraged her in her spiritual direction of the students and the younger sisters who continued to enter the community. With Bruté's support Seton maintained a constant correspondence with many of her former students, as well as with several of the young men who were her son's classmates at nearby St. Mary's College. The priest felt these letters were salutary not only for the young people but also for Seton, for they kept her from having the time to review the grim details of her daughter's

final illness and death. Bruté had a great respect for Seton's eloquence and wit, and he recognized her ability to influence those around her as a positive attribute to be nurtured, not a vice to be controlled. In fact it was Bruté who assured that all Seton's papers were preserved after her death.

During the last decade of Seton's life the school and novitiate in Emmitsburg became firmly established, and daughter communities of the Sisters of Charity were founded in New York and Pennsylvania. Both these communities ran diocesan-sponsored orphanages engaged in work on which Seton herself had longed to focus.

The death of Anna Maria was followed just three years later by that of Elizabeth Seton's youngest child, Rebecca. Seton's concerns were divided between resolving ecclesiastical disputes involving the authority of the community and providing for the settlement of her surviving children. Her letters to her sons, William and Richard, reflect her concern for their spiritual and temporal welfare. Neither son evidenced much interest in business, nor had either embraced Seton's religious beliefs as her daughters had. Both eventually persuaded their mother to help them enter the navy. Seton continued to correspond with both sons, but she never saw either of them again. Seton's surviving daughter, Catherine, remained with her mother until her death, and eventually entered the Sisters of Mercy. Catherine Seton lived to be ninety-one years old, dying on 23 April 1891 at St. Catherine's Convent in New York City.

During the last three years of her life, Elizabeth Seton realized that she had successfully provided for the security of her only surviving daughter and derived great comfort from Catherine's strong religious convictions. Likewise, she was pleased that her sons had begun the life's work they had chosen, even though she continued to fear for their spiritual well-being. Finally she was assured of the great success of the school at Emmitsburg and the stability and growth of the religious order she had founded. Even as her labors prospered and her work flourished, her health began a steady decline. She died on 4 January 1821.

During her decline Seton was able to write brief letters to some of her correspondents. These letters include an episodic memoir, "Dear Remembrances," which record Seton's impressionistic memories of how she had felt God's presence at crucial moments in her life. It was written for her religious sisters at the request of her spiritual director. The form and tone of this text, clearly affected by her physical limitations as well as her mental fatigue, unfortunately became the formal model used by the earliest editors of her writings. Transcribed and extensively quoted in the earliest biographies by the Reverend Charles I. White and Madame Hélène Bailly de Barberey, as well as in later biographies by Monsignor Joseph B. Code and the Reverend Joseph I. Dirvin, these writings became a rich resource and model for late-nineteenth- and early-twentieth-century Catholic spirituality. White, Code, and Dirvin presented Seton as an intensely spiritual, albeit fragmented, writer whose thoughts come across as impressionistic and incomplete. Of the early works, only de Barberey's biography presents generous selections of Seton's writings without heavily interpolated commentary on her religious piety. Unfortunately Dirvin and Code seem to have relied more heavily on White's biography than on de Barberey's, and consequently they created a rather stiff picture of a woman of single-minded religiosity. Later in the twentieth century, however, with the publication of biographies by Annabelle Melville and Sister Marie Celeste, Seton's true ability as a storyteller and her power as a witty and sometimes even ironic commentator on the events around her came to the forefront. Melville and Sister Marie Celeste returned to the original manuscripts to create a fuller portrait of their subject, and they presented more of Seton's own writing. While earlier biographers were generally intent on proving Seton's worth as a true daughter of the Catholic Church and advancing the cause of her canonization, later biographers seemed more dedicated to showing that this acknowledged exemplar and saint was also a vibrant and human woman of strong personal will and fortitude.

Since Seton's canonization in 1975, several books have been published that collect representations of writing from Seton's letters and journals, all of which have been emended less heavily than earlier editions of her writings. These works allow Seton's writing to stand on its own, and they reveal not only the piety and fortitude of the saint portrayed in the early biographies, but also Seton's real skill as a reporter and commentator on early American life.

Biographies:

Hélène Bailly de Barberey, *Seton,* translated by Monseigneur Joseph B. Code (New York: Macmillan, 1927);

Leonard Feeney, SJ, *Seton: An American Woman* (New York: America Press, 1938); republished as *Mother Seton, An American Woman* (New York: Dodd, Mead, 1947);

Katherine Burton, *His Dear Persuasion: The Life of Elizabeth Ann Seton* (New York: Longmans, Green, 1940);

Annabelle M. Melville, *Elizabeth Bayley Seton: 1774–1821* (New York: Scribners, 1951);

Reverend Charles I. White, *Mother Seton: Mother of Many Daughters,* revised edition (Emmitsburg, Md.: Mother Seton Guild, 1953);

Sister Rose Maria Laverty, SC, *Loom of Many Threads* (New York: Sisters of Charity, 1958);

Joseph I. Dirvin, C.M., *Mrs. Seton: Foundress of the American Sisters of Charity* (New York: Farrar, Strauss & Cudahy, 1962);

Sister Marie Celeste, SC, *Elizabeth Ann Seton: A Self-Portrait* (Libertyville, Ill.: Franciscan Marytown Press, 1986);

Sister Marie Celeste, SC, *The Intimate Friendships of Elizabeth Ann Bayley Seton, First Native-Born American Saint (1774–1821)* (New York: Society of St. Paul, 1989).

References:

Margaret Alderman and Josephine Burns, *Praying with Seton* (Winona, Minn.: St. Mary's Press/Christian Brothers Publications, 1992);

Sister Mary Electa Boyle, *Mother Seton's Sisters of Charity in Western Pennsylvania* (Greensburg, Pa.: Sisters of Charity, 1946).

Papers:

Seton's letters are scattered in archives throughout the United States, including those at Georgetown University; Mount Saint Mary's College in Emmitsburg, Maryland; Saint Joseph's Central House in Emmitsburg; the Sisters of Charity of Mount Saint Vincent-on-Hudson, New York; the University of Notre Dame; the Baltimore Cathedral Archives; and the Sisters of Charity of Seton Hill in Greensburg, Pennsylvania. The Sisters of Charity of Mount Saint Vincent-on-Hudson, New York, have Seton's diary.

Eunice Smith

(1757 – 29 October 1823)

Rosemary Fithian Guruswamy
Radford University

BOOKS: *Some Arguments against Worldly-Mindedness, & Needless Care & Trouble, with Some Other Useful Instructions Represented by Way of a Dialogue or, Discourse between Mary & Martha* (Boston: Printed by E. Russell for Zadok King, 1791); republished as *A Dialogue or, Discourse between Mary & Martha* (Boston: Printed by E. Russell for Zadok King, 1791);

Practical Language Interpreted, in a Dialogue between a Believer and Unbeliever, in Two Parts (Boston: Printed by E. Russell for Zadok King, 1792);

Some of the Exercises of a Believing Soul Described in a Short Answer to 12 Serious & Important Questions (Boston: Printed by E. Russell for Zadok King, 1792);

Some Motives to Engage Those Who Have Professed the Name of the Lord Jesus to Depart from All Iniquity and Study a Close Walk with God: to Which Are Affixed a Number of Songs Presented to Those Who Love the Lord (Greenfield, Mass., 1798).

The evangelistic consciousness that seized early American religious life from the time of the first Great Awakening in the 1740s provided an opening for women of all denominations, including Baptist Eunice Smith of Ashfield, Massachusetts, to express their faith publicly, allowing them to find a public identity and a community through speaking and writing. Drawing sanction mainly from the letters of Paul in the New Testament, the early Protestant religious establishment in America had cautioned women to remain silent and submissive to male directives in the conduct of their spiritual lives and to stay in the private sphere of the home, tending to the moral direction of their children and the physical sustenance of their husbands so that the men could actively confront rigors of spiritual life in the wilderness. Thus, in seventeenth-century New England women such as Anne Bradstreet and Margaret Tyndal Winthrop produced writings more concerned with family spiritual life than with communal struggle with religious issues. Although both these women were well aware of the contro-

versy surrounding Anne Hutchinson, whose public emphasis on the individual experience of grace was considered too radical by the early Puritan community, neither Bradstreet nor Winthrop mentioned Hutchinson in their writings. By the years of the early republic, however, the dimensions of women's religious experience had widened, mainly because the male-sanctioned emphasis on the individual's direct confrontation with salvation allowed oral and written testimony of how the naturally pious woman should conduct herself privately and publicly.

Women from various sects, particularly those known as "Separates" or "New Lights," published diaries, conversion narratives, and religious essays to guide and edify other women. The focus of many of these writings was the conversion process—a journey from a self-centered life, often characterized by close flirtation with sinfulness, through realization of its shortcomings and dangers, to an acceptance of Jesus Christ as the actual center of one's existence. Such a religious experience had special significance in the life of a woman as she grew out of the youthful frivolities of the single state, anticipated marriage, and faced the important task of raising Christian children.

Eunice Smith was one of the few Baptist women in New England to publish her writings for public reading. During the last decade of the eighteenth century she became popular as a writer of religious advice and as an exhorter who spoke about the conversion process so crucial to women as they grew from adolescence to adulthood.

Smith's prose evinces more concern for the religious than the political, a reflection of the necessity—even in a radical religious family—for a woman to stay out of the public eye except when edifying her readers' spirituality. Two of Smith's essays feature acrostic poems that spell her name, a device used often in earlier religious texts to suggest the author's decorous reticence about revealing his or her name. This reserve is echoed by Smith's pronouncements in her prefaces that she wrote mainly for her own spiritual health and published her writings only from concern for the welfare of her fellow Christians. Like many women writers before and after her, she also mentioned the weakness of her writing skills and expressed the certainty that her thoughts would be overlooked because of her inadequacies with the pen. Yet, unlike many of her modest female contemporaries who published their works anonymously or used pseudonyms, all four of her published essays bear her name and city on their title pages.

Eunice Smith was born in 1757 in the frontier community of Ashfield, Massachusetts, in the Berkshire Mountains. The daughter of Chileab Smith (1708–1800) and Sarah Moody Smith (1709–1789), she was the youngest of twelve children and the only one born after the family's move to Ashfield from South Hadley, Massachusetts. Smith's father had started out as a Congregationalist deacon in South Hadley, but on hearing the sermons of the leading ministers of the Great Awakening, most notably Jonathan Edwards, he followed the enthusiastic religion of Edwards's Northampton church. After finding the doctrine of acceptance into church fellowship of the unconverted, introduced by Edwards's Puritan grandfather, Solomon Stoddard, incompatible with his interpretation of Scripture, Chileab Smith became a New Light Separate early in 1751. Shortly thereafter, he moved his family to Ashfield (then Huntstown), a remote settlement where only two other families lived and where the Smiths subsequently converted to the Baptist faith in 1761, when Eunice was only four. Her oldest brother, Ebenezer Smith (1734–1824), then twenty-seven, became the first pastor of the First Church of Baptized Believers in Ashfield, a small church that the Smith family was instrumental in founding.

Chileab Smith and several of his Baptist colleagues in Massachusetts, including Isaac Backus and John Davis, frequently produced pamphlets protesting the dominance of the Congregationalists. In one of these works, *An Answer to Many Slanderous Reports Cast on the Baptists, at Ashfield* (1774), Chileab Smith used Revolutionary-era rhetoric of slavery and freedom in combination with biblical imagery to explain his exodus from the Boston area in pursuit of his own religious liberty from Congregationalist strictures and to make the case for the Baptists' freedom to worship according to their own principles. Eunice Smith's brother Ebenezer was an unpublished poet and is credited with writing the only Baptist antislavery work, which called on the church in which he was pastor to support the abolition of slavery. The publication and dissemination of his statement to the New England Baptist community in 1773 occurred several months in advance of the better-known early abolitionist writings of John Woolman and other Quakers.

As the youngest member of the family, Eunice Smith was not old enough to have been embroiled in the struggles of her family to settle Ashfield and to combat the subsequent encroachment of the Congregationalists. Her name is absent from the documents that chronicle the troubles and the social and political commitments of the Ashfield Baptists. The tradition of writing in her family, however, apparently encouraged her to develop her potential as a religious writer once she became an adult.

As a child Smith experienced the rigors of frontier life and observed her family's defense of its Baptist principles against the attempts of the state-sanctioned and more-liberal Congregationalists to establish the primacy of their church. She spent the first six years of her life behind a barrier of logs that formed a twelve-foot bullet-proof fort around the Smith homestead to protect them during an often bloody seven-year war with the local Native American tribes. This experience might help to explain Smith's use of conventional religio-military imagery in her essays and her depiction of earthly life as a state of war. Once the settlers triumphed over the Native Americans, a Congregationalist Church was established in Ashfield and, ignoring the claims of priority voiced by the Baptist congregation, declared itself the established church in town. This declaration, protected by a 1692 Massachusetts law, obligated the Baptist community to pay taxes to support the Congregational Church and its pastor. When the Baptists refused to do so, the Congregationalists took them to court.

One of the Congregationalists' central objections against the dissenting sects who were beginning to dominate the frontier was that their ministers lacked formal theological training. Ebenezer Smith, for example, did not have a college degree, but in 1769 the Warren, Rhode Island, Baptist Association—the first permanent regional meeting of Baptists in New England, formed in 1767—granted him its official seal, legitimatizing his ordination. The Congregationalists looked down on the less intellectual and more affective evangelical Baptists and referred to Ebenezer Smith as a "hedge priest." The Baptists' lack of intellectualism is apparent in Eunice Smith's simple style, which, as Katherine Hall Molumby has suggested, appeals to the uneducated lay reader of the Bible.

Despite the Congregationalists' representation of them as unschooled people, the Ashfield Baptists were not anti-education. They had founded a common school in Ashfield as early as 1766, when

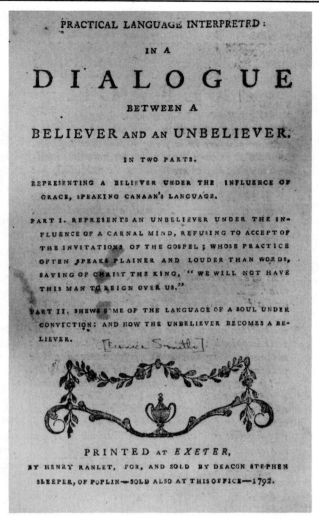

PRACTICAL LANGUAGE INTERPRETED:

IN A

DIALOGUE

BETWEEN A

BELIEVER AND AN UNBELIEVER.

IN TWO PARTS.

REPRESENTING A BELIEVER UNDER THE INFLUENCE OF
GRACE, SPEAKING CANAAN'S LANGUAGE.

PART I. REPRESENTS AN UNBELIEVER UNDER THE IN-
FLUENCE OF A CARNAL MIND, REFUSING TO ACCEPT OF
THE INVITATIONS OF THE GOSPEL; WHOSE PRACTICE
OFTEN SPEAKS PLAINER AND LOUDER THAN WORDS,
SAYING OF CHRIST THE KING, "WE WILL NOT HAVE
THIS MAN TO REIGN OVER US."

PART II. SHEWS SOME OF THE LANGUAGE OF A SOUL UNDER
CONVICTION: AND HOW THE UNBELIEVER BECOMES A BE-
LIEVER.

[Eunice Smith]

PRINTED AT EXETER,
BY HENRY RANLET, FOR, AND SOLD BY DEACON STEPHEN
SLEEPER, OF POPLIN—SOLD ALSO AT THIS OFFICE—1792.

*Title page for one of several 1792 editions of Eunice Smith's popular pamphlet on the necessity for
individual conversion (courtesy of the American Antiquarian Society)*

Eunice Smith was nine. She may well have learned to read and write in this school along with the other young Baptists in town. A commitment to the education of the socially disadvantaged continued to flourish in the Smith family. Eunice Smith's older sister Jemima was the grandmother of Mary Lyon, who founded the Mount Holyoke Female Seminary in 1837.

The struggle to defend their young minister and their faith did not go well for the Ashfield Baptists. Their petitions to the local authorities were at first ignored and then backfired on them. The Massachusetts legislature eventually responded to their complaint in 1768 by passing the Ashfield law, which required the Baptists specifically to support the Congregational Church and its minister, Jacob Sherwin, a graduate of Yale University. During 1769 and 1770, when the Baptists still refused to pay, the government auctioned off most of their land, with the proceeds going to Sherwin's support. Chileab Smith's family lost their or-

chard, their church's burial ground (which was on their property), and a small house. Ebenezer Smith's family had ten acres of their land sold for less than a quarter of its worth.

The Baptists then threatened to take their grievance to the king. At first the situation looked favorable for them because of the political competition between the colonists and the loyalists in Boston. After Ebenezer wrote some articles for local newspapers that called prominent Congregationalists liars, however, the Baptists' request was immediately rejected, and Chileab Smith was arrested on specious charges of counterfeiting, which were later dropped for lack of evidence.

In 1774 the Warren Baptist Association joined with several Quakers to bring the general issue of the abuse of non-Congregationalist denominations in Massachusetts to the attention of the First Continental Congress in Philadelphia. The Ashfield case was cited as the most dramatic example, and Chileab Smith attended the legislative session with other major Baptist leaders, including James Manning, who soon became the first president of Brown University. They did not get much satisfaction in Philadelphia, being dismissed as "not regular Baptists" and viewed as enthusiasts and fanatics. The issue was thus further deferred, and the taxation of other denominations for support of Congregationalism was not outlawed until 1833.

The alliance with the Quakers against the mainstream religion and the designation of the Smith family's New Light theology as fanatic seem to have affected Eunice Smith's religious thinking and the subjects of her four popular pamphlets, written many years later. All her writing clearly reflects the New Light belief in the spiritual centrality of the individual's personal confrontation with his or her own wickedness, followed by the necessary acts of repentance and a conversion that would result in a palpable perception of the sweetness of Jesus, portrayed as an experience of the inner light radiating a changed appearance to reality. While the Quakers also emphasized the experience of this inner light, Molumby has also pointed out parallels between this emphasis in Smith's writing and Jonathan Edwards's *Faithful Narrative of the Surprizing Work of God In The Conversion of Many Hundred Souls* (revised edition, 1737).

Eunice Smith was baptized on 13 January 1771 at the age of fourteen, in accordance with her family's radical Baptist opposition to infant baptism on the grounds that the child could not yet have undergone the necessary conversion experience that had to precede church membership. Smith was accepted into the covenant of the Ashfield Baptist Church the same year.

Smith's most popular pamphlet, *Some Arguments against Worldly-Mindedness, & Needless Care & Trouble, with Some Other Useful Instructions Represented by Way of a Dialogue or, Discourse between Mary & Martha* confronts the dilemma many women of her generation were experiencing, even after religious conversion, as they tried to balance their spiritual lives with their domestic responsibilities. It was published in Boston in 1791 and reprinted in the same year as *A Dialogue or, Discourse between Mary & Martha,* perhaps to increase its attractiveness to women readers. A second edition of this work followed in 1791 with printings in Boston, Springfield, and Warren, Rhode Island. The conversation between the biblical sisters Martha and Mary moves from a concern for one another's physical health to Mary's query about Martha's spiritual health, which is held to be much more important by both women. Smith

used Martha's washing of Christ's feet, her action of devotion to him as he conversed with the more intellectual Mary, as a strong metaphor for the humility Smith recommended to her readers. Mary, who is extremely conscious of and verbose about her own wickedness, contrasts humility to the selfishness that might develop when one becomes too concerned about daily affairs. She assures Martha that "Self is an unpleasant field for meditation," leading to a discussion of the proper focus for meditation: the life and suffering of Christ. Several times in the piece Mary and Martha burst spontaneously into song, as their discussion of Christ and conversion leads them to emotional excitation. The essay ends with the standard evangelistic call for redemption and deliverance from sin. Several editions of the essay also include Smith's poem "Youth Cut Down in the Flower of Age." Eleven editions of this work were published between 1791 and 1802. A 1797 edition includes this commentary on the text's popularity and utility: "The rapid sale of a late Edition of this useful and ingenious Pamphlet, has encouraged this Impression. This is the fourth Edition from this Press, and waits the reception of its former favours."

The use of the biblical characters of Mary and Martha must have appealed to female readers not only because they understood how Martha's domestic concerns could distract her from focusing on spirituality but also because of the social emphasis on the need for evangelistic conversion as a woman moved from the single state to the married state. Whether women were beset by selfishness of a frivolous kind, such as preoccupation with appearance and possessions, or of the kind depicted in Martha's preoccupation with family and household, the overriding concern of the pious woman was that her commitment to Christ should have priority over anything else. Smith clearly spoke to this societal emphasis in her dialogue.

Two more of Smith's essays were published in 1792. *Practical Language Interpreted, in a Dialogue between a Believer and Unbeliever, in Two Parts* uses the dialogue format to illustrate the importance of the spiritual dialectic to personal conversion. This essay is reminiscent of Anne Bradstreet's dialogue poem "The Flesh and the Spirit," but Smith's work has a more urgent tone as the Believer voices shock and issues a stern warning to caution the Unbeliever about her backsliding sinfulness. As Jacqueline Hornstein noted in *American Women Writers* (1982), Smith's "revivalist metaphors" clearly show the evangelistic spirit of the frontier. Emphasizing the necessity of actual heartfelt conversion, Smith employed a vivid depiction of hellfire that has a much different tone than the idealistic theology of Bradstreet's Renaissance-inspired poem. Yet despite the tone of Smith's pamphlet, at the end of the Believer's descriptions of the horrible fate that awaits unrepentant sinners, the Unbeliever finally hears a "still small voice" that forgives her. This gentle ending suggests the influence of the Quakers, who often use this phrase to portray the action of the inner light, the spirit of Christ that lives in everyone. Indeed, Smith seems to use the phrase in the same sense. This dialogue was reprinted eight times through 1816 in various New England cities.

Smith's other 1792 pamphlet, *Some of the Exercises of a Believing Soul Described in a Short Answer to 12 Serious & Important Questions,* seems to be written from the viewpoint of the converted Unbeliever in the previous essay to express the results of her conversion. In this work Smith used the popular question-and-answer technique reminiscent of catechisms and sermon literature. Each answer concludes with a short poem. The new Believer, who answers the questions, maintains a constant narrative posture of mourning for the hurt she has unwittingly done to Christ as well as an aura of astonishment at the freeness of his gift of grace. Like Mary and Martha, she also views the world and the flesh (as well as the devil) as a person's chief enemies. Starting with her answer to Question IX, the narrator begins using military metaphors, stating a few pages later that "the present life is a state of war." To come to a state of peace the reader needs to submit to the grace of Christ, who "is my strength and song." The text ends with a poem, "An Invitation to be Constant in Running the Christian Race." This tract was apparently not as popular as Smith's others. Only one edition is extant. It ends with an advertisement for the earlier works of "the ingenious Miss Eunice Smith."

Smith's final work is *Some Motives to Engage Those Who Have Professed the Name of the Lord Jesus to Depart from All Iniquity and Study a Close Walk with God: to Which Are Affixed a Number of Songs Presented to Those Who Love the Lord* (1798), which suggests reasons why Christians should be diligent in maintaining the spiritual power they first experienced at the moment of conversion. This essay was published in Greenfield, Massachusetts, in 1798, but it may have been written earlier. In it Smith used the image of Lot's wife looking back at Sodom to urge her readers to continue turning away from worldly cares and sin. Of all the motives for forsaking sin, meditation on Christ's suffering seems to be central. This essay also includes poems after each numbered section and concludes with ten songs presented as a gift from a "loving sister" to those who worship Jesus. Smith's use of verse and song to enhance her religious presentation—as well as her frequent citation of passages from the Book of Psalms and her call in this final essay to make the most of hymn singing as a form of praise—indicate that she shared the artistic leanings of her eldest brother and was sensitive to the central role hymnody and psalmody played in the life of seventeenth- and eighteenth-century Christians. This essay appeared in only one edition, suggesting that Smith's contemporaries preferred her dialogues.

Modern scholars and anthologists who mention Smith usually call her an advice writer or a religious conduct-book writer who encouraged her contemporaries to behave well, to exploit their natural feminine talent for piety, and to avoid the corrupting influence of the flesh. Her self-effacement in her prefaces speaks to eighteenth-century attitudes about women writers as much as to her own humility about addressing spiritual subjects. The picture of a well-dressed, kneeling woman contemplating a book, most probably the Bible, that appears on the title page of the first edition of *Some of the Exercises of a Believing Soul* points to the use of her texts in a woman's religious sphere where such humility was expected. Except for her employment of Martha and Mary in her first essay, however, none of Smith's rhetoric seems particularly focused on domesticity or women's peculiar concerns. The sinner and the believer she depicted could be either male or female, and the trajectory of conversion she described is the same as that in the works of such diverse evangelical writers as Jonathan Edwards and Olaudah Equiano.

All Smith's writing was published with the help of the Warren Baptist Association, which had been constantly solicitous to the religious needs of her family. Although many more-radical Baptists were skeptical about the need for a hierarchical organization, the Ashfield incident and others like it convinced many that central leadership was needed to present grievances to the authorities. In addition to its support for the Baptist petition to the First Continental Congress, the Warren Association was conscientious about the religious education of its membership and worked to counteract the popular opinion that Baptists were illiterate. Its home church in Warren founded Rhode Island College (later Brown University) in 1765, and in 1791 the Warren Association petitioned Congress to license the publication of all U.S. Bibles. The association subsequently sponsored the publication of much religious literature, including the essays of Smith.

On 10 January 1792, at the time when her pamphlets were reaching the peak of their popularity, Smith married Benjamin Randall (also spelled "Randal," "Randol," and "Randoll") of nearby Shelburne,

Massachusetts. Records indicate that in March 1799 she resigned her church membership in Ashfield and was subsequently accepted into the First Baptist Church of Christ in Deerfield/Shelburne. Her seven-year wait before transferring her membership to her husband's church and before publishing her final pamphlet (written just before or just after her marriage) may have been because of a theological disagreement that developed among her family members, resulting in her father's founding a second Baptist church in Ashfield with her brother Enos as pastor. This quarrel was resolved in 1798. When her father died, her brother Ebenezer moved to western New York, and the two Baptist churches were reunited under Enos's leadership. With peace in the family once more, she no doubt felt secure in transferring her allegiance to her husband's church.

Smith ceased to write in the mid 1790s. Upon her marriage she had become the stepmother of her husband's nine children by his first wife, who had died in 1791, only four months before he married the thirty-five-year-old Smith. Eunice and Benjamin Randall had one son, Joseph, born in 1795. No information exists about the rest of her life. She died on 29 October 1823 in Shelburne. Her gravestone in the Shelburne Baptist Church burial ground reads:

In life or death Christ's image she display'd.
For him she wrote exorted sang or pray'd.
To live to God her ever constant care,
If she has fail'd mortals may all despair.

By the end of the eighteenth century, women were regularly reading the works of female devotional writers who gave them religious advice on achieving the true Christian character. Spiritual conduct-books proliferated, and women considered such writing and reading part of their duty to be models—or to learn to be models—of moral rectitude for those over whom they might have influence. Eunice Smith's focus on the emotional richness and passion of the evangelistic conversion experience reached the mainstream of theological concern among her fellow Baptists.

References:
Martha Tomhave Blauvelt, "Women and Revivalism," in *Women and Religion in America, Volume I: The Nineteenth Century,* edited by Rosemary Radford Ruether and Rosemary Skinner Keller (San Francisco: Harper & Row, 1981), pp. 1–45;
Nancy F. Cott, *The Bonds of Womanhood: Women's Sphere in New England, 1780–1835* (New Haven: Yale University Press, 1977), pp. 138–144;
Sharon M. Harris, ed. *American Women Writers to 1800* (New York: Oxford University Press, 1996), pp. 14–19, 31–39;
Katherine Hall Molumby, *"For Him She Wrote Exorted Sang or Pray'd": The Eighteenth Century Religious Pamphlets of Eunice Smith of Ashfield, Massachusetts* (Deerfield, Mass.: Historic Deerfield Summer Fellowship Program, 1993).

Sarah Pogson Smith

(17 September 1774 – 24 July 1870)

Kirstin R. Wilcox
Columbia University

BOOKS: *The Female Enthusiast* (Charleston, S.C.: Printed for the Author by J. Hoff, 1807);
The Power of Christianity, or Abdallah and Sabat (Charleston, S.C.: Printed by J. Hoff for the Benefit of the Ladies Benevolent and Protestant Episcopal Societies, 1814); revised as *The Arabians; or, The Power of Christianity,* Published in Aid of the Funds of the Seamen's Floating Church (Philadelphia: Herman Hooker, 1844);
Essays, Religious, Moral, Dramatic and Poetical: addressed to youth and published for a benevolent purpose (Charleston, S.C.: Printed by Archibald E. Miller, 1818);
Daughters of Eve (Schenectady, N.Y.: G. Ritchie Jr., 1826);
Zerah, The Believing Jew (New York: Printed by the New York Protestant Episcopal Press, 1837).

SELECTED PERIODICAL PUBLICATION–UNCOLLECTED: "On Gratitude," *Monthly Register, Magazine, and Review of the United States,* 2 (April 1807): 319–330.

Sarah Pogson Smith's drama, poetry, and prose explored issues in theology, history, and anthropology. Her books frequently address cross-cultural encounters between Christians and adherents of other religions, particularly Islam. As she moved up and down the eastern seaboard, she wrote almost exclusively to benefit her favorite charities. While she followed the career of her stepson, the influential reformer and philanthropist Gerrit Smith, during the last half of her life, she took little interest in abolition and woman suffrage, the causes for which he became well known.

Facts about the first fifty years of Sarah Pogson's life are scant. She was born on 17 September 1774 in Essex, England, to John Pogson and his second wife, Ann Wood Pogson. John Pogson, who had inherited several plantations in the West Indies, was renting Woodside House in Essex at the time that Sarah Pogson and most of her siblings

were born. Shortly after her birth the family moved to West Molesley, Surrey, a mile from Hampton Court. The only information about Sarah Pogson's early education comes from her 11 February 1867 letter to Gerrit Smith, in which she wrote, "My school years were at Hampton and school walks in the court gardens."

In 1793 Sarah Pogson immigrated to Charleston, South Carolina, where she lived for the next thirty years with her brother, the Reverend Milward Pogson, the sometime rector of St. James Goose Creek Parish. Though she returned to England only once, for a visit in 1830, Sarah Pogson Smith regarded herself as English until the end of her long life. "Song" in her *Essays, Religious, Moral, Dramatic and Poetical* (1818) expresses her lasting affection for "The island encircl'd by glory / My own native England."

Sarah Pogson's earliest publications were a blank-verse play, *The Female Enthusiast* (1807), and a long poem, "On Gratitude," published in the April 1807 issue of *The Monthly Register.* Published with the title-page notation that its author was "A Lady," *The Female Enthusiast* has received the most attention of any of her work. Set in France, the play freely interprets the story of Charlotte Corday, the assassin of the radical French revolutionary Jean-Paul Marat. Pogson's representation of the "enthusiastic" Charlotte Corday is remarkable. Corday stoutly asserts her political convictions to the audience, and she acts on them, undeterred by her awareness that in killing Marat she renounces "all the softness of a woman's name." Her actions result in the deaths of her father and brother and the suicide of the man who loves her; yet she is unrepentant at her execution. The play also includes a conventional courtship plot that mitigates the unhappy ending of the main plot and makes possible a denouement in which the remaining characters decide to immigrate to America. In choosing her subject Pogson may have been trying to appeal to the large French immigrant population in Charleston

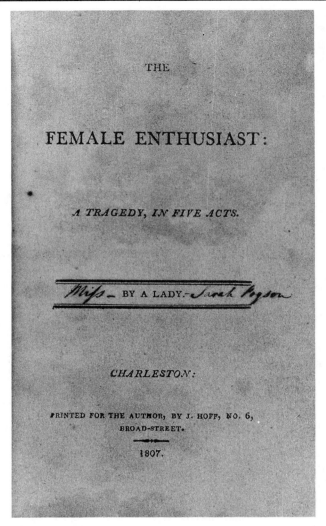

THE

FEMALE ENTHUSIAST:

A TRAGEDY, IN FIVE ACTS.

BY A LADY.

CHARLESTON:

PRINTED FOR THE AUTHOR, BY J. HOFF, NO. 6,
BROAD-STREET.

1807.

Title page for Sarah Pogson Smith's first book, a play about Charlotte Corday, the Frenchwoman who assassinated the revolutionary Jean-Paul Marat (courtesy of the South Caroliniana Library, University of South Carolina)

at the time. There is no evidence that the play was ever performed.

"On Gratitude" displays many of the themes of Pogson's later work and has been attributed to her on that basis. Manifesting her lifelong fascination with the differences between the ethical tenets of Christianity and those of other religions, it tells the story of an encounter between a young Italian man and the Moslem he befriends in his travels. As in her later play *The Young Carolinians* (1818), the plot of this poem turns on the enslavement of whites in the Middle East. The same exotic settings are featured in *The Power of Christianity, or Abdallah and Sabat* (1814), and *Zerah, The Believing Jew* (1837).

After the appearance of her first two works in 1807, Pogson is not known to have published any of

her writings for the next seven years. When she did publish her next work, and for the rest of her life, she did so for the benefit of specific charitable organizations, donating all the proceeds to the charities mentioned prominently on the title pages. *The Power of Christianity, or Abdallah and Sabat,* a long narrative poem, was published to raise money for two Charleston, South Carolina, charities: the Ladies Benevolent Society and the Protestant Episcopal Society. The lengthy subscription list for the slim volume shows that Pogson was well-connected to Charleston society. Among the prominent subscribers were the Misses Pinckney, who ordered ten copies; members of the Middleton and Izard families; and several of the Grimkés, including Sarah Grimké, later known for her abolitionist activities. The poem recounts the travels and fortunes of two

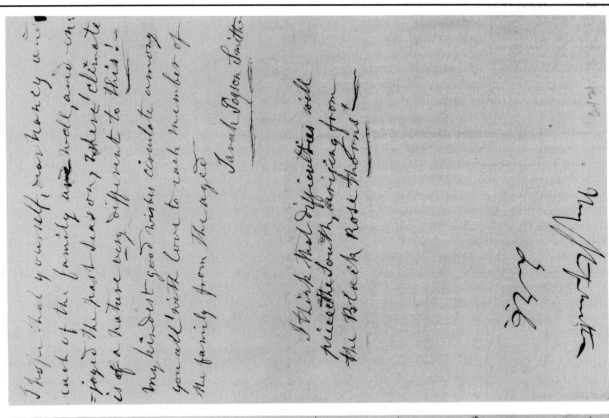

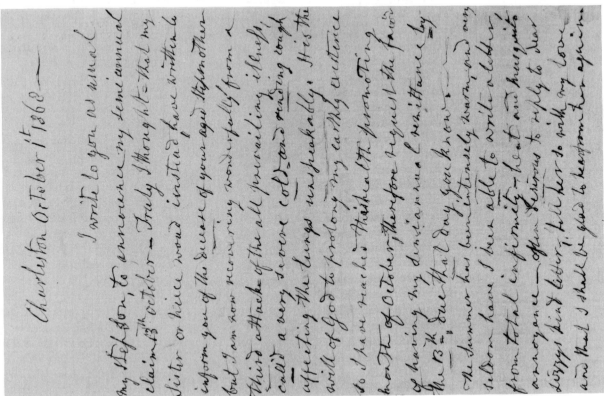

Letter from Sarah Pogson Smith to her stepson, Gerrit Smith, reminding him to make the semi-annual payment of the annuity left to her by her husband, Peter Smith (Gerrit Smith Papers, Special Collections, Syracuse University Library)

Muslim friends, one of whom converts to Christianity early in the poem. It also displays the influence of Pogson's wide-ranging reading. The preface credits Dr. Claudius Buchanan's Asiatic research for the knowledge of Hindu and Moslem religious practices displayed in the poem, and Pogson supports her narrative with footnotes to Isaac Newton and Hugh Knox and frequent biblical references.

Pogson's next publication shows the full range of her belletristic versatility with essays on religious themes, three full-length plays, and lyric and elegiac poetry. The book also reveals her ease with a variety of secular and religious themes. Incorrectly ascribed to Maria Henrietta Pinckney in many bibliographies, *Essays, Religious, Moral, Dramatic and Poetical* was published in 1818 "to contribute to the means of extricating a widow from embarrassed circumstances and declining health, occasioned by the encumbrance of debts most painfully incurred," according to Pogson's preface. There is no reason to think that the widow in question was Pogson herself, particularly as she used her maiden name when she applied for the copyright. A short but impressive subscription list documents Pogson's standing in the community, as does the dedication of the volume to Maria Middleton and of one of the plays to Edward Pinckney.

As the title suggests, the volume is an eclectic collection, which according to Pogson's preface, was intended for young readers. The seven expository essays that begin the volume (Pogson's only known nonfiction prose) are sprinkled with poems and narrative vignettes. Two of the seven essays forthrightly express the religious doctrines that inform Pogson's other literary writing: her preference for steady and uncharismatic Episcopalian practice, her conviction of the self-evident truth of Scripture, and her interest in the range of intellectual inquiry made available through scriptural study. The other five essays are first-person narratives describing the vicissitudes of upper-class individuals that the narrator encounters in her movements around Charleston and its environs. She tells two conventional stories in these essays. One is an account of a rakish young man who perceives his errors too late; the other describes two sisters whose marital choices portray the limits of male vice and virtue.

Of greatest interest are Essays VI and VII, occasioned by a journey from Charleston to a country plantation for an extended summer visit. Composed of assorted vignettes, the essays include a diatribe against revivalist camp meetings and a portrait of the odd personalities assembled at the country house. These last two essays also introduce a lengthy poetic fragment, "Hubert of Carolina," in-

volving an Indian hero and a band of escaped slaves, and the first of three plays in the volume, *The Young Carolinians, or Americans in Algiers*. Pogson presents the poem and the play as the productions of young women discussed in the essay, a device that helps her to weave these thematically unrelated texts into her narrative. She incorporates each work into the essay by describing a scene in which the putative author has been induced to entertain the assembled company by sharing her belletristic efforts, which Pogson in turn shares with her readers. The device hints at the ubiquity of women's literary creativity at the same time that it distances Pogson from her work.

The narrative frame also distances Pogson from the affirmation of slavery that is expressed in the poem and the play. In "Hubert of Carolina" some escaped slaves discuss their motives for running away and agree that they would have gladly remained in servitude if their absentee masters had lived on the plantation or if their cruel masters had been kinder. This image of benign slavery is affirmed in *The Young Carolinians*, which centers on the plight of several Americans enslaved by Algerian pirates. The Americans finally escape with the help of sympathetic Algerians and return to the United States. A monologue by the black slave Cudjo is apparently intended to forestall the obvious comparison between his situation and that of the enslaved white Carolinians. Cudjo claims that his servitude under the care of a kind mistress is preferable to impoverished freedom. Pogson accepted the practices and racist myths of Southern culture. After the Civil War and the emancipation of her own household slaves, she continued to voice her belief that slavery was beneficial for African Americans.

The other two plays in the volume are *A Tyrant's Victims*, a blank-verse play that tells the story of Agathocles, tyrant of Syracuse in the third century B.C., and *The Orphans*, set in contemporary England. A lengthy preface to *A Tyrant's Victims* announces Pogson's intention of presenting "a strong conviction, that such monsters are permitted to rule with unlimited sway, for a while, that mankind may abhor their enormities, and by contrasting the illustrious qualities of a Scipio, a Paulus Aemelius, an Alfred, a Washington, with an Agathocles, a Nero, or a Napoleon Buonoparte, love true virtue and magnanimity." *The Orphans* explores tyranny of a different sort, that of a wealthy and aristocratic English woman who casts her three orphaned sisters-in-law out of her house. They are rescued by a seafaring brother, who finds occasion along the way to heap praise on the United States. This celebration of Pogson's adopted country gives the play a patriotic flavor similar to that of *The Female Enthusiast*. There is no evidence that any of these plays were ever performed publicly. Indeed, *The Young Carolinians* is virtually impossible to stage. The stage directions call for the enactment of sea battles, and the action alternates between Carolina and Algiers with a rapidity that would require multiple set changes in the middle of acts. All three plays are of interest, however, in their display of Pogson's imaginative scope and their cross-cultural representations of class differences.

A series of lyric and elegiac poems completes the collection. Most of them celebrate the pleasures of friendship and the promise of an afterlife, and they include references to members of Pogson's social circle, designated with initials and asterisks.

As of 1821 Pogson was still living in Charleston. She was in Baltimore by 1823, when she married Peter Smith of New York after a whirlwind courtship that surprised Smith's family. His previous wife had died in 1818, leaving six grown children. At the time of his marriage to Pogson, Smith had sold his extensive business and real-estate operations to his son Gerrit, who later served in Congress and became known for his abolitionist activities. Though he had relinquished control of his business activities as a step toward retirement, Smith was rapidly building another fortune by engaging in new business ventures at the time he married Sarah Pogson. Smith's piety (he was active in distributing religious tracts) and his respect for Pogson's intelligence drew them together, but disagreements about money, his wife's independence, and his reclusiveness and devotion to business matters quickly drove them apart. As early as 1824 Smith was writing to his son of marital trouble, and Pogson Smith was spending the summer traveling through New York with her sister. The Smiths formally separated in 1826, with Smith agreeing to give his wife an annuity of $700.

Marital difficulties did not interrupt Sarah Pogson Smith's writing or interfere with her charitable activities. Despite the upheavals occasioned by the separation, she published *Daughters of Eve* in 1826. This series of thirteen poems appeared in Schenectady, New York, "in aid of the New York Female Association, for the support and instruction of the indigent deaf and dumb." Only the first of the poems in the collection discusses the difficulties of the deaf and dumb. The others address a wide variety of topics, including missionary work, contemporary women writers, biblical themes, and tales of antiquity. The lengthy subscription list for the volume includes subscribers from Boston, Salem, Philadelphia, Baltimore, Annapolis, Fredericksburg, and Charleston, but none from anywhere in New York State. Pogson Smith solicited subscriptions from her stepdaughter-in-law, the only mention of her writing in any of the Smith family correspondence. Apparently she was not successful in getting her new family involved in her charitable activities.

Though she still had family in South Carolina and England and many friends in Philadelphia, where she considered living, Pogson Smith took lodgings in New York and traveled intermittently to visit friends. She attempted several reconciliations with her husband, but none of their efforts to live together was successful. In 1830 she made a trip to England, where she visited several of her brothers and sisters. She and Smith exchanged cordial letters while she was abroad, inspiring her to return to the United States in October of that year rather than remaining until the spring as her family wished. The Smiths' last attempt at cohabitation proved unsuccessful, and there was little contact between husband and wife thereafter, although she remained in New York and was still professing wifely devotion in an 1835 letter to her husband.

In 1836 Peter Smith died. Pogson Smith agreed to his son's proposal that she renounce her dower rights in exchange for an increased annuity of $1,200. In the following year Pogson Smith's only novel was published in New York. *Zerah, The Believing Jew* was published in 1837 for the charitable purpose of "laying the cornerstone of Jesus' Church, a Protestant Church in the Valley of the Mississippi." In this historical novel Zerah is the unidentified man in the Gospels of Mark and Luke who leads the disciples to the location of the Last Supper. Zerah serves as a fictional eyewitness to the biblical and historical events that are the focus of the book. He is present in the final days of Jesus' life and at the Resurrection (recounted with much direct quotation from the Bible), the conversion of Paul, the development of the early Christians, and a sum of Roman history. The novel aroused enough interest as a pedagogical tool to warrant a second edition in South Carolina twenty years later.

Pogson Smith's financial arrangements with her stepson make it possible to compile an unusually detailed chronicle of the last decades of her life. Gerrit Smith asked her to write him twice a year to remind him to deposit her annuity; he preserved these letters, which record Pogson Smith's movements for the next thirty-four years. In the years immediately following Peter Smith's death, Pogson Smith had no fixed residence. She wrote to her stepson from Charleston, Connecticut, New York, and Philadelphia, where she published *The*

Arabians; or, the Power of Christianity in 1844. This poem is a slightly revised version of *The Power of Christianity,* with a lengthy introduction describing the Seamen's Floating Church, the charity she hoped to benefit by republishing the poem. By the outbreak of the Civil War, Pogson Smith was settled in Charleston, sharing the household of her widowed sister, Frances Blamyer. Too enfeebled to flee the city, she endured the shelling of Charleston. An increase in her annuity from her stepson and a $1,000 bequest from a deceased friend helped to ease some of the privations of the postwar years. After several years of increasingly ill health and several bouts of rheumatic fever, Pogson Smith died in Charleston on 24 July 1870.

There has been little critical attention to Pogson Smith's work aside from passing discussion of her early, best-crafted, and most overtly critical verse plays, *The Female Enthusiast* and *The Tyrant's Victims.* Her poetry, essays, novel, and prose play have gone almost entirely unnoticed, but they reveal the imaginative possibilities opened up by Smith's intellectual curiosity and her deep commitment to Episcopalian belief and practice. The issues that interested Pogson Smith most and the kinds of charitable concerns that prompted her literary activity were the impetus for a wide-ranging body of writing far removed from the domestic themes and settings conventionally associated with women writers of the nineteenth century. Her letters are strikingly open about marital politics in the nineteenth century and the significance of domestic life for a financially independent and creative woman. Pogson Smith's life and work warrant further study.

References:

Nina Baym, *American Women Writers and the Work of History, 1790–1860* (New Brunswick, N.J.: Rutgers University Press, 1995);

Ralph Volney Harlow, *Gerrit Smith: Philanthropist and Reformer* (New York: Holt, 1939);

William S. Kable, "South Carolina District Copyrights: 1794–1820," *Proof: The Yearbook of American Bibliographical and Textual Studies,* 1 (1971): 180–198;

Amelia Howe Kritzer, *Plays by Early American Women, 1775–1850* (Ann Arbor: University of Michigan Press, 1995).

Papers:

Letters by and relating to Sarah Pogson Smith are in the Gerrit Smith Papers at the Library of Syracuse University. They are available on microfilm.

Tabitha Gilman Tenney

(7 April 1762 – 2 May 1837)

Joseph Fichtelberg
Hofstra University

See also the Tenney entry in *DLB 37: American Writers of the Early Republic.*

BOOK: *Female Quixotism: Exhibited in the Romantic Opinions and Extravagant Adventures of Dorcasina Sheldon* (Boston: Printed by Isaiah Thomas & E. T. Andrews, 1801).

OTHER: *The New Pleasing Instructor: or, Young Lady's Guide to Virtue and Happiness,* edited by Tenney (Boston: Printed by Isaiah Thomas & E. T. Andrews, 1799).

During a period when the American social landscape was rapidly changing, Tabitha Gilman Tenney, like Hannah Webster Foster and Susanna Haswell Rowson, examined the relation between private and public virtue, stressing women's crucial role as guardians of family virtue and molders of republican citizens. Tenney's schoolbook, *The New Pleasing Instructor* (1799), and her novel, *Female Quixotism* (1801), are indictments of moral peril in Jeffersonian America, at a time when many Americans saw their new nation as plagued by avarice and self-interest. Tenney warned women that to give way to these vices was to strike a blow at the republic itself.

Tabitha Gilman was born and raised in Exeter, New Hampshire, where her family was active in politics. Her father, Samuel Gilman, was an old-line New Englander whose ancestors had arrived in 1638. Her mother, Lydia Robinson Giddings (or Giddinge) Gilman, was said to be forceful and educated, and she raised Tabitha, the eldest child, in an atmosphere that stressed belles lettres and religious propriety. In 1788, at the age of twenty-six, Tabitha married forty-year-old Dr. Samuel Tenney, a Revolutionary War surgeon who was returning to private practice in Exeter. In 1799 Tenney edited *The New Pleasing Instructor: or, Young Lady's Guide to Virtue and Happiness.* The text was aimed at affluent girls in the many "female academies" that had proliferated in the larger cities of the early republic, but it was also used by less wealthy students. In 1800 Samuel

Tenney was elected as a Federalist to the U.S. House of Representatives, and the Tenneys lived in Washington, D.C., for the next seven years.

Tenney's choice of works to include in *The New Pleasing Instructor* reflects moral and critical concerns of the day. Education and the diffusion of knowledge were widely heralded as the chief means of preserving that virtuous citizenry so crucial to a thriving republic. The cornerstone of that project, in turn, was mothers and wives who would raise morally scrupulous families. Tenney articulated a social role for women in which moderation, politeness, and deference would stimulate familial harmony throughout the republic.

The textbook is divided into four parts, exhibiting the principal kinds of belles lettres published in popular journals of the period. Tenney first laid out her instructional principles in a series of addresses on subjects such as grammar, geography, and music—all designed to promote virtuous conduct. She then illustrated these principles through moral tales, "elegant and entertaining letters," and excerpts from drama and poetry. Female decorum had wide-ranging cultural implications. Like the rising middle class of many Western societies, Tenney's readers were urged to equate civility with social order. A compassionate society based on the mutual exchange of affection was far superior to one driven by avarice and interest. In "Against Cruelty to Animals," for example, a sister pleads with her brother not to torture a field mouse even though the animal eats crops; allowing the female to return to "its children" would preserve the familial order of nature. Similarly, idleness is attacked not for its effect on industry but for its numbing of "the strong but fine affections of love, pity, compassion, sorrow, sympathy." Mourning is commended for the poignant immediacy of its passions. As in a scene of private grief, which touches the reader more than one of national mourning, the feelings are best cultivated when they are appropriately constrained. The filial devotion of a beautiful daughter sacrificing herself to care for an aging father is much more inspiring than an act of martial heroism, precisely because the daughter can expect no grand public acclaim. Conversely, young women who indulge the dangerous passions of self-interest weaken the lines of paternal authority. "A father and a parson may preach as they please," contends one fashionable daughter, "but are to be followed only according to the inclination of their audience."

As in *Female Quixotism* two years later, the homilies of *The New Pleasing Instructor* were meant to alert readers to threats to social order arising from their behavior. A young woman's dress should be modest and appropriate to her station; individuals should desire only an elegant sufficiency and exhibit "a just proportion to . . . fortune and rank." An Eastern tale by Susanna Rowson, "Urganda and Fatima," points to the moral by borrowing a plot line from Charles-Louis de Secondat, Baron de Montesquieu's *Persian Letters* (1721). A poor young girl who has wished to live in the greatest splendor imaginable laments getting her wish after she becomes empress to a grizzled sultan; she falls in love with a much younger suitor and is executed. In "Economy" the young reader is warned against social climbing: "to go beyond your sphere, either in dress, or in the appearance of your table, indicates a greater fault in your character than to be too much within it." In "Dialogue . . . On Different Stations in Life" Little Sally Meanwell is made to understand the wisdom of social classes: "why should not papa be as rich as any body else?" she asks. Her mother wisely responds, "Every thing ought to be suited to the station in which we live," and adds that ostentation is never appropriate to those of modest means.

"The Danger of Dissimulation" shows how even the slightest pretense poisons families. Charlotte is compelled to marry Sir James Forrest after a poorer suitor, Captain Freeman, is rejected by her father. When Freeman and Lady Forrest later meet on a brief excursion, Charlotte's muddled attempt to acknowledge but conceal her tenderness for Freeman leads to mounting complications that end in the suspicion of adultery and a duel in which Sir James kills Freeman. Sir James voices the inevitable moral, claiming that dissimulation ends in "misery and confusion." The social tragedies of deceit—including the literary deceit that produced novels—soon became the focus of Tenney's own art.

Another recurrent message in *The New Pleasing Instructor* is the moral perils of public display. In depicting characters who submit to the public gaze, Tenney explored the perils of ostentation. People who lived only for admiration were justly reprehensible. One young girl entertains the fantasy of a life of dissipation in which she becomes a gaudy butterfly spreading her charms "before admiring spectators." Another young letter writer stricken by smallpox rues the day when she lived only for superficial beauty and the esteem of "gazers in the Mall." More commendable is the virtuous gaze of a traveler who secretly witnesses the transports of a debtor restored to his family. In all cases, though, the public gaze is linked to luxury and fortune and to the wider problem of avoiding the temptations of the market, the subject of satire in *Female Quixotism*.

Female Quixotism may be divided into three episodes, each focusing on a cluster of characters. In each, suitors largely take their cues from Dorcasina Sheldon, the young woman they are courting, acting out theatrical metaphors that threaten to enmesh them as well. The first sequence involves Lysander, Patrick O'Connor, and the young scholar Philander, to whom is attached a fourth suitor, a barber who makes a brief appearance in Dorcasina's village of L___. The action is motivated by the most powerful of Dorcasina's illusions—that true love invariably arises at first sight. Replying to Lysander's sensible and prudent proposal of marriage, she sends a formal note laying out her romantic assumptions. Although she is aware of his virtues, she confesses, she has not "experienced . . . that violent emotion, at first sight of you" that marks true love.

Tenney properly scorned such passion, but she was actually more concerned with the theatrical implications of mutual spectatorship, which has unsettling implications for all social roles. Portraying the characters as obsessed with luxury and show, as if they were constantly onstage, the novel is echoing a common theme of eighteenth-century writers, who used metaphors of the theater and performance to explore the rapidly changing roles in a competitive society. The idea of actors donning and doffing disguises and of spectators sympathetic to the performance yet isolated from each other in a darkened room seemed to capture contemporary anxieties over the contradictory pressures of a new competitive order. As capitalism came to dominate everyday life, people struggled to adapt to its demands for individualism, suspicion, and constant change even as they professed to be drawn together by the ties of cooperation and concern. The eyeing and role-playing with which *Female Quixotism* abounds is more than simple satire: it represents Tenney's attempt to examine the consequences of possessive individualism.

As role-playing becomes ever more elaborate in the novel, the fictions generated by Dorcasina and her suitors acquire a life of their own, threatening to spin out of control. The shrewd O'Connor at once grasps the rules of the game, although he initially applies them to the wrong target. Glimpsing an abandoned woman he takes to be Dorcasina, he "lifted up his eyes and appeared lost in astonishment," frozen like a statue. When O'Connor finally meets Dorcasina, his seduction unfolds as an elaborate series of fixed glances, languishing gazes, and eyes straining for every lingering trace of his departing lover. When he urges Dorcasina to intercede for him with her skeptical father, he manages a look of such "extreme tenderness" as to enter her soul. How greatly Dorcasina is devoted to him is indicated by her early avowal that not even the appearance of a real ghost could keep her from meeting him in the grove.

Yet the shadowy line between reality and illusion becomes increasingly difficult to maintain. When Dorcasina, eager to comfort her lover after he is injured in a late-night tryst, disguises herself to visit him at his inn, she is shrewdly observed by a servant, who accosts her as a loose woman and sets the neighborhood boys on her. Her misfortune merely complements that of O'Connor, who, intending to meet her late in her garden, is mistaken for a thief and beaten. As stratagem is heaped on stratagem, the weight of his fictions becomes so great that he must precipitately leave. Yet his influence persists in a lengthening train of miscalculations. Trying to recapture her lost affair, Dorcasina has Betty dress up in Mr. Sheldon's clothing and impersonate O'Connor in the grove. There Betty is beset by the family servants who take her for a thief, is inundated in a storm while hiding from further persecution, and is chased by a white cat that she imagines to be a fearful specter. Although the narrator confines such superstitious terrors to the most gullible characters, they are like the more refined illusions in which all eventually participate. While Dorcasina fashions one community through her unfailing benevolence, she helps to distort another through an ardent, if muddled, theatricality.

The infection is evident in Philander's manipulation of the barber Puff. After toying with Dorcasina—once again allowing that the mere sight of her has robbed him of all repose—Philander tricks the fatuous Puff into representing him in the grove. Stimulated, like O'Connor, by the prospect of possessing her fortune, Puff unsuccessfully accosts her, is attacked by Betty, and takes his revenge by tying up and kidnapping the two women. Almost overlooked in the hijinks is the characters' rootless isolation. Philander is spirited into town, toys briefly with Dorcasina, and is spirited out again. Puff barely arrives in the area when, in an attempt to hush up the entire affair, Mr. Sheldon pays him to

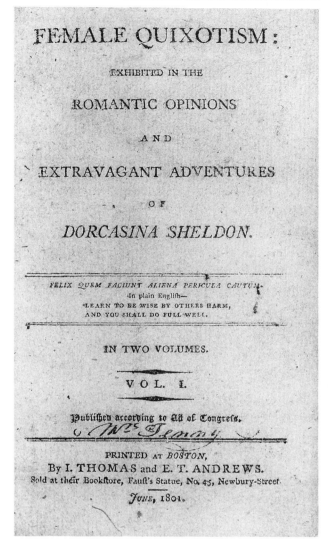

Title page for Tabitha Tenney's only novel, a satire on the breakdown of traditional American values (courtesy of the Lilly Library, Indiana University)

leave. Paradoxically only Dorcasina, with her deeply distorted attachments, preserves something like genuine feeling, lamenting in a supposititious farewell letter to her father that she should be "torn from the best and tenderest parent that ever lived." It is fitting that her final disillusionment comes through the eye: a scene of public humiliation in which O'Connor, apprehended for theft, is whipped in a Philadelphia square. Although the rogue is justly isolated and punished, his lover also withdraws, succumbing to a fit that keeps her confined for some time. Restoration to her tender father prepares her only for renewed despair.

If the home is the center of moral authority in *Female Quixotism,* that integrity is increasingly threatened in book two as various boarders bring illusion to Dorcasina's doorstep. The irritant is Captain Barry and his servant, refugees from Gen. Arthur St. Clair's dramatic wilderness defeat by the Indians in 1791. Certainly there is cause to fault Dorcasina's extravagant benevolence and her equally extravagant assumption that her charity guarantees marriage. Yet the presentation of Barry suggests that the captain is theatrical, drawing his dramatic power from external conditions as much as from Dorcasina's mind. St. Clair took his troops into Ohio with hopes of quick success. Instead he suffered the most humiliating defeat of any American officer to that time, a defeat that precipitated national anguish. Spokesmen lamented the spilled "blood of our defenceless frontier people," sacrificed to "savages" who "scattered their flesh to fatten the unclean birds of the wilderness." A Philadelphia paper noted how "universally lamented" were the soldiers' early deaths, a fate that "fills our hearts with sorrow." Tenney imported that pathos to the village of L___, where Barry, barely healed from life-threatening injuries, collapses by the Sheldon house, with his wounds reopening in the midst of a January storm. Tenney thus presented Dorcasina with the exact sort of romantic situation she is accused of manufacturing: can she be blamed for succumbing to the national obsession?

Dorcasina plays the role to the hilt, bedecking herself for one dinner in such hopelessly bad taste that she becomes a caricature of sentimental excess. Yet the scrupulous Barry is not entirely innocent in the matter either. Having fantasized that the daughter of such an imposing man as Mr. Sheldon would be well worth his attention, he is chagrined to find her old enough to be his mother and covers his embarrassment by allowing his servant, James, to impersonate him. Thus follows a familiar train of circumstances in which Betty, Dorcasina, and the household servants are caught up in artifice. At one point, for example, James must fake an assault on Betty to cover his tracks, causing the servants to think that ghosts were responsible. When James finally convinces Dorcasina to elope and she is disabused of her illusions, the satire turns almost savage—the woman shivering and, after the carriage overturns, making her way alone to a neighboring cottage. It is more difficult to fault her this time because her motives are so utterly unselfish and the deception has been so assured. Dorcasina may still be absorbed in narcissistic fantasy, but a predatory world seems to support her. As her home becomes more vulnerable, the boundaries between integrity and deception also seem to dissolve.

Age also makes Dorcasina vulnerable, as her father becomes almost desperately pragmatic. When a Philadelphia merchant named Cumberland solicits her hand and pays a visit, his lack of poetic fire makes her rejection of him far more palatable than was the case with Lysander. Referring to his courtship as "business"—a term that Dorcasina rightly labels "mercantile"—Cumberland impatiently weathers her rejection and submits to the trickery of the family slave, Scipio, before storming off. Though Dorcasina is somewhat justified in resisting him, the failure of the affair marks a poignant moment, one in which her desire to assert herself is hampered not only by her fatuousness but also by the incursions and fantasies of others. Despite her rejection of Cumberland, for example, Scipio keeps him lingering on by practicing the same sort of masquerade between the suitor and Betty as James practised with Dorcasina. Illusion has now become so natural to the Sheldon household that there seems to be little difference between Dorcasina's principles and the infatuations of those around her.

The dividing line becomes even more blurred after Mr. Sheldon's death, when Dorcasina must assert a thwarted independence. Imagining her common servant, John Brown, to be a gentleman in disguise, she becomes increasingly taken in by the disguises that surround her. Once again resisting all advice from her prudent neighbors, the Stanlys, Dorcasina engages in an elaborate domestic charade, not only dressing herself in youthful fashion but also urging Brown to dress in her father's clothes. So desperate does the illusion appear that the Stanlys can think to combat it only with more comprehensive illusions that seem to confirm Dorcasina's most deeply held beliefs. When Brown resists Scipio's pranks, which turn Mr. Sheldon's old room into a haunted chamber, young Harriot Stanly decides to don a costume as outlandish as any worn by Dorcasina. Finding her father's old military uniform and painting her face, Harriot becomes Montague, a dashing soldier smitten by one glimpse of Dorcasina. Although she connives with Scipio and brandishes her sword at every opportunity, Harriot succeeds merely in delaying, not in halting, Dorcasina's intended wedding with Brown. At this point Harriot draws in her father, who had solemnly promised Mr. Sheldon to look after Dorcasina. Seeing no other expedient, the two decide to kidnap her, transport her to one of Stanly's farms, and keep her there until the danger with Brown has passed. Although there is a certain ironic justice in answering Dorcasina's illusions with a more powerful one of their own, they also demonstrate a cynical cruelty in reinforcing the fantasies they oppose. However Dorcasina is deluded, there remains a genuine pathos in her protest against being torn away from all she finds familiar as the "unfeeling wretch" ties a handkerchief over her mouth and forces her into a coach. Once again illusion isolates her; yet her imprisonment far from home exposes Dorcasina to further and more sinister manipulation. While the Stanlys had hoped to administer a bracing tonic for her disease, they succeed only in worsening the symptoms.

As Dorcasina lingers for months on the farm without any word from Mr. Stanly, she becomes, for the first time in the novel, a figure of potentially tragic depth. In a poignant letter to the supposed Montague, she charges him with the most un-American of crimes, urging that her further "detention" will not win her love, and entreating him "to grant me my liberty." At this point Tenney introduces the last and most sinister impostor in the novel, Seymore, a wastrel from South Carolina who, having resided in France, has absorbed all its corrupting radicalism. Setting his sights on Dorcasina, Seymore not only insinuates himself into her company but also into the nearby village, where he is taken to be a worthy schoolteacher who lived with a clergyman, attended church, and was universally regarded as "a man of piety." Seymore finally discloses the truth to Dorcasina, declaring that she has displayed "Ridiculous vanity" in imagining that an aging woman could still make conquests and asserting that suitors were only after her money. Why this plain talk should succeed where all other instances of it have failed is not entirely clear—unless Dorcasina needs to hear truth from the mouth of an impostor. Nevertheless her recovery also exposes a more serious social problem that may not be so simply cured. In a culture that promotes the romance of social mobility and unrestrained choice, the modest fantasies of an elderly maiden may be the least threatening of all forms of empowerment.

When Tenney completed her book in Washington, D.C., early in 1801, she did so as a political outsider. Jefferson had won the presidential election of 1800, and the Federalists wasted no time in predicting disaster, playing on many of the latent class tensions that had long marked their contest with Jefferson's Democratic Republicans. He was widely charged with rousing "the mechanics of this country" into "paroxysms of rage" and with encouraging "the general ascendency of the worthless, the dishonest, the rapacious, the vile, the merciless, and the ungodly." Such shadowy figures stalked *Female Quixotism* as well. Beneath its mockery of fashionable reading is a far more subtle and serious plea for a Federalist ethos that was fast receding before the vigor of Jeffersonian democracy. Tenney not only

expressed her uneasiness through the imagery of class conflict but also trained her sights on the market revolution that was transforming all class relations. Her novel is thus a conservative protest against an emerging liberal order.

To explore this aspect of the novel it is necessary to recall some of the links between sentiment and the market. Although the language of sentiment is often thought to be far removed from the cold calculations of the marketplace, the eighteenth-century market may have actually promoted a certain kind of humanitarian sensibility. Market relations involve trust in the promises of associates—promises that allow traders to make extended calculations over time. In the late eighteenth century the complex network of such promises in the international marketplace brought the world much closer than ever before, allowing individuals to be ardently concerned about conditions far distant from them. Benevolent undertakings such as the antislavery movement were greatly stimulated by market behavior. At the same time, however, the orderly stimulations of the market promoted other more private and less predictable effects, encouraging the expectation that not only economic transactions, but ultimately all interactions, would be the occasion for infinite gain or infinite loss. Through this "threshold mentality," one's expectations for reward and deficit became ever present and as boundless as the market itself. The almost limitless hopes of a rapidly expanding marketplace, stimulated by a consumer revolution in the late eighteenth century, which brought a new fluidity to social relations, concerned many conservatives of the period. Tenney was perhaps unusual in using the suspect form of the novel as the means to reflect on this wider array of social problems.

Viewed from this angle, *Female Quixotism* presents the reader with a series of structural alternatives, all devolving on the explosive new relations unleashed by the Jeffersonian revolution of 1800. Despite her frivolity, Dorcasina is not the helpless plaything of romantic urges. Rather, she is a woman of great integrity and considerable social power threatened by a predatory milieu. The novel confronts her with a series of stark choices: How can she honor the promises she makes while she is subject to and even cultivates such a riot of passions? How can she manage a handsome estate when she is surrounded by deception, wracked by insomnia, and exposed to a relentlessly competitive and vicious social order? On the one hand, the novel presents the reader with a relatively stable, if fractious, paternal estate marked by loyalty, civility, and benevolence. On the other hand, just beyond the bounds of the Sheldon and Stanly property lies a jostling democracy full of social climbers, misfits, and impostors. Between them, as if in suspended animation, stands Dorcasina herself, a character who, like every sentimental heroine facing marriage, must negotiate that competitive world with only the equipment of the patriarchal one. The great irony of the novel is that, with her utter absorption in the fantasy world of fiction, Dorcasina has already incorporated the threshold mentality of the market, even as she feebly attempts to oppose it. Ultimately, it is left to others to preserve the older patrician world from the assaults of a new mentality.

The essential humanity of that older world comes through early in the novel. Despite Dorcasina's vagaries, she is pious—so pious that her father's estate becomes a magnet for the poor. Anyone "for many miles round" can find relief there, "for it was her invariable rule to send none away empty hand." Recognizing his own youthful enthusiasm in his daughter's conduct, the sober Mr. Sheldon permits an extravagance in charity that he otherwise seeks to banish from his life.

That benevolent stewardship of the poor is part of a wider pattern of conduct captured in the equation between benevolence and promise keeping. No matter how outrageously Dorcasina conducts herself, she sees her behavior as part of a sacred code whereby a lover's glances are as binding as a father's exactions. Promise keeping in *Female Quixotism* takes two forms. Like some latter-day Cordelia, Dorcasina is unafraid to act according to her bond, even if it works to the sacrifice of her happiness. Indeed the record of some of her courtships is little more than a sequence of increasingly restricting promises. For example, when her ailing father misses her late one evening and discovers she has been in the grove, he extracts a promise that she not venture out at night. Later, when Mr. Sheldon discovers her interest in O'Connor, she must promise not to marry without her father's consent, just as she promises O'Connor to marry no one else. That promise becomes a source of both rectitude and doubt when Dorcasina is tempted by Philander, and she insists that she was bound never to admit another love. So ardent is this rectitude that she refuses to be swayed even as evidence mounts against O'Connor, as she maintains that all attacks on his character are plots by his enemies. Although the narrator suggests that such reactions are signs of her fatal weakness for sentimental fiction, they may also be signs of a rare strength. It is not by accident that her subsequent affairs all seem to gather in a noose of conflicting promises. Indeed, in one sense Dorcasina is entirely correct: the clamorous and self-seeking world beyond her estate conspires against

such conscientious promise keeping, just as O'Connor exacts vengeance on Mr. Sheldon through Dorcasina's vow to remain single—a vow she ultimately keeps. Dorcasina is too good, as well as too foolish, for the world.

In another sense, though, her courtships are the model of worldly, market-driven behavior. Like any conscientious entrepreneur, Dorcasina is punctual, insists on a reciprocal punctuality, and suffers when such arrangements are breached. Her meetings with O'Connor in the grove and later in the house proceed like clockwork, and even their clandestine interviews come off "punctually at the hour" prescribed. It is a quality Philander recognizes and exploits, promising Puff that he will arrange the time of an early meeting with her and warning him not to make her wait. This advice is both prudent and shrewd, of course, since it stimulates a woman craving constant reinforcement. Yet it is also, once again, a recognition of an essential strength. No matter how arrogant are the rogues besetting her, all must acknowledge that Dorcasina injects a vital order into an otherwise riotous world. It is the same passion for punctuality that Harriot Stanly, in the guise of Montague, exploits when she makes Dorcasina pledge to wait for one month before publishing the banns on her marriage to John Brown. The woman who takes such stock in the printed word may also be expected to value her own.

Yet Dorcasina's rectitude also conceals an irony. Promise keeping was one of the engines of a market threatening Federalist hegemony—the predatory forces that Dorcasina confronts in making her marriage choice. The operation of the market vastly expanded the venues for sensibility, a sensibility that endangers the heroine. Although Dorcasina's benevolence and punctuality suggest the expansive self-discipline required of market participants, her exquisite sensibility implies a fatal exposure, as if she cannot defend herself against the demands of the world. While the market requires punctuality and order, it also requires an openness to others quite close to the generous sympathy Dorcasina displays. As one Federalist orator later put it, commerce carried the mind "out of its own little circle for a while, . . . kindl[ing] a sympathetic concern for the remotest borderer or seaman on the ocean." The sympathy that Adam Smith, in *The Theory of Moral Sentiments* (1759), saw as an indispensable moral tool was also the lubricant in a market-driven world.

Given the ever-expanding influence of the market, Dorcasina's sympathy knows no bounds. Though she may be manipulated by knaves and fortune hunters, she nevertheless feels for the plight of an Irish vagrant, a captain retired in disgrace from the defeat of St. Clair's army, and migrants from Rhode Island and Carolina. Perhaps the greatest conflict between patriarchal benevolence and market responsiveness comes in her reaction to Captain Barry, whom Dorcasina so seductively nurses, claiming to feel "a thrill of pleasure" from hand to heart as she exchanges delicious emotions. The Stanlys stare in disbelief as she sympathizes not only with the squirming Barry but also with his muddy dog; yet the extremity of her behavior may mask an uncomfortable reality. Federalists had long been insisting on a culture of deference wherein, to cite *The Federalist* (1787–1788), citizens ought to be "knit together . . . by so many cords of affection" that they would "live together as members of the same family." With claimants invading her estate, Dorcasina is forced to exploit those sentiments in unanticipated and dangerous ways. To read about the passions of lovers had once been her particular delight, but falling victim to the importunities of strangers now exposes Dorcasina to the distressing urgencies of a contentious liberal order. The fact that she could not prudently express benevolence and affection may be as much an indictment of the times as of her own judgment.

The toll that Dorcasina's mixed duties exacts may be seen in two linked responses. As the suitors for her fortune become more numerous and demanding, she finds the discipline of her paternal estate increasingly affected. One consequence is that her internal order is disrupted, and sleeping becomes almost impossible. When she receives a note concerning O'Connor's pursuit of a loose woman whom he has taken for Dorcasina, she stays up the whole night awaiting a meeting with him. She has equal trouble sleeping after Scipio roughs up O'Connor in the garden, after Barry arrives, after her elopement with Barry's servant, and when she meets Cumberland. Such frequent bouts are in one sense a widening of the satire against overt sentimentalism, but the fact that nearly every character in the novel suffers the same symptoms—including the sober Barry and Mr. Sheldon—suggests that the problem is deeper. The universal insomnia may also be understood as a sign of the threshold state into which market incursions have thrown the principals in the novel—a sense of being suspended between powerful but unattainable alternatives. Just as Mr. Sheldon, on returning from the grove after discovering O'Connor's lovemaking, faints at his own doorstep, so characters are overcome by a variety of emotions so intense that even to entertain them exacts a severe penalty. What so tortures such characters is often the prospect of infinite gain and infinite loss.

Dorcasina focuses these conflicts. When O'Connor woos her, he recounts how his initial siege in the grove was attended by "vain hopes, and disappointed expectations," but after one glimpse of her he discovered a woman "a thousand times" more charming than his fantasy. Similarly, Philander imparts that Dorcasina has given him "the bitterest pangs and the sweetest joys," and Barry imagines that the heiress to the Sheldon estate must have "a thousand attractions." That expectation, innocent enough in a man of Barry's stature, exposes the crucial link between threshold psychology and the alluring world of commodities that Dorcasina represents. For Barry she displays herself in all the fashions of the day, choosing and rejecting "a white lustring jacket; then a purple satin; then a blue, and lastly a pink." Later she wears an elaborate jacket and skirt of blue satin with silver trim, covered by a wrapper of embroidered India muslin. Her extravagant dress is the sign of a far more subtle and extensive market penetration, one in which luxuries had become commonplace. Dorcasina's voracious desire to read every novel she can lay her hands on is matched by John Brown's fascination for her father's wardrobe of fine coats, linen underclothes, silk stockings, and holland shirts, which he spreads out on the bed while overcome with "boundless" joy. Even the humble farmhouse to which Dorcasina is led after being kidnapped has tea and butter, and there seems to be little difference between the modest desires of commoners and the more ardent speculations of their betters. All are caught in a dizzying web of commodities.

Threats to control take on other, starker attitudes long associated with conservative depictions of the market. Some of the most disturbing offenses in the novel involve the desires of inferiors to displace their betters. When Puff, duped by Philander, imagines that he will soon wed Dorcasina and control her estate, he immediately begins to insult his customers and narrowly escapes being beaten. Betty coldly dismisses her mistress when she imagines herself to be the object of Cumberland's attentions, only to regret her impertinence later. John Brown is the most serious and absurd of social climbers—an illiterate rustic who spends many a sleepless night imagining how to turn himself into Dorcasina's ideal gentleman. "Better stick to your own kind, John," Betty warns him, but John insists on clothing himself in the finery of a higher class and is humiliated for his pretensions when one of Scipio's tricks forces him to crawl back home in his underclothes. When one adds to his depredations those of the outright knaves O'Connor and Seymore, it becomes apparent that the target of *Female Quixotism* is more than one woman's fanciful imagination. It is an indictment of a culture prone to stimulate such excesses in almost all its subjects.

The device Tenney most often used to convey this cultural infection is disguise. Writers of this period were preoccupied with the need for social masks, a consequence, in part, of a market order that demanded increasingly plastic responses to its ever-changing conditions. Appropriately, then, nearly all of the characters in the novel, from the sober Stanlys to the most ardent carpetbaggers, embrace deception and disguise. Here Tenney gave full expression to the menaces of a surging democracy. O'Connor, the son of an Irish steward, was successively scholar, gambler, highwayman, and convict before alighting in America as a pretended gentleman. Seymore is even more sinister, having defrauded several creditors in Charleston before leaving his wife and children for Philadelphia, where he masqueraded as a pious scholar. Appropriately, he is captured while disguised as a woman. Indeed, in one regard *Female Quixotism* seems to be little more than an account of the donning and doffing of disguises. A short catalogue included Dorcasina's masquerading as Betty, Betty's masquerading as O'Connor, the village scholar's masquerading as Philander, Puff's masquerading as Philander's spurned lover, James's masquerading as his master, and Harriot Stanly's masquerading as Montague. From one perspective such universal role-playing serves to reinforce the romantic excesses from which Dorcasina suffers; yet the excesses are clearly not confined to her. They suggest a wider pattern of irresistible deception that threatens to overwhelm even the benevolent Stanlys, who can no longer maintain a deferential social order. The lean and hungry Seymores of the world have come to dominate the landscape, further isolating Dorcasina's embattled benevolence. Such a character, unconscious of the market forces in which she participates, makes the saddest and most ridiculous of displays.

Female Quixotism proved popular enough to warrant several reprintings. A second edition was published in Newburyport, Massachusetts, in 1808, and others followed in Boston in 1825, 1829, and 1841. When Samuel Tenney retired from Congress in 1807, the childless couple remained in Washington, D.C., until his death in 1816. Thereafter, Tenney returned to Exeter, where she died on 2 May 1837.

Like *The New Pleasing Instructor*, *Female Quixotism* attempted to oppose a rigorous standard of female propriety against a rapidly changing world. Whereas the school text inculcated virtue through an interplay of dramatic homilies, the novel revealed the strains of a nation undergoing rapid modernization, one in which conservative elites were being rapidly displaced. Conservative readers turned to satire to restore their sense of moral order, and Tenney provided them a vigorous platform for their concerns. *Female Quixotism* remains one of the most significant social critiques of the early national period.

References:

Donna R. Bontatibus, "The Seduction Novel of the Early Nation: A Call for Socio-Political Reform," dissertation, University of Rhode Island, 1995;

Herbert Ross Brown, *The Sentimental Novel in America, 1789–1860* (Durham, N.C.: Duke University Press, 1940);

Sevda Caliskan, "The Coded Language of *Female Quixotism*," *Studies in American Humor,* 3, no. 2 (1995): 23–35;

Cathy N. Davidson, *Revolution and the Word: The Rise of the Novel in America* (New York: Oxford University Press, 1986), pp. 186–192;

Linda Frost, "The Body Politic in Tabitha Tenney's *Female Quixotism*," *Early American Literature,* 32 (1997): 113–134;

Sharon M. Harris, "Lost Boundaries: The Use of the Carnivalesque in Tabitha Tenney's *Female Quixotism*," in *Speaking the Other Self: American Women Writers,* edited by Jeanne Campbell Reesman (Athens: University of Georgia Press, 1997), pp. 213–228;

Sally C. Hoople, "The Spanish, English, and American Quixotes," *Annales Cervantinos,* 22 (1984): 119–142;

Hoople, "Tabitha Tenney: Female Quixotism," dissertation, Fordham University, 1984;

Lillie Deming Loshe, *The Early American Novel, 1789–1830* (New York: Columbia University Press, 1907), pp. 19–20;

Candace K. Matzke, "'The Woman Writes as if the Devil Was in Her': A Rhetorical Approach to Three Early American Novels," dissertation, University of Oregon, 1983;

Cynthia J. Miecznikowski, "The Parodic Mode and the Patriarchal Imperative: Reading the Female Reader(s) in Tabitha Tenney's *Female Quixotism*," *Early American Literature,* 25 (1990): 34–45;

Michael Thomas Newman, "Variations on a Theme: 'Don Quixote' in Eighteenth-Century English Literature," dissertation, Georgia State University, 1996;

Henri Petter, *The Early American Novel* (Columbus: Ohio State University Press, 1971), pp. 46–59, 300–301.

Caroline Matilda Warren Thayer

(21 February 1785 – 1844)

Mark L. Kamrath
University of Central Florida

BOOKS: *The Gamesters; or, Ruins of Innocence. An Original Novel, Founded in Truth,* 1 volume (Boston: Printed for Thomas & Andrews by David Carlisle, 1805); republished as *Conrade; or the Gamesters. A Novel Founded on Facts,* 2 volumes (London: Lane, Newman & Co., 1806);

Religion Recommended to Youth, in a Series of Letters, Addressed to a Young Lady. To Which are Added, Poems on Various Occasions (New York: Published by Thomas Bakewell, printed by Abraham Paul, 1817; Dublin: R. Napper for the Methodist Book-Room, 1820);

Letter to the Members of the Methodist Episcopal Church in the City of New York, Stating the Reasons of the Writer for Withdrawing from that Church and the Circumstances of Her Subsequent Dismission from the Wesleyan Seminary (New York: Printed for the Publisher, 1821; London: T. Goydner, 1824);

First Lessons in the History of the United States: Compiled for the Use of the Junior Classes in Joseph Hoxie's Academy (New York: D. Fanshaw, 1823);

Poems, on Various Occasions (Ravenna, Ohio: Office of the Ohio Star, 1840).

OTHER: Harriet Muzzy, *Poems, Moral and Sentimental by Mrs. Harriet Muzzy,* compiled, with contributions, by Thayer (New York: F. W. Ritter, 1821);

"Ode," in *An Oration, Delivered in the First Baptist Meeting-house, in Providence, at the Celebration, February 23, A.D. 1824, in Commemoration of the Birth-day of Washington, and in Aid of the Cause of the Greeks,* by Solomon Drowne (Providence, R.I.: Printed by Brown & Danforth, 1824).

SELECTED PERIODICAL PUBLICATIONS— UNCOLLECTED: Antoinette Legroing-La Maisonneuve, "Female Education," translated by Thayer, *New-York Mirror, and Ladies' Literary Gazette,* 21 February 1824, pp. 236–237;

"Letter from Mrs. C. M. Thayer," *Methodist Magazine,* 8 (February 1825): 229–235.

Caroline Matilda Warren Thayer's novel and religious writings reveal changing attitudes toward American republicanism and the role of "virtue" in an atmosphere of liberal individualism at the end of the eighteenth century and the beginning of the nineteenth century. Her themes are contemporary cultural issues, including authorship and novel reading, male conduct and female morals and manners, domestic violence and dueling, the relationship of familial duty, class or social rank, and the politics of nation building. In addition her letters and other writings offer revealing insights into Calvinistic doctrines of the time and testify to her leadership in educating youth and improving public attitudes toward female education. They not only call attention to prevailing attitudes toward private education and issues of religious and civil liberty but also chart one woman's commitment to—and questioning of—early Methodism and rival secular and religious ideologies as they existed in early-nineteenth-century rural and urban America.

While biographical information is limited, records show that Thayer was born in Watertown, Massachusetts, on 21 February 1785 and educated in the Boston area. She was one of several children born to William Warren and Rebecca Roby Hathaway Warren and was the granddaughter of Gen. Joseph Warren, a hero in the Battle of Bunker Hill. After living briefly in New Hampshire, she married Dr. James Thayer of Rehoboth, Massachusetts, on 10 April 1809 in Sutton, Massachusetts. The Thayers appear to have settled in the wilderness of west central New York. Remarks from her early works and later elegies indicate that three infant children, two of whom were girls, died sometime before 1814. It is not clear whether the death of the first child on or before 15 November 1809 indicates that she had a miscarriage or that she was already pregnant when she married. She had two more sons, Henry and Fisher D., before her husband's death at an early age.

Republicanism, as a set of cultural values that led to the American Revolution in 1776, was in a state of crisis by the end of the eighteenth century. Instead of promoting a rational commonwealth that honored self-sacrifice and civic community, the republican model of politics increasingly favored self-interest and values that were seen as materialistic and licentious. Amid this development of emerging liberal values and the decline of patriarchical authority, Protestant moralism and Scottish common-sense philosophy combined with evolving commercial values to form a bourgeois ethic of self-control. In response to this ideological shifting, republican mothers increasingly sought to inculcate in their families republican principles such as duty to parents and country, prudence, benevolence, and justice, thereby preserving the virtue and morality of the new nation. In this cultural atmosphere views of narrative fiction also began to change. Instead of being viewed as evil or undermining the status quo, novels, if they were sufficiently didactic, were increasingly seen as aids to the cause of virtue. The author of such novels was therefore fulfilling a patriotic duty.

Written under her maiden name, Thayer's first publication, *The Gamesters; or, Ruins of Innocence. An Original Novel, Founded in Truth* (1805), is a sentimental novel that attempted to counter perceived threats to the status quo by gambling or gaming. As Thayer noted in her preface, many fashionable foibles of the day were linked to novel writing, and publications by women were subject to close scrutiny. Although she expressed concerns that her work would be judged unfairly by prejudiced critics, she combined instruction and amusement to promote human "feeling" or "sympathy" and to discourage gaming and its pernicious effects on domestic life. Like many writers in her day, she was influenced by Laurence Sterne and Hannah More and believed that if her novel were devoted to the cause of "virtue," it would be regarded as a useful "moral lesson" in the service of God, family, and country. Indeed, like Hannah Foster's *The Coquette* (1797), Thayer's work seems to draw on truth or lived experience in an attempt to distance itself from the sensationalism of earlier novels.

Thayer's focus on the "manners of an American village" outside a major metropolitan area in Massachusetts anticipates elements of rural life in Caroline Kirkland's *A New Home—Who'll Follow?* (1839). Thayer's novel begins by briefly sketching the education Leander Anderson received from his parents and the manner in which later circumstances led to his spiritual and social ruin. Underscoring the family's commitment to moral virtue, the novel relates how Leander's parents had married for love, not the conventional ideals of wealth and beauty,

and how his upbringing had enabled him to return from the university "uncorrupted in his morals." While the deaths of his mother and then his father make him rich, they also make him prey to his libertine classmate, Edward Somerton. It becomes clear early on that Somerton's moral education was deficient and that because he had no parents and no "culture of the heart," he felt a moral inferiority and the need to reduce Leander to his level. The novel also establishes that a second, though no less important, motive for plotting against Leander is Somerton's own self-interest—his desire for financial gain and his reluctance to "improve his fortune by ordinary methods."

The orphaned Leander is cared for by his father's brother-in-law, whose two daughters, Harriot and Eliza, introduce Leander to Amelia Stanhope, a woman with whom he falls in love and later marries. During this period he participates in lively evening discussions about the role of the family in educating youth in republican principles, and he earnestly listens to the reformation tale of Old Williamson, a former gardener for Leander's uncle. Thayer's blending of familial imagery and political discourse in the early parts of the novel is especially interesting. By having Leander declare himself to be of "Neither party" and say that "We all sprang from the same common parent, we are all members of one common family," Thayer used romantic and didactic discourse in ways that address the increasing political fighting and self-interest of her time. Although her comparison of a republican model of family and order with a global or universal one seems to comment on contemporary political faction, it is not always clear, especially later in the story, whether she was endorsing a particular brand of political liberalism or promoting "moderation" and defending the status quo.

After Leander eventually moves to Philadelphia to study law, his foes intercept letters to his fiancée, Amelia, and spread rumors about her moral and physical subversion. Amelia is kidnapped and brutalized by Somerton's friend Evander Ebbert, but she is eventually rescued by Tom Tarpulin, an honest sailor who returns her to her parents. Leander gains his inheritance from his uncle. No sooner does he receive it, however, than Somerton takes advantage of Leander's passion for gambling and causes him to neglect his duty as a husband, father, and friend. With the assistance of his uncle and, later, the moral example of Old Williamson, Leander momentarily regains the "path of virtue," but he eventually lets his passions rule, slips back into the "slavery of vice," and is ruined financially. He falls further into moral degeneracy and abuses his wife.

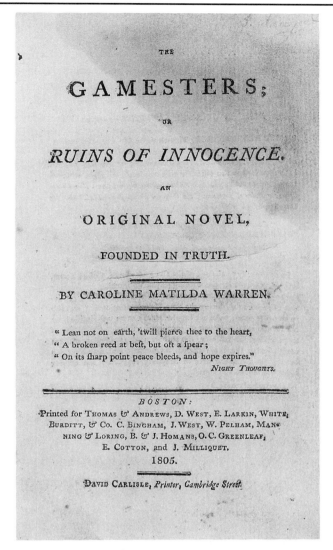

THE

GAMESTERS;

OR

RUINS OF INNOCENCE.

AN

ORIGINAL NOVEL,

FOUNDED IN TRUTH.

BY CAROLINE MATILDA WARREN.

" Lean not on earth, 'twill pierce thee to the heart,
" A broken reed at beſt, but oft a ſpear;
" On its ſharp point peace bleeds, and hope expires."
NIGHT THOUGHTS.

BOSTON:
Printed for THOMAS & ANDREWS, D. WEST, E. LARKIN, WHITE,
BURDITT, & Co. C. BINGHAM, J. WEST, W. PELHAM, MAN-
NING & LORING, B. & J. HOMANS, O. C. GREENLEAF,
E. COTTON, and J. MILLIQUET.
1805.

DAVID CARLISLE, *Printer, Cambridge Street.*

*Title page for Caroline Thayer's only novel, a warning against
the immorality of gambling (courtesy of the Lilly Library,
Indiana University)*

Finally, after Somerton ruins Eliza, Leander recognizes his friend's corrupt nature, becomes overwhelmed by guilt and despair, and commits suicide by jumping into a nearby river. Thayer's seemingly apologetic view of suicide at the end of the novel has been construed by some readers as morally or theologically compromising. Other readers view it as evidence of a marked tension between early-nineteenth-century Calvinistic doctrine and increasingly liberal values.

While the main plot concerns Leander's struggle to avoid gambling and increasing financial debt and his growing recognition of the way he has mistreated his family, the story of Old Williamson and several related subplots underscore this theme. Old Williamson, for example, appreciates Leander's willingness to listen to his tale and admires Leander's capacity for "feeling," especially in light of his rank and the attitudes then fashionable toward the lower class. Old Williamson's history with dissolute companions and his drift from virtue serve as a moral guidance and prompt Leander not only to be "all sensibility" but also to act benevolently, especially toward the less fortunate. (Other subplots involve Somerton's seduction and ruin of Herbert's daughter Eliza and Ebbert's seduction of Celestia, the daughter of Old Williamson, who is also driven to commit suicide, bringing shame to her family.) One of the few redeeming parts of the novel concerns Lorenzo, Amelia's brother, who marries Harriet and whose enterprising and industrious ways enable him to

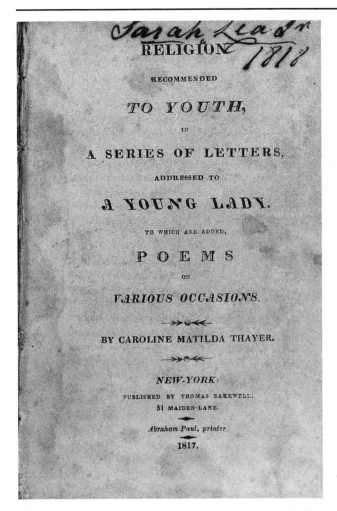

Title page for Thayer's attempt to counter "much of the frivolity,
discoverable in the manners and fashions of modern females"
(courtesy of Special Collections, Thomas Cooper Library,
University of South Carolina)

help his sister and her child avoid financial ruin. These various subplots comment on the importance of educating sons and daughters of the early republic according to the "dictates of reason" and established "precepts of religion" and warn the reader about how the love of virtue can be undermined by immoral sexual and social behavior.

Thayer's incorporation of multiple genres in the novel may be seen as an attempt to capitalize on the growing popularity of periodical literature, which also offered an appealing blend of literary genres and topics. For example, Thayer integrates epistolary techniques and writings from Hannah More and other popular writers, and she included poetry she had published in the *Worcester National Aegis*. She also used moral maxims to defend the "emotions of sensibility" as a type of knowledge, saying that "Critics have laboured much to demon-

strate the impropriety of tears of joy, and have considered the *sigh of rapture,* as contrary to the order of nature." In addition to her use of various Gothic elements, allegorical or stage figures such as "Christopher Dilemma," and many classical allusions, Thayer self-consciously commented on a variety of issues ranging from authorship in the early national period to social ills such as dueling and domestic violence.

Thayer's novel received its share of criticism, some of which may have been unduly harsh. A 14 December 1805 review in *The Boston Magazine* remarked that her novel lacked originality and that some of her scenes were implausible. The writer also observed, however: "Considering the age of the female who wrote it, the benevolent purpose and the good intention for which it is published, it would be illiberal and unjust to treat it with that severity and malignity so common with *Reviewers.*" While Thayer used conventional phrases and quotations, the reviewer added, she also demonstrated "lively imagination" and a style that is for the most part "destitute of simplicity." More-modern critics concur, suggesting that while the novel may sacrifice suspense for didacticism, Thayer nevertheless attempted to combine the elements of seduction and suicide in thematically engaging ways. Indeed, Thayer's novel was reprinted several times up to 1828, suggesting that *The Gamesters* not only was commercially successful but also continued to be relevant to Americans' moral and political concerns over a period of two decades.

Thayer's next published work, *Religion Recommended to Youth, in a Series of Letters, Addressed to a Young Lady. To Which are Added, Poems on Various Occasions* (1817), also proved successful and remained in print even longer—well into the 1850s. The letters were written from places as far west as Canandaigua, New York, near Rochester, and show a decided shift from male conduct to female morals and manners. Using Julia, a former student, as the vehicle of her advice to other women, Thayer later claimed that she had hoped to counter "much of the frivolity, discoverable in the manners and fashions of modern females," especially as a result of their reading habits. She attempted to "present the youth of her own sex a succedaneum to the fascinating page of Romance, and the dangerous luxury of Novels." As suggested elsewhere in her preface, however, she had a more personal reason for writing the piece. She missed the familiar places of her youth and the company of her relations, and she had recently endured the deaths of her three children.

During this era Methodist revivalist meetings were frequent and attracted many followers. Beyond acknowledging that her religious beliefs afforded her a certain measure of consolation, Thayer confesses that earlier in her life she had absorbed the writings and religious skepticism of Voltaire and that she could not always distinguish between competing systems of thought. Thomas Paine, Mary Wollstonecraft, and Constantin-François Chasseboeuf, Comte de Volney, she admitted, also contributed to her moral decline. In the course of her letters, however, she tells Julia of her conversion experience at a Methodist meeting and how—at age twenty—she met a nineteen-year-old man who helped her accept the love of Christ. Thayer appended letters that recount Julia's triumphant death and her acceptance of the "Religion of Jesus." The various poetic reflections in the book include verse about the deaths of her children. Stylistically, *Religion Recommended to Youth* resembles conversion narratives of the period, particularly in its use of personal testimony, emotional appeals, extended analogies, and rhetorical questions. Yet, just as Thayer integrated material from Hannah More and some of her own meditative verse, so her letters, as the Reverend John Newland Maffit observed, "differ from the productions of most females in their argumentative style—containing as they do the irresistible arguments of our holy faith against infidelity" or natural religion. The letters offer a penetrating critique of Calvinistic doctrine, that "preposterous system, called the doctrine of election," and the manner in which it has contributed to skepticism. *Religion Recommended to Youth* went through four editions by 1821 and at least two more by 1831. It continued to be published in the 1840s and 1850s.

Shortly after the publication of *Religion Recommended to Youth,* Thayer became the superintendent of the female department of New York City Wesleyan Seminary, a private school organized by Methodists in 1818 and located in lower Manhattan. Little is known about Thayer's specific responsibilities or life at this time. By 1821 she had embraced the doctrines of Emanuel Swedenborg and the New Jerusalem Church and was consequently forced to resign her position at Wesleyan Seminary. Offended by the actions taken against her, she published *Letter to the Members of the Methodist Episcopal Church in the City of New York, Stating the Reasons of the Writer for Withdrawing from that Church and the Circumstances of Her Subsequent Dismission from the Wesleyan Seminary* (1821).

Addressed to her Christian friends, the letter reflects her disappointment over their various nega-

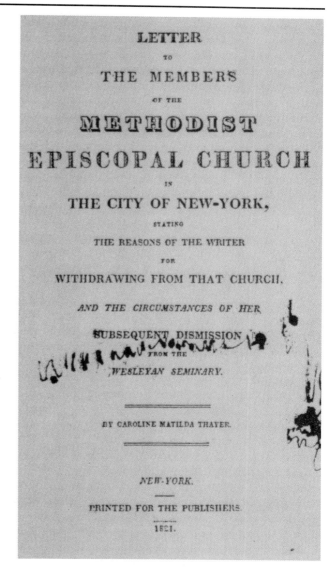

Title page for Thayer's response to her forced resignation as superintendent of the female department at the Wesleyan Seminary in New York after she embraced Swedenborgianism

tive reactions to her changing belief system. In narrating the various stages of her religious pilgrimage, including her initial conversion from religious skepticism to the writings of John Wesley and John William Fletcher, Thayer explained how her habit of intellectual inquiry had led her to embrace the teachings of Swedenborg. This action, she claimed, caused her to be "branded with the Unitarian heresies" and, without warning from her peers or superiors at the seminary, she had been made to feel that she should resign her position. Thayer supported her argument not only by using appeals to conscience and other rhetorical strategies but also by giving a detailed account of how her superiors had misrepresented their evaluation of her performance and reasons for dismissal. While the letter was published in the United States, England, and Ireland, it seems to have generated interest primarily in the way it brought attention to the motives and procedures for academic dismissal at the seminary and questioned the Methodist commitment to religious toleration or, in Wesley's words, "liberty of conscience." As Thayer saw it at the time, her dismissal gave reason to question the "principles of toleration" within the church and was closely connected with issues of religious, moral, and civil liberty.

After publishing her letter to Methodists of New York City, Thayer remained in the New York area and found employment as the superintendent of the female department at Joseph Hoxie's Academy, later known as the Academy at St. Matthews. Also located in lower Manhattan, first on William Street and later in the basement of a Lutheran church on Walker Street, Hoxie's schoolroom provided instruction primarily to boys, many of whom became leading merchants and professional men in the area. During this time Thayer edited Harriet Muzzy's *Poems, Moral and Sentimental* (1821) and produced a history text, *First Lessons in the History of the United States: Compiled for the Use of the Junior Classes in Joseph Hoxie's Academy* (1823). The collection of poems was designed to relieve the monetary difficulties of the widowed Muzzy. In the preface Thayer remarked that she and Muzzy had similar life experiences, such as the early deaths of their husbands, and that Thayer's own misfortunes prevented her from assisting her friend more fully. The collection also includes verse Thayer published in periodicals and poems she addressed to Muzzy on the topics of friendship and faith.

With *First Lessons in the History of the United States,* Thayer's primary aim was to provide a history of the United States that could be easily recalled by children and would fill their leisure time with instruction and pleasure. While it was designed initially only for Hoxie's classes, he encouraged her to publish it for use in other schools. Based, as Thayer noted in her preface, on William Grimshaw's *History of the United States* (1819), the narrative adheres to a traditional form of history writing, outlining the role of Providence in the exploration and settlement of America from Columbus to the cession of Florida in 1818. The book also includes questions at the end of each lesson as well as appended letters of recommendation from area school principals, many of whom lauded the arrangement of information and the appropriate-

ness of style for younger readers. In one such letter, for example, the writer was pleased to find "the intelligent author a person who gives credit to the navigators of the North, the Ericksons, and others, worthy of higher praise than they have generally received." In *The New-York Mirror, and Ladies' Literary Gazette* (9 August 1823) a reviewer summed up the reception of the work by remarking, "Mrs. Thayer has conferred an invaluable benefit on the rising generation. No *school* or *family* ought to be without it."

While Thayer's history text has long since been superseded, her narrative remains an important source of cultural information. Her remarks, for example, on the evils of slavery and on the often-violent displacement of native populations indicate her acceptance of and resistance to predominant constructions of racial others. Moreover, the concluding remarks record contemporary attitudes advocating democracy, capitalism, and the role of revolution—and "American enterprise"—in the South American republics.

After having lived and taught in New York City for several years, Thayer moved briefly to Green River, Kentucky, to teach school with the Reverend Valentine Cook, a local Methodist circuit rider. During this time she translated for *The New-York Mirror, and Ladies' Literary Gazette* (21 February 1824) material on female education from Antoinette Legroing-La Maisonneuve's *Essai sur le genre d'instruction qui paroit le plus analogue à la destination Des femmes* (1801; Essay on the Type of Instruction that Appears Most Suitable for the Purposes of Women).

Before moving to Mississippi in 1825, she visited or briefly lived at Adena, Ohio, near Chillicothe, and experienced what appears to be a final evolution in her thinking. At that time Adena, a Hebrew word meaning "places remarkable for the delightfulness of their situations," was the wealthy estate of Thomas Worthington, one of the original trustees of the local Methodist Church and the sixth governor of Ohio (1814–1818). Worthington received many visitors at Adena, some of whom stayed for extended periods of time. It is likely that Thayer's past association with the Methodist Church or the revivals led by Edward Tiffin, the lay-minister brother-in-law of Worthington, and circuit-riding bishops at the time had something to do with her visit. Indeed, many of the preachers whose names are associated with early Methodism were stationed in Chillicothe.

Whatever Thayer's reasons were for being at Adena in February 1825, in a letter to the

Adena, the house near Chillicothe, Ohio, where Thayer wrote the letter recanting her Swedenborgian beliefs (Ohio Historical Society)

Reverend Nathan Bangs, one of the editors of the sober-minded monthly *The Methodist Magazine* (and an individual who seems to have been involved in her dismissal from Wesleyan Seminary), she renounced her previous belief in the teachings of Swedenborg, a move that did not go unnoticed in Nathaniel Holley's New Jerusalem publication, *The Herald of Truth*. In the first part of the letter, dated 14 March, Thayer expresses her desire to make her return to the church as public as had been her earlier separation. The "whole system," she wrote, "of that extraordinary man now appears to me like a kind of *fairy vision*. The explanations which I have been able to obtain of his doctrines remind me of what seamen term '*point no point!*'" In addition to recanting her Swedenborgian beliefs she acknowledged to the ministers and members of the Methodist Church in New York that she had rashly thrown away their friendship. Accompanying her brief letter to Bangs is a longer, more substantial letter to the members of the Methodist Episcopal Church in Chillicothe, Ohio. Also autobiographical in content, it outlines her earlier departure from Methodism and her subsequent reasons for returning to the church. Significantly, she admitted

that she had reconciled the one significant point of difference—the doctrine of atonement— and had come to embrace orthodox views of the subject. Beyond articulating her acceptance of previous theological differences, she admitted that she misunderstood the reasons of those who dismissed her from the Wesleyan Seminary. As in her first letter, however, she did not offer an outright apology; rather, she told how further reflection on her earlier motives enabled her to progress to a higher level of religious—and rational—conviction.

After leaving Adena, Thayer published little about her Methodist beliefs and largely devoted her energies to the education of female students in the west central Mississippi area, first at the Elizabeth Female Academy in Washington, Mississippi, six miles east of Natchez, and later at Mississippi College in Clinton, Mississippi. Established in honor of Mrs. Elizabeth Rouch, the Elizabeth Female Academy was the first preparatory school in the state devoted to the education of adolescent girls and one of the first institutions of its kind established in the South. Methodist in denomination, the academy initially hired Thayer in fall 1825 because of her reputation as an author and teacher. Her talent for administration quickly displayed itself, and over the next several years her leadership in female education marked an era. While the administration clearly valued Thayer's presence at the academy, Thayer felt gratified by the accomplishments of her female students and the slowly improving climate for educating young women. For example, in addition to recording the progress of the academy, Thayer noted in a December 1829 annual report to the board of trustees that despite the lack of a suitable history book for her female students, she had been able to teach them the subject and that, happily for the present age as well as posterity, "the public sentiment has undergone an important change in favor of female education." "Without undervaluing personal accomplishments," she remarked, "or disregarding domestic duties, we are permitted to aspire to the dignity of intellectual beings. . . ."

In addition to her duties as a teacher and administrator, Thayer also worked with other women in the city of Washington, Mississippi, to form the Female Assistance Society, which sought to raise money outside regular church donations to supplement the salaries of preachers who worked the poorer circuits. She remained in her position until 1832, when she became the head of the female department at nearby Mississippi College in Clinton, Mississippi.

At Mississippi College, Thayer's career as an educator and administrator seemingly reached its apex. Under Thayer's direction the female department apparently led the way for the new college and continued to teach substantial numbers of female students. By all accounts she was extremely successful in her management of the department. On 16 July 1836 Thayer informed her friends and the public that repairs on the building assigned to her by the board of trustees would necessitate in-

structing pupils at her own home, and in October 1836 she started her own private school. Thayer left Clinton the following year, and there is little information about where she went. Census and other records indicate that by 1840 she was living in Ascension Parish, Louisiana, and that she died in 1844, possibly in the Catahoula Parish area.

It is generally thought that the literary merit of Thayer's work lies mostly in the way she voiced her concerns as a religious teacher. To a large extent this evaluation is true. Yet as a woman who variously embraced secular and orthodox belief systems, Thayer's importance also lies in her willingness to use the sentimental novel as a means of grappling with important contemporary social and moral issues as well as in the manner her various writings respond to cultural and ideological change. Beyond providing academic and administrative leadership for the education of young women, Thayer's willingness to question patriarchical codes and to accept Methodist doctrine on her own terms testifies to her lifelong habit of intellectual inquiry and self-reflection—the manner in which she employed independent thought as a means of self-definition and to benefit the lives of individuals in the communities in which she lived.

References:

Herbert Ross Brown, *The Sentimental Novel in America 1789–1860* (New York: Pageant Book, 1959);

Alexander Cowie, *The Rise of the American Novel* (New York: American Book Company, 1948), pp. 19–21;

Reverend John Newland Maffitt, "Mrs. Caroline Matilda Thayer," *Cabinet of Religion, Education, Literature, Science and Intelligence,* 5 (1831): 195–196;

Henri Petter, *The Early American Novel* (Athens: Ohio State University Press, 1971), pp. 225–231.

Mary Palmer Tyler

(1 March 1775 – 6 July 1866)

Marilyn S. Blackwell
Community College of Vermont

BOOKS: *The Maternal Physician: A Treatise on the Nurture and Management of Infants From the Birth Until Two Years Old. Being the Result of Sixteen Years' Experience in the Nursery. Illustrated By Extracts From The Most Approved Medical Authors. By An American Matron* (New York: Isaac Riley, 1811);

Grandmother Tyler's Book: The Recollections of Mary Palmer Tyler (Mrs. Royall Tyler) 1775–1866, edited by Helen Tyler Brown and Frederick Tupper (New York: Putnam, 1925).

Mary Palmer Tyler

In *The Maternal Physician* (1811), one of the earliest comprehensive childcare manuals by an American woman, Mary Palmer Tyler articulated an expanded role for mothers in child rearing and argued that mothers' authority in the physical care and mental development of children is superior to that of physicians or fathers. A daughter of the Revolutionary generation in Massachusetts, Tyler filtered Enlightenment thought through her experience as a mother to formulate a systematic approach to raising successful citizens for the new republic. Tyler's understanding of a mother's role in the formation of responsible citizens represents a classic example of what historians have labeled "republican motherhood." By 1858, when she began writing a memoir, Tyler had reformulated her patriotism. Published as *Grandmother Tyler's Book* (1925), this book is a romantic adventure story of her marriage to playwright Royall Tyler (1757–1826) in which her domestic skills and Christian motherhood prevailed in frontier Vermont.

Born in Watertown, Massachusetts, on the eve of the Battles of Lexington and Concord (19 April 1775), Mary Hunt Palmer entered a world in the process of revolutionary upheaval that eroded her family's wealth and status. Her grandfather Joseph Palmer (1716–1788) and her Harvard-educated father, Joseph Pearse Palmer (1750–1797), served briefly local militias, and they fought at Bunker Hill on 17 June 1775. During the war, inflation and their donations to the war effort diminished the family's capital. The eldest daughter, Mary Hunt Palmer spent her early childhood at her grandfather's estate, where she experienced the privileges and affectionate childcare characteristic of many upper-class families. Her mother, Elizabeth Hunt Palmer (1755–1838), the daughter of storekeeper John Hunt of Watertown, Massachusetts, taught her daughters to read and, according to Mary Palmer, followed John Locke's advice about child rearing. In *Some Thoughts Concerning Education* (1693) Locke stressed the importance of childhood health and learning through experience, not harsh discipline, and argued that parents could channel their children's natural goodness through regular discipline into the patterns of self-control necessary for good citizenship.

Mary Palmer benefited from this regime. After the war, however, family needs limited her freedom and took precedence over education. Burdened with eight children by 1788, Elizabeth Palmer began taking in boarders and enlisted the help of her eldest daughter for housekeeping. With a large family and no funds for secondary schooling, the Palmers were unable to supply their children with further formal education, but Joseph Pearse Palmer, who took literacy for women seriously, encouraged his daughter to read extensively and to write as well. In 1789 he apprenticed Mary Palmer as a mother's helper to wealthy friends, who took her to New York City, where she experienced the mortification of servant status. All the while, however, her father bolstered her spirits with affectionate letters filled with praise for her natural writing style and concern about excessive novel reading.

From age fifteen until her marriage Mary Palmer's future remained uncertain as her family sought ways to provide for their children in Framingham, Massachusetts, where Joseph Palmer leased a farm, and his wife ran a small tavern. The Palmers felt isolated from Boston cultural life and abandoned by former friends, except Royall Tyler, who had developed a close association with Joseph Palmer in the mid 1780s. Famous as the author of the comedy *The Contrast,* which had its premiere in New York in 1787, Tyler had a reputation as a dandy who had squandered his wealth and been jilted by his fiancée, John Adams's daughter Abigail. Seeking new opportunity as a lawyer in Vermont, Tyler repeatedly visited the Palmers in rural Framingham, where he began courting Mary Palmer in the winter of 1793.

Their marriage date remains uncertain. In her memoir Mary Palmer Tyler maintained that because Royall Tyler's mother objected to their union, the couple had married secretly in May 1794 and that their first child, Royall Jr., was born prematurely on 1 December 1794. While Mary needed to announce the marriage because of her early pregnancy, Royall Tyler might have wanted to delay it because he lacked the resources to establish a family in the style to which he was accustomed. He and Mary were certainly husband and wife by February 1796, when Royall took his wife and young child to live with him in Guilford, Vermont. Eighteen years his wife's senior, Royall Tyler treated Mary with affectionate paternalism while she found a sense of security with her husband, who had rescued her from an uncertain future.

Mary Tyler's early years as a parent in Vermont provided her with the experience of mother-

hood that informs *The Maternal Physician.* Between 1796 and 1810, when she began writing the book, she gave birth to two daughters and five sons, all of whom survived infancy. By 1818 she had nurtured a total of eleven children. After 1801, when the family moved to Brattleboro, Vermont, and her husband was elected to the Vermont Supreme Court, Mary Tyler managed her household with intermittent help from hired servants. The Tylers associated with a lively literary group in Guilford, but their move to Brattleboro represented a retreat to rural life. Mary Tyler had insisted that they purchase a farm as a means of supplementing the family's income. While she enjoyed supervising the production of butter and cheese and believed their location sheltered her young sons from the unhealthy influence of village life, Royall Tyler had little time or inclination to improve the farm, which barely sustained itself. With her husband either away at court for nearly six months at a time or preoccupied with writing poetry and witty essays for literary magazines, Mary Tyler developed her domestic skills and her methods of nurturing and training her children despite a chronic lack of funds. Royall's affectionate letters bolstered Mary's spirits during her many pregnancies, and his absence reduced the tensions that arose at home. Moody by temperament, Royall Tyler sometimes did not speak for days. Mary tolerated his long silences, but she challenged his inconsistent behavior with the children. In her memoir she claimed that her husband's oscillation between indulgence and strict discipline would have resulted in grave consequences for the children "had it not been for his frequent absences from home when we could do as we pleased."

Building on the Lockean methods she had learned as a child, her practical experience, and her reading of British health-care manuals, Mary Tyler formulated a child-rearing philosophy that reflects her expanding role in the Tyler household. Removed from her mother and other traditional sources of infant health care, she sought information from British books such as William Buchan's *Domestic Medicine* (1769) and William Cadogan's *Essay upon Nursing* (1750). Steeped in Enlightenment thought, these writers hoped to reform the domestic practices of elite women, especially the hiring of wet nurses, whom physicians believed harbored disease. They encouraged parents to prevent disease and infant death through close attention to their children and improved health practices, thereby charging parents with responsibility for the well-being and usefulness of future generations. Integrating this philosophy with her own experiences in breast-feeding and experiments with herbal medicines, Mary

Tyler increasingly felt as competent as any doctor to treat her children's illnesses. She detailed her child-care techniques in *The Maternal Physician,* which she dedicated to her mother, to whom she credited much of her knowledge. Yet the book is informed as well by the wisdom Mary Tyler gained through experience and reading. In the tradition of many women writers and perhaps to avoid criticism from physicians, Tyler's book appeared anonymously, brought out by one of Royall Tyler's publishing contacts.

Mary Tyler addressed her advice to literate, middle-class women who presumably had the leisure time to read and wealth enough to hire servants but who lacked the "power or inclination to consult" extensive health-care manuals. *The Maternal Physician* challenges physicians' claims to authority over routine child health care while also announcing Tyler's membership in the class of intellectual and social elite who dictate social standards. She not only explained her treatment of childhood diseases and her approach to education and discipline but also argued that a mother's daily experience with children is more valuable as a guide to their care than a physician's scientific knowledge. This claim distinguishes her approach to child rearing from Lockean educational theory and from the eighteenth-century writings of the British physicians on whom she relied for advice.

In six chapters Tyler dealt with problems of feeding, teething, and childhood disease. Mirroring British physicians' arguments, she encouraged mothers not to abandon an infant to "attendants" who might "cram its little stomach with pap." Instead she urged mothers to breast-feed their babies and to prevent illness through cleanliness and attention to early symptoms. Unlike her male sources, however, Tyler promoted breast-feeding not only to prevent infection from food contamination but also to establish female authority over children by grounding a mother's nurturing role in her biological function. Only a mother who breast-feeds and bathes her infant on a daily basis, she stressed, can detect "any latent symptoms of disease" that might "baffle the physician's skill." Citing examples from her own experience with infants, Tyler asserted "that a mother is her child's best physician, in all ordinary cases."

Throughout her book she displayed an ambiguous attitude toward the emerging medical profession. While she identified herself with "so much real humanity, learning and experience" by citing doctors' advice for smallpox and other serious diseases and while she repeated their treatments and procedures, Tyler claimed authority for the inti-

Royall Tyler

mate knowledge that only mothers can bring to childcare. By cloaking her reasonable approach to childcare in sentimental language and including quotations from Alexander Pope and other eighteenth-century British poets, Tyler expressed the powerful emotions underlying mother-child relationships. She described her children as "sweet pledges of connubial love," a mother's "pure unadulterated cup of joy." Affirming a woman's nurturing role as the source of her personal happiness and her familial and moral authority, Tyler asserted that mothers' naturally tender feelings for their children justify their dominion over childcare.

The Maternal Physician differs from American health-care manuals published before 1811 because Mary Tyler not only stressed a mother's responsibility for her children's physical care and offered an extensive list of herbal remedies, but she also emphasized her control over their intellectual and moral training. Asserting the connection between the physical and mental well-being of children, she also urged that mothers should play a dominant role in creating rational, self-disciplined citizens and in preserving the family as the foundation of society. In a chapter on the "early Regulation of the infant Temper and Disposition," Tyler argued that mothers should not only exercise their babies every day to stimulate their physical growth but also talk to them frequently to encourage their mental development. Because they learn through experience, she insisted, their "passions and desires" can be controlled through affectionate persuasion and regular

Pages from Mary Tyler's memoir, published in 1925 as Grandmother Tyler's Book *(Vermont Historical Society Library)*

225

that the Judge had been appointed Judge of Probate—and he wanted not to urge your Father to become Register, who finally succeeded as I have said—even after he persuaded your Father to sell our farm pay off all the little demands yet unsettled and finally we removed to this village—hiring the house then owned by General Elias Lyman—near the Insane Asylum—this was however many years before that Institution was thought of. We afterwards as you all know lived in various houses in this place during which time our dear boys in Boston, and New York (there in stores as apprentices with my brother) William & Edward were for some time grew in age, and strength and were all our dependence John especially, who in time became connected in business with Mr Wheelock whose daughter he became attached and at length married but before that interesting event took place he told her In the he was resolved never to marry till he had provided a home for us—a resolution he kept and finally purchased this place where we now live—At this time his Father began to be seriously afflicted by the awful disease which finally occasioned his death. he lived however several years but lost all inclination to go from home—and for that reason declined John's invitation to his wedding—but insisted upon my going—which I did—and then I first saw Miss W. then a very lovely young Lady and still living his faithful and affectionate Wife—Their only Child Lucina now Mrs George Hunter the joy and pride of her Fathers heart we all know and appreciate—she has two Daughters—the eldest now, Mrs Pearson & her sister Emily—my great Grandchildren
                                 Mary

            Now I think I have written enough—I began with an account of my birth, and the great Revolution—the birth of the American Nation, And now, I have lived to see her struggling for life with her own rebellious Children—What will be the final issue is known only to Him who has right to rule we joyfully acknowledge—and whose wisdom we implicitly trust—If I should attempt to record all the incidents and events of the last fifty years of my life my strength and your patience would be exhausted therefore I bid you adieu I am now eighty eight years & eight months old— - - - - - -

Mary Tyler late in life

discipline. An eight- or nine-month-old is not too young to learn obedience, she instructed, and for mothers "to acquire that ascendency" over children's minds necessary to ensure "a due degree of influence over them through life." While Tyler advocated expanding the mother's influence over her children, she refrained from explaining how fathers should behave, sensing that her husband, whom she portrayed in the manual as an indulgent father, "might esteem it too presuming." *The Maternal Physician* equates affectionate family relations with rational child rearing, resting responsibility for the physical, mental, and emotional development of children nearly exclusively with their mothers. Indeed, for Tyler the "future beauty, health, and happiness of the rising generation, and, eventually, the welfare of the community at large" depend on the proper discharge of a mother's duties. Her argument, arising from her expanded role in the home, matched that of post-Revolutionary advocates for female education, who sought to prepare women to train virtuous and useful citizens for the new republic.

The Maternal Physician is part of the abundant early-nineteenth-century British and American lit-

erature on the health and education of children. Addressed to the expanding population of middle-class women, maternal-advice and home-management manuals helped to redefine and elevate the cultural role of mothers and set new standards for domestic practice. As the commercial economy drew fathers' attention outside the household and as the emphasis on raising educated citizenry heightened, mothers' supervision of children and domestic life gained in significance. American women began writing prescriptive literature shortly before 1800, but none of the early manuals appears to combine advice about children's health and education in as comprehensive a manner as *The Maternal Physician,* nor do they challenge the authority of physicians as directly. In *Maternal Solicitude, or, Lady's Manual* (1809) midwife Mary Watkins, for example, offered advice only about the naturalness and pleasures derived from maternal breast-feeding and the importance of infant exercise; she rested the ultimate responsibility to ensure proper care with fathers. Other female writers provided instructional techniques for early-childhood education. Compared with later comprehensive advice books, Tyler's work adheres more closely to Enlightenment rationalism than to the sentimental maternal religiosity that predominated in advice literature by the 1830s, but *The Maternal Physician* parallels this literature in its emphasis on a mother's influence in family life. As an anonymous author, Tyler never received recognition for her work, but Dr. James Thacher cited her advice on breast-feeding in his *American Modern Practice* (1817, 1826) and extolled the author as "a fascinating American writer."

The Tylers' family life changed dramatically after 1813, when Royall Tyler lost his position as a jurist, creditors rendered him nearly bankrupt, and their eldest son died of typhus. After selling their farm and moving into rented quarters in Brattleboro village Mary Tyler nursed her husband's psychological and physical distress. As his health soon deteriorated, she sought to keep her family solvent and to find a means of educating her sons. While the family's dismal finances dominated her concerns, she also worried about her sons' behavior away from home. Apprenticed to a relative in Boston, her son John managed to avoid the dangers of the city and to send money home to support the family, but Mary worried excessively about her poverty and her ability to ensure her children's good fortune.

She turned to religion for consolation and guidance. Her desperate personal circumstances coincided with the rise of religious revivalism in New England, which led several of her sons into ministerial training and Tyler into church membership. By instilling religious principles in her sons, she hoped that religious values would guide their behavior away from home and ensure their devotion to supporting the family. In this way she shifted the basis for her child-rearing philosophy from rationalism and maternal solicitude to evangelical piety. Tyler's sense of responsibility for her children's future evolved into a desire to direct their spiritual development as the chief means of achieving self-control, family survival, and civic, as well as religious, virtue. After her husband died in 1826, Tyler was extraordinarily successful in sustaining her household because her children continued to support her with money and labor. Her sons also upheld their civic duty, for several served as civil or military officers, and to their mother's delight four became ministers. As for her daughters, Tyler elicited housekeeping services from the eldest and helped her younger daughter, Amelia, open a school in their home. Ironically, her obsessive control over her daughters prevented them from fulfilling her ideal of motherhood, for neither married.

As a widow in the 1830s and 1840s, Mary Tyler extended her female influence through religious and benevolent activities in Brattleboro. While she clung to the Episcopalian Church, she also assumed an evangelical stance in her community, helping to organize a local maternal society and supporting temperance activities. Amelia Tyler's private school helped to educate local boys as well as some of Mary Tyler's grandchildren. In 1858 Mary Tyler began her memoir, which was eventually published by her great-granddaughter as *Grandmother Tyler's Book* (1925).

Dedicated to her children and probably not intended for publication, the narrative reaffirms the Tylers' elite status as descendants of American patriots and Mary Tyler's role in sustaining that class identity by upholding her duties as daughter, wife, and mother. The book juxtaposes Tyler's story with that of her mother, Elizabeth Palmer, who had come to live with her daughter briefly before her death in 1838. Both women portrayed their marriages as the dramatic centers of their lives, and both took pride in their connections to heroes of Revolutionary Boston. Whereas Palmer's marriage was the beginning of "a life of sorrow and trials," Tyler's became a romantic adventure. Relating her birth to the birth of the nation, Tyler paralleled her "rescue" by her husband and her life in frontier Vermont with the growth of America and the promise of opportunity. She did not mention her accomplishments as a writer, her skill in medical care, and her nearly life-long poverty, focusing instead on her domestic skills and her piety. Without taking deserved credit for her achievements Tyler ended her story with praise for her son John, who shouldered family burdens with diligence and virtue. The narrative prominently features women's domestic work, showing how American women adhered to the values of industry and frugality and spurned excessive luxury. Yet the story also includes many anecdotes about other women in financial distress, revealing an underlying tension between the ideal marriage and the reality of female dependence. In keeping with her growing piety Tyler extolled the role of minister's wife and recounted a conversion experience from the period of her first pregnancy. She stressed the importance of Scripture readings with her young children, an activity not mentioned in her childcare manual. While her shift toward religion had reshaped her relationship with her children at midlife, by the time of her old age sentimental religiosity was not only a dominant mode of middle-class, female expression but also a means to maintain a passive voice in her own story.

Mary Palmer Tyler's writings helped to establish the "republican mother" ideal, articulating the expanded domestic authority mothers assumed in the nineteenth century. *The Maternal Physician* can also be seen as an effort to reshape Lockean educational philosophy to accommodate traditional female knowledge and to suit the needs of literate women of the early nineteenth century.

References:

Marilyn S. Blackwell, "The Republican Vision of Mary Palmer Tyler," *Journal of the Early Republic,* 12 (1992): 11–35;

Ruth H. Bloch, "American Feminine Ideals in Transition: The Rise of the Moral Mother, 1785–1815," *Feminist Studies,* 4 (1978): 101–126;

Christina Gibbons, "Mary Tyler and *The Maternal Physician,*" *Journal of Regional Cultures,* 3 (1983): 33–45;

Jacqueline S. Reinier, "Rearing the Republican Child: Attitudes and Practices in Post-Revolutionary Philadelphia," *William and Mary Quarterly,* 39 (1982): 150–163;

G. Thomas Tanselle, *Royall Tyler* (Cambridge, Mass.: Harvard University Press, 1967).

Papers:

The largest collection of Mary Palmer Tyler's papers is in the Royall Tyler Collection at the Vermont Historical Society in Montpelier, Vermont.

Sukey Vickery

(12 June 1779 – 17 June 1821)

Amy E. Winans
Susquehanna University

BOOK: *Emily Hamilton, a Novel. Founded on Incidents in Real Life* (Worcester, Mass.: Printed & sold by Isaiah Thomas Jr., 1803).

As the American Revolution drew to a close, women increasingly found themselves at the center of debates about the direction and character of the emerging nation. According to many writers, the same women who had gone off to war or run family businesses during the Revolution needed to return to their homes and assume responsibility for molding their husbands and children into solid citizens. As John Adams had insisted in 1778, the "foundation of national morality must be laid in private families." Much of the literature published during the decades immediately following the Revolution addressed this concern by linking the future of the nation with women's behavior and influence in the home. Sentimental novels, in particular, centered on the issues of marriage and family and thus offered young women readers guidance about the sometimes contradictory expectations and assumptions they might later face as wives and mothers.

Sukey Vickery was already known for her poetry when she published her first and only sentimental novel, *Emily Hamilton,* in 1803 and thus entered an increasingly vociferous discussion about women's roles in the new republic. The issues Vickery explored in her epistolary novel—the possibilities of women's friendships; parents' influence or control over their children; the bounds of acceptable conduct, especially for young women and men; and the rituals surrounding courtship—were of particular importance to unmarried women readers, many of whom would face weighty expectations as wives and mothers. In *Emily Hamilton* the discussion of these expectations takes place in letters exchanged among women friends and questions the double standard for male and female conduct with a directness that is distinctive for its era. Although in many ways Vickery affirmed rather traditional assumptions about women and women's conduct, the novel provides an intriguing examination of the discursive freedom available among unmarried female letter writers.

Sukey Vickery was born on 12 June 1779 to Benjamin and Susannah Barter Vickery in Leicester, Massachusetts, where she would live most of her life. She had one sibling. By the time Sukey was nine, her father's income as a tailor was apparently sufficient to allow her to attend Leicester Academy, a coeducational school, for at least one summer term. School records are unclear, but it is possible that she continued to attend the academy through 1795. Vickery's educational background might explain the familiarity with the classics exhibited in her literary works, one that was unusual for many women of her day. Her early writings also suggest that close female friendship and letter writing played an important role in her life, as they do in the lives of her characters. In fact, Vickery's correspondence with her friend Adelide Hartwell illustrates the central position that women assumed in each other's emotional lives during Vickery's day.

While she was in her early twenties, Vickery began to publish poetry in Isaiah Thomas's Worcester newspaper, *The Massachusetts Spy,* using the pseudonym "Fidelia." Published between 1801 and 1803 in the column "Blossoms of Parnassus," her poetry was rather conventional in form, but it was quite well received. In their own admiring verse, fellow poets "Frederic," "Theodorus," and "Eugene" praised "Fidelia" in *The Massachusetts Spy,* expressing hope that she would "never cease" her "charming strain."

At approximately the same time that she was writing and publishing poetry, Vickery was also hard at work on her novel. By 1802 she had shown her manuscript to Thomas and had begun to discuss its publication with him. Vickery's correspondence with Thomas illustrates that she, like many women novelists of her day, was sensitive to criticism about a literary genre that was often judged morally suspect. Her concern is apparent in a 13 February 1802 letter, which demonstrates that despite her clear wish to circulate her novel publicly, she was adamantly opposed to being identified as its author either by her given name or by her pseudonym Fidelia. While writing poetry was an acceptable, even admirable, activity for a young woman of Vickery's class and social background, writing a novel was not. Novels were frequently viewed with suspicion, and women novelists were considered particularly questionable. Vickery responded to the challenges she confronted as a woman novelist both by concealing her identity and by anticipating charges that novel writing had taken her away from her household duties. She carefully assured Thomas that her writing was done exclusively during her leisure hours in the evening. Like many novelists—both men and women—Vickery also asserted the moral usefulness of her novel by explaining that it was "founded primarily on facts" and that she had "been careful not to write anything that could have a tendency to injure the mind of the young and inexperienced." Vickery's claim that her novel was based on "facts, some of which I have heard from persons with whom I am connected," is not merely a rhetorical convention. As her biographer John Barnard Bennett notes, much of Vickery's lengthy 1799 letter to her friend Adelaide Hartwell, which describes the troubled life of a woman married to an alcoholic, appears almost verbatim in *Emily Hamilton*. Indeed, Vickery's concerns about women's characters, lives, and conduct echoes throughout much of her extant writing, both public and private.

Vickery and Thomas seem to have perceived the didactic nature of the novel as important to purchasers and readers. Claims similar to those in her letter to Thomas appear in the preface to *Emily Hamilton* and in advertisements for the novel printed by Thomas. In the preface Vickery defended her novel as a means of instruction and amusement, clearly distinguishing it from novels whose romantic, overly dramatic plots might create unrealistic expectations for young readers. Vickery's defense of her novel is ironic, however, because its plot in fact suggests that a faith in the value of romance is one of the things young readers might learn from the text. A central character in *Emily Hamilton* agrees to an inappropriate marriage in part because he does not believe that he will ever have the romantic feelings he reads about in novels. Later experience proves him wrong, and he suffers greatly for his mistake. Like most novelists of her day, Vickery proposed that reading novels could help young people make appropriate decisions about their futures, decisions

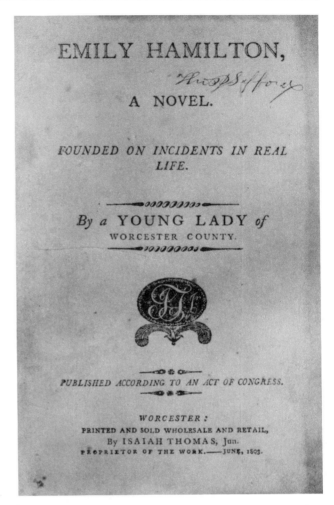

Title page for Sukey Vickery's only novel, which examines the dual standards of conduct for young men and women and concludes "that the world has been too rigid, much too rigid, as respects the female sex" (courtesy of the American Antiquarian Society)

that are both emotionally sensible and socially acceptable.

Published in 1803, *Emily Hamilton* explores courtship and young women's conduct in relationships with friends and parents, as well as with potential lovers. The novel tells the story of three young women's evolving friendships and courtships through seventy letters, written principally by Emily Hamilton, Mary Carter, and Eliza Anderson. Through their letters the young New Englanders, particularly Emily Hamilton and her close friend Mary Carter, explore the emotional and practical options available to young women who are arriving at a turning point in their adult lives. The primary correspondents in the novel are Emily and Mary, and the principal actor is Emily, who introduces Mary to her eventual husband, Mr. Gray, after his first fiancée (a close friend of Emily's) dies of consumption. Mary's side of the correspondence dwindles after she marries Mr. Gray, and the plot increasingly focuses on Emily's romantic pursuits. Amid letter writing, reading, trips to the theater, and continual visits to friends, Emily explores three possible romantic relationships, all of which she recounts in detail to her women friends. She rejects her first suitor, Lambert, after learning he has impregnated and deserted a young woman. She later struggles to reciprocate the feelings of Charles Devas, a respectable, loving young man, but she finds herself distracted by her feelings for a married man, Edward Belmont. In the end Emily is "rewarded" for being faithful to Charles, whom she has agreed to marry. The reward she gains, in an ironic twist, is Belmont's hand in marriage. Shortly after Mrs. Belmont dies, Charles dies at sea, leaving Emily free to marry Belmont. Their marriage concludes the novel.

Although many of the events described in the letters concern courtship and marriage, the structure of the novel and the emotions described in many of the letters demonstrate the centrality of women (particularly women friends) to each other's lives. Although men clearly have the ability to change women's lives dramatically, throughout much of the novel men function principally as the object of women's conversations. In their letters young women explore conflicts that emerge as they are torn between their duty to parents and their own desires. As was typical in many epistolary exchanges of the era, correspondents remind each other of the standards of acceptable behavior, sometimes by means of religious references. Yet the correspondents continue to explore socially unacceptable feelings in their letters, including Emily's love for the married Edward Belmont, suggesting less that the friends are expected to provide each other with appropriate conduct lessons and more that they offer each other a forum for exploring their feelings and eventually reconciling them with their duties to their family and the larger society. The young women not only exchange letters directly with each other but also copy and enclose additional letters they have received from others, actions that illustrate the range of connections among friends and the importance of epistolary culture to young women.

In fact, the prominent role of women's friendship in *Emily Hamilton* represents larger cultural shifts taking place during the postrevolutionary era. As historian Nancy Cott notes in *The Bonds of Wom-*

anhood (1977), orderly relationships between people who recognized themselves as either superiors or inferiors had guided familial and political relationships during much of the colonial era. Surviving texts from the latter part of the eighteenth century, however, suggest that increasingly attention was drawn to "peer relationships," or relationships among people of similar ages and social backgrounds. Changes in the meaning of the word *friend* reflect the shifting importance of different types of relationships. Previously *friend* had been used to describe a range of relationships, including those among family members. Although it continued to be used to identify relationships between husbands and wives, in the second half of the eighteenth century *friend* increasingly referred to relationships outside familial bonds. Friendship became idealized because it was a chosen relationship typically formed among equals and was thus distinct from the comparatively unequal parent-child or husband-wife relationships. The way the young women in *Emily Hamilton* negotiate their courtships reflects the growing role of women friends in each other's lives during this era, often at the expense of relationships between parents and children. In the novel some of the best marriages are those actively encouraged and supported by friends. Mary's marriage to Mr. Gray is brought about not by her grandparents (her parents are dead) but by her friend Emily. It is Emily who arranges for Mary and Mr. Gray to meet and Emily who offers her approval for the match. And although Emily's eventual marriage to Mr. Belmont is a foregone conclusion—the emotional and social compatibility of the pair is made quite clear—he acknowledges that she will want to ask for her friends' approval before committing to him.

The role that parents play or should play in their daughters' decisions regarding marriage is less clear in the world of the novel. Like many contemporary periodicals and novels, *Emily Hamilton* is filled with stories of parents who prove more interested in negotiating sound financial matches for their children than in helping them establish loving, egalitarian marriages. One of the most disastrous marriages in the novel, that of Clara Belknap and Edward Belmont, was arranged by Clara's elderly uncle and Edward's elderly father, both of whom were interested in their children's achieving a financially advantageous match. Yet older male relatives who overemphasize the importance of money are not the only parental figures to intervene negatively in the younger generations' romantic lives. Even Emily's devoted parents come dangerously close to encouraging her to marry a man who at first appears quite suitable but is later found to be a liar, a gambler, and a drunk. Yet the novel does not seem to propose that young women should overlook their parents' ideas or wishes. Rather, the novel manages to avoid addressing directly the roles of parents in their daughters' decisions about marriage. Conveniently, the most appropriate suitors seek the parents' or grandparents' blessings before beginning their courtships.

Emily Hamilton is quite explicit about what constitutes an appropriate marriage. As Emily and Mary repeatedly remind one another, a desirable marriage consists of two partners who love each other and who share common interests. Their unstated assumption that the partners will share a similar—and elevated—class position simply reflects the elite background of the characters in the novel. Although a potential husband need not be wealthy, a supportive, loving wife should be able to cultivate her husband's industry in ways that will encourage, though not ensure, financial prosperity. The novel makes clear that finding an appropriate mate is not a simple task. Although some characters make unfortunate mistakes in courtship and marriage, the admirable ones recover because they take active steps in assessing their options realistically. As Cathy N. Davidson has argued in *Revolution and the Word* (1986), the novel teaches its young readers that "good will, common sense, mutual esteem, and a realistic appraisal of possible marriage partners can promote personal happiness; whereas impossible dreams, proper passivity, necessary disappointment, and sentimental sorrow do not." Although *Emily Hamilton* focuses on the lives and decisions of young women, it suggests that both young women and young men must be active, realistic, and relatively independent of the influence of parents or older relatives when making romantic matches.

Because by the end of the novel all the main characters marry "appropriate" men, the outcome might be termed conservative. Yet the novel does confront the limitations placed on women, both in terms of socially acceptable sexual behavior and in terms of the admittedly unequal role a young woman will assume once she is married. More directly than most contemporary novels, *Emily Hamilton* examines the double standard for women and men. As they exchange stories of young women abandoned by their seducers, both Emily and Mary lament the fact that in the public eye women are judged more harshly for sexual liaisons than are men. Emily explains to Mary that "It has ever been my opinion that the world has been too rigid, much too rigid, as respects the female sex." While one

"false step forever blasts the same [reputation] of a woman . . . . the men are suffered to proceed in their licentiousness unpunished." The novel proposes that women might sometimes be judged more harshly by other women than by men. Clara's sister-in-law, Matilda, criticizes Clara sharply for her continued allegiance to her former lover after her marriage to Edward Belmont. In contrast, Clara's husband comments more sympathetically on her social transgression; those who would judge Clara, he suggests, should realize that Clara was forced into a marriage she did not want by an uncle who sabotaged her letters and held her physically captive. Curiously, in the end neither Emily nor Mary criticize the constraints on sexual behavior per se; rather they criticize the fact that men do not face the same constraints and judgment as women. In so doing they appear to seek stricter social standards and—in a conservative sense—to limit the behavior of elite-class people more generally.

The young women in *Emily Hamilton* also talk openly about the changes they will encounter as married women when relationships with husbands will take priority over relationships with treasured women friends. Mary Carter, for example, expresses reluctance when encouraged to marry quickly because she recognizes that marriage will curtail her social and personal freedom. She explains in part, "When I am married I expect to submit to his [her husband's] authority, but surely I ought to exercise my power as long as possible now." As an unmarried woman her primary relationships with her women friends are figured in egalitarian terms. Once she becomes a wife, even within a loving, affectional marriage, she will not be the equal of her husband and instead will submit to him. The little the reader sees of Mary after her marriage suggests that she is happily married. Yet she writes seldom because she is busy with "domestic duties." Like her friend Mary, Emily also finds herself hurried into marriage. Mr. Belmont is eager to make Emily his wife because he wants his two motherless young children to have a loving caretaker. As Emily awaits her wedding, Mary reminds her that "a wife ought to find her highest happiness at home." Each young woman eagerly anticipates marriage, even as she recognizes that it will bring an end to the primacy of her egalitarian relationships with her friends. Instead, her relationship with her husband, one that is based on mutuality but not on equality, will take precedence. Marriage marks the end of the prolific epistolary exchange between Emily and Mary and of their frequent extended visits to one another. The trepidation with which Emily and Mary confront marriage would not prove unfamiliar to their female contemporaries, who were themselves quite aware of the legal disadvantages that accompanied marriage for women and of the real threats of death that women faced during childbirth.

Vickery's novel, expensively priced at seventy-five cents, did not sell well and was not reprinted. Isaiah Thomas seems to have sought to increase sales of the novel by enclosing a note that created a sympathetic image of the author when he sent a copy to *The Monthly Anthology and Boston Review.* His inventive note describes the novel as the work of "a country girl, about eighteen years of age, residing in an obscure town, and by her needle maintaining her aged parents." Davidson notes that although the anonymous reviewer was rather dismissive of the novel and women authors in general, Thomas's portrait of the author did gain some sympathy from the reviewer. The 1805 review explained that "we are not disposed to encourage the exertions of females to become known as authors . . . . Considering, however, the age at which it was written, and the peculiar embarrassments of the author, the novel before us is deserving of commendation."

The focus on courtship to the exclusion of marriage reflects Vickery's own experience. In 1804, the year after the novel was published, she married Samuel Watson, who operated a clothier's shop in Leicester. Although her husband later achieved some financial and political success, during Vickery's lifetime the couple's finances were often quite precarious. Samuel Watson struggled to expand his business, introducing the manufacture of woolen cloth to the area, while the couple raised two sons and seven daughters. As literary historians have noted, an unpublished diary excerpt from 1815 illustrates that Sukey Vickery Watson was concerned about providing for her daughters' education, arranging their schedules to ensure that their household duties allowed sufficient time for their lessons. Commenting on the happiness she felt while instructing her children, she wrote on 18 December 1815, "could the dear creatures know the interest I feel in all that concerns them, and my anxious wishes for their improvement and future use-

fulness, it would be sufficient stimulus to their ambition." Just as the young women in *Emily Hamilton* appear to have ceased most personal writing after marriage, Sukey Vickery Watson appears to have ceased at least her public writing as poet and novelist and to have turned her attention to her children. She died in Leicester on 17 June 1821, one year after giving birth to her last child.

Vickery's life and works illustrate the possibilities and the obstacles facing women writers of her day. While the young elite women in *Emily Hamilton* accept marriage as their certain future, the novel does show them assuming an active role in selecting appropriate mates. Although the marriages chosen by the main characters in the novel are finally rather conventional, the conversations that precede them question the public treatment of women's sexuality and explore the conflicts between personal desire and socially acceptable behavior in important ways. Within the context of egalitarian relationships among women, Vickery suggests, women friends can speak with a freedom unavailable elsewhere.

Biography:

John Barnard Bennett, "A Young Lady of Worcester County," Wesleyan University, master's thesis, 1942.

References:

Henry Ross Brown, *The Sentimental Novel in America* (Durham: Duke University Press, 1940), pp. 11–12, 38–41, 160;

Cathy N. Davidson, "Female Authorship and Authority: The Case of Sukey Vickery," *Early American Literature,* 21 (Spring 1986): 4–28;

Davidson, *Revolution and the Word* (New York: Oxford University Press, 1986);

Henri Petter, *The Early American Novel* (Columbus: Ohio State University Press, 1971), pp. 108–182, 188, 417–418.

Papers:

Vickery's papers, including letters, poetry, and a brief diary fragment, are at the American Antiquarian Society in Worcester, Massachusetts.

Mercy Otis Warren

(25 September 1728 – 19 October 1814)

Jeffrey H. Richards
Old Dominion University

See also the Warren entry in *DLB 31: American Colonial Writers, 1735–1781.*

BOOKS: *The Adulateur. A Tragedy, As it is now acted in Upper Servia* (Boston: Printed & sold at the New Printing-Office, 1773);
The Group, As lately acted, and to be re-acted to the wonder of all superior intelligences, nigh head-quarters at Amboyne (Boston: Printed & sold by Edes & Gill, 1775);
Observations on the New Constitution, and on the Federal and State Conventions (Boston, 1788);
Poems, Dramatic and Miscellaneous (Boston: Printed by I. Thomas & E. T. Andrews, 1790);
History of the Rise, Progress and Termination of the American Revolution. Interspersed with Biographical, Political and Moral Observations, 3 volumes (Boston: Printed by Manning & Loring for E. Larkin, 1805).
Edition: *The Plays and Poems of Mercy Otis Warren,* edited by Benjamin Franklin V (Delmar, N.Y.: Scholars Facsimiles, 1980).

OTHER: Catharine Macaulay Graham, *Observations on the Reflections of the Right Hon. Edmund Burke,* introduction by Warren (Boston: Printed by I. Thomas & E. T. Andrews, 1791).

Mercy Otis Warren, circa 1763 (portrait by John Singleton Copley; Museum of Fine Arts, Boston; Bequest of Winslow Warren)

As a writer of poetry, satiric plays, tragic dramas, letters to public and private figures, and a major history of the American Revolution, Mercy Otis Warren stood out among Americans of her time as virtually the only person of letters to work in all those genres. An exemplar for many modern historians of the "Republican Mother," she sought to explain the significance of the American Revolution and her own Stoic brand of republicanism to rising generations of young people. She believed with many of her time that women are primarily responsible for transmitting the values of culture to youth, but at the same time she affirmed through her work that women have a right to teach not only in the pri-

vacy of the domestic sphere but also in the arena of public discourse. With a life that spanned three wars and the deaths of three sons and a husband, Warren remained undeterred in her pursuit of the intellectual life. Nearly until her death she continued to write to generals and presidents and to share her thoughts on the meaning of a republic.

Mercy Otis was born in Barnstable, Massachusetts, on 25 September 1728, the first daughter of James and Mary Allyne Otis, merchant-class parents who were able to provide her with a comfortable if not lavish upbringing. With her older brothers James Jr. and Joseph, who were preparing to attend Harvard, she was tutored by the Reverend Jonathan Russell, who introduced her to Walter Ralegh's *History of the World* (1614) and gave to her the essentials of a precollegiate education. On 14 November 1754 she married James Warren (1726–1808) and settled in Plymouth, Massachusetts, where she would live for most of the rest of her life. Her marriage was marked by amiability and mutual respect. Warren was a minor officeholder in Plymouth, a farmer, and later a prominent figure in Massachusetts politics. Like Mercy and her brothers, he was a fifth-generation descendant of *Mayflower* passengers, and like her brother James, he was a Harvard graduate. Mercy and James Warren spent their time in Plymouth at two households, one in town and the other on a farm outside Clifford, an old Warren family property. Between 1756 and 1766 Mercy and James had five sons: James Jr., Winslow, Charles, Henry, and George.

While her children were still young, Mercy Otis Warren began to write poems, often addressed to her husband or other family members or descriptive of natural phenomena. Her personal poems display control and fluidity of lines, but her talents suited her more for other genres. With an unusual education for a woman and with a gift for philosophical and political thinking, she began to reach out to the world through letters, of which some three hundred or more are extant. Although few letters survive from before 1770, her poems from the 1760s indicate interests in nature, family, and philosophical explorations of death.

A turning point in her life occurred in 1769, when her brother James Otis was beaten severely in an altercation with a political opponent, John Robinson. When word of the event reached her in Plymouth, Warren's September letter to James phrased her worries in the high style later used by Whig orators in their speeches on the Boston Massacre (5 March 1770): "You know not what I have suffered for you within the last twenty four hours—I saw you fallen—slain by the hands of merciless men—I saw your wife a widow, your children orphans." From this point on, Warren added politics to her list of topics, and policy makers became recipients of her letters.

An important experience in fixing her direction toward public discourse was meeting John Adams. In 1772 he, James Warren, and Samuel Adams gathered at the Warren home in Plymouth to discuss the formation of the committees of correspondence, radical Whig organizations created to guard against intrusions of Tory policy into the lives of citizens. From 1772 until her death in 1814—with

one major hiatus—Mercy Warren maintained a correspondence with John Adams and his wife, Abigail Smith Adams, on matters literary, political, and personal.

Her style with John Adams is sometimes playful, but for the most part she adopted a formality that seems intended to preserve the moment for history. For example, in a 5 July 1775 letter to John Adams, written immediately following the Battle of Bunker Hill, she described the cause of Boston's present ills in dire terms, lamenting "the Corruption Duplicity And meaness" of the governor as "He sends out his Ruffians to Butcher their Brethren, And wrap in flames the Neighboring towns." As her letter makes quite clear, she believed that all human action is subject to the scrutiny of universal laws; when that action fails the test, as did that of Gen. Thomas Gage, who was royal governor of Massachusetts in 1774–1775, it must be condemned in the sternest possible terms. This sense of being always under the watch of the universal guided Mercy Otis Warren's own actions and writing for the remainder of her life.

Even before she began her correspondence with Adams, Warren had published her first work, a play called *The Adulateur,* which was published in *The Massachusetts Spy* on 26 March and 23 April 1772. Republished in 1773 as a pamphlet with additions by an unknown hand, *The Adulateur,* a blankverse satire, criticizes the administration of Thomas Hutchinson, who was royal governor of Massachusetts in 1771–1774. She depicts him as the villain Rapatio and his followers as self-serving toadies whose personal greed or desire for royal preferment leads them to despise the people and undo the ancient liberties that Whig political philosophers were claiming as rights of the English. *The Adulateur* is also the first play published by a woman born and residing in English America. Two other satiric plays in blank verse followed; *The Defeat,* partially published in 24 May and 19 July 1773 issues of the *Boston Gazette,* is also an attack on Rapatio, and her best-known play, *The Group* (1775), is a critique of Hutchinson's political allies. Since Hutchinson himself felt compelled by the mounting political pressure against his regime to leave for England in June 1774, Mercy Otis Warren may be said to have had a hand in his abdication.

Warren's satiric verse plays are important to the history of Whig resistance and to the development of the drama in America. Their writing inspired several comments by Warren in her correspondence with John and Abigail Adams. As a satirist, Warren wondered how far a woman could go in attacking and making fun of public (male) figures.

In one exchange Abigail and Mercy discoursed on Molière, with the former criticizing the heartlessness of the French playwright's attitude toward his subjects and the latter defending his method. While she granted to her friend some justice in her remarks, Warren argued in a 19 January 1774 letter that the French playwright sat higher in the estimation of one who had already taken up the pen to ridicule:

> when Vice is held up at once in a detestable and Ridiculous Light, and the Windings of the Human Heart which lead to self deciption unfolded it Certainly points us to the path Reason and Rectitude. And if we do not Embrace the amiable image of Virtue we must Exculpate the Moniter and Attribute the Fault to the Wrong biass of our own Clamorous and ungovernd passions.

For Warren, satire as a form could be justified as a publicly useful genre if it caused readers to see evil as something to be despised. Virtue, then, should follow from reason. While many Americans in the late eighteenth century turned to satire to mock their enemies, few went about it as deliberately as Mercy Warren.

That deliberation can be seen in a later exchange with John Adams. After publishing some scenes from *The Group,* she wrote to Adams for some reassurance that what she was doing was within the sphere of socially sanctioned activity for a woman. She worried that the "Female Character" might "suffer" if a woman expressed herself through "acrimony." While Adams did give his correspondent the reassurance for which she asked, the fact remains that she had already written and published three satires on the Hutchinson and Gage administrations. Whether Adams approved or not, Warren had determined for herself that a woman could keep her domestic amiability and denounce vice in the press at the same time.

With the outbreak of military conflict between Britain and the newly confederated colonies, James Warren became an active participant as a representative to and speaker of the Massachusetts provincial assembly. Mercy Warren had opportunities to meet and write to the emerging leaders of the patriot movement. George and Martha Washington became acquaintances and correspondents, and over time other American luminaries, including Thomas Jefferson, Alexander Hamilton, Elbridge Gerry, Jabez Bowen, James Bowdoin, and Joel Barlow, joined the ranks of those to whom she wrote. The war also put her in contact with important women, notably Janet Montgomery, wife of the slain war hero Richard Montgomery; Hannah Winthrop; and Ann Gerry, among others. Commiserating with others'

James Warren, who married Mercy Otis in 1754 (portrait by John Singleton Copley; Museum of Fine Arts, Boston; Bequest of Winslow Warren)

losses, as with Janet Montgomery, or sharing stories of wartime privation, as with Hannah Winthrop, or offering political observations, as with many of her male correspondents, Mercy Warren expressed her thoughts and feelings through crafted, sometimes rhetorically high-flown letters.

With the outbreak of war in April 1775 she felt that the need for satire had come to an end but not the need for commentary on unfolding events. Consequently, she turned her attention to another project, a history of the revolution that was just in its early stages. Through her brother James and John Adams, Mercy Warren began an extensive correspondence with the English writer Catharine Macaulay (later Graham), the noted Whig author of *The History of England from the Accession of James I to the Elevation of the House of Hanover* (1763–1783) and, indeed, the rare model for the American woman of a female historian. Warren and Macaulay kept up their exchange of letters on political matters well into wartime, until the dangers of conveying letters between patriot America and England became too overwhelming. As with her letter to Adams on satire, Warren's letters to Macaulay show that the American is seeking affirmation about the propriety of a woman's writing in a genre traditionally domi-

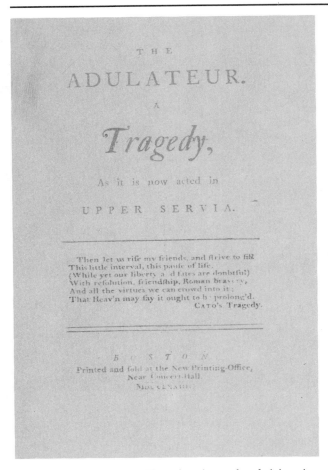

Title page for Mercy Otis Warren's satire on the administration of Royal Governor Thomas Hutchinson

the expense of the greater good was an ever-present danger. Although imagining a successful conclusion to the Revolution, Warren worried what independence would mean for the young.

A commonly known and controversial symbol of the potential corruption that awaited young Americans was the published edition (1774) of Philip Dormer Stanhope, Lord Chesterfield's letters to his son. Ever alert to cultural trends, Warren recognized the dangers to youthful minds. In 1779 she set down her thoughts in a long letter to her son Winslow, and copies of the letter began to circulate privately. At the behest of Abigail Adams, Warren's letter appeared in the *Independent Chronicle* on 18 January 1781 and was republished and admired by many for its advice to the rising generation. For Mercy Warren, Chesterfield erred on two significant accounts. She had, she said, "no quarrel with the graces." Chesterfield's much admired style and emphasis on personal polish was not in itself detestable, but his first mistake was to allow style to become the sole arbiter in life's decisions. As Warren explained,

> for however much I admire the innocent arts of engaging the esteem, I love better that frankness and sincerity, which bespeak a soul above dissimulation; that generous, resolute, manly fortitude, that equally despises and resists the temptations to vice in the Purlieu's of the Brothel, or the anti chamber of the Princess, in the arms of the emaciated, distemper'd prostitute, or beneath the smiles of the painted Courtezan, who decorates her guilty charms even with the blandishments of honour.

Although technically a letter, Warren's piece is really an essay on style and substance, written in cascading, parallel phrases and clauses. In as polished a style as she herself was capable of writing she attempted to assert the necessity for moral behavior at all times.

Chesterfield's second major error, Warren argued, was to assume that women are a subordinate and exploitable element among human beings. Warren's denunciation of his antifeminism is one of her most forthright statements on the perceptions of women in culture. His "contempt" for women, she remarked, is "trite, hackney'd, vulgar"—and thus the species of sentiment destined to undermine the moral authority of women in a republic. Indeed, his remarks on women

> are as much beneath the resentment of a woman of education and reflection, as derogatory to the candor and generosity of a writer of his acknowledged abilities and fame; . . . I ever considered human nature as the same in both sexes, not perhaps is the soul very differently modified by the vehicle in which it is placed; the foibles,

nated by men. Singing Macaulay's praises, she noted in a 19 December 1774 letter that no male political thinker had ever achieved perfection; therefore, she asked why women should be held to a different standard. Besides, she continued, "When the observations are just and honorary to the heart and character, I think it very immaterial whether they flow from a female lip in the soft whispers of private friendship or whether thundered in the Senate in the bolden language of the other sex." Within a year Warren was writing her own history of her time and was far more assured that a woman had every right, indeed every duty, to address the nation in print.

As active as she was in the political affairs of her time, Mercy Warren did not neglect her sons. James Jr. and Charles both attended Harvard, getting steady doses of motherly advice. Like some other patriots, she worried not only about outcomes of battles or debates in legislative bodies but also about the direction the country would take once the war was over. War profiteering was only one sign that making money or pursuing one's self-interest at

the passions, the vices, and the virtues, appear to spring from the same scource [sic], and under similar advantages, frequently reach the same degree of perfection, or sink to the same stages of pravity which so often stamp disgrace on the human form.

In terms as explicit as those of her younger contemporary and admirer Judith Sargent Murray, and with implications more far-reaching for the possibilities of her sex, Mercy Otis Warren used the opportunity of warning her son about vice to express the full equality of women.

In 1781, at the end of the Revolution, the Warrens moved to Milton, Massachusetts, living in the former home of their one-time enemy, Governor Hutchinson. There, Mercy and James received distinguished visitors, including Catharine Macaulay and her young husband, William Graham. Yet the years of living closer to Boston were not especially happy ones. Warren was productive, writing two verse dramas at Milton Hill, but a pall was cast by the death of her son Charles in 1785. Realizing that their lives were centered on the town that had been home to them for years, the Warrens moved back to Plymouth in 1788.

Following the completion of most of the poems and the two verse dramas that were collected in her *Poems, Dramatic and Miscellaneous* (1790), Mercy Otis Warren found herself keenly interested in the debate over the new Constitution. Her husband and their close political friend Elbridge Gerry had already weighed in with complaints about the Federalist direction of the document coming out of the convention. For the radical republicans the biggest danger under the new government was a return to the conditions maintained under British rule, namely that centralized authority would play too large a role in the governance of citizens. Having fought Hutchinson and Prime Minister Frederick, Lord North, Warren felt that this battle was too important to sit out. Because she was too late to influence the Philadelphia convention, she decided to aim her critique at those state legislators who would be voting to ratify.

Her pamphlet, *Observations on the New Constitution, and on the Federal and State Conventions,* was published in February 1788 under the pseudonym "A Columbian Patriot," and copies were sent to the New York delegates who would vote on ratification. While her work does not seem to have made a major difference in the debate—the Federalists still carried the vote—Warren's essay has the distinction of being the only major anti-Federalist publication by a female writer. Her basic theme remained Jeffersonian: that human beings have "certain unalien-

Mercy Warren's brother James Otis Jr., a prominent Whig whose beating at the hands of a political rival in 1769 intensified his sister's political loyalties (portrait by Jonathan B. Blackburn; from Jean Fritz, Cast for a Revolution, *1972)*

able rights" and that "the origin of all power is in the people." Many of her concerns reemerged in the late-twentieth-century debates over the limits of government. She argued, for instance, that elected officials should have one-year terms to make them more accountable and easier to recall. She also maintained that ultimate veto authority over government lay in the hands of citizenry. Although some New Yorkers criticized the work as too affected in style to be effective political rhetoric, Mercy Warren had articulated in elevated terms the obligations of government to preserve the liberties of the people. In this way she became a voice for a style of democracy that gave more credit to the intelligence and wisdom of the populace than most American political theorists and architects would bestow.

In 1790 she published her major volume of belles lettres, *Poems, Dramatic and Miscellaneous,* comprising two verse dramas and eighteen shorter poems as well as some prose introductions to the plays and a dedicatory letter to George Washington. The letter alludes to her prior correspondence and acquaintance with Washington, who at that time was president; it also expresses the author's hope for a great person's "approbation." Yet she also used the

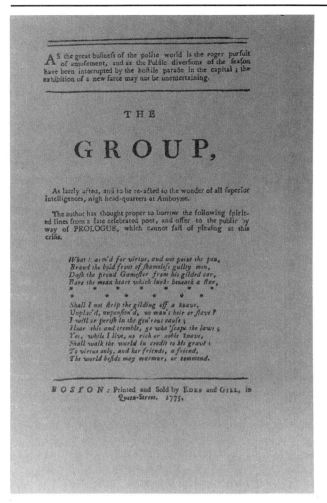

Title page for Warren's best-known play, a satire on the royal governor's political allies

occasion to talk about another project—her history of the Revolution. She noted that she had tracked the war from the beginning and that in her writing she had been just in assessing good characters and bad. Her appeal to Washington is as to an equal, presenting herself as one who, like the president, has taken the keenest interest in the fate of the country. Although Washington was well known as a patron of the theater and a subscriber to plays, Warren mentioned not a word about her dramas or her poems. Instead she used the occasion of her first book published under her own name to prepare the way for a succeeding one. Little could she have expected that Washington would be dead before her story of the Revolution reached the shelves.

Appearing first in the book is *The Sack of Rome,* a play that examines the fifth-century history of that city as the Vandals prepare to overrun the capital of the empire. In her introduction to the play Warren cited the long history of using Rome as a literary

subject, but it is apparent that for her, ancient Rome had a modern application. "In tracing the rise, the character, the revolutions, and the fall of the most politic and brave, the most insolent and selfish people, the world ever exhibited," she wrote, one could find examples of heroic virtue and perfidious vice—examples that could be made contemporary by finding analogues in recent history. One need only translate her description into recent events in American history, where heroes and villains people the Revolution, to see where Warren's heart lay. The overall point is "moral improvement," but she also confronted the seeming anomaly of pursuing that end in the form of a play. Her response to the potential criticism of using a play for moral purposes illustrates the shifting attitudes toward the stage in postwar culture: "Theatrical amusements may, sometimes, have been prostituted to the purposes of vice; yet, in an age of taste and refinement, lessons of morality, and the consequences of deviation, may perhaps, be as successfully enforced from the stage, as by modes of instruction, less censured by the severe." Warren turned the tables on critics, arguing in effect for a republican stage and drama, another tool in the arsenal of the writer dedicated to teaching citizens about the essential qualities and characters required in the new political order.

The introduction to *The Ladies of Castile,* the other play in *Poems, Dramatic and Miscellaneous,* is dated 20 February 1784, which indicates that it was her first verse drama. In a dedicatory letter to her son Winslow, the mother writer responds to her reader child, who had apparently suggested that she create plays on any subject but an American one. In compliance Mercy Warren chose a moment in the history of Spain when a popular force challenged the imperial government of the country and lost. As with Rome, the connection to her own country is intentional. She based her play on an event in the sixteenth century, when the Spanish legislature, the Cortes, declared its independence from imperial oversight. Such a moment, she remarked, "will ever be interesting to an American ear," since Americans are motivated by the same desire for liberty and by the same valor in their heroes, as the Spaniards of two-and-a-half centuries earlier.

Yet more than a mere analogy is at issue. By writing in play form, Warren planned to meet her intended audience, the young, at its level of interest. In her introduction she expressed the hope that the "conduct" of the young people of America might "never contradict the professions of the patriots who have asserted the rights of human nature; nor cause a blush to pervade the cheek of the children of the martyrs who have fallen in defence of the liber-

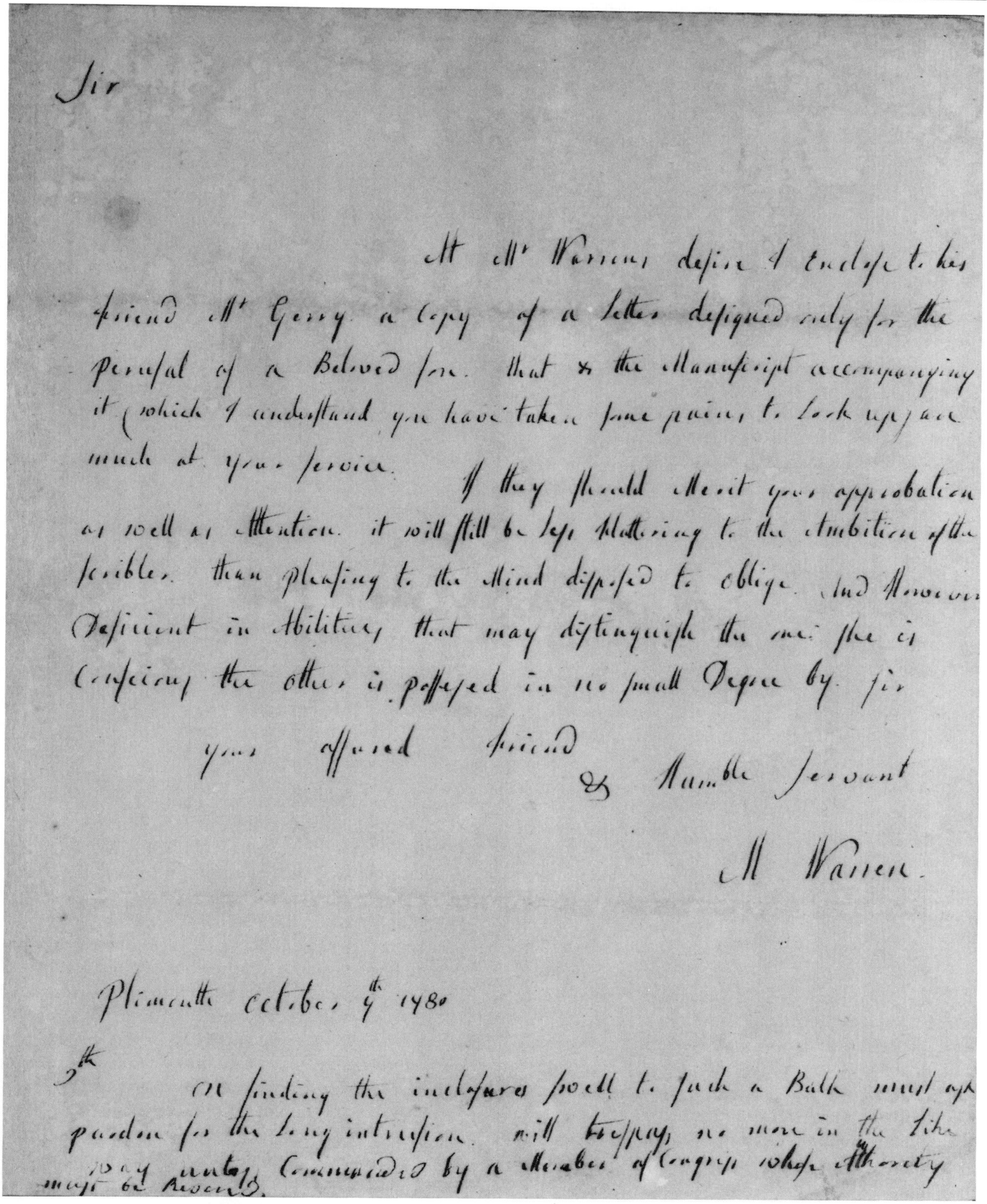

Sir

At Mr Warrens desire I enclose to his friend Mr Gerry a copy of a letter designed only for the perusal of a Beloved son. that & the Manuscript accompanying it (which I understand you have taken some pains to look up) are much at your service.

If they should Merit your approbation as well as attention. it will still be less flattering to the Ambition of the scribbler. than pleasing to the Mind disposed to oblige. And However deficient in Abilities, that may distinguish the one, she is Conscious the other is possessed in no small Degree by, Sir

your Assured friend

& Humble Servant

M Warren.

Plimouth October 4th 1780

5th On finding the inclosure swell to such a Bulk must ask pardon for the long intrusion. will trespass no more in the like way unless Commanded by a Member of Congress whose Authority must be Revered.

Letter from Warren to Elbridge Gerry, delegate to the Continental Congress, 4 October 1780 (Henry E. Huntington Library and Art Gallery)

The house in Milton, Massachusetts, that the Warrens bought in 1781. Formerly the country house of Royal Governor Hutchinson, it was confiscated along with his other property in the colonies soon after the beginning of the Revolution

ties of their country." Seeing her own son as at once gifted and ripe for corruption in the postwar demand for worldly goods and foreign fashion, Warren subordinated her aesthetic to an overall purpose of civic and moral education. Indeed, her writing takes on the sort of urgency that arises from an author who imagines herself almost single-handedly standing between the dark forces of self-interest and the enlightened virtues of Stoic sacrifice in the republican cause.

In the year following the publication of *Poems, Dramatic and Miscellaneous* Warren obtained a copy of *Observations on the Reflections of the Right Hon. Edmund Burke* (1790), a work by her longtime correspondent Catharine Macaulay Graham, who took Burke to task for his thoroughgoing attack on the French Revolution, published in 1789 as *Reflections on the Revolution in France*. Burke, who had sometimes supported the American cause, found the French Revolution too threatening to be encouraged, and he feared that its importation into Britain would destabilize the country. Some Americans also condemned the French, while the Jeffersonians, or Democratic Republicans, were more hopeful. In autumn 1791, after several people, including John Adams, pressed to borrow her copy, Warren persuaded Isaiah Thomas and E. T. Andrews to publish an American edition with an introduction by Warren, who was no great lover of French intellectual culture. (While she admired Molière, she remained a persistent critic of Voltaire.) Warren agreed with Macaulay Graham that Burke had been intemperate, and in her intro-

duction to the American edition, the Plymouth writer expressed her view that the French Revolution would necessarily have a salutary effect on politics "by agitating questions which have for a time lain dormant in England and have been almost forgotten, or *artfully disguised,* in America." In short, although well into her sixties, Warren felt that radical ideas were valuable for a complaisant society, if for no other reason than to stir debate on important issues that were being ignored. At a time when many Americans in the new republic felt threatened or uneasy with the major changes they had witnessed, Warren expressed continued interest in change until such time as the proper delegation of authority to the people could be maintained.

An event in late 1791 forced Warren into semiretirement as a writer for the public. Having returned home after several undistinguished years in Europe, Winslow Warren had joined the army and set out on an expedition to Ohio, where he was killed in the defeat of Gen. Arthur St. Clair's forces by Native Americans. As the inspiration for much of her work, Winslow had an importance to Mercy Warren beyond any significance he seems to have had outside her sphere. His death was a serious blow to a woman who had already lost one son. She continued to work on her history and wrote letters, many of them giving advice to young women, but the world was changing for her. The deaths of her friends John and Hannah Winthrop, strained relations with the Adamses, the ascendancy in political power of the Federalists, not to mention her grief over her sons, gave a check to Mercy Warren as a public literary figure. In 1800, the year in which Thomas Jefferson, supported publicly by James Warren, defeated their one-time ally John Adams in the presidential election, the Warrens lost still another son, George.

In late 1805 the first of three volumes of Warren's *History of the Rise, Progress and Termination of the American Revolution* appeared under the imprint of Ebenezer Larkin in Boston. A book over which she had labored since the beginning of the conflict, this history remains Warren's most significant prose work. In writing it she had the standard published documents written from British and American perspectives, but she also had access to private correspondence: her own, her husband's, and that of friends such as John Adams. As the only full-length history of the Revolution by a contemporary woman, her history allows the modern reader a view of the conflict that is more attentive to the sufferings of the innocent than other histories of her time.

In its day the *History of the Rise, Progress and Termination of the American Revolution* had the power to inspire lengthy reviews and scathing commentary. While the *Panoplist* reviewer (January and February 1807) found her very act of writing transgressed biblically established gender distinctions and criticized Warren for going public with her book, the Worcester *National Aegis* reviewer (10 January – 28 February 1810) found it fully justifiable for a woman to write history and to write it well. Yet overall, the timing of its release could not have been worse. It appeared just after early volumes of John Marshall's *Life of George Washington* (1804–1807), a direct competitor for the subscription market in Revolutionary War histories. Other histories had already appeared, notably those by David Ramsay and William Gordon. Warren's main audience would have been in Massachusetts, where she was best known, but as her Boston subscription solicitor, Judith Sargent Murray, reported, the people she canvassed (and she herself) were of Federalist persuasion while Warren was a firm Jeffersonian. Indeed, the respect accorded female authors during the Revolution and in the decade after was waning as well. As a woman, as a Democratic Republican, as a person of a dying generation, and as an author whose near blindness left her dependent on the agency of family and friends to get her work to press, Warren could not command the readership that other writers and works could muster.

Nevertheless, Warren's perspective on the Revolution, and on American history in general, is unmatched among her contemporaries. To compre-

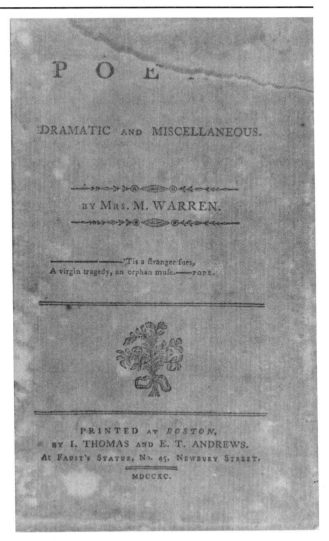

Title page for the volume that includes Warren's verse dramas The Sack of Rome *and* The Ladies of Castile, *both written as warnings against "corruption" among the postrevolutionary generation of Americans (courtesy of Special Collections, Thomas Cooper Library, University of South Carolina)*

hend her method, one must pay close attention to the subtitle: *Interspersed with Biographical, Political and Moral Observations.* Warren had little patience for or interest in military history in the traditional sense. Her history dutifully follows the course of the various campaigns; yet it rarely goes into any special detail on topics such as troop movements, formations, strategies, and fortifications. Instead her history is resolutely human, connected to character and issues of human nature; it also devotes considerable space to political questions, notably those philosophical points tied to the nature of a republic. One is more likely to "drop the tear of compassion" over the suffering of a civilian than to find catalogues of casualties among the soldiers. Thus it is important to note

Needlepoint tabletop embroidered by Warren (Pilgrim Society, Plymouth, Massachusetts)

the role of style and conceptual framework in evaluating Warren's history.

She began the narrative portion with a survey of American history that includes the arrival of the Calvinists. While acknowledging their contribution to the settlement of the country, the history notes among the Puritans and some of their antagonists, including the Massachusetts Quakers, a spirit of intolerance and extremism that defies a rational apprehension of the universe. Thus, her reading of American history is tied early in the book to a liberalizing of thought; true progress has been marked by the increased tolerance for diversity that the republic ought to foster. "It is rational to believe," she explained, "that the benevolent Author of nature designed universal happiness as the basis of his works. Nor is it unphilosophical to suppose the difference in human sentiment, and the variety of opinions among mankind, may conduce to this end." Her own history is in some ways a testament to the liberality that she celebrated; for she wrote against suppression of her own views. "The contemplative and liberal minded man must, therefore, blush for the weakness of his own species, when he sees any of them endeavouring to circumscribe the limits of virtue and happiness within his own contracted sphere, too often darkened by superstition and bigotry."

The act of a liberal-minded woman writing a lesson in history to her country becomes a theme that rivals some of the political and military themes in the book.

In surveying events that lead to war, Warren introduced another theme that pervades her book: the proclivity of human beings to cling to self-interest, even in the face of threats to the larger interests of the people. As she remarked in chapter two, the populace as a group is always in danger of "supineness," a kind of lassitude brought about by habit and an unhealthy trust in government. People tend to give up their claim on governance when in a state of "inglorious ease," as if prosperity makes cowards of citizens. Yet once awakened to their state, those same beings will rise up and denounce or overthrow their oppressors; it is in the nature of humankind to rebel at the idea of being made into perpetual slaves. For Warren the Revolution was not simply an historical event of significance in the life of the country but also an opportunity to test certain theories about the operation of moral character. Thus the tension between self-interested behavior, which tends to "supineness," and self-sacrificing dedication to cause, which inspires the free-minded to revolt, is the real battleground of the republic.

In addition to the large philosophical and moral questions she raised, the writing of the history gave Mercy Warren an opportunity to elevate old prejudices and wounds to the status of national lesson. Her longtime resentment of Thomas Hutchinson reveals itself in her character sketch of the one-time royal governor. For Warren, Hutchinson was a Machiavel of the first order, a rival to the scheming European political operators in whose history she had been schooled. "He was," she wrote, "dark, intriguing, insinuating, haughty and ambitious, while the extreme of avarice marked each feature of his character."

Pitted against the designing governor is her brother James Otis Jr. Styling his beating in 1769 by John Robinson as an attempted "assassination," Warren noted the contrast of character between an early opponent of crown policy and its chief supporter in Massachusetts. Where Hutchinson lived largely as a tool of the court in London, spinning plots in which to trap republican-leaning Americans, Otis spoke from "the fire of eloquence" and demonstrated a character in which "His humanity was conspicuous, his sincerity acknowledged, his integrity unimpeached, his honor unblemished, and his patriotism marked with the disinterestedness of the Spartan." Thus throughout her history Warren gave the advantage to the patriot side by virtue of its superior characters as much as by any particular political principle.

By making character a measure of the war, Warren shaped her history according to a natural drama in which certain individuals on both sides would be put to the test. After the portrait of Hutchinson, one expects Warren to shape the narrative around patriot virtue and loyalist vice. Yet the author does not give in readily to so monolithic a reading of the war. Indeed, not every character on the American side passes the test of character. Warren created dramatic tension by noting within American ranks certain flawed patriots, whose blemished characters threatened the success of republican partisans in wartime and the ability of the independent nation to thrive in peace.

For Warren one such problematic patriot was Gen. Charles Lee. Third in command in 1776, Lee served an historical—perhaps even providential—role as one of the few men early in the war capable of battlefield command. Yet for Warren his virtues in battle could not overcome his vices in peace: "Without religion or country, principle, or attachment, gold was his deity, and liberty the idol of his fancy." Lee, she argued, fought for the glory and potential remuneration he might achieve, not for principle. His disavowal of the spur of fame only

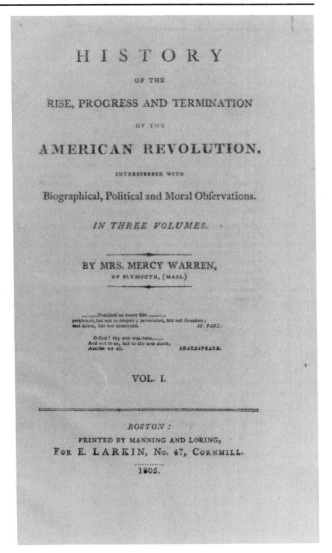

Title page for volume one of Warren's best-known book, which, unlike Revolutionary War histories by her contemporaries, focuses on moral issues and the characters of leaders, rather than battles and military strategy (courtesy of Special Collections, Thomas Cooper Library, University of South Carolina)

exposed his dependence on it for motivation. Warren went so far as to denigrate his attempts to appear dignified, reducing his actions outside the public arena as the actions of a "clown." Although Warren's summary of Lee's character had been determined early in the writing of her history, she may have seen its significance only later. Her purpose in writing, after all, was to acquaint the rising generations with the principles and actions of their predecessors, with an additional hope that if the spirit of the Revolution were recognized and vigorously maintained, the vices of peacetime—excessive prosperity, luxury, corruption, self-interest—could be kept in check. It matters, then, what heroes one finds. As an epicurean, Lee had no place in Warren's pantheon of model, "Spartan" Americans.

Another strategy beyond the character sketch was to center British or Tory brutality as images of the perversion of ideals in wartime. An example of this tactic occurs in her depiction of the Battles of Lexington and Concord, which seems to impugn Hugh, Lord Percy, who, after rescuing the entrapped troops of Col. Francis Smith, led the British on a rampage against civilians. Their burning of houses and verbal abuse of defenseless families was bad enough; worse, Warren wrote, "the aged and infirm fell under the sword of the ruffian; women, with their new-born infants, were obliged to fly naked, to escape the fury of the flames in which their houses were enwrapped." This ravaging of domestic spaces—a theme repeated throughout Warren's volumes, with many examples—puts the war on a different footing. Not simply an ideological contention over the rights of sovereign and subject, the American Revolution pits antidomestic redcoat savages against patriotic upholders of the hearth. For Nina Baym this violation of the home produced a "gendered melodrama"; in fact, Warren simply recast familiar Whig tropes of resistance in a language sure to engage the sensibilities of young readers. She brought the "blood of the slain" imagery, which pervades prewar orations commemorating the Boston Massacre, into the larger and more momentous conflict of the war. Since Warren's intention was to bring home the lessons of the patriots to rising and future generations of young people, the focus on mothers and children as particular victims of antipatriot violence intensifies the message and gives a telling lesson to the message bearers, the republican mothers who interpret the Revolution for their children.

There are many other stories and images worth mentioning: Warren's emblems of Stoic sacrifice, as in the suffering troops at Valley Forge; the creation of early heroes in Joseph Warren, who died at Bunker Hill, and Richard Montgomery, who was killed in the assault on Montreal; continued violence against civilians, including the butchering of Loyalist Jane McCrea; the deliberations of Congress; the gallantry of the French allies; and the final victories and postwar negotiations. All these people and events are presented in brief narratives, many of which offer pictures of violence against the domestic and the innocence of families trapped by war.

Nevertheless, Warren's narratives are largely subordinate to philosophic and critical ends. After all, the subtitle of her history advertises that it is replete with "observations," which for Warren were the point of writing. By the conclusion of her work

Warren's purpose is quite clearly something besides illustrating war. Rather, it is the peacetime progress of the new republic. She looked at other republics and took her story nearly to the present of her own time. As she announced early in the book, the fate of republican government depends on the continued virtue of the people and the responsibility of political leaders to respect the freedom of conscience of citizens. That theme, the definition of a republic, is often rendered abstractly as a topic of political philosophy. Yet much of this theme can be detected by looking at another story to which Warren frequently, if obscurely, alluded. Her history is also about her disintegrating friendship with John Adams.

When she began writing in 1775, she wrote with the intention, perhaps, of pleasing John and Abigail Adams, then her most important friends. By the time the volumes emerged from the printer, the Adamses and Warrens stood on opposite sides of a wide gulf. Indeed, in 1807, when John Adams finally received his volumes of Warren's book, the rift that had never been fully acknowledged spread even wider. In a series of ten long, pained, angry letters, Adams wrote how much Madame Warren had abused him and belittled his accomplishments. Although the historian held her own against the senior statesman in the epistolary exchange, the fact remains that the diminution of Adams does play a significant part in the shape of the history as a whole.

One of Adams's complaints centered on the lateness with which he is introduced in Warren's history. Not mentioned outright until her discussion of the Massachusetts elections of May 1774, Adams appears thus: "John Adams, a barrister at law of rising abilities; his appearance on the theatre of politics commenced at this period; we shall meet him again in still more dignified stations." As Warren well knew, Adams had been active in public affairs long before this election, but even in the context of her discussion—elected representatives who were denied seats by the royal governor—others stand above him, notably future governor James Bowdoin and the astronomer John Winthrop.

Mercy Warren's complaint against Adams rested on his activities and attitudes after the war. Adams spent several years abroad, in Holland, France, and England, in various treaty and economic negotiations. During this period Shays's Rebellion (1786–1787), an uprising of debt-ridden farmers in western Massachusetts against what they saw as an oppressive new state apparatus, divided the loyalties of many former revolutionaries. For John Adams the rebellion needed to be crushed. For James Warren, as well as for his wife, the farmers deserved sympathy. This split between the men exacerbated some other tensions between the families as a whole. From the time that Adams entered national administration, first as George Washington's vice president, then as president (1797–1801), the Warrens viewed his assertion of a strong central government and his clear distaste for popular authority—evident in his promotion of restrictions on the press in the Alien and Sedition Acts of 1798—as antirepublican.

At the end of her *History of the Rise, Progress and Termination of the American Revolution* Warren surveyed postwar trends and, finally, after pointedly understating the significance of one of the chief architects of the nation, she assessed Adams's character. Even at this point in her writing, with Adams already out of office, the wounds of betrayal that she felt are apparent: "The veracity of an historian requires, that all those who have been distinguished, either by their abilities or their elevated rank, should be exhibited through every period of public life with impartiality and truth. But," she continued, "the heart of the annalist may sometimes be hurt by political deviations which the pen of the historian is obliged to record." This passage means, in essence, that she felt obliged to expose her old friend as dangerous to the republic.

In summary, these are the charges she leveled against Adams: that he was more choleric than rational in his approach to policy; that during his time in England on government business he became attracted to monarchy; and that by the time he came back to the United States, he had forgotten the principles for which the Warrens and the Adamses had originally risked their lives and careers. In effect, Warren argued that if a man such as Adams can be corrupted by monarchy and systems of preference, then the rest of the nation is chronically at risk of setting aside the essential principles for which the Revolution was fought. Strangely, then, while her early motivation to begin her *History of the Rise, Progress and Termination of the American Revolution* was inspired by Adams's friendship and firm patriotism, her motivation to complete the book—when age, loss of children, and increasing blindness were taking their tolls—stemmed from her desire to explain the flight from principle by the same individual who once supplied her with eyewitness accounts of momentous events. Keeping John Adams in his place was necessary so that rising generations would not be misled by his straying from the democratic republicanism that Warren felt was essential for the system of checks on tyranny.

History of the Rise, Progress and Termination of the American Revolution was the last work Warren published in her lifetime. By 1800 her eyesight had become so diminished that she conducted her correspondence through an amanuensis, her son James, who had lost a leg in the war. Following the exchange in 1807 with Adams, her remaining prose works are letters to friends, largely of a personal nature. With the death of her husband in 1808, and with only one of her two surviving sons married and a father, she needed those letters to keep up her commerce with the world. One of those friends, Elbridge Gerry, effected a reconciliation between the Adamses and Mercy Warren in late 1812. In October 1814, following a visit from another valued correspondent, Sarah Gray Cary, Mercy Otis Warren became violently ill. Apparently lucid to the end, she died on 19 October 1814 and was buried next to her husband in the Plymouth cemetery. In that grave were deposited the remains of the most important female author from the era of the Revolution.

As a prose writer, Mercy Otis Warren produced one great published work, the *History of the Rise, Progress and Termination of the American Revolution*. In addition, her letters, though occasionally florid or even sententious, provide an often elegant illumination of one woman's attempt at discourse, with men and women alike, on the major issues of the day. Her other works, her introductions and her critique of the Constitution, help flesh out Warren's literary and political attitudes. Taken together, her prose works represent a significant body of political, moral, and philosophical reflections on a key era in American history. Those writings, along with her poetical and dramatic works, have largely determined her lasting reputation as a significant cultural figure in eighteenth-century America.

Letters:

Warren-Adams Letters: Being chiefly a correspondence among John Adams, Samuel Adams, and James Warren, 2 volumes (Boston: Massachusetts Historical Society, 1917);

The Adams Papers: Adams Family Correspondence, 1761–1782, edited by L. H. Butterfield and others, 4 volumes (Cambridge, Mass.: Harvard University Press, 1963, 1973); *The Adams Papers: Adams Family Correspondence, 1782–1785,* edited by Richard Alan Ryerson and others, 2 volumes (Cambridge, Mass.: Harvard University Press, 1993);

A Study in Dissent: The Warren-Gerry Correspondence, 1776–1792, edited by C. Harvey Gardiner (Carbondale: Southern Illinois University Press, 1968);

Correspondence between John Adams and Mercy Warren, edited by Charles F. Adams (New York: Arno, 1972).

Biographies:

Alice Brown, *Mercy Warren* (New York: Scribners, 1896);

Katherine Anthony, *First Lady of the Revolution: The Life of Mercy Otis Warren* (Garden City, N.Y.: Doubleday, 1958);

Jean Fritz, *Cast for a Revolution: Some American Friends and Enemies, 1728–1814* (Boston: Houghton Mifflin, 1972);

Rosemarie Zagarri, *A Woman's Dilemma: Mercy Otis Warren and the American Revolution* (Wheeling, Ill.: Harlan Davidson, 1995).

References:

Nina Baym, "Mercy Otis Warren's Gendered Melodrama of Revolution," *South Atlantic Quarterly,* 90 (1991): 531–554;

Lester H. Cohen, "Explaining the Revolution: Ideology and Ethics in Mercy Otis Warren's Historical Theory," *William and Mary Quarterly,* 37 (1980): 200–218;

Cohen, "Mercy Otis Warren: The Politics of Language and the Aesthetics of Self," *American Quarterly,* 35 (1983): 481–498;

Cohen, *The Revolutionary Histories: Contemporary Narratives of the American Revolution* (Ithaca, N.Y.: Cornell University Press, 1980);

Elizabeth F. Ellet, *The Women of the American Revolution,* volume 1 (New York: Baker & Scribner, 1848);

Lawrence J. Friedman and Arthur J. Shaffer, "Mercy Otis Warren and the Politics of Historical Nationalism," *New England Quarterly,* 48 (1975): 194–215;

Edmund M. Hayes, "Mercy Otis Warren: *The Defeat,*" *New England Quarterly,* 49 (1976): 440–458;

Hayes, "Mercy Otis Warren versus Lord Chesterfield, 1779," *William and Mary Quarterly,* 40 (1983): 616–621;

Hayes, "The Private Poems of Mercy Otis Warren," *New England Quarterly,* 54 (1981): 199–224;

Maud Macdonald Hutcheson, "Mercy Warren, 1728–1814," *William and Mary Quarterly,* 10 (1953): 378–402;

Judith B. Markovitz, "Radical and Feminist: Mercy Otis Warren and the Historiographers," *Peace and Change,* 4 (1977): 10–20;

Janis L. McDonald, "The Need for Contextual Revision: Mercy Otis Warren, a Case in Point," *Yale Journal of Law and Feminism,* 5 (1992): 183–215;

Cheryl Oreovicz, "Mercy Otis Warren (1728–1814)," *Legacy,* 13 (1996): 54–64;

Oreovicz, "Mercy Warren and Freedom's Genius," *University of Mississippi Studies in English,* 5 (1984–1987): 215–230;

Jeffrey H. Richards, *Mercy Otis Warren* (New York: Twayne/Simon & Schuster, 1995);

Richards, *Theater Enough: American Culture and the Metaphor of the World Stage, 1607–1789* (Durham, N.C.: Duke University Press, 1991);

Frank Shuffelton, "In Different Voices: Gender in the American Republic of Letters," *Early American Literature,* 25 (1990): 289–304;

Charles Warren, "Elbridge Gerry, James Warren, Mercy Warren, and the Ratification of the Federal Constitution in Massachusetts," *Massachusetts Historical Society Proceedings,* 60 (1926–1927): 143–164.

Papers:

The main repository of Warren letters and papers is the Massachusetts Historical Society in Boston, with the largest collection being the Mercy Warren Papers. This collection is divided into two parts, each available on a separate roll of microfilm: the "Letterbook," copies of letters she sent; and loose papers and letters, including fair copies by Warren. The Pilgrim Society in Plymouth has a typescript of many of the items in the Mercy Warren Papers at the Massachusetts Historical Society. Scattered letters can be found in several other collections, most notably those at the Boston Public Library and the Houghton and Schlesinger Libraries at Harvard University. In addition, the Houghton Library has a manuscript for Warren's *History of the Rise, Progress and Termination of the American Revolution* and another with texts of her three satiric plays and some poems. Other manuscript versions of the *History of the Rise, Progress and Termination of the American Revolution* can be found at the Library of Congress, along with a few letters.

Helena Wells
(1758? – 6 July 1824)

Steven Hamelman
Coastal Carolina University

BOOKS: *The Step-Mother: A Domestic Tale, from Real Life,* 2 volumes (London: Printed for T. N. Longman, 1798);
Letters on Subjects of Importance to the Happiness of Young Females, Addressed by a Governess to Her Pupils, Chiefly While They Were under Her Immediate Tuition: to Which is Added, a Few Practical Lessons in the Improprieties of Language, and Errors of Pronunciation, Which Frequently Occur in Common Conversation (London: L. Peacock / Edinburgh: W. Creech, 1799);
Constantia Neville; or, The West Indian. A Novel, 3 volumes (London: Printed by C. Whittingham for T. Cadell Jr. & W. Davies & W. Creech, Edinburgh, 1800);
Thoughts and Remarks on Establishing an Institution, for the Support and Education of Unportioned Respectable Females (London: Printed for Longman, Hurst, Rees & Orme, Cadell & Davies / York: T. Wilson & Son, 1809).

Helena Wells is an early example of a transplanted American writer. During adolescence she went to England, where, during a ten-year period beginning in 1798, she completed and published two multivolume novels, a guidebook on the education of young females, and a treatise advocating social reform on behalf of destitute women. These four works reveal an author concerned about women's struggles to live decently in late-eighteenth-century England. Thematically, Wells focused on proper child rearing and education as the essential means of social reform and domestic happiness, the need to help "unportioned respectable females," rational management of one's financial resources, and behavior modeled on patience, modesty, humility, honesty, and faith. Although Wells's writings do not comment on the American Revolution in any significant way, the war and her family's attitudes toward it did contribute to the views expressed in her books.

Helena Wells's parents, Robert and Mary Wells, came to South Carolina from their native Scotland in 1753, eventually settling in Charleston, where Robert soon succeeded as a bookbinder and bookseller, and as the printer of *The South-Carolina and American General Gazette* in 1758. These and other enterprises gained him considerable stature and wealth.

Helena Wells was born in Charleston, probably between 1758 and 1765. Her birth is undocumented, but in "A Memoir of His Life" (1818) her brother Dr. William Charles Wells, who was born in 1757, wrote that Helena was the youngest surviving Wells child, which means she was born no earlier than 1758. On the other hand, Helena's sister Louisa (born in 1755) recalled in *The Journal of a Voyage from Charlestown, S.C., to London* (written in 1779) that at age ten she helped take care of two sick infant sisters. If one of these infants was Helena, she might have been born around 1764. (One or both of the babies mentioned must not have survived infancy.)

Helena Wells enjoyed a privileged childhood in Charleston. In addition to being a successful businessman, her father was a cultured man who provided his two sons with excellent educations in Scotland and who apparently encouraged learning in his three daughters. Robert Wells wrote poetry, edited his newspaper judiciously, inspired respect for his forthright behavior, and raised children who inherited his literary skills and pro-British perspective. Historians characterize Robert Wells as a man of staunch Old World demeanor and ideology who was committed to resourceful business practices.

The works that Helena Wells wrote in the late eighteenth and early nineteenth centuries might not reflect the upheavals caused by the American Revolution, but they certainly resulted from her wartime living situation. Because he was an outspoken and inflexible Loyalist, Robert Wells found himself unable to remain in South Carolina. In 1777 he and Mary Wells moved to England, taking their daughters Griselda and Helena. At some point they were joined by their daughter Louisa.

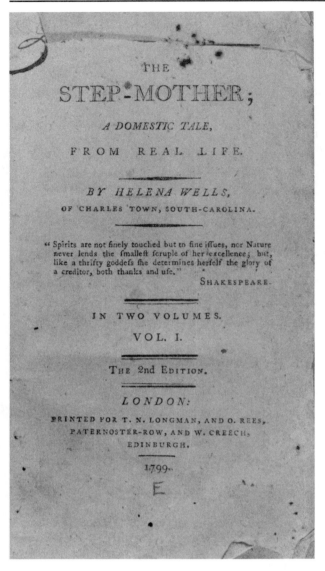

Title page for Helena Wells's first book, a sentimental novel about a woman of exemplary manners and morals (courtesy of the South Caroliniana Library, University of South Carolina)

For the next few years Robert continued to succeed financially. He amassed £20,000 as a trader in wartime London. In 1779 Helena was living in London with her family. They had a lease of twenty-one years on a house in Salisbury Square, which was being renovated. Louisa reported in her journal that she and Helena spent each day superintending the carpenters, masons, and other laborers. Yet despite Robert Wells's commercial success, questions of money soon became more urgent for the family.

After the peace treaties were signed in 1783, financial reversal began to plague the Wellses. The government of South Carolina had confiscated much of Robert Wells's colonial property, giving him insufficient compensation for it. Because the reparations paid by England were equally insufficient, the family's financial needs increased over the next five years. In 1789, with no other options available to women of their class, breeding, and prospects, Helena and Griselda opened a boarding school. In *Thoughts and Remarks on Establishing an Institution, for the Support and Education of Unportioned Respectable Females* (1809) Helena Wells wrote, "It was in the prime of my life (past thirty), that I attempted to place myself at the head of an establishment to board and educate Young Ladies." (If this passage refers to the project she undertook in 1789, her birth year might be 1758.) Supervising this institution was a rude awakening for Helena, a woman who had enjoyed the benefits of an excellent education and strict moral inculcation at home and had never attended a school. At some time during this period she was also employed as a governess.

Helena Wells also began to write seriously, thereby upholding her family's reputation for literary productivity. (Her two brothers, her father, and her sister Louisa were all published authors. The most successful writer was William, whose papers on dew and vision were considered groundbreaking in the science community.) She may also have turned to writing for a practical reason: to supplement her meagre earnings as a teacher. Robert Wells died insolvent in 1794, another terrible blow to the financial security of the Wells women.

By 1791 Helena Wells had completed the first volume of *The Step-Mother* (1798), or at least a draft of it. While continuing to work on this novel and while she was still teaching, she was also writing *Letters on Subjects of Importance to the Happiness of Young Females* (1799). The first letter in this book is dated 10 March 1794, and the last is dated 20 January 1799. *The Step-Mother* was popular enough to warrant another edition in 1799.

The protagonist of this novel is Caroline Williams, the daughter of a retired rural clergyman. Lacking other options, fourteen-year-old Caroline enters the home of the upper-class Glanviles a few years after her mother's death. Three years later Caroline assumes the duties of governess to the two Glanvile girls. Taking exciting trips to London and interacting with local nobility, who admire her exemplary manners and behavior, Caroline has a happy life. Romantic complications arise when her employer's son Edward, two years her senior, declares his love, which she is unable to reciprocate. Caroline's sense of duty and station is unyielding:

Had I been the daughter of a duke, I should have been proud to share my rank and fortune with Edward Glanvile: but, unfortunately, I was only the *humble éleve* of his father and mother. I dared to refuse his proferred hand, when it was inconsistent with my honour to accept it.

Caroline's decision devastates Edward. Mrs. Belton, a distant relation, becomes Caroline's next guardian, through whom she meets other admirers. In her early twenties Caroline marries the widower Captain Wentworth. Called away to the American war, he dies at sea, leaving Caroline to be stepmother to his four girls.

Volume two of *The Step-Mother* is largely epistolary. The novel becomes more diffuse as it traces new courtships and depicts Caroline's rational management of financial, legal, and maternal matters (such as overseeing the marriages of her stepdaughters). Several subplots are intended to enrich the narrative texture and to gird Wells's didacticism. Projecting her own ideas through Caroline, Wells covered much moral ground. For example, the novel celebrates the esteem and affection that derive from well-trained intelligence and sensibility; it praises a rational and enlightened government; and it denounces the kind of innovative, specious thinking that leads to the spread of vice. The ending of *The Step-Mother*—which features reconciliation, marriages, and even an appropriate death—demonstrates that virtue is the key to personal, domestic, and communal happiness.

Overall, the contemporary reviews of *The Step-Mother* were positive, with the *Historical Magazine* (1799) declaring it one of the best novels of that year. Most reviewers also appreciated the morality of the novel, even though, as one writer asserted in *The Gentleman's Magazine* (June 1798), its morality detracted at times from the development of an exciting plot.

In their studies of the early American novel, formalist critics of the twentieth century regularly commented on *The Step-Mother*. Employing standards based on aesthetic assumptions far different from those of Wells's era, these New Critics concluded that *The Step-Mother* was excessively sentimental and didactic, and, despite the favor it found in her day, they judged it less kindly than Wells's readers did. More-recent evaluations of the American novel, especially feminist and new historicist, suggest fresh interpretations of Wells's output based on her commanding presence as a novelist-cum-preceptor. It was as a preceptor that Wells encapsulated her philosophies in her second book, *Letters on Subjects of Importance,* published in 1799.

Wells's years of experience as a governess and teacher inform this collection of letters, which are addressed to pupils whose academic instruction and moral behavior she supervised for ten years. Twelve letters rail against luxury, laziness (moral, mental, and physical), superficial attainments, excessive emotion, godlessness, boisterousness, gabbing, uncleanliness, and snobbery toward (as well as familiarity with) servants. The letters also condemn affectation, empty banter, romantic exuberance, nail biting and other "low" habits, vanity, and infidelity. The "moral fiber" revealed in this work shows the influence of the Scottish commonsense thinking engrained in Wells years earlier by her father.

Wells's earnestness is enhanced by her felicitous prose. Writing that sufficient recompense for her efforts would be success "in drawing the attention of the younger part of my own sex from frivolous pursuits," she sounded a note consistent not only with all her work but also with her family's reputation for conforming to a rigid moral code. In *Letters on Subjects of Importance* Wells sought specifically to instill in her pupils the powers of rational reflection and judgment. Education based on sound religious principles, upright manners, self-discipline, even irreproachable grammar and usage (covered in an appendix), would empower young women to lead fulfilling lives, no matter what afflictions the future may hold.

Wells's own hardships are mentioned briefly. The seventh letter, written in 1796 to fifteen-year-old Harriet, alludes to Wells's transatlantic voyage, taken "at an earlier age than you will undertake one" (suggesting that Wells, emigrating in 1777, could have been born in 1763 and departed Charleston at the age of fourteen). The eighth letter bemoans the "disastrous effects of the American war" on Wells's family.

Letters on Subjects of Importance is a platform for Wells's beliefs. In this book sincerity and purity of purpose are allowed free rein without being embedded in, and thereby diluted by, a fictional context. In fact, the first letter attacks novels, endorsing Homer, Virgil, Edmund Spenser, and John Dryden while arguing that novels of imagination and frivolity (but apparently, not of utility) should be avoided:

> Novel reading tends to enervate the mind. We rise from the perusal of even the best writer languid and fatigued; such overcharged pictures of life and manners as they generally draw, make us sick of ourselves, and the homely beings with whom we are compelled to associate.

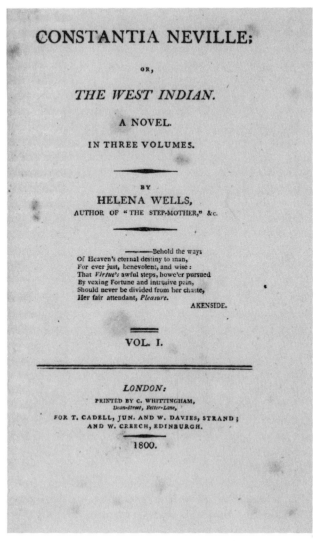

CONSTANTIA NEVILLE;

OR,

THE WEST INDIAN.

A NOVEL.

IN THREE VOLUMES.

BY

HELENA WELLS,

AUTHOR OF "THE STEP-MOTHER," &c.

————Behold the ways
Of Heaven's eternal destiny to man,
For ever just, benevolent, and wise:
That *Virtue's* awful steps, howe'er pursued
By vexing Fortune and intrusive pain,
Should never be divided from her chaste,
Her fair attendant, *Pleasure*.

AKENSIDE.

VOL. I.

LONDON:

PRINTED BY C. WHITTINGHAM,
Dean-Street, Fetter-Lane,
FOR T. CADELL, JUN. AND W. DAVIES, STRAND;
AND W. CREECH, EDINBURGH.

1800.

Title page for Wells's second novel, which laments the plight of the "unportioned female," who has neither family nor inheritance to support her (courtesy of the Special Collections Department, University of Virginia Library)

This statement—a conventional eighteenth-century view of fiction—is not articulated with such clarity anywhere else in Wells's cannon.

Most critics of the day recommended *Letters on Subjects of Importance.* As one reviewer claimed in the *Anti-Jacobin Review* (July 1799), Wells's guidelines displayed a genuine desire to sow in the minds of impressionable females the virtues of self-discipline, religious veneration, justice, parental respect and love, and related traits. Conversely, twentieth-century critics have ignored this contribution to a genre that includes the letters of Michel-Guillaume-Jean de Crèvecoeur in America and Philip Dormer Stanhope, Lord Chesterfield, in England. Wells's *Letters on Subjects of Importance* not only provides

modern readers with an insight into the morality, psychology, and aesthetic philosophy of a representative eighteenth-century teacher, but it also provides an appendix that deserves separate commentary. This appendix, filled with examples from contemporary speech, reveals much about the eighteenth-century attitude toward an intriguing pedagogical concept: the interrelationship between morality and the proper use of language.

In *Constantia Neville,* published in April 1800 with a second edition in August, Wells sustained her moralistic tone while restraining her imagination, as if to exemplify her conception of what the ideal novelist could achieve. Constantia is the child of an English merchant and his wife in Barbados, where Constantia's father and brother maintain the family mercantile house. Also set in Hamburg, England, and Puerto Rico, the novel devotes hundreds of pages to Constantia's life after the age of thirteen, when she moves to England and begins traveling from one country home to another while interacting with an array of aristocratic matrons and aggressive gentlemen. After a series of remarkable shifts in plot, Constantia finds love and prosperity. For most of the novel, however, she embodies the "unportioned young female" Wells lamented throughout her writings. In one passage Wells directly addressed the problem:

> Until the chief glory of women consists in protecting and supporting each other in what is laudable, so long may we despair of a reformation in morals. The delicately brought up unportioned female, is truly an object of commiseration; most fervently does the writer . . . dedicate her feeble powers to their cause. . . .

Didactic interludes such as this one buttress a drawn-out plot that ends happily. (The novel exceeds one thousand pages.)

One intriguing aspect of the novel is Wells's brief use of American Indians, the captors of Constantia's future husband. She also commented on slavery, a subject she touched on in *The Step-Mother* and *Thoughts and Remarks on Establishing an Institution* (1809). Although she opposed slavery, she was ambivalent about "negroes," whom she identified, along with hot weather and mosquitoes, as unbearable grievances indigenous to Barbados.

Since it is arguable that Wells's writings shine brightest in their didactic asides, it is perhaps to her advantage that *Constantia Neville* is saturated with them. Though in terms of plot *Constantia Neville* is livelier than *The Step-Mother,* its strengths and weaknesses—and the critical responses to them—resemble those of her earlier texts. Relishing Wells's blend of morality and incident, contemporary reviewers were almost unanimous in their recommendations of the novel, but twentieth-century scholars tend to criticize its diffuse plot, thin characterization, and overt didacticism. *Constantia Neville* was Wells's last attempt at integrating didactic reflections into a fictional work.

In November 1801 Wells married a Mr. Whitford, who seems not to have improved her standard of living to any great extent. It is possible that Dr. William Wells, who lived nearby, paid her income and property tax, as well as giving her an annuity of £20. His memoir alludes to the hardship of paying these monies to a female relation from 1806 to 1816. This woman could not have been Louisa Wells, who had embarked for Kingston, Jamaica, sometime between 1779 and 1782. Helena Wells was certainly in her brother's mind. In the same memoir he mentioned that apoplexy, which killed his father and brother, had almost killed Helena, who suffered an attack after giving birth to a child.

Wells's marriage to Whitford interrupted her writing career. Bearing and then raising four children (while living, at least part of the time, in Yorkshire) delayed the composition and publication of *Thoughts and Remarks on Establishing an Institution*. Calling for the establishment of a "Protestant nunnery" as a way to solve the problems facing women without means, Wells assumed her strongest religious and feminist (that is, conservative and liberal) voices. In her final extant work she spoke both as a devout Christian mother and wife who feared radical politics and social upheaval and as a progressive woman dedicated to reforming institutions that fostered discrimination against her sisters. She conceded that "to pursue objects, though laudable in themselves, ought ever to be subservient to those superior claims of Husband and Children." At the same time she pondered the severe difficulty for industrious women of her class to gain respectful, meaningful employment: "for does not man bar every avenue to successful enterprize, by engrossing almost every employment, by which she might be enabled to render herself independent?" An impassioned, eloquent, and practical yet visionary essay written on behalf of a dispossessed group, *Thoughts and Remarks on Establishing an Institution* boldly criticizes what Wells considered a defective educational system that did not prepare single or widowed women for economic hardship and the false social values that allowed such a system to flourish.

As a girl Helena Wells was nurtured on the example of a father who had used his newspaper as a forum to defy the colonial spirit of independence,

even though such defiance doomed him and his family to losing everything in defense of those principles. In 1809 Robert Wells's daughter assumed a similar stance for a different cause. Adopting the tone of a fearless reformer who had carefully observed English society and law, Helena Wells committed herself to rooting out the causes of evils that no one seemed willing to identify or remedy. *Thoughts and Remarks on Establishing an Institution* is the pinnacle of Wells's literary mission to raise the character, status, and material condition of women by liberating them from frivolity and folly and by outlining concrete ways in which they might attain happiness for themselves and, thus, contribute to a better society for all. Wells named the main oppressor of women: "her spoiler, her avowed enemy? Man!" She did not flinch when suggesting that Parliament, having emancipated "the African Negroes" by abolishing the slave trade, should extend the same "commiseration" to her "suffering Sisters." Wells condemned the tragic consequences of the French Revolution, and she scoffed at the sophistry of male authority figures who, with all their learning, failed to rectify social abuses. She pointed to poor parenting, the infamy of divorce, women "debased . . . by their communication with men, whose only desire is to allure them to their destruction," ignorant teachers, and the profligacy of husbands.

In *Thoughts and Remarks on Establishing an Institution* Wells articulated the Anglophilia on which she was raised by her Loyalist parents. Despite the flaws she observed in English society, her loyalty to England did not abate. With the exception of her brother John, a respected printer and newspaper owner in the West Indies, Anglophilia ran deep among all the Wellses. In *Thoughts and Remarks on Establishing an Institution* Wells declared:

> When I first trod the verdant grass and sweet humidity which bedews this favoured island . . . then was I tempted to exclaim, 'What country on the habitable globe is equal to that which now gladdens the sight! Our Sea-girt Island is surely the favourite abode of benevolence!'

Given such nostalgia, perhaps it is no surprise that in the same work Wells mentioned her father. Recalling his exemplary character, she alluded to Robert Wells twice as her "ever to be revered father." Yet she did depart from him on one significant issue: she supported emancipation while her father owned and traded slaves. It is obvious, however, that his influence on her values, expressed clearly in her four books, was lifelong and incalculable.

Wells's frankness extended to herself in *Thoughts and Remarks on Establishing an Institution,* at once her most polemical and most autobiographical book. Mentioning her "long detention from indisposition" in Yorkshire, her four children, her American birth, and her serious illness and long convalescence following her fourth delivery, it also includes a few anecdotes about running a boarding school. Because she did not shift her personal beliefs onto a fictional alter ego, *Thoughts and Remarks on Establishing an Institution* is as close as readers will get to the "real" Helena Wells, whose voice is refreshing, candid, sympathetic, rational, and engaging throughout. Except for one good review *Thoughts and Remarks on Establishing an Institution* received no critical attention, and modern critics have maintained that silence.

During the next fifteen years Helena Wells published nothing else. Before her obituary appeared in 1824, the only sure biographical fact about her (found in her brother William's memoir) is that in 1818 she was living in London, presumably attending to the needs of her family.

Who should claim Helena Wells—England or the United States? In the second edition of *The Step-Mother* she is called "Helena Wells of Charles Town, South Carolina," and in *Constantia Neville* the West Indies bears a striking resemblance to the American South. Yet her settings, characters, and plots are indubitably English. At her best, however, Wells probed issues—such as class, child rearing, education, gender politics, and greed—that continue to challenge both England and America, and her solutions, based on timeless precepts, yet imbued with commonplaces of feminism, still hold validity. In her novels and tracts Helena Wells demonstrated innovative thinking, vigorous prose, moral tenacity, and selfless commitment to the amelioration of injustices suffered by women who, mainly because of flawed economic and educational systems, lack the opportunity to achieve self-fulfillment.

References:

Elisha Bartlett, *A Brief Sketch of the Life, Character, and Writings: William Charles Wells, M.D., F.R.S. An Address Delivered Before the Louisville Medical Society, December 7th, 1849* (Louisville, Ky.: Prentice & Weissinger, 1849);

David Moltke-Hansen, "A World Introduced: The Writings of Helena Wells of Charles Town, South Carolina's First Novelist," in *South Carolina Women Writers,* edited by James B. Meriwether (Spartanburg, S.C.: Reprint Company, 1979), pp. 61–81;

Henri Petter, *The Early American Novel* (Columbus: Ohio State University Press, 1971);

Frances M. Ponick, "Helena Wells and Her Family: Loyalist Writers and Printers of Colonial Charleston," master's thesis, University of South Carolina, 1975;

Lorenzo Sabine, *Biographical Sketches of Loyalists of the American Revolution with an Historical Essay,* 2 volumes (Baltimore: Genealogical Publishing Co., 1979);

Louisa Susannah Wells, *The Journal of a Voyage from Charlestown, S.C., to London Undertaken during the American Revolution by a Daughter of an Eminent American Loyalist [Louisa Susannah Wells] in the Year 1778 and Written from Memory Only in 1779* (New York: New-York Historical Society, 1906);

William Charles Wells, "A Memoir of His Life," in *Two Essays: One upon Single Vision with Two Eyes; the Other on Dew. A Letter to the Right Hon. Lloyd, Lord Kenyon and an Account of a Female of the White Race of Mankind, Part of Whose Skin Resembles That of a Negro, with Some Observations of the Causes of the Differences in Colour and Form between the White and Negro Races of Men* (London: Constable, 1818), pp. vii–lxi.

Eliza Yonge Wilkinson

(7 February 1757 – circa 1813)

C. P. Seabrook Wilkinson
University of South Carolina

BOOK: *Letters of Eliza Wilkinson During the Invasion and Possession of Charlestown, S. C. by the British in the Revolutionary War,* edited by Caroline Gilman (New York: Published by Samuel Colman, 1839).

OTHER: Letter to Mary Porcher, in *The Writers of South Carolina,* edited by George Armstrong Wauchope (Columbia, S.C.: The State, 1910).

The letters of Eliza Yonge Wilkinson constitute one of the most vivid accounts of life during the American Revolution. Like her celebrated South Carolina contemporary Eliza Lucas Pinckney, she wrote not for publication but for the amusement of herself and her intimates. Unlike Pinckney, however, Wilkinson was also conscious of creating an historical record of the unprecedented social and political upheaval that occurred during the period when the Revolution reached its crisis in the South. Private and public considerations occur side by side throughout her letters as they bring her readers into the midst of events far removed from their own experiences. Creating characters and investing them with distinctive speech, she displayed a wide range of emotions as she narrated a variety of incidents. The letters are important as historical documents, as personal testaments to human resourcefulness in adversity, and as attempts to turn the horrors of war to artistic account in carefully crafted prose.

Elizabeth Yonge was born in St. Paul's Parish, South Carolina, on 7 February 1757, the third child of Francis Yonge of Yonge's Island and his first wife, Sarah Clifford. Elizabeth's paternal grandfather was Robert Yonge, an English gentleman who became a successful Carolina planter and member of the provincial Commons Assembly. Always called "Eliza," she was married, probably early in 1774, to Joseph Wilkinson, a man a decade her senior. From a family of transplanted Yorkshire gentry who had become leading planters in the parishes south of Charleston, Joseph Wilkinson was a fourth son, and he had not shared in the 1765 inheritance

of lands from his great-uncle the third Landgrave Morton, property that made his elder brothers prodigiously wealthy. Joseph Wilkinson died within the year of their marriage, and their only son, Joseph Morton Wilkinson, born 10 March 1775, died soon after birth. Having no establishment and no husband, Eliza Wilkinson returned to Yonge's Island. Francis Yonge gave her land, making her a gentlewoman of independent means. In 1788 she inherited her elder brother's plantation on Wadmalaw Island.

Eliza Wilkinson is remembered for her letters, the best of which are distinguished by an immediacy that makes the reader an eyewitness, as when she broke off Letter X by exclaiming: "Bless me! here is a whole troop of British horse coming up to the house; get into my bosom, letter." Caroline Gilman published selections from Wilkinson's letters serially in the *Rose-Bud* and then in book form in 1839. She portrayed Wilkinson as an attractive and vivacious heroine who painted "a most living picture." Regrettably Gilman heavily edited the original letters, not only regularizing spelling and punctuation, repunctuating dialogue, and dividing long passages into paragraphs but also "correcting" grammar, altering vocabulary, and adding passages to make Wilkinson sound more patriotic.

Gilman shaped her selections from the original letter-book into twelve letters, creating a more or less continuous narrative from the spring of 1779 until the surrender of Charles, Lord Cornwallis, in October 1781. At that time Charleston was still in British hands, and skirmishes continued in Wilkinson's part of the country. The "Miss M– P–" to whom they are addressed is almost certainly Mary Porcher, daughter of a Huguenot family in an adjoining parish. Letters I and II describe a period of alarms and anxious waiting. The Yonges and Wilkinsons are directly touched by war in Letters III–VI. Repeatedly plundered, insulted, threatened, and forced to retreat from one plantation to another, they at length sought refuge in the one village in the area, Willtown. The final group of letters, VIII–XII,

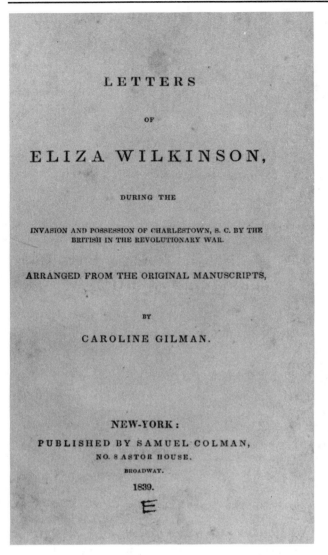

Title page for the collection of letters in which Eliza Younge Wilkinson described her experiences during the American Revolution (courtesy of the South Caroliniana Library, University of South Carolina)

describes life in occupied South Carolina. Letter XI conveys the eerie unreality of the times, describing how Eliza, visiting Charleston, enjoyed a sociable coffee party with American officers on a British prison ship and seemed to think there was nothing unusual in the event. In course of the letters several officers on both sides attain the "high favor" of Eliza Wilkinson. Hints of coquetry in the twelve published letters are confirmed in the 70 percent of the letter-book that remains unpublished. The unpublished letters—to a variety of male and female correspondents in Carolina and Philadelphia—are largely concerned with social life in occupied Charleston and with Eliza's private campaign to find a suitable second husband.

Gilman's reordering of the letters does help to show the quality of much of Eliza Wilkinson's remarkably lifelike dialogue. She had a fine ear for idiosyncrasies of speech, even slave dialect in Letter VI. Her mastery of the details of speech is complemented by a considerable skill in scene painting, notably in the nocturnal flight through marsh and woods described in Letter VI. Her account is not merely incidental or anecdotal; she was also able to orchestrate a chapter-length scene. An element of suspense, partly attributable to the difficulty of distinguishing enemies from friends (even the uniforms were often misleading), pervades the letters. For most of the occasion described in Letter V, convinced that visiting officers were British, she was evasive and defiantly rude by turns, attempting to keep all useful information from them until she finally came to suspect that they were her "countrymen."

Although the letters are historically interesting for Wilkinson's description of military engagements and the Southern campaign of Gen. Benjamin Lincoln, they are most significant because they document the Americanization of an upper-class Anglophile. Not without wrenching did Eliza Wilkinson turn patriot. She could not credit reports of British savagery and disregard for property (a constant concern of hers) until she saw atrocities with her own eyes. In Letter I she suggested that she was being punished for her earlier reluctance to believe reports of British cruelty. Even with the enemy scorching neighboring earth, she supposes there must be some misunderstanding: "Surely, if the British knew the misery they occasion, they would abate their rigor, and blush to think that the name of Englishman, (once so famous among the Fair,) should now produce terror and dismay in every female breast." The letters that follow are largely a record of the re-education of the young widow of a Tory whose family had close ties of blood, affinity, and education to England, as did the Yonges. The political shift in the author's beliefs provides a curve of continuity to a narrative filled with sudden reversals of fortune.

Irony is a major feature of the letters from the first line, which declares Wilkinson's purpose in narrating the events of the 1779 campaign: "As I mean never to forget the *loving-kindness and tender mercies* of the renowned Britons while among us. . . ." Nothing is safe or sacred from her all-embracing irony. When the language of the drawing room is redeployed, the shift in usage is emblematic of the upheaval in her world: "The enemy were all around my Father's, but had not as yet been so *complaisant* as to visit him." The vocabulary of military maneuvers was also adapted with ironic effect, as when she described a plundering party who "presently laid siege to a bee-hive, which they soon brought to terms." Irony speaks most clearly, and most necessarily, from her darkest experiences, as in the report of her bout with smallpox in 1781: after giving thanks to God for safe delivery from this dangerous illness, she observed piquantly, "My face is finely ornamented, and my nose *honored with thirteen spots.* I must add, that I am pleased they will not pit, for as much as I revere the number, I would not choose to have so conspicuous a mark." A young lady of a decidedly literary bent, she frequently quoted from her reading, but she wore her learning lightly, often affecting or confessing ignorance of the sources of her quotations. She was familiar with classical literature, at least in translation, referring to Ovid and Homer. Pope's translation of Homer appears to have been a favorite; she quoted from the same passage in his *Iliad* twice, in Letters I and IV. A quotation from Edward Young in Letter VII attests her acquaintance with modern British poetry.

Throughout her letters Wilkinson was highly self-conscious of her role as writer and historian. Advising of her intention to be as methodical as possible, she cautioned Mary Porcher not to ridicule her "historical manner" of relating the events around her. Pledged to keep her narrative dispassionate and factually accurate, Wilkinson found her prejudices and private opinions irrepressible: "I had determined not to make a digression or observation, and before I am aware, it flies from matters of fact or plain narration, and introduces my poor opinion on the stage." She was acutely aware that recollection of violent events in tranquillity transforms them. The letters display a recurrent sharp sense of her psychological state at the time and an awareness of the fragmentary nature of what memory salvages from the shocks of wartime events. Wilkinson often chafed at the limited perspective her sex and social status afforded. Writing of a major engagement at nearby Stono Ferry, she allowed that she had to employ her imagination to take her to the field of battle. By interpolating the accounts of other eyewitnesses, such as her stepmother, Wilkinson continually sought to extend the range of her eyewitness account without compromising its authenticity.

Wilkinson sometimes cast an ironic eye on her authorial pretensions, frequently confessing incapacity to convey events or to describe her feelings and poking fun at her sententiousness: "But you will conclude I've turned quaker, and the spirit has just moved me to preach you a sermon on the instability of sublunary enjoyments." Sometimes she wrote not for posterity but simply to gratify a curious friend.

In one account of the genesis of her letters, Wilkinson ascribed the impulse to write about the wrenching confrontations of the war not for the purpose of historical truth but to ease her boredom in a quiet country location at which nothing interesting was happening at present. Oscillating between self-importance and extreme self-deprecation, she often questioned the worth of her enterprise: "Well, I have composed a long letter out of nothing; pardon the subject. I am on this lonely island, and have nothing to inspire my pen."

Wilkinson's fluctuating sense of self-worth reflects the feminist simmering beneath the conventional contours of the life of a young gentlewoman who had been taught to discount efforts of women to break into male preserves such as history and literature. In some arresting moments her feminism does surface, assuming ironic guise as she characterized the transformation of the tea table by rumors of invasion. Putting aside discussion of the latest fashions, the ladies turned their attention to military and political events, with such success that Wilkinson archly commented that they might soon be mistaken for statesmen or even "qualified for prime ministers." One of her most eloquent passages, in Letter VI, is an earnest plea for intellectual autonomy:

> I won't have it thought, that because we are the weaker sex as to *bodily* strength, my dear, we are capable of nothing more than minding the dairy, visiting the poultry-house, and all such domestic concerns; our thoughts can soar aloft, we can form conceptions of things of higher nature; and have as just a sense of honor, glory, and great actions, as these "Lords of the Creation." What contemptible *earth worms* these authors make us! They won't even allow us the liberty of thought, and that is all I want.

What emerges in these letters is a self-portrait of Eliza Wilkinson as a candid, charming, resourceful, and high-minded woman whose sense of fun was never extinguished by the terrifying events she narrated. She was at once of her time and, especially in her attitude toward rights for women, far in advance of it. She did not spare herself in her self-presentation, allowing foolishness and cowardice to alternate with courage and ready wit. Wilkinson was also candid about her religious lapses. After a band of British irregulars insulted her aged father, she remembered that Christians are commanded to pray for their enemies, but she confessed that in the heat of indignation all charity vanished from her heart. After her attack of smallpox, she announced with humor and courage, "I intend, in a few days, to introduce my spotted face in Charlestown." She perfectly described herself in a report on the morale of the American officers on the

British prison ship in Charleston harbor: "I am very much pleased to see by their style, that they bear all with fortitude, and are still in high spirits." High spirits distinguish almost all her letters. Exuberant and feisty, she was ever willing to do verbal battle with the invaders even though she knew that other outspoken ladies, such as her correspondent Mrs. Brewton, had been exiled for a single nerve-tweaking witticism. Detained by a British patrol, she observed with evident satisfaction, "I recovered my reason and sauciness at once." Her sense of humor is a constant ally in trying times, as in describing how plundering Loyalists, who had just ripped the buckles from her shoes, left the plantation: "Each wretch's bosom stuffed so full, they appeared to be all afflicted with some dropsical disorder." Sometimes there is a hint of acerbity in remarks that bespeak the frayed tempers of such uncertain times: "the cry from every trembling mouth, 'Where is Lincoln?' but rather, said I, where's the *Lord God of Israel?* Will he indeed deliver us into the hands of these Philistines?"

If at times she was mesmerized by the social rounds, Eliza Wilkinson also had a large fund of compassion, which extended to Tory slaves as well as to dashing officers. In one of the most dramatic scenes, the flight from Yonge's Island across the causeway by night (Letter VI), she reacted in horror to the brutality of one of her father's servants toward a slave belonging to the British. Curtailing the beating of the slave who blundered across their retreat, she attempted to comfort the petrified man, and to reassure him she ran alongside him for the remainder of the journey. When a British officer made a fool of himself by pursuing her through the millinery shops of Broad Street in Charleston, she confessed that his good nature excited pity rather than contempt, confiding to Mary Porcher that she could not find it in herself to resent his clumsy and unwanted attentions.

After the war ended, Wilkinson married the eldest half brother of her chief correspondent, Peter Porcher Sr. of St. Peter's Parish (born circa 1751), on 4 January 1786, and went to live on his plantation at Black Swamp near the Savannah River. Retiring from the gay round of Charleston, which she had loved so well and described so memorably, she also retired from literary history into domesticity and maternity as she turned her attention to the four children of her second marriage. If she wrote anything else, it has not survived. The date of her death is uncertain, but it occurred sometime between 1812 and 1820.

In his 1910 anthology *The Writers of South Carolina,* George Armstrong Wauchope published one additional letter to Mary Porcher, which is punctuated almost exactly as Wilkinson wrote it. Since then no more of the unpublished letters have been made available, but several of the published letters have been included in anthologies of women writers and American literature in general. While they do not deal directly with the momentous events of the British campaign that led to brutal enemy occupation of the Carolina Low Country, the unpublished letters do fill out the self-portrait of the author. A new complete edition of the letters, now in preparation, will present a much fuller picture of Eliza Wilkinson and her times and also restore her authentic authorial voice, so that she no longer sounds like a refined lady of the 1830s but speaks as the altogether racier product of half a century earlier.

The eyewitness account of the Revolution will always be the primary reason for reading Eliza Wilkinson's letters, but they are also valuable for the important light they cast on the role of women, on social conditions in eighteenth-century South Carolina, and on developments in material culture. The letters also possess genuine literary merit, exhibiting many of the features that distinguish much later Southern fiction: vivid appreciation of the landscape, a sure eye for social comedy, and a sense of the bizarre and of the strange juxtaposition of comedy and tragedy in Southern life. Wilkinson was equally adept at narrating the events of war and at conveying the texture of the social life that went on even in the midst of the most desperate conflict. With artistry one does not often find in the private letters of a young gentlewoman, she conveyed the complexity of her feelings and the lights and shades of the uneasy peace within war, creating in her self-portrait a rounded, believable, engaging, and admirable character worthy of the fiction her narrative and descriptive talents might have equipped her to write.

References:

Elizabeth Fries Lummis Ellet, "Heroic Women of the Revolution—Mrs. Eliza Wilkinson," *Godey's Lady's Magazine,* 35 (May 1848): 300–302;

Sharon M. Harris, "WHOSE PAST IS IT? Women Writers in Early America," *Early American Literature,* 30 (1995): 175–181.

Papers:

Eliza Wilkinson's manuscript letter-book remains in the possession of her Porcher descendants; in 1997 it was publicly exhibited for the first time at the Charleston Museum. A careful transcript of the entire volume, made for Professor Yates Snowden in 1905, is among his papers in the South Caroliniana Library at the University of South Carolina.

Anna Green Winslow

(29 November 1759 – 19 July 1780)

Ann E. Green
St. Joseph's University

BOOK: *Diary of Anna Green Winslow, A Boston School Girl of 1771,* edited by Alice Morse Earle (Boston & New York: Houghton, Mifflin, 1894).

OTHER: Pattie Cowell, ed., *Women Poets in Pre-Revolutionary America, 1650–1775: An Anthology,* includes poems by Winslow (Troy, N.Y.: Whitston, 1981), pp. 279–280.

Anna Green Winslow, diarist, schoolgirl, and self-proclaimed "daughter of liberty," lived and wrote in Boston between 1771 and 1773, keeping a letter-diary that is one of the few records of the daily life of a young girl during the prerevolutionary period. Her accounts of education, social events, reading, and daily work provide a thorough picture of Boston life for a young girl of her time and useful documentation of women's writing, education, and socialization just prior to the American Revolution.

Anna Green Winslow came from a long line of prestigious, upper-class British colonists. Her relatives included *Mayflower* passengers, and many were established in Boston society and members of the congregation of Old South Church. Her father, Joshua Winslow, who was baptized at Old South Church on 23 January 1727, served in the British army. In 1745 he was appointed commissary-general of the British forces in Nova Scotia. The records he kept there indicate that he was well educated and a good writer. He married his cousin, Anna Green, on 3 January 1759, and their daughter, Anna Green Winslow, was born there on 29 November 1759. The Winslows subsequently had two sons, neither of whom survived childhood. In 1771, at age eleven, Anna was sent to Boston to attend school. Living with an aunt, she attended dancing and penmanship classes and recorded the details of her life in a letter-dairy for her parents. Joshua Winslow remained in Nova Scotia until 1773, when he reunited his family in Marshfield, Massachusetts. By 1775, however, his Loyalist sympathies caused his exile from the colonies. After some time in England, he became paymaster general for the British

forces in Quebec, a job he held for the remainder of his life.

There are few records of how Anna Green Winslow spent the rest of her life after she stopped keeping her diary in 1773. It is known that Joshua Winslow was separated from his wife and daughter for about eight years, and a journal kept by Anna Green Winslow's mother in Marshfield, Massachusetts, during 1773 includes some information on her daughter's daily life and declining health as well as notes on sermons and other religious musings. Winslow died of what seems to have been tuberculosis on 19 July 1780, when she was twenty years old. In 1783 her mother joined her husband in Quebec.

While in Boston, Anna lived with her aunt and uncle, Sarah and John Deming, and was surrounded by other aunts and uncles in a large, extended family. It was fairly typical for a young, upper-middle-class woman to be sent away to school, and it was also common for a "gentlewoman" such as Winslow's Aunt Deming to take in schoolgirls as boarders in order to earn some additional income. Winslow's parents wanted her to be educated in an appropriate manner for young women of her class. Thus, she studied sewing and helped her aunt with housework, learning skills that prepared her for marriage and running a household. She also learned the arts considered most useful to women of her class, dancing and penmanship, while developing social connections that gave her opportunities to meet eligible young men. In contrast to Loyalist and conservative Nova Scotia, Boston was liberal and prorebellion. (The Sons of Liberty were meeting there daily.) The impact of her father's Loyalist sympathies on Winslow during her stay in Boston is unclear. Her diary rarely mentions politics directly, but she did record sermon notes that include veiled references to rebellion. It is clear that she had ambivalent feelings about the differing attitudes of Bostonians and Nova Scotians.

Winslow began keeping her diary at her aunt's suggestion that she do so to practice her penmanship and to show her the progress she was making in

Anna Green Winslow (from Alice Morse Earle, ed., Diary of
Anna Green Winslow, A Boston School Girl of
1771, *1894)*

her education. During the eighteenth century, diaries were often shared with family members and friends. Anna's aunt seems to have read her diary regularly and recommended what Anna should write about and what she should omit. In addition, her parents responded to her diary in their letters. Throughout the diary she mentioned her various readers, sometimes writing a passage that she hoped her mother would not show to her father and sometimes mentioning her grief that her father did not seem to respond to her remarks, no matter what she wrote. When he finally did read her journal and wrote that he "approv'd some part of them," Winslow recorded her happiness. While Winslow almost always appears to have been cheerful, even when she was sick or recording sad events, she occasionally mentioned her homesickness.

A typical day for Winslow involved attending penmanship, dancing, or sewing school (sometimes more than one), visiting a Boston relative, sewing and mending for her aunt and uncle, and reading the Bible to her aunt. On days when the weather was too bad for her to attend school or when she was ill with boils and colds during the winter, Winslow read, wrote, and sewed. Her entry for 22 February 1772 records a typical day's work:

> I have spun 30 knots of linning yarn, and (partly) new footed a pair of stockings for Lucinda, read a part of the pilgrim's progress, coppied part of my text journal . . . play'd some, tuck'd a great deal . . . laugh'd enough.

Winslow's sense of humor is apparent throughout her diary, as is the sense of her identity as connected to her household tasks. Although Winslow was exempted from some of the harsh work that rural and poor women did, she was still expected to sew, to bake pies occasionally, and generally to participate in the running of the household.

Winslow wrote about funeral processions and other public events and recorded celebrations of holidays such as Valentine's Day and other entertainments and diversions. (True to their Puritan heritage, Bostonians still refused to celebrate Christmas.) Like many other diarists of this period, Winslow took detailed notes on sermons and religious talks that she heard while attending Old South Church with her aunt. Her aunt, however, advised her to stop such detailed note taking, telling Anna that it seemed inappropriate for a girl of twelve to take such an interest in religion. Since Anna's parents encouraged her religious meditations, the real reason for her aunt's advice seems to have been that the sermons included references to revolution and politics. Aunt Deming probably did not consider these texts appropriate subjects for Anna's contemplation and did not want her Loyalist parents to become concerned that their daughter was being exposed to too much talk about rebellion.

While primarily concerned with happenings within the family, Winslow described the punishment of criminals at the public whipping post and wrote about military, religious, and political events, such as the celebration of the anniversary of the Boston Massacre at the Old South Church. Aunt Deming instructed her niece not to go into detail about this celebration, probably for the same reasons she told her to omit some of her notes on sermons. Winslow also watched troops practicing on election day.

Public punishment of criminals was common at that time, and Winslow wrote about the case of Betty Smith, whom Winslow's mother might have known. According to Winslow, Smith, who lived with the troops in Boston, was accused of stealing. She was publicly whipped and jailed, but once in jail she set it on fire in an attempt to escape. Later, Winslow wrote that Smith was "set upon the gallows" and "behav'd with great impudence." This story stands out in the diary because Winslow seems to have been fascinated with such a "bad woman," who developed a "bad" character because she did not conform to societal norms. Clearly this event was also part of Winslow's education, intended to show her the kind of woman she should not become and the violent repercussions of acting in ways that did not meet societal standards.

Among Winslow's reports of family events is a description of a visit to her "Aunt Sukey's." There she celebrated the birth of a baby by buying cakes from the nurse, which she "took care to eat" before paying for them. Other occasions involved parties for young women only, social affairs that were intended to introduce Winslow to others in her class and to socialize her in the conventions of dress and behavior necessary for a good marriage. She started attending these parties around the time of her twelfth birthday. At these parties the Demings' slave, Lucinda, played a flute while the young women danced, played games, and drank wine and punch. Adults were present at these gatherings, but they did not participate in the girls' games and dancing. At one of these parties a man explained to Winslow the difference between Whigs and Tories, but in her diary she did not elaborate on what he told her.

During the colonial period a woman's interests were supposed to be limited to her household tasks and her immediate family circle. She was not to be concerned with politics (although this attitude was beginning to change during the prerevolutionary and Revolutionary period). Winslow's role was further limited by the Congregationalist traditions of her Puritan ancestors. She was expected to be modest, delicate, passive, pious, and virtuous, and the purpose of her education was to promote these aspects of her character. Winslow illustrated her virtue in the diary by recording her household chores and her church attendance. In keeping with the Puritan belief that idleness would encourage sin, she was constantly sewing or knitting.

Sent to Boston so that she could be "finished," Winslow wrote diary entries that provide insights into the conflict between the Puritan ideal of modesty and her concerns about fashion and about fitting in with her peers in the cultural center of Boston. The passage most often quoted from Winslow's diary concerns her worries over her clothing and her wish to look like everyone else:

I hope aunt wont let me wear the black hatt with the red Dominie—for the people will ask me what I have got to sell as I go along street if I do, or, how the folks at New guinie do? Dear mamma, you don't know the fation here—I beg you to look like other folk. You don't know what a stir would be made in sudbury street, were I to make my appearance there in my red Dominie & black Hatt.

Writing in *The Atlantic Monthly* in 1894, the editor of Winslow's diary, Alice Morse Earle, stated that "no feminine reader" could think of this passage "without a thrill of sympathy." Winslow's appeal to nineteenth-century readers was largely based on such accounts, which Earle emphasized to her nineteenth-century readers. In early 1772 Winslow recorded in detail the clothing that she wore, adding: "And I would tell you, that *for the first time, they all lik'd my dress very much.*" Her clothes were a part of her identity and her attempts to become the

I hope aunt wont let one
wear the black hatt with the red Dominie— for the
people will afk one what I have got to fell as I
go along ftreet if I do. or, how the folk at Newgu=
nie do? Dear mamma, you dont know the fation
here— I beg to look like other folk., You dont kno
what a ftir would be made in fudbury ftreet
were I to make my appearance there in my red Domi
nie & black Hatt. But the old cloak & bonnett together
will make me a decent Bonnet for common ocation
(I like that aunt fays, its a putty fome of the ribbin
you fent wont do for the Bonnet— I muft now
clofe up this Journal. With Duty. Love. & Comple=
ments as due, perticularly to my Dear little brother,
(I long to fee him) & Mrs Law, I will write to her foon
I am Honᵈ Pᴬpa & mama,
Yʳ ever Dutiful Daughter
Anna Green Winflow.

N. B. my aunt Deming,
dont approve of my Englifh.
& has not the fear that you will think her concern'd in the
Dution

A page from Winslow's letter-diary, written to her parents in Nova Scotia while she was attending school in Boston during the years 1771–1773 (from Diary of Anna Green Winslow, *1894)*

woman her parents wanted her to be, one who was suited for a good marriage to an appropriate man.

Prior to the Revolution women's education was not considered important, and it was sporadic at best. Reading and writing were taught as separate skills. While reading was seen as necessary so that each church member could read and interpret the Bible, writing was a more specialized skill and was taught less frequently, particularly to women. Before learning to write, the student was expected to have mastered reading. Reading was also necessary for women so that they could educate their children. While women were not taught to write as often as men were, writing a "good" letter—one without misspellings and in a neat script—was a valued skill for an upper-class or upper-middle-class woman. It was much more common for women to attend sewing schools than writing schools, one reason that diaries like Winslow's are rare.

Winslow did not record the specifics of what she learned or did at her dancing, penmanship, and sewing schools, but she did record her reasons for attempting to write daily. On 17 April 1772 she wrote: "You see, Momma, I comply with your orders . . . of writing in my journal every day tho' my matters are of little importance & I have nothing at present to communicate." She also listed some of the books she read, including John Bunyan's *The Pilgrim's Progress* (1678), Jonathan Swift's *Gulliver's Travels* (1726), Alexander Pope's *The Dunciad* (1728), and books that she sometimes borrowed from one of her cousins. Although Earle found Winslow's handwriting and spelling to be exceptional for her time, Winslow often recorded her aunt's dissatisfaction with the diary entries and her comments on Winslow's poor diction. While some of Winslow's text was copied from newspapers or other materials, Winslow also wrote two poems, which have been collected in *Women Poets in Pre-Revolutionary America* (1981).

The boycott on imported goods from England is also mentioned in the diary. In one entry Winslow remarked that she is "(as we say) a daughter of liberty," adding "I chuse to wear as much of our own manufactory as possible. But my aunt says, I have wrote this account very badly." Aunt Deming was probably encouraging her niece to write less on this subject for the same reason that she discouraged reports on sermons with revolutionary undertones. Prior to this passage Winslow had described a new hat that was evidently not made in America, and she thanked her father for her allowance, with which she bought the hat. In other places in the diary Winslow described the amount she spun in a day, emphasizing that she was participating in the production of homespun, which would lessen the dependence on British goods. Spinning parties, where young women gathered together to spin for an entire day, played an important part in promoting homespun over imported British goods, and they were widely reported in newspapers. While Winslow was interested in promoting American materials, she recorded drinking tea and made no mention of the boycott on it.

Anna Green Winslow's diary is one of the few records by a young girl from a Loyalist family growing up in liberal surroundings. Winslow was much more than a "whimsical child," as her aunt called her. She was a young woman becoming increasingly aware of the social, cultural, and political tensions surrounding Bostonians in the 1770s. Facsimiles of the 1894 edition of her diary were published in 1970 and 1996. The location of the original manuscript for the diary is unknown.

Reference:

Alice Morse Earle, "A Boston School Girl in 1771," *Atlantic Monthly,* 72 (August 1893): 218–224.

Margaret Tyndal Winthrop

(circa 1591 – 14 June 1647)

Rosemary Fithian Guruswamy
Radford University

WORKS: *Some Old Puritan Love Letters: John and Margaret Winthrop, 1618–1638,* edited by Joseph Hopkins Twichell (New York: Dodd, Mead, 1893; London: B. F. Stevens, 1893);

Letters in *Winthrop Papers,* 5 volumes (Boston: Massachusetts Historical Society, 1929–1947).

A New England Puritan woman lived with a constant sense of her role as moral center of her family, helpmate to a Christian husband, and wife to him and Christ. The writings of Margaret Tyndal Winthrop, wife of the first governor of the Massachusetts Bay Colony, reveal her acceptance, and even joy, at how this idealized role anchored her life. In her writing, which consists of letters to relatives, the reader discovers her attempts to forge a strong domestic network on both sides of the Atlantic Ocean in the face of lengthy separations and wilderness adventures. In fact many scholars have concluded that her strength and steadiness made her the social center of the early Massachusetts Bay Colony and the religious model that other Puritan wives emulated.

Margaret Tyndal was born in about 1591 at Chelmshey House, a country estate in Great Maplestead, Essex, England. She was the fourth child and second daughter of Sir John and Lady Anne Egerton Tyndal. In 1616, as Master of Chancery, John Tyndal made an adverse financial judgment against a man who was subsequently ruined. The man then ambushed, shot, and killed Tyndal. The solicitous tone of many of Margaret Tyndal Winthrop's later letters to her husband, especially when he was in the midst of important political decisions, reflects her realization of the sometimes tragic consequences of a public person's professional judgment.

Not much has been recorded about Margaret Tyndal's childhood, her education, or her life before 1618, when the Puritan country squire and justice of the peace John Winthrop (1588–1649) began to court her. The two were married on 24 or 29

April 1618 and went to live at Groton Manor in Suffolk with his parents, Adam and Anne Browne Winthrop; John's younger sister, Lucy, who was not yet married to Emmanuel Downing; nine servants; and John's four surviving children by his first wife, Mary Forth Winthrop: John Jr., Henry, Forth, and Mary. Her new husband's third wife, Margaret Winthrop assumed a stepmother's responsibility with grace and ease, as many second and third wives must have done during an era when death in childbirth was so common. John Winthrop commented in his journal about the same quality in his second wife, Thomasine Clopton Winthrop, who had died giving birth to her first child, who also did not survive. Margaret Winthrop herself nearly died giving birth to her first son, Stephen, in 1619.

Perhaps the hardest part of the Winthrops' marriage was John Winthrop's frequent trips from home to pursue his career in London while leaving his wife at Groton. Their separations became even more frequent after he was appointed common attorney in His Majesty's Court of Wards and Liveries in 1627. Several letters also reveal that Margaret Winthrop left Groton Manor to attend to her mother during her final illness.

As Edmund S. Morgan says, John Winthrop would rather have spent every day close to his wife, but their loss has been posterity's gain. Joseph Hopkins Twichell collected ninety-five of their early letters in *Some Old Puritan Love Letters: John and Margaret Winthrop, 1618–1638* (1893). The majority of these letters were written in England, and many are undated. Several of them are short and devoted to domestic commonplaces. Because no regular postal service existed between London and Suffolk in the early seventeenth century, the Winthrops had to depend on friends and relatives to deliver their communications to one another. Often the announcements that someone was journeying to London must have caught Margaret Winthrop at a bad time, because more than once she admitted that she had more to say but no time in which to say it. Her first

Letter from Margaret Tyndal Winthrop to her husband, John Winthrop (early June 1627), expressing her loneliness while he was in London (Massachusetts Historical Society)

extant letter is undated, but internal evidence suggests that it was written some six years after their marriage, probably in 1624 or 1625. John Winthrop's earliest letters allude to several of his wife's previous missives that have apparently been lost. As Twichell explains, many of the Winthrop family papers, which are now at the Massachusetts Historical Society, suffered from the ravages of time and neglect over the years, especially between 1817 and 1860, when William Henry Winthrop zealously guarded them from the eyes of scholars but did nothing to preserve them himself. The surviving papers were published in five volumes as *Winthrop Papers* (1929–1947), and Francis J. Bremer is preparing a new edition.

The letters that remain create a picture of a loving relationship that persevered despite separations, a marriage in which both partners participated equally in domestic concerns and shared a spiritual affinity. Margaret Winthrop's early voice manifests many of the commonplaces of Puritan womanhood. She often assumed a stance of submissiveness and meekness toward her husband, always bowing to his judgment even when solicited for her opinion. In a letter dated 22 November 1627 she expressed her humility by quoting Abigail's speech to David about the gratification she received from washing her beloved's feet. Margaret Winthrop also used the sort of self-deprecation found in many early American religious writings by women, as in her circa October 1627 letter to her husband, in which she wrote: "I can not expres my love to you as I desire in theese poore livelesse lines. . . ." She never expressed desire without a conscious reminder that Christ was at the center of their marriage and that Jesus was her spiritual husband who could tend to her needs when her earthly spouse was away. The Winthrop's separations did not hamper their marital relations. By the time Margaret Winthrop was ready to join her husband in the Massachusetts Bay Colony in 1631, she had borne six children: Stephen, Adam, Deane, Nathaniel, Samuel, and Anne. (Nathaniel died in infancy.)

Margaret Winthrop's letters always expressed support for her husband's dream to establish a "city on a hill," a perfect Christian community in the New World that he described so vividly in his 1630 sermon "A Model of Christian Charity." When he began to write to her about the expedition to establish the Massachusetts Bay Colony, she spoke of the mission, in a letter dated 13 October 1629, as "our intended purpose." This sort of support was expected of a Puritan wife, of course, but John Winthrop's letters to her about his hopes for New England are detailed and vivid, and he expressed a conscientious desire that she be apprised of all the developments in the plans. He trusted his wife's intelligence and spiritual steadfastness and considered her as much a participant in the founding of Christ's kingdom on earth as he was himself.

Margaret Winthrop was unable to join her husband when he sailed for America in April 1630 to found the Massachusetts Bay Colony. Though she had expressed a desire to accompany him in a letter dated 5 November 1629, she was pregnant with her first daughter, Anne, and had the extra responsibility of looking after her stepson Henry's wife, Bess, who was also pregnant. While Margaret Winthrop's letters expressed trepidation about the immense distance of this new separation, they also show the priority she gave her domestic responsibilities, a sense of duty that grew stronger when she finally joined her husband in the New World. In a 31 January 1630 letter, one of the last letters she wrote to her husband before his departure, she assured him that she longed to join him and looked forward to meeting him again in New England. Like many lovers before and since, the Winthrops devised a plan by which they would meet in spirit by thinking of one another and engaging in prayer every Monday and Friday at five o'clock in the afternoon. John Winthrop suggested this plan in a letter dated 28 March 1630, but he later admitted that he was often too busy to remember.

When John Winthrop set sail for New England aboard the *Arbella* on 8 April 1630, he took his two eldest sons by Margaret Winthrop—Stephen, who was eleven, and Adam, who was nine—as well as Henry, his twenty-three-year-old son by Mary Forth. Henry was accidentally left behind when the *Arbella* stopped at the Isle of Wight and did not reach New England until a few weeks after the others. He drowned in Salem, Massachusetts, on the day he arrived, increasing his stepmother's sense of responsibility to his wife.

While still in England, Margaret Winthrop also maintained a correspondence with her stepson John Winthrop Jr. and his wife, Martha Fones Winthrop, who were preparing to sail with Margaret to join the elder John Winthrop in the Massachusetts Bay Colony. These letters, written between March 1630 and May 1631, evince her customary warmth toward them, addressing them as her beloved children. In late November 1630 she had the painful task of conveying to John Winthrop Jr. the news of his brother Forth's death of natural causes just after his graduation from Cambridge. In these letters Margaret Winthrop strengthened their resolve to join her in the journey to New England by assuring them of her certainty of God's providence and bind-

*John Winthrop, who married Margaret Tyndal in 1618 (The State
House, Boston)*

ing them, as she wrote in late April 1631, in "an intercorce of love."

In autumn 1631, several months after her husband had hoped she would join him, Margaret Winthrop sailed for New England, taking her infant daughter, Anne, who was still nursing, but leaving behind her sons Deane and Stephen. She and Anne, who died during the journey, boarded the ship *Lyon* with John Jr. and his wife. John Winthrop was reunited with his wife and son when the ship finally stopped at Long Island, and they sailed together as far as Boston. On her arrival the governor's wife was greeted with a royal welcome including volleys of musket fire and many gifts. On 11 November the colony observed a day of thanksgiving for her safe arrival, and among her many visitors was Gov. William Bradford of the Plymouth Colony, who came on 17 November to pay his respects. The Winthrops settled in Boston, on what is now Washington Street near the site of the Old South Church, and in close proximity to the home of Anne Hutch-

inson. Margaret Winthrop apparently became the center of a Boston social circle that included many families originally from Suffolk and Essex, the majority of whom she had known in England. While in New England, Margaret Winthrop bore two more children, William and Sarah, who did not live beyond infancy.

In New England, Margaret Winthrop wrote fewer letters. Scholars have made much of the letter dated only 1637, but probably written in November of that year, and sent from "Sad Boston" while Winthrop was participating in the trial of Anne Hutchinson for preaching her Antinomian beliefs, perhaps because this letter is one of the few in which Margaret Winthrop displayed any political consciousness. In the letter she mentioned a "trembling hart" that was finding it difficult to submit to God's will in this situation. Expressing a fear that God might be using Hutchinson to end abruptly the errand into the wilderness, she expressed more concern for the possible collapse of her husband's idealism than for the woman who was her neighbor. Like Anne Bradstreet, she left no written evidence that she knew Anne Hutchinson, and this letter is the only indication of her concern about the Antinomian Controversy that rocked the colony and subsequently made her husband more staunchly conservative than he had ever been before. Still, the phrasing of the letter, the admission that she was finding it difficult to submit to her spiritual husband, suggests a trace of reluctance to agree with an establishment that was trying a woman for following her own conscience in interpreting complex religious doctrine. Most of the time, however, Winthrop, like Bradstreet, avoided comment on the many colonial controversies that must have been discussed at length in her home.

Instead, as a good Puritan wife, Margaret Winthrop assumed a social and domestic position befitting the first lady of the Massachusetts Bay Colony, supporting and comforting her husband as he attempted to perpetuate the mission of the Puritan colony. Her central concern seems to have been the smooth operation of her home and the female community, as well as upholding the class structure that the colonists had brought with them from England.

In the summer of 1647, just as Winthrop was about to start his eleventh term as governor, Margaret Winthrop became ill with influenza, which reached epidemic proportions throughout New England that year, and she died the next day. Her burial place is not marked, but according to popular tradition, she is buried beside her husband in the King's Chapel or Stone Chapel churchyard in Boston. Shortly after her death John Winthrop married Martha Rainsborough Coytmore, who bore him one son before his death in 1649.

Margaret Winthrop emerges from the silence of history in a way that other Puritan women do not. Her letters have been included in various volumes, and a fictional character in Catharine Maria Sedgwick's novel *Hope Leslie* (1827) is based on her. In 1980 Stephen Paulus used one of her letters—along with texts by Sarah Kemble Knight, Samuel Sewall, and John Winthrop—as the libretto for *Letters for the Times: for Chorus and Chamber Ensemble*. The continued interest in her letters is a testament to the aesthetic legitimacy of women's letter literature and to the validity of the domestic sphere as a field worthy of study as modern scholars try to reconstruct the identity of Puritan New England.

Biographies:

Alice Morse Earle, *Margaret Winthrop* (New York: Scribners, 1895);

Edmund S. Morgan, *The Puritan Dilemma: The Story of John Winthrop* (Boston: Little, Brown, 1958);

Mary Ann Groves, *Most Sweet Friend: A Brief Biography of Margaret Winthrop* (Greenville, Ill.: National Society of the Colonial Daughters of the Seventeenth Century, 1977).

Papers:

Margaret Winthrop's surviving letters are at the Massachusetts Historical Society.

Sarah Wister
(20 July 1761 – 21 April 1804)

Etta M. Madden
Southwest Missouri State University

BOOKS: *Sally Wister's Journal,* edited, with an introduction, by Albert Cook Myers (Philadelphia: Ferris & Leach, 1902);

The Journal and Occasional Writings of Sarah Wister, edited, with an introduction, by Kathryn Zabelle Derounian (Rutherford, N.J.: Fairleigh Dickinson University Press, 1987).

Sarah Wister, best known for her account of household events during the British occupation of Philadelphia, continued to use journal, letter, and verse writing as a means of reflection throughout her life in the early republic. Her writings present a view of domestic, political, and religious life not available in formal histories and belles lettres of that period. In particular Wister's Revolutionary War journal, forty-eight manuscript pages that record her life from 25 September 1777 through June 1778, has fascinated historians and literary critics. In lively prose and with vigorous wit and humor, it reveals the self-centered interests of a well-read, observant, and gregarious sixteen-year-old who had been torn from her social circle in the city and sequestered at a relative's farm. Wister's Revolutionary War narrative displays a sense of self and of audience comparable to the writings of the mature Quaker Elizabeth Ashbridge and female novelists of the period such as Hannah Foster and Susanna Rowson. Wister's later writings reveal the further development of this self-consciousness and deliberation. Though the tenor of her poems, prose, and journal entries darkens somewhat and her visions become more subdued, she tempers them with a clearly spiritual light drawn from years of participating in the practices of the Society of Friends (Quakers).

Born on 20 July 1761, Wister was the first child of Lowry Jones Wister (1742–1804) and Daniel Wister (1739–1805), whose German father (born Johannes Wüster) had arrived in Philadelphia in the early eighteenth century and had established a successful business as a wine merchant. Daniel and

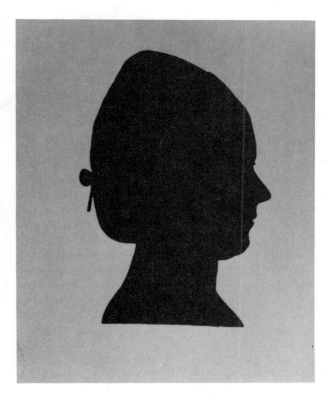

Silhouette of Sarah Wister (The Historical Society of Pennsylvania)

Lowry Wister had seven children after Sarah: Elizabeth (1764–1812), Hannah (1767–1862), Susannah (1773–1862), John (1776–1862), William (1778–1781), Charles Jones (1782–1865), and William Wynne (1784–1866). Most of their lives were spent at 141 Market Street, just across from Benjamin Franklin's house, and they generally summered at Grumblethorpe, their countryhouse in Germantown. As a member of a well-to-do family, Sarah Wister attended a local dame school, where she learned reading, writing, and arithmetic as well as domestic arts such as needlework. Because of her family's socioeconomic status, Wister was later able to attend philanthropist Anthony Benezet's Quaker Girls' School in Philadelphia. During her enrollment there she de-

Sampler embroidered by Wister in 1773 (Philadelphia Museum of Art, Gift of Sally Wister Ingersoll Fox)

veloped friendships with Deborah Norris (later Deborah Norris Logan) and Sally Jones, who was Wister's aunt though less than a year her senior.

Knowledge of Wister's education under Benezet's guidance emerges not only from an understanding of his educational theories but also from references she made in her journal. Along with needlework, penmanship, recreation, and reading, Benezet's curriculum included a sampling of classical and modern languages. Thus it is not surprising that Wister mentioned and cited Cicero's life and Homer's works, as well as those of eighteenth-century writers Alexander Pope and William Collins. In an early February 1778 entry, soon after complaining of boredom because "nothing happen'd all January that was uncommon," she acknowledged being given "a charming collection of book[s]," including Henry Fielding's *Joseph Andrews* (1742), Henry Brooke's *Juliet Grenville* (1774), So-

phia Briscoe's *Miss Melmoth; or the New Clarissa* (1771), and several volumes of *The Lady's Magazine,* a popular eighteenth-century periodical. Certainly Wister's schooling encouraged her love of language, which was fostered by the gifts of friends and family in her later life.

On 25 September 1777, the day Wister began her journal, the British army entered Germantown, the location of the Wister family's summer home. During the summer months the family had not used this home, nor were they at their city house in Philadelphia. Although the official British military entry into Philadelphia occurred on 26 September 1777, since 1775 political leaders had made life increasingly difficult for Quakers, who refused to profess partisanship with either the British or the rebels. At least nine months prior to September 1777, the Wisters had found refuge from the difficult conditions in the city at the home of Hannah Foulke, a recently widowed relative by marriage, who resided on a farm in Gwynedd, Pennsylvania, fifteen miles from Philadelphia. Foulke's three unmarried children—a son, Jesse, and daughters Priscilla and Lydia—became Wister's new companions, but their companionship did not fill Wister's need for self-expression and the company of her childhood friends. Thus Wister began to compose her Revolutionary journal.

One of the most remarkable aspects of this journal is Wister's sense of audience. Addressing her journal to "Debby" Norris, who had remained in Philadelphia, Wister set out her purpose in the opening lines: "Tho' I have not the least shadow of an opportunity to send a letter if I do write I will keep a sort of journal of the time that may expire before I see thee, the perusal of it may some time hence give pleasure in a solitary hour to thee and our Sally Jones." According to this passage, the motivation for the humorous style and for invoking this audience is pragmatic enough: accustomed to speaking frequently with Norris and Jones, Wister picked up her pen to continue the conversations she had engaged in for years. In fact, the three young women had already corresponded while Wister was at Gwynedd. Unable to chat with her friends, Wister channeled the conversation onto paper but refused to relinquish the supportive ears and advice of a female friend. Wister claimed that she wanted to "give pleasure" as much as to inform her friends of the rural battles or to work through her own anxieties. Nothing indicates, however, that she shared this writing with them after she and her family returned to Philadelphia in the summer of 1778 and the friendships were renewed. The journal undoubtedly offered a healthy outlet for Wister's emotions during the nine-month period, which included several major military events of the Revolution in addition to the British entry into Philadelphia: Washington's bitter winter encampment at Valley Forge and the French acknowledgment of American independence influenced the emotions of all with whom Wister came in contact. The Foulke farmhouse, in fact, was headquarters and a haven from battle for a network of American military officers. Sarah Wister met military leaders such as Gen. William Smallwood of Maryland, Col. James Wood of Virginia, and Maj. Aaron Ogden of New Jersey, who later became governors of their respective states. Wister was in the thick of the excitement, though also distant from it. Her writing during this period is characterized by a paradoxical, almost dreamlike theatricality and a heightened sensibility, undoubtedly influenced by her age: no longer a child, she was not yet fully an adult.

Wister's sense of audience and her self-awareness as a writer and female subject are demonstrated in three aspects of the journal: her uses of conversation, her character analysis, and her implicit references to performance and spectacle through explicit and frequent comments on clothing or costume. These qualities give her prose the sophistication of some epistolary novels and autobiographies of the period. Like contemporary fiction writers such as William Hill Brown and Hannah Webster Foster, Wister anticipated and inscribed her audience's replies, creating fictional dialogues that increase in frequency and length as the journal progresses. On the first of these occasions, for example, Wister cut short a vivid description of her interactions with military men at the Foulke farm, concluding: "Oh Debby I have a thousand things to tell thee. I shall give thee so droll an account of my adventures that thee will smile, no occasion of that sally methinks I hear thee say. for thee tells me every triffle, but child thee is mistaken for I have not told thee half the civil things that are said of us *sweet* creatures at General Smallwoods quarters." Phrases such as the qualifying "*methinks* I hear thee say" disappear as the imagined conversations with her friend continue; Wister appears to have gained a complete belief in her fictionalized versions of conversation. In most of these passages she used Debby Norris's imagined voice to reprimand herself and to celebrate her self-confidence, perhaps reflecting ambivalence toward Quaker teachings and acceptable practices. After describing how Virginian Alexander Spotswood Dandridge, who claimed he abhorred excesses of energy placed upon dress, appeared "powder'd very white" and made "a truly elegant figure," Wister asked to be excused for interpreting the man's fine appearance as a compliment to her own presence. In the constructed conversation Debby approves, with mockery, and Sally calls her "saucy" in return. Wister also used an imagined conversation to remind herself and Debby that she was a Philadelphian who, in spite of a twenty-month absence, would leave Foulke Farm without having become a country bumpkin in dress and manners.

Though Wister claims that Norris was her audience, Wister wrote as much for her own purposes as for Norris. The journal occupied her time and helped her endure a period of dramatic change and uncertainty. Anxious and unable to sleep, she arose at 4:30 on one June morning, perhaps influenced as much by the summer solstice as fear. As in the journals of Philadelphia Quakers Elizabeth Drinker and Sarah Logan Fisher, her words reveal her unsettling position as a pacifist Quaker who was

The Foulke farmhouse in Gwynedd, Pennsylvania, where Wister wrote most of her Revolutionary War journal (from Charles Jones Wister Jr., The Labour of a Long Life, *1866, 1886)*

challenged by Tories and rebels alike. When Dandridge, for example, teased her about being a Tory, she insisted that she was not. Although she leaned toward the rebel cause, Wister's uncertainty about the behavior of these men, their power against the redcoats, and her ignorance of men in general underlie her prose. She might even have doubted whether Logan would ever be able to see her lengthy epistle. Wister's fears emerged explicitly in the early entries as she described the first appearance of about three hundred military men at Foulke Farm and herself "all in a shake with fear"—her "teeth rattled" and her "hand shook like an aspin leaf." Although the men "beg'd for drink" and one "was a little tipsy and had a mind to be saucy," they were not all so. Calling "reason" to her aid, Wister decided she need not worry.

With her fear of American soldiers allayed, she still worried about the Hessians and the redcoats. When she heard of their troops moving toward Philadelphia, she advised Debby Norris with a string of imperatives: "summon up all your resolution call Fortitude to your aid dont suffer your spirits to sink." Along with Wister's fear of the unknown, such passages reveal her ability to adjust. Adults such as Drinker endured the chaos, existing through rituals and routines that included writing journal entries. The young, adaptable Wister, however, thrived by visualizing the chaotic house as a kind of carnival and by participating in it. She uses

her journal entries primarily to record that carnival, giving attention to dress, conversation, humor, spectacle, and the art of deception.

The most frequently quoted passages from Wister's writings exhibit these characteristics. After a morning of watching troops approach from several miles away, Wister became excited about the quartering of American soldiers and returned to the house to breakfast and wait. Becoming accustomed to being so near soldiers, she referred to herself as entering the battle—albeit a sexual rather than a national contest. Wister set the stage for the Foulke farm theatrics by referring to her dress, "a green skirt dark short gown, &c.," in the first sentence. In words reminiscent of Pope's *The Rape of the Lock* (1712), Wister wrote, "when we were alone our dress and lips were put in order for conquest." When General Smallwood and his men arrived later in the evening, she described the place as "glitterd with military equipments." Such delight with the ongoing spectacle at the farm appears throughout the later entries of the journal.

Wister thrived on her participation in the show. Like Foster's Eliza Wharton or Royall Tyler's Charlotte, she explained her roles—opportunities "of seeing and being seen." She concluded one such journal entry by revealing her own un-Quaker-like desires. In the journal passage that is most often quoted she wrote: "adieu I am going to my chamber to dream I suppose of bayonets and swords, sashes, guns, and epaulets." Here the bayonets, swords, and guns have been transformed from the fearful to the playful—items associated with costume. No different from sashes and epaulets, they mark Wister's visual reception of and participation in an excess of clothing not generally a part of the Quaker life.

Wister also described and analyzed character, both physical qualities and personalities, as did the novelists she read. Foreshadowing James Fenimore Cooper's *The Spy* (1821) or Washington Irving's *Sketchbook* (1819–1820), she described with humor a military parson "near seven foot high thin and meagre not a single personal charm very few mental ones. he fell violently in love with liddy at first sight, the first discover'd conquest that has been made since the arrival of the Genl." She wrote of Dr. Enoch Edwards's cleverness and ongoing "clack" and derided what she saw as the uncouth Southern style of lieutenants Lee and Warring, who talked of "turkey hash and fry'd hominy."

Only occasionally did Wister's Quaker consciousness call her back from the character analysis and attention to costume and spectacle. One such expression of a guilty conscience and grief followed Wister's participation in a practical joke that made one officer, Maj. William Stoddard, look good in the women's eyes and another, Virginian Robert Tilly, look like a dolt. Using a six-foot image of a British grenadier painted on wood and placing living servants around the room as well, Stoddard and the young women of the farm created a spectacle of the British arriving, a scene that frightened Tilly. Wister's account of their practical joke moves from comical to poignant: "figure to thyself this Tilly of a snowy even: no hat shoes down at heel, hair unty'd, flying across meadows creeks and mud-holes flying from what—why a bit of painted wood." When Tilly returned and after the girls and other officers had a good laugh, however, she explained, "the greatest part of my risibility turn'd into pity, inexpressible confusion had taken intire possession of his countenance, his fine hair hanging dishevell'd down his shoulders. all splash'd with mud yet his fright confusion and race had not divested him of his beauty." Of course, Tilly was humiliated and angry and, to make matters worse, the men would not let the joke die.

Accounts such as the one about tricking Tilly demonstrate that up to that point Wister looked at men as playthings, objects of delight not associated with politics, fear of death, or imprisonment. When Tilly and the other soldiers left in early December, Wister expressed her new emotions, "I feel sorry at their departure yet 'tis a different kind from what I felt some time since, we had not contracted so great an intimacy with those last." Most of the military men and officers had moved into winter quarters at Valley Forge. Wister's desire for friendship and playfulness had not dissipated, and the winter and spring months of 1778 were almost without interest to her. When Dandridge arrived in June, Wister was ripe for interaction. The man earned more of her attention and affection—marked by more titillating journal entries and attention to her clothing—than any other. On his departure she confessed, "he is gone and I think as I have escapd thus far safe I am quite a heroine, and need not be fearful of any of the lords of the creation for the future." Her entries make it quite clear that she enjoyed his company, but she knew he was not a suitable marriage partner because he was not a Quaker.

The excitement and energy so common in the entries of the first section almost entirely disappear from the briefer second section. Less than three weeks after Dandridge's departure, Wister learned that General Washington had regained Philadelphia and abruptly concludes the first section of her journal, avoiding revelation of any additional emotions and probably shifting her attention back to life in the city. Even the next year, in an undated entry written between January and August of 1779, she remembered her friend of the previous summer: "Dandrige the gay the gallant roving Dandrige is at last bound or on the verge of being bound in hymens fetters. I hope the lady may possess prudence and discretion sufficient to effect a reformation in his principles," which included swearing and being playful with language. The next entry recorded her grief on learning that "the amiable, worthy General Smallwood in full possession of the goods of this world and in the vigour of life fell in the battle with Cornwallis." Appalled by the British soldiers' "savage cruelty" in destroying "his breathless corse" with their bayonets, she exclaimed, "I ardently hope and make no doubt that the General whose soul I am confident was a stranger to such vices is enjoying happyness inexpressible in the mansion of eternal felicity" and prays that "all those brave men who were companions in war and death with General Smallwood enjoy eternal happiness." Although Wister learned later that word of his death was premature, the entry shows the serious and dismal tone of the few entries that follow.

The poems, letters, and prose pieces Wister wrote later continue in this serious and reflective tone, only occasionally breaking from it with touches of wit or humor. These works present Wister's worldview and personality as an adult and provide a few glimpses of her daily affairs. In 1781, for

First page of Wister's Revolutionary War journal, which she started in September 1777 (The Historical Society of Pennsylvania)

example, Wister wrote a brief prose reflection on her three-year-old brother William's death on 7 October. The piece follows the typical elegiac conventions of using the young man's life and imagined eternal salvation as a motive for the writer's religious improvement through imitation. Perhaps the war joined with the death of a sibling to bring mortality forcefully to Wister's mind.

Poetry writing appears to have been a creative outlet for Wister during her late twenties and early thirties. Among the dated poems she wrote between 1790 and 1793, Wister devoted several to her mother, including "To my Beloved Mother" and

"To my Mother with a rose." Typical of Augustan neoclassical verse in their regular rhythm and rhyme, these poems demonstrate her dedication to her mother's virtues and her guilt at falling short in her own. Wister signed these and other poems with the pen name "Laura" for reasons of convention rather than for any desire of anonymity. Although she did not seek to publish, as her sister Elizabeth had, Wister wrote for at least a handful of readers. Family members and friends knew she composed verse. Thomas B. Adams, a son of John and Abigail Adams, for example, asked Wister to write an ode for his birthday. In this poem, stylistically similar to

Phillis Wheatley's verses, Wister at length pleads humility and points to her lack of association with the Muses before extending a blessing of friendship and happiness to the president's son. In this poem, as in others, Wister's themes of virtue and goodness are almost secularized, reflecting the type of religious life Quakerism had taught her and a romantic sensibility akin to that of Philip Freneau. In a poem dedicated to George Bensell, a family friend and physician mentioned in letters to Benjamin Rush, Wister asks for calm and peace. She appeals to Bensell for aid "As thro' the devious maze of life" she "stray[s]," "sinking with distress" and living with "griefs deep wounds." She proclaims that wealth, learning, and even "glowing Science" pale in comparison to the longstanding bliss that "Virtue alone" bestows. The poem concludes:

> When yon bright Orb, which gives the golden Day,
> Shall lose its light–and set, no more to rise;
> Virtue and Peace shall 'scape the general wreck,
> And mount, triumphant, to their native Skies.–

The movement from despair, which provoked the piece, to hope is repeated in Wister's devotional journal. Comparable to the Revolutionary journal in length (forty-two manuscript pages), the devotional journal documents the period between June 1796 and May 1797, first at Germantown and then in Philadelphia. While in the early journal Wister devoted her attention to recording and responding to external events, in this journal she recorded responses and transcendent goals without indicating external provocations. More than the poems and letters of this period, this journal is highly personal. Wister appears to have written it only for herself, although many Quakers such as Elizabeth Ashbridge and John Woolman wrote spiritual autobiographies for circulation within the Society of Friends. Wister's journal notes spiritual crises without revealing the causes. One possible cause was her sister Susannah's marriage to someone outside the Society of Friends; another could have been Wister's struggle to accept single life as other women her age married and began families. Quakers' marriages were to be approved by the local monthly meeting, and some historians have suggested that the increasing number of single women in the faith during the late eighteenth and early nineteenth centuries reflects the low number of men eligible for approved lifetime partnerships with these women. Certainly, as Mary Maples Dunn has remarked, it is surprising to many readers of Wister's Revolutionary journal that the energetic young woman never married. Yet the later writings of a single woman in midlife re-count a dedication to a spiritual journey. An entry dated 11 June 1796, for example, begins with a confession and moves, quite typically, to pleas for forgiveness and strength:

> O! Lord Thou knowest all my foolishness, and my varied weakness: o strengthen me according to Thy power. . . . O! why is it so with me, where is another shield or reward: Oh that I had wings like a dove for then would I flee away and escape, from these vain fears from those frailties of my nature–then would I hasten my escape from the windy storm and tempest–from the vain wanderings of my imagination, from the tempest of my passions and unsubdued nature.

The journal never reveals exactly what caused "the tempest" of her "passions" nor which part of her nature was unsubdued. Even when she began her 9 August 1796 entry, "Abington Quarterly meeting," a note that might suggest her motivation for writing, she moved quickly into commentary: "That a christian life is a continual warfare, I cannot doubt, but if I am at all favor'd to be in the Christian path, I can scarcely tell: 'but the troubles of my heart are enlarged.'" The quotation of Scripture (in this case Psalms 25:17) is typical of her writing and of contemplative autobiographies throughout centuries preceding hers. Was the main message of the meeting recorded in her comment, or did the meeting provoke these uncertainties?

Occasionally, however, a clear reference to public events intercedes, as in the entry of 23 August 1796. Yet Wister colored the entry with spiritual vision and glossed it with judgment: "A great evil hath been committed in my native City–the public preaching of the Unitarian doctrines–by one in whom the light has become darkness." The reference, probably to Elias Hicks, a liberal Quaker whose teachings contributed to a formal split in the Society in 1827, demonstrates Wister's struggles with spiritual truth and its application in her life. The final passage of the journal reiterates her desire for transcendence and spiritual perfection, an existence far above "the most desirable terrestrial situation" and removed from even "The happiest bonds of relationship."

Letters written between 1794 and 1803 help to fill in some gaps of the spiritual journal. Written to her uncle Owen Jones; her aunt Hannah Foulke; her friend the physician, reformer, and philosopher Benjamin Rush; and Quaker leader Isaac Pennington, the letters discuss–in terms much more specific than the journal–family members, Wister's emotional state, her responses to texts she has read, and her thoughts on romances and the theater. Wister's

The last page of Wister's Revolutionary War journal (August 1781), which she kept sporadically after returning to Philadelphia in summer 1778 (The Historical Society of Pennsylvania)

lessons on reading in these letters include examples of what should be read for moral improvement and comments about what women should not read. Her 24 May 1800 letter to Isaac Pennington provides Wister's response to reading his wife's spiritual narrative. Wister extolled Mary Pennington's virtues, which "irradiated the whole tenor of her life" and encouraged the living to imitate her. A November 1802 letter of thanks to Rush accompanied the fourth volume of Erasmus Middleton's *Biographia Evangelica* (1786), which he had lent to Wister. In

contrast to these examples, other letters explicitly comment on reading and morality. Wister copied a passage from Armand de Bourbon, Prince of Conti's *Extracts from Several Treatises . . . Concerning Stage Plays* (1754) in a letter to her sister-in-law, Rebecca Bullock. The excerpt claims that plays and romances "extinguish the love of the Word of God" and cause women, when they return to the realities of their houses, to "find every thing there disagreeable." On 20 January 1802 Wister wrote to Hannah Foulke that Hannah More's *Considerations on Religion*

Grumblethorpe, the house in Germantown, Pennsylvania, where Wister wrote most of her devotional journal (from Charles Jones Wister Jr., The Labour of a Long Life, *1866, 1886)*

and Public Education (1794) encouraged women to develop themselves intellectually and morally rather than "wasting invaluable time in frivolous empty pursuits on dress, at the Theater and the card table."

These letters reflect the physical demands of Wister's life as an adult caregiver to her aging mother and four other unmarried adults who remained within the household. In a few letters, such as one to Foulke on 31 May 1803, she commented obliquely on marriage—the improbability of her own and the possibilities of her sister Susannah's. At times household labor might have caused her to struggle with despair and exhaustion. She wrote to Owen Jones on 19 August 1796 of "mental inertia [such] as to be scarcely capable of any good." Nonetheless the adult Wister chose to devote her life to care for her family and to intellectual and spiritual development.

Sarah Wister died on 21 April 1804, only two months after the death of her mother. Sarah's nephew, Charles Jones Wister Jr., claimed that Lowry Wister's death affected Sarah so deeply that she failed to recover physically and departed to join her mother in an eternal state. Certainly her poems and letters indicate such a powerful attachment. Sarah Wister's obituary, written by Benjamin Rush and published in the *Pennsylvania Gazette,* linked both women as "shining examples of prudence, virtue, piety, and eminent acquirements," characteristics far different from those revealed in the early writing of

the young Quaker who had observed the sparkling uniforms of the Revolutionary military men.

Wister's writings have been recognized as important to social and literary history for the information they provide about the lives of women during the Revolution and the early republic. As Kathryn Zabelle Derounian has noted, Wister's work has until recently received attention from those with extremely specialized interests such as colonial history, Quaker life and culture, women of the Revolution, and Philadelphia history. Such readers first referred to and published excerpts from Wister's Revolutionary journal in the early nineteenth century, only twenty-five years after her death. The ongoing interest in the nineteenth century, demonstrated by many references to and partial publications of Wister's work, culminated in the publication of her Revolutionary journal as *Sally Wister's Journal* in 1902. Interests in women's rights and roles, including ways in which females develop from girlhood to adulthood, have contributed to republications of Wister's work and to references to it in women's and literary studies during the twentieth century. In 1987 Derounian published a scholarly edition of all Wister's extant writings along with bibliographic information. Derounian's edition also includes a thorough biographical and critical introduction and useful notes to the prose and poetry.

Wister's writings also shed light on other works composed during the formation of the American republic. Most important, Wister's narrative voice in her Revolutionary journal, that of a sixteen-year-old female under the duress of immediate domestic changes brought on by war, adds an informative link to several literary works of the late-eighteenth and early nineteenth centuries, including Hannah Webster Foster's *The Coquette* (1797), Michel Guillaume Jean de Crevecoeur's *Letters from an American Farmer* (1782), Susanna Rowson's *Charlotte: A Tale of Truth* (1791), Royall Tyler's *The Contrast* (1790), and James Fenimore Cooper's *The Spy* (1821). Joined with her later occasional writing, Wister's Revolutionary journal illuminates readings of Quaker autobiographical pieces by John Woolman, Elizabeth Ashbridge, and Elizabeth Drinker that illustrate the development of a female subject. The reader marvels at the power of Wister's words to do more than reflect an historical period; they have the ability to create life and to give meaning to an otherwise chaotic existence.

References:

Richard Bauman, *Let Your Words Be Few: Symbolism of Speaking and Silence among Seventeenth-Century Quakers* (New York: Cambridge University Press, 1983);

Kathryn Zabelle Derounian, Introduction to *The Journal and Occasional Writings of Sarah Wister,* edited by Derounian (Rutherford, N.J.: Fairleigh Dickinson University Press, 1987);

Mary Maples Dunn, "Latest Light on Women of Light," in *Witnesses for Change: Quaker Women over Three Centuries,* edited by Elisabeth Potts Brown and Susan Mosher Stuard (New Brunswick, N.J.: Rutgers University Press, 1985), pp. 71–85;

Amelia Mott Gummere, *The Quaker: A Study in Costume* (Philadelphia: Ferris & Leach, 1901);

Wendy Martin, "Women and the American Revolution," *Early American Literature,* 3 (1976–1977): 322–335;

Albert Cook Myers, Introduction to *Sally Wister's Journal,* edited by Myers (Philadelphia: Ferris & Leach, 1902);

Milton Rubincam, "The Wistar-Wister Family: A Pennsylvania Family's Contributions toward American Cultural History," *Pennsylvania History,* 20 (1953): 142–164;

Judith Van Buskirk, "They Didn't Join the Band: Disaffected Women in Revolutionary Philadelphia," *Pennsylvania History,* 62 (1995): 306–329.

Papers:

Most of Sarah Wister's extant papers are in Philadelphia. The manuscript for the Revolutionary journal, her correspondence for 1777–1779, and the manuscript for her journal of 1796–1797 are included in the Wister Family Papers at the Historical Society of Pennsylvania. Ten letters, thirteen poems, a fragment on the death of her brother, an essay on happiness, and another fragment of a poem are part of the Eastwick Collection of the American Philosophical Society. The letters Wister wrote to Benjamin Rush are with the Rush Manuscripts at the Library Company of Philadelphia.

Sally Sayward Barrell Keating Wood

(1 October 1759 – 6 January 1855)

Doreen Alvarez Saar
Drexel University

BOOKS: *Julia and the Illuminated Baron. A Novel Founded on Recent Facts Which Have Transpired in the Course of the Late Revolution of Moral Principles in France* (Portsmouth, N.H.: Printed at the United States Oracle Press by Charles Peirce, 1800);

Dorval; or, The Speculator (Portsmouth, N.H.: Printed at the Ledger Press by Nutting & Whitelock, 1801);

Amelia; or, The Influence of Virtue. An Old Man's Story (Portsmouth, N.H.: Printed at the United States Oracle Press by William Treadwell, 1802);

Ferdinand and Elmira: A Russian Story (Baltimore: Printed for Samuel Butler by J. W. Butler, 1804);

Tales of the Night (Portland: Thomas Todd, 1827).

OTHER: *The Little Hymn Book; Compiled for The Moral and Religious Instruction of Children, At Home and in Sunday School,* edited by Wood (Worcester, Mass., 1850);

"War, the Parent of Domestic Calamity: A Tale of the Revolution," edited by Hilda M. Fife, in *A Handful of Spice: A Miscellany of Maine Literature and History,* edited by Richard S. Sprague, University of Maine Studies, second series, no. 88 (Orono: University of Maine Press, 1968).

Sally Sayward Barrell Keating Wood

One of the earliest women novelists in the new republic, Sally Sayward Barrell Keating Wood is generally considered the first American woman writer of Gothic fiction. Also recognized as the first woman writer of Maine, she has been praised for her depiction of local scenes of her native state. Her reputation as an American reworker of Anne Radcliffe's Gothic fiction is somewhat mistaken because it is based only on her first novel, *Julia and the Illuminated Baron* (1800). Although she also used some Gothic motifs in her later novels, as Henri Petter has shown, the novels vary in style. Early critics described Wood as one of a group of women novelists who imitated the work of Susanna Rowson, an American popularizer of the Richardsonian style. In the late twentieth century, critics have reevaluated Wood's fiction.

To understand Sally Wood's history and her work, it is necessary to examine her social position in colonial and postrevolutionary society. Sarah (Sally) Sayward Barrell was born on 1 October 1759 in the town of York in what is now the state of Maine. (Maine was part of Massachusetts until 1820.) She was the first child of Sarah Sayward Barrell and Nathaniel Barrell, who were both from prominent Massachusetts families. The aspirations and allegiances of her family played an important role in Sally's life. Always particularly proud of her mother's family, she wrote to a relative in 1842: "I look upon my grandparents as belonging to the highest order of Nobility and the best wishes I can form for there descendants that they may imitate every estimable virtue and shrink with horror from everything like vice or meanness as a reflection upon there memories and render them unworthy of their ancestors." Mingled with her respect for her grandparents' personal traits was her pride in their aristocratic lineage: on her maternal side Wood could trace her family back to the English Lord Cutts, Baron of Girondale.

Although little is known of Wood's early years, most scholars agree that Wood's grandfather Jonathan Sayward was the most important figure in the life of her family, in part because of his wealth and social position but also because of his character. Called by his granddaughter "one of Nature's nobility" and "beloved by all who knew him," Sayward was the richest man in York and, by some accounts, in all of Maine. An exemplar of the self-made American, Sayward rose from a relatively humble status to become a wealthy merchant, shipowner, and landowner. While Wood was a child in the 1760s and 1770s, Sayward held several important colonial posts, including Justice of the Quorum, Justice of the Court of Common Pleas, and Judge of Probate. These appointments were probably rewards for his loyal support of the Crown, a loyalty that led to his political ostracism during the American Revolution. Sayward is likely to be the original of many of the noble male characters in Wood's fiction.

While Wood's father, Nathaniel Barrell, was as prominent as Sayward, he appears to have been eclipsed by his father-in-law for most of his life, not only in the eyes of society but also in the eyes of his daughter. In the same letter that described her grandparents as a pattern of virtue, Wood was circumspect about her father. She did not grant him the same unstinting praise she had given her grandparents, but she did acknowledge: "Few men have made greater sacrifices to religion than my Father—he was in the high road to wealth and honor a perfect gentleman, a respected merchant, honored by the King . . . he is now receiving a rich reward where 'neither moth nor rust can corrupt, nor thieves break through and steal.'"

Like his father-in-law, Nathaniel Barrell seemed destined for success. Raised in a wealthy Boston family, he became an officer in the British army. In fact, Sally Barrell was born while her father was serving with Gen. James Wolfe in Quebec. It is not clear why Barrell gave up his military career in 1763 and established himself as a merchant in Portsmouth, New Hampshire. At first he was part of the political and social inner circle there and served as a member of Gov. Benning Wentworth's council. Religion, however, became a bar to Barrell's advancement. He and his family were followers of the Reverend Robert Sandeman, the American representative of the Scottish theologian John Glass. The Sandemanians followed a policy of civil obedience, which made the group politically unpopular. When Sally was six, during the crisis over the Stamp Act (1765–1766), she probably saw the Barrells' church in Portsmouth being burned by rioters. By 1766 the Barrells were bankrupt, in part because of money Nathaniel Barrell had donated to the church. Soon after, the family retired to Barrell Grove, their farm in York. Although Nathaniel Barrell was never prosecuted for his Tory leanings during the Revolution, he and his family were suspected of disloyalty and shunned by many.

On 23 October 1778 Sally Barrell married Richard Keating, a native of Kittery and a clerk in Jonathan Sayward's office. Sayward was fond of the couple and gave them a house as a wedding present. Sally's first child, Elizabeth Walker Keating, was born on 7 November 1779. Her next child, Sally Sayward Barrell Keating, was born on 29 July 1781. Richard Keating died of a fever before the birth of their son, Richard Keating, in 1783. Sally Keating was left a twenty-four-year-old widow with three small children. Four years later her father again courted general contempt for following his own personal and moral inclinations. Elected by the townspeople of York to represent their anti-Federalist views at the Constitutional Convention, Barrell was converted to a supporter for the Constitution during the convention. The townspeople of York did not appreciate his change of heart.

Only after Richard Keating's death did Sally Keating begin to write. Her only surviving letter from this period (written to her father in 1794) indicated that she had read and had a lively interest in novels by women:

> I have seen advertised in a Late Paper by Miss Charlott Smith, the author of Cellestine which you were so much Pleasd with, a New Performance, the title of which was Ethelinda, or the recluse of the Lake. I dare say Mrs. Jervis has it and I do not doubt she would lend it to you, Do, my dear Sir, try to borrow it. . . .

Sally Keating's first literary effort was a poem written in 1797 as condolence to parents on the drowning of their son. Her writing, she claimed, "soothed many melancholy, and sweetened many bitter hours." Beginning in 1800 she published four novels before her marriage to Gen. Abiel Wood in 1804.

Wood's novels are unified by their focus on the interests of her social class rather than by a stylistic unity. Her didactic themes seem to be the occasion for telling a story rather than the reason for the story, and often they have little to do with the mechanics of the plot. While she favored intricate devices, particularly the kidnapping and imprisonment of her heroines, Wood's plots are well within the traditions of the popular romances and Gothics of the eighteenth century.

Unlike novels by American women writers such as Rowson and Foster, Wood's books are generally not critical of women's social position. Her heroines are paragons of virtue who resist their seducers and remain pure. They are often members of the aristocracy whose identities have been kept hidden, and their adventures are usually set in foreign locales. Unlike other seducers, Wood's villains are not average men run amok but personifications of evil who are never remorseful and must be killed. All Wood's works end in a happy marriage, and generally this nuptial bliss is extended to more than just the main characters.

Wood's first and best-known novel, *Julia and the Illuminated Baron,* demonstrates the relationship between the concerns of Wood's social class and her novelistic imagination. Most scholars consider the work a response to the fears raised by the French Revolution and, in particular, to the alleged existence of a secret society of enlightened freethinkers and political radicals known as the Illuminati. In fact, the Illuminati probably never existed and were invented by conservative elements in Europe and America as a kind of political bogeyman. Yet Wood was not politically sophisticated, a fact she acknowledges in her preface to the novel:

> I am apprehensive from the perusal of the title page that Julia may, by some be considered a political work as I have ever hated female politicians I think it absolutely necessary to declare it is not intirely unacquainted with politics. . . . But when we see the greatest part of the world throwing off the shackles of religion, and becoming by profession as well as by precepts, infidels, it is impossible not to consider it as a revolution from piety, and from morality; and leaving politics intirely out of sight, we shudder at the present view, and shrink from the distant prospect.

The threat of the French Revolution is subsumed in the fight over Julia's virtue, and politics becomes merely a mechanism to summon up fear rather than to develop a social critique.

Julia and the Illuminated Baron takes place in the French countryside and falls into the general Gothic plot category of "virgin defends virtue against villain." Julia, an orphan, is befriended by the Countess De Launa, who introduces Julia to the rest of the De Launa family. The countess's nephew, Baron De

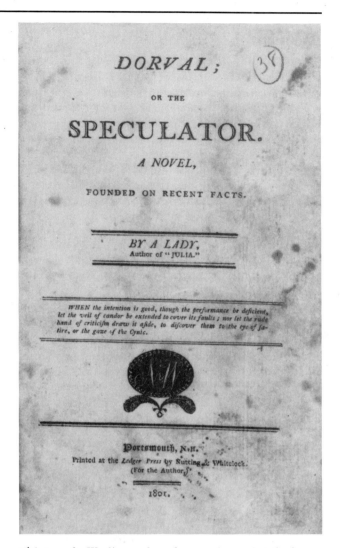

Title page for Wood's second novel, a warning against the dangers of land speculation (courtesy of the Special Collections Department, University of Virginia Library)

Launa, has been raised by a tutor who is a member of the atheistic Illuminati, and he is a secret adherent of the sect. While under the countess's protection, Julia meets and becomes engaged to Francis Colwort, an Englishman. At the same time, however, the baron plots to seduce Julia. In a subplot, while Colwort is absent on business, Julia is abducted and taken to Spain, where she is mistaken for another woman and is put on trial for murder. After this error is corrected and Julia is being returned to France, she is kidnapped by the baron's men and held at his house. When the baron comes to force himself on her, Julia is rescued by Colwort. She escapes, but Colwort is captured and held for the baron's murder. After other plot twists Julia is recognized as the daughter of the Marquis De Launa. Colwort is rescued, and he is discovered to be the countess's son by her first husband. Julia and Colwort marry and return to England.

In *Julia and the Illuminated Baron* the Gothic structure works to reinforce Wood's socially conservative message. The novel presents a society in which inequality is a natural fact of life and the lower classes benefit from the class system because the true aristocrat practices a general policy of benevolence. The orphaned Julia is both good and recognized for her good qualities because, although no one knows that she is an aristocrat, good blood tells. The French Revolution is bad in part because it makes the sons of good families into villains and encourages the seduction of maidens as a matter of right. The setting of the novel also suggests Wood's political inclinations: France is portrayed as the source of political upheaval, while England is considered the home of reason.

Wood's second novel, *Dorval; or, The Speculator* (1801), is completely American in theme and setting. In the preface Wood asked, "Why must the amusements of our leisure hours cross the Atlantic? Why should we not wait on ourselves? Why can not we aim at independence?" Disassociating her work from radical politics, she defended the practice of novel writing as an antidote to the dissipation in which some women indulge: "no one will find, upon perusal, a lesson or even a sentence that could authorize vice or sanction immorality" in her work. Like Wood's first novel, *Dorval* speaks to the concerns of the period and of Wood's class. Unlike the situations of *Julia and the Illuminated Baron,* the dangers in this novel are immediate and specifically American. *Dorval* warns against the dangers of speculation and paper money.

Set in New York, the novel introduces the Morely family: Colonel Morely, late of the American army; the frivolous Mrs. Morely; the virtuous Aurelia; and Miss Woodley, Aurelia's aunt whose sole interest is making Aurelia into a sensible person. Like Nathaniel Barrell, Colonel Morely was a delegate to the Constitutional Convention; unlike Barrell, Morely has made a great deal of money by speculating in soldier's certificates. Aurelia's father and Dunbar, the father of Aurelia's friend Elizabeth, are persuaded by Dorval, an acquaintance, to invest in land speculation. Elizabeth disappears at the same time as Burlington, Aurelia's fiancé, and it is rumored that they have eloped. The land speculation goes bust, and the Morelys and the Dunbars are ruined. Imprisoned for debt, Morely, who is nursed unstintingly by Aurelia, dies. Having unsuccessfully pursued Aurelia, Dorval marries Mrs. Morely. Aurelia then discovers that she was adopted and that she is actually the child of her aunt and Seymour, a

British soldier. Dorval's true nature is revealed: he has killed his uncle, tried to kill his first wife's father, and eloped with Elizabeth. If these crimes are not enough to convince the reader of his villainy, he then drives Mrs. Morely crazy and kills her.

Trying to discover the truth, Aurelia visits Dorval in jail, where he attempts to kill her but is stopped by a man who turns out to be Seymour's son. Aurelia is subsequently reunited with Seymour, her wealthy British father. Burlington, who had been tricked into believing that Aurelia married Dorval, returns a wealthy man and marries Aurelia.

Petter classifies *Dorval* as a novel of suspense in which the reader waits to see what new and unexpected horrors the villain can produce. The real horror in *Dorval,* however, is the terror of financial and resulting social instability. The novel warns the reader that desire to make money quickly has deleterious effects on the social order, causing disruptions that eventually hurt the women who are dependent on the risk takers. Wood did not disapprove of financial success in general, however. She favored wealth acquired in a traditional manner, once again revealing her links to the conservative landowning merchant class. The other themes of *Dorval* underpin this message of fiscal and social responsibility. The novel disparages the love of entertainment and dissipation in the American upper class and supports the notion that "good" people recognize their responsibility to the lower class. (One of Dorval's many negative traits is his mistreatment of slaves.) *Dorval* anticipates Wood's next novel in its brief mention of female emancipation: one of the characters says, "I consider Wollstonecraft's 'Rights of Woman' as injurious to female happiness as Tom Paine's 'Age of Reason' is to the cause of religion."

Having written two novels on the theme that female virtue is rewarded by marriage, in *Amelia; or, The Influence of Virtue* (1802) Wood turned her attention to show how a wife could prove her virtue within marriage. *Amelia* was likely written in reaction to the furor over the influence of Mary Wollstonecraft's *A Vindication of the Rights of Woman* (1792) on the behavior of women and on the institution of marriage. Wood's heroine, Amelia, is "not a disciple or pupil of Mary Wollstonecraft. . . . she was not a woman of fashion, nor a woman of spirit. She was an old-fashioned wife." To prove her virtue and her worthiness as an object of love, Amelia suffers endless indignities. Cathy N. Davidson postulates that the novel undercuts Wood's intention because it shows how dreadful most women's lives were. As Petter notes, *Amelia* is a novel of domestic victimization.

Amelia is set in England, where Amelia, an orphan, is taken into the protection of a wealthy aristocrat, Lady Stanly, who intends that her son, Sir William, should marry Amelia. Amelia, however, loves Lord Barrymore, and Sir William is smitten by his mother's adopted niece, Harriot. In a display of worthiness Amelia renounces Barrymore, a Catholic, because she will not convert to his religion. On her deathbed Lady Stanly asks her son and Amelia to marry. In respect for her goodness, they do as Lady Stanly has requested, but their marriage remains unconsummated. Still infatuated with Harriot, William believes that he does not love Amelia and offers her a divorce, but Amelia intends to be faithful to her duty and her sacred vows. Meanwhile, the scheming Harriot entices Barrymore to marry her. Harriot and William become lovers. Barrymore discovers the affair and divorces Harriot. Amelia demonstrates her virtue by raising Harriot and William's son while keeping the child's identity hidden from William. Wood addresses her reader's apprehension that Amelia is suffering too much with this explanation: "She was an old fashioned wife, and . . . meant to do her duty in the strictest sense of the word. To perform it cheerfully would perhaps be painful, but in the end, it would most assuredly be best."

Just as William seems about to recognize and reward Amelia's virtue, she is abducted, as part of a plot originated by her uncle Volpoon, who hates her because she is the child of his half-brother and the woman Volpoon loved. He believed he had killed Amelia earlier, and, discovering her existence, he tries to finish her off again. Eventually William and Barrymore rescue Amelia, and Volpoon is killed. The novel concludes with William accepting Amelia as his wife because of her innate goodness. Barrymore marries Volpoon's wife, who turns out to be Barrymore's long-lost love, and Harriot dies in poverty, disgrace, and pain.

Amelia is perhaps the best written of Wood's works. Petter finds "energy and purposefulness" in its "design and execution." In this novel Wood created a central character who engages the reader's sympathies in a way her previous heroines do not, even though the novel violates the modern notion that love redeems all. Amelia's virtue grows out of duty, and the modern reader may find Amelia's scruples excessive, as when she marries a man she does not love because of her respect for the wishes of her aunt. Many of the themes of Wood's earlier works are repeated in slightly altered forms in this novel: Amelia is the unrecognized child of aristocratic parents; her virtue is rewarded; and France is once again the locus of evil.

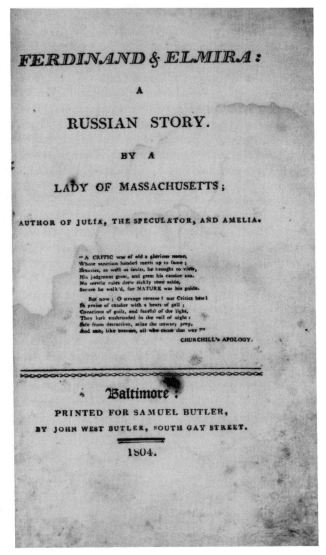

Title page for Wood's fourth novel, which examines "the consequences of arbitrary power, and despotic government" (courtesy of the Special Collections Department, University of Virginia Library)

Ferdinand and Elmira: A Russian Story (1804) is perhaps the most thematically elusive and the most structurally convoluted of Wood's novels. Petter classifies it as a novel of adventure because the lives of the main characters are essentially "Fortune's Football." Most of the novel is taken up with retelling the main characters' family histories. Early in the novel the author remarks on "the consequences of arbitrary power, and despotic government." The evil of unregulated monarchy was still of interest to Americans at the beginning of the nineteenth century, and Russia was a model of despotic excess.

Ferdinand and Elmira opens in a large house in Poland, where Elmira is being held against her will. In a plot device that Wood first used in *Julia and the*

Illuminated Baron, Elmira has been kidnapped by mistake. She is freed and led away by "a man in a gown." The reader then learns the history of her family. Her mother, Emma, was the daughter of the Russian Count Laprochin, and Emma's older sister, the Countess Laprochin, has had an affair with an Englishman, Oldham. They eventually married, but Oldham returned to England with their child, Ferdinand. Meanwhile, Emma has secretly married the Polish ambassador, Count Peletre. After their lives are threatened by the irrational Czarina Elizabeth, who has decided that she must marry Peletre, Emma and Peletre flee to Poland. Enraged by Peletre's actions, the czarina has the Laprochin family and Peletre accused of treason, and they are subjected to all sorts of unspeakable punishments. Mrs. Oldham (Countess Laprochin) takes the brunt of the czarina's wrath and is sent to Siberia. The Peletres also feel the czarina's imperial wrath because she has convinced the Polish court that it must stand with a fellow monarch. The Peletres leave the Polish court and go into hiding in the countryside, where Elmira is born. Eventually, Peletre tries to find Oldham and fails, but he does locate Ferdinand and returns with him to Poland. Considering the danger and foolishness of the nobility, the Peletres raise Elmira and Ferdinand in ignorance of their elevated status. After escaping from Russia, Mrs. Oldham happens upon their cottage.

Time passes, and the children grow up and fall in love. Fate allows Ferdinand to learn of his background, and he joins the Prussian army during the Seven Years' War to avenge himself against the Russians. At this point the portion of the novel that links the opening chapter with the rest of the novel finally begins. Accompanied by the man in the gown, Elmira happens upon Ferdinand, who has returned home to announce that he will be executed. Ferdinand tells his beloved Elmira that, while in the army, he became friends with an American named Lawrence, who was engaged to Maria, the daughter of the general's mistress. Discovering the vicious colonel attempting to seduce Maria, Ferdinand knocked the colonel down. In reprisal the colonel had Ferdinand arrested and condemned to death. The man in the gown promises to ask General Brunsdel, Ferdinand's commander, to intercede in the case. On the way to Warsaw they learn that all the Peletres and Lapochins have been pardoned by the new ruler of Russia. This revelation leads the man in the gown to reveal that he is Oldham, Ferdinand's father. At the last minute Brunsdel intervenes and prevents Ferdinand's execution. The novel concludes with the marriages of Lawrence and Maria and Ferdinand and Elmira. The Peletre

and Lapochin estates are sold, and the parents and children all move to England, realizing that absolute monarchs are not to be trusted.

Ferdinand and Elmira differs from Wood's other novels in its lack of a single central female character and, consequently, in its lack of tight moral economy. In covering an entire extended family, it is more complexly patterned than Wood's other works. For example, the arbitrary nature of Ferdinand's punishment echoes the punishment suffered by his entire family. Yet overall the novel lacks structure, perhaps indicative of Wood's inability to control a novelistic world in which virtue is not central. Indeed, the novel presents a world that is, by Wood's standards, completely dissipated.

Wood's spurt of publication ended with her marriage on 28 October 1804 to Gen. Abiel Wood of Wiscasset, Maine, a wealthy shipbuilder and merchant. Some fifteen years older than his new bride, Abiel Wood was a family friend of the Saywards and the Barrells and had been a brigadier general in the Massachusetts militia. He was also an irascible and determined person: in 1773, when a customs agent seized a vessel that belonged to Wood, the agent was tarred and feathered. According to historians, Wood was actively Tory and exhibited contempt for the Continental Congress. Like the Barrell and Sayward men, General Wood was not prosecuted for disloyalty during the Revolution. Sally Wood was genuinely attached to him, writing in an 1808 letter, "I can in truth say my own attachments are as strong and as fervent as ever, my Husband is still kind and affectionate & perhaps I Love him more tenderly for the Perplexetys he encounters." After General Wood's death in 1811 she wrote to her brother expressing her affection for the general ("I shall always set down the Seven years I have passed with him as some of the happiest of my life") while carefully setting down the details of her large inheritance from her husband's estate.

The details of Wood's life after the general's death are not fully documented. At some point she moved to Portland, Maine, and resumed her writing. In 1827 she published *Tales of the Night,* which comprises two stories, both with American settings. In this book Wood enhanced her plots by incorporating accurate social details.

The first story, "Storms and Sunshine," is a romance. Henry Arnold, a Massachusetts native living in Great Britain, returns to Maine to settle the estate his uncle has willed to him. Caught in a terrible snowstorm on the way to Maine, Arnold, his wife, and his daughters, Cornelia and Emma, find shelter in an empty house. As a result of their ordeal, Mrs. Arnold falls desperately ill, and Cornelia bravely nurses her mother until a local doctor, Mr. Barton, and Mr. Howard, the owner of the house, find the Arnolds. News arrives that the Arnolds have lost their fortune. Howard proposes to Cornelia, but she refuses him because she must remain with her destitute family. Then a series of fortunate discoveries results in the Arnolds' winning their case to regain the uncle's inheritance, and all their other misfortunes are righted. Cornelia marries Mr. Howard, and Emma marries the doctor. The story is notable for its depiction of local scenes and the realities of travel in early America.

The second story in *Tales of the Night,* "The Hermitage," is a Cinderella story. Because of his medical condition, the elderly Governor Wellington and his wife take in a servant, Marcia Vernon, who is "merry as a cricket, as nimble as a bee and as industrious." When Marcia is fifteen, the Wellingtons house a mysterious stranger, whose presence must be kept a secret. Stunned by Marcia's innocence and beauty, the stranger falls in love with her but cannot marry her because of his personal misfortune. As he leaves, he tells Marcia that if she does not hear from him, she must assume he has died. In Marcia's eighteenth year, the dying Mrs. Wellington makes a deathbed request that Marcia continue to minister to the governor's needs, and about a year later the governor realizes that he must marry Marcia or let her go. Thinking of her promise to Mrs. Wellington, Marcia agrees to the marriage. Ten years later Marcia has become a respected member of society, and the mysterious stranger, now identified as Colonel Mortimer, returns. Mortimer and Marcia realize that they still love one another, but Mortimer leaves. Soon after, Wellington dies, telling Marcia that she must marry a year after his death. Mortimer returns in good time and the two marry. While the plot is fantastic, "The Hermitage" is an excellent study of the relationship between servant and master.

Eventually Wood settled in Portland with the family of her son, Richard Keating, a sea captain. After he was accidentally drowned in 1833, Wood remained with his family for some time and then moved to Kennebunkport, Maine, to live with a widowed granddaughter and great-grandson. A contemporary commentator remarked that Wood was a conspicuous figure during that period because of her peculiar style of dress, "one owing much to the last century." According to Doris R. Marston, at age ninety-one Wood edited *The Little Hymn Book; Compiled for The Moral and Religious Instruction of Children, At Home and in Sunday School.* She died on 6 January 1855 in Kennebunkport.

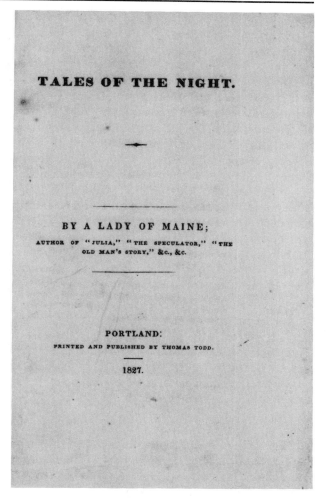

TALES OF THE NIGHT.

BY A LADY OF MAINE;
AUTHOR OF "JULIA," "THE SPECULATOR," "THE OLD MAN'S STORY," &c., &c.

PORTLAND:
PRINTED AND PUBLISHED BY THOMAS TODD.
1827.

Title page for two stories Wood set in her native New England, notable for their depictions of local scenes (courtesy of the Special Collections Department, University of Virginia Library)

After her death other works by Wood were discovered. In 1903 the Portsmouth, New Hampshire, newspaper published letters written by Wood in 1842. Intended for a relative, Mrs. Cushing, the letters recall various local historical events. These letters were used by Hilda Fife to support her argument that Nathaniel Hawthorne and others read and adapted Wood's writings. The manuscript for "War, the Parent of Domestic Calamity: A Tale of the Revolution" was found in the library of the Maine Historical Society and published in 1968. Based on internal evidence, it is believed that the story dates from some time after 1815. Unlike Wood's other works, "War" is a tragedy, the story of the ill-fated love of Julia Ann Fitsbriant, the child of an Englishman living in America, and Alexander Campbell, a British officer. Julia meets Campbell at the home of her aunt in England and then returns home to Wolfborough, New Hampshire, at the outbreak of the Revolution. Two years later Julia is in Portsmouth, where she meets Campbell, who has become a prisoner of war. With the aid of her father, who is also a British officer, Julia and Campbell elope. Julia's brothers, both ardent American soldiers, discover that Julia is eloping with a British officer and decide to intervene. When they come upon Julia with her father and Campbell, they mistakenly shoot their father, whom they think is Campbell, as well as their sister. Campbell, who is standing nearby, kills and is killed by Julia's younger brother. In the coda to this tragedy Julia's elder brother is killed in battle, and their mother, worn down by grief, quickly follows him in death. As Fife has noted, this work is initially well developed but essentially weak in structure. The achievement of the tale lies in its simple moral: good people on both sides suffer, often needlessly, in war.

Like many women writers of the early national period, Wood was generally ignored by critics. Early assessments of her novels tend to be comments in general studies of the novel as a type or in surveys of women writers. Generally her books were treated as literary curiosities. Most scholars found Wood to be socially ambivalent, drawing on English literary tradition, as personified by the works of Rowson and Radcliffe, but returning to patriotic American themes. Most critical attention was focused on *Julia and the Illuminated Baron,* which was judged to be second-rate as were the novels of most women of the period. With the beginning of the women's movement and the consequent growth of feminist criticism, Wood and the other writers of the early national period garnered more attention. Yet her reputation did not significantly change as a result of this attention. Studies of the early American novel usually describe Wood as a weak stylist with an inability to create a well-structured plot. Many modern feminist critics consider Wood a conservative who—in the words of Sharon M. Harris—"perpetuated patriarchal ideals of women's second-class citizenship." Other recent critics have shed new light on Wood's fiction. Anne Dalke, for example, theorizes that, like other American women novelists of her time, Wood used the incest theme to express a widespread fear about the apparent instability of the new class structure in America, while William Scheick emphasizes the theme of education in *Julia and the Illuminated Baron,* arguing that the protagonists are examples of the Jeffersonian ideal, people who, through education, are able to become Republicans despite their aristocratic origins.

An important figure in the development of the American novel, Sally Sayward Barrell Keating Wood chronicled Maine life in novels that anticipate the work of regional writers such as Sarah Orne Jewett. As a conservative writer, she created a world of melodrama and fantasy that deserves more critical attention.

References:

Anne Dalke, "Original Vice: The Political Implications of Incest in the Early American Novel," *Early American Literature,* 23 (1988): 188–201;

Cathy N. Davidson, *Revolution and the Word: the Rise of the Novel in America* (New York: Oxford University Press, 1986);

Hilda Fife, "Madam Wood's Recollections," *Colby Library Quarterly,* 7 (1965): 88–115;

Doris R. Marston, "A Lady of Maine: Sally Barrell Keating Wood," master's thesis, University of New Hampshire, 1970;

Henri Petter, *The Early American Novel* (Columbus: Ohio State University Press, 1971);

Doreen Alvarez Saar, "Sally Barrell Keating Wood," in *Eighteenth-Century Anglo-American Women Novelists: A Reference Guide,* edited by Saar and Mary Anne Schofield (New York: G. K. Hall / London: Prentice Hall International, 1996);

William Scheick, "Education, Class, and the French Revolution in Sarah Wood's *Julia,*" *Studies in American Fiction,* 6, no. 1 (1990): 111–118.

Appendix

Women's Work, Women's Sphere: Selected Comments from Women Writers

Women's Work, Women's Sphere: Selected Comments from Women Writers

To appreciate fully the complexity of the writings and biographies of early American women, it is necessary to understand the social conditions of their lives. What was life like for these women, and what was considered acceptable behavior for them? Some answers to these questions may be found in the writings of women themselves. The question of women's roles in society was by no means a new one; debates on the topic appear as early as ancient Greece and Rome. For American colonists during the mid to late eighteenth century, however, the issue of women's proper roles, or "spheres" of activity, was a frequent topic in literary discourse. Increased leisure, improved education, and greater circulation of printed materials made it possible for these discussions to take place more publicly and for women's writings on the question of their own status to be preserved. While their writings do not always agree, most women shared several assumptions based on a common experience (and a long history) that defined "woman's sphere" as the domain of home and family.

From the time of the first arrival of English colonists in North America to the establishment of the American republic, women's essential work and women's spheres of activity were defined within domestic spaces. For early American women, including many of the women treated in this volume, daily work encompassed a set of tasks focused around family and the home: household maintenance and cleaning, preparation of meals, making clothing and other products for family use, tending a family garden, caring for and educating children, supervising servants, and nursing the sick. A frequent motif in women's writing of the era is the difficulty of finding time to write after fulfilling these primary duties. Indeed many women described themselves as writing late at night, after completing the day's work and while the rest of the family was asleep. Writing and other intellectual pursuits were viewed as leisure activities. Formal education for women was limited: most middle- and upper-class women learned to read, but they often were not taught to write. They learned needlework and other domestic skills while their brothers were sent to writing teachers.

During the eighteenth century, however, several factors converged to make women's work and social roles the subject for debate and discussion. Competing definitions of women's "proper sphere" emerged. In the literary world, colonists, influenced by debates among English writers, continued lines of argument that can be traced to classical writers. While some British writers—both men and women—were calling for improved female education, others discounted the value of educating women, either because "learned ladies" would no longer be suited for their domestic duties or because women were naturally inferior, as Jonathan Swift (1667–1745) argued when he said that no amount of reading could bring a woman up to the level of "a common school-boy." Other popular writers, including Alexander Pope (1688–1744) and Philip Dormer Stanhope, Lord Chesterfield (1694–1773), outlined in detail the failings of women, which they attributed to the female sex rather than cultural influences. According to the negative side of the argument, women were vain and capricious; they loved fashion and gossip; and they were ruled by emotion, not reason. Other writers, including Joseph Addison (1672–1717) and Richard Steele (1672–1729), following a line of argument taken up by Daniel Defoe (1660–1731) before them, argued that women's faults could be improved by better education. American readers were interested in both sides of the debates, sometimes characterized as the battle of the sexes.

On a broader scale, definitions of what came to be called the "woman's sphere" were also influenced by the philosophical movement now called the Enlightenment, which stressed the human capacity for rationality. Philosophers such as John Locke were developing new theories about human development and behavior that suggested education, not nature, was central to forming character. If this theory were true, some argued, differences between men and women were caused not by inherently different male and female natures but by the different educations received by men and women. Moreover, Enlightenment philosophers argued that government was a matter not of the divine right of kings but of mutual benefit for citizens. This argument was also later used to attempt to redefine women's proper roles: If man should obey government based on rationality rather than blind obedience to a monarch, should women be required to submit without question to a husband or father? Or was men's right to govern their families dependent on their reasonable behavior? Some women, such as the British writer Mary Wollstonecraft, used Enlightenment ideas about government to argue that women should not be required to submit blindly to men's authority.

Perhaps the most important influence in the American context, however, was the Revolutionary War. In justifying their separation from England, Americans made claims about human rights, most famously in the announcement of the "self-evident" truth that "all men are created equal." Such claims led some people to question the validity of slavery and other forms of servitude as well as the legal and political status of women. At the same time, in the aftermath of the Revolution, many Americans came to believe that their culture was superior to European culture because Americans, whose lives were more free of the deleterious effects of luxury, lived closer to the natural world. Americans also argued that they were living in the freest country in the world. One result of freedom was the need for well-educated citizens; that is, because all citizens participated in government, their education was more important than it was for subjects under a monarch. Since mothers were usually responsible for their children's earliest education, the American concern for a virtuous citizenry led to an interest in improving women's education because educated mothers could best train the nation's youth.

Women took part in defining their appropriate spheres of activity. By their examples, women who engaged in activities not usually defined as part of the domestic sphere demonstrated that women were capable of performing business dealings and other "masculine" activities and should not be uniformly excluded from them. Particularly in the later part of the eighteenth century, talented women accomplished much in traditionally male areas. Mary Katherine Goddard was publisher of two newspapers, the official and first printer of the Declaration of Independence, and postmistress of Baltimore during the American Revolution. Eliza Lucas Pinckney conducted significant horticultural research and ran three family plantations. Mercy Otis Warren wrote political plays, a pamphlet critiquing the Federal Constitution, and a major history of the Revolution. These women's lives and accomplishments illustrate that the definition of women's work was not inflexible.

Women also wrote about their proper work and spheres of activity. The selections from women's writings collected here demonstrate a range of ideas about women's work as mothers and wives, women's education and friendship, and their intellectual capacity and political rights. Because of the limitations of many women's education, the writers represented here are from the upper classes, and because there is a larger body of literature by women from the Middle and Northeastern colonies, these are the women represented. Although their backgrounds are in some ways similar, these women's attitudes and arguments are by no means uniform.

The earliest of the selections, a diary entry by Esther Edwards Burr (1732–1758), might seem somewhat conventional in its focus on women's friendship. Yet it is worth noting that Burr, daughter of the well-known minister Jonathan Edwards (1703–1758) and prominent socially as the wife of a college president, Aaron Burr Sr., felt strongly enough about the issue to enter into what seems to have been a heated debate with a college tutor. The letters written by Abigail Adams (1744–1818) during the Revolutionary War are explicitly political in that she asked her husband, John Adams (1735–1826), who was then involved in the Continental Congress, to make some legal considerations for women; yet, in some ways, Adams seems to have deferred more to male authority than did Burr several decades earlier. Adams accepted her husband's joking reply to her letter, and then recounted the exchange to Mercy Otis Warren in a similarly light tone.

The selections from the 1790s all deal in one way or another with education, the topic that had come by then to dominate discussion of women's sphere. Judith Sargent Murray (1751–1820), herself an especially well-educated woman, asserted that all branches of education should be open to women. Her arguments in many ways resemble those that Mary Wollstonecraft (1759–1797) made a few years later. In a letter to her daughter Annis Boudinot Stockton (1736–1801) commented on Wollstonecraft's ideas. Stockton agreed on the need for improved women's education, but she worried that Wollstonecraft's ideas, especially her religious views, were too radical. The selection from *The Boarding-School,* by Hannah Webster Foster (1758–1840), focuses on specific aspects of female education, suggesting that women's education should enable them to support their families if necessary—a surprising idea if women's sphere is defined as domestic.

The last two selections, both from 1818, offer somewhat different perspectives from those of the 1790s. Hannah Mather Crocker (1752–1829), though arguing for women's right to education, claims that American women were already more free and thus more accomplished than European women. Mary Palmer Tyler (1775–1866) stressed the most practical side of women's education: the care of children. She represented child care as a woman's most important duty and especially important in a republic. In these final two selections, then, there is a greater emphasis on the special nature of American womanhood and a greater assertion of national pride.

There is no neat chronological progression of ideas in these selections, a fact that reflects the nature of the debates about women's roles in society, which tended to shift along with political and social needs rather than progress in a straight line. Taken as a group, these writings offer a window into the varieties of women's roles in early America and the ways in which women themselves helped to define those roles.

—Angela Vietto

Esther Edwards Burr (1732–1758)

Esther Edwards Burr, a devout Puritan, lived most of her life in the public eye, first as the daughter of the famous minister Jonathan Edwards and then as the wife of Princeton president Aaron Burr Jr. Like many pious women, she recorded her religious life and details of her daily life in a journal. From 1754 until 1757 Burr exchanged her journal regularly with her friend Sarah Prince. The journal reveals the value Burr placed on female friendship, especially with Prince but also with other women.

In the following selection from her journal, Burr recounts a discussion about female friendship that indicates some of the typical lines taken in debates about women's nature. Burr's partner in this battle of wits, John Ewing, was a tutor at the College of New Jersey (now Princeton University). Ewing presented an argument that relied on old stereotypes about gender differences: men are controlled and rational, while women are erratic and ruled by emotion. Such ideas date back to classical writers such as Aristotle and Juvenal. In Esther Burr's day, however, these ideas were also available in the writings of authors such as Alexander Pope, whose *Rape of the Lock* (1712) and "Epistle to a Lady" (1735) characterized women as vain, unbalanced, and silly and discouraged women from demonstrating their learning.

By recording this discussion, Burr provided not just insight into how American men could make use of the old stereotypes of women but also a view of how such ideas were debated and the extent to which at least some women felt comfortable defending their sex. The fact that the discussion took place in Burr's home, where she often entertained tutors from the college as well as visiting dignitaries, indicates that the domestic sphere was not isolated from intellectual or moral discussions.

from *The Journal of Esther Edwards Burr*[1]

(April 12, 1757)
Teusday A.M. 10. o'Clock.

I have had a smart Combat with Mr Ewing about our sex—he is a man of good parts and Lerning but has mean thoughts of Women—he began the dispute in this Manner. Speaking of Miss Boudanot[2] I said she was a sociable friendly creture. A Gentleman seting by joined with me, but Mr Ewing says—*she and the Stocktons are full of talk about Friendship and society and such stuff*—and made up a Mouth as if much disgusted—I asked what he would have 'em talk about—whether he chose they should talk about fashions and dress—*he said things that they understood. He did not think women knew what Friendship was. They were hardly capable of anything so cool and rational as friendship*—(My tongue, you know, hangs pretty loose, thoughts Crouded in—so I sputtered away for dear life.) You may Guss what a large field this speach opened for me—I retorted several severe things upon him before he had time to speak again. He Blushed and seemed confused. The Gentleman seting by said little but when did speak it was to my purpose and we carried on the dispute for an hour—I talked him quite silent. He got up and said your servant and went off—I dont know that ever I meet with one that was so openly and fully in Mr Pop[e's] sordid scheam—One of the last things that he said was that he never in all his life knew or hear[d] of a woman that had a little more lerning then [common?] but it made her proud to such a degree that she was disgusfull [to] all her acquaintance.

1. Burr's diary was not published during her lifetime. An abridged version appeared in 1901 as *Esther Burr's Journal,* edited by Jeremiah Eames Rankin (Washington, D.C.: Howard University). The entire diary appeared in 1984 as *The Journal of Esther Edwards Burr, 1754–1757,* edited by Carol F. Karlsen and Laurie Crumpacker (New Haven: Yale University Press).

2. Annis Boudinot (later Stockton) was a young poet whose family had recently moved to the Princeton area. Boudinot was a frequent visitor at the Burr home in 1756–1757 and had given several poems to Burr, including one about their friendship. See *Only for the Eye of a Friend: The Poems of Annis Boudinot Stockton,* edited by Carla Mulford (Charlottesville: University Press of Virginia, 1995).

Abigail Adams (1744–1818)

Letters to John Adams (31 March 1776) and to Mercy Otis Warren (27 April 1776)[1]

It would perhaps be surprising if Abigail Adams had not written to her husband about women's legal rights. In 1776 she was functioning as the head of her family in Braintree, Massachusetts, while her husband was away serving in the Continental Congress. In his absence Abigail Adams was responsible for managing property and business as well as caring for her family, while spending occasional sleepless nights listening to cannon fire from occupied Boston. Surely this experience had something to do with Adams's sense that women's legal status ought to be improved. Although Abigail and John Adams seem to have had a happy marriage, Abigail Adams still recognized that there was an incompatibility between women's legal status and the philosophical and political claims of the American Revolution. Under English law, women were subordinated legally to their fathers and husbands. A married woman could not own property or conduct business without her husband's permission. It is most likely these sorts of restrictions, rather than political rights such as enfranchisement, that Adams had in mind when she asked John Adams to "Remember the Ladies" as the Continental Congress constructed a new code of law. Her letter is one of the earliest recorded statements of this apparent contradiction. The light tone of her letter recounting the incident to her friend Mercy Otis Warren suggests that Adams did not really expect much to come of her suggestion.

Though the passage in which Adams asks her husband to "Remember the Ladies" has become famous, it is interesting to read this passage in the larger context of Abigail Adams's letters, noting her sense of her own marriage as a partnership as well as her sense of a shared interest among women in her letter to her friend Mercy Otis Warren. The letters also give hints of the kinds of work that fell to Abigail Adams during the Revolution. From managing property to making soap, Abigail Adams, like many women, faced new challenges on the home front that demonstrated the importance of their roles in American economic and social life.

Abigail Adams to John Adams
Braintree March 31 1776

I wish you would ever write me a Letter half as long as I write you; and tell me if you may where your Fleet are gone? What sort of Defence Virginia can make against our common Enemy? Whether it is so situated as to make an able Defence? Are not the Gentery Lords and the common people vassals, are they not like the uncivilized natives Brittain represents us to be? I hope their Riffel Men who have shewen themselves very savage and even Blood thirsty; are not a specimen of the Generality of the people. . . .

I have sometimes been ready to think that the passion for Liberty cannot be Eaquelly Strong in the Breasts of those who have been accustomed to deprive their fellow Creatures of theirs. Of this I am certain that it is not founded upon that generous and christian principal of doing to others as we would that others should do unto us.

Do not you want to see Boston; I am fearfull of the small pox, or I should have been in before this time. I got Mr. Crane[2] to go to our House and see what state it was in. I find it has been occupied by one of the Doctors of a regiment, very dirty, but no other damage has been done to it. The few things which were left in it are all gone. [Crane] has the key which he never deliverd up. I have wrote to him for it and am determined to get it cleand as soon as possible and shut it up. I look upon it a new acquisition of property, a property which one month ago I did not value at a single Shilling, and could with pleasure have seen it in flames.[3]

The Town in General is left in a better state than we expected, more oweing to a percipitate flight than any Regard to the inhabitants, tho some individuals discoverd a sense of honour and justice and have left the rent of the Houses in which they were, for the owners and the furniture unhurt, or if damaged sufficent to make it good.

Others have committed abominable Ravages. The Mansion House of your President[4] is safe and the furniture unhurt whilst both the House and Furniture of the Solisiter General[5] have fallen a prey to their own merciless party. Surely the very Fiends feel a Reverential awe for Virtue and patriotism, whilst they Detest the paricide and traitor.

I feel very differently at the approach of spring to what I did a month ago. We knew not then whether we could plant or sow with safety, whether when we had toild we could reap the fruits of our own industery, whether we could rest in our own Cottages, or whether we should not be driven from the sea coasts to seek shelter in the wilderness, but now we feel as if we might sit under our own vine and eat the good of the land.

I feel a gaieti de Coar[6] to which before I was a stranger. I think the Sun looks brighter, the Birds sing more melodiously, and Nature puts on a more chearfull countanance. We feel a temporary peace, and the poor fugitives are returning to their deserted habitations.

Tho we felicitate ourselves, we sympathize with those who are trembling least the Lot of Boston should be theirs. But they cannot be in similar circumstances unless pusilanimity and cowardise should take possession of them. They have time and warning given them to see the Evil and shun it.—I long to hear that you have declared an independancy—and by the way in the new Code of Laws which I suppose it will be necessary for you to make I desire you would Remember the Ladies, and be more generous and favourable to them than your ancestors. Do not put such unlimited power into the hands of the Husbands. Remember all Men would be tyrants if they could. If perticuliar care and attention is not paid to the Laidies we are determined to foment a Rebelion, and will not hold ourselves bound by any Laws in which we have no voice, or Representation.

That your Sex are naturally Tyrannical is a Truth so thoroughly established as to admit of no dispute, but such of you as wish to be happy willingly give up the harsh title of Master for the more tender and endearing one of Friend. Why then, not put it out of the power of the vicious and the Lawless to use us with cruelty and indignity with impunity. Men of Sense in all Ages abhor those customs which treat us only as the vassals of your Sex. Regard us then as Beings placed by providence under your protection and in immitation of the Supreem Being make use of that power only for our happiness.

April 5

Not having an opportunity of sending this I shall add a few lines more;

. . .

I want to hear much oftener from you than I do. March 8 was the last date of any that I have yet had.—You inquire of whether I am making Salt peter.[7] I have not yet attempted it, but after Soap making believe I shall make the experiment. I find as much as I can do to manufacture cloathing for my family which would else be Naked. I know of but one person in this part of the Town who has made any, that is Mr. Tertias Bass as he is calld who has got very near an hundred weight which has been found to be very good. I have heard of some others in the other parishes. Mr. Reed of Weymouth has been applied to, to go to Andover to the mills which are now at work, and has gone. I have lately seen a small Manuscrip de[s]cribing the proportions for the various sorts of powder, fit for cannon, small arms and pistols. If it would be of any Service your way I will get it transcribed and send it to you.—Every one of your Friend[s] send their Regards, and all the little ones. . . . Adieu. I need not say how much I am Your ever faithfull Friend.

Abigail Adams to Mercy Otis Warren

Braintree April 27 1776

I set myself down to comply with my Friends request, who I think seem's rather low spiritted.

I did write last week, but not meeting with an early conveyance I thought the Letter of But little importance and tos'd it away. I acknowledg my Thanks due to my Friend for the entertainment she so kindly afforded me in the Characters drawn in her Last Letter, and if coveting my Neighbours Goods was not prohibited by the Sacred law, I should be most certainly tempted to envy her the happy talant she possesses above the rest of her Sex, by adorning with her pen even trivial occurances, as well as dignifying the most important. Cannot you communicate some of those Graces to your Friend and suffer her to pass them upon the World for her own that she may feel a little more upon an Eaquality with you?—Tis true I often receive large packages from P[hiladelphi]a.[8] They contain as I said before more News papers than Letters, tho they are not forgotton. It would be hard indeed if absence had not some alleviations.

I dare say he writes to no one unless to Portia[9] oftner than to your Friend,[10] because I know there is no one besides in whom he has an eaquel confidence. His Letters to me have been generally short, but he pleads in Excuse the critical state of affairs and the Multiplicity of avocations and says further that he has been very Busy, and writ near ten Sheets of paper, about some affairs which he does not chuse to Mention for fear of accident.

He is very sausy to me in return for a List of Female Grievances which I transmitted to him. I think I will get you to join me in a petition to Congress. I thought it was very probable our wise Statesmen would erect a new Goverment and form a new code of Laws. I ventured to speak a word in behalf of our Sex, who are rather hardly dealt with by the Laws of England which gives such unlimitted power to the Husband to use his wife Ill.

I requested that our Legislators would consider our case and as all men of delicacy and Sentiment are averse to Excercising the power they possess, yet as there is a natural propensity in Humane Nature to domination, I thought the most generous plan was to put it out of the power of the Arbitary and tyranick to injure us with impunity by Establishing some Laws in our favour upon just and Liberal principals.

I believe I even threatned fomenting a Rebellion in case we were not considerd, and assured him we would not hold ourselves bound by any Laws in which we had neither a voice, nor representation.

In return he tells me he cannot but Laugh at My Extrodonary Code of Laws. That he had heard their Struggle had loosned the bands of Goverment, that children and apprentices were dissabedient, that Schools and Colledges were grown turbulant, that Indians slighted their Guardians, and Negroes grew insolent to their Masters. But my letter was the first intimation that another Tribe more numerous and powerfull than all the rest were grown discontented. This is rather too coarse a complement, he adds, but that I am so sausy he wont blot it out.

So I have help'd the Sex abundantly, but I will tell him I have only been making trial of the Disintresstedness of his Virtue, and when weigh'd in the balance have found it wanting.

It would be bad policy to grant us greater power say they since under all the disadvantages we Labour we have the assendancy over their Hearts

And charm by accepting, by submitting sway.

I wonder Apollo and the Muses could not have indulged me with a poetical Genious. I have always been a votary to her charms but never could assend Parnassus myself.

I am very sorry to hear of the indisposition of your Friend. I am affraid it will hasten his return, and I do not think he can be spared.

"Though certain pains attend the cares of State
A Good man owes his Country to be great
Should act abroad the high distinguishd part
or shew at least the purpose of his heart."

Good Night my Friend. You will be so good as to remember me to our worthy Friend Mrs. W————e[11] when you see her and write soon to your
Portia

---

1. The first collection of Abigail Adams's letters appeared in 1840, edited by her grandson Charles Francis Adams. A more complete collection of Adams's letters is in *The Adams Family Correspondence*, edited by L. H. Butterfield and others (1963–).

2. Abigail Adams's agent in Boston.

3. British troops occupying Boston had evacuated the city on 17 March 1776, following an American siege on 5 March.

4. John Hancock, then president of the Continental Congress.

5. Samuel Quincy, a royal official.

6. Lightness of heart.

7. Potassium nitrate, used in making gunpowder.

8. From her husband, John Adams.

9. Portia was a pen name Abigail Adams used in correspondence with friends.

10. Warren's husband, James Warren, was at this time Speaker of the House in the Massachusetts provincial government.

11. Mrs. John Winthrop.

Judith Sargent Murray (1751–1820)

Like several other women writers of her era, Judith Sargent Murray had an unusually thorough education, sharing her brother's preparation for Harvard. Although she was not alone in stressing the importance of women's education, Murray was unusual in proposing that all branches of learning be open to women. Astronomy and natural science were rarely considered suitable subjects for women, though a few notable female botanists did produce scientific texts during the eighteenth century. Murray's argument that scientific study would help women appreciate God's greatness makes use of positions offered by early scientists such as Isaac Newton, who claimed that studying the natural world would lead to greater understanding of the nature of God, and by theologians such as Jonathan Edwards, who sought in the natural world scientific answers to spiritual questions. Murray's argument that improved education would not only make women happier but also make them better companions for men anticipates later, similar arguments on behalf of women's education.

The letter that is appended to the original essay is also interesting in its approach to religious claims about the status of women. One of the few areas in which women could write without criticism, from the Middle Ages on, was biblical exegesis. Murray thus followed a tradition of women's writing and at the same time transformed it by claiming that the story of the Fall does not prove women's greater weakness. Murray's reinterpretation of the story of Adam and Eve anticipated many such scriptural interpretations by women in the nineteenth century, most notably suffragist Elizabeth Cady Stanton's *The Woman's Bible* (1895). Murray's essay as a whole lays out basic principles that later became part of more-radical arguments.

On the Equality of the Sexes (1790)[1]

That minds are not alike, full well I know,
This truth each day's experience will show;
To heights surprising some great spirits soar,
With inborn strength mysterious depths explore;
Their eager gaze surveys the path of light,
Confessed it stood to Newton's piercing sight.
Deep science, like a bashful maid retires,
And but the *ardent* breast her worth inspires;

By perseverance the coy fair is won.
And Genius, led by Study, wears the crown.
But some there are who wish not to improve,
Who never can the path of knowledge love,
Whose soul's almost with the dull body one,
With anxious care each mental pleasure shun;
Weak is the leveled, enervated mind,
And but while here to vegetate designed.
The torpid spirit mingling with its clod,
Can scarcely boast its origin from God;
Stupidly dull—they move progressing on—
They eat, and drink and all their work is done.
While others, emulous of sweet applause,
Industrious seek for each event a cause,
Tracing the hidden spring whence knowledge flows,
Which nature all in beauteous order shows.
Yet cannot I their sentiments imbibe,
who this distinction to the sex ascribe,
As if a woman's form must needs enroll,
A weak, a servile, an inferior soul;
And that the guise of man must still proclaim,
Greatness of mind, and him, to be the same:
Yet as the hours revolve fair proofs arise,
Which the bright wreath of growing fame supplies;
And in past times some men have *sunk* so *low*,
That female records nothing *less* can show.
But imbecility is still confined,
And by the lordly sex to us consigned;
They rob us of the power t'improve,
And then declare we only trifles love;
Yet haste the era, when the world shall know,
That such distinctions only dwell below;
The soul unfettered, to no sex confined,
Was for the abodes of cloudless day designed.
Meantime we emulate their manly fires,
Though erudition all their thoughts inspires,
Yet nature with *equality* imparts,
And *noble passions,* swell e'en *female hearts.*

Is it upon mature consideration we adopt the idea, that nature is thus partial in her distributions? Is it indeed a fact, that she hath yielded to one half of the human species so unquestionable a mental superiority? I know that to both sexes elevated understandings, and the reverse, are common. But, suffer me to ask, in what the minds of females are so notoriously deficient, or unequal. May not the intellectual powers be ranged under their four heads—imagination, reason, memory and judgement. The province of imagination has long since been surrendered up to us, and we have been crowned undoubted sovereigns of the regions of fancy. Invention is perhaps the most arduous effort of the mind; this branch of imagination hath been particularly ceded to us, and we have been time out of mind invested with that creative faculty. Observe the variety of fashions (here I bar the contemptuous smile) which distinguish and adorn the female world; how continually are they changing, insomuch that they almost render the whole man's assertion problematical, and we are ready to say, *there is something new under the sun.* Now, what a playfulness, what an exuberance of fancy, what strength of inventive imagination, doth this continual variation discover? Again, it hath been observed, that if the turpitude of the conduct of our sex, hath been ever so enormous, so extremely ready are we that the very first thought presents us with an apology so plausible, as to produce our actions even in an amiable light. Another instance of our creative powers is our talent for slander; how ingenious are we at inventive scandal? What a formidable story can we in a moment fabricate merely from the force of a prolifick imagination? How many reputations, in the fertile brain of a female, have been utterly despoiled? How industrious are we at improving a hint? Suspicion how easily do we convert into conviction, and conviction, embellished by the power of eloquence, stalks abroad to the surprise and confusion of unsuspecting innocence. Perhaps it will be asked if I furnish these facts as instances of excellency in our sex. Certainly not; but as proofs of a creative faculty, of a lively imagination. Assuredly great activity of mind is thereby discovered, and was this activity properly directed, what beneficial effects would follow. Is the needle and kitchen sufficient to employ the operations of a soul thus organized? I should conceive not. Nay, it is a truth that those very departments leave the intelligent principle vacant, and at liberty for speculation. Are we deficient in reason? We can only reason from what we know, and if opportunity of acquiring knowledge hath been denied us, the inferiority of our sex cannot fairly be deduced from thence. Memory, I believe, will be allowed us in common, since every one's experience must testify, that a loquacious old woman is as frequently met with, as a communicative old man; their subjects are alike drawn from the fund of other times, and the transactions of their youth, or of maturer life, entertain, or perhaps fatigue you, in the evening of their lives. "But our judgment is not so strong—we do not distinguish so well." Yet it may be questioned, from what doth this superiority, in this discriminating fac-

ulty of the soul, proceed. May we not trace its source in the difference of education, and continued advantages? Will it be said that the judgment of a male of two years old, is more sage than that of a female's of the same age? I believe the reverse is generally observed to be true. But from that period what partiality! how is the one exalted and the other depressed, by the contrary modes of education which are adopted! The one is taught to aspire, and the other is early confined and limited. As their years increase, the sister must be wholly domesticated, while the brother is led by the hand through all the flowery paths of science. Grant that their minds are by nature equal, yet who shall wonder at the *apparent* superiority, if indeed custom becomes *second nature;* nay if it taketh place of nature, and that it doth the experience of each day will evince. At length arrived at womanhood, the uncultivated fair one feels a void, which the employments allotted her are by no means capable of filling. What can she do? To books, she may not apply; or if she doth, *to those only of the novel kind,* lest she merit the appellation of a *learned lady;* and what ideas have been affixed to this term, the observation of many can testify. Fashion, scandal and sometimes what is still more reprehensible, are then called in to her relief; and who can say to what lengths the liberties she takes may proceed. Meantime she herself is most unhappy; she feels the want of a cultivated mind. Is she single, she in vain seeks to fill up time from sexual employments or amusements. Is she united to a person whose soul nature made equal to her own, education hath set him so far above her, that in those entertainments which are productive of such rational felicity, she is not qualified to accompany him. She experiences a mortifying consciousness of inferiority, which embitters every enjoyment. Doth the person to whom her adverse fate hath consigned her, possess a mind incapable of improvement, she is equally wretched, in being so closely connected with an individual whom she cannot but despise. Now, was she permitted the same instructors as her brother, (with an eye however to their particular departments) for the employment of a rational mind an ample field would be opened. In astronomy she might catch a glimpse of the immensity of the Deity, and thense she would form amazing conceptions of the august and supreme Intelligence. In geography she would admire Jehovah in the midst of his benevolence; thus adapting this globe to the various wants and amusements of its inhabitants. In natural philosophy she would adore the infinite majesty of heaven, clothed in condescension; and as she traversed the reptile world, she would hail the goodness of a creating God. A mind, thus filled, would have little room for the trifles with which our sex are, with too much justice, accused of amusing themselves, and they would thus be rendered fit companions for those, who should one day wear them as their crown. Fashions, in their variety, would then give place to conjectures, which might perhaps conduce to the improvement of the literary world; and there would be no leisure for slander or detraction. Reputation would not then be blasted, but serious speculations would occupy the lively imaginations of the sex. Unnecessary visits would be precluded, and that customs would only be indulged by way of relaxation, or to answer the demands of consanguinity and friendship. Females would become discreet, their judgments would be invigorated, and their partners for life being circumspectly chosen, an unhappy Hymen would then be as rare, as is now the reverse.

Will it be urged that those acquirements would supersede our domestick duties, I answer that every requisite in female economy is easily attained; and, with truth I can add, that when once attained they require no further *mental attention*. Nay, while we are pursuing the needle, or the superintendency of the family, I repeat, that our minds are at full liberty for reflection; that imagination may exert itself in full vigor; and that if a just foundation is early laid, our ideas will then be worthy of rational beings. If we were industrious we might easily find time to arrange them upon paper, or should avocations press too hard for such an indulgence, the hours allotted for conversation would at least become more refined and rational. Should it still be vociferated, "Your domestick employments are sufficient"—I would calmly ask, is it reasonable, that a candidate for immortality, for the joys of heaven, an intelligent being, who is to spend an eternity in contemplating the works of Deity, should at present be so degraded, as to be allowed no other ideas, than those which are suggested by the mechanism of a pudding, or the sewing of the seams of a garment? Pity that all such censurers of female improvement do not go one step further, and deny their future existence; to be consistent they surely ought.

Yes, ye lordly, ye haughty sex, our souls are by nature *equal* to yours; the same breath of God animates, enlivens, and invigorates us; and that we are not fallen lower than yourselves, let those witness who have greatly towered above the various discouragements by which they have been so heavily oppressed; and though I am unacquainted with the list of celebrated characters on either side, yet from the observations I have made in the contracted circle in which I have moved, I dare confidently believe, that from the commencement of time to the present day, there hath been as many females, as males, who by the *mere force of natural powers,* have merited the crown of applause; who *thus unassisted,* have seized the wreath of fame. I know there are those who assert, that as the animal powers of the one sex are superiour, of course their mental faculties also must be stronger; thus attributing strength of mind to the transient organization of this earth born tenement. But if this reasoning is just, man must be content to yield the palm to many of the brute creation, since by not a few of his breathren of the field, he is far surpassed in bodily strength. Moreover, was this argument admitted, it would prove too much, for occular demonstration evinceth, that there are many robust masculine ladies, and effeminate gentlemen. Yet I fancy that Mr. Pope, though clogged with an enervated body, and distinguished by a diminutive stature, could nevertheless lay claim to greatness of soul; and perhaps there are many other instances which might be adduced to combat so unphilosophical an opinion. Do we not often see, that when the clay built tabernacle is well nigh dissolved, when it is just ready to mingle with the parent soil, the immortal inhabitant aspires to, and even attaineth heights the most sublime, and which were before wholly unexplored. Besides, were we to grant that animal strength proved anything, taking into consideration the accustomed impartiality of nature, we should be induced to imagine, that she had invested the female mind with superiour strength as an equivalent for the bodily powers of man. But waving this however palpable advantage, for *equality* only, we wish to contend.

I am aware that there are many passages in the sacred oracles which seem to give the advantage to the other sex; but I consider all these as wholly metaphorical. Thus David was a man after God's own heart, yet see him enervated by his licentious passions! Behold him following Uriah to the death, and shew me wherein could consist the immaculate Being's complacency. Listen to the curses which Job bestoweth upon the day of his nativity, and tell me where is his perfection, where his patience—*literally* it existed not. David and Job were types of him who was to come; and the superiority of man, as exhibited in scripture, being also emblematical, all arguments deduced from thence, of course fall to the ground. The exquisite delicacy of the female mind proclaimeth the exactness of its texture, while its nice sense of honor announceth its innate, its native grandeur. And indeed, in one respect, the preeminence seems to be tacitly allowed us, for after an education which limits and confines, and employments and recreations which naturally tend to enervate the body and debilitate the mind; after we have from early youth been adorned with ribbons and other gewgaws, dressed out like the ancient victims previous to a sacrifice, being taught by the care of our parents in collecting the most showy materials that the ornamenting our exterior ought to be the principal object of our attention; after, I say, fifteen years thus spent, we are introduced into the world, amid the united adulation of every beholder. Praise is sweet to the soul; we are immediately intoxicated by large draughts of flattery, which, being plentifully administered, is to the pride of our hearts the most acceptable incense. It is expected that with the other sex we should commence immediate war, and that we should triumph over the machinations of the most artful. We must be constantly upon our guard; prudence and discretion must be our characteristics; and we must rise superior to, and obtain a complete victory over those who have been long adding to the native strength of their minds by an unremitted study of men and books, and who have, moreover, conceived from the loose characters which they have seen portrayed in the extensive variety of their reading, a most contemptible opinion of the sex. Thus unequal, we are, nothwithstanding, forced to the combat, and the infamy which is consequent upon the smallest deviation in our conduct, proclaims the high idea which was formed of our native strength; and thus, indirectly at least, is the preference acknowledged to be our due. And if we are allowed an equality of acquirement, let serious studies equally employ our minds, and we will bid our souls arise to equal strength. We will meet upon even ground, the despot man; we will rush with alacrity to the combat, and, crowned by success, we shall then answer the exalted expectations which are formed. Though sensibility, soft compassion, and gentle commiseration are inmates in the female bosom, yet against every deep-laid art, altogether fearless of the event, we will set them in array; for assuredly the wreath of victory will encircle the spotless brow. If we meet an equal, a sensible friend, we will reward him with the hand of amity, and through life we will be assiduous to promote his happiness; but from every deep-laid scheme for our ruin, retiring into ourselves, amid the flowery paths of science, we will indulge in all the refined and sentimental pleasures of contemplation. And should it still be urged that the studies thus insisted upon would interfere with our more peculiar department, I must further reply that *early hours,* and close application, will do wonders; and to her who is from the first dawn of reason taught to fill up time rationally, both the requisites will be easy. I grant that niggard fortune is too generally unfriendly to the mind, and that much of the valuable treasure, time, is necessarily expended upon the wants of the body; but it should be remembered, that in embarrassed circumstances our companions have as little leisure for literary improvement as is afforded to us; for most certainly their provident care is at least as requisite as our exertions. Nay, we have even more leisure for sedentary pleasures, as our avocations are more retired, much less laborious, and, as hath been observed, by no means require that avidity of attention which is proper to the employments of the other sex. In high life, or, in other words, where the parties are in possession of affluence, the objection respecting time is wholly obviated, and of course falls to the ground; and it may also be repeated that many of those hours which are at present swallowed up in fashion and scandal might be redeemed, were we habituated to useful reflections. But in one respect, O ye arbiters of our fate! We confess that the superiority is undubitably yours; you are by nature formed for our protectors; we pretend not to vie with you in bodily strength; upon this point we will never contend for victory. Shield us then, we beseech you, from external evils, and in return we will transact *your* domestic affairs. Yes, *your,* for are you not equally interested in those matters with ourselves? Is not the elegancy of neatness as agreeable to your sight as to ours, is not the well favored viand equally delightful to your taste; and doth not your sense of hearing suffer as much from the discordant sounds prevalent in an ill regulated family, produced by the voices of children and many *et ceteras*?

Constantia.[2]

By way of supplement to the forgoing pages, I subjoin the following extract from a letter wrote to a friend in the December of 1780.

And now assist me, O thou genius of my sex, while I undertake the arduous task of endeavouring to combat that vulgar, that almost universal errour, which hath, it seems enlisted even Mr. P—— under its banners. The superiority of your sex hath, I grant, been time out of mind esteemed a truth incontrovertible; in consequence of which persuasion, every plan of education hath been calculated to establish this favourite tenet. Not long since, weak and presuming as I was, I amused myself with selecting some arguments from nature, reason and experience, against this so generally received idea. I confess that to sacred testimonies I had not recourse. I held them to be merely metaphorical, and thus regarding them, I could not persuade myself that there was any propriety in bringing them to decide in this *very important debate.* However, as you, sir, confine yourself entirely to the sacred oracles, I mean to bend the whole of my artillery against those supposed proofs, which you have from thence provided, and from which you have formed an intrenchment *apparently* so invulnerable. And first, to begin with our great progenitors; but here, suffer me to promise, that it is for mental strength I mean to contend, for with respect to animal powers, I yield them undisputed to that sex, which enjoys them in common with the lion, the tyger, and many other beast of prey; therefore your observations respecting *the rib, under the arm, at a distance from the head, & c.&c.* in no sort militate against my view. Well, but the woman was first in the transgression. Strange how blind *self love* renders you men; were you not wholly absorbed in a partial admiration of your own abilities, you would long since have acknowledged the force of what I am now going to urge. It is true some ignoramuses have, absurdly enough informed us, that the beauteous fair of paradise, was seduced from her obedience, by a malignant demon, *in the guise of a baleful serpent;* but we, who are better informed, know that the fallen spirit presented himself to her view, *a shining angel* still; for thus, saith the criticks in the Hebrew tongue, ought the word to be rendered. Let us examine her motive–Hark! The seraph declares that she shall attain a perfection of knowledge; for is there aught which is not comprehended under one or other of the terms *good* and *evil*. It doth not appear that she was governed by any one sensual appetite; but merely by a desire of adorning her mind; a laudable ambition fired her soul, and a thirst for knowledge impelled the predilection so fatal in its consequences. Adam could not plead the same deception; assuredly he was not deceived; nor ought we to admire his superiour strength, or wonder at his sagacity, when we so often confess that example is much more influential than precept. His gentle partner stood before him, a melancholy instance of the direful effects of disobedience; he saw her not possessed of that wisdom which she had fondly hoped to obtain, but he beheld the once blooming female, disrobed of that innocence, which had heretofore rendered her so lovely. To him then deception became impossible, as he had proof positive of the fallacy of the argument, which the deceiver had suggested. What then could be his inducement to burst the barriers, and to fly directly in the face of that command, which *immediately* from the mouth of Deity *he* had received, since, I say, he could not plead the fascinating stimulus, the accumulation of knowledge, as indisputable conviction was so visibly portrayed before him. What mighty cause impelled him to sacrifice myriads of beings yet unborn, and by one impious act, which *he saw* would be productive of such fatal effect, entail undistinguished ruin upon a race of beings, which he was yet to produce. Blush, ye vaunters of fortitude; ye boasters of resolution; ye haughty lords of the creation; blush when ye remember, that he was influenced by no other motive than a bare pusillanimous attachment to a woman! By sentiments so exquisitely soft, that all his sons have, from that period, when they have designed to degrade them, described as highly feminine. Thus it should seem, that all the arts of the grand deceiver (since means adequate to the purpose are, I conceive, invariably pursued) were requisite to mis-lead our general mother, while the father of mankind forfeited his own, and relinquished the happiness of posterity, merely in compliance with the blandishments of a female. The subsequent subjection the apostle Paul explains as a figure; after enlarging upon the subject, he adds, "*This is a great mystery; but I speak concerning Christ and the church.*" Now we know with what consummate wisdom the unerring father of eternity hath formed his plans; all the types which he hath displayed, he hath permitted *materially* to fail, in the very virtue for which *they* were famed. The reason for this is obvious, we might otherwise mistake his economy, and render that honor to the creature which is due only to the creator. I know that Adam was a figure of him who was to come. The grace contained in this figure is the reason of my rejoicing, and while I am very far from prostrating before the shadow, I yield joyfully in all things the preeminence to the second federal head. Confiding faith is prefigured by Abraham, yet he exhibits a contrast to affiance, when he says of his fair companion, she is my sister. Gentleness was the characteristic of Moses, yet he hesitated not to reply to Jehovah himself; with unsaintlike tongue he murmured at the waters of strife, and with rash hands he brake the tables, which were inscribed by the finger of divinity. David, dignified with the title of the man after God's own heart, and yet how stained was his life. Solomon was celebrated for wisdom, but folly is wrote in legible characters upon his almost every action. Lastly, let us turn our eyes to man in the aggregate. He is manifested as the figure of strength, but that we may not regard him as anything more than a figure, his soul is formed in no sort superior, but every way equal to the mind of her, who is the emblem of weakness, and whom he hails the gentle companion of his better days.

---

1. Originally published in the *Massachusetts Magazine (March–April 1799):* 132–135, 223–226; republished in *American Women Writers to 1800,* edited by Sharon Harris (New York: Oxford University Press, 1996).

2. Constantia was the pseudonym under which Murray published many of her writings.

Annis Boudinot Stockton (1736–1801)

From references in diaries, letters, and novels it is clear that literate women often read to each other or shared their opinions about authors. Yet it is unusual to find preserved such a detailed reading response as one that poet Annis Boudinot Stockton sent to her married daughter, critiquing a new book on women that was causing quite a stir: Mary Wollstonecraft's *A Vindication of the Rights of Woman* (1792).

Stockton was an accomplished poet, well known in literary and social circles in the Middle and Southern colonies. By the time she wrote the following letter she had written a large body of verse, including poems to George Washington and other statesmen, and her reputation as a woman of letters was well established. The following letter is notable, therefore, as the sentiments of one accomplished woman writer on the work of another woman.

Wollstonecraft claimed that women's moral and intellectual capacities equal those of men and that improved education would allow women to equal men's accomplishments. In commenting on Wollstonecraft's book, Stockton also reflected on the superior social and educational status of women as compared to that of European women. This letter demonstrates Stockton's interest in women's education but also her sense that women's sphere of influence was and should be separate, but complementary to, that of men. The letter also provides a glimpse into the intellectual community of women inhabited by Stockton and her daughter, Julia Stockton Rush, the recipient of the letter and the spouse of Benjamin Rush, who considered himself an important innovator in women's education.

Letter to Julia Stockton Rush (22 March 1793)[1]

Morven 22d of March

My dear Julia

I have been engaged these two days with reading the rights of women, which I never could procure before, tho it has been much longer in the neighbourhood. I have been musing upon the subject over my solitary fire till I took up the resolution to give you my sentiments upon it tho I suppose it is an old thing with you—I wonder you never Sent me your Critique—I am much pleased with her strength of reasoning, and her sentiment in general—but think that she like many other great geniuses—establish an hypothesis and lay

such a weight upon it as to cause the superstructure to destroy the foundation.—and I am sorry to find a woman capable to write such strictures should Complement Roussaus nonesense so much as to make his Ideas of women the criterion of the rank they hold in society.[2]—I think we need go no farther, than his Confessions, to discover that he had some defect in his brain, or that he was a refined Idiot, rather than an enlightened philosopher. I have always contended that the education of women was not made a matter of that importance, which it ought to be—but we see that error daily Correcting—and in this Country, the Empire of reason, is not monopolized by men, there is great pains taken to improve our sex, and store their minds with that knowledge best adapted, to make them useful in the situation that their creator has placed them—and we do not often see those efforts opposed by the other sex, but rather disposed to asist them by every means in their power, and men of sense generally prefer such women, as Companions thro life—the state of society may be different in Europe from what it is in America—but from the observation I have been able to make in my own Country, I do not think any of that Slavish obedience exists, that She talks so much of—I think the women have their equal right of everything, Latin and Greek excepted.—and I believe women of the most exalted minds, and the most improved understanding, will be most likly to practice that Conciliating mode of Conduct, which She seems to condemn, as blind Obedience, and Slavish Submission, to the Caprice of an arbitrary tyrant, which character she seems to apply to men as a sex.—but certainly exercising the virtues of moderation and forbearence—and avoiding desputes as much as possible, can easily be distinguished from Slavish fear—and must certainly tend to strengthen the mind, and give it a degree of fortitude, in accomodating ourselves to our situation, that adds dignity to the human character.—because this is necessesary, not only with a husband, that one has chosen for a Companion thro life—but with every other person, that we are obliged to be in the habits of strict intimacy—you know that it is a favourite tenet with me, that there is no sex in Soul—I believe it as firmly as I do my existance—but at the same time I do not think that the sexes were made to be independent of each other—I believe that our creator intended us for different walks in life—and that it takes equal powers of mind, and understanding, properly to fulfil the duties that he has marked out for

us—as it does for the other sex, to gain a knowledge
of the arts and Sciences, and if our education was
the same, our improvement would be the same—but
there is no occasion for exactly the same education.
I think we may draw the Conclusion that there is no
sex in soul, from the following illustrations—that
there are many men, that have been taught, and
have *not* obtained any great degree of knowledge in the
circle of the Sciences—and that there *have* been women
who have excelled in every branch, when they have
had an opportunity of instruction, and I have no doubt
if those advantages were oftener to occur, we should
see more instances.—one argument brought to prove
the inferiority of the mind of a woman, is that the organs of her body are weaker than mens, and that her
constitution is not so strong—now I know a great
number of women, who have much stronger organs of
body, and twice the strength of Constitution, that as
great a number of men, and men of genius too, can
boast of—or that from their infancy, they ever did enjoy—and it does not follow, that their souls are inferior,
or that they are women instead of men.

I am much pleased with her remarks upon Doctor Gregory[3]—I have many a time drawn upon my self a
sneer, for venturing to desent from that amiable man,
for one of his sentiments—respecting the reserve, which
a woman should treat her husband with on the Subject
of her affection for him—I allway thought it a little art,
and such a want of Confidence unbecoming a woman
of Sense. I Confess I have a nobler opinion of men than
our author appears to have—I dare say there are many
who answer her description—but happily for me, those
that I have had an opportunity to risk my opinion on,
have had as high ideas of the rationality of women—and
there equal right to the exertion of the immortal mind,
as the most tenacious of our sex could be—

She has some most charming remarks on education and her observation on some of the faults of her
sex are good, but her whole chapter on modesty is admirable, and has some marks of originallity. But I

must Confess that not withstanding the appearance
of piety in her ejaculatory addresses to the supreme
being, interspersed thro the book—I am not pleased
with the bold, indeed I may say, almost presumptious
manner, in which She speaks of the Diety—it too much
partakes of the spirit of the whole work—which I think
is written in a style that does not accord with the nature
of our intercourse with each other—or with the imperfection of our state.—we are all beings dependant on
one another, and therefore must often expect the inconveniences that must necessarily arise from the weakness of human nature, and the imperfection of some of
those with whom we are Connected. And we must
make the best of it.—and some of her expressions are by
far, too strong for my Ideas.—but *she* writes like a philosopher, and *I* think as a novice.—yet to sum up my
poor Judgement upon this wonderful book, I do really
think a great deal of instruction may be gathered from
it—and I am sure that no one, can read it, but they may
find something or other, that will Correct their Conduct and enlarge their Ideas.—

I am frightened at the length of my letter—and
more when I look at the watch and see the hour of the
night—it is past one oclock, and not a creature upon in
the house but my self—but you will say, it is my custon
to keep the vigils of the night.

Adieu my love, may heaven bless you and yours
and protect you this night, prays your ever affectionate
mother A Stockton—

1. This letter, probably written in 1793, was published in *Only for the Eye of a Friend: The Poems of Annis Boudinot Stockton,* edited by Carla Mulford (Charlottesville: University Press of Virginia, 1995).

2. In *A Vindication of the Rights of Woman* Wollstonecraft agreed with Jean-Jacques Rousseau (1712–1778) that society (not God) is the ori-gin of evil in the world. Rousseau's *Confessions* (1782), to which Stock-ton refers, gave him a scandalous reputation.

3. Dr. John Gregory (1724–1773), a Scottish physician, wrote a popu-lar women's advice book, *A Father's Legacy to His Daughters* (1774).

Hannah Webster Foster (1758–1840)

Many writers of the eighteenth century went
beyond arguing for the importance of women's education in general to giving specific advice about the
best methods of education—which subjects to study
and how much time was appropriate to devote to
each. While Hannah Webster Foster's *The Boarding
School* uses a fictional framework, its primary subject
matter is detailed instructions on women's educa-

tion, accompanied by short, parable-like stories designed to demonstrate the value of specific recommendations.

The Boarding School was Foster's second novel.
Her first, *The Coquette* (1797), is a cautionary story
that illustrates the dangers of seduction. In *The
Boarding School* Foster turned to an explicitly educational method, presenting her novel as a series of

lectures by the headmistress of a boarding school and letters from the pupils recounting their experiences after leaving school.

The selection included here discusses the importance of writing and arithmetic in women's education. The instructive stories that the headmistress uses to illustrate her points also suggest some of the expectations for young women of the middle and upper classes, including the need for women to be able to manage household accounts and even conduct business when necessary. The importance of arithmetic in Foster's plan of women's education points out that the domestic sphere had significant economic dimensions.

from *The Boarding School* (1798)[1]

Writing and Arithmetic

The young ladies being seated, this morning, their Preceptress addressed them as follows.

"Writing is productive both of pleasure and improvement. It is a source of entertainment which enlarges the mental powers more, perhaps, than any other. The mind is obliged to exertion for materials to supply the pen. Hence it collects new stores of knowledge, and is enriched by its own labours. It imperceptibly treasures up the ideas, which the hand impresses. An opportunity is furnished of reviewing our sentiments before they are exposed; and we have the privilege of correcting or expunging such as are erroneous. For this purpose, you will find it a good method to collect and write your thoughts upon any subject that occurs; for by repeatedly arranging and revising your expressions and opinions, you may daily improve them, and learn to think and reason properly on every occasion. By this mean you may likewise provide yourselves with a fund of matter for future use, which, without this assistance, the memory would not retain. It will be of great service to note down in your common-place book such particulars as you may judge worth remembering, with your own observations upon them. This will be a kind of amusement which will exercise your thinking powers at the time, and, by recurring to it afterwards, it may afford you many useful hints.

"The frequent use of the pen is calculated to refine and enlarge your understandings. Have you any talent at composition? it will be increased by cultivation.

"Neglect no opportunity, therefore, which your leisure affords, of delighting your friends, and accomplishing yourselves by the exercise of your genius in this way.

"Thrice blessed are we, the happy daughters of this land of liberty, where the female mind is unshackled by the restraints of tyrannical custom, which in many other regions confines the exertions of genius to the usurped powers of lordly man! Here virtue, merit, and abilities are properly estimated under whatever form they appear. Here the widely extended fields of literature court attention; and the American fair are invited to cull the flowers, and cultivate the expanding laurel.

"But the species of writing, which is open to every capacity, and ornamental to every station, is the epistolary.[2] This, between particular friends, is highly agreeable and interesting. It is a method of interchanging sentiments, and of enjoying intercourse with those from whom you are far removed, which is a happy substitute for personal conversation. In a correspondence of this sort, all affectation, formality, and bombast should be laid aside.

"Ease, frankness, simplicity, and sincerity should be its leading traits. Yet let not your letters be composed of mere sounding terms, and verbose egotism; but intermix sentiment with expression, in such a manner as may be improving as well as pleasing. Letters of friendship should conduce no less to the advantage than entertainment of the person addressed; and mere cursory letters, of general acquaintance, must, at least, be written with propriety and accuracy. The formation of the characters, the spelling, the punctuation, as well as the style and sense, must be attended to.

"Never omit noticing the receipt of letters, unless you mean to affront the writers. Not to answer a letter, without being able to assign some special reason for the neglect, is equally unpardonable as to keep silence when conversation is addressed to you in person.

"By habituating yourselves to writing, what may, at first, appear a task, will become extremely pleasant. Refuse not, then, to improve this part of your education, especially by your frequent and dutifully affectionate epistles to your parents, when absent from them. Express your gratitude for their care, and convince them it has not been lost upon you.

"Always employ your pens upon something useful and refined. Let no light or loose compositions occupy your time and thoughts; but remember that what you utter in this way is in some measure the picture of your hearts. Virtue forbid, that this favourite employment should be disgraced by impurity, indelicacy, or the communication of vicious and ignoble sentiments!

"One of the sages of antiquity being asked why he was so long in writing his opinion, replied, "I am writing for futurity."

"Your characters during life, and even when you shall sleep in the dust, may rest on the efforts of your pens. Beware then how you employ them. Let not the merit of your attainments in this noble art be degraded by improper subjects for its exercise. Suffer not the expectation of secrecy to induce you to indulge your pens upon subjects, which you would blush to have exposed. In this way your characters may be injured, and your happiness destroyed.

"Celia and Cecilia were companions at a boarding school. When separated, they commenced an epistolary correspondence, on which each valued herself. Their former intimacy, which they termed friendship, prompted them to write with unlimited confidence; and, without the least reserve, to reveal every dictate of levity and thoughtless folly. They imagined themselves perfectly secure from the censure of the critic. Their education had not taught them, that a virtuous mind should shrink even from ideal indelicacy. Celia was courted by Silvander, a young man of whom she was passionately fond; but she had art and resolution enough to conceal her letters from his inspection, though he often solicited a communication of her correspondence. At length he became impatient for a perusal of letters which appeared so pleasing and interesting to the parties, and suspicious that some particular cause directed their privacy. Influenced by these motives, Silvander bribed a market-boy, who came from the village where Cecilia lived, and always conveyed the letters to and from her, to give them first into his hand. How astonished was he to find the lightness of mind exemplified in them! Purity of sentiment, delicacy of thought, and refinement of taste were entirely laid aside; and illiberal wit, frothy jests, double entendres, and ridiculous love-tales were substituted in their place. His name was used with so much freedom, and every circumstance relative to his intercourse, and proposed connexion with Celia, was bandied with such familiarity, that he was mortified, disgusted, and chagrined, in the extreme. He had the policy, however, to conceal the discovery until he had copied a considerable number of Celia's letters, leaving out whatever had reference to his own affairs. He then revenged himself by disclosing his knowledge to her, avowing his indignation at her weakness, duplicity and folly, and taking an immediate and final leave. Not content with this, he even circulated her letters among his acquaintance. This fixed the stamp of ignominy on the correspondents; and their names and characters were rendered as ridiculous as scandal and malicious wit could desire.

"Celia was almost distracted at the loss of her lover; but when she found the method he had taken to punish her indiscretion, and that her reputation was thus materially injured, she secluded herself, in a great measure, from society. Her sensibility received a wound which could never be healed; and she lived and died in melancholy, regret, and obscurity.

"However censurable the unjust and ungenerous conduct of Silvander may be deemed, yet no adequate excuse can be offered for the young ladies, who dishonored their pens and their talents by a most improper and unbecoming use of both.

"Next to writing, arithmetic usually claims attention. This is absolutely necessary in every department, and in every stage of life. Even in youth, the proper arrangement of your expenses will conduce greatly to your advantage; and when placed at the head of families, it will be very friendly to the order and economy of your domestic affairs. But, leaving your matronal conduct to future admonition, many benefits result from keeping regular accounts in a single state. Your parents allow you a certain sum for your own private use. Fashion and folly are always busy in creating innumerable imaginary wants, which must exceed your finances, if you do not attend to an exact adjustment of your expenditures. For this purpose, always calculate your immediate and most necessary demands. Let these be first supplied, and then, if your funds be not exhausted, more superfluous ones may occupy your thoughts. There is one claim, however, which must not be neglected, and that is CHARITY. You will, therefore, manage your expenses in such a manner as to reserve some portion of your income for the necessitous. Should you think your allowance insufficient to admit the children of want to a share, let your benevolence plead for the retrenchment of some trifling article which you may dispense with, without much inconvenience; and the exquisite pleasure resulting from the bestowment, will more than counterbalance the sacrifice. In these, and many other particulars, a knowledge of arithmetic will enable you to conduct the affairs of youth with ease, advantage, and usefulness. And, perhaps, as you advance in years, and are called to fill more important stations, you may find it of still greater utility.

"The father of Lucinda was in easy circumstances, while he could perform the duties and enjoy the profits of a lucrative business. He was the affectionate parent of a numerous family, to whose education and improvement he attended with unwearied diligence and pleasure; till repeated losses in trade, and disappointments in his worldly expectations embarrassed his affairs, depressed his spirits, and impaired his health. In the midst of these difficulties, his amiable and beloved wife was removed by death. This trial was greater than he could support. He sunk under the affliction, and lost his reason. Lucinda was the eldest of six children, the care of whom, with the melancholy task of attending and ministering to the necessities of her unhappy father, devolved on her. She looked upon the woe-fraught scene, and wept. Her heart was sinking under the weight of grief; and hope, the best soother of the unfortunate, had nearly abandoned her. She advised with her friends, who proposed to relieve the family by means of a subscription. Lucinda thanked them for their proffered kindness, and returned to her disconsolate habitation. She deliberated on the projected measure; which she considered must be slow, uncertain, and, at any rate, inadequate to their future exigences. She could not reconcile herself to the idea of her father's depending on charity for subsistence. Yet what could be done? One resource only remained;—her own exertions. By these she flattered herself, that she might save the family from suffering want, and discharge the obligations she owed to her revered parent. Her education, by which, among other branches of learning, she had been well instructed in arithmetic, (that being her father's favourite study) qualified her for this undertaking. She therefore devoted herself to the business with

out delay; examined her father's accounts, collected whatever remained that was valuable; sold the superfluous moveables, and purchased a small stock for trade. All who knew her motives and merit frequented her shop, and encouraged her by their custom and kindness. By this mean, together with her judicious management, and engaging behaviour, she increased her business to such a degree, as to support the family with ease and reputation.

"Her discreet and dutiful conduct to her father, soon restored him to his reason.

"When he found how prudently and affectionately Lucinda had exerted herself in his behalf, he exclaimed, "Many daughters have done virtuously, but thou excellest them all!"

"He resumed his former business, and lived to see his children all well provided for, and happily settled around him."

---

1. *The Boarding School; or, Lessons of a Preceptress to Her Pupils* was originally published anonymously "By a Lady of Massachusetts" (Boston: Printed by I. Thomas & E. T. Andrews, 1798).

2. Epistolary, or letter, writing was one of the most popular genres for women in the eighteenth century. As Foster's discussion demonstrates, letter writing was seen in important ways as a substitute for personal presence and was believed to reflect the writer's true, unmediated self.

Hannah Mather Crocker (1752–1829)

As did other writers in these selections, Hannah Mather Crocker had a somewhat unusual educational background, having founded before her marriage a female Masonic lodge for the purpose of education. While her earliest writing focused on the need for women's education, in her best-known work Crocker took up the issue of rights. Like Abigail Adams before her though, Crocker did not argue for the specific political rights that suffragists demanded later in the century. Rather, Crocker argued that women's rights have their basis in women's observable achievements, biblical authority, and common sense. Moreover, she claimed that women's equality had never been a matter of much debate in the freedom-loving United States.

In the following selection from her *Observations on the Real Rights of Women,* Crocker made use of a common rhetorical strategy for writers on women's ability: a catalogue of the achievements of women in the past and present. Her catalogue of successful

women writers includes both Europeans and Americans, suggesting that Crocker read widely and that there was some connection between women writers despite differences of nationality. At the same time, however, Crocker expressed a distinctively American point of view in stressing the freedom of American women to pursue intellectual achievements. Crocker also stressed the American perspective that women's efforts to educate children were particularly crucial in a republic, where each citizen's virtue is important to the functioning of society.

from *Observations on the Real Rights of Women* (1818)[1]

CHAP. IV

The female character and writings are equal in the present day to any former period; and some miscellaneous sentiments respecting the sex.

Madam De Staal,[2] for strength of mind, true magnanimity, patriotism and independence, as well as her literary talents and acquirements, shines unequalled. Her late work of the Influence of Literature on Society, would do honour to the able pen of a man. She can have no rival.

For poetic fancy and genius few have ever excelled Lucy Akin.[3] Her Epistles on Women, and other poems, do honour to her pen. We give a further specimen of the general spirit of the author.

"Does history speak; drink in her loftiest tone
And make Cornelia's virtues all thy own.
Thus self endow'd, thus arm'd for every state,
Improve, excel, surmount, subdue your fate;
So shall enlighten'd man at length efface,
That slavish stigma, sear'd on half the race;
His rude forefather's shame, and please'd confess,
Tis your's to elevate, tis your's to bless.
Your interest, one with his, your hope the same,
Fair peace on earth, in death undying fame,
And bliss in words, beyond the species general aim,
Rise shall he say, O woman, rise, be free,
My life's associate, now partake with me.
Rouse thy keen energies, expand thy soul,
And see and feel, and comprehend the whole.
My deepest thoughts intelligent divide;
When right confirm me, and when erring guide;
Sooth all my cares, in all my virtues blend,
And be my sister, be at length my friend."
Epist. On Women.

Many other authors could be produced who have done honour to the female pen and character in their writings.

We must now say of the amiable Miss H. More,[4] "many daughters have done virtuously, but thou hast excelled them all." Her works from the smallest grade to the most important, are all calculated to improve the mind, and mend the heart.

American Character noticed.

America, though as yet but young in the arts and sciences, will not long remain in the back ground, as she can now claim the birth-right of many respectable female writers, both in prose and verse.

The lovely Morton[5] may vie with many in Europe for her sublime and poetic fancy. She, with many other respectable writers, who have not been sufficiently appreciated, still shine with the lustre of the aurora borealis in the northern hemisphere.

Among the most distinguished historians are seen a Warren, and an Adams,[6] who have done honour to themselves, their country and sex, as faithful compilers of history. Mrs. Warren, in her History of the American Revolution, (vol. I. page 4) observes.

There are appropriate duties assigned to each sex, and surely it is the peculiar province of masculine strength, not only to repulse the bold invader of his country's rights, but in the nervous style of manly eloquence, describe the blood stained field, and relate the story of slaughtered armies.

In vol. II. page 30, she mentions Mrs. Ackland, who was a British officer's lady, as a pattern of female heroism and conjugal affection: She came with her husband to America, and shared with him all the hardships of the camp life; he was badly wounded and taken prisoner by the Americans; she knew his situation, and left him not a moment, but joins herself a prisoner, and by her fortitude supported him, as she lost not her resolution or usual spirits. The American commander, pleased with her firmness, gave orders that she should have every attention paid to her rank, character, and sex.

There might now be recorded a number of American ladies, who left domestic peace and retirement, to share with the partners of their affections, all the trials and fatigue of a camp life; suffice it to notice two in particular, Mrs. Washington, and Mrs. Jackson, who with six little boys, left her rural retreat to accompany the Colonel to the field of battle. She partook with him in the fatigues and inconveniences of the camp life; he was soon commissioned as a general officer: Under her own guardian eye she had these sons trained and disciplined, till they were efficient to become respectable officers, which they all were in the American army.

Mrs. Washington shone a bright example of female excellence; she followed the foot paths of her beloved hero, by her firmness and christian fortitude; with affection she soothed every care of his long war-worn life. She has left a bright example, of every virtue that adorns the christian of female character. Mrs. Warren says, Having personally known her I can say, her whole deportment was blended with such sweetness of manners, that she not only engaged the affection of her intimates, but of all who had the felicity of knowing her, and even strangers were captivated with her mild and affectionate address. To every child of sorrow and affliction, she lent a listening ear, and often extended the hand of meek charity, to alleviate the cruel anguish of poverty. She shone as the patriotic wife, the meek christian, and the truly upright in heart. She was like her Fabius, modest, but not timid. She may with propriety be esteemed a model of female perfection, and highly worthy the imitation of the American fair. May her memory, with her virtues, be engraven on the tablet of every female's heart. She has erected a temple of virtue and fame, for the female standard.

By the mutual virtue, energy, and fortitude of the sexes, the freedom and independence of the United States were attained and secured. The same virtue, energy, and fortitude, must be called into continual exercise, as long as we continue a free, federal, independent nation. The culture and improvement of the female understanding will strengthen the mental faculties, and give vigour to their councils, which will give a weight to any argument used for their mutual defence and safety. No nation nor republic ever fell a prey to despotism, till by indolence and dissipation, it neglected the arts and sciences, and the love of literature. They then became effeminate and degraded; and by them the female character was degraded. As long as the German women were free and honoured by the men, it acted as a stimulus to their ambition. On the value and integrity of both sexes their success and independence very much depended.

If we take a retrospect of the world, from the creation, it will be found, that in every age where ignorance prevailed most, women were most degraded. Before the christian era, and through the dark ages, very little light was thrown upon their characters. They were supposed to have the command of Pandora's iron box, which contained all the accumulated evils incident to human nature. Some authors say, from the circumstance attending this box, at that period, that age was called the iron age, and has been known by that name ever since.

There are some excellent sentiments respecting women in a small treatise, entitled, The Friend of Women, by De Villamont, in French, translated by Maurice.[7] He says, every one speaks of women according to the disposition of his heart; and the most vicious men are most disposed to paint them in the most odious colours. He says, whatever we meet with in the different opinions of men with regard to women, the lively interest they regard them with, is always the principal.

Every thing which this lovely half of the human race does, has a right to interest us; we are born the friends of women, and not their rivals, still less their tyrants. Let women then, who lead in our first circles, condescend to cultivate their minds, and encourage useful reading; their merit will cause a swarm of thoughtless beaux to disappear from their presence, and men of more merit will form a circle about them, more worthy the name of good company; in this new circle they will join on the score of friendship, without losing any thing in point of cheerfulness; merit is not naturally gloomy, on the contrary, there is generally found among polite people, who are well bred, a mild serenity far preferable to bursts of stupid and ignorant merriment. Happily

for us, the day is past that condemned women, as well as the nobility, to rustic ignorance, though there has always been some women found, who dared to think, and speak reasonably. We have in the present day, many who do not blush to be better informed than many of our court gentry, or petit-maitres are.

But of all studies most necessary and most natural to women is the study of men, as their government must be that of persuasion; it is necessary for them to know the main springs by which men are actuated. If any thing can add to the pleasure derived from a select society, it is the charms of friendship. The injustice they have done women by excluding them the privilege of being friends, they cannot account for on any principle, as women are born with more sensibility than men, and are capable of being friends.

I shall not enlarge on the advantage of friendship, which may be called a double life, as each lives in his friend. I shall give you Pliny's receipt for making friendship. From Pliny's Natural history we find this curious receipt, for making Roman friendship.

The principal ingredients were, union of hearts, a flower that grew in several parts of the empire, sincerity, frankness, disinterestedness, pity and tenderness, of each an equal quantity; these made up together with a rich oil, which they called perpetual good wishes, and serenity of temper, and the whole was strongly perfumed with the desire of pleasing, which gave it a most grateful smell, and was a sure restorative against vapours of every kind. The cordial thus prepared was of so durable a nature, that length of time could not waste it. What is more remarkable, says our author, it increases in value the longer it is kept.

That women are capable of friendship there can be no doubt. There is no deficiency in the female mind, either as to talent or disposition. Women are more sensible than men to all moral distinction: They do not indeed class the virtues in the same order, but they give the highest importance to the comprehensive virtue of temperance. But it is christianity, undoubtedly, which has seated woman on her true throne. Bound to the same duties, and candidates for the same happiness, as soon as a woman wishes to raise herself above all the trifling objects that debase her, her mind will find itself capable of the same strength as that of men. Mind has no sex, and women cannot be made too frequently to recollect this truth, to preserve them from all those frivolities in which they place too much happiness. Oh, that women would but keep their rights, and improve them to their and our advantage. For women have not degenerated; there are many among us at this time, whose success has made them sufficiently known, without my naming them; and who comparatively with us, have reaped the golden harvest in the fertile field of history and philosophy. Their powers and intellects are equal with the men, but their mode of education often checks their progress in learning.—*So says Villamont.*

We must join with him in thinking their powers of mind are very equal. Still it might be thought an unequal right, to profess or claim any knowledge of the masonic art; for it seems really man's prerogative to bear the hod, or mould the mortar.

But females may erect a temple of fame, and support it by virtue, wisdom, strength, and beauty, and perfect rectitude. Let then the mysteries of the craft remain profoundly secret to the female ken, till time shall unfold the hidden mysteries of all ancient knowledge and science. Then may the master mason display his skill and talent in architecture, and lay the corner-stone in rectitude and justice, and by his skill draw the parallel line correct, that shall encompass the views of the sexes to their mutual satisfaction and happiness. It cannot be expected the views of females will exactly correspond with the men, respecting the masonic art, as they are debarred the investigation of its principles in some measure. Yet in the present day, there ought to be that harmony and mutual confidence, respecting the system, as shall effectually eradicate any old prejudices respecting the powers of females being unequal to comprehend the incomprehensible mysteries of the masonic art. Let females then retire within the vail, and in the Sanctum Sanctorum, study the beauty of holiness, and endeavour to follow the example of their king and master, Solomon, by praying for an understanding heart, and seeking that wisdom which is from above, and can direct our moral and religious course through life.

CHAP. VII

Treats of the beauty and good order that may accrue to society, by the united fidelity of the sexes in performing their appropriate duties.

As it appears from scripture and reason there is just, and right equality of the sexes, common sense must teach the propriety of a union of the sexes in sentiments and opinions respecting the rights of women. Very little has been written on the subject in America; and perhaps it has not been necessary in a land where the rights of women have never appeared a bone of much contention. It may naturally be supposed, the ideas of a free independent people, will be more liberal and expanded respecting the sexual rights.

Under this impression, the writer has ventured to pen this small system or statement of the mutual rights and appropriate duties of the sexes with the most philanthropic wish, that the parties concerned may mutually agree to support the real orthodox principle of a mutual dependence on each other, which will promote peace, harmony and happiness; for without harmony and affection subsist between the sexes, society must soon become a mere nuisance to itself.

Our venerable ancestors, soon after they came to this country, framed laws and regulations for the general utility, and made ample provision for the happiness of every class of the citizens, including equal rights for the female sex. They soon as possible instituted schools, churches, and colleges, and the best mode of promoting the interest of their country; and females partook of the advantage of education, and some made a wise improvement of it.

Among some of the early instructors of writing may be found Mrs. Sarah Knights,[8] in the year 1706. She was famous in her day for teaching to write. Most of the letters on business, and notes of hand, and letters on friendship were wrote by her. She was a smart, witty, sensible woman, and had considerable influence at that period.

The first characters for learning and knowledge at that time certainly had an exalted opinion of the female character and abilities, and fully appreciated their rights and judgment, as they were often consulted on important subjects both in church and state. From that time they have often been consulted on important occasions.

In the important struggle for the independence of the American States, some females embarked in the cause of freedom, both by their writings and advice; and ever since the establishment of independence, it has been an invariable fixed principle in the female character to pray for the peace of our American Israel. And they must have an equal right to enjoy, with mutual satisfaction, all the blessings, tranquillity, freedom, and peace can bestow on a free and happy people.

It is almost impossible that those, who reside under a despotic or monarchical government, can imbibe as liberal sentiments as those, who reside under the more temperate zone of a free, federal republican government, which admits of free discussion of sentiments among all classes of the citizens. Such a government requires more sense and judgment to preserve it from disorder and disunion; therefore the union and right understanding of the sexes will have a tendency to strengthen, confirm and support such a government, and common sense must allow women the right of mutual judgment, and joining with the other sex in every prudent measure for their mutual defence and safety.

It may be seen by the fatal fall of Greece and Rome how much depends on public faith and confidence in the government, which must commence in the private faith and confidence of individuals.

From the universal benevolence, conspicuous in every section of the union, there is reason to anticipate our future greatness and respectability. The various institutions, for benevolent and charitable purposes, have a tendency to promote the kind affection, and make man mild and sociable to man; women shine preeminent in most of them, and have an equal right to establish schools of industry and economy, which must have a happy effect on the community. There is nothing can make better subjects for a republican government, than to give children an early education, and train them in habits of prudence and industry. Every day produces some proofs how much we are the creatures of habit; the juvenile mind requires continual occupation, for the vivacity of youth is such, that if not constantly employed in some valuable pursuit, there is danger of their resorting to some evil propensity, for want of regular occupation; for such is the natural depravity of the human heart. As women generally have the forming of the infant mind, it is necessary their own minds should be cultivated, that they may be capable of enlarging the mind of their pupils; as the first seeds implanted in their breast, if virtuous and noble, will prepare them for some important station in life. Children's constitution and capacities differ so very much, that it requires the affection, tenderness and care of a prudent woman to mould and model the tender olive-branch, as there is hardly a human being, though of very inferior abilities, but will discover a genius should be always consistent; for of those, who set out wrong in life, there are few who ever clear the rocks and ledges, and very seldom arrive at plain sailing; the whole voyage of life will prove rough and boisterous, if it is not commenced right. This may often be seen in the common course of human life, if the compass of genius is not regulated by learning, prudence, discretion and religion.

A religious, steady, rational course of living will be found the safest pilot to the haven of rest and perfect happiness. It is faith in the divine promises that can alone give peace of mind and great joy in believing. It is that which only can give that calm serenity of mind, which will support us under all the vicissitudes of this transitory state. There is no path can be pursued more likely to promote this calmness and serenity of mind, than to appropriate a certain space of our time every day for meditation; as every rational being, who reflects at all, must be sensible

there is a wise governing providence that superintends the affairs of men, kingdoms, nations and states. It is most undoubtedly the duty of every individual to commit every event of their lives to his care and disposal, for he who can take into view and comprehend the whole plan of creation, must know what is best for his dependent creatures.

Therefore unerring wisdom can do no wrong. We may safely trust in his protecting care, and when called to affliction in the course of divine providence, if we receive the chastisement with the spirit of meekness, and bear it with christian fortitude, it may prove the brightest epoch in human life.

The minds of the sexes are equally capable of making a wise improvement of the various dispensations of divine providence; they all have equal need, and equal right, to seek the divine favour, aid, protection and consolation; and without the support, hope, trust and confidence in the promises of divine grace, they must both be equally unhappy. How vain and inconsistent are those, who flee from trouble to drown sorrow in dissipation! Oh foolish and inconsiderate mortals, why will you involve yourselves in greater troubles and tenfold misery, by adding to your sorrow the bitter sting of perhaps a too late death-bed repentance!

But let us turn the scene, and view the calm sedate christian, who, through the whole passage of life, is resigned to the divine direction and guidance, in the firm faith, that all the dispensations of providence are perfectly consistent with divine rectitude, and goodness. Under such impressions, the real christian will most fervently say, not my will, but thine be done, heavenly Father.

Scripture, reason and common sense dictates the divine right is in women, to promote those fine sympathetic affections that will have a tendency to assist, harmonize and sweeten a religious course of life. The power of friendship can sooth the cares of this transitory state, and meliorate the greatest miseries of human woe. Love is the sacred bond of mutual friendship, and promotes a reciprocal intercourse of kind affection.

Good humour, Dr. Johnson says, may be defined a habit of being pleased; a constant and perennial softness of manners, easiness of approach, and serenity of disposition, like that which every man perceives in himself, when sided, and his thoughts are only kept in motion by a slow succession of soft impulses. Good humour is a state between gaiety and unconcern, the act of emanation of mind at leisure to regard the gratification of another.

It has been justly observed that discord generally operates in little things. It is inflamed to its utmost vehemence by contrariety of talk oftener than of principle; and might therefore commonly be avoided by innocent conformity, which, if it was not at first the motive, ought always to be the consequence, of indissoluble union.

The great remedy which heaven has put in our hands is patience; by which, though we cannot lessen the torments of the body, we can in a great measure, preserve the peace of the mind, and shall suffer only the natural and genuine force of an evil, without heightening its acrimony or prolonging its effects. When patience has performed its perfect work, it is the right of every female to have ready the mantle of meek charity, to gently cover the faults of her domestic circle.

---

1. *Observations on the Real Rights of Women, with Their Appropriate Duties, Agreeable to Scripture, Reason and Common Sense* by H. Mather Crocker was published in Boston (Printed for the Author, 1818).

2. Anne-Louise Germaine, Madame de Staël (1766–1817) was an internationally known French woman of letters. Her book *The Influence of Literature on Society* was first published in Paris in 1800; an English translation was published in Boston in 1813.

3. Lucy Aiken (1781–1864) published *Epistles on Women, Exemplifying their Character and Condition in Various Ages and Nations* in London in 1810. It was republished in Boston by W. Wells and T. B. Wait in the same year.

4. Hannah More (1745–1833) was a well-known British writer on women's conduct and education. "A Comparative View of the Sexes" was part of chapter twelve of her book *Strictures on the Modern System of Female Education,* originally published in London in 1799 and republished in New York by Evert Duyckinck in 1813. Crocker dedicated her *Observations on the Real Rights of Women* to More.

5. Sarah Wentworth Morton (1759–1846) was a well-known Boston poet who published poems and verse plays with distinctly American themes–such as Native American/European contact, slavery, and Revolutionary battles–in the 1790s.

6. Poet, dramatist, and historian Mercy Otis Warren (1728– 1814) was a longtime friend of Abigail Adams (1744–1818), and both women were well known because of their close ties to Revolutionary leaders.

7. Pierre-Joseph Boudier de Vellemert (1716–1801) published his book *The Friend of Women* (more often translated as *The Ladies Friend*) anonymously in Paris in 1758; the book went through several American editions beginning in 1784 but was first translated under the title Crocker uses here in an 1803 Philadelphia printing.

8. Sarah Kemble Knight (1666–1727) wrote a travel diary and was rumored to have kept a writing school where Benjamin Franklin was a pupil; there seems today to be no truth to this claim, but the rumor may have augmented Knight's reputation for Crocker's readers.

Mary Palmer Tyler (1775–1866)

Mary Palmer Tyler's book on child rearing is the first such work by an American woman. The mother of eleven children, Tyler presents her book as an effort to educate other mothers in the best ways to care for young children. Motherhood consistently held an important place in most conceptions of women's sphere throughout the early period. Advocates for women's education argued that mothers needed to be well educated in a variety of fields in order properly to fulfill their maternal duties.

For Tyler an essential component of education for motherhood was medical knowledge. Her book, *The Maternal Physician,* is filled with practical advice for keeping children healthy and for treating common childhood illnesses with herbal medication and other remedies. A well-informed mother need not, Tyler suggested, be entirely dependent on professional (male) physicians, whose popularity was on the rise at the time. In the selections below, Tyler argues for the importance of motherhood and the value of medical knowledge for successful motherhood. Tyler's writing is just one example of the frequent emphasis on the responsibilities and duties of motherhood, an emphasis that would continue throughout the nineteenth century.

from *The Maternal Physician* (1818)[1]

INTRODUCTION.

EVERY MOTHER HER CHILD'S BEST PHYSICIAN.

Some time since, while looking over a file of old newspapers, I cast my eyes upon the obituaries, and was forcibly impressed with the great proportion of children who are yearly consigned to the relentless grave under the age of two years. I revolved in my mind why it was so, and could not avoid concluding that it must be in a great measure occasioned by some gross mismanagement in mothers or nurses, or perhaps both. Involuntarily I looked around upon my children, and my heart swelled with gratitude to heaven for hitherto averting the shafts of the fell destroyer from them, and permitting the roses of health to bloom on their cheeks with almost uninterrupted continuity.

Deeply impressed by this invaluable blessing of a merciful Providence, I felt an irresistible desire to see the same felicity pervade every maternal bosom. But alas! Imagination presented to my view the sick or the dying babe, and the anxious or distracted mother, and I ardently wished to extend my hand, feeble thought it might be, to their relief. And why, thought I, may not this be done. I remembered, when my first child was an infant, how easily I was alarmed if he was ill, and how eagerly I caught at every glimpse of light that promised to direct me in the management of him; I recollected the words of an eminent physician, whom I was in the habit of summoning every time my babe looked paler than usual. "You may yourself be your child's best physician," said this excellent man, "if you only will attend to a few general directions." I promised faithful obedience; and heaven has crowned my endeavours with success: why then may I not show my gratitude, by presenting to the matrons of my country the fruits of my experience, in the pleasing hope that I may be instrumental in directing them in the all-important and delightful task of nursing those sweet pledges of connubial love, over whom every good mother watches with tremulous anxiety, and almost painful affection. A very near and dear friend, not entirely unknown in the literary world, approving my plan, I have resolved on the attempt, and if I can happily aid in preserving but one lovely babe from fell disease, in averting the deadliest arrow of affliction from the bosom of but one mother, great will be my reward. I am well aware how much has been written on this subject by the most able physicians, to whom I acknowledge my self indebted for many useful hints; but these gentlemen must pardon me if I think, after all, that a mother is her child's best physician, in all ordinary cases; and that none but a mother can tell how to *nurse* an infant as it ought to be nursed. Who but a mother can possibly feel interest enough in a helpless new born babe to pay it that unwearied, uninterrupted attention necessary to detect in season any latent symptoms of disease lurking in its tender frame, and which, if neglected, or injudiciously treated at first, might in a few hours baffle the physician's skill, and consign it to the grave?

And believe me, my fair friends, this is not a labour. What can so sweetly relieve the tedium of three or four weeks' confinement to a sick room, as to watch with unremitting care, and mark with enraptured eye, the opening beauties of the dear innocent cause of such confinement? Or what can equal a mother's ecstasy when she catches the first emanation of mind in the mantling smile of her babe? Kotzebue little knew the mother's heart when he

makes Cora place her first joy after birth, "When first the white blossoms of his teeth appear, breaking the crimson buds that did encase them." Ten thousand raptures thrill her bosom before a tooth is formed. How dead to the finest feelings of our nature must that mother be, who can voluntarily banish her infant from her bosom, and thus forego the exquisite delight attending the first development of its rational faculties. O fashion! arbitrary tyrant, of what hours of heartfelt bliss dost thou deprive thy votary—

> "One lovely babe her fostering care demands;
> "And can she trust it to a hireling's hands?"

Far distant, I trust, from our beloved country, is the period when it shall be accounted disgraceful for a mother to nurse her own babe. When that time arrives my system must fall to the ground. It is upon the presumption, that my readers are among those who glory in the sweetest privilege of nature, and are never more blest

> "Than whilst their babe, with unpolluted lips,
> "As nature asks, the vital fountain sips."

that I presume to offer my advice; for it is under such circumstances only that a mother can observe all the minutiæ of her child's state of health.

Experience has taught me that the babe who was to all appearance well in the morning may droop in the afternoon, be very ill at night, and yet, by proper care and attention, again be well the next morning; when, perhaps, the same babe if neglected or improperly treated, would have been seized with fits, or some equally fatal complaint, and possibly have died in less time. For the truth of this statement, I appeal to those who are skilled in those dreadful disorders the quinsy and the croup. It is upon cases similar to this, that I ground my hypothesis that every mother is her child's best physician; and how can a mother reconcile her conscience when she consigns this precious little being, given her by Providence to her comfort through life, and the staff of her declining age, to the care of a stranger, when assured that one day's neglect might deprive her of it for ever, and blast her fondest hopes.

> "Ah then, by duty led, ye nuptial fair,
> "Let the sweet office be your constant care;
> "With peace and health in humblest station blest,
> "Give to the smiling babe the fostering breast;
> "Nor if by prosperous fortune placed on high,
> "Think aught superior to the dear employ."
> "Not half a mother she, whose pride denies
> "The streaming beverage to her infant's cries,

"Admits another in her rights to share,
"Or trusts its nurture to a stranger's care."

That there are many instances when the mother's health will not permit her to suckle her child I will allow; but I must believe those cases would less frequently occur if the attempt were persevered in. This I assert from experience in one remarkable instance. My first child had the thrush when about a fortnight old. I had previously suffered great pain from an exuberant flow of milk, and was greatly weakened by it. Now I took the humour from his mouth, and for two months he seldom sucked without throwing up fresh blood afterwards, which he had swallowed with his milk. The torture I endured can better be conceived than described. Many of my friends with tears entreated me to wean my child, and dry away my milk, which, owing to loss of appetite, and fever, occasioned by excess of suffering, might then have been done with ease; but my own mother, who watched over me and my babe with more than maternal tenderness, and who, I am convinced, felt all I suffered with redoubled anguish, constantly exhorted me to persevere with fortitude, nor let any thing I endured tempt me to tear my babe from the breast, and by improper food occasion ill health, if not endanger his life; for amidst all my distress I had the inexpressible delight of seeing him thrive surprisingly. I listened to my mother, for my judgment was on her side, and had abundant cause to rejoice that I did so, for the days of affliction passed away as a dream, and left the sweet consciousness of having done my duty as a recompense for suffering; a recompense, how rich, how lasting, how consoling! Had I weakly yielded in the hour of pain, and dried away my milk, it is more than probable, from the bad state the humours were then in, some unnatural contractions would have taken place, and not only that child but all my succeeding family would have suffered from it. Therefore I entreat every mother to undergo every thing short of death of lasting disease, rather than refuse to suckle her child. There are now many useful inventions for drawing out the milk, which were not in general use when I was so afflicted; and if it can be drawn out with sucking glasses, and the babe fed with it for a few days in cases similar to the one related above, it will without a doubt be far better both for mother and child: upon this plan the milk may be preserved; for it is a fact, that while the babe is nourished by it, it will continue to flow, let it be obtained from the breast how it may; whereas, if it is drawn out and thrown away, the mother will have less and less until it eventually dries away entirely.[2] It may not be amiss to mention here, for the benefit of the afflicted, that the remedy I eventually found most efficacious in this distressing complaint was *white lead*. After trying various applications, and employing several physicians, in vain, this was accidentally recommended by a lady who had herself experienced the same affliction. The cooling qualities of the ceruse appeared to allay the distressing heat of the humour, and, by its absorbency to heal and sooth the part. Great care, however, must be taken when using it, carefully to wash the breast with warm milk and water before the child is permitted to suck.

But if, after all, my amiable friends, you should actually be so unhappy as to be obliged to permit your infant to draw its first nourishment from a stranger, let me advise you to have your nurse under your own roof if possible. Notwithstanding all the horrors so poetically described in an elegant little poem already quoted in the preceding pages, called "The Nurse," translated from the Italian by that learned and fascinating writer, William Roscoe, of Liverpool, (and which I would recommend to the perusal of every lady who hesitates for a moment whether to nurse her infant herself or not, from a blind devotedness to fashion, or still more reprehensible indolence of disposition,) if your babe is in the house with you, you can with ease pay it every attention requisite to its health, and thus discharge the only remaining duty in your power. You can observe, and by your authority oblige your nurse to observe, the state of its bowels, and other indications of disease.

"Sick, pale and languid, when your infant's moans
"Speaks its soft sufferings in pathetic tones,
"When nature asks a purer lymph, subdued
"By needful physic and by temperate food,"

it must be your care to see the proper regimen adopted and medicine taken. You will also have it in your power to prevent the attendants from crowding its little stomach with pap and other crudities, which I fear are too often given, from a mistaken tenderness, to the great injury of the child. You will likewise be able to watch that your babe is not exposed to every change of atmosphere. I have known a fine healthy child seized with a violent quinsy, owing to carelessness in exposing it to the evening air after a sultry day. Indifferent persons are apt to forget that an infant in arms, from inactivity, is much more sensible of the cold than those who attend it, who from that very exertion keep up a brisk circulation of blood, which renders them less obnoxious to the deleterious effects of any sudden change in the air. For this reason a mother is her child's best physician, as it is better by care to prevent disease, than to be ever so well skilled in curing it.

"Once exiled from your breast, and doomed to bring
"His daily nurture from a stranger spring,
"Ah who can tell the dangers that await
"Your infant, thus abandoned to his fate?"

Let your tenderness, then, render you tremblingly alive to every appearance of danger. Do not, however, imagine, from what is here said, that I mean to advocate a too delicate regimen for infants. The following pages, if they respond to my wishes, will fully prove the contrary. I only wish such care to be taken of them, as their extreme tenderness evidently demands. If a child is properly and faithfully nursed the first year, it will have gained such a portion of health and strength by that time, as will enable it to bear all the exercise in the open air which its age will admit; and then the more it is carried abroad the better, when the weather is fair. When

"The rural wilds
"Invite; the mountains call you, and the vales,
"The woods, the streams, and each ambrosial breeze
"That fans the ever undulating sky;
"A kindly sky! whose fostering power regales
"Man, beast, and all the vegetable reign."
ARMSTRONG.

Eight lovely and beloved children, who have all (except the three youngest) passed through the usual epidemics of our country, and now enjoy an unusual proportion of health and strength, are the best apologies I can offer for thus presuming to give my advice unasked, and perhaps undesired, to my fair country-women. The motive, I trust, will insure my pardon for any traits of egotism, which must unavoidably appear while recommending a mode of treatment founded chiefly upon my own experience; but which, nevertheless, the better to enforce, I intend to enrich with casual extracts from the most approved medical authorities.

In the following work I propose to take the babe from the birth, and attend it through every stage until it is two years old; after which period children in general, having cut all their teeth, grow more robust, (that is, if they have been properly managed,) and will increase in health and strength without any attention except the ordinary care conducive to cleanliness and exercise, two points never to be dispensed with through life.

That I may not tire your patience, and in the pleasing hope that from what has been said, you will be inclined to believe the mother may be her child's best physician, if she is desirous to be so, I shall en-

deavour to enable her to manage her babe from the birth until it is four months old; the time when they generally begin to breed teeth, and consequently require an appropriate treatment. And I do verily believe, if the directions I shall give are faithfully attended to, many a fond mother will have reason to rejoice in the experiment.

"Think not that I would forbid your softness share
"Undue fatigue, and every grosser care;
"Another's toils may here supply your own,
"But be the task of *nurture* yours alone;
"Nor from a stranger let your offspring prove
"The fond endearments of a parent's love—
"So shall your child in manhood's riper day,
"With warm affection all your cares repay."

CHESNUT HILL,
June, 1810.

. . .

CHAPTER VI
CONCLUSION.
"But trust me, when you have done all this,
"Much will be missing still, and much will be amiss"
MILTON'S ODES.

I have thus, to the best of my abilities, fulfilled my promise, and endeavoured to enable my fair readers to nurse their lovely offspring *from the birth until two years old,* or till they arrive at an age requiring *comparatively* less attention. And if my plan is adopted, I flatter my self, they will acquire such a stock of health and strength by that time, as with only common care through the remainder of their childhood, will ensure their exemption from the various complaints, arising from debility, weakness of body, and relaxation of the nervous system, such as convulsions, epilepsies, fevers, consumptions, king's evil, rickets, and many others, too numerous to mention; and which, for want of proper attention to their first complaints, and sufficient exercise in the open air, to frequently afflict them to an early grave. Therefore, let me once more entreat for my young friends who have arrived at an age when nature prompts them to seek health and happiness in sportive gambols suited to their age, that they may not be confined to the house, to their infinite vexation, and the imminent danger of undoing all you have hitherto done. Surely it is wrong to immure *boys,* from a desire to see them look fair and delicate, whose chief attraction, both now and in after life, must consist in their courage, strength, and activity. To say nothing of our duty, as *citizens,* while forming the future guardians of our beloved country, it is undoubtedly our duty, as *mothers,* to bring up our sons in such a manner as shall render them most useful and happy; and one of the most effectual steps towards this desirable end, is to let them have the free use of their limbs during this active period of their lives, and restricting them to the most simple and nutritious diet—

"By arts like these,
"Laconia nursed of old her hardy sons,
"And Rome's unconquer'd legions urged their way,
"Unhurt, through every toil, in every clime."
                                        ARMSTRONG.

And even our lovely and interesting daughters will be more lovely and more interesting, if adorned with the roses of health, entwined with the lilies of innocence and delicacy. And this is the time to strengthen their constitutions, and give grace and activity to their limbs, by frequent exercise in the open air. Now, before female vanity begins to operate, and teaches them to shun the light kisses of the passing zephyr, lest they should leave the unseemly traces of the rude salute on the damask cheek, or lily neck: now, while the infant heart, elate with joy and unconscious of remark, bounds with delight at every change of scene, eagerly springing from object to object, ever seeking and ever finding new and innocent enjoyments, while indulgent Nature seems to say—

"For *thee* my borders nurse the fragrant wreath,
"My fountains murmur and my zephyrs breathe;
"Slow slides the painted snail—the gilded fly
"Smooths his fine down to charm thy curious eye;
"On twinkling fins my pearly nations play,
"Or win with sinuous train their trackless way;
"My plumy pairs in gay embroidery drest,
"Form with ingenious bill the pensile nest,
"To love's soft notes attune the listening dell,
"And Echo sounds her soft symphonious shell."

And surely parents ought to coincide with their benign Creator, and permit them to enjoy for a few years the various delights he has prepared for them, and which appear almost necessary to their existence. The time will soon arrive when they must be confined to different studies and occupations, and then they will infalliby sicken and decay, unless the *mind* and *body* have both been duly invigorated, the one by early precept and admonition, the other by abundant exercise in sports and amusements such as all-wise Nature excites them to delight in.

The complexions of your daughters may be as well guarded as you please from the rude effects of the elements: this done, let them run and enjoy themselves in full liberty, for a few hours every day, being properly attended by some faithful domestic,

and they will inhale health and beauty from every breeze.

And as for your sons, let me entreat you to reflect upon what manner of men you will wish to see them in after life, and as you determine, so regulate your conduct now. Do you wish to see them effeminate and pusillanimous, then be it your care to guard their complexions, to instil into their tender minds the love of dress and show, to lead their attention to the best drest guest, and most splendid equipage—teach them to believe true excellence consists in sporting with superior grace and lily hand and diamond ring—

"Betwixt the finger and the thumb to hold
"The pouncet box"—

The poison will quickly pervade the whole soul of your children, and they will grow up the *things* you wish them. But if, on the other hand, you wish to rear the hero and the sage, teach them betimes to set no more than their just value on the trappings of fashion, the mere escutcheons to adorn, and set off to advantage the nobler part, altogether beneath the anxious notice of an immortal being, born to high honours, and capable of vast attainments. Teach them to exclaim with gallant Hotspur—

"By Heaven! methinks it were an easy leap
"To pluck bright honour from the pale face moon,
"Or dive into the bottom of the deep,
"Where fathom line could never touch the ground,
"And pluck up drowned honour by the locks!
"So he that doth redeem her thence, might wear
"Without co-rival all her dignities."
                                        SHAKSPEARE.

At the same time that you insensibly instil into their youthful minds such just ideas of right and wrong, as shall "grow with their growth, and strengthen with their strength," enabling them through life to distinguish between that well earned *honour* which is at once the basis and reward of true courage and real merit, and that *air bubble* which owes its existence to the breath of the multitude, and which a rude puff may elevate on high or sink into insignificance, and from that barbarous, blood-thirsty sentiment, which aims the deadly weapon at the loved bosom of a darling, perhaps, an only friend.

But I am wandering beyond my bounds. Pardon, gentle reader, my zeal on this important subject, and impute it to the real and sole cause, a desire to promote the best interests of your lovely and beloved children.

I must now take my leave, with the sincere hope that this little volume may answer the end for which it is presented to the public, and assist the young and inexperienced mother in the discharge of duties, on the due fulfilment of which depend the future beauty, health, and happiness of rising generation, and, eventually, the welfare of the community at large.

It will be observed, as respects the medical part of this work, I have confined myself chiefly to those disorders which few children escape, and every mother may be called upon to nurse and prescribe for; and, if I have in any material degree deviated from the most approved methods of treatment, I must beg the gentlemen of the faculty, if any such should honour my book with a perusal, to believe me open to conviction, and erring through ignorance or inexperience, not from vanity or empiricism.

1. *The Maternal Physician; A Treatise on the Nurture and Management of Infants* was originally published in 1818 (Philadelphia: Lewis &

Adams). It was reprinted in 1972 with an introduction by Charles E. Rosenberg (New York: Arno Press/*New York Times,* 1972).

2. [Tyler's Note]: This statement may perhaps excite a smile of incredulity in the learned reader, because the fact cannot be accounted for on any known principles. Facts, however, are not made by theory, but theory created by facts. If the fact that a mother's milk will cease to flow when it is thrown away, and continue to flow when given to her babe, is derided by the learned, it will only meet the fate of discoveries every way more important. The same thing has always happened. An operation of nature is noticed by the vulgar: if the learned cannot account for it, those who credit it are derided as weak and credulous, and its existence is denied; but when it can be no longer denied, the learned set down seriously to account for it; they publish their reveries; and this is called theory. The sneer of derision is then on the other side; and those who do not at once admit the fact and the theory, are ranked among the weak and the vulgar. I believe in the existence of *this* fact; and if it can derive support from analogy, I appeal to every observing dairy woman if the same does not happen in the management of her milch-kine.

Books for Further Reading

Andrews, William L., gen. ed. *Journeys in New Worlds: Early American Women's Narratives*. Madison: University of Wisconsin Press, 1990.

Armstrong, Nancy. *Desire and Domestic Fiction: A Political History of the Novel*. New York & Oxford: Oxford University Press, 1987.

Armstrong, and Leonard Tennenhouse, eds. *The Ideology of Conduct: Essays in the Literature and the History of Sexuality*. New York: Methuen, 1987.

Bacon, Margaret Hope. *Mothers of Feminism: The Story of Quaker Women in America*. San Francisco: Harper & Row, 1986.

Bacon, ed. *Wilt Thou Go on My Errand? Journals of Three Eighteenth-Century Quaker Women Ministers*. Wallingford, Pa.: Pendle Hill Publications, 1994.

Barker-Benfield, G. J. *The Culture of Sensibility: Sex and Society in Eighteenth-Century Britain*. Chicago & London: University of Chicago Press, 1992.

Baym, Nina. *American Women Writers and the Work of History, 1790–1860*. New Brunswick, N.J.: Rutgers University Press, 1995.

Benson, Mary Sumner. *Women in Eighteenth-Century America: A Study of Opinion and Social Usage*. New York: Columbia University Press, 1935.

Berkin, Carol. *First Generations: Women in Colonial America*. New York: Hill & Wang, 1996.

Berkin, and Mary Beth Norton, eds. *Women of America: A History*. Boston: Houghton Mifflin, 1979.

Berlin, Ira, and Ronald Hoffman, eds. *Slavery and Freedom in the Age of the American Revolution*. Charlottesville: University Press of Virginia for the U.S. Capitol Historical Society, 1983.

Bonta, Marcia Myers. *Women in the Field: America's Pioneering Women Naturalists*. College Station: Texas A&M University Press, 1991.

Boydston, Jeanne. *Home and Work: Housework, Wages, and the Ideology of Labor in the Early Republic*. New York: Oxford University Press, 1990.

Brown, Elizabeth Potts, and Susan Mosher Stuard, eds. *Witnesses for Change: Quaker Women over Three Centuries*. New Brunswick, N.J.: Rutgers University Press, 1985.

Brown, Herbert Ross. *The Sentimental Novel in America*. Durham, N.C.: Duke University Press, 1940.

Brown, Kathleen M. *Good Wives, Nasty Wenches, and Anxious Patriarchs: Gender, Race, and Power in Colonial Virginia*. Chapel Hill: University of North Carolina Press, 1996.

Buel, Joy Day, and Richard Buel Jr. *The Way of Duty: A Woman and Her Family in Revolutionary America*. New York: Norton, 1984.

Bunkers, Suzanne, and Cynthia Huff, eds. *Inscribing the Daily: Critical Essays on Women's Diaries*. Amherst: University of Massachusetts Press, 1996.

Bush, Barbara. *Slave Women in Caribbean Society, 1650–1838*. Bloomington: Indiana University Press, 1990.

Castiglia, Christopher. *Bound and Determined: Captivity, Culture, and White Womanhood from Mary Rowlandson to Patty Hearst*. Chicago: University of Chicago Press, 1996.

Chambers-Schiller, Lee Virginia. *Liberty, a Better Husband: Single Women in America, the Generations of 1780–1840*. New Haven, Conn.: Yale University Press, 1984.

Cline, Cheryl. *Women's Diaries, Journals, and Letters: An Annotated Bibliography*. New York: Garland, 1989.

Cohen, Daniel A. *Pillars of Salt, Monuments of Grace: New England Crime Literature and the Origins of American Popular Culture, 1674–1860*. New York: Oxford University Press, 1993.

Cott, Nancy F. *The Bonds of Womanhood: "Women's Sphere" in New England, 1780–1835*. New Haven, Conn.: Yale University Press, 1977.

Cowell, Pattie, ed. *Women Poets in Pre-Revolutionary America, 1650–1775: An Anthology*. Troy, N.Y.: Whitston, 1981.

Culley, Margo, ed. *American Women's Autobiography: Fea(s)ts of Memory*. Madison: University of Wisconsin Press, 1992.

Culley, ed. *A Day at a Time: The Diary Literature of American Women from 1764 to the Present*. New York: Feminist Press, 1985.

Davidson, Cathy N. *Revolution and the Word: The Rise of the Novel in America*. New York: Oxford University Press, 1986.

Davidson, ed. *Reading in America: Literature and Social History*. Baltimore: Johns Hopkins University Press, 1989.

Davidson, and Linda Wagner-Martin, eds. *The Oxford Companion to Women's Writing in the United States*. New York: Oxford University Press, 1995.

Derounian-Stodola, Kathryn Zabelle, and James Arthur Levernier. *The Indian Captivity Narrative, 1550–1900*. New York: Twayne, 1993.

Eldridge, Larry D., ed. *Women and Freedom in Early America*. New York: New York University Press, 1997.

Ellet, Elizabeth. *The Women of the American Revolution*, 3 volumes. New York: Baker & Scribner, 1848–1850.

Evans, Elizabeth. *Weathering the Storm: Women of the American Revolution*. New York: Scribners, 1975.

Ferguson, Moira. *Subject to Others: British Women Writers and Colonial Slavery, 1670–1834*. New York & London: Routledge, 1992.

Goodfriend, Joyce D. *The Published Diaries and Letters of American Women: An Annotated Bibliography*. Boston: G. K. Hall, 1987.

Hanaford, Phebe A. *Daughters of America, or Women of the Century*. Augusta, Maine: True, 1883.

Harris, Sharon M., ed. *American Women Writers to 1800*. New York: Oxford University Press, 1996.

Hindle, Brooke. *The Pursuit of Science in Revolutionary America, 1735–1789.* Chapel Hill: University of North Carolina Press, 1956.

Hoffman, Ronald, and Peter J. Albert, eds. *Women in the Age of the American Revolution.* Charlottesville: University Press of Virginia, 1989.

Jelinek, Estelle C., ed. *Women's Autobiography: Essays in Criticism.* Bloomington: Indiana University Press, 1980.

Kagle, Steven E. *American Diary Literature: 1620–1799.* Boston: G. K. Hall, 1979.

Kerber, Linda K. *Women of the Republic: Intellect and Ideology in Revolutionary America.* Chapel Hill: University of North Carolina Press, 1980.

Kolodny, Annette. *The Land Before Her: Fantasy and Experience of the American Frontiers, 1630–1860.* Chapel Hill: University of North Carolina Press, 1984.

Kritzer, Amelia Howe. *Plays by Early American Women, 1775–1850,* 3 volumes. Ann Arbor: University of Michigan Press, 1995.

Levenduski, Cristine. *Peculiar Power: A Quaker Woman Preacher in Eighteenth-Century America.* Washington, D.C.: Smithsonian Institution Press, 1996.

Levernier, James A., and Douglas R. Wilmes. *American Writers before 1800, A Biographical and Critical Dictionary,* 3 volumes. Westport, Conn.: Greenwood Press, 1983.

Loshe, Lillie Deming. *The Early American Novel, 1789–1830.* New York: Columbia University Press, 1907.

Mack, Phyllis. *Visionary Women: Gender and Prophecy in Seventeenth-Century England.* Berkeley: University of California Press, 1992.

Mainiero, Lina, ed. *American Women Writers: A Critical Reference Source from Colonial Times to the Present,* 4 volumes. New York: Ungar, 1979–1982.

Morrissey, Marietta. *Slave Women in the New World: Gender Stratification in the Caribbean.* Lawrence: University of Kansas Press, 1989.

Newman, Shirley, ed. *Autobiography and Questions of Gender.* London: Frank Cass, 1991.

Norton, Mary Beth. *Founding Mothers and Fathers: Gendered Power and the Forming of American Society.* New York: Knopf, 1996.

Norton. *Liberty's Daughters: The Revolutionary Experience of American Women, 1750–1800.* Boston: Little, Brown, 1980.

Parker, Patricia L., comp. *Early American Fiction: A Reference Guide.* Boston: G. K. Hall, 1984.

Petter, Henri. *The Early American Novel.* Columbus: Ohio State University Press, 1971.

Porterfield, Amanda. *Female Spirituality in America: From Sarah Edwards to Martha Graham.* Philadelphia: Temple University Press, 1980.

Sabine, Lorenzo. *Biographical Sketches of Loyalists of the American Revolution, with an Historical Essay,* 2 volumes. Boston: Little, Brown, 1864.

Salmon, Marylynn. *Women and the Law of Property in Early America*. Chapel Hill: University of North Carolina Press, 1986.

Scarry, Elaine, ed. *Literature and the Body: Essays on Populations and Persons*. Baltimore: Johns Hopkins University Press, 1988.

Schiebinger, Londa. *The Mind Has No Sex?: Women in the Origins of Modern Science*. Cambridge, Mass.: Harvard University Press, 1989.

Schteir, Ann B. *Cultivating Women, Cultivating Science: Flora's Daughters and Botany in England*. Baltimore: Johns Hopkins University Press, 1996.

Seelye, John. *Prophetic Waters: The River in Early American Life and Literature*. New York: Oxford University Press, 1977.

Shea, Daniel B. *Spiritual Autobiography in Early America*. Madison: University of Wisconsin Press, 1988.

Spengemann, William. *The Adventurous Muse: The Poetics of American Fiction, 1789–1900*. New Haven, Conn.: Yale University Press, 1977.

Spruill, Julia Cherry. *Women's Life and Work in the Southern Colonies*. Chapel Hill: University of North Carolina Press, 1938.

Stearns, Raymond Phineas. *Science in the British Colonies of North America*. Urbana: University of Illinois Press, 1970.

Stoneburner, Carol and John Stoneburner, eds. *The Influence of Quaker Women on American History*. Lewiston, N.Y.: Edwin Mellen, 1986.

Todd, Janet, ed. *A Dictionary of British and American Women Writers, 1660–1800*. Totawa, N.J.: Rowman & Allanheld, 1985.

Trevett, Christine. *Women and Quakerism in the Seventeenth Century*. York, U.K.: Ebor Press, 1991.

Ulrich, Laurel Thatcher. *Good Wives: Image and Reality in the Lives of Women in Northern New England, 1650–1750*. New York: Oxford University Press, 1982.

Verhoeven, W. M. and A. Robert Lee, eds. *Making America / Making American Literature: Franklin to Cooper*. Amsterdam & Atlanta: Rodopi, 1996.

Williams, Selma. *Demeter's Daughters: The Women Who Founded America, 1587–1787*. New York: Atheneum, 1976.

Woloch, Nancy. *Women and the American Experience*. New York: Knopf, 1984.

Wright, Luella. *The Literary Life of Early Friends, 1650–1725*. New York: Columbia University Press, 1932.

Contributors

Jennifer Jordan Baker ....*University of Pennsylvania*
Marilyn S. Blackwell ....*Community College of Vermont*
Lee S. Burchfield ....*Louisville Free Public Library*
Pattie Cowell ....*Colorado State Uniersity*
Laurie Crumpacker ....*Susquehanna University*
Deborah Dietrich ....*California State University, Fullerton*
Ellen Butler Donovan ....*Middle Tennessee State University*
Janice Durbin ....*University of Missouri–Columbia*
Joseph Fichtelberg ....*Hofstra University*
Edward J. Gallagher ....*Lehigh University*
Edith B. Gelles ....*Stanford University*
Allison Giffen ....*New Mexico State University*
Joanna B. Gillespie ....*University of Arizona, Tucson*
Amanda Gilroy ....*University of Groningen*
Joyce D. Goodfriend ....*University of Denver*
Philip Gould ....*Brown University*
Lorenza Gramegna ....*Illinois State University*
Ann E. Green ....*St. Joseph's University*
Rosemary Fithian Guruswamy ....*Radford University*
Sandra M. Gustafson ....*University of Notre Dame*
Thomas Hallock .... *Valdosta State University*
Steven Hamelman ....*Coastal Carolina University*
Mark L. Kamrath ....*University of Central Florida*
Cynthia A. Kierner ....*University of North Carolina at Charlotte*
Erika M. Kreger ....*University of California, Davis*
Amy Schrager Lang ....*Emory University*
Cristine Levenduski ....*Emory University*
James A. Levernier ....*University of Arkansas at Little Rock*
Lisa M. Logan ....*University of Central Florida*
Etta M. Madden .... *Southwest Missouri State University*
Dana D. Nelson ....*University of Kentucky*
Amy K. Ott ....*University of Delaware*
Patricia L. Parker ....*Salem State College*
David H. Payne..*University of Georgia*
Sandra Harbert Petrulionis ....*Pennsylvania State University, The Altoona College*
Karen M. Poremski ....*Emory University*
Constance J. Post ....*Iowa State University*
Donald R. Reese ....*University of New Mexico*
Jeffrey H. Richards ....*Old Dominion University*
Nicholas Rombes ....*University of Detroit Mercy*
Doreen Alvarez Saar ....*Drexel University*
John Saillant..*Western Michigan University*

George S. Scouten ....*University of South Carolina*

Sheila L. Skemp ....*University of Mississippi*

Gail K. Smith ....*Marquette University*

Michele Lise Tarter ....*Eastern Illinois University*

Ann Taves ....*Claremont School of Theology*

Michael W. Vella ....*Indiana University of Pennsylvania*

W. M. Verhoeven ....*University of Groningen*

Angela Vietto ....*Pennsylvania State University*

Kirsten R. Wilcox ....*Columbia University*

C. P. Seabrook Wilkinson ....*University of South Carolina*

Amy E. Winans ....*Susquehanna University*

Frances Murphy Zauhar ....*Saint Vincent College*

Cumulative Index

Dictionary of Literary Biography, Volumes 1-200
Dictionary of Literary Biography Yearbook, 1980-1997
Dictionary of Literary Biography Documentary Series, Volumes 1-18

Cumulative Index

DLB before number: *Dictionary of Literary Biography,* Volumes 1-200
Y before number: *Dictionary of Literary Biography Yearbook,* 1980-1997
DS before number: *Dictionary of Literary Biography Documentary Series,* Volumes 1-18

A

Abbey, Edwin Austin 1852–1911 . . . . DLB-188

Abbey Press DLB-49

The Abbey Theatre and Irish Drama,
1900-1945 . . . . DLB-10

Abbot, Willis J. 1863-1934 . . . . DLB-29

Abbott, Jacob 1803-1879 . . . . DLB-1

Abbott, Lee K. 1947- DLB-130

Abbott, Lyman 1835-1922 . . . . DLB-79

Abbott, Robert S. 1868-1940 . . . . DLB-29, 91

Abe, Kōbō 1924-1993 . . . . DLB-182

Abelard, Peter circa 1079-1142 . . . . . DLB-115

Abelard-Schuman DLB-46

Abell, Arunah S. 1806-1888 . . . . . . DLB-43

Abercrombie, Lascelles 1881-1938 . . . . DLB-19

Aberdeen University Press
Limited DLB-106

Abish, Walter 1931- DLB-130

Ablesimov, Aleksandr Onisimovich
1742-1783 . . . . DLB-150

Abraham à Sancta Clara
1644-1709 . . . . DLB-168

Abrahams, Peter 1919- DLB-117

Abrams, M. H. 1912- DLB-67

Abrogans circa 790-800 . . . . DLB-148

Abschatz, Hans Aßmann von
1646-1699 . . . . DLB-168

Abse, Dannie 1923- DLB-27

Academy Chicago Publishers DLB-46

Accrocca, Elio Filippo 1923- DLB-128

Ace Books DLB-46

Achebe, Chinua 1930- DLB-117

Achtenberg, Herbert 1938- DLB-124

Ackerman, Diane 1948- DLB-120

Ackroyd, Peter 1949- DLB-155

Acorn, Milton 1923-1986 . . . . DLB-53

Acosta, Oscar Zeta 1935?- DLB-82

Actors Theatre of Louisville DLB-7

Adair, Gilbert 1944- DLB-194

Adair, James 1709?-1783? DLB-30

Adam, Graeme Mercer 1839-1912 . . . . DLB-99

Adam, Robert Borthwick II
1863-1940 . . . . DLB-187

Adame, Leonard 1947- DLB-82

Adamic, Louis 1898-1951 . . . . DLB-9

Adams, Abigail 1744-1818 . . . . DLB-200

Adams, Alice 1926- Y-86

Adams, Brooks 1848-1927 . . . . DLB-47

Adams, Charles Francis, Jr.
1835-1915 . . . . DLB-47

Adams, Douglas 1952- Y-83

Adams, Franklin P. 1881-1960 . . . . . DLB-29

Adams, Hannah 1755-1832 . . . . . . DLB-200

Adams, Henry 1838-1918 . . . DLB-12, 47, 189

Adams, Herbert Baxter 1850-1901 . . . . DLB-47

Adams, J. S. and C.
[publishing house] DLB-49

Adams, James Truslow
1878-1949 . . . . DLB-17; DS-17

Adams, John 1735-1826 . . . . . . DLB-31, 183

Adams, John 1735-1826 and
Adams, Abigail 1744-1818 . . . . . DLB-183

Adams, John Quincy 1767-1848 . . . . . DLB-37

Adams, Léonie 1899-1988 . . . . DLB-48

Adams, Levi 1802-1832 . . . . DLB-99

Adams, Samuel 1722-1803 . . . . . DLB-31, 43

Adams, Sarah Fuller Flower
1805-1848 . . . . DLB-199

Adams, Thomas
1582 or 1583-1652 . . . . DLB-151

Adams, William Taylor 1822-1897 . . . . DLB-42

Adamson, Sir John 1867-1950 . . . . . DLB-98

Adcock, Arthur St. John
1864-1930 . . . . DLB-135

Adcock, Betty 1938- DLB-105

Adcock, Fleur 1934- DLB-40

Addison, Joseph 1672-1719 . . . . . . DLB-101

Ade, George 1866-1944 . . . . . DLB-11, 25

Adeler, Max (see Clark, Charles Heber)

Adonias Filho 1915-1990 . . . . DLB-145

Advance Publishing Company DLB-49

AE 1867-1935 . . . . DLB-19

Ælfric circa 955-circa 1010 . . . . . . DLB-146

Aeschines circa 390 B.C.-circa 320 B.C.
. . . . DLB-176

Aeschylus
525-524 B.C.-456-455 B.C. DLB-176

Aesthetic Poetry (1873), by
Walter Pater DLB-35

After Dinner Opera Company Y-92

Afro-American Literary Critics:
An Introduction DLB-33

Agassiz, Elizabeth Cary 1822-1907 . . . DLB-189

Agassiz, Jean Louis Rodolphe
1807-1873 . . . . DLB-1

Agee, James 1909-1955 . . . . . DLB-2, 26, 152

The Agee Legacy: A Conference at
the University of Tennessee
at Knoxville Y-89

Aguilera Malta, Demetrio
1909-1981 . . . . DLB-145

Ai 1947- DLB-120

Aichinger, Ilse 1921- DLB-85

Aidoo, Ama Ata 1942- DLB-117

Aiken, Conrad
1889-1973 . . . . DLB-9, 45, 102

Aiken, Joan 1924- DLB-161

Aikin, Lucy 1781-1864 . . . . . . DLB-144, 163

Ainsworth, William Harrison
1805-1882 . . . . DLB-21

Aitken, George A. 1860-1917 . . . . . DLB-149

Aitken, Robert [publishing house] DLB-49

Akenside, Mark 1721-1770 . . . . . . DLB-109

Akins, Zoë 1886-1958 . . . . DLB-26

Aksahov, Sergei Timofeevich
1791-1859 . . . . DLB-198

Akutagawa, Ryūnsuke
1892-1927 . . . . DLB-180

Alabaster, William 1568-1640 . . . . . DLB-132

Alain-Fournier 1886-1914 . . . . DLB-65

Alarcón, Francisco X. 1954- DLB-122

Alba, Nanina 1915-1968 . . . . DLB-41

Albee, Edward 1928- DLB-7

Albert the Great circa 1200-1280 . . . . DLB-115

Alberti, Rafael 1902- DLB-108

Albertinus, Aegidius
circa 1560-1620 . . . . DLB-164

Alcaeus born circa 620 B.C. DLB-176

Alcott, Amos Bronson 1799-1888 . . . . . DLB-1

Alcott, Louisa May
    1832-1888 . . . . . . DLB-1, 42, 79; DS-14

Alcott, William Andrus 1798-1859 . . . . DLB-1

Alcuin circa 732-804 . . . . DLB-148

Alden, Henry Mills 1836-1919 . . . . . DLB-79

Alden, Isabella 1841-1930 . . . . DLB-42

Alden, John B. [publishing house] DLB-49

Alden, Beardsley and Company DLB-49

Aldington, Richard
    1892-1962 . . . . . . DLB-20, 36, 100, 149

Aldis, Dorothy 1896-1966 . . . . DLB-22

Aldis, H. G. 1863-1919 . . . . DLB-184

Aldiss, Brian W. 1925- DLB-14

Aldrich, Thomas Bailey
    1836-1907 . . . . DLB-42, 71, 74, 79

Alegría, Ciro 1909-1967 . . . . DLB-113

Alegría, Claribel 1924- DLB-145

Aleixandre, Vicente 1898-1984 . . . . . DLB-108

Aleksandrov, Aleksandr Andreevich (see Durova,
    Nadezhda Andreevna)

Aleramo, Sibilla 1876-1960 . . . . . . DLB-114

Alexander, Cecil Frances 1818-1895 . . DLB-199

Alexander, Charles 1868-1923 . . . . . DLB-91

Alexander, Charles Wesley
    [publishing house] DLB-49

Alexander, James 1691-1756 . . . . . . DLB-24

Alexander, Lloyd 1924- DLB-52

Alexander, Sir William, Earl of Stirling
    1577?-1640 . . . . DLB-121

Alexie, Sherman 1966- DLB-175

Alexis, Willibald 1798-1871 . . . . . . DLB-133

Alfred, King 849-899 . . . . DLB-146

Alger, Horatio, Jr. 1832-1899 . . . . . . DLB-42

Algonquin Books of Chapel Hill DLB-46

Algren, Nelson 1909-1981 . . . . DLB-9; Y-81, Y-82

Allan, Andrew 1907-1974 . . . . DLB-88

Allan, Ted 1916- DLB-68

Allbeury, Ted 1917- DLB-87

Alldritt, Keith 1935- DLB-14

Allen, Ethan 1738-1789 . . . . DLB-31

Allen, Frederick Lewis 1890-1954 . . . . DLB-137

Allen, Gay Wilson
    1903-1995 . . . . DLB-103; Y-95

Allen, George 1808-1876 . . . . DLB-59

Allen, George [publishing house] DLB-106

Allen, George, and Unwin
    Limited DLB-112

Allen, Grant 1848-1899 . . . . DLB-70, 92, 178

Allen, Henry W. 1912- Y-85

Allen, Hervey 1889-1949 . . . . . . DLB-9, 45

Allen, James 1739-1808 . . . . DLB-31

Allen, James Lane 1849-1925 . . . . . . DLB-71

Allen, Jay Presson 1922- DLB-26

Allen, John, and Company DLB-49

Allen, Paula Gunn 1939- DLB-175

Allen, Samuel W. 1917- DLB-41

Allen, Woody 1935- DLB-44

Allende, Isabel 1942- DLB-145

Alline, Henry 1748-1784 . . . . DLB-99

Allingham, Margery 1904-1966 . . . . . DLB-77

Allingham, William 1824-1889 . . . . . DLB-35

Allison, W. L.
    [publishing house] DLB-49

The *Alliterative Morte Arthure* and
    the *Stanzaic Morte Arthur*
    circa 1350-1400 . . . . DLB-146

Allott, Kenneth 1912-1973 . . . . DLB-20

Allston, Washington 1779-1843 . . . . . DLB-1

Almon, John [publishing house] DLB-154

Alonzo, Dámaso 1898-1990 . . . . . . DLB-108

Alsop, George 1636-post 1673 . . . . . DLB-24

Alsop, Richard 1761-1815 . . . . DLB-37

Altemus, Henry, and Company DLB-49

Altenberg, Peter 1885-1919 . . . . . . DLB-81

Altolaguirre, Manuel 1905-1959 . . . . DLB-108

Aluko, T. M. 1918- DLB-117

Alurista 1947- DLB-82

Alvarez, A. 1929- DLB-14, 40

Amadi, Elechi 1934- DLB-117

Amado, Jorge 1912- DLB-113

Ambler, Eric 1909- DLB-77

*America: or, a Poem on the Settlement of the
    British Colonies* (1780?), by Timothy
    Dwight DLB-37

American Conservatory Theatre DLB-7

American Fiction and the 1930s DLB-9

American Humor: A Historical Survey
    East and Northeast
    South and Southwest
    Midwest
    West DLB-11

The American Library in Paris Y-93

American News Company DLB-49

The American Poets' Corner: The First
    Three Years (1983-1986) Y-86

American Proletarian Culture:
    The 1930s DS-11

American Publishing Company DLB-49

American Stationers' Company DLB-49

American Sunday-School Union DLB-49

American Temperance Union DLB-49

American Tract Society DLB-49

The American Trust for the
    British Library Y-96

The American Writers Congress
    (9-12 October 1981) Y-81

The American Writers Congress: A Report
    on Continuing Business Y-81

Ames, Fisher 1758-1808 . . . . DLB-37

Ames, Mary Clemmer 1831-1884 . . . . DLB-23

Amini, Johari M. 1935- DLB-41

Amis, Kingsley
    1922-1995 . . . . DLB-15, 27, 100, 139, Y-96

Amis, Martin 1949- DLB-194

Ammons, A. R. 1926- DLB-5, 165

Amory, Thomas 1691?-1788 . . . . . . DLB-39

Anania, Michael 1939- DLB-193

Anaya, Rudolfo A. 1937- DLB-82

Ancrene Riwle circa 1200-1225 . . . . . DLB-146

Andersch, Alfred 1914-1980 . . . . . . DLB-69

Anderson, Alexander 1775-1870 . . . . DLB-188

Anderson, Margaret 1886-1973 . . . DLB-4, 91

Anderson, Maxwell 1888-1959 . . . . . DLB-7

Anderson, Patrick 1915-1979 . . . . . . DLB-68

Anderson, Paul Y. 1893-1938 . . . . . DLB-29

Anderson, Poul 1926- DLB-8

Anderson, Robert 1750-1830 . . . . . DLB-142

Anderson, Robert 1917- DLB-7

Anderson, Sherwood
    1876-1941 . . . . DLB-4, 9, 86; DS-1

Andreae, Johann Valentin
    1586-1654 . . . . DLB-164

Andreas-Salomé, Lou 1861-1937 . . . . DLB-66

Andres, Stefan 1906-1970 . . . . DLB-69

Andreu, Blanca 1959- DLB-134

Andrewes, Lancelot
    1555-1626 . . . . DLB-151, 172

Andrews, Charles M. 1863-1943 . . . . DLB-17

Andrews, Miles Peter ?-1814 . . . . . . DLB-89

Andrian, Leopold von 1875-1951 . . . . DLB-81

Andrić, Ivo 1892-1975 . . . . DLB-147

Andrieux, Louis (see Aragon, Louis)

Andrus, Silas, and Son DLB-49

Angell, James Burrill 1829-1916 . . . . DLB-64

Angell, Roger 1920- DLB-171, 185

Angelou, Maya 1928- DLB-38

Anger, Jane flourished 1589 . . . . . . DLB-136

Angers, Félicité (see Conan, Laure)

Anglo-Norman Literature in the
    Development of Middle English
    Literature DLB-146

The Anglo-Saxon Chronicle
    circa 890-1154 . . . . DLB-146

The "Angry Young Men" DLB-15

Angus and Robertson (UK)
    Limited DLB-112

Anhalt, Edward 1914- DLB-26

Anners, Henry F.
    [publishing house] DLB-49

Annolied between 1077
  and 1081. . . . . and DLB-148

Anselm of Canterbury
  1033-1109 . . . . DLB-115

Anstey, F. 1856-1934. . . . . . . DLB-141, 178

Anthony, Michael 1932- DLB-125

Anthony, Piers 1934- DLB-8

Anthony, Susanna 1726-1791 . . . . . DLB-200

Anthony Burgess's *99 Novels:*
  An Opinion Poll Y-84

Antin, David 1932- DLB-169

Antin, Mary 1881-1949. . . . . Y-84

Anton Ulrich, Duke of Brunswick-Lüneburg
  1633-1714 . . . . DLB-168

Antschel, Paul (see Celan, Paul)

Anyidoho, Kofi 1947- DLB-157

Anzaldúa, Gloria 1942- DLB-122

Anzengruber, Ludwig
  1839-1889 . . . . DLB-129

Apess, William 1798-1839. . . . . . . DLB-175

Apodaca, Rudy S. 1939- DLB-82

Apollonius Rhodius third century B.C.
  . . . . DLB-176

Apple, Max 1941- DLB-130

Appleton, D., and Company DLB-49

Appleton-Century-Crofts. DLB-46

Applewhite, James 1935- DLB-105

Apple-wood Books DLB-46

Aquin, Hubert 1929-1977. . . . . . . DLB-53

Aquinas, Thomas 1224 or
  1225-1274 . . . . DLB-115

Aragon, Louis 1897-1982. . . . . DLB-72

Aralica, Ivan 1930- DLB-181

Aratus of Soli circa 315 B.C.-circa 239 B.C.
  . . . . DLB-176

Arbasino, Alberto 1930- DLB-196

Arbor House Publishing
  Company DLB-46

Arbuthnot, John 1667-1735 . . . . . . DLB-101

Arcadia House. DLB-46

Arce, Julio G. (see Ulica, Jorge)

Archer, William 1856-1924 . . . . DLB-10

Archilochhus mid seventh century B.C.E.
  . . . . DLB-176

The Archpoet circa 1130?-?. DLB-148

Archpriest Avvakum (Petrovich)
  1620?-1682 . . . . DLB-150

Arden, John 1930- DLB-13

Arden of Faversham DLB-62

Ardis Publishers. Y-89

Ardizzone, Edward 1900-1979. . . . . DLB-160

Arellano, Juan Estevan 1947- DLB-122

The Arena Publishing Company. DLB-49

Arena Stage. DLB-7

Arenas, Reinaldo 1943-1990. . . . . . DLB-145

Arensberg, Ann 1937- Y-82

Arguedas, José María 1911-1969 . . . . DLB-113

Argueta, Manlio 1936- DLB-145

Arias, Ron 1941- DLB-82

Arishima, Takeo 1878-1923 . . . . . . DLB-180

Aristophanes
  circa 446 B.C.-circa 386 B.C. . . . DLB-176

Aristotle 384 B.C.-322 B.C. DLB-176

Ariyoshi, Sawako 1931-1984 . . . . . DLB-182

Arland, Marcel 1899-1986 . . . . . . DLB-72

Arlen, Michael
  1895-1956 . . . . DLB-36, 77, 162

Armah, Ayi Kwei 1939- DLB-117

Armantrout, Rae 1947- DLB-193

Der arme Hartmann
  ?-after 1150 . . . . DLB-148

Armed Services Editions DLB-46

Armstrong, Martin Donisthorpe 1882-1974
  . . . . DLB-197

Armstrong, Richard 1903- DLB-160

Arndt, Ernst Moritz 1769-1860. . . . . DLB-90

Arnim, Achim von 1781-1831 . . . . . DLB-90

Arnim, Bettina von 1785-1859 . . . . DLB-90

Arnim, Elizabeth von (Countess Mary Annette
  Beauchamp Russell) 1866-1941 . . . DLB-197

Arno Press. DLB-46

Arnold, Edwin 1832-1904. . . . . . . DLB-35

Arnold, Edwin L. 1857-1935 . . . . . DLB-178

Arnold, Matthew 1822-1888 . . . . DLB-32, 57

Arnold, Thomas 1795-1842. . . . . . . DLB-55

Arnold, Edward
  [publishing house] DLB-112

Arnow, Harriette Simpson
  1908-1986. . . . . DLB-6

Arp, Bill (see Smith, Charles Henry)

Arpino, Giovanni 1927-1987 . . . . . DLB-177

Arreola, Juan José 1918- DLB-113

Arrian circa 89-circa 155 . . . . DLB-176

Arrowsmith, J. W.
  [publishing house] DLB-106

The Art and Mystery of Publishing:
  Interviews. Y-97

Arthur, Timothy Shay
  1809-1885 . . . . . . DLB-3, 42, 79; DS-13

The Arthurian Tradition and Its European
  Context. DLB-138

Artmann, H. C. 1921- DLB-85

Arvin, Newton 1900-1963. . . . . . . DLB-103

As I See It, by
  Carolyn Cassady DLB-16

Asch, Nathan 1902-1964. . . . . . . DLB-4, 28

Ash, John 1948- DLB-40

Ashbery, John 1927- DLB-5, 165; Y-81

Ashbridge, Elizabeth 1713-1755 . . . . DLB-200

Ashburnham, Bertram Lord
  1797-1878 . . . . DLB-184

Ashendene Press. DLB-112

Asher, Sandy 1942- Y-83

Ashton, Winifred (see Dane, Clemence)

Asimov, Isaac 1920-1992 . . . . . DLB-8; Y-92

Askew, Anne circa 1521-1546. . . . . DLB-136

Asselin, Olivar 1874-1937. . . . . . . DLB-92

Asturias, Miguel Angel
  1899-1974 . . . . DLB-113

Atheneum Publishers DLB-46

Atherton, Gertrude 1857-1948. . DLB-9, 78, 186

Athlone Press. DLB-112

Atkins, Josiah circa 1755-1781 . . . . . DLB-31

Atkins, Russell 1926- DLB-41

The Atlantic Monthly Press DLB-46

Attaway, William 1911-1986 . . . . . DLB-76

Atwood, Margaret 1939- DLB-53

Aubert, Alvin 1930- DLB-41

Aubert de Gaspé, Phillipe-Ignace-François
  1814-1841 . . . . DLB-99

Aubert de Gaspé, Phillipe-Joseph
  1786-1871 . . . . DLB-99

Aubin, Napoléon 1812-1890 . . . . . DLB-99

Aubin, Penelope 1685-circa 1731. . . . DLB-39

Aubrey-Fletcher, Henry Lancelot
  (see Wade, Henry)

Auchincloss, Louis 1917- DLB-2; Y-80

Auden, W. H. 1907-1973 . . . . . DLB-10, 20

Audio Art in America: A Personal
  Memoir Y-85

Audubon, John Woodhouse
  1812-1862 . . . . DLB-183

Auerbach, Berthold 1812-1882 . . . . DLB-133

Auernheimer, Raoul 1876-1948. . . . . DLB-81

Augier, Emile 1820-1889 . . . . DLB-192

Augustine 354-430 . . . . DLB-115

Austen, Jane 1775-1817 . . . . DLB-116

Austin, Alfred 1835-1913 . . . . DLB-35

Austin, Mary 1868-1934. . . . . . DLB-9, 78

Austin, William 1778-1841 . . . . . . DLB-74

Author-Printers, 1476–1599 . . . . . DLB-167

Author Websites Y-97

The Author's Apology for His Book
  (1684), by John Bunyan DLB-39

An Author's Response, by
  Ronald Sukenick Y-82

Authors and Newspapers
  Association DLB-46

Authors' Publishing Company DLB-49

Avalon Books DLB-46

Avancini, Nicolaus 1611-1686 . . . . . DLB-164

Avendaño, Fausto 1941- DLB-82

Averroëó 1126-1198 . . . . DLB-115

Avery, Gillian 1926- DLB-161

Avicenna 980-1037 . . . . DLB-115

Avison, Margaret 1918- DLB-53

Avon Books DLB-46

Awdry, Wilbert Vere 1911- DLB-160

Awoonor, Kofi 1935- DLB-117

Ayckbourn, Alan 1939- DLB-13

Aymé, Marcel 1902-1967 . . . . DLB-72

Aytoun, Sir Robert 1570-1638 . . . . . DLB-121

Aytoun, William Edmondstoune
1813-1865 . . . . DLB-32, 159

B

B. V. (see Thomson, James)

Babbitt, Irving 1865-1933 . . . . DLB-63

Babbitt, Natalie 1932- DLB-52

Babcock, John [publishing house] DLB-49

Babrius circa 150-200 . . . . DLB-176

Baca, Jimmy Santiago 1952- DLB-122

Bache, Benjamin Franklin
1769-1798 . . . . DLB-43

Bachmann, Ingeborg 1926-1973 . . . . DLB-85

Bacon, Delia 1811-1859 . . . . DLB-1

Bacon, Francis 1561-1626 . . . . DLB-151

Bacon, Roger circa
1214/1220-1292 . . . . DLB-115

Bacon, Sir Nicholas
circa 1510-1579 . . . . DLB-132

Bacon, Thomas circa 1700-1768 . . . . . DLB-31

Badger, Richard G.,
and Company. DLB-49

Bage, Robert 1728-1801. . . . . DLB-39

Bagehot, Walter 1826-1877 . . . . DLB-55

Bagley, Desmond 1923-1983 . . . . . . DLB-87

Bagnold, Enid 1889-1981 . . . DLB-13, 160, 191

Bagryana, Elisaveta 1893-1991 . . . . . DLB-147

Bahr, Hermann 1863-1934 . . . . . DLB-81, 118

Bailey, Abigail Abbot 1746-1815 . . . . DLB-200

Bailey, Alfred Goldsworthy
1905- DLB-68

Bailey, Francis
[publishing house]. DLB-49

Bailey, H. C. 1878-1961 . . . . DLB-77

Bailey, Jacob 1731-1808. . . . . DLB-99

Bailey, Paul 1937- DLB-14

Bailey, Philip James 1816-1902 . . . . . DLB-32

Baillargeon, Pierre 1916-1967 . . . . . . DLB-88

Baillie, Hugh 1890-1966 . . . . DLB-29

Baillie, Joanna 1762-1851 . . . . DLB-93

Bailyn, Bernard 1922- DLB-17

Bainbridge, Beryl 1933- DLB-14

Baird, Irene 1901-1981 . . . . DLB-68

Baker, Augustine 1575-1641 . . . . . . DLB-151

Baker, Carlos 1909-1987 . . . . DLB-103

Baker, David 1954- DLB-120

Baker, Herschel C. 1914-1990 . . . . . DLB-111

Baker, Houston A., Jr. 1943- DLB-67

Baker, Samuel White 1821-1893 . . . . DLB-166

Baker, Walter H., Company
("Baker's Plays") DLB-49

The Baker and Taylor
Company DLB-49

Balaban, John 1943- DLB-120

Bald, Wambly 1902- DLB-4

Balde, Jacob 1604-1668 . . . . DLB-164

Balderston, John 1889-1954 . . . . DLB-26

Baldwin, James
1924-1987 . . . . DLB-2, 7, 33; Y-87

Baldwin, Joseph Glover
1815-1864 . . . . DLB-3, 11

Baldwin, Richard and Anne
[publishing house] DLB-170

Baldwin, William
circa 1515-1563 . . . . DLB-132

Bale, John 1495-1563 . . . . DLB-132

Balestrini, Nanni 1935- DLB-128, 196

Balfour, Arthur James 1848-1930 . . . . DLB-190

Ballantine Books. DLB-46

Ballantyne, R. M. 1825-1894 . . . . . . DLB-163

Ballard, J. G. 1930- DLB-14

Ballard, Martha Moore 1735-1812 . . . DLB-200

Ballerini, Luigi 1940- DLB-128

Ballou, Maturin Murray
1820-1895 . . . . DLB-79, 189

Ballou, Robert O.
[publishing house] DLB-46

Balzac, Honoré de 1799-1855 . . . . . DLB-119

Bambara, Toni Cade 1939- DLB-38

Bamford, Samuel 1788-1872 . . . . . . DLB-190

Bancroft, A. L., and
Company DLB-49

Bancroft, George
1800-1891 . . . . DLB-1, 30, 59

Bancroft, Hubert Howe
1832-1918 . . . . DLB-47, 140

Bandelier, Adolph F. 1840-1914 . . . . DLB-186

Bangs, John Kendrick
1862-1922 . . . . DLB-11, 79

Banim, John
1798-1842 . . . . DLB-116, 158, 159

Banim, Michael 1796-1874 . . . . DLB-158, 159

Banks, Iain 1954- DLB-194

Banks, John circa 1653-1706 . . . . . . DLB-80

Banks, Russell 1940- DLB-130

Bannerman, Helen 1862-1946 . . . . . DLB-141

Bantam Books. DLB-46

Banti, Anna 1895-1985 . . . . DLB-177

Banville, John 1945- DLB-14

Baraka, Amiri
1934- DLB-5, 7, 16, 38; DS-8

Barbauld, Anna Laetitia
1743-1825 . . . . . DLB-107, 109, 142, 158

Barbeau, Marius 1883-1969 . . . . DLB-92

Barber, John Warner 1798-1885 . . . . . DLB-30

Bàrberi Squarotti, Giorgio
1929- DLB-128

Barbey d'Aurevilly, Jules-Amédée
1808-1889 . . . . DLB-119

Barbour, John circa 1316-1395 . . . . . DLB-146

Barbour, Ralph Henry
1870-1944 . . . . DLB-22

Barbusse, Henri 1873-1935 . . . . DLB-65

Barclay, Alexander
circa 1475-1552 . . . . DLB-132

Barclay, E. E., and Company DLB-49

Bardeen, C. W.
[publishing house]. DLB-49

Barham, Richard Harris
1788-1845 . . . . DLB-159

Barich, Bill 1943- DLB-185

Baring, Maurice 1874-1945 . . . . DLB-34

Baring-Gould, Sabine
1834-1924. . . . . DLB-156, 190

Barker, A. L. 1918- DLB-14, 139

Barker, George 1913-1991 . . . . DLB-20

Barker, Harley Granville
1877-1946 . . . . DLB-10

Barker, Howard 1946- DLB-13

Barker, James Nelson 1784-1858 . . . . DLB-37

Barker, Jane 1652-1727 . . . . . . DLB-39, 131

Barker, Lady Mary Anne
1831-1911 . . . . DLB-166

Barker, William
circa 1520-after 1576 . . . . DLB-132

Barker, Arthur, Limited DLB-112

Barkov, Ivan Semenovich
1732-1768 . . . . DLB-150

Barks, Coleman 1937- DLB-5

Barlach, Ernst 1870-1938 . . . . . DLB-56, 118

Barlow, Joel 1754-1812 . . . . DLB-37

Barnard, John 1681-1770 . . . . DLB-24

Barne, Kitty (Mary Catherine Barne)
1883-1957 . . . . DLB-160

Barnes, Barnabe 1571-1609 . . . . . . DLB-132

Barnes, Djuna 1892-1982 . . . . . DLB-4, 9, 45

Barnes, Jim 1933- DLB-175

Barnes, Julian 1946- DLB-194; Y-93

Barnes, Margaret Ayer 1886-1967 . . . . . DLB-9

Barnes, Peter 1931- DLB-13

Barnes, William 1801-1886 . . . . DLB-32

Barnes, A. S., and Company. DLB-49

Barnes and Noble Books DLB-46

Barnet, Miguel 1940- DLB-145

Barney, Natalie 1876-1972 . . . . DLB-4

Barnfield, Richard 1574-1627 . . . . . . DLB-172

Baron, Richard W.,
　　Publishing Company DLB-46

Barr, Robert 1850-1912 . . . . DLB-70, 92

Barral, Carlos 1928-1989 . . . . DLB-134

Barrax, Gerald William
　　1933- DLB-41, 120

Barrès, Maurice 1862-1923 . . . . . . DLB-123

Barrett, Eaton Stannard
　　1786-1820 . . . . DLB-116

Barrie, J. M. 1860-1937 . . . . DLB-10, 141, 156

Barrie and Jenkins DLB-112

Barrio, Raymond 1921- DLB-82

Barrios, Gregg 1945- DLB-122

Barry, Philip 1896-1949 . . . . DLB-7

Barry, Robertine (see Françoise)

Barse and Hopkins DLB-46

Barstow, Stan 1928- DLB-14, 139

Barth, John 1930- DLB-2

Barthelme, Donald
　　1931-1989 . . . . DLB-2; Y-80, Y-89

Barthelme, Frederick 1943- Y-85

Bartholomew, Frank 1898-1985 . . . . . DLB-127

Bartlett, John 1820-1905 . . . . DLB-1

Bartol, Cyrus Augustus 1813-1900 . . . . DLB-1

Barton, Bernard 1784-1849 . . . . DLB-96

Barton, Thomas Pennant
　　1803-1869 . . . . DLB-140

Bartram, John 1699-1777 . . . . DLB-31

Bartram, William 1739-1823 . . . . DLB-37

Basic Books DLB-46

Basille, Theodore (see Becon, Thomas)

Bass, T. J. 1932- Y-81

Bassani, Giorgio 1916- DLB-128, 177

Basse, William circa 1583-1653 . . . . . DLB-121

Bassett, John Spencer 1867-1928 . . . . . DLB-17

Bassler, Thomas Joseph (see Bass, T. J.)

Bate, Walter Jackson
　　1918- DLB-67, 103

Bateman, Christopher
　　[publishing house] DLB-170

Bateman, Stephen
　　circa 1510-1584 . . . . DLB-136

Bates, H. E. 1905-1974 . . . . . DLB-162, 191

Bates, Katharine Lee 1859-1929 . . . . . DLB-71

Batsford, B. T.
　　[publishing house] DLB-106

Battiscombe, Georgina 1905- DLB-155

The Battle of Maldon circa 1000 . . . . DLB-146

Bauer, Bruno 1809-1882 . . . . DLB-133

Bauer, Wolfgang 1941- DLB-124

Baum, L. Frank 1856-1919 . . . . . . DLB-22

Baum, Vicki 1888-1960 . . . . DLB-85

Baumbach, Jonathan 1933- Y-80

Bausch, Richard 1945- DLB-130

Bawden, Nina 1925- DLB-14, 161

Bax, Clifford 1886-1962 . . . . . . DLB-10, 100

Baxter, Charles 1947- DLB-130

Bayer, Eleanor (see Perry, Eleanor)

Bayer, Konrad 1932-1964 . . . . DLB-85

Baynes, Pauline 1922- DLB-160

Bazin, Hervé 1911- DLB-83

Beach, Sylvia 1887-1962 . . . . . DLB-4; DS-15

Beacon Press DLB-49

Beadle and Adams DLB-49

Beagle, Peter S. 1939- Y-80

Beal, M. F. 1937- Y-81

Beale, Howard K. 1899-1959 . . . . . . DLB-17

Beard, Charles A. 1874-1948 . . . . . . DLB-17

A Beat Chronology: The First Twenty-five
　　Years, 1944-1969 . . . . DLB-16

Beattie, Ann 1947- Y-82

Beattie, James 1735-1803 . . . . . . DLB-109

Beauchemin, Nérée 1850-1931 . . . . . DLB-92

Beauchemin, Yves 1941- DLB-60

Beaugrand, Honoré 1848-1906 . . . . . DLB-99

Beaulieu, Victor-Lévy 1945- DLB-53

Beaumont, Francis circa 1584-1616
　　and Fletcher, John 1579-1625 . . . . DLB-58

Beaumont, Sir John 1583?-1627 . . . . . DLB-121

Beaumont, Joseph 1616–1699 . . . . . DLB-126

Beauvoir, Simone de
　　1908-1986 . . . . DLB-72; Y-86

Becher, Ulrich 1910- DLB-69

Becker, Carl 1873-1945 . . . . DLB-17

Becker, Jurek 1937- DLB-75

Becker, Jurgen 1932- DLB-75

Beckett, Samuel
　　1906-1989 . . . . DLB-13, 15; Y-90

Beckford, William 1760-1844 . . . . . DLB-39

Beckham, Barry 1944- DLB-33

Becon, Thomas circa 1512-1567 . . . . DLB-136

Becque, Henry 1837-1899 . . . . . . DLB-192

Bećković, Matija 1939- DLB-181

Beddoes, Thomas 1760-1808 . . . . . DLB-158

Beddoes, Thomas Lovell
　　1803-1849 . . . . DLB-96

Bede circa 673-735 . . . . DLB-146

Beecher, Catharine Esther
　　1800-1878 . . . . DLB-1

Beecher, Henry Ward
　　1813-1887 . . . . DLB-3, 43

Beer, George L. 1872-1920 . . . . DLB-47

Beer, Johann 1655-1700 . . . . DLB-168

Beer, Patricia 1919- DLB-40

Beerbohm, Max 1872-1956 . . . . DLB-34, 100

Beer-Hofmann, Richard
　　1866-1945 . . . . DLB-81

Beers, Henry A. 1847-1926 . . . . DLB-71

Beeton, S. O.
　　[publishing house] DLB-106

Bégon, Elisabeth 1696-1755 . . . . DLB-99

Behan, Brendan 1923-1964 . . . . DLB-13

Behn, Aphra
　　1640?-1689 . . . . DLB-39, 80, 131

Behn, Harry 1898-1973 . . . . DLB-61

Behrman, S. N. 1893-1973 . . . . . . DLB-7, 44

Belaney, Archibald Stansfeld (see Grey Owl)

Belasco, David 1853-1931 . . . . DLB-7

Belford, Clarke and Company DLB-49

Belinksy, Vissarion Grigor'evich
　　1811-1848 . . . . DLB-198

Belitt, Ben 1911- DLB-5

Belknap, Jeremy 1744-1798 . . . . . DLB-30, 37

Bell, Adrian 1901-1980 . . . . DLB-191

Bell, Clive 1881-1964 . . . . DS-10

Bell, Gertrude Margaret Lowthian
　　1868-1926 . . . . DLB-174

Bell, James Madison 1826-1902 . . . . . DLB-50

Bell, Marvin 1937- DLB-5

Bell, Millicent 1919- DLB-111

Bell, Quentin 1910- DLB-155

Bell, Vanessa 1879-1961 . . . . DS-10

Bell, George, and Sons DLB-106

Bell, Robert [publishing house] DLB-49

Bellamy, Edward 1850-1898 . . . . . . DLB-12

Bellamy, John [publishing house] DLB-170

Bellamy, Joseph 1719-1790 . . . . . . DLB-31

Bellezza, Dario 1944- DLB-128

La Belle Assemblée 1806-1837 . . . . . . DLB-110

Belloc, Hilaire
　　1870-1953 . . . . . DLB-19, 100, 141, 174

Bellonci, Maria 1902-1986 . . . . . . DLB-196

Bellow, Saul
　　1915- DLB-2, 28; Y-82; DS-3

Belmont Productions DLB-46

Bemelmans, Ludwig 1898-1962 . . . . . DLB-22

Bemis, Samuel Flagg 1891-1973 . . . . . DLB-17

Bemrose, William
　　[publishing house] DLB-106

Benchley, Robert 1889-1945 . . . . . . DLB-11

Benedetti, Mario 1920- DLB-113

Benedictus, David 1938- DLB-14

Benedikt, Michael 1935- DLB-5

Benét, Stephen Vincent
1898-1943. . . . . DLB-4, 48, 102

Benét, William Rose 1886-1950 . . . . . DLB-45

Benford, Gregory 1941- Y-82

Benjamin, Park 1809-1864 . . . . DLB-3, 59, 73

Benjamin, S. G. W. 1837-1914 . . . . . DLB-189

Benlowes, Edward 1602-1676 . . . . . . DLB-126

Benn, Gottfried 1886-1956 . . . . DLB-56

Benn Brothers Limited DLB-106

Bennett, Arnold
1867-1931 . . . . DLB-10, 34, 98, 135

Bennett, Charles 1899- DLB-44

Bennett, Gwendolyn 1902- DLB-51

Bennett, Hal 1930- DLB-33

Bennett, James Gordon 1795-1872 . . . . DLB-43

Bennett, James Gordon, Jr.
1841-1918 . . . . DLB-23

Bennett, John 1865-1956 . . . . DLB-42

Bennett, Louise 1919- DLB-117

Benni, Stefano 1947- DLB-196

Benoit, Jacques 1941- DLB-60

Benson, A. C. 1862-1925 . . . . DLB-98

Benson, E. F. 1867-1940 . . . . . DLB-135, 153

Benson, Jackson J. 1930- DLB-111

Benson, Robert Hugh
1871-1914 . . . . DLB-153

Benson, Stella 1892-1933 . . . . . DLB-36, 162

Bent, James Theodore 1852-1897 . . . . DLB-174

Bent, Mabel Virginia Anna ?-? DLB-174

Bentham, Jeremy
1748-1832 . . . . DLB-107, 158

Bentley, E. C. 1875-1956 . . . . DLB-70

Bentley, Phyllis 1894-1977 . . . . DLB-191

Bentley, Richard
[publishing house] DLB-106

Benton, Robert 1932- and Newman,
David 1937- DLB-44

Benziger Brothers DLB-49

Beowulf circa 900-1000
or 790-825 . . . . DLB-146

Beresford, Anne 1929- DLB-40

Beresford, John Davys
1873-1947 . . . . DLB-162, 178, 197

Beresford-Howe, Constance
1922- DLB-88

Berford, R. G., Company DLB-49

Berg, Stephen 1934- DLB-5

Bergengruen, Werner 1892-1964 . . . . DLB-56

Berger, John 1926- DLB-14

Berger, Meyer 1898-1959 . . . . DLB-29

Berger, Thomas 1924- DLB-2; Y-80

Berkeley, Anthony 1893-1971 . . . . . DLB-77

Berkeley, George 1685-1753 . . . . DLB-31, 101

The Berkley Publishing
Corporation DLB-46

Berlin, Lucia 1936- DLB-130

Bernal, Vicente J. 1888-1915 . . . . . . DLB-82

Bernanos, Georges 1888-1948 . . . . . DLB-72

Bernard, Harry 1898-1979 . . . . DLB-92

Bernard, John 1756-1828 . . . . DLB-37

Bernard of Chartres
circa 1060-1124? DLB-115

Bernari, Carlo 1909-1992 . . . . DLB-177

Bernhard, Thomas
1931-1989 . . . . DLB-85, 124

Bernstein, Charles 1950- DLB-169

Berriault, Gina 1926- DLB-130

Berrigan, Daniel 1921- DLB-5

Berrigan, Ted 1934-1983 . . . . . DLB-5, 169

Berry, Wendell 1934- DLB-5, 6

Berryman, John 1914-1972 . . . . DLB-48

Bersianik, Louky 1930- DLB-60

Berthelet, Thomas
[publishing house] DLB-170

Berto, Giuseppe 1914-1978 . . . . DLB-177

Bertolucci, Attilio 1911- DLB-128

Berton, Pierre 1920- DLB-68

Besant, Sir Walter 1836-1901 . . . DLB-135, 190

Bessette, Gerard 1920- DLB-53

Bessie, Alvah 1904-1985 . . . . DLB-26

Bester, Alfred 1913-1987 . . . . DLB-8

The Bestseller Lists: An Assessment Y-84

Bestuzhev, Aleksandr Aleksandrovich (Marlinsky)
1797-1837 . . . . DLB-198

Bestuzhev, Nikolai Aleksandrovich
1791-1855 . . . . DLB-198

Betham-Edwards, Matilda Barbara (see Edwards,
Matilda Barbara Betham-)

Betjeman, John 1906-1984 . . . . . DLB-20; Y-84

Betocchi, Carlo 1899-1986 . . . . DLB-128

Bettarini, Mariella 1942- DLB-128

Betts, Doris 1932- Y-82

Beveridge, Albert J. 1862-1927 . . . . . DLB-17

Beverley, Robert
circa 1673-1722 . . . . DLB-24, 30

Bevilacqua, Alberto 1934- DLB-196

Bevington, Louisa Sarah 1845-1895 . . . DLB-199

Beyle, Marie-Henri (see Stendhal)

Bianco, Margery Williams
1881-1944 . . . . DLB-160

Bibaud, Adèle 1854-1941 . . . . DLB-92

Bibaud, Michel 1782-1857 . . . . DLB-99

Bibliographical and Textual Scholarship
Since World War II Y-89

The Bicentennial of James Fenimore
Cooper: An International
Celebration Y-89

Bichsel, Peter 1935- DLB-75

Bickerstaff, Isaac John
1733-circa 1808 . . . . DLB-89

Biddle, Drexel [publishing house] DLB-49

Bidermann, Jacob
1577 or 1578-1639 . . . . DLB-164

Bidwell, Walter Hilliard
1798-1881 . . . . DLB-79

Bienek, Horst 1930- DLB-75

Bierbaum, Otto Julius 1865-1910 . . . . . DLB-66

Bierce, Ambrose
1842-1914? . . . DLB-11, 12, 23, 71, 74, 186

Bigelow, William F. 1879-1966 . . . . . DLB-91

Biggle, Lloyd, Jr. 1923- DLB-8

Bigiaretti, Libero 1905-1993 . . . . . . DLB-177

Bigland, Eileen 1898-1970 . . . . DLB-195

Biglow, Hosea (see Lowell, James Russell)

Bigongiari, Piero 1914- DLB-128

Billinger, Richard 1890-1965 . . . . . DLB-124

Billings, Hammatt 1818-1874 . . . . . DLB-188

Billings, John Shaw 1898-1975 . . . . . DLB-137

Billings, Josh (see Shaw, Henry Wheeler)

Binding, Rudolf G. 1867-1938 . . . . . DLB-66

Bingham, Caleb 1757-1817 . . . . DLB-42

Bingham, George Barry
1906-1988 . . . . DLB-127

Bingley, William
[publishing house] DLB-154

Binyon, Laurence 1869-1943 . . . . . . DLB-19

Biographia Brittanica DLB-142

Biographical Documents I Y-84

Biographical Documents II Y-85

Bioren, John [publishing house] . . . DLB-49

Bioy Casares, Adolfo 1914- DLB-113

Bird, Isabella Lucy 1831-1904 . . . . . . DLB-166

Bird, William 1888-1963 . . . . . DLB-4; DS-15

Birken, Sigmund von 1626-1681 . . . . DLB-164

Birney, Earle 1904- DLB-88

Birrell, Augustine 1850-1933 . . . . . . DLB-98

Bisher, Furman 1918- DLB-171

Bishop, Elizabeth 1911-1979 . . . . . DLB-5, 169

Bishop, John Peale 1892-1944 . . . DLB-4, 9, 45

Bismarck, Otto von 1815-1898 . . . . . DLB-129

Bisset, Robert 1759-1805 . . . . DLB-142

Bissett, Bill 1939- DLB-53

Bitzius, Albert (see Gotthelf, Jeremias)

Black, David (D. M.) 1941- DLB-40

Black, Winifred 1863-1936 . . . . DLB-25

Black, Walter J.
  [publishing house]. DLB-46

The Black Aesthetic: Background. DS-8

The Black Arts Movement, by
  Larry Neal DLB-38

Black Theaters and Theater Organizations in
  America, 1961-1982:
  A Research List. DLB-38

Black Theatre: A Forum
  [excerpts] DLB-38

Blackamore, Arthur 1679-? DLB-24, 39

Blackburn, Alexander L. 1929- Y-85

Blackburn, Paul 1926-1971 . . . . DLB-16; Y-81

Blackburn, Thomas 1916-1977 . . . . . DLB-27

Blackmore, R. D. 1825-1900 . . . . . . DLB-18

Blackmore, Sir Richard
  1654-1729 . . . . DLB-131

Blackmur, R. P. 1904-1965. . . . . . DLB-63

Blackwell, Basil, Publisher. DLB-106

Blackwood, Algernon Henry
  1869-1951. . . . . . . DLB-153, 156, 178

Blackwood, Caroline 1931- DLB-14

Blackwood, William, and
  Sons, Ltd. DLB-154

Blackwood's Edinburgh Magazine
  1817-1980 . . . . DLB-110

Blades, William 1824-1890 . . . . . . DLB-184

Blagden, Isabella 1817?-1873 . . . . . DLB-199

Blair, Eric Arthur (see Orwell, George)

Blair, Francis Preston 1791-1876 . . . . DLB-43

Blair, James circa 1655-1743 . . . . . . DLB-24

Blair, John Durburrow 1759-1823 . . . . DLB-37

Blais, Marie-Claire 1939- DLB-53

Blaise, Clark 1940- DLB-53

Blake, George 1893-1961 . . . . . . DLB-191

Blake, Nicholas 1904-1972 . . . . . . DLB-77
  (see Day Lewis, C.)

Blake, William
  1757-1827 . . . . DLB-93, 154, 163

The Blakiston Company DLB-49

Blanchot, Maurice 1907- DLB-72

Blanckenburg, Christian Friedrich von
  1744-1796 . . . . DLB-94

Blaser, Robin 1925- DLB-165

Bledsoe, Albert Taylor
  1809-1877 . . . . DLB-3, 79

Bleecker, Ann Eliza 1752-1783 . . . . DLB-200

Blelock and Company DLB-49

Blennerhassett, Margaret Agnew
  1773-1842 . . . . DLB-99

Bles, Geoffrey
  [publishing house] DLB-112

Blessington, Marguerite, Countess of
  1789-1849 . . . . DLB-166

The Blickling Homilies
  circa 971 . . . . DLB-146

Blind, Mathilde 1841-1896. . . . . . DLB-199

Blish, James 1921-1975. . . . . DLB-8

Bliss, E., and E. White
  [publishing house]. DLB-49

Bliven, Bruce 1889-1977. . . . . . . DLB-137

Bloch, Robert 1917-1994 . . . . . . DLB-44

Block, Rudolph (see Lessing, Bruno)

Blondal, Patricia 1926-1959 . . . . . . DLB-88

Bloom, Harold 1930- DLB-67

Bloomer, Amelia 1818-1894 . . . . . DLB-79

Bloomfield, Robert 1766-1823 . . . . DLB-93

Bloomsbury Group DS-10

Blotner, Joseph 1923- DLB-111

Bloy, Léon 1846-1917 . . . . DLB-123

Blume, Judy 1938- DLB-52

Blunck, Hans Friedrich 1888-1961 . . . DLB-66

Blunden, Edmund
  1896-1974 . . . . DLB-20, 100, 155

Blunt, Lady Anne Isabella Noel
  1837-1917 . . . . DLB-174

Blunt, Wilfrid Scawen
  1840-1922 . . . . DLB-19, 174

Bly, Nellie (see Cochrane, Elizabeth)

Bly, Robert 1926- DLB-5

Blyton, Enid 1897-1968 . . . . DLB-160

Boaden, James 1762-1839. . . . . . . DLB-89

Boas, Frederick S. 1862-1957 . . . . . DLB-149

The Bobbs-Merrill Archive at the
  Lilly Library, Indiana University Y-90

The Bobbs-Merrill Company. DLB-46

Bobrov, Semen Sergeevich
  1763?-1810. . . . . DLB-150

Bobrowski, Johannes 1917-1965 . . . . DLB-75

Bodenheim, Maxwell 1892-1954 . . . DLB-9, 45

Bodenstedt, Friedrich von
  1819-1892 . . . . DLB-129

Bodini, Vittorio 1914-1970 . . . . . . DLB-128

Bodkin, M. McDonnell
  1850-1933 . . . . DLB-70

Bodley Head. DLB-112

Bodmer, Johann Jakob 1698-1783 . . . . DLB-97

Bodmershof, Imma von 1895-1982 . . . DLB-85

Bodsworth, Fred 1918- DLB-68

Boehm, Sydney 1908- DLB-44

Boer, Charles 1939- DLB-5

Boethius circa 480-circa 524. . . . . . DLB-115

Boethius of Dacia circa 1240-? DLB-115

Bogan, Louise 1897-1970 . . . . DLB-45, 169

Bogarde, Dirk 1921- DLB-14

Bogdanovich, Ippolit Fedorovich
  circa 1743-1803 . . . . DLB-150

Bogue, David [publishing house] . . . DLB-106

Böhme, Jakob 1575-1624 . . . . . . DLB-164

Bohn, H. G. [publishing house] DLB-106

Bohse, August 1661-1742 . . . . . . DLB-168

Boie, Heinrich Christian
  1744-1806 . . . . DLB-94

Bok, Edward W. 1863-1930. . . DLB-91; DS-16

Boland, Eavan 1944- DLB-40

Bolingbroke, Henry St. John, Viscount
  1678-1751 . . . . DLB-101

Böll, Heinrich 1917-1985. . . . DLB-69; Y-85

Bolling, Robert 1738-1775 . . . . . . DLB-31

Bolotov, Andrei Timofeevich
  1738-1833 . . . . DLB-150

Bolt, Carol 1941- DLB-60

Bolt, Robert 1924- DLB-13

Bolton, Herbert E. 1870-1953 . . . . . DLB-17

Bonaventura DLB-90

Bonaventure circa 1217-1274 . . . . . DLB-115

Bonaviri, Giuseppe 1924- DLB-177

Bond, Edward 1934- DLB-13

Bond, Michael 1926- DLB-161

Boni, Albert and Charles
  [publishing house]. DLB-46

Boni and Liveright DLB-46

Bonner, Paul Hyde 1893-1968. . . . . DS-17

Robert Bonner's Sons. DLB-49

Bonnin, Gertrude Simmons (see Zitkala-Ša)

Bonsanti, Alessandro 1904-1984. . . . DLB-177

Bontemps, Arna 1902-1973. . . . . DLB-48, 51

The Book Arts Press at the University
  of Virginia Y-96

The Book League of America. DLB-46

Book Reviewing in America: I Y-87

Book Reviewing in America: II Y-88

Book Reviewing in America: III. Y-89

Book Reviewing in America: IV Y-90

Book Reviewing in America: V. Y-91

Book Reviewing in America: VI Y-92

Book Reviewing in America: VII Y-93

Book Reviewing in America: VIII. . . . Y-94

Book Reviewing in America and the
  Literary Scene Y-95

Book Reviewing and the
  Literary Scene Y-96, Y-97

Book Supply Company. DLB-49

The Book Trade History Group Y-93

The Booker Prize. Y-96

The Booker Prize
  Address by Anthony Thwaite,
  Chairman of the Booker Prize Judges
  Comments from Former Booker
  Prize Winners Y-86

Boorde, Andrew circa 1490-1549 . . . DLB-136

Boorstin, Daniel J. 1914- DLB-17

Booth, Mary L. 1831-1889 . . . . . . DLB-79

Booth, Franklin 1874-1948 . . . . . . DLB-188

Booth, Philip 1925- Y-82

Booth, Wayne C. 1921- DLB-67

Booth, William 1829-1912. . . . . . DLB-190

Borchardt, Rudolf 1877-1945. . . . . . DLB-66

Borchert, Wolfgang
1921-1947 . . . . DLB-69, 124

Borel, Pétrus 1809-1859 . . . . DLB-119

Borges, Jorge Luis
1899-1986 . . . . DLB-113; Y-86

Börne, Ludwig 1786-1837 . . . . DLB-90

Borrow, George
1803-1881 . . . . DLB-21, 55, 166

Bosch, Juan 1909- DLB-145

Bosco, Henri 1888-1976 . . . . DLB-72

Bosco, Monique 1927- DLB-53

Boston, Lucy M. 1892-1990. . . . . . DLB-161

Boswell, James 1740-1795 . . . . DLB-104, 142

Botev, Khristo 1847-1876 . . . . DLB-147

Bote, Hermann
circa 1460-circa 1520 . . . . DLB-179

Botta, Anne C. Lynch 1815-1891 . . . . . DLB-3

Bottome, Phyllis 1882-1963 . . . . . . DLB-197

Bottomley, Gordon 1874-1948 . . . . . DLB-10

Bottoms, David 1949- DLB-120; Y-83

Bottrall, Ronald 1906- DLB-20

Bouchardy, Joseph 1810-1870 . . . . . DLB-192

Boucher, Anthony 1911-1968 . . . . . . DLB-8

Boucher, Jonathan 1738-1804. . . . . . DLB-31

Boucher de Boucherville, George
1814-1894 . . . . DLB-99

Boudreau, Daniel (see Coste, Donat)

Bourassa, Napoléon 1827-1916 . . . . . DLB-99

Bourget, Paul 1852-1935. . . . . DLB-123

Bourinot, John George 1837-1902 . . . . DLB-99

Bourjaily, Vance 1922- DLB-2, 143

Bourne, Edward Gaylord
1860-1908 . . . . DLB-47

Bourne, Randolph 1886-1918. . . . . . DLB-63

Bousoño, Carlos 1923- DLB-108

Bousquet, Joë 1897-1950 . . . . DLB-72

Bova, Ben 1932- Y-81

Bovard, Oliver K. 1872-1945. . . . . . DLB-25

Bove, Emmanuel 1898-1945 . . . . . . DLB-72

Bowen, Elizabeth 1899-1973 . . . . DLB-15, 162

Bowen, Francis 1811-1890. . . . . . DLB-1, 59

Bowen, John 1924- DLB-13

Bowen, Marjorie 1886-1952 . . . . . . DLB-153

Bowen-Merrill Company DLB-49

Bowering, George 1935- DLB-53

Bowers, Bathsheba 1671-1718 . . . . . DLB-200

Bowers, Claude G. 1878-1958 . . . . . DLB-17

Bowers, Edgar 1924- DLB-5

Bowers, Fredson Thayer
1905-1991 . . . . DLB-140; Y-91

Bowles, Paul 1910- DLB-5, 6

Bowles, Samuel III 1826-1878 . . . . . DLB-43

Bowles, William Lisles 1762-1850 . . . . DLB-93

Bowman, Louise Morey
1882-1944 . . . . DLB-68

Boyd, James 1888-1944 . . . . . DLB-9; DS-16

Boyd, John 1919- DLB-8

Boyd, Thomas 1898-1935 . . . . . DLB-9; DS-16

Boyesen, Hjalmar Hjorth
1848-1895. . . . . DLB-12, 71; DS-13

Boyle, Kay
1902-1992 . . . . . DLB-4, 9, 48, 86; Y-93

Boyle, Roger, Earl of Orrery
1621-1679 . . . . DLB-80

Boyle, T. Coraghessan 1948- Y-86

Božić, Mirko 1919- DLB-181

Brackenbury, Alison 1953- DLB-40

Brackenridge, Hugh Henry
1748-1816. . . . . DLB-11, 37

Brackett, Charles 1892-1969 . . . . . . DLB-26

Brackett, Leigh 1915-1978 . . . . . DLB-8, 26

Bradburn, John
[publishing house]. DLB-49

Bradbury, Malcolm 1932- DLB-14

Bradbury, Ray 1920- DLB-2, 8

Bradbury and Evans. DLB-106

Braddon, Mary Elizabeth
1835-1915 . . . . DLB-18, 70, 156

Bradford, Andrew 1686-1742 . . . DLB-43, 73

Bradford, Gamaliel 1863-1932 . . . . . DLB-17

Bradford, John 1749-1830. . . . . DLB-43

Bradford, Roark 1896-1948. . . . . . . DLB-86

Bradford, William 1590-1657 . . . DLB-24, 30

Bradford, William III
1719-1791 . . . . DLB-43, 73

Bradlaugh, Charles 1833-1891 . . . . . DLB-57

Bradley, David 1950- DLB-33

Bradley, Marion Zimmer 1930- DLB-8

Bradley, William Aspenwall
1878-1939. . . . . DLB-4

Bradley, Ira, and Company DLB-49

Bradley, J. W., and Company. DLB-49

Bradshaw, Henry 1831-1886 . . . . . . DLB-184

Bradstreet, Anne
1612 or 1613-1672 . . . . DLB-24

Bradwardine, Thomas circa
1295-1349 . . . . DLB-115

Brady, Frank 1924-1986. . . . . DLB-111

Brady, Frederic A.
[publishing house]. DLB-49

Bragg, Melvyn 1939- DLB-14

Brainard, Charles H.
[publishing house]. DLB-49

Braine, John 1922-1986 . . . . . DLB-15; Y-86

Braithwait, Richard 1588-1673 . . . . . DLB-151

Braithwaite, William Stanley
1878-1962. . . . . DLB-50, 54

Braker, Ulrich 1735-1798. . . . . DLB-94

Bramah, Ernest 1868-1942 . . . . DLB-70

Branagan, Thomas 1774-1843 . . . . . DLB-37

Branch, William Blackwell
1927- DLB-76

Branden Press. DLB-46

Brant, Sebastian 1457-1521 . . . . . . DLB-179

Brassey, Lady Annie (Allnutt)
1839-1887 . . . . DLB-166

Brathwaite, Edward Kamau
1930- DLB-125

Brault, Jacques 1933- DLB-53

Braun, Volker 1939- DLB-75

Brautigan, Richard
1935-1984 . . . . . . DLB-2, 5; Y-80, Y-84

Braxton, Joanne M. 1950- DLB-41

Bray, Anne Eliza 1790-1883. . . . . . DLB-116

Bray, Thomas 1656-1730. . . . . DLB-24

Braziller, George
[publishing house] DLB-46

The Bread Loaf Writers'
Conference 1983 . . . . Y-84

The Break-Up of the Novel (1922),
by John Middleton Murry. DLB-36

Breasted, James Henry 1865-1935 . . . . DLB-47

Brecht, Bertolt 1898-1956 . . . . . DLB-56, 124

Bredel, Willi 1901-1964. . . . . DLB-56

Breitinger, Johann Jakob
1701-1776 . . . . DLB-97

Bremser, Bonnie 1939- DLB-16

Bremser, Ray 1934- DLB-16

Brentano, Bernard von
1901-1964 . . . . DLB-56

Brentano, Clemens 1778-1842 . . . . . DLB-90

Brentano's DLB-49

Brenton, Howard 1942- DLB-13

Breslin, Jimmy 1929- DLB-185

Breton, André 1896-1966. . . . . DLB-65

Breton, Nicholas
circa 1555-circa 1626 . . . . DLB-136

The Breton Lays
1300-early fifteenth century DLB-146

Brewer, Luther A. 1858-1933 . . . . . DLB-187

Brewer, Warren and Putnam DLB-46

Brewster, Elizabeth 1922- DLB-60

Bridge, Ann (Lady Mary Dolling Sanders
O'Malley) 1889-1974 . . . . DLB-191

Bridge, Horatio 1806-1893. . . . . . . DLB-183

Bridgers, Sue Ellen 1942- DLB-52

Bridges, Robert 1844-1930 . . . . . DLB-19, 98

Bridie, James 1888-1951 . . . . DLB-10

Brieux, Eugene 1858-1932 . . . . DLB-192

Bright, Mary Chavelita Dunne
(see Egerton, George)

Brimmer, B. J., Company DLB-46

Brines, Francisco 1932- DLB-134

Brinley, George, Jr. 1817-1875 . . . . . DLB-140

Brinnin, John Malcolm 1916- DLB-48

Brisbane, Albert 1809-1890 . . . . DLB-3

Brisbane, Arthur 1864-1936 . . . . . . DLB-25

British Academy DLB-112

The British Library and the Regular
Readers' Group Y-91

The British Critic 1793-1843 . . . . DLB-110

*The British Review and London
Critical Journal* 1811-1825 . . . . . . DLB-110

Brito, Aristeo 1942- DLB-122

Brittain, Vera 1893-1970 . . . . DLB-191

Broadway Publishing Company DLB-46

Broch, Hermann 1886-1951 . . . . DLB-85, 124

Brochu, André 1942- DLB-53

Brock, Edwin 1927- DLB-40

Brockes, Barthold Heinrich
1680-1747 . . . . DLB-168

Brod, Max 1884-1968 . . . . DLB-81

Brodber, Erna 1940- DLB-157

Brodhead, John R. 1814-1873 . . . . . DLB-30

Brodkey, Harold 1930- DLB-130

Brodsky, Joseph 1940-1996 . . . . Y-87

Broeg, Bob 1918- DLB-171

Brome, Richard circa 1590-1652 . . . . DLB-58

Brome, Vincent 1910- DLB-155

Bromfield, Louis 1896-1956 . . . . DLB-4, 9, 86

Bromige, David 1933- DLB-193

Broner, E. M. 1930- DLB-28

Bronk, William 1918- DLB-165

Bronnen, Arnolt 1895-1959 . . . . . . DLB-124

Brontë, Anne 1820-1849 . . . . . DLB-21, 199

Brontë, Charlotte
1816-1855 . . . . DLB-21, 159, 199

Brontë, Emily 1818-1848 . . . . DLB-21, 32, 199

Brooke, Frances 1724-1789 . . . . . DLB-39, 99

Brooke, Henry 1703?-1783 . . . . DLB-39

Brooke, L. Leslie 1862-1940 . . . . . . DLB-141

Brooke, Margaret, Ranee of Sarawak
1849-1936 . . . . DLB-174

Brooke, Rupert 1887-1915 . . . . DLB-19

Brooker, Bertram 1888-1955 . . . . . . DLB-88

Brooke-Rose, Christine 1926- DLB-14

Brookner, Anita 1928- DLB-194; Y-87

Brooks, Charles Timothy
1813-1883 . . . . DLB-1

Brooks, Cleanth 1906-1994 . . . . DLB-63; Y-94

Brooks, Gwendolyn
1917- DLB-5, 76, 165

Brooks, Jeremy 1926- DLB-14

Brooks, Mel 1926- DLB-26

Brooks, Noah 1830-1903 . . . . DLB-42; DS-13

Brooks, Richard 1912-1992 . . . . . . DLB-44

Brooks, Van Wyck
1886-1963 . . . . DLB-45, 63, 103

Brophy, Brigid 1929- DLB-14

Brophy, John 1899-1965 . . . . DLB-191

Brossard, Chandler 1922-1993 . . . . . DLB-16

Brossard, Nicole 1943- DLB-53

Broster, Dorothy Kathleen
1877-1950 . . . . DLB-160

Brother Antoninus (see Everson, William)

Brotherton, Lord 1856-1930 . . . . . . DLB-184

Brougham and Vaux, Henry Peter
Brougham, Baron
1778-1868 . . . . DLB-110, 158

Brougham, John 1810-1880 . . . . DLB-11

Broughton, James 1913- DLB-5

Broughton, Rhoda 1840-1920 . . . . . . DLB-18

Broun, Heywood 1888-1939 . . . . DLB-29, 171

Brown, Alice 1856-1948 . . . . DLB-78

Brown, Bob 1886-1959 . . . . DLB-4, 45

Brown, Cecil 1943- DLB-33

Brown, Charles Brockden
1771-1810 . . . . DLB-37, 59, 73

Brown, Christy 1932-1981 . . . . DLB-14

Brown, Dee 1908- Y-80

Brown, Frank London 1927-1962 . . . . DLB-76

Brown, Fredric 1906-1972 . . . . DLB-8

Brown, George Mackay
1921- DLB-14, 27, 139

Brown, Harry 1917-1986 . . . . DLB-26

Brown, Marcia 1918- DLB-61

Brown, Margaret Wise
1910-1952 . . . . DLB-22

Brown, Morna Doris (see Ferrars, Elizabeth)

Brown, Oliver Madox
1855-1874 . . . . DLB-21

Brown, Sterling
1901-1989 . . . . DLB-48, 51, 63

Brown, T. E. 1830-1897 . . . . DLB-35

Brown, William Hill 1765-1793 . . . . DLB-37

Brown, William Wells
1814-1884 . . . . DLB-3, 50, 183

Browne, Charles Farrar
1834-1867 . . . . DLB-11

Browne, Frances 1816-1879 . . . . . . DLB-199

Browne, Francis Fisher
1843-1913 . . . . DLB-79

Browne, Michael Dennis
1940- DLB-40

Browne, Sir Thomas 1605-1682 . . . . DLB-151

Browne, William, of Tavistock
1590-1645 . . . . DLB-121

Browne, Wynyard 1911-1964 . . . . . . DLB-13

Browne and Nolan DLB-106

Brownell, W. C. 1851-1928 . . . . DLB-71

Browning, Elizabeth Barrett
1806-1861 . . . . DLB-32, 199

Browning, Robert
1812-1889 . . . . DLB-32, 163

Brownjohn, Allan 1931- DLB-40

Brownson, Orestes Augustus
1803-1876 . . . . DLB-1, 59, 73

Bruccoli, Matthew J. 1931- DLB-103

Bruce, Charles 1906-1971 . . . . DLB-68

Bruce, Leo 1903-1979 . . . . DLB-77

Bruce, Philip Alexander
1856-1933 . . . . DLB-47

Bruce Humphries
[publishing house] DLB-46

Bruce-Novoa, Juan 1944- DLB-82

Bruckman, Clyde 1894-1955 . . . . . . DLB-26

Bruckner, Ferdinand 1891-1958 . . . . DLB-118

Brundage, John Herbert (see Herbert, John)

Brutus, Dennis 1924- DLB-117

Bryan, C. D. B. 1936- DLB-185

Bryant, Arthur 1899-1985 . . . . DLB-149

Bryant, William Cullen
1794-1878 . . . . DLB-3, 43, 59, 189

Bryce Echenique, Alfredo
1939- DLB-145

Bryce, James 1838-1922 . . . . . . DLB-166, 190

Brydges, Sir Samuel Egerton
1762-1837 . . . . DLB-107

Bryskett, Lodowick 1546?-1612 . . . . . DLB-167

Buchan, John 1875-1940 . . . . DLB-34, 70, 156

Buchanan, George 1506-1582 . . . . . . DLB-132

Buchanan, Robert 1841-1901 . . . . DLB-18, 35

Buchman, Sidney 1902-1975 . . . . . . DLB-26

Buchner, Augustus 1591-1661 . . . . . DLB-164

Büchner, Georg 1813-1837 . . . . DLB-133

Bucholtz, Andreas Heinrich
1607-1671 . . . . DLB-168

Buck, Pearl S. 1892-1973 . . . . . . DLB-9, 102

Bucke, Charles 1781-1846 . . . . DLB-110

Bucke, Richard Maurice
1837-1902 . . . . DLB-99

Buckingham, Joseph Tinker 1779-1861 and
Buckingham, Edwin
1810-1833 . . . . DLB-73

Buckler, Ernest 1908-1984 . . . . DLB-68

Buckley, William F., Jr.
1925- DLB-137; Y-80

Buckminster, Joseph Stevens
1784-1812 . . . . DLB-37

Buckner, Robert 1906- DLB-26

Budd, Thomas ?-1698 . . . . DLB-24

Budrys, A. J. 1931- DLB-8

Buechner, Frederick 1926- Y-80

Buell, John 1927- DLB-53

Bufalino, Gesualdo 1920-1996 . . . . . DLB-196

Buffum, Job [publishing house] DLB-49

Bugnet, Georges 1879-1981 . . . . DLB-92

Buies, Arthur 1840-1901 . . . . DLB-99

Building the New British Library
    at St Pancras Y-94

Bukowski, Charles
    1920-1994 . . . . DLB-5, 130, 169

Bulatović, Miodrag 1930-1991 . . . . . DLB-181

Bulgarin, Faddei Venediktovich
    1789-1859 . . . . DLB-198

Bulger, Bozeman 1877-1932 . . . . . . DLB-171

Bullein, William
    between 1520 and 1530-1576 . . . . DLB-167

Bullins, Ed 1935- DLB-7, 38

Bulwer-Lytton, Edward (also Edward Bulwer)
    1803-1873 . . . . DLB-21

Bumpus, Jerry 1937- Y-81

Bunce and Brother DLB-49

Bunner, H. C. 1855-1896 . . . . . DLB-78, 79

Bunting, Basil 1900-1985 . . . . DLB-20

Buntline, Ned (Edward Zane Carroll Judson)
    1821-1886 . . . . DLB-186

Bunyan, John 1628-1688 . . . . DLB-39

Burch, Robert 1925- DLB-52

Burciaga, José Antonio 1940- DLB-82

Bürger, Gottfried August
    1747-1794 . . . . DLB-94

Burgess, Anthony 1917-1993 . . . . DLB-14, 194

Burgess, Gelett 1866-1951 . . . . DLB-11

Burgess, John W. 1844-1931 . . . . . . DLB-47

Burgess, Thornton W.
    1874-1965 . . . . DLB-22

Burgess, Stringer and Company DLB-49

Burick, Si 1909-1986 . . . . DLB-171

Burk, John Daly circa 1772-1808 . . . . DLB-37

Burke, Edmund 1729?-1797 . . . . . . DLB-104

Burke, Kenneth 1897-1993 . . . . . DLB-45, 63

Burke, Thomas 1886-1945 . . . . DLB-197

Burlingame, Edward Livermore
    1848-1922 . . . . DLB-79

Burnet, Gilbert 1643-1715 . . . . DLB-101

Burnett, Frances Hodgson
    1849-1924 . . . . . DLB-42, 141; DS-13, 14

Burnett, W. R. 1899-1982 . . . . DLB-9

Burnett, Whit 1899-1973 and
    Martha Foley 1897-1977 . . . . . DLB-137

Burney, Fanny 1752-1840 . . . . DLB-39

Burns, Alan 1929- DLB-14, 194

Burns, John Horne 1916-1953 . . . . Y-85

Burns, Robert 1759-1796 . . . . DLB-109

Burns and Oates DLB-106

Burnshaw, Stanley 1906- DLB-48

Burr, C. Chauncey 1815?-1883 . . . . DLB-79

Burr, Esther Edwards 1732-1758 . . . DLB-200

Burroughs, Edgar Rice 1875-1950 . . . . DLB-8

Burroughs, John 1837-1921 . . . . . . DLB-64

Burroughs, Margaret T. G.
    1917- DLB-41

Burroughs, William S., Jr.
    1947-1981 . . . . DLB-16

Burroughs, William Seward
    1914- DLB-2, 8, 16, 152; Y-81, Y-97

Burroway, Janet 1936- DLB-6

Burt, Maxwell Struthers
    1882-1954 . . . . DLB-86; DS-16

Burt, A. L., and Company DLB-49

Burton, Hester 1913- DLB-161

Burton, Isabel Arundell
    1831-1896 . . . . DLB-166

Burton, Miles (see Rhode, John)

Burton, Richard Francis
    1821-1890 . . . . DLB-55, 166, 184

Burton, Robert 1577-1640 . . . . DLB-151

Burton, Virginia Lee 1909-1968 . . . . . DLB-22

Burton, William Evans
    1804-1860 . . . . DLB-73

Burwell, Adam Hood 1790-1849 . . . . . DLB-99

Bury, Lady Charlotte
    1775-1861 . . . . DLB-116

Busch, Frederick 1941- DLB-6

Busch, Niven 1903-1991 . . . . DLB-44

Bushnell, Horace 1802-1876 . . . . . . DS-13

Bussieres, Arthur de 1877-1913 . . . . DLB-92

Butler, Josephine Elizabeth
    1828-1906 . . . . DLB-190

Butler, Juan 1942-1981 . . . . DLB-53

Butler, Octavia E. 1947- DLB-33

Butler, Pierce 1884-1953 . . . . DLB-187

Butler, Robert Olen 1945- DLB-173

Butler, Samuel 1613-1680 . . . . DLB-101, 126

Butler, Samuel 1835-1902 . . . DLB-18, 57, 174

Butler, William Francis
    1838-1910 . . . . DLB-166

Butler, E. H., and Company DLB-49

Butor, Michel 1926- DLB-83

Butter, Nathaniel
    [publishing house] DLB-170

Butterworth, Hezekiah 1839-1905 . . . DLB-42

Buttitta, Ignazio 1899- DLB-114

Buzzati, Dino 1906-1972 . . . . DLB-177

Byars, Betsy 1928- DLB-52

Byatt, A. S. 1936- DLB-14, 194

Byles, Mather 1707-1788 . . . . DLB-24

Bynneman, Henry
    [publishing house] DLB-170

Bynner, Witter 1881-1968 . . . . DLB-54

Byrd, William circa 1543-1623 . . . . DLB-172

Byrd, William II 1674-1744 . . . . DLB-24, 140

Byrne, John Keyes (see Leonard, Hugh)

Byron, George Gordon, Lord
    1788-1824 . . . . DLB-96, 110

Byron, Robert 1905-1941 . . . . DLB-195

C

Caballero Bonald, José Manuel
    1926- DLB-108

Cabañero, Eladio 1930- DLB-134

Cabell, James Branch
    1879-1958 . . . . DLB-9, 78

Cabeza de Baca, Manuel
    1853-1915 . . . . DLB-122

Cabeza de Baca Gilbert, Fabiola
    1898- DLB-122

Cable, George Washington
    1844-1925 . . . . DLB-12, 74; DS-13

Cable, Mildred 1878-1952 . . . . DLB-195

Cabrera, Lydia 1900-1991 . . . . DLB-145

Cabrera Infante, Guillermo
    1929- DLB-113

Cadell [publishing house] DLB-154

Cady, Edwin H. 1917- DLB-103

Caedmon flourished 658-680 . . . . . DLB-146

Caedmon School circa 660-899 . . . . DLB-146

Cafés, Brasseries, and Bistros DS-15

Cage, John 1912-1992 . . . . DLB-193

Cahan, Abraham
    1860-1951 . . . . DLB-9, 25, 28

Cain, George 1943- DLB-33

Caird, Mona 1854-1932 . . . . DLB-197

Caldecott, Randolph 1846-1886 . . . . DLB-163

Calder, John
    (Publishers), Limited DLB-112

Calderón de la Barca, Fanny
    1804-1882 . . . . DLB-183

Caldwell, Ben 1937- DLB-38

Caldwell, Erskine 1903-1987 . . . . DLB-9, 86

Caldwell, H. M., Company DLB-49

Caldwell, Taylor 1900-1985 . . . . . . DS-17

Calhoun, John C. 1782-1850 . . . . . . DLB-3

Calisher, Hortense 1911- DLB-2

A Call to Letters and an Invitation
    to the Electric Chair,
    by Siegfried Mandel DLB-75

Callaghan, Morley 1903-1990 . . . . . DLB-68

Callahan, S. Alice 1868-1894 . . . . . DLB-175

Callaloo Y-87

Callimachus circa 305 B.C.-240 B.C.
. . . . DLB-176

Calmer, Edgar 1907- DLB-4

Calverley, C. S. 1831-1884. . . . . . . DLB-35

Calvert, George Henry
1803-1889 . . . . DLB-1, 64

Calvino, Italo 1923-1985. . . . . DLB-196

Cambridge Press DLB-49

Cambridge Songs (Carmina Cantabrigensia)
circa 1050 . . . . DLB-148

Cambridge University Press. DLB-170

Camden, William 1551-1623 . . . . . DLB-172

Camden House: An Interview with
James Hardin. Y-92

Cameron, Eleanor 1912- DLB-52

Cameron, George Frederick
1854-1885 . . . . DLB-99

Cameron, Lucy Lyttelton
1781-1858 . . . . DLB-163

Cameron, William Bleasdell
1862-1951 . . . . DLB-99

Camm, John 1718-1778. . . . . DLB-31

Camon, Ferdinando 1935- DLB-196

Campana, Dino 1885-1932 . . . . . . DLB-114

Campbell, Gabrielle Margaret Vere
(see Shearing, Joseph, and Bowen, Marjorie)

Campbell, James Dykes
1838-1895 . . . . DLB-144

Campbell, James Edwin
1867-1896 . . . . DLB-50

Campbell, John 1653-1728 . . . . . . DLB-43

Campbell, John W., Jr.
1910-1971 . . . . DLB-8

Campbell, Roy 1901-1957 . . . . DLB-20

Campbell, Thomas
1777-1844 . . . . DLB-93, 144

Campbell, William Wilfred
1858-1918 . . . . DLB-92

Campion, Edmund 1539-1581 . . . . . DLB-167

Campion, Thomas
1567-1620 . . . . DLB-58, 172

Camus, Albert 1913-1960. . . . . . . DLB-72

The Canadian Publishers' Records
Database Y-96

Canby, Henry Seidel 1878-1961 . . . . DLB-91

Candelaria, Cordelia 1943- DLB-82

Candelaria, Nash 1928- DLB-82

Candour in English Fiction (1890),
by Thomas Hardy DLB-18

Canetti, Elias 1905-1994. . . . . . DLB-85, 124

Canham, Erwin Dain
1904-1982 . . . . DLB-127

Canitz, Friedrich Rudolph Ludwig von
1654-1699 . . . . DLB-168

Cankar, Ivan 1876-1918. . . . . DLB-147

Cannan, Gilbert 1884-1955 . . . . . DLB-10, 197

Cannan, Joanna 1896-1961 . . . . . . DLB-191

Cannell, Kathleen 1891-1974. . . . . . DLB-4

Cannell, Skipwith 1887-1957 . . . . . DLB-45

Canning, George 1770-1827. . . . . . DLB-158

Cannon, Jimmy 1910-1973 . . . . . . DLB-171

Cantwell, Robert 1908-1978 . . . . . . DLB-9

Cape, Jonathan, and Harrison Smith
[publishing house]. DLB-46

Cape, Jonathan, Limited. DLB-112

Capen, Joseph 1658-1725 . . . . DLB-24

Capes, Bernard 1854-1918. . . . . . . DLB-156

Capote, Truman
1924-1984 . . . . . DLB-2, 185; Y-80, Y-84

Caproni, Giorgio 1912-1990. . . . . . DLB-128

Cardarelli, Vincenzo 1887-1959 . . . . DLB-114

Cárdenas, Reyes 1948- DLB-122

Cardinal, Marie 1929- DLB-83

Carew, Jan 1920- DLB-157

Carew, Thomas
1594 or 1595-1640 . . . . DLB-126

Carey, Henry
circa 1687-1689-1743 . . . . DLB-84

Carey, Mathew 1760-1839 . . . . . DLB-37, 73

Carey and Hart. DLB-49

Carey, M., and Company DLB-49

Carlell, Lodowick 1602-1675 . . . . . DLB-58

Carleton, William 1794-1869 . . . . . DLB-159

Carleton, G. W.
[publishing house]. DLB-49

Carlile, Richard 1790-1843 . . . . DLB-110, 158

Carlyle, Jane Welsh 1801-1866. . . . . DLB-55

Carlyle, Thomas 1795-1881. . . . . DLB-55, 144

Carman, Bliss 1861-1929 . . . . DLB-92

Carmina Burana circa 1230 . . . . . . DLB-138

Carnero, Guillermo 1947- DLB-108

Carossa, Hans 1878-1956. . . . . . . DLB-66

Carpenter, Humphrey 1946- DLB-155

Carpenter, Stephen Cullen ?-1820? . . . DLB-73

Carpentier, Alejo 1904-1980. . . . . . DLB-113

Carrier, Roch 1937- DLB-53

Carrillo, Adolfo 1855-1926 . . . . . . DLB-122

Carroll, Gladys Hasty 1904- DLB-9

Carroll, John 1735-1815 . . . . DLB-37

Carroll, John 1809-1884 . . . . DLB-99

Carroll, Lewis
1832-1898 . . . . DLB-18, 163, 178

Carroll, Paul 1927- DLB-16

Carroll, Paul Vincent 1900-1968. . . . DLB-10

Carroll and Graf Publishers DLB-46

Carruth, Hayden 1921- DLB-5, 165

Carryl, Charles E. 1841-1920 . . . . . DLB-42

Carson, Anne 1950- DLB-193

Carswell, Catherine 1879-1946 . . . . . DLB-36

Carter, Angela 1940-1992. . . . . . . DLB-14

Carter, Elizabeth 1717-1806 . . . . . . DLB-109

Carter, Henry (see Leslie, Frank)

Carter, Hodding, Jr. 1907-1972 . . . . DLB-127

Carter, Landon 1710-1778 . . . . . . DLB-31

Carter, Lin 1930- Y-81

Carter, Martin 1927- DLB-117

Carter and Hendee DLB-49

Carter, Robert, and Brothers. DLB-49

Cartwright, John 1740-1824 . . . . . . DLB-158

Cartwright, William circa
1611-1643 . . . . DLB-126

Caruthers, William Alexander
1802-1846. . . . . DLB-3

Carver, Jonathan 1710-1780 . . . . . . DLB-31

Carver, Raymond
1938-1988. . . . . . DLB-130; Y-84, Y-88

Cary, Joyce 1888-1957 . . . . . . DLB-15, 100

Cary, Patrick 1623?-1657 . . . . DLB-131

Casey, Juanita 1925- DLB-14

Casey, Michael 1947- DLB-5

Cassady, Carolyn 1923- DLB-16

Cassady, Neal 1926-1968 . . . . DLB-16

Cassell and Company DLB-106

Cassell Publishing Company DLB-49

Cassill, R. V. 1919- DLB-6

Cassity, Turner 1929- DLB-105

Cassius Dio circa 155/164-post 229
. . . . DLB-176

Cassola, Carlo 1917-1987 . . . . DLB-177

The Castle of Perseverance
circa 1400-1425 . . . . DLB-146

Castellano, Olivia 1944- DLB-122

Castellanos, Rosario 1925-1974 . . . . DLB-113

Castillo, Ana 1953- DLB-122

Castlemon, Harry (see Fosdick, Charles Austin)

Čašule, Kole 1921- DLB-181

Caswall, Edward 1814-1878 . . . . . . DLB-32

Catacalos, Rosemary 1944- DLB-122

Cather, Willa
1873-1947. . . . . . . DLB-9, 54, 78; DS-1

Catherine II (Ekaterina Alekseevna), "The
Great," Empress of Russia
1729-1796 . . . . DLB-150

Catherwood, Mary Hartwell
1847-1902 . . . . DLB-78

Catledge, Turner 1901-1983. . . . . . DLB-127

Catlin, George 1796-1872 . . . . . DLB-186, 189

Cattafi, Bartolo 1922-1979. . . . . . . DLB-128

Catton, Bruce 1899-1978 . . . . DLB-17

Causley, Charles 1917- DLB-27

Caute, David 1936- DLB-14

Cavendish, Duchess of Newcastle,
    Margaret Lucas 1623-1673 . . . . DLB-131

Cawein, Madison 1865-1914 . . . . . . DLB-54

The Caxton Printers, Limited DLB-46

Caxton, William
    [publishing house] DLB-170

Cayrol, Jean 1911- DLB-83

Cecil, Lord David 1902-1986 . . . . . DLB-155

Cela, Camilo José 1916- Y-89

Celan, Paul 1920-1970 . . . . DLB-69

Celati, Gianni 1937- DLB-196

Celaya, Gabriel 1911-1991 . . . . DLB-108

Céline, Louis-Ferdinand
    1894-1961 . . . . DLB-72

The Celtic Background to Medieval English
    Literature DLB-146

Celtis, Conrad 1459-1508 . . . . DLB-179

Center for Bibliographical Studies and
    Research at the University of
    California, Riverside Y-91

The Center for the Book in the Library
    of Congress Y-93

Center for the Book Research Y-84

Centlivre, Susanna 1669?-1723 . . . . . DLB-84

The Century Company DLB-49

Cernuda, Luis 1902-1963 . . . . DLB-134

"Certain Gifts," by Betty Adcock DLB-105

Cervantes, Lorna Dee 1954- DLB-82

Chaadaev, Petr Iakovlevich
    1794-1856 . . . . DLB-198

Chacel, Rosa 1898- DLB-134

Chacón, Eusebio 1869-1948 . . . . . . DLB-82

Chacón, Felipe Maximiliano
    1873-? DLB-82

Chadwyck-Healey's Full-Text Literary Data-bases:
    Editing Commercial Databases of
    Primary Literary Texts Y-95

Challans, Eileen Mary (see Renault, Mary)

Chalmers, George 1742-1825 . . . . . . DLB-30

Chaloner, Sir Thomas
    1520-1565 . . . . DLB-167

Chamberlain, Samuel S.
    1851-1916 . . . . DLB-25

Chamberland, Paul 1939- DLB-60

Chamberlin, William Henry
    1897-1969 . . . . DLB-29

Chambers, Charles Haddon
    1860-1921 . . . . DLB-10

Chambers, W. and R.
    [publishing house] DLB-106

Chamisso, Albert von
    1781-1838 . . . . DLB-90

Champfleury 1821-1889 . . . . DLB-119

Chandler, Harry 1864-1944 . . . . . . DLB-29

Chandler, Norman 1899-1973 . . . . . DLB-127

Chandler, Otis 1927- DLB-127

Chandler, Raymond 1888-1959 . . . . . DS-6

Channing, Edward 1856-1931 . . . . . DLB-17

Channing, Edward Tyrrell
    1790-1856 . . . . DLB-1, 59

Channing, William Ellery
    1780-1842 . . . . DLB-1, 59

Channing, William Ellery, II
    1817-1901 . . . . DLB-1

Channing, William Henry
    1810-1884 . . . . DLB-1, 59

Chaplin, Charlie 1889-1977 . . . . . . DLB-44

Chapman, George
    1559 or 1560 - 1634 . . . . . DLB-62, 121

Chapman, John DLB-106

Chapman, Olive Murray
    1892-1977 . . . . DLB-195

Chapman, William 1850-1917 . . . . . DLB-99

Chapman and Hall DLB-106

Chappell, Fred 1936- DLB-6, 105

Charbonneau, Jean 1875-1960 . . . . . DLB-92

Charbonneau, Robert 1911-1967 . . . . DLB-68

Charles, Gerda 1914- DLB-14

Charles, William
    [publishing house] DLB-49

The Charles Wood Affair:
    A Playwright Revived Y-83

Charlotte Forten: Pages from
    her Diary DLB-50

Charteris, Leslie 1907-1993 . . . . . . DLB-77

Charyn, Jerome 1937- Y-83

Chase, Borden 1900-1971 . . . . DLB-26

Chase, Edna Woolman
    1877-1957 . . . . DLB-91

Chase-Riboud, Barbara 1936- DLB-33

Chateaubriand, François-René de
    1768-1848 . . . . DLB-119

Chatterton, Thomas 1752-1770 . . . . DLB-109

Chatto and Windus DLB-106

Chatwin, Bruce 1940-1989 . . . . . . DLB-194

Chaucer, Geoffrey 1340?-1400 . . . . . DLB-146

Chauncy, Charles 1705-1787 . . . . . . DLB-24

Chauveau, Pierre-Joseph-Olivier
    1820-1890 . . . . DLB-99

Chávez, Denise 1948- DLB-122

Chávez, Fray Angélico 1910- DLB-82

Chayefsky, Paddy
    1923-1981 . . . . DLB-7, 44; Y-81

Cheesman, Evelyn 1881-1969 . . . . . DLB-195

Cheever, Ezekiel 1615-1708 . . . . . . DLB-24

Cheever, George Barrell
    1807-1890 . . . . DLB-59

Cheever, John
    1912-1982 . . . . . DLB-2, 102; Y-80, Y-82

Cheever, Susan 1943- Y-82

Cheke, Sir John 1514-1557 . . . . . . DLB-132

Chelsea House DLB-46

Cheney, Ednah Dow (Littlehale)
    1824-1904 . . . . DLB-1

Cheney, Harriet Vaughn
    1796-1889 . . . . DLB-99

Chénier, Marie-Joseph 1764-1811 . . . . DLB-192

Cherry, Kelly 1940- Y-83

Cherryh, C. J. 1942- Y-80

Chesnutt, Charles Waddell
    1858-1932 . . . . DLB-12, 50, 78

Chesney, Sir George Tomkyns
    1830-1895 . . . . DLB-190

Chester, Alfred 1928-1971 . . . . DLB-130

Chester, George Randolph
    1869-1924 . . . . DLB-78

The Chester Plays circa 1505-1532;
    revisions until 1575 . . . . DLB-146

Chesterfield, Philip Dormer Stanhope,
    Fourth Earl of 1694-1773 . . . . . . DLB-104

Chesterton, G. K. 1874-1936
    . . . . . DLB-10, 19, 34, 70, 98, 149, 178

Chettle, Henry
    circa 1560-circa 1607 . . . . DLB-136

Chew, Ada Nield 1870-1945 . . . . . . DLB-135

Cheyney, Edward P. 1861-1947 . . . . . DLB-47

Chiara, Piero 1913-1986 . . . . DLB-177

Chicano History DLB-82

Chicano Language DLB-82

Child, Francis James
    1825-1896 . . . . DLB-1, 64

Child, Lydia Maria
    1802-1880 . . . . DLB-1, 74

Child, Philip 1898-1978 . . . . DLB-68

Childers, Erskine 1870-1922 . . . . . . DLB-70

Children's Book Awards
    and Prizes DLB-61

Children's Illustrators,
    1800-1880 . . . . DLB-163

Childress, Alice 1920-1994 . . . . . . DLB-7, 38

Childs, George W. 1829-1894 . . . . . DLB-23

Chilton Book Company DLB-46

Chinweizu 1943- DLB-157

Chitham, Edward 1932- DLB-155

Chittenden, Hiram Martin
    1858-1917 . . . . DLB-47

Chivers, Thomas Holley
    1809-1858 . . . . DLB-3

Cholmondeley, Mary 1859-1925 . . . . DLB-197

Chopin, Kate 1850-1904 . . . . DLB-12, 78

Chopin, Rene 1885-1953 . . . . DLB-92

Choquette, Adrienne 1915-1973 . . . . DLB-68

Choquette, Robert 1905- DLB-68

The Christian Publishing
    Company DLB-49

Christie, Agatha 1890-1976. . . . . DLB-13, 77

Christus und die Samariterin
circa 950 . . . . DLB-148

Christy, Howard Chandler 1873-1952 . DLB-188

Chulkov, Mikhail Dmitrievich
1743?-1792 . . . . DLB-150

Church, Benjamin 1734-1778 . . . . . . DLB-31

Church, Francis Pharcellus
1839-1906 . . . . DLB-79

Church, Richard 1893-1972 . . . . DLB-191

Church, William Conant
1836-1917 . . . . DLB-79

Churchill, Caryl 1938- DLB-13

Churchill, Charles
1731-1764 . . . . DLB-109

Churchill, Sir Winston
1874-1965 . . . . DLB-100; DS-16

Churchyard, Thomas
1520?-1604 . . . . DLB-132

Churton, E., and Company DLB-106

Chute, Marchette 1909-1994 . . . . . DLB-103

Ciardi, John 1916-1986 . . . . DLB-5; Y-86

Cibber, Colley 1671-1757 . . . . DLB-84

Cima, Annalisa 1941- DLB-128

Čingo, Živko 1935-1987 . . . . DLB-181

Cirese, Eugenio 1884-1955 . . . . . . DLB-114

Cisneros, Sandra 1954- DLB-122, 152

City Lights Books DLB-46

Cixous, Hélène 1937- DLB-83

Clampitt, Amy 1920-1994 . . . . DLB-105

Clapper, Raymond 1892-1944 . . . . . DLB-29

Clare, John 1793-1864 . . . . DLB-55, 96

Clarendon, Edward Hyde, Earl of
1609-1674 . . . . DLB-101

Clark, Alfred Alexander Gordon
(see Hare, Cyril)

Clark, Ann Nolan 1896- DLB-52

Clark, C. E. Frazer Jr. 1925- DLB-187

Clark, C. M., Publishing
Company DLB-46

Clark, Catherine Anthony
1892-1977 . . . . DLB-68

Clark, Charles Heber
1841-1915 . . . . DLB-11

Clark, Davis Wasgatt 1812-1871 . . . . DLB-79

Clark, Eleanor 1913- DLB-6

Clark, J. P. 1935- DLB-117

Clark, Lewis Gaylord
1808-1873 . . . . DLB-3, 64, 73

Clark, Walter Van Tilburg
1909-1971 . . . . DLB-9

Clark, William (see Lewis, Meriwether)

Clark, William Andrews Jr.
1877-1934 . . . . DLB-187

Clarke, Austin 1896-1974 . . . . . DLB-10, 20

Clarke, Austin C. 1934- DLB-53, 125

Clarke, Gillian 1937- DLB-40

Clarke, James Freeman
1810-1888 . . . . DLB-1, 59

Clarke, Pauline 1921- DLB-161

Clarke, Rebecca Sophia
1833-1906 . . . . DLB-42

Clarke, Robert, and Company DLB-49

Clarkson, Thomas 1760-1846 . . . . . DLB-158

Claudel, Paul 1868-1955 . . . . DLB-192

Claudius, Matthias 1740-1815 . . . . . DLB-97

Clausen, Andy 1943- DLB-16

Clawson, John L. 1865-1933 . . . . . DLB-187

Claxton, Remsen and
Haffelfinger DLB-49

Clay, Cassius Marcellus
1810-1903 . . . . DLB-43

Cleary, Beverly 1916- DLB-52

Cleaver, Vera 1919- and
Cleaver, Bill 1920-1981 . . . . DLB-52

Cleland, John 1710-1789 . . . . DLB-39

Clemens, Samuel Langhorne (Mark Twain) 1835-1910
. . . . . DLB-11, 12, 23, 64, 74, 186, 189

Clement, Hal 1922- DLB-8

Clemo, Jack 1916- DLB-27

Clephane, Elizabeth Cecilia
1830-1869 . . . . DLB-199

Cleveland, John 1613-1658 . . . . . DLB-126

Cliff, Michelle 1946- DLB-157

Clifford, Lady Anne 1590-1676 . . . . DLB-151

Clifford, James L. 1901-1978 . . . . . DLB-103

Clifford, Lucy 1853?-1929 . . . DLB-135, 141, 197

Clifton, Lucille 1936- DLB-5, 41

Clines, Francis X. 1938- DLB-185

Clive, Caroline (V) 1801-1873 . . . . DLB-199

Clode, Edward J.
[publishing house] DLB-46

Clough, Arthur Hugh 1819-1861 . . . DLB-32

Cloutier, Cécile 1930- DLB-60

Clutton-Brock, Arthur
1868-1924 . . . . DLB-98

Coates, Robert M.
1897-1973 . . . . DLB-4, 9, 102

Coatsworth, Elizabeth 1893- DLB-22

Cobb, Charles E., Jr. 1943- DLB-41

Cobb, Frank I. 1869-1923 . . . . DLB-25

Cobb, Irvin S.
1876-1944 . . . . DLB-11, 25, 86

Cobbe, Frances Power 1822-1904 . . . DLB-190

Cobbett, William 1763-1835 . . . . DLB-43, 107

Cobbledick, Gordon 1898-1969 . . . . DLB-171

Cochran, Thomas C. 1902- DLB-17

Cochrane, Elizabeth 1867-1922 . . . DLB-25, 189

Cockerill, John A. 1845-1896 . . . . . DLB-23

Cocteau, Jean 1889-1963 . . . . DLB-65

Coderre, Emile (see Jean Narrache)

Coffee, Lenore J. 1900?-1984 . . . . . DLB-44

Coffin, Robert P. Tristram
1892-1955 . . . . DLB-45

Cogswell, Fred 1917- DLB-60

Cogswell, Mason Fitch
1761-1830 . . . . DLB-37

Cohen, Arthur A. 1928-1986 . . . . . DLB-28

Cohen, Leonard 1934- DLB-53

Cohen, Matt 1942- DLB-53

Colden, Cadwallader
1688-1776 . . . . DLB-24, 30

Colden, Jane 1724-1766 . . . . DLB-200

Cole, Barry 1936- DLB-14

Cole, George Watson
1850-1939 . . . . DLB-140

Colegate, Isabel 1931- DLB-14

Coleman, Emily Holmes
1899-1974 . . . . DLB-4

Coleman, Wanda 1946- DLB-130

Coleridge, Hartley 1796-1849 . . . . . DLB-96

Coleridge, Mary 1861-1907 . . . . DLB-19, 98

Coleridge, Samuel Taylor
1772-1834 . . . . DLB-93, 107

Coleridge, Sara 1802-1852 . . . . . . DLB-199

Colet, John 1467-1519 . . . . DLB-132

Colette 1873-1954 . . . . DLB-65

Colette, Sidonie Gabrielle (see Colette)

Colinas, Antonio 1946- DLB-134

Coll, Joseph Clement 1881-1921 . . . DLB-188

Collier, John 1901-1980 . . . . DLB-77

Collier, John Payne 1789-1883 . . . . DLB-184

Collier, Mary 1690-1762 . . . . DLB-95

Collier, Robert J. 1876-1918 . . . . . DLB-91

Collier, P. F. [publishing house] DLB-49

Collin and Small DLB-49

Collingwood, W. G. 1854-1932 . . . . DLB-149

Collins, An floruit circa 1653 . . . . . DLB-131

Collins, Merle 1950- DLB-157

Collins, Mortimer 1827-1876 . . . . DLB-21, 35

Collins, Wilkie 1824-1889 . . . DLB-18, 70, 159

Collins, William 1721-1759 . . . . . DLB-109

Collins, William, Sons and
Company DLB-154

Collins, Isaac [publishing house] . . . DLB-49

Collis, Maurice 1889-1973 . . . . . . DLB-195

Collyer, Mary 1716?-1763? DLB-39

Colman, Benjamin 1673-1747 . . . . . DLB-24

Colman, George, the Elder
1732-1794 . . . . DLB-89

Colman, George, the Younger
1762-1836 . . . . DLB-89

Colman, S. [publishing house] DLB-49

Colombo, John Robert 1936- DLB-53

Colquhoun, Patrick 1745-1820 . . . . . DLB-158

Colter, Cyrus 1910- DLB-33

Colum, Padraic 1881-1972 . . . . DLB-19

Colvin, Sir Sidney 1845-1927 . . . . . DLB-149

Colwin, Laurie 1944-1992 . . . . Y-80

Comden, Betty 1919- and Green,
    Adolph 1918- DLB-44

Comi, Girolamo 1890-1968 . . . . . . DLB-114

The Comic Tradition Continued
    [in the British Novel] DLB-15

Commager, Henry Steele
    1902- DLB-17

The Commercialization of the Image of
    Revolt, by Kenneth Rexroth DLB-16

Community and Commentators: Black
    Theatre and Its Critics DLB-38

Compton-Burnett, Ivy
    1884?-1969 . . . . DLB-36

Conan, Laure 1845-1924 . . . . DLB-99

Conde, Carmen 1901- DLB-108

Conference on Modern Biography Y-85

Congreve, William
    1670-1729 . . . . DLB-39, 84

Conkey, W. B., Company DLB-49

Connell, Evan S., Jr. 1924- DLB-2; Y-81

Connelly, Marc 1890-1980 . . . . . DLB-7; Y-80

Connolly, Cyril 1903-1974 . . . . . . DLB-98

Connolly, James B. 1868-1957 . . . . . DLB-78

Connor, Ralph 1860-1937 . . . . DLB-92

Connor, Tony 1930- DLB-40

Conquest, Robert 1917- DLB-27

Conrad, Joseph
    1857-1924 . . . . DLB-10, 34, 98, 156

Conrad, John, and Company DLB-49

Conroy, Jack 1899-1990 . . . . Y-81

Conroy, Pat 1945- DLB-6

The Consolidation of Opinion: Critical
    Responses to the Modernists DLB-36

Consolo, Vincenzo 1933- DLB-196

Constable, Henry 1562-1613 . . . . . DLB-136

Constable and Company
    Limited DLB-112

Constable, Archibald, and
    Company DLB-154

Constant, Benjamin 1767-1830 . . . . . DLB-119

Constant de Rebecque, Henri-Benjamin de
    (see Constant, Benjamin)

Constantine, David 1944- DLB-40

Constantin-Weyer, Maurice
    1881-1964 . . . . DLB-92

Contempo Caravan: Kites in
    a Windstorm Y-85

A Contemporary Flourescence of Chicano
    Literature Y-84

"Contemporary Verse Story-telling,"
    by Jonathan Holden. DLB-105

The Continental Publishing
    Company DLB-49

A Conversation with Chaim Potok Y-84

Conversations with Editors. Y-95

Conversations with Publishers I: An Interview
    with Patrick O'Connor Y-84

Conversations with Publishers II: An Interview
    with Charles Scribner III Y-94

Conversations with Publishers III: An Interview
    with Donald Lamm Y-95

Conversations with Publishers IV: An Interview
    with James Laughlin Y-96

Conversations with Rare Book Dealers I: An
    Interview with Glenn Horowitz Y-90

Conversations with Rare Book Dealers II: An
    Interview with Ralph Sipper Y-94

Conversations with Rare Book Dealers
    (Publishers) III: An Interview with
    Otto Penzler Y-96

The Conversion of an Unpolitical Man,
    by W. H. Bruford DLB-66

Conway, Moncure Daniel
    1832-1907 . . . . DLB-1

Cook, Ebenezer
    circa 1667-circa 1732 . . . . DLB-24

Cook, Edward Tyas 1857-1919 . . . . . DLB-149

Cook, Eliza 1818-1889 . . . . DLB-199

Cook, Michael 1933- DLB-53

Cook, David C., Publishing
    Company DLB-49

Cooke, George Willis 1848-1923 . . . . . DLB-71

Cooke, Increase, and Company DLB-49

Cooke, John Esten 1830-1886 . . . . . . DLB-3

Cooke, Philip Pendleton
    1816-1850 . . . . DLB-3, 59

Cooke, Rose Terry
    1827-1892 . . . . DLB-12, 74

Cook-Lynn, Elizabeth 1930- DLB-175

Coolbrith, Ina 1841-1928 . . . . . DLB-54, 186

Cooley, Peter 1940- DLB-105

Coolidge, Clark 1939- DLB-193

Coolidge, Susan (see Woolsey, Sarah Chauncy)

Coolidge, George
    [publishing house] DLB-49

Cooper, Giles 1918-1966 . . . . DLB-13

Cooper, James Fenimore
    1789-1851 . . . . DLB-3, 183

Cooper, Kent 1880-1965 . . . . DLB-29

Cooper, Susan 1935- DLB-161

Cooper, William
    [publishing house] DLB-170

Coote, J. [publishing house] DLB-154

Coover, Robert 1932- DLB-2; Y-81

Copeland and Day DLB-49

Ćopić, Branko 1915-1984 . . . . DLB-181

Copland, Robert 1470?-1548 . . . . . DLB-136

Coppard, A. E. 1878-1957 . . . . DLB-162

Coppel, Alfred 1921- Y-83

Coppola, Francis Ford 1939- DLB-44

Copway, George (Kah-ge-ga-gah-bowh)
    1818-1869 . . . . DLB-175, 183

Corazzini, Sergio 1886-1907 . . . . . . DLB-114

Corbett, Richard 1582-1635 . . . . . . DLB-121

Corcoran, Barbara 1911- DLB-52

Cordelli, Franco 1943- DLB-196

Corelli, Marie 1855-1924 . . . . . DLB-34, 156

Corle, Edwin 1906-1956 . . . . Y-85

Corman, Cid 1924- DLB-5, 193

Cormier, Robert 1925- DLB-52

Corn, Alfred 1943- DLB-120; Y-80

Cornish, Sam 1935- DLB-41

Cornish, William
    circa 1465-circa 1524 . . . . DLB-132

Cornwall, Barry (see Procter, Bryan Waller)

Cornwallis, Sir William, the Younger
    circa 1579-1614 . . . . DLB-151

Cornwell, David John Moore
    (see le Carré, John)

Corpi, Lucha 1945- DLB-82

Corrington, John William 1932- DLB-6

Corrothers, James D. 1869-1917 . . . . . DLB-50

Corso, Gregory 1930- DLB-5, 16

Cortázar, Julio 1914-1984 . . . . DLB-113

Cortez, Jayne 1936- DLB-41

Corvinus, Gottlieb Siegmund
    1677-1746 . . . . DLB-168

Corvo, Baron (see Rolfe, Frederick William)

Cory, Annie Sophie (see Cross, Victoria)

Cory, William Johnson
    1823-1892 . . . . DLB-35

Coryate, Thomas
    1577?-1617 . . . . DLB-151, 172

Ćosić, Dobrica 1921- DLB-181

Cosin, John 1595-1672 . . . . DLB-151

Cosmopolitan Book Corporation DLB-46

Costain, Thomas B. 1885-1965 . . . . . . DLB-9

Coste, Donat 1912-1957 . . . . DLB-88

Costello, Louisa Stuart 1799-1870 . . . DLB-166

Cota-Cárdenas, Margarita
    1941- DLB-122

Cotten, Bruce 1873-1954 . . . . DLB-187

Cotter, Joseph Seamon, Sr.
    1861-1949 . . . . DLB-50

Cotter, Joseph Seamon, Jr.
    1895-1919 . . . . DLB-50

Cottle, Joseph [publishing house] DLB-154

Cotton, Charles 1630-1687 . . . . DLB-131

Cotton, John 1584-1652. . . . . DLB-24

Coulter, John 1888-1980 . . . . DLB-68

Cournos, John 1881-1966. . . . . DLB-54

Courteline, Georges 1858-1929 . . . . . DLB-192

Cousins, Margaret 1905- DLB-137

Cousins, Norman 1915-1990 . . . . . . DLB-137

Coventry, Francis 1725-1754 . . . . . . DLB-39

Coverdale, Miles
1487 or 1488-1569 . . . . DLB-167

Coverly, N. [publishing house]. DLB-49

Covici-Friede. DLB-46

Coward, Noel 1899-1973 . . . . DLB-10

Coward, McCann and
Geoghegan DLB-46

Cowles, Gardner 1861-1946 . . . . DLB-29

Cowles, Gardner ("Mike"), Jr.
1903-1985. . . . . DLB-127, 137

Cowley, Abraham
1618-1667. . . . . DLB-131, 151

Cowley, Hannah 1743-1809 . . . . DLB-89

Cowley, Malcolm
1898-1989. . . . . . DLB-4, 48; Y-81, Y-89

Cowper, William
1731-1800. . . . . DLB-104, 109

Cox, A. B. (see Berkeley, Anthony)

Cox, James McMahon
1903-1974 . . . . DLB-127

Cox, James Middleton
1870-1957 . . . . DLB-127

Cox, Palmer 1840-1924. . . . . DLB-42

Coxe, Louis 1918-1993. . . . . DLB-5

Coxe, Tench 1755-1824 . . . . DLB-37

Cozzens, James Gould
1903-1978. . . . . DLB-9; Y-84; DS-2

Cozzens's *Michael Scarlett* Y-97

Crabbe, George 1754-1832 . . . . DLB-93

Crackanthorpe, Hubert
1870-1896. . . . . DLB-135

Craddock, Charles Egbert
(see Murfree, Mary N.)

Cradock, Thomas 1718-1770 . . . . . . DLB-31

Craig, Daniel H. 1811-1895 . . . . DLB-43

Craik, Dinah Maria
1826-1887 . . . . DLB-35, 136

Cramer, Richard Ben 1950- DLB-185

Cranch, Christopher Pearse
1813-1892 . . . . DLB-1, 42

Crane, Hart 1899-1932 . . . . DLB-4, 48

Crane, R. S. 1886-1967. . . . . DLB-63

Crane, Stephen 1871-1900 . . . . DLB-12, 54, 78

Crane, Walter 1845-1915 . . . . DLB-163

Cranmer, Thomas 1489-1556 . . . . . . DLB-132

Crapsey, Adelaide 1878-1914 . . . . . . DLB-54

Crashaw, Richard
1612 or 1613-1649 . . . . DLB-126

Craven, Avery 1885-1980 . . . . DLB-17

Crawford, Charles
1752-circa 1815 . . . . DLB-31

Crawford, F. Marion 1854-1909 . . . . DLB-71

Crawford, Isabel Valancy
1850-1887 . . . . DLB-92

Crawley, Alan 1887-1975. . . . . DLB-68

Crayon, Geoffrey (see Irving, Washington)

Creamer, Robert W. 1922- DLB-171

Creasey, John 1908-1973 . . . . DLB-77

Creative Age Press DLB-46

Creech, William
[publishing house] DLB-154

Creede, Thomas
[publishing house] DLB-170

Creel, George 1876-1953 . . . . DLB-25

Creeley, Robert
1926- DLB-5, 16, 169; DS-17

Creelman, James 1859-1915 . . . . . . DLB-23

Cregan, David 1931- DLB-13

Creighton, Donald Grant
1902-1979 . . . . DLB-88

Cremazie, Octave 1827-1879 . . . . . . DLB-99

Crémer, Victoriano 1909?- DLB-108

Crescas, Hasdai
circa 1340-1412? DLB-115

Crespo, Angel 1926- DLB-134

Cresset Press DLB-112

Cresswell, Helen 1934- DLB-161

Crèvecoeur, Michel Guillaume Jean de
1735-1813 . . . . DLB-37

Crews, Harry 1935- DLB-6, 143, 185

Crichton, Michael 1942- Y-81

A Crisis of Culture: The Changing Role
of Religion in the New Republic
. . . . DLB-37

Crispin, Edmund 1921-1978 . . . . . . DLB-87

Cristofer, Michael 1946- DLB-7

"The Critic as Artist" (1891), by
Oscar Wilde DLB-57

"Criticism In Relation To Novels" (1863),
by G. H. Lewes DLB-21

Crnjanski, Miloš 1893-1977 . . . . . . DLB-147

Crocker, Hannah Mather 1752-1829 . . DLB-200

Crockett, David (Davy)
1786-1836. . . . . DLB-3, 11, 183

Croft-Cooke, Rupert (see Bruce, Leo)

Crofts, Freeman Wills
1879-1957 . . . . DLB-77

Croker, John Wilson
1780-1857 . . . . DLB-110

Croly, George 1780-1860 . . . . DLB-159

Croly, Herbert 1869-1930 . . . . DLB-91

Croly, Jane Cunningham
1829-1901 . . . . DLB-23

Crompton, Richmal 1890-1969 . . . . . DLB-160

Cronin, A. J. 1896-1981. . . . . DLB-191

Crosby, Caresse 1892-1970. . . . . DLB-48

Crosby, Caresse 1892-1970 and Crosby,
Harry 1898-1929. . . . . DLB-4; DS-15

Crosby, Harry 1898-1929. . . . . DLB-48

Cross, Gillian 1945- DLB-161

Cross, Victoria 1868-1952 . . . . . DLB-135, 197

Crossley-Holland, Kevin
1941- DLB-40, 161

Crothers, Rachel 1878-1958 . . . . DLB-7

Crowell, Thomas Y., Company DLB-49

Crowley, John 1942- Y-82

Crowley, Mart 1935- DLB-7

Crown Publishers DLB-46

Crowne, John 1641-1712 . . . . DLB-80

Crowninshield, Edward Augustus
1817-1859 . . . . DLB-140

Crowninshield, Frank 1872-1947 . . . . . DLB-91

Croy, Homer 1883-1965. . . . . DLB-4

Crumley, James 1939- Y-84

Cruz, Victor Hernández 1949- DLB-41

Csokor, Franz Theodor
1885-1969 . . . . DLB-81

Cuala Press. DLB-112

Cullen, Countee
1903-1946 . . . . DLB-4, 48, 51

Culler, Jonathan D. 1944- DLB-67

The Cult of Biography
Excerpts from the Second Folio Debate:
"Biographies are generally a disease of
English Literature" – Germaine Greer,
Victoria Glendinning, Auberon Waugh,
and Richard Holmes Y-86

Cumberland, Richard 1732-1811 . . . . . DLB-89

Cummings, Constance Gordon
1837-1924 . . . . DLB-174

Cummings, E. E. 1894-1962 . . . . . DLB-4, 48

Cummings, Ray 1887-1957 . . . . DLB-8

Cummings and Hilliard. DLB-49

Cummins, Maria Susanna
1827-1866 . . . . DLB-42

Cundall, Joseph
[publishing house] DLB-106

Cuney, Waring 1906-1976 . . . . DLB-51

Cuney-Hare, Maude 1874-1936 . . . . . DLB-52

Cunningham, Allan 1784-1842 . . DLB-116, 144

Cunningham, J. V. 1911- DLB-5

Cunningham, Peter F.
[publishing house]. DLB-49

Cunquiero, Alvaro 1911-1981 . . . . . . DLB-134

Cuomo, George 1929- Y-80

Cupples and Leon DLB-46

Cupples, Upham and Company DLB-49

Cuppy, Will 1884-1949 . . . . DLB-11

Curll, Edmund
[publishing house] DLB-154

Currie, James 1756-1805 . . . . DLB-142

Currie, Mary Montgomerie Lamb Singleton,
Lady Currie (see Fane, Violet)

Cursor Mundi circa 1300 . . . . DLB-146

Curti, Merle E. 1897- DLB-17

Curtis, Anthony 1926- DLB-155

Curtis, Cyrus H. K. 1850-1933 . . . . . DLB-91

Curtis, George William
1824-1892 . . . . DLB-1, 43

Curzon, Robert 1810-1873 . . . . DLB-166

Curzon, Sarah Anne
1833-1898 . . . . DLB-99

Cushing, Harvey 1869-1939 . . . . DLB-187

Cynewulf circa 770-840 . . . . DLB-146

Czepko, Daniel 1605-1660 . . . . DLB-164

D

D. M. Thomas: The Plagiarism
Controversy Y-82

Dabit, Eugène 1898-1936 . . . . DLB-65

Daborne, Robert circa 1580-1628 . . . . DLB-58

Dacey, Philip 1939- DLB-105

Dach, Simon 1605-1659 . . . . DLB-164

Daggett, Rollin M. 1831-1901 . . . . . DLB-79

D'Aguiar, Fred 1960- DLB-157

Dahl, Roald 1916-1990 . . . . DLB-139

Dahlberg, Edward 1900-1977 . . . . . . DLB-48

Dahn, Felix 1834-1912 . . . . DLB-129

Dal', Vladimir Ivanovich (Kazak Vladimir
Lugansky) 1801-1872 . . . . DLB-198

Dale, Peter 1938- DLB-40

Daley, Arthur 1904-1974 . . . . DLB-171

Dall, Caroline Wells (Healey)
1822-1912 . . . . DLB-1

Dallas, E. S. 1828-1879 . . . . DLB-55

The Dallas Theater Center DLB-7

D'Alton, Louis 1900-1951 . . . . DLB-10

Daly, T. A. 1871-1948 . . . . DLB-11

Damon, S. Foster 1893-1971 . . . . . . DLB-45

Damrell, William S.
[publishing house] DLB-49

Dana, Charles A. 1819-1897 . . . . . DLB-3, 23

Dana, Richard Henry, Jr.
1815-1882 . . . . DLB-1, 183

Dandridge, Ray Garfield DLB-51

Dane, Clemence 1887-1965 . . . . DLB-10, 197

Danforth, John 1660-1730 . . . . DLB-24

Danforth, Samuel, I 1626-1674 . . . . . DLB-24

Danforth, Samuel, II 1666-1727 . . . . . DLB-24

Dangerous Years: London Theater,
1939-1945 . . . . DLB-10

Daniel, John M. 1825-1865 . . . . DLB-43

Daniel, Samuel
1562 or 1563-1619 . . . . DLB-62

Daniel Press DLB-106

Daniells, Roy 1902-1979 . . . . DLB-68

Daniels, Jim 1956- DLB-120

Daniels, Jonathan 1902-1981 . . . . . . DLB-127

Daniels, Josephus 1862-1948 . . . . . . DLB-29

Danis Rose and the Rendering
of *Ulysses* Y-97

Dannay, Frederic 1905-1982 and
Manfred B. Lee 1905-1971 . . . . . DLB-137

Danner, Margaret Esse 1915- DLB-41

Danter, John [publishing house] DLB-170

Dantin, Louis 1865-1945 . . . . DLB-92

Danzig, Allison 1898-1987 . . . . DLB-171

D'Arcy, Ella circa 1857-1937 . . . . . . DLB-135

Darley, Felix Octavious Carr
1822-1888 . . . . DLB-188

Darley, George 1795-1846 . . . . DLB-96

Darwin, Charles 1809-1882 . . . . . DLB-57, 166

Darwin, Erasmus 1731-1802 . . . . . . DLB-93

Daryush, Elizabeth 1887-1977 . . . . . DLB-20

Dashkova, Ekaterina Romanovna
(née Vorontsova) 1743-1810 . . . . DLB-150

Dashwood, Edmée Elizabeth Monica
de la Pasture (see Delafield, E. M.)

Daudet, Alphonse 1840-1897 . . . . . . DLB-123

d'Aulaire, Edgar Parin 1898- and
d'Aulaire, Ingri 1904- DLB-22

Davenant, Sir William
1606-1668 . . . . DLB-58, 126

Davenport, Guy 1927- DLB-130

Davenport, Marcia 1903-1996 . . . . . . DS-17

Davenport, Robert ?-? DLB-58

Daves, Delmer 1904-1977 . . . . DLB-26

Davey, Frank 1940- DLB-53

Davidson, Avram 1923-1993 . . . . DLB-8

Davidson, Donald 1893-1968 . . . . . . DLB-45

Davidson, John 1857-1909 . . . . DLB-19

Davidson, Lionel 1922- DLB-14

Davidson, Sara 1943- DLB-185

Davie, Donald 1922- DLB-27

Davie, Elspeth 1919- DLB-139

Davies, Sir John 1569-1626 . . . . . . DLB-172

Davies, John, of Hereford
1565?-1618 . . . . DLB-121

Davies, Rhys 1901-1978 . . . . . DLB-139, 191

Davies, Robertson 1913- DLB-68

Davies, Samuel 1723-1761 . . . . DLB-31

Davies, Thomas 1712?-1785 . . . . DLB-142, 154

Davies, W. H. 1871-1940 . . . . . DLB-19, 174

Davies, Peter, Limited DLB-112

Daviot, Gordon 1896?-1952 . . . . DLB-10
(see also Tey, Josephine)

Davis, Charles A. 1795-1867 . . . . . . DLB-11

Davis, Clyde Brion 1894-1962 . . . . . . DLB-9

Davis, Dick 1945- DLB-40

Davis, Frank Marshall 1905-? DLB-51

Davis, H. L. 1894-1960 . . . . DLB-9

Davis, John 1774-1854 . . . . DLB-37

Davis, Lydia 1947- DLB-130

Davis, Margaret Thomson 1926- DLB-14

Davis, Ossie 1917- DLB-7, 38

Davis, Paxton 1925-1994 . . . . Y-94

Davis, Rebecca Harding
1831-1910 . . . . DLB-74

Davis, Richard Harding 1864-1916
. . . . . . DLB-12, 23, 78, 79, 189; DS-13

Davis, Samuel Cole 1764-1809 . . . . . DLB-37

Davison, Peter 1928- DLB-5

Davys, Mary 1674-1732 . . . . DLB-39

DAW Books DLB-46

Dawn Powell, Where Have You Been All
Our lives? Y-97

Dawson, Ernest 1882-1947 . . . . DLB-140

Dawson, Fielding 1930- DLB-130

Dawson, William 1704-1752 . . . . . . DLB-31

Day, Angel flourished 1586 . . . . DLB-167

Day, Benjamin Henry 1810-1889 . . . . DLB-43

Day, Clarence 1874-1935 . . . . DLB-11

Day, Dorothy 1897-1980 . . . . DLB-29

Day, Frank Parker 1881-1950 . . . . . . DLB-92

Day, John circa 1574-circa 1640 . . . . DLB-62

Day, John [publishing house] DLB-170

Day Lewis, C. 1904-1972 . . . . . DLB-15, 20
(see also Blake, Nicholas)

Day, Thomas 1748-1789 . . . . DLB-39

Day, The John, Company DLB-46

Day, Mahlon [publishing house] DLB-49

Dazai, Osamu 1909-1948 . . . . DLB-182

Deacon, William Arthur
1890-1977 . . . . DLB-68

Deal, Borden 1922-1985 . . . . DLB-6

de Angeli, Marguerite 1889-1987 . . . . . DLB-22

De Angelis, Milo 1951- DLB-128

De Bow, James Dunwoody Brownson
1820-1867 . . . . DLB-3, 79

de Bruyn, Günter 1926- DLB-75

de Camp, L. Sprague 1907- DLB-8

De Carlo, Andrea 1952- DLB-196

The Decay of Lying (1889),
by Oscar Wilde [excerpt] DLB-18

Dechert, Robert 1895-1975 . . . . . . DLB-187

Dedication, *Ferdinand Count Fathom* (1753),
by Tobias Smollett DLB-39

Dedication, *The History of Pompey the Little*
(1751), by Francis Coventry DLB-39

Dedication, *Lasselia* (1723), by Eliza
Haywood [excerpt] DLB-39

Dedication, *The Wanderer* (1814),
by Fanny Burney. DLB-39

Dee, John 1527-1609. . . . . DLB-136

Deeping, George Warwick
1877-1950 . . . . DLB 153

Defense of *Amelia* (1752), by
Henry Fielding DLB-39

Defoe, Daniel 1660-1731 . . . . DLB-39, 95, 101

de Fontaine, Felix Gregory
1834-1896 . . . . DLB-43

De Forest, John William
1826-1906 . . . . DLB-12, 189

DeFrees, Madeline 1919- DLB-105

DeGolyer, Everette Lee 1886-1956 . . . DLB-187

de Graff, Robert 1895-1981 . . . . Y-81

de Graft, Joe 1924-1978 . . . . DLB-117

De Heinrico circa 980? DLB-148

Deighton, Len 1929- DLB-87

DeJong, Meindert 1906-1991 . . . . . . DLB-52

Dekker, Thomas
circa 1572-1632 . . . . DLB-62, 172

Delacorte, Jr., George T.
1894-1991 . . . . DLB-91

Delafield, E. M. 1890-1943 . . . . . . DLB-34

Delahaye, Guy 1888-1969 . . . . DLB-92

de la Mare, Walter
1873-1956 . . . . . . DLB-19, 153, 162

Deland, Margaret 1857-1945 . . . . . . DLB-78

Delaney, Shelagh 1939- DLB-13

Delano, Amasa 1763-1823. . . . . . . DLB-183

Delany, Martin Robinson
1812-1885 . . . . DLB-50

Delany, Samuel R. 1942- DLB-8, 33

de la Roche, Mazo 1879-1961 . . . . . DLB-68

Delavigne, Jean François Casimir 1793-1843
. . . . DLB-192

Delbanco, Nicholas 1942- DLB-6

De León, Nephtalí 1945- DLB-82

Delgado, Abelardo Barrientos
1931- DLB-82

Del Giudice, Daniele 1949- DLB-196

De Libero, Libero 1906-1981 . . . . . DLB-114

DeLillo, Don 1936- DLB-6, 173

de Lisser H. G. 1878-1944 . . . . . . DLB-117

Dell, Floyd 1887-1969 . . . . DLB-9

Dell Publishing Company DLB-46

delle Grazie, Marie Eugene
1864-1931 . . . . DLB-81

Deloney, Thomas died 1600 . . . . . DLB-167

Deloria, Ella C. 1889-1971 . . . . . . DLB-175

Deloria, Vine, Jr. 1933- DLB-175

del Rey, Lester 1915-1993 . . . . DLB-8

Del Vecchio, John M. 1947- DS-9

de Man, Paul 1919-1983 . . . . DLB-67

Demby, William 1922- DLB-33

Deming, Philander 1829-1915 . . . . . DLB-74

Demorest, William Jennings
1822-1895 . . . . DLB-79

De Morgan, William 1839-1917 . . . . DLB-153

Demosthenes 384 B.C.-322 B.C. DLB-176

Denham, Henry
[publishing house] DLB-170

Denham, Sir John
1615-1669 . . . . DLB-58, 126

Denison, Merrill 1893-1975. . . . . . DLB-92

Denison, T. S., and Company. DLB-49

Dennery, Adolphe Philippe 1811-1899 . . . DLB-192

Dennie, Joseph
1768-1812 . . . . . . DLB-37, 43, 59, 73

Dennis, John 1658-1734 . . . . DLB-101

Dennis, Nigel 1912-1989 . . . . . . DLB-13, 15

Denslow, W. W. 1856-1915 . . . . . . DLB-188

Dent, Tom 1932- DLB-38

Dent, J. M., and Sons. DLB-112

Denton, Daniel circa 1626-1703 . . . . DLB-24

DePaola, Tomie 1934- DLB-61

Department of Library, Archives, and Institutional
Research, American Bible Society. . . . Y-97

De Quille, Dan 1829-1898 . . . . . . DLB-186

De Quincey, Thomas
1785-1859. . . . . DLB-110, 144

Derby, George Horatio
1823-1861 . . . . DLB-11

Derby, J. C., and Company DLB-49

Derby and Miller DLB-49

Derleth, August 1909-1971 . . . . DLB-9; DS-17

The Derrydale Press DLB-46

Derzhavin, Gavriil Romanovich
1743-1816 . . . . DLB-150

Desaulniers, Gonsalve
1863-1934 . . . . DLB-92

Desbiens, Jean-Paul 1927- DLB-53

des Forêts, Louis-Rene 1918- DLB-83

Desiato, Luca 1941- DLB-196

Desnica, Vladan 1905-1967 . . . . . . DLB-181

DesRochers, Alfred 1901-1978 . . . . . DLB-68

Desrosiers, Léo-Paul 1896-1967. . . . . DLB-68

Dessì, Giuseppe 1909-1977 . . . . . . DLB-177

Destouches, Louis-Ferdinand
(see Céline, Louis-Ferdinand)

De Tabley, Lord 1835-1895 . . . . . . DLB-35

"A Detail in a Poem,"
by Fred Chappell DLB-105

Deutsch, Babette 1895-1982. . . . . . DLB-45

Deutsch, Niklaus Manuel (see Manuel, Niklaus)

Deutsch, André, Limited DLB-112

Deveaux, Alexis 1948- DLB-38

The Development of the Author's Copyright
in Britain. DLB-154

The Development of Lighting in the Staging
of Drama, 1900-1945 . . . . DLB-10

The Development of Meiji Japan. . . . DLB-180

De Vere, Aubrey 1814-1902 . . . . . . DLB-35

Devereux, second Earl of Essex, Robert
1565-1601 . . . . DLB-136

The Devin-Adair Company DLB-46

De Vinne, Theodore Low
1828-1914 . . . . DLB-187

De Voto, Bernard 1897-1955 . . . . . . DLB-9

De Vries, Peter 1910-1993 . . . . DLB-6; Y-82

Dewdney, Christopher 1951- DLB-60

Dewdney, Selwyn 1909-1979 . . . . . DLB-68

DeWitt, Robert M., Publisher DLB-49

DeWolfe, Fiske and Company. DLB-49

Dexter, Colin 1930- DLB-87

de Young, M. H. 1849-1925. . . . . . DLB-25

Dhlomo, H. I. E. 1903-1956 . . . . . DLB-157

Dhuoda circa 803-after 843 . . . . . . DLB-148

The Dial Press DLB-46

Diamond, I. A. L. 1920-1988 . . . . . DLB-26

Dibdin, Thomas Frognall
1776-1847 . . . . DLB-184

Di Cicco, Pier Giorgio 1949- DLB-60

Dick, Philip K. 1928-1982 . . . . DLB-8

Dick and Fitzgerald DLB-49

Dickens, Charles
1812-1870 . . . . DLB-21, 55, 70, 159, 166

Dickinson, Peter 1927- DLB-161

Dickey, James 1923-1997
. . . . DLB-5, 193; Y-82, Y-93, Y-96; DS-7

Dickey, William 1928-1994 . . . . DLB-5

Dickinson, Emily 1830-1886 . . . . . . DLB-1

Dickinson, John 1732-1808 . . . . . . DLB-31

Dickinson, Jonathan 1688-1747 . . . . DLB-24

Dickinson, Patric 1914- DLB-27

Dickinson, Peter 1927- DLB-87

Dicks, John [publishing house] DLB-106

Dickson, Gordon R. 1923- DLB-8

*Dictionary of Literary Biography
Yearbook* Awards Y-92, Y-93

The Dictionary of National Biography
. . . . DLB-144

Didion, Joan
1934- DLB-2, 173, 185; Y-81, Y-86

Di Donato, Pietro 1911- DLB-9

Die Fürstliche Bibliothek Corvey Y-96

Diego, Gerardo 1896-1987 . . . . DLB-134

Digges, Thomas circa 1546-1595 . . . . DLB-136

Dillard, Annie 1945- Y-80

Dillard, R. H. W. 1937- DLB-5

Dillingham, Charles T.,
    Company DLB-49

The Dillingham, G. W.,
    Company DLB-49

Dilly, Edward and Charles
    [publishing house] DLB-154

Dilthey, Wilhelm 1833-1911 . . . . . . DLB-129

Dimitrova, Blaga 1922- DLB-181

Dimov, Dimitŭr 1909-1966 . . . . . . DLB-181

Dimsdale, Thomas J. 1831?-1866 . . . . DLB-186

Dingelstedt, Franz von
    1814-1881 . . . . DLB-133

Dintenfass, Mark 1941- Y-84

Diogenes, Jr. (see Brougham, John)

Diogenes Laertius circa 200 . . . . DLB-176

DiPrima, Diane 1934- DLB-5, 16

Disch, Thomas M. 1940- DLB-8

Disney, Walt 1901-1966 . . . . DLB-22

Disraeli, Benjamin 1804-1881 . . . . DLB-21, 55

D'Israeli, Isaac 1766-1848 . . . . DLB-107

Ditzen, Rudolf (see Fallada, Hans)

Dix, Dorothea Lynde 1802-1887 . . . . . DLB-1

Dix, Dorothy (see Gilmer,
    Elizabeth Meriwether)

Dix, Edwards and Company DLB-49

Dix, Gertrude circa 1874–? DLB-197

Dixie, Florence Douglas
    1857-1905 . . . . DLB-174

Dixon, Ella Hepworth 1855 or
    1857-1932 . . . . DLB-197

Dixon, Paige (see Corcoran, Barbara)

Dixon, Richard Watson
    1833-1900 . . . . DLB-19

Dixon, Stephen 1936- DLB-130

Dmitriev, Ivan Ivanovich
    1760-1837 . . . . DLB-150

Dobell, Bertram 1842-1914 . . . . . . DLB-184

Dobell, Sydney 1824-1874 . . . . DLB-32

Döblin, Alfred 1878-1957 . . . . DLB-66

Dobson, Austin
    1840-1921 . . . . DLB-35, 144

Doctorow, E. L.
    1931- DLB-2, 28, 173; Y-80

Documents on Sixteenth-Century
    Literature DLB-167, 172

Dodd, William E. 1869-1940 . . . . . . DLB-17

Dodd, Anne [publishing house] DLB-154

Dodd, Mead and Company DLB-49

Doderer, Heimito von 1896-1968 . . . . DLB-85

Dodge, Mary Mapes
    1831?-1905 . . . . DLB-42, 79; DS-13

Dodge, B. W., and Company DLB-46

Dodge Publishing Company DLB-49

Dodgson, Charles Lutwidge
    (see Carroll, Lewis)

Dodsley, Robert 1703-1764 . . . . . . DLB-95

Dodsley, R. [publishing house] DLB-154

Dodson, Owen 1914-1983 . . . . DLB-76

Doesticks, Q. K. Philander, P. B.
    (see Thomson, Mortimer)

Doheny, Carrie Estelle
    1875-1958 . . . . DLB-140

Doherty, John 1798?-1854 . . . . DLB-190

Domínguez, Sylvia Maida
    1935- DLB-122

Donahoe, Patrick
    [publishing house] DLB-49

Donald, David H. 1920- DLB-17

Donaldson, Scott 1928- DLB-111

Doni, Rodolfo 1919- DLB-177

Donleavy, J. P. 1926- DLB-6, 173

Donnadieu, Marguerite (see Duras,
    Marguerite)

Donne, John 1572-1631 . . . . . DLB-121, 151

Donnelley, R. R., and Sons
    Company DLB-49

Donnelly, Ignatius 1831-1901 . . . . . DLB-12

Donohue and Henneberry DLB-49

Donoso, José 1924- DLB-113

Doolady, M. [publishing house] DLB-49

Dooley, Ebon (see Ebon)

Doolittle, Hilda 1886-1961 . . . . . . DLB-4, 45

Doplicher, Fabio 1938- DLB-128

Dor, Milo 1923- DLB-85

Doran, George H., Company DLB-46

Dorgelès, Roland 1886-1973 . . . . . DLB-65

Dorn, Edward 1929- DLB-5

Dorr, Rheta Childe 1866-1948 . . . . . DLB-25

Dorris, Michael 1945-1997 . . . . . . DLB-175

Dorset and Middlesex, Charles Sackville,
    Lord Buckhurst,
    Earl of 1643-1706 . . . . DLB-131

Dorst, Tankred 1925- DLB-75, 124

Dos Passos, John
    1896-1970 . . . . . DLB-4, 9; DS-1, DS-15

John Dos Passos: A Centennial
    Commemoration Y-96

Doubleday and Company DLB-49

Dougall, Lily 1858-1923 . . . . DLB-92

Doughty, Charles M.
    1843-1926 . . . . DLB-19, 57, 174

Douglas, Gavin 1476-1522 . . . . . . DLB-132

Douglas, Keith 1920-1944 . . . . DLB-27

Douglas, Norman 1868-1952 . . . . DLB-34, 195

Douglass, Frederick
    1817?-1895 . . . . DLB-1, 43, 50, 79

Douglass, William circa
    1691-1752 . . . . DLB-24

Dourado, Autran 1926- DLB-145

Dove, Arthur G. 1880-1946 . . . . . . DLB-188

Dove, Rita 1952- DLB-120

Dover Publications DLB-46

Doves Press DLB-112

Dowden, Edward 1843-1913 . . . . DLB-35, 149

Dowell, Coleman 1925-1985 . . . . . . DLB-130

Dowland, John 1563-1626 . . . . DLB-172

Downes, Gwladys 1915- DLB-88

Downing, J., Major (see Davis, Charles A.)

Downing, Major Jack (see Smith, Seba)

Dowriche, Anne
    before 1560-after 1613 . . . . DLB-172

Dowson, Ernest 1867-1900 . . . . . DLB-19, 135

Doxey, William
    [publishing house] DLB-49

Doyle, Sir Arthur Conan
    1859-1930 . . . . . . DLB-18, 70, 156, 178

Doyle, Kirby 1932- DLB-16

Doyle, Roddy 1958- DLB-194

Drabble, Margaret 1939- DLB-14, 155

Drach, Albert 1902- DLB-85

Dragojević, Danijel 1934- DLB-181

Drake, Samuel Gardner 1798-1875 . . . DLB-187

The Dramatic Publishing
    Company DLB-49

Dramatists Play Service DLB-46

Drant, Thomas
    early 1540s?-1578 . . . . DLB-167

Draper, John W. 1811-1882 . . . . . . DLB-30

Draper, Lyman C. 1815-1891 . . . . . DLB-30

Drayton, Michael 1563-1631 . . . . . DLB-121

Dreiser, Theodore
    1871-1945 . . . . DLB-9, 12, 102, 137; DS-1

Drewitz, Ingeborg 1923-1986 . . . . . . DLB-75

Drieu La Rochelle, Pierre
    1893-1945 . . . . DLB-72

Drinker, Elizabeth 1735-1807 . . . . . DLB-200

Drinkwater, John 1882-1937
    . . . . DLB-10, 19, 149

Droste-Hülshoff, Annette von
    1797-1848 . . . . DLB-133

The Drue Heinz Literature Prize
    Excerpt from "Excerpts from a Report
    of the Commission," in David
    Bosworth's *The Death of Descartes*
    An Interview with David
    Bosworth Y-82

Drummond, William Henry
    1854-1907 . . . . DLB-92

Drummond, William, of Hawthornden 1585-1649 . . . . DLB-121

Dryden, Charles 1860?-1931 . . . . . DLB-171

Dryden, John 1631-1700 . . . DLB-80, 101, 131

Držić, Marin circa 1508-1567 . . . . . DLB-147

Duane, William 1760-1835 . . . . DLB-43

Dubé, Marcel 1930- DLB-53

Dubé, Rodolphe (see Hertel, François)

Dubie, Norman 1945- DLB-120

Du Bois, W. E. B. 1868-1963 . . . . DLB-47, 50, 91

Du Bois, William Pène 1916- DLB-61

Dubus, Andre 1936- DLB-130

Ducange, Victor 1783-1833 . . . . . . DLB-192

Du Chaillu, Paul Belloni 1831?-1903 . . . . DLB-189

Ducharme, Réjean 1941- DLB-60

Dučić, Jovan 1871-1943 . . . . DLB-147

Duck, Stephen 1705?-1756 . . . . . DLB-95

Duckworth, Gerald, and Company Limited DLB-112

Dudek, Louis 1918- DLB-88

Duell, Sloan and Pearce DLB-46

Duerer, Albrecht 1471-1528 . . . . . . DLB-179

Dufief, Nicholas Gouin 1776-1834 . . . DLB-187

Duff Gordon, Lucie 1821-1869 . . . . . DLB-166

Dufferin, Helen Lady, Countess of Gifford 1807-1867 . . . . DLB-199

Duffield and Green DLB-46

Duffy, Maureen 1933- DLB-14

Dugan, Alan 1923- DLB-5

Dugard, William [publishing house] DLB-170

Dugas, Marcel 1883-1947 . . . . DLB-92

Dugdale, William [publishing house] DLB-106

Duhamel, Georges 1884-1966 . . . . . DLB-65

Dujardin, Edouard 1861-1949 . . . . . DLB-123

Dukes, Ashley 1885-1959 . . . . DLB-10

du Maurier, Daphne 1907-1989 . . . . DLB-191

Du Maurier, George 1834-1896 . . . . DLB-153, 178

Dumas, Alexandre *fils* 1824–1895 . . . . DLB-192

Dumas, Alexandre *père* 1802-1870 . . . . DLB-119, 192

Dumas, Henry 1934-1968 . . . . DLB-41

Dunbar, Paul Laurence 1872-1906 . . . . DLB-50, 54, 78

Dunbar, William circa 1460-circa 1522 . . . . DLB-132, 146

Duncan, Norman 1871-1916 . . . . . . DLB-92

Duncan, Quince 1940- DLB-145

Duncan, Robert 1919-1988 . . . DLB-5, 16, 193

Duncan, Ronald 1914-1982 . . . . . . DLB-13

Duncan, Sara Jeannette 1861-1922 . . . . DLB-92

Dunigan, Edward, and Brother DLB-49

Dunlap, John 1747-1812 . . . . DLB-43

Dunlap, William 1766-1839 . . . . DLB-30, 37, 59

Dunn, Douglas 1942- DLB-40

Dunn, Harvey Thomas 1884-1952 . . . DLB-188

Dunn, Stephen 1939- DLB-105

Dunne, Finley Peter 1867-1936 . . . . DLB-11, 23

Dunne, John Gregory 1932- Y-80

Dunne, Philip 1908-1992 . . . . DLB-26

Dunning, Ralph Cheever 1878-1930 . . . . DLB-4

Dunning, William A. 1857-1922 . . . . DLB-17

Duns Scotus, John circa 1266-1308 . . . . DLB-115

Dunsany, Lord (Edward John Moreton Drax Plunkett, Baron Dunsany) 1878-1957 . . . . . . DLB-10, 77, 153, 156

Dunton, John [publishing house] DLB-170

Dunton, W. Herbert 1878-1936 . . . . DLB-188

Dupin, Amantine-Aurore-Lucile (see Sand, George)

Durand, Lucile (see Bersianik, Louky)

Duranti, Francesca 1935- DLB-196

Duranty, Walter 1884-1957 . . . . DLB-29

Duras, Marguerite 1914- DLB-83

Durfey, Thomas 1653-1723 . . . . DLB-80

Durova, Nadezhda Andreevna (Aleksandr Andreevich Aleksandrov) 1783-1866 . . . . DLB-198

Durrell, Lawrence 1912-1990 . . . . DLB-15, 27; Y-90

Durrell, William [publishing house] DLB-49

Dürrenmatt, Friedrich 1921-1990 . . . . DLB-69, 124

Duston, Hannah 1657-1737 . . . . . . DLB-200

Dutton, E. P., and Company DLB-49

Duvoisin, Roger 1904-1980 . . . . . . DLB-61

Duyckinck, Evert Augustus 1816-1878 . . . . DLB-3, 64

Duyckinck, George L. 1823-1863 . . . . DLB-3

Duyckinck and Company DLB-49

Dwight, John Sullivan 1813-1893 . . . . DLB-1

Dwight, Timothy 1752-1817 . . . . . . DLB-37

Dybek, Stuart 1942- DLB-130

Dyer, Charles 1928- DLB-13

Dyer, George 1755-1841 . . . . DLB-93

Dyer, John 1699-1757 . . . . DLB-95

Dyer, Sir Edward 1543-1607 . . . . . DLB-136

Dylan, Bob 1941- DLB-16

E

Eager, Edward 1911-1964 . . . . DLB-22

Eames, Wilberforce 1855-1937 . . . . DLB-140

Earle, James H., and Company DLB-49

Earle, John 1600 or 1601-1665 . . . . . DLB-151

Early American Book Illustration, by Sinclair Hamilton DLB-49

Eastlake, William 1917- DLB-6

Eastman, Carol ?- DLB-44

Eastman, Charles A. (Ohiyesa) 1858-1939 . . . . DLB-175

Eastman, Max 1883-1969 . . . . DLB-91

Eaton, Daniel Isaac 1753-1814 . . . . . DLB-158

Eberhart, Richard 1904- DLB-48

Ebner, Jeannie 1918- DLB-85

Ebner-Eschenbach, Marie von 1830-1916 . . . . DLB-81

Ebon 1942- DLB-41

Ecbasis Captivi circa 1045 . . . . DLB-148

Ecco Press DLB-46

Eckhart, Meister circa 1260-circa 1328 . . . . DLB-115

The Eclectic Review 1805-1868 . . . . . DLB-110

Eco, Umberto 1932- DLB-196

Edel, Leon 1907- DLB-103

Edes, Benjamin 1732-1803 . . . . DLB-43

Edgar, David 1948- DLB-13

Edgeworth, Maria 1768-1849 . . . . DLB-116, 159, 163

The Edinburgh Review 1802-1929 . . . . DLB-110

Edinburgh University Press DLB-112

The Editor Publishing Company DLB-49

Editorial Statements DLB-137

Edmonds, Randolph 1900- DLB-51

Edmonds, Walter D. 1903- DLB-9

Edschmid, Kasimir 1890-1966 . . . . . DLB-56

Edwards, Amelia Anne Blandford 1831-1892 . . . . DLB-174

Edwards, Edward 1812-1886 . . . . . DLB-184

Edwards, Jonathan 1703-1758 . . . . . DLB-24

Edwards, Jonathan, Jr. 1745-1801 . . . . DLB-37

Edwards, Junius 1929- DLB-33

Edwards, Matilda Barbara Betham- 1836-1919 . . . . DLB-174

Edwards, Richard 1524-1566 . . . . . DLB-62

Edwards, James [publishing house] DLB-154

Edwards, Sarah Pierpont 1710-1758 . . DLB-200

Effinger, George Alec 1947- DLB-8

Egerton, George 1859-1945 . . . . . . DLB-135

Eggleston, Edward 1837-1902 . . . . . DLB-12

Eggleston, Wilfred 1901-1986 . . . . . DLB-92

Ehrenstein, Albert 1886-1950 . . . . . . DLB-81

Ehrhart, W. D. 1948- DS-9

Eich, Günter 1907-1972 . . . . . . DLB-69, 124

Eichendorff, Joseph Freiherr von
1788-1857 . . . . DLB-90

1873 Publishers' Catalogues DLB-49

Eighteenth-Century Aesthetic
Theories DLB-31

Eighteenth-Century Philosophical
Background DLB-31

Eigner, Larry 1926-1996 . . . . . . DLB-5, 193

Eikon Basilike 1649 . . . . DLB-151

Eilhart von Oberge
circa 1140-circa 1195 . . . . DLB-148

Einhard circa 770-840 . . . . DLB-148

Eiseley, Loren 1907-1977 . . . . DS-17

Eisenreich, Herbert 1925-1986 . . . . . DLB-85

Eisner, Kurt 1867-1919 . . . . DLB-66

Eklund, Gordon 1945- Y-83

Ekwensi, Cyprian 1921- DLB-117

Eld, George
[publishing house] DLB-170

Elder, Lonne III 1931- DLB-7, 38, 44

Elder, Paul, and Company DLB-49

Elements of Rhetoric (1828; revised, 1846),
by Richard Whately [excerpt] DLB-57

Elie, Robert 1915-1973 . . . . DLB-88

Elin Pelin 1877-1949 . . . . DLB-147

Eliot, George 1819-1880 . . . . . DLB-21, 35, 55

Eliot, John 1604-1690 . . . . DLB-24

Eliot, T. S. 1888-1965 . . . . DLB-7, 10, 45, 63

Eliot's Court Press DLB-170

Elizabeth I 1533-1603 . . . . DLB-136

Elizabeth of Nassau-Saarbrücken
after 1393-1456 . . . . DLB-179

Elizondo, Salvador 1932- DLB-145

Elizondo, Sergio 1930- DLB-82

Elkin, Stanley 1930- DLB-2, 28; Y-80

Elles, Dora Amy (see Wentworth, Patricia)

Ellet, Elizabeth F. 1818?-1877 . . . . . DLB-30

Elliot, Ebenezer 1781-1849 . . . . . DLB-96, 190

Elliot, Frances Minto (Dickinson)
1820-1898 . . . . DLB-166

Elliott, Charlotte 1789-1871 . . . . . . DLB-199

Elliott, George 1923- DLB-68

Elliott, Janice 1931- DLB-14

Elliott, William 1788-1863 . . . . DLB-3

Elliott, Thomes and Talbot DLB-49

Ellis, Alice Thomas (Anna Margaret Haycraft)
1932- DLB-194

Ellis, Edward S. 1840-1916 . . . . DLB-42

Ellis, Frederick Staridge
[publishing house] DLB-106

The George H. Ellis Company DLB-49

Ellis, Havelock 1859-1939 . . . . DLB-190

Ellison, Harlan 1934- DLB-8

Ellison, Ralph Waldo
1914-1994 . . . . DLB-2, 76; Y-94

Ellmann, Richard
1918-1987 . . . . DLB-103; Y-87

The Elmer Holmes Bobst Awards in Arts
and Letters Y-87

Elyot, Thomas 1490?-1546 . . . . DLB-136

Emanuel, James Andrew 1921- DLB-41

Emecheta, Buchi 1944- DLB-117

The Emergence of Black Women
Writers DS-8

Emerson, Ralph Waldo
1803-1882 . . . . DLB-1, 59, 73, 183

Emerson, William 1769-1811 . . . . . . DLB-37

Emerson, William 1923-1997 . . . . Y-97

Emin, Fedor Aleksandrovich
circa 1735-1770 . . . . DLB-150

Empedocles fifth century B.C. DLB-176

Empson, William 1906-1984 . . . . . . DLB-20

Enchi, Fumiko 1905-1986 . . . . DLB-182

Encounter with the West DLB-180

The End of English Stage Censorship,
1945-1968 . . . . DLB-13

Ende, Michael 1929- DLB-75

Endō, Shūsaku 1923-1996 . . . . DLB-182

Engel, Marian 1933-1985 . . . . DLB-53

Engels, Friedrich 1820-1895 . . . . . . DLB-129

Engle, Paul 1908- DLB-48

English Composition and Rhetoric (1866),
by Alexander Bain [excerpt] DLB-57

The English Language:
410 to 1500 . . . . DLB-146

The English Renaissance of Art (1908),
by Oscar Wilde DLB-35

Enright, D. J. 1920- DLB-27

Enright, Elizabeth 1909-1968 . . . . . . DLB-22

L'Envoi (1882), by Oscar Wilde DLB-35

Epictetus circa 55-circa 125-130 . . . . DLB-176

Epicurus 342/341 B.C.-271/270 B.C.
. . . . DLB-176

Epps, Bernard 1936- DLB-53

Epstein, Julius 1909- and
Epstein, Philip 1909-1952 . . . . . . DLB-26

Equiano, Olaudah
circa 1745-1797 . . . . DLB-37, 50

Eragny Press DLB-112

Erasmus, Desiderius 1467-1536 . . . . . DLB-136

Erba, Luciano 1922- DLB-128

Erdrich, Louise 1954- DLB-152, 175

Erichsen-Brown, Gwethalyn Graham
(see Graham, Gwethalyn)

Eriugena, John Scottus
circa 810-877 . . . . DLB-115

Ernest Hemingway's Toronto Journalism
Revisited: With Three Previously
Unrecorded Stories Y-92

Ernst, Paul 1866-1933 . . . . DLB-66, 118

Erskine, Albert 1911-1993 . . . . Y-93

Erskine, John 1879-1951 . . . . . . DLB-9, 102

Erskine, Mrs. Steuart ?-1948 . . . . . DLB-195

Ervine, St. John Greer 1883-1971 . . . . DLB-10

Eschenburg, Johann Joachim 1743-č820 . . . DLB-97

Escoto, Julio 1944- DLB-145

Eshleman, Clayton 1935- DLB-5

Espriu, Salvador 1913-1985 . . . . . . DLB-134

Ess Ess Publishing Company DLB-49

Essay on Chatterton (1842), by
Robert Browning DLB-32

Essex House Press DLB-112

Estes, Eleanor 1906-1988 . . . . DLB-22

Eszterhas, Joe 1944- DLB-185

Estes and Lauriat DLB-49

Etherege, George 1636-circa 1692 . . . . DLB-80

Ethridge, Mark, Sr. 1896-1981 . . . . . DLB-127

Ets, Marie Hall 1893- DLB-22

Etter, David 1928- DLB-105

Ettner, Johann Christoph
1654-1724 . . . . DLB-168

Eudora Welty: Eye of the Storyteller Y-87

Eugene O'Neill Memorial Theater
Center DLB-7

Eugene O'Neill's Letters: A Review Y-88

Eupolemius
flourished circa 1095 . . . . DLB-148

Euripides circa 484 B.C.-407/406 B.C.
. . . . DLB-176

Evans, Caradoc 1878-1945 . . . . DLB-162

Evans, Charles 1850-1935 . . . . DLB-187

Evans, Donald 1884-1921 . . . . DLB-54

Evans, George Henry 1805-1856 . . . . . DLB-43

Evans, Hubert 1892-1986 . . . . DLB-92

Evans, Mari 1923- DLB-41

Evans, Mary Ann (see Eliot, George)

Evans, Nathaniel 1742-1767 . . . . DLB-31

Evans, Sebastian 1830-1909 . . . . DLB-35

Evans, M., and Company DLB-46

Everett, Alexander Hill 1790-1847 . . . . DLB-59

Everett, Edward 1794-1865 . . . . . . DLB-1, 59

Everson, R. G. 1903- DLB-88

Everson, William 1912-1994 . . . . . . DLB-5, 16

Every Man His Own Poet; or, The
Inspired Singer's Recipe Book (1877),
by W. H. Mallock DLB-35

Ewart, Gavin 1916- DLB-40

Ewing, Juliana Horatia
1841-1885 . . . . DLB-21, 163

The Examiner 1808-1881 . . . . DLB-110

Exley, Frederick
1929-1992 . . . . DLB-143; Y-81

Experiment in the Novel (1929),
by John D. Beresford DLB-36

von Eyb, Albrecht 1420-1475 . . . . . DLB-179

"Eyes Across Centuries: Contemporary
Poetry and 'That Vision Thing,'"
by Philip Dacey DLB-105

Eyre and Spottiswoode DLB-106

Ezzo ?-after 1065. . . . . DLB-148

F

"F. Scott Fitzgerald: St. Paul's Native Son
and Distinguished American Writer":
University of Minnesota Conference,
29-31 October 1982 . . . . Y-82

Faber, Frederick William
1814-1863 . . . . DLB-32

Faber and Faber Limited DLB-112

Faccio, Rena (see Aleramo, Sibilla)

Fagundo, Ana María 1938- DLB-134

Fair, Ronald L. 1932- DLB-33

Fairfax, Beatrice (see Manning, Marie)

Fairlie, Gerard 1899-1983 . . . . DLB-77

Fallada, Hans 1893-1947 . . . . DLB-56

Falsifying Hemingway Y-96

Fancher, Betsy 1928- Y-83

Fane, Violet 1843-1905 . . . . DLB-35

Fanfrolico Press DLB-112

Fanning, Katherine 1927 . . . . DLB-127

Fanshawe, Sir Richard
1608-1666 . . . . DLB-126

Fantasy Press Publishers DLB-46

Fante, John 1909-1983 . . . . . DLB-130; Y-83

Al-Farabi circa 870-950 . . . . DLB-115

Farah, Nuruddin 1945- DLB-125

Farber, Norma 1909-1984 . . . . DLB-61

Farigoule, Louis (see Romains, Jules)

Farjeon, Eleanor 1881-1965 . . . . . . DLB-160

Farley, Walter 1920-1989 . . . . DLB-22

Farmer, Penelope 1939- DLB-161

Farmer, Philip José 1918- DLB-8

Farquhar, George circa 1677-1707 . . . . DLB-84

Farquharson, Martha (see Finley, Martha)

Farrar, Frederic William
1831-1903 . . . . DLB-163

Farrar and Rinehart. DLB-46

Farrar, Straus and Giroux DLB-46

Farrell, James T.
1904-1979 . . . . . . DLB-4, 9, 86; DS-2

Farrell, J. G. 1935-1979 . . . . DLB-14

Fast, Howard 1914- DLB-9

Faulkner and Yoknapatawpha Conference,
Oxford, Mississippi. Y-97

"Faulkner 100—Celebrating the Work," University
of South Carolina, Columbia Y-97

Faulkner, William 1897-1962
. . . . . . DLB-9, 11, 44, 102; DS-2; Y-86

Faulkner, George
[publishing house] DLB-154

Fauset, Jessie Redmon 1882-1961 . . . . DLB-51

Faust, Irvin 1924- DLB-2, 28; Y-80

Fawcett Books. DLB-46

Fawcett, Millicent Garrett 1847-1929 . . DLB-190

Fearing, Kenneth 1902-1961 . . . . DLB-9

Federal Writers' Project. DLB-46

Federman, Raymond 1928- Y-80

Feiffer, Jules 1929- DLB-7, 44

Feinberg, Charles E.
1899-1988 . . . . DLB-187; Y-88

Feind, Barthold 1678-1721. . . . . . . DLB-168

Feinstein, Elaine 1930- DLB-14, 40

Feiss, Paul Louis 1875-1952. . . . . . . DLB-187

Feldman, Irving 1928- DLB-169

Felipe, Léon 1884-1968 . . . . DLB-108

Fell, Frederick, Publishers. DLB-46

Felltham, Owen 1602?-1668. . . . DLB-126, 151

Fels, Ludwig 1946- DLB-75

Felton, Cornelius Conway
1807-1862. . . . . DLB-1

Fenn, Harry 1837-1911 . . . . DLB-188

Fennario, David 1947- DLB-60

Fenno, Jenny 1765?-1803 . . . . DLB-200

Fenno, John 1751-1798 . . . . DLB-43

Fenno, R. F., and Company DLB-49

Fenoglio, Beppe 1922-1963 . . . . . . DLB-177

Fenton, Geoffrey 1539?-1608 . . . . . DLB-136

Fenton, James 1949- DLB-40

Ferber, Edna 1885-1968 . . . . . DLB-9, 28, 86

Ferdinand, Vallery III (see Salaam, Kalamu ya)

Ferguson, Sir Samuel 1810-1886 . . . . . DLB-32

Ferguson, William Scott
1875-1954 . . . . DLB-47

Fergusson, Robert 1750-1774 . . . . . DLB-109

Ferland, Albert 1872-1943 . . . . DLB-92

Ferlinghetti, Lawrence 1919- DLB-5, 16

Fern, Fanny (see Parton, Sara Payson Willis)

Ferrars, Elizabeth 1907- DLB-87

Ferré, Rosario 1942- DLB-145

Ferret, E., and Company. DLB-49

Ferrier, Susan 1782-1854 . . . . DLB-116

Ferrini, Vincent 1913- DLB-48

Ferron, Jacques 1921-1985 . . . . DLB-60

Ferron, Madeleine 1922- DLB-53

Ferrucci, Franco 1936- DLB-196

Fetridge and Company DLB-49

Feuchtersleben, Ernst Freiherr von
1806-1849 . . . . DLB-133

Feuchtwanger, Lion 1884-1958 . . . . . DLB-66

Feuerbach, Ludwig 1804-1872. . . . . DLB-133

Feuillet, Octave 1821-1890. . . . . . . DLB-192

Feydeau, Georges 1862-1921 . . . . . DLB-192

Fichte, Johann Gottlieb
1762-1814 . . . . DLB-90

Ficke, Arthur Davison 1883-1945 . . . . DLB-54

Fiction Best-Sellers, 1910-1945 . . . . . . DLB-9

Fiction into Film, 1928-1975: A List of Movies
Based on the Works of Authors in
British Novelists, 1930-1959 . . . . . DLB-15

Fiedler, Leslie A. 1917- DLB-28, 67

Field, Edward 1924- DLB-105

Field, Eugene
1850-1895. . . . . DLB-23, 42, 140; DS-13

Field, John 1545?-1588. . . . . DLB-167

Field, Marshall, III 1893-1956. . . . . DLB-127

Field, Marshall, IV 1916-1965 . . . . . DLB-127

Field, Marshall, V 1941- DLB-127

Field, Nathan 1587-1619 or 1620 . . . . DLB-58

Field, Rachel 1894-1942 . . . . DLB-9, 22

A Field Guide to Recent Schools of American
Poetry. Y-86

Fielding, Henry
1707-1754 . . . . DLB-39, 84, 101

Fielding, Sarah 1710-1768. . . . . DLB-39

Fields, James Thomas 1817-1881 . . . . . DLB-1

Fields, Julia 1938- DLB-41

Fields, W. C. 1880-1946 . . . . DLB-44

Fields, Osgood and Company DLB-49

Fifty Penguin Years. Y-85

Figes, Eva 1932- DLB-14

Figuera, Angela 1902-1984 . . . . . . DLB-108

Filmer, Sir Robert 1586-1653 . . . . . DLB-151

Filson, John circa 1753-1788 . . . . . . DLB-37

Finch, Anne, Countess of Winchilsea
1661-1720 . . . . DLB-95

Finch, Robert 1900- DLB-88

"Finding, Losing, Reclaiming: A Note on My
Poems," by Robert Phillips. DLB-105

Findley, Timothy 1930- DLB-53

Finlay, Ian Hamilton 1925- DLB-40

Finley, Martha 1828-1909. . . . . DLB-42

Finn, Elizabeth Anne (McCaul)
1825-1921 . . . . DLB-166

Finney, Jack 1911- DLB-8

Finney, Walter Braden (see Finney, Jack)

Firbank, Ronald 1886-1926 . . . . DLB-36

Firmin, Giles 1615-1697 . . . . DLB-24

Fischart, Johann
1546 or 1547-1590 or 1591 . . . . DLB-179

First Edition Library/Collectors'
Reprints, Inc. Y-91

First International F. Scott Fitzgerald
Conference Y-92

First Strauss "Livings" Awarded to Cynthia
Ozick and Raymond Carver
An Interview with Cynthia Ozick
An Interview with Raymond
Carver Y-83

Fischer, Karoline Auguste Fernandine
1764-1842 . . . . DLB-94

Fish, Stanley 1938- DLB-67

Fishacre, Richard 1205-1248 . . . . . . DLB-115

Fisher, Clay (see Allen, Henry W.)

Fisher, Dorothy Canfield
1879-1958 . . . . DLB-9, 102

Fisher, Leonard Everett 1924- DLB-61

Fisher, Roy 1930- DLB-40

Fisher, Rudolph 1897-1934 . . . . DLB-51, 102

Fisher, Sydney George 1856-1927 . . . . DLB-47

Fisher, Vardis 1895-1968 . . . . DLB-9

Fiske, John 1608-1677 . . . . DLB-24

Fiske, John 1842-1901 . . . . DLB-47, 64

Fitch, Thomas circa 1700-1774 . . . . . DLB-31

Fitch, William Clyde 1865-1909 . . . . . DLB-7

FitzGerald, Edward 1809-1883 . . . . . DLB-32

Fitzgerald, F. Scott 1896-1940
. . . . . DLB-4, 9, 86; Y-81; DS-1, 15, 16

F. Scott Fitzgerald Centenary
Celebrations Y-96

Fitzgerald, Penelope 1916- DLB-14, 194

Fitzgerald, Robert 1910-1985 . . . . Y-80

Fitzgerald, Thomas 1819-1891 . . . . . DLB-23

Fitzgerald, Zelda Sayre 1900-1948 . . . . . Y-84

Fitzhugh, Louise 1928-1974 . . . . DLB-52

Fitzhugh, William
circa 1651-1701 . . . . DLB-24

Flagg, James Montgomery 1877-1960 . . DLB-188

Flanagan, Thomas 1923- Y-80

Flanner, Hildegarde 1899-1987 . . . . . DLB-48

Flanner, Janet 1892-1978 . . . . DLB-4

Flaubert, Gustave 1821-1880 . . . . . DLB-119

Flavin, Martin 1883-1967 . . . . DLB-9

Fleck, Konrad (flourished circa 1220)
. . . . DLB-138

Flecker, James Elroy 1884-1915 . . . DLB-10, 19

Fleeson, Doris 1901-1970 . . . . DLB-29

Fleißer, Marieluise 1901-1974 . . . . DLB-56, 124

Fleming, Ian 1908-1964 . . . . DLB-87

Fleming, Paul 1609-1640 . . . . DLB-164

Fleming, Peter 1907-1971 . . . . DLB-195

The Fleshly School of Poetry and Other
Phenomena of the Day (1872), by Robert
Buchanan DLB-35

The Fleshly School of Poetry: Mr. D. G.
Rossetti (1871), by Thomas Maitland
(Robert Buchanan) DLB-35

Fletcher, Giles, the Elder
1546-1611 . . . . DLB-136

Fletcher, Giles, the Younger
1585 or 1586-1623 . . . . DLB-121

Fletcher, J. S. 1863-1935 . . . . DLB-70

Fletcher, John (see Beaumont, Francis)

Fletcher, John Gould 1886-1950 . . . DLB-4, 45

Fletcher, Phineas 1582-1650 . . . . . . DLB-121

Flieg, Helmut (see Heym, Stefan)

Flint, F. S. 1885-1960 . . . . DLB-19

Flint, Timothy 1780-1840 . . . . . DLB-73, 186

Florio, John 1553?-1625 . . . . DLB-172

Fo, Dario 1926- Y-97

Foix, J. V. 1893-1987 . . . . DLB-134

Foley, Martha (see Burnett, Whit, and
Martha Foley)

Folger, Henry Clay 1857-1930 . . . . . DLB-140

Folio Society DLB-112

Follen, Eliza Lee (Cabot) 1787-1860 . . . DLB-1

Follett, Ken 1949- DLB-87; Y-81

Follett Publishing Company DLB-46

Folsom, John West
[publishing house] DLB-49

Folz, Hans
between 1435 and 1440-1513 . . . . DLB-179

Fontane, Theodor 1819-1898 . . . . . DLB-129

Fonvisin, Denis Ivanovich
1744 or 1745-1792 . . . . DLB-150

Foote, Horton 1916- DLB-26

Foote, Mary Hallock 1847-1938 . . DLB-186, 188

Foote, Samuel 1721-1777 . . . . DLB-89

Foote, Shelby 1916- DLB-2, 17

Forbes, Calvin 1945- DLB-41

Forbes, Ester 1891-1967 . . . . DLB-22

Forbes, Rosita 1893?-1967 . . . . DLB-195

Forbes and Company DLB-49

Force, Peter 1790-1868 . . . . DLB-30

Forché, Carolyn 1950- DLB-5, 193

Ford, Charles Henri 1913- DLB-4, 48

Ford, Corey 1902-1969 . . . . DLB-11

Ford, Ford Madox
1873-1939 . . . . DLB-34, 98, 162

Ford, Jesse Hill 1928- DLB-6

Ford, John 1586-? DLB-58

Ford, R. A. D. 1915- DLB-88

Ford, Worthington C. 1858-1941 . . . . DLB-47

Ford, J. B., and Company DLB-49

Fords, Howard, and Hulbert DLB-49

Foreman, Carl 1914-1984 . . . . DLB-26

Forester, C. S. 1899-1966 . . . . DLB-191

Forester, Frank (see Herbert, Henry William)

"Foreword to Ludwig of Bavaria," by
Robert Peters DLB-105

Forman, Harry Buxton 1842-1917 . . . DLB-184

Fornés, María Irene 1930- DLB-7

Forrest, Leon 1937- DLB-33

Forster, E. M. 1879-1970
. . . . DLB-34, 98, 162, 178, 195; DS-10

Forster, Georg 1754-1794 . . . . DLB-94

Forster, John 1812-1876 . . . . DLB-144

Forster, Margaret 1938- DLB-155

Forsyth, Frederick 1938- DLB-87

Forten, Charlotte L. 1837-1914 . . . . . DLB-50

Fortini, Franco 1917- DLB-128

Fortune, T. Thomas 1856-1928 . . . . DLB-23

Fosdick, Charles Austin
1842-1915 . . . . DLB-42

Foster, Genevieve 1893-1979 . . . . . . DLB-61

Foster, Hannah Webster
1758-1840 . . . . DLB-37, 200

Foster, John 1648-1681 . . . . DLB-24

Foster, Michael 1904-1956 . . . . DLB-9

Foster, Myles Birket 1825-1899 . . . . DLB-184

Foulis, Robert and Andrew / R. and A.
[publishing house] DLB-154

Fouqué, Caroline de la Motte
1774-1831 . . . . DLB-90

Fouqué, Friedrich de la Motte
1777-1843 . . . . DLB-90

Four Essays on the Beat Generation,
by John Clellon Holmes DLB-16

Four Seas Company DLB-46

Four Winds Press DLB-46

Fournier, Henri Alban (see Alain-Fournier)

Fowler and Wells Company DLB-49

Fowles, John 1926- DLB-14, 139

Fox, John, Jr. 1862 or 1863-1919 DLB-9; DS-13

Fox, Paula 1923- DLB-52

Fox, Richard Kyle 1846-1922 . . . . . DLB-79

Fox, William Price 1926- DLB-2; Y-81

Fox, Richard K.
[publishing house] DLB-49

Foxe, John 1517-1587 . . . . DLB-132

Fraenkel, Michael 1896-1957 . . . . . . DLB-4

France, Anatole 1844-1924 . . . . . . DLB-123

France, Richard 1938- DLB-7

Francis, Convers 1795-1863 . . . . . . DLB-1

Francis, Dick 1920- DLB-87

Francis, Jeffrey, Lord 1773-1850 . . . DLB-107

Francis, C. S. [publishing house] DLB-49

François 1863-1910 . . . . DLB-92

François, Louise von 1817-1893 . . . . DLB-129

Franck, Sebastian 1499-1542 . . . . DLB-179

Francke, Kuno 1855-1930 . . . . DLB-71

Frank, Bruno 1887-1945 . . . . DLB-118

Frank, Leonhard 1882-1961 . . . . DLB-56, 118

Frank, Melvin (see Panama, Norman)

Frank, Waldo 1889-1967 . . . . . . DLB-9, 63

Franken, Rose 1895?-1988 . . . . Y-84

Franklin, Benjamin
1706-1790 . . . . DLB-24, 43, 73, 183

Franklin, James 1697-1735 . . . . DLB-43

Franklin Library DLB-46

Frantz, Ralph Jules 1902-1979 . . . . . . DLB-4

Franzos, Karl Emil 1848-1904 . . . . . DLB-129

Fraser, G. S. 1915-1980 . . . . DLB-27

Fraser, Kathleen 1935- DLB-169

Frattini, Alberto 1922- DLB-128

Frau Ava ?-1127 . . . . DLB-148

Frayn, Michael 1933- DLB-13, 14, 194

Frederic, Harold
1856-1898 . . . . DLB-12, 23; DS-13

Freeling, Nicolas 1927- DLB-87

Freeman, Douglas Southall
1886-1953 . . . . DLB-17; DS-17

Freeman, Legh Richmond
1842-1915 . . . . DLB-23

Freeman, Mary E. Wilkins
1852-1930 . . . . DLB-12, 78

Freeman, R. Austin 1862-1943 . . . . . DLB-70

Freidank circa 117?-circa 1233 . . . . . DLB-138

Freiligrath, Ferdinand 1810-1876 . . . . DLB-133

Frémont, John Charles 1813-1890 . . . DLB-186

Frémont, John Charles 1813-1890
and Frémont, Jessie Benton
1834-1902 . . . . DLB-183

French, Alice 1850-1934 . . . . DLB-74; DS-13

French, David 1939- DLB-53

French, Evangeline 1869-1960 . . . . . DLB-195

French, Francesca 1871-1960 . . . . . . DLB-195

French, James [publishing house] DLB-49

French, Samuel [publishing house] . . . DLB-49

Samuel French, Limited DLB-106

Freneau, Philip 1752-1832 . . . . . DLB-37, 43

Freni, Melo 1934- DLB-128

Freshfield, Douglas W.
1845-1934 . . . . DLB-174

Freytag, Gustav 1816-1895 . . . . DLB-129

Fried, Erich 1921-1988 . . . . DLB-85

Friedman, Bruce Jay 1930- DLB-2, 28

Friedrich von Hausen
circa 1171-1190 . . . . DLB-138

Friel, Brian 1929- DLB-13

Friend, Krebs 1895?-1967? DLB-4

Fries, Fritz Rudolf 1935- DLB-75

Fringe and Alternative Theater
in Great Britain DLB-13

Frisch, Max 1911-1991 . . . . . . DLB-69, 124

Frischlin, Nicodemus 1547-1590 . . . . DLB-179

Frischmuth, Barbara 1941- DLB-85

Fritz, Jean 1915- DLB-52

Fromentin, Eugene 1820-1876 . . . . . DLB-123

From *The Gay Science,* by
E. S. Dallas DLB-21

Frost, A. B. 1851-1928 . . . . . DLB-188; DS-13

Frost, Robert 1874-1963 . . . . . DLB-54; DS-7

Frothingham, Octavius Brooks
1822-1895 . . . . DLB-1

Froude, James Anthony
1818-1894 . . . . DLB-18, 57, 144

Fry, Christopher 1907- DLB-13

Fry, Roger 1866-1934 . . . . DS-10

Frye, Northrop 1912-1991 . . . . . DLB-67, 68

Fuchs, Daniel
1909-1993 . . . . DLB-9, 26, 28; Y-93

Fuentes, Carlos 1928- DLB-113

Fuertes, Gloria 1918- DLB-108

The Fugitives and the Agrarians:
The First Exhibition Y-85

Fulbecke, William 1560-1603? DLB-172

Fuller, Charles H., Jr. 1939- DLB-38

Fuller, Henry Blake 1857-1929 . . . . . DLB-12

Fuller, John 1937- DLB-40

Fuller, Margaret (see Fuller, Sarah Margaret,
Marchesa D'Ossoli)

Fuller, Roy 1912-1991 . . . . . . DLB-15, 20

Fuller, Samuel 1912- DLB-26

Fuller, Sarah Margaret, Marchesa
D'Ossoli 1810-1850 . . . DLB-1, 59, 73, 183

Fuller, Thomas 1608-1661 . . . . DLB-151

Fullerton, Hugh 1873-1945 . . . . DLB-171

Fulton, Alice 1952- DLB-193

Fulton, Len 1934- Y-86

Fulton, Robin 1937- DLB-40

Furbank, P. N. 1920- DLB-155

Furman, Laura 1945- Y-86

Furness, Horace Howard
1833-1912 . . . . DLB-64

Furness, William Henry 1802-1896 . . . . DLB-1

Furnivall, Frederick James
1825-1910 . . . . DLB-184

Furthman, Jules 1888-1966 . . . . DLB-26

Furui, Yoshikichi 1937- DLB-182

Futabatei, Shimei (Hasegawa Tatsunosuke)
1864-1909 . . . . DLB-180

The Future of the Novel (1899), by
Henry James DLB-18

Fyleman, Rose 1877-1957 . . . . DLB-160

G

The G. Ross Roy Scottish Poetry
Collection at the University of
South Carolina Y-89

Gadda, Carlo Emilio 1893-1973 . . . . DLB-177

Gaddis, William 1922- DLB-2

Gág, Wanda 1893-1946 . . . . DLB-22

Gagarin, Ivan Sergeevich 1814-1882 . . DLB-198

Gagnon, Madeleine 1938- DLB-60

Gaine, Hugh 1726-1807 . . . . DLB-43

Gaine, Hugh [publishing house] DLB-49

Gaines, Ernest J.
1933- DLB-2, 33, 152; Y-80

Gaiser, Gerd 1908-1976 . . . . DLB-69

Galarza, Ernesto 1905-1984 . . . . . . DLB-122

Galaxy Science Fiction Novels DLB-46

Gale, Zona 1874-1938 . . . . DLB-9, 78

Galen of Pergamon 129-after 210 . . . DLB-176

Gales, Winifred Marshall
1761-1839 . . . . DLB-200

Gall, Louise von 1815-1855 . . . . . . DLB-133

Gallagher, Tess 1943- DLB-120

Gallagher, Wes 1911- DLB-127

Gallagher, William Davis
1808-1894 . . . . DLB-73

Gallant, Mavis 1922- DLB-53

Gallico, Paul 1897-1976 . . . . . . DLB-9, 171

Galloway, Grace Growden
1727-1782 . . . . DLB-200

Gallup, Donald 1913- DLB-187

Galsworthy, John
1867-1933 . . . DLB-10, 34, 98, 162; DS-16

Galt, John 1779-1839 . . . . . . DLB-99, 116

Galton, Sir Francis 1822-1911 . . . . . DLB-166

Galvin, Brendan 1938- DLB-5

Gambit DLB-46

Gamboa, Reymundo 1948- DLB-122

Gammer Gurton's Needle DLB-62

Gan, Elena Andreevna (Zeneida R-va)
1814-1842 . . . . DLB-198

Gannett, Frank E. 1876-1957 . . . . . . DLB-29

Gaos, Vicente 1919-1980 . . . . DLB-134

García, Lionel G. 1935- DLB-82

García Lorca, Federico
1898-1936 . . . . DLB-108

García Márquez, Gabriel
1928- DLB-113; Y-82

Gardam, Jane 1928- DLB-14, 161

Garden, Alexander
circa 1685-1756 . . . . DLB-31

Gardiner, Margaret Power Farmer (see
Blessington, Marguerite, Countess of)

Gardner, John 1933-1982 . . . . . DLB-2; Y-82

Garfield, Leon 1921- DLB-161

Garis, Howard R. 1873-1962. . . . . . DLB-22

Garland, Hamlin
1860-1940. . . . . . . DLB-12, 71, 78, 186

Garneau, Francis-Xavier
1809-1866 . . . . DLB-99

Garneau, Hector de Saint-Denys
1912-1943 . . . . DLB-88

Garneau, Michel 1939- DLB-53

Garner, Alan 1934- DLB-161

Garner, Hugh 1913-1979 . . . . DLB-68

Garnett, David 1892-1981 . . . . DLB-34

Garnett, Eve 1900-1991 . . . . DLB-160

Garnett, Richard 1835-1906. . . . . . . DLB-184

Garrard, Lewis H. 1829-1887. . . . . . DLB-186

Garraty, John A. 1920- DLB-17

Garrett, George
1929- DLB-2, 5, 130, 152; Y-83

Garrett, John Work 1872-1942 . . . . . DLB-187

Garrick, David 1717-1779 . . . . DLB-84

Garrison, William Lloyd
1805-1879 . . . . DLB-1, 43

Garro, Elena 1920- DLB-145

Garth, Samuel 1661-1719. . . . . DLB-95

Garve, Andrew 1908- DLB-87

Gary, Romain 1914-1980. . . . . DLB-83

Gascoigne, George 1539?-1577 . . . . . DLB-136

Gascoyne, David 1916- DLB-20

Gaskell, Elizabeth Cleghorn
1810-1865 . . . . DLB-21, 144, 159

Gaspey, Thomas 1788-1871. . . . . . . DLB-116

Gass, William Howard 1924- DLB-2

Gates, Doris 1901- DLB-22

Gates, Henry Louis, Jr. 1950- DLB-67

Gates, Lewis E. 1860-1924 . . . . DLB-71

Gatto, Alfonso 1909-1976 . . . . DLB-114

Gaunt, Mary 1861-1942. . . . . DLB-174

Gautier, Théophile 1811-1872. . . . . . DLB-119

Gauvreau, Claude 1925-1971. . . . . . DLB-88

The *Gawain*-Poet
flourished circa 1350-1400 . . . . . DLB-146

Gay, Ebenezer 1696-1787. . . . . DLB-24

Gay, John 1685-1732. . . . . DLB-84, 95

The Gay Science (1866), by E. S. Dallas [excerpt]
. . . . DLB-21

Gayarré, Charles E. A. 1805-1895. . . . DLB-30

Gaylord, Edward King
1873-1974 . . . . DLB-127

Gaylord, Edward Lewis 1919- DLB-127

Gaylord, Charles
[publishing house]. DLB-49

Geddes, Gary 1940- DLB-60

Geddes, Virgil 1897- DLB-4

Gedeon (Georgii Andreevich Krinovsky)
circa 1730-1763 . . . . DLB-150

Geibel, Emanuel 1815-1884 . . . . DLB-129

Geiogamah, Hanay 1945- DLB-175

Geis, Bernard, Associates DLB-46

Geisel, Theodor Seuss
1904-1991 . . . . DLB-61; Y-91

Gelb, Arthur 1924- DLB-103

Gelb, Barbara 1926- DLB-103

Gelber, Jack 1932- DLB-7

Gelinas, Gratien 1909- DLB-88

Gellert, Christian Füerchtegott
1715-1769 . . . . DLB-97

Gellhorn, Martha 1908- Y-82

Gems, Pam 1925- DLB-13

A General Idea of the College of Mirania (1753),
by William Smith [excerpts] DLB-31

Genet, Jean 1910-1986 . . . . . . DLB-72; Y-86

Genevoix, Maurice 1890-1980 . . . . . DLB-65

Genovese, Eugene D. 1930- DLB-17

Gent, Peter 1942- Y-82

Geoffrey of Monmouth
circa 1100-1155 . . . . DLB-146

George, Henry 1839-1897 . . . . DLB-23

George, Jean Craighead 1919- DLB-52

George, W. L. 1882-1926. . . . . DLB-197

Georgslied 896? DLB-148

Gerhardie, William 1895-1977 . . . . . DLB-36

Gerhardt, Paul 1607-1676. . . . . DLB-164

Gérin, Winifred 1901-1981 . . . . DLB-155

Gérin-Lajoie, Antoine 1824-1882 . . . . DLB-99

German Drama 800-1280 . . . . DLB-138

German Drama from Naturalism
to Fascism: 1889-1933. . . . . . . DLB-118

German Literature and Culture from
Charlemagne to the Early Courtly
Period DLB-148

German Radio Play, The DLB-124

German Transformation from the Baroque
to the Enlightenment, The. DLB-97

The Germanic Epic and Old English Heroic
Poetry: *Widseth, Waldere,* and *The
Fight at Finnsburg*. DLB-146

Germanophilism, by Hans Kohn. . . . DLB-66

Gernsback, Hugo 1884-1967 . . . . DLB-8, 137

Gerould, Katharine Fullerton
1879-1944 . . . . DLB-78

Gerrish, Samuel [publishing house] . . . DLB-49

Gerrold, David 1944- DLB-8

The Ira Gershwin Centenary Y-96

Gersonides 1288-1344 . . . . DLB-115

Gerstäcker, Friedrich 1816-1872. . . . . DLB-129

Gerstenberg, Heinrich Wilhelm von
1737-1823 . . . . DLB-97

Gervinus, Georg Gottfried
1805-1871 . . . . DLB-133

Geßner, Salomon 1730-1788 . . . . . . DLB-97

Geston, Mark S. 1946- DLB-8

"Getting Started: Accepting the Regions You
Own—or Which Own You," by Walter
McDonald DLB-105

Al-Ghazali 1058-1111. . . . . DLB-115

Gibbings, Robert 1889-1958. . . . . . . DLB-195

Gibbon, Edward 1737-1794 . . . . . . DLB-104

Gibbon, John Murray 1875-1952 . . . . DLB-92

Gibbon, Lewis Grassic (see Mitchell,
James Leslie)

Gibbons, Floyd 1887-1939 . . . . DLB-25

Gibbons, Reginald 1947- DLB-120

Gibbons, William ?-? DLB-73

Gibson, Charles Dana 1867-1944 . . . . DS-13

Gibson, Charles Dana
1867-1944 . . . . DLB-188; DS-13

Gibson, Graeme 1934- DLB-53

Gibson, Margaret 1944- DLB-120

Gibson, Margaret Dunlop
1843-1920 . . . . DLB-174

Gibson, Wilfrid 1878-1962 . . . . DLB-19

Gibson, William 1914- DLB-7

Gide, André 1869-1951. . . . . DLB-65

Giguère, Diane 1937- DLB-53

Giguère, Roland 1929- DLB-60

Gil de Biedma, Jaime 1929-1990 . . . . DLB-108

Gil-Albert, Juan 1906- DLB-134

Gilbert, Anthony 1899-1973 . . . . . . DLB-77

Gilbert, Michael 1912- DLB-87

Gilbert, Sandra M. 1936- DLB-120

Gilbert, Sir Humphrey
1537-1583 . . . . DLB-136

Gilchrist, Alexander
1828-1861 . . . . DLB-144

Gilchrist, Ellen 1935- DLB-130

Gilder, Jeannette L. 1849-1916 . . . . . DLB-79

Gilder, Richard Watson
1844-1909 . . . . DLB-64, 79

Gildersleeve, Basil 1831-1924 . . . . . . DLB-71

Giles, Henry 1809-1882. . . . . DLB-64

Giles of Rome circa 1243-1316 . . . . . DLB-115

Gilfillan, George 1813-1878 . . . . DLB-144

Gill, Eric 1882-1940. . . . . DLB-98

Gill, Sarah Prince 1728-1771 . . . . . . DLB-200

Gill, William F., Company. DLB-49

Gillespie, A. Lincoln, Jr.
1895-1950. . . . . DLB-4

Gilliam, Florence ?-? DLB-4

Gilliatt, Penelope 1932-1993 . . . . . . DLB-14

Gillott, Jacky 1939-1980. . . . . DLB-14

Gilman, Caroline H. 1794-1888. . . . DLB-3, 73

Gilman, W. and J.
[publishing house]. DLB-49

Gilmer, Elizabeth Meriwether
1861-1951 . . . . DLB-29

Gilmer, Francis Walker
1790-1826 . . . . DLB-37

Gilroy, Frank D. 1925- DLB-7

Gimferrer, Pere (Pedro) 1945- DLB-134

Gingrich, Arnold 1903-1976. . . . . . DLB-137

Ginsberg, Allen 1926- DLB-5, 16, 169

Ginzburg, Natalia 1916-1991 . . . . . DLB-177

Ginzkey, Franz Karl 1871-1963 . . . . DLB-81

Gioia, Dana 1950- DLB-120

Giono, Jean 1895-1970 . . . . DLB-72

Giotti, Virgilio 1885-1957 . . . . DLB-114

Giovanni, Nikki 1943- DLB-5, 41

Gipson, Lawrence Henry
1880-1971 . . . . DLB-17

Girard, Rodolphe 1879-1956 . . . . . . DLB-92

Giraudoux, Jean 1882-1944. . . . . . . DLB-65

Gissing, George 1857-1903 . . DLB-18, 135, 184

Giudici, Giovanni 1924- DLB-128

Giuliani, Alfredo 1924- DLB-128

Glackens, William J. 1870-1938. . . . . DLB-188

Gladstone, William Ewart
1809-1898 . . . . DLB-57, 184

Glaeser, Ernst 1902-1963 . . . . DLB-69

Glancy, Diane 1941- DLB-175

Glanville, Brian 1931- DLB-15, 139

Glapthorne, Henry 1610-1643?. DLB-58

Glasgow, Ellen 1873-1945 . . . . . . DLB-9, 12

Glasier, Katharine Bruce 1867-1950 . . DLB-190

Glaspell, Susan 1876-1948 . . . . DLB-7, 9, 78

Glass, Montague 1877-1934 . . . . . . DLB-11

The Glass Key and Other Dashiell Hammett
Mysteries Y-96

Glassco, John 1909-1981 . . . . DLB-68

Glauser, Friedrich 1896-1938 . . . . . . DLB-56

F. Gleason's Publishing Hall DLB-49

Gleim, Johann Wilhelm Ludwig
1719-1803 . . . . DLB-97

Glendinning, Victoria 1937- DLB-155

Glover, Richard 1712-1785 . . . . DLB-95

Glück, Louise 1943- DLB-5

Glyn, Elinor 1864-1943 . . . . DLB-153

Gobineau, Joseph-Arthur de
1816-1882 . . . . DLB-123

Godbout, Jacques 1933- DLB-53

Goddard, Morrill 1865-1937 . . . . . . DLB-25

Goddard, William 1740-1817. . . . . . DLB-43

Godden, Rumer 1907- DLB-161

Godey, Louis A. 1804-1878 . . . . . . DLB-73

Godey and McMichael DLB-49

Godfrey, Dave 1938- DLB-60

Godfrey, Thomas 1736-1763 . . . . . . DLB-31

Godine, David R., Publisher DLB-46

Godkin, E. L. 1831-1902 . . . . DLB-79

Godolphin, Sidney 1610-1643 . . . . . DLB-126

Godwin, Gail 1937- DLB-6

Godwin, Mary Jane Clairmont
1766-1841 . . . . DLB-163

Godwin, Parke 1816-1904 . . . . . . DLB-3, 64

Godwin, William
1756-1836. . . . DLB-39, 104, 142, 158, 163

Godwin, M. J., and Company DLB-154

Goering, Reinhard 1887-1936 . . . . . DLB-118

Goes, Albrecht 1908- DLB-69

Goethe, Johann Wolfgang von
1749-1832 . . . . DLB-94

Goetz, Curt 1888-1960 . . . . DLB-124

Goffe, Thomas circa 1592-1629 . . . . DLB-58

Goffstein, M. B. 1940- DLB-61

Gogarty, Oliver St. John
1878-1957 . . . . DLB-15, 19

Gogol, Nikolai Vasil'evich
1809-1852 . . . . DLB-198

Goines, Donald 1937-1974 . . . . DLB-33

Gold, Herbert 1924- DLB-2; Y-81

Gold, Michael 1893-1967 . . . . . . DLB-9, 28

Goldbarth, Albert 1948- DLB-120

Goldberg, Dick 1947- DLB-7

Golden Cockerel Press DLB-112

Golding, Arthur 1536-1606 . . . . . . DLB-136

Golding, Louis 1895-1958 . . . . DLB-195

Golding, William 1911-1993 . DLB-15, 100; Y-83

Goldman, William 1931- DLB-44

Goldring, Douglas 1887-1960 . . . . . DLB-197

Goldsmith, Oliver
1730?-1774 . . . . DLB-39, 89, 104, 109, 142

Goldsmith, Oliver 1794-1861 . . . . . DLB-99

Goldsmith Publishing Company DLB-46

Goldstein, Richard 1944- DLB-185

Gollancz, Victor, Limited DLB-112

Gómez-Quiñones, Juan 1942- DLB-122

Gomme, Laurence James
[publishing house]. DLB-46

Goncourt, Edmond de 1822-1896 . . DLB-123

Goncourt, Jules de 1830-1870 . . . . . DLB-123

Gonzales, Rodolfo "Corky"
1928- DLB-122

González, Angel 1925- DLB-108

Gonzalez, Genaro 1949- DLB-122

Gonzalez, Ray 1952- DLB-122

González de Mireles, Jovita
1899-1983 . . . . DLB-122

González-T., César A. 1931- DLB-82

"The Good, The Not So Good," by
Stephen Dunn DLB-105

Goodbye, Gutenberg? A Lecture at
the New York Public Library,
18 April 1995 . . . . Y-95

Goodison, Lorna 1947- DLB-157

Goodman, Paul 1911-1972 . . . . . . DLB-130

The Goodman Theatre DLB-7

Goodrich, Frances 1891-1984 and
Hackett, Albert 1900- DLB-26

Goodrich, Samuel Griswold
1793-1860 . . . . DLB-1, 42, 73

Goodrich, S. G. [publishing house] . . . DLB-49

Goodspeed, C. E., and Company DLB-49

Goodwin, Stephen 1943- Y-82

Googe, Barnabe 1540-1594 . . . . . . DLB-132

Gookin, Daniel 1612-1687 . . . . DLB-24

Gordimer, Nadine 1923- Y-91

Gordon, Caroline
1895-1981. . . . DLB-4, 9, 102; DS-17; Y-81

Gordon, Giles 1940- DLB-14, 139

Gordon, Helen Cameron, Lady Russell
1867-1949 . . . . DLB-195

Gordon, Lyndall 1941- DLB-155

Gordon, Mary 1949- DLB-6; Y-81

Gordone, Charles 1925- DLB-7

Gore, Catherine 1800-1861 . . . . . . DLB-116

Gorey, Edward 1925- DLB-61

Gorgias of Leontini circa 485 B.C.-376 B.C.
. . . . DLB-176

Görres, Joseph 1776-1848. . . . . . . DLB-90

Gosse, Edmund 1849-1928 . . DLB-57, 144, 184

Gosson, Stephen 1554-1624 . . . . . . DLB-172

Gotlieb, Phyllis 1926- DLB-88

Gottfried von Straßburg
died before 1230 . . . . DLB-138

Gotthelf, Jeremias 1797-1854 . . . . . DLB-133

Gottschalk circa 804/808-869 . . . . . DLB-148

Gottsched, Johann Christoph
1700-1766 . . . . DLB-97

Götz, Johann Nikolaus
1721-1781 . . . . DLB-97

Goudge, Elizabeth 1900-1984 . . . . . DLB-191

Gould, Wallace 1882-1940 . . . . DLB-54

Govoni, Corrado 1884-1965. . . . . . DLB-114

Gower, John circa 1330-1408 . . . . . DLB-146

Goyen, William 1915-1983 . . . . DLB-2; Y-83

Goytisolo, José Augustín 1928- DLB-134

Gozzano, Guido 1883-1916 . . . . . . DLB-114

Grabbe, Christian Dietrich
1801-1836 . . . . DLB-133

Gracq, Julien 1910- DLB-83

Grady, Henry W. 1850-1889. . . . . . DLB-23

Graf, Oskar Maria 1894-1967 . . . . . . DLB-56

Graf Rudolf between circa 1170
  and circa 1185. . . . . DLB-148

Grafton, Richard
  [publishing house] DLB-170

Graham, George Rex
  1813-1894 . . . . DLB-73

Graham, Gwethalyn 1913-1965. . . . . . DLB-88

Graham, Jorie 1951- DLB-120

Graham, Katharine 1917- DLB-127

Graham, Lorenz 1902-1989. . . . . . . DLB-76

Graham, Philip 1915-1963. . . . . . . DLB-127

Graham, R. B. Cunninghame
  1852-1936 . . . . DLB-98, 135, 174

Graham, Shirley 1896-1977. . . . . . . DLB-76

Graham, Stephen 1884-1975. . . . . . DLB-195

Graham, W. S. 1918- DLB-20

Graham, William H.
  [publishing house]. DLB-49

Graham, Winston 1910- DLB-77

Grahame, Kenneth
  1859-1932 . . . . DLB-34, 141, 178

Grainger, Martin Allerdale
  1874-1941 . . . . DLB-92

Gramatky, Hardie 1907-1979. . . . . . DLB-22

Grand, Sarah 1854-1943 . . . . . DLB-135, 197

Grandbois, Alain 1900-1975 . . . . . . DLB-92

Grange, John circa 1556-?. DLB-136

Granich, Irwin (see Gold, Michael)

Granovsky, Timofei Nikolaevich
  1813-1855 . . . . DLB-198

Grant, Anne MacVicar 1755-1838 . . . DLB-200

Grant, Duncan 1885-1978 . . . . DS-10

Grant, George 1918-1988. . . . . DLB-88

Grant, George Monro 1835-1902 . . . . DLB-99

Grant, Harry J. 1881-1963 . . . . . . DLB-29

Grant, James Edward 1905-1966. . . . . DLB-26

Grass, Günter 1927- DLB-75, 124

Grasty, Charles H. 1863-1924 . . . . . DLB-25

Grau, Shirley Ann 1929- DLB-2

Graves, John 1920- Y-83

Graves, Richard 1715-1804 . . . . DLB-39

Graves, Robert 1895-1985
  . . . . . . DLB-20, 100, 191; DS-18; Y-85

Gray, Alasdair 1934- DLB-194

Gray, Asa 1810-1888. . . . . DLB-1

Gray, David 1838-1861. . . . . DLB-32

Gray, Simon 1936- DLB-13

Gray, Thomas 1716-1771 . . . . DLB-109

Grayson, William J. 1788-1863 . . . . DLB-3, 64

The Great Bibliographers Series Y-93

The Great War and the Theater, 1914-1918
  [Great Britain]. DLB-10

The Great War Exhibition and Symposium at the
  University of South Carolina Y-97

Grech, Nikolai Ivanovich 1787-1867 . . DLB-198

Greeley, Horace 1811-1872 . . . DLB-3, 43, 189

Green, Adolph (see Comden, Betty)

Green, Duff 1791-1875 . . . . DLB-43

Green, Elizabeth Shippen 1871-1954 . . DLB-188

Green, Gerald 1922- DLB-28

Green, Henry 1905-1973 . . . . DLB-15

Green, Jonas 1712-1767. . . . . DLB-31

Green, Joseph 1706-1780 . . . . DLB-31

Green, Julien 1900- DLB-4, 72

Green, Paul 1894-1981. . . . . DLB-7, 9; Y-81

Green, T. and S.
  [publishing house]. DLB-49

Green, Thomas Hill 1836-1882. . . . . DLB-190

Green, Timothy
  [publishing house]. DLB-49

Greenaway, Kate 1846-1901. . . . . . DLB-141

Greenberg: Publisher DLB-46

Green Tiger Press. DLB-46

Greene, Asa 1789-1838 . . . . DLB-11

Greene, Belle da Costa 1883-1950 . . . DLB-187

Greene, Benjamin H.
  [publishing house]. DLB-49

Greene, Graham 1904-1991
  . . . DLB-13, 15, 77, 100, 162; Y-85, Y-91

Greene, Robert 1558-1592 . . . . DLB-62, 167

Greene Jr., Robert Bernard (Bob)
  1947- DLB-185

Greenhow, Robert 1800-1854 . . . . . DLB-30

Greenlee, William B. 1872-1953 . . . . DLB-187

Greenough, Horatio 1805-1852 . . . . . DLB-1

Greenwell, Dora 1821-1882 . . . . DLB-35, 199

Greenwillow Books DLB-46

Greenwood, Grace (see Lippincott, Sara Jane
  Clarke)

Greenwood, Walter 1903-1974 . . . DLB-10, 191

Greer, Ben 1948- DLB-6

Greflinger, Georg 1620?-1677 . . . . . DLB-164

Greg, W. R. 1809-1881. . . . . DLB-55

Gregg, Josiah 1806-1850 . . . . . DLB-183, 186

Gregg Press DLB-46

Gregory, Isabella Augusta
  Persse, Lady 1852-1932 . . . . DLB-10

Gregory, Horace 1898-1982 . . . . . . DLB-48

Gregory of Rimini
  circa 1300-1358 . . . . DLB-115

Gregynog Press DLB-112

Greiffenberg, Catharina Regina von
  1633-1694 . . . . DLB-168

Grenfell, Wilfred Thomason
  1865-1940 . . . . DLB-92

Greve, Felix Paul (see Grove, Frederick Philip)

Greville, Fulke, First Lord Brooke
  1554-1628 . . . . DLB-62, 172

Grey, Sir George, K.C.B.
  1812-1898 . . . . DLB-184

Grey, Lady Jane 1537-1554 . . . . . . DLB-132

Grey Owl 1888-1938 . . . . DLB-92; DS-17

Grey, Zane 1872-1939 . . . . DLB-9

Grey Walls Press DLB-112

Grier, Eldon 1917- DLB-88

Grieve, C. M. (see MacDiarmid, Hugh)

Griffin, Bartholomew
  flourished 1596 . . . . DLB-172

Griffin, Gerald 1803-1840 . . . . DLB-159

Griffith, Elizabeth 1727?-1793 . . . . DLB-39, 89

Griffith, George 1857-1906 . . . . . . DLB-178

Griffiths, Trevor 1935- DLB-13

Griffiths, Ralph
  [publishing house] DLB-154

Griggs, S. C., and Company. DLB-49

Griggs, Sutton Elbert
  1872-1930 . . . . DLB-50

Grignon, Claude-Henri 1894-1976 . . . DLB-68

Grigson, Geoffrey 1905- DLB-27

Grillparzer, Franz 1791-1872 . . . . . DLB-133

Grimald, Nicholas
  circa 1519-circa 1562 . . . . DLB-136

Grimké, Angelina Weld
  1880-1958. . . . . DLB-50, 54

Grimm, Hans 1875-1959 . . . . DLB-66

Grimm, Jacob 1785-1863 . . . . DLB-90

Grimm, Wilhelm 1786-1859 . . . . . . DLB-90

Grimmelshausen, Johann Jacob Christoffel von
  1621 or 1622-1676 . . . . DLB-168

Grimshaw, Beatrice Ethel
  1871-1953 . . . . DLB-174

Grindal, Edmund
  1519 or 1520-1583 . . . . DLB-132

Griswold, Rufus Wilmot
  1815-1857 . . . . DLB-3, 59

Grosart, Alexander Balloch
  1827-1899 . . . . DLB-184

Gross, Milt 1895-1953 . . . . DLB-11

Grosset and Dunlap. DLB-49

Grossman, Allen 1932- DLB-193

Grossman Publishers DLB-46

Grosseteste, Robert
  circa 1160-1253 . . . . DLB-115

Grosvenor, Gilbert H. 1875-1966 . . . . DLB-91

Groth, Klaus 1819-1899 . . . . DLB-129

Groulx, Lionel 1878-1967 . . . . DLB-68

Grove, Frederick Philip 1879-1949 . . . . DLB-92

Grove Press DLB-46

Grubb, Davis 1919-1980 . . . . DLB-6

Gruelle, Johnny 1880-1938 . . . . . . DLB-22

von Grumbach, Argula
  1492-after 1563? DLB-179

Grymeston, Elizabeth
  before 1563-before 1604 . . . . DLB-136

Gryphius, Andreas 1616-1664 . . . . . DLB-164

Gryphius, Christian 1649-1706 . . . . DLB-168

Guare, John 1938- DLB-7

Guerra, Tonino 1920- DLB-128

Guest, Barbara 1920- DLB-5, 193

Guèvremont, Germaine
  1893-1968 . . . . DLB-68

Guidacci, Margherita 1921-1992 . . . . DLB-128

Guide to the Archives of Publishers, Journals, and
  Literary Agents in North American Libraries
  . . . . Y-93

Guillén, Jorge 1893-1984 . . . . DLB-108

Guilloux, Louis 1899-1980 . . . . DLB-72

Guilpin, Everard
  circa 1572-after 1608? DLB-136

Guiney, Louise Imogen 1861-1920 . . . . DLB-54

Guiterman, Arthur 1871-1943 . . . . . . DLB-11

Günderrode, Caroline von
  1780-1806 . . . . DLB-90

Gundulić, Ivan 1589-1638 . . . . DLB-147

Gunn, Bill 1934-1989 . . . . DLB-38

Gunn, James E. 1923- DLB-8

Gunn, Neil M. 1891-1973 . . . . DLB-15

Gunn, Thom 1929- DLB-27

Gunnars, Kristjana 1948- DLB-60

Günther, Johann Christian
  1695-1723 . . . . DLB-168

Gurik, Robert 1932- DLB-60

Gustafson, Ralph 1909- DLB-88

Gütersloh, Albert Paris 1887-1973 . . . . DLB-81

Guthrie, A. B., Jr. 1901- DLB-6

Guthrie, Ramon 1896-1973 . . . . DLB-4

The Guthrie Theater DLB-7

Guthrie, Thomas Anstey (see Anstey, FC)

Gutzkow, Karl 1811-1878 . . . . DLB-133

Guy, Ray 1939- DLB-60

Guy, Rosa 1925- DLB-33

Guyot, Arnold 1807-1884 . . . . DS-13

Gwynne, Erskine 1898-1948 . . . . DLB-4

Gyles, John 1680-1755 . . . . DLB-99

Gysin, Brion 1916- DLB-16

                    H

H. D. (see Doolittle, Hilda)

Habington, William 1605-1654 . . . . . DLB-126

Hacker, Marilyn 1942- DLB-120

Hackett, Albert (see Goodrich, Frances)

Hacks, Peter 1928- DLB-124

Hadas, Rachel 1948- DLB-120

Hadden, Briton 1898-1929 . . . . DLB-91

Hagedorn, Friedrich von
  1708-1754 . . . . DLB-168

Hagelstange, Rudolf 1912-1984 . . . . . DLB-69

Haggard, H. Rider
  1856-1925 . . . . . . DLB-70, 156, 174, 178

Haggard, William 1907-1993 . . . . Y-93

Hahn-Hahn, Ida Gräfin von
  1805-1880 . . . . DLB-133

Haig-Brown, Roderick 1908-1976 . . . . DLB-88

Haight, Gordon S. 1901-1985 . . . . . . DLB-103

Hailey, Arthur 1920- DLB-88; Y-82

Haines, John 1924- DLB-5

Hake, Edward
  flourished 1566-1604 . . . . DLB-136

Hake, Thomas Gordon 1809-1895 . . . . DLB-32

Hakluyt, Richard 1552?-1616 . . . . . . DLB-136

Halbe, Max 1865-1944 . . . . DLB-118

Haldone, Charlotte 1894-1969 . . . . . DLB-191

Haldane, J. B. S. 1892-1964 . . . . . . DLB-160

Haldeman, Joe 1943- DLB-8

Haldeman-Julius Company DLB-46

Hale, E. J., and Son DLB-49

Hale, Edward Everett
  1822-1909 . . . . DLB-1, 42, 74

Hale, Janet Campbell 1946- DLB-175

Hale, Kathleen 1898- DLB-160

Hale, Leo Thomas (see Ebon)

Hale, Lucretia Peabody
  1820-1900 . . . . DLB-42

Hale, Nancy
  1908-1988 . . . . DLB-86; DS-17; Y-80, Y-88

Hale, Sarah Josepha (Buell)
  1788-1879 . . . . DLB-1, 42, 73

Hales, John 1584-1656 . . . . DLB-151

Halévy, Ludovic 1834-1908 . . . . DLB-192

Haley, Alex 1921-1992 . . . . DLB-38

Haliburton, Thomas Chandler
  1796-1865 . . . . DLB-11, 99

Hall, Anna Maria 1800-1881 . . . . . . DLB-159

Hall, Donald 1928- DLB-5

Hall, Edward 1497-1547 . . . . DLB-132

Hall, James 1793-1868 . . . . DLB-73, 74

Hall, Joseph 1574-1656 . . . . . . DLB-121, 151

Hall, Radclyffe 1880-1943 . . . . DLB-191

Hall, Sarah Ewing 1761-1830 . . . . . . DLB-200

Hall, Samuel [publishing house] DLB-49

Hallam, Arthur Henry 1811-1833 . . . . DLB-32

Halleck, Fitz-Greene 1790-1867 . . . . . DLB-3

Haller, Albrecht von 1708-1777 . . . . . DLB-168

Halliwell-Phillipps, James Orchard
  1820-1889 . . . . DLB-184

Hallmann, Johann Christian
  1640-1704 or 1716? DLB-168

Hallmark Editions DLB-46

Halper, Albert 1904-1984 . . . . DLB-9

Halperin, John William 1941- DLB-111

Halstead, Murat 1829-1908 . . . . DLB-23

Hamann, Johann Georg 1730-1788 . . . DLB-97

Hamburger, Michael 1924- DLB-27

Hamilton, Alexander 1712-1756 . . . . . DLB-31

Hamilton, Alexander 1755?-1804 . . . . DLB-37

Hamilton, Cicely 1872-1952 . . . . DLB-10, 197

Hamilton, Edmond 1904-1977 . . . . . . DLB-8

Hamilton, Elizabeth 1758-1816 . . . . DLB-116, 158

Hamilton, Gail (see Corcoran, Barbara)

Hamilton, Ian 1938- DLB-40, 155

Hamilton, Janet 1795-1873 . . . . . . DLB-199

Hamilton, Mary Agnes 1884-1962 . . . DLB-197

Hamilton, Patrick 1904-1962 . . . . DLB-10, 191

Hamilton, Virginia 1936- DLB-33, 52

Hamilton, Hamish, Limited DLB-112

Hammett, Dashiell 1894-1961 . . . . . . DS-6

Dashiell Hammett:
  An Appeal in TAC Y-91

Hammon, Jupiter 1711-died between
  1790 and 1806 . . . . DLB-31, 50

Hammond, John ?-1663 . . . . DLB-24

Hamner, Earl 1923- DLB-6

Hampson, John 1901-1955 . . . . DLB-191

Hampton, Christopher 1946- DLB-13

Handel-Mazzetti, Enrica von
  1871-1955 . . . . DLB-81

Handke, Peter 1942- DLB-85, 124

Handlin, Oscar 1915- DLB-17

Hankin, St. John 1869-1909 . . . . . . DLB-10

Hanley, Clifford 1922- DLB-14

Hanley, James 1901-1985 . . . . DLB-191

Hannah, Barry 1942- DLB-6

Hannay, James 1827-1873 . . . . DLB-21

Hansberry, Lorraine 1930-1965 . . . . DLB-7, 38

Hanson, Elizabeth 1684-1737 . . . . . DLB-200

Hapgood, Norman 1868-1937 . . . . . DLB-91

Happel, Eberhard Werner
  1647-1690 . . . . DLB-168

Harcourt Brace Jovanovich DLB-46

Hardenberg, Friedrich von (see Novalis)

Harding, Walter 1917- DLB-111

Hardwick, Elizabeth 1916- DLB-6

Hardy, Thomas 1840-1928 . . . DLB-18, 19, 135

Hare, Cyril 1900-1958 . . . . DLB-77

Hare, David 1947- DLB-13

Hargrove, Marion 1919- DLB-11

Häring, Georg Wilhelm Heinrich (see Alexis, Willibald)

Harington, Donald 1935- DLB-152

Harington, Sir John 1560-1612 . . . . . DLB-136

Harjo, Joy 1951- DLB-120, 175

Harkness, Margaret (John Law)
1854-1923 . . . . DLB-197

Harlow, Robert 1923- DLB-60

Harman, Thomas
flourished 1566-1573 . . . . DLB-136

Harness, Charles L. 1915- DLB-8

Harnett, Cynthia 1893-1981 . . . . . . DLB-161

Harper, Fletcher 1806-1877 . . . . DLB-79

Harper, Frances Ellen Watkins
1825-1911 . . . . DLB-50

Harper, Michael S. 1938- DLB-41

Harper and Brothers DLB-49

Harraden, Beatrice 1864-1943 . . . . . DLB-153

Harrap, George G., and Company
Limited DLB-112

Harriot, Thomas 1560-1621 . . . . . . DLB-136

Harris, Benjamin ?-circa 1720 . . . DLB-42, 43

Harris, Christie 1907- DLB-88

Harris, Frank 1856-1931 . . . . . DLB-156, 197

Harris, George Washington
1814-1869 . . . . DLB-3, 11

Harris, Joel Chandler
1848-1908 . . . . . DLB-11, 23, 42, 78, 91

Harris, Mark 1922- DLB-2; Y-80

Harris, Wilson 1921- DLB-117

Harrison, Charles Yale
1898-1954 . . . . DLB-68

Harrison, Frederic 1831-1923 . . . . DLB-57, 190

Harrison, Harry 1925- DLB-8

Harrison, Jim 1937- Y-82

Harrison, Mary St. Leger Kingsley
(see Malet, Lucas)

Harrison, Paul Carter 1936- DLB-38

Harrison, Susan Frances
1859-1935 . . . . DLB-99

Harrison, Tony 1937- DLB-40

Harrison, William 1535-1593 . . . . . DLB-136

Harrison, James P., Company DLB-49

Harrisse, Henry 1829-1910 . . . . DLB-47

Harryman, Carla 1952- DLB-193

Harsdörffer, Georg Philipp
1607-1658 . . . . DLB-164

Harsent, David 1942- DLB-40

Hart, Albert Bushnell 1854-1943 . . . . DLB-17

Hart, Anne 1768-1834 . . . . DLB-200

Hart, Elizabeth 1771-1833 . . . . DLB-200

Hart, Julia Catherine 1796-1867 . . . . DLB-99

The Lorenz Hart Centenary Y-95

Hart, Moss 1904-1961 . . . . DLB-7

Hart, Oliver 1723-1795 . . . . DLB-31

Hart-Davis, Rupert, Limited DLB-112

Harte, Bret
1836-1902 . . . . DLB-12, 64, 74, 79, 186

Harte, Edward Holmead 1922- DLB-127

Harte, Houston Harriman 1927- DLB-127

Hartlaub, Felix 1913-1945 . . . . DLB-56

Hartleben, Otto Erich
1864-1905 . . . . DLB-118

Hartley, L. P. 1895-1972 . . . . . DLB-15, 139

Hartley, Marsden 1877-1943 . . . . . . DLB-54

Hartling, Peter 1933- DLB-75

Hartman, Geoffrey H. 1929- DLB-67

Hartmann, Sadakichi 1867-1944 . . . . DLB-54

Hartmann von Aue
circa 1160-circa 1205 . . . . DLB-138

Harvey, Gabriel 1550?-1631 . . . . . . DLB-167

Harvey, Jean-Charles 1891-1967 . . . . DLB-88

Harvill Press Limited DLB-112

Harwood, Lee 1939- DLB-40

Harwood, Ronald 1934- DLB-13

Haskins, Charles Homer
1870-1937 . . . . DLB-47

Hass, Robert 1941- DLB-105

The Hatch-Billops Collection DLB-76

Hathaway, William 1944- DLB-120

Hauff, Wilhelm 1802-1827 . . . . DLB-90

A Haughty and Proud Generation (1922),
by Ford Madox Hueffer DLB-36

Haugwitz, August Adolph von
1647-1706 . . . . DLB-168

Hauptmann, Carl
1858-1921 . . . . DLB-66, 118

Hauptmann, Gerhart
1862-1946 . . . . DLB-66, 118

Hauser, Marianne 1910- Y-83

Havergal, Frances Ridley 1836-1879 . . DLB-199

Hawes, Stephen
1475?-before 1529 . . . . DLB-132

Hawker, Robert Stephen
1803-1875 . . . . DLB-32

Hawkes, John 1925- DLB-2, 7; Y-80

Hawkesworth, John 1720-1773 . . . . DLB-142

Hawkins, Sir Anthony Hope (see Hope, Anthony)

Hawkins, Sir John
1719-1789 . . . . DLB-104, 142

Hawkins, Walter Everette 1883-? DLB-50

Hawthorne, Nathaniel
1804-1864 . . . . DLB-1, 74, 183

Hawthorne, Nathaniel 1804-1864 and
Hawthorne, Sophia Peabody
1809-1871 . . . . DLB-183

Hay, John 1835-1905 . . . . . DLB-12, 47, 189

Hayashi, Fumiko 1903-1951 . . . . . . DLB-180

Haycraft, Anna Margaret (see Ellis, Alice Thomas)

Hayden, Robert 1913-1980 . . . . . DLB-5, 76

Haydon, Benjamin Robert
1786-1846 . . . . DLB-110

Hayes, John Michael 1919- DLB-26

Hayley, William 1745-1820 . . . . DLB-93, 142

Haym, Rudolf 1821-1901 . . . . DLB-129

Hayman, Robert 1575-1629 . . . . . . DLB-99

Hayman, Ronald 1932- DLB-155

Hayne, Paul Hamilton
1830-1886 . . . . DLB-3, 64, 79

Hays, Mary 1760-1843 . . . . . DLB-142, 158

Haywood, Eliza 1693?-1756 . . . . . . DLB-39

Hazard, Willis P. [publishing house] DLB-49

Hazlitt, William 1778-1830 . . . . DLB-110, 158

Hazzard, Shirley 1931- Y-82

Head, Bessie 1937-1986 . . . . DLB-117

Headley, Joel T.
1813-1897 . . . . DLB-30, 183; DS-13

Heaney, Seamus 1939- DLB-40; Y-95

Heard, Nathan C. 1936- DLB-33

Hearn, Lafcadio 1850-1904 . . . DLB-12, 78, 189

Hearne, John 1926- DLB-117

Hearne, Samuel 1745-1792 . . . . DLB-99

Hearst, William Randolph
1863-1951 . . . . DLB-25

Hearst, William Randolph, Jr
1908-1993 . . . . DLB-127

Heartman, Charles Frederick
1883-1953 . . . . DLB-187

Heath, Catherine 1924- DLB-14

Heath, Roy A. K. 1926- DLB-117

Heath-Stubbs, John 1918- DLB-27

Heavysege, Charles 1816-1876 . . . . . DLB-99

Hebbel, Friedrich 1813-1863 . . . . . . DLB-129

Hebel, Johann Peter 1760-1826 . . . . . DLB-90

Heber, Richard 1774-1833 . . . . DLB-184

Hébert, Anne 1916- DLB-68

Hébert, Jacques 1923- DLB-53

Hecht, Anthony 1923- DLB-5, 169

Hecht, Ben 1894-1964
. . . . DLB-7, 9, 25, 26, 28, 86

Hecker, Isaac Thomas 1819-1888 . . . . DLB-1

Hedge, Frederic Henry
1805-1890 . . . . DLB-1, 59

Hefner, Hugh M. 1926- DLB-137

Hegel, Georg Wilhelm Friedrich
1770-1831 . . . . DLB-90

Heidish, Marcy 1947- Y-82

Heißenbüttel 1921- DLB-75

Hein, Christoph 1944- DLB-124

Heine, Heinrich 1797-1856 . . . . DLB-90

Heinemann, Larry 1944- DS-9

Heinemann, William, Limited DLB-112

Heinlein, Robert A. 1907-1988 . . . . . . DLB-8

Heinrich Julius of Brunswick
1564-1613 . . . . DLB-164

Heinrich von dem Türlin
flourished circa 1230 . . . . DLB-138

Heinrich von Melk
flourished after 1160 . . . . DLB-148

Heinrich von Veldeke
circa 1145-circa 1190 . . . . DLB-138

Heinrich, Willi 1920- DLB-75

Heiskell, John 1872-1972 . . . . DLB-127

Heinse, Wilhelm 1746-1803 . . . . . . DLB-94

Heinz, W. C. 1915- DLB-171

Hejinian, Lyn 1941- DLB-165

Heliand circa 850 . . . . DLB-148

Heller, Joseph 1923- DLB-2, 28; Y-80

Heller, Michael 1937- DLB-165

Hellman, Lillian 1906-1984 . . . . . DLB-7; Y-84

Hellwig, Johann 1609-1674 . . . . DLB-164

Helprin, Mark 1947- Y-85

Helwig, David 1938- DLB-60

Hemans, Felicia 1793-1835 . . . . DLB-96

Hemingway, Ernest 1899-1961 . . DLB-4, 9, 102;
Y-81, Y-87; DS-1, DS-15, DS-16

Hemingway: Twenty-Five Years
Later Y-85

Hémon, Louis 1880-1913 . . . . DLB-92

Hemphill, Paul 1936- Y-87

Hénault, Gilles 1920- DLB-88

Henchman, Daniel 1689-1761 . . . . . . DLB-24

Henderson, Alice Corbin
1881-1949 . . . . DLB-54

Henderson, Archibald
1877-1963 . . . . DLB-103

Henderson, David 1942- DLB-41

Henderson, George Wylie
1904- DLB-51

Henderson, Zenna 1917-1983 . . . . DLB-8

Henisch, Peter 1943- DLB-85

Henley, Beth 1952- Y-86

Henley, William Ernest
1849-1903 . . . . DLB-19

Henniker, Florence 1855-1923 . . . . . DLB-135

Henry, Alexander 1739-1824 . . . . . . DLB-99

Henry, Buck 1930- DLB-26

Henry VIII of England
1491-1547 . . . . DLB-132

Henry, Marguerite 1902- DLB-22

Henry, O. (see Porter, William Sydney)

Henry of Ghent
circa 1217-1229 - 1293 . . . . . . DLB-115

Henry, Robert Selph 1889-1970 . . . . DLB-17

Henry, Will (see Allen, Henry W.)

Henryson, Robert
1420s or 1430s-circa 1505 . . . . . DLB-146

Henschke, Alfred (see Klabund)

Hensley, Sophie Almon 1866-1946 . . . . DLB-99

Henson, Lance 1944- DLB-175

Henty, G. A. 1832?-1902 . . . . . DLB-18, 141

Hentz, Caroline Lee 1800-1856 . . . . . . DLB-3

Heraclitus flourished circa 500 B.C.
. . . . DLB-176

Herbert, Agnes circa 1880-1960 . . . . . DLB-174

Herbert, Alan Patrick 1890-1971 . . DLB-10, 191

Herbert, Edward, Lord, of Cherbury
1582-1648 . . . . DLB-121, 151

Herbert, Frank 1920-1986 . . . . DLB-8

Herbert, George 1593-1633 . . . . DLB-126

Herbert, Henry William
1807-1858 . . . . DLB-3, 73

Herbert, John 1926- DLB-53

Herbert, Mary Sidney, Countess of Pembroke
(see Sidney, Mary)

Herbst, Josephine 1892-1969 . . . . DLB-9

Herburger, Gunter 1932- DLB-75, 124

Êercules, Frank E. M. 1917- DLB-33

Herder, Johann Gottfried
1744-1803 . . . . DLB-97

Herder, B., Book Company DLB-49

Herford, Charles Harold
1853-1931 . . . . DLB-149

Hergesheimer, Joseph
1880-1954 . . . . DLB-9, 102

Heritage Press DLB-46

Hermann the Lame 1013-1054 . . . . . DLB-148

Hermes, Johann Timotheus
1738-1821 . . . . DLB-97

Hermlin, Stephan 1915- DLB-69

Hernández, Alfonso C. 1938- DLB-122

Hernández, Inés 1947- DLB-122

Hernández, Miguel 1910-1942 . . . . DLB-134

Hernton, Calvin C. 1932- DLB-38

"The Hero as Man of Letters: Johnson,
Rousseau, Burns" (1841), by Thomas
Carlyle [excerpt] DLB-57

The Hero as Poet. Dante; Shakspeare (1841),
by Thomas Carlyle DLB-32

Herodotus circa 484 B.C.-circa 420 B.C.
. . . . DLB-176

Heron, Robert 1764-1807 . . . . DLB-142

Herr, Michael 1940- DLB-185

Herrera, Juan Felipe 1948- DLB-122

Herrick, Robert 1591-1674 . . . . . . DLB-126

Herrick, Robert 1868-1938 . . . . DLB-9, 12, 78

Herrick, William 1915- Y-83

Herrick, E. R., and Company DLB-49

Herrmann, John 1900-1959 . . . . DLB-4

Hersey, John 1914-1993 . . . . . . DLB-6, 185

Hertel, François 1905-1985 . . . . DLB-68

Hervé-Bazin, Jean Pierre Marie (see Bazin, Hervé)

Hervey, John, Lord 1696-1743 . . . . . DLB-101

Herwig, Georg 1817-1875 . . . . DLB-133

Herzog, Emile Salomon Wilhelm (see Maurois, André)

Hesiod eighth century B.C. DLB-176

Hesse, Hermann 1877-1962 . . . . . . DLB-66

Hessus, Helius Eobanus
1488-1540 . . . . DLB-179

Hewat, Alexander
circa 1743-circa 1824 . . . . DLB-30

Hewitt, John 1907- DLB-27

Hewlett, Maurice 1861-1923 . . . . DLB-34, 156

Heyen, William 1940- DLB-5

Heyer, Georgette 1902-1974 . . . . DLB-77, 191

Heym, Stefan 1913- DLB-69

Heyse, Paul 1830-1914 . . . . DLB-129

Heytesbury, William
circa 1310-1372 or 1373 . . . . . . DLB-115

Heyward, Dorothy 1890-1961 . . . . . . DLB-7

Heyward, DuBose
1885-1940 . . . . DLB-7, 9, 45

Heywood, John 1497?-1580? DLB-136

Heywood, Thomas
1573 or 1574-1641 . . . . DLB-62

Hibbs, Ben 1901-1975 . . . . DLB-137

Hichens, Robert S. 1864-1950 . . . . . DLB-153

Hickey, Emily 1845-1924 . . . . DLB-199

Hickman, William Albert
1877-1957 . . . . DLB-92

Hidalgo, José Luis 1919-1947 . . . . . DLB-108

Hiebert, Paul 1892-1987 . . . . DLB-68

Hieng, Andrej 1925- DLB-181

Hierro, José 1922- DLB-108

Higgins, Aidan 1927- DLB-14

Higgins, Colin 1941-1988 . . . . DLB-26

Higgins, George V. 1939- DLB-2; Y-81

Higginson, Thomas Wentworth
1823-1911 . . . . DLB-1, 64

Highwater, Jamake 1942?- DLB-52; Y-85

Hijuelos, Oscar 1951- DLB-145

Hildegard von Bingen
1098-1179 . . . . DLB-148

Das Hildesbrandslied circa 820 . . . . . DLB-148

Hildesheimer, Wolfgang
1916-1991 . . . . DLB-69, 124

Hildreth, Richard
1807-1865 . . . . DLB-1, 30, 59

Hill, Aaron 1685-1750 . . . . DLB-84

Hill, Geoffrey 1932- DLB-40

Hill, "Sir" John 1714?-1775 . . . . . . DLB-39

Hill, Leslie 1880-1960 . . . . DLB-51

Hill, Susan 1942- DLB-14, 139

Hill, Walter 1942- DLB-44

Hill and Wang DLB-46

Hill, George M., Company. DLB-49

Hill, Lawrence, and Company,
Publishers DLB-46

Hillberry, Conrad 1928- DLB-120

Hilliard, Gray and Company DLB-49

Hills, Lee 1906- DLB-127

Hillyer, Robert 1895-1961 . . . . DLB-54

Hilton, James 1900-1954 . . . . . . DLB-34, 77

Hilton, Walter died 1396 . . . . DLB-146

Hilton and Company DLB-49

Himes, Chester
1909-1984. . . . . DLB-2, 76, 143

Hindmarsh, Joseph
[publishing house] DLB-170

Hine, Daryl 1936- DLB-60

Hingley, Ronald 1920- DLB-155

Hinojosa-Smith, Rolando
1929- DLB-82

Hippel, Theodor Gottlieb von
1741-1796 . . . . DLB-97

Hippocrates of Cos flourished circa 425 B.C.
. . . . DLB-176

Hirabayashi, Taiko 1905-1972 . . . . . DLB-180

Hirsch, E. D., Jr. 1928- DLB-67

Hirsch, Edward 1950- DLB-120 *The History of the
Adventures of Joseph Andrews*
(1742), by Henry Fielding
[excerpt] DLB-39

Hoagland, Edward 1932- DLB-6

Hoagland, Everett H., III 1942- DLB-41

Hoban, Russell 1925- DLB-52

Hobbes, Thomas 1588-1679. . . . . . . DLB-151

Hobby, Oveta 1905- DLB-127

Hobby, William 1878-1964 . . . . . . DLB-127

Hobsbaum, Philip 1932- DLB-40

Hobson, Laura Z. 1900- DLB-28

Hoby, Thomas 1530-1566. . . . . DLB-132

Hoccleve, Thomas
circa 1368-circa 1437 . . . . DLB-146

Hochhuth, Rolf 1931- DLB-124

Hochman, Sandra 1936- DLB-5

Hocken, Thomas Morland
1836-1910 . . . . DLB-184

Hodder and Stoughton, Limited DLB-106

Hodgins, Jack 1938- DLB-60

Hodgman, Helen 1945- DLB-14

Hodgskin, Thomas 1787-1869 . . . . . DLB-158

Hodgson, Ralph 1871-1962. . . . . . . DLB-19

Hodgson, William Hope
1877-1918 . . . . . DLB-70, 153, 156, 178

Hoe, Robert III 1839-1909 . . . . . . DLB-187

Hoffenstein, Samuel 1890-1947 . . . . . DLB-11

Hoffman, Charles Fenno
1806-1884. . . . . DLB-3

Hoffman, Daniel 1923- DLB-5

Hoffmann, E. T. A. 1776-1822 . . . . DLB-90

Hoffman, Frank B. 1888-1958 . . . . DLB-188

Hoffmanswaldau, Christian Hoffman von
1616-1679 . . . . DLB-168

Hofmann, Michael 1957- DLB-40

Hofmannsthal, Hugo von
1874-1929 . . . . DLB-81, 118

Hofstadter, Richard 1916-1970 . . . . . DLB-17

Hogan, Desmond 1950- DLB-14

Hogan, Linda 1947- DLB-175

Hogan and Thompson DLB-49

Hogarth Press DLB-112

Hogg, James 1770-1835 . . . . DLB-93, 116, 159

Hohberg, Wolfgang Helmhard Freiherr von
1612-1688 . . . . DLB-168

von Hohenheim, Philippus Aureolus
Theophrastus Bombastus (see Paracelsus)

Hohl, Ludwig 1904-1980 . . . . DLB-56

Holbrook, David 1923- DLB-14, 40

Holcroft, Thomas
1745-1809 . . . . DLB-39, 89, 158

Holden, Jonathan 1941- DLB-105

Holden, Molly 1927-1981. . . . . DLB-40

Hölderlin, Friedrich 1770-1843 . . . . DLB-90

Holiday House DLB-46

Holinshed, Raphael died 1580 . . . . DLB-167

Holland, J. G. 1819-1881. . . . . DS-13

Holland, Norman N. 1927- DLB-67

Hollander, John 1929- DLB-5

Holley, Marietta 1836-1926. . . . . . . DLB-11

Hollingsworth, Margaret 1940- DLB-60

Hollo, Anselm 1934- DLB-40

Holloway, Emory 1885-1977 . . . . . DLB-103

Holloway, John 1920- DLB-27

Holloway House Publishing
Company DLB-46

Holme, Constance 1880-1955. . . . . . DLB-34

Holmes, Abraham S. 1821?-1908 . . . . DLB-99

Holmes, John Clellon 1926-1988 . . . . DLB-16

Holmes, Oliver Wendell
1809-1894. . . . . DLB-1, 189

Holmes, Richard 1945- DLB-155

Holmes, Thomas James 1874-1959 . . . DLB-187

Holroyd, Michael 1935- DLB-155

Holst, Hermann E. von
1841-1904 . . . . DLB-47

Holt, John 1721-1784 . . . . DLB-43

Holt, Henry, and Company DLB-49

Holt, Rinehart and Winston DLB-46

Holtby, Winifred 1898-1935. . . . . . . DLB-191

Holthusen, Hans Egon 1913- DLB-69

Hölty, Ludwig Christoph Heinrich
1748-1776 . . . . DLB-94

Holz, Arno 1863-1929 . . . . DLB-118

Home, Henry, Lord Kames (see Kames, Henry
Home, Lord)

Home, John 1722-1808 . . . . DLB-84

Home, William Douglas 1912- DLB-13

Home Publishing Company DLB-49

Homer circa eighth-seventh centuries B.C.
. . . . DLB-176

Homer, Winslow 1836-1910 . . . . . DLB-188

Homes, Geoffrey (see Mainwaring, Daniel)

Honan, Park 1928- DLB-111

Hone, William 1780-1842 . . . . DLB-110, 158

Hongo, Garrett Kaoru 1951- DLB-120

Honig, Edwin 1919- DLB-5

Hood, Hugh 1928- DLB-53

Hood, Thomas 1799-1845 . . . . DLB-96

Hook, Theodore 1788-1841. . . . . . . DLB-116

Hooker, Jeremy 1941- DLB-40

Hooker, Richard 1554-1600. . . . . . . DLB-132

Hooker, Thomas 1586-1647 . . . . . . DLB-24

Hooper, Johnson Jones
1815-1862 . . . . DLB-3, 11

Hope, Anthony 1863-1933. . . . . DLB-153, 156

Hopkins, Ellice 1836-1904 . . . . . . DLB-190

Hopkins, Gerard Manley
1844-1889. . . . . DLB-35, 57

Hopkins, John (see Sternhold, Thomas)

Hopkins, Lemuel 1750-1801 . . . . . . DLB-37

Hopkins, Pauline Elizabeth
1859-1930 . . . . DLB-50

Hopkins, Samuel 1721-1803 . . . . . . DLB-31

Hopkins, John H., and Son DLB-46

Hopkinson, Francis 1737-1791 . . . . . DLB-31

Hoppin, Augustus 1828-1896 . . . . . DLB-188

Horgan, Paul 1903- DLB-102; Y-85

Horizon Press DLB-46

Horne, Frank 1899-1974 . . . . DLB-51

Horne, Richard Henry (Hengist)
1802 or 1803-1884 . . . . DLB-32

Hornung, E. W. 1866-1921 . . . . . . DLB-70

Horovitz, Israel 1939- DLB-7

Horton, George Moses
1797?-1883? DLB-50

Horváth, Ödön von
1901-1938 . . . . DLB-85, 124

Horwood, Harold 1923- DLB-60

Hosford, E. and E.
[publishing house] DLB-49

Hoskens, Jane Fenn 1693-1770? DLB-200

Hoskyns, John 1566-1638 . . . . DLB-121

Hotchkiss and Company DLB-49

Hough, Emerson 1857-1923 . . . . DLB-9

Houghton Mifflin Company DLB-49

Houghton, Stanley 1881-1913 . . . . . DLB-10

Household, Geoffrey 1900-1988 . . . . DLB-87

Housman, A. E. 1859-1936. . . . . . . DLB-19

Housman, Laurence 1865-1959. . . . . DLB-10

Houwald, Ernst von 1778-1845 . . . . . DLB-90

Hovey, Richard 1864-1900 . . . . DLB-54

Howard, Donald R. 1927-1987 . . . . . DLB-111

Howard, Maureen 1930- Y-83

Howard, Richard 1929- DLB-5

Howard, Roy W. 1883-1964. . . . . . . DLB-29

Howard, Sidney 1891-1939 . . . . . DLB-7, 26

Howe, E. W. 1853-1937 . . . . . . DLB-12, 25

Howe, Henry 1816-1893 . . . . DLB-30

Howe, Irving 1920-1993 . . . . DLB-67

Howe, Joseph 1804-1873 . . . . DLB-99

Howe, Julia Ward 1819-1910 . . . . DLB-1, 189

Howe, Percival Presland
1886-1944 . . . . DLB-149

Howe, Susan 1937- DLB-120

Howell, Clark, Sr. 1863-1936. . . . . . DLB-25

Howell, Evan P. 1839-1905 . . . . . . DLB-23

Howell, James 1594?-1666. . . . . . . DLB-151

Howell, Warren Richardson
1912-1984 . . . . DLB-140

Howell, Soskin and Company DLB-46

Howells, William Dean
1837-1920 . . . . . DLB-12, 64, 74, 79, 189

Howitt, Mary 1799-1888. . . . . DLB-110, 199

Howitt, William 1792-1879 and
Howitt, Mary 1799-1888 . . . . . . DLB-110

Hoyem, Andrew 1935- DLB-5

Hoyers, Anna Ovena 1584-1655 . . . . DLB-164

Hoyos, Angela de 1940- DLB-82

Hoyt, Palmer 1897-1979. . . . . DLB-127

Hoyt, Henry [publishing house] DLB-49

Hrabanus Maurus 776?-856. . . . . . . DLB-148

Hrotsvit of Gandersheim
circa 935-circa 1000 . . . . DLB-148

Hubbard, Elbert 1856-1915. . . . . . . DLB-91

Hubbard, Kin 1868-1930 . . . . DLB-11

Hubbard, William circa 1621-1704. . . . DLB-24

Huber, Therese 1764-1829 . . . . DLB-90

Huch, Friedrich 1873-1913 . . . . DLB-66

Huch, Ricarda 1864-1947. . . . . DLB-66

Huck at 100: How Old Is
Huckleberry Finn? Y-85

Huddle, David 1942- DLB-130

Hudgins, Andrew 1951- DLB-120

Hudson, Henry Norman
1814-1886 . . . . DLB-64

Hudson, Stephen 1868?-1944 . . . . . DLB-197

Hudson, W. H.
1841-1922 . . . . DLB-98, 153, 174

Hudson and Goodwin DLB-49

Huebsch, B. W.
[publishing house]. DLB-46

Hueffer, Oliver Madox 1876-1931 . . . DLB-197

Hughes, David 1930- DLB-14

Hughes, John 1677-1720 . . . . DLB-84

Hughes, Langston
1902-1967 . . . . . . DLB-4, 7, 48, 51, 86

Hughes, Richard 1900-1976. . . . . DLB-15, 161

Hughes, Ted 1930- DLB-40, 161

Hughes, Thomas 1822-1896 . . . DLB-18, 163

Hugo, Richard 1923-1982 . . . . DLB-5

Hugo, Victor 1802-1885 . . . . . DLB-119, 192

Hugo Awards and Nebula Awards DLB-8

Hull, Richard 1896-1973 . . . . DLB-77

Hulme, T. E. 1883-1917 . . . . DLB-19

Hulton, Anne ?-1779? DLB-200

Humboldt, Alexander von
1769-1859 . . . . DLB-90

Humboldt, Wilhelm von
1767-1835 . . . . DLB-90

Hume, David 1711-1776 . . . . DLB-104

Hume, Fergus 1859-1932. . . . . DLB-70

Hume, Sophia 1702-1774 . . . . DLB-200

Hummer, T. R. 1950- DLB-120

Humorous Book Illustration DLB-11

Humphrey, William 1924- DLB-6

Humphreys, David 1752-1818 . . . . . DLB-37

Humphreys, Emyr 1919- DLB-15

Huncke, Herbert 1915- DLB-16

Huneker, James Gibbons
1857-1921 . . . . DLB-71

Hunold, Christian Friedrich
1681-1721 . . . . DLB-168

Hunt, Irene 1907- DLB-52

Hunt, Leigh 1784-1859 . . . DLB-96, 110, 144

Hunt, Violet 1862-1942 . . . . . DLB-162, 197

Hunt, William Gibbes 1791-1833 . . . . DLB-73

Hunter, Evan 1926- Y-82

Hunter, Jim 1939- DLB-14

Hunter, Kristin 1931- DLB-33

Hunter, Mollie 1922- DLB-161

Hunter, N. C. 1908-1971. . . . . DLB-10

Hunter-Duvar, John 1821-1899 . . . . DLB-99

Huntington, Henry E.
1850-1927 . . . . DLB-140

Huntington, Susan Mansfield
1791-1823 . . . . DLB-200

Hurd and Houghton DLB-49

Hurst, Fannie 1889-1968 . . . . DLB-86

Hurst and Blackett. DLB-106

Hurst and Company DLB-49

Hurston, Zora Neale
1901?-1960 . . . . DLB-51, 86

Husson, Jules-François-Félix (see Champfleury)

Huston, John 1906-1987 . . . . DLB-26

Hutcheson, Francis 1694-1746 . . . . . DLB-31

Hutchinson, R. C. 1907-1975 . . . . . DLB-191

Hutchinson, Thomas
1711-1780. . . . . DLB-30, 31

Hutchinson and Company
(Publishers) Limited DLB-112

von Hutton, Ulrich 1488-1523 . . . . . DLB-179

Hutton, Richard Holt 1826-1897. . . . . DLB-57

Huxley, Aldous
1894-1963 . . . . . DLB-36, 100, 162, 195

Huxley, Elspeth Josceline 1907- DLB-77

Huxley, T. H. 1825-1895. . . . . DLB-57

Huyghue, Douglas Smith
1816-1891 . . . . DLB-99

Huysmans, Joris-Karl 1848-1907 . . . . DLB-123

Hyde, Donald 1909-1966 and
Hyde, Mary 1912- DLB-187

Hyman, Trina Schart 1939- DLB-61

I

Iavorsky, Stefan 1658-1722 . . . . . . DLB-150

Ibn Bajja circa 1077-1138 . . . . DLB-115

Ibn Gabirol, Solomon
circa 1021-circa 1058 . . . . DLB-115

Ibuse, Masuji 1898-1993. . . . . DLB-180

The Iconography of Science-Fiction
Art DLB-8

Iffland, August Wilhelm
1759-1814 . . . . DLB-94

Ignatow, David 1914- DLB-5

Ike, Chukwuemeka 1931- DLB-157

Iles, Francis (see Berkeley, Anthony)

The Illustration of Early German
Literary Manuscripts,
circa 1150-circa 1300 . . . . DLB-148

"Images and 'Images,'" by
Charles Simic DLB-105

Imbs, Bravig 1904-1946 . . . . DLB-4

Imbuga, Francis D. 1947- DLB-157

Immermann, Karl 1796-1840 . . . . . DLB-133

Impressions of William Faulkner Y-97

Inchbald, Elizabeth 1753-1821 . . . . DLB-39, 89

Inge, William 1913-1973 . . . . DLB-7

Ingelow, Jean 1820-1897 . . . . . DLB-35, 163

Ingersoll, Ralph 1900-1985 . . . . . . DLB-127

The Ingersoll Prizes Y-84

Ingoldsby, Thomas (see Barham, Richard Harris)

Ingraham, Joseph Holt 1809-1860 . . . . . DLB-3

Inman, John 1805-1850 . . . . DLB-73

Innerhofer, Franz 1944- DLB-85

Innis, Harold Adams 1894-1952 . . . . . DLB-88

Innis, Mary Quayle 1899-1972 . . . . . DLB-88

Inoue, Yasushi 1907-1991 . . . . DLB-181

International Publishers Company DLB-46

An Interview with David Rabe Y-91

An Interview with George Greenfield, Literary Agent Y-91

An Interview with James Ellroy Y-91

Interview with Norman Mailer Y-97

An Interview with Peter S. Prescott Y-86

An Interview with Russell Hoban Y-90

Interview with Stanley Burnshaw Y-97

An Interview with Tom Jenks Y-86

"Into the Mirror," by Peter Cooley DLB-105

Introduction to Paul Laurence Dunbar, Lyrics of Lowly Life (1896), by William Dean Howells DLB-50

Introductory Essay: *Letters of Percy Bysshe Shelley* (1852), by Robert Browning DLB-32

Introductory Letters from the Second Edition of *Pamela* (1741), by Samuel Richardson DLB-39

Irving, John 1942- DLB-6; Y-82

Irving, Washington 1783-1859 . . . . DLB-3, 11, 30, 59, 73, 74, 183, 186

Irwin, Grace 1907- DLB-68

Irwin, Will 1873-1948 . . . . DLB-25

Isherwood, Christopher 1904-1986 . . . . DLB-15, 195; Y-86

Ishiguro, Kazuo 1954- DLB-194

Ishikawa, Jun 1899-1987 . . . . DLB-182

The Island Trees Case: A Symposium on School Library Censorship
An Interview with Judith Krug
An Interview with Phyllis Schlafly
An Interview with Edward B. Jenkinson
An Interview with Lamarr Mooneyham
An Interview with Harriet Bernstein Y-82

Islas, Arturo 1938-1991 . . . . DLB-122

Ivaniševič, Drago 1907-1981 . . . . . . DLB-181

Ivers, M. J., and Company DLB-49

Iwano, Hōmei 1873-1920 . . . . DLB-180

Iyayi, Festus 1947- DLB-157

Izumi, Kyōka 1873-1939 . . . . DLB-180

J

Jackmon, Marvin E. (see Marvin X)

Jacks, L. P. 1860-1955 . . . . DLB-135

Jackson, Angela 1951- DLB-41

Jackson, Helen Hunt 1830-1885 . . . . . . DLB-42, 47, 186, 189

Jackson, Holbrook 1874-1948 . . . . . . DLB-98

Jackson, Laura Riding 1901-1991 . . . . DLB-48

Jackson, Shirley 1919-1965 . . . . DLB-6

Jacob, Naomi 1884?-1964 . . . . DLB-191

Jacob, Piers Anthony Dillingham (see Anthony, Piers)

Jacobi, Friedrich Heinrich 1743-1819 . . . . DLB-94

Jacobi, Johann Georg 1740-1841 . . . . DLB-97

Jacobs, Joseph 1854-1916 . . . . DLB-141

Jacobs, W. W. 1863-1943 . . . . DLB-135

Jacobs, George W., and Company . . . DLB-49

Jacobson, Dan 1929- DLB-14

Jaggard, William [publishing house] DLB-170

Jahier, Piero 1884-1966 . . . . DLB-114

Jahnn, Hans Henny 1894-1959 . . . . DLB-56, 124

Jakes, John 1932- Y-83

James, C. L. R. 1901-1989 . . . . . . DLB-125

James Dickey Tributes Y-97

James, George P. R. 1801-1860 . . . . . DLB-116

James Gould Cozzens–A View from Afar Y-97

James Gould Cozzens Case Re-opened . . . Y-97

James Gould Cozzens: How to Read Him Y-97

James, Henry 1843-1916 . . . DLB-12, 71, 74, 189; DS-13

James, John circa 1633-1729 . . . . . . DLB-24

The James Jones Society Y-92

James Laughlin Tributes Y-97

James, M. R. 1862-1936 . . . . DLB-156

James, P. D. 1920- DLB-87; DS-17

James, Will 1892-1942 . . . . DS-16

James Joyce Centenary: Dublin, 1982 . . . . Y-82

James Joyce Conference Y-85

James VI of Scotland, I of England 1566-1625 . . . . DLB-151, 172

James, U. P. [publishing house] DLB-49

Jameson, Anna 1794-1860 . . . . . DLB-99, 166

Jameson, Fredric 1934- DLB-67

Jameson, J. Franklin 1859-1937 . . . . . DLB-17

Jameson, Storm 1891-1986 . . . . DLB-36

Jančar, Drago 1948- DLB-181

Janés, Clara 1940- DLB-134

Janevski, Slavko 1920- DLB-181

Jaramillo, Cleofas M. 1878-1956 . . . . DLB-122

Jarman, Mark 1952- DLB-120

Jarrell, Randall 1914-1965 . . . . . DLB-48, 52

Jarrold and Sons DLB-106

Jarry, Alfred 1873-1907 . . . . DLB-192

Jarves, James Jackson 1818-1888 . . . . DLB-189

Jasmin, Claude 1930- DLB-60

Jay, John 1745-1829 . . . . DLB-31

Jefferies, Richard 1848-1887 . . . . . DLB-98, 141

Jeffers, Lance 1919-1985 . . . . DLB-41

Jeffers, Robinson 1887-1962 . . . . . . DLB-45

Jefferson, Thomas 1743-1826 . . . . DLB-31, 183

Jelinek, Elfriede 1946- DLB-85

Jellicoe, Ann 1927- DLB-13

Jenkins, Elizabeth 1905- DLB-155

Jenkins, Robin 1912- DLB-14

Jenkins, William Fitzgerald (see Leinster, Murray)

Jenkins, Herbert, Limited DLB-112

Jennings, Elizabeth 1926- DLB-27

Jens, Walter 1923- DLB-69

Jensen, Merrill 1905-1980 . . . . DLB-17

Jephson, Robert 1736-1803 . . . . DLB-89

Jerome, Jerome K. 1859-1927 . . . . DLB-10, 34, 135

Jerome, Judson 1927-1991 . . . . DLB-105

Jerrold, Douglas 1803-1857 . . . . DLB-158, 159

Jesse, F. Tennyson 1888-1958 . . . . . . DLB-77

Jewett, Sarah Orne 1849-1909 . . . . DLB-12, 74

Jewett, John P., and Company DLB-49

The Jewish Publication Society DLB-49

Jewitt, John Rodgers 1783-1821 . . . . . DLB-99

Jewsbury, Geraldine 1812-1880 . . . . . DLB-21

Jewsbury, Maria Jane 1800-1833 . . . . DLB-199

Jhabvala, Ruth Prawer 1927- . . DLB-139, 194

Jiménez, Juan Ramón 1881-1958 . . . . DLB-134

Joans, Ted 1928- DLB-16, 41

John, Eugenie (see Marlitt, E.)

John of Dumbleton circa 1310-circa 1349 . . . . DLB-115

John Edward Bruce: Three Documents DLB-50

John O'Hara's Pottsville Journalism Y-88

John Steinbeck Research Center Y-85

John Updike on the Internet Y-97

John Webster: The Melbourne Manuscript Y-86

Johns, Captain W. E. 1893-1968 . . . . DLB-160

Johnson, B. S. 1933-1973 . . . . . DLB-14, 40

Johnson, Charles 1679-1748 . . . . . . DLB-84

Johnson, Charles R. 1948- DLB-33

Johnson, Charles S. 1893-1956. . . . . DLB-51, 91

Johnson, Denis 1949- DLB-120

Johnson, Diane 1934- Y-80

Johnson, Edgar 1901- DLB-103

Johnson, Edward 1598-1672 . . . . DLB-24

Johnson E. Pauline (Tekahionwake)
    1861-1913 . . . . DLB-175

Johnson, Fenton 1888-1958. . . . . DLB-45, 50

Johnson, Georgia Douglas
    1886-1966 . . . . DLB-51

Johnson, Gerald W. 1890-1980 . . . . . DLB-29

Johnson, Helene 1907- DLB-51

Johnson, James Weldon
    1871-1938 . . . . DLB-51

Johnson, John H. 1918- DLB-137

Johnson, Linton Kwesi 1952- DLB-157

Johnson, Lionel 1867-1902 . . . . DLB-19

Johnson, Nunnally 1897-1977 . . . . . DLB-26

Johnson, Owen 1878-1952 . . . . Y-87

Johnson, Pamela Hansford
    1912- DLB-15

Johnson, Pauline 1861-1913 . . . . DLB-92

Johnson, Ronald 1935- DLB-169

Johnson, Samuel 1696-1772. . . . . . . DLB-24

Johnson, Samuel
    1709-1784 . . . . . . DLB-39, 95, 104, 142

Johnson, Samuel 1822-1882 . . . . DLB-1

Johnson, Susanna 1730-1810 . . . . . DLB-200

Johnson, Uwe 1934-1984 . . . . DLB-75

Johnson, Benjamin
    [publishing house]. DLB-49

Johnson, Benjamin, Jacob, and
    Robert [publishing house] DLB-49

Johnson, Jacob, and Company DLB-49

Johnson, Joseph [publishing house] DLB-154

Johnston, Annie Fellows 1863-1931 . . . DLB-42

Johnston, David Claypole 1798?-1865 . DLB-188

Johnston, Basil H. 1929- DLB-60

Johnston, Denis 1901-1984 . . . . DLB-10

Johnston, Ellen 1835-1873 . . . . DLB-199

Johnston, George 1913- DLB-88

Johnston, Sir Harry 1858-1927 . . . . DLB-174

Johnston, Jennifer 1930- DLB-14

Johnston, Mary 1870-1936 . . . . DLB-9

Johnston, Richard Malcolm
    1822-1898 . . . . DLB-74

Johnstone, Charles 1719?-1800? DLB-39

Johst, Hanns 1890-1978 . . . . . . DLB-124

Jolas, Eugene 1894-1952 . . . . . . DLB-4, 45

Jones, Alice C. 1853-1933 . . . . DLB-92

Jones, Charles C., Jr. 1831-1893 . . . . DLB-30

Jones, D. G. 1929- DLB-53

Jones, David 1895-1974 . . . . . DLB-20, 100

Jones, Diana Wynne 1934- DLB-161

Jones, Ebenezer 1820-1860 . . . . DLB-32

Jones, Ernest 1819-1868. . . . . DLB-32

Jones, Gayl 1949- DLB-33

Jones, George 1800-1870 . . . . DLB-183

Jones, Glyn 1905- DLB-15

Jones, Gwyn 1907- DLB-15, 139

Jones, Henry Arthur 1851-1929 . . . . DLB-10

Jones, Hugh circa 1692-1760 . . . . . . DLB-24

Jones, James 1921-1977 . . . DLB-2, 143; DS-17

Jones, Jenkin Lloyd 1911- DLB-127

Jones, LeRoi (see Baraka, Amiri)

Jones, Lewis 1897-1939 . . . . DLB-15

Jones, Madison 1925- DLB-152

Jones, Major Joseph (see Thompson, William
    Tappan)

Jones, Preston 1936-1979. . . . . DLB-7

Jones, Rodney 1950- DLB-120

Jones, Sir William 1746-1794 . . . . . DLB-109

Jones, William Alfred 1817-1900 . . . . DLB-59

Jones's Publishing House DLB-49

Jong, Erica 1942- DLB-2, 5, 28, 152

Jonke, Gert F. 1946- DLB-85

Jonson, Ben 1572?-1637 . . . . . . DLB-62, 121

Jordan, June 1936- DLB-38

Joseph, Jenny 1932- DLB-40

Joseph, Michael, Limited DLB-112

Josephson, Matthew 1899-1978 . . . . . DLB-4

Josephus, Flavius 37-100 . . . . DLB-176

Josiah Allen's Wife (see Holley, Marietta)

Josipovici, Gabriel 1940- DLB-14

Josselyn, John ?-1675 . . . . DLB-24

Joudry, Patricia 1921- DLB-88

Jovine, Giuseppe 1922- DLB-128

Joyaux, Philippe (see Sollers, Philippe)

Joyce, Adrien (see Eastman, Carol)

A Joyce (Con)Text: Danis Rose and the Remaking
    of *Ulysses* Y-97

Joyce, James
    1882-1941 . . . . . . DLB-10, 19, 36, 162

Judd, Sylvester 1813-1853 . . . . DLB-1

Judd, Orange, Publishing
    Company DLB-49

Judith circa 930 . . . . DLB-146

Julian of Norwich
    1342-circa 1420 . . . . DLB-1146

Julian Symons at Eighty Y-92

June, Jennie (see Croly, Jane Cunningham)

Jung, Franz 1888-1963 . . . . DLB-118

Jünger, Ernst 1895- DLB-56

Der jüngere Titurel circa 1275 . . . . . DLB-138

Jung-Stilling, Johann Heinrich
    1740-1817 . . . . DLB-94

Justice, Donald 1925- Y-83

The Juvenile Library (see Godwin, M. J., and
    Company)

K

Kacew, Romain (see Gary, Romain)

Kafka, Franz 1883-1924 . . . . DLB-81

Kahn, Roger 1927- DLB-171

Kaikō, Takeshi 1939-1989 . . . . DLB-182

Kaiser, Georg 1878-1945 . . . . DLB-124

Kaiserchronik circca 1147 . . . . DLB-148

Kaleb, Vjekoslav 1905- DLB-181

Kalechofsky, Roberta 1931- DLB-28

Kaler, James Otis 1848-1912 . . . . . . DLB-12

Kames, Henry Home, Lord
    1696-1782 . . . . DLB-31, 104

Kandel, Lenore 1932- DLB-16

Kanin, Garson 1912- DLB-7

Kant, Hermann 1926- DLB-75

Kant, Immanuel 1724-1804 . . . . DLB-94

Kantemir, Antiokh Dmitrievich
    1708-1744 . . . . DLB-150

Kantor, Mackinlay 1904-1977 . . . . DLB-9, 102

Kaplan, Fred 1937- DLB-111

Kaplan, Johanna 1942- DLB-28

Kaplan, Justin 1925- DLB-111

Kapnist, Vasilii Vasilevich
    1758?-1823 . . . . DLB-150

Karadžić, Vuk Stefanović
    1787-1864 . . . . DLB-147

Karamzin, Nikolai Mikhailovich
    1766-1826 . . . . DLB-150

Karsch, Anna Louisa 1722-1791 . . . . . DLB-97

Kasack, Hermann 1896-1966 . . . . . . DLB-69

Kasai, Zenzō 1887-1927 . . . . DLB-180

Kaschnitz, Marie Luise 1901-1974 . . . DLB-69

Kaštelan, Jure 1919-1990 . . . . DLB-147

Kästner, Erich 1899-1974 . . . . DLB-56

Kattan, Naim 1928- DLB-53

Katz, Steve 1935- Y-83

Kauffman, Janet 1945- Y-86

Kauffmann, Samuel 1898-1971 . . . . . DLB-127

Kaufman, Bob 1925- DLB-16, 41

Kaufman, George S. 1889-1961 . . . . . DLB-7

Kavanagh, P. J. 1931- DLB-40

Kavanagh, Patrick 1904-1967 . . . . DLB-15, 20

Kawabata, Yasunari 1899-1972 . . . . . DLB-180

Kaye-Smith, Sheila 1887-1956 . . . . . . DLB-36

Kazin, Alfred 1915- DLB-67

Keane, John B. 1928- DLB-13

Keary, Annie 1825-1879 . . . . DLB-163

Keating, H. R. F. 1926- DLB-87

Keats, Ezra Jack 1916-1983 . . . . DLB-61

Keats, John 1795-1821 . . . . . . DLB-96, 110

Keble, John 1792-1866 . . . . DLB-32, 55

Keeble, John 1944- Y-83

Keeffe, Barrie 1945- DLB-13

Keeley, James 1867-1934 . . . . DLB-25

W. B. Keen, Cooke
and Company DLB-49

Keillor, Garrison 1942- Y-87

Keith, Marian 1874?-1961 . . . . DLB-92

Keller, Gary D. 1943- DLB-82

Keller, Gottfried 1819-1890 . . . . . . DLB-129

Kelley, Edith Summers 1884-1956 . . . . DLB-9

Kelley, William Melvin 1937- DLB-33

Kellogg, Ansel Nash 1832-1886 . . . . DLB-23

Kellogg, Steven 1941- DLB-61

Kelly, George 1887-1974 . . . . DLB-7

Kelly, Hugh 1739-1777 . . . . DLB-89

Kelly, Robert 1935- DLB-5, 130, 165

Kelly, Piet and Company DLB-49

Kelman, James 1946- DLB-194

Kelmscott Press DLB-112

Kemble, E. W. 1861-1933 . . . . DLB-188

Kemble, Fanny 1809-1893 . . . . DLB-32

Kemelman, Harry 1908- DLB-28

Kempe, Margery circa 1373-1438 . . . . DLB-146

Kempner, Friederike 1836-1904 . . . . DLB-129

Kempowski, Walter 1929- DLB-75

Kendall, Claude [publishing company] . . DLB-46

Kendell, George 1809-1867 . . . . DLB-43

Kenedy, P. J., and Sons DLB-49

Kennan, George 1845-1924 . . . . . . DLB-189

Kennedy, Adrienne 1931- DLB-38

Kennedy, John Pendleton 1795-1870 . . . DLB-3

Kennedy, Leo 1907- DLB-88

Kennedy, Margaret 1896-1967 . . . . . DLB-36

Kennedy, Patrick 1801-1873 . . . . . . DLB-159

Kennedy, Richard S. 1920- DLB-111

Kennedy, William 1928- DLB-143; Y-85

Kennedy, X. J. 1929- DLB-5

Kennelly, Brendan 1936- DLB-40

Kenner, Hugh 1923- DLB-67

Kennerley, Mitchell
[publishing house] DLB-46

Kenneth Dale McCormick Tributes Y-97

Kenny, Maurice 1929- DLB-175

Kent, Frank R. 1877-1958 . . . . DLB-29

Kenyon, Jane 1947- DLB-120

Keough, Hugh Edmund 1864-1912 . . . DLB-171

Keppler and Schwartzmann DLB-49

Kerlan, Irvin 1912-1963 . . . . DLB-187

Kern, Jerome 1885-1945 . . . . DLB-187

Kerner, Justinus 1776-1862 . . . . DLB-90

Kerouac, Jack 1922-1969 . . . . DLB-2, 16; DS-3

The Jack Kerouac Revival Y-95

Kerouac, Jan 1952- DLB-16

Kerr, Orpheus C. (see Newell, Robert Henry)

Kerr, Charles H., and Company . . . DLB-49

Kesey, Ken 1935- DLB-2, 16

Kessel, Joseph 1898-1979 . . . . DLB-72

Kessel, Martin 1901- DLB-56

Kesten, Hermann 1900- DLB-56

Keun, Irmgard 1905-1982 . . . . DLB-69

Key and Biddle DLB-49

Keynes, John Maynard 1883-1946 . . . . DS-10

Keyserling, Eduard von 1855-1918 . . . DLB-66

Khan, Ismith 1925- DLB-125

Khaytov, Nikolay 1919- DLB-181

Khemnitser, Ivan Ivanovich
1745-1784 . . . . DLB-150

Kheraskov, Mikhail Matveevich
1733-1807 . . . . DLB-150

Khristov, Boris 1945- DLB-181

Khvostov, Dmitrii Ivanovich
1757-1835 . . . . DLB-150

Kidd, Adam 1802?-1831 . . . . DLB-99

Kidd, William
[publishing house] DLB-106

Kidder, Tracy 1945- DLB-185

Kiely, Benedict 1919- DLB-15

Kieran, John 1892-1981 . . . . DLB-171

Kiggins and Kellogg DLB-49

Kiley, Jed 1889-1962 . . . . DLB-4

Kilgore, Bernard 1908-1967 . . . . . DLB-127

Killens, John Oliver 1916- DLB-33

Killigrew, Anne 1660-1685 . . . . . . DLB-131

Killigrew, Thomas 1612-1683 . . . . . DLB-58

Kilmer, Joyce 1886-1918 . . . . DLB-45

Kilwardby, Robert
circa 1215-1279 . . . . DLB-115

Kincaid, Jamaica 1949- DLB-157

King, Charles 1844-1933 . . . . DLB-186

King, Clarence 1842-1901 . . . . DLB-12

King, Florence 1936 . . . . Y-85

King, Francis 1923- DLB-15, 139

King, Grace 1852-1932 . . . . DLB-12, 78

King, Harriet Hamilton 1840-1920 . . . DLB-199

King, Henry 1592-1669 . . . . DLB-126

King, Stephen 1947- DLB-143; Y-80

King, Thomas 1943- DLB-175

King, Woodie, Jr. 1937- DLB-38

King, Solomon [publishing house] DLB-49

Kinglake, Alexander William
1809-1891 . . . . DLB-55, 166

Kingsley, Charles
1819-1875 . . . . DLB-21, 32, 163, 178, 190

Kingsley, Mary Henrietta
1862-1900 . . . . DLB-174

Kingsley, Henry 1830-1876 . . . . DLB-21

Kingsley, Sidney 1906- DLB-7

Kingsmill, Hugh 1889-1949 . . . . . . DLB-149

Kingston, Maxine Hong
1940- DLB-173; Y-80

Kingston, William Henry Giles
1814-1880 . . . . DLB-163

Kinnan, Mary Lewis 1763-1848 . . . . DLB-200

Kinnell, Galway 1927- DLB-5; Y-87

Kinsella, Thomas 1928- DLB-27

Kipling, Rudyard
1865-1936 . . . . . . DLB-19, 34, 141, 156

Kipphardt, Heinar 1922-1982 . . . . . DLB-124

Kirby, William 1817-1906 . . . . DLB-99

Kircher, Athanasius 1602-1680 . . . . DLB-164

Kireevsky, Ivan Vasil'evich
1806-1856 . . . . DLB-198

Kirk, John Foster 1824-1904 . . . . . . DLB-79

Kirkconnell, Watson 1895-1977 . . . . DLB-68

Kirkland, Caroline M.
1801-1864 . . . . . . DLB-3, 73, 74; DS-13

Kirkland, Joseph 1830-1893 . . . . . . DLB-12

Kirkman, Francis
[publishing house] DLB-170

Kirkpatrick, Clayton 1915- DLB-127

Kirkup, James 1918- DLB-27

Kirouac, Conrad (see Marie-Victorin, Frère)

Kirsch, Sarah 1935- DLB-75

Kirst, Hans Hellmut 1914-1989 . . . . DLB-69

Kiš, Danilo 1935-1989 . . . . DLB-181

Kita, Morio 1927- DLB-182

Kitcat, Mabel Greenhow
1859-1922 . . . . DLB-135

Kitchin, C. H. B. 1895-1967 . . . . . . DLB-77

Kizer, Carolyn 1925- DLB-5, 169

Klabund 1890-1928 . . . . DLB-66

Klaj, Johann 1616-1656 . . . . DLB-164

Klappert, Peter 1942- DLB-5

Klass, Philip (see Tenn, William)

Klein, A. M. 1909-1972 . . . . DLB-68

Kleist, Ewald von 1715-1759 . . . . . . DLB-97

Kleist, Heinrich von 1777-1811 . . . . . DLB-90

Klinger, Friedrich Maximilian
1752-1831 . . . . DLB-94

Klopstock, Friedrich Gottlieb
1724-1803 . . . . DLB-97

Klopstock, Meta 1728-1758 . . . . DLB-97

Kluge, Alexander 1932- DLB-75

Knapp, Joseph Palmer 1864-1951 . . . . DLB-91

Knapp, Samuel Lorenzo
1783-1838 . . . . DLB-59

Knapton, J. J. and P.
[publishing house] DLB-154

Kniazhnin, Iakov Borisovich
1740-1791 . . . . DLB-150

Knickerbocker, Diedrich (see Irving,
Washington)

Knigge, Adolph Franz Friedrich Ludwig,
Freiherr von 1752-1796 . . . . DLB-94

Knight, Damon 1922- DLB-8

Knight, Etheridge 1931-1992 . . . . . . DLB-41

Knight, John S. 1894-1981 . . . . DLB-29

Knight, Sarah Kemble
1666-1727 . . . . DLB-24, 200

Knight, Charles, and Company DLB-106

Knight-Bruce, G. W. H.
1852-1896 . . . . DLB-174

Knister, Raymond 1899-1932 . . . . . . DLB-68

Knoblock, Edward 1874-1945 . . . . . . DLB-10

Knopf, Alfred A. 1892-1984 . . . . Y-84

Knopf, Alfred A.
[publishing house] DLB-46

Knorr von Rosenroth, Christian
1636-1689 . . . . DLB-168

"Knots into Webs: Some Autobiographical
Sources," by Dabney Stuart DLB-105

Knowles, John 1926- DLB-6

Knox, Frank 1874-1944 . . . . DLB-29

Knox, John circa 1514-1572 . . . . . . DLB-132

Knox, John Armoy 1850-1906 . . . . . . DLB-23

Knox, Ronald Arbuthnott
1888-1957 . . . . DLB-77

Knox, Thomas Wallace 1835-1896 . . . DLB-189

Kobayashi, Takiji 1903-1933 . . . . . . DLB-180

Kober, Arthur 1900-1975 . . . . DLB-11

Kocbek, Edvard 1904-1981 . . . . DLB-147

Koch, Howard 1902- DLB-26

Koch, Kenneth 1925- DLB-5

Kōda, Rohan 1867-1947 . . . . DLB-180

Koenigsberg, Moses 1879-1945 . . . . . DLB-25

Koeppen, Wolfgang 1906- DLB-69

Koertge, Ronald 1940- DLB-105

Koestler, Arthur 1905-1983 . . . . Y-83

Kohn, John S. Van E. 1906-1976 and
Papantonio, Michael 1907-1978 . . . DLB-187

Kokoschka, Oskar 1886-1980 . . . . . . DLB-124

Kolb, Annette 1870-1967 . . . . DLB-66

Kolbenheyer, Erwin Guido
1878-1962 . . . . DLB-66, 124

Kolleritsch, Alfred 1931- DLB-85

Kolodny, Annette 1941- DLB-67

Komarov, Matvei
circa 1730-1812 . . . . DLB-150

Komroff, Manuel 1890-1974 . . . . DLB-4

Komunyakaa, Yusef 1947- DLB-120

Koneski, Blaže 1921-1993 . . . . DLB-181

Konigsburg, E. L. 1930- DLB-52

Konrad von Würzburg
circa 1230-1287 . . . . DLB-138

Konstantinov, Aleko 1863-1897 . . . . . DLB-147

Kooser, Ted 1939- DLB-105

Kopit, Arthur 1937- DLB-7

Kops, Bernard 1926?- DLB-13

Kornbluth, C. M. 1923-1958 . . . . . . DLB-8

Körner, Theodor 1791-1813 . . . . . . DLB-90

Kornfeld, Paul 1889-1942 . . . . DLB-118

Kosinski, Jerzy 1933-1991 . . . . . DLB-2; Y-82

Kosmač, Ciril 1910-1980 . . . . DLB-181

Kosovel, Srečko 1904-1926 . . . . . . DLB-147

Kostrov, Ermil Ivanovich
1755-1796 . . . . DLB-150

Kotzebue, August von 1761-1819 . . . . DLB-94

Kotzwinkle, William 1938- DLB-173

Kovačić, Ante 1854-1889 . . . . DLB-147

Kovič, Kajetan 1931- DLB-181

Kraf, Elaine 1946- Y-81

Kramer, Jane 1938- DLB-185

Kramer, Mark 1944- DLB-185

Kranjčević, Silvije Strahimir
1865-1908 . . . . DLB-147

Krasna, Norman 1909-1984 . . . . . . DLB-26

Kraus, Hans Peter 1907-1988 . . . . . DLB-187

Kraus, Karl 1874-1936 . . . . DLB-118

Krauss, Ruth 1911-1993 . . . . DLB-52

Kreisel, Henry 1922- DLB-88

Kreuder, Ernst 1903-1972 . . . . DLB-69

Kreymborg, Alfred 1883-1966 . . . . DLB-4, 54

Krieger, Murray 1923- DLB-67

Krim, Seymour 1922-1989 . . . . DLB-16

Krleža, Miroslav 1893-1981 . . . . . . DLB-147

Krock, Arthur 1886-1974 . . . . DLB-29

Kroetsch, Robert 1927- ‰DLB-53

Krutch, Joseph Wood 1893-1970 . . . . DLB-63

Krylov, Ivan Andreevich
1769-1844 . . . . DLB-150

Kubin, Alfred 1877-1959 . . . . DLB-81

Kubrick, Stanley 1928- DLB-26

Kudrun circa 1230-1240 . . . . DLB-138

Kuffstein, Hans Ludwig von
1582-1656 . . . . DLB-164

Kuhlmann, Quirinus 1651-1689 . . . . DLB-168

Kuhnau, Johann 1660-1722 . . . . . . DLB-168

Kumin, Maxine 1925- DLB-5

Kunene, Mazisi 1930- DLB-117

Kunikida, Doppo 1869-1908 . . . . . . DLB-180

Kunitz, Stanley 1905- DLB-48

Kunjufu, Johari M. (see Amini, Johari M.)

Kunnert, Gunter 1929- DLB-75

Kunze, Reiner 1933- DLB-75

Kupferberg, Tuli 1923- DLB-16

Kurahashi, Yumiko 1935- DLB-182

Kureishi, Hanif 1954- DLB-194

Kürnberger, Ferdinand
1821-1879 . . . . DLB-129

Kurz, Isolde 1853-1944 . . . . DLB-66

Kusenberg, Kurt 1904-1983 . . . . . . DLB-69

Kuttner, Henry 1915-1958 . . . . DLB-8

Kyd, Thomas 1558-1594 . . . . DLB-62

Kyffin, Maurice
circa 1560?-1598 . . . . DLB-136

Kyger, Joanne 1934- DLB-16

Kyne, Peter B. 1880-1957 . . . . DLB-78

L

L. E. L. (see Landon, Letitia Elizabeth)

Laberge, Albert 1871-1960 . . . . DLB-68

Laberge, Marie 1950- DLB-60

Labiche, Eugène 1815-1888 . . . . . . DLB-192

La Capria, Raffaele 1922- DLB-196

Lacombe, Patrice (see Trullier-Lacombe,
Joseph Patrice)

Lacretelle, Jacques de 1888-1985 . . . . DLB-65

Lacy, Sam 1903- DLB-171

Ladd, Joseph Brown 1764-1786 . . . . DLB-37

La Farge, Oliver 1901-1963 . . . . . . DLB-9

Lafferty, R. A. 1914- DLB-8

La Flesche, Francis 1857-1932 . . . . . DLB-175

Lagorio, Gina 1922- DLB-196

La Guma, Alex 1925-1985 . . . . . . DLB-117

Lahaise, Guillaume (see Delahaye, Guy)

Lahontan, Louis-Armand de Lom d'Arce,
Baron de 1666-1715? DLB-99

Laing, Kojo 1946- DLB-157

Laird, Carobeth 1895- Y-82

Laird and Lee DLB-49

Lalić, Ivan V. 1931-1996 . . . . DLB-181

Lalić, Mihailo 1914-1992 . . . . DLB-181

Lalonde, Michèle 1937- DLB-60

Lamantia, Philip 1927- DLB-16

Lamb, Charles
1775-1834 . . . . DLB-93, 107, 163

Lamb, Lady Caroline 1785-1828 . . . DLB-116

Lamb, Mary 1764-1874 . . . . DLB-163

Lambert, Betty 1933-1983 . . . . DLB-60

Lamming, George 1927- DLB-125

L'Amour, Louis 1908?- Y-80

Lampman, Archibald 1861-1899 . . . . DLB-92

Lamson, Wolffe and Company DLB-49

Lancer Books DLB-46

Landesman, Jay 1919- and
    Landesman, Fran 1927- DLB-16

Landolfi, Tommaso 1908-1979 . . . . . DLB-177

Landon, Letitia Elizabeth 1802-1838 . . . DLB-96

Landor, Walter Savage
    1775-1864 . . . . DLB-93, 107

Landry, Napoléon-P. 1884-1956 . . . . . DLB-92

Lane, Charles 1800-1870 . . . . DLB-1

Lane, Laurence W. 1890-1967 . . . . . . DLB-91

Lane, M. Travis 1934- DLB-60

Lane, Patrick 1939- DLB-53

Lane, Pinkie Gordon 1923- DLB-41

Lane, John, Company DLB-49

Laney, Al 1896-1988 . . . . DLB-4, 171

Lang, Andrew 1844-1912 . . . DLB-98, 141, 184

Langevin, André 1927- DLB-60

Langgässer, Elisabeth 1899-1950 . . . . DLB-69

Langhorne, John 1735-1779 . . . . . . DLB-109

Langland, William
    circa 1330-circa 1400 . . . . DLB-146

Langton, Anna 1804-1893 . . . . DLB-99

Lanham, Edwin 1904-1979 . . . . DLB-4

Lanier, Sidney 1842-1881 . . . . DLB-64; DS-13

Lanyer, Aemilia 1569-1645 . . . . . . DLB-121

Lapointe, Gatien 1931-1983 . . . . . . DLB-88

Lapointe, Paul-Marie 1929- DLB-88

Lardner, John 1912-1960 . . . . . . DLB-171

Lardner, Ring
    1885-1933 . . . DLB-11, 25, 86, 171; DS-16

Lardner, Ring, Jr. 1915- DLB-26

Lardner 100: Ring Lardner
    Centennial Symposium. Y-85

Larkin, Philip 1922-1985 . . . . DLB-27

La Roche, Sophie von 1730-1807 . . . . DLB-94

La Rocque, Gilbert 1943-1984 . . . . . . DLB-60

Laroque de Roquebrune, Robert (see Roquebrune,
    Robert de)

Larrick, Nancy 1910- DLB-61

Larsen, Nella 1893-1964 . . . . DLB-51

Lasker-Schüler, Else
    1869-1945 . . . . DLB-66, 124

Lasnier, Rina 1915- DLB-88

Lassalle, Ferdinand 1825-1864 . . . . . DLB-129

Lathrop, Dorothy P. 1891-1980 . . . . . DLB-22

Lathrop, George Parsons
    1851-1898 . . . . DLB-71

Lathrop, John, Jr. 1772-1820 . . . . . . DLB-37

Latimer, Hugh 1492?-1555 . . . . . . DLB-136

Latimore, Jewel Christine McLawler
    (see Amini, Johari M.)

Latymer, William 1498-1583 . . . . . DLB-132

Laube, Heinrich 1806-1884 . . . . . . DLB-133

Laughlin, James 1914- DLB-48

Laumer, Keith 1925- DLB-8

Lauremberg, Johann 1590-1658 . . . . DLB-164

Laurence, Margaret 1926-1987 . . . . . DLB-53

Laurentius von Schnüffis
    1633-1702 . . . . DLB-168

Laurents, Arthur 1918- DLB-26

Laurie, Annie (see Black, Winifred)

Laut, Agnes Christiana 1871-1936 . . . . DLB-92

Lauterbach, Ann 1942- DLB-193

Lavater, Johann Kaspar 1741-1801 . . . . DLB-97

Lavin, Mary 1912- DLB-15

Law, John (see Harkness, Margaret)

Lawes, Henry 1596-1662 . . . . DLB-126

Lawless, Anthony (see MacDonald, Philip)

Lawrence, D. H.
    1885-1930 . . . DLB-10, 19, 36, 98, 162, 195

Lawrence, David 1888-1973 . . . . . . DLB-29

Lawrence, Seymour 1926-1994 . . . . . . Y-94

Lawrence, T. E. 1888-1935 . . . . . . DLB-195

Lawson, John ?-1711 . . . . DLB-24

Lawson, Robert 1892-1957 . . . . DLB-22

Lawson, Victor F. 1850-1925 . . . . . . DLB-25

Layard, Sir Austen Henry
    1817-1894 . . . . DLB-166

Layton, Irving 1912- DLB-88

LaZamon flourished circa 1200 . . . . DLB-146

Lazarević, Laza K. 1851-1890 . . . . . DLB-147

Lazhechnikov, Ivan Ivanovich
    1792-1869 . . . . DLB-198

Lea, Henry Charles 1825-1909 . . . . . DLB-47

Lea, Sydney 1942- DLB-120

Lea, Tom 1907- DLB-6

Leacock, John 1729-1802 . . . . DLB-31

Leacock, Stephen 1869-1944 . . . . . . DLB-92

Lead, Jane Ward 1623-1704 . . . . . DLB-131

Leadenhall Press DLB-106

Leapor, Mary 1722-1746 . . . . DLB-109

Lear, Edward 1812-1888 . . . DLB-32, 163, 166

Leary, Timothy 1920-1996 . . . . DLB-16

Leary, W. A., and Company DLB-49

Léautaud, Paul 1872-1956 . . . . . . DLB-65

Leavitt, David 1961- DLB-130

Leavitt and Allen DLB-49

Le Blond, Mrs. Aubrey
    1861-1934 . . . . DLB-174

le Carré, John 1931- DLB-87

Lécavelé, Roland (see Dorgeles, Roland)

Lechlitner, Ruth 1901- DLB-48

Leclerc, Félix 1914- DLB-60

Le Clézio, J. M. G. 1940- DLB-83

Lectures on Rhetoric and Belles Lettres (1783),
    by Hugh Blair [excerpts] DLB-31

Leder, Rudolf (see Hermlin, Stephan)

Lederer, Charles 1910-1976 . . . . . . DLB-26

Ledwidge, Francis 1887-1917 . . . . . . DLB-20

Lee, Dennis 1939- DLB-53

Lee, Don L. (see Madhubuti, Haki R.)

Lee, George W. 1894-1976 . . . . DLB-51

Lee, Harper 1926- DLB-6

Lee, Harriet (1757-1851) and
    Lee, Sophia (1750-1824) DLB-39

Lee, Laurie 1914- DLB-27

Lee, Li-Young 1957- DLB-165

Lee, Manfred B. (see Dannay, Frederic, and
    Manfred B. Lee)

Lee, Nathaniel circa 1645 - 1692 . . . . DLB-80

Lee, Sir Sidney 1859-1926 . . . . . DLB-149, 184

Lee, Sir Sidney, "Principles of Biography," in
    Elizabethan and Other Essays DLB-149

Lee, Vernon
    1856-1935 . . . DLB-57, 153, 156, 174, 178

Lee and Shepard DLB-49

Le Fanu, Joseph Sheridan
    1814-1873 . . . . DLB-21, 70, 159, 178

Leffland, Ella 1931- Y-84

le Fort, Gertrud von 1876-1971 . . . . . DLB-66

Le Gallienne, Richard 1866-1947 . . . . . DLB-4

Legaré, Hugh Swinton
    1797-1843 . . . . DLB-3, 59, 73

Legaré, James M. 1823-1859 . . . . DLB-3

The Legends of the Saints and a Medieval
    Christian Worldview DLB-148

Léger, Antoine-J. 1880-1950 . . . . . . DLB-88

Le Guin, Ursula K. 1929- DLB-8, 52

Lehman, Ernest 1920- DLB-44

Lehmann, John 1907- DLB-27, 100

Lehmann, Rosamond 1901-1990 . . . . DLB-15

Lehmann, Wilhelm 1882-1968 . . . . . DLB-56

Lehmann, John, Limited DLB-112

Leiber, Fritz 1910-1992 . . . . DLB-8

Leibniz, Gottfried Wilhelm
    1646-1716 . . . . DLB-168

Leicester University Press DLB-112

Leigh, W. R. 1866-1955 . . . . DLB-188

Leinster, Murray 1896-1975 . . . . . . DLB-8

Leisewitz, Johann Anton
    1752-1806 . . . . DLB-94

Leitch, Maurice 1933- DLB-14

Leithauser, Brad 1943- DLB-120

Leland, Charles G. 1824-1903 . . . . . DLB-11

Leland, John 1503?-1552 . . . . DLB-136

Lemay, Pamphile 1837-1918 . . . . . . DLB-99

Lemelin, Roger 1919- DLB-88

Lemercier, Louis-Jean-Népomucène
1771-1840 . . . . DLB-192

Lemon, Mark 1809-1870 . . . . DLB-163

Le Moine, James MacPherson
1825-1912 . . . . DLB-99

Le Moyne, Jean 1913- DLB-88

Lemperly, Paul 1858-1939. . . . . . . DLB-187

L'Engle, Madeleine 1918- DLB-52

Lennart, Isobel 1915-1971 . . . . DLB-44

Lennox, Charlotte
1729 or 1730-1804 . . . . DLB-39

Lenox, James 1800-1880. . . . . DLB-140

Lenski, Lois 1893-1974 . . . . DLB-22

Lenz, Hermann 1913- DLB-69

Lenz, J. M. R. 1751-1792 . . . . DLB-94

Lenz, Siegfried 1926- DLB-75

Leonard, Elmore 1925- DLB-173

Leonard, Hugh 1926- DLB-13

Leonard, William Ellery
1876-1944 . . . . DLB-54

Leonowens, Anna 1834-1914 . . . . DLB-99, 166

LePan, Douglas 1914- DLB-88

Leprohon, Rosanna Eleanor
1829-1879 . . . . DLB-99

Le Queux, William 1864-1927 . . . . . DLB-70

Lerner, Max 1902-1992 . . . . DLB-29

Lernet-Holenia, Alexander
1897-1976 . . . . DLB-85

Le Rossignol, James 1866-1969 . . . . . DLB-92

Lescarbot, Marc circa 1570-1642 . . . . DLB-99

LeSeur, William Dawson
1840-1917 . . . . DLB-92

LeSieg, Theo. (see Geisel, Theodor Seuss)

Leslie, Doris before 1902-1982 . . . . DLB-191

Leslie, Frank 1821-1880 . . . . DLB-43, 79

Leslie, Frank, Publishing House DLB-49

Lesperance, John 1835?-1891 . . . . . . DLB-99

Lessing, Bruno 1870-1940 . . . . DLB-28

Lessing, Doris 1919- DLB-15, 139; Y-85

Lessing, Gotthold Ephraim
1729-1781 . . . . DLB-97

Lettau, Reinhard 1929- DLB-75

Letter from Japan. Y-94

Letter from London Y-96

Letter to [Samuel] Richardson on *Clarissa*
(1748), by Henry Fielding DLB-39

A Letter to the Editor of *The Irish
Times* Y-97

Lever, Charles 1806-1872. . . . . DLB-21

Leverson, Ada 1862-1933 . . . . DLB-153

Levertov, Denise 1923- DLB-5, 165

Levi, Peter 1931- DLB-40

Levi, Primo 1919-1987 . . . . DLB-177

Levien, Sonya 1888-1960 . . . . DLB-44

Levin, Meyer 1905-1981 . . . . DLB-9, 28; Y-81

Levine, Norman 1923- DLB-88

Levine, Philip 1928- DLB-5

Levis, Larry 1946- DLB-120

Levy, Amy 1861-1889 . . . . DLB-156

Levy, Benn Wolfe
1900-1973 . . . . DLB-13; Y-81

Lewald, Fanny 1811-1889 . . . . DLB-129

Lewes, George Henry
1817-1878 . . . . DLB-55, 144

Lewis, Agnes Smith 1843-1926 . . . . DLB-174

Lewis, Alfred H. 1857-1914 . . . . DLB-25, 186

Lewis, Alun 1915-1944 . . . . . . DLB-20, 162

Lewis, C. Day (see Day Lewis, C.)

Lewis, C. S. 1898-1963 . . . . DLB-15, 100, 160

Lewis, Charles B. 1842-1924 . . . . . . DLB-11

Lewis, Henry Clay 1825-1850 . . . . . . DLB-3

Lewis, Janet 1899- Y-87

Lewis, Matthew Gregory
1775-1818 . . . . DLB-39, 158, 178

Lewis, Meriwether 1774-1809 and
Clark, William 1770-1838. . . DLB-183, 186

Lewis, R. W. B. 1917- DLB-111

Lewis, Richard circa 1700-1734 . . . . DLB-24

Lewis, Sinclair
1885-1951 . . . . DLB-9, 102; DS-1

Lewis, Wilmarth Sheldon
1895-1979 . . . . DLB-140

Lewis, Wyndham 1882-1957 . . . . . . DLB-15

Lewisohn, Ludwig
1882-1955 . . . . DLB-4, 9, 28, 102

Leyendecker, J. C. 1874-1951 . . . . . DLB-188

Lezama Lima, José 1910-1976 . . . . . DLB-113

The Library of America DLB-46

The Licensing Act of 1737 . . . . DLB-84

Lichfield, Leonard I
[publishing house] DLB-170

Lichtenberg, Georg Christoph
1742-1799 . . . . DLB-94

The Liddle Collection Y-97

Lieb, Fred 1888-1980 . . . . DLB-171

Liebling, A. J. 1904-1963 . . . . . . DLB-4, 171

Lieutenant Murray (see Ballou, Maturin
Murray)

Lighthall, William Douw
1857-1954 . . . . DLB-92

Lilar, Françoise (see Mallet-Joris, Françoise)

Lillo, George 1691-1739 . . . . DLB-84

Lilly, J. K., Jr. 1893-1966 . . . . DLB-140

Lilly, Wait and Company DLB-49

Lily, William circa 1468-1522. . . . . . DLB-132

Limited Editions Club DLB-46

Lincoln and Edmands DLB-49

Lindesay, Ethel Forence (see Richardson, Henry
Handel)

Lindsay, Alexander William, Twenty-fifth Earl
of Crawford 1812-1880 . . . . DLB-184

Lindsay, Sir David
circa 1485-1555 . . . . DLB-132

Lindsay, Jack 1900- Y-84

Lindsay, Lady (Caroline Blanche Elizabeth Fitzroy
Lindsay) 1844-1912 . . . . DLB-199

Lindsay, Vachel 1879-1931 . . . . DLB-54

Linebarger, Paul Myron Anthony (see Smith,
Cordwainer)

Link, Arthur S. 1920- DLB-17

Linn, John Blair 1777-1804. . . . . . . DLB-37

Lins, Osman 1924-1978 . . . . DLB-145

Linton, Eliza Lynn 1822-1898 . . . . . DLB-18

Linton, William James 1812-1897 . . . . DLB-32

Lintot, Barnaby Bernard
[publishing house] DLB-170

Lion Books DLB-46

Lionni, Leo 1910- DLB-61

Lippincott, Sara Jane Clarke
1823-1904 . . . . DLB-43

Lippincott, J. B., Company DLB-49

Lippmann, Walter 1889-1974 . . . . . . DLB-29

Lipton, Lawrence 1898-1975 . . . . . . DLB-16

Liscow, Christian Ludwig
1701-1760 . . . . DLB-97

Lish, Gordon 1934- DLB-130

Lispector, Clarice 1925-1977 . . . . . . DLB-113

The Literary Chronicle and Weekly Review
1819-1828 . . . . DLB-110

Literary Documents: William Faulkner
and the People-to-People
Program. Y-86

Literary Documents II: *Library Journal*
Statements and Questionnaires from
First Novelists Y-87

Literary Effects of World War II
[British novel]. DLB-15

Literary Prizes [British] DLB-15

Literary Research Archives: The Humanities
Research Center, University of
Texas Y-82

Literary Research Archives II: Berg
Collection of English and American
Literature of the New York Public
Library Y-83

Literary Research Archives III:
The Lilly Library Y-84

Literary Research Archives IV:
The John Carter Brown Library Y-85

Literary Research Archives V:
Kent State Special Collections Y-86

Literary Research Archives VI: The Modern
Literary Manuscripts Collection in the
Special Collections of the Washington
University Libraries Y-87

Literary Research Archives VII:
The University of Virginia
Libraries. Y-91

Literary Research Archives VIII:
The Henry E. Huntington
Library Y-92

"Literary Style" (1857), by William
Forsyth [excerpt] DLB-57

Literatura Chicanesca: The View From Without
. . . . DLB-82

Literature at Nurse, or Circulating Morals (1885),
by George Moore DLB-18

Littell, Eliakim 1797-1870. . . . . . . DLB-79

Littell, Robert S. 1831-1896 . . . . . . DLB-79

Little, Brown and Company DLB-49

Little Magazines and Newspapers DS-15

The Little Review 1914-1929 . . . . DS-15

Littlewood, Joan 1914- DLB-13

Lively, Penelope 1933- DLB-14, 161

Liverpool University Press DLB-112

The Lives of the Poets DLB-142

Livesay, Dorothy 1909- DLB-68

Livesay, Florence Randal
1874-1953 . . . . DLB-92

"Living in Ruin," by Gerald Stern . . . DLB-105

Livings, Henry 1929- DLB-13

Livingston, Anne Howe
1763-1841 . . . . DLB-37, 200

Livingston, Myra Cohn 1926- DLB-61

Livingston, William 1723-1790 . . . . . DLB-31

Livingstone, David 1813-1873 . . . . . DLB-166

Liyong, Taban lo (see Taban lo Liyong)

Lizárraga, Sylvia S. 1925- DLB-82

Llewellyn, Richard 1906-1983 . . . . . DLB-15

Lloyd, Edward
[publishing house] DLB-106

Lobel, Arnold 1933- DLB-61

Lochridge, Betsy Hopkins (see Fancher, Betsy)

Locke, David Ross 1833-1888 . . . . DLB-11, 23

Locke, John 1632-1704 . . . . . . DLB-31, 101

Locke, Richard Adams 1800-1871 . . . . DLB-43

Locker-Lampson, Frederick
1821-1895 . . . . DLB-35, 184

Lockhart, John Gibson
1794-1854 . . . . DLB-110, 116 144

Lockridge, Ross, Jr.
1914-1948 . . . . DLB-143; Y-80

Locrine and *Selimus* DLB-62

Lodge, David 1935- DLB-14, 194

Lodge, George Cabot 1873-1909. . . . . DLB-54

Lodge, Henry Cabot 1850-1924 . . . . DLB-47

Lodge, Thomas 1558-1625 . . . . . . DLB-172

Loeb, Harold 1891-1974 . . . . DLB-4

Loeb, William 1905-1981 . . . . DLB-127

Lofting, Hugh 1886-1947 . . . . DLB-160

Logan, Deborah Norris 1761-1839 . . . DLB-200

Logan, James 1674-1751 . . . . . DLB-24, 140

Logan, John 1923- DLB-5

Logan, Martha Daniell 1704?-1779 . . . DLB-200

Logan, William 1950- DLB-120

Logau, Friedrich von 1605-1655 . . . . DLB-164

Logue, Christopher 1926- DLB-27

Lohenstein, Daniel Casper von
1635-1683 . . . . DLB-168

Lomonosov, Mikhail Vasil'evich
1711-1765 . . . . DLB-150

London, Jack 1876-1916 . . . . . DLB-8, 12, 78

The London Magazine 1820-1829 . . . . DLB-110

Long, Haniel 1888-1956 . . . . DLB-45

Long, Ray 1878-1935 . . . . DLB-137

Long, H., and Brother DLB-49

Longfellow, Henry Wadsworth
1807-1882 . . . . DLB-1, 59

Longfellow, Samuel 1819-1892 . . . . . DLB-1

Longford, Elizabeth 1906- DLB-155

Longinus circa first century DLB-176

Longley, Michael 1939- DLB-40

Longman, T. [publishing house] DLB-154

Longmans, Green and Company DLB-49

Longmore, George 1793?-1867 . . . . . DLB-99

Longstreet, Augustus Baldwin
1790-1870 . . . . DLB-3, 11, 74

Longworth, D. [publishing house] . . . DLB-49

Lonsdale, Frederick 1881-1954 . . . . . DLB-10

A Look at the Contemporary Black Theatre
Movement DLB-38

Loos, Anita 1893-1981 . . . . . DLB-11, 26; Y-81

Lopate, Phillip 1943- Y-80

López, Diana (see Isabella, Ríos)

Loranger, Jean-Aubert 1896-1942 . . . . DLB-92

Lorca, Federico García 1898-1936 . . . DLB-108

Lord, John Keast 1818-1872 . . . . . . DLB-99

The Lord Chamberlain's Office and Stage
Censorship in England DLB-10

Lorde, Audre 1934-1992 . . . . DLB-41

Lorimer, George Horace
1867-1939 . . . . DLB-91

Loring, A. K. [publishing house] DLB-49

Loring and Mussey DLB-46

Lossing, Benson J. 1813-1891 . . . . . DLB-30

Lothar, Ernst 1890-1974 . . . . DLB-81

Lothrop, Harriet M. 1844-1924 . . . . DLB-42

Lothrop, D., and Company DLB-49

Loti, Pierre 1850-1923 . . . . DLB-123

Lotichius Secundus, Petrus
1528-1560 . . . . DLB-179

Lott, Emeline ?-? DLB-166

The Lounger, no. 20 (1785), by Henry
Mackenzie DLB-39

Louisiana State University Press Y-97

Lounsbury, Thomas R. 1838-1915. . . . DLB-71

Louÿs, Pierre 1870-1925 . . . . DLB-123

Lovelace, Earl 1935- DLB-125

Lovelace, Richard 1618-1657 . . . . . DLB-131

Lovell, Coryell and Company DLB-49

Lovell, John W., Company DLB-49

Lover, Samuel 1797-1868 . . . . DLB-159, 190

Lovesey, Peter 1936- DLB-87

Lovingood, Sut (see Harris,
George Washington)

Low, Samuel 1765-? DLB-37

Lowell, Amy 1874-1925. . . . . . DLB-54, 140

Lowell, James Russell
1819-1891 . . . . . DLB-1, 11, 64, 79, 189

Lowell, Robert 1917-1977 . . . . . DLB-5, 169

Lowenfels, Walter 1897-1976 . . . . . . DLB-4

Lowndes, Marie Belloc 1868-1947 . . . . DLB-70

Lowndes, William Thomas
1798-1843 . . . . DLB-184

Lownes, Humphrey
[publishing house] DLB-170

Lowry, Lois 1937- DLB-52

Lowry, Malcolm 1909-1957 . . . . . . DLB-15

Lowther, Pat 1935-1975. . . . . DLB-53

Loy, Mina 1882-1966 . . . . DLB-4, 54

Lozeau, Albert 1878-1924 . . . . DLB-92

Lubbock, Percy 1879-1965 . . . . . . DLB-149

Lucas, E. V. 1868-1938 . . . . DLB-98, 149, 153

Lucas, Fielding, Jr.
[publishing house] DLB-49

Luce, Henry R. 1898-1967 . . . . . . DLB-91

Luce, John W., and Company. DLB-46

Lucian circa 120-180 . . . . DLB-176

Lucie-Smith, Edward 1933- DLB-40

Lucini, Gian Pietro 1867-1914 . . . . . DLB-114

Luder, Peter circa 1415-1472 . . . . . DLB-179

Ludlum, Robert 1927- Y-82

Ludus de Antichristo circa 1160 . . . . . DLB-148

Ludvigson, Susan 1942- DLB-120

Ludwig, Jack 1922- DLB-60

Ludwig, Otto 1813-1865 . . . . DLB-129

Ludwigslied 881 or 882 . . . . DLB-148

Luera, Yolanda 1953- DLB-122

Luft, Lya 1938- DLB-145

Lugansky, Kazak Vladimir (see Dal', Vladimir Ivanovich)

Luke, Peter 1919- DLB-13

Lummis, Charles F. 1859-1928 . . . . DLB-186

Lupton, F. M., Company DLB-49

Lupus of Ferrières
circa 805-circa 862. . . . . DLB-148

Lurie, Alison 1926- DLB-2

Luther, Martin 1483-1546 . . . . . . DLB-179

Luzi, Mario 1914- DLB-128

L'vov, Nikolai Aleksandrovich
1751-1803 . . . . DLB-150

Lyall, Gavin 1932- DLB-87

Lydgate, John circa 1370-1450 . . . . DLB-146

Lyly, John circa 1554-1606 . . . . DLB-62, 167

Lynch, Patricia 1898-1972 . . . . DLB-160

Lynch, Richard
flourished 1596-1601 . . . . DLB-172

Lynd, Robert 1879-1949 . . . . DLB-98

Lyon, Matthew 1749-1822 . . . . DLB-43

Lysias circa 459 B.C.-circa 380 B.C.
. . . . DLB-176

Lytle, Andrew 1902-1995 . . . . . DLB-6; Y-95

Lytton, Edward (see Bulwer-Lytton, Edward)

Lytton, Edward Robert Bulwer
1831-1891 . . . . DLB-32

M

Maass, Joachim 1901-1972 . . . . DLB-69

Mabie, Hamilton Wright
1845-1916 . . . . DLB-71

Mac A'Ghobhainn, Iain (see Smith, Iain Crichton)

MacArthur, Charles
1895-1956 . . . . DLB-7, 25, 44

Macaulay, Catherine 1731-1791 . . . . . DLB-104

Macaulay, David 1945- DLB-61

Macaulay, Rose 1881-1958 . . . . DLB-36

Macaulay, Thomas Babington
1800-1859 . . . . DLB-32, 55

Macaulay Company DLB-46

MacBeth, George 1932- DLB-40

Macbeth, Madge 1880-1965 . . . . DLB-92

MacCaig, Norman 1910- DLB-27

MacDiarmid, Hugh 1892-1978 . . . . . DLB-20

MacDonald, Cynthia 1928- DLB-105

MacDonald, George
1824-1905 . . . . DLB-18, 163, 178

MacDonald, John D.
1916-1986 . . . . DLB-8; Y-86

MacDonald, Philip 1899?-1980 . . . . . DLB-77

Macdonald, Ross (see Millar, Kenneth)

MacDonald, Wilson 1880-1967 . . . . . DLB-92

Macdonald and Company
(Publishers) DLB-112

MacEwen, Gwendolyn 1941- DLB-53

Macfadden, Bernarr
1868-1955 . . . . DLB-25, 91

MacGregor, John 1825-1892 . . . . . . DLB-166

MacGregor, Mary Esther (see Keith, Marian)

Machado, Antonio 1875-1939 . . . . . DLB-108

Machado, Manuel 1874-1947 . . . . . DLB-108

Machar, Agnes Maule 1837-1927 . . . . DLB-92

Machen, Arthur Llewelyn Jones
1863-1947 . . . . DLB-36, 156, 178

MacInnes, Colin 1914-1976. . . . . . . DLB-14

MacInnes, Helen 1907-1985 . . . . . . DLB-87

Mack, Maynard 1909- DLB-111

Mackall, Leonard L. 1879-1937 . . . . DLB-140

MacKaye, Percy 1875-1956 . . . . DLB-54

Macken, Walter 1915-1967 . . . . DLB-13

Mackenzie, Alexander 1763-1820 . . . . DLB-99

Mackenzie, Alexander Slidell
1803-1848 . . . . DLB-183

Mackenzie, Compton
1883-1972 . . . . DLB-34, 100

Mackenzie, Henry 1745-1831 . . . . . . DLB-39

Mackenzie, William 1758-1828 . . . . . DLB-187

Mackey, Nathaniel 1947- DLB-169

Mackey, William Wellington
1937- DLB-38

Mackintosh, Elizabeth (see Tey, Josephine)

Mackintosh, Sir James
1765-1832 . . . . DLB-158

Maclaren, Ian (see Watson, John)

Macklin, Charles 1699-1797 . . . . . . DLB-89

MacLean, Katherine Anne 1925- DLB-8

MacLeish, Archibald
1892-1982 . . . . DLB-4, 7, 45; Y-82

MacLennan, Hugh 1907-1990 . . . . . DLB-68

Macleod, Fiona (see Sharp, William)

MacLeod, Alistair 1936- DLB-60

Macleod, Norman 1906-1985 . . . . . DLB-4

Mac Low, Jackson 1922- DLB-193

Macmillan and Company DLB-106

The Macmillan Company DLB-49

Macmillan's English Men of Letters,
First Series (1878-1892) DLB-144

MacNamara, Brinsley 1890-1963 . . . . DLB-10

MacNeice, Louis 1907-1963 . . . . DLB-10, 20

MacPhail, Andrew 1864-1938 . . . . . DLB-92

Macpherson, James 1736-1796 . . . . DLB-109

Macpherson, Jay 1931- DLB-53

Macpherson, Jeanie 1884-1946 . . . . . DLB-44

Macrae Smith Company DLB-46

Macrone, John
[publishing house] DLB-106

MacShane, Frank 1927- DLB-111

Macy-Masius. DLB-46

Madden, David 1933- DLB-6

Madden, Sir Frederic 1801-1873 . . . . DLB-184

Maddow, Ben 1909-1992 . . . . DLB-44

Maddux, Rachel 1912-1983 . . . . Y-93

Madgett, Naomi Long 1923- DLB-76

Madhubuti, Haki R.
1942- DLB-5, 41; DS-8

Madison, James 1751-1836 . . . . DLB-37

Maeterlinck, Maurice 1862-1949 . . . . DLB-192

Magee, David 1905-1977 . . . . DLB-187

Maginn, William 1794-1842 . . . . DLB-110, 159

Mahan, Alfred Thayer 1840-1914 . . . . DLB-47

Maheux-Forcier, Louise 1929- DLB-60

Mafūz, Najīb 1911- Y-88

Mahin, John Lee 1902-1984 . . . . . . DLB-44

Mahon, Derek 1941- DLB-40

Maikov, Vasilii Ivanovich
1728-1778 . . . . DLB-150

Mailer, Norman 1923- . . . .
DLB-2, 16, 28, 185; Y-80, Y-83; DS-3

Maillart, Ella 1903-1997 . . . . DLB-195

Maillet, Adrienne 1885-1963 . . . . . . DLB-68

Maimonides, Moses 1138-1204 . . . . DLB-115

Maillet, Antonine 1929- DLB-60

Maillu, David G. 1939- DLB-157

Main Selections of the Book-of-the-Month
Club, 1926-1945 . . . . DLB-9

Main Trends in Twentieth-Century Book Clubs
. . . . DLB-46

Mainwaring, Daniel 1902-1977 . . . . . DLB-44

Mair, Charles 1838-1927 . . . . DLB-99

Mais, Roger 1905-1955 . . . . DLB-125

Major, Andre 1942- DLB-60

Major, Clarence 1936- DLB-33

Major, Kevin 1949- DLB-60

Major Books. DLB-46

Makemie, Francis circa 1658-1708 . . . . DLB-24

The Making of a People, by
J. M. Ritchie DLB-66

Maksimović, Desanka 1898-1993 . . . . DLB-147

Malamud, Bernard
1914-1986 . . . . DLB-2, 28, 152; Y-80, Y-86

Malerba, Luigi 1927- DLB-196

Malet, Lucas 1852-1931 . . . . DLB-153

Malleson, Lucy Beatrice (see Gilbert, Anthony)

Mallet-Joris, Françoise 1930- DLB-83

Mallock, W. H. 1849-1923. . . . . DLB-18, 57

Malone, Dumas 1892-1986 . . . . DLB-17

Malone, Edmond 1741-1812 . . . . . . DLB-142

Malory, Sir Thomas
circa 1400-1410 - 1471 . . . . DLB-146

Malraux, André 1901-1976 . . . . DLB-72

Malthus, Thomas Robert
1766-1834. . . . . DLB-107, 158

Maltz, Albert 1908-1985 . . . . DLB-102

Malzberg, Barry N. 1939- DLB-8

Mamet, David 1947- DLB-7

Manaka, Matsemela 1956- DLB-157

Manchester University Press DLB-112

Mandel, Eli 1922- DLB-53

Mandeville, Bernard 1670-1733 . . . . DLB-101

Mandeville, Sir John
mid fourteenth century DLB-146

Mandiargues, André Pieyre de
1909- DLB-83

Manfred, Frederick 1912-1994 . . . . . . DLB-6

Manfredi, Gianfranco 1948- DLB-196

Mangan, Sherry 1904-1961 . . . . DLB-4

Manganelli, Giorgio 1922-1990 . . . . . DLB-196

Mankiewicz, Herman 1897-1953 . . . . . DLB-26

Mankiewicz, Joseph L. 1909-1993 . . . . DLB-44

Mankowitz, Wolf 1924- DLB-15

Manley, Delarivière
1672?-1724 . . . . DLB-39, 80

Mann, Abby 1927- DLB-44

Mann, Heinrich 1871-1950 . . . . . DLB-66, 118

Mann, Horace 1796-1859 . . . . DLB-1

Mann, Klaus 1906-1949 . . . . DLB-56

Mann, Thomas 1875-1955 . . . . . : . DLB-66

Mann, William D'Alton
1839-1920 . . . . DLB-137

Mannin, Ethel 1900-1984 . . . . DLB-191, 195

Manning, Marie 1873?-1945 . . . . . . DLB-29

Manning and Loring DLB-49

Mannyng, Robert
flourished 1303-1338 . . . . DLB-146

Mano, D. Keith 1942- DLB-6

Manor Books DLB-46

Mansfield, Katherine 1888-1923 . . . . DLB-162

Manuel, Niklaus circa 1484-1530 . . . . DLB-179

Manzini, Gianna 1896-1974 . . . . . . DLB-177

Mapanje, Jack 1944- DLB-157

Maraini, Dacia 1936- DLB-196

March, William 1893-1954 . . . . . DLB-9, 86

Marchand, Leslie A. 1900- DLB-103

Marchant, Bessie 1862-1941 . . . . . . DLB-160

Marchessault, Jovette 1938- DLB-60

Marcus, Frank 1928- DLB-13

Marden, Orison Swett
1850-1924 . . . . DLB-137

Marechera, Dambudzo
1952-1987 . . . . DLB-157

Marek, Richard, Books DLB-46

Mares, E. A. 1938- DLB-122

Mariani, Paul 1940- DLB-111

Marie-Victorin, Frère 1885-1944 . . . . DLB-92

Marin, Biagio 1891-1985 . . . . DLB-128

Marincović, Ranko 1913- DLB-147

Marinetti, Filippo Tommaso
1876-1944 . . . . DLB-114

Marion, Frances 1886-1973 . . . . . . DLB-44

Marius, Richard C. 1933- Y-85

The Mark Taper Forum DLB-7

Mark Twain on Perpetual Copyright Y-92

Markfield, Wallace 1926- DLB-2, 28

Markham, Edwin 1852-1940 . . . . DLB-54, 186

Markle, Fletcher 1921-1991 . . . . DLB-68; Y-91

Marlatt, Daphne 1942- DLB-60

Marlitt, E. 1825-1887 . . . . DLB-129

Marlowe, Christopher 1564-1593 . . . . DLB-62

Marlyn, John 1912- DLB-88

Marmion, Shakerley 1603-1639 . . . . . DLB-58

Der Marner
before 1230-circa 1287 . . . . DLB-138

The *Marprelate Tracts* 1588-1589 . . . . DLB-132

Marquand, John P. 1893-1960 . . . . DLB-9, 102

Marqués, René 1919-1979 . . . . DLB-113

Marquis, Don 1878-1937 . . . . . . DLB-11, 25

Marriott, Anne 1913- DLB-68

Marryat, Frederick 1792-1848 . . . . DLB-21, 163

Marsh, George Perkins
1801-1882 . . . . DLB-1, 64

Marsh, James 1794-1842 . . . . . . DLB-1, 59

Marsh, Capen, Lyon and Webb DLB-49

Marsh, Ngaio 1899-1982 . . . . DLB-77

Marshall, Edison 1894-1967 . . . . . . DLB-102

Marshall, Edward 1932- DLB-16

Marshall, Emma 1828-1899 . . . . . . DLB-163

Marshall, James 1942-1992 . . . . . . DLB-61

Marshall, Joyce 1913- DLB-88

Marshall, Paule 1929- DLB-33, 157

Marshall, Tom 1938- DLB-60

Marsilius of Padua
circa 1275-circa 1342 . . . . DLB-115

Marson, Una 1905-1965 . . . . DLB-157

Marston, John 1576-1634 . . . . . DLB-58, 172

Marston, Philip Bourke 1850-1887 . . . . DLB-35

Martens, Kurt 1870-1945 . . . . DLB-66

Martien, William S.
[publishing house] DLB-49

Martin, Abe (see Hubbard, Kin)

Martin, Charles 1942- DLB-120

Martin, Claire 1914- DLB-60

Martin, Jay 1935- DLB-111

Martin, Johann (see Laurentius von Schnüffis)

Martin, Violet Florence (see Ross, Martin)

Martin du Gard, Roger
1881-1958 . . . . DLB-65

Martineau, Harriet 1802-1876
. . . . . . DLB-21, 55, 159, 163, 166, 190

Martínez, Eliud 1935- DLB-122

Martínez, Max 1943- DLB-82

Martyn, Edward 1859-1923 . . . . . . DLB-10

Marvell, Andrew 1621-1678 . . . . . . DLB-131

Marvin X 1944- DLB-38

Marx, Karl 1818-1883 . . . . DLB-129

Marzials, Theo 1850-1920 . . . . DLB-35

Masefield, John
1878-1967 . . . . . . DLB-10, 19, 153, 160

Mason, A. E. W. 1865-1948 . . . . . . DLB-70

Mason, Bobbie Ann
1940- DLB-173; Y-87

Mason, William 1725-1797 . . . . . . DLB-142

Mason Brothers DLB-49

Massey, Gerald 1828-1907 . . . . DLB-32

Massey, Linton R. 1900-1974 . . . . . . DLB-187

Massinger, Philip 1583-1640 . . . . . . DLB-58

Masson, David 1822-1907 . . . . DLB-144

Masters, Edgar Lee 1868-1950 . . . . . DLB-54

Mastronardi, Lucio 1930-1979 . . . . . DLB-177

Matevski, Mateja 1929- DLB-181

Mather, Cotton
1663-1728 . . . . DLB-24, 30, 140

Mather, Increase 1639-1723 . . . . . . DLB-24

Mather, Richard 1596-1669 . . . . . . DLB-24

Matheson, Richard 1926- DLB-8, 44

Matheus, John F. 1887- DLB-51

Mathews, Cornelius
1817?-1889 . . . . DLB-3, 64

Mathews, John Joseph
1894-1979 . . . . DLB-175

Mathews, Elkin
[publishing house] DLB-112

Mathias, Roland 1915- DLB-27

Mathis, June 1892-1927 . . . . DLB-44

Mathis, Sharon Bell 1937- DLB-33

Matković, Marijan 1915-1985 . . . . . . DLB-181

Matoš, Antun Gustav 1873-1914 . . . . DLB-147

Matsumoto, Seichō 1909-1992 . . . . . DLB-182

The Matter of England
1240-1400 . . . . DLB-146

The Matter of Rome
early twelfth to late fifteenth
century DLB-146

Matthews, Brander
1852-1929 . . . . DLB-71, 78; DS-13

Matthews, Jack 1925- DLB-6

Matthews, William 1942- DLB-5

Matthiessen, F. O. 1902-1950 . . . . . DLB-63

Maturin, Charles Robert
    1780-1824 . . . . DLB-178

Matthiessen, Peter 1927- DLB-6, 173

Maugham, W. Somerset
    1874-1965 . . DLB-10, 36, 77, 100, 162, 195

Maupassant, Guy de 1850-1893 . . . . DLB-123

Mauriac, Claude 1914- DLB-83

Mauriac, François 1885-1970 . . . . . . DLB-65

Maurice, Frederick Denison
    1805-1872 . . . . DLB-55

Maurois, André 1885-1967 . . . . DLB-65

Maury, James 1718-1769 . . . . DLB-31

Mavor, Elizabeth 1927- DLB-14

Mavor, Osborne Henry (see Bridie, James)

Maxwell, William 1908- Y-80

Maxwell, H. [publishing house] DLB-49

Maxwell, John [publishing house]. . . . DLB-106

May, Elaine 1932- DLB-44

May, Karl 1842-1912 . . . . DLB-129

May, Thomas 1595 or 1596-1650 . . . . DLB-58

Mayer, Bernadette 1945- DLB-165

Mayer, Mercer 1943- DLB-61

Mayer, O. B. 1818-1891 . . . . DLB-3

Mayes, Herbert R. 1900-1987 . . . . . DLB-137

Mayes, Wendell 1919-1992 . . . . DLB-26

Mayfield, Julian 1928-1984 . . . . DLB-33; Y-84

Mayhew, Henry 1812-1887 . . DLB-18, 55, 190

Mayhew, Jonathan 1720-1766 . . . . . . DLB-31

Mayne, Ethel Colburn 1865-1941 . . . DLB-197

Mayne, Jasper 1604-1672 . . . . DLB-126

Mayne, Seymour 1944- DLB-60

Mayor, Flora Macdonald
    1872-1932 . . . . DLB-36

Mayröcker, Friederike 1924- DLB-85

Mazrui, Ali A. 1933- DLB-125

Mažuranić, Ivan 1814-1890 . . . . . . DLB-147

Mazursky, Paul 1930- DLB-44

McAlmon, Robert
    1896-1956 . . . . DLB-4, 45; DS-15

McArthur, Peter 1866-1924 . . . . DLB-92

McBride, Robert M., and
    Company DLB-46

McCabe, Patrick 1955- DLB-194

McCaffrey, Anne 1926- DLB-8

McCarthy, Cormac 1933- DLB-6, 143

McCarthy, Mary 1912-1989 . . . . DLB-2; Y-81

McCay, Winsor 1871-1934 . . . . DLB-22

McClane, Albert Jules 1922-1991 . . . . DLB-171

McClatchy, C. K. 1858-1936 . . . . . . DLB-25

McClellan, George Marion
    1860-1934 . . . . DLB-50

McCloskey, Robert 1914- DLB-22

McClung, Nellie Letitia 1873-1951 . . . DLB-92

McClure, Joanna 1930- DLB-16

McClure, Michael 1932- DLB-16

McClure, Phillips and Company. DLB-46

McClure, S. S. 1857-1949 . . . . DLB-91

McClurg, A. C., and Company DLB-49

McCluskey, John A., Jr. 1944- DLB-33

McCollum, Michael A. 1946- Y-87

McConnell, William C. 1917- DLB-88

McCord, David 1897- DLB-61

McCorkle, Jill 1958- Y-87

McCorkle, Samuel Eusebius
    1746-1811 . . . . DLB-37

McCormick, Anne O'Hare
    1880-1954 . . . . DLB-29

McCormick, Robert R. 1880-1955 . . . . DLB-29

McCourt, Edward 1907-1972 . . . . . . DLB-88

McCoy, Horace 1897-1955 . . . . DLB-9

McCrae, John 1872-1918 . . . . DLB-92

McCullagh, Joseph B. 1842-1896 . . . . DLB-23

McCullers, Carson
    1917-1967 . . . . DLB-2, 7, 173

McCulloch, Thomas 1776-1843 . . . . . DLB-99

McDonald, Forrest 1927- DLB-17

McDonald, Walter
    1934- DLB-105, DS-9

McDougall, Colin 1917-1984 . . . . . . DLB-68

McDowell, Obolensky DLB-46

McEwan, Ian 1948- DLB-14, 194

McFadden, David 1940- DLB-60

McFall, Frances Elizabeth Clarke
    (see Grand, Sarah)

McFarlane, Leslie 1902-1977 . . . . . . DLB-88

McFee, William 1881-1966 . . . . . . DLB-153

McGahern, John 1934- DLB-14

McGee, Thomas D'Arcy
    1825-1868 . . . . DLB-99

McGeehan, W. O. 1879-1933 . . . DLB-25, 171

McGill, Ralph 1898-1969 . . . . DLB-29

McGinley, Phyllis 1905-1978 . . . . DLB-11, 48

McGinniss, Joe 1942- DLB-185

McGirt, James E. 1874-1930 . . . . . . DLB-50

McGlashan and Gill DLB-106

McGough, Roger 1937- DLB-40

McGraw-Hill. DLB-46

McGuane, Thomas 1939- DLB-2; Y-80

McGuckian, Medbh 1950- DLB-40

McGuffey, William Holmes
    1800-1873 . . . . DLB-42

McIlvanney, William 1936- DLB-14

McIlwraith, Jean Newton
    1859-1938 . . . . DLB-92

McIntyre, James 1827-1906 . . . . . . DLB-99

McIntyre, O. O. 1884-1938 . . . . . . DLB-25

McKay, Claude
    1889-1948 . . . . DLB-4, 45, 51, 117

The David McKay Company DLB-49

McKean, William V. 1820-1903 . . . . DLB-23

McKenna, Stephen 1888-1967 . . . . . DLB-197

The McKenzie Trust Y-96

McKinley, Robin 1952- DLB-52

McLachlan, Alexander 1818-1896 . . . . DLB-99

McLaren, Floris Clark 1904-1978 . . . . DLB-68

McLaverty, Michael 1907- DLB-15

McLean, John R. 1848-1916 . . . . . . DLB-23

McLean, William L. 1852-1931 . . . . . DLB-25

McLennan, William 1856-1904 . . . . . DLB-92

McLoughlin Brothers DLB-49

McLuhan, Marshall 1911-1980 . . . . . DLB-88

McMaster, John Bach 1852-1932 . . . . DLB-47

McMurtry, Larry
    1936- DLB-2, 143; Y-80, Y-87

McNally, Terrence 1939- DLB-7

McNeil, Florence 1937- DLB-60

McNeile, Herman Cyril
    1888-1937 . . . . DLB-77

McNickle, D'Arcy 1904-1977 . . . . . DLB-175

McPhee, John 1931- DLB-185

McPherson, James Alan 1943- DLB-38

McPherson, Sandra 1943- Y-86

McWhirter, George 1939- DLB-60

McWilliams, Carey 1905-1980 . . . . DLB-137

Mead, L. T. 1844-1914 . . . . DLB-141

Mead, Matthew 1924- DLB-40

Mead, Taylor ?- DLB-16

Meany, Tom 1903-1964 . . . . DLB-171

Mechthild von Magdeburg
    circa 1207-circa 1282 . . . . DLB-138

Medill, Joseph 1823-1899 . . . . DLB-43

Medoff, Mark 1940- DLB-7

Meek, Alexander Beaufort
    1814-1865 . . . . DLB-3

Meeke, Mary ?-1816? DLB-116

Meinke, Peter 1932- DLB-5

Mejia Vallejo, Manuel 1923- . . . DLB-113

Melanchthon, Philipp 1497-1560 . . . . DLB-179

Melançon, Robert 1947- DLB-60

Mell, Max 1882-1971 . . . . DLB-81, 124

Mellow, James R. 1926- DLB-111

Meltzer, David 1937- DLB-16

Meltzer, Milton 1915- DLB-61

Melville, Elizabeth, Lady Culross
    circa 1585-1640 . . . . DLB-172

Melville, Herman 1819-1891 . . . . DLB-3, 74

Memoirs of Life and Literature (1920),
    by W. H. Mallock [excerpt] DLB-57

Menander 342-341 B.C.-circa 292-291 B.C.
. . . . DLB-176

Menantes (see Hunold, Christian Friedrich)

Mencke, Johann Burckhard
1674-1732 . . . . DLB-168

Mencken, H. L.
1880-1956. . . . . . . DLB-11, 29, 63, 137

Mencken and Nietzsche: An Unpublished Excerpt
from H. L. Mencken's *My Life
as Author and Editor*. Y-93

Mendelssohn, Moses 1729-1786 . . . . . DLB-97

Méndez M., Miguel 1930- DLB-82

Mens Rea (or Something). Y-97

The Mercantile Library of
New York Y-96

Mercer, Cecil William (see Yates, Dornford)

Mercer, David 1928-1980. . . . . DLB-13

Mercer, John 1704-1768 . . . . DLB-31

Meredith, George
1828-1909. . . . . . . DLB-18, 35, 57, 159

Meredith, Louisa Anne
1812-1895 . . . . DLB-166

Meredith, Owen (see Lytton, Edward Robert Bulwer)

Meredith, William 1919- DLB-5

Mergerle, Johann Ulrich
(see Abraham ä Sancta Clara)

Mérimée, Prosper 1803-1870 . . . DLB-119, 192

Merivale, John Herman
1779-1844 . . . . DLB-96

Meriwether, Louise 1923- DLB-33

Merlin Press DLB-112

Merriam, Eve 1916-1992 . . . . DLB-61

The Merriam Company DLB-49

Merrill, James
1926-1995 . . . . DLB-5, 165; Y-85

Merrill and Baker. DLB-49

The Mershon Company DLB-49

Merton, Thomas 1915-1968 . . . . DLB-48; Y-81

Merwin, W. S. 1927- DLB-5, 169

Messner, Julian [publishing house] DLB-46

Metcalf, J. [publishing house]. DLB-49

Metcalf, John 1938- DLB-60

The Methodist Book Concern DLB-49

Methuen and Company. DLB-112

Mew, Charlotte 1869-1928 . . . . DLB-19, 135

Mewshaw, Michael 1943- Y-80

Meyer, Conrad Ferdinand 1825-1898 . . . DLB-129

Meyer, E. Y. 1946- DLB-75

Meyer, Eugene 1875-1959 . . . . DLB-29

Meyer, Michael 1921- DLB-155

Meyers, Jeffrey 1939- DLB-111

Meynell, Alice 1847-1922. . . . . . DLB-19, 98

Meynell, Viola 1885-1956 . . . . DLB-153

Meyrink, Gustav 1868-1932 . . . . . . DLB-81

Michael M. Rea and the Rea Award for the
Short Story Y-97

Michaels, Leonard 1933- DLB-130

Micheaux, Oscar 1884-1951 . . . . . . DLB-50

Michel of Northgate, Dan
circa 1265-circa 1340 . . . . DLB-146

Micheline, Jack 1929- DLB-16

Michener, James A. 1907?- DLB-6

Micklejohn, George
circa 1717-1818 . . . . DLB-31

Middle English Literature:
An Introduction DLB-146

The Middle English Lyric. DLB-146

Middle Hill Press DLB-106

Middleton, Christopher 1926- DLB-40

Middleton, Richard 1882-1911 . . . . DLB-156

Middleton, Stanley 1919- DLB-14

Middleton, Thomas 1580-1627. . . . . DLB-58

Miegel, Agnes 1879-1964 . . . . DLB-56

Mihailović, Dragoslav 1930- DLB-181

Mihalić, Slavko 1928- DLB-181

Miles, Josephine 1911-1985 . . . . . . DLB-48

Miliković, Branko 1934-1961 . . . . . DLB-181

Milius, John 1944- DLB-44

Mill, James 1773-1836 . . . . . . DLB-107, 158

Mill, John Stuart 1806-1873 . . . . DLB-55, 190

Millar, Kenneth
1915-1983. . . . . DLB-2; Y-83; DS-6

Millar, Andrew
[publishing house] DLB-154

Millay, Edna St. Vincent
1892-1950 . . . . DLB-45

Miller, Arthur 1915- DLB-7

Miller, Caroline 1903-1992. . . . . . . DLB-9

Miller, Eugene Ethelbert 1950- DLB-41

Miller, Heather Ross 1939- DLB-120

Miller, Henry 1891-1980. . . . . DLB-4, 9; Y-80

Miller, Hugh 1802-1856 . . . . DLB-190

Miller, J. Hillis 1928- DLB-67

Miller, James [publishing house] DLB-49

Miller, Jason 1939- DLB-7

Miller, Joaquin 1839-1913 . . . . . . DLB-186

Miller, May 1899- DLB-41

Miller, Paul 1906-1991. . . . . DLB-127

Miller, Perry 1905-1963 . . . . . . DLB-17, 63

Miller, Sue 1943- DLB-143

Miller, Vassar 1924- DLB-105

Miller, Walter M., Jr. 1923- DLB-8

Miller, Webb 1892-1940 . . . . DLB-29

Millhauser, Steven 1943- DLB-2

Millican, Arthenia J. Bates
1920- DLB-38

Mills and Boon DLB-112

Milman, Henry Hart 1796-1868 . . . . DLB-96

Milne, A. A.
1882-1956 . . . . . . DLB-10, 77, 100, 160

Milner, Ron 1938- DLB-38

Milner, William
[publishing house] DLB-106

Milnes, Richard Monckton (Lord Houghton)
1809-1885 . . . . DLB-32, 184

Milton, John 1608-1674 . . . . . . DLB-131, 151

Minakami, Tsutomu 1919- DLB-182

The Minerva Press DLB-154

Minnesang circa 1150-1280 . . . . DLB-138

Minns, Susan 1839-1938. . . . . DLB-140

Minor Illustrators, 1880-1914 . . . . . DLB-141

Minor Poets of the Earlier Seventeenth
Century DLB-121

Minton, Balch and Company DLB-46

Mirbeau, Octave 1848-1917 . . . . DLB-123, 192

Mirk, John died after 1414? DLB-146

Miron, Gaston 1928- DLB-60

A Mirror for Magistrates. DLB-167

Mishima, Yukio 1925-1970 . . . . . . DLB-182

Mitchel, Jonathan 1624-1668 . . . . . DLB-24

Mitchell, Adrian 1932- DLB-40

Mitchell, Donald Grant
1822-1908 . . . . DLB-1; DS-13

Mitchell, Gladys 1901-1983. . . . . . . DLB-77

Mitchell, James Leslie 1901-1935. . . . DLB-15

Mitchell, John (see Slater, Patrick)

Mitchell, John Ames 1845-1918 . . . . DLB-79

Mitchell, Joseph 1908-1996 . . . . DLB-185; Y-96

Mitchell, Julian 1935- DLB-14

Mitchell, Ken 1940- DLB-60

Mitchell, Langdon 1862-1935 . . . . . . DLB-7

Mitchell, Loften 1919- DLB-38

Mitchell, Margaret 1900-1949 . . . . . DLB-9

Mitchell, W. O. 1914- DLB-88

Mitchison, Naomi Margaret (Haldane)
1897- DLB-160, 191

Mitford, Mary Russell
1787-1855. . . . . DLB-110, 116

Mitford, Nancy 1904-1973. . . . . . . DLB-191

Mittelholzer, Edgar 1909-1965. . . . . DLB-117

Mitterer, Erika 1906- DLB-85

Mitterer, Felix 1948- DLB-124

Mitternacht, Johann Sebastian
1613-1679 . . . . DLB-168

Miyamoto, Yuriko 1899-1951 . . . . . DLB-180

Mizener, Arthur 1907-1988 . . . . . . DLB-103

Mo, Timothy 1950- DLB-194

Modern Age Books. DLB-46

"Modern English Prose" (1876),
by George Saintsbury DLB-57

The Modern Language Association of America
Celebrates Its Centennial Y-84

The Modern Library DLB-46

"Modern Novelists – Great and Small" (1855), by
Margaret Oliphant DLB-21

"Modern Style" (1857), by Cockburn
Thomson [excerpt] DLB-57

The Modernists (1932),
by Joseph Warren Beach DLB-36

Modiano, Patrick 1945- DLB-83

Moffat, Yard and Company DLB-46

Moffet, Thomas 1553-1604 . . . . . . DLB-136

Mohr, Nicholasa 1938- DLB-145

Moix, Ana María 1947- DLB-134

Molesworth, Louisa 1839-1921 . . . . DLB-135

Möllhausen, Balduin 1825-1905 . . . . DLB-129

Momaday, N. Scott 1934- DLB-143, 175

Monkhouse, Allan 1858-1936 . . . . . . DLB-10

Monro, Harold 1879-1932 . . . . DLB-19

Monroe, Harriet 1860-1936 . . . . DLB-54, 91

Monsarrat, Nicholas 1910-1979 . . . . . DLB-15

Montagu, Lady Mary Wortley
1689-1762 . . . . DLB-95, 101

Montague, C. E. 1867-1928 . . . . . . DLB-197

Montague, John 1929- DLB-40

Montale, Eugenio 1896-1981 . . . . . DLB-114

Monterroso, Augusto 1921- DLB-145

Montgomerie, Alexander
circa 1550?-1598 . . . . DLB-167

Montgomery, James
1771-1854 . . . . DLB-93, 158

Montgomery, John 1919- DLB-16

Montgomery, Lucy Maud
1874-1942 . . . . DLB-92; DS-14

Montgomery, Marion 1925- DLB-6

Montgomery, Robert Bruce (see Crispin, Edmund)

Montherlant, Henry de 1896-1972 . . . . DLB-72

The Monthly Review 1749-1844 . . . . . DLB-110

Montigny, Louvigny de 1876-1955 . . . DLB-92

Montoya, José 1932- DLB-122

Moodie, John Wedderburn Dunbar
1797-1869 . . . . DLB-99

Moodie, Susanna 1803-1885 . . . . . . DLB-99

Moody, Joshua circa 1633-1697 . . . . DLB-24

Moody, William Vaughn
1869-1910 . . . . DLB-7, 54

Moorcock, Michael 1939- DLB-14

Moore, Catherine L. 1911- DLB-8

Moore, Clement Clarke 1779-1863 . . . DLB-42

Moore, Dora Mavor 1888-1979 . . . . DLB-92

Moore, George
1852-1933 . . . . DLB-10, 18, 57, 135

Moore, Marianne
1887-1972 . . . . DLB-45; DS-7

Moore, Mavor 1919- DLB-88

Moore, Richard 1927- DLB-105

Moore, T. Sturge 1870-1944 . . . . . . DLB-19

Moore, Thomas 1779-1852 . . . . DLB-96, 144

Moore, Ward 1903-1978 . . . . DLB-8

Moore, Wilstach, Keys and
Company DLB-49

The Moorland-Spingarn Research
Center DLB-76

Moorman, Mary C. 1905-1994 . . . . DLB-155

Moraga, Cherríe 1952- DLB-82

Morales, Alejandro 1944- DLB-82

Morales, Mario Roberto 1947- DLB-145

Morales, Rafael 1919- DLB-108

Morality Plays: *Mankind* circa 1450-1500 and
Everyman circa 1500 . . . . DLB-146

Morante, Elsa 1912-1985 . . . . DLB-177

Morata, Olympia Fulvia
1526-1555 . . . . DLB-179

Moravia, Alberto 1907-1990 . . . . . . DLB-177

Mordaunt, Elinor 1872-1942 . . . . . DLB-174

More, Hannah
1745-1833 . . . . . DLB-107, 109, 116, 158

More, Henry 1614-1687 . . . . DLB-126

More, Sir Thomas
1477 or 1478-1535 . . . . DLB-136

Moreno, Dorinda 1939- DLB-122

Morency, Pierre 1942- DLB-60

Moretti, Marino 1885-1979 . . . . . . DLB-114

Morgan, Berry 1919- DLB-6

Morgan, Charles 1894-1958 . . . . DLB-34, 100

Morgan, Edmund S. 1916- DLB-17

Morgan, Edwin 1920- DLB-27

Morgan, John Pierpont
1837-1913 . . . . DLB-140

Morgan, John Pierpont, Jr.
1867-1943 . . . . DLB-140

Morgan, Robert 1944- DLB-120

Morgan, Sydney Owenson, Lady
1776?-1859 . . . . DLB-116, 158

Morgner, Irmtraud 1933- DLB-75

Morhof, Daniel Georg
1639-1691 . . . . DLB-164

Mori, Ōgai 1862-1922 . . . . DLB-180

Morier, James Justinian
1782 or 1783?-1849 . . . . DLB-116

Mörike, Eduard 1804-1875 . . . . . . DLB-133

Morin, Paul 1889-1963 . . . . DLB-92

Morison, Richard 1514?-1556 . . . . . DLB-136

Morison, Samuel Eliot 1887-1976 . . . DLB-17

Moritz, Karl Philipp 1756-1793 . . . . DLB-94

Moriz von Craûn
circa 1220-1230 . . . . DLB-138

Morley, Christopher 1890-1957 . . . . . DLB-9

Morley, John 1838-1923 . . . . DLB-57, 144, 190

Morris, George Pope 1802-1864 . . . . DLB-73

Morris, Lewis 1833-1907 . . . . DLB-35

Morris, Margaret 1737-1816 . . . . . DLB-200

Morris, Richard B. 1904-1989 . . . . . DLB-17

Morris, William
1834-1896 . . DLB-18, 35, 57, 156, 178, 184

Morris, Willie 1934- Y-80

Morris, Wright 1910- DLB-2; Y-81

Morrison, Arthur
1863-1945 . . . . DLB-70, 135, 197

Morrison, Charles Clayton
1874-1966 . . . . DLB-91

Morrison, Toni
1931- DLB-6, 33, 143; Y-81, Y-93

Morrow, William, and Company DLB-46

Morse, James Herbert 1841-1923 . . . . DLB-71

Morse, Jedidiah 1761-1826 . . . . DLB-37

Morse, John T., Jr. 1840-1937 . . . . . DLB-47

Morselli, Guido 1912-1973 . . . . . . DLB-177

Mortimer, Favell Lee 1802-1878 . . . . DLB-163

Mortimer, John 1923- DLB-13

Morton, Carlos 1942- DLB-122

Morton, H. V. 1892-1979 . . . . DLB-195

Morton, John P., and Company DLB-49

Morton, Nathaniel 1613-1685 . . . . . . DLB-24

Morton, Sarah Wentworth
1759-1846 . . . . DLB-37

Morton, Thomas
circa 1579-circa 1647 . . . . DLB-24

Moscherosch, Johann Michael
1601-1669 . . . . DLB-164

Moseley, Humphrey
[publishing house] DLB-170

Möser, Justus 1720-1794 . . . . DLB-97

Mosley, Nicholas 1923- DLB-14

Moss, Arthur 1889-1969 . . . . DLB-4

Moss, Howard 1922-1987 . . . . DLB-5

Moss, Thylias 1954- DLB-120

The Most Powerful Book Review in America
[*New York Times Book Review*] Y-82

Motion, Andrew 1952- DLB-40

Motley, John Lothrop
1814-1877 . . . . DLB-1, 30, 59

Motley, Willard 1909-1965 . . . . DLB-76, 143

Motte, Benjamin Jr.
[publishing house] DLB-154

Motteux, Peter Anthony
1663-1718 . . . . DLB-80

Mottram, R. H. 1883-1971 . . . . DLB-36

Mouré, Erin 1955- DLB-60

Mourning Dove (Humishuma)
   between 1882 and 1888?-1936 . . . . DLB-175

Movies from Books, 1920-1974 . . . . . . DLB-9

Mowat, Farley 1921- DLB-68

Mowbray, A. R., and Company,
   Limited. DLB-106

Mowrer, Edgar Ansel 1892-1977. . . . . DLB-29

Mowrer, Paul Scott 1887-1971 . . . . . . DLB-29

Moxon, Edward
   [publishing house] DLB-106

Moxon, Joseph
   [publishing house] DLB-170

Mphahlele, Es'kia (Ezekiel)
   1919- DLB-125

Mtshali, Oswald Mbuyiseni
   1940- DLB-125

Mucedorus. DLB-62

Mudford, William 1782-1848 . . . . . . DLB-159

Mueller, Lisel 1924- DLB-105

Muhajir, El (see Marvin X)

Muhajir, Nazzam Al Fitnah (see Marvin X)

Mühlbach, Luise 1814-1873 . . . . DLB-133

Muir, Edwin 1887-1959 . . . . DLB-20, 100, 191

Muir, Helen 1937- DLB-14

Muir, John 1838-1914 . . . . DLB-186

Mukherjee, Bharati 1940- DLB-60

Mulcaster, Richard
   1531 or 1532-1611 . . . . DLB-167

Muldoon, Paul 1951- DLB-40

Müller, Friedrich (see Müller, Maler)

Müller, Heiner 1929- DLB-124

Müller, Maler 1749-1825 . . . . DLB-94

Müller, Wilhelm 1794-1827. . . . . . . DLB-90

Mumford, Lewis 1895-1990 . . . . . . DLB-63

Munby, Arthur Joseph 1828-1910 . . . . DLB-35

Munday, Anthony 1560-1633. . . . DLB-62, 172

Mundt, Clara (see Mühlbach, Luise)

Mundt, Theodore 1808-1861 . . . . . . DLB-133

Munford, Robert circa 1737-1783 . . . . DLB-31

Mungoshi, Charles 1947- DLB-157

Munonye, John 1929- DLB-117

Munro, Alice 1931- DLB-53

Munro, H. H. 1870-1916. . . . . DLB-34, 162

Munro, Neil 1864-1930 . . . . DLB-156

Munro, George
   [publishing house]. DLB-49

Munro, Norman L.
   [publishing house]. DLB-49

Munroe, James, and Company. DLB-49

Munroe, Kirk 1850-1930 . . . . DLB-42

Munroe and Francis DLB-49

Munsell, Joel [publishing house] DLB-49

Munsey, Frank A. 1854-1925 . . . . DLB-25, 91

Murakami, Haruki 1949- DLB-182

Munsey, Frank A., and
   Company DLB-49

Murav'ev, Mikhail Nikitich
   1757-1807 . . . . DLB-150

Murdoch, Iris 1919- DLB-14, 194

Murdoch, Rupert 1931- DLB-127

Murfree, Mary N. 1850-1922 . . . . DLB-12, 74

Murger, Henry 1822-1861. . . . . . . DLB-119

Murger, Louis-Henri (see Murger, Henry)

Murner, Thomas 1475-1537 . . . . . . DLB-179

Muro, Amado 1915-1971. . . . . DLB-82

Murphy, Arthur 1727-1805 . . . . DLB-89, 142

Murphy, Beatrice M. 1908- DLB-76

Murphy, Emily 1868-1933 . . . . DLB-99

Murphy, John H., III 1916- DLB-127

Murphy, John, and Company DLB-49

Murphy, Richard 1927-1993 . . . . . . DLB-40

Murray, Albert L. 1916- DLB-38

Murray, Gilbert 1866-1957 . . . . DLB-10

Murray, Judith Sargent
   1751-1820 . . . . DLB-37, 200

Murray, Pauli 1910-1985 . . . . DLB-41

Murray, John [publishing house] DLB-154

Murry, John Middleton
   1889-1957 . . . . DLB-149

Musäus, Johann Karl August
   1735-1787 . . . . DLB-97

Muschg, Adolf 1934- DLB-75

The Music of Minnesang DLB-138

Musil, Robert 1880-1942 . . . . . DLB-81, 124

Muspilli circa 790-circa 850 . . . . . . DLB-148

Musset, Alfred de 1810-1857 . . . . . . DLB-192

Mussey, Benjamin B., and
   Company DLB-49

Mutafchieva, Vera 1929- DLB-181

Mwangi, Meja 1948- DLB-125

Myers, Frederic W. H. 1843-1901 . . . DLB-190

Myers, Gustavus 1872-1942 . . . . . . DLB-47

Myers, L. H. 1881-1944 . . . . DLB-15

Myers, Walter Dean 1937- DLB-33

Myles, Eileen 1949- DLB-193

N

Nabl, Franz 1883-1974 . . . . DLB-81

Nabokov, Vladimir
   1899-1977 . . . . . DLB-2; Y-80, Y-91; DS-3

Nabokov Festival at Cornell Y-83

The Vladimir Nabokov Archive
   in the Berg Collection Y-91

Naden, Constance 1858-1889 . . . . . DLB-199

Nadezhdin, Nikolai Ivanovich
   1804-1856 . . . . DLB-198

Nafis and Cornish DLB-49

Nagai, Kafū 1879-1959 . . . . DLB-180

Naipaul, Shiva 1945-1985. . . . . DLB-157; Y-85

Naipaul, V. S. 1932- DLB-125; Y-85

Nakagami, Kenji 1946-1992 . . . . . . DLB-182

Nancrede, Joseph
   [publishing house]. DLB-49

Naranjo, Carmen 1930- DLB-145

Narezhny, Vasilii Trofimovich
   1780-1825 . . . . DLB-198

Narrache, Jean 1893-1970. . . . . . . DLB-92

Nasby, Petroleum Vesuvius (see Locke, David
   Ross)

Nash, Ogden 1902-1971 . . . . DLB-11

Nash, Eveleigh
   [publishing house] DLB-112

Nashe, Thomas 1567-1601? DLB-167

Nast, Conde 1873-1942. . . . . DLB-91

Nast, Thomas 1840-1902 . . . . DLB-188

Nastasijević, Momčilo 1894-1938 . . . . DLB-147

Nathan, George Jean 1882-1958 . . . . DLB-137

Nathan, Robert 1894-1985 . . . . DLB-9

The National Jewish Book Awards Y-85

The National Theatre and the Royal
   Shakespeare Company: The
   National Companies DLB-13

Natsume, Sōseki 1867-1916 . . . . . . DLB-180

Naughton, Bill 1910- DLB-13

Naylor, Gloria 1950- DLB-173

Nazor, Vladimir 1876-1949 . . . . . . DLB-147

Ndebele, Njabulo 1948- DLB-157

Neagoe, Peter 1881-1960. . . . . DLB-4

Neal, John 1793-1876 . . . . . . DLB-1, 59

Neal, Joseph C. 1807-1847 . . . . DLB-11

Neal, Larry 1937-1981 . . . . DLB-38

The Neale Publishing Company DLB-49

Neely, F. Tennyson
   [publishing house]. DLB-49

Negri, Ada 1870-1945 . . . . DLB-114

"The Negro as a Writer," by
   G. M. McClellan DLB-50

"Negro Poets and Their Poetry," by
   Wallace Thurman DLB-50

Neidhart von Reuental
   circa 1185-circa 1240 . . . . DLB-138

Neihardt, John G. 1881-1973 . . . . DLB-9, 54

Neledinsky-Meletsky, Iurii Aleksandrovich
   1752-1828 . . . . DLB-150

Nelligan, Emile 1879-1941 . . . . DLB-92

Nelson, Alice Moore Dunbar
   1875-1935 . . . . DLB-50

Nelson, Thomas, and Sons [U.S.] DLB-49

Nelson, Thomas, and Sons [U.K.] . . . DLB-106

Nelson, William 1908-1978 . . . . . . DLB-103

Nelson, William Rockhill
1841-1915 . . . . DLB-23

Nemerov, Howard 1920-1991 . . . DLB-5, 6; Y-83

Nesbit, E. 1858-1924 . . . . . DLB-141, 153, 178

Ness, Evaline 1911-1986 . . . . DLB-61

Nestroy, Johann 1801-1862 . . . . DLB-133

Neukirch, Benjamin 1655-1729 . . . . . DLB-168

Neugeboren, Jay 1938- DLB-28

Neumann, Alfred 1895-1952 . . . . . . DLB-56

Neumark, Georg 1621-1681 . . . . DLB-164

Neumeister, Erdmann 1671-1756 . . . . DLB-168

Nevins, Allan 1890-1971 . . . . . DLB-17; DS-17

Nevinson, Henry Woodd
1856-1941 . . . . DLB-135

The New American Library DLB-46

New Approaches to Biography: Challenges
from Critical Theory, USC Conference
on Literary Studies, 1990 . . . . Y-90

New Directions Publishing
Corporation DLB-46

A New Edition of *Huck Finn* Y-85

New Forces at Work in the American Theatre:
1915-1925 . . . . DLB-7

New Literary Periodicals:
A Report for 1987 . . . . Y-87

New Literary Periodicals:
A Report for 1988 . . . . Y-88

New Literary Periodicals:
A Report for 1989 . . . . Y-89

New Literary Periodicals:
A Report for 1990 . . . . Y-90

New Literary Periodicals:
A Report for 1991 . . . . Y-91

New Literary Periodicals:
A Report for 1992 . . . . Y-92

New Literary Periodicals:
A Report for 1993 . . . . Y-93

The New Monthly Magazine
1814-1884 . . . . DLB-110

The New *Ulysses* Y-84

The New Variorum Shakespeare Y-85

A New Voice: The Center for the Book's First
Five Years Y-83

The New Wave [Science Fiction] DLB-8

New York City Bookshops in the 1930s and
1940s: The Recollections of Walter
Goldwater Y-93

Newbery, John
[publishing house] DLB-154

Newbolt, Henry 1862-1938 . . . . DLB-19

Newbound, Bernard Slade (see Slade, Bernard)

Newby, P. H. 1918- DLB-15

Newby, Thomas Cautley
[publishing house] DLB-106

Newcomb, Charles King 1820-1894 . . . . DLB-1

Newell, Peter 1862-1924 . . . . DLB-42

Newell, Robert Henry 1836-1901 . . . . DLB-11

Newhouse, Samuel I. 1895-1979 . . . . DLB-127

Newman, Cecil Earl 1903-1976 . . . . . DLB-127

Newman, David (see Benton, Robert)

Newman, Frances 1883-1928 . . . . Y-80

Newman, Francis William
1805-1897 . . . . DLB-190

Newman, John Henry
1801-1890 . . . . DLB-18, 32, 55

Newman, Mark [publishing house] DLB-49

Newnes, George, Limited DLB-112

Newsome, Effie Lee 1885-1979 . . . . . DLB-76

Newspaper Syndication of American
Humor DLB-11

Newton, A. Edward 1864-1940 . . . . . DLB-140

Ngugi wa Thiong'o 1938- DLB-125

Niatum, Duane 1938- DLB-175

The *Nibelungenlied* and the *Klage*
circa 1200 . . . . DLB-138

Nichol, B. P. 1944- DLB-53

Nicholas of Cusa 1401-1464 . . . . . . DLB-115

Nichols, Beverly 1898-1983 . . . . . . DLB-191

Nichols, Dudley 1895-1960 . . . . DLB-26

Nichols, Grace 1950- DLB-157

Nichols, John 1940- Y-82

Nichols, Mary Sargeant (Neal) Gove
1810-1884 . . . . DLB-1

Nichols, Peter 1927- DLB-13

Nichols, Roy F. 1896-1973 . . . . DLB-17

Nichols, Ruth 1948- DLB-60

Nicholson, Edward Williams Byron
1849-1912 . . . . DLB-184

Nicholson, Norman 1914- DLB-27

Nicholson, William 1872-1949 . . . . . DLB-141

Ní Chuilleanáin, Eiléan 1942- DLB-40

Nicol, Eric 1919- DLB-68

Nicolai, Friedrich 1733-1811 . . . . . . DLB-97

Nicolay, John G. 1832-1901 and
Hay, John 1838-1905 . . . . DLB-47

Nicolson, Harold 1886-1968 . . . . DLB-100, 149

Nicolson, Nigel 1917- DLB-155

Niebuhr, Reinhold 1892-1971 . . DLB-17; DS-17

Niedecker, Lorine 1903-1970 . . . . . . DLB-48

Nieman, Lucius W. 1857-1935 . . . . . DLB-25

Nietzsche, Friedrich 1844-1900 . . . . . DLB-129

Nievo, Stanislao 1928- DLB-196

Niggli, Josefina 1910- Y-80

Nightingale, Florence 1820-1910 . . . . DLB-166

Nikolev, Nikolai Petrovich
1758-1815 . . . . DLB-150

Niles, Hezekiah 1777-1839 . . . . DLB-43

Nims, John Frederick 1913- DLB-5

Nin, Anaïs 1903-1977 . . . . DLB-2, 4, 152

1985: The Year of the Mystery:
A Symposium Y-85

The 1997 Booker Prize Y-97

Nissenson, Hugh 1933- DLB-28

Niven, Frederick John 1878-1944 . . . . DLB-92

Niven, Larry 1938- DLB-8

Nizan, Paul 1905-1940 . . . . DLB-72

Njegoš, Petar II Petrović
1813-1851 . . . . DLB-147

Nkosi, Lewis 1936- DLB-157

"The No Self, the Little Self, and the Poets,"
by Richard Moore DLB-105

Nobel Peace Prize

The 1986 Nobel Peace Prize:
Elie Wiesel Y-86

The Nobel Prize and Literary Politics . . . Y-86

Nobel Prize in Literature

The 1982 Nobel Prize in Literature:
Gabriel García Márquez Y-82

The 1983 Nobel Prize in Literature:
William Golding Y-83

The 1984 Nobel Prize in Literature:
Jaroslav Seifert Y-84

The 1985 Nobel Prize in Literature:
Claude Simon Y-85

The 1986 Nobel Prize in Literature:
Wole Soyinka Y-86

The 1987 Nobel Prize in Literature:
Joseph Brodsky Y-87

The 1988 Nobel Prize in Literature:
Najīb Mahfūz Y-88

The 1989 Nobel Prize in Literature:
Camilo José Cela Y-89

The 1990 Nobel Prize in Literature:
Octavio Paz Y-90

The 1991 Nobel Prize in Literature:
Nadine Gordimer Y-91

The 1992 Nobel Prize in Literature:
Derek Walcott Y-92

The 1993 Nobel Prize in Literature:
Toni Morrison Y-93

The 1994 Nobel Prize in Literature:
Kenzaburō Ōe Y-94

The 1995 Nobel Prize in Literature:
Seamus Heaney Y-95

The 1996 Nobel Prize in Literature:
Wisława Szymborska Y-96

The 1997 Nobel Prize in Literature:
Dario Fo Y-97

Nodier, Charles 1780-1844 . . . . DLB-119

Noel, Roden 1834-1894 . . . . DLB-35

Nogami, Yaeko 1885-1985 . . . . DLB-180

Nogo, Rajko Petrov 1945- DLB-181

Nolan, William F. 1928- DLB-8

Noland, C. F. M. 1810?-1858 . . . . . . DLB-11

Noma, Hiroshi 1915-1991 . . . . DLB-182

Nonesuch Press DLB-112

Noonan, Robert Phillipe (see Tressell, Robert)

Noonday Press DLB-46

Noone, John 1936- DLB-14

Nora, Eugenio de 1923- DLB-134

Nordhoff, Charles 1887-1947 . . . . . . DLB-9

Norman, Charles 1904- DLB-111

Norman, Marsha 1947- Y-84

Norris, Charles G. 1881-1945 . . . . . . DLB-9

Norris, Frank 1870-1902 . . . . DLB-12, 71, 186

Norris, Leslie 1921- DLB-27

Norse, Harold 1916- DLB-16

North, Marianne 1830-1890 . . . . . . DLB-174

North Point Press DLB-46

Nortje, Arthur 1942-1970 . . . . DLB-125

Norton, Alice Mary (see Norton, Andre)

Norton, Andre 1912- DLB-8, 52

Norton, Andrews 1786-1853 . . . . DLB-1

Norton, Caroline
1808-1877 . . . . DLB-21, 159, 199

Norton, Charles Eliot 1827-1908 . . . DLB-1, 64

Norton, John 1606-1663 . . . . DLB-24

Norton, Mary 1903-1992 . . . . DLB-160

Norton, Thomas (see Sackville, Thomas)

Norton, W. W., and Company DLB-46

Norwood, Robert 1874-1932 . . . . . . DLB-92

Nosaka, Akiyuki 1930- DLB-182

Nossack, Hans Erich 1901-1977 . . . . . DLB-69

A Note on Technique (1926), by
Elizabeth A. Drew [excerpts] DLB-36

Notker Balbulus circa 840-912 . . . . . DLB-148

Notker III of Saint Gall
circa 950-1022 . . . . DLB-148

Notker von Zweifalten ?-1095 . . . . . DLB-148

Nourse, Alan E. 1928- DLB-8

Novak, Slobodan 1924- DLB-181

Novak, Vjenceslav 1859-1905 . . . . . . DLB-147

Novalis 1772-1801 . . . . DLB-90

Novaro, Mario 1868-1944 . . . . DLB-114

Novás Calvo, Lino 1903-1983 . . . . . DLB-145

"The Novel in [Robert Browning's] 'The Ring
and the Book' " (1912), by
Henry James DLB-32

The Novel of Impressionism,
by Jethro Bithell DLB-66

Novel-Reading: The Works of Charles Dickens,
The Works of W. Makepeace Thackeray
(1879), by Anthony Trollope DLB-21

Novels for Grown-Ups Y-97

The Novels of Dorothy Richardson (1918),
by May Sinclair DLB-36

Novels with a Purpose (1864), by
Justin M'Carthy DLB-21

Noventa, Giacomo 1898-1960 . . . . . DLB-114

Novikov, Nikolai Ivanovich
1744-1818 . . . . DLB-150

Nowlan, Alden 1933-1983 . . . . DLB-53

Noyes, Alfred 1880-1958 . . . . DLB-20

Noyes, Crosby S. 1825-1908 . . . . . . DLB-23

Noyes, Nicholas 1647-1717 . . . . DLB-24

Noyes, Theodore W. 1858-1946 . . . . . DLB-29

N-Town Plays circa 1468 to early
sixteenth century DLB-146

Nugent, Frank 1908-1965 . . . . DLB-44

Nugent, Richard Bruce 1906- DLB-151

Nušić, Branislav 1864-1938 . . . . . . DLB-147

Nutt, David [publishing house] DLB-106

Nwapa, Flora 1931- DLB-125

Nye, Bill 1850-1896 . . . . DLB-186

Nye, Edgar Wilson (Bill)
1850-1896 . . . . DLB-11, 23

Nye, Naomi Shihab 1952- DLB-120

Nye, Robert 1939- DLB-14

O

Oakes, Urian circa 1631-1681 . . . . . . DLB-24

Oakley, Violet 1874-1961 . . . . DLB-188

Oates, Joyce Carol
1938- DLB-2, 5, 130; Y-81

Ōba, Minako 1930- DLB-182

Ober, Frederick Albion 1849-1913 . . . DLB-189

Ober, William 1920-1993 . . . . Y-93

Oberholtzer, Ellis Paxson
1868-1936 . . . . DLB-47

Obradović, Dositej 1740?-1811 . . . . . DLB-147

O'Brien, Edna 1932- DLB-14

O'Brien, Fitz-James 1828-1862 . . . . . DLB-74

O'Brien, Kate 1897-1974 . . . . DLB-15

O'Brien, Tim
1946- DLB-152; Y-80; DS-9

O'Casey, Sean 1880-1964 . . . . DLB-10

Occom, Samson 1723-1792 . . . . . . DLB-175

Ochs, Adolph S. 1858-1935 . . . . . . DLB-25

Ochs-Oakes, George Washington
1861-1931 . . . . DLB-137

O'Connor, Flannery
1925-1964 . . . . . DLB-2, 152; Y-80; DS-12

O'Connor, Frank 1903-1966 . . . . . . DLB-162

Octopus Publishing Group DLB-112

Oda, Sakunosuke 1913-1947 . . . . . . DLB-182

Odell, Jonathan 1737-1818 . . . . . DLB-31, 99

O'Dell, Scott 1903-1989 . . . . DLB-52

Odets, Clifford 1906-1963 . . . . . . DLB-7, 26

Odhams Press Limited DLB-112

Odoevsky, Vladimir Fedorovich
1804 or 1803-1869 . . . . DLB-198

O'Donnell, Peter 1920- DLB-87

O'Donovan, Michael (see O'Connor, Frank)

Ōe, Kenzaburō 1935- DLB-182; Y-94

O'Faolain, Julia 1932- DLB-14

O'Faolain, Sean 1900- DLB-15, 162

Off Broadway and Off-Off Broadway . . DLB-7

Off-Loop Theatres DLB-7

Offord, Carl Ruthven 1910- DLB-76

O'Flaherty, Liam
1896-1984 . . . . DLB-36, 162; Y-84

Ogilvie, J. S., and Company DLB-49

Ogilvy, Eliza 1822-1912 . . . . DLB-199

Ogot, Grace 1930- DLB-125

O'Grady, Desmond 1935- DLB-40

Ogunyemi, Wale 1939- DLB-157

O'Hagan, Howard 1902-1982 . . . . . . DLB-68

O'Hara, Frank 1926-1966 . . . DLB-5, 16, 193

O'Hara, John 1905-1970 . . . . DLB-9, 86; DS-2

Okara, Gabriel 1921- DLB-125

O'Keeffe, John 1747-1833 . . . . DLB-89

Okes, Nicholas
[publishing house] DLB-170

Okigbo, Christopher 1930-1967 . . . . . DLB-125

Okot p'Bitek 1931-1982 . . . . DLB-125

Okpewho, Isidore 1941- DLB-157

Okri, Ben 1959- DLB-157

Olaudah Equiano and Unfinished Journeys:
The Slave-Narrative Tradition and
Twentieth-Century Continuities, by
Paul Edwards and Pauline T.
Wangman DLB-117

Old English Literature:
An Introduction DLB-146

Old English Riddles
eighth to tenth centuries DLB-146

Old Franklin Publishing House DLB-49

Old German Genesis and Old German Exodus
circa 1050-circa 1130 . . . . DLB-148

Old High German Charms and
Blessings DLB-148

The Old High German Isidor
circa 790-800 . . . . DLB-148

Older, Fremont 1856-1935 . . . . DLB-25

Oldham, John 1653-1683 . . . . DLB-131

Olds, Sharon 1942- DLB-120

Olearius, Adam 1599-1671 . . . . . . DLB-164

Oliphant, Laurence
1829?-1888 . . . . DLB-18, 166

Oliphant, Margaret 1828-1897 . . . DLB-18, 190

Oliver, Chad 1928- DLB-8

Oliver, Mary 1935- DLB-5, 193

Ollier, Claude 1922- DLB-83

Olsen, Tillie 1913?- DLB-28; Y-80

Olson, Charles 1910-1970 . . . . DLB-5, 16, 193

Olson, Elder 1909- DLB-48, 63

Omotoso, Kole 1943- DLB-125

"On Art in Fiction "(1838),
    by Edward Bulwer DLB-21

On Learning to Write Y-88

On Some of the Characteristics of Modern
    Poetry and On the Lyrical Poems of
    Alfred Tennyson (1831), by Arthur
    Henry Hallam DLB-32

"On Style in English Prose" (1898), by
    Frederic Harrison DLB-57

"On Style in Literature: Its Technical
    Elements" (1885), by Robert Louis
    Stevenson DLB-57

"On the Writing of Essays" (1862),
    by Alexander Smith DLB-57

Ondaatje, Michael 1943- DLB-60

O'Neill, Eugene 1888-1953 . . . . DLB-7

Onetti, Juan Carlos 1909-1994 . . . . DLB-113

Onions, George Oliver
    1872-1961 . . . . DLB-153

Onofri, Arturo 1885-1928 . . . . DLB-114

Opie, Amelia 1769-1853 . . . . . DLB-116, 159

Opitz, Martin 1597-1639 . . . . DLB-164

Oppen, George 1908-1984 . . . . . DLB-5, 165

Oppenheim, E. Phillips 1866-1946 . . . . DLB-70

Oppenheim, James 1882-1932 . . . . . . DLB-28

Oppenheimer, Joel 1930-1988 . . . DLB-5, 193

Optic, Oliver (see Adams, William Taylor)

Oral History Interview with Donald S.
    Klopfer Y-97

Orczy, Emma, Baroness
    1865-1947 . . . . DLB-70

Origo, Iris 1902-1988 . . . . DLB-155

Orlovitz, Gil 1918-1973 . . . . DLB-2, 5

Orlovsky, Peter 1933- DLB-16

Ormond, John 1923- DLB-27

Ornitz, Samuel 1890-1957 . . . . . DLB-28, 44

O'Rourke, P. J. 1947- DLB-185

Ortese, Anna Maria 1914- DLB-177

Ortiz, Simon J. 1941- DLB-120, 175

Ortnit and *Wolfdietrich*
    circa 1225-1250 . . . . DLB-138

Orton, Joe 1933-1967 . . . . DLB-13

Orwell, George 1903-1950 . . . DLB-15, 98, 195

The Orwell Year Y-84

Ory, Carlos Edmundo de 1923- . . . DLB-134

Osbey, Brenda Marie 1957- DLB-120

Osbon, B. S. 1827-1912 . . . . DLB-43

Osborn, Sarah 1714-1796 . . . . DLB-200

Osborne, John 1929-1994 . . . . DLB-13

Osgood, Herbert L. 1855-1918 . . . . . DLB-47

Osgood, James R., and
    Company DLB-49

Osgood, McIlvaine and
    Company DLB-112

O'Shaughnessy, Arthur
    1844-1881 . . . . DLB-35

O'Shea, Patrick
    [publishing house] DLB-49

Osipov, Nikolai Petrovich
    1751-1799 . . . . DLB-150

Oskison, John Milton 1879-1947 . . . . DLB-175

Osler, Sir William 1849-1919 . . . . . DLB-184

Osofisan, Femi 1946- DLB-125

Ostenso, Martha 1900-1963 . . . . DLB-92

Ostriker, Alicia 1937- DLB-120

Osundare, Niyi 1947- DLB-157

Oswald, Eleazer 1755-1795 . . . . DLB-43

Oswald von Wolkenstein
    1376 or 1377-1445 . . . . DLB-179

Otero, Blas de 1916-1979 . . . . DLB-134

Otero, Miguel Antonio
    1859-1944 . . . . DLB-82

Otero Silva, Miguel 1908-1985 . . . . . DLB-145

Otfried von Weißenburg
    circa 800-circa 875? DLB-148

Otis, James (see Kaler, James Otis)

Otis, James, Jr. 1725-1783 . . . . DLB-31

Otis, Broaders and Company DLB-49

Ottaway, James 1911- DLB-127

Ottendorfer, Oswald 1826-1900 . . . . DLB-23

Ottieri, Ottiero 1924- DLB-177

Otto-Peters, Louise 1819-1895 . . . . . DLB-129

Otway, Thomas 1652-1685 . . . . DLB-80

Ouellette, Fernand 1930- DLB-60

Ouida 1839-1908 . . . . DLB-18, 156

Outing Publishing Company DLB-46

Outlaw Days, by Joyce Johnson DLB-16

Overbury, Sir Thomas
    circa 1581-1613 . . . . DLB-151

The Overlook Press DLB-46

Overview of U.S. Book Publishing,
    1910-1945 . . . . DLB-9

Owen, Guy 1925- DLB-5

Owen, John 1564-1622 . . . . DLB-121

Owen, John [publishing house] DLB-49

Owen, Robert 1771-1858 . . . . DLB-107, 158

Owen, Wilfred 1893-1918 . . . . DLB-20; DS-18

Owen, Peter, Limited DLB-112

The Owl and the Nightingale
    circa 1189-1199 . . . . DLB-146

Owsley, Frank L. 1890-1956 . . . . . . DLB-17

Oxford, Seventeenth Earl of, Edward de Vere
    1550-1604 . . . . DLB-172

Ozerov, Vladislav Aleksandrovich
    1769-1816 . . . . DLB-150

Ozick, Cynthia 1928- DLB-28, 152; Y-82

P

Pace, Richard 1482?-1536 . . . . DLB-167

Pacey, Desmond 1917-1975 . . . . . . DLB-88

Pack, Robert 1929- DLB-5

Packaging Papa: *The Garden of Eden* Y-86

Padell Publishing Company DLB-46

Padgett, Ron 1942- DLB-5

Padilla, Ernesto Chávez 1944- DLB-122

Page, L. C., and Company DLB-49

Page, P. K. 1916- DLB-68

Page, Thomas Nelson
    1853-1922 . . . . DLB-12, 78; DS-13

Page, Walter Hines 1855-1918 . . . . DLB-71, 91

Paget, Francis Edward
    1806-1882 . . . . DLB-163

Paget, Violet (see Lee, Vernon)

Pagliarani, Elio 1927- DLB-128

Pain, Barry 1864-1928 . . . . DLB-135, 197

Pain, Philip ?-circa 1666 . . . . DLB-24

Paine, Robert Treat, Jr. 1773-1811 . . . DLB-37

Paine, Thomas
    1737-1809 . . . . DLB-31, 43, 73, 158

Painter, George D. 1914- DLB-155

Painter, William 1540?-1594 . . . . . . DLB-136

Palazzeschi, Aldo 1885-1974 . . . . . . DLB-114

Paley, Grace 1922- DLB-28

Palfrey, John Gorham
    1796-1881 . . . . DLB-1, 30

Palgrave, Francis Turner
    1824-1897 . . . . DLB-35

Palmer, Joe H. 1904-1952 . . . . DLB-171

Palmer, Michael 1943- DLB-169

Paltock, Robert 1697-1767 . . . . DLB-39

Pan Books Limited DLB-112

Panama, Norman 1914- and
    Frank, Melvin 1913-1988 . . . . . . DLB-26

Panaev, Ivan Ivanovich 1812-1862 . . . DLB-198

Pancake, Breece D'J 1952-1979 . . . . DLB-130

Panero, Leopoldo 1909-1962 . . . . . DLB-108

Pangborn, Edgar 1909-1976 . . . . DLB-8

"Panic Among the Philistines": A Postscript,
    An Interview with Bryan Griffin Y-81

Panizzi, Sir Anthony 1797-1879 . . . . DLB-184

Panneton, Philippe (see Ringuet)

Panshin, Alexei 1940- DLB-8

Pansy (see Alden, Isabella)

Pantheon Books DLB-46

Papantonio, Michael (see Kohn, John S. Van E.)

Paperback Library. DLB-46

Paperback Science Fiction DLB-8

Paquet, Alfons 1881-1944. . . . . DLB-66

Paracelsus 1493-1541. . . . . DLB-179

Paradis, Suzanne 1936- DLB-53

Pareja Diezcanseco, Alfredo
  1908-1993 . . . . DLB-145

Pardoe, Julia 1804-1862 . . . . DLB-166

Parents' Magazine Press DLB-46

Parise, Goffredo 1929-1986 . . . . . . DLB-177

Parisian Theater, Fall 1984: Toward
  A New Baroque Y-85

Parizeau, Alice 1930- DLB-60

Parke, John 1754-1789 . . . . DLB-31

Parker, Dorothy
  1893-1967. . . . . DLB-11, 45, 86

Parker, Gilbert 1860-1932. . . . . DLB-99

Parker, James 1714-1770 . . . . DLB-43

Parker, Theodore 1810-1860. . . . . . . DLB-1

Parker, William Riley 1906-1968 . . . . DLB-103

Parker, J. H. [publishing house] DLB-106

Parker, John [publishing house] DLB-106

Parkman, Francis, Jr.
  1823-1893 . . . . DLB-1, 30, 183, 186

Parks, Gordon 1912- DLB-33

Parks, William 1698-1750. . . . . DLB-43

Parks, William [publishing house] DLB-49

Parley, Peter (see Goodrich, Samuel Griswold)

Parmenides late sixth-fifth century B.C.
  . . . . DLB-176

Parnell, Thomas 1679-1718. . . . . . . DLB-95

Parr, Catherine 1513?-1548 . . . . DLB-136

Parrington, Vernon L.
  1871-1929 . . . . DLB-17, 63

Parrish, Maxfield 1870-1966. . . . . . . DLB-188

Parronchi, Alessandro 1914- DLB-128

Partridge, S. W., and Company DLB-106

Parton, James 1822-1891 . . . . DLB-30

Parton, Sara Payson Willis
  1811-1872. . . . . DLB-43, 74

Parun, Vesna 1922- DLB-181

Pasinetti, Pier Maria 1913- DLB-177

Pasolini, Pier Paolo 1922- DLB-128, 177

Pastan, Linda 1932- DLB-5

Paston, George (Emily Morse Symonds)
  1860-1936. . . . . DLB-149, 197

The *Paston Letters* 1422-1509. . . . . . DLB-146

Pastorius, Francis Daniel
  1651-circa 1720 . . . . DLB-24

Patchen, Kenneth 1911-1972. . . . . DLB-16, 48

Pater, Walter 1839-1894 . . . . . DLB-57, 156

Paterson, Katherine 1932- DLB-52

Patmore, Coventry 1823-1896 . . . . DLB-35, 98

Paton, Alan 1903-1988 . . . . DS-17

Paton, Joseph Noel 1821-1901 . . . . . DLB-35

Paton Walsh, Jill 1937- DLB-161

Patrick, Edwin Hill ("Ted")
  1901-1964 . . . . DLB-137

Patrick, John 1906- DLB-7

Pattee, Fred Lewis 1863-1950 . . . . . DLB-71

Pattern and Paradigm: History as
  Design, by Judith Ryan DLB-75

Patterson, Alicia 1906-1963 . . . . . . DLB-127

Patterson, Eleanor Medill
  1881-1948 . . . . DLB-29

Patterson, Eugene 1923- DLB-127

Patterson, Joseph Medill
  1879-1946 . . . . DLB-29

Pattillo, Henry 1726-1801. . . . . DLB-37

Paul, Elliot 1891-1958 . . . . DLB-4

Paul, Jean (see Richter, Johann Paul Friedrich)

Paul, Kegan, Trench, Trubner and Company
  Limited. DLB-106

Paul, Peter, Book Company DLB-49

Paul, Stanley, and Company
  Limited. DLB-112

Paulding, James Kirke
  1778-1860 . . . . DLB-3, 59, 74

Paulin, Tom 1949- DLB-40

Pauper, Peter, Press. DLB-46

Pavese, Cesare 1908-1950 . . . . DLB-128, 177

Pavić, Milorad 1929- DLB-181

Pavlov, Konstantin 1933- DLB-181

Pavlov, Nikolai Filippovich
  1803-1864 . . . . DLB-198

Pavlović, Miodrag 1928- DLB-181

Paxton, John 1911-1985. . . . . DLB-44

Payn, James 1830-1898 . . . . DLB-18

Payne, John 1842-1916 . . . . DLB-35

Payne, John Howard 1791-1852 . . . . DLB-37

Payson and Clarke DLB-46

Paz, Octavio 1914-1998 . . . . Y-90

Pazzi, Roberto 1946- DLB-196

Peabody, Elizabeth Palmer
  1804-1894. . . . . DLB-1

Peabody, Elizabeth Palmer
  [publishing house] DLB-49

Peabody, Oliver William Bourn
  1799-1848 . . . . DLB-59

Peace, Roger 1899-1968 . . . . DLB-127

Peacham, Henry 1578-1644? DLB-151

Peacham, Henry, the Elder
  1547-1634 . . . . DLB-172

Peachtree Publishers, Limited. DLB-46

Peacock, Molly 1947- DLB-120

Peacock, Thomas Love
  1785-1866 . . . . DLB-96, 116

Pead, Deuel ?-1727 . . . . DLB-24

Peake, Mervyn 1911-1968 . . . . DLB-15, 160

Peale, Rembrandt 1778-1860 . . . . . DLB-183

Pear Tree Press DLB-112

Pearce, Philippa 1920- DLB-161

Pearson, H. B. [publishing house] DLB-49

Pearson, Hesketh 1887-1964. . . . . . DLB-149

Peck, George W. 1840-1916. . . . DLB-23, 42

Peck, H. C., and Theo. Bliss
  [publishing house]. DLB-49

Peck, Harry Thurston
  1856-1914. . . . . DLB-71, 91

Peele, George 1556-1596 . . . . DLB-62, 167

Pegler, Westbrook 1894-1969 . . . . . DLB-171

Pekić, Borislav 1930-1992 . . . . DLB-181

Pelletier, Aimé (see Vac, Bertrand)

Pellegrini and Cudahy DLB-46

Pemberton, Sir Max 1863-1950 . . . . DLB-70

Penfield, Edward 1866-1925. . . . . . DLB-188

Penguin Books [U.S.] DLB-46

Penguin Books [U.K.] DLB-112

Penn Publishing Company DLB-49

Penn, William 1644-1718. . . . . DLB-24

Penna, Sandro 1906-1977 . . . . DLB-114

Pennell, Joseph 1857-1926. . . . . . . DLB-188

Penner, Jonathan 1940- Y-83

Pennington, Lee 1939- Y-82

Pepys, Samuel 1633-1703 . . . . DLB-101

Percy, Thomas 1729-1811. . . . . . . DLB-104

Percy, Walker 1916-1990. . . DLB-2; Y-80, Y-90

Percy, William 1575-1648. . . . . . . DLB-172

Perec, Georges 1936-1982. . . . . . . DLB-83

Perelman, Bob 1947- DLB-193

Perelman, S. J. 1904-1979 . . . . . DLB-11, 44

Perez, Raymundo "Tigre"
  1946- DLB-122

Peri Rossi, Cristina 1941- DLB-145

Periodicals of the Beat Generation. . . . DLB-16

Perkins, Eugene 1932- DLB-41

Perkoff, Stuart Z. 1930-1974 . . . . . . DLB-16

Perley, Moses Henry 1804-1862 . . . . DLB-99

Permabooks DLB-46

Perovsky, Aleksei Alekseevich (Antonii Pogorel'sky)
  1787-1836 . . . . DLB-198

Perrin, Alice 1867-1934 . . . . DLB-156

Perry, Bliss 1860-1954 . . . . DLB-71

Perry, Eleanor 1915-1981. . . . . . . DLB-44

Perry, Matthew 1794-1858 . . . . . . DLB-183

Perry, Sampson 1747-1823 . . . . . . DLB-158

"Personal Style" (1890), by John Addington
  Symonds. DLB-57

Perutz, Leo 1882-1957 . . . . DLB-81

Pesetsky, Bette 1932- DLB-130

Pestalozzi, Johann Heinrich
  1746-1827 . . . . DLB-94

Peter, Laurence J. 1919-1990 . . . . . . DLB-53

Peter of Spain circa 1205-1277 . . . . . DLB-115

Peterkin, Julia 1880-1961. . . . . DLB-9

Peters, Lenrie 1932- DLB-117

Peters, Robert 1924- DLB-105

Petersham, Maud 1889-1971 and
  Petersham, Miska 1888-1960. . . . . DLB-22

Peterson, Charles Jacobs
  1819-1887 . . . . DLB-79

Peterson, Len 1917- DLB-88

Peterson, Louis 1922- DLB-76

Peterson, T. B., and Brothers DLB-49

Petitclair, Pierre 1813-1860 . . . . . . DLB-99

Petrov, Aleksandar 1938- DLB-181

Petrov, Gavriil 1730-1801 . . . . DLB-150

Petrov, Vasilii Petrovich
  1736-1799 . . . . DLB-150

Petrov, Valeri 1920- DLB-181

Petrović, Rastko 1898-1949 . . . . . . DLB-147

Petruslied circa 854?. DLB-148

Petry, Ann 1908- DLB-76

Pettie, George circa 1548-1589 . . . . . DLB-136

Peyton, K. M. 1929- DLB-161

Pfaffe Konrad
  flourished circa 1172 . . . . DLB-148

Pfaffe Lamprecht
  flourished circa 1150 . . . . DLB-148

Pfeiffer, Emily 1827-1890 . . . . DLB-199

Pforzheimer, Carl H. 1879-1957 . . . . DLB-140

Phaer, Thomas 1510?-1560 . . . . . . DLB-167

Phaidon Press Limited. DLB-112

Pharr, Robert Deane 1916-1992 . . . . DLB-33

Phelps, Elizabeth Stuart
  1844-1911 . . . . DLB-74

Philander von der Linde
  (see Mencke, Johann Burckhard)

Philby, H. St. John B. 1885-1960. . . . DLB-195

Philip, Marlene Nourbese
  1947- DLB-157

Philippe, Charles-Louis
  1874-1909 . . . . DLB-65

Phillipps, Sir Thomas 1792-1872 . . . . DLB-184

Philips, John 1676-1708 . . . . DLB-95

Philips, Katherine 1632-1664 . . . . . DLB-131

Phillips, Caryl 1958- DLB-157

Phillips, David Graham
  1867-1911 . . . . DLB-9, 12

Phillips, Jayne Anne 1952- Y-80

Phillips, Robert 1938- DLB-105

Phillips, Stephen 1864-1915. . . . . . . DLB-10

Phillips, Ulrich B. 1877-1934. . . . . . DLB-17

Phillips, Willard 1784-1873 . . . . . . DLB-59

Phillips, William 1907- DLB-137

Phillips, Sampson and Company. DLB-49

Phillpotts, Adelaide Eden (Adelaide Ross)
  1896-1993 . . . . DLB-191

Phillpotts, Eden
  1862-1960 . . . . . . DLB-10, 70, 135, 153

Philo circa 20-15 B.C.-circa A.D. 50
  . . . . DLB-176

Philosophical Library DLB-46

"The Philosophy of Style" (1852), by
  Herbert Spencer. DLB-57

Phinney, Elihu [publishing house] DLB-49

Phoenix, John (see Derby, George Horatio)

PHYLON (Fourth Quarter, 1950),
  The Negro in Literature:
  The Current Scene DLB-76

Physiologus
  circa 1070-circa 1150 . . . . DLB-148

Piccolo, Lucio 1903-1969 . . . . DLB-114

Pickard, Tom 1946- DLB-40

Pickering, William
  [publishing house] DLB-106

Pickthall, Marjorie 1883-1922. . . . . . DLB-92

Pictorial Printing Company. DLB-49

Piercy, Marge 1936- DLB-120

Pierro, Albino 1916- DLB-128

Pignotti, Lamberto 1926- DLB-128

Pike, Albert 1809-1891 . . . . DLB-74

Pike, Zebulon Montgomery 1779-1813 . . DLB-183

Pilon, Jean-Guy 1930- DLB-60

Pinckney, Eliza Lucas 1722-1793 . . . . DLB-200

Pinckney, Josephine 1895-1957 . . . . . DLB-6

Pindar circa 518 B.C.-circa 438 B.C.
  . . . . DLB-176

Pindar, Peter (see Wolcot, John)

Pinero, Arthur Wing 1855-1934 . . . . . DLB-10

Pinget, Robert 1919- DLB-83

Pinnacle Books DLB-46

Piñon, Nélida 1935- DLB-145

Pinsky, Robert 1940- Y-82

Pinter, Harold 1930- DLB-13

Piontek, Heinz 1925- DLB-75

Piozzi, Hester Lynch [Thrale]
  1741-1821. . . . . DLB-104, 142

Piper, H. Beam 1904-1964. . . . . DLB-8

Piper, Watty. DLB-22

Pirckheimer, Caritas 1467-1532 . . . . . DLB-179

Pirckheimer, Willibald
  1470-1530 . . . . DLB-179

Pisar, Samuel 1929- Y-83

Pitkin, Timothy 1766-1847 . . . . DLB-30

The Pitt Poetry Series: Poetry Publishing Today
  . . . . Y-85

Pitter, Ruth 1897- DLB-20

Pix, Mary 1666-1709 . . . . DLB-80

Pixerécourt, René Charles Guilbert de
  1773-1844 . . . . DLB-192

Plaatje, Sol T. 1876-1932 . . . . DLB-125

The Place of Realism in Fiction (1895), by
  George Gissing DLB-18

Plante, David 1940- Y-83

Platen, August von 1796-1835 . . . . . DLB-90

Plath, Sylvia 1932-1963 . . . . . DLB-5, 6, 152

Plato circa 428 B.C.-348-347 B.C.
  . . . . DLB-176

Platon 1737-1812. . . . . DLB-150

Platt and Munk Company DLB-46

Playboy Press DLB-46

Playford, John
  [publishing house] DLB-170

Plays, Playwrights, and Playgoers DLB-84

Playwrights and Professors, by
  Tom Stoppard DLB-13

Playwrights on the Theater DLB-80

Der Pleier flourished circa 1250 . . . . DLB-138

Plenzdorf, Ulrich 1934- DLB-75

Plessen, Elizabeth 1944- DLB-75

Plievier, Theodor 1892-1955 . . . . . . DLB-69

Plimpton, George 1927- DLB-185

Plomer, William 1903-1973 . . DLB-20, 162, 191

Plotinus 204-270 . . . . DLB-176

Plumly, Stanley 1939- DLB-5, 193

Plumpp, Sterling D. 1940- DLB-41

Plunkett, James 1920- DLB-14

Plutarch circa 46-circa 120 . . . . . . DLB-176

Plymell, Charles 1935- DLB-16

Pocket Books DLB-46

Poe, Edgar Allan
  1809-1849 . . . . DLB-3, 59, 73, 74

Poe, James 1921-1980. . . . . DLB-44

The Poet Laureate of the United States
  Statements from Former Consultants
  in Poetry Y-86

"The Poet's Kaleidoscope: The Element of Surprise
  in the Making of the Poem," by Madeline De-
  Frees DLB-105

"The Poetry File," by
  Edward Field DLB-105

Pogodin, Mikhail Petrovich
  1800-1875 . . . . DLB-198

Pogorel'sky, Antonii (see Perovsky, Aleksei Alekseevich)

Pohl, Frederik 1919- DLB-8

Poirier, Louis (see Gracq, Julien)

Polanyi, Michael 1891-1976 . . . . . . DLB-100

Pole, Reginald 1500-1558 . . . . DLB-132

Polevoi, Nikolai Alekseevich
1796-1846 . . . . DLB-198

Polidori, John William
1795-1821 . . . . DLB-116

Polite, Carlene Hatcher 1932- DLB-33

Pollard, Edward A. 1832-1872 . . . . . DLB-30

Pollard, Percival 1869-1911 . . . . DLB-71

Pollard and Moss DLB-49

Pollock, Sharon 1936- DLB-60

Polonsky, Abraham 1910- DLB-26

Polotsky, Simeon 1629-1680 . . . . . . DLB-150

Polybius circa 200 B.C.-118 B.C. DLB-176

Pomilio, Mario 1921-1990 . . . . DLB-177

Ponce, Mary Helen 1938- DLB-122

Ponce-Montoya, Juanita 1949- DLB-122

Ponet, John 1516?-1556 . . . . DLB-132

Poniatowski, Elena 1933- DLB-113

Ponsard, François 1814-1867 . . . . . . DLB-192

Ponsonby, William
[publishing house] DLB-170

Pontiggia, Giuseppe 1934- DLB-196

Pony Stories DLB-160

Poole, Ernest 1880-1950 . . . . DLB-9

Poole, Sophia 1804-1891 . . . . DLB-166

Poore, Benjamin Perley
1820-1887 . . . . DLB-23

Popa, Vasko 1922-1991 . . . . DLB-181

Pope, Abbie Hanscom
1858-1894 . . . . DLB-140

Pope, Alexander 1688-1744 . . . . DLB-95, 101

Popov, Mikhail Ivanovich
1742-circa 1790 . . . . DLB-150

Popović, Aleksandar 1929-1996 . . . . DLB-181

Popular Library DLB-46

Porlock, Martin (see MacDonald, Philip)

Porpoise Press DLB-112

Porta, Antonio 1935-1989 . . . . DLB-128

Porter, Anna Maria
1780-1832 . . . . DLB-116, 159

Porter, David 1780-1843 . . . . DLB-183

Porter, Eleanor H. 1868-1920 . . . . . . DLB-9

Porter, Gene Stratton (see Stratton-Porter, Gene)

Porter, Henry ?-? DLB-62

Porter, Jane 1776-1850 . . . . . . DLB-116, 159

Porter, Katherine Anne
1890-1980 . . . DLB-4, 9, 102; Y-80; DS-12

Porter, Peter 1929- DLB-40

Porter, William Sydney
1862-1910 . . . . DLB-12, 78, 79

Porter, William T. 1809-1858 . . . . . DLB-3, 43

Porter and Coates DLB-49

Portis, Charles 1933- DLB-6

Posey, Alexander 1873-1908 . . . . . . DLB-175

Postans, Marianne
circa 1810-1865 . . . . DLB-166

Postl, Carl (see Sealsfield, Carl)

Poston, Ted 1906-1974 . . . . DLB-51

Postscript to [the Third Edition of] Clarissa
(1751), by Samuel Richardson DLB-39

Potok, Chaim 1929- DLB-28, 152; Y-84

Potter, Beatrix 1866-1943 . . . . DLB-141

Potter, David M. 1910-1971 . . . . . . DLB-17

Potter, John E., and Company DLB-49

Pottle, Frederick A.
1897-1987 . . . . DLB-103; Y-87

Poulin, Jacques 1937- DLB-60

Pound, Ezra 1885-1972 . . DLB-4, 45, 63; DS-15

Povich, Shirley 1905- DLB-171

Powell, Anthony 1905- DLB-15

Powell, John Wesley 1834-1902 . . . . DLB-186

Powers, J. F. 1917- DLB-130

Pownall, David 1938- DLB-14

Powys, John Cowper 1872-1963 . . . . DLB-15

Powys, Llewelyn 1884-1939 . . . . . . DLB-98

Powys, T. F. 1875-1953 . . . . . DLB-36, 162

Poynter, Nelson 1903-1978 . . . . . . DLB-127

The Practice of Biography: An Interview
with Stanley Weintraub Y-82

The Practice of Biography II: An Interview
with B. L. Reid Y-83

The Practice of Biography III: An Interview
with Humphrey Carpenter Y-84

The Practice of Biography IV: An Interview with
William Manchester Y-85

The Practice of Biography V: An Interview
with Justin Kaplan Y-86

The Practice of Biography VI: An Interview with
David Herbert Donald Y-87

The Practice of Biography VII: An Interview with
John Caldwell Guilds Y-92

The Practice of Biography VIII: An Interview
with Joan Mellen Y-94

The Practice of Biography IX: An Interview
with Michael Reynolds Y-95

Prados, Emilio 1899-1962 . . . . DLB-134

Praed, Winthrop Mackworth
1802-1839 . . . . DLB-96

Praeger Publishers DLB-46

Praetorius, Johannes 1630-1680 . . . . DLB-168

Pratolini, Vasco 1913—1991 . . . . . . DLB-177

Pratt, E. J. 1882-1964 . . . . DLB-92

Pratt, Samuel Jackson 1749-1814 . . . . DLB-39

Preface to Alwyn (1780), by
Thomas Holcroft DLB-39

Preface to Colonel Jack (1722), by
Daniel Defoe DLB-39

Preface to Evelina (1778), by
Fanny Burney DLB-39

Preface to Ferdinand Count Fathom (1753), by
Tobias Smollett DLB-39

Preface to Incognita (1692), by
William Congreve DLB-39

Preface to Joseph Andrews (1742), by
Henry Fielding DLB-39

Preface to Moll Flanders (1722), by
Daniel Defoe DLB-39

Preface to Poems (1853), by
Matthew Arnold DLB-32

Preface to Robinson Crusoe (1719), by
Daniel Defoe DLB-39

Preface to Roderick Random (1748), by
Tobias Smollett DLB-39

Preface to Roxana (1724), by
Daniel Defoe DLB-39

Preface to St. Leon (1799), by
William Godwin DLB-39

Preface to Sarah Fielding's Familiar Letters
(1747), by Henry Fielding
[excerpt] DLB-39

Preface to Sarah Fielding's The Adventures of
David Simple (1744), by
Henry Fielding DLB-39

Preface to The Cry (1754), by
Sarah Fielding DLB-39

Preface to The Delicate Distress (1769), by
Elizabeth Griffin DLB-39

Preface to The Disguis'd Prince (1733), by
Eliza Haywood [excerpt] DLB-39

Preface to The Farther Adventures of Robinson
Crusoe (1719), by Daniel Defoe . . . DLB-39

Preface to the First Edition of Pamela (1740), by
Samuel Richardson DLB-39

Preface to the First Edition of The Castle of
Otranto (1764), by
Horace Walpole DLB-39

Preface to The History of Romances (1715), by
Pierre Daniel Huet [excerpts] DLB-39

Preface to The Life of Charlotta du Pont (1723),
by Penelope Aubin DLB-39

Preface to The Old English Baron (1778), by
Clara Reeve DLB-39

Preface to the Second Edition of The Castle of
Otranto (1765), by Horace
Walpole DLB-39

Preface to The Secret History, of Queen Zarah,
and the Zarazians (1705), by Delariviere
Manley DLB-39

Preface to the Third Edition of Clarissa (1751),
by Samuel Richardson
[excerpt] DLB-39

Preface to The Works of Mrs. Davys (1725), by
Mary Davys DLB-39

Preface to Volume 1 of Clarissa (1747), by
Samuel Richardson DLB-39

Preface to Volume 3 of Clarissa (1748), by
Samuel Richardson DLB-39

Préfontaine, Yves 1937- DLB-53

Prelutsky, Jack 1940- DLB-61

Premisses, by Michael Hamburger. . . . DLB-66

Prentice, George D. 1802-1870. . . . . . DLB-43

Prentice-Hall DLB-46

Prescott, Orville 1906-1996. . . . . Y-96

Prescott, William Hickling
1796-1859 . . . . DLB-1, 30, 59

The Present State of the English Novel (1892),
by George Saintsbury DLB-18

Prešeren, Francè 1800-1849 . . . . . . DLB-147

Preston, May Wilson 1873-1949 . . . . DLB-188

Preston, Thomas 1537-1598 . . . . DLB-62

Price, Reynolds 1933- DLB-2

Price, Richard 1723-1791 . . . . DLB-158

Price, Richard 1949- Y-81

Priest, Christopher 1943- DLB-14

Priestley, J. B. 1894-1984
. . . . . . DLB-10, 34, 77, 100, 139; Y-84

Primary Bibliography: A
Retrospective Y-95

Prime, Benjamin Young 1733-1791 . . . DLB-31

Primrose, Diana
floruit circa 1630 . . . . DLB-126

Prince, F. T. 1912- DLB-20

Prince, Thomas 1687-1758 . . . . DLB-24, 140

The Principles of Success in Literature (1865), by
George Henry Lewes [excerpt] . . . DLB-57

Printz, Wolfgang Casper
1641-1717 . . . . DLB-168

Prior, Matthew 1664-1721 . . . . DLB-95

Prisco, Michele 1920- DLB-177

Pritchard, William H. 1932- DLB-111

Pritchett, V. S. 1900- DLB-15, 139

Probyn, May 1856 or 1857-1909 . . . . DLB-199

Procter, Adelaide Anne
1825-1864 . . . . DLB-32, 199

Procter, Bryan Waller
1787-1874 . . . . DLB-96, 144

Proctor, Robert 1868-1903. . . . . . . DLB-184

Producing Dear Bunny, Dear Volodya: The Friendship
and the Feud. Y-97

The Profession of Authorship:
Scribblers for Bread Y-89

The Progress of Romance (1785), by Clara Reeve
[excerpt] DLB-39

Prokopovich, Feofan 1681?-1736 . . . . DLB-150

Prokosch, Frederic 1906-1989 . . . . . DLB-48

The Proletarian Novel DLB-9

Propper, Dan 1937- DLB-16

The Prospect of Peace (1778), by
Joel Barlow DLB-37

Protagoras circa 490 B.C.-420 B.C.
. . . . DLB-176

Proud, Robert 1728-1813 . . . . DLB-30

Proust, Marcel 1871-1922. . . . . DLB-65

Prynne, J. H. 1936- DLB-40

Przybyszewski, Stanislaw
1868-1927 . . . . DLB-66

Pseudo-Dionysius the Areopagite floruit
circa 500 . . . . DLB-115

Public Domain and the Violation of
Texts Y-97

The Public Lending Right in America
Statement by Sen. Charles McC.
Mathias, Jr. PLR and the Meaning
of Literary Property Statements on
PLR by American Writers Y-83

The Public Lending Right in the United Kingdom
Public Lending Right: The First Year in the
United Kingdom Y-83

The Publication of English
Renaissance Plays. DLB-62

Publications and Social Movements
[Transcendentalism] DLB-1

Publishers and Agents: The Columbia
Connection Y-87

A Publisher's Archives: G. P. Putnam . . . Y-92

Publishing Fiction at LSU Press. Y-87

Pückler-Muskau, Hermann von
1785-1871 . . . . DLB-133

Pufendorf, Samuel von
1632-1694 . . . . DLB-168

Pugh, Edwin William 1874-1930 . . . . DLB-135

Pugin, A. Welby 1812-1852 . . . . DLB-55

Puig, Manuel 1932-1990. . . . . DLB-113

Pulitzer, Joseph 1847-1911 . . . . DLB-23

Pulitzer, Joseph, Jr. 1885-1955 . . . . . DLB-29

Pulitzer Prizes for the Novel,
1917-1945. . . . . DLB-9

Pulliam, Eugene 1889-1975 . . . . . . DLB-127

Purchas, Samuel 1577?-1626 . . . . . DLB-151

Purdy, Al 1918- DLB-88

Purdy, James 1923- DLB-2

Purdy, Ken W. 1913-1972 . . . . . . DLB-137

Pusey, Edward Bouverie
1800-1882 . . . . DLB-55

Putnam, George Palmer
1814-1872 . . . . DLB-3, 79

Putnam, Samuel 1892-1950 . . . . DLB-4

G. P. Putnam's Sons [U.S.] DLB-49

G. P. Putnam's Sons [U.K.] DLB-106

Puzo, Mario 1920- DLB-6

Pyle, Ernie 1900-1945. . . . . DLB-29

Pyle, Howard
1853-1911 . . . . DLB-42, 188; DS-13

Pym, Barbara 1913-1980. . . . . DLB-14; Y-87

Pynchon, Thomas 1937- DLB-2, 173

Pyramid Books DLB-46

Pyrnelle, Louise-Clarke 1850-1907 . . . DLB-42

Pythagoras circa 570 B.C.-? DLB-176

Q

Quad, M. (see Lewis, Charles B.)

Quaritch, Bernard 1819-1899 . . . . . DLB-184

Quarles, Francis 1592-1644 . . . . . . DLB-126

The Quarterly Review
1809-1967 . . . . DLB-110

Quasimodo, Salvatore 190è-1968 . . . . DLB-114

Queen, Ellery (see Dannay, Frederic, and
Manfred B. Lee)

The Queen City Publishing House . . . DLB-49

Queneau, Raymond 1903-1976. . . . . DLB-72

Quennell, Sir Peter 1905-1993. . . DLB-155, 195

Quesnel, Joseph 1746-1809 . . . . DLB-99

The Question of American Copyright
in the Nineteenth Century
Headnote
Preface, by George Haven Putnam
The Evolution of Copyright, by Brander
Matthews
Summary of Copyright Legislation in
the United States, by R. R. Bowker
Analysis oœ the Provisions of the
Copyright Law of 1891, by
George Haven Putnam
The Contest for International Copyright,
by George Haven Putnam
Cheap Books and Good Books,
by Brander Matthews DLB-49

Quiller-Couch, Sir Arthur Thomas
1863-1944 . . . . DLB-135, 153, 190

Quin, Ann 1936-1973. . . . . DLB-14

Quincy, Samuel, of Georgia ?-? DLB-31

Quincy, Samuel, of Massachusetts
1734-1789 . . . . DLB-31

Quinn, Anthony 1915- DLB-122

Quinn, John 1870-1924 . . . . DLB-187

Quintana, Leroy V. 1944- DLB-82

Quintana, Miguel de 1671-1748
A Forerunner of Chicano
Literature DLB-122

Quist, Harlin, Books DLB-46

Quoirez, Françoise (see Sagan, Françoise)

R

R-va, Zeneida (see Gan, Elena Andreevna)

Raabe, Wilhelm 1831-1910 . . . . . . DLB-129

Rabe, David 1940- DLB-7

Raboni, Giovanni 1932-. DLB-128

Rachilde 1860-1953. . . . . DLB-123, 192

Racin, Kočo 1908-1943 . . . . DLB-147

Rackham, Arthur 1867-1939 . . . . . . DLB-141

Radcliffe, Ann 1764-1823 . . . . . DLB-39, 178

Raddall, Thomas 1903- DLB-68

Radichkov, Yordan 1929- DLB-181

Radiguet, Raymond 1903-1923 . . . . . DLB-65

Radishchev, Aleksandr Nikolaevich
  1749-1802 . . . . DLB-150

Radványi, Netty Reiling (see Seghers, Anna)

Rahv, Philip 1908-1973 . . . . DLB-137

Raičković, Stevan 1928- DLB-181

Raimund, Ferdinand Jakob
  1790-1836 . . . . DLB-90

Raine, Craig 1944- DLB-40

Raine, Kathleen 1908- DLB-20

Rainolde, Richard
  circa 1530-1606 . . . . DLB-136

Rakić, Milan 1876-1938 . . . . DLB-147

Rakosi, Carl 1903- DLB-193

Ralegh, Sir Walter 1554?-1618 . . . . . DLB-172

Ralin, Radoy 1923- DLB-181

Ralph, Julian 1853-1903 . . . . DLB-23

Ralph Waldo Emerson in 1982 . . . . . . Y-82

Ramat, Silvio 1939- DLB-128

Rambler, no. 4 (1750), by Samuel Johnson
  [excerpt] DLB-39

Ramée, Marie Louise de la (see Ouida)

Ramírez, Sergío 1942- DLB-145

Ramke, Bin 1947- DLB-120

Ramler, Karl Wilhelm 1725-1798 . . . . DLB-97

Ramon Ribeyro, Julio 1929- DLB-145

Ramous, Mario 1924- DLB-128

Rampersad, Arnold 1941- DLB-111

Ramsay, Allan 1684 or 1685-1758 . . . . DLB-95

Ramsay, David 1749-1815 . . . . DLB-30

Ramsay, Martha Laurens 1759-1811 . . DLB-200

Ranck, Katherine Quintana
  1942- DLB-122

Rand, Avery and Company DLB-49

Rand McNally and Company DLB-49

Randall, David Anton
  1905-1975 . . . . DLB-140

Randall, Dudley 1914- DLB-41

Randall, Henry S. 1811-1876 . . . . . . DLB-30

Randall, James G. 1881-1953 . . . . . . DLB-17

The Randall Jarrell Symposium: A Small
  Collection of Randall Jarrells
    Excerpts From Papers Delivered at
    the Randall Jarrel Symposium Y-86

Randolph, A. Philip 1889-1979 . . . . . DLB-91

Randolph, Anson D. F.
  [publishing house] DLB-49

Randolph, Thomas 1605-1635 . . . DLB-58, 126

Random House DLB-46

Ranlet, Henry [publishing house] DLB-49

Ransom, Harry 1908-1976 . . . . DLB-187

Ransom, John Crowe
  1888-1974 . . . . DLB-45, 63

Ransome, Arthur 1884-1967 . . . . . . DLB-160

Raphael, Frederic 1931- DLB-14

Raphaelson, Samson 1896-1983 . . . . DLB-44

Raskin, Ellen 1928-1984 . . . . DLB-52

Rastell, John 1475?-1536 . . . . . DLB-136, 170

Rattigan, Terence 1911-1977 . . . . . . DLB-13

Rawlings, Marjorie Kinnan
  1896-1953 . . . . . DLB-9, 22, 102; DS-17

Raworth, Tom 1938- DLB-40

Ray, David 1932- DLB-5

Ray, Gordon Norton
  1915-1986. . . . . DLB-103, 140

Ray, Henrietta Cordelia
  1849-1916 . . . . DLB-50

Raymond, Ernest 1888-1974 . . . . DLB-191

Raymond, Henry J. 1820-1869 . . . DLB-43, 79

Raymond Chandler Centenary Tributes
  from Michael Avallone, James Elroy, Joe
  Gores,
  and William F. Nolan Y-88

Reach, Angus 1821-1856 . . . . DLB-70

Read, Herbert 1893-1968 . . . . . . DLB-20, 149

Read, Herbert, "The Practice of Biography," in
  The English Sense of Humour and Other
  Essays DLB-149

Read, Martha Meredith DLB-200

Read, Opie 1852-1939 . . . . DLB-23

Read, Piers Paul 1941- DLB-14

Reade, Charles 1814-1884 . . . . DLB-21

Reader's Digest Condensed
  Books DLB-46

Readers Ulysses Symposium Y-97

Reading, Peter 1946- DLB-40

Reading Series in New York City Y-96

Reaney, James 1926- DLB-68

Rebhun, Paul 1500?-1546 . . . . DLB-179

Rèbora, Clemente 1885-1957 . . . . . DLB-114

Rechy, John 1934- DLB-122; Y-82

The Recovery of Literature: Criticism in the
  1990s: A Symposium Y-91

Redding, J. Saunders
  1906-1988 . . . . DLB-63, 76

Redfield, J. S. [publishing house] DLB-49

Redgrove, Peter 1932- DLB-40

Redmon, Anne 1943- Y-86

Redmond, Eugene B. 1937- DLB-41

Redpath, James [publishing house] DLB-49

Reed, Henry 1808-1854 . . . . DLB-59

Reed, Henry 1914- DLB-27

Reed, Ishmael
  1938- DLB-2, 5, 33, 169; DS-8

Reed, Rex 1938- DLB-185

Reed, Sampson 1800-1880 . . . . DLB-1

Reed, Talbot Baines 1852-1893 . . . . DLB-141

Reedy, William Marion 1862-1920 . . . DLB-91

Reese, Lizette Woodworth
  1856-1935 . . . . DLB-54

Reese, Thomas 1742-1796 . . . . DLB-37

Reeve, Clara 1729-1807 . . . . DLB-39

Reeves, James 1909-1978 . . . . . . DLB-161

Reeves, John 1926- DLB-88

"Reflections: After a Tornado,"
  by Judson Jerome DLB-105

Regnery, Henry, Company DLB-46

Rehberg, Hans 1901-1963 . . . . DLB-124

Rehfisch, Hans José 1891-1960 . . . . DLB-124

Reid, Alastair 1926- DLB-27

Reid, B. L. 1918-1990 . . . . DLB-111

Reid, Christopher 1949- DLB-40

Reid, Forrest 1875-1947 . . . . DLB-153

Reid, Helen Rogers 1882-1970 . . . . . DLB-29

Reid, James ?-? DLB-31

Reid, Mayne 1818-1883 . . . . . . DLB-21, 163

Reid, Thomas 1710-1796 . . . . DLB-31

Reid, V. S. (Vic) 1913-1987 . . . . . DLB-125

Reid, Whitelaw 1837-1912 . . . . DLB-23

Reilly and Lee Publishing
  Company DLB-46

Reimann, Brigitte 1933-1973 . . . . . . DLB-75

Reinmar der Alte
  circa 1165-circa 1205 . . . . DLB-138

Reinmar von Zweter
  circa 1200-circa 1250 . . . . DLB-138

Reisch, Walter 1903-1983 . . . . DLB-44

Remarque, Erich Maria 1898-1970 . . . . DLB-56

"Re-meeting of Old Friends": The Jack
  Kerouac Conference Y-82

Reminiscences, by Charles Scribner Jr. . . . DS-17

Remington, Frederic
  1861-1909 . . . . DLB-12, 186, 188

Renaud, Jacques 1943- DLB-60

Renault, Mary 1905-1983 . . . . Y-83

Rendell, Ruth 1930- DLB-87

Rensselaer, Maria van Cortlandt van
  1645-1689 . . . . DLB-200

Representative Men and Women: A Historical
  Perspective on the British Novel,
  1930-1960 . . . . DLB-15

(Re-)Publishing Orwell Y-86

Research in the American Antiquarian Book
  Trade Y-97

Responses to Ken Auletta Y-97

Rettenbacher, Simon 1634-1706 . . . . DLB-168

Reuchlin, Johannes 1455-1522 . . . . . DLB-179

Reuter, Christian 1665-after 1712 . . . . DLB-168

Reuter, Fritz 1810-1874 . . . . DLB-129

Reuter, Gabriele 1859-1941 . . . . . . DLB-66

Revell, Fleming H., Company DLB-49

Reventlow, Franziska Gräfin zu
  1871-1918 . . . . DLB-66

Review of Reviews Office DLB-112

Review of [Samuel Richardson's] *Clarissa* (1748),
  by Henry Fielding DLB-39

The Revolt (1937), by Mary Colum
  [excerpts] DLB-36

Rexroth, Kenneth
  1905-1982 . . . . . DLB-16, 48, 165; Y-82

Rey, H. A. 1898-1977 . . . . DLB-22

Reynal and Hitchcock DLB-46

Reynolds, G. W. M. 1814-1879 . . . . . DLB-21

Reynolds, John Hamilton
  1794-1852 . . . . DLB-96

Reynolds, Mack 1917- DLB-8

Reynolds, Sir Joshua 1723-1792 . . . . DLB-104

Reznikoff, Charles 1894-1976 . . . . DLB-28, 45

"Rhetoric" (1828; revised, 1859), by
  Thomas de Quincey [excerpt] DLB-57

Rhett, Robert Barnwell 1800-1876 . . . . DLB-43

Rhode, John 1884-1964 . . . . DLB-77

Rhodes, James Ford 1848-1927 . . . . . DLB-47

Rhodes, Richard 1937- DLB-185

Rhys, Jean 1890-1979 . . . . DLB-36, 117, 162

Ricardo, David 1772-1823 . . . . . DLB-107, 158

Ricardou, Jean 1932- DLB-83

Rice, Elmer 1892-1967 . . . . DLB-4, 7

Rice, Grantland 1880-1954 . . . . DLB-29, 171

Rich, Adrienne 1929- DLB-5, 67

Richards, David Adams 1950- DLB-53

Richards, George circa 1760-1814 . . . . DLB-37

Richards, I. A. 1893-1979 . . . . DLB-27

Richards, Laura E. 1850-1943 . . . . . DLB-42

Richards, William Carey
  1818-1892 . . . . DLB-73

Richards, Grant
  [publishing house] DLB-112

Richardson, Charles F. 1851-1913 . . . . DLB-71

Richardson, Dorothy M.
  1873-1957 . . . . DLB-36

Richardson, Henry Handel (Ethel Florence
  Lindesay) 1870-1946 . . . . DLB-197

Richardson, Jack 1935- DLB-7

Richardson, John 1796-1852 . . . . . . DLB-99

Richardson, Samuel
  1689-1761 . . . . DLB-39, 154

Richardson, Willis 1889-1977 . . . . . DLB-51

Riche, Barnabe 1542-1617 . . . . DLB-136

Richepin, Jean 1849-1926 . . . . DLB-192

Richler, Mordecai 1931- DLB-53

Richter, Conrad 1890-1968 . . . . DLB-9

Richter, Hans Werner 1908- DLB-69

Richter, Johann Paul Friedrich
  1763-1825 . . . . DLB-94

Rickerby, Joseph
  [publishing house] DLB-106

Rickword, Edgell 1898-1982 . . . . . . DLB-20

Riddell, Charlotte 1832-1906 . . . . . DLB-156

Riddell, John (see Ford, Corey)

Ridge, John Rollin 1827-1867 . . . . . DLB-175

Ridge, Lola 1873-1941 . . . . DLB-54

Ridge, William Pett 1859-1930 . . . . DLB-135

Riding, Laura (see Jackson, Laura Riding)

Ridler, Anne 1912- DLB-27

Ridruejo, Dionisio 1912-1975 . . . . . DLB-108

Riel, Louis 1844-1885 . . . . DLB-99

Riemer, Johannes 1648-1714 . . . . . DLB-168

Riffaterre, Michael 1924- DLB-67

Riggs, Lynn 1899-1954 . . . . DLB-175

Riis, Jacob 1849-1914 . . . . DLB-23

Riker, John C. [publishing house] DLB-49

Riley, James 1777-1840 . . . . DLB-183

Riley, John 1938-1978 . . . . DLB-40

Rilke, Rainer Maria 1875-1926 . . . . . DLB-81

Rimanelli, Giose 1926- DLB-177

Rinehart and Company DLB-46

Ringuet 1895-1960 . . . . DLB-68

Ringwood, Gwen Pharis
  1910-1984 . . . . DLB-88

Rinser, Luise 1911- DLB-69

Ríos, Alberto 1952- DLB-122

Ríos, Isabella 1948- DLB-82

Ripley, Arthur 1895-1961 . . . . DLB-44

Ripley, George 1802-1880 . . . . DLB-1, 64, 73

The Rising Glory of America:
  Three Poems DLB-37

The Rising Glory of America: Written in 1771
  (1786), by Hugh Henry Brackenridge and
  Philip Freneau DLB-37

Riskin, Robert 1897-1955 . . . . DLB-26

Risse, Heinz 1898- DLB-69

Rist, Johann 1607-1667 . . . . DLB-164

Ritchie, Anna Mowatt 1819-1870 . . . . DLB-3

Ritchie, Anne Thackeray
  1837-1919 . . . . DLB-18

Ritchie, Thomas 1778-1854 . . . . . . DLB-43

Rites of Passage
  [on William Saroyan] Y-83

The Ritz Paris Hemingway Award Y-85

Rivard, Adjutor 1868-1945 . . . . DLB-92

Rive, Richard 1931-1989 . . . . DLB-125

Rivera, Marina 1942- DLB-122

Rivera, Tomás 1935-1984 . . . . DLB-82

Rivers, Conrad Kent 1933-1968 . . . . DLB-41

Riverside Press DLB-49

Rivington, James circa 1724-1802 . . . . DLB-43

Rivington, Charles
  [publishing house] DLB-154

Rivkin, Allen 1903-1990 . . . . DLB-26

Roa Bastos, Augusto 1917- DLB-113

Robbe-Grillet, Alain 1922- DLB-83

Robbins, Tom 1936- Y-80

Roberts, Charles G. D. 1860-1943 . . . . DLB-92

Roberts, Dorothy 1906-1993 . . . . . . DLB-88

Roberts, Elizabeth Madox
  1881-1941 . . . . DLB-9, 54, 102

Roberts, Kenneth 1885-1957 . . . . . . DLB-9

Roberts, William 1767-1849 . . . . . . DLB-142

Roberts Brothers DLB-49

Roberts, James [publishing house] . . . DLB-154

Robertson, A. M., and Company DLB-49

Robertson, William 1721-1793 . . . . . DLB-104

Robins, Elizabeth 1862-1952 . . . . . DLB-197

Robinson, Casey 1903-1979 . . . . . . DLB-44

Robinson, Edwin Arlington
  1869-1935 . . . . DLB-54

Robinson, Henry Crabb
  1775-1867 . . . . DLB-107

Robinson, James Harvey
  1863-1936 . . . . DLB-47

Robinson, Lennox 1886-1958 . . . . . . DLB-10

Robinson, Mabel Louise
  1874-1962 . . . . DLB-22

Robinson, Mary 1758-1800 . . . . . . DLB-158

Robinson, Richard
  circa 1545-1607 . . . . DLB-167

Robinson, Therese
  1797-1870 . . . . DLB-59, 133

Robison, Mary 1949- DLB-130

Roblès, Emmanuel 1914- DLB-83

Roccatagliata Ceccardi, Ceccardo
  1871-1919 . . . . DLB-114

Rochester, John Wilmot, Earl of
  1647-1680 . . . . DLB-131

Rock, Howard 1911-1976 . . . . DLB-127

Rockwell, Norman Perceval
  1894-1978 . . . . DLB-188

Rodgers, Carolyn M. 1945- DLB-41

Rodgers, W. R. 1909-1969 . . . . DLB-20

Rodríguez, Claudio 1934- DLB-134

Rodriguez, Richard 1944- DLB-82

Rodríguez Julia, Edgardo
  1946- DLB-145

Roethke, Theodore 1908-1963 . . . . . DLB-5

Rogers, Jane 1952- DLB-194

Rogers, Pattiann 1940- DLB-105

Rogers, Samuel 1763-1855 . . . . DLB-93

Rogers, Will 1879-1935 . . . . DLB-11

Rohmer, Sax 1883-1959 . . . . DLB-70

Roiphe, Anne 1935- Y-80

Rojas, Arnold R. 1896-1988 . . . . . . DLB-82

Rolfe, Frederick William
1860-1913 . . . . DLB-34, 156

Rolland, Romain 1866-1944 . . . . DLB-65

Rolle, Richard
circa 1290-1300 - 1340 . . . . . . DLB-146

Rölvaag, O. E. 1876-1931 . . . . DLB-9

Romains, Jules 1885-1972. . . . . DLB-65

Roman, A., and Company DLB-49

Romano, Lalla 1906- DLB-177

Romano, Octavio 1923- DLB-122

Romero, Leo 1950- DLB-122

Romero, Lin 1947- DLB-122

Romero, Orlando 1945- DLB-82

Rook, Clarence 1863-1915 . . . . . . DLB-135

Roosevelt, Theodore 1858-1919 . . DLB-47, 186

Root, Waverley 1903-1982. . . . . DLB-4

Root, William Pitt 1941- DLB-120

Roquebrune, Robert de 1889-1978. . . . DLB-68

Rosa, João Guimarães
1908-1967 . . . . DLB-113

Rosales, Luis 1910-1992 . . . . DLB-134

Roscoe, William 1753-1831 . . . . . . DLB-163

Rose, Reginald 1920- DLB-26

Rose, Wendy 1948- DLB-175

Rosegger, Peter 1843-1918. . . . . . . DLB-129

Rosei, Peter 1946- DLB-85

Rosen, Norma 1925- DLB-28

Rosenbach, A. S. W. 1876-1952 . . . . DLB-140

Rosenbaum, Ron 1946- DLB-185

Rosenberg, Isaac 1890-1918. . . . . . . DLB-20

Rosenfeld, Isaac 1918-1956 . . . . . . DLB-28

Rosenthal, M. L. 1917- DLB-5

Rosenwald, Lessing J. 1891-1979 . . . . DLB-187

Ross, Alexander 1591-1654 . . . . . . DLB-151

Ross, Harold 1892-1951. . . . . DLB-137

Ross, Leonard Q. (see Rosten, Leo)

Ross, Lillian 1927- DLB-185

Ross, Martin 1862-1915 . . . . DLB-135

Ross, Sinclair 1908- DLB-88

Ross, W. W. E. 1894-1966 . . . . DLB-88

Rosselli, Amelia 1930- DLB-128

Rossen, Robert 1908-1966 . . . . DLB-26

Rossetti, Christina Georgina
1830-1894 . . . . DLB-35, 163

Rossetti, Dante Gabriel 1828-1882 . . . . DLB-35

Rossner, Judith 1935- DLB-6

Rostand, Edmond 1868-1918 . . . . . DLB-192

Rosten, Leo 1908- DLB-11

Rostenberg, Leona 1908- DLB-140

Rostovsky, Dimitrii 1651-1709 . . . . DLB-150

Bertram Rota and His Bookshop Y-91

Roth, Gerhard 1942- DLB-85, 124

Roth, Henry 1906?- DLB-28

Roth, Joseph 1894-1939. . . . . DLB-85

Roth, Philip 1933- DLB-2, 28, 173; Y-82

Rothenberg, Jerome 1931- DLB-5, 193

Rothschild Family DLB-184

Rotimi, Ola 1938- DLB-125

Routhier, Adolphe-Basile
1839-1920 . . . . DLB-99

Routier, Simone 1901-1987 . . . . DLB-88

Routledge, George, and Sons DLB-106

Roversi, Roberto 1923- DLB-128

Rowe, Elizabeth Singer
1674-1737 . . . . DLB-39, 95

Rowe, Nicholas 1674-1718 . . . . DLB-84

Rowlands, Samuel
circa 1570-1630 . . . . DLB-121

Rowlandson, Mary
circa 1637-circa 1711 . . . . . DLB-24, 200

Rowley, William circa 1585-1626 . . . . DLB-58

Rowse, A. L. 1903- DLB-155

Rowson, Susanna Haswell
circa 1762-1824 . . . . DLB-37, 200

Roy, Camille 1870-1943 . . . . DLB-92

Roy, Gabrielle 1909-1983 . . . . DLB-68

Roy, Jules 1907- DLB-83

The Royal Court Theatre and the English
Stage Company DLB-13

The Royal Court Theatre and the New Drama
. . . . DLB-10

The Royal Shakespeare Company
at the Swan Y-88

Royall, Anne 1769-1854 . . . . DLB-43

The Roycroft Printing Shop DLB-49

Royde-Smith, Naomi 1875-1964. . . . . DLB-191

Royster, Vermont 1914- DLB-127

Royston, Richard
[publishing house] DLB-170

Ruark, Gibbons 1941- DLB-120

Ruban, Vasilii Grigorevich
1742-1795 . . . . DLB-150

Rubens, Bernice 1928- DLB-14

Rudd and Carleton DLB-49

Rudkin, David 1936- DLB-13

Rudolf von Ems
circa 1200-circa 1254 . . . . DLB-138

Ruffin, Josephine St. Pierre
1842-1924 . . . . DLB-79

Ruganda, John 1941- DLB-157

Ruggles, Henry Joseph 1813-1906 . . . . DLB-64

Rukeyser, Muriel 1913-1980 . . . . . . DLB-48

Rule, Jane 1931- DLB-60

Rulfo, Juan 1918-1986 . . . . DLB-113

Rumaker, Michael 1932- DLB-16

Rumens, Carol 1944- DLB-40

Runyon, Damon 1880-1946 . . DLB-11, 86, 171

Ruodlieb circa 1050-1075 . . . . DLB-148

Rush, Benjamin 1746-1813 . . . . DLB-37

Rush, Rebecca 1779-? DLB-200

Rushdie, Salman 1947- DLB-194

Rusk, Ralph L. 1888-1962 . . . . DLB-103

Ruskin, John 1819-1900 . . . . DLB-55, 163, 190

Russ, Joanna 1937- DLB-8

Russell, B. B., and Company DLB-49

Russell, Benjamin 1761-1845 . . . . . . DLB-43

Russell, Bertrand 1872-1970. . . . . . DLB-100

Russell, Charles Edward
1860-1941 . . . . DLB-25

Russell, Charles M. 1864-1926 . . . . . DLB-188

Russell, Countess Mary Annette Beauchamp (see
Arnim, Elizabeth von)

Russell, George William (see AE)

Russell, R. H., and Son DLB-49

Rutherford, Mark 1831-1913 . . . . . . DLB-18

Ruxton, George Frederick
1821-1848 . . . . DLB-186

Ryan, Michael 1946- Y-82

Ryan, Oscar 1904- DLB-68

Ryga, George 1932- DLB-60

Rylands, Enriqueta Augustina Tennant
1843-1908 . . . . DLB-184

Rylands, John 1801-1888 . . . . DLB-184

Rymer, Thomas 1643?-1713 . . . . . . DLB-101

Ryskind, Morrie 1895-1985. . . . . . . DLB-26

Rzhevsky, Aleksei Andreevich
1737-1804 . . . . DLB-150

S

The Saalfield Publishing
Company DLB-46

Saba, Umberto 1883-1957 . . . . DLB-114

Sábato, Ernesto 1911- DLB-145

Saberhagen, Fred 1930- DLB-8

Sabin, Joseph 1821-1881 . . . . DLB-187

Sacer, Gottfried Wilhelm
1635-1699 . . . . DLB-168

Sachs, Hans 1494-1576 . . . . DLB-179

Sack, John 1930- DLB-185

Sackler, Howard 1929-1982 . . . . DLB-7

Sackville, Thomas 1536-1608 . . . . . . DLB-132

Sackville, Thomas 1536-1608
and Norton, Thomas
1532-1584 . . . . DLB-62

Sackville-West, Edward 1901-1965 . . . DLB-191

Sackville-West, V. 1892-1962 . . . . DLB-34, 195

Sadlier, D. and J., and Company DLB-49

Sadlier, Mary Anne 1820-1903 . . . . . DLB-99

Sadoff, Ira 1945- DLB-120

Saenz, Jaime 1921-1986 . . . . DLB-145

Saffin, John circa 1626-1710 . . . . . . DLB-24

Sagan, Françoise 1935- DLB-83

Sage, Robert 1899-1962 . . . . DLB-4

Sagel, Jim 1947- DLB-82

Sagendorph, Robb Hansell
1900-1970 . . . . DLB-137

Sahagún, Carlos 1938- DLB-108

Sahkomaapii, Piitai (see Highwater, Jamake)

Sahl, Hans 1902- DLB-69

Said, Edward W. 1935- DLB-67

Saiko, George 1892-1962 . . . . DLB-85

St. Dominic's Press DLB-112

Saint-Exupéry, Antoine de
1900-1944 . . . . DLB-72

St. John, J. Allen 1872-1957 . . . . . . DLB-188

St. Johns, Adela Rogers 1894-1988 . . . DLB-29

The St. John's College Robert
Graves Trust Y-96

St. Martin's Press DLB-46

St. Omer, Garth 1931- DLB-117

Saint Pierre, Michel de 1916-1987 . . . . DLB-83

Saintsbury, George
1845-1933 . . . . DLB-57, 149

Saki (see Munro, H. H.)

Salaam, Kalamu ya 1947- DLB-38

Šalamun, Tomaž 1941- DLB-181

Salas, Floyd 1931- DLB-82

Sálaz-Marquez, Rubén 1935- DLB-122

Salemson, Harold J. 1910-1988 . . . . . DLB-4

Salinas, Luis Omar 1937- DLB-82

Salinas, Pedro 1891-1951 . . . . DLB-134

Salinger, J. D. 1919- DLB-2, 102, 173

Salkey, Andrew 1928- DLB-125

Salt, Waldo 1914- DLB-44

Salter, James 1925- DLB-130

Salter, Mary Jo 1954- DLB-120

Salustri, Carlo Alberto (see Trilussa)

Salverson, Laura Goodman
1890-1970 . . . . DLB-92

Sampson, Richard Henry (see Hull, Richard)

Samuels, Ernest 1903- DLB-111

Sanborn, Franklin Benjamin
1831-1917 . . . . DLB-1

Sánchez, Luis Rafael 1936- DLB-145

Sánchez, Philomeno "Phil"
1917- DLB-122

Sánchez, Ricardo 1941- DLB-82

Sanchez, Sonia 1934- DLB-41; DS-8

Sand, George 1804-1876 . . . . . DLB-119, 192

Sandburg, Carl 1878-1967 . . . . . DLB-17, 54

Sanders, Ed 1939- DLB-16

Sandoz, Mari 1896-1966 . . . . DLB-9

Sandwell, B. K. 1876-1954 . . . . DLB-92

Sandy, Stephen 1934- DLB-165

Sandys, George 1578-1644 . . . . DLB-24, 121

Sangster, Charles 1822-1893 . . . . . . DLB-99

Sanguineti, Edoardo 1930- DLB-128

Sansay, Leonora ?-after 1823 . . . . . DLB-200

Sansom, William 1912-1976 . . . . . . DLB-139

Santayana, George
1863-1952 . . . . DLB-54, 71; DS-13

Santiago, Danny 1911-1988 . . . . . . DLB-122

Santmyer, Helen Hooven 1895-1986 . . . . Y-84

Sanvitale, Francesca 1928- DLB-196

Sapidus, Joannes 1490-1561 . . . . . . DLB-179

Sapir, Edward 1884-1939 . . . . DLB-92

Sapper (see McNeile, Herman Cyril)

Sappho circa 620 B.C.-circa 550 B.C.
. . . . DLB-176

Sardou, Victorien 1831-1908 . . . . . DLB-192

Sarduy, Severo 1937- DLB-113

Sargent, Pamela 1948- DLB-8

Saro-Wiwa, Ken 1941- DLB-157

Saroyan, William
1908-1981 . . . . DLB-7, 9, 86; Y-81

Sarraute, Nathalie 1900- DLB-83

Sarrazin, Albertine 1937-1967 . . . . . . DLB-83

Sarris, Greg 1952- DLB-175

Sarton, May 1912- DLB-48; Y-81

Sartre, Jean-Paul 1905-1980 . . . . DLB-72

Sassoon, Siegfried
1886-1967 . . . . DLB-20, 191; DS-18

Sata, Ineko 1904- DLB-180

Saturday Review Press DLB-46

Saunders, James 1925- DLB-13

Saunders, John Monk 1897-1940 . . . . DLB-26

Saunders, Margaret Marshall
1861-1947 . . . . DLB-92

Saunders and Otley DLB-106

Savage, James 1784-1873 . . . . DLB-30

Savage, Marmion W. 1803?-1872 . . . . DLB-21

Savage, Richard 1697?-1743 . . . . . . DLB-95

Savard, Félix-Antoine 1896-1982 . . . . DLB-68

Saville, (Leonard) Malcolm
1901-1982 . . . . DLB-160

Sawyer, Ruth 1880-1970 . . . . DLB-22

Sayers, Dorothy L.
1893-1957 . . . . DLB-10, 36, 77, 100

Sayle, Charles Edward 1864-1924 . . . DLB-184

Sayles, John Thomas 1950- DLB-44

Sbarbaro, Camillo 1888-1967 . . . . . DLB-114

Scalapino, Leslie 1947- DLB-193

Scannell, Vernon 1922- DLB-27

Scarry, Richard 1919-1994 . . . . DLB-61

Schaeffer, Albrecht 1885-1950 . . . . . DLB-66

Schaeffer, Susan Fromberg 1941- DLB-28

Schaff, Philip 1819-1893 . . . . DS-13

Schaper, Edzard 1908-1984 . . . . DLB-69

Scharf, J. Thomas 1843-1898 . . . . . . DLB-47

Schede, Paul Melissus 1539-1602 . . . . DLB-179

Scheffel, Joseph Viktor von
1826-1886 . . . . DLB-129

Scheffler, Johann 1624-1677 . . . . . . DLB-164

Schelling, Friedrich Wilhelm Joseph von
1775-1854 . . . . DLB-90

Scherer, Wilhelm 1841-1886 . . . . . . DLB-129

Schickele, René 1883-1940 . . . . DLB-66

Schiff, Dorothy 1903-1989 . . . . DLB-127

Schiller, Friedrich 1759-1805 . . . . . . DLB-94

Schirmer, David 1623-1687 . . . . . . DLB-164

Schlaf, Johannes 1862-1941 . . . . . . DLB-118

Schlegel, August Wilhelm
1767-1845 . . . . DLB-94

Schlegel, Dorothea 1763-1839 . . . . . DLB-90

Schlegel, Friedrich 1772-1829 . . . . . DLB-90

Schleiermacher, Friedrich
1768-1834 . . . . DLB-90

Schlesinger, Arthur M., Jr. 1917- DLB-17

Schlumberger, Jean 1877-1968 . . . . . DLB-65

Schmid, Eduard Hermann Wilhelm (see
Edschmid, Kasimir)

Schmidt, Arno 1914-1979 . . . . DLB-69

Schmidt, Johann Kaspar (see Stirner, Max)

Schmidt, Michael 1947- DLB-40

Schmidtbonn, Wilhelm August
1876-1952 . . . . DLB-118

Schmitz, James H. 1911- DLB-8

Schnabel, Johann Gottfried
1692-1760 . . . . DLB-168

Schnackenberg, Gjertrud 1953- DLB-120

Schnitzler, Arthur 1862-1931 . . . . DLB-81, 118

Schnurre, Wolfdietrich 1920- DLB-69

Schocken Books DLB-46

Scholartis Press DLB-112

The Schomburg Center for Research
in Black Culture DLB-76

Schönbeck, Virgilio (see Giotti, Virgilio)

Schönherr, Karl 1867-1943 . . . . . . DLB-118

Schoolcraft, Jane Johnston
1800-1841 . . . . DLB-175

School Stories, 1914-1960 . . . . DLB-160

Schopenhauer, Arthur 1788-1860 . . . . DLB-90

Schopenhauer, Johanna 1766-1838 . . . DLB-90

Schorer, Mark 1908-1977 . . . . DLB-103

Schottelius, Justus Georg
1612-1676 . . . . DLB-164

Schouler, James 1839-1920 . . . . DLB-47

Schrader, Paul 1946- DLB-44

Schreiner, Olive 1855-1920 . . DLB-18, 156, 190

Schroeder, Andreas 1946- DLB-53

Schubart, Christian Friedrich Daniel
1739-1791 . . . . DLB-97

Schubert, Gotthilf Heinrich
1780-1860 . . . . DLB-90

Schücking, Levin 1814-1883 . . . . . . DLB-133

Schulberg, Budd 1914- . . DLB-6, 26, 28; Y-81

Schulte, F. J., and Company DLB-49

Schulze, Hans (see Praetorius, Johannes)

Schupp, Johann Balthasar
1610-1661 . . . . DLB-164

Schurz, Carl 1829-1906 . . . . DLB-23

Schuyler, George S. 1895-1977 . . . DLB-29, 51

Schuyler, James 1923-1991 . . . . . DLB-5, 169

Schwartz, Delmore 1913-1966 . . . . DLB-28, 48

Schwartz, Jonathan 1938- Y-82

Schwarz, Sibylle 1621-1638 . . . . . . DLB-164

Schwerner, Armand 1927- DLB-165

Schwob, Marcel 1867-1905 . . . . . . DLB-123

Sciascia, Leonardo 1921-1989 . . . . . DLB-177

Science Fantasy DLB-8

Science-Fiction Fandom and
Conventions DLB-8

Science-Fiction Fanzines: The Time
Binders DLB-8

Science-Fiction Films DLB-8

Science Fiction Writers of America and the
Nebula Awards. DLB-8

Scot, Reginald circa 1538-1599 . . . . DLB-136

Scotellaro, Rocco 1923-1953 . . . . . . DLB-128

Scott, Dennis 1939-1991 . . . . DLB-125

Scott, Dixon 1881-1915 . . . . DLB-98

Scott, Duncan Campbell 1862-1947 . . . DLB-92

Scott, Evelyn 1893-1963 . . . . DLB-9, 48

Scott, F. R. 1899-1985 . . . . DLB-88

Scott, Frederick George 1861-1944 . . . . DLB-92

Scott, Geoffrey 1884-1929 . . . . DLB-149

Scott, Harvey W. 1838-1910 . . . . . . DLB-23

Scott, Paul 1920-1978 . . . . DLB-14

Scott, Sarah 1723-1795 . . . . DLB-39

Scott, Tom 1918- DLB-27

Scott, Sir Walter
1771-1832. . . . DLB-93, 107, 116, 144, 159

Scott, William Bell 1811-1890 . . . . . . DLB-32

Scott, Walter, Publishing
Company Limited. DLB-112

Scott, William R.
[publishing house]. DLB-46

Scott-Heron, Gil 1949- DLB-41

Scribe, Eugene 1791-1861 . . . . DLB-192

Scribner, Arthur Hawley
1859-1932 . . . . DS-13, 16

Scribner, Charles 1854-1930 . . . . . DS-13, 16

Scribner, Charles, Jr. 1921-1995 . . . . . . Y-95

Charles Scribner's
Sons DLB-49; DS-13, 16, 17

Scripps, E. W. 1854-1926. . . . . DLB-25

Scudder, Horace Elisha
1838-1902 . . . . DLB-42, 71

Scudder, Vida Dutton 1861-1954 . . . . DLB-71

Scupham, Peter 1933- DLB-40

Seabrook, William 1886-1945 . . . . . . DLB-4

Seabury, Samuel 1729-1796. . . . . . . DLB-31

Seacole, Mary Jane Grant
1805-1881 . . . . DLB-166

The Seafarer circa 970 . . . . DLB-146

Sealsfield, Charles (Carl Postl)
1793-1864. . . . . DLB-133, 186

Sears, Edward I. 1819?-1876 . . . . . . DLB-79

Sears Publishing Company DLB-46

Seaton, George 1911-1979 . . . . DLB-44

Seaton, William Winston
1785-1866 . . . . DLB-43

Secker, Martin, and Warburg
Limited. DLB-112

Secker, Martin [publishing house]. . . . DLB-112

Second-Generation Minor Poets of the
Seventeenth Century. DLB-126

Sedgwick, Arthur George
1844-1915 . . . . DLB-64

Sedgwick, Catharine Maria
1789-1867. . . . . DLB-1, 74, 183

Sedgwick, Ellery 1872-1930. . . . . . . DLB-91

Sedley, Sir Charles 1639-1701. . . . . . DLB-131

Seeger, Alan 1888-1916 . . . . DLB-45

Seers, Eugene (see Dantin, Louis)

Segal, Erich 1937- Y-86

Šegedin, Petar 1909- DLB-181

Seghers, Anna 1900-1983 . . . . DLB-69

Seid, Ruth (see Sinclair, Jo)

Seidel, Frederick Lewis 1936- Y-84

Seidel, Ina 1885-1974 . . . . DLB-56

Seifert, Jaroslav 1901- Y-84

Seigenthaler, John 1927- DLB-127

Seizin Press. DLB-112

Séjour, Victor 1817-1874 . . . . DLB-50

Séjour Marcou et Ferrand, Juan Victor (see Séjour,
Victor)

Sekowski, Józef-Julian, Baron Brambeus (see
Senkovsky, Osip Ivanovich)

Selby, Hubert, Jr. 1928- DLB-2

Selden, George 1929-1989 . . . . DLB-52

Selected English-Language Little Magazines
and Newspapers [France,
1920-1939] DLB-4

Selected Humorous Magazines
(1820-1950) DLB-11

Selected Science-Fiction Magazines and
Anthologies DLB-8

Selenić, Slobodan 1933-1995. . . . . . DLB-181

Self, Edwin F. 1920- DLB-137

Seligman, Edwin R. A. 1861-1939 . . . . DLB-47

Selimović, Meša 1910-1982 . . . . . . DLB-181

Selous, Frederick Courteney
1851-1917 . . . . DLB-174

Seltzer, Chester E. (see Muro, Amado)

Seltzer, Thomas
[publishing house]. DLB-46

Selvon, Sam 1923-1994 . . . . DLB-125

Semmes, Raphael 1809-1877 . . . . . . DLB-189

Senancour, Etienne de 1770-1846. . . . DLB-119

Sendak, Maurice 1928- DLB-61

Senécal, Eva 1905- DLB-92

Sengstacke, John 1912- DLB-127

Senior, Olive 1941- DLB-157

Senkovsky, Osip Ivanovich (Józef-Julian Sekowski,
Baron Brambeus) 1800-1858 . . . . DLB-198

Šenoa, August 1838-1881 . . . . DLB-147

"Sensation Novels" (1863), by
H. L. Manse DLB-21

Sepamla, Sipho 1932- DLB-157

Seredy, Kate 1899-1975. . . . . DLB-22

Sereni, Vittorio 1913-1983 . . . . DLB-128

Seres, William
[publishing house] DLB-170

Serling, Rod 1924-1975 . . . . DLB-26

Serote, Mongane Wally 1944- DLB-125

Serraillier, Ian 1912-1994 . . . . DLB-161

Serrano, Nina 1934- DLB-122

Service, Robert 1874-1958 . . . . DLB-92

Sessler, Charles 1854-1935. . . . . . . DLB-187

Seth, Vikram 1952- DLB-120

Seton, Elizabeth Ann 1774-1821 . . . . DLB-200

Seton, Ernest Thompson
1860-1942 . . . . DLB-92; DS-13

Setouchi, Harumi 1922- DLB-182

Settle, Mary Lee 1918- DLB-6

Seume, Johann Gottfried
1763-1810 . . . . DLB-94

Seuse, Heinrich 1295?-1366 . . . . . . DLB-179

Seuss, Dr. (see Geisel, Theodor Seuss)

The Seventy-fifth Anniversary of the Armistice:
The Wilfred Owen Centenary and the Great
War Exhibit at the University of
Virginia Y-93

Sewall, Joseph 1688-1769 . . . . DLB-24

Sewall, Richard B. 1908- DLB-111

Sewell, Anna 1820-1878 . . . . DLB-163

Sewell, Samuel 1652-1730. . . . . DLB-24

Sex, Class, Politics, and Religion [in the
    British Novel, 1930-1959] DLB-15

Sexton, Anne 1928-1974 . . . . . . DLB-5, 169

Seymour-Smith, Martin 1928- DLB-155

Sgorlon, Carlo 1930- DLB-196

Shaara, Michael 1929-1988 . . . . Y-83

Shadwell, Thomas 1641?-1692 . . . . . DLB-80

Shaffer, Anthony 1926- DLB-13

Shaffer, Peter 1926- DLB-13

Shaftesbury, Anthony Ashley Cooper,
    Third Earl of 1671-1713 . . . . . . DLB-101

Shairp, Mordaunt 1887-1939 . . . . DLB-10

Shakespeare, William
    1564-1616 . . . . DLB-62, 172

The Shakespeare Globe Trust Y-93

Shakespeare Head Press DLB-112

Shakhovskoi, Aleksandr Aleksandrovich
    1777-1846 . . . . DLB-150

Shange, Ntozake 1948- DLB-38

Shapiro, Karl 1913- DLB-48

Sharon Publications DLB-46

Sharp, Margery 1905-1991 . . . . DLB-161

Sharp, William 1855-1905 . . . . DLB-156

Sharpe, Tom 1928- DLB-14

Shaw, Albert 1857-1947 . . . . DLB-91

Shaw, George Bernard
    1856-1950 . . . . DLB-10, 57, 190

Shaw, Henry Wheeler 1818-1885 . . . . DLB-11

Shaw, Joseph T. 1874-1952 . . . . DLB-137

Shaw, Irwin 1913-1984 . . . . DLB-6, 102; Y-84

Shaw, Robert 1927-1978 . . . . . . DLB-13, 14

Shaw, Robert B. 1947- DLB-120

Shawn, William 1907-1992 . . . . DLB-137

Shay, Frank [publishing house] DLB-46

Shea, John Gilmary 1824-1892 . . . . . DLB-30

Sheaffer, Louis 1912-1993 . . . . DLB-103

Shearing, Joseph 1886-1952 . . . . . . DLB-70

Shebbeare, John 1709-1788 . . . . DLB-39

Sheckley, Robert 1928- DLB-8

Shedd, William G. T. 1820-1894 . . . . DLB-64

Sheed, Wilfred 1930- DLB-6

Sheed and Ward [U.S.] DLB-46

Sheed and Ward Limited [U.K.] DLB-112

Sheldon, Alice B. (see Tiptree, James, Jr.)

Sheldon, Edward 1886-1946 . . . . DLB-7

Sheldon and Company DLB-49

Shelley, Mary Wollstonecraft
    1797-1851 . . . . . DLB-110, 116, 159, 178

Shelley, Percy Bysshe
    1792-1822 . . . . DLB-96, 110, 158

Shelnutt, Eve 1941- DLB-130

Shenstone, William 1714-1763 . . . . . DLB-95

Shepard, Ernest Howard
    1879-1976 . . . . DLB-160

Shepard, Sam 1943- DLB-7

Shepard, Thomas I,
    1604 or 1605-1649 . . . . DLB-24

Shepard, Thomas II, 1635-1677 . . . . . DLB-24

Shepard, Clark and Brown DLB-49

Shepherd, Luke
    flourished 1547-1554 . . . . DLB-136

Sherburne, Edward 1616-1702 . . . . . DLB-131

Sheridan, Frances 1724-1766 . . . . . DLB-39, 84

Sheridan, Richard Brinsley
    1751-1816 . . . . DLB-89

Sherman, Francis 1871-1926 . . . . DLB-92

Sherriff, R. C. 1896-1975 . . . . . DLB-10, 191

Sherry, Norman 1935- DLB-155

Sherwood, Mary Martha
    1775-1851 . . . . DLB-163

Sherwood, Robert 1896-1955 . . . . DLB-7, 26

Shiel, M. P. 1865-1947 . . . . DLB-153

Shiels, George 1886-1949 . . . . DLB-10

Shiga, Naoya 1883-1971 . . . . DLB-180

Shiina, Rinzō 1911-1973 . . . . DLB-182

Shillaber, B.[enjamin] P.[enhallow]
    1814-1890 . . . . DLB-1, 11

Shimao, Toshio 1917-1986 . . . . . . DLB-182

Shimazaki, Tōson 1872-1943 . . . . . DLB-180

Shine, Ted 1931- DLB-38

Ship, Reuben 1915-1975 . . . . DLB-88

Shirer, William L. 1904-1993 . . . . . . DLB-4

Shirinsky-Shikhmatov, Sergii Aleksandrovich
    1783-1837 . . . . DLB-150

Shirley, James 1596-1666 . . . . DLB-58

Shishkov, Aleksandr Semenovich
    1753-1841 . . . . DLB-150

Shockley, Ann Allen 1927- DLB-33

Shōno, Junzō 1921- DLB-182

Shore, Arabella 1820?-1901 and
    Shore, Louisa 1824-1895 . . . . . . DLB-199

Short, Peter
    [publishing house] DLB-170

Shorthouse, Joseph Henry
    1834-1903 . . . . DLB-18

Showalter, Elaine 1941- DLB-67

Shulevitz, Uri 1935- DLB-61

Shulman, Max 1919-1988 . . . . DLB-11

Shute, Henry A. 1856-1943 . . . . DLB-9

Shuttle, Penelope 1947- DLB-14, 40

Sibbes, Richard 1577-1635 . . . . DLB-151

Siddal, Elizabeth Eleanor
    1829-1862 . . . . DLB-199

Sidgwick, Ethel 1877-1970 . . . . DLB-197

Sidgwick and Jackson Limited DLB-112

Sidney, Margaret (see Lothrop, Harriet M.)

Sidney, Mary 1561-1621 . . . . DLB-167

Sidney, Sir Philip 1554-1586 . . . . . DLB-167

Sidney's Press DLB-49

Siegfried Loraine Sassoon: A Centenary Essay
    Tributes from Vivien F. Clarke and
    Michael Thorpe Y-86

Sierra, Rubén 1946- DLB-122

Sierra Club Books DLB-49

Siger of Brabant
    circa 1240-circa 1284 . . . . DLB-115

Sigourney, Lydia Howard (Huntley)
    1791-1865 . . . . DLB-1, 42, 73, 183

Silkin, Jon 1930- DLB-27

Silko, Leslie Marmon
    1948- DLB-143, 175

Silliman, Benjamin 1779-1864 . . . . . . DLB-183

Silliman, Ron 1946- DLB-169

Silliphant, Stirling 1918- DLB-26

Sillitoe, Alan 1928- DLB-14, 139

Silman, Roberta 1934- DLB-28

Silva, Beverly 1930- DLB-122

Silverberg, Robert 1935- DLB-8

Silverman, Kenneth 1936- DLB-111

Simak, Clifford D. 1904-1988 . . . . . . DLB-8

Simcoe, Elizabeth 1762-1850 . . . . . . DLB-99

Simcox, Edith Jemima 1844-1901 . . . . DLB-190

Simcox, George Augustus
    1841-1905 . . . . DLB-35

Sime, Jessie Georgina 1868-1958 . . . . . DLB-92

Simenon, Georges
    1903-1989 . . . . DLB-72; Y-89

Simic, Charles 1938- DLB-105

Simmel, Johannes Mario 1924- DLB-69

Simmes, Valentine
    [publishing house] DLB-170

Simmons, Ernest J. 1903-1972 . . . . . DLB-103

Simmons, Herbert Alfred 1930- DLB-33

Simmons, James 1933- DLB-40

Simms, William Gilmore
    1806-1870 . . . . DLB-3, 30, 59, 73

Simms and M'Intyre DLB-106

Simon, Claude 1913- DLB-83; Y-85

Simon, Neil 1927- DLB-7

Simon and Schuster DLB-46

Simons, Katherine Drayton Mayrant
    1890-1969 . . . . Y-83

Simović, Ljubomir 1935- DLB-181

Simpkin and Marshall
    [publishing house] DLB-154

Simpson, Helen 1897-1940 . . . . DLB-77

Simpson, Louis 1923- DLB-5

Simpson, N. F. 1919- DLB-13

Sims, George 1923- DLB-87

Sims, George Robert 1847-1922 . . . . DLB-35, 70, 135

Sinán, Rogelio 1904- DLB-145

Sinclair, Andrew 1935- DLB-14

Sinclair, Bertrand William 1881-1972 . . . . DLB-92

Sinclair, Catherine 1800-1864 . . . . DLB-163

Sinclair, Jo 1913- DLB-28

Sinclair Lewis Centennial Conference Y-85

Sinclair, Lister 1921- DLB-88

Sinclair, May 1863-1946. . . . . . DLB-36, 135

Sinclair, Upton 1878-1968 . . . . DLB-9

Sinclair, Upton [publishing house] DLB-46

Singer, Isaac Bashevis 1904-1991 . . . . DLB-6, 28, 52; Y-91

Singer, Mark 1950- DLB-185

Singmaster, Elsie 1879-1958 . . . . DLB-9

Sinisgalli, Leonardo 1908-1981 . . . . . DLB-114

Siodmak, Curt 1902- DLB-44

Siringo, Charles A. 1855-1928 . . . . . DLB-186

Sissman, L. E. 1928-1976 . . . . DLB-5

Sisson, C. H. 1914- DLB-27

Sitwell, Edith 1887-1964 . . . . DLB-20

Sitwell, Osbert 1892-1969 . . . . DLB-100, 195

Skármeta, Antonio 1940- DLB-145

Skeat, Walter W. 1835-1912 . . . . . DLB-184

Skeffington, William [publishing house] DLB-106

Skelton, John 1463-1529 . . . . DLB-136

Skelton, Robin 1925- DLB-27, 53

Skinner, Constance Lindsay 1877-1939 . . . . DLB-92

Skinner, John Stuart 1788-1851 . . . . DLB-73

Skipsey, Joseph 1832-1903 . . . . DLB-35

Slade, Bernard 1930- DLB-53

Slamnig, Ivan 1930- DLB-181

Slater, Patrick 1880-1951 . . . . DLB-68

Slaveykov, Pencho 1866-1912 . . . . . . DLB-147

Slaviček, Milivoj 1929- DLB-181

Slavitt, David 1935- DLB-5, 6

Sleigh, Burrows Willcocks Arthur 1821-1869 . . . . DLB-99

A Slender Thread of Hope: The Kennedy Center Black Theatre Project DLB-38

Slesinger, Tess 1905-1945 . . . . DLB-102

Slick, Sam (see Haliburton, Thomas Chandler)

Sloan, John 1871-1951 . . . . DLB-188

Sloane, William, Associates DLB-46

Small, Maynard and Company DLB-49

Small Presses in Great Britain and Ireland, 1960-1985 . . . . DLB-40

Small Presses I: Jargon Society Y-84

Small Presses II: The Spirit That Moves Us Press Y-85

Small Presses III: Pushcart Press Y-87

Smart, Christopher 1722-1771. . . . . DLB-109

Smart, David A. 1892-1957 . . . . . . DLB-137

Smart, Elizabeth 1913-1986 . . . . DLB-88

Smedley, Menella Bute 1820?-1877 . . . DLB-199

Smellie, William [publishing house] DLB-154

Smiles, Samuel 1812-1904 . . . . DLB-55

Smith, A. J. M. 1902-1980 . . . . DLB-88

Smith, Adam 1723-1790 . . . . DLB-104

Smith, Adam (George Jerome Waldo Goodman) 1930- DLB-185

Smith, Alexander 1829-1867 . . . . DLB-32, 55

Smith, Betty 1896-1972 . . . . Y-82

Smith, Carol Sturm 1938- Y-81

Smith, Charles Henry 1826-1903 . . . . DLB-11

Smith, Charlotte 1749-1806 . . . . . DLB-39, 109

Smith, Chet 1899-1973 . . . . DLB-171

Smith, Cordwainer 1913-1966 . . . . . . DLB-8

Smith, Dave 1942- DLB-5

Smith, Dodie 1896- DLB-10

Smith, Doris Buchanan 1934- DLB-52

Smith, E. E. 1890-1965 . . . . DLB-8

Smith, Elihu Hubbard 1771-1798 . . . DLB-37

Smith, Elizabeth Oakes (Prince) 1806-1893 . . . . DLB-1

Smith, Eunice 1757-1823 . . . . DLB-200

Smith, F. Hopkinson 1838-1915 . . . . . DS-13

Smith, George D. 1870-1920 . . . . . DLB-140

Smith, George O. 1911-1981 . . . . DLB-8

Smith, Goldwin 1823-1910 . . . . DLB-99

Smith, H. Allen 1907-1976 . . . . DLB-11, 29

Smith, Harry B. 1860-1936 . . . . . . DLB-187

Smith, Hazel Brannon 1914- DLB-127

Smith, Henry circa 1560-circa 1591 . . . . DLB-136

Smith, Horatio (Horace) 1779-1849 . . . . DLB-116

Smith, Horatio (Horace) 1779-1849 and James Smith 1775-1839 . . . . DLB-96

Smith, Iain Crichton 1928- DLB-40, 139

Smith, J. Allen 1860-1924 . . . . DLB-47

Smith, Jessie Willcox 1863-1935 . . . . DLB-188

Smith, John 1580-1631 . . . . DLB-24, 30

Smith, Josiah 1704-1781 . . . . DLB-24

Smith, Ken 1938- DLB-40

Smith, Lee 1944- DLB-143; Y-83

Smith, Logan Pearsall 1865-1946 . . . . DLB-98

Smith, Mark 1935- Y-82

Smith, Michael 1698-circa 1771 . . . . DLB-31

Smith, Red 1905-1982 . . . . DLB-29, 171

Smith, Roswell 1829-1892 . . . . DLB-79

Smith, Samuel Harrison 1772-1845 . . . . DLB-43

Smith, Samuel Stanhope 1751-1819 . . . . DLB-37

Smith, Sarah (see Stretton, Hesba)

Smith, Sarah Pogson 1774-1870 . . . . . DLB-200

Smith, Seba 1792-1868 . . . . DLB-1, 11

Smith, Sir Thomas 1513-1577 . . . . . DLB-132

Smith, Stevie 1902-1971 . . . . DLB-20

Smith, Sydney 1771-1845 . . . . DLB-107

Smith, Sydney Goodsir 1915-1975 . . . . DLB-27

Smith, Wendell 1914-1972 . . . . DLB-171

Smith, William flourished 1595-1597 . . . . DLB-136

Smith, William 1727-1803 . . . . DLB-31

Smith, William 1728-1793 . . . . DLB-30

Smith, William Gardner 1927-1974 . . . . DLB-76

Smith, William Henry 1808-1872 . . . . DLB-159

Smith, William Jay 1918- DLB-5

Smith, Elder and Company DLB-154

Smith, Harrison, and Robert Haas [publishing house] DLB-46

Smith, J. Stilman, and Company DLB-49

Smith, W. B., and Company DLB-49

Smith, W. H., and Son DLB-106

Smithers, Leonard [publishing house] DLB-112

Smollett, Tobias 1721-1771 . . . . . DLB-39, 104

Smythe, Francis Sydney 1900-1949 . . . . DLB-195

Snellings, Rolland (see Touré, Askia Muhammad)

Snodgrass, W. D. 1926- DLB-5

Snow, C. P. 1905-1980 . . . DLB-15, 77; DS-17

Snyder, Gary 1930- DLB-5, 16, 165

Sobiloff, Hy 1912-1970 . . . . DLB-48

The Society for Textual Scholarship and TEXT Y-87

The Society for the History of Authorship, Reading and Publishing Y-92

Soffici, Ardengo 1879-1964 . . . . . . DLB-114

Sofola, 'Zulu 1938- DLB-157

Solano, Solita 1888-1975 . . . . DLB-4

Soldati, Mario 1906- DLB-177

Šoljan, Antun 1932-1993 . . . . DLB-181

Sollers, Philippe 1936- DLB-83

Sollogub, Vladimir Aleksandrovich 1813-1882 . . . . DLB-198

Solmi, Sergio 1899-1981 . . . . DLB-114

Solomon, Carl 1928- DLB-16

Solway, David 1941- DLB-53

Solzhenitsyn and America Y-85

Somerville, Edith Œnone
1858-1949 . . . . DLB-135

Somov, Orest Mikhailovich
1793-1833 . . . . DLB-198

Song, Cathy 1955- DLB-169

Sono, Ayako 1931- DLB-182

Sontag, Susan 1933- DLB-2, 67

Sophocles 497/496 B.C.-406/405 B.C.
. . . . DLB-176

Šopov, Aco 1923-1982. . . . . DLB-181

Sorge, Reinhard Johannes
1892-1916 . . . . DLB-118

Sorrentino, Gilbert
1929- DLB-5, 173; Y-80

Sotheby, William 1757-1833 . . . . DLB-93

Soto, Gary 1952- DLB-82

Sources for the Study of Tudor and Stuart Drama
DLB-62

Souster, Raymond 1921- DLB-88

The South English Legendary
circa thirteenth-fifteenth
centuries DLB-146

Southerland, Ellease 1943- DLB-33

Southern Illinois University Press Y-95

Southern, Terry 1924- DLB-2

Southern Writers Between the
Wars DLB-9

Southerne, Thomas 1659-1746 . . . . DLB-80

Southey, Caroline Anne Bowles
1786-1854 . . . . DLB-116

Southey, Robert
1774-1843 . . . . . . DLB-93, 107, 142

Southwell, Robert 1561?-1595. . . . . DLB-167

Sowande, Bode 1948- DLB-157

Sowle, Tace
[publishing house] DLB-170

Soyfer, Jura 1912-1939. . . . . DLB-124

Soyinka, Wole 1934- . . . DLB-125; Y-86, Y-87

Spacks, Barry 1931- DLB-105

Spalding, Frances 1950- DLB-155

Spark, Muriel 1918- DLB-15, 139

Sparke, Michael
[publishing house] DLB-170

Sparks, Jared 1789-1866 . . . . . . DLB-1, 30

Sparshott, Francis 1926- DLB-60

Späth, Gerold 1939- DLB-75

Spatola, Adriano 1941-1988 . . . . . . DLB-128

Spaziani, Maria Luisa 1924- DLB-128

The Spectator 1828- DLB-110

Spedding, James 1808-1881 . . . . . . DLB-144

Spee von Langenfeld, Friedrich
1591-1635 . . . . DLB-164

Speght, Rachel 1597-after 1630 . . . . DLB-126

Speke, John Hanning 1827-1864 . . . . DLB-166

Spellman, A. B. 1935- DLB-41

Spence, Thomas 1750-1814 . . . . . . DLB-158

Spencer, Anne 1882-1975. . . . . . DLB-51, 54

Spencer, Elizabeth 1921- DLB-6

Spencer, George John, Second Earl Spencer
1758-1834 . . . . DLB-184

Spencer, Herbert 1820-1903 . . . . . DLB-57

Spencer, Scott 1945- Y-86

Spender, J. A. 1862-1942 . . . . DLB-98

Spender, Stephen 1909-. DLB-20

Spener, Philipp Jakob 1635-1705 . . . . DLB-164

Spenser, Edmund circa 1552-1599 . . . DLB-167

Sperr, Martin 1944- DLB-124

Spicer, Jack 1925-1965 . . . . . DLB-5, 16, 193

Spielberg, Peter 1929- Y-81

Spielhagen, Friedrich 1829-1911. . . . DLB-129

"Spielmannsepen"
(circa 1152-circa 1500) DLB-148

Spier, Peter 1927- DLB-61

Spinrad, Norman 1940- DLB-8

Spires, Elizabeth 1952- DLB-120

Spitteler, Carl 1845-1924. . . . . . . DLB-129

Spivak, Lawrence E. 1900- DLB-137

Spofford, Harriet Prescott
1835-1921 . . . . DLB-74

Spring, Howard 1889-1965 . . . . . . DLB-191

Squier, E. G. 1821-1888. . . . . . . DLB-189

Squibob (see Derby, George Horatio)

Stacpoole, H. de Vere
1863-1951 . . . . DLB-153

Staël, Germaine de 1766-1817. . . DLB-119, 192

Staël-Holstein, Anne-Louise Germaine de
(see Staël, Germaine de)

Stafford, Jean 1915-1979 . . . . . . DLB-2, 173

Stafford, William 1914- DLB-5

Stage Censorship: "The Rejected Statement"
(1911), by Bernard Shaw
[excerpts] DLB-10

Stallings, Laurence 1894-1968 . . . . DLB-7, 44

Stallworthy, Jon 1935- DLB-40

Stampp, Kenneth M. 1912- DLB-17

Stanev, Emiliyan 1907-1979 . . . . . DLB-181

Stanford, Ann 1916- DLB-5

Stankevich, Nikolai Vladimirovich
1813-1840 . . . . DLB-198

Stanković, Borisav ("Bora")
1876-1927 . . . . DLB-147

Stanley, Henry M. 1841-1904 . DLB-189; DS-13

Stanley, Thomas 1625-1678 . . . . . DLB-131

Stannard, Martin 1947- DLB-155

Stansby, William
[publishing house]. DLB-170

Stanton, Elizabeth Cady 1815-1902 . . DLB-79

Stanton, Frank L. 1857-1927 . . . . . DLB-25

Stanton, Maura 1946- DLB-120

Stapledon, Olaf 1886-1950 . . . . . DLB-15

Star Spangled Banner Office DLB-49

Stark, Freya 1893-1993 . . . . . . DLB-195

Starkey, Thomas circa 1499-1538. . . . DLB-132

Starkie, Walter 1894-1976. . . . . . DLB-195

Starkweather, David 1935- DLB-7

Starrett, Vincent 1886-1974 . . . . . DLB-187

Statements on the Art of Poetry. . . . DLB-54

The State of Publishing Y-97

Stationers' Company of
London, The DLB-170

Stead, Robert J. C. 1880-1959 . . . . . DLB-92

Steadman, Mark 1930- DLB-6

The Stealthy School of Criticism (1871), by
Dante Gabriel Rossetti DLB-35

Stearns, Harold E. 1891-1943 . . . . . DLB-4

Stedman, Edmund Clarence
1833-1908 . . . . DLB-64

Steegmuller, Francis 1906-1994 . . . . DLB-111

Steel, Flora Annie 1847-1929 . . . DLB-153, 156

Steele, Max 1922- Y-80

Steele, Richard 1672-1729. . . . . DLB-84, 101

Steele, Timothy 1948- DLB-120

Steele, Wilbur Daniel 1886-1970 . . . . DLB-86

Steere, Richard circa 1643-1721 . . . . DLB-24

Stefanovski, Goran 1952- DLB-181

Stegner, Wallace 1909-1993 . . . . DLB-9; Y-93

Stehr, Hermann 1864-1940 . . . . . DLB-66

Steig, William 1907- DLB-61

Stein, Gertrude
1874-1946 . . . . . . DLB-4, 54, 86; DS-15

Stein, Leo 1872-1947. . . . . DLB-4

Stein and Day Publishers. DLB-46

Steinbeck, John 1902-1968 . . . . DLB-7, 9; DS-2

Steiner, George 1929- DLB-67

Steinhoewel, Heinrich
1411/1412-1479 . . . . DLB-179

Steloff, Ida Frances 1887-1989 . . . . DLB-187

Stendhal 1783-1842 . . . . DLB-119

Stephen Crane: A Revaluation Virginia
Tech Conference, 1989 . . . . Y-89

Stephen, Leslie 1832-1904. . . DLB-57, 144, 190

Stephen Vincent Benét Centenary. Y-97

Stephens, Alexander H. 1812-1883. . . . DLB-47

Stephens, Alice Barber 1858-1932. . . . DLB-188

Stephens, Ann 1810-1886 . . . . . DLB-3, 73

Stephens, Charles Asbury
1844?-1931 . . . . DLB-42

Stephens, James
   1882?-1950. . . . . DLB-19, 153, 162

Stephens, John Lloyd 1805-1852 . . . . DLB-183

Sterling, George 1869-1926 . . . . DLB-54

Sterling, James 1701-1763. . . . . DLB-24

Sterling, John 1806-1844. . . . . DLB-116

Stern, Gerald 1925- DLB-105

Stern, Gladys B. 1890-1973 . . . . . . DLB-197

Stern, Madeleine B. 1912- DLB-111, 140

Stern, Richard 1928- Y-87

Stern, Stewart 1922- DLB-26

Sterne, Laurence 1713-1768. . . . . . . DLB-39

Sternheim, Carl 1878-1942 . . . . DLB-56, 118

Sternhold, Thomas ?-1549 and
   John Hopkins ?-1570 . . . . DLB-132

Stevens, Henry 1819-1886. . . . . . . DLB-140

Stevens, Wallace 1879-1955. . . . . . . DLB-54

Stevenson, Anne 1933- DLB-40

Stevenson, D. E. 1892-1973. . . . . . DLB-191

Stevenson, Lionel 1902-1973 . . . . . DLB-155

Stevenson, Robert Louis 1850-1894
   . . . . DLB-18, 57, 141, 156, 174; DS-13

Stewart, Donald Ogden
   1894-1980 . . . . DLB-4, 11, 26

Stewart, Dugald 1753-1828 . . . . DLB-31

Stewart, George, Jr. 1848-1906 . . . . . DLB-99

Stewart, George R. 1895-1980 . . . . . . DLB-8

Stewart and Kidd Company DLB-46

Stewart, Randall 1896-1964 . . . . . . DLB-103

Stickney, Trumbull 1874-1904 . . . . . DLB-54

Stieler, Caspar 1632-1707 . . . . DLB-164

Stifter, Adalbert 1805-1868 . . . . . . DLB-133

Stiles, Ezra 1727-1795. . . . . DLB-31

Still, James 1906- DLB-9

Stirner, Max 1806-1856 . . . . DLB-129

Stith, William 1707-1755 . . . . DLB-31

Stock, Elliot [publishing house] DLB-106

Stockton, Frank R.
   1834-1902. . . . . DLB-42, 74; DS-13

Stoddard, Ashbel
   [publishing house]. DLB-49

Stoddard, Charles Warren
   1843-1909 . . . . DLB-186

Stoddard, Richard Henry
   1825-1903 . . . . DLB-3, 64; DS-13

Stoddard, Solomon 1643-1729 . . . . . DLB-24

Stoker, Bram 1847-1912 . . . . DLB-36, 70, 178

Stokes, Frederick A., Company DLB-49

Stokes, Thomas L. 1898-1958 . . . . . . DLB-29

Stokesbury, Leon 1945- DLB-120

Stolberg, Christian Graf zu
   1748-1821 . . . . DLB-94

Stolberg, Friedrich Leopold Graf zu
   1750-1819 . . . . DLB-94

Stone, Herbert S., and Company DLB-49

Stone, Lucy 1818-1893 . . . . DLB-79

Stone, Melville 1848-1929. . . . . DLB-25

Stone, Robert 1937- DLB-152

Stone, Ruth 1915- DLB-105

Stone, Samuel 1602-1663 . . . . DLB-24

Stone and Kimball DLB-49

Stoppard, Tom 1937- DLB-13; Y-85

Storey, Anthony 1928- DLB-14

Storey, David 1933- DLB-13, 14

Storm, Theodor 1817-1888 . . . . . . DLB-129

Story, Thomas circa 1670-1742 . . . . . DLB-31

Story, William Wetmore 1819-1895. . . . DLB-1

Storytelling: A Contemporary
   Renaissance. Y-84

Stoughton, William 1631-1701 . . . . . DLB-24

Stow, John 1525-1605 . . . . DLB-132

Stowe, Harriet Beecher
   1811-1896 . . . . . DLB-1, 12, 42, 74, 189

Stowe, Leland 1899- DLB-29

Stoyanov, Dimitŭr Ivanov (see Elin Pelin)

Strabo 64 or 63 B.C.-circa A.D. 25
   . . . . DLB-176

Strachey, Lytton
   1880-1932 . . . . DLB-149; DS-10

Strachey, Lytton, Preface to Eminent
   Victorians DLB-149

Strahan and Company DLB-106

Strahan, William
   [publishing house] DLB-154

Strand, Mark 1934- DLB-5

The Strasbourg Oaths 842 . . . . . . DLB-148

Stratemeyer, Edward 1862-1930 . . . . DLB-42

Strati, Saverio 1924- DLB-177

Stratton and Barnard DLB-49

Stratton-Porter, Gene 1863-1924 . . . . . DS-14

Straub, Peter 1943- Y-84

Strauß, Botho 1944- DLB-124

Strauß, David Friedrich
   1808-1874 . . . . DLB-133

The Strawberry Hill Press DLB-154

Streatfeild, Noel 1895-1986 . . . . . . DLB-160

Street, Cecil John Charles (see Rhode, John)

Street, G. S. 1867-1936 . . . . DLB-135

Street and Smith DLB-49

Streeter, Edward 1891-1976. . . . . . . DLB-11

Streeter, Thomas Winthrop
   1883-1965 . . . . DLB-140

Stretton, Hesba 1832-1911 . . . . . DLB-163, 190

Stribling, T. S. 1881-1965 . . . . DLB-9

Der Stricker circa 1190-circa 1250 . . . DLB-138

Strickland, Samuel 1804-1867. . . . . . DLB-99

Stringer and Townsend. DLB-49

Stringer, Arthur 1874-1950 . . . . DLB-92

Strittmatter, Erwin 1912- DLB-69

Strniša, Gregor 1930-1987 . . . . DLB-181

Strode, William 1630-1645 . . . . . . DLB-126

Strong, L. A. G. 1896-1958. . . . . . . DLB-191

Strother, David Hunter 1816-1888 . . . . DLB-3

Strouse, Jean 1945- DLB-111

Stuart, Dabney 1937- DLB-105

Stuart, Jesse
   1906-1984 . . . . . . DLB-9, 48, 102; Y-84

Stuart, Lyle [publishing house] DLB-46

Stubbs, Harry Clement (see Clement, Hal)

Stubenberg, Johann Wilhelm von
   1619-1663 . . . . DLB-164

Studio. DLB-112

The Study of Poetry (1880), by
   Matthew Arnold DLB-35

Sturgeon, Theodore
   1918-1985 . . . . DLB-8; Y-85

Sturges, Preston 1898-1959 . . . . DLB-26

"Style" (1840; revised, 1859), by
   Thomas de Quincey [excerpt] DLB-57

"Style" (1888), by Walter Pater DLB-57

Style (1897), by Walter Raleigh
   [excerpt] DLB-57

"Style" (1877), by T. H. Wright
   [excerpt] DLB-57

"Le Style c'est l'homme" (1892), by
   W. H. Mallock. DLB-57

Styron, William 1925- DLB-2, 143; Y-80

Suárez, Mario 1925- DLB-82

Such, Peter 1939- DLB-60

Suckling, Sir John 1609-1641? . . . DLB-58, 126

Suckow, Ruth 1892-1960. . . . . . . DLB-9, 102

Sudermann, Hermann 1857-1928 . . . . DLB-118

Sue, Eugène 1804-1857 . . . . DLB-119

Sue, Marie-Joseph (see Sue, Eugène)

Suggs, Simon (see Hooper, Johnson Jones)

Sukenick, Ronald 1932- DLB-173; Y-81

Suknaski, Andrew 1942- DLB-53

Sullivan, Alan 1868-1947 . . . . DLB-92

Sullivan, C. Gardner 1886-1965 . . . . . DLB-26

Sullivan, Frank 1892-1976 . . . . DLB-11

Sulte, Benjamin 1841-1923 . . . . DLB-99

Sulzberger, Arthur Hays
   1891-1968 . . . . DLB-127

Sulzberger, Arthur Ochs 1926- DLB-127

Sulzer, Johann Georg 1720-1779 . . . . DLB-97

Sumarokov, Aleksandr Petrovich
   1717-1777 . . . . DLB-150

Summers, Hollis 1916- DLB-6

Sumner, Henry A.
[publishing house]. DLB-49

Surtees, Robert Smith 1803-1864. . . . . DLB-21

Surveys: Japanese Literature,
1987-1995 . . . . DLB-182

A Survey of Poetry Anthologies,
1879-1960 . . . . DLB-54

Surveys of the Year's Biographies

A Transit of Poets and Others: American
Biography in 1982 . . . . Y-82

The Year in Literary Biography . . . Y-83–Y-96

Survey of the Year's Book Publishing

The Year in Book Publishing Y-86

Survey of the Year's Children's Books

The Year in Children's Books
. . . . Y-92–Y-96

Surveys of the Year's Drama

The Year in Drama
. . . . Y-82–Y-85, Y-87–Y-96

The Year in London Theatre Y-92

Surveys of the Year's Fiction

The Year's Work in Fiction:
A Survey Y-82

The Year in Fiction: A Biased View Y-83

The Year in
Fiction. Y-84–Y-86, Y-89, Y-94–Y-96

The Year in the
Novel Y-87, Y-88, Y-90–Y-93

The Year in Short Stories Y-87

The Year in the
Short Story Y-88, Y-90–Y-93

Survey of the Year's Literary Theory

The Year in Literary Theory Y-92–Y-93

Surveys of the Year's Poetry

The Year's Work in American
Poetry. Y-82

The Year in Poetry Y-83–Y-92, Y-94–Y-96

Sutherland, Efua Theodora
1924- DLB-117

Sutherland, John 1919-1956. . . . . . . DLB-68

Sutro, Alfred 1863-1933. . . . . DLB-10

Swados, Harvey 1920-1972 . . . . DLB-2

Swain, Charles 1801-1874 . . . . DLB-32

Swallow Press DLB-46

Swan Sonnenschein Limited. DLB-106

Swanberg, W. A. 1907- DLB-103

Swenson, May 1919-1989 . . . . DLB-5

Swerling, Jo 1897- DLB-44

Swift, Graham 1949- DLB-194

Swift, Jonathan 1667-1745 . . . DLB-39, 95, 101

Swinburne, A. C. 1837-1909. . . . . DLB-35, 57

Swineshead, Richard floruit
circa 1350 . . . . DLB-115

Swinnerton, Frank 1884-1982. . . . . . DLB-34

Swisshelm, Jane Grey 1815-1884. . . . DLB-43

Swope, Herbert Bayard 1882-1958. . . . DLB-25

Swords, T. and J., and Company DLB-49

Swords, Thomas 1763-1843 and
Swords, James ?-1844 . . . . DLB-73

Sykes, Ella C. ?-1939 . . . . DLB-174

Sylvester, Josuah
1562 or 1563 - 1618 . . . . DLB-121

Symonds, Emily Morse (see Paston, George)

Symonds, John Addington
1840-1893 . . . . DLB-57, 144

Symons, A. J. A. 1900-1941 . . . . . DLB-149

Symons, Arthur 1865-1945. . . DLB-19, 57, 149

Symons, Julian 1912-1994 . . DLB-87, 155; Y-92

Symons, Scott 1933- DLB-53

A Symposium on *The Columbia History of
the Novel*. Y-92

Synge, John Millington
1871-1909. . . . . DLB-10, 19

Synge Summer School: J. M. Synge and the Irish
Theater, Rathdrum, County Wiclow, Ireland
. . . . Y-93

Syrett, Netta 1865-1943 . . . . . DLB-135, 197

Szymborska, Wisława 1923- Y-96

T

Taban lo Liyong 1939?- DLB-125

Tabucchi, Antonio 1943- DLB-196

Taché, Joseph-Charles 1820-1894. . . . DLB-99

Tachihara, Masaaki 1926-1980 . . . . DLB-182

Tadijanović, Dragutin 1905- DLB-181

Tafolla, Carmen 1951- DLB-82

Taggard, Genevieve 1894-1948. . . . . DLB-45

Taggart, John 1942- DLB-193

Tagger, Theodor (see Bruckner, Ferdinand)

Tait, J. Selwin, and Sons DLB-49

Tait's Edinburgh Magazine
1832-1861 . . . . DLB-110

The Takarazaka Revue Company Y-91

Talander (see Bohse, August)

Talese, Gay 1932- DLB-185

Talev, Dimitŭr 1898-1966. . . . . . . DLB-181

Tallent, Elizabeth 1954- DLB-130

TallMountain, Mary 1918-1994 . . . . DLB-193

Talvj 1797-1870 . . . . DLB-59, 133

Tan, Amy 1952- DLB-173

Tanizaki, Jun'ichirō 1886-1965 . . . . DLB-180

Tapahonso, Luci 1953- DLB-175

Taradash, Daniel 1913- DLB-44

Tarbell, Ida M. 1857-1944 . . . . . . DLB-47

Tardivel, Jules-Paul 1851-1905 . . . . DLB-99

Targan, Barry 1932- DLB-130

Tarkington, Booth 1869-1946 . . . . DLB-9, 102

Tashlin, Frank 1913-1972. . . . . . . DLB-44

Tate, Allen 1899-1979 . . DLB-4, 45, 63; DS-17

Tate, James 1943- DLB-5, 169

Tate, Nahum circa 1652-1715 . . . . . DLB-80

Tatian circa 830 . . . . DLB-148

Taufer, Veno 1933- DLB-181

Tauler, Johannes circa 1300-1361. . . . DLB-179

Tavčar, Ivan 1851-1923 . . . . DLB-147

Taylor, Ann 1782-1866 . . . . DLB-163

Taylor, Bayard 1825-1878 . . . . . DLB-3, 189

Taylor, Bert Leston 1866-1921. . . . . DLB-25

Taylor, Charles H. 1846-1921 . . . . . DLB-25

Taylor, Edward circa 1642-1729 . . . . DLB-24

Taylor, Elizabeth 1912-1975. . . . . . DLB-139

Taylor, Henry 1942- DLB-5

Taylor, Sir Henry 1800-1886. . . . . . DLB-32

Taylor, Jane 1783-1824 . . . . DLB-163

Taylor, Jeremy circa 1613-1667. . . . . DLB-151

Taylor, John 1577 or 1578 - 1653. . . DLB-121

Taylor, Mildred D. ?- DLB-52

Taylor, Peter 1917-1994. . . . . . . Y-81, Y-94

Taylor, William, and Company DLB-49

Taylor-Made Shakespeare? Or Is
"Shall I Die?" the Long-Lost Text
of Bottom's Dream? Y-85

Teasdale, Sara 1884-1933. . . . . . . DLB-45

The Tea-Table (1725), by Eliza Haywood [excerpt]
DLB-39

Telles, Lygia Fagundes 1924- DLB-113

Temple, Sir William 1628-1699. . . . . DLB-101

Tenn, William 1919- DLB-8

Tennant, Emma 1937- DLB-14

Tenney, Tabitha Gilman
1762-1837 . . . . DLB-37, 200

Tennyson, Alfred 1809-1892 . . . . . . DLB-32

Tennyson, Frederick 1807-1898 . . . . . DLB-32

Terhune, Albert Payson 1872-1942 . . . . DLB-9

Terhune, Mary Virginia
1830-1922 . . . . DS-13, DS-16

Terry, Megan 1932- DLB-7

Terson, Peter 1932- DLB-13

Tesich, Steve 1943- Y-83

Tessa, Delio 1886-1939 . . . . DLB-114

Testori, Giovanni 1923-1993 . . . DLB-128, 177

Tey, Josephine 1896?-1952 . . . . . . DLB-77

Thacher, James 1754-1844 . . . . . . DLB-37

Thackeray, William Makepeace
1811-1863 . . . . . . DLB-21, 55, 159, 163

Thames and Hudson Limited. DLB-112

Thanet, Octave (see French, Alice)

Thatcher, John Boyd 1847-1909 . . . . DLB-187

Thayer, Caroline Matilda Warren
    1785-1844 . . . . DLB-200

The Theater in Shakespeare's Time . . . DLB-62

The Theatre Guild. DLB-7

Thegan and the Astronomer
    flourished circa 850 . . . . DLB-148

Thelwall, John 1764-1834. . . . . DLB-93, 158

Theocritus circa 300 B.C.-260 B.C.
    . . . . DLB-176

Theodulf circa 760-circa 821 . . . . . . DLB-148

Theophrastus circa 371 B.C.-287 B.C.
    . . . . DLB-176

Theriault, Yves 1915-1983 . . . . DLB-88

Thério, Adrien 1925- DLB-53

Theroux, Paul 1941- DLB-2

They All Came to Paris DS-16

Thibaudeau, Colleen 1925- DLB-88

Thielen, Benedict 1903-1965. . . . . . DLB-102

Thiong'o Ngugi wa (see Ngugi wa Thiong'o)

Third-Generation Minor Poets of the
    Seventeenth Century DLB-131

This Quarter 1925-1927, 1929-1932 . . . . DS-15

Thoma, Ludwig 1867-1921. . . . . . . DLB-66

Thoma, Richard 1902- DLB-4

Thomas, Audrey 1935- DLB-60

Thomas, D. M. 1935- DLB-40

Thomas, Dylan
    1914-1953 . . . . DLB-13, 20, 139

Thomas, Edward
    1878-1917 . . . . DLB-19, 98, 156

Thomas, Gwyn 1913-1981 . . . . DLB-15

Thomas, Isaiah 1750-1831 . . . DLB-43, 73, 187

Thomas, Isaiah [publishing house]. . . . DLB-49

Thomas, Johann 1624-1679 . . . . . . DLB-168

Thomas, John 1900-1932 . . . . DLB-4

Thomas, Joyce Carol 1938- DLB-33

Thomas, Lorenzo 1944- DLB-41

Thomas, R. S. 1915- DLB-27

The Thomas Wolfe Collection at the University of
    North Carolina at Chapel Hill Y-97

The Thomas Wolfe Society Y-97

Thomasîn von Zerclære
    circa 1186-circa 1259 . . . . DLB-138

Thomasius, Christian 1655-1728 . . . . DLB-168

Thompson, David 1770-1857. . . . . . DLB-99

Thompson, Dorothy 1893-1961 . . . . DLB-29

Thompson, Francis 1859-1907 . . . . . DLB-19

Thompson, George Selden (see Selden, George)

Thompson, Henry Yates 1838-1928 . . DLB-184

Thompson, Hunter S. 1939- DLB-185

Thompson, John 1938-1976 . . . . . . DLB-60

Thompson, John R. 1823-1873 . . . . DLB-3, 73

Thompson, Lawrance 1906-1973 . . . . DLB-103

Thompson, Maurice 1844-1901 . . . DLB-71, 74

Thompson, Ruth Plumly
    1891-1976 . . . . DLB-22

Thompson, Thomas Phillips
    1843-1933 . . . . DLB-99

Thompson, William 1775-1833 . . . . . DLB-158

Thompson, William Tappan
    1812-1882 . . . . DLB-3, 11

Thomson, Edward William
    1849-1924 . . . . DLB-92

Thomson, James 1700-1748 . . . . . . DLB-95

Thomson, James 1834-1882 . . . . . . DLB-35

Thomson, Joseph 1858-1895 . . . . . . DLB-174

Thomson, Mortimer 1831-1875 . . . . DLB-11

Thoreau, Henry David
    1817-1862. . . . . DLB-1, 183

Thornton Wilder Centenary at Yale Y-97

Thorpe, Thomas Bangs
    1815-1878 . . . . DLB-3, 11

Thoughts on Poetry and Its Varieties (1833),
    by John Stuart Mill DLB-32

Thrale, Hester Lynch (see Piozzi, Hester
    Lynch [Thrale])

Thucydides circa 455 B.C.-circa 395 B.C.
    . . . . DLB-176

Thulstrup, Thure de 1848-1930 . . . . DLB-188

Thümmel, Moritz August von
    1738-1817 . . . . DLB-97

Thurber, James
    1894-1961 . . . . DLB-4, 11, 22, 102

Thurman, Wallace 1902-1934 . . . . . DLB-51

Thwaite, Anthony 1930- DLB-40

Thwaites, Reuben Gold
    1853-1913 . . . . DLB-47

Ticknor, George
    1791-1871. . . . . DLB-1, 59, 140

Ticknor and Fields DLB-49

Ticknor and Fields (revived) DLB-46

Tieck, Ludwig 1773-1853 . . . . DLB-90

Tietjens, Eunice 1884-1944 . . . . . . DLB-54

Tilney, Edmund circa 1536-1610 . . . . DLB-136

Tilt, Charles [publishing house]. DLB-106

Tilton, J. E., and Company DLB-49

Time and Western Man (1927), by Wyndham
    Lewis [excerpts]. DLB-36

Time-Life Books. DLB-46

Times Books DLB-46

Timothy, Peter circa 1725-1782 . . . . DLB-43

Timrod, Henry 1828-1867 . . . . DLB-3

Tindal, Henrietta 1818?-1879 . . . . . DLB-199

Tinker, Chauncey Brewster
    1876-1963 . . . . DLB-140

Tinsley Brothers DLB-106

Tiptree, James, Jr. 1915-1987 . . . . . DLB-8

Tišma, Aleksandar 1924- DLB-181

Titus, Edward William
    1870-1952 . . . . DLB-4; DS-15

Tlali, Miriam 1933- DLB-157

Todd, Barbara Euphan
    1890-1976 . . . . DLB-160

Tofte, Robert
    1561 or 1562-1619 or 1620 . . . . DLB-172

Toklas, Alice B. 1877-1967 . . . . DLB-4

Tokuda, Shūsei 1872-1943 . . . . . . DLB-180

Tolkien, J. R. R. 1892-1973 . . . . DLB-15, 160

Toller, Ernst 1893-1939 . . . . DLB-124

Tollet, Elizabeth 1694-1754 . . . . DLB-95

Tolson, Melvin B. 1898-1966 . . . . DLB-48, 76

Tom Jones (1749), by Henry Fielding
    [excerpt] DLB-39

Tomalin, Claire 1933- DLB-155

Tomasi di Lampedusa,
    Giuseppe 1896-1957 . . . . DLB-177

Tomlinson, Charles 1927- DLB-40

Tomlinson, H. M. 1873-1958
    . . . . DLB-36, 100, 195

Tompkins, Abel [publishing house] . . . DLB-49

Tompson, Benjamin 1642-1714. . . . . DLB-24

Tondelli, Pier Vittorio 1955-1991 . . . . DLB-196

Tonks, Rosemary 1932- DLB-14

Tonna, Charlotte Elizabeth
    1790-1846 . . . . DLB-163

Tonson, Jacob the Elder
    [publishing house] DLB-170

Toole, John Kennedy 1937-1969 . . . . . Y-81

Toomer, Jean 1894-1967 . . . . . . DLB-45, 51

Tor Books DLB-46

Torberg, Friedrich 1908-1979. . . . . . DLB-85

Torrence, Ridgely 1874-1950 . . . . . . DLB-54

Torres-Metzger, Joseph V.
    1933- DLB-122

Toth, Susan Allen 1940- Y-86

Tottell, Richard
    [publishing house] DLB-170

Tough-Guy Literature DLB-9

Touré, Askia Muhammad 1938- DLB-41

Tourgée, Albion W. 1838-1905 . . . . . DLB-79

Tourneur, Cyril circa 1580-1626 . . . . . DLB-58

Tournier, Michel 1924- DLB-83

Tousey, Frank [publishing house] DLB-49

Tower Publications DLB-46

Towne, Benjamin circa 1740-1793 . . . . DLB-43

Towne, Robert 1936- DLB-44

The Townely Plays
    fifteenth and sixteenth
    centuries DLB-146

Townshend, Aurelian
    by 1583 - circa 1651 . . . . DLB-121

Tracy, Honor 1913- DLB-15

Traherne, Thomas 1637?-1674 . . . . . DLB-131

Traill, Catharine Parr 1802-1899. . . . . DLB-99

Train, Arthur 1875-1945 . . . . . DLB-86; DS-16

The Transatlantic Publishing
  Company DLB-49

The Transatlantic Review 1924-1925 . . . . . DS-15

Transcendentalists, American. DS-5

transition 1927-1938. . . . . DS-15

Translators of the Twelfth Century:
  Literary Issues Raised and Impact
  Created. DLB-115

Travel Writing, 1837-1875 . . . . . . DLB-166

Travel Writing, 1876-1909 . . . . . . DLB-174

Traven, B.
  1882? or 1890?-1969? DLB-9, 56

Travers, Ben 1886-1980 . . . . DLB-10

Travers, P. L. (Pamela Lyndon)
  1899- DLB-160

Trediakovsky, Vasilii Kirillovich
  1703-1769 . . . . DLB-150

Treece, Henry 1911-1966 . . . . DLB-160

Trejo, Ernesto 1950- DLB-122

Trelawny, Edward John
  1792-1881. . . . . DLB-110, 116, 144

Tremain, Rose 1943- DLB-14

Tremblay, Michel 1942- DLB-60

Trends in Twentieth-Century
  Mass Market Publishing DLB-46

Trent, William P. 1862-1939 . . . . . . DLB-47

Trescot, William Henry
  1822-1898 . . . . DLB-30

Tressell, Robert (Robert Phillipe Noonan)
  1870-1911 . . . . DLB-197

Trevelyan, Sir George Otto
  1838-1928 . . . . DLB-144

Trevisa, John
  circa 1342-circa 1402 . . . . DLB-146

Trevor, William 1928- DLB-14, 139

Trierer Floyris circa 1170-1180 . . . . . DLB-138

Trillin, Calvin 1935- DLB-185

Trilling, Lionel 1905-1975 . . . . . DLB-28, 63

Trilussa 1871-1950. . . . . DLB-114

Trimmer, Sarah 1741-1810 . . . . . . DLB-158

Triolet, Elsa 1896-1970 . . . . DLB-72

Tripp, John 1927- DLB-40

Trocchi, Alexander 1925- DLB-15

Troisi, Dante 1920-1989 . . . . DLB-196

Trollope, Anthony
  1815-1882 . . . . DLB-21, 57, 159

Trollope, Frances 1779-1863 . . . . DLB-21, 166

Troop, Elizabeth 1931- DLB-14

Trotter, Catharine 1679-1749 . . . . . . DLB-84

Trotti, Lamar 1898-1952 . . . . DLB-44

Trottier, Pierre 1925- DLB-60

Troupe, Quincy Thomas, Jr. 1943- . . DLB-41

Trow, John F., and Company DLB-49

Truillier-Lacombe, Joseph-Patrice
  1807-1863 . . . . DLB-99

Trumbo, Dalton 1905-1976. . . . . . . DLB-26

Trumbull, Benjamin 1735-1820. . . . . DLB-30

Trumbull, John 1750-1831 . . . . DLB-31

Trumbull, John 1756-1843 . . . . DLB-183

Tscherning, Andreas 1611-1659 . . . . . DLB-164

T. S. Eliot Centennial Y-88

Tsubouchi, Shōyō 1859-1935 . . . . . DLB-180

Tucholsky, Kurt 1890-1935. . . . . . . DLB-56

Tucker, Charlotte Maria
  1821-1893. . . . . DLB-163, 190

Tucker, George 1775-1861 . . . . . DLB-3, 30

Tucker, Nathaniel Beverley
  1784-1851. . . . . DLB-3

Tucker, St. George 1752-1827 . . . . . DLB-37

Tuckerman, Henry Theodore
  1813-1871 . . . . DLB-64

Tunis, John R. 1889-1975 . . . . . DLB-22, 171

Tunstall, Cuthbert 1474-1559 . . . . . DLB-132

Tuohy, Frank 1925- DLB-14, 139

Tupper, Martin F. 1810-1889 . . . . . DLB-32

Turbyfill, Mark 1896- DLB-45

Turco, Lewis 1934- Y-84

Turgenev, Aleksandr Ivanovich
  1784-1845 . . . . DLB-198

Turnball, Alexander H. 1868-1918 . . . DLB-184

Turnbull, Andrew 1921-1970 . . . . . DLB-103

Turnbull, Gael 1928- DLB-40

Turner, Arlin 1909-1980. . . . . DLB-103

Turner, Charles (Tennyson)
  1808-1879 . . . . DLB-32

Turner, Frederick 1943- DLB-40

Turner, Frederick Jackson
  1861-1932 . . . . DLB-17, 186

Turner, Joseph Addison
  1826-1868 . . . . DLB-79

Turpin, Waters Edward
  1910-1968 . . . . DLB-51

Turrini, Peter 1944- DLB-124

Tutuola, Amos 1920- DLB-125

Twain, Mark (see Clemens, Samuel Langhorne)

Tweedie, Ethel Brilliana
  circa 1860-1940 . . . . DLB-174

The 'Twenties and Berlin, by
  Alex Natan DLB-66

Tyler, Anne 1941- DLB-6, 143; Y-82

Tyler, Mary Palmer 1775-1866 . . . . . DLB-200

Tyler, Moses Coit 1835-1900 . . . . DLB-47, 64

Tyler, Royall 1757-1826 . . . . DLB-37

Tylor, Edward Burnett 1832-1917 . . . . DLB-57

Tynan, Katharine 1861-1931 . . . . . DLB-153

Tyndale, William
  circa 1494-1536 . . . . DLB-132

U

Udall, Nicholas 1504-1556 . . . . DLB-62

Ugrěsić, Dubravka 1949- DLB-181

Uhland, Ludwig 1787-1862 . . . . . . DLB-90

Uhse, Bodo 1904-1963 . . . . DLB-69

Ujević, Augustin ("Tin")
  1891-1955 . . . . DLB-147

Ulenhart, Niclas
  flourished circa 1600 . . . . DLB-164

Ulibarrí, Sabine R. 1919- DLB-82

Ulica, Jorge 1870-1926 . . . . DLB-82

Ulivi, Ferruccio 1912- DLB-196

Ulizio, B. George 1889-1969 . . . . . DLB-140

Ulrich von Liechtenstein
  circa 1200-circa 1275 . . . . DLB-138

Ulrich von Zatzikhoven
  before 1194-after 1214 . . . . DLB-138

Ulysses, Reader's Edition Y-97

Unamuno, Miguel de 1864-1936 . . . . DLB-108

Under the Microscope (1872), by
  A. C. Swinburne DLB-35

Unger, Friederike Helene
  1741-1813 . . . . DLB-94

Ungaretti, Giuseppe 1888-1970 . . . . . DLB-114

United States Book Company DLB-49

Universal Publishing and Distributing
  Corporation DLB-46

The University of Iowa Writers'
  Workshop Golden Jubilee Y-86

The University of South Carolina
  Press Y-94

University of Wales Press. DLB-112

"The Unknown Public" (1858), by
  Wilkie Collins [excerpt] DLB-57

Uno, Chiyo 1897-1996 . . . . DLB-180

Unruh, Fritz von 1885-1970 . . . . DLB-56, 118

Unspeakable Practices II: The Festival of
  Vanguard Narrative at Brown
  University. Y-93

Unsworth, Barry 1930- DLB-194

Unwin, T. Fisher
  [publishing house] DLB-106

Upchurch, Boyd B. (see Boyd, John)

Updike, John
  1932- . . . DLB-2, 5, 143; Y-80, Y-82; DS-3

Upton, Bertha 1849-1912 . . . . DLB-141

Upton, Charles 1948- DLB-16

Upton, Florence K. 1873-1922 . . . . . DLB-141

Upward, Allen 1863-1926. . . . . DLB-36

Urista, Alberto Baltazar (see Alurista)

Urzidil, Johannes 1896-1976 . . . . . . DLB-85

Urquhart, Fred 1912- DLB-139

The Uses of Facsimile Y-90

Usk, Thomas died 1388 . . . . DLB-146

Uslar Pietri, Arturo 1906- DLB-113

Ustinov, Peter 1921- DLB-13

Uttley, Alison 1884-1976 . . . . DLB-160

Uz, Johann Peter 1720-1796 . . . . . . DLB-97

V

Vac, Bertrand 1914- DLB-88

Vail, Laurence 1891-1968 . . . . DLB-4

Vailland, Roger 1907-1965 . . . . DLB-83

Vajda, Ernest 1887-1954 . . . . DLB-44

Valdés, Gina 1943- DLB-122

Valdez, Luis Miguel 1940- DLB-122

Valduga, Patrizia 1953- DLB-128

Valente, José Angel 1929- DLB-108

Valenzuela, Luisa 1938- DLB-113

Valeri, Diego 1887-1976 . . . . DLB-128

Valesio, Paolo 1939- DLB-196

Valgardson, W. D. 1939- DLB-60

Valle, Víctor Manuel 1950- DLB-122

Valle-Inclán, Ramón del 1866-1936 . . . . DLB-134

Vallejo, Armando 1949- DLB-122

Vallès, Jules 1832-1885 . . . . DLB-123

Vallette, Marguerite Eymery (see Rachilde)

Valverde, José María 1926- DLB-108

Van Allsburg, Chris 1949- DLB-61

Van Anda, Carr 1864-1945 . . . . . . DLB-25

Van Dine, S. S. (see Wright, Williard Huntington)

Van Doren, Mark 1894-1972 . . . . . DLB-45

van Druten, John 1901-1957 . . . . . . DLB-10

Van Duyn, Mona 1921- DLB-5

Van Dyke, Henry 1852-1933 . . . . DLB-71; DS-13

Van Dyke, John C. 1856-1932 . . . . DLB-186

Van Dyke, Henry 1928- DLB-33

van Gulik, Robert Hans 1910-1967 . . . . DS-17

van Itallie, Jean-Claude 1936- DLB-7

Van Loan, Charles E. 1876-1919 . . . . DLB-171

Van Rensselaer, Mariana Griswold 1851-1934 . . . . DLB-47

Van Rensselaer, Mrs. Schuyler (see Van Rensselaer, Mariana Griswold)

Van Vechten, Carl 1880-1964 . . . . . DLB-4, 9

van Vogt, A. E. 1912- DLB-8

Vanbrugh, Sir John 1664-1726 . . . . . DLB-80

Vance, Jack 1916?- DLB-8

Vane, Sutton 1888-1963 . . . . DLB-10

Vanguard Press DLB-46

Vann, Robert L. 1879-1940 . . . . . . DLB-29

Vargas, Llosa, Mario 1936- DLB-145

Varley, John 1947- Y-81

Varnhagen von Ense, Karl August 1785-1858 . . . . DLB-90

Varnhagen von Ense, Rahel 1771-1833 . . . . DLB-90

Vásquez Montalbán, Manuel 1939- DLB-134

Vassa, Gustavus (see Equiano, Olaudah)

Vassalli, Sebastiano 1941- DLB-128, 196

Vaughan, Henry 1621-1695 . . . . . . DLB-131

Vaughan, Thomas 1621-1666 . . . . . DLB-131

Vaux, Thomas, Lord 1509-1556 . . . . DLB-132

Vazov, Ivan 1850-1921 . . . . DLB-147

Vega, Janine Pommy 1942- DLB-16

Veiller, Anthony 1903-1965 . . . . . . DLB-44

Velásquez-Trevino, Gloria 1949- DLB-122

Veley, Margaret 1843-1887 . . . . . . DLB-199

Veloz Maggiolo, Marcio 1936- DLB-145

Vel'tman Aleksandr Fomich 1800-1870 . . . . DLB-198

Venegas, Daniel ?-? DLB-82

Vergil, Polydore circa 1470-1555 . . . . DLB-132

Veríssimo, Erico 1905-1975 . . . . . . DLB-145

Verne, Jules 1828-1905 . . . . DLB-123

Verplanck, Gulian C. 1786-1870 . . . . DLB-59

Very, Jones 1813-1880 . . . . DLB-1

Vian, Boris 1920-1959 . . . . DLB-72

Vickers, Roy 1888?-1965 . . . . DLB-77

Vickery, Sukey 1779-1821 . . . . DLB-200

Victoria 1819-1901 . . . . DLB-55

Victoria Press DLB-106

Vidal, Gore 1925- DLB-6, 152

Viebig, Clara 1860-1952 . . . . DLB-66

Viereck, George Sylvester 1884-1962 . . . . DLB-54

Viereck, Peter 1916- DLB-5

Viets, Roger 1738-1811 . . . . DLB-99

Viewpoint: Politics and Performance, by David Edgar DLB-13

Vigil-Piñon, Evangelina 1949- DLB-122

Vigneault, Gilles 1928- DLB-60

Vigny, Alfred de 1797-1863 . . . . DLB-119, 192

Vigolo, Giorgio 1894-1983 . . . . . . DLB-114

The Viking Press DLB-46

Villanueva, Alma Luz 1944- DLB-122

Villanueva, Tino 1941- DLB-82

Villard, Henry 1835-1900 . . . . DLB-23

Villard, Oswald Garrison 1872-1949 . . . . DLB-25, 91

Villarreal, José Antonio 1924- DLB-82

Villegas de Magnón, Leonor 1876-1955 . . . . DLB-122

Villemaire, Yolande 1949- DLB-60

Villena, Luis Antonio de 1951- DLB-134

Villiers de l'Isle-Adam, Jean-Marie Mathias Philippe-Auguste, Comte de 1838-1889 . . . . DLB-123, 192

Villiers, George, Second Duke of Buckingham 1628-1687 . . . . . DLB-80

Vine Press DLB-112

Viorst, Judith ?- DLB-52

Vipont, Elfrida (Elfrida Vipont Foulds, Charles Vipont) 1902-1992 . . . . DLB-160

Viramontes, Helena María 1954- DLB-122

Vischer, Friedrich Theodor 1807-1887 . . . . DLB-133

Vivanco, Luis Felipe 1907-1975 . . . . DLB-108

Viviani, Cesare 1947- DLB-128

Vizenor, Gerald 1934- DLB-175

Vizetelly and Company DLB-106

Voaden, Herman 1903- DLB-88

Voigt, Ellen Bryant 1943- DLB-120

Vojnović, Ivo 1857-1929 . . . . DLB-147

Volkoff, Vladimir 1932- DLB-83

Volland, P. F., Company DLB-46

Vollbehr, Otto H. F. 1872?-1945 or 1946 . . . . DLB-187

Volponi, Paolo 1924- DLB-177

von der Grün, Max 1926- DLB-75

Vonnegut, Kurt 1922- DLB-2, 8, 152; Y-80; DS-3

Voranc, Prežihov 1893-1950 . . . . . . DLB-147

Voß, Johann Heinrich 1751-1826 . . . . DLB-90

Voynich, E. L. 1864-1960 . . . . DLB-197

Vroman, Mary Elizabeth circa 1924-1967 . . . . DLB-33

W

Wace, Robert ("Maistre") circa 1100-circa 1175 . . . . DLB-146

Wackenroder, Wilhelm Heinrich 1773-1798 . . . . DLB-90

Wackernagel, Wilhelm 1806-1869 . . . . DLB-133

Waddington, Miriam 1917- DLB-68

Wade, Henry 1887-1969 . . . . DLB-77

Wagenknecht, Edward 1900- DLB-103

Wagner, Heinrich Leopold 1747-1779 . . . . DLB-94

Wagner, Henry R. 1862-1957 . . . . . DLB-140

Wagner, Richard 1813-1883. . . . . . . DLB-129

Wagoner, David 1926- DLB-5

Wah, Fred 1939- DLB-60

Waiblinger, Wilhelm 1804-1830 . . . . DLB-90

Wain, John
1925-1994 . . . . . . DLB-15, 27, 139, 155

Wainwright, Jeffrey 1944- DLB-40

Waite, Peirce and Company DLB-49

Wakeman, Stephen H. 1859-1924 . . . DLB-187

Wakoski, Diane 1937- DLB-5

Walahfrid Strabo circa 808-849 . . . . . DLB-148

Walck, Henry Z. DLB-46

Walcott, Derek 1930- . . . DLB-117; Y-81, Y-92

Waldegrave, Robert
[publishing house] DLB-170

Waldman, Anne 1945- DLB-16

Waldrop, Rosmarie 1935- DLB-169

Walker, Alice 1944- DLB-6, 33, 143

Walker, George F. 1947- DLB-60

Walker, Joseph A. 1935- DLB-38

Walker, Margaret 1915- DLB-76, 152

Walker, Ted 1934- DLB-40

Walker and Company DLB-49

Walker, Evans and Cogswell
Company DLB-49

Walker, John Brisben 1847-1931 . . . . DLB-79

Wallace, Alfred Russel 1823-1913 . . . DLB-190

Wallace, Dewitt 1889-1981 and
Lila Acheson Wallace
1889-1984 . . . . DLB-137

Wallace, Edgar 1875-1932 . . . . DLB-70

Wallace, Lila Acheson (see Wallace, Dewitt,
and Lila Acheson Wallace)

Wallant, Edward Lewis
1926-1962 . . . . DLB-2, 28, 143

Waller, Edmund 1606-1687 . . . . . . DLB-126

Walpole, Horace 1717-1797 . . . . DLB-39, 104

Walpole, Hugh 1884-1941 . . . . DLB-34

Walrond, Eric 1898-1966 . . . . DLB-51

Walser, Martin 1927- DLB-75, 124

Walser, Robert 1878-1956 . . . . DLB-66

Walsh, Ernest 1895-1926 . . . . . DLB-4, 45

Walsh, Robert 1784-1859 . . . . DLB-59

Waltharius circa 825 . . . . DLB-148

Walters, Henry 1848-1931 . . . . . . DLB-140

Walther von der Vogelweide
circa 1170-circa 1230 . . . . DLB-138

Walton, Izaak 1593-1683 . . . . DLB-151

Wambaugh, Joseph 1937- DLB-6; Y-83

Waniek, Marilyn Nelson 1946- . . . DLB-120

Warburton, William 1698-1779 . . . . DLB-104

Ward, Aileen 1919- DLB-111

Ward, Artemus (see Browne, Charles Farrar)

Ward, Arthur Henry Sarsfield
(see Rohmer, Sax)

Ward, Douglas Turner 1930- DLB-7, 38

Ward, Lynd 1905-1985 . . . . DLB-22

Ward, Lock and Company DLB-106

Ward, Mrs. Humphry 1851-1920 . . . . DLB-18

Ward, Nathaniel circa 1578-1652 . . . . DLB-24

Ward, Theodore 1902-1983 . . . . DLB-76

Wardle, Ralph 1909-1988 . . . . DLB-103

Ware, William 1797-1852 . . . . DLB-1

Warne, Frederick, and
Company [U.S.]. DLB-49

Warne, Frederick, and
Company [U.K.]. DLB-106

Warner, Charles Dudley
1829-1900 . . . . DLB-64

Warner, Marina 1946- DLB-194

Warner, Rex 1905- DLB-15

Warner, Susan Bogert
1819-1885 . . . . DLB-3, 42

Warner, Sylvia Townsend
1893-1978 . . . . DLB-34, 139

Warner, William 1558-1609 . . . . . . DLB-172

Warner Books DLB-46

Warr, Bertram 1917-1943 . . . . DLB-88

Warren, John Byrne Leicester
(see De Tabley, Lord)

Warren, Lella 1899-1982 . . . . Y-83

Warren, Mercy Otis 1728-1814 . . DLB-31, 200

Warren, Robert Penn
1905-1989 . . . . DLB-2, 48, 152; Y-80, Y-89

Warren, Samuel 1807-1877 . . . . . . DLB-190

Die Wartburgkrieg
circa 1230-circa 1280 . . . . DLB-138

Warton, Joseph 1722-1800 . . . . DLB-104, 109

Warton, Thomas 1728-1790 . . . DLB-104, 109

Washington, George 1732-1799 . . . . DLB-31

Wassermann, Jakob 1873-1934 . . . . . DLB-66

Wasson, David Atwood 1823-1887 . . . . DLB-1

Waterhouse, Keith 1929- DLB-13, 15

Waterman, Andrew 1940- DLB-40

Waters, Frank 1902- Y-86

Waters, Michael 1949- DLB-120

Watkins, Tobias 1780-1855 . . . . . . DLB-73

Watkins, Vernon 1906-1967 . . . . . . DLB-20

Watmough, David 1926- DLB-53

Watson, James Wreford (see Wreford, James)

Watson, John 1850-1907 . . . . DLB-156

Watson, Sheila 1909- DLB-60

Watson, Thomas 1545?-1592 . . . . . . DLB-132

Watson, Wilfred 1911- DLB-60

Watt, W. J., and Company DLB-46

Watten, Barrett 1948- DLB-193

Watterson, Henry 1840-1921 . . . . . . DLB-25

Watts, Alan 1915-1973 . . . . DLB-16

Watts, Franklin [publishing house] DLB-46

Watts, Isaac 1674-1748 . . . . DLB-95

Wand, Alfred Rudolph 1828-1891 . . . DLB-188

Waugh, Alec 1898-1981 . . . . DLB-191

Waugh, Auberon 1939- DLB-14, 194

Waugh, Evelyn 1903-1966 . . DLB-15, 162, 195

Way and Williams DLB-49

Wayman, Tom 1945- DLB-53

Weatherly, Tom 1942- DLB-41

Weaver, Gordon 1937- DLB-130

Weaver, Robert 1921- DLB-88

Webb, Beatrice 1858-1943 and
Webb, Sidney 1859-1947 . . . . . . DLB-190

Webb, Frank J. ?-? DLB-50

Webb, James Watson 1802-1884 . . . . . DLB-43

Webb, Mary 1881-1927 . . . . DLB-34

Webb, Phyllis 1927- DLB-53

Webb, Walter Prescott 1888-1963 . . . . DLB-17

Webbe, William ?-1591 . . . . DLB-132

Webster, Augusta 1837-1894 . . . . . . DLB-35

Webster, Charles L.,
and Company. DLB-49

Webster, John
1579 or 1580-1634? DLB-58

Webster, Noah
1758-1843 . . . . . . DLB-1, 37, 42, 43, 73

Weckherlin, Georg Rodolf
1584-1653 . . . . DLB-164

Wedekind, Frank 1864-1918 . . . . . DLB-118

Weeks, Edward Augustus, Jr.
1898-1989 . . . . DLB-137

Weeks, Stephen B. 1865-1918 . . . . . DLB-187

Weems, Mason Locke
1759-1825 . . . . DLB-30, 37, 42

Weerth, Georg 1822-1856 . . . . DLB-129

Weidenfeld and Nicolson DLB-112

Weidman, Jerome 1913- DLB-28

Weigl, Bruce 1949- DLB-120

Weinbaum, Stanley Grauman
1902-1935 . . . . DLB-8

Weintraub, Stanley 1929- DLB-111

Weise, Christian 1642-1708 . . . . . . DLB-168

Weisenborn, Gunther
1902-1969 . . . . DLB-69, 124

Weiß, Ernst 1882-1940 . . . . DLB-81

Weiss, John 1818-1879 . . . . DLB-1

Weiss, Peter 1916-1982 . . . . DLB-69, 124

Weiss, Theodore 1916- DLB-5

Weisse, Christian Felix 1726-1804 . . . . DLB-97

Weitling, Wilhelm 1808-1871 . . . . . . DLB-129

Welch, James 1940- DLB-175

Welch, Lew 1926-1971? DLB-16

Weldon, Fay 1931- DLB-14, 194

Wellek, René 1903- DLB-63

Wells, Carolyn 1862-1942 . . . . DLB-11

Wells, Charles Jeremiah
circa 1800-1879 . . . . DLB-32

Wells, Gabriel 1862-1946 . . . . DLB-140

Wells, H. G.
1866-1946 . . . . . . DLB-34, 70, 156, 178

Wells, Helena 1758?-1824 . . . . DLB-200

Wells, Robert 1947- DLB-40

Wells-Barnett, Ida B. 1862-1931 . . . . . DLB-23

Welty, Eudora
1909- DLB-2, 102, 143; Y-87; DS-12

Wendell, Barrett 1855-1921. . . . . . . DLB-71

Wentworth, Patricia 1878-1961 . . . . . DLB-77

Werder, Diederich von dem
1584-1657 . . . . DLB-164

Werfel, Franz 1890-1945 . . . . . DLB-81, 124

The Werner Company DLB-49

Werner, Zacharias 1768-1823. . . . . . DLB-94

Wersba, Barbara 1932- DLB-52

Wescott, Glenway 1901- DLB-4, 9, 102

We See the Editor at Work. Y-97

Wesker, Arnold 1932- DLB-13

Wesley, Charles 1707-1788. . . . . . . DLB-95

Wesley, John 1703-1791. . . . . DLB-104

Wesley, Richard 1945- DLB-38

Wessels, A., and Company DLB-46

Wessobrunner Gebet
circa 787-815. . . . . DLB-148

West, Anthony 1914-1988 . . . . DLB-15

West, Dorothy 1907- DLB-76

West, Jessamyn 1902-1984 . . . . DLB-6; Y-84

West, Mae 1892-1980. . . . . DLB-44

West, Nathanael 1903-1940 . . . . DLB-4, 9, 28

West, Paul 1930- DLB-14

West, Rebecca 1892-1983 . . . . . DLB-36; Y-83

West, Richard 1941- DLB-185

West and Johnson DLB-49

Western Publishing Company DLB-46

The Westminster Review 1824-1914 . . . . DLB-110

Weston, Elizabeth Jane
circa 1582-1612 . . . . DLB-172

Wetherald, Agnes Ethelwyn
1857-1940 . . . . DLB-99

Wetherell, Elizabeth (see Warner, Susan Bogert)

Wetzel, Friedrich Gottlob
1779-1819 . . . . DLB-90

Weyman, Stanley J. 1855-1928 . . DLB-141, 156

Wezel, Johann Karl 1747-1819 . . . . . DLB-94

Whalen, Philip 1923- DLB-16

Whalley, George 1915-1983 . . . . . . DLB-88

Wharton, Edith
1862-1937. . . DLB-4, 9, 12, 78, 189; DS-13

Wharton, William 1920s?- Y-80

Whately, Mary Louisa
1824-1889 . . . . DLB-166

Whately, Richard 1787-1863 . . . . . DLB-190

What's Really Wrong With Bestseller
Lists. Y-84

Wheatley, Dennis Yates
1897-1977 . . . . DLB-77

Wheatley, Phillis
circa 1754-1784. . . . . DLB-31, 50

Wheeler, Anna Doyle
1785-1848? DLB-158

Wheeler, Charles Stearns
1816-1843. . . . . DLB-1

Wheeler, Monroe 1900-1988. . . . . . . DLB-4

Wheelock, John Hall 1886-1978 . . . . DLB-45

Wheelwright, John
circa 1592-1679 . . . . DLB-24

Wheelwright, J. B. 1897-1940 . . . . . DLB-45

Whetstone, Colonel Pete (see Noland, C. F. M.)

Whetstone, George 1550-1587 . . . . DLB-136

Whicher, Stephen E. 1915-1961 . . . . DLB-111

Whipple, Edwin Percy 1819-1886 . . DLB-1, 64

Whitaker, Alexander 1585-1617 . . . . DLB-24

Whitaker, Daniel K. 1801-1881 . . . . DLB-73

Whitcher, Frances Miriam
1814-1852 . . . . DLB-11

White, Andrew 1579-1656 . . . . DLB-24

White, Andrew Dickson
1832-1918 . . . . DLB-47

White, E. B. 1899-1985 . . . . . . DLB-11, 22

White, Edgar B. 1947- DLB-38

White, Ethel Lina 1887-1944. . . . . . DLB-77

White, Henry Kirke 1785-1806 . . . . DLB-96

White, Horace 1834-1916. . . . . DLB-23

White, Phyllis Dorothy James
(see James, P. D.)

White, Richard Grant 1821-1885 . . . . DLB-64

White, T. H. 1906-1964. . . . . DLB-160

White, Walter 1893-1955. . . . . DLB-51

White, William, and Company DLB-49

White, William Allen 1868-1944 . . . DLB-9, 25

White, William Anthony Parker
(see Boucher, Anthony)

White, William Hale (see Rutherford, Mark)

Whitechurch, Victor L. 1868-1933. . . . DLB-70

Whitehead, Alfred North
1861-1947 . . . . DLB-100

Whitehead, James 1936- Y-81

Whitehead, William 1715-1785. . . DLB-84, 109

Whitfield, James Monroe 1822-1871 . . . DLB-50

Whitgift, John circa 1533-1604 . . . . DLB-132

Whiting, John 1917-1963 . . . . DLB-13

Whiting, Samuel 1597-1679. . . . . . . DLB-24

Whitlock, Brand 1869-1934. . . . . . . DLB-12

Whitman, Albert, and Company. DLB-46

Whitman, Albery Allson
1851-1901 . . . . DLB-50

Whitman, Alden 1913-1990 . . . . Y-91

Whitman, Sarah Helen (Power)
1803-1878. . . . . DLB-1

Whitman, Walt 1819-1892 . . . . . DLB-3, 64

Whitman Publishing Company. DLB-46

Whitney, Geoffrey
1548 or 1552?-1601 . . . . DLB-136

Whitney, Isabella
flourished 1566-1573 . . . . DLB-136

Whitney, John Hay 1904-1982 . . . . DLB-127

Whittemore, Reed 1919- DLB-5

Whittier, John Greenleaf 1807-1892. . . DLB-1

Whittlesey House DLB-46

Who Runs American Literature? Y-94

Whose *Ulysses?* The Function of
Editing Y-97

Wideman, John Edgar 1941- . . . DLB-33, 143

Widener, Harry Elkins 1885-1912 . . . DLB-140

Wiebe, Rudy 1934- DLB-60

Wiechert, Ernst 1887-1950 . . . . . . DLB-56

Wied, Martina 1882-1957. . . . . DLB-85

Wiehe, Evelyn May Clowes (see Mordaunt,
Elinor)

Wieland, Christoph Martin
1733-1813 . . . . DLB-97

Wienbarg, Ludolf 1802-1872 . . . . . DLB-133

Wieners, John 1934- DLB-16

Wier, Ester 1910- DLB-52

Wiesel, Elie 1928- DLB-83; Y-86, Y-87

Wiggin, Kate Douglas 1856-1923 . . . DLB-42

Wigglesworth, Michael 1631-1705 . . . DLB-24

Wilberforce, William 1759-1833. . . . DLB-158

Wilbrandt, Adolf 1837-1911. . . . . . DLB-129

Wilbur, Richard 1921- DLB-5, 169

Wild, Peter 1940- DLB-5

Wilde, Lady Jane Francesca Elgee
1821?-1896. . . . . DLB-199

Wilde, Oscar 1854-1900
. . . . . DLB-10, 19, 34, 57, 141, 156, 190

Wilde, Richard Henry
1789-1847 . . . . DLB-3, 59

Wilde, W. A., Company. DLB-49

Wilder, Billy 1906- DLB-26

Wilder, Laura Ingalls 1867-1957 . . . . DLB-22

Wilder, Thornton 1897-1975 . . . DLB-4, 7, 9

Wildgans, Anton 1881-1932. . . . . . DLB-118

Wiley, Bell Irvin 1906-1980 . . . . . . DLB-17

Wiley, John, and Sons DLB-49

Wilhelm, Kate 1928- DLB-8

Wilkes, Charles 1798-1877 . . . . DLB-183

Wilkes, George 1817-1885 . . . . DLB-79

Wilkinson, Anne 1910-1961 . . . . DLB-88

Wilkinson, Eliza Yonge
1757-circa 1813 . . . . DLB-200

Wilkinson, Sylvia 1940- Y-86

Wilkinson, William Cleaver
1833-1920 . . . . DLB-71

Willard, Barbara 1909-1994 . . . . DLB-161

Willard, L. [publishing house] DLB-49

Willard, Nancy 1936- DLB-5, 52

Willard, Samuel 1640-1707 . . . . DLB-24

William of Auvergne 1190-1249 . . . . DLB-115

William of Conches
circa 1090-circa 1154 . . . . DLB-115

William of Ockham
circa 1285-1347 . . . . DLB-115

William of Sherwood
1200/1205 - 1266/1271 . . . . DLB-115

The William Chavrat American Fiction
Collection at the Ohio State University
Libraries. Y-92

William Faulkner Centenary. Y-97

Williams, A., and Company DLB-49

Williams, Ben Ames 1889-1953 . . . . . DLB-102

Williams, C. K. 1936- DLB-5

Williams, Chancellor 1905- DLB-76

Williams, Charles
1886-1945. . . . . DLB-100, 153

Williams, Denis 1923- DLB-117

Williams, Emlyn 1905- DLB-10, 77

Williams, Garth 1912- DLB-22

Williams, George Washington
1849-1891 . . . . DLB-47

Williams, Heathcote 1941- DLB-13

Williams, Helen Maria
1761-1827 . . . . DLB-158

Williams, Hugo 1942- DLB-40

Williams, Isaac 1802-1865 . . . . DLB-32

Williams, Joan 1928- DLB-6

Williams, John A. 1925- DLB-2, 33

Williams, John E. 1922-1994 . . . . . . DLB-6

Williams, Jonathan 1929- DLB-5

Williams, Miller 1930- DLB-105

Williams, Raymond 1921- DLB-14

Williams, Roger circa 1603-1683 . . . . DLB-24

Williams, Rowland 1817-1870 . . . . . DLB-184

Williams, Samm-Art 1946- DLB-38

Williams, Sherley Anne 1944- DLB-41

Williams, T. Harry 1909-1979 . . . . . DLB-17

Williams, Tennessee
1911-1983. . . . . DLB-7; Y-83; DS-4

Williams, Ursula Moray 1911- DLB-160

Williams, Valentine 1883-1946 . . . . . DLB-77

Williams, William Appleman
1921- DLB-17

Williams, William Carlos
1883-1963 . . . . DLB-4, 16, 54, 86

Williams, Wirt 1921- DLB-6

Williams Brothers DLB-49

Williamson, Henry 1895-1977 . . . . . DLB-191

Williamson, Jack 1908- DLB-8

Willingham, Calder Baynard, Jr.
1922- DLB-2, 44

Williram of Ebersberg
circa 1020-1085 . . . . DLB-148

Willis, Nathaniel Parker
1806-1867 . . . DLB-3, 59, 73, 74, 183; DS-13

Willkomm, Ernst 1810-1886. . . . . . DLB-133

Wilmer, Clive 1945- DLB-40

Wilson, A. N. 1950- DLB-14, 155, 194

Wilson, Angus
1913-1991 . . . . DLB-15, 139, 155

Wilson, Arthur 1595-1652 . . . . . . DLB-58

Wilson, Augusta Jane Evans
1835-1909 . . . . DLB-42

Wilson, Colin 1931- DLB-14, 194

Wilson, Edmund 1895-1972 . . . . . . DLB-63

Wilson, Ethel 1888-1980 . . . . DLB-68

Wilson, Harriet E. Adams
1828?-1863?. DLB-50

Wilson, Harry Leon 1867-1939 . . . . . DLB-9

Wilson, John 1588-1667 . . . . DLB-24

Wilson, John 1785-1854. . . . . DLB-110

Wilson, Lanford 1937- DLB-7

Wilson, Margaret 1882-1973. . . . . . . DLB-9

Wilson, Michael 1914-1978. . . . . . . DLB-44

Wilson, Mona 1872-1954 . . . . DLB-149

Wilson, Romer 1891-1930. . . . . . . DLB-191

Wilson, Thomas
1523 or 1524-1581 . . . . DLB-132

Wilson, Woodrow 1856-1924 . . . . . DLB-47

Wilson, Effingham
[publishing house] DLB-154

Wimsatt, William K., Jr.
1907-1975 . . . . DLB-63

Winchell, Walter 1897-1972 . . . . . . DLB-29

Winchester, J. [publishing house]. DLB-49

Winckelmann, Johann Joachim
1717-1768 . . . . DLB-97

Winckler, Paul 1630-1686 . . . . DLB-164

Wind, Herbert Warren 1916- DLB-171

Windet, John [publishing house] DLB-170

Windham, Donald 1920- DLB-6

Wing, Donald Goddard 1904-1972. . . DLB-187

Wing, John M. 1844-1917 . . . . DLB-187

Wingate, Allan [publishing house] . . . DLB-112

Winnemucca, Sarah 1844-1921 . . . . . DLB-175

Winnifrith, Tom 1938- DLB-155

Winsloe, Christa 1888-1944 . . . . . . DLB-124

Winslow, Anna Green 1759-1780 . . . DLB-200

Winsor, Justin 1831-1897 . . . . DLB-47

John C. Winston Company DLB-49

Winters, Yvor 1900-1968 . . . . DLB-48

Winthrop, John 1588-1649 . . . . DLB-24, 30

Winthrop, John, Jr. 1606-1676 . . . . . DLB-24

Winthrop, Margaret Tyndal
1591-1647 . . . . DLB-200

Wirt, William 1772-1834 . . . . DLB-37

Wise, John 1652-1725. . . . . DLB-24

Wise, Thomas James 1859-1937 . . . . DLB-184

Wiseman, Adele 1928- DLB-88

Wishart and Company DLB-112

Wisner, George 1812-1849 . . . . DLB-43

Wister, Owen 1860-1938 . . . . DLB-9, 78, 186

Wister, Sarah 1761-1804. . . . . DLB-200

Wither, George 1588-1667 . . . . DLB-121

Witherspoon, John 1723-1794 . . . . . DLB-31

Withrow, William Henry 1839-1908. . . DLB-99

Wittig, Monique 1935- DLB-83

Wodehouse, P. G.
1881-1975 . . . . DLB-34, 162

Wohmann, Gabriele 1932- DLB-75

Woiwode, Larry 1941- DLB-6

Wolcot, John 1738-1819 . . . . DLB-109

Wolcott, Roger 1679-1767 . . . . DLB-24

Wolf, Christa 1929- DLB-75

Wolf, Friedrich 1888-1953 . . . . DLB-124

Wolfe, Gene 1931- DLB-8

Wolfe, John [publishing house] DLB-170

Wolfe, Reyner (Reginald)
[publishing house] DLB-170

Wolfe, Thomas
1900-1938. . DLB-9, 102; Y-85; DS-2, DS-16

Wolfe, Tom 1931- DLB-152, 185

Wolff, Helen 1906-1994 . . . . Y-94

Wolff, Tobias 1945- DLB-130

Wolfram von Eschenbach
circa 1170-after 1220 . . . . DLB-138

Wolfram von Eschenbach's *Parzival*:
Prologue and Book 3 . . . . DLB-138

Wollstonecraft, Mary
1759-1797 . . . . DLB-39, 104, 158

Wondratschek, Wolf 1943- DLB-75

Wood, Benjamin 1820-1900 . . . . . . DLB-23

Wood, Charles 1932- DLB-13

Wood, Mrs. Henry 1814-1887 . . . . . DLB-18

Wood, Joanna E. 1867-1927 . . . . . . DLB-92

Wood, Sally Sayward Barrell Keating
1751-1855 . . . . DLB-200

Wood, Samuel [publishing house] DLB-49

Wood, William ?-? DLB-24

Woodberry, George Edward
1855-1930 . . . . DLB-71, 103

Woodbridge, Benjamin 1622-1684 . . . . DLB-24

Woodcock, George 1912- DLB-88

Woodhull, Victoria C. 1838-1927 . . . . DLB-79

Woodmason, Charles circa 1720-? DLB-31

Woodress, Jr., James Leslie 1916- . . . DLB-111

Woodson, Carter G. 1875-1950 . . . . . DLB-17

Woodward, C. Vann 1908- DLB-17

Woodward, Stanley 1895-1965 . . . . . DLB-171

Wooler, Thomas
1785 or 1786-1853 . . . . DLB-158

Woolf, David (see Maddow, Ben)

Woolf, Leonard 1880-1969 . . . . DLB-100; DS-10

Woolf, Virginia
1882-1941 . . . . . DLB-36, 100, 162; DS-10

Woolf, Virginia, "The New Biography," *New York
Herald Tribune,* 30 October 1927
. . . . DLB-149

Woollcott, Alexander 1887-1943 . . . . . DLB-29

Woolman, John 1720-1772 . . . . DLB-31

Woolner, Thomas 1825-1892 . . . . . . DLB-35

Woolsey, Sarah Chauncy 1835-1905 . . . DLB-42

Woolson, Constance Fenimore
1840-1894 . . . . DLB-12, 74, 189

Worcester, Joseph Emerson
1784-1865 . . . . DLB-1

Worde, Wynkyn de
[publishing house] DLB-170

Wordsworth, Christopher 1807-1885 . . DLB-166

Wordsworth, Dorothy 1771-1855 . . . . DLB-107

Wordsworth, Elizabeth 1840-1932 . . . . DLB-98

Wordsworth, William 1770-1850 . . DLB-93, 107

Workman, Fanny Bullock 1859-1925 . . DLB-189

The Works of the Rev. John Witherspoon
(1800-1801) [excerpts] DLB-31

A World Chronology of Important Science
Fiction Works (1818-1979) DLB-8

World Publishing Company DLB-46

World War II Writers Symposium at the
University of South Carolina,
12–14 April 1995 . . . . Y-95

Worthington, R., and Company DLB-49

Wotton, Sir Henry 1568-1639 . . . . . DLB-121

Wouk, Herman 1915- Y-82

Wreford, James 1915- DLB-88

Wren, Percival Christopher 1885-1941 . . DLB-153

Wrenn, John Henry 1841-1911 . . . . DLB-140

Wright, C. D. 1949- DLB-120

Wright, Charles 1935- DLB-165; Y-82

Wright, Charles Stevenson 1932- DLB-33

Wright, Frances 1795-1852 . . . . DLB-73

Wright, Harold Bell 1872-1944 . . . . . DLB-9

Wright, James 1927-1980 . . . . . DLB-5, 169

Wright, Jay 1935- DLB-41

Wright, Louis B. 1899-1984 . . . . . . DLB-17

Wright, Richard 1908-1960 . . DLB-76, 102; DS-2

Wright, Richard B. 1937- DLB-53

Wright, Sarah Elizabeth 1928- DLB-33

Wright, Willard Huntington ("S. S. Van Dine")
1888-1939 . . . . DS-16

Writers and Politics: 1871-1918,
by Ronald Gray DLB-66

Writers and their Copyright Holders:
the WATCH Project Y-94

Writers' Forum Y-85

Writing for the Theatre, by
Harold Pinter DLB-13

Wroth, Lady Mary 1587-1653 . . . . . DLB-121

Wroth, Lawrence C. 1884-1970 . . . . DLB-187

Wurlitzer, Rudolph 1937- DLB-173

Wyatt, Sir Thomas
circa 1503-1542 . . . . DLB-132

Wycherley, William 1641-1715 . . . . . DLB-80

Wyclif, John
circa 1335-31 December 1384 . . . DLB-146

Wyeth, N. C.
1882-1945 . . . . DLB-188; DS-16

Wylie, Elinor 1885-1928 . . . . DLB-9, 45

Wylie, Philip 1902-1971 . . . . DLB-9

Wyllie, John Cook
1908-1968 . . . . DLB-140

Wynne-Tyson, Esmé 1898-1972 . . . . DLB-191

X

Xenophon circa 430 B.C.-circa 356 B.C.
. . . . DLB-176

Y

Yasuoka, Shōtarō 1920- DLB-182

Yates, Dornford 1885-1960 . . . . DLB-77, 153

Yates, J. Michael 1938- DLB-60

Yates, Richard 1926-1992 . . DLB-2; Y-81, Y-92

Yavorov, Peyo 1878-1914 . . . . DLB-147

Yearsley, Ann 1753-1806 . . . . DLB-109

Yeats, William Butler
1865-1939 . . . . DLB-10, 19, 98, 156

Yep, Laurence 1948- DLB-52

Yerby, Frank 1916-1991 . . . . DLB-76

Yezierska, Anzia 1885-1970 . . . . . . DLB-28

Yolen, Jane 1939- DLB-52

Yonge, Charlotte Mary
1823-1901 . . . . DLB-18, 163

The York Cycle
circa 1376-circa 1569 . . . . DLB-146

A Yorkshire Tragedy DLB-58

Yoseloff, Thomas
[publishing house] DLB-46

Young, Al 1939- DLB-33

Young, Arthur 1741-1820 . . . . DLB-158

Young, Dick
1917 or 1918 - 1987 . . . . DLB-171

Young, Edward 1683-1765 . . . . DLB-95

Young, Francis Brett 1884-1954 . . . . DLB-191

Young, Stark 1881-1963 . . . DLB-9, 102; DS-16

Young, Waldeman 1880-1938 . . . . . DLB-26

Young, William [publishing house] . . . DLB-49

Young Bear, Ray A. 1950- DLB-175

Yourcenar, Marguerite
1903-1987 . . . . DLB-72; Y-88

"You've Never Had It So Good," Gusted by
"Winds of Change": British Fiction in the
1950s, 1960s, and After DLB-14

Yovkov, Yordan 1880-1937 . . . . . . DLB-147

Z

Zachariä, Friedrich Wilhelm
1726-1777 . . . . DLB-97

Zagoskin, Mikhail Nikolaevich
1789-1852 . . . . DLB-198

Zajc, Dane 1929- DLB-181

Zamora, Bernice 1938- DLB-82

Zand, Herbert 1923-1970 . . . . DLB-85

Zangwill, Israel 1864-1926 . . DLB-10, 135, 197

Zanzotto, Andrea 1921- DLB-128

Zapata Olivella, Manuel 1920- DLB-113

Zebra Books DLB-46

Zebrowski, George 1945- DLB-8

Zech, Paul 1881-1946 . . . . DLB-56

Zepheria DLB-172

Zeidner, Lisa 1955- DLB-120

Zelazny, Roger 1937-1995 . . . . DLB-8

Zenger, John Peter 1697-1746 . . . DLB-24, 43

Zesen, Philipp von 1619-1689 . . . . . DLB-164

Zieber, G. B., and Company DLB-49

Zieroth, Dale 1946- DLB-60

Zigler und Kliphausen, Heinrich Anshelm von
1663-1697 . . . . DLB-168

Zimmer, Paul 1934- DLB-5

Zingref, Julius Wilhelm
1591-1635 . . . . DLB-164

Zindel, Paul 1936- DLB-7, 52

Zinnes, Harriet 1919- DLB-193

Zinzendorf, Nikolaus Ludwig von
    1700-1760 . . . . DLB-168

Zitkala-Ša 1876-1938 . . . . DLB-175

Zola, Emile 1840-1902 . . . . DLB-123

Zolla, Elémire 1926- DLB-196

Zolotow, Charlotte 1915- DLB-52

Zschokke, Heinrich 1771-1848 . . . . . . DLB-94

Zubly, John Joachim 1724-1781 . . . . . DLB-31

Zu-Bolton II, Ahmos 1936- DLB-41

Zuckmayer, Carl 1896-1977 . . . . DLB-56, 124

Zukofsky, Louis 1904-1978 . . . . . DLB-5, 165

Zupan, Vitomil 1914-1987 . . . . DLB-181

Župančič, Oton 1878-1949 . . . . . . DLB-147

zur Mühlen, Hermynia 1883-1951 . . . . DLB-56

Zweig, Arnold 1887-1968 . . . . DLB-66

Zweig, Stefan 1881-1942 . . . . . . DLB-81, 118